Milton Friedman

AND ECONOMIC DEBATE IN
THE UNITED STATES, 1932–1972

Milton Friedman

AND ECONOMIC DEBATE IN
THE UNITED STATES, 1932–1972

VOLUME 1

Edward Nelson

THE UNIVERSITY OF CHICAGO PRESS
CHICAGO AND LONDON

The University of Chicago Press, Chicago 60637
The University of Chicago Press, Ltd., London
© 2020 by The University of Chicago
All rights reserved. No part of this book may be used or
reproduced in any manner whatsoever without written
permission, except in the case of brief quotations in critical
articles and reviews. For more information, contact the
University of Chicago Press, 1427 E. 60th St., Chicago, IL 60637.
Published 2020
Printed in the United States of America

29 28 27 26 25 24 23 22 21 20   1 2 3 4 5

ISBN-13: 978-0-226-68377-5 (cloth)
ISBN-13: 978-0-226-68380-5 (e-book)
DOI: https://doi.org/10.7208/chicago/9780226683805.001.0001

Library of Congress Cataloging-in-Publication Data

Names: Nelson, Edward, 1971– author.
Title: Milton Friedman and economic debate in the
United States, 1932–1972 / Edward Nelson.
Description: Chicago ; London : University of Chicago Press,
2020. | Includes bibliographical references and index.
Identifiers: LCCN 2019046214 | ISBN 9780226683775 (v. 1 ;
cloth) | ISBN 9780226684895 (v. 2 ; cloth) | ISBN 9780226683805
(v. 1 ; ebook) | ISBN 9780226684925 (v. 2 ; ebook)
Subjects: LCSH: Friedman, Milton, 1912–2006. | Economists—
United States—Biography. | Economics—United States—
History—20th century. | Chicago school of economics.
Classification: LCC HB119.F84 N45 2020 |
DDC 330.15/53092 [B]—dc23
LC record available at https://lccn.loc.gov/2019046214

♾ This paper meets the requirements of
ANSI/NISO Z39.48-1992 (Permanence of Paper).

TO MY FATHER, MICHAEL NELSON

Contents

Part 2: Friedman's Framework

Part 3: Friedman's Monetarist Years, 1951 to 1972

Introduction

The objective of this study is to provide an account of Milton Friedman's role in several major economic debates that took place in the United States from 1932 through the end of 1972.[1] The debates considered include both those that were largely carried out in the economic-research literature and those that primarily proceeded in the media or in policy forums. But the fact that this book's coverage extends through 1972 does mean that the book's narrative encompasses Friedman's main years of activity in economic research. For, although Friedman continued to be an active participant in economic discourse after 1972 (from his bases of the University of Chicago up to the 1976–77 academic year and of the Hoover Institution, Stanford University, thereafter), a very large amount of this post-1972 participation was via public policy and popular forums rather than via contributions to the research literature.

The perspective provided in this book is that of an author who specializes in the same field of research that Friedman did: that is, monetary economics. This is not a standpoint from which previous books on Friedman have been written. The earlier books have overwhelmingly tended to come from non-economists, from economists who have not engaged extensively in journal-oriented economic research, or from economists who have been specialized in research in the field of the history of economic thought rather than in the field of monetary economics.

It is true that historians of economic thought would seem to be the most natural authors on the topic of Milton Friedman and economic debate. It is also true that valuable work has indeed been done about Friedman by historians of economic thought. At the same time, it is fair to say that, on balance, the state of the existing literature prompts the same question regarding Friedman's contributions that Harrod (1970, 617) asked in connection with Keynes's work: "But can historians of thought be relied on to get things straight?"

A thorough discussion of the prior literature on Friedman is beyond the scope of this introduction—and indeed of this book.[2] But a number of recurring features of the existing literature pointed to the likelihood that an evaluation of Friedman's work from a monetary-economics perspective could add value. First, many authors cited unpublished items (such as correspondence) from the Hoover Institution's Friedman archives to document points about Friedman's views that could readily have been established by reference to Friedman's published writings. This practice suggested an insufficient familiarity with Friedman's body of publications. Second, all too often Friedman's views were taken as interchangeable with those of his University of Chicago colleagues—and particularly with those of George Stigler. This practice overlooked major differences between Friedman and other figures in the Chicago School. Third, the existing literature contained a good many statements about monetary analysis that would not have been made by those more familiar with that topic.

What follows in this book is therefore a monetary economist's attempt to provide an analytical narrative of Friedman's career from 1932 to 1972 (with the narrative organized primarily in terms of key economic debates), together with an exposition of Friedman's economic framework.

Three major limitations of this book's scope should be given at the outset.

The first limitation is that, as already indicated, this book covers only the period up to 1972. Post-1972 events are brought into the narrative primarily to make more complete the book's account of specific debates. A byproduct of this limit on the chronology is that this book does not cover two of the most controversial debates in which Friedman was involved. One of these omissions concerns his advocacy of drug legalization. Although Friedman voiced this advocacy in the early 1970s, prolonged engagement on his part in the debate on narcotic drugs began only in the 1980s. The other omission concerns Friedman's 1975 visit to Chile and the subsequent highly charged exchanges over the topic summarized in a *New York Times* headline of May 22, 1977: "Milton Friedman, the Chilean Junta and the Matter of Their Association." These topics would be among those considered in the event of a continuation volume, which would extend the narrative of volumes 1 and 2 to cover the period from the beginning of 1973 until Friedman's death in November 2006.[3]

Second, the book has no specific section or chapter devoted to Friedman's case for floating exchange rates or to the open-economy aspects of his economic framework. These are matters that are covered—occasionally in detail—at various points in the course of the present book's discussion. But a more systematic treatment of them is reserved for a projected companion volume that will cover Friedman and economic debate in the United Kingdom. For a number of reasons, the Friedman case for floating exchange rates is more readily discussed in the context of an examination of an economy that is smaller and more open than the US economy.[4] Indeed, Friedman's 1953 paper on floating exchange rates explicitly applied the case for floating rates to the UK economy.

Third, Friedman's interventions in debates on education and conscription are not included here. As these debates were largely separate from the macroeconomic debates that were the focus of Friedman's research, and key developments in the debates occurred after 1972, it was judged that these subjects could be excluded from the present book while leaving open the possibility of giving them full coverage in an account that took up the narrative beyond 1972.[5]

Acknowledgments

The author is grateful for the guidance and encouragement of current and former editors at the University of Chicago Press, in particular Joe Jackson, who organized the commissioning of the book, and Jane Macdonald and Alan Thomas, who have seen the project through to completion. The author is also indebted to Kathleen Kageff for meticulous copyediting and to Mark Reschke and Alicia Sparrow for their production advice.

The author is grateful also to a number of people for providing comments on drafts of this book. In many cases, the comments pertained to drafts of specific chapters. Accordingly, each of the individual chapters of this book contains an acknowledgments paragraph recognizing feedback received on earlier versions of those chapters. In addition, the author is grateful to Michael Bordo, Charles Goodhart, David Laidler, and David Lindsey for remarks on the whole of the manuscript and to William A. Allen, Russell Boyer, Thomas Humphrey, Douglas Irwin, James Lothian, Ann-Marie Meulendyke, the late Allan Meltzer, Michael Parkin, Charles Steindel, George Tavlas, Roy Weintraub, and the late Donald Winch for supplying comments on a large number of chapters. The late Julio Rotemberg provided much advice and encouragement concerning the writing of this book and also supplied detailed comments on several chapters.

Furthermore, in the years prior to starting this book, the author benefited from extensive discussions with a number of individuals concerning Friedman's place in monetary economics. These individuals include Michael Bordo, Tim Congdon, Robert Hetzel, Bennett McCallum, the late Allan Meltzer, Christina Romer, David Romer, the late Anna Schwartz, George Tavlas, and John Taylor; as well as current and former colleagues at the Federal Reserve Board, including Mark Carlson, Burcu Duygan-Bump, Neil Ericsson, Jon Faust, Christopher Gust, Andrew Levin, David López-Salido, John Maggs, Ellen Meade, Jonathan Rose, Jeremy Rudd, and Robert

Tetlow; former colleagues at the Federal Reserve Bank of St. Louis, including James Bullard, Riccardo DiCecio, William Gavin, and David Wheelock; and former colleagues at the Bank of England, including Christopher Allsopp, Nicholas Oulton, and Geoffrey Wood. In more recent years, the author has benefited from discussions on the matter with former colleagues at the University of Sydney, including Colin Cameron, Daniel Hamermesh, and Colm Harmon.

For research assistance on various matters, the author is grateful to Miguel Acosta, George Fenton, William Gamber, Christine Garnier, and Andrew Giffin. For help in finding and obtaining archival material and related information, the author is indebted to Riccardo DiCecio, Andrew Ewing, Johanna Francis, Kurt Gooch, Daniel Hammond, Özer Karagedikli, Stephen Kirchner, Levis Kochin, Terry Metter, Eric Monnet, Charles Palm, Jeremy Piger, Marcel Priebsch, Hugh Rockoff, Glenn Rudebusch, Bernd Schlusche, Tara Sinclair, David Small, Katrina Stierholz, Paolo Surico, Gloria Valentine, Mark Wynne, and the staffs of the libraries of Duke University, the Federal Reserve Board, the Federal Reserve Bank of Dallas, the Federal Reserve Bank of San Francisco, the Federal Reserve Bank of St. Louis, and the University of Sydney. In addition, the following individuals kindly shared material from their own collections: Douglas Adie, James Bullard, Nigel Duck, Claire Friedland, John Greenwood, Christopher Gust, R. W. (Rik) Hafer, Robert Hall, Rudolf Hauser, James Heckman, Douglas Irwin, Michael Keran, David Laidler, Leo Melamed, Ann-Marie Meulendyke, Michael Mork, Charles Nelson, Gerald O'Driscoll, Pascal Salin, Roger Sandilands, the late Anna Schwartz, Christopher Sims, Stephen Stigler, and Lester Telser. The author is also indebted to Milton Friedman's daughter, Janet Martel, for providing clearances and for making herself available for a conversation with the author in September 2016 about her father. The author extends sincere apologies to any individuals who also provided help for this project but who have inadvertently not been mentioned in the preceding acknowledgments.

Notwithstanding the acknowledgments given above, the views and conclusions expressed in this study are the author's alone, and the author is solely responsible for errors in this study. In addition, the views expressed in this book should not be interpreted as those of the Federal Reserve Board or the Federal Reserve System.

Interviews

Many people kindly made themselves available for interviews with the author for this project. The interviews conducted since 2012 are listed below. In many cases, the coverage of the interview mainly involved topics that were ultimately reserved for a later book—either because those topics are intended for the project on 1973–2006 US economic debate or because they will be covered in the companion project that concerns Friedman and economic debate in the United Kingdom. However, even those interviews not explicitly cited in later chapters proved extremely helpful in shaping the present book.

Andrew Abel	October 14, 2014
Joshua Aizenman	June 30, 2016
Roger Alford	January 23, 2014
Robert Aliber	May 1, 2013, and May 3, 2013
William A. Allen	December 13, 2013
William R. Allen	March 14, 2014
Christopher Allsopp	December 9, 2013, and April 10, 2015
Richard Anderson	November 14, 2013
Kenneth Arrow	December 7, 2013
Alan J. Auerbach	May 18, 2015
Kathy Axilrod	April 25, 2013, and June 26, 2014
Stephen Axilrod	April 24, 2013
David Backus	April 16, 2014
Robert Barro	June 4, 2013
Roy Batchelor	November 8, 2013
Francis Bator	January 6, 2015, and March 16, 2015
William Baumol	January 23, 2014
Gary Becker	December 13, 2013
Michael Beenstock	September 26, 2013
Geoffrey Bell	November 5, 2013
Esra Bennathan	April 1, 2015
Ben Bernanke	February 19, 2014
Alan Blinder	December 6, 2013
Christopher Bliss	January 2, 2015
Ronald Bodkin	November 17, 2015
Michael Bordo	July 24, 2013
Michael Boskin	July 3, 2013
William Brainard	March 5, 2014
Donald Brash	July 9, 2013
Arturo Brillembourg	September 30, 2015
Samuel Brittan	April 18, 2013
Charles H. Brunie	July 15, 2013
Sir Alan Budd	October 7, 2013, and October 8, 2013
Edwin Burmeister	November 20, 2014
Lord (Terence) Burns	September 18, 2013
Joseph Burns	September 12, 2013
Guillermo A. Calvo	April 1, 2014
Thomas Campbell	August 19, 2015
Michael Canes	November 7, 2013
Victor Canto	September 11, 2015

Thomas Cargill	April 17, 2015
Jack Carr	July 29, 2013
Victoria Chick	January 13, 2015
A. Lawrence (Lawry) Chickering	March 24, 2015, and March 27, 2015
Robert Chitester	July 9, 2013
Gregory Chow	July 1, 2013
Carl Christ	May 1, 2013, and August 15, 2015
Lars Christensen	August 9, 2013
Kenneth Clements	September 26, 2013
Warren Coats	October 21, 2013
Tim Congdon	November 25, 2013
Michael Connolly	May 13, 2015
J. Phillip Cooper	September 17, 2015
Charles Cox	November 5, 2013
Francis Cripps	January 22, 2015
Dewey Daane	May 8, 2015
Michael Darby	October 15, 2013
Sir Partha Dasgupta	February 27, 2014
James Davidson	February 12, 2015
Paul Davidson	May 3, 2013
Sir Roderick Deane	August 14, 2013
Lord (Meghnad) Desai	January 9, 2015
William Dewald	April 25, 2013
Peter Diamond	November 19, 2014
Avinash Dixit	June 10, 2015
Lord (Bernard) Donoughue	February 3, 2015
William Dougan	September 19, 2013
Gerald Dwyer	August 20, 2013
Lord (John) Eatwell	January 4, 2015
Benjamin Eden	March 14, 2014
Barry Eichengreen	April 3, 2014
Kenneth Elzinga	March 10, 2015
Paul Evans	February 26, 2013
Eugene Fama	September 11, 2013
Martin Feldstein	November 21, 2013
Christopher Fildes	December 9, 2015
Stanley Fischer	August 30, 2013
Franklin Fisher	January 16, 2015, and January 21, 2015
Duncan Foley	October 2, 2014
Claire Friedland	October 27, 2014
Benjamin Friedman	May 10, 2013, and July 23, 2013
Roman Frydman	March 2, 2015
Mark Gertler	September 26, 2014
William Gibson	March 6, 2013
Christopher Gilbert	November 21, 2014
Claudia Goldin	September 20, 2013
Charles Goodhart	July 3, 2013
Robert Gordon	March 21, 2013

John P. (Jack) Gould	March 20, 2015
Lyle Gramley	April 2, 2013; April 10, 2013; and June 24, 2013
Jo Anna Gray	August 8, 2013
Alan Greenspan	August 19, 2013
Lord (Brian) Griffiths	September 23, 2013, and October 7, 2013
Arthur Grimes	September 17, 2013
Herbert Grubel	May 19, 2015
Graham Hacche	November 14, 2014, and December 9, 2014
R. W. (Rik) Hafer	August 29, 2013
Robert Hall	May 31, 2013
Lars Peter Hansen	March 11, 2014
Arnold Harberger	April 12, 2013; May 2, 2013; December 9, 2013; and September 12, 2014
Geoffrey Harcourt	July 7, 2014
Laurence Harris	October 30, 2015
Oliver Hart	December 29, 2014
Andrew Harvey	December 18, 2014
Rudolf Hauser	June 22, 2012, and July 15, 2013
Robert Heller	September 9, 2013
Dieter Helm	January 14, 2015
Robert Hodrick	January 23, 2016
Lord (David) Howell	September 4, 2015
Thomas M. Humphrey	July 10, 2013
Otmar Issing	October 11, 2013
Richard Jackman	November 4, 2014
Sir Antony Jay	May 29, 2013
Peter Jay	May 8, 2013
Peter Jonson	November 14, 2013
Lars Jonung	September 8, 2014
Jerry Jordan	June 5, 2013
Thomas (Tom) Jordan	June 24, 2013
Dale Jorgenson	September 12, 2014
Peter Jovanovich	March 24, 2015
Edward Kane	June 24, 2015
George Kaufman	November 12, 2013
Henry Kaufman	October 14, 2014, and January 22, 2015
William Keegan	January 9, 2014
Michael Keran	March 7, 2013
Mohsin Khan	December 18, 2015
Lord (Mervyn) King	August 15, 2016, and August 16, 2016
Benjamin Klein	March 4, 2013
Levis Kochin	April 23, 2013
Laurence Kotlikoff	May 26, 2015
Arthur Laffer	June 10, 2013, and August 11, 2014
David Laidler	June 3, 2013; June 19, 2013; and November 6, 2014
Lord (Richard) Layard	February 7, 2014
Eugene Lerner	July 29, 2016
Fred Levin	March 10, 2014

Peter Lilley	October 28, 2014
David Lindsey	May 2, 2013
Richard Lipsey	June 17, 2015
Rachel Lomax	March 25, 2014
James Lothian	October 24, 2013
Robert Lucas	March 12, 2013
George Macesich	May 28, 2013
Gregory Mankiw	September 24, 2013
Henry G. Manne	April 30, 2014
Harry Markowitz	February 23, 2016
Thomas Mayer	October 16, 2013
Bennett McCallum	June 13, 2013
Deirdre McCloskey	August 21, 2013, and August 17, 2015
Rachel McCulloch	October 4, 2013
Ronald McKinnon	January 23, 2014
Sir Christopher (Kit) McMahon	February 14, 2014
Philip Meguire	November 19, 2013
David Meiselman	April 30, 2013, and July 16, 2014
Leo Melamed	June 19, 2013
Allan Meltzer	April 21, 2013, and April 8, 2015
Ann-Marie Meulendyke	April 29, 2013
Marc A. Miles	February 20, 2014
Murray Milgate	January 22, 2015
Marcus Miller	April 16, 2014
Patrick Minford	October 4, 2013, and March 27, 2015
Jeffrey Miron	June 20, 2013
James Mirrlees	January 6, 2015
Frederic Mishkin	June 18, 2013
John H. Moore	April 29, 2014
Michael Mork	June 5, 2013
Richard Muth	May 20, 2015
Robert Neild	November 6, 2013
Charles Nelson	September 9, 2013
Marc Nerlove	September 13, 2013; September 18, 2013; and September 26, 2013
David Newbery	October 10, 2014
Maurice Newman	September 18, 2013
Stephen Nickell	December 6, 2013
Robert Nobay	December 3, 2013
Coleman Nutter	April 18, 2014
Jane Nutter	April 23, 2014
Gerald O'Driscoll	April 24, 2015
Lawrence Officer	January 10, 2016
Lee Ohanian	September 26, 2013
Peter Oppenheimer	December 29, 2014
Athanasios Orphanides	June 27, 2014
Adrian Pagan	January 8, 2015
Michael Parkin	May 29, 2013

John Paulus	February 28, 2014
Sam Peltzman	March 1, 2013, and June 22, 2015
John Pencavel	May 12, 2014
Gordon Pepper	October 21, 2013
Edmund Phelps	May 16, 2013
Charles Plosser	April 2, 2015
William Poole	March 25, 2013, and April 30, 2013
Richard Posner	October 27, 2014
Edward Prescott	February 16, 2016
Lionel Price	December 12, 2014
R. David Ranson	April 30, 2014, and September 22, 2014
Robert Rasche	May 6, 2013
Brian Reading	November 28, 2013
Hugh Rockoff	August 29, 2013
Harold Rose	October 11, 2013
Julio Rotemberg	September 5, 2014
Robert Rowthorn	December 17, 2014
John Rutledge	November 14, 2014
Michael Salemi	November 12, 2014
Pascal Salin	November 4, 2015
J. R. (Dick) Sargent	April 15, 2015
Thomas Sargent	January 24, 2014, and March 26, 2014
Thomas Saving	June 9, 2014
José Scheinkman	March 13, 2014
George Shultz	May 22, 2013
Charles Schultze	July 9, 2013
Matthew Shapiro	November 14, 2013
William F. Sharpe	February 6, 2016
Robert Shiller	September 26, 2014
George Shultz	May 22, 2013
Jeremy Siegel	September 17, 2013
William E. (Bill) Simon Jr.	September 25, 2015
Thomas Simpson	May 9, 2013
Christopher Sims	March 15, 2013, and September 20, 2013
Allen Sinai	May 7, 2015
Peter Sinclair	November 13, 2014
Lord (Robert) Skidelsky	November 27, 2013
Robert Solow	December 2, 2013; December 31, 2013; July 7, 2014; and April 3, 2015
Aris Spanos	March 26, 2014
Ben Stein	March 18, 2015
Charles Steindel	December 3, 2015
Arlie Sterling	October 9, 2015
Max Steuer	December 8, 2015
Stephen Stigler	November 6, 2013
Houston Stokes	May 12, 2015
Lawrence Summers	November 22, 2013
Alexander Swoboda	September 10, 2014

Vito Tanzi	April 15, 2014
George Tauchen	November 13, 2014
John Taylor	July 2, 2013
Lester Telser	October 8, 2013, and November 18, 2014
A. P. (Tony) Thirlwall	October 1, 2013
Jim Thomas	January 7, 2015
Niels Thygesen	February 10, 2015
Nicolaus Tideman	May 15, 2015
Richard Timberlake	September 10, 2014
George Tolley	November 14, 2014
Juan J. Toribio	November 14, 2013
Robert Townsend	November 14, 2014
Stephen Turnovsky	April 28, 2014
Charles Upton	January 8, 2015
Gloria Valentine	April 1, 2013; May 8, 2013; and December 5, 2013
Paul Volcker	October 16, 2013
Michael Walker	June 21, 2013
Neil Wallace	March 15, 2013
T. Dudley Wallace	July 20, 2015
Kenneth Wallis	January 29, 2015
Glen Weyl	June 17, 2015
William R. (Bill) White	May 5, 2015
Donald Winch	September 22, 2014
Paul Wonnacott	May 12, 2014
Geoffrey Wood	November 14, 2013, and September 8, 2014
Clifford Wymer	April 17, 2014
Leland Yeager	August 8, 2013
Richard Zecher	September 3, 2013

In addition to the above, the author interviewed Milton Friedman, Phillip Cagan, John Scadding, and Sir Alan Walters (all in 1992); Anna Schwartz (in 1992 and 2003); and Alvin Marty (in 2008).

Conventions Used
in This Book

1. The chronological chapters in this book (those that cover blocks of years, i.e., chapters 2–4 and 10–15) are divided into sections titled "Events and Activities," "Issues," and "Personalities" (with the latter two sections in turn broken into subsections). The "Events and Activities" section covers some of Friedman's main engagements in economic debate over the years considered in the chapter; this section, however, omits those topics subsequently covered in the "Issues" and "Personalities" sections. The "Issues" sections cover major policy or research issues in which Friedman was involved during the years in question: for example, chapter 3, which covers the years 1940–43, includes under "Issues" the question of how to pay for wartime government spending. The "Personalities" section is of the same format as the "Issues" section, except that it is more closely focused on an individual with whom Friedman interacted (or to whom Friedman reacted) in the years covered in the chapter. In each case, no attempt is made to provide a complete picture of the work of the individual considered in the "Personalities" section. The aim of the discussion is, instead, to bring out the activities and work of Friedman that reflected his overlap of interests with the individual in question.

The motivation for the "Events and Activities"/"Issues"/"Personalities" division of each chapter is that Friedman's activities covered several different areas in each block of years considered. Consequently, an explicit demarcation of each chapter by topic seemed preferable to a strictly chronological format.

2. References are described in the past tense ("Romer and Romer [2002a] argued . . .") for publications that appeared during (or prior to) Friedman's lifetime, and in the present tense ("Romer and Romer [2013a] argue . . .") for post-2006 articles.[1] An exception to the latter practice is made for cases in which items published after 2006 were by authors who are now deceased (for example, Anna Schwartz and Gary Becker). In those cases, even post-2006 articles by the authors are referred to in the past tense.

3. Except when quoting others, or when using standard terminology (for example, "the Chicago School"), the term "Chicago," appearing by itself, refers to the city of Chicago. It is not used as shorthand for the University of Chicago.

4. Articles cited in this book that appeared in newspapers or news or public-affairs periodicals are referenced in the main text or endnotes by their publication title and date (for example, "*New York Times*, January 25, 1970"). Fuller bibliographical details for these articles (including article title and, where given, article author, as well as page number, where known) appear in section I of the bibliography, in which the news articles are listed in chronological order. (Section II of the bibliography covers books, as well as articles that were published in research journals. This section of the bibliography gives articles in alphabetical order, arranged by author.)

5. To limit the extent to which the flow of sentences in the main text is interrupted by bibliographical references, and to contain the number of times that the word "Friedman" appears in any sentence in the main text, citations of Friedman's writings appear in notes rather than in the main text. Accordingly, it is in the text of endnotes that one will find citation of the Friedman items to which reference is made in the main text (with such endnotes typically reading "See Friedman [(1973a, 1973b] . . ."). References to authors, other than Milton Friedman, with the surname Friedman are identified by both the author's first initial and surname.

6. Interviews conducted specifically for this book are indicated in the main text or endnotes by the name of the interview subject and the date of the interview. Interviews quoted or cited in the main text or endnotes that appeared in research journals are cited using the name of the interviewer (not the interviewee).[2] Thus, John Taylor's interview with Milton Friedman, published in 2001 in *Macroeconomic Dynamics*, is cited as Taylor (2001) and not as a Friedman-authored article.

PART 1

Friedman's Pre-monetarist Period, 1932 to 1950

CHAPTER 1

1942 and 1995

I. 1942

"Mr. Ruml, come up here and sit down, will you please? And everybody better move in a little closer." Senator Bennett Champ Clark, acting chairman of a subcommittee of the US Senate Committee on Finance, was opening a lightly attended hearing in room 312 of the Senate Office Building at 10 a.m. on August 19, 1942. Only two senators other than Clark were in attendance; they were outnumbered by the six witnesses for the session.[1] The first witness was Beardsley Ruml, of Macy's.[2] The second witness was Milton Friedman of the US Department of the Treasury.

Friedman, recently turned thirty, was appearing in his capacity as an economist in the US Treasury's Division of Tax Research. His location in that division of the Treasury meant that he could keep his distance from what he regarded as the less edifying activities in which the US Treasury was engaging during the war. In particular, Friedman, who had first cited Irving Fisher in print while he was in his midtwenties, looked askance at the debt-management activities of the Treasury, which included marketing bonds at 3 percent interest rates. Friedman would later recall being "shocked" at the ethics of presenting a 3 percent per year longer-term rate as a good investment when that rate was manifestly below the inflation rate likely to prevail for much of the investment horizon. Indeed, an appreciably positive real return on such an investment could realistically be expected only in the event of a serious postwar deflation—in the event, that is, of precisely the sort of postwar economic downturn that Friedman and his divi-

The views expressed in this study are those of the author alone and should not be interpreted as those of the Federal Reserve Board or the Federal Reserve System. The author received valuable comments on an earlier draft of this chapter from Miguel Acosta, George Fenton, Andrew Giffin, Herbert Grubel, Robert Hetzel, Douglas Irwin, the late Allan Meltzer, the late Julio Rotemberg, David Wilcox, and four anonymous reviewers. See the introduction for a full list of acknowledgments for this book. The author regrets to note that, in the period since the research for this chapter was conducted, Charles H. Brunie, whose interview with the author is drawn on below, has passed away.

sional colleagues' efforts were directed at avoiding. By confining himself to US Treasury activity that did not involve the bond drives, Friedman could, as he put it in one retrospective, "by my standards, be an honest man."[3]

Friedman had been asked to testify at the subcommittee's hearing, whose formal title was "Data Relative to Withholding Provisions of the 1942 Revenue Act" but whose content was better encapsulated by the shorthand title for the hearing, "Withholding Tax." Friedman and the higher-ranked Treasury official present, General Counsel Randolph Paul, were attending to give the Treasury's analysis of the "Ruml Plan"—a tax reform proposal that incorporated a move to withholding-at-source arrangements for income tax collection. The US Treasury would indeed come to introduce tax withholding during World War II. Friedman later noted that he "played a part in the United States in designing our system . . . and I may say my wife has never forgiven me."[4] But, as between different methods for withdrawing income at source, the Ruml Plan was not the Treasury's preferred template, and Friedman had been assigned the legwork of undertaking a detailed analysis of the Ruml Plan. Friedman's function at the hearing was to offer a critique of the Ruml Plan based on this analysis. Well before Friedman had been formally called as a witness, he jumped the gun with critical interjections during Ruml's testimony, leading Ruml to complain that Friedman's characterization of the plan was making it "sound more complicated than it is."[5]

Once Ruml had been excused as a witness, Senator Clark turned to the senior Treasury representative. "Mr. Paul, will you tell us about the effect on the revenue? We are all very much concerned about that." Paul replied, "Well, I think this estimate that has just been made by Mr. Friedman is pertinent, and I think he might be in a better position to summarize it than I. . . . Suppose you summarize that, Mr. Friedman."[6]

That was Friedman's cue to discuss the revenue effects of the Ruml Plan and to lay out the Treasury's proposed modification of it. The Treasury version of withholding, according to Friedman's projections, would yield more revenue than Ruml's proposal. Friedman's preamble to the presentation of numbers underscored the uncertainties involved in making projections: "it is awfully hard, now, to estimate what income will be in '44 and '45."[7] In subsequent decades, the degree of uncertainty associated with forecasts would be a recurring theme in Friedman's work on economic policy.

If that aspect of Friedman's testimony could be said to foreshadow his positions in subsequent years, just the opposite was true of a portion of his testimony that followed almost immediately. This occurred in an exchange with Senator Clark. Friedman clarified that in his estimates of revenue, he was counting income as having been collected as taxes the moment it was withdrawn at source by the employer, even if the funds had yet to be handed over to the Treasury. Friedman argued that "so long as the employers have withdrawn it . . . it is practically equivalent to having it in the Treasury." "So far as the employees are concerned, anyway," Clark observed. "And certainly so far as the inflationary problem is concerned," Friedman concurred.[8] Underlying this reply was the view that tax policy, by altering disposable income and thereby household spending, offered a way of controlling inflation. The reply thus bears unwitting testament to the distance that Friedman's thinking would later travel. In the years to come, few economists would be less enamored of the notion that consumer spending depends on current disposable income than Milton Friedman. And the position that tax increases were the key to restraining inflation would have no more prominent a critic than Milton Friedman.

II. 1995

Fifty-two and a half years later, Milton Friedman began his final testimony to a congressional committee hearing by observing: "I am delighted that the miracle of interactive TV enables me to be with the Committee when I could not be there physically."[9]

The occasion, as well as the committee's treatment of Friedman, now eighty-two, had a considerably grander scale than the hearing in 1942. In 1942, the session at which Friedman had testified had been of a small subcommittee, and he had been the junior Treasury representative; in 1995, he was testifying on his own at a full hearing of the Joint Economic Committee. His testimony, beamed into Washington from Friedman's location in the Bay Area, served to cap off the day's proceedings. This star treatment reflected the reality that a great deal had happened since Friedman's wartime days as a legman at the US Treasury. He had left the Treasury in 1943 and—consultancy work and positions on commissions and advisory boards aside—had never returned to government service after World War II. But his analysis of economic policy in the intervening five decades had had a profound effect in policy circles, and Friedman's fame preceded him when at this hearing, on January 20, 1995, he gave testimony on the Balanced Budget Amendment, the latest of many proposed constitutional amendments of that name.

Though ostensibly testifying in favor of the amendment, Friedman in his opening statement provided a clear demonstration of how far his position had shifted, since the 1940s, from a belief in the significance of the budget deficit. "The real problem, the basic problem, is not the deficit," Friedman testified. "The basic problem is government spending. . . . So the fundamental problem is, how do we get spending cut?"[10] In proceeding to answer that question, Friedman transitioned from his position about the economic effects of fiscal policy to his position on the policy maker re-action function. "History has shown us that under the present arrangements, government will spend whatever the tax system will raise, plus as much more as they think they can get away with. The only way to stop that is by making it hard to raise taxes."[11] Friedman had taken a long time to reach this position—which became familiar as the "starve-the-beast" view of government-spending determination, although Friedman himself rarely used that term. Until the early 1960s, he had viewed getting community acceptance of lower government spending as a necessary precondition for tax reduction. Since then, the evolution of his views about the relationship between deficit spending and monetary control, and about the dynamics of the fiscal policy process, had led him to a much more sanguine position regarding fiscal deficits.

Having made his opening statement, Friedman said: "I should be delighted to answer questions on anything at all."[12] In the spirit of that invitation, the final question posed to Friedman at the hearing, from Representative James Saxton, was not on the Balanced Budget Amendment but instead concerned the role of monetary policy. In his reply, Friedman stated: "The role of the Fed should be very simple—to stabilize the price level, prevent inflation."[13] In a sense, nobody had pushed this recommendation as much as Friedman had, and no one more deserved to be associated with it. Friedman's answer at the hearing nevertheless represented a step away from his most familiar prescription for monetary policy. It constituted a distinct change in emphasis from that in past statements—such as one in November 1958, when Friedman had characterized "the best policy we could follow at the present time" as one in which the Federal Reserve was instructed "that it has one job and one job only; namely, to see that the money supply or the stock of money in the United States rises by a fixed percentage annually."[14] At that time, unlike in 1995, Friedman had not been willing to have the Federal Reserve directly assigned responsibility for price-level developments.

III. The Challenge

The matter of whether the assignment to a central bank of responsibility for price stability should be regarded as discordant with, or an affirmation of, Friedman's long-standing position is not one on which economists agree. The disagreement on this matter illustrates the problem of providing a simple characterization of Friedman's status in the economics profession, and it underscores the dissent that exists about how to view his legacy. Friedman was one of several of his generation who came to be hailed for having made a lasting contribution to the way economists and policy makers view economic policy. But Friedman is the only one of these who has prompted such a distinct countermovement: there exists a very large number of articles downplaying his influence on modern economics and modern economic policy, or trying to establish that Friedman's economics was not internally consistent—especially if his popular and research writings are considered as a whole—or arguing that, even if consistent, his economic viewpoint should now be considered hopelessly outmoded or proven invalid.

The years highlighted in this chapter, 1942 and 1995, provide a useful contrast that is helpful for an evaluation of Friedman's contribution, influence, and legacy. In 1942 Friedman, although he had already gone on record with a string of publications, had yet to arrive at most of the positions on economic policy with which he would become associated. By 1995, on the other hand, Friedman had taken a back seat and had largely confined himself to occasional commentaries on current events.[15] In this capacity, he contributed observations that were often pointed and topical but, equally, were rarely a surprise to those familiar with his prior body of public statements. It is in the years between 1942 and 1995 that the development of Friedman's worldview, the crystallization of his economic analysis, and the heyday of his critique of economic policy are all to be found. A great deal of the challenge in analyzing Friedman's positions on economic matters lies in tracking the development of his positions over this period and in obtaining an accurate characterization of the economic framework to which Friedman converged.

By the early 1950s, the economics profession surely thought it knew the sort of work Friedman did and the direction in which his research was going. His work had had, by and large, a highly favorable reception—as reflected in the conferring, in 1951, of the John Bates Clark Medal to Friedman by the American Economic Association. On that occasion, the Clark medal had been awarded to an economist who had built bridges between mathematical statistics and economics and who had used statistical theory to generalize the analysis of utility to a world of uncertainty.[16] What caught Friedman's peers off guard is that, just as he was being awarded for these achievements, his research—together with, in large measure, his overall approach to economics—was changing direction. In effect, he gave up his old life as a distinguished mathematical statistician and contributor to price theory, instead venturing into the unpopular field of advocacy of the strong effectiveness of monetary policy. For good measure, he discarded much of the economic analysis to which he had adhered during his years at the US Treasury and that had been reflected in his research contributions to the Keynesian analysis of inflation. Indeed, he became a strong critic of those who stuck to that approach.

In Friedman's new research pursuits, his way of conducting empirical work eschewed large-scale econometric models and instead focused on reduced-form relationships among small numbers of variables and on inferences from historical episodes. On many occasions, he did not lay out an explicit model at all. An exception to this approach—his work on consumption—was well received in the profession, but it represented a separate enterprise from what he regarded as his main line of research.[17] Many terms were used to describe Friedman's new status within the economics profession—including iconoclast, intellectual provocateur, and resident critic—but that these terms needed to be used at all was testament to Friedman's newfound estrangement from his own profession. From being hailed in the Clark award for his "most significant contribution to economic thought and knowledge," Friedman had experienced a remarkably rapid decline in prestige among his fellow economists.[18]

That prestige would be regained in due course, on the basis of his later body of work, but it would be a long time coming. By the end of the 1950s, Friedman had been publishing for nearly a quarter century and had been working continuously in the monetary field for a decade, but he was perceived as having taken a wayward path and encountered resistance and suspicion. Sam Peltzman, a student in Friedman's Price Theory class at the University of Chicago in 1960–61, recalls that Friedman's image at this point was that of a "nut" (Sam Peltzman, interview, March 1, 2013). Correspondingly, Davis (1969, 119) noted that, as strong proponents of money materialized with Friedman in the lead, "economists regarded this group—when they regarded it at all—as a mildly amusing, not quite respectable collection of eccentrics." But, by virtue of stubborn perseverance, reflected in a prolific research output, Friedman's work maintained some kind of profile in the economics profession, and it did so via a number of routes: by informal circulation of manuscripts after rough-and-ready mimeograph or stencil reproduction, by printed articles in University of Chicago Press publications and a few other outlets, by congressional testimony, and by the hitting of the seminar circuit by himself and a small band of students and associates. Friedman also continued his practice, begun during World War II, of advocating market solutions to popular audiences. A national radio discussion program on which he appeared sporadically had stopped in 1955, but he used other outlets: op-ed writing, television appearances, and public-speaking tours.

A turning point came in the early 1960s with the appearance of Friedman's *Capitalism and Freedom* and Friedman and Anna Schwartz's *A Monetary History of the United States*.[19] These books, published in 1962 and 1963, respectively, but largely reflecting work done in the 1950s, became essential parts of the Friedman canon on monetarism (in the case of *A Mone-*

tary History) and market economics (which, despite some coverage of his monetary work, formed the bulk of *Capitalism and Freedom*). Friedman over the 1960s hit his stride with what one periodical later called "a prolific outpouring of books, pamphlets, papers and popular articles" (*National Journal*, January 13, 1973). The 1960s closed with Friedman on the front cover of *Time* magazine—notwithstanding Friedman being a columnist for the rival magazine *Newsweek*.[20] Friedman's higher profile was reflected also in the *New York Times*: having declined to review *Capitalism and Freedom* in 1962, that newspaper ended up devoting a large amount of column inches to Friedman over the subsequent decades, with a long profile of Friedman appearing in 1970 (*New York Times*, January 25, 1970). Likewise, a great number of pages of economics journals in the 1960s and 1970s came to be devoted to debating Friedman's views. And in the quarter century from 1962 to 1986, not a year passed in which a new book by Friedman did not appear.[21]

Friedman wrote prolifically—and yet he produced nothing that consolidated his views into a single definitive statement. This is true even if one leaves to one side Friedman's monetary work and considers solely his position on free markets. Friedman would irreverently say that *Capitalism and Freedom* was the Old Testament and the book version of *Free to Choose* was the New Testament.[22] But these books were not by any means the entirety of the Friedman canon on market economics and did not distill all the major messages contained in that larger body of work. Indeed, Friedman's views on many public policy issues cannot be coaxed out of these volumes. Many important aspects of Friedman's market economics were scattered across other books and articles, in both popular and research outlets, as well as in interviews and speeches, and an integrated picture of his views on nonmonetary economic issues is obtainable only after pooling and synthesizing these various writings.

Friedman's statements of his monetary position took an even more scattered form. Although monetary economics was his area of specialty, the only textbook (actually, lecture notes turned into prose) he produced was outside that field—although, consistent with his view of the interconnections between different fields of economics, that text, *Price Theory*, did trespass on some areas of monetary economics, especially in its revised edition.[23] But Friedman produced no comprehensive statement on his position: no monograph that could be regarded as a compendium of his monetary views.[24] An implicit economic model underlay Friedman and Schwartz's *Monetary History*, but a systematic theoretical statement was notably absent from their study.[25] Friedman's 1969 book *The Optimum Quantity of Money* was said on the dust jacket of its first edition to be a "comprehensive presentation of the body of monetary thought of one of the world's leading monetary economists," a description that failed to make clear that the book consisted mostly of reprints, and also a description that conflicts with the fact that key aspects of Friedman's monetary thought were to be found in items not in the collection.[26] The comprehensive-sounding "A Theoretical Framework for Monetary Analysis" Friedman article of 1970 proved, in fact, to be far from comprehensive, its focus being mainly on a narrow set of aggregate-supply issues and on economic behavior in depression conditions, to the exclusion of a more general presentation of Friedman's framework.[27] Indeed, that 1970 exposition proved so lacking in comprehensiveness that Friedman had to add some new paragraphs to a reprint to make its coverage of aggregate-demand determination somewhat more complete, while Bernanke (2004), in a speech entitled "Friedman's Monetary Framework: Some Lessons," chose a *different* 1970 Friedman article to stand in as the encapsulation of Friedman's framework.[28]

There is no escaping the conclusion that Friedman often made his readers work hard to track down his views on key subjects—a tendency reflected in Harry Johnson's (1974, 346) reference to Friedman's "lifelong habit of scattering his new empirical results and ideas in unlikely places."

Yet despite the seemingly haphazard and scattered fashion in which it was placed into the public record, a clear Friedman position did emerge. And that position in turn changed the views of the economics profession. Consequently, notwithstanding the fact that Friedman never wrote a textbook in the monetary field, his contributions to that field succeeded in rendering obsolete the coverage of monetary matters provided in textbooks written before the 1970s. The textbooks emerging from the economics department of the Massachusetts Institute of Technology (MIT) provide a microcosm of this phenomenon. From its initial edition in 1948 suggesting the powerlessness of monetary policy in Great Depression–like circumstances, Paul Samuelson's celebrated textbook *Economics* had in successive editions assigned incrementally greater importance for monetary policy, leading Friedman in the early 1970s to suggest that a comparison of "the first edition and the eighth or ninth edition of the leading economic principles book" would bring out the scale of the change in Samuelson's position.[29]

Samuelson nevertheless tried to hold the line against Friedman's research: while Friedman's work on the consumption function was rapidly integrated into the book's presentations, Samuelson would largely refrain from making other concessions to Friedman's framework. His textbook in its 1970s editions continued to reject the primacy of monetary policy for inflation determination while also reaffirming the notion of a long-run nonvertical Phillips curve. In 1978, Samuelson's coverage of monetary issues was left in the dust by the appearance of the first edition of the textbook

Macroeconomics by his MIT colleagues Rudiger Dornbusch and Stanley Fischer. Dornbusch and Fischer copiously cited Friedman's research and popular writings, and they incorporated large amounts of his analysis into their presentation, observing: "Much of the analysis of this book would, a few years ago, have been considered monetarist."[30] Dornbusch and Fischer's saturation coverage of Friedman's work was reflected in their book's index, for which the entry for Friedman ran ten lines. In contrast, the one-line index entry for Samuelson recorded only a solitary page reference.[31]

As of 1986, Milton Friedman had been publishing research articles for over fifty years and regarded his scope to make further contributions as largely exhausted: "people's capacities to do scientific work decline with age" (*Los Angeles Times*, December 14, 1986, 14). But his influence continued to make itself felt in the agenda of the economics profession, as evidenced by two landmark articles appearing that year. An article by Olivier Blanchard of MIT and Lawrence Summers of Harvard University, "Hysteresis and the European Unemployment Problem," was used to launch the new journal *NBER Macroeconomics Annual*. The opening of Blanchard and Summers's article noted "the premise of most macroeconomic theories that there exists some 'natural' or 'non-accelerating inflation' rate of unemployment toward which the economy tends to gravitate and at which the level of inflation remains constant."[32] In effect, the authors were using as their jumping-off point a consensus grounded in Friedman's work—and the contribution of that work now so permeated the discourse of economics that Blanchard and Summers did not actually cite or mention Friedman in their article.[33]

Another prominent 1986 article, authored by Ben Bernanke of Princeton University and titled "Alternative Explanations of the Money-Income Correlation," prepared for the Carnegie-Rochester Conference series, made overt its connections with Friedman's work. "By now it should be unnecessary to motivate a study of the statistical correlation between the money stock and national income," Bernanke observed at the beginning of his article. "At least since the work of Friedman and Schwartz (1963[a]), this stylized fact has been considered among the most important in macroeconomics; at times, its explication has nearly defined the field."[34]

Friedman had also helped shape the terms of the debate even in fields outside his own area of specialty. He was not a specialist in international economics. Yet, in a 1953 article that applied his monetary analysis to the field of international monetary arrangements, he had set out the definitive case for floating exchange rates.[35] That paper achieved immortality in the research literature on international economics. Furthermore, as of 1995, floating exchange rates had been part of everyday reality for over two decades—a clear-cut example of one of Friedman's recommendations being put into practice. By 1995, a number of the arguments Friedman had made for floating rates—that they would not be associated with large short-term capital flows, that they would discourage destabilizing speculation, that they would imply instability of exchange rates only if internal economic policies were unstable—had fallen by the wayside, as experience with floating rates had rendered these arguments fragile if not outright untenable. But the paramount argument in Friedman's advocacy of floating rates—that they alone gave a country the wherewithal to follow policies directed at domestic economic stabilization—had proved durable, and it underpinned the consensus in favor of floating exchange rates that, by the end of the twentieth century, was entrenched across the English-speaking world.

Friedman was by his own description "a rank amateur in the field of labor economics."[36] But that did not prevent him from laying out, in two crucial paragraphs of the 1962 edition of *Price Theory*, the notion of intertemporal substitution in labor that became a cornerstone of the modern literature on labor supply.[37] And, in other writings, Friedman propagated and developed terms and concepts that would pervade the idiom of labor economics: human capital; the natural rate of unemployment.[38] The latter term became a staple also of monetary economics. So did another word—"monetarism." This was not a term that Friedman coined, and it was one that he claimed to dislike. But it became almost synonymous with him.

These terms moved outside academic economics, coming into use in broader public discussion. Friedman himself likewise acquired a fame that eventually stretched outside the economics profession. Anna Schwartz has observed that when she first met Friedman, "he had not yet become a world celebrity. What has always fascinated me about Milton's life is how and why this transformation occurred."[39] It is little wonder that Schwartz had cause to reflect on these questions: one of the reasons her final book with Friedman—*Monetary Trends in the United States and the United Kingdom*, the capstone of their work on money—came out nearly twenty years after *Monetary History* is because Friedman was so frequently tied up with other activities in the intervening years, including hosting a television series. Friedman's status as a celebrity was acknowledged in the structure that Alan Walters chose for his entry on Friedman in the 1987 *New Palgrave* economics dictionary: Walters ended with a section titled "The Public Image of Friedman."[40]

That public image was so prominent from the 1970s onward that references to Friedman could be found in the most incongruous locations. In the first half of the 1980s, mentions of Friedman appeared not only in books and journals in the economics field, but also in books with such titles as *The*

Secret Life of Girls and *The Year in Rock 1981–82* and in periodicals such as *Car and Driver* and *Professional Engineer*.[41] Friedman was interviewed by *Playboy* magazine and *People Weekly* in the 1970s, while in the 1980s *Penthouse* magazine included him in a profile of the twenty-five most influential Americans.[42] On one surreal evening in Los Angeles in 1977, Friedman shared the platform of an awards ceremony with John Wayne and Frank Sinatra.[43] And while James Tobin could claim to have been immortalized in fiction well ahead of Friedman—as Herman Wouk had put a character who was based on, and a near-namesake of, Tobin into his novel *The Caine Mutiny*—Friedman's eminence would reach such a degree that he found himself written into the story lines of television series. An early installment of the situation comedy *Family Ties*, an episode regarded as setting the seal on Michael J. Fox's status as the star of that program, made Friedman a character in the story line, not seen on-screen but weaved heavily into the narrative.[44] In the mid-1990s, a recurring on-screen character in *Beverly Hills 90210* was clearly modeled after Friedman; and just in case the inspiration for the character wasn't clear enough, the program's writers gave the character the name "Milton."

Friedman's fame also stretched beyond the frontiers of the United States. A London newspaper in the 1980s noted of Friedman and John Kenneth Galbraith that "both achieved a superstar status in Europe that far exceeded their celebrity at home" (*Daily Telegraph*, June 30, 1986).[45] Friedman's international impact was felt in a string of books cataloguing his various tours—including *Milton Friedman in Australia 1975*, *Milton Friedman in South Africa*, and *Friedman in China*—whose titles might leave the uninitiated under the impression that he was a travel writer rather than an economist.[46] Friedman spoke on these tours about both monetary policy and on markets, and a University of Chicago faculty member, Sam Peltzman, has judged that Friedman became a better-known advocate of free markets than Hayek as well as the world face of the Chicago School (Sam Peltzman, interview, March 1, 2013).

Friedman's image on the national and world stage was not only as an abstract thinker and advocate of reform but also as an academic willing to engage in current economic commentary. Friedman's various economic commentaries utilized and illuminated his economic framework. His opposition to the imposition in 1971 of wage and price controls by the Nixon administration contrasted with the endorsement of that move given by Paul Samuelson and others. In late 1976, Friedman stuck his neck out again when, against a background of placid inflation projections from professional economic forecasters, and with bond market indicators suggesting blue skies ahead on the inflation front, he predicted that inflation would shortly start rising again and that 7 to 9 percent inflation could be expected over 1977 and 1978. In late 1977, again well ahead of the bond market and other forecasts, he further indicated that a return of inflation to the double-digit range was in prospect for 1979 and 1980. These judgments about inflation prospects would, like Friedman's opposition to wage/price controls, be vindicated. But a string of serious overpredictions of inflation in the 1980s did little to enhance his reputation.[47]

Those well-publicized errors reinforced the difficulties that his fellow economists had always had in reaching an overall assessment of Friedman. His status in the profession was paradoxical and ambiguous, even after his monetary work had given him unquestioned prominence. He was not "an economist's economist," notwithstanding Samuelson's and John Taylor's use of that description in their tributes to Friedman, if that term implies that Friedman provided a template that the economics profession could follow.[48] Quite the contrary: no one who eschewed explicit mathematical modeling so much could claim to be setting the pattern for a profession in which formal models were used by so many. Likewise, Friedman could not claim, despite his empirical orientation and his work on methodology, to have led the way in which the profession carried out empirical work; he had forgone any claim to that mantle via his distrust of large-scale econometric models and his aversion, especially after the 1940s, to formal testing and forecasting techniques. Friedman was one of the most read academic economists among business and financial market economists, and he played a key role in promoting the development of futures markets and markets for indexed government securities. But Friedman had disdain for what he called "the jargon of Wall Street."[49] This perspective, combined with his position that financial markets were often shortsighted—not to mention his contention that research in finance could barely be considered economics—set Friedman apart from the mainstream of economists in the financial markets and in the nonfinancial private sector.

Yet the outstanding fact remains that Friedman had a profound effect on economics, an effect felt not only throughout discussions in present-day textbooks but also in the shaping of the modern economics agenda. He was at the center of economic debates in research and policy circles in the 1960s and 1970s. Subsequently, as already indicated, the Friedman and Friedman-Schwartz positions played a large role in shaping the terms of economists' debates on real business cycle theory, New Keynesian economics, monetary policy rules, and the vector-autoregression analysis of monetary policy. An upshot of this was that in the 1980s and 1990s Friedman and his writings were mentioned prominently in a large number of leading research articles—the bulk of which Friedman probably never read. By this stage, Friedman did not have to participate to make his presence felt in the debates. His earlier writings had left an enduring imprint.

But deciphering that imprint in detail is not a straightforward undertaking. Naturally, with Friedman having produced such a vast amount of work over a long career, not every contribution he made to the public record proved to be enduring. In some cases, the fading into obscurity of certain contributions no doubt reflects a negative judgment on the merits of those particular efforts. In this vein, McCallum (1990a, 167) argued that with respect to some of the Friedman contributions that are little cited in the modern literature, "this neglect is probably warranted." But a corollary of the fact that Friedman's writings and statements were so voluminous and so widely dispersed is that much of his work has become largely unknown. This was a sore point for Friedman, who cited an example of a paper that he regarded as an important contribution but that had "sunk into complete oblivion."[50] And even in the cases of work of Friedman's that is unambiguously well known, it seems evident that there remains a large amount of misinterpretation and misunderstanding of that work on the part of the economics profession—a situation that may in part account for the considerable disagreement about Friedman's legacy.

The scale of the task involved in ascertaining Friedman's economics and in evaluating his legacy is underlined by considering the seemingly contrasting facts about Friedman and the perceptions to which they gave rise. Friedman was a student of business cycles who was prone to say that he did not believe there was a business cycle. He was a trenchant critic of reserve requirements as a monetary policy tool and a strong advocate of financial deregulation, yet he had many favorable things to say about moving to a regime of 100 percent reserve requirements. He stressed the looseness of the relationship between money and the economy, yet critics saw his policy prescriptions as predicated on a tight relationship. He criticized in detail the way the Federal Reserve allowed the money stock to adjust to the state of the economy, yet he was often characterized as treating empirical money-stock behavior as exogenous. He made fundamental contributions to the development of Phillips-curve theory, yet he was averse to conducting discussion of inflation prospects using Phillips-curve analysis.[51] He spent much of his first two decades as a researcher working on labor unions and the use of market power in setting prices, yet for the subsequent five decades he found himself accused by critics of predicating his economic analysis on an atomistic labor market, a one-good model, or perfectly competitive firms. He was a strong advocate of free markets, and consequently he was frequently portrayed as an apologist for greed, yet he also said that the problem of any society was to find arrangements that kept greed in check. He authored highly cited journal articles and several leading books in economic research, yet in debates with other researchers he was quite likely to point to one of his newspaper op-eds, a *Newsweek* column, a pamphlet, or an obscure speech for documentation of a position he was taking. He lived to see the day when policy makers' views on monetary policy reflected his influence more than they did that of any other person. Yet at the same time he would watch the study of money-stock behavior become peripheral to both the analysis and making of monetary policy, with the consideration of the role of money in monetary policy a more desolate pursuit than it had ever been earlier in his lifetime.

We are therefore confronted with someone whose way of thinking about the economy contained many easily overlooked and easily misunderstood subtleties, a problem compounded by the fact that Friedman was not given to consolidating his views into a single publication. Friedman's views require sifting through and organization if they are to be treated as an overall body of thought. Yet once this is done, the framework that emerges is internally consistent. As Friedman put it in describing his monetary work: "The picture as a whole, as I see it, fits together."[52] It is possible to reconcile Friedman's statements in various outlets, and the result of considering them as a group yields insights not available from considering each in isolation. The contradictions in his writings that have been alleged over the years reflect, to some extent, the development of Friedman's views: most notably, Friedman's monetary position did not crystallize into its recognizable monetarist form until the early 1950s. Other apparent contradictions prove not to be so, instead forming compatible pieces of Friedman's worldview.

To ascertain this worldview, one cannot just skim the surface. Friedman's major works are and should be the focus. But a focus is not the same thing as tunnel vision, and we miss a great amount of fleshing out of details, clarifications, and insights if we neglect the more obscure material available in the Friedman canon. As Friedman's own frequent recourse to little-known items in his catalogue of writings illustrates, one needs to cast a very wide net over Friedman's publications, interviews, and other public statements to obtain the complete picture of his conceptual framework. As already indicated, considering little-known items helps draw out his views on issues not covered in his major writings. Just as Friedman's major and minor works gel together, so, too, his popular and research writings can and should be treated as of a piece. Friedman's view of monetary economics is an intricately woven and cohesive tapestry, every stitch of which requires attention.

Friedman's vision of microeconomics—or, as he preferred to call it, price theory—is consistent with his view of monetary economics. But his positive economics in the microeconomics field did not amount to a challenge to the professional mainstream in the way that his monetary work did. Friedman regarded microeconomic theory as more settled than macroeconomic theory, and his work in the former area reflected this view.[53] He was perceived as a critic of the theory of imperfect competition, but even here his disagreement largely amounted to a resistance to the notion that the advent of a detailed theory of imperfect competition implied that the prior body of price theory needed to be thrown out.[54] Indeed, his own view of how monetary policy worked its way through the economy would involve synthesizing some of the features stressed by writers on imperfect competition, notably the notion that many firms were price setters rather than price takers.

The normative side of Friedman's approach to microeconomics—his advocacy of free markets—was something that Friedman prided on being separable from his monetary analysis.[55] Economists could and did accept many of Friedman's propositions about the Phillips curve, the potency of monetary policy, and the desirability of a rule-based framework for monetary policy without subscribing to the chapter and verse of Friedman's recommendations concerning the role of government in labor and goods markets. Friedman's free-market advocacy and his monetary analysis did intersect on such matters as the desirability of flexible exchange rates and the case against wage and price controls; in addition, his argument for monetary rules rested on confidence in the market system, for he saw rules as providing a stable background against which the private sector could make decisions. But the positions that Friedman took on monetary policy did amount to granting a major role for government: he had little sympathy for proposals for private-sector-issued currency, and his perception that the government's monetary responsibilities went beyond its provision of currency was manifested in his and Schwartz's citation of the absence of an official rescue of the Bank of United States in 1930 as a major policy mistake, and in his endorsement of the official rescue of Continental Illinois Bank in 1984.

Outside the monetary sphere, Friedman was far less enamored of government intervention. This standpoint stemmed partly from a strong philosophical dislike of anything that could be regarded as paternalism by the government. However, much of his free-market advocacy can be viewed as stemming from his theoretical framework. In particular, two cases in which Friedman took a far more libertarian line than that of the general community and most economists—Social Security and consumer protection—can be regarded as stemming from an underlying model that includes his proposed consumption function: a model in which the bulk of the population is well approximated as highly informed, long-horizon households. In such a setting, the market failures cited as the basis for mandatory retirement plans and product-safety regulations are likely to figure less prominently. Friedman did, however, recognize the existence of externalities and accepted them in principle as the basis for government action, while remaining skeptical in many cases about whether government intervention would succeed in producing a better outcome. One instance in which he conceded a role for government was in the area of environmental protection. Here, Friedman took what was, for economists, a highly conventional position, as he advocated a Pigovian tax on pollution. In some areas, such as antitrust policy, disillusionment with government regulation made Friedman take a less interventionist posture over time. In the area of health insurance, however, Friedman would become persuaded by the early 1990s that the laissez-faire position that he initially took was no longer tenable.

To distill and systematize Friedman's conceptual framework, covering both monetary and price-theoretical matters, is a major aim of the present study. This book will reassemble, interpret, and reconcile Friedman's scattered writings and statements, using them to lay out Friedman's theory and to place his work in the context of both other economists' work and historical developments. And, having ascertained that worldview, one needs to examine very broadly both the economic-research literature and the historical record to get an accurate picture of Friedman's activities and influence. It is the aim of the present volume to accomplish this task, too. In sum, this study aims to construct a composite picture of Friedman's theoretical positions and policy conclusions and to show how these informed his interactions with both other economists and policy makers and shaped his commentary on economic policy in the United States.

Much of the period considered in this study is bracketed by the 1942 and 1995 points that began this chapter. But the narrative of this study begins earlier than 1942—specifically in 1932, when Friedman completed undergraduate study—and ends earlier than 1995—specifically at the end of 1972, by which time Friedman had completed his principal research contributions.

The 1930s represent both the decade in which Friedman entered the world of economics and a period that his later research studied in detail. That decade is covered in the next chapter. Chapter 3 covers 1940 to 1943, while chapter 4 considers 1944 to 1950, the years that constitute the transitional period of Friedman's thinking, especially with regard to monetary matters. Then part 2 steps back and analyzes, in chapters 5 through 9, Friedman's economic framework, which had largely emerged by 1951 and which formed the basis for Friedman's work on economic matters for the rest of his life. Then part 3, spanning chapters 10 (in volume 1) and chapters 11 to 15 (the whole of volume 2), considers US economic debate, and Friedman's participation in it, in the years from 1951 to 1972—the first two decades of Friedman's "monetarist period."

· CHAPTER 2 ·

Starting Out,
1932 to 1939

I. Events and Activities, 1932–39

Appearing on the television talk show *Donahue* in 1984, Milton Friedman faced a hostile question from a member of the studio audience, who cast doubt on his credentials for making recommendations about the financing of university education. "I think you're a bit out of touch," the audience member stated. "Because when you were in college or you received your scholarship, more than likely your father could pay his mortgage and your mother stayed at home. In today's economy, it takes two people working— just to keep up."

Although his facial expression during the question registered anger, Friedman delivered most of his reply in a nearly flat tone. "First of all, you're quite wrong about myself," he responded. "My parents were very poor; they never had an income which today would qualify as [above] poverty. My father died when I was fifteen. My mother supported the family thereafter by running a small retail store. . . . I never got a penny from my parents. I worked my way through college. . . . I went to college between 1929 and 1932, the greatest depression in our history."[1]

Friedman's undergraduate years had been at Rutgers University, New Jersey—his studies there commencing in 1928, rather than the 1929 date that he implied in his television appearance.[2] The degree was a bachelor of arts.[3] In the course of his study for this degree, Friedman initially majored in mathematics, then added an economics major, taking his first economics courses in 1930 and 1931.[4] As he later described things, however, Friedman envisioned a career in actuarial studies, involving "a lot of fancy mathe-

The views expressed in this study are those of the author alone and should not be interpreted as those of the Federal Reserve Board or the Federal Reserve System. The author thanks Miguel Acosta, William A. Allen, Michael Bordo, Andrew Giffin, Douglas Irwin, David Laidler, Ann-Marie Meulendyke, Gerald O'Driscoll, Michael Parkin, Julio Rotemberg, and Rajat Sood for comments on an earlier draft of this chapter, and Ricardo Nunes for useful conversations on subjects covered in this chapter. See the introduction for a full list of acknowledgments for this book.

matics."[5] When in 1987 he looked back on this plan, it was with scorn. That scorn most likely did not reflect a negative judgment on the idea of a career outside economics. On the contrary, in the 1980s Friedman conjectured that he might well have equally enjoyed a non-economics career (G. Martin 1983, 53). More probably, his retrospective attitude toward his early career plans was an outgrowth of Friedman's disdain, by 1987, for mathematical sophistication.

Friedman's experience at Rutgers University would not lead him away from mathematical modeling—that shift would instead take decades to occur—but did switch him from actuaries to economics as a career. The instructors whom Friedman would repeatedly cite as focusing him on economics were two of his teachers at Rutgers University: Arthur Burns—about whom more presently—and Homer Jones. Jones had a temporary teaching job at the Rutgers University economics department.[6]

Friedman took several courses with Jones, including in insurance and statistics.[7] Jones would have a meager output of credited research publications in economics but could claim to have helped set in motion two key elements of the postwar monetarist juggernaut. The first of these was Friedman himself. Jones was a not-yet-graduated student of the University of Chicago.[8] He therefore had connections with the economics department, and Friedman would credit Jones both with encouraging Friedman to take graduate study in economics at the University of Chicago, and with writing a recommendation that helped secure Friedman's admission.[9] The second monetarist institution influenced by Jones was the Federal Reserve Bank of St. Louis, which became the principal voice of monetarism within the Federal Reserve System during Jones's years (1958 to 1971) as the bank's research director.[10] In recognition of Jones's dual roles, Friedman would later give two public tributes to Jones after Jones's retirement. One was an article in the *Journal of Monetary Economics* in 1976 that mainly concerned Jones's teaching years. The other tribute was a lunch talk Friedman gave at a Federal Reserve Bank of St. Louis conference in 1984, in which Friedman concentrated on Jones's contribution to monetary policy discussions in the Federal Reserve System (R. W. Hafer, interview, August 29, 2013).

The connection with Arthur Burns also stretched beyond Friedman's Rutgers University years. Indeed, Friedman went so far as to describe Burns in his memoirs as a "surrogate father" over much of his career— even though Burns was slightly less than eight years older than Friedman.[11] Burns's involvement in Friedman's life after undergraduate study included having Friedman on the National Bureau of Economic Research (NBER) staff from 1937 to 1940, heavy interaction with Friedman during Friedman's PhD dissertation work through the mid-1940s, and service once more as one of Friedman's employers when, from the late 1940s to the late

1960s, Burns, on and off, headed the NBER during Friedman's renewed affiliation with the institution. Later still, Friedman had a professional affiliation of sorts with Burns when Friedman served as an academic consultant to the Federal Reserve Board during Burns's tenure as Board chairman from 1970 to 1978. A far more prominent aspect of his relations with Burns during those years, however, was the severe criticism of Burns's monetary policy that Friedman gave in his *Newsweek* column and other public outlets.

The Problem of Establishing Early Influences on Friedman

The presence of figures such as Burns and Jones in Friedman's undergraduate education makes it tempting to see all kinds of anticipations of Friedman's later monetary work in his undergraduate activities. That temptation should be resisted. Friedman's focus on money from the late 1940s onward represented a break from his prior interests and, as suggested in chapter 1, it clearly reflected a largely different mindset from that he had in the 1930s.[12]

The existence of that break in Friedman's views has to be coupled with another caveat. This is that, in considering the influence of Friedman's teachers on his development as an economist, it is important to be on guard against generalities. Generalities on this matter have been prevalent in previous studies of Friedman's views. For example, one of the earliest accounts, Breit and Ransom (1971, 226), listed a number of Rutgers University and University of Chicago economics teachers alongside the attributes that Breit and Ransom alleged that Friedman acquired from each, stating, for example, "From Simons and Knight, he developed his philosophy of classical liberalism." Over the years Friedman himself would, in paying tribute to his teachers, occasionally attribute some broad characteristic of his own approach to a particular instructor. But on other occasions he was more cautious, warning that "no man can say precisely whence his beliefs and his values come."[13] In the same vein, Friedman also observed that he could not say with confidence what had been the main influences on his thinking (G. Martin 1983, 50–51). Friedman no doubt did assimilate many different influences. But to regard, in the manner of the Breit-Ransom account just quoted, anyone, Friedman included, as having acquired characteristic A from individual X, characteristic B from individual Y, and characteristic C from individual Z, as though taking items from a menu, does not seem plausible as a description of how a real person's views evolve.[14]

Some idea of the problems and ambiguities involved in attempting to establish a direct lineage between Friedman's views and those of his teachers is brought out by running ahead of our story somewhat and considering the case of Jacob Viner, one of Friedman's teachers at the University of

Chicago in the 1932–33 academic year. In his belief in the scope for monetary expansion to revive the economy in the 1930s and in being critical of Keynes's *General Theory*, Viner was an antecedent of Friedman. Friedman emphasized this point in 1972 when he stated that the impact in the 1930s of the *General Theory* was muted for "those of us who had sat at the feet of Simons, Mints, Knight, and Viner."[15] These University of Chicago economists had emphasized deficient aggregate demand as a key problem in the 1930s. On this matter, therefore, the *General Theory* did not amount to a challenge to the view prevailing among key University of Chicago economists. Where these economists differed with Keynes was on whether monetary expansion had been discredited as a means of providing stimulus.[16] The upshot was that Friedman would characterize his teachers, especially Viner, as having been broadly correct in their analysis of the Great Depression.

At the same time, however, it would not seem appropriate to conclude that Friedman simply absorbed Viner's analysis as a student and elaborated on it when the Depression became a key research interest of his own. On the contrary, there is evidence that Friedman was not someone who kept close tabs on Viner's monetary writings. Only in retrospect did Friedman appreciate the strength of the links between Viner's arguments in the 1930s and those in the Friedman-Schwartz *Monetary History* of 1963. It was not until the early 1970s that Friedman reread Viner (1933) and, upon noting the similarities with the *Monetary History*, was prompted to observe that he was "embarrassed that we [he and Schwartz] made no reference to it in our account."[17]

Nor is there a seamless link between Viner and Friedman when it comes to views about market economics. Viner and Friedman were both admirers of Adam Smith, but Viner made observations on Smith that would be greatly at variance with Friedman's interpretation of Smith. For example, Viner (1927) made the observation that businessmen favored free markets in general but wanted government privileges in their own industry. Here Viner anticipated a complaint Friedman himself frequently made about the business community.[18] But Viner (1927, 219) went on to say that Adam Smith also was "fully capable of this type of inconsistency," which contrasted with Friedman's own interpretation of Smith as offering a consistent approach to economic matters except in very specific areas such as usury.[19] Likewise, Viner (1927) has been cited as a key reference supportive of the view that Smith was not an advocate of economic liberalism, and as such Viner's work is at odds with Friedman's interpretation of Adam Smith.[20]

As these examples show, Friedman's own reading evidently led him to dissent in important respects from the interpretations and positions advanced by his teachers.

Indeed, in the present writer's judgment, a strong emphasis on teachers as influences is greatly inconsistent with the sizable role that the written word tends to play in the shaping of a researcher's views. While Friedman in a CSPAN interview weighted the role of living people somewhat above books in his assessment of people's process of education, he added: "Books influence you. There's no doubt about it. They make a great difference."[21] To take one example of the role that printed material played in the formation of Friedman's thinking: Friedman's own written output in the 1930s referred to the "admiration for Professor Pigou's work which I share with all students of economics," and he never met Pigou.[22]

Even if we take Friedman's glowing testimonials to his teachers literally, we do not thereby obtain a satisfactory basis for ascertaining his influences. In 1976 Friedman credited Burns and Jones with "opening my eyes to the broader reaches of economics and to the beauties and intricacies of economic theory."[23] Consider, however, his 1967 recollection of Jacob Viner's graduate course in economic theory at the University of Chicago: "This opened my eyes to a world I had not realized existed. I was made aware of both the beauty and the power of formal economic theory."[24] The quotation regarding Viner has the effect of throwing into question the credit that Friedman gave to Burns and Jones.

Further doubt on the extent to which Burns and Jones shaped Friedman's economics is cast by Anna Schwartz's judgment concerning Friedman: "Only as a graduate student did he discover economics as an empire to be conquered."[25] Schwartz really should have said "focus on" rather than "discover," as Friedman did, of course, study economics in his undergraduate years, and his decision to pursue economics as a career was, after all, embedded in his taking graduate study at the University of Chicago. Furthermore, at his graduation ceremony at Rutgers University, Friedman, while receiving the Bradley Mathematical Prize, was also commended for "honors in special subjects," the special subject in his case being economics (*New York Times*, June 11, 1932). And, as noted, Friedman gave credit to Burns and Jones for setting him on the path of graduate economics study and, in Jones's case, for helping arrange his scholarship for graduate studies at the University of Chicago.[26] But Schwartz's observation deserves weight, especially as it is buttressed by Friedman's own statement that, as late as his undergraduate period, "I never dreamed I'd go into economics" (in *Philadelphia Sunday Bulletin*, March 2, 1975) and his observation that, notwithstanding Jones's and Burns's influence, even in 1932 he still felt tempted to pursue an education and career in a non-economics field.[27] Taken together, these statements underscore the messages that one should not overemphasize Burns's and Jones's role in shaping Friedman's economics, and that one should be vigilant against accepting every particular of the generous testimonials Friedman provided about them and other teachers in later years. Consistent with this judgment, Joseph Burns (personal communication, December 18, 2014) has expressed the view that his father's principal impact on Friedman during Friedman's years at Rutgers University was in steering him toward economics. Joseph Burns downplayed Burns's role, in those years, in shaping Friedman's specific positions on subjects in economics.

It seems much more fruitful, instead of making generalizations about individuals' influences, to identify specific, concrete issues on which Friedman's views seemed to reflect the mark of an early teacher. The principal aim in this book's treatment of the matter will be to isolate cases in which Friedman's position on a *particular* issue reflected and echoed (or, in some cases, was at odds with) those of an early teacher or mentor. To that end, before we leave the Rutgers University years, let us try to be as concrete as possible about the links between Friedman's later work and his Rutgers University teachers Jones and Burns.

Specific Influences on Friedman Arising from His Teachers

In the case of Homer Jones, the links are straightforward to discern, because Friedman did not claim that Jones was an outstanding source of original material. Instead, he credited Jones with exposing Friedman to others' work through his teaching—specifically, Frank Knight's writings.[28] As already noted, Jones was a far from prolific author. It also appears that Jones was not a particularly skilled composer of words: Jones's later employee at the Federal Reserve Bank of St. Louis Jerry Jordan observed that Jones's pieces typically did not read well, and that items going out under Jones's name typically required considerable restructuring by other bank staff ahead of publication (Jerry Jordan, interview, June 5, 2013). But Jones was credited by Jordan and others who served at the Federal Reserve Bank of St. Louis with setting a tone conducive to a vibrant research atmosphere. This approach on Jones's part is evident also in Friedman's portrait of Jones as someone who read widely and who encouraged Friedman to do so. At the same time, the interest in monetary economics on the part of both Friedman and Jones is clearly something that predominantly manifested itself after the 1930s rather than in their years of overlap at Rutgers University. As indicated above, with respect to the University of Chicago, Friedman confirmed that Jones was in effect an early liaison for Friedman: evidently, it was primarily Jones who exposed him to Chicago School writings, and, via Jones's contacts with the University of Chicago (especially Frank Knight), it was Jones who set in motion Friedman's master's degree study at the University of Chicago for the 1932–33 academic year.

With respect to Arthur Burns, a more clear-cut influence on Friedman's research can be inferred because, unlike Jones, Burns was a prolific writer and researcher. In addition, there are aspects of Burns's teaching that have a counterpart in Friedman's later interests and practices. Joseph Burns observed of his father: "He spent a huge amount of time in his classes going over Alfred Marshall" (Joseph Burns, personal communication, December 18, 2014). Joseph Burns further recounted that the class discussion of Marshall's work would include line-by-line analysis of Marshall's *Principles*, a volume that Friedman would return to many times in later years.[29]

Furthermore, during his studies at Rutgers University Friedman received what he would describe as "probably the best research training I ever got" in the form of a seminar conducted by Burns, which consisted of very detailed study of Burns's PhD dissertation.[30] In addition, the NBER approach to business cycle analysis, exemplified by Burns and Mitchell (1946), would leave an imprint on Friedman and Schwartz's *Monetary History of the United States* and *Monetary Trends in the United States and the United Kingdom*, including in the approaches that the latter book took to the dating of business cycles and to the transformation of data.

Another element common to Burns and Friedman is that each would become known as critics of the Keynesian revolution. Burns (1929) had actually written a detailed defense of the quantity theory of money in response to the writings of a critic, Benjamin M. Anderson (and in particular, to a 1929 Anderson article). Burns's 1929 piece could not, of course, be considered a criticism of the Keynesian movement, as the article preceded the *General Theory* and Burns's discussion actually named Keynes as a leading advocate of the quantity theory.[31] But in the post–*General Theory* period, and especially until he became Federal Reserve chairman, Burns was, like Friedman, associated with the view that much pre-Keynesian economic analysis deserved to be restored to economists' thinking about the determination of output and prices. And an observation with which Friedman became associated—that all economists used Keynesian language but that they did not necessarily accept the economic analysis underlying the type of Keynesianism embedded in the *General Theory*—was likely something he had picked up from Burns (1947).[32]

These parallels notwithstanding, Burns's and Friedman's respective bodies of work have significant dissimilarities in both style and substance. Friedman's writing style was quite unlike that of Burns.[33] Furthermore, despite Friedman's use of the Burns-Mitchell procedures in much of his NBER-commissioned work, a good deal of Friedman's approach to statistics was not derived from Burns's research. With regard to economic theory, both Burns and Friedman would be characterized by some critics as being atheoretical and as lacking an economic model.[34] This characterization, however, does neither of these economists justice. Each of them had a theoretical framework. But their respective frameworks did not coincide. Burns was a critic of Keynesianism in the 1940s and in subsequent decades. However, he did not subscribe to the monetarist position with which Friedman would become associated. In particular, it will be argued in chapters 11 and 15 that, by the late 1960s, Burns had absorbed and accepted the validity of a number of Friedman's positions, but by no means all of them. Burns would later describe his specialty as "business cycle theory," and he would characterize that theory as different from both Keynesianism and monetarism (*Newsweek*, May 14, 1979).

There are elements of Burns's theoretical framework that Friedman does seem to have absorbed into his own belief system. In particular, the notion of inherent persistence in output dynamics was a finding from the NBER's business cycle researches that Friedman embraced.[35] What is more, Burns's belief in the greater importance of longer-term interest rates than short-term rates for the behavior of aggregate demand was shared by Friedman, and it provided a rare area of agreement between Burns and Friedman during the mid-1970s, by which time their frameworks had diverged considerably.[36]

As for Friedman's designation of Burns as his surrogate father, this may be largely an ex post characterization on Friedman's part. Burns was a confidante and mentor of Friedman's and was clearly a major source of advice on research and career matters. Their face-to-face encounters also remained very frequent even after the Rutgers University years, while their correspondence was copious. But to assign Burns a surrogate-father status would seem to overstate Burns's influence on Friedman. The two had considerable differences in outlook even in the 1930s. For example, Burns had a strong religious faith throughout his life, while Friedman had dropped religious beliefs in his early teenage years and never went back to them.[37] And two figures in the best position to observe the Burns/Friedman connections—Burns's son Joseph, and Anna Schwartz—did not regard a father/son-type relationship as the natural way of viewing their interaction. Joseph Burns, in an interview for this book, did not recall Friedman referring to Arthur Burns as his surrogate father in the many Friedman/Joseph Burns conversations during Arthur Burns's lifetime. And Anna Schwartz suggested to the present author that a different figure was really Friedman's surrogate father: Aaron Director—Friedman's brother-in-law after Friedman and Rose Director married in 1938. Schwartz observed of Director: "He was really the head of the family and they [Milton and Rose Friedman] enormously admired him" (conversation with Anna J. Schwartz, September 18, 2009).

Graduate Study

After his Rutgers University years, the next stage of Friedman's education was the start of his graduate studies in economics at the University of Chicago. As he recounted many times, Friedman faced the choice between two offers of graduate study, each with payment of tuition as part of the offered package: economics at the University of Chicago and mathematics at Brown University.[38] Friedman was not consistent in his accounts of how he weighed the two alternatives. His recollection in the mid-1980s was that the decision was "close to a toss of a coin," but his memoirs suggested that the choice of economics over mathematics was a foregone conclusion.[39] Something that is more clear-cut, and that was stressed in the accounts given by both Milton and Rose Friedman, is that the advent of the Great Depression was important in convincing Milton Friedman that economics was the field that he wanted to pursue.[40]

The same need stressed above to guard against generalities applies to the issue of determining the influence of the University of Chicago on Friedman. There is much evidence that Friedman's views underwent considerable change well after he had finished taking classes at the University of Chicago. But before we come to this, some effort is required to get the facts straight about Friedman's activities at the University of Chicago and elsewhere from 1932 onward.

There are convoluted elements in Friedman's movements from 1932 through the end of the decade because he went to the University of Chicago, left, came back, and left again, and correspondingly he went to Columbia University, left, and came back. Friedman's locations and activities between 1933 and 1935 can nevertheless be stated concisely: (1) 1932–33 academic year, graduate studies in economics at the University of Chicago, culminating in receipt of an AM (master of arts) degree in 1933;[41] (2) 1933–34 academic year, fellowship at Columbia University and PhD coursework studies in economics at the university; (3) 1934–35 academic year, back at the University of Chicago as a research assistant to the economics department's Professor Henry Schultz.

In the fifty years after these events, despite several attempts in print to chronicle Friedman's career, accounts that got this sequence exactly right were few and far between.[42] For example, a profile of Friedman in the *New York Times* (January 25, 1970) made no mention of his Columbia University studies and created the impression, albeit without actually saying so, that Friedman received a PhD from the University of Chicago in the mid-1930s.[43] But if this account overstated Friedman's connections with the University of Chicago, other accounts understated it. A lengthy biographical essay concerning Friedman by Silk (1976) made clear that Friedman was a Columbia University PhD graduate, only to create confusion because of a different omission: although Silk mentioned (53) that Friedman departed from the University of Chicago and moved to Columbia University following the conclusion of the 1932–33 academic year, he did not refer to Friedman's year back at the University of Chicago in the 1934–35 academic year.[44]

Friedman himself contributed to the confusion about his early activities through errors and omissions in the biographical data that he supplied during the 1970s and 1980s. For example, his *Who's Who in America 1976/1977* entry correctly gave his receipt of the AM from the University of Chicago in 1933 but then had him serving in the years 1933 to 1937 as an associate economist for the National Resources Committee.[45] On the other hand, Friedman's entries for the 1970 American Economic Association Directory of Members and for the 1986 *Who's Who in Economics* provided correct but incomplete information about Friedman's 1930s activities. Both entries gave the correct date for his years of National Resources Commission employment (1935 to 1937), but they listed that position as Friedman's first job as an economist, omitting his year as a research assistant in 1934–35 at the University of Chicago and, indeed, any information about Friedman's activities between 1933 and 1935.[46]

Walters's (1987) biographical entry for Friedman in the *New Palgrave* dictionary of economics represented an early case in the modern literature in which Friedman's return to the University of Chicago in 1934–35 was registered.[47] As it happens, the fact of Friedman's presence in 1934–35 at the University of Chicago, although obscured by the inaccurate accounts that appeared between the 1930s and the 1980s, could have been found in the acknowledgments of H. Schultz (1938, xi).

One of the enduring testaments to Friedman's mid-1930s stint at the University of Chicago was a book that consisted of a selection of key articles by the economics department's Frank Knight. This book, published in 1935, was coedited by Friedman and several other graduate students.[48] In 1998, Friedman's memoirs further elaborated on his activities at the University of Chicago in 1934–35 by indicating that, in addition to serving as Schultz's assistant, he took all the remaining coursework necessary for him to proceed to PhD dissertation work at the University of Chicago.[49] Indeed, as of 1937, Friedman still regarded himself as on a path that might lead to a University of Chicago PhD, as he described his dissertation in progress as: "*The economic theory of commodity stocks*. 1937. Chicago or Columbia" (American Economic Association 1937, 639).

In sum, although he was not present at the University of Chicago for consecutive academic years, and he emerged with a master's degree and not a PhD, Friedman could accurately claim to have been a PhD student at the University of Chicago, and one who reached what is sometimes called "all-but-dissertation" status.

It is possible that the widespread perception to the contrary—that is, that Friedman was a student at the University of Chicago for a single year only, and that his studies did not encompass the PhD coursework component— played a part in the backlash that occurred when, in later years, Friedman claimed to be speaking in the University of Chicago's monetary tradition. There were issues of economic substance in this debate, in which Friedman's interpretation of the older University of Chicago position was challenged by Patinkin (1969, 1972a). But one factor in that debate may have been a view on the part of Friedman's critics that he lacked the credentials to talk firsthand about the University of Chicago's monetary tradition, and that others' misconception that Friedman had a University of Chicago PhD was contributing to the weight given to Friedman's discussions of pre-1946 University of Chicago monetary economics.[50]

Friedman indeed did not have a University of Chicago PhD, but he had more economics training at the university than that associated with a master's degree only. Master's degree and PhD students, although classified collectively as graduate students and often overlapping in their teachers and course material, are not known for enjoying a great degree of camaraderie with one another. It is likely that the erroneous belief that Friedman's University of Chicago education consisted solely of a master's degree contributed to the groundswell of skepticism that he would encounter regarding his qualifications to speak authoritatively on the university's monetary-economics tradition.[51]

Friedman made his own contribution to a rapprochement between master's and PhD students in economics when, in June 1938, he married Rose Director. Rose Director had been a classmate of Friedman's in the graduate program at the University of Chicago in the 1932–33 academic year but did not make it to a completed PhD dissertation.[52] Friedman in 1938 was, in contrast, well into his dissertation work at Columbia University and also teaching part time at that institution.[53] He had also completed two years working for the National Resources Committee in Washington, DC. The commission was, as discussed below, a New Deal initiative in which Friedman's work had involved constructing estimates of consumer spending. Following his work at the commission, Friedman had been employed, starting in 1937, by the National Bureau of Economic Research in New York City. In practice, the NBER employment had largely meant carrying out his Columbia University dissertation work, conducted in collaboration with Simon Kuznets. This work is discussed at the end of this chapter.

The University of Chicago and the Shaping of Friedman's Views

With the chronology of Friedman's 1930s activities now laid out, it is worthwhile spending some more time on the role that his activities following completion of undergraduate education played in shaping his monetarist and free-market economics of later years. The appropriate conclusion parallels that already made about the influence of the Rutgers University years on Friedman: the influence was not decisive or clear-cut. The fact is that Friedman's views in the area of monetary analysis were sharply different during the 1940-48 period from those that he held from the late 1940s onward—too different to justify confidence in the notion that Friedman's later, familiar positions were shaped decisively by his exposure to economics during the years 1933-39.

In reaching this judgment, one has to balance the fact that Friedman stated that "very few people change their basic philosophy after they are 25 years of age" against the considerable evidence that this characterization is not true of his own intellectual development.[54] Rather, Friedman's adoption of the positions made familiar by his activities of later decades became recognizable only in the period beyond the 1930s. To look back to his 1930s activities for anticipations of his later work is to give insufficient credit to his own later research, and that of others, in reshaping his views. In 1991, when asked by the present author to account for a discrepancy between analyses he had given in the first and second halves of the 1980s, Friedman answered that the difference reflected developments in his thinking that had occurred "as I have worked more with the data and have read what other people have done."[55] Likewise, in an appearance on *Meet the Press* in 1970, Friedman had occasion to mention that "I have since gone back and looked at a lot of past experience" and that he had evaluated recent monetary relationships in that light.[56]

For the period prior to 1970, too, Friedman's exposure to evidence is again a critical factor in obtaining an understanding of the development of his views on monetary matters. In particular, Friedman's subscription to monetarist positions—a clear feature of his writings from the early 1950s onward—reflected the fact that he was much more familiar with the empirical evidence on the relationship between money, output, and prices in 1950 than he was in 1940. To attribute Friedman's postwar positions to what he learned in the 1930s would be to overlook this critical point.

Indeed, there is abundant basis—as will be detailed in the following chapters—for regarding Friedman's move to monetarism and to advocacy of market economics as a response, as suggested by Schwartz (1992), to empirical evidence—consisting of historical evidence as well as the new evidence generated by World War II and the early postwar experience—and to research findings from his own work and to his study of research undertaken by others. It seems inappropriate, therefore, to treat Friedman's postwar views on money and markets as essentially preordained—as having been locked in by his education and very early career.

Accordingly, tempting though it may be to perceive close connections between Friedman's 1930s activities and his later work, that is *not* the perspective taken in this book. A brief catalogue of specific elements of Friedman's positions reinforces this judgment:

(*i*) As noted above, Friedman's Rutgers University experience no doubt steered him away from non-economics pursuits—but it did not do so sufficiently to prevent him from spending much of his early research career on studies in mathematical statistics that had very little economic content.

(*ii*) Friedman's University of Chicago education, as well as giving him excellent training, no doubt pointed him in the direction of economic liberalism, and he later credited his education at the University of Chicago with having played this role.[57] But until the early 1940s, he appears to have had a more favorable perspective on the role of the public sector than was the typical Chicago School line.

(*iii*) With respect to monetary issues, Friedman studied monetary theory in a course taught by Lloyd Mints during Friedman's 1932–33 year at the University of Chicago.[58] But that course must be discounted as a decisive influence on Friedman's monetary views: for the emphasis on the quantity theory in Mints's course was not sufficient to stop Friedman from taking, as we shall see in the next chapter, a strongly negative perspective on the quantity theory in his writings in the early 1940s.

(*iv*) A further monetary-economics example is the prescription of 100 percent reserve banking. Friedman, like key members of the prior generation of University of Chicago economists, was an advocate of this arrangement. But his support for 100 percent reserves rested largely on arguments different from those advanced by his predecessors. These differences are discussed in section III of this chapter, when Henry Simons's monetary economics is considered.

(*v*) Friedman's studies of consumption during his 1935–37 Washington, DC, employment gave him familiarity with the data—but his permanent-income perspective on the consumption function was not yet apparent, as the 1939 write-up of the consumption work endorsed the pre-permanent-income-hypothesis consumption function of Keynes's (1936) *General Theory*.[59]

(*vi*) Friedman would state that Frank Knight "perhaps had the greatest influence on my general philosophy" (*Wall Street Journal*, November 4, 1969, 1), and he would recommend Knight's (1933) *The Economic Organization* for its exposition of the virtues of the market economy (G. Martin 1983,

61). But Baumol's (1983, 1081) observation that it is "hardly appropriate" to regard Friedman as a Knight disciple is well taken. Friedman and Knight differed on many areas of market economics.[60] Friedman himself implied that his views did not coincide with Knight's when it came to what constituted the appropriate areas of state intervention in the economy.[61] Furthermore, Friedman broke sharply with a key aspect of Knight's capital theory, rejecting Knight's distinction between risk and uncertainty.[62]

(vii) Friedman's University of Chicago background surely made him receptive to the notion, expressed in reviews of the *General Theory* by Chicago School members (such as Viner 1936; and especially Knight 1937), that it was not appropriate to regard Keynes, in presenting an account of the Depression that was oriented on deficient aggregate demand, as having achieved a theoretical breakthrough.[63] But the position initially taken by such reviewers as Knight—that there was something fundamentally wrong in Keynes's argument—was clearly not something Friedman accepted, for Friedman himself expounded some of the more hard-line Keynesian positions in the early 1940s. And when, in the postwar period, Friedman did become a vocal critic of the *General Theory*'s arguments, he nevertheless accepted that Keynes had provided a coherent theoretical explanation for deep slumps, one that had not been present in the earlier literature. Friedman's position was, rather, that he did not regard Keynes's explanation, with its emphasis on absolute liquidity preference, as empirically compelling.[64] And it would be wrong, in considering the monetarist Friedman who emerged in the early 1950s, to regard Friedman as simply reverting to what he had been taught at the University of Chicago in the 1930s. Instead, his move to monetarism came in light of his study of empirical evidence, as well as his reconsideration of a large body of literature, including that of monetary economists, like Fisher and Pigou, whom Friedman never encountered in person.[65]

The final item in the preceding catalogue raises a matter that has been stressed at earlier points in this book and that will feature heavily in the next two chapters: Friedman's fundamental reassessment, well after his years as a student, of his own positions. The extent to which the period 1948–51 witnessed a shake-up in Friedman's thinking, especially with respect to monetary economics, is difficult to overstate. And what emerged from this shake-up was not—as has been claimed by such critics as Patinkin (1972a)—a minor variant on the *General Theory*'s approach to monetary analysis. But Friedman's position from 1951 onward did not correspond to 1930s-vintage University of Chicago monetary analysis either. Thus, while Friedman would observe (*Boston Globe*, April 3, 1983, 20) that the "main influences on me undoubtedly were from the University of Chicago," he would part company, even after his late-1940s embrace of the quantity

theory, with many of the specific positions that University of Chicago economics department members had held in the 1930s.

Entering the Research Debate

In the 1930s, with the aforementioned shake-up still some time off, Friedman was very far from what can today be regarded as his fully considered
position on economic matters. Nonetheless, as will now be discussed,
Friedman was an energetic participant in a number of economic debates
that took place in print during the second half of the 1930s.

Friedman first entered the fray with an article in the area of applied
price theory. His article, "Professor Pigou's Method for Measuring Elasticities of Demand from Budgetary Data," appeared in the *Quarterly Journal
of Economics* in November 1935, when Friedman was 23.[66] The paper was
one Friedman apparently drafted while he was bedridden with a cold.[67]
The impetus for the paper came from the research assistance that Friedman provided to Henry Schultz when the latter was writing his monograph
The Theory and Measurement of Demand.[68] In the course of his discussion,
Schultz outlined a procedure for estimating demand elasticities that had
been proposed by A. C. Pigou in a 1910 article. Friedman was moved to
undertake a critical examination of Pigou's procedure.[69] Friedman showed
that Pigou's method of obtaining a compact expression for the ratio of price
elasticities of demand for two goods "is either invalid or of very limited applicability."[70]

Six months later, a follow-up to Friedman's comment appeared in the
form of a symposium, again in the *Quarterly Journal of Economics*, with
brief contributions from Pigou and Friedman, and a longer one from
N. Georgescu-Roegen, who had been brought into the debate to serve as a
third-party arbitrator (Georgescu-Roegen 1988, 27). A word about the title
under which this symposium appeared—"Marginal Utility of Money and
Elasticities of Demand"—is warranted. If one were trying to establish when
Friedman first ventured into print in the area of monetary economics, a
read-through of the list of article titles in Friedman's bibliography might
lead to the conclusion that he did so in this 1936 symposium. After all, the
symposium has the word "money" in it, and "marginal utility of money"
is certainly a term prevalent in monetary economics. A conclusion of this
kind has in fact been drawn by Ruger (2011, 26), who gives this symposium
as marking Friedman's entry into the monetary field.

That conclusion, however, is incorrect. The problem is, of course, that
"money" is used in many senses in economics: when Friedman appeared
on television in 1968, he clarified his discussion by noting that "by 'money'
here I mean the quantity of money, not income."[71] In the 1936 symposium,

however, "money" meant income. In particular, that discussion followed Marshall's practice of taking the marginal utility of wealth or income, that is, what in modern practice corresponds to the variable denoted λ, U_C, or $U'(C)$. "Marginal utility of money" in this context did *not* connote the marginal utility of real money balances—the variable often denoted $U'(M/P)$ or $U_{M/P}$. The "marginal utility of money" terminology for consumption or wealth utility did not become outmoded until well after the 1936 symposium, and much credit for the change in terminology should go to Don Patinkin's *Money, Interest, and Prices*, which stated: "Marshall's 'marginal utility of money' . . . is more appropriately termed the 'marginal utility of money income,' or even better, 'of money wealth.'"[72]

By the 1970s, the published version of a dissertation supervised by Friedman was able to classify the practice under which "λ is sometimes called 'the marginal utility of money'" as "incorrect."[73] Friedman himself used the "marginal utility of money" phrase in the Marshallian sense in his price-theory discussions in the 1940s and 1950s and even in the first edition of *Price Theory*.[74] But, in light of the tension that had emerged from the term's usage in monetary economics, he added a footnote to the 1976 revision of *Price Theory* stating that the "marginal utility of money" terminology was misleading when applied outside monetary-economics contexts, and that the term should be reserved for the marginal utility from holding cash balances.[75] In any event, however, the 1936 exchange did not initiate Friedman's publications in monetary economics. These would not begin until the 1940s.

Although Pigou declined to reply in detail to Friedman's criticism, instead claiming that it rested on a misconception—a claim that Friedman's brief reply made clear was not accurate—Georgescu-Roegen did provide a detailed analysis of Friedman's argument. Georgescu-Roegen's conclusion was that, although Friedman had indeed established that Pigou's result was not a general one, this result did not constitute a devastating criticism of Pigou's method for obtaining elasticities. Rather, the Pigou method could still be defended as an approximation.[76]

Friedman's criticism of Pigou received further publicity later in the 1930s with the publication of the Henry Schultz text, which included an exposition of Pigou's method and Friedman's critique thereof (H. Schultz 1938, 110-11). Friedman would observe in 1988 of Schultz: "His book on the *Theory and Measurement of Demand* is a great book—even the parts I didn't write" (Hammond 1992, 98). One might infer from this statement that Friedman was implying that his research assistance to Schultz slipped into substantial ghostwriting of Schultz's book, and that the prominence given to Friedman's debate with Pigou reflected that ghostwriting. However, Schultz explicitly credited Friedman with coauthorship of the successive chapters "The Special Theory of Related Demands" and "The General Theory of Related Demands" late in the book, stating: "I am profoundly grateful to Mr. Milton Friedman for invaluable assistance in the preparation and writing of these chapters."[77] Indeed, Kenneth Arrow would recall a conversation with Allen Wallis in which Wallis noted that Friedman was primarily responsible for these key theoretical sections, with Wallis going on to relate that "he [Friedman] doubted seriously that Schultz ever even understood them."[78] Considerable confidence is warranted in the conclusion that Friedman was not responsible for the section of Schultz's book that advertised Friedman's 1935 criticism of Pigou, because that discussion occurs much earlier in the book and is written in a writing style dissimilar to Friedman's.[79]

To have one's work discussed at length in a major economics book, and to be portrayed in that book as having bested a giant of the profession like Pigou, was heady stuff for someone just turning twenty-six.[80] Nonetheless, the position Friedman took in his debate with Pigou in 1935–36 was not something he could take complete pride in later, as it amounted to a stand that conflicted with his later approach to economic research. As Georgescu-Roegen's analysis made clear, Friedman had established the invalidity of the strict applicability of Pigou's approach. But the Friedman critique had not undermined the status of Pigou's approach as a reasonable approximation.[81] In time, that state of affairs would justify second thoughts on Friedman's part about the merits of the challenge he had offered to Pigou's analysis. Friedman would eventually use approximations aplenty in his monetary research and would come to see theoretical findings that rested on exact parameter restrictions, and focuses by researchers on very special cases, as often lacking in practical value.[82]

Once he had adopted that perspective, Friedman could hardly begrudge economists' use of approximations. On the contrary, his own approach to economic analysis became much more in line with the aphorism that approximation is the soul of science.[83] Friedman would insist that exact parameter restrictions were appropriate if they had a strong economic basis—for example, the imposition of homogeneity restrictions on demand functions. In this connection, he certainly regarded price-level homogeneity of the demand for nominal money balances as an important theory-based restriction. But he otherwise took a pragmatic approach to model parameterization, a key aim being to make the analysis straightforward: for example, he set the real income elasticity of the demand for real money balances to unity on the grounds that it was a reasonable approximation, even if the data suggested that that restriction was formally rejected.[84] Therefore, although (or "altho," as Friedman mostly spelled that word in his 1935 debut article) his critique of Pigou was formally valid,

Friedman's later approach to economic research would cast doubt on the economic substance of that critique.

Another indication of the shift in Friedman's perspective away from that underlying his 1930s price-theory research comes in the reference in one of the Friedman-Schultz coauthored chapters of H. Schultz (1938) to a January 1934 Friedman paper titled "The Fitting of Indifference Curves as a Method of Deriving Statistical Demand Curves."[85] In the event, the paper apparently never made it into print. And an insight into Friedman's subsequent negative verdict on the value of the research reported in the paper comes from his observation in 1967, "economists cannot just stand aside and lose themselves in indifference curves. Their ideas do have practical consequences and when things are going wrong they should speak up" (*Fortune*, June 1, 1967, 148).

Friedman's changed outlook to economics, and the accompanying transformation in his attitude to his earliest published work, is reflected in the fact that his 1935 paper and its 1936 follow-up were not reprinted in any of his various book collections and did not appear in his list of selected publications in his self-authored entry for *Who's Who in Economics* 1986.[86] Furthermore, the impact of these articles on the field of research was muted, as is illustrated by the fact that a collection in 1972 titled *The Evolution of Modern Demand Theory* included Friedman's 1949 article on the Marshallian demand curve but not his 1935 article.[87] Friedman's critical analysis of Pigou received coverage in Paul Samuelson's *Foundations of Economic Analysis* (Samuelson 1947, 180–82) but in a discussion that cast doubt on the importance of Friedman's critique.

It is unlikely that the later Friedman would have had much disagreement with Samuelson's judgment.[88] Indeed, in the postwar period Friedman would write to Pigou of his "youthful indiscretion" in making the critique.[89] In addition, he would concede to Georgescu-Roegen the substance of the latter's argument. For when Friedman introduced Georgescu-Roegen at a University of Chicago event, he referred to Georgescu-Roegen as the only economist who had proven him wrong.[90]

The fact that Friedman repudiated the spirit but not the letter of his early work, and the distance of that work from his later interests, bring out the dilemma of studying the main policy issues that arose in the 1930s. The abstract price-theory research that Friedman published in the 1930s was far removed from the serious national economic problems prevalent at the time. Friedman's later criticism of the economics profession's conduct in the 1930s—that is, that it focused insufficient attention on the most serious economic problems of the period—applies to his mid-1930s publications (as well as to his 1933 master's dissertation, which was on railroad earnings).[91] That criticism underscores the contrast between this work and the key motivation for his 1932 pursuit of graduate economics study—which was, as noted above, to gain insight into the nation's urgent economic problems.[92]

The Friedman article from the 1930s whose perspective most lines up with that of the later Friedman—albeit an article whose subject matter is also very far removed from that of his later work—is a critique he published in 1938 of a procedure to estimate demand curves. A theme in this analysis was one that Friedman would stick to right up to his last truly significant research paper, in the 1990s: the danger of obtaining apparently economically interpretable results that are in fact due to a statistical artifact, in this case excessive smoothing of the data.[93] The 1938 article's tone also anticipated Friedman's later work. Whereas Friedman's 1935–36 critique of Pigou had been careful to record how highly he rated Pigou, the more combative Friedman of later debates came out more clearly in his 1938 critique, directed at E. J. Broster: "It is evident that Mr. Broster's technique is worthless for deriving statistical demand curves: it will yield 'good' results even when there is no 'real' demand curve underlying the data and may distort this underlying curve even if it exists."[94]

The National Resources Committee

In the mid-1980s, fifty years after the event, Friedman would note that he owed his first job to the New Deal.[95] The work that Friedman did in Washington, DC, during his years (1935 to 1937) as an associate economist for the National Resources Committee (NRC), a New Deal–related federal government venture, moved him closer in subject matter to his later research, as his responsibilities at the NRC involved the study of consumer spending.[96] Friedman's specific role was to serve in the Consumption Research Staff of the Industrial Section of the NRC.[97] The survey data that the team collected resulted in the government-published 1939 book *Consumer Expenditures in the United States: Estimates for 1935–1936*.[98] It would be wrong to overstate the importance of Friedman's role in the project. The project was, in fact, at the direction of Hildegarde Kneeland, not Friedman.[99] Consistent with Friedman's subordinate role, his name appeared last (and out of alphabetical order) in the authors' name listing in a 1936 article announcing plans for the consumer-spending study.[100] When, in 1941, Paul Samuelson cited the project's book, he referenced it as a "National Resources Committee and W.P.A. [Works Progress Administration] study," without mentioning Friedman or the other authors' names.[101]

Samuelson's citation practice underlined the fact that the book was the product of a committee. In later decades, Friedman would be very reluctant to add his name to items such as petitions or committee reports that were a product of many hands. Conversely, when he would serve on government committees in the postwar period—as he did for investigations of conscription and of monetary statistics—he dominated proceedings to such an extent that the final report of the committee largely read like a solo-authored Friedman product. The 1939 report, however, is more clearly the outcome of a collaborative process. Furthermore, the consumer-survey work carried out by the NRC differed from the work of those later committees in being essentially fact-finding: a report on the data by government employees, rather than a prescription for policy by outside experts commissioned by the government to write a report. And, again in contrast to the case of later committees, Friedman had left the project before the report was finalized.

It is also important, as indicated above, not to view this work as a major step toward the consumption-function literature of the 1950s to which Friedman was a premier contributor. Friedman's wife's work in the 1940s was a far more important antecedent of the 1950s research (including Milton Friedman's) than anything the NRC produced, and this fact is reflected in the citations of Brady and R. D. Friedman (1947) by Friedman and Modigliani in their postwar work.[102] The work by Friedman and his NRC colleagues on consumer spending certainly did not anticipate his permanent income hypothesis. On the contrary, in a paper written in 1935 in connection with the project, Friedman expressed the view that tastes (i.e., the specification of the utility function) will change with income—in contrast to the permanent income hypothesis's prediction that household preferences are stable as income changes.[103] Furthermore, the official 1939 write-up of the NRC's consumer-survey work stated that "the proportion of income saved appears to increase as total income expands" (Kneeland et al. 1939, 171).

It would be remiss not to mention here one aspect of Friedman's 1930s consumption work that Anna Schwartz underscored to the present author in late 2010.[104] Schwartz observed that, even before she started collaborating with him, Friedman was noted for working with women. Friedman observed in 1965: "I am a feminist, among other things."[105] His coauthorship with women for his first two books (*Consumer Expenditures in the United States* in 1939 and *Taxing to Prevent Inflation* in 1943) bears this out.[106]

Empirical Analysis and Columbia University

Friedman would view himself as having become data oriented even before his years with the National Resources Committee, crediting his year of graduate classes at Columbia University in 1933-34 with being "heavy on statistical and empirical evidence."[107] Friedman's suggestion that Columbia University was less theoretically oriented than the University of Chicago was likely based mainly on the basis of the presence at the former institution of Wesley Mitchell. Friedman's memoirs, while stating his appreciation for Mitchell's business cycle course, were critical of Mitchell's coverage of economic theory in his other teaching, and after Mitchell's death Friedman would take it on himself to work out the theory that underlay Mitchell's very data-oriented published work.[108] It would be incorrect, however, to characterize Friedman's exposure to economics during his classes in the 1933–34 academic year as lacking theoretical content. To do so would do an injustice to the person whom Friedman credited as most influencing him in that year, Harold Hotelling.[109]

A member of a later cohort of Columbia University's graduate classes, Kenneth Arrow, has observed of Hotelling: "You know, he was a theorist and economist, as well as a statistician. A very good economist, in fact" (Kenneth Arrow, interview, December 7, 2013). Friedman himself also pointed out on many occasions that Hotelling was a "mathematical economist" and not simply a statistician.[110] Furthermore, Friedman stressed the economic substance involved in Hotelling's theoretical contributions: after the first OPEC oil price shock of 1973–74, both Rose and Milton Friedman would note the relevance of Hotelling's 1931 study of resource use.[111] And, although he only rarely mentioned it in print, Friedman was very familiar with, and impressed by the wide applicability of, a 1929 Hotelling study advancing a theory of retailer/customer behavior—a study that Friedman felt helped explain the tendency of opposing political parties to arrive at similar policy platforms.[112]

It was, however, Friedman's increased exposure to statistical theory through Hotelling, along with the applications of statistics associated with Friedman's NRC work, that set in train an increased interest in mathematical statistics on his part and led him to make a major contribution to the statistical literature. Friedman's paper in the December 1937 issue of the *Journal of the American Statistical Association*, "The Use of Ranks to Avoid the Assumption of Normality Implicit in the Analysis of Variance," introduced what is known, in scores of statistical textbooks, as the "Friedman test." The *Los Angeles Times* (December 14, 1986, 14) reported that the test was known by that name in statistical software packages, with generation of the test statistic part of the packages' automatic routines; and Friedman took pride in this fact in his memoirs.[113]

The Friedman test is heavily covered in statistical textbooks and is embedded in statistical packages to this day. It is, however, little known and little used in the economic-research literature.[114] Consequently, while the test built Friedman's reputation as a mathematical statistician, his work on the test again falls into the category of 1930s activity that had very little relation to his later research. Indeed, because the Friedman test was not one designed for time-series data, while Friedman's quantitative empirical research in the postwar period was predominantly time-series analysis, there was little occasion for synergies to emerge between Friedman's 1930s work on statistical testing and his later research. The part of Friedman's statistical work that has left a major impression on economic research is instead, as Beveridge and C. R. Nelson (1981) stressed, his permanent-transitory decomposition of series. This contribution, however, was the outgrowth of research that Friedman was only just beginning in 1937: his study with Simon Kuznets of professional incomes, discussed later in this chapter.

The activities of Friedman from 1932 to 1939 occurred against a national background that has so far been discussed only in passing: the 1930-33 banking catastrophe—which Friedman would describe as the near-collapse of the monetary system, or even simply as the collapse of the monetary system—followed by the New Deal. The next section, "Issues, 1932-39," will consider Friedman's perspective on those events. The Friedman perspective that is considered will predominantly correspond to that he voiced in his monetarist period, 1951 to 2006, *not* the viewpoint he held as the events of the 1930s unfolded. This approach to the discussion reflects the fact that most of Friedman's analysis of the economic events of the 1930s was written in the postwar period, as well as the consideration that his statements in the later period offer the more definitive Friedman view on the events of the 1930s—a view arrived at in the wake of his epochal 1948-51 rethinking of monetary matters. Instances in which Friedman's 1951-2006 perspective on the events of the 1930s represented a clear break with the views he held during the 1930s will, however, be noted.[115]

II. Issues, 1933–39

Friedman in the postwar period would contrast himself with "the people who want to conserve the New Deal" (*Speaking Freely*, WNBC, May 4, 1969, p. 2 of transcript). And he would lament the fact that the Roosevelt administration had ushered in an era of "active intervention by government" in the economy.[116] Nonetheless, Friedman would not become an unconditional critic of the measures introduced in the New Deal. Indeed, he would name Franklin Delano Roosevelt as one of the historical figures who had contributed positively to world civilization (G. Martin 1983, 56), and it is clear that Roosevelt's wartime leadership was not the sole basis on which Friedman reached this judgment. For, asked in 1979 whether Roosevelt's victory in the 1932 presidential election had been a desirable development, Friedman replied that it was a very difficult question to answer because there were some good, and some undesirable, aspects of Roosevelt's changes to economic policy.[117]

In the Friedman-Schwartz account of the 1930s, the desirable and undesirable aspects of the New Deal can be partitioned in a straightforward manner: the favorable effects on the economy of the reforms to monetary policy and monetary arrangements, and what Friedman and Schwartz perceived as the unfavorable effects on the economy of changes that the Roosevelt administration imposed on US aggregate-supply conditions.[118] These two categories of changes are now considered in turn.

THE NEW DEAL: MONETARY CHANGES

As he would recall much later, Friedman's conviction in 1933 was that the economic situation was so parlous that the government had to step in.[119] That was not a position from which Friedman departed in subsequent years: while, by 1987, Friedman ascribed blame to the government for the economic collapse, he nevertheless expressed the view that, in the state that the economy had reached by the start of the Roosevelt administration, it was an appropriate time for concerted government measures (Idea Channel, 1987).[120]

Friedman approved, in the main, of the monetary and banking reforms associated with the New Deal that were introduced in response to the final phase (that is, 1932–33) of the crisis in the US banking system. Among these reforms were the introduction of deposit insurance, and the recapitalization of the banking system via the Reconstruction Finance Corporation, which was given clear power to make capital injections into banks by the Emergency Banking Act of March 1933.[121]

Friedman was consistently in favor of the banking reforms over the years, but his research with Schwartz altered the prism through which he viewed those reforms. He came to see the stabilizing effects conferred by the New Deal banking reforms as largely arising from the way in which they reversed the prior decline in the money stock, defined to include currency and bank deposits. Many of the key New Deal financial reforms could be viewed as having this effect, but the reform on which Friedman and Schwartz put greatest emphasis was the introduction of deposit insurance, which they called the "most important structural change in the banking system to result from the 1933 panic."[122] A judgment that Friedman stated repeatedly over the years was that the most important monetary reform in the United States was not the creation of the Federal Reserve System in 1913–14 but, instead, that of the Federal Deposit Insurance Corporation in 1933.[123] This judgment underlay his statement in 1962 that "if Hoover in 1929 had inherited the present financial structure, we would not have had the Great Depression."[124]

Deposit insurance ended the bank runs that had been contracting the money stock. Household money holdings that had been transferred into currency now flowed back into commercial banks, terminating what Friedman and Schwartz had called "the famous multiple expansion process of the banking system in vicious reverse."[125] This reversal in the direction of household money flows implied an enlarged stock of bank reserves (for given high-powered money), removing a key source of monetary contraction and, indeed, creating favorable conditions for a rebound in both bank deposits and the overall stock of money.

Deposit insurance also implied a more stable monetary environment beyond 1933. Runs on an individual bank were made less likely by deposit insurance, and cases in which individual banks did have difficulties were much less prone to provoke wider banking problems. For distress withdrawals of deposits from a bank would henceforth predominantly take the form of transfers of funds to other commercial banks, rather than conversion of deposits into currency. Consequently, the currency-deposit ratio was given enhanced stability by the reform. This in turn implied that the money stock would have greater built-in stability. One of the reasons that Friedman and Schwartz were critical of Federal Reserve performance between 1930 and 1933 was that the authorities did not increase high-powered money on a scale sufficient to meet US households' wish to hold more money in the form of currency. The surge in currency had therefore been allowed to lower the stock of bank reserves, prompting the overall money stock to decline.[126]

Deposit insurance greatly reduced the likelihood of events that called for Federal Reserve intervention of the kind that Friedman and Schwartz advocated. Therefore, not only did the advent of deposit insurance facilitate a rebound in bank deposits in 1933; it also installed an institutional environment that was more conducive to monetary stability in the future. A more stable regime for the creation of money had therefore been achieved via the New Deal reforms. This was the case even though, as Friedman and Schwartz noted, those reforms proceeded in an environment in which policy makers continued—as they had during the 1929-33 Great Contraction—to downplay the importance of monetary policy for the behavior of economic activity.[127]

One aspect of the New Deal's domestic monetary reforms of which Friedman and Schwartz were critical was the prohibition of payment on interest on demand deposits and the introduction of ceilings on commercial bank time-deposit rates. In their view, these measures reflected a misdiagnosis on the part of policy makers of the reasons for the financial collapse: specifically, a misguided belief that the 1930s bank failures arose largely from unsound lending made possible by aggressive bank bidding for deposits.[128] However, Friedman did not consider the implications of the prohibitions to be appreciable for the decade of the 1930s. He viewed bank earnings as so weak that rates paid on demand deposits would likely have been low in any event, and he regarded the time-deposit interest-rate ceilings as not binding in the 1930s, and rarely binding on a protracted basis until the 1960s.[129] Friedman would also give considerable credence to the view that banks were able to evade the interest-rate ceilings, except perhaps in the short run, by a variety of indirect means of remunerating deposits.[130]

These considerations meant that, although Friedman opposed the interest-rate ceilings—largely embodied in the Federal Reserve Board's Regulation Q—because they were a case of "government intervention where it has no business intervening" (Instructional Dynamics Economics Cassette Tape 16, February 1969), he viewed Regulation Q's practical implications as initially very limited. Interest-rate ceilings played a truly major part in Friedman's analysis of the behavior of monetary aggregates only in the period beyond the 1960 cutoff date of the Friedman-Schwartz *Monetary History*.[131]

The New Deal actions on the international front—the limits imposed in March 1933 on US citizens' use of gold and the broadening of these limits in April and December, exchange-rate flexibility over much of 1933, then a dollar devaluation enshrined in the fixing of the price of gold at $35 per ounce in January 1934—were also conducive to monetary stabilization, as they made it more straightforward for the Federal Reserve to exercise control over the money stock.[132]

Friedman and Schwartz argued that, even under pre-1933 arrangements, the United States' international obligations did not prevent considerable autonomy of the US authorities with respect to the setting of the US money stock. In particular, they noted that the Federal Reserve in the 1920s had prevented disequilibria in the US balance of payments from being passed through into the money stock.[133] Friedman acknowledged, in line with the *Monetary History*'s account, that "the desire to stay on gold" played a role in explaining the Federal Reserve's behavior during the period 1929–33.[134] But he and Schwartz argued that options other than a domestic monetary tightening remained available as ways of continuing to satisfy the United States' international obligations in the early 1930s.[135]

The 1933–34 change in the United States' international monetary arrangements put the US monetary authorities in a much more clear-cut position to call the shots on US domestic monetary conditions, irrespective of the United States' international obligations and of the US balance-of-payments situation. The initial New Deal monetary measures in 1933 were associated with a gold inflow that shored up bank reserves and the money stock.[136] But the longer-term impact of the 1933–34 New Deal changes was to disconnect variations in the money stock from international payments flows. As Friedman implied (Instructional Dynamics Economics Cassette Tape 50, May 16, 1970), hereafter Federal Reserve open-market purchases would serve the function that gold inflows did in the early Roosevelt period of creating monetary ease. The US government's pegging from the mid-1930s onward of the price of gold at $35 was, on this view, akin to a commodity-price support program, rather than an arrangement that determined the stance of US monetary policy.[137]

As far as Friedman and Schwartz were concerned, the boost to the money stock begun in 1933, together with the US monetary policy autonomy that was instituted thereafter, constituted the most important aspects of the New Deal–era changes to international economic policy—far exceeding in importance any change induced in the US price level by the devaluation of the dollar. Friedman and Schwartz noted that the devaluation was designed explicitly to raise prices, but Friedman would conclude that the implications of the devaluation for prices were quite limited and did not involve the kind of broad-based increase in the national price level envisioned by some versions of the law of one price.[138] Nor, as we shall see in the next subsection, was Friedman amenable to the notion that a large increase in the US price level was an essential component of a successful monetary stimulus.

The changes to the United States' domestic and international monetary arrangements in 1933 were associated with a major rebound in monetary growth—whether measured by M1 or M2—and in nominal and real income growth. These patterns are recorded in table 2.1 (in which the use of annual averages means that the monetary and economic rebounds occur in 1934).

The rapid expansion in money that occurred basically lined up with the prescriptions Friedman gave, after becoming a monetarist, for the type of situation the US economy faced in 1933. For Friedman, the fact that the United States had just undergone a severe monetary and economic contraction meant that his favored monetary policy of a steady M2 growth rate of around 3 to 5 percent per year should not be adopted immediately. Rather, he believed that this constant rate of monetary growth should be reached gradually from above, and that a monetary contraction, if it had been allowed to occur, should be followed by a catch-up period of rapid monetary growth.

The preceding portrayal of Friedman's position is at variance with the characterization of Modigliani (1988, 4), who stated that the "only exception" to a constant-monetary-growth rule allowed for in the monetarist prescription was that in which the economy started from a situation of high inflation. Modigliani's characterization was inaccurate, as in one of Friedman's earliest statements in favor of a constant-monetary-growth rule, Friedman indicated that it was not appropriate to start immediately

TABLE 2.1. Behavior of the Money Stock, Nominal Income, Real Income, and Prices, 1929–36

			Percentage change in annual average of:		
Year	M1	M2	Nominal GNP	Real GNP	GNP Deflator
1929	0.4	0.2	6.4	6.6	−0.1
1930	−4.0	−2.2	−12.3	−9.6	−3.1
1931	−8.0	−7.7	−16.1	−7.7	−9.1
1932	−11.8	−16.5	−23.4	−13.8	−11.1
1933	−5.2	−11.7	−4.3	−2.2	−2.1
1934	13.3	8.4	16.9	7.6	8.6
1935	18.2	15.1	11.1	8.8	2.1
1936	13.8	11.9	14.2	13.7	0.4

Source: Computed from the annual-data tables in Balke and Gordon (1986).

at the constant growth rate after a deep recession.[139] Friedman elaborated on this point in 1972, when he stated that a monetary-growth policy that started from initial conditions like those in 1933 should incorporate a catch-up period of rapid monetary growth ahead of the shift to a constant growth rate.[140] And in 1975 Friedman described as an "excellent and correct statement" the expression of the position that, during the transition to a monetary-growth rate that is consistent with long-run noninflationary economic growth, a period of above-normal monetary growth should be permitted if the economy is starting from a position of resource slack (*Wall Street Journal*, August 21, 1975).[141]

The gradualist approach embodied in these statements can be viewed as reflecting an expectations-augmented Phillips-curve analysis—which, of course, was a fundamental part of Friedman's framework.[142] When an expectational Phillips curve governs inflation dynamics, the closure of the output gap associated with rapid economic growth will likely be helpful in achieving an inflation objective, because it will aid in eliminating expectations of deflation or of below-target inflation. Expectational-Phillips-curve analysis is also relevant to a discussion of the supply-side aspects of the New Deal, to which the discussion now turns.

THE NEW DEAL: THE SUPPLY SIDE

In a retrospective that he provided on US economic performance after the Great Contraction, Friedman noted that there was a "massive expansion in nominal aggregate demand" from 1933.[143] This is evident in the data on nominal GNP growth in table 2.1. Friedman pointed to the shift in monetary behavior—from sharply negative rates of change in the quantity of money, to strongly positive monetary growth—as the factor behind this phenomenon. He would observe that "expansionary monetary policy" was "what really brought us out" of the 1933 trough.[144] The grounds for believing in a connection between monetary growth and nominal income growth will be considered below. But en route to that discussion, which really pertains to aggregate-demand determination, it is useful to consider first a matter that relates primarily to the state of aggregate supply in the 1930s. In particular, let us consider how the expansion in US nominal income that took place from 1933 onward was divided between increases in aggregate real output and changes in the price level.

The split of nominal income growth during the 1930s had unusual features. Friedman and Schwartz noted that, generally, nominal income growth and real income growth tended to move together from one year to the other—a phenomenon consistent with the existence of short-run effects of monetary policy on real output.[145] Comovement of real income growth and nominal income growth was also a feature of the 1930s recovery. However, one anomaly in the annual-average data of table 2.1 is that more than half of the initial rebound in nominal income growth in 1934 is absorbed by increases in prices. Indeed, although nominal income growth peaks in 1934, the strongest year of real output growth (13.7 percent) is not until 1936, when real income growth accounts for the lion's share of the rise in nominal income.

The fact that double-digit growth in real output was possible in 1936 raises the question of whether the prior years' recovery in real output could have been improved on even if nominal GNP growth were no different from that shown in table 2.1. The debate on that question may be seen as a dispute regarding the implications for real growth of the supply-side measures of the Roosevelt administration. The various stands taken in the dispute may be divided into three basic positions: the monetarist line taken by Friedman and Schwartz; the real business cycle (RBC)–oriented interpretation of Cole and Ohanian (2004, 2013); and the New Keynesian perspective of Eggertsson (2008, 2012). The recent literature has contrasted the latter two positions. The aim of this subsection is to show that the Friedman-Schwartz position is a plausible alternative that incorporates parts of the other two positions while also having its own distinct features.

There is some common ground, across the three schools of thought, concerning some key matters. The monetarist, RBC, and New Keynesian accounts all agree that the measures taken to raise US wages and prices and control important parts of US output in key economic sectors from 1933 onward had the effect of putting upward pressure on wages and prices and downward pressure on aggregate US potential output. The specific measures early in the Roosevelt administration cited by Friedman and Schwartz and others as having had these effects are the "codes" of the National Industrial Recovery Act; the Guffey Coal Act; and agricultural production controls and price supports.[146] There is, furthermore, wide agreement across studies of this period that, notwithstanding the fact that US Supreme Court rulings formally unwound some of the legislation underlying these industrial policy measures, the restrictions on production and official impetus for higher wages and prices continued after these rulings, thanks to new measures by the Roosevelt administration that substituted for the actions that had been ruled unconstitutional.[147]

According to his later recollection, Friedman was a critic of the price- and cost-raising aspects of New Deal controls even in the 1930s.[148] He made public criticisms of farm-price supports and other cartelization measures as early as 1948 (*New York Times*, January 11, 1948). He repeated these criticisms on many occasions. For example, in a 1970 discussion Friedman criticized the National Recovery Administration as well as "the Agricultural Adjustment Act and its successors."[149] But it was the *Monetary History* that put his criticism of the Roosevelt administration's supply-side (or industrial policy) measures within a monetarist framework. Friedman and Schwartz's monetarist analysis of the administration-imposed changes to the supply side in the 1930s contrasts both with New Keynesian analyses— which see these measures as providing a stimulus to economic activity that monetary policy might be unable to provide (Eggertsson 2012)—and real business cycle analyses—which see the measures as contractionary irrespective of monetary policy (Cole and Ohanian 2004, 2013).

Although the discussion below will go into considerable detail about the distinctions between the Friedman-Schwartz account and its two rivals, the Friedman-Schwartz account's key elements can be summarized very briefly. They are as follows. The shift in monetary growth (that is, growth in an M2-type aggregate) in the mid-1930s, from negative rates of change to double-digit rates of increase, created the conditions for nominal income growth to do the same. With the nominal GDP growth rebound so obtained, the question remained how much of that rebound would take the form of output growth and how much of inflation. Friedman and Schwartz's position was that a larger share of the observed nominal income growth could have taken the form of real growth and less the form of inflation in 1933 and 1934 if the US federal government's industrial policy had not pushed up the inflation component of spending growth in those years. In what follows, this monetarist position will be fleshed out in a way that brings out its differences from the New Keynesian and RBC positions.

A Phillips-Curve Perspective

Each interpretation of the recovery can be viewed in terms of a New Keynesian Phillips curve. Although, as will be discussed in chapter 7, the price-setting equation in Friedman's framework did not coincide fully with the New Keynesian Phillips curve, enough common ground is shared by these two perspectives on inflation behavior that no damage is done to his and Schwartz's account of the recovery by considering it with the use of a New Keynesian Phillips curve. The specific version of the Phillips curve to be considered is:

$$\pi_t = \beta E_t \pi_{t+1} + \alpha(y_t - y_t^*) + u_t. \tag{1}$$

In equation (1), π_t is inflation in period t, y_t is log real output in period t, y_t^* is log potential real output in period t, β is at or near unity, α is strictly positive, and u_t is a "cost-push" shock that, for given expected future inflation ($E_t \pi_{t+1}$) and the current value of the output gap, raises inflation in period t.[150] u_t is assumed to be a first-order autoregressive process, with an autoregressive coefficient in the range $0 \leq \rho_u < 1$.

For most analyses of historical inflation developments, it would be possible to say that the monetarist, RBC, and New Keynesian hypotheses share the position that inflation is a monetary phenomenon, and we would be able to represent this common position as the restrictions that $E[u_t]$ is zero, that it has negligible persistence ($\rho_u = 0$) and that α is positive. Differences between the RBC and the other two accounts (monetarist and New Keynesian) would then boil down to differences about the size of α, with the monetarist and New Keynesian hypotheses allowing for gradual price adjustment by making α strictly positive but finite. In fact, however, the special circumstances of the 1930s mean that there are further differences between the RBC account, in particular, and those associated with the monetarist and New Keynesian stories.

The RBC account's restrictions on the preceding Phillips curve are the same as those that would apply in RBC analysis of other periods: $u_t = 0$ for all t, and $\alpha = \infty$. Under those restrictions, prices are fully flexible, and the key RBC proposition, that output and potential output coincide, prevails. The supply-side measures of the Roosevelt administration in that case unambiguously reduced actual output.

For the analysis of the 1930s, the monetarist hypothesis and New Keynesian hypothesis, although dissimilar to one another in a number of respects, impose the same restrictions on the Phillips curve above. Both hypotheses specify $0 < \alpha < \infty$, so that price adjustment is gradual and the course of monetary policy makes a difference to the short-run behavior of output. In addition, *for the 1933–37 recovery*, these hypotheses take the mean of u_t to be positive and its serial correlation as also positive ($0 < \rho_u < 1$).

It is worth underscoring how different Friedman's analysis of 1933–37 price behavior was from his analysis of nearly any other historical episode. Friedman's position was that "almost all inflations have been demand-pull" (Instructional Dynamics Economics Cassette Tape 182, December 1975), and he regarded most alleged cases of cost-push inflation as instances in which a demand-pull inflation had been misdiagnosed.[151] But Friedman repeatedly singled out the 1933 to 1937 period as an important exception to this generalization.[152]

Friedman's emphasis on the exceptional nature of this period has been represented above as amounting to a position that the cost-push shock in equation (1) was positive and persistent. To be sure, Friedman viewed part of the consequence of the Roosevelt administration's supply-side measures as amounting to a reduction in potential output rather than as actions that, like u_t in equation (1), raised inflation for a given level of the output gap. But his acceptance that potential output declined would not, in itself, make his treatment of 1930s developments very different from his coverage of other historical periods. For a decline in potential output can be regarded as a factor making for excess demand and as such is a source of demand-pull inflation.

Consequently, Friedman readily acknowledged that changes in potential output could be a source of variation in the price level in a quantity-theory framework.[153] What, however, made the 1930s episode unusual in Friedman's discussions of price-level behavior was the importance he assigned to a cost-push shock. Friedman normally contended that autonomous forces making for higher prices could be a source of only transitory fluctuations in inflation: that is, they were factors that averaged out to zero and were not capable of being a source of ongoing inflation or of inflationary expectations in the absence of monetary accommodation. He made an exception, however, in his accounts of US developments in the 1933–37 period. Friedman regarded this period as one characterized by concerted government measures, which amounted to a sequence of positive shocks to the price level and inflation—shocks that put upward pressure on inflation and inflation expectations for a given output gap.

Eggertsson's (2008, 2012) New Keynesian account of the 1930s is entirely consistent with the Friedman position described in the preceding paragraph, yet it reaches a conclusion opposite to Friedman and Schwartz on whether the supply-side measures were supportive of *actual* output (as opposed to potential output, on which no one disputes the Roosevelt administration's industrial policy measures had an adverse effect).

Monetarist and New Keynesian Accounts

We come therefore to the divergence between the New Keynesian and monetarist accounts of the New Deal era's supply-side measures. Although the two accounts concur that these measures implied a succession of positive cost-push shocks—that is, positive values for u_t in the Phillips curve above—and thereby pushed up inflation, they disagree on whether this inflationary pressure provided, on net, a boost to real aggregate demand.

The New Keynesian position is that when—as likely was the case in the early 1930s—the expected path of the short-term nominal interest rate is flat and at a low level, industrial policy measures of the New Deal kind that systematically raise the path of the inflation rate (and thus expected inflation) are unambiguously stimulative for real aggregate demand and hence output. The reason is that, in the basic New Keynesian framework, the variable that is crucial for real spending decisions is the expected path of the real short-term interest rate. A rise in expected inflation reduces the path of the short-term real interest rate, and so, in this framework, it necessarily boosts real spending.[154] And, if the scope to reduce the expected path of the short-term nominal interest rate has been exhausted, there is no way, in this New Keynesian baseline, of providing a stimulus to nominal or real aggregate demand via monetary policy. Recourse to nonmonetary measures such as industrial policy to boost spending would then appear to be essential.

The monetarist view, in contrast, does not regard the scope that monetary policy has to boost nominal or real aggregate demand as having been exhausted once it is no longer possible to lower the expected path of the short-term nominal interest rate. Nor does the monetarist account accept that boosting expectations of inflation to high values—as opposed to simply removing expectations of deflation—is a necessary part of monetary policy measures to create recovery in a situation in which the short-term nominal interest rate is at its lower bound.

To bring this monetarist view out, it is worth proceeding in two stages. In the first stage, let us discuss the respect in which Friedman and Schwartz saw the industrial policy measures as having an adverse effect on the recovery of real output. For this discussion, it will be provisionally taken for granted that a boost to nominal monetary growth tends to raise nominal income growth, even when the path of the main short-term nominal interest rate is frozen—with an outline of the grounds for expecting this outcome deferred until the second stage.

As already indicated, Friedman traced the rapid nominal income growth in table 2.1 to rapid monetary growth.[155] This rise in monetary growth would, he stressed, have occurred without the industrial policy measures, being attributable instead to the 1933 monetary reforms.[156]

When the fact that the higher monetary growth would have emerged irrespective of the developments in industrial policy is combined with the premise that the surge in nominal income growth flowed from the upturn in monetary growth, the conclusion that the industrial policy actions worked against economic recovery follows naturally. For given nominal income growth, measures that directly raise inflation leave less room for real income growth. Friedman and Schwartz argued that downward pressure on output growth of this kind was indeed a feature of the high-inflation recovery year of 1934. On this interpretation, the New Deal's supply-side measures prevented 1934 from being a year like 1936, in which inflation took up a much smaller fraction of the rapid nominal income growth that occurred. The Friedman-Schwartz contention was that the price measures were counterproductive, in the sense that they tended to remove some of the stimulus to real output that would otherwise have come from the expansion of the money stock. This contention had, as they noted, also been advanced by Roose (1954, 143–44). Other proponents of the position have included A. Hart (1948, 323) and Weinstein (1980).[157] Also in line with the monetarist position was the study of Bordo, Erceg, and Evans (2000). On the basis of results from a quantitative business cycle model with nominal rigidities, Bordo, Erceg, and Evans suggested that the New Deal supply-side reforms made the recovery in real output considerably weaker than it would have otherwise been.

With the monetarist account of the 1930s recovery expressed in this way, one can see an area of agreement between that account and the RBC account, that area being the effects of the industrial policy measures on output. Although the monetarist account does, and the RBC account does not, see monetary policy as having short-run effects on output, both accounts agree that output would have been higher in the absence of the industrial policy shocks. In the RBC story, this is so because the reduction in potential output produced by the industrial policies ipso facto reduced actual output. In the monetarist story, on the other hand, it is because the inflation engendered by the industrial shocks absorbed nominal income growth and so reduced the boost to real output implied by the New Deal era's monetary expansion. This argument concerning the New Deal's policy mix surely underlay Friedman's 2003 assessment that "the New Deal hampered recovery from the contraction, [and] prolonged and added to unemployment."[158] In keeping with this assessment, Friedman expressed a degree of agreement with the Cole-Ohanian research on the New Deal industrial policies when discussing that research with Ohanian at a University of Chicago conference in Friedman's honor in November 2002.[159]

It is the area of disagreement between the monetarist and New Keynesian position on which the discussion will now focus. For this purpose, let us now proceed to the second stage of our discussion and consider the reasons why, in the monetarist view, policies that stimulate nominal monetary growth tend to promote stronger nominal income growth.

To start with, it should be emphasized that the monetarist view of transmission is *not* based on a direct role for the money stock in the determination of nominal or real spending. On the contrary, like the New Keynesian account, the monetarist view rests on an interest-rate transmission channel. Both accounts depict the 1933 regime change as successful in boosting real output because the measures lowered real interest rates. But beyond this, the monetarist view parts company with the New Keynesian framework: for, in the monetarist account, raising expected inflation to above-normal levels is inessential for getting real yields down. The basis for this position is the monetarist contention that, even with the short-term nominal interest rate at its lower bound, and all scope for reducing expected future riskless rates having been exhausted, there is still scope for monetary policy to place downward pressure on important interest rates. Many yields matter for aggregate demand in the monetarist account, and this account holds that the fact that some of these yields were still positive in nominal terms when the short-term riskless rate had been brought to near zero implied continued scope for expansion of the money stock to lower real and nominal yields.

Friedman and Schwartz saw measures that expanded the supply of money, not measures that reduced the potential supply of goods and services, as the vehicle through which aggregate-demand stimulus could and should be provided. They contended that this was the case even when policy makers were faced with the zero bound on short-term nominal interest rates on riskless assets. In the environment of the 1930s, yields that were likely candidates for being susceptible to downward pressure were the prominent interest rates that remained positive: yields on short-term private-sector-issued paper and yields on longer-term government and nongovernment securities. Friedman and Schwartz saw the monetary contraction of 1929–33 as raising risk premiums and term premiums via adverse portfolio-balance effects. A monetary expansion could be expected to have the opposite effect.[160] Admittedly, this view of the transmission mechanism was expressed more explicitly in Friedman and Schwartz's other joint work than it is in the *Monetary History*.[161] But it can be regarded as a view that underlies the account of the 1930s in the *Monetary History*.

That said, Friedman's framework does include an acceptance that removing expectations of *deflation* was an important stabilizing action of the New Deal reforms. Friedman's writings repeatedly underlined the potentially damaging repercussions of deflation for output stabilization.[162] True, Friedman and Schwartz noted in their *Monetary History* that the predominantly positive US economic growth of the pre–World War I period 1879–1914 had featured deflation (of a little over 1 percent per year on average) for the first eighteen years, 1879–97.[163] They also noted, however, that this earlier period had included depressed economic activity and deflation during 1893–96, and that there was evidence that the conditions for economic growth had been better in the years 1897–1914, with 2 percent average inflation, than in the 1879–97 deflationary period.[164]

Furthermore, although ex post real interest rates were high in the deflationary 1879–97 period, Friedman and Schwartz felt that ex ante real interest rates were well below ex post rates.[165] During what they called the "great monetary uncertainty in the early nineties," the silver movement promoted expectations of long-term inflation, even as the US economy experienced deflation.[166] These qualifications implied that the late nineteenth-century experience did not in fact offer valid evidence that expected deflation was not harmful to output.[167] Indeed, Friedman's post-*Monetary History* work reaffirmed the message that prolonged deflation—although in principle something to which economic agents could acclimatize themselves—tended in practice to be harmful for the economy. Revisiting the nineteenth century, he argued that had the push for a silver standard been adopted, the price level would have been steadier, expectations of deflation would have been further warded off, and the path of output would have been more stable, with the major output contractions in the late nineteenth century avoided.[168] The fact that the *Monetary History* account is consistent with the harm to output arising from expected deflation has been stressed by Bordo, Choudhri, and Schwartz (1995) and Romer and Romer (2013a) in these authors' consideration of the Friedman-Schwartz account of the early-1930s contraction.[169]

Ending expectations of deflation was, accordingly, important in the Friedman-Schwartz account of the 1930s recovery, and that emphasis constitutes common ground with the New Keynesian position outlined in Eggertsson (2008). But if one accepts the monetarist view that the riskless short-term interest rate is not the only yield appearing in the IS equation, the expectations channel is not the be-all and end-all as a means of providing monetary stimulus in a situation like that the US economy faced in early 1933. An expansion of the nominal money stock, even in circumstances in which the short-term riskless rate is near its floor and expectations of inflation do not exceed rates consistent with price stability, can stimulate nominal and real aggregate spending by creating downward pressure on a host of nominal interest rates that are still above their floor.

Accordingly, when the 1930s are viewed from the perspective taken by Friedman and Schwartz, the key message is that a policy that rids the economy of expectations of deflation is necessary for recovery, but actually pro-

moting rapid inflation is not. All real interest rates would be raised if expected deflation were allowed to occur, but key real interest rates could be
reduced without resorting to inflation. The downward pressure on these
yields is greater, the more that an increase in the nominal money stock
translates into an expansion of the real money stock. Price rises are not
a satisfactory substitute for monetary expansion in this situation. An increase in the price level in the face of a constant nominal money stock is
unlikely to provide stimulus to real aggregate demand. And when the nominal money stock *is* expanded, increases in the price level are not needed for
the monetary expansion to exert expansionary effects on real spending. Indeed, price rises might well reduce those effects by containing the rise in
the real money stock. The industrial policy measures of the 1930s, from this
perspective, had the undesirable effect of reducing the increase in the real
money stock implied by any given increase in the nominal money stock.

There is some evidence that the multiple-yield view of the monetary
transmission mechanism is an important element in an understanding
of the 1930s recovery. In particular, several studies that have attempted
to link, via reduced-form regression equations, the behavior of output or
nominal spending in the 1930s to the behavior of monetary aggregates
have found a significant relationship. For example, McCallum (1990b, 9)
found that M1 growth, lagged one quarter, appeared significantly, with sizable positive coefficient, in a regression of nominal GNP growth on three
lags of itself for 1922:Q1–1941:Q4, while Bernanke (1982, 148), also using
measures of monetary growth derived from M1, reported regressions for
growth in industrial production that "support the Friedman-Schwartz view
that money was an important source of output variation in the Great Depression."[170] Bernanke also noted that the monetary-growth terms in his
estimated equations actually had higher and more significant coefficients
in a sample (January 1919–December 1941) that included the New Deal
period than in a subsample (January 1921–January 1933) that ended prior
to the New Deal. Likewise, Bordo, Choudhri, and Schwartz (1995, 494–95)
found that M2 growth was highly significant in predicting output behavior
during the interwar period.

In contrast, Eggertsson (2008, 1477) argues that the "turning point [in
the economy in 1933] cannot be explained by contemporaneous changes
in the money supply." But Eggertsson's discussion seems to be defining
money as the monetary base, rather than M1 or M2, and consequently his
description of monetary-aggregate behavior lacks force as a critique of the
monetarist account of the 1930s, which emphasizes instead the behavior
of deposit-inclusive aggregates.[171] Eggertsson's (2008, 1477) position that
"the money supply did not change around the turning point" in the economy is not valid when M1 or M2 is considered to be the money-supply mea-

sure.[172] The timing evidence that links the monetary turnaround and the economic turnaround is buttressed by the reduced-form econometric estimates discussed in the previous paragraph.

The reduced-form evidence on money/output patterns would appear to be consistent with the broad-based transmission mechanism that Friedman and Schwartz stressed. This evidence supports the notion that measures that boosted the money stock could and did provide stimulus to real and nominal aggregate spending during the New Deal years. Pointing instead to industrial policy as the source of the expansion in aggregate demand neglects the importance of measures to boost the quantity of money. And to suggest that industrial policy was a boost to aggregate demand is to overlook the point that the price rises associated with the industrial policy measures had the effect of reducing the downward pressure that faster nominal monetary growth could exert on key nominal interest rates.

The supply-side dimension of the Friedman-Schwartz account also provides insight into the relationship between the monetarist explanations for the post-1933 recovery and accounts that emphasize the role of the veterans' bonus of 1936. Specifically, both Telser (2003) and Hausman (2016) have pointed to the strengthening of US real output growth in 1936 in the wake of the veterans' bonus. Both these accounts have suggested that this fiscal policy initiative, rather than monetary policy, is the source of the boost to output in 1936 (a sharp output rise that comes out clearly in table 2.1).

Lester Telser engaged Friedman extensively on this topic. It will come as no surprise that Friedman viewed the veterans' bonus as a contributing factor to the economic expansion but mainly via its status as a source of upward pressure on monetary growth. He regarded the veterans' bonus as making for higher deficit spending by the federal government, spending that the Federal Reserve accommodated with money creation. Indeed, in this spirit, Sargent and Wallace (1973, 1044) earlier cited a veterans' bonus as a factor that might trigger a once-and-for-all increase in the money stock.

Because the veterans' bonus occurred alongside monetary expansion, it is little wonder that Friedman viewed the bonus as working on aggregate demand via its monetary effects, instead of accepting it as an example of the influence on total spending of fiscal policy for given monetary policy. Again, we can understand his viewpoint by considering a simplified case in which the nominal income path is fixed by the policies determining the quantity of money (in combination with largely separate factors determining velocity), with the short-run breakdown of nominal income between output and prices in turn influenced heavily by supply-side factors.[173] From this perspective, the fact that nominal income growth was roughly the same in 1936 as its average rate in 1934 and 1935, together with the fact that rapid monetary growth prevailed throughout the period from 1934 to

1936, is evidence that the veterans' bonus had little independent influence on nominal income growth in 1936. And the fact that real income sped up in 1936 without a corresponding rise in nominal spending supports the notion that the strengthening in real spending came not from a change in monetary or fiscal policy, but from the better aggregate-supply conditions: as the price shocks associated with the New Deal supply-side measures receded, real output growth in 1936 could form a larger share of the rise in nominal spending.

The same verdict on the veterans' bonus can be arrived at if we allow for more structure and consider a situation in which nominal income is determined simultaneously with its components (real income and prices). In particular, consider the case in which real aggregate demand is driven by a set of real yields, and—as in the monetarist transmission mechanism sketched earlier—the nominal yields that are counterparts to these real yields are influenced by the real stock of M2 outstanding. Under these conditions, it is plausible that real income growth strengthened in 1936 because the absence of a major price-level shock in that year allowed more of the expansion of the nominal money stock in 1936 to pass through into real money, compared with the situation in 1934–35. The rapid growth in the real money stock in turn put greater downward pressure on nominal yields and therefore on real yields, and the lowering of real yields served to boost real aggregate demand.

Either in its money-to-nominal-income shorthand version or in the more structural version that features portfolio-balance effects, the bottom line in the monetarist story is the same. The monetarist account emphasizes that the veterans' bonus provided upward pressure on the nominal money stock because the higher level of deficit spending associated with the bonus was monetized—thus allowing the rapid monetary expansion observed since 1933 to continue. The veterans' bonus stimulated output, but the stimulus should, according to the monetarist account, primarily be seen as having worked via the increase in the money stock. The real money stock also expanded, as there were no longer large price-level shocks that stopped the rise in nominal money from being felt in a higher real money stock. The strengthening of real GDP growth, on this view, reflected the impact on yields of the boost to the real money stock. One does not need to point to the veterans' bonus as a separate source of stimulus to aggregate demand.

An encapsulation of the Friedman position on the New Deal supply-side changes can be obtained by considering a judgment that James Tobin gave in 1989. Tobin stated that "in the 1930's one of the first objectives of the Roosevelt Administration was to get prices to rise and to stop the deflation. . . . It worked and it arrested the severe decline."[174] To Friedman, the undoubted contribution that this part of the New Deal policies made to recovery stemmed from their "stop the deflation" element. Whether measures "to get prices to rise" were beneficial for output, on net, was much more questionable in Friedman's view.

III. Personalities, 1932–39

HENRY SIMONS

Henry Simons, who joined the University of Chicago in 1927 (*New York Times*, June 20, 1946) and worked in the fields of both law and economics, was not the teacher of Friedman's monetary-theory class—that was instead Lloyd Mints—and Friedman dated Simons's monetary writings as mostly in the period from 1933 onward, after Friedman's studies at the University of Chicago had begun.[175] Once Simons had shifted his focus to monetary matters, he evolved into the principal representative of the University of Chicago's positions on money until his death in 1946. This role led Friedman, who would remember Simons as "my teacher and my friend—and above all, a shaper of my ideas," to devote a lecture, "The Monetary Theory and Policy of Henry Simons," to him in 1967.[176] In his post-1967 research and statements, Friedman would emphatically reaffirm the links between Simons's work and his own. It is not the case, as has been claimed, that Friedman dropped references to Simons in his later monetary writings or that he omitted to mention Simons in his memoirs' (brief) account of monetary thought at the University of Chicago.[177]

A debt to Simons undoubtedly existed and was repeatedly acknowledged by Friedman. There is, however, room for disagreement on the amount of continuity that existed between Friedman and Simons in regard to monetary issues. A whole subliterature has developed on the extent to which Friedman carried the mantle of the pre-Friedman Chicago School, and of Simons in particular, on matters of monetary theory and policy. In this connection, Patinkin (1969, 1979) questioned whether Friedman's emphasis on the demand for money in his presentation of the quantity theory of money can be considered a development of Simons's framework. This subliterature has been the subject of a two-volume analysis and readings collection (see Leeson 2003b, 2003c) and much of the debate documented therein is tangential to the present book. The discussion that follows will therefore not be concerned with this debate. Nor will a comprehensive picture of Simons's monetary views be attempted: see Tavlas (1977a, 2015) and Rockoff (2015) on that score. Instead, the discussion here will focus on what Friedman in his 1967 lecture specified as one area of *disagreement* with Simons: Simons's proposals for monetary reform, which Friedman concluded were "largely irrelevant and wrong."[178]

Let us consider, in particular, Simons's and Friedman's views on 100 percent reserve requirements. Both Simons and Friedman favored this institutional change, but the 100 percent reserves proposal became less central to Friedman's monetary-reform agenda after the 1950s, and his advocacy of 100 percent reserves rested on a different perspective on financial intermediation from that to which Simons subscribed. It happens that a remark that Friedman made in other connection—when he was discussing an aspect of John Kenneth Galbraith's policy recommendations—captures succinctly the role that 100 percent reserve requirements played in Friedman's own reform proposals: "You can subtract it and leave his position unaltered."[179]

Simons did not originate the 100 percent reserve-requirement scheme, variants of which had been proposed prior to the 1930s. Furthermore, figures not at the University of Chicago also proposed the scheme during the 1930s, including Lauchlin Currie and Yale University's Irving Fisher (1935) (see Sandilands 1990, 52; Laidler 1993a, 1095; and Laidler 1999, 240–41). But Simons became a leading advocate of the reform, notably in Simons (1934) and in a joint statement with other University of Chicago economists issued in 1933.[180] The University of Chicago variant of the 100 percent proposal received the label of the "Chicago Plan" (A. Hart 1935), a term Friedman himself would occasionally use when referring to the proposal in his postwar writings.[181]

Friedman's early work on policy rules gave a prominent place to Simons's 100 percent reserves proposal. In particular, the package of reforms advocated for the United States in Friedman's 1948 article "A Monetary and Fiscal Framework for Economic Stability" included a move to 100 percent reserve requirements.[182] Furthermore, the principal rationale that Friedman advanced for this move was the same as that advanced by Simons and other authors. This was that a 100 percent reserve-requirement arrangement would eliminate any slippage between actions by the monetary authority on the monetary base and the behavior of aggregate commercial bank deposits. Friedman's 1948 package also reflected other aspects of Simons's position. As Friedman later noted, Simons, like Keynes (1936), viewed the private sector as treating short-term securities and money balances as largely interchangeable assets.[183] The perception of short-term securities as money-like led Simons to recommend elimination of Treasury bills as a public-debt instrument, with the government's interest-bearing debt restricted to bonds of the consol type.[184] Friedman's 1948 reform agenda followed this template, as his 1948 article proposed that the outstanding stock of government debt be completely converted into consols.[185]

Friedman's 1948 proposal, however, proved to be the high-water mark of the agreement between his and Simons's framework. As has already been stressed, and as discussed in more detail in chapter 4, Friedman's monetary thinking underwent a major change between 1948 and 1951. With a lag, this transformation in thinking altered Friedman's perspective on the appropriate reforms to US monetary arrangements and most preferable rule for policy conduct.

Once Friedman's thinking on rules had changed, the significance of 100 percent reserve requirements in his reform agenda diminished. Friedman's advocacy of 100 percent reserve banking is *not* a critical component of his post-1951 monetary economics. Accordingly, as Friedman was a key monetarist from 1951 onward, it would be inappropriate to depict 100 percent reserve requirements as a cornerstone of the monetarist position. Williamson and Wright's (2011) attempt to make their rejection of 100 percent reserve banking a selling point for their own approach to monetary analysis, and to juxtapose this "New Monetarism" against an "Old Monetarism" in which 100 percent reserve requirements figure prominently, is therefore misplaced.[186]

After Friedman began advocating a rule of constant monetary growth, he frequently proposed that rule without including 100 percent reserve banking as part of the necessary reforms.[187] Indeed, he would state specifically that 100 percent reserves were less essential than other reforms that he recommended.[188] A key feature that Friedman stressed was the achievement of arrangements under which monetary policy ensured that the money stock should be maintained in the face of disruption to the credit market. As Friedman stressed even in his 1960 *Program for Monetary Stability*, in which his reform package *did* include 100 percent reserves, 100 percent reserve requirements were not essential for achieving these arrangements.[189]

This position contrasts sharply with Simons's stress on 100 percent reserve requirements. The reason why Friedman eventually came to downplay the importance of the 100 percent reserve scheme is twofold. First, Friedman from the 1950s disagreed with the Simons position on the tools of monetary control. Second, Friedman developed a different perspective on the transmission mechanism from Simons, leading him to depart from Simons's position regarding the degree of control of financial intermediation that the monetary authorities needed to exert. Each of these points is now elaborated on.

With regard to monetary control, Friedman shared with Simons a concern that there were potential instabilities in the deposit-creation process that needed to be offset or overridden by government actions. But, as indicated above, Friedman and Schwartz saw one of these instabilities (that associated with the currency-deposit ratio) as having been greatly ameliorated by the advent of deposit insurance. Friedman stressed that open market operations *could* achieve the goal of maintaining the money stock:

private-sector-generated movements in the money multiplier could and should be offset by open market operations.[190] Indeed, *Program for Monetary Stability* did not contend that a 100 percent reserve system was essential, but rather that variations in reserve requirements did not deliver anything that open market operations could not accomplish.

In addition, in Friedman's view, reserve-requirement changes were less efficient than open market operations: the latter actions bore on all depository institutions, including those that were not subject to reserve requirements. And reserve requirements were an awkward policy tool even for influencing the behavior of institutions that were subject to reserve requirements, a source of complication being the fact that different requirement ratios applied to different categories of bank deposits.[191] In any event, for much of the time, as Friedman observed, the Federal Reserve routinely undid with open market operations the pressure on bank reserves that it had created with changes in reserve requirements.[192]

For all these reasons, Friedman felt that it was desirable to "rationalize" reserve requirements by making them uniform across deposits and constant over time.[193] The sort of streamlining of reserve requirements that he advocated did not necessarily involve imposition of a 100 percent reserves system. Indeed, it is insufficiently recognized that Friedman put forward alternatives to 100 percent reserve banking. *A Program for Monetary Stability* acknowledged that zero reserve requirements could achieve monetary control just as 100 percent reserve requirements could. And, in that exposition and subsequently, Friedman presented the zero percent and 100 percent alternatives as equally attractive.[194] In this connection, Friedman affirmed in 1992: "You ought to have reserve requirements of either zero or 100 percent. Either extreme makes sense" (Milton Friedman, interview, January 22, 1992).

It is clear, therefore, that although Friedman's vision of a fundamental monetary overhaul would involve a shift to 100 percent reserve requirements, in making policy recommendations he frequently took for granted the continuation of a fractional reserve system. The 100 percent reserve-requirement scheme was not central to Friedman's position on monetary control, whereas it *had* been central in Simons's reform proposals.

The second part of the difference between Simons and Friedman on the 100 percent reserve scheme relates to their distinct perspectives on financial intermediation. As noted, Simons saw deposit money and short-term securities as largely serving the same function for their holders. In contrast, Friedman from the 1950s onward saw an open-market sale that replaced reserves with bills as a demonetizing operation, and he viewed the contraction in bank deposits that occurred in the wake of this operation as materially reducing the liquidity of the nonbank private sector. Provided that interest rates were allowed to fluctuate, Treasury or commercial bills would not be regarded by the private sector as equivalent to money, and the fact that those securities could not be redeemed (prior to maturity) at face value helped break the equivalence of bills and money. The implication was that control of the money stock, not of all short-term financial assets, was key to policy makers' control of aggregate demand.[195]

This different conception of the asset structure led to a contrast between Simons and Friedman on the issue of what control powers were needed to secure the effectiveness of monetary policy. For Simons, meaningful control by the authorities entailed not only control of the money stock but also a curb on the wherewithal of the Treasury and the private sector to issue short-term securities, as he regarded these securities as de facto money. Accordingly, Simons's reform package involved, in addition to 100 percent reserve requirements, a prohibition on the issuance of short-term securities by both the Treasury and the private sector. To this end, Simons advocated the "abolition . . . of all special institutional arrangements for large-scale financing at short term" and a prohibition on short-term lending by commercial banks, supplemented by "drastic limitation upon the powers of corporations" to borrow.[196]

Simons's reputation was as an advocate of free markets—a status reflected in the *University of Chicago Magazine*'s observation (July 1946) that Simons was the voice of the "cause of economic freedom," and in Aaron Director's indication that Simons was emerging as the new leader of the Chicago School at the time of his death.[197] However, the recommendations Simons made in favor of market economics pertained primarily to the nonfinancial sector. In the financial sphere, his prescriptions were different: Simons envisioned that the government's exercise of monetary control would take place in the context of institutional arrangements that heavily restricted the scope for private-sector activity in the credit market.

Simons's stand on the credit market contrasted markedly with Friedman's position from the 1950s onward. Friedman would drop his 1948 proposals that issuance of Treasury bills be discontinued and that the existing stock of bills be withdrawn from the market. Friedman's endorsement of 100 percent reserve requirements did amount to advocacy of a system in which commercial banks could not use their deposit liabilities as a source of funds for their loans to the private sector. But he had no interest in imposing wide-ranging additional restrictions on the terms of private borrowing and lending. Friedman did not concur with Simons's advocacy of a prohibition of a market for short-term private securities. They had in common the belief in the desirability of laissez-faire arrangements as far as possible in the nonfinancial sector, but Friedman would part company with Simons's anti-free-market prescriptions regarding the credit market.[198]

Thus, the areas of the economy in which Friedman viewed it as desirable to have what he called "free and flexible private markets" included the credit market.[199] To this end, Friedman sought a reduction in government regulations of the issuance of securities by private corporations.[200] Friedman further believed that if strict limits were to be imposed on the terms of the private sector's scope to issue debt and equity, this "would probably greatly reduce the economy's productivity and efficiency."[201] As a more general matter, Friedman advocated reducing "government interference with lending and borrowing."[202]

Friedman's advocacy of a free credit market was not based on a view that the credit market could invariably be counted on to function well and behave in a stable manner. On the contrary, Friedman saw the demand function for credit as liable to exhibit considerable instability.[203] His advocacy of laissez-faire in securities markets arose instead from doubts that regulation could remove the instabilities and failures of the credit system. What the authorities should instead make their priority, in his view, was the creation of arrangements under which credit market instabilities did not spill over into fluctuations in the money stock. A major attraction to Friedman of a 100 percent reserve system was, as noted above, that it could automatically separate deposit creation from developments in the credit market.[204] Friedman viewed such a separation as an important function of monetary policy, even absent 100 percent reserves. Most importantly, even in a zero or fractional reserve-requirement regime, the option was open to the authorities to carry out open market operations on a scale sufficient to insulate the money stock from a collapse in the volume of credit. Friedman suggested that the Federal Reserve should have done this, but did not do so, in the 1929–33 period, as well as in the 1980 credit-controls episode.

Let us move away, temporarily, from the issue of reserve requirements, to another respect in which Friedman and Simons parted company: namely, on their recommended target. Simons favored using a system under which the authorities used their control of the money stock to target a general price index.[205] Friedman himself made a similar recommendation in his very early monetarist years, until he switched to the constant-monetary-growth rule in 1956. In the 1990s and 2000s he was again amenable to a direct price stability goal but did not fully repudiate the constant-monetary-growth rule. However, the position that Friedman took in his main years of activity was that the lack of knowledge about the short- and intermediate-run connections between monetary policy and the economy made it inappropriate to hold the monetary authorities accountable for price-level outcomes. This model-uncertainty consideration and the need for central-bank accountability instead pointed, in his view, to the constant-monetary-growth rule as the appropriate policy.

Confronted with this recommendation, Friedman's critics would throw in his face a Simons quotation, which Friedman had himself used in his 1967 lecture, that stressed the reality of "sharp changes on the velocity side."[206] For his part, Friedman acknowledged that the period with which Simons was most concerned, namely the 1930s, did feature sizable fluctuations in velocity, but Friedman did not see that experience as the basis for a strong case against constant growth in the money stock.

The 1929–33 period had indeed seen sharp changes in velocity: Friedman and Schwartz reported a 29 percent decline in the velocity of their measure of the money stock.[207] But Friedman and Schwartz's interpretation of this velocity decline did not support the position implicit in Simons's rejection of fixed-quantity rules (which is to say, the position that large velocity fluctuations tended to be opposite in sign to those of the money stock—and so worked to undo the connection between monetary changes and changes in nominal income). Rather, as Friedman and Schwartz viewed matters, households' demand for real money holdings arose partly from money's status as a source of funds in emergencies. Accordingly, the demand for real money balances was an increasing function of economic uncertainty. From this it followed that the monetary contraction—a decline in nominal money—of the 1929–33 period produced an economic contraction whose depth was reinforced by the uncertainty-induced decline in velocity—a rise in desired and actual real money balances.

On this interpretation—which subsequently received support from Christiano, Motto, and Rostagno's (2003) quantitative dynamic general equilibrium analysis of the US Great Depression—the sharp velocity contraction amounted to a propagation of the monetary contraction rather than testimony against the stabilizing properties of a fixed-monetary-growth rule. This propagation also implied that, although both money-supply increases and deflation in principle added to the real money stock, and so both measures might appear to be a source of stimulus to aggregate demand, only money-supply increases could be counted on to be stimulative. Rather than serving to boost real spending via its impact on real money balances, deflation might trigger such economic disruption that the associated boost to real money supply was swamped by a boost to real money demand. It was precisely the latter scenario that Friedman and Schwartz believed to have described the period 1929–33: as the increases in real money balances in that period occurred alongside monetary contraction, they were a sign of tight, not easy, money.[208]

Indeed, Friedman and Schwartz believed that the monetary contraction might have given rise to a still-larger velocity decline, had it not been for the fact of the banking failures, which reduced confidence in bank deposits and so constrained the private sector's tendency to raise their holding of money balances. Friedman and Schwartz pointed to the example of Canada, which had avoided major bank failures in the early 1930s. For this country, there had not been the negative influence on real money demand arising from bank failures to work against the positive influence on money demand that was arising from increased uncertainty.[209] In line with this reasoning, Canadian velocity fell much more between 1929 and 1933 than US velocity—by 41 percent.[210]

Friedman and Schwartz regarded the Depression-era decline in US velocity as part of a phenomenon that they viewed as being in operation, on a smaller scale, in other historical episodes. Typically, velocity did not behave in such a way that nominal income fluctuations were dissimilar to those of money. Rather, the norm that Friedman and Schwartz found was that nominal income and the money stock moved in the same direction, and the role played by velocity was that it *amplified* the movement of nominal income. Or, as Friedman put it shortly after the release of the *Monetary History*: "On the average, velocity tends to move in the same direction as the quantity of money and not in the opposite direction."[211]

This process, in which the behavior of velocity reinforces the behavior of the money stock instead of counteracting it, was also in evidence in the recovery phase of the 1930s. McCallum (1990b, 9) found that, while monetary growth was highly significant in accounting for the behavior of nominal income growth in the 1930s, the monetary-growth terms were boosted further in significance if allowance was made for a shift to a higher velocity level in 1933:Q2 and 1933:Q3 as the New Deal banking reforms were put into effect.[212] A rise in monetary velocity during the New Deal is consistent with the reduction in uncertainty as well as with Friedman and Schwartz's generalization that velocity movements can largely be regarded as "set in train" by prior monetary change.[213]

The fact of sizable variations in velocity was therefore acknowledged in monetarist analysis. But that analysis went on to argue that it remained valid, even in the presence of such velocity variations, to view monetary factors as an important source of business cycle fluctuations. In the 1930s, the monetary reforms generated more stable conditions for the creation of *nominal* money, and they produced the confidence required for a flight by the private sector out of money into other assets, and so a reduction in *real* money balances.[214] In sum, for Friedman, the fact of sharp changes in velocity during the Great Contraction was not evidence against a nonmonetary interpretation of the Great Contraction, nor did it provide a sound basis for opposition to a constant-monetary-growth rule.

There is, however, an important respect in which Friedman's advocacy of a 100 percent reserve requirement left him vulnerable to the criticism that his rule would provoke (to use the Simons phrase quoted above) "sharp changes on the velocity side." Neither Friedman nor Simons seems to have adequately appreciated the extent to which a regime of 100 percent reserve requirements might promote the creation of deposit substitutes. As critics of 100 percent reserve arrangements such as Schlesinger (1960), Mishkin (1989), Benston and Kaufman (1993), and Laurent (2000) have stressed, while a 100 percent reserve-requirement system would make it illegal for banks to issue fixed-value liabilities as a way of financing loans to the private sector, it might well create new incentives for unregulated intermediaries to step in and do so.[215] As a result, the monetary control provided by 100 percent reserve requirements might be illusory, as the economically relevant money stock could be one that included the unregulated institutions' liabilities, and the officially controlled money stock might consequently be a series whose velocity had considerable instability.

Friedman recognized that financial intermediaries had incentives to evade reserve requirements as well as other direct controls on their activities.[216] He further acknowledged that banks were a "very efficient and sensible mechanism" for financial intermediation (Instructional Dynamics Economics Cassette Tape 16, February 1969). It was precisely this institutional fact that led Benston and Kaufman (1993, 42–44) to argue that imposition of a 100 percent reserves system would lead to a proliferation of deposit-taking-and-lending activities by unregulated, yet bank-like, institutions.

Friedman himself was aware that evasion along these lines had flowed from the existing fractional reserve-requirement arrangements in the US system, and that such evasion had given rise to the creation of deposit-like assets that were not included in the official US monetary aggregates. Yet he does not seem to have fully confronted the tension between this realization and his occasional advocacy of 100 percent reserve requirements. It might be argued that, since Friedman from 1960 onward paired his 100 percent reserve-requirement proposal with a recommendation that bank reserves receive interest, he envisioned reforms under which the incentive to evade reserve requirements was held down. But a system consisting of interest payments on bank reserves and 100 percent reserve requirements is still likely to imply substantial incentives to bypass the requirements. Banks' intermediation frequently involves riding the yield curve and lending to risky, but bank-screened, private-enterprise projects. A 100 percent reserve system in which banks earn the riskless-asset interest rate on their reserve balances would likely leave banks with lower returns on their portfolio than they would receive if they could use their deposit liabilities to finance private loans.

Friedman continued his advocacy of 100 percent reserve requirements in the 1980s and 1990s. For example, in April 1981, Friedman stated, "If I could really be as radical as I wanted to be, I would abolish a [*sic*; the] fractional reserve banking system and have a 100 percent reserve system," while in his 1992 preface to a reissue of *A Program for Monetary Stability* he reaffirmed the merits of 100 percent reserve requirements.[217] More than likely, however, 100 percent reserve requirements amount to an impractical reform that would not achieve the intended aim of improved monetary control. Friedman did not explicitly absorb this point in print. But, unlike Simons, he did acknowledge that several of the main aims of the 100 percent reserves scheme—in particular, central-bank control of bank deposits and insulation of the money stock from credit-market disturbances—could be achieved by other means. Reflecting these acknowledgments, Friedman underlined the point that the adoption of 100 percent reserve requirements was not an essential reform.

It is convenient to conclude this section by considering another issue connected to reserve requirements that was brought up by the 1930s experience: namely, the effects of the Federal Reserve's moves to increase reserve requirements in 1936 and 1937. Until quite recently, it was not very controversial to suggest that the Federal Reserve's increase in reserve requirements made monetary conditions more contractionary and helped set back the US economy in 1937 and 1938. This was the *Monetary History*'s position, and Meltzer (2003, 518–21) reached a similar conclusion. In contrast, Goodhart (2005, 273) expressed skepticism, and he suggested instead that commercial banks might well shrug off reserve-requirement increases. And Hanes (2006, 189), while emphasizing the importance of another US monetary action—the cutback in commercial bank reserves associated with the US Treasury's sales of its gold holdings—as a factor behind monetary and economic contraction in the later 1930s, concluded that "the reserve requirement changes did not matter" in the creation of the conditions that led to the late-1930s downturn.

A very straightforward demonstration that the reserve-requirement increases of 1936 and 1937 likely amounted to a significant contractionary measure is provided by table 2.2, which presents the correlations, for the post-1933 recovery period, of M2 growth and nominal income growth with two measures of monetary base growth: one adjusted for changes in reserve requirements, and one that does not have this adjustment. The two base series, although derived from somewhat different definitions of currency and bank reserves, have essentially the same growth rates for the 1930s, except for the years 1935–38. The material differences between the two series therefore overwhelmingly reflect the increases in reserve requirements in 1936 and 1937.

The table shows that both M2 growth and nominal income growth are clearly more closely related to (prior) adjusted base growth than to the unadjusted series. This finding has negative implications for the sanguine interpretation of reserve-requirement changes that Goodhart (2005) sketched. That interpretation essentially relies on commercial banks' behavior (in particular, their deposit creation) being neutral with respect to the increases in reserve requirements. One condition under which such neutrality might prevail would be if the increase was not binding on commercial banks because banks in the late 1930s were indifferent between holding their abundant reserve balances as excess reserves or as required reserves. The fact that M2 contracted in response to the reserve-requirement increases is inconsistent with this view, as the monetary contraction suggests that the reserve-requirement increase prompted retrenchment on the part of the banking sector.[218] In a similar vein, the contraction in nominal income growth in the wake of the reserve-requirement increases does not seem consistent with the notion that the changes in reserve requirements were innocuous.

Another scenario in which reserve requirements could have a neutral effect would involve the unadjusted base being raised by an amount that offsets the impact on money of the reserve-requirement increase. However, both the reduction in the adjusted monetary base and the contraction in M2 provide evidence against this scenario.

Table 2.2 is also inconsistent with Hanes's (2006) dismissal of the 1936–37 changes in reserve requirements. If the reserve-requirement increases were of no consequence, growth in the adjusted monetary base should not be better correlated with M2 growth (and nominal income growth) than is growth in the unadjusted base—yet it is. The changes in reserve requirements therefore do seem to have played an important role in producing a renewed downturn in money and the associated 1937–38 downturn in the economy. Recognition of the importance of this action should not be regarded as implying a denial that other contractionary monetary policy actions were present over the period. In particular, as Hanes (2006) emphasized, and as Friedman also recognized, the US Treasury dominated the behavior of commercial bank reserves in the late 1930s, its sterilization of gold inflows reducing the stock of reserves.[219] But the increases in reserve requirements evidently reinforced this contractionary measure.

SIMON KUZNETS

Over the years, some of the more visceral critics of the Keynesian revolution have taken umbrage at the suggestion, often advanced, that Keynes's *General Theory* initiated—or was the major spur to—the development of national income accounting.[220] For example, in the late 1950s Henry Hazlitt, Milton Friedman's predecessor as a *Newsweek* economics columnist, wrote a book-length critique of the *General Theory* in which he dismissed

TABLE 2.2. Correlations of Monetary Base Growth with Current and Future
Nominal Income Growth and with Current and Future Monetary Growth, 1934–41

| | Correlation for 1934–41 of row variable with: | | | |
| | Monetary base growth (not adjusted for changes in reserve requirements) | | Monetary base growth (adjusted for changes in reserve requirements) | |
	Of same year	Of prior year	Of same year	Of prior year
Nominal GNP growth	−0.08	0.41	−0.17	0.73
M2 growth	0.45	0.47	0.28	0.87

Note: Nominal GNP and M2 series are obtained from Balke and Gordon's (1986) annual-data tables. Annual averages of the monetary base (not adjusted for changes in reserve requirements) are computed from the quarterly average series on high-powered money in McCallum (1990b) (itself derived from data in Friedman and Schwartz 1963a). Annual data on the monetary base adjusted for reserve-requirement changes are obtained from the monthly data on the Federal Reserve Bank of St. Louis Adjusted Monetary Base series, available in the Federal Reserve Bank of St. Louis's FRED portal. In all cases, growth rates are computed from the annual series on levels.

as "pure fantasy" the notion that it was "Keynes who created the 'national income concept'" (Hazlitt 1959, 409). Around the same time, Clark Warburton—the economist who, as discussed in detail in the next chapter, foreshadowed Friedman in many of his writings on monetary policy and criticisms of Keynes—expressed a similar complaint. Warburton (1958, 211) observed: "In the United States, at least, both the theory and methodology of national income and product tabulations . . . are more closely linked with economic thought and work in this field prior to publication of the *General Theory* than to the work of Keynes and his followers." Like Hazlitt, Warburton went on to cite late-1930s work with which Simon Kuznets was primarily associated, specifically volumes 1 to 3 (1937 to 1939) of the National Bureau of Economic Research's conference series *Studies in Income and Wealth*.[221]

Friedman, however, was more circumspect when he considered this topic. "The stress on national income estimation," he wrote in 1961, "though not its initial development, derived largely from the Keynesian revolution in economic theory."[222] Friedman's measured response is notable because it comes from someone who was, by 1961, a critic of the Keynesian revolution. It is notable also because Friedman had a further incentive to downplay the impetus provided by Keynesianism to the development of national income accounting. During the late 1930s, Friedman had been a student/

assistant of Kuznets, the developer of national accounts, and Kuznets had assigned Friedman some of the research involved in the national accounts compilations. Indeed, the three late-1930s NBER volumes on national accounts data that Clark Warburton cited in the discussion mentioned above were edited by none other than Milton Friedman.[223]

One of Friedman's earliest publications was a favorable review, published during Friedman's 1930s spell in Washington, DC, of a Kuznets book—a review that was Friedman's first-ever article in the *Journal of Political Economy*.[224] Friedman's recollection, however, was that he did not know Kuznets at this time and probably did not meet him until early 1937.[225] It was from then until 1940 that Friedman worked with Kuznets as a combination of salaried assistant to Kuznets at the National Bureau and, in effect, PhD student of Kuznets.[226] Consequently, Friedman found himself almost at the ground floor of a major breakthrough in economics: the development of national income accounting. Friedman's assistance on this endeavor was acknowledged in Kuznets's 1941 work, *National Income and Its Composition, 1919–1938*, in which Kuznets noted: "I have especially profited from the comments by Milton Friedman" (xxix); in addition, calculations made by Friedman were noted as such in Kuznets's discussion (441).[227]

Consistent with the statements quoted above, this work on national accounts was set in train before the appearance of the *General Theory*. Furthermore, work on national accounts is not an area of research that is amenable to Keynesian economic analysis alone. After all, national income accounts provided measurement of the right-hand-side components of the income form of the equation of exchange—that is, $MV = Py$; and, after he became a monetarist, Friedman would point to the development of national accounts as an argument for favoring the income form of the equation of exchange over the transactions form.[228]

Nevertheless, Friedman's assessment that the Keynesian revolution was a major catalyst for work on national accounts seems appropriate. And it is consistent with Burns's (1952a, 6) observation that the Keynesian revolution was "the most important single factor in shifting the emphasis of economic theory from prices to incomes." With this change of emphasis, detailed measurement of income flows had become more imperative. What is more, the Keynesian revolution facilitated the drive for comprehensive national accounts because of the Keynesian emphasis on the breakdown of total spending among its components.[229]

It was, in fact, a study of such spending breakdowns that would be a major part of the evidence that inspired Friedman's later work on consumption. Kuznets's finding in the 1940s that the ratio of consumption to income had exhibited considerable historical stability in the United States would have a profound effect on Friedman's research. The finding contrasted with the *General Theory*'s hypothesis that the ratio would decline as national income rose. The doubt thereby cast on the original Keynesian consumption function would help motivate Friedman's development of the permanent income hypothesis.[230]

In the late 1930s, however, the issue of consumption behavior was not at the forefront of Friedman's research agenda. Indeed, with his move from his NRC position in Washington, DC, to work at the NBER in New York City, Friedman moved his focus away from the area of consumption. And the work on national income accounting that Friedman carried out in the late 1930s was only a subsidiary part of his research during those years. The expertise he had acquired on national accounts would serve Friedman well within a few years when, as a Treasury employee, he would serve as an informal tutor to US senator Robert Taft on the subject (*Chicago Tribune*, November 28, 1976).[231] But from his beginning at the NBER in September 1937 until his departure for new employment in 1940, Friedman's principal concern was his development of a project that he had inherited from Kuznets.[232] As with Kuznets's other work, this project involved studying income data. However, it was a research enterprise that was distant from the study of national-spending totals and also far removed from theories of aggregate behavior of either the Keynesian or quantity-theory type. Instead, the Friedman-Kuznets project was—to use a term not in circulation during the 1930s, and one that Friedman disliked once it did emerge—a study of microeconomic data.

The research that Friedman conducted under Kuznets's supervision consisted of a study of professional incomes. That research provides a counterexample to the claim—which would be commonly made about Friedman in his monetarist years—that he saw perfect competition wherever he looked and had no interest in, or appreciation of, the extent to which monopolistic power was exercised in the pricing of goods and services. While ostensibly this project studied the behavior of the income of five professional categories—medical doctors, dentists, certified public accountants, lawyers, and consulting engineers—the findings that emerged from the project led Friedman, once he took it over, to make it, in effect, a critique of the medical profession. Friedman's comparisons of incomes across professions suggested that barriers to entry into the medical profession were elevating doctors' incomes. The fact that the research ended up focusing on health-care costs means that Friedman's interest in this subject matter bookended his career: his work in the 1930s and 1940s on the cost pressures arising from the supply side of the health-care market had a counterpart to his work in the 1990s and 2000s on health insurance, in which he focused on cost pressures arising from the market's demand side.[233]

A version of the Friedman-Kuznets work went public in 1939 in the form of a lengthy (sixteen-page, double-columned, and small-print) research report in the February 5, 1939, double-issue of the *National Bureau of Economic Research Bulletin*.[234] This ephemeral version of the Friedman-Kuznets work has become so obscure that it is infrequently cited or mentioned in published discussions of the professional-incomes project. Yet the publication of this pamphlet would be the first of many occasions on which Friedman's research would make headlines, as the *New York Times* (February 5, 1939) provided a news report about the 1939 version of the Kuznets-Friedman work on the day of its release.[235] The 1939 study also received an entry, as though it was a book in its own right, in the book review section of one journal (University of Chicago Press 1941). And Friedman himself cited the 1939 Kuznets-Friedman pamphlet in some of his contemporaneous published work.[236]

The title of the 1939 report, "Incomes from Independent Professional Practice, 1929–1936," differed from that of Friedman and Kuznets's later full-length book only in the features that the latter dropped the years from the title and changed "Incomes" to singular.[237] Although the NBER report listed Kuznets as the first author, the NBER's preamble acknowledged that Friedman had directed the research since 1937, Kuznets having become occupied with other projects. Indeed, both the 1939 and later versions of the study were essentially Friedman's product. Friedman would later recall that his inheritance of the project led eventually to a "completely rewritten manuscript."[238] And Anna Schwartz, who joined the NBER in 1941, would note: "I will say that Friedman had recast the manuscript that he and Kuznets had prepared in such fundamental ways that it was truly more Friedman's dissertation than it was Kuznets'."[239]

Friedman's influence is also clear in the readable quality of the final version of the study: the book version that appeared in 1945.[240] Its readability did not derive from the conciseness of the author's presentation, as the book stretched to over six hundred pages. As might be expected, the length of the book drew criticism from reviewers, with the *American Economic Review*'s appraisal of the book (Yntema 1946, 682) expressing reservations about the "sheer length of a volume that is spun from so limited a central subject matter."

In the course of its sprawling analysis, the Friedman-Kuznets book features many Friedman hallmarks in its turns of phrase, including repeated use of the term "free to choose" (vi, 88, 89). A quotation from Adam Smith also provides a recognizable Friedman touch (129). On the other hand, the book's concern with the need for a "realistic assumption" indicates that Friedman's approach to economic methodology was still in flux (159). Furthermore, it should be emphasized, as some readers did (Muttitt 1948, 538), that the whole Friedman-Kuznets investigation was based on an analysis of responses to questionnaires. Obtaining conclusions from the study of questionnaire evidence was a practice about which Friedman would later be skeptical, and this skepticism would prompt him to make, by the early 1950s, caustic remarks about questionnaire-based evidence.[241] In fairness, however, his later skepticism could be construed as a warning to be careful in using that evidence, rather than a stricture against using such evidence; and one reason why the Friedman-Kuznets study ultimately took such a lengthy form is because the authors attempted to make an exhaustive search for possible biases in their survey data. Perhaps most importantly, Friedman's doubts regarding questionnaires centered on the use of them by economists to deduce the reasons underlying agents' decisions. This criticism did not apply to the reliance on questionnaires for quantitative information (which was Friedman and Kuznets's primary concern).[242]

In terms of its lasting contribution to the economic literature, the *Income* study is notable on two counts. First, it included the permanent-income/transitory-income distinction that would feature prominently in Friedman's work on consumption, which is discussed in later chapters (see especially chapters 3 and 5 below).

Second, it was a study that emphasized and developed the concept of human capital. The "human capital" concept and terminology were not due to Friedman and Kuznets. Blaug (1976) emphasized the prevalence of the concept in early economics writings, while the term "human capital," employed in a way that essentially coincides with that of modern usage, appeared in some pre-1940s articles. For example, an article by Harold Boag, "Human Capital and the Cost of the War," appeared in the January 1916 issue of the *Journal of the Royal Statistical Society* and referred (7) to the "question, often debated by political economists, of the valuation as a form of capital of the skill and knowledge embodied in the workers of a country." The Friedman-Kuznets book nevertheless deserves credit for bringing the study of human capital into systematic economic research. Ahead of the publication of *Income*, Friedman used the term "human capital" in print in his 1943 article on the expenditure tax.[243] He would claim for his study with Kuznets the status of being "one of the earliest empirical studies" of human capital.[244] Anna Schwartz (1992) credited Friedman with an enormous influence on the human-capital literature. More surprisingly, perhaps, Paul Samuelson (in *Newsweek*, October 25, 1976a) gave Friedman similar credit, observing that "Friedman (with Simon Kuznets, Nobel Laureate 1971) first analyzed and measured 'human capital,' the investment we make in our medical and other education and the interest return on this investment."

The Friedman-Kuznets study also contributed to the *theory* of human capital, being credited by Blaug (1976, 827) with providing "some of the key elements of the new theory" of human capital. That said, the "new theory" of human capital was developed largely by others in Friedman and Kuznets's wake. In particular, Blaug (1976) singled out Theodore Schultz and Gary Becker, and it is their work (T. Schultz 1963; and Becker 1964) that Lucas (1988a) cited when referring to human capital and adding it to his model of economic growth.[245] Indeed, Becker's (2007, 182–83) assessment of the Friedman-Kuznets volume concentrated on its introduction on permanent/transitory-income decomposition, although his discussion did acknowledge that the book was also an early analysis of human capital.[246]

Friedman would list "theory of capital" as one of his research areas in his *Who's Who in Economics* 1986 entry (Blaug 1986, 293), although what Friedman may have had principally in mind here was the capital theory (the theory of interest) of his *Price Theory* texts rather than his human-capital research. When asked in 1981 to predict future Nobel laureates in economics, Friedman predicted that Becker's research on the theory of human capital would lead Becker to receive the prize—as Becker indeed did, in 1992.[247]

In the postwar period, Friedman would return to the subject of human capital in his price-theory course at the University of Chicago and occasionally in his discussions of various economic topics. For example, in an interview on UK radio in 1973, Friedman remarked that the "great misunderstanding" underlying proposals to tax capital was their neglect of a key fact: "Most capital is human capital" (*Listener*, May 30, 1974, 688).[248] In more recent years, this property of the total capital stock has been stressed in the literature on optimal taxation, with L. Jones and Manuelli (2001), for example, reconsidering results concerning the taxation of capital once human capital is admitted into the analysis.[249]

The *New York Times* report on the 1939 version of the Friedman-Kuznets study (which listed the pamphlet as by "Dr. Simon Kuznets and Milton Friedman") identified the controversy that the work would generate. In particular, the *New York Times* coverage, after noting that the authors had explicitly stated that they were not attributing to doctors a deliberate attempt to raise their incomes through restrictions on entry to the medical profession, went on to quote a passage from the report that carried precisely that implication.

The same implication came through clearly in the 1945 version of the Friedman-Kuznets work, despite the abundance of technical material in the book (including an appendix of no fewer than seventy-five pages titled "The Reliability of the Department of Commerce Samples"). The study's bottom line and the prepublication reaction to it among NBER officials were well encapsulated in *Newsweek*'s observation that the release of the complete Friedman-Kuznets study was "delayed for four years because he [Friedman] had the temerity to suggest that the high income of doctors might reflect a deliberate effort to restrict entry to the profession."[250]

Friedman's memoirs indicated that the Friedman-Kuznets manuscript was "essentially complete" by 1941, although that statement should not be taken as implying that the published version in 1945 was identical to the 1941 draft.[251] On the contrary, as Friedman acknowledged, he and Kuznets had to make numerous rewrites—in the direction of softening the discussion—after a pharmaceutical official on the NBER board had raised objections to the imputations contained in the draft about the medical profession's practices. The initial objections by the official were in October 1941, and the rewrites took place in the subsequent three years.[252]

The delay also pushed out the date of Friedman's receipt of a doctorate. Friedman's road to a PhD in economics is testimony to the changes in the positions taken by universities over the years regarding the protocol for publishing dissertation work. Today, research work might appear in print only well after it had been used as the basis for a PhD dissertation, and the form of publication that is most encouraged for such work would correspond to an article in a research journal. In his student days, however, the rule that Friedman faced was that a dissertation had to be published as a book before a PhD could be conferred (Silk 1976, 60; *Margin*, January 1986). In these circumstances, it was a portion of his 1945 book with Kuznets that was deemed to be Friedman's doctoral dissertation. This dissertation, in turn, underlay the PhD in economics that Friedman was granted by Columbia University in 1946.[253] And, although it had been toned down by the qualifications added during the long revision process, "the original position of Friedman and Kuznets is certainly still in the published version," as Anna Schwartz would observe.[254]

In his memoirs, Friedman credited Wesley Mitchell—head of the NBER at the time—with helping steer the *Income* study through the various controversies of the review process into publication, and so allowing Friedman to receive a doctorate.[255] Matters were more complicated than that, however, for the archive of Arthur Burns's correspondence shows that Mitchell had grave reservations about the thesis.[256] Indeed, during the 1970s, after Friedman had given a withering critique of Burns's monetary policy at a Federal Reserve Board consultants' meeting, Burns wryly commented to his staff and fellow Board governors that perhaps he should have gone along with Mitchell's advice not to approve Friedman's doctoral dissertation (John Scadding, interview, January 7, 1992).

Friedman's resentment at being delayed and being partially muzzled in the course of the Friedman-Kuznets project likely prompted him to go out of his way in subsequent years to repeat and underscore the controversial findings of the Friedman-Kuznets study. For example, when studying data concerning labor unions for a 1951 study, Friedman remarked that a shortcoming of the data was its failure to classify the American Medical

Association (AMA) as a trade union.[257] He used his dissertation research on the medical profession's restrictive practices to argue against medical licensure in *Capitalism and Freedom* in 1962. It was this link between *Income* and *Capitalism and Freedom* that prompted Bernanke's (2004, 207) observation, "Milton has never been a big fan of government licensing of professionals."

With respect to Friedman's stand on licensure, William Baumol observed:

Well, Milton was at the extreme end of many of these things. I once met an attorney who had cross-examined Milton when he was on the witness stand. And I said, "You know, he's a great debater, you must have had terrible trouble cross-examining him." And the lawyer said, "Not at all, I just asked him, 'Professor Friedman, do you believe that doctors should be licensed?' And he would simply say, 'Of course not.'" And he'd asked two or three more questions of that sort. And then the lawyer said, "I would just say to him, 'Thank you, sir. No further questions.'" (William Baumol, interview, January 23, 2014)

In his audiotaped and videotaped series in the 1970s, Friedman made criticisms of the medical profession like those he had expressed in prior decades. He did so again in the book version of *Free to Choose*, which cited the Friedman-Kuznets study and suggested that its argument remained valid.[258] By the 1990s, however, Friedman believed that the AMA's power to restrict supply had diminished significantly.[259] And, as already noted, he was at that time concentrating on the demand side of the health-care market in his public policy work.

Friedman was not entirely to blame for the unwieldy length of the Friedman-Kuznets study. As part of the compromise brokered to get *Income* into print, the authors' concluding chapter was immediately followed by a six-page "Director's Comment" from C. Reinold Noyes, the NBER director who had blocked approval of the 1941 draft. This critical comment began (Noyes 1945, 405): "Certain reservations seem to me to be required with regard to the scientific validity of some of the points made in this study." It went on from there. The fact that the NBER had had to publish more than its usual disclaimer when publishing Friedman's work was a sign of things to come. In 1963, in releasing the Friedman-Schwartz *Monetary History*, with its blunt description of Federal Reserve policy in the early 1930s as "inept," the NBER was once more prompted to include a "Director's Comment" at the end of the book, thereby establishing daylight between the bureau and Friedman.[260]

Friedman's tendency to zero in on policy implications of an economic-research issue clashed with the bureau's tradition.[261] By NBER rules, he could not put policy prescriptions into a bureau study. But that state of affairs left Friedman with considerable leeway to present findings that seemed to carry obvious policy implications. Friedman could also, in items published in non-NBER outlets, cite research findings he had made under the NBER's auspices as the basis for strong policy prescriptions. He did just this in discussion of licensure in *Capitalism and Freedom* and in advocating the constant-monetary-growth rule in *Program for Monetary Stability* (which cited the then-forthcoming *Monetary History*).[262]

The tension inherent in this situation was magnified in the later 1960s as Friedman's fame grew and the Friedman name threatened to overshadow, or become interchangeable with, that of the NBER. It was a problem the NBER struggled with openly, as in 1967 when John Meyer, the head of research at the NBER at that time, urged that the bureau not be treated synonymously with Friedman, "just because Friedman speaks out so strongly."[263] The NBER's goal of having economists classified by their expertise in particular fields, and its insistence on refraining from policy recommendations, sat uneasily with the presence among its affiliates of Friedman, who seemed to have a strong opinion on almost everything, and who could regularly be found in the national media offering views and policy recommendations on matters that traversed many areas of economics. The conflict between Friedman's approach and the NBER's sensibility would remain until Friedman's name left the NBER's rolls in 1981.

Becker (2007, 183) judged that the "Director's Comment" that accompanied the publication of *Income* was "largely irrelevant."[264] For Friedman, in the late 1930s, it may well have seemed that the same might be said of the Friedman-Kuznets study itself. Friedman was well aware that the subject matter of the Friedman-Kuznets work was dwarfed in significance by what he described in 1938 correspondence with his future wife as "this damn European situation."[265] Friedman would look with dismay at the inactivity exhibited over much of the 1930s by the major democracies when they were confronted with the behavior of Germany. This inactivity led, Friedman would later observe, "to the consequences which are only too tragically familiar."[266]

CHAPTER 3

Economic Policy on the Home Front, 1940 to 1943

I. Events and Activities, 1940–43

At the start of the 1940–41 academic year, Friedman joined the Department of Economics at the University of Wisconsin as a visiting professor of economics.[1] At the end of the same year, Friedman left the University of Wisconsin. Friedman's exit came in the wake of a decision by the university not to offer Friedman a permanent position. The events leading to this decision received extensive coverage in chapter 6 of the Friedmans' memoirs. In light of that detailed treatment and the fact that the reasons for Friedman's departure did not much involve the subject of economics, no detailed account of the episode is required here. A brief discussion is, however, necessary, owing to the great importance of the change in career direction that the events at the University of Wisconsin set in motion. It was only with Friedman's exit from the University of Wisconsin that he really took to writing articles and commentary on national economic policy and macroeconomics—an activity that he never left.

Part of the reason for Friedman's departure from the University of Wisconsin was that he ruffled feathers among other academic staff with his attempt to revamp the teaching of statistics at the university.[2] As discussed below, it is far from accurate to characterize Friedman in the early 1940s as disengaged from economics and focused solely on mathematical statistics. That said, there is merit in Becker's (1991a, 138) characterization that

The views expressed in this study are those of the author alone and should not be interpreted as those of the Federal Reserve Board or the Federal Reserve System. The author received valuable comments on an earlier draft of this chapter from Miguel Acosta, William A. Allen, Alan Auerbach, Andrew Giffin, David Laidler, Ann-Marie Meulendyke, Michael Parkin, and the late Julio Rotemberg. Thanks also go to Robert Barro for useful discussions on some of the topics discussed in this chapter. See the introduction for a full list of acknowledgments for this book. The author regrets to note that, in the period since the research for this chapter was begun, David Meiselman and Leland Yeager (whose interviews with the author are quoted below) have passed away.

Friedman was not very widely known in the economics profession even by the mid-1940s (although Becker's suggestion that Friedman did not have many publications by that point was certainly not valid). By the start of the 1940s, Friedman had, however, established a name for himself in the area of statistics, notably via his 1937 article on the analysis of ranks. Thus, Paul Samuelson (*Newsweek*, October 25, 1976a) would note that Friedman in his early career "made his mark in statistics and mathematical economics," while Anna Schwartz would recall of first meeting Friedman, in New York City in 1943: "At that point Friedman was regarded as a statistician, and not particularly an up-and-coming economist."[3] Testament to Friedman's visibility in the field of statistics by the end of the 1930s comes in the fact that he was acknowledged in print by the eminent statistician Jerzy Neyman. Neyman opened a 1938 article by indicating that he had been stimulated in his recent research by a question about sampling that "Mr. Milton Friedman" had asked at an April 1937 conference.[4]

These observations underscore the distance Friedman traveled over the 1940s. By the end of the decade, the area of statistics had essentially become a past interest for him. So too, for the most part, was mathematical economics, and in 1970 Friedman would describe Paul Samuelson as a "mathematical economist," no doubt conscious that that label was no longer applicable to himself.[5] In 1940 and 1941, however, Friedman's high level of interest in the study of statistics was manifested in his zeal to update the teaching of the subject—an effort that plainly left some other University of Wisconsin statistics teachers disgruntled.

Another reason for Friedman's departure from the University of Wisconsin, evidently, was anti-Semitism.[6] Friedman had lost interest in Judaism and religion by his early teenage years and, indeed, enthusiastically celebrated Christmas as an adult.[7] But he would describe himself as having a "Talmudic cast of mind."[8] And he proudly kept close ties with the Jewish community throughout his life, including during the horrific years of 1933–45.[9] "He was not very much in contact with the religious aspects of Judaism," recalled Leo Melamed, a refugee from Nazi persecution in the 1930s who became a close friend of Friedman's in the postwar period. But, Melamed added, "clearly he knew he was a Jew, and that was very important to him" (Leo Melamed, interview, June 19, 2013). Friedman would regard the events of the 1930s and 1940s in Europe as having had the effect of reducing the prevalence of, and tolerance for, anti-Semitism in the United States in the postwar period.[10] In the meantime, however, anti-Semitism continued to be pervasive in the United States, and Friedman would cite it as an obstacle to his employment opportunities during both the 1930s and 1940s. Defying the caricature of himself as someone who saw nothing good in the public sector, Friedman in his 1998 memoirs credited federal government agencies in the 1930s with providing employment opportunities to Jews at a time when discrimination was prevalent elsewhere.[11]

Friedman's Wartime Activities

With his stint at the University of Wisconsin ending, in 1941 Friedman was looking for a new job. He obtained one at the US Treasury, and he had been installed in Washington, DC, for several months when in December 1941 the United States entered combat in the Second World War. Before we consider Friedman's Treasury experiences in detail, a few words are needed about Friedman's activities during World War II, as past accounts have given the wrong perspective on this matter. Ebenstein (2007, 50) uncritically quotes a statement, originally from Leeson (1998), regarding Friedman: "For most of the war years, at least, he was exclusively concerned with mathematical statistics."[12] This observation jars so severely with the record of Friedman's activities during the war that it must be considered a considerable overstatement, and to accept this overstatement as valid is to put the discussion on the wrong basis. In the US war years (December 1941–August 1945), Friedman was successively at the Treasury (1941 to early 1943) and the Statistics Research Group of Columbia University (March 1943 to summer 1945).[13]

At the Treasury, Friedman's work was on economic matters—specifically, the tax structure and inflation analysis.[14] Although Friedman's main line of 1943–45 employment was indeed in the field of statistics (with some of his work also trespassing into the field of metallurgy), he was not away from economics in those years. Far from it. He continued to revise his PhD dissertation. He served occasionally as a consultant to the Treasury.[15] And he published a book review that Brunner and Meltzer (1993, 18) would consider Friedman's first challenge to Keynesian economics.[16] Furthermore, as discussed below, in June 1943, in a radio discussion of inflation (NBC 1943), Friedman entered the sphere of national popular debate on economic matters.[17]

To suggest that mathematical statistics was Friedman's exclusive concern for most of the war years is, therefore, not a fruitful way of characterizing Friedman's wartime activities. Rather, what is striking is the heterogeneity of Friedman's wartime activities in the years from December 1941 through 1945: in addition to his work in two successive jobs and his dabbling in broadcasting, he published several journal articles. Most notable of these were articles on inflation and taxation in the *American Economic Review*.[18] He also wrote a book chapter with Allen Wallis on empirical analysis of indifference curves.[19] He produced his second book (*Taxing to Prevent Inflation* in 1943).[20] Then came his third book (*Income from Inde-*

pendent Professional Practice, discussed in the previous chapter, published in 1945).[21]

The *American Economic Review* articles in 1942 and 1943 stemmed from Friedman's work at the US Treasury. It is this employment—in which he served as a principal economist at the Division of Tax Research—that is now considered.

Friedman's Work at the US Treasury

Friedman would describe his period at the Treasury as his "first real involvement in government policy" (*Chicago Tribune*, November 28, 1976). He had, of course, served in the government from 1935 to 1937 at the National Resources Committee, but that had essentially been an applied research position. In contrast, his Treasury employment—albeit, as Friedman acknowledged, in a "junior" position—routinely involved him in major issues of domestic political debate and put him in regular contact with members of Congress.[22] It would also immerse him in the subjects of inflation, taxation, and fiscal policy, on which he would be engaged for the rest of his life.

Friedman's assignment to the sensitive area of tax policy meant that he worked in a division of the Treasury in which there was considerable congressional interest. As noted in chapter 1 and discussed further below, Friedman himself testified to congressional committees during 1942. Near the end of his period at the Treasury, Friedman's name came up again at a congressional hearing on January 8, 1943, when the director of his division, Roy Blough, was required to explain the functions of the Division of Tax Research. Blough found himself called on to go, one by one, through the names of his technical staff members and explain the qualifications that each had for working at the Treasury. The tone of the questions faced by Blough suggested that training in economics was not high among the criteria considered essential for tax research at the Treasury. Rather, the strong presumption on the part of Blough's interlocutors seemed to be that business experience was considered vital. Congressman Malcolm Taber (Georgia) repeatedly asked, "Has he ever had any business experience?," as Blough provided biographical sketches of his staff.[23] By the time he reached Friedman, Blough did not need to be asked about his employee's business experience, volunteering, "He has had some business experience. He comes from a family of retailers, and I think the experience he has had has been in that business." Blough was reaching back into Friedman's teenage years—when Friedman helped with the operation of his parents' grocery store—to establish Friedman's "business experience"!

In subsequent years, Friedman would be highly critical of the presumption that business experience made one qualified to speak authoritatively about economic policy. In a television appearance in 1975, when an audience member challenged him on whether he had business experience, Friedman responded sharply:

> I'd like to ask this gentleman if he thinks that no physician is capable of prescribing for cancer unless he's had cancer. . . . [Economics] is a science and a discipline, and we have something to say independently of whether we've been businessmen.[24]

Friedman added a few years later: "Every businessman deals with dollars, so he believes that he is an economist."[25] To Friedman, however, analysis of the national economy drew on a different set of skills from those involved in either analyzing or running a business.[26] It followed that businessmen were not economic experts. Conversely, expertise on the behavior of the national economy did not imply expertise in business analysis. "I'm not a business expert," Friedman answered in 1979 when called on to explain the rise of K-Mart.[27] Furthermore, what Friedman called "the confusion between business and economics" was liable to create a serious problem, namely, the misguided applications of corporate-management principles to economic policy.[28] In later life, Friedman emphasized this problem repeatedly, in the context of international economics: he would criticize analyses that likened different countries to rival firms and that applied concepts like competitiveness and profit-and-loss accounts to a nation's trade performance.[29]

The need to justify Friedman's qualifications for a government position would not arise again, because the Treasury position proved to be Friedman's final full-time position in government.[30] Although he later indicated that his time working at the Treasury was "extremely fascinating" (*Margin*, January 1986, 4) and credited it with opening his eyes about the process by which draft legislation evolved into acts passed by Congress (Instructional Dynamics Economics Cassette Tape 32, August 7, 1969), Friedman also had occasion to refer to the "supercharged political atmosphere of Washington" (Instructional Dynamics Economics Cassette Tape 83, October 6, 1971) as well as what he perceived as the District's atmosphere of unreality and lack of time perspective.[31] Friedman would cite as a reason for his 1943 departure from the Treasury the desire to avoid staying long enough to catch "Potomac Fever."[32] When, in the early 1970s, Friedman's former student William Gibson had an opportunity to work in Washington, DC, Friedman, Gibson recalled, "said everybody should spend a year in Washington"—which Gibson took to imply that they should not spend more than a year there (William Gibson, interview, March 7, 2013). Friedman himself would likewise recall telling students not to spend more than a year in Washington (see R. Roberts 2006).

In his own case, Friedman left the US Treasury several months ahead of the second anniversary of his arrival. In the postwar decades, he would turn down offers to return to government as a full-time formal adviser (*Chicago Tribune*, November 28, 1976). "Milton never wanted a policy position," Anna Schwartz would recall.[33] The opportunities to serve in government that Friedman turned down during the postwar period included offers to be a member of the Council of Economic Advisers (*California*, October 1984, 79), of which at least one was made during the Eisenhower administration (*Chicago Tribune*, April 12, 1964; *Los Angeles Times*, December 14, 1986, 17; Burgin 2012, 177).

Alongside his reluctance to reenter the Washington atmosphere, a further factor motivated Friedman's latter-day disinclination to serve in government. He would come to the conclusion, once he had reached prominence, that he could exert more influence on policy makers as an outside commentator (*Chicago Tribune*, November 28, 1976). "I believe I can be much more useful on the outside," he affirmed in 1984 (*California*, October 1984, 79). Indeed, one of Friedman's academic colleagues during the 1960s and 1970s, Robert Gordon, would express the view that "the fact that he had all the influence he did" on national policy in the postwar period confirms that "often you can have more influence by staying away [from Washington] and just becoming a respected intellectual voice" (Robert Gordon, interview, March 21, 2013).

Friedman was likewise not attracted to the idea of seeking an elected post. Bill Simon, who had Friedman as an economic adviser during Simon's 2002 California gubernatorial campaign, said: "I remember I once asked Milton, 'Have you ever thought about running for public office?' He said, 'No. I think that my service is really in serving up ideas for people to use and then keeping my fingers crossed that, if they get elected, they actually follow through on the promises that they made during the campaign'" (William E. Simon Jr., interview, September 25, 2015).[34] Along similar lines, Herbert Grubel, a one-time University of Chicago colleague of Friedman's who participated in Canadian federal politics, recalled that Friedman "put much stock in the ability to increase his influence on economic thought and policy by having students become professors, or employees in government, business, and the media, after they had absorbed his ideas" (Herbert Grubel, personal communication, May 25, 2015).

Friedman's Embrace of Free-Market Economics

As well as shaping his view of the role that he should play, the war years also saw a change in Friedman's perspective on the appropriate role of government in the economy. Friedman assessed in retrospect that "I was mildly socialistic" prior to graduate study (*Newsweek*, June 15, 1998, 45) and that he was persuaded of the merits of free-market ideas through what he learned from teachers at the University of Chicago in 1932–33.[35] Friedman's memoirs suggested, however, that yet another change in view subsequently occurred and that, as of the mid- to late 1930s, Friedman approved of a good deal of the extensions of state involvement in the economy associated with the New Deal.[36] As detailed in the previous chapter, Friedman—including in his years as a famous free-market advocate—*always* approved of *portions* of the reforms embodied in the New Deal. But the degree of his approval of the New Deal reform package in toto likely peaked in the second half of the 1930s.

During the early 1940s, Friedman moved back to a free-market position and never left it. His reconversion may be dated to this period because, by the time he read Hayek's (1944) *Road to Serfdom*, Friedman was, by his own account, already persuaded of the desirability of a relatively laissez-faire economic system.[37] And, indeed, the public record of the early to mid-1940s is replete with evidence of Friedman's move back to a free-market position.[38] To take two examples: In his *American Economic Review* article on the expenditure tax, published in early 1943, Friedman stated that "minimizing the role of government intervention into the details of the economic system" was one desirable property of the tax; and the Friedman-Kuznets *Income* monograph had stated of the framework that guided the authors: "This approach treats professional activity as taking place in an economy best described as a free enterprise system in which the production of goods and distribution of incomes are regulated primarily by the impersonal mechanism of the market."[39]

The war experience had a different effect on many others' perspective on government. The move to a war footing took the United States out of depressed economic conditions and was associated with a degree of output expansion so great that Alvin Hansen (1951a, 3) could observe of the US economy: "Its performance in the Second World War amazed the entire world." In the book version of *Free to Choose* in 1980, the Friedmans would acknowledge that the buoyancy of the US economy observed during the 1941–45 period of heavy federal government control, coming in the wake of the Depression years, increased the community's willingness to confer a permanently greater role to the state in economic matters.[40]

In his own explanation for the strength of the wartime economy, however, Friedman would cite the change in *monetary* conditions associated with the war, and he would reject explanations that traced the economic expansion to the intrinsic power of fiscal policy. And he would see the success of the war effort as testament not to the general validity of heavy government involvement in the economy, but to the fact that a centrally directed economy was workable if the whole community had a common objective. That condition was not transferable to peacetime conditions, he believed, because in peacetime the community could not unite in pursuit of a single, overriding goal as it did during a full-scale war.[41]

One way in which Friedman articulated his renewed doubts about government economic intervention was by opposing wartime price controls. Friedman attended congressional hearings on inflation and taxation in 1942. He also submitted a solo-authored memorandum on the subject to the House of Representatives Committee on Ways and Means in May 1942.[42] In this memorandum, which compared taxation with other methods of controlling inflation, Friedman included price controls in a list of the "most important other methods that are now being employed."[43] Ruger (2011, 22, 34) interprets the fact that Friedman, in his 1942 submission, mentioned price control as an anti-inflation tool as implying Friedman's support for "illiberal policy prescriptions" (34) during the war.[44] Price controls, however, had already been introduced in the United States by May 1942 and became wider ranging in that month (P. Evans 1982a, 955). Furthermore, the May 1942 broadening of price controls had been announced the previous month (Rockoff 1984, 92–93).[45] In imputing Friedman's personal support for controls from a statement that Friedman gave in May 1942 as a US government representative, Ruger seems to be under the impression that government employees, when writing or testifying in their official capacity, have the option open to them of criticizing official policy. They do not. If Friedman had expressed outright opposition to price controls in his congressional submission, such an expression would have been grounds for his dismissal.[46]

The tack that Friedman instead took in his May 1942 submission was to downplay the role that controls should be given in the formation of policy. He stated that "in the absence of additional taxation . . . pressure on prices would be so great as to make direct price control and rationing unenforceable," and he warned that imposing controls in a situation of excess demand would promote violations and an underground economy.[47] In addition, in his interactions with members of Congress at the May 1942 hearing—not recorded in his published testimony but recounted by Friedman later—he urged repeal of wage and price controls.[48] Prior to this, in a restricted-circulation 1941 memo, Friedman and his coauthors argued that draining aggregate demand constituted an "efficient" way of stabilizing prices that, in contrast to price controls, was an approach that operated "within the framework of accepted government function."[49]

In economic-research journals, Friedman could write more freely, reflecting those journals' narrow professional audience and the presence of a formal disclaimer in the articles. His 1942 article in the *American Economic*

Review was categorical in opposing controls: "The price system seems the least undesirable method of allocating the limited resources that will be available for the production of civilian goods."[50] Friedman immediately went on to cite the likelihood that controls would distort the relative-price structure.

Once he had left the Treasury, Friedman was free to speak publicly against controls, and he did so to a wide audience in an appearance on NBC radio in June 1943. The radio series *University of Chicago Round Table* showcased University of Chicago academic staff as panelists but also featured guest panelists. In the case of the June 1943 program, the guest panelists included Friedman, by then employed at Columbia University, while the University of Chicago was represented by George Stigler (at the time a visiting professor with the economics department).[51]

In his contribution to the panel discussion, Friedman emphasized that, taking as given the government's call on resources that was associated with the defense effort, the market should allocate consumer goods, and management of aggregate expenditure should be the method used to control price pressures. Rather than "concentrate on the symptoms" in relying on price controls, economic policy, he argued, should "go to the fundamental cause and remove the excess purchasing power."[52]

This appearance on a national radio program marked Friedman's first foray into the advocacy of market solutions to general audiences. The claim made by Krugman (2007), and echoed by Ruger (2011, 127), that Friedman inaugurated this practice only in 1946 (with the Friedman-Stigler pamphlet *Roofs or Ceilings?*) is not correct.[53]

Tax Withholding

One respect in which Friedman's wartime activities have been alleged to have led, albeit unintentionally, the United States away from the direction of a private-enterprise economy, concerns his participation in the federal government's switch to a system of income tax collection based on withdrawal-at-source. Friedman was, it should be underscored, a junior employee, and he was not the principal public spokesperson regarding the Treasury's work in this area.[54] That role was instead taken by Randolph Paul, the secretary of the treasury's tax adviser.[55] As Roy Blough described the situation in his testimony in early 1943, the Division of Tax Research did not make policy decisions, which were instead made by the secretary of the treasury and his special tax adviser (that is, Paul), while Friedman was "not so much a tax man, but he is an economist."[56]

As noted in chapter 1, Friedman was involved in the development of the withholding system. The specifics of his work on the proposed system included conducting interviews with current and former tax personnel from countries that did have withholding, working out a critique of the Ruml Plan for withholding as well as devising an alternative, and testifying on these matters to Congress.[57] In his memoirs, Friedman gave something of a mea culpa for his role in shaping the withholding system that resulted, stating that, as he now saw it, "I was helping to develop machinery that would make possible a government that I would come to criticize severely as too large, too intrusive, too destructive of freedom."[58]

This judgment reflected the fact that, in the postwar period, Friedman would conclude that taxes were most likely to be tolerated by the community at large if they were partially hidden and did not involve a conscious payment on the part of the taxpayer. Furthermore, from the early 1960s, Friedman would see the fiscal policy-making process as one in which the level of tax revenues largely determined the level of government spending. According to this "starve-the-beast" view, a more efficient tax-collection system might well imply higher government spending. From these positions flowed his conclusion that tax withholding had fostered the growth of government—a conclusion Friedman voiced as early as 1967 (*Fortune*, June 1, 1967, 147).

Friedman's admission in his memoirs has been much quoted, particularly by libertarian critics. It is, however, unlikely that Friedman regretted his involvement to the point of wishing that withholding had not been introduced.[59] As he testified in 1942, the introduction of general income tax withholding did not amount to the federal government's first use of withholding, which was already present in Social Security tax collections. Furthermore, Friedman exhibited pride in the extension of withholding to income tax payments even when discussing the matter in the mid-1980s. In this later discussion, Friedman affirmed that the practice of income tax withholding had vindicated his position, against Internal Revenue System opposition, that income tax withholding was administratively feasible.[60] And however much Friedman regarded withholding as a reason for the increase in the size of government, its abolition did not figure prominently in his proposed measures to reduce the role of the public sector. He did not press hard for the abolition of withholding. Instead, Friedman emphasized tax cuts and constitutional limitations on the federal budget as the key changes to fiscal policy arrangements.

Asked point-blank in 1969 by NBC's Edwin Newman whether he had "since come to regret" his involvement in the advent of withholding, Friedman's answer was far from an unequivocal "yes":

Well (laughs), that's a very, very hard question. I think that withholding was absolutely essential during the war to raise the kind of taxes we did. But I also do believe that it would be impossible today to have the level of taxation we have if it weren't made largely painless through withholding. So I have had very mixed feelings about whether I (laughs) contributed to a good thing or a bad thing. I have no doubt that it was good from the short-term point of view. (*Speaking Freely*, WNBC, May 4, 1969, pp. 38–39 of transcript)

In a similar vein, when again confronted on the issue of withholding in the mid-1990s, Friedman stated that he had no apologies to make about his part in the introduction of withholding, again declaring that the measure was necessary (*Reason*, June 1995). In mid-1996, he once more defended the introduction of withholding as a correct wartime action while stating that withholding had had a "very bad effect" in the peacetime period due to its status as a nontransparent form of taxation.[61]

One point that deserves emphasis is that the criticism of income tax withholding rests basically on libertarian or political-economy arguments. According to these arguments, the improvements in the efficiency of tax collection engendered by withholding had the by-product of facilitating growth in the overall levels of taxes and government spending. The economic case for withholding, however, was and remains sound, and it is likely that most economists today would strongly support withholding. One prominent virtue of withholding is that it makes tax revenues highly sensitive to the state of the economy and allows the operation of automatic fiscal stabilizers. Friedman highlighted this implication of withholding in the mid-1950s, when he noted that, with tax collection methods having been "radically reformed" by withholding, the United States now featured a "greatly increased . . . sensitivity of tax payments to changes in economic conditions."[62] Even in later years, when he downplayed the significance of fiscal deficits, Friedman continued to see the sensitivity of tax revenue to the business cycle as a desirable state of affairs.[63]

There was one by-product of the advent of tax withholding in which Friedman could take great satisfaction: the support it gave to the permanent-income view of consumption behavior that he developed after the war. In 1972, Friedman considered the case of taxpayers whose disposable income was temporarily held down by overpayment of federal taxes that they could expect to get back the following year as a tax refund. These taxpayers, Friedman contended, would "continue their spending as if they weren't being overwithheld," because "the idea that people are simply mechanical, stupid fools, who spend as dollars come into their pocket and don't spend if dollars don't come into their pocket, simply does not fit with the facts of consumer expenditures over a long period."[64] Rather, consumers seemed to smooth their consumption in the face of the variations in disposable income produced by the vagaries of the withholding process.

II. Issues, 1940–43

PAYING FOR WORLD WAR II

The control of inflation was a recurring theme in Friedman's writings in the sixty-five years from 1941 to 2006. Among his earliest writings on the subject were items composed during his years at the US Treasury. In addition to the May 1942 memorandum discussed previously, Friedman coauthored a restricted-circulation Treasury staff memorandum in 1941, produced a solo-authored journal article in 1942, and collaborated on the book *Taxing to Prevent Inflation* that appeared in 1943.[65] But although the control of inflation was an abiding interest of Friedman's, his approach to the subject underwent profound changes over the years. These changes are reflected in the contrast between Friedman's contemporaneous views on how the United States should pay for its defense spending in World War II and his later perspective on war finance.

For all the changes that took place in Friedman's views after the early 1940s, however, some elements of Friedman's position on war finance did not change. These were that inflation was a bad form of taxation, one that in ordinary times should be avoided altogether; that the occasion of war did provide some basis for a policy in which inflation was allowed to exceed its peacetime norms, so that inflation became one of the means used to divert resources from the consumer goods sector to the defense effort; that, because of the impediments that inflation imposed on the efficient working of the market system, the amount of inflation permitted during wartime should be contained to the low single-digit range—no more than 5 percent; and that, in the face of wartime pressure on aggregate demand, price controls concealed rather than removed inflationary pressures and were more damaging to the operation of the economy than was the alternative of open (that is, unsuppressed) inflation.

But beyond these tenets, Friedman's views during the Second World War on inflation were markedly different from those he took during the postwar period. The differences are best brought out by considering Friedman's views during the war, then those after the war. The discussion below proceeds along those lines. Then Friedman's views in both eras are compared with those prevalent in the modern literature on public finance.

Friedman's Views during the Second World War

According to Friedman's later accounts, his Treasury colleagues and superiors saw him as falling into the category of "starry-eyed theorists."[66] This being the case, it was as a Keynesian theorist, for Friedman had largely accepted the theoretical contribution of the *General Theory*.[67] In particular, he embraced the book's negative perspective regarding the power of monetary policy as well as its emphasis on fiscal policy. The Keynesian outlook is so clear in Friedman's early 1940s writings that monetarists such as Laidler (2012) have marveled at the contrast with Friedman's later work. It might seem that an element of dissent from Keynesianism on Friedman's part was evident even in the early 1940s in the fact that, by the time he joined the Treasury, Friedman had criticized Tinbergen's (1939) econometric model in a book review.[68] But, in contrast to Lucas (1996, 669–70), who would criticize Tinbergen for neglecting insights from pre-Keynesian monetary theory, Friedman's contemporaneous critique of Tinbergen's approach concentrated on Tinbergen's model-selection criteria rather than on the Keynesian theory that Tinbergen used as his framework.[69]

In later decades, Friedman would express disdain for much of his own early-1940s work and the extent to which it had taken the validity of Keynesian economics for granted. When David Meiselman, who had been one of Friedman's students at the University of Chicago, was working in the federal government during the first half of the 1960s, he received a visit from Friedman. Meiselman had come across one of Friedman's Treasury memos from the early 1940s. "I showed him the memo, and he didn't want to talk about it. It was quite Keynesian. He was acting like it was an early part of his life that he did not want to touch" (David Meiselman, interview, April 30, 2013).[70]

Several years after this conversation, Friedman broached the subject publicly, this time focusing on his published early 1940s work. "One score and seven years ago, I was the joint author of a book entitled *Taxing to Prevent Inflation*," he told an audience at MIT in 1969. "So you can see that in my younger days I, too, was beguiled by the Keynesian revolution to believe that fiscal policy was *the* key in controlling aggregate demand" (in *The Great Economics Debate*, WGBH Boston, May 22, 1969). In a similar vein, Friedman was retrospectively critical of his *American Economic Review* article on inflation. "In a note on the inflationary gap that I published in 1942," Friedman observed in a November 1971 talk, "I never mentioned the quantity of money or monetary factors at all!"[71] And a further three decades on, early in the new century, Friedman was still reproaching himself about his wartime economic analysis: "I look back at that and say, how the hell could I have done that?"[72] Consciously echoing the verdict that Paul Samuelson (1968) retrospectively delivered on his own mindset during Samuelson's *pre*-Keynesian period, Friedman would once declare that his younger self had been a "jackass" in accepting the positions of early Keynesianism on fiscal and monetary policy.[73]

Friedman attempted to characterize his wartime views in a television interview in 1994. "When I was at the Treasury, I was essentially a Keynesian," he observed, "as I believed that the way to control inflation was by controlling government spending. I paid very little attention to money."[74] This recollection fell somewhat short as an accurate encapsulation of the position Friedman took during the 1941–43 period. In the face of the United States' defense needs, "controlling government spending" was not an option. A rising trend in government spending had to be taken as given. What instead occupied Friedman and his colleagues over this period was the task of getting taxes to keep pace with government spending.

And it was here that the Keynesian influence on Friedman manifested itself. In his 1940s writings, including those in research outlets, he would repeatedly state the view that deficit spending was an important influence on nominal and real total spending. In 1982 Friedman contended that he had never argued that fiscal policy, given monetary policy, was important for cyclical fluctuations.[75] Friedman's wartime analyses of national income and inflation fluctuations belie this contention. Indeed, these writings serve to underline how greatly Friedman's views underwent a shakeup after the war (in particular, as will be argued in the next chapter, during the years from 1948 to 1951). On occasion, Friedman would provide a more careful characterization of the evolution of his own views—for example, in late 1968, when he stated, "we also have found that increased taxation has a negligible effect on inflation. I have believed that for twenty years" (*St. Louis Post-Dispatch*, November 11, 1968). But, as we have just seen, on other occasions Friedman gave a number of categorical statements that ignored the positions he had taken ahead of the late 1940s. A caution, therefore, in interpreting the accounts that Friedman gave in later life about the evolution of his views is that in these accounts, "I have never . . ." often meant "Since 1951, I have never . . ."[76]

Examples of Friedman statements from the early 1940s in which he trumpeted the importance of fiscal policy are legion. In 1941, Friedman stated: "The prevention of a substantial increase in the cost of living is, therefore, a prerequisite to any equitable distribution of the defense burden; it is the major objective of fiscal policy today."[77] In his August 1942 congressional testimony he talked of the need for an "adequate and flexible fiscal policy."[78] In his June 1943 radio broadcast, Friedman said that the "basic solution [to inflation] . . . is a strong fiscal policy" (NBC 1943, 19). Little wonder that Friedman's 1953 collection, *Essays in Positive Economics*, reprinted only one pre-1945 reference—and even that article, the 1942 piece on the inflationary gap (that is, the excess of total nominal spending over the level consistent with price stability), became notorious for the changes Friedman made to it for the 1953 collection.[79] The inflationary-gap article appeared along with five other papers in a section of the 1953 collection titled "Monetary Theory and Policy." For the collection, Friedman inserted new paragraphs into the gap paper so that it qualified—as the 1942 original version had not—as an exercise in monetary theory, and also so that it lined up with Friedman's newly monetarist views.[80] He opened the article by noting the "serious error of omission" (namely, of money) in the original version, and along with the new material, Friedman included a self-reproving footnote, which concluded: "As I trust the new material makes clear, the omission from that version of monetary effects is a serious error which is not excused but may perhaps be explained by the prevailing Keynesian temper of the times."[81]

A discussion provided in Grossman and Van Huyck (1986, 21) brings out the change in the substance of Friedman's inflation discussion that his 1953 insertion of the extra paragraphs created. These authors cited the 1942 Friedman paper as an example of an "old strategy . . . [that] treats the expected inflation rate, Ep, as a policy variable, and assumes that the sovereign issues money at the rate that validates its choice of Ep."[82] The description the authors gave to Friedman's "strategy" is applicable to the 1942 article only once the 1953 additions to that article are considered. It does not apply to the original, unamended discussion, in which government issuance of money did not feature at all.[83] Friedman was conscious in the early 1940s of the possible role that inflation might provide as a revenue source for the government, but that was not the concern of his 1942 paper. What is more, as of the early 1940s Friedman regarded the aggregate-demand tool with which the government could reliably affect inflation to be fiscal policy, not monetary policy.

Of Friedman's writings in the early 1940s, only a 1940 book review, in which Friedman expressed doubts about Tinbergen's (1939) attempt to build a Keynesian econometric model, could really be put forward as a fore-runner of the critiques of Keynesianism that would be prevalent in his work from 1944 onward.[84] And, as already indicated, the status of that review as an anti-Keynesian article is tenuous. The content of the book review reflected less an emergence on Friedman's part as a skeptic about Keynesianism than it did his deep background in statistics: the review was, as many pieces by statisticians would be in later years, highly critical of econometricians' approach to structural model building.[85] Friedman's ideas expressed elsewhere around the time of the review were Keynesian: as discussed in the previous chapter, his first book, the coauthored report on consumer behavior published in 1939, reflected *General Theory* ideas. Furthermore, a course that Friedman taught in 1940s devoted "class period after class period" to Keynesian postulates (*National Review*, June 16, 1989a, 25).

Friedman therefore came to the US Treasury already having a Keynesian perspective. But Friedman's employment at the Treasury surely reinforced his Keynesianism. To be sure, the notion of a countercyclical role for US economic policy was not an innovation of the 1930s or 1940s. With respect to monetary policy, Friedman and Schwartz's *Monetary History* emphasized that the Federal Reserve's statement of its goals during the 1920s included a responsibility for minimizing cyclical fluctuations.[86]

Friedman added in 1982 that every recession during his lifetime had prompted calls for an employment-creating government spending program.[87] But Friedman also ascribed importance to the New Deal in magnifying the tendency of the government to take responsibility for the economy, and to the Keynesian revolution in providing a formal rationale for a demand-management system oriented on fiscal policy. According to a US Treasury economist whose service in the Treasury encompassed Friedman's years there, the Treasury mindset transformed after the mid-1930s, from an outlook in which fiscal policy was dictated by public-finance considerations to an acceptance of fiscal policy as a tool for the management of aggregate demand: "Keynes' ideas were picked up rapidly" (*South China Morning Post*, January 29, 1971, 1).[88] Friedman, who would later reflect that "none of us can help being affected by the intellectual atmosphere that we breathe," came to the Treasury after this change in mindset had become entrenched.[89]

The task of developing fiscal policy as a demand-management tool fell into the laps of Friedman and two colleagues in the Treasury's Division of Tax Research, Carl Shoup and Ruth Mack, in 1941. The economic situation that they faced was characterized not by the Depression conditions that were the focus of the *General Theory* but, instead, by the emergence of inflation from excess demand. In this connection, in their first report in October 1941, the authors noted: "The cost of living in the United States has been rising during the past few months almost as fast as it did during the first world war."[90]

The authors' proposed policy measures were Keynesian but, reflecting the situation of economic overheating, were different in sign from those prescribed for Depression conditions. This analysis, and to a considerable extent the actual policies followed by the federal government from 1941 onward, represented an early conscious application of Keynesian principles by US economic officials. This wartime experience with Keynesian policies would seem to conflict with the chronology given in Friedman's later accounts: he would date the pressure to implement Keynesian policies as beginning just after World War II (*Newsweek*, December 6, 1976), and he would see the Employment Act of 1946 as enshrining this movement toward Keynesian policies.[91] But, in these retrospectives, Friedman likely had in mind policy makers' desire to use *General Theory*-inspired expansionary policies to bear when unemployment threatened to rise above a certain rate.[92] As the pressure of aggregate demand built up in the United States in 1940 and 1941, the task faced by policy makers was not one of preventing a deficiency in demand but instead one of finding a way to contain aggregate demand while facilitating the transfer of resources to the defense sector.

The Keynesian analysis that Friedman and his coauthors deployed was less that of the *General Theory* than it was of Keynes's more recent book. In *How to Pay for the War* (1940), Keynes had provided an analysis directly concerned with wartime excess demand conditions. Friedman does not appear to have cited this book until 1983 (*Economist*, June 4, 1983). The absence of references to it in the 1941 Shoup-Friedman-Mack memorandum and the authors' 1943 book, and the similar lack of mention of Keynes (1940) in Friedman's 1942 article on the inflationary gap, would seem to leave open the issue of whether Friedman was actually familiar with Keynes's book when he was a US Treasury economist.

The weight of the evidence suggests that Friedman did read *How to Pay for the War* soon after its publication and that he was consciously following in its footsteps with his own analysis. One indirect piece of evidence for this conclusion comes from Friedman's tendency to use turns of phrase that he had picked up from books he had read. For example, the formulation, "to mention only the most conspicuous cases," used in Jacob Viner's book *The United States in a Multi-national Economy* (1945, 84), likely sank into Friedman's consciousness: Friedman later echoed Viner's wording in an early draft of his and Meiselman's paper on monetary and fiscal policy.[93] Likewise, when, in a 1950 radio broadcast, Friedman remarked, "You need something more than vague generalities" (NBC 1950, 7), he may have been unconsciously paraphrasing a passage of Keynes (1940, 27) in which Keynes had stated, "if I restrict myself to generalities, I do not give the reader enough to bite on."[94]

Other pieces of evidence confirm that, notwithstanding the paucity of direct citations of Keynes (1940) in Friedman's writings, Friedman was aware that, in his "inflationary gap" analysis of 1942 and 1943, he was embracing some of Keynes's post–*General Theory* ideas, notably those on inflation. Friedman's contribution to *Taxing to Prevent Inflation* revealed that he followed UK developments closely, in keeping with the later assessment Friedman gave that the United Kingdom remained, at that time, the world's center of economic research.[95]

Specifically, Friedman's solo-authored chapter in that book discussed "recent English discussion of fiscal policy [that] has centered on the so-called 'inflationary gap,'" and in this light discussed UK gap estimates made by UK economist Frank Paish.[96] Paish's (1941, 43) article explicitly referred to the Keynes Plan given in Keynes (1940). Indeed, one contribution to a

US symposium on war finance stated that "the whole world now knows" about the Keynes Plan.[97] Furthermore, Friedman's 1943 chapter also cited as a reference on the inflationary gap a 1941 House of Commons speech by the UK Chancellor of the Exchequer, Kingsley Wood.[98] That speech, which delivered the United Kingdom's budget for 1941, was well understood even at the time as having been largely drafted by Keynes (Samuelson 1946, 191; see also Skidelsky 2000, 84). It is therefore wholly appropriate that Okun's (1981, 262) retrospective on the inflationary-gap approach traced the analysis to Keynes (1940) and cited *Taxing to Prevent Inflation* as an "important application" of Keynes's analysis.

Some aspects of the inflationary-gap analysis were not a source of embarrassment to the later Friedman. Parts of the 1940s inflationary-gap analysis carried through to his later work, consistent with Friedman's latter-day praise (in the *Economist*, June 4, 1983, 37) for Keynes's "important pamphlet" *How to Pay for the War*. Like his later monetarist self, the wartime Friedman emphasized the demand-pull nature of inflation, and, with it, the notion that the key to inflation control lay in a demand-management scheme in which policy makers kept the path for nominal spending close to the feasible path for real spending.

True, the inflationary-gap analysis of Keynes and Friedman in the 1940s emphasized a full-employment *ceiling* for output, above which essentially all nominal spending would be translated into inflation immediately.[99] In the postwar decades, in contrast, Friedman would come to see an excess demand situation as capable of being manifested in above-normal output in the short run. But that modification of inflation analysis would be common ground among Friedman and those postwar Keynesians who adopted the original, nonaugmented Phillips-curve approach. Consequently, the use of a maximum-output concept does not constitute a strong basis for the monetarist Friedman to have looked back with disdain at his wartime analysis.

The basis for the negative retrospective judgment that Friedman, nevertheless, made regarding his 1940s inflation analysis, and the grounds for his judgment in 1953 that that analysis had been plagued by an error of omission, lay in the roles he had assigned in his wartime writings to monetary and fiscal policy.

The heart of the problem was that Friedman's 1940s inflationary-gap analysis treated fiscal deficits as ipso facto a stimulant to aggregate demand. In that analysis, an accommodative monetary policy stance was *not* a key part of the sequence in which deficit spending generated an increase in nominal aggregate demand. It followed that, in Friedman's wartime analysis, lower deficit spending was crucial to restraining inflationary pressure in a way that monetary restraint was not. There was an irony in the fact that Keynesian principles were introduced in the conditions of war-time in the United States. Keynesian ideas were often later judged to have made deficit spending acceptable in the United States. However, the early applications, including Friedman's, of Keynesian policies to US fiscal policy were in the direction of promoting deficit *control* in a situation—wartime— that had hitherto been regarded in US policy practice as one in which large-scale deficit spending was appropriate.

Friedman's Keynesianism was reflected not only in his belief in the effectiveness of fiscal policy but also in his dismissal of the possible effectiveness of monetary policy. Formally, the *General Theory* had centered its case for the ineffectiveness of monetary policy in Depression circumstances, in which, Keynes hypothesized, the long-term interest rate (assumed to be the key variable through which monetary policy affected the economy) might reach a floor, and additions to the money stock would not succeed in stimulating spending; that is, the economy would be in a liquidity trap. In retrospect, Friedman would interpret early Keynesianism as extrapolating "money doesn't matter" results to conditions beyond the Depression scenario. In his view, Keynesians would reach this more comprehensive dismissal of the importance of monetary policy by either one of two means. One was by inferring that aggregate demand was largely or wholly interest inelastic (itself a possibility to which Keynes gave some credence in the *General Theory*).[100] The other means was by suggesting that the floor on long-term interest rates implied by the liquidity trap might hold even when the economy was not in a depressed state.[101]

In the early 1940s, Friedman's own analysis of monetary policy adhered closely to the dismissive tone prevalent in much other Keynesian literature of that vintage. His solo-authored contribution to 1943's *Taxing to Prevent Inflation*, written while he was at the Treasury, plotted growth rates of the nominal money stock and nominal income for the United States for the period 1899–1929.[102] To the modern reader, the scatter plot in Friedman's paper indicates that the monetary growth/income growth relationship is clearly positive, and reasonably tight by the standards of rate-of-change data. That was not, however, the judgment Friedman reached in his 1943 paper, in which he concluded instead that the relationship was "extremely unstable."[103]

Two important points must be noted about Friedman's dismissal of the money/income relationship, both of which sharpen the contrast with his later views.

First, because he was considering pre-1929 data, his verdict against the usefulness of money was applied to a context broader than Depression conditions. One cannot argue that Friedman's 1940s-vintage doubts about monetary policy applied only to circumstances of Depression.

Second, it is not possible to rescue Friedman's 1940s-era emphasis on fiscal deficits by pointing to the fact that during the war, and especially from 1942, the Federal Reserve was pegging short- and long-term interest rates. As discussed in more detail in the next chapter, an interest-rate peg would appear to justify some skepticism about the value of monetary aggregates as indicators—and certainly should foster doubts about the indicator value of the monetary base. The reason is that an interest-rate peg blurs the distinction between base money and the assets whose rates are subject to the peg by making the latter assets closer substitutes for money. Furthermore, as emphasized in both IS-LM and modern economic analysis, interest-rate pegging tends to tighten and magnify the link between fiscal deficits and total spending by creating conditions in which deficit spending is automatically accommodated by monetary policy (i.e., in which budget deficits lead to creation of money).[104] Under these conditions, a monetarist perspective on inflation control might lead to emphasis on restraint in deficit spending, as this prescription provides a means of restraining monetary growth.[105] One cannot contend, however, that this position underlay Friedman's 1943 emphasis on deficit control, because his analysis rejected the money/spending link and, by necessity, the monetary growth/inflation link that underlies the monetarist perspective. In addition, Friedman did not see a situation in which fiscal policy was a key driver of inflation as prevailing only in conditions of an interest-rate peg. Rather, he was putting forward his fiscal-policy-oriented approach to studying inflation as a general analysis. Friedman at this point did not see monetary policy's response to deficit spending as decisive in determining whether deficit spending raised the price level.

Friedman's Later Views on War Finance

What position on war finance did Friedman reach in his later analysis? As a starting point in answering this question, it is worthwhile quoting a provocative passage on this subject from a critic of Friedman's, Charles Kindleberger:

> I do not know if the remark appears in print, but there is an oral tradition that Friedman has said that it would have been possible for the United States to finance the war with an equilibrium amount of money, a balanced budget, and a constant price level. (Kindleberger 1985, 291)

Kindleberger acknowledged that Friedman may not have actually made the claim attributed to him. But the claim, even in the unsourced form given by Kindleberger, provides a useful basis for laying out Friedman's views on war finance in his later, post-1950, monetarist period.

Kindleberger was correct to suggest that Friedman in his monetarist period thought that price-level stability was achievable in war conditions. In particular, Friedman viewed such a state as attainable via monetary policy—implying that the balanced-budget condition given in the Kindleberger quotation above would *not* be an essential requirement for stabilizing the price level. Deficit spending not accommodated by money creation might put upward pressure on the price level by increasing the opportunity cost of holding money and so raising velocity. Even then, however, an appropriately chosen "equilibrium" money stock (to use Kindleberger's terminology) could in principle generate a constant price level.

However, Friedman's doubts in the fine-tuning skill of the authorities led him to regard them as unlikely to calculate the appropriate level for the money stock that would exactly deliver price stability. These doubts prompted him, from the later 1950s, to look suspiciously on monetary policy schemes that were designed to offset the effect of shifts in velocity on nominal income and prices. But in contrast to his wartime writings, the later Friedman did see monetary policy as able to dominate the behavior of inflation irrespective of the behavior of the fiscal deficit. Friedman's postwar position was therefore even stronger than Kindleberger conjectured: whereas the Kindleberger representation of Friedman's position implies that fiscal balance might be necessary for a constant price level, Friedman viewed price-level stabilization as possible even in conditions of large budget deficits. From this perspective flowed Friedman's statement in 1970: "By itself, it [fiscal policy] is not important for inflation."[106]

In light of the fact that he saw price-level stability, in the face of budget deficits, as something that was achievable in principle even in wartime, what did Friedman actually prescribe as appropriate wartime economic policy? Did he regard deficit spending as appropriate in war conditions, and did he view above-normal inflation as appropriate in wartime? These questions will be considered in what follows.

On the issue of permitting deficits, Friedman from an early stage advocated the principle of allowing budget deficits to vary over the cycle, and he continued in later years to regard this as a valuable principle.[107] Such a principle would not, however, point to the desirability of deficit spending in wartime. Friedman would nonetheless come to take a more favorable attitude toward allowing temporary deficit spending even in conditions of economic expansion, because of two other considerations. First, as noted, he believed that low inflation could be secured by monetary policy, in the presence of unbalanced budgets. Second, Friedman's "starve-the-beast" perspective, which he adopted in the 1960s, meant that he came to see tax increases as leading, with a lag, to permanent increases in government spending. That being so, tax increases would only temporarily reduce deficits and would lead—in Friedman's view, undesirably—to a permanently higher plateau for state spending. This consideration alone would tend to support deficit spending in wartime, as it suggested that that tax increases to finance wartime spending would lead to permanently higher peacetime spending, probably in the nondefense spending category.

Notwithstanding the more sanguine attitude that he had adopted toward budget deficits, Friedman would voice his support in the 1980s for proposals to impose by constitutional amendment the goal of ex ante budget balance. His basis for supporting the proposed amendment was that, as it included clauses that made it difficult to use tax increases as a way of achieving balance, the amendment would serve in effect as a restriction on the growth of federal spending.[108] The form of this proposed amendment, along with Friedman's writings in support of it and related proposals, sheds light on his later perspective on appropriate wartime fiscal policy. In these writings, Friedman would characterize US history before the 1930s as featuring "an unwritten constitutional prohibition on deficit budgets."[109] In thus characterizing the historical record, however, Friedman may have had in mind peacetime periods only; for, even before the 1930s, the US Treasury granted that deficit spending was necessary during wars.[110] The balanced-budget amendment that Friedman favored in the 1980s made an explicit allowance for deficit spending in times of war.[111] Friedman in his later work therefore *did* grant the desirability of very substantial wartime deficit spending. This was in contrast to the stand that he had taken during World War II, when he had urged that deficit financing be avoided to the extent practicable.[112]

The desirability of deficit spending during wartime is also a key message of the modern literature on public finance and tax smoothing, as advanced by Barro (1979a, 1987) and applied to US data by Barro (1986), Bohn (1998), and Ohanian (1998), among others.[113] As stressed in that literature, the fact that major wars are associated with high deficit spending can be regarded as a good thing—a practical application of the principles that only permanent increases in government spending should be financed by increases in taxation, and that tax schedules should be kept stable in the face of temporary changes in public spending.

In this connection, Cooley and Ohanian (1997) and Ohanian (1998) were highly critical of Keynes's (1940) advocacy of wartime tax measures. Some of their critique of Keynes's book applied to the specific taxes that Keynes recommended, rather than to the inflationary-gap-based analysis of deficit spending to which Friedman subscribed. But Ohanian's (1998) critique applied to the latter component of Keynes's analysis too. In Ohanian's assessment, the United States relied too little during the Second World War on deficit finance, while US practice during the First World War featured a more appropriate financing of defense expenditures. And here a clash between Ohanian's findings and the wartime-era analysis of Friedman materializes: for, as already indicated, the financing of wartime spending by current taxes was the key element of Keynes's (1940) prescriptions that Friedman adopted in the 1940s.[114]

As we have seen, in later years Friedman became more relaxed about temporary budget deficits and he accepted the necessity of wartime deficit spending in particular. Furthermore, the modern literature has underscored the desirability of deficit spending in wartime—and has done so in part by appealing to arguments with which Friedman had much sympathy, including those that stress the desirability of stable tax schedules. Can it therefore be concluded that the later Friedman would have favored, as this later literature did, deficit financing on a *much* larger scale, and much less reliance on taxes, during World War II than actually occurred? The appropriate answer would appear to be no. The reason is that, although Friedman's views on wartime deficit spending changed substantially, his position on the desirability of wartime *inflation* did not undergo a comparably large shift, and his views on inflation and deflation remained different from those expressed in the public-finance literature.

In contrast to his views about deficit spending, Friedman's position on the use of inflation as a way of financing wartime expenditures exhibited considerable continuity over the years. In 1983 he approvingly quoted Keynes's (1940) statement that while inflation was one way of financing government expenditures, it was "the worst possible solution."[115] And in the period between 1940 and 1983, Friedman was outspoken on many occasions about inflation's status as a particularly disruptive tax. He wrote in 1943 that, once inflation reached a certain rate, it distorted resource allocation in a way that was inconsistent with "the effective utilization of that output for war purposes."[116] On many occasions in the 1940s and subsequent decades, Friedman stressed that price controls did not remove these distortions and that, on the contrary, they led to a suppressed inflation that Friedman considered "vastly more harmful" in its distortion to resource allocation than open inflation.[117]

Friedman's ideal, it is true, was zero inflation.[118] Along this line, he once stated that he would like a move back to a world in which 3 percent inflation was regarded as "terrible" (Instructional Dynamics Economics Cassette Tape 57, August 20, 1970). But he acknowledged that the point at which inflation rates started to generate severe inefficiencies was somewhere above the low single-digit range. He observed that inflation in the range of 2 or 3 percent amounted to reasonable price stability (Instructional Dynamics Economics Cassette Tape 27, May 29, 1969) and did not correspond to rates for which there would be much incentive for indexation of contracts (American Enterprise Institute 1974, 51).[119]

It is in this context that Friedman's views on the role of inflation in war finance should be seen. In his public-finance-based analysis, Barro (1986, 362) stated that "there seems to be no reason to give special treatment to the inflation tax." This perspective contrasts with Friedman's own position. To be sure, Friedman was amenable to the notion that, as war conditions meant that resources had to be transferred to the public sector one way or the other, inflation might be one of the taxes that might be deployed to finance war spending. For example, in a 1965 memorandum to the Federal Reserve Board, Friedman granted that inflation was "generally a desirable component of wartime taxation."[120] But it was not a component that should figure heavily in relation to most other taxes. Both during the war and afterward, Friedman shared Keynes's position that high inflation was a particularly distortionary tax. Consequently, inflation should not, even in wartime, be moved into a range in which it generated major economic costs.

This imperative implied, for Friedman, avoiding policies that raised inflation into the high single-digit range or beyond. Accordingly, in 1941 he and his Treasury colleagues argued that, while inflation "may well have a function to perform" in transferring resources from the household sector toward use in national defense, the recourse to inflation for this purpose should be limited, and that economic policy should seek "the prevention of significant price changes—say a rise of 5 percent or more a year."[121] If anything, the rate that Friedman regarded as the threshold for significant price changes would fall a percentage point or two in later years, making him inclined to tolerate inflation of no more than about 3 percent and to reject proposals that relied on large-scale money creation for war financing.

Friedman's consistent opposition to wartime inflation has another dimension: a belief in the costs of deflation. Again, this outlook contrasts with the public-finance literature, which has prescribed wartime inflation followed by deflation. This literature has largely used flexible-price analyses in which expected deflation is costless. For example, Ohanian (1998, 65) judged that the US price-level pattern of the 1940s—in which a permanent upward shift in the price index occurred—was less desirable than the corresponding pattern during and after World War I—when wartime inflation was followed by a policy of "deflating the economy back to the prewar price level." Likewise, Barro (1979b, 20) stated that "there would seem to be no objection to . . . systematic—and hence, anticipated—deflation on business cycle grounds." A framework in which prices are sticky and anticipated declines in the price level are not—or cannot practicably be—built fully into contracts for financial and nonfinancial transactions provides a basis for objecting to a policy of systematic deflation.

And such a framework underlay Friedman's opposition to deflation.

During the war years, his view was that prices had considerable downward rigidity and that output might be permanently kept down in the presence of deflation. Later on, Friedman would come to see prices as temporarily sticky in both directions, with this stickiness leading to short-run deviations of output from its potential value. Although not identical to one another, his wartime and postwar perspectives on nominal rigidities both had the implication that deflation was not costless and that a policy aimed at driving the price level down would be inconsistent with stable output patterns. In light of this judgment, part of his wartime analysis at the Treasury, as discussed in chapter 1, was directed at forestalling a postwar economic slump, and in 1943 he wrote about the need to keep output equal to potential after the war.[122] This position necessarily entailed a hostility to a major postwar deflation. The upshot is that the public-finance literature's proposal of inflation followed by deflation was an undesirable prescription, both in the analytical framework that Friedman used during the war and in his much-revised postwar framework.

The conclusion that emerges from the preceding discussion is that Friedman's monetarist position did not move him very far away from his wartime disposition to shun large deficits. As just indicated, Friedman regarded inflation and deflation alike as more costly than the public-finance literature would suppose, and he wanted to avoid both. His later position on inflation did differ sharply from his wartime view, because he would come to regard control of monetary growth as central for avoiding inflation. But applying this principle to the conditions of World War II still leads to a support for limitation of deficits, because the monetary policy regime of interest-rate pegging in force during World War II implied that control of monetary growth required deficit limitation.

We are therefore back where we began: notwithstanding the shake-up in his views that occurred in the postwar years, the later Friedman would still have favored a very sizable amount of tax financing of the temporary wartime spending. In 1970 he stated that it would be "a mistake" to insist that in war conditions the maximum tax rate on income be the same as would be appropriate in peacetime (*Chicago Daily News*, July 29, 1970, 4), and in 1995 Friedman referred to "the need to collect extremely high rates of taxation [receipts] to help finance World War II" (*Reason*, November 1995). Against this must be weighed some Friedman statements—albeit made in a peacetime context—that went in the direction of tax smoothing, such as his observation in 1972 that "we ought to set our tax rates and keep them stable" and that government spending should be aligned with longer-term revenue behavior rather than current revenue.[123] Once he had become a monetarist, the ideal fiscal policy response to a World War II scenario in Friedman's view would likely have involved a larger deficit, in order to facilitate more constant tax schedules—so some tax smoothing was implied.[124] It would also have involved a nonaccommodative monetary policy that kept inflation at single-digit rates. In contrast to the public-finance literature, he would not have recommended monetization of wartime budget deficits.

In the event of an interest-rate pegging policy by the monetary authorities, deficit control was necessary and desirable, according to Friedman's later framework, to ensure containment of the money stock and therefore price stability.[125] And low inflation was unquestionably desirable, he concluded, even in wartime. The public-finance literature's idea of leaning heavily on the inflation tax in wartime and deflating afterward had no appeal to him.

In choosing between different taxes, however, a couple of percentage points of price rise had some appeal to Friedman as a resource-shifting measure. Indeed, even in a peacetime context, Friedman would observe that while inflation was a "very undesirable" tax (Instructional Dynamics Economics Cassette Tape 171, July 1975, part 1), a case existed for a mild amount of inflation if that was the only alternative to raising the tax revenue by imposing extra taxes on producers of output (see also Instructional Dynamics Economics Cassette Tape 162, January 1975, part 2). Friedman's rationale was that inflation was an implicit tax on spending. This discussion, however, took place in a context in which production taxes and the inflation tax were the only taxes being considered.[126] As discussed in the next subsection, Friedman preferred to tax spending directly rather than resort to inflation to do so.

In the event, World War II featured both a sharp increase in explicit taxes and considerable use of the inflation tax. The *Monetary History* would judge that 48 percent of the wartime expenditures was financed by ordinary tax revenues.[127] Accompanying this increase in revenues were strong increases in tax rates: for example, Joines's (1981, table 2) estimates imply that the marginal tax rate on labor roughly doubled from 1940 to 1945.

Figure 3.1, in contrast, plots two dimensions of the *inflation* tax during World War II: monetary growth (figure 3.1 [*a*]) and inflation (figure 3.1 [*b*]). As figure 3.1 (*a*) shows, both M1 and M2 growth reached high double-digit rates during the war, each series averaging about 20 percent in the 1942–45 period. Figure 3.1 (*b*) plots recorded inflation in the GNP deflator, from Balke and Gordon (1986), as well as the growth in a deflator series adjusted for wartime price controls. The latter series was constructed by Friedman and Schwartz for their 1982 *Monetary Trends* and it was designed to have the same average growth rate as the measured price level. But their adjustment reallocated the pattern of price rises over time, in a way intended to display the inflationary pressure that was disguised by the wartime controls.[128] In effect, the adjustment for controls moves the double-digit in-

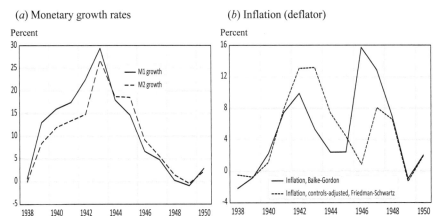

FIGURE 3.1. Monetary growth and inflation in World War II. *Sources*: Percentage change in M1, M2, and GNP deflator from Balke and Gordon (1986) annual tables. Controls-adjusted inflation computed from Friedman and Schwartz (1982a) price-controls-adjusted price-level series for the United States.

flation observed in 1946–47 back to the 1942–43 period. The Friedman-Schwartz adjustment likely shifted the inflation peak too far back in time. But the basic message suggested by that adjustment—that true inflation peaked *during* the war, not after it—is likely to be robust.[129]

The behavior of both monetary growth and inflation indicates that the US government's reliance on the inflation tax was substantial during the war, notwithstanding the increase in official taxes.

Friedman believed that the amount of inflationary pressure that the price controls had to contain had been made lower by patriotism (*Newsweek*, August 30, 1971, 22; *Wall Street Journal*, February 12, 1987). With a money-financed eruption in defense spending and the shift of the US economy to a war footing, aggregate nominal spending was bound to surge. But a degree of voluntary restraint by households in their purchases of goods, alongside a large take-up by the private sector of low-coupon war bonds, had the effect of making the rise in aggregate nominal spending lower than it otherwise would have been. Consequently, in financing the expansion of the defense effort, the United States was able to rely on money creation, yet a good deal of the inflation that would ordinarily be associated with such money creation was avoided.

THE SPENDINGS TAX

In March 1943, Friedman published an article in the *American Economic Review* titled "The Spendings Tax as a Wartime Fiscal Measure," in which he pressed the case for a tax on consumer expenditure as a way of containing inflationary pressure. The paper was formally a follow-up to an article on the subject by Allen Wallis in the September 1942 issue of the *American Economic Review*, and Friedman's paper was accompanied by the standard disclaimer, "The opinions expressed are the author's personal views and do not necessarily reflect those of the Treasury Department."[130]

Ostensibly, therefore, Friedman's paper was only a contribution to an exchange of views in a research forum. In fact, however, the material relayed in the paper had helped form the basis for a push by the Treasury to have an expenditure tax introduced in the United States. That effort was unsuccessful (Prest 1956, 36)—"it never got anywhere," Friedman would recall fifty years later (CSPAN, May 7, 1993). The failure of the expenditure tax initiative was no doubt a factor that would lead Friedman to describe his period at the US Treasury as an experience that disabused him of the notion that a well-argued memorandum would be decisive in making the case for a tax reform (Instructional Dynamics Economics Cassette Tape 23, April 1969).

Friedman never reprinted the 1943 item in his later book collections, perhaps because the reference to war conditions in the paper's text and title reduced the relevance of the paper to a postwar readership. The paper is nonetheless notable for bearing many of the hallmarks of later Friedman writings. There is considerable emphasis on the need to rely on market forces. Although, as noted earlier, Friedman acknowledged that patriotism was a factor that had facilitated the diversion of resources to government use, he had no doubt about the need to send price signals that generated the spending and supply patterns consistent with a large-scale defense effort. An expenditure tax, under which consumers would have an incentive to postpone spending until after the war, was offered by Friedman as a way of facilitating the needed demand adjustments without recourse to direct physical controls (such as rationing).

The article did not refer to Keynes or his work, but Friedman proposed the spendings tax explicitly as an alternative to the Keynes (1940) proposal of compulsory "lending"—that is to say, tax payments reimbursed after the war via tax rebates—from households to the government. Friedman rejected this proposal as administratively infeasible and unlikely to be successful in restraining spending.[131]

A stronger indictment of the Keynes scheme was later made by Cooley and Ohanian (1997), who suggested that the compulsory-lending arrangements had produced severely adverse supply-side effects when they were partially implemented in the United Kingdom. In its own analysis of the supply side, Friedman's 1943 paper recognized the importance of incentives, arguing that the "spendings tax would help to maximize total output by enabling income to operate effectively as a device for organizing the use of resources" and also by reducing the need to rely on taxes on income.[132] Friedman insisted that after-tax income was an important driver of the private sector's supply decisions, even in wartime. This attitude was manifested in his observation: "Some device must be used to stimulate individuals to work, to work harder and longer, and to move from one type of work to another."[133] That observation presaged his remark (discussed in chapter 1) in his price-theory course and text, in which Friedman indicated that one reason for the rise in nonmilitary labor supply in the United States during World War II was that households responded to temporarily high real wages.

The spendings tax paper also contained an early hint of Friedman's work on consumption in its suggestion that household expenditure was more closely related to wealth than to income: "the individual of large wealth may be able and willing to maintain his spending at a higher level than an individual with the same income but less wealth either because he is under less pressure to save or because he can draw on his capital."[134] It is thus seen that part of Friedman's rationale for the expenditure tax was a permanent-income view of consumption behavior (albeit not yet called that). This position contrasted markedly with the confidence Friedman expressed in *Taxing to Prevent Inflation*, published the same year, on the reliability of the relationship between consumption and (current) income.[135] It also clashed with the analysis underlying Friedman's 1942 congressional testimony concerning tax withholding.[136]

It would be wrong to suggest that Friedman was squarely and irrevocably a subscriber to the permanent income hypothesis as of 1943. On the contrary, as discussed in the next chapter, remarks that Friedman made in a 1946 radio appearance seemed to reaffirm the notion that short-term fluctuations in current disposable income figured powerfully in household spending decisions. Rather, it seems that Friedman's views were in flux. His 1943 reliance on permanent-income-type arguments may perhaps indicate exposure to, and attempts to account for, the findings of the kind published in Kuznets (1946) of a steady consumption/income ratio in the United States. However, in the later 1940s, it is possible that Friedman reverted to a more traditional Keynesian consumption function because he was prepared to accept the arguments, advanced by Alvin Hansen, that attempted to reconcile Kuznets's findings with the Keynesian, diminishing-marginal-propensity-to-consume, consumption function.[137] If so, Friedman may have put to one side the line of argument that was pointing toward the permanent income hypothesis. The rest of the 1940s would, in any event, give Friedman little opportunity to develop his thinking on aggregate consumption behavior, as he would be preoccupied with topics in other areas of research and policy. But Friedman would return to the issue of the consumption function in 1951.

The literature on the expenditure tax predated Friedman, as he acknowledged in his reference to Allen Wallis's paper as well as his indication that the proposal had been made for peacetime conditions by "C. A. Jordan, Irving Fisher and others."[138] After Friedman, a substantial literature on the expenditure tax developed, especially in the United Kingdom. Among these later contributions was Kaldor (1955), whose advocacy of the tax, like Friedman's, particularly emphasized what would now be considered a form of the permanent-income perspective on consumption decisions. Although the literature on the expenditure tax would mushroom, the bibliographical practice of this literature suggests that Friedman's 1943 *American Economic Review* paper, although occasionally cited, was not considered a basic reference in the immediate decades after World War II.[139] In part, this practice may reflect the fact that the 1943 paper's fundamental rationale for an expenditure tax in terms of the permanent income hypothesis was somewhat lost among the arguments in the paper that applied only to wartime conditions. In more recent decades, however, Friedman's study has received greater appreciation, as Michael Boskin relates: "To academic public-finance economists of my generation and a little older, he had a remarkably influential paper he wrote, while at the Treasury in World War II, on consumption taxes, and the case for a consumption tax" (Michael Boskin, interview, July 3, 2013).

For his part, Friedman largely stayed on the sidelines of the postwar debate on the expenditure tax, and he turned to other tax-reform proposals—in particular those involving a flat income tax. Friedman's occasional interventions on the matter, however, indicated that he had not abandoned his belief in the merits of an expenditure tax, and that he thought it would be a worthwhile peacetime tax reform. His work, he acknowledged, had been done "for wartime, but ever since [1942] I have supported taxing consumption rather than income" (*Reason*, November 1995).[140]

As this quotation indicates, in contrast to a great deal of his other World War II–era views on fiscal policy, Friedman was willing to stand by his advocacy of the expenditure tax fifty years after the fact. Indeed, far from disowning the proposal, he linked it up to his latter-day advocacy of a flat tax. Speaking at a retreat for Republican members of Congress in May 1993, Friedman stated, "The ideal flat tax in my system would be a flat tax not on income, but on spending," implemented using "the present type of income tax form, in which, however, you are allowed as deductions all additions to assets . . . [net] of all additions to liabilities" (CSPAN, May 7, 1993).[141]

III. Personalities, 1940–43

ALVIN HANSEN

Alvin Hansen of Harvard University was, in Friedman's assessment, "the leading propagator of Keynes's views in the United States," a judgment widely shared both in the 1940s and since.[142] Although it was not until 1953 that Hansen published a book under the title *A Guide to Keynes*, Hansen had by then been performing the role of explaining, applying, and developing Keynes's work for over a dozen years. Friedman believed that one reason that Hansen played a major role in shaping US economists' opinions about the *General Theory* was that Hansen was a well-established economist by 1936. Indeed, most of the references to Hansen in Friedman and Schwartz's *Monetary History* were to his 1932 book on business cycles.[143] In Friedman's view, the Keynesian revolution acquired prestige and credibility in the United States from the fact that someone of Hansen's eminence had—after initial skepticism—undergone such a "sharp conversion" to Keynesianism in the late 1930s. Partly for this reason, Friedman credited Hansen with a "really important" part in changing academic thinking in the United States.[144] Indeed, the impact that Hansen made on economists' attitudes toward the Keynesian revolution was probably greater on the profession on the whole than on his own department: Robert Solow, who was an undergraduate and subsequently graduate student at Harvard University in the 1940s, has remarked that it is "absolutely wrong" to think of Harvard as being the center of US Keynesianism at that time.[145] But Hansen made a profound impact on economic opinion outside the Harvard environs via his prolific writings on Keynesian economics in the 1940s and early 1950s.

It was perhaps as a developer, as opposed to expositor and propagator, of Keynes's work that Hansen may have been underrated in retrospect, for Hansen played a large role in translating ideas from the *General Theory* into clear, usable formal models. Many economists, including Robert Lucas, Bennett McCallum, Charles Plosser, and Paul Samuelson, have suggested that it is the formal mathematical development of Keynes's (1936) ideas that really made Keynesian economics catch on in the economics profession—a view with which Friedman also expressed sympathy.[146] Although Lucas (1994a, 154–55) named John Hicks and Franco Modigliani as the economists who "showed us how to distill intelligible equation systems out of the confusions of Keynes's *General Theory*," Hansen also made contributions on this score. Indeed, Hansen's work can be viewed as a purer distillation of Keynes's ideas. Hicksian IS-LM analysis was not inherently Keynesian, as that analysis allowed the primacy of monetary policy over fiscal policy for the determination of nominal aggregate demand, as well as "classical dichotomy" results in which real and nominal variables were determined by different forces, to emerge as special cases. Hansen, in contrast, developed the income-expenditure model, which emphasized the importance of the fiscal multiplier and abstracted from price-level movements. It was this income-expenditure model that Friedman came to identify specifically with Keynesianism.[147]

In defending Keynesian economics, Hansen had skirmishes in print with several of those in whose footsteps Friedman followed. A case in point was a 1946 discussion by Alvin Hansen (1946, 69). In replying to Friedman's former teacher Lloyd Mints, Hansen made clear at the outset that he believed that both Mints and Henry Simons had too much confidence in monetary policy. Simons himself had described his own inclination, in correspondence with Keynes, as "bitterly anti-Hansen" in light of "the extreme 'American Keynesism' [sic; Keynesianism]" that Hansen was propagating (Patinkin 1979, 232).[148] In 1947, with Simons gone from the scene, Arthur Burns was emerging as a new critic of the Keynesian movement, and Hansen offered vigorous ripostes to Burns in multiple articles that Hansen published that year.[149]

Friedman's own emergence as a critic of Keynesian economics came too late to give rise to significant direct, published exchanges between himself and Hansen, although the two did know each other and were co-attendees of various conferences, including two forums on inflation held in 1951.[150] In addition, each of them would be invited contributors to a 1951 journal symposium on monetary policy. However, on this occasion, no direct exchange saw print, Friedman instead being assigned to be the discussant of Hansen's Harvard University colleague Seymour Harris.[151]

Nor did Friedman's writings provide detailed critiques of Alvin Hansen's work. Hansen served a different function in Friedman's research output. Friedman consistently treated Hansen as a key authority on Keynesian economics, but the context in which Hansen's name was mentioned would undergo a distinct change that paralleled Friedman's transformation in views. In the early 1940s, Friedman was an analyst of fiscal policy, and Hansen's work served as a key reference on fiscal matters—being cited by Friedman in *Taxing to Prevent Inflation*.[152] In particular, Hansen's (1941) study of fiscal policy—which was treated with disdain by Henry Simons—received a respectful, though brief, mention in Friedman's 1943 analysis. After the 1940s, however—indeed, right into the 1980s and 1990s—Friedman would cite Hansen repeatedly as an example of the extreme nature of Keynesian economics.[153] In effect, these citations served as proof that early Keynesianism really was as hard-line as Friedman said it was.[154] And in their discussions of both fiscal and monetary policy, Hansen's writings provided a treasure trove of militantly Keynesian statements on which Friedman could draw.

With respect to fiscal policy, a passage from Hansen's 1941 book *Fiscal Policy and Business Cycles* provides a snapshot of the Hansen perspective: "a new aim of fiscal policy" was "the aim of ensuring the full employment of the factors of production." At the time Hansen's book appeared, Friedman would very likely have concurred with this sentiment. Even in the early 1940s, however, Friedman would likely have had reservations about Hansen's next sentence, insofar as it was intended to apply to peacetime conditions: "This policy involves greatly enlarged governmental expenditures" (Alvin Hansen 1941, 117). The 1941 statement just quoted lends support to Friedman's later judgment that the position that "deficits . . . were a way of expanding the economy" had helped to promote a "tremendous growth in government spending."[155] This was the case even though, as Friedman acknowledged, Keynesian analysis itself suggested that a tax cut of an appropriate magnitude could deliver the same amount of stimulus to national income as an increase in public spending.[156]

An underpinning of Alvin Hansen's support for fiscal policy was his emphasis on the Keynesian consumption function. In particular, Hansen (1947c, 135) contended: "It has been my conviction for many years that the great contribution of Keynes' *General Theory* was the clear and specific formulation of the consumption function." Friedman, even in his years as a critic of Keynesian economics, did not altogether contest the importance of Keynes's contribution to the consumption function. Friedman would regard his own 1957 development of the consumption function as a refinement, rather than a thoroughgoing refutation, of the *General Theory*'s analysis of consumer spending. But it happens that Friedman's refinement eliminated just the aspect of Keynes's consumption function on which Hansen put great emphasis: the notion that the marginal propensity to consume would decline as households' income rose. Hansen's 1941 book on fiscal policy had a diagram and table displaying hypothetical values of income and consumption, in a manner designed to highlight this aspect of the consumption function. In these tabulations, the consumption/income ratio declined from 1.036 to 0.925 as hypothetical income rose from 56 to 80 (Alvin Hansen 1941, 229).

Later—indeed, before Friedman had published his main permanent-income work, but in the wake of widespread discussion of Kuznets's (1946) findings on the consumption-function ratio—Hansen seemed to soften his position, as he acknowledged the possibility that consumption and income moved commensurately in the long run.[157] In the meantime, however, Hansen had advocated the old-style Keynesian consumption function for medium- and longer-run policy analysis. In the course of this advocacy,

Hansen came to be credited by Friedman and others with what was variously called the "underconsumption" or "paradox-of-thrift" hypothesis, and which Hansen labeled the "secular-stagnation" thesis.[158]

According to the secular-stagnation thesis, the dilemma that faced policy makers once the economy returned to peacetime conditions was a situation of chronically low aggregate demand. The thesis suggested that the prospect of a rising real national income path for the United States was jeopardized by the likelihood that the increments in real income would not prompt extra flows of real spending of the magnitude needed to sustain economic expansion. This scenario was seen as pointing to the need for the kind of "greatly enlarged" government spending to which Hansen referred, as the public sector could shift the economy to a sustained high level of economic activity by stepping in with its own spending. Teaching of the secular-stagnation hypothesis occupied a great deal of Friedman's business cycles course in 1940 (National Review, June 16, 1989a, 25). Soon after the war, however, the secular-stagnation hypothesis would become one of the most widely criticized Keynesian ideas and, as we shall see, it would draw criticism from Friedman by the end of the 1940s.

With respect to monetary policy, Alvin Hansen's interpretation of the line taken by the General Theory closely coincided with that Friedman would lay out when, in his monetarist period, he endeavored to provide a sketch of Keynes's main points. Hansen's (1947a, 140) view that Keynes "rests his case heavily on the liquidity preference analysis, from which it follows that the economy does not tend toward full employment" lined up very closely with Friedman's position a quarter century later: "Time and again[,] when Keynes must face up to precisely what it is that prevents a full-employment equilibrium, his final line of defense is absolute liquidity preference."[159] Indeed, one of the ironies of the position on Keynes that Friedman repeatedly articulated in his monetarist period is that although Friedman's views on monetary policy differed more sharply from early Keynesians like Alvin Hansen and Roy Harrod than they did from those of later Keynesians like Tobin and Patinkin, Friedman's interpretation of what Keynes had said matched up neatly with Hansen and Harrod's interpretation and deviated from the perspective of many of the major Keynesians of Friedman's own generation.[160]

The difference between Friedman and Hansen—once Friedman became a monetarist—lay not in their interpretation of what Keynes had said about monetary policy, but in their evaluation of the consistency of Keynes's position with experience. In contrast to the subsequent Friedman-Schwartz account of the Great Contraction, Hansen regarded the experience of the 1930s as having confirmed Keynes's liquidity-trap scenario.

Nor did Alvin Hansen soften his position over time. Friedman would come to characterize economic opinion in the United States in the initial postwar period as featuring the earliest stirrings of a revival of belief in monetary policy.[161] The title of a book that Hansen published in 1949, *Monetary Theory and Fiscal Policy*, might sound like a concession to this trend. But the contents of the book indicated otherwise, and a generation after the book appeared Friedman would cite it as a demonstration of the extreme positions that had once been part of Keynesian monetary analysis.[162] The editor's introduction to Hansen's book cited as a virtue of the book the fact that that "unlike numerous modern writings . . . [it] avoids overemphasizing the importance of money."[163] Overemphasis on money was indeed not something of which Hansen's (1949) work could be accused.[164] The book argued that the "quantity of money may indeed affect the level of income, but the connection is a tenuous one" (6). Furthermore, Hansen cast the 1930s as a "vast laboratory demonstration" of the liquidity trap (191), and he regarded monetary control as an ineffective tool for a wide range of interest-rate values (194), leading to his judgment that "fiscal policy, and in emergency conditions direct controls, are however the appropriate tools for *cyclical control*" (194, emphasis in original).

Alvin Hansen's disdain for money did not boil down to an "interest rate vs. money" issue. In proclaiming that the "generally accepted doctrine that the rate of interest should be varied as a means of stabilizing the cycle" had been superseded by the Keynesian revolution, Hansen (1945, 250) was taking a position inconsistent with any kind of advocacy of the importance of monetary policy.[165] Hansen was inclined to characterize monetary policy in terms of interest-rate policy rather than in terms of monetary totals, but he was dismissive of the importance of interest rates for spending determination. He regarded both consumption and investment as highly interest inelastic.

Friedman accordingly saw Alvin Hansen, much like Keynes, as embracing the degenerate case in which the IS curve was vertical. This perceived property of the IS function provided a basis for believing that the ineffectiveness of monetary policy—already established as applying in cases in which the Keynesian liquidity-trap result held—might prevail more generally. As Friedman put it, monetary policy was "twice damned" in the Keynesian view.[166] In this vein, a book that Friedman would repeatedly cite in later years was Hansen's contribution to a 1945 symposium (*Financing American Prosperity*). Hansen's (1945, 218–27) lengthy coverage of the determination of saving and investment had, Friedman observed, found no "need to use the words 'interest rate' or any close facsimile thereto."[167] Friedman later acknowledged that Hansen *did* mention the interest rate in a later passage of the same piece—but in a context that only confirmed the irrelevance of interest rates, for Hansen had written that "both theoretical analysis and practical case studies indicate that the volume of real investment made by business is but little affected by the interest rate."[168]

The upshot, as Friedman also noted, was that Alvin Hansen thought that monetary policy had very little influence on aggregate demand, short of policies that moved interest rates to extremely high levels.[169] In this connection, Hansen's (1947a) book *Economic Policy and Full Employment* had a short chapter titled "Interest-Rate Policy" that declared (148): "Modern economic analysis favors the maintenance of a low rate of interest." Hansen supplemented this observation by accurately noting, "This also is the announced policy of all modern democracies." This policy of cheap money, along with Friedman's battle against it, is considered in the next chapter.

As has already been indicated, Alvin Hansen and Friedman had only a modest amount of one-on-one confrontations on the matter of monetary policy. By the time Friedman was concentrating on monetary matters, Hansen had made many of his principal contributions. And by the time Friedman's most prominent findings appeared in the 1960s, Hansen had become an emeritus at Harvard University. Friedman did have Hansen as a speaker in his money workshop at the University of Chicago in the early 1960s. But ahead of that appearance—in which Hansen affirmed the validity of Keynes's analysis—Friedman indicated to his students that the workshop discussion would need to be less aggressive than usual, in deference to Hansen's advancing age (David Laidler, personal communication, November 6, 2014). This strategy lined up with Friedman's typical approach to Hansen in his written work. In these writings, Hansen was treated not as contemporary to be debated but instead as a spokesman for the economic consensus of an earlier age.

It is useful to consider one of the final occasions on which Friedman quoted Alvin Hansen, as it throws into the spotlight a difference between Keynesianism and the quantity theory that is basic but in some respects surprising. In 1982's *Monetary Trends*, Friedman and Schwartz quoted Hansen (1957, 50) saying: "I think we should do well to eliminate, once and for all, the phrase 'velocity of circulation' from our vocabulary."[170] The surprising aspect of Hansen's position is that Keynesianism, in its early Keynes-Hansen form, would seem to place velocity at center stage. After all, it was that brand of Keynesianism that emphasized instances in which policies that altered the quantity of money were an ineffective means of influencing national income. Yet it was Hansen and other Keynesians who urged for an analysis that did not refer to velocity, while it was the quantity theorists, especially those of the monetarist vintage, who, in contrast, devoted great attention to velocity behavior.

Velocity analysis was a fundamental part of Friedman's monetary work. As he put it in 1964: "I have examined intensively the behavior of the velocity of circulation. . . . I have studied its secular and cyclical behavior, and [I] have tried to present some theoretical explanation of why velocity behaves as it does."[171] In keeping with this characterization, the Friedman-Schwartz *Monetary History* had a chapter with "velocity" in the title, while *Monetary Trends* would have two.

An understanding of why Keynesians thought velocity often dominated income fluctuations yet shunned analyses that referred to velocity, while quantity theorists emphasized money yet focused much of their research on velocity, lies in the structural significance assigned to velocity behavior in the two schools of thought.

Keynesianism, especially in Hansen's income-expenditure form, offered a way of looking at nominal income fluctuations in which the money/velocity division was unhelpful. The Hansen-style framework cast certain classes of nominal spending (such as government purchases) as giving rise, via the Keynesian multiplier, to further flows of spending, and it depicted the behavior of the money stock as having little or no importance in shaping this behavior of income. The ratio of that stock to income, or its reciprocal (velocity), was therefore not deemed a useful variable through which to view the behavior of spending.

The way Alvin Hansen (1949, 118) characterized this result was that "in the income theory M and V are regarded as changing *in response to* changes in aggregate outlays." Although Hansen's formulation might suggest otherwise, the Keynesian account was not really an account centered on an endogenous-money story. For Hansen contended that even if money were held constant when the multiplier process was in motion, the same nominal spending path would be the outcome: a constant money stock would simply raise the amount of income variation that could be attributed to velocity.[172] The terminology Friedman and Schwartz offered for the Hansen/ *General Theory* view of velocity was that it was a "will o' the wisp."[173] Robert Solow also gave an astute perspective on the early Keynesian position: that view saw "no structure to velocity."[174] In contrast, the monetarist position that Friedman and others would lay out contended that velocity *was* governed by a structural relationship, and that, furthermore, it was frequently possible to understand national income fluctuations in terms of money-stock variations and to see velocity fluctuations as reinforcing rather than offsetting the money movement.[175] The hypothesized behavioral stability of velocity meant that the money/income ratio was a key variable in monetarist analysis, whereas it did not have that status in Keynesian analysis.[176]

Analyses that downplay the role of money tend also, therefore, to be analyses that eschew explicit consideration of velocity. This was true not only of early Keynesian analysis, but also of the largely non-Keynesian, but also largely nonmonetary, approach to analyzing economic fluctuations that was prevalent at the Federal Reserve during the Great Depression. Hence, after examining the Federal Reserve internal documents available to them for the 1930-40 period, the point on which Friedman and Schwartz took the discussions of monetary policy to task was that "we have noted only one explicit discussion of the quantity of money and its velocity."[177]

As the preceding discussion indicates, Hansen's views provide a contrast with those that Friedman, in his monetarist period, advocated in a host of areas: the role of fiscal policy, the role of monetary policy, the consumption function, the IS function, and the money demand or velocity function—so many areas, in fact, that it is easy to overlook still another crucial topic on which Hansen staked out a position distinctly different from Friedman's: that of price setting and aggregate supply.

In a tribute to Hansen after his death, Paul Samuelson observed: "Hansen was one of the first to discern—no less than 30 years ago!—that no mixed economy can simultaneously have full employment, steady price levels and free-market wage and price determination."[178] Hansen's work therefore lent support to specifications of economic behavior that included two prominent features in the aggregate-supply process: a long-run negative relationship between inflation and unemployment (i.e., a permanently nonvertical—in particular, permanently downward-sloping—Phillips curve); and a cost-push term, of positive average value, in the equation describing inflation behavior (implying that business costs had an inherent tendency to rise and to place upward pressure on the trend of prices). As discussed in later chapters, in many of his discussions of monetary policy in the 1960s and 1970s, Friedman would challenge economists who emphasized these two features of inflation behavior. His opponents in these debates would be Hansen's successors as champions of the Keynesian position, including Samuelson.

CLARK WARBURTON

The vast majority of people are likely to come across Clark Warburton's name only after they are already familiar with Milton Friedman's views on monetary economics. When they do encounter Warburton's work, or others' discussions of it (especially those of Cargill 1979, and Bordo and Schwartz 1979, 1983), few cannot be struck by the extent to which Warburton anticipated Milton Friedman's work on matters relating to monetary policy. On the interpretation of the Great Depression, the advocacy of constant monetary growth, and several other matters, Warburton—an economist at the Federal Deposit Insurance Corporation—was taking a stand during the war and the early postwar period that Friedman would take up only after 1948.[179] His writings well justify Phillip Cagan's retrospective evaluation that the Friedman-Schwartz project was "an extension of Warburton's work."[180] They also underlie Friedman and Schwartz's much-quoted statement at the start of *Monetary History* that "time and again, as we came to some conclusion that seemed to us novel and original, we found he had been there before."[181] This was a degree of praise that Friedman normally reserved for former teachers and for venerable predecessors in the monetary field like Hume, Jevons, and Fisher.

Warburton's writings on inflation during World War II put to shame Friedman's contemporaneous writings on the same subject.[182] Three pieces Warburton published in the *American Economic Review* in 1943 and 1944 on the inflationary gap were part of a sequence of articles on that topic that, of course, had included Friedman's 1942 contribution.[183] In contrast to Friedman's piece—which Warburton did not mention—Warburton centered squarely on the quantity of money as the decisive factor for the path of inflation. Warburton's 1944 article—a reply (albeit in the form of a full-length article) to a critical comment on his work by Ensley and Goode (1943)—is particularly notable. In that article, just as Friedman would do in the 1950s and 1960s, Warburton juxtaposed a quantity-theory-based analysis of inflation and an income-flow-based analysis of the Keynesian type, and he portrayed the issue at stake as being which of the two approaches proved empirically useful. Just as Friedman would argue subsequently, Warburton held that the money/spending relationship had proved more resilient in wartime than the Keynesian consumption function.[184] In summarizing his analysis of the early war years, Warburton was defiant:

> These facts are in perfect accord with the quantity theory of money, defined as the belief that changes in the price level are primarily due to changes in the volume of money relative to the need for money. . . . Modern economists who observe the facts around them have no more reason to disavow this old-fashioned theory, as Messrs. Ensley and Goode describe it ([1943,] 897), than modern physicians have to discard the equally old-fashioned theories of transmission of disease by infection and contagion. (Warburton 1944, 323-24)

A few paragraphs later, Warburton added for good measure, "The cause of the great depression of the early 1930's was monetary deficiency" (Warburton 1944, 325).

Warburton's affiliation was listed in Warburton (1946a) as "Division of Research and Statistics, Federal Deposit Insurance Corporation." Several other Warburton papers simply gave his affiliation as "Washington, D.C." or "FDIC." As indicated in Yeager (1981), Warburton's position at the FDIC was a factor holding back his scope to contribute to the research literature. For one thing, the FDIC had less of an embedded research tradition than institutions like the Federal Reserve.[185] For another, Warburton's research on money—particularly in connection with the Great Depression—was a source of agitation. Warburton put the blame for 1929-33 squarely on monetary policy—an accusation that the Federal Reserve's own accounts of the Depression did not accept until well beyond the 1940s. Warburton's acquaintance, Leland Yeager, would recall that Warburton "was made to feel that that publication, particularly publication that seemed critical of the Federal Reserve—and, of course, his work was implicitly quite critical of the Federal Reserve—was unwelcome, or undesired. . . . And he mentioned this: he did feel gagged, or restrained, against publishing for a few years" (Leland Yeager, interview, August 8, 2013).[186] So, although Warburton's contrarian views on money led Walters (1987, 424) to refer to "the irrepressible Clark Warburton," Walters's label is not wholly accurate with respect to Warburton's publishing record, which was stifled, or repressed, in the wake of his employer's edict.

Leland Yeager's position was that, notwithstanding the recognition Friedman and Schwartz gave Warburton in the *Monetary History*, "I think he deserves more credit than he got." Yeager added, "I, at one time, or maybe several times, asked him the obvious question of whether he felt that he had scooped Friedman and Schwartz. And 'scooped' is my word, not his. He did recognize that he had been working along the same lines before Friedman apparently took up interest in those matters, and he regretted, perhaps, that Friedman hadn't given him enough credit, although Friedman certainly mentions Warburton. But Warburton did not seem at all bitter to me about it, [instead taking the view that] it's just one of those facts" (Leland Yeager, interview, August 8, 2013).

Prior to the employer-issued gag order, Warburton had produced seminal work on the Depression and the wartime inflation, as indicated above. But a proposal that Warburton laid out for monetary policy after the war was of more questionable merit. In a July 1946 manuscript, "Effect of Wartime Monetary Expansion on the Postwar Price Level," Warburton started out his discussion with an observation that still resonates today: that price-level control was the "basic function of monetary policy" (Warburton 1946a, i). But he went on to make a recommendation that looks jarring from a modern-day perspective: that the monetary authorities claw back the wartime rise in prices via a deliberate policy of deflation.

The proposal for a managed postwar deflation rested on the dubious premise that it was desirable to return to a "normal" price level. It is very doubtful whether Friedman would have agreed with this proposal even in 1946. Rather, as suggested in the previous chapter and section II of this chapter, Friedman seems to have arrived at the judgment that deflation was costly at an early point in his career and to have maintained that judgment thereafter. It is true that, in an April 1946 radio appearance, Friedman said that "if possible," the money stock should be lowered from its existing level, but Friedman advanced this recommendation in the context of a discussion of measures to reduce inflation. It was not put forward with the aim of actually generating deflation.[187] And, within a few years of that 1946 statement, Friedman became more clear-cut in declaring policies that entailed a major deflation as undesirable in practice. By 1949, he was openly critical of the path of deflation, and in the early 1950s he referred to the "twin evils of inflation and deflation."[188]

As already noted, Friedman had by this stage come to the conclusion that, even though a managed deflation could generate some benefits under idealized conditions, output costs were likely to result from an attempt to deflate in practice. That remained Friedman's position in later postwar decades.[189] Even a relatively benign statement about deflation that Friedman made in 1984—that the economy might function smoothly with 1 or 2 percent deflation—was given alongside a reaffirmation of his own preference for a zero inflation rate. Furthermore, the 1984 remark came in the wake of comments in which Friedman noted the damage done by high rates of deflation in the 1930s.[190]

In fairness to Warburton, it should be mentioned that his 1946 proposal stressed that the proposed deflation had to proceed gradually in order to minimize disruption to real output. Furthermore, Warburton's attachment to the notion that there existed a normal price level to which the economy should return was one that both economists and laypeople seemed to find hard to shake off. As discussed in chapter 10 below, some residues of this notion lingered even in Friedman's discussions of US monetary conditions until well into the 1960s.

Putting particular policy prescriptions aside, the basic monetary analysis brought out in Warburton's writings has so many similarities to Friedman's that it is easier to focus on the differences. The remaining discussion in this chapter will highlight two differences between Warburton's analysis and Friedman's monetarism.[191]

As a preliminary matter, it is worth indicating why one difference suggested by Cargill (1979, 444) is not accepted in the present analysis. Cargill argued that Warburton did, and modern monetarism did not, use the equation of exchange when providing monetary analysis.[192] Velocity was referred to very frequently in Friedman's work, as well as in that of Brunner and Meltzer (for example, in their 1963 paper). Consequently, the Cargill characterization is, in the view of the present author, not sustainable. As the preceding discussion of Alvin Hansen indicated, explicit analyses of velocity behavior pervaded the quantity-theory literature, including the monetarist literature—a fact recognized in Friedman's remark that the analysis of fiscal policy can be put "in monetarist terms" by referring to the implied behavior of velocity.[193] True, Friedman did not write out the $MV = Py$ equation (or a variant of it) in his 1956 "restatement" of the quantity theory.[194] He did do so in many other writings both before and after 1956, however, including in a 1952 submission to Congress on the quantity theory of money and in his 1968 and 1974 encyclopedia entries on the quantity theory.[195]

Friedman's affinity with the equation of exchange was also conveyed in his two contributions to the 1987 New Palgrave dictionary of economics. His entry on the quantity theory of money used the equation of exchange as a way of organizing the discussion. His other contribution to the New Palgrave dictionary was an entry on Simon Newcomb, whom Friedman felt deserved greater recognition among economists as a creator of the equation of exchange. That an entry appeared in the New Palgrave on Newcomb reflected Friedman's suggestion to the editors. Having made the suggestion, Friedman volunteered to write the entry on Newcomb (Lord [John] Eatwell, interview, January 4, 2015).[196] Friedman also was enthusiastic about Bordo's (1987) New Palgrave entry on the equation of exchange.

In relying on the equation of exchange in his presentations of the quantity theory of money, Friedman did not, of course, treat the equation of exchange as *implying* quantity-theory results without the imposition of restrictions on the behavior of the variables in the equation appearing alongside the money stock.[197] But neither did Warburton. As Brunner (1960, 606) put it, "even the crudest quantity theory is more significant than any quantity equation."[198]

One must look elsewhere to locate the key differences between Friedman and Warburton. To the present author, two such differences stand out. The first difference is that Friedman was more willing than Warburton to spell out the transmission mechanism. This difference was felt in their analysis of both aggregate demand and aggregate supply. On the aggregate-demand side, Friedman laid out his specification of the IS equation, whereas Warburton did not provide a correspondingly explicit treatment. The multiple-interest-rate view of the transmission process that Friedman articulated (see chapter 6) was more explicit than was typical in the approach of Warburton. Warburton instead focused on the tendency of household behavior to make the money-income ratio stationary and did not specify in detail the adjustment of spending to an injection of money. Warburton could therefore be regarded as relying to a greater degree than Friedman did on "high-level assumptions" about private-sector behavior. True, Friedman for the most part did not provide rigorous microfoundations for his modeling, and a good deal of his theoretical analysis of aggregate demand behavior was verbal. All the same, however, Friedman's theoretical analysis of aggregate demand determination was more detailed and precise than what was available in Warburton's discussions.[199]

On the aggregate-supply side, Warburton did not lay out an analogue to the natural-rate hypothesis.[200] Warburton did bring a rudimentary form of Phillips-curve analysis into his work when he specified in his 1944 paper that the adjustment of prices to variations in the money stock worked via an output gap channel. In addition, Warburton's 1946 admonition against a too-rapid deflation seems to suggest an understanding that keeping expected inflation lined up with actual inflation helps minimize output-gap fluctuations—a message that is consistent with the Friedman-Phelps expectations-augmented Phillips curve.[201] But Warburton failed to pull together his ideas about price adjustment in the way that Friedman did in his 1967 presidential address to the American Economic Association.[202]

On the other hand, Warburton devoted more attention than Friedman to fleshing out particular aspects of the money-supply process. Both Friedman and Warburton emphasized the link between reserve creation and money creation, with Warburton (1943b, 609) stating that commercial bankers' "decisions are profoundly influenced, at times almost completely dominated, by their reserve position." But—fittingly, in light of his FDIC affiliation—Warburton was more inclined to write at length about bank regulation (other than reserve requirements) as a factor that bore on the behavior of the money multiplier (that is, the ratio of the money stock to base money), and more specifically on the behavior of the deposit-to-reserve ratio.

This is not to say that the connection between the money multiplier and regulatory policy was absent from Friedman's own research. Indeed, when he began his work with Schwartz in 1948, Friedman listed the "condition of banks" as one aspect of their research undertaking (American Economic Association 1948, 64). And so it proved: the link between regulatory policy and the multiplier was recognized by Friedman and Schwartz in their discussion of the Great Contraction. They saw the imposition by regulators of strict mark-to-market-style rules as a reason why commercial banks, in the face of a major bond price decline, felt obliged to engage in a massive reduction in their holdings of earning assets (both loans and securities).[203]

Warburton, however, discussed this aspect of multiplier determination at greater length in his writings. Although he continued to emphasize the stock of bank reserves as a factor in deposit creation, he also noted: "Bank supervisory officials doubtless have some influence on the volume of bank credit and hence on the volume of circulating media through the standards which they use in examining bank portfolios and judging the adequacy of bank capital, particularly in the case of temporary relaxation, during a period of crisis, of customary standards."[204] In remarks published in 1951 that Warburton used to close his 1966 collection of articles, *Depression, Inflation, and Monetary Policy*, Warburton indicated that one reason an equity-capital requirement on banks was desirable was to forestall the monetary disturbances that were associated with bank failures.[205] While not extensive, the coverage that Warburton gave to bank regulation and bank equity as factors entering the determination of the money multiplier exceeded that found in Friedman's main works. In this coverage, Warburton foreshadowed modern research such as Kashyap and Stein (2000) in which bank capital is a critical element behind banks' decisions concerning their total asset holdings.[206]

Despite publishing prolifically in major economics journals both during and after the war, Warburton found his work "largely neglected" and "ignored" by the profession, in the words of Brunner and Meltzer (1993, 18).[207] The appearance of the Friedman-Schwartz *Monetary History* promoted belated interest in Warburton's work, stimulating the release of the 1966 collection mentioned above.[208] That book was not an exhaustive volume of collected works. Instead, it consisted of only a portion of the Warburton canon. As was reflected in its subtitle, *Selected Papers, 1945–1953*, the book concentrated heavily on materials from the second half of the 1940s, in which Warburton's activity in the field of monetary research peaked.

As it happened, in the same late-1940s period in which Warburton's monetary work reached its zenith, a profound change was occurring in Milton Friedman's views on monetary matters. The result of this change was that, by the early 1950s, Friedman had shed the decidedly Keynesian positions to which he had held allegiance for the balance of the war years, and he was poised to take from Warburton the mantle as the principal defender of the quantity theory of money. The crucial years from 1944 to 1950—during which this change in Friedman's thinking occurred—are considered in the next chapter.

CHAPTER 4

Money Changes Everything, 1944 to 1950

I. Events and Activities, 1944–50

In early 1943, Friedman left the US Treasury and moved to the Statistical Research Group (SRG).[1] The assignments for the SRG consisted of government-contracted work and involved access to classified military information.[2] Reflecting the war-related nature of its activities, the SRG was reduced to a skeletal staff (which did not include Friedman) once the war was over.[3] Friedman's move from the Treasury to the SRG nonetheless amounted to a return to an academic position. The SRG was a Columbia University organization, not a governmental unit. Accordingly, two books showcasing the SRG's research output had "Statistical Research Group, Columbia University" on the title page.[4] And it was simply an affiliation of "Columbia University" that accompanied a most notable book review that Friedman published in the *Review of Economics and Statistics* in May 1944, during his employment at the SRG.[5]

That review, of the book *Saving, Investment, and National Income* by Oscar L. Altman, has lasting significance as the occasion on which Friedman first laid down a marker as a critic of Keynesian economics. Most likely, it was this review that he remembered a half century later as being "very critical of the Keynesian analysis."[6] Friedman put distance between himself and the Keynesian revolution from the first paragraph, in which he

The views expressed in this study are those of the author alone and should not be interpreted as those of the Federal Reserve Board or the Federal Reserve System. The author received valuable comments on drafts of this chapter from Miguel Acosta, Michael Bordo, Douglas Irwin, David Laidler, Ann-Marie Meulendyke, Gerald O'Driscoll, Michael Parkin, and the late Julio Rotemberg. Thanks also go to Robert Lucas and Michael Woodford for useful discussions on some of the topics discussed in this chapter. See the introduction for a full list of acknowledgments for this book. The author regrets to note that, in the period since the research for this chapter was begun, six of the individuals whose interviews with the author are quoted in this chapter—Kenneth Arrow, William Baumol, Carl Christ, Sir Antony Jay, David Meiselman, and Richard Muth—have passed away.

designated the book under review "an expression of the Keynesian saving-investment theory which has had such vogue in recent years."[7] In 1970, Friedman would comment that one of the appeals of Keynesian analysis was that, after some training with the associated apparatus, it provided a straightforward, mechanical, and widely applicable means of conducting analysis of the determination of national income.[8] He made the same observation in that 1944 review. After a problem had been stated in terms of the Keynesian apparatus, Friedman wrote, "it is only necessary to crank the handle . . . apply the proper multipliers, and out comes the answer. And this answer will appear certain and will seem to prescribe definite action."[9]

Friedman concluded that the Altman book brought little evidence that bore directly on its "central thesis, namely, that (*ex ante*) investment is the major dynamic variable which determines the aggregate level of income and employment over both short and long periods."[10] Nearly twenty years later, he would have occasion to apply this criticism to the economics profession in general, when he and Meiselman would argue that there had still been "almost no systematic attempt to assess the relevant empirical evidence" on the Keynesian spending multiplier.[11] A major difference between the criticism that Friedman advanced in 1944 and that he made in 1963 was that, by the time of the later statement, Friedman had lived up to his dictum that "you cannot beat a theory without a theory."[12] To this end, the later work put up the quantity theory of money as the alternative to the Keynesian multiplier theory of national income determination. In contrast, apart from a fleeting reference to liquidity preference, discussion of money was notably absent from Friedman's 1944 criticism of Keynesian economics. He was a skeptic about Keynesianism, but he had not yet become a monetarist.

Friedman's Attitude to Regression Analysis

Friedman's work during his years at the SRG would play a part in the American Statistical Association's appointment of him as a fellow in December 1949. The SRG work would be summarized in the latter half of the citation for Friedman's fellowship: "MILTON FRIEDMAN, economist who has skillfully applied both quantitative and other methods, not only to add to the science of economics, but under the call of wartime urgency, to help design metallurgical experiments and participate in the design of weapons and tactics."[13] It was largely this work in connection with weapon design that underlay Friedman's subsequent summary of his assignment at the SRG as "war research."[14] Such work included the development of sampling inspection. The SRG's research in this field helped provide a more efficient way for the military to allow for the likelihood of faults in its munitions supplies.

Other SRG work involved the design of anti-aircraft shells and bomb fuses, in the course of which military personnel met with Friedman for advice.[15] It was, however, an incident in connection with Friedman's work in the field of metallurgy that would, according to his later accounts, have lasting significance in his approach to economics, because of its alleged role in shaping Friedman's attitude to econometric modeling.

As Friedman later recalled it, in 1944 or 1945 he had been charged with the task of helping to design alloys that would be resilient in the face of heat pressure. The basis Friedman used for guiding his design of alloys was a multiple regression, with time-to-fracture as the dependent variable. Friedman found that although the regression had high explanatory power "and it satisfied every other test statistic that I knew of," the alloys produced from his proposals turned out to be highly susceptible to heat.[16] That experience, Friedman would claim, was what convinced him that out-of-sample performance, not in-sample fit, is the true measure of success of a model.[17]

There is considerable reason to believe that this experience, which Friedman summarized as a "cautionary tale about multiple regressions" on one of the occasions that he recounted it, had a less decisive influence on Friedman's attitude to econometrics than he would later remember.[18] This incident does not, in fact, make a particularly striking anecdote, as many others have related similar stories about multiple-regression analysis in print.[19] And it is, in any event, very unlikely that the incident really provided the genesis for Friedman's skepticism about multiple regressions, as he would claim.[20] Friedman had *already* put on record, in his 1940 evaluation of Tinbergen's econometric model, his doubts about multiple regression analysis and his belief in the need for out-of-sample validation.[21] That review made it clear that Friedman's early enthusiasm for multiple regressions—exemplified by his observation in 1935 about the "excellent possibilities" offered by the extension of multiple regression analysis to a broader range of economic topics—had, following the additional experience Friedman acquired over the rest of the 1930s in both the statistical and economic-research fields, been replaced with a jaded attitude.[22]

Indeed, the message that Friedman in 1991 stated that he had learned from his SRG experience—that "any hypothesis must be tested with data or nonquantitative evidence other than that used in deriving the regression or available when the regression was derived"—had already been embodied in his 1940 complaint that "Tinbergen makes no attempt to determine whether his equations agree with data other than those which they translate."[23]

The alloy anecdote seems to have been on Friedman's mind in the 1980s, in the wake of Hendry and Ericsson's (1983) critique of his empirical work with Anna Schwartz: Friedman told the SRG-era story in a 1985 talk, for example.[24] In reconstructing the story from that late vantage point, Friedman seems to have overrated the role that the SRG incident played in shaping his thinking on econometrics. That said, although the alloy incident did not mark the onset of Friedman's doubts about multiple-regression analysis, it may well have decisively confirmed his preexisting doubts. Certainly, there is no question that Friedman was very ill-disposed toward multiple-regression analysis in the postwar period—a posture reflected in his proclamation that "the more complex the regression, the more skeptical I am."[25]

This perspective toward multivariate analysis was confirmed not only in Friedman's empirical work but also in the emphasis on parsimony that permeated his theoretical research on structural economic relationships. With respect to the latter, the theoretical refinements that Friedman advanced in postwar decades to the consumption function and the Phillips curve made them more defensible as structural relationships, yet they did so without adding a multiplicity of variables to the specifications. On the empirical side, his work with Meiselman would attempt to boil down the Keynesian and quantity-theory models to hypotheses that could each be represented by a single, two-variable equation. Friedman's skepticism about econometric model-building also led him, after some interaction, to keep his distance from the major projects of the University of Chicago's Cowles Commission in the late 1940s and early 1950s.[26]

One of the reasons why Friedman might initially have seemed a natural for involvement in the Cowles Commission's activities is that he had deepened his involvement in statistics during his period with the SRG. In particular, Friedman played a key role in the development of sequential analysis and in the production of a book on the subject, *Sampling Inspection*. The book appeared in 1948, but it reflected work from earlier years, with Allen Wallis's introduction, written from his new base of the University of Chicago, bearing a date of December 1946.[27] Friedman and Wallis were among the author-editors listed on the cover page. Although not listed on the cover page, L. J. (Jimmie) Savage—whose later work with Friedman is discussed below—was identified in Wallis's introduction as another author of the book, as was one David H. Schwartz. The latter's presence among the book's contributors led, incidentally, to the use in Wallis's introduction of the phrase "Friedman and Schwartz" (W. A. Wallis 1948, vii), years before that phrase had become the shorthand for the collaborations of Friedman and Anna Schwartz.

Friedman's Place in Statistical Analysis

It was on the basis of Friedman's work on sequential analysis—not his statistical work in economics or his development of the ranks test—that Friedman's name was invoked at a major conference held in 1970 on the history of statistics. At that conference, Jerzy Neyman (1971, 6) noted the credit that Wald (1947, v, 2) gave to Friedman and Wallis for highlighting the importance of sequential analysis when Wald was a consultant to the SRG—an action that helped set in motion a course of events in which Wald wrote a classified memorandum on the subject (in 1943) and then published a major monograph in the area (in 1947).[28] As of May 1945, Friedman was planning to make sequential analysis a major research activity of his own in the postwar period, and he included his ability to teach a course on the subject among the credentials he gave when seeking employment at the University of Minnesota (Hammond and Hammond 2006, 16). Friedman indeed secured the University of Minnesota position, but his interest in sequential analysis did not prove enduring. Indeed, even though, as we shall see, statistical theory figured heavily in Friedman's early postwar economic research, he would retrospectively view his interest in, and aptitude for, the whole field of mathematical statistics as having peaked with the end of his time at the SRG and as having declined progressively thereafter.[29]

Joining the University of Chicago's Economics Department

The *University of Chicago Magazine*, keeping track of alumni, noted in its January 1946 issue that Friedman had recently left Columbia University for a position at the University of Minnesota (*University of Chicago Magazine*, January 1946, 28). Five months later, the magazine provided an update: "Milton Friedman, AM '35 [*sic*; 1933], associate professor of economics and statistics at the University of Minnesota, has been made an Associate Professor of Economics [at the University of Chicago]" (*University of Chicago Magazine*, June 1946, 13).[30] The item also indicated that Friedman's appointments would become effective the following fall. Accordingly, later in 1946, after his one academic year at the University of Minnesota, Friedman moved to the Department of Economics of the University of Chicago.

And so Friedman reentered the rough-and-tumble world of the University of Chicago economics scene. Robert Lucas, who in the 1960s and 1970s would be a PhD student and professor, respectively, in the economics department at the University of Chicago, and who would interact with Friedman at the university in both these capacities, has observed: "His courtesy was remarkable."[31] If this observation does not seem to fit altogether comfortably with Friedman's aggressive image, it should be said by way of reconciliation that (*a*) the combative University of Chicago atmosphere probably implied a fairly low bar in defining courtesy, and (*b*) Lucas knew Friedman only after the latter had been joined at the University of Chicago by George Stigler.[32] Stigler's gift for devastating one-liners raised the standard of wit at the university, but perhaps it had the further effect of setting the bar for the definition of courtesy still lower.[33]

It is also true that Friedman was typically courteous with members of the public (one manifestation of which was his practice, even after obtaining celebrity status, of replying personally to correspondence) and that he was noted by PhD students to be very generous with his time.[34] Friedman himself recalled a "highly collegial atmosphere" at the University of Chicago when he was a teacher in the economics department.[35] However, he would also come to observe that one characteristic of the Chicago School was that its members did not take themselves seriously (Instructional Dynamics Economics Cassette Tape 110, November 1, 1972). This irreverent outlook was reflected in the fact that department members could be forensic and ultracritical about one another's work—a situation that was brought out in the numerous instances in which the acknowledgments in Friedman's papers thanked readers for "criticism," as though that term was synonymous with "comments."[36]

This critical outlook was evident not only in the department members' interaction with one another, but also in many of the department members' interaction with economists from outside the university. Friedman was not exactly a shrinking violet before he joined the staff of the University of Chicago. Indeed, Nicholas Georgescu-Roegen, one of his antagonists in Friedman's first exchange in print in 1935-36, would cite that early exchange as exemplifying the fact that "if you disagree with him[,] however little, Milton Friedman would clobber you."[37] Friedman's pre-1946 writings include a number of acerbic remarks, including his observation, in the aforementioned book review, that the Altman (1941) application of Keynesian analysis was unbelievably simple and simply unbelievable.[38] And it was noted in chapter 2 that Friedman could be abrasive with Henry Schultz when working with the latter in the mid-1930s.

But Friedman's tongue sharpened further in his years as a teacher in the University of Chicago, and his catalogue of sharp remarks in print also increased. "He was certainly a very nice person," observed Carl Christ, who was a graduate student at the University of Chicago from 1946 to 1950 and was a member of the department from 1955 to 1961. "Even when debating people with whom he disagreed . . . he could be relentless intellectually but not personally."[39] Consistent with this characterization, at the end of Friedman's thirty years at the university a *Newsweek* profile (October 25, 1976b, 89, 86) described him both as "unfailingly cheerful, witty and courteous" and as "acerbic."[40] Against this backdrop, Franco Modigliani approached a January 1977 public debate with Friedman with a heavy amount of preparation. "I knew that he is tough and very fast and dangerous."[41]

As Modigliani's remark makes clear, Friedman became well known in the University of Chicago years for his withering comments in written and spoken exchanges. Some flavor of these is given by the following sample:

"I enjoyed reading it and am glad to report that in my opinion its conclusions are utterly fallacious." (August 6, 1971, comments in a letter to Fischer Black on a paper of Black's, quoted in Mehrling 2005, 155)

"So often in the past what they've [the Federal Reserve] said they were going to do, and what they actually did, were quite different—not because they didn't have integrity, but because they didn't have competence, which is a quite different thing." (Instructional Dynamics Economics Cassette Tape 138, January 16, 1974)

"I had not read or seen [his] paper and know nothing about the method of estimation but I am confident that the advice he gave you was bad advice." (Communication with Federal Reserve Board staff in connection with the Bach Committee, September 27, 1976, Federal Reserve Board records)

"Let us try to see if we can get out the little element of your comment which is really relevant to our discussion here." (*Milton Friedman Speaks*, episode 11, "Putting Learning Back in the Classroom," taped September 15, 1977, p. 22 of transcript)

"And there has been no shortage of proposed explanations. The trouble is, all of them are wrong." (*Newsweek*, September 21, 1981)

"Whether our foreign policy is sensible or not: I'm not an expert on that. Neither are you, frankly." (to Phil Donahue on *Donahue*, NBC, April 25, 1984)

"Then I believe you're utterly inconsistent." (to George Will on *This Week with David Brinkley*, ABC, December 17, 1989, p. 6 of transcript)

"That question simply reflects a misunderstanding of what the facts are." (November 21, 1996, talk at Indiana University, broadcast on CSPAN, December 1, 1996)

The Friedman-Stigler Pamphlet

An experience that gave Friedman good preparation for the combative atmosphere of the University of Chicago was that surrounding the production and release of his pamphlet *Roofs or Ceilings?*, written jointly with George Stigler. This pamphlet went into print just as Friedman was relocating to Chicago in August–September 1946.[42]

As discussed presently, by that point the text of the Friedman-Stigler analysis had produced a dispute between the pamphlet's authors and its publishers. Even putting this aspect of the controversy to one side, however, the pamphlet was bound to cause a stir because of its advocacy of the abolition of rent control. The pamphlet's stand on rent control continued the hostile position toward wage and price controls that Friedman had held during the war. But the question at issue did not—as discussions of price and wage control after the 1970s typically would—come down to a disagreement between pro-controls non-economists and an anti-controls economics profession. Rather, the Keynesian revolution had brought with it not only an emphasis on demand management, but also a case for wage and price controls.[43] That case arose from the notion, embedded in the *General Theory* but particularly emphasized by Keynes and others after 1936, that control of aggregate demand was not sufficient for price stability. According to the cost-push view endorsed in the Keynesian approach, autonomous forces could trigger a wage/price spiral, and direct wage and price controls or other forms of incomes policy could be used to hold these forces in check. Along these lines, Alvin Hansen (1947a, 314) had written that the degree of moderation in wage growth observed of late in the United States "could never have been achieved except against the background of continued price control."

Friedman and Stigler broke with positions of this kind. Their line of argument, which Friedman would restate and elaborate on many times in later writings, was that resort to price controls, including rent controls, meant "dealing clumsily and ineffectively with the symptoms and results of inflation" instead of the cause: excessive aggregate demand.[44]

With concern about inflation therefore rejected as a basis for maintaining rent control, most of the Friedman-Stigler pamphlet was directed toward the additions to rental supply that would flow in the residential sector from abolition of rent control. Would rent decontrol mean a rise in rental costs for housing tenants? "Absolutely!" Friedman answered in a radio appearance a few months after the pamphlet was released (NBC 1947b, 4). But, he stressed, the addition to supply associated with higher rents would provide housing access to low-income families.

Despite their common ground with Friedman and Stigler on the undesirability of rent control, the editor and publishers of the pamphlet did not see eye to eye with the authors about the draft. They took exception to Friedman and Stigler's statement: "For those, like us, who would like even more equality than there is at present . . . it is surely better to attack directly existing inequalities in income and wealth at their source than to ration each of the hundreds of commodities and services that compose our standard of living."[45] The acrimonious correspondence that took place between the authors and the editor, who wanted the statement deleted, would occupy a good part of Hammond and Hammond's (2006) book of Friedman-Stigler correspondence.[46] In the event, the passage was let through into the published version of Friedman and Stigler's piece, accompanied by an editorial disclaimer. It subsequently became one of the passages that libertarian writers would seize on in later years as evidence that Friedman was not one of their number (for example, Rothbard 1971).

In light of the travails that Friedman went through in 1946 to preserve the passage in the published version of the pamphlet, and the backlash he thereby provoked from libertarians, an irony is that the sentiment expressed in the statement was not one that Friedman would likely have reaffirmed in the 1970s. Indeed, in a 1974 radio appearance Friedman stated: "I think that economic inequality in the United States and Britain is highly tolerable."[47]

The change in circumstances that prompted this revised judgment on Friedman's part had not, as he saw it, primarily arisen from the tax and welfare policies pursued in both countries between the 1940s and the 1970s. On the contrary, Friedman argued that US and UK tax policies of the postwar decades had produced a "vast reshuffling" of wealth but that it was not clear that they had produced a redistribution of wealth in a more equitable direction.[48] Friedman further contended that tax policies had been steered in directions that could not be rationalized by a community desire to redistribute wealth (*Financial Times*, January 6, 1977). What had been more important in changing his view concerning whether greater income equality was imperative was the rise in *absolute* incomes over the postwar period. As incomes had risen over time, the official definition used in the United States as the minimal above-poverty income came to exceed levels that, he said, the Friedman family had earned during his childhood—years that he recalled as financially difficult ones for his family but generally not featuring outright distress.[49]

Consequently, Friedman would come to regard it as useful to distinguish low income from poverty and, in view of this distinction, he saw a role for government policy in supplementing very low incomes but without using the official definition of poverty as the criterion.[50] In that connection, he would concentrate on the virtues of a government-provided floor on absolute income for US households, with the aim of mitigating distress, rather than endorse more wide-ranging proposals for reducing disparities in incomes.[51] However, it was not the case that Friedman's move from supporting wide-ranging income redistribution to a focus on distress cases was a shift that repaired his rift with the libertarians. To the contrary: when, in the 1960s, he advanced his negative income tax proposal as a way of providing a guaranteed income and serving a distress-relief function, Friedman would infuriate libertarians all over again.

Friedman and Popular Debate

As noted in the previous chapter, the *Roofs or Ceilings?* experience did not constitute Friedman's debut as an advocate of market solutions to popular audiences, for he had already played this role as a guest panelist in 1943 on an edition of the NBC radio series *University of Chicago Round Table*. In 1968, Friedman would recall that "in the old days" he had been a regular radio debater; here he was recalling his stint as a recurring panelist on the same *Round Table* series from 1946 onward.[52]

An early Friedman appearance as a regular on the program, in December 1946, brought out both his research in human capital for the Friedman-Kuznets study and his status as a free marketer. In his contribution to the panel discussion, Friedman used the term "human capital" and elaborated that "the thing which really makes us rich—the great, important wealth—is a wealth in our human resources, our wealth of technology and of skill and of know-how" (NBC 1946b, 8). Friedman regarded his emphasis on human capital as underscoring the importance of education and training, but not as pointing toward an expanded role for the public sector. Rather, he cited the nineteenth century as a period of "great development of economic well-being in the Western world" (8) in which a framework oriented on democracy, free markets, and a limited state role had allowed institutions to emerge that developed human capital (8–9).[53]

Friedman's conviction that the promotion of markets, and not a larger role for the state, provided the key to economic advance was reinforced by a trip that he and Stigler made in 1947 to the United Kingdom and France—both nations in which the government was assuming a greater role in the economy than was the case in the United States.[54]

Research on Decision Theory

Friedman's appointment to the University of Chicago's economics department was as associate professor; promotion to full professor occurred in 1948.[55] The initial appointment came after Stigler, who was his colleague at the University of Minnesota, had been turned down for the post. The reasoning behind the latter decision was that Stigler was perceived as too empirical (Kitch 1983, 180; G. Stigler 1988, 40; Coase 1991, 470). Evidently, therefore, Friedman was hired in the belief that, as in much of his research to date, he would be theoretically oriented. It transpired that Friedman did not long continue in this direction. He would produce a large body of empirical work in the postwar decades. The resulting perception among economists, succinctly captured by Michael Evans (1983, 122), was that Friedman "was, and in fact, remains, the supreme empiricist." However, at the time of Friedman's University of Chicago appointment, and in the initial few years thereafter, his research agenda was largely concerned with theory, and it seemed to conform to a call to action that he and Allen Wallis had made in 1942—that future research needed to include "concentrating some heavy theoretical artillery" on issues in consumer behavior.[56]

Wallis and Friedman were speaking with particular reference to the study of indifference curves. It was, however, instead the topic of utility functions to which Friedman in the later 1940s would apply "theoretical artillery." The resulting papers, with L. J. Savage, would do more than anything else Friedman wrote prior to the 1950s to make his reputation among economists, even though these papers had very little to do with Friedman's principal research endeavors after the mid-1950s.

In the view of Mervyn King (1977, 128), "the rigorous extension of economic theory to a world of uncertainty was developed by Arrow (1964) and Debreu (1959)." When, however, Friedman and Savage were carrying out their joint research in the late 1940s, they probably saw themselves as contributing to the effort that King would see as starting only in the late 1950s. Friedman and Savage's collaborations built on the work of von Neumann and Morgenstern (1944) in applying utility analysis to a stochastic environment. The King interpretation of the literature can be defended, however, because it was the Arrow-Debreu contributions, rather than those of von Neumann and Morgenstern or Friedman and Savage, that put uncertainty into a general equilibrium framework. And Morgenstern himself may have been acknowledging the importance of the Arrow-Debreu work when in 1971 he referred to the "almost explosive development" of the analysis of utility in the last "few decades" (most of which postdated his work with von Neumann and that of Friedman and Savage).[57]

Friedman and Savage's work was presented in a 1948 *Journal of Political Economy* article and a 1952 follow-up in the same journal.[58] Their concern was to bring "choices involving risk," and particularly activities involving insurance and gambling, into a framework in which households maximized expected utility. The 1948 article was essentially a theoretical paper, even though only a few numbered equations appeared in it. Notwithstanding the motivation that the authors offered with pieces of information about existing lottery and insurance arrangements, their paper was *not* a piece of applied research into consumer behavior—a fact consistent with Friedman's later observation that he had not worked with consumption data at all from 1937 until his research on consumption in the 1950s.[59]

The paper's concern with reconciling gambling activity with maximizing household behavior reflected the dissonance between gambling and ordinary utility analysis: diminishing marginal utility implied that households would refrain from gambling in circumstances in which their odds of a positive dollar outcome were only 50/50, yet there was evidence that households did partake in gambles with these, or worse, odds. Friedman and Savage's proposed reconciliation was to suggest that diminishing marginal utility was not a global property of the utility function, and that, instead, the utility function contained a region over which increasing marginal utility prevailed.[60]

Insofar as the Friedman-Savage work aimed to widen the applicability of orthodox economic tools (in particular, utility theory), it anticipated Friedman's subsequent position that a wide range of firm and household behavior was conducive to standard economic analysis (in particular, to a Marshallian approach to demand). Indeed, the 1952 follow-up paper, in which Friedman and Savage replied to a critique by Baumol (1951), was a vigorous defense of the expected-utility approach. The defense of their 1948 extension of that approach played only an ancillary role in their discussion. As Friedman would emphasize, another respect in which the Friedman-Savage work affirmed economic orthodoxy—and in so doing broke with one strand of University of Chicago thinking—consisted of its rejection of the case, advanced by Frank Knight, for distinguishing between the concepts of risk and uncertainty.[61] Indeed, Friedman's rejection of Knightian uncertainty not only contrasted him with a key member of the prior generation of University of Chicago economists; it would also be a factor that set him apart from several later economists at the university, who did attach considerable importance to the concept of Knightian uncertainty—including Lester Telser, Richard Posner, and Lars Hansen.[62]

The last of these authors has considered Friedman's approach to uncertainty on several occasions, including in Lars Hansen and Thomas Sargent (2014). Hansen and Sargent emphasize that the Bayesian approach to decision theory underlying this price-theory work also manifested itself in Friedman's subsequent approach to monetary policy rules. In particular, model uncertainty was a major consideration underlying Friedman's case against activist stabilization policy, and in the face of that uncertainty, Friedman adopted what Hansen and Sargent (2014, 5) call "Friedman's Bayesian decision rule" in his work in the early 1950s on destabilizing stabilization policy.[63]

Friedman's advocacy, beginning later in the 1950s, of a constant-monetary-growth rule likewise stemmed from model-uncertainty considerations—see chapter 8—although it did not flow from a formal analysis of policy making under uncertainty. Even though, as Lars Hansen and Thomas Sargent stress, the Bayesian approach informed his perspective on both decision theory and policy rules, it would be an exaggeration to suggest that Friedman fully embraced Bayesian techniques. In particular, although—as noted earlier in this chapter—Friedman had many skeptical remarks to make about mainstream econometrics, he did not follow the Bayesian alternative systematically in his empirical work.[64]

As of the 1950s, the Friedman-Savage work was regarded as a seminal piece of research, a judgment reflected in Friedman's Clark prize—discussed at the end of this chapter—and in the reprinting of the 1948 Friedman-Savage article in the American Economic Association's 1952 collection *Readings in Price Theory* (Boulding and Stigler 1952). Indeed, Frank Hahn, who was not well-disposed toward much of Friedman's work (especially that in monetary economics), admired the Friedman-Savage papers.[65]

But whether the Friedman-Savage joint work left an appreciable, *durable* imprint on the economic literature is questionable. Friedman himself would later take nonexclusive credit for the term "maximization of utility under conditions of risk."[66] In this spirit, some treatments (such as S. Weintraub 1964, 155; Fishburn 1970, 103; McCloskey 1985, 64; Zellner 1985, 254; Machina 1987, 235; and Lars Hansen and Thomas Sargent 2011, 1104) have cited Friedman and Savage's work as part of the research that linked up the study of utility with statistical theory, thereby setting up the expected-utility-maximizing approach of the type routinely used in dynamic optimizing models.[67] But citation of their work in that context is rare, and the development of expected-utility theory is much more widely credited to von Neumann and Morgenstern, with Arrow and Debreu then providing much of the remaining apparatus necessary to apply the theory to a stochastic general equilibrium model. Furthermore, Savage's solo-authored work involving subjective probabilities (Savage 1954), including the axioms laid out therein, is considered a far more fundamental generalization of the von Neumann-Morgenstern expected-utility foundations than either Friedman and Savage's joint work or Friedman's early-1950s solo-authored work on utility.[68] Friedman's own literature discussion in *Price Theory* seemed to reflect an acceptance that this was the case.[69] Friedman was a subscriber to Savage's subjective-probability concept, but he was not a collaborator on Savage's outline of it.[70]

Furthermore, the later research on a specific activity to which Friedman and Savage applied their extension of utility theory—gambling—reached a generally unfavorable verdict on the Friedman-Savage proposal. An early critique came from Harry Markowitz, shortly after he completed graduate studies at the University of Chicago. His criticisms of the Friedman-Savage approach notwithstanding, Markowitz's (1952, 155) analysis led him to endorse the basic Friedman-Savage approach of specifying a utility function that was concave and convex in different regions. The subsequent literature suggested, however, that the explanation for the phenomenon of gambling lay elsewhere. This was the message that emerged especially clearly from a critique of Friedman and Savage's work by Bailey, Olson, and Wonnacott (1980). Although the 1980 critique was itself challenged by Hartley and Farrell (2002), this later study ultimately also registered a negative verdict on Friedman and Savage's proposed explanation for gambling. The fact that later studies of gambling have generally eschewed the Friedman-Savage approach is also evident in the literature of "superstars." In this literature, such papers as Rosen (1981) and Murphy and Wolfson (2013) have acknowledged but rejected the Friedman-Savage explanation for gambling.[71]

"It was very ingenious," Kenneth Arrow recalled of the Friedman-Savage approach, "changing the slope so that you had increasing and decreasing marginal utility." But Arrow affirmed that the joint Friedman-Savage work did not match, in its influence and importance, Savage's other research on utility (Kenneth Arrow, interview, December 7, 2013).[72] The Friedman-Savage research has not faded into obscurity, but neither is it generally regarded as a fundamental reference in the area of expected utility.[73]

In the field of macroeconomics, the generalization of the utility function proposed by Friedman and Savage has made essentially no impact. The notion of specifying a utility function that is occasionally convex has not caught on at all in mainstream work. The condition that the representative agent has a globally concave utility function is pervasive in macroeconomic theory—being essentially a sine qua non—and empirical findings of preferences outside the strictly concave region are viewed as uninterpretable and as evidence against the representative-agent, expected-utility framework.[74] One could, however, view the celebrated work of Epstein and Zin (1989), who proposed a utility function in which high risk aversion and high intertemporal substitution can coexist, as having some parallels to the Friedman-Savage approach: both pairs of authors advanced a utility function that encompassed two properties that were normally seen as not amenable to being captured by a single function. But the Epstein-Zin utility function is much more conducive to obvious macroeconomic applications than the Friedman-Savage specification. In keeping with this assessment, John Taylor (2001, 101) classified the Friedman-Savage work among Friedman's contributions to mathematical statistics rather than to economics.[75]

In later life, Friedman gave much credit to Savage for their joint work, describing Savage as an "honest-to-God genius" and judging that without Savage's input he could not have produced research of the kind presented in their collaborations (see Hammond 1989, 44).[76] "I had a lot of interaction with Savage—well, interaction is probably the wrong word," Kenneth Arrow observed about the period in the late 1940s when Arrow was at the University of Chicago.[77] "I was just listening and admiring it, being privy to it [Savage's work-in-progress]. But I did know Savage very well, at that time. We were good friends. And I heard him develop these theories, and I was really amazed" (Kenneth Arrow, interview, December 7, 2013).

Arrow characterized the late 1940s and early 1950s as a period in which he, Friedman, and Savage, as well as others such as William Baumol and Maurice Allais, were "in the uncertainty business" (interview, December 7, 2013). Beyond this period, uncertainty continued to play an important role in Friedman's analysis of economic problems. He pressed the case for adding important stochastic elements to key macroeconomic relationships by introducing the permanent-income/transitory-income distinction into the consumption function, replacing inflation in the Phillips curve with the inflation/expected-inflation discrepancy, emphasizing the role of inflation expectations in the determination of the nominal interest rate, and defining the natural rate of unemployment in terms of the outcomes of a stochastic flexible-price economy.[78] The existence of uncertainty also shaped Friedman's policy prescriptions, as discussed below and in chapter 8.

In addition, the subject of uncertainty helped shape Friedman's monetary theory. His contention was that it was not possible to rationalize a positive demand for real money balances without appeal to uncertainty.[79] Furthermore, Friedman believed that fluctuations in uncertainty were an important source of variations in the amount of real money demanded.[80] This position was exemplified by his statement to the present author: "I am absolutely sure that the degree of uncertainty is a very important factor in the demand for money" (Milton Friedman, interview, January 22, 1992). This conviction led Friedman to search for proxies for economic uncertainty. A remark he gave in 1983 on the outcome of his search serves as a poignant sign of his times: "Unfortunately, I have never been able to find a good empirical proxy for the degree of uncertainty, and hence I do not have any way to estimate the quantitative importance of this factor" (*Wall Street Journal*, September 1, 1983). This gap has been filled in recent years with the development of operational empirical measures of uncertainty by Nicholas Bloom and his coauthors.[81]

The fact remains, however, that Friedman's interest in the formal modeling of uncertainty declined after he wound up his research into utility functions. Other than in his work on consumption, he rarely entered stochastic terms directly on those occasions when he laid out explicit models. Friedman's move away from formally allowing for uncertainty is reflected in his 1972 remark that uncertainty was "taken for granted throughout [my] analysis" even when the analysis did not include disturbance terms.[82]

Friedman's work on utility in the late 1940s and early 1950s also had little traceable effect on his later discussions of public policy issues. He was hesitant to draw policy implications from his research into utility, and he stated in 1964 that it had taken the form of an "entirely abstract analysis" that was hard to apply directly to policy discussions.[83]

To locate the main element of Friedman's research on utility that endured in his later work, one needs to consider not the specifics of the Friedman-Savage papers but the general posture taken toward economic analysis in those papers. As already indicated, the Friedman-Savage work shared with Friedman's later research—including his study of labor unions with the use of Marshallian tools, much of *Price Theory*'s approach to various problems, and even the analysis of *Free to Choose*—the approach of seeking to view a very large range of private-sector activity as arising from self-interested optimizing behavior.[84]

It is true that, as stressed by Hirsch and de Marchi (1990), Friedman was a critic of nineteenth-century and early twentieth-century price theory in certain respects. It is also true, however, that the implication of much of Friedman's criticism was that economists had underestimated the variety of decisions by the private sector that was susceptible to analysis using orthodox economic theoretical approaches based on utility maximization.[85] The generalization of economic analysis to the study of areas other than traditional market activity did not feature particularly heavily in Friedman's main lines of research after the early 1950s: such work was identified instead with other researchers. Friedman was an outspoken admirer of some of these researchers, including Gary Becker and key contributors to the public-choice literature (that is, the economic analysis of politics). But the approach associated with this work was prevalent in much of Friedman's teaching and his popular writings.[86]

Friedman and Savage's paper had also certainly been in the same spirit as that approach. Their introduction presented their work as a "rather simple extension of orthodox utility analysis" that permitted the application of household optimization to areas like gambling that had previously been thought difficult to reconcile with standard economic modeling.[87] As they saw it, their extension allowed for a wider degree of agreement of observed behavior "with the body of economic theory."[88] The notion that private-sector behavior could be treated "as if" it arose from utility maximization was pressed by Friedman and Savage (including the use of the term "as if").[89] This approach prefigured Friedman's 1953 article on methodology. Indeed, the Friedman-Savage work contains a statement of the "billiard-ball" analogy that Friedman later reused in his methodology essay and that then caught readers' imaginations.[90] The line of argument implied by that analogy was that it was reasonable to attribute optimizing behavior to the agents under study even when agents were not actually carrying out a formal mathematical optimization exercise.

Research on the Marshallian Demand Curve

Along with his studies with Savage, another element of Friedman's price-theory research during the late 1940s was his work on modeling the demand curve for a product. This research reached print in the form of Friedman's paper "The Marshallian Demand Curve" in 1949, again in the *Journal of Political Economy*. Although the elaboration of the argument in Friedman's article was lengthy and accompanied by textual evidence from Marshall (whom Friedman credited with the argument), the basic message relayed in the paper was simple: The demand curve for an individual good should be viewed as drawn on the assumption of constant real income. This contrasted with a situation in which *nominal* income was held constant and, consequently, changes in the price of the good in question altered the overall value of the consumer price index, in turn necessarily altering real income. Friedman offered his constant-purchasing-power interpretation of the demand curve as one that reconciled various discussions of the demand curve in Marshall's work. This contrasted with interpretations offered in the existing literature, which Friedman said had judged Marshall guilty of "logical inconsistency and mathematical error."[91] It was also an interpretation that aligned Marshall's treatment of consumer demand with the writings of Eugen Slutsky.[92]

As an interpretation of Alfred Marshall's work, Friedman's paper remains open to question. Friedman reported that most colleagues who had read his draft had disagreed with his interpretation—including George Stigler, who was also unconvinced by the published version.[93] Likewise, Baumol (1954) and Alford (1956) provided telling textual evidence against Friedman's interpretation of Marshall.[94] In the dispute over Marshall's own intended meaning, Friedman probably came off second best to his critics.

But irrespective of its validity as a representation of Marshall, Friedman's proposal did—as his paper also argued—provide a framework for demand analysis that was useful in its own right. In particular, contrary to Yeager's (1960, 64) position that no "substantive issue is involved" in deciding between Friedman's suggested demand function and those that did not specify the demand function in real terms, Friedman's proposal allowed for a clearer demarcation between monetary theory and those issues that Friedman considered could be analyzed in a "nonmonetary context."[95] In particular, the specification that Friedman advanced permitted a *consideration of the behavior of relative prices*—an enterprise that he saw as vital to what he called price theory, and that others, to his disapproval, were beginning to call "microeconomics"—that was separate from *monetary theory*. It therefore allowed for the price level to be treated, when the demand for a particular product was being analyzed, as a "scale factor" rather than a variable whose movements automatically altered real income.[96]

At the same time, there was a macroeconomic dimension to Friedman's analysis of the demand function—consistent with his observation: "Though price theory and monetary theory can be separated, they are not basically independent."[97] His proposed specification, in which household behavioral functions were cast in real terms, permitted the study of the interaction between real and nominal variables.[98] Allowing for real/nominal interaction did not require real and nominal variables to be treated—as in 1940s Keynesian analysis that treated the price level as frozen or externally given—as essentially one and the same. Nor did it require demand functions to involve a mix of nominal and real variables—as in others' interpretation of Marshall's framework.[99] Rather, a model in which households' demands for assets and goods were embodied in functions expressed in real terms, goods prices were endogenous but not perfectly flexible in the short run, and policy makers' behavior set a course for nominal money, provided a setting in which real/monetary interaction could be studied.

It was against this background that Friedman later cast the demand function for money as a demand for real purchasing power, with a real scale variable and real opportunity-cost variables as arguments.[100] This perspective also lined up with Friedman's long-standing emphasis on the role of relative prices in private-sector spending and production decisions and on the severe costs that both inflation and price controls generated via the distortions they created in the structure of relative prices.[101] Friedman's endeavor to find a means of reconciling price theory and monetary theory, but in a manner in which the former could be studied without reference to nominal prices, found favor with Don Patinkin, who was engaged in a far more rigorous effort to combine the two—an effort that culminated in his 1956 book, *Money, Interest, and Prices*.[102] Patinkin's book, although lukewarm toward Friedman's contribution as interpretation of Marshall, was highly consistent with Friedman's basic approach of characterizing private-sector decisions as the outcome of problems that were expressed in real terms, with the behavior of the monetary authority serving to pin down a nominal variable.[103]

Monetary Analysis

The integration of price theory and monetary theory could not fail to interest Friedman in the late 1940s, for it was in these early postwar years that he devoted his energies to both areas, before settling into a situation he later described as "working primarily in the monetary area."[104]

In "A Monetary and Fiscal Framework for Economic Stability," published in the June 1948 *American Economic Review*, Friedman advocated that the United States adopt 100 percent reserve requirements. He further urged that the US government have a cyclically adjusted balanced budget, with the associated cyclical deficits and surpluses being monetized.[105]

This article definitely marked Friedman's permanent move into monetary economics. But it should not be regarded as a paper that expounded the monetarist position. Phillip Cagan would later portray the 1948 Friedman paper as part of the monetarist literature.[106] But this was not the view of Anna Schwartz.[107] And James Tobin (1981b, 35) astutely observed that Friedman wrote the 1948 paper "before he became so exclusively monetarist."[108] As detailed below, the rule advocated in the 1948 paper contrasts with Friedman's later proposal of a constant rate of monetary growth.[109] That difference does not, however, provide the basis for regarding the 1948 paper as outside the monetarist literature: for as Friedman later noted, monetarist theory does not inexorably lead one to an endorsement of the constant-money-growth prescription.[110] Indeed, Friedman continued to advocate the 1948 rule in the early 1950s while also extolling the virtues of the quantity theory of money and discussing the support for the quantity theory that had come from his early findings with Schwartz.[111]

In fact, the basis for denying the 1948 paper monetarist status is precisely that it does not use monetarist theory.[112] Instead, the 1948 article's analysis is one that takes policy-induced changes in the quantity of money as having their effects on the economy via the fiscal-multiplier effect of deficit spending and not via reactions of yields.[113] The multiple-interest-rate channel of monetary policy transmission that Friedman emphasized from the 1950s onward is absent from this analysis, as Friedman explicitly stated that he was not relying crucially on "changes in relative prices and interest rates."[114] The 1948 paper did, however, contain an acknowledgment on Friedman's part that money-financed deficits had greater repercussions for spending than deficits financed by issuance of longer-term securities.[115] This feature does not actually represent a difference from *General Theory*–style Keynesianism, which acknowledged a distinction between the properties of money and long-maturity bonds. But that early Keynesian analysis glossed over the money/bonds distinction for the case in which bonds were short-term securities. In the spirit of that analysis, in his 1948 discussion Friedman did not sharply distinguish between money and other short-term financial assets, as he would in his later work on deficit spending.[116] Rather, Friedman's 1948 rule can be seen as one that aims to maximize the value of the fiscal multiplier by ensuring that deficits are monetized instead of being financed by the issuance of longer-term securities.[117] Underlying that proposal is a position that increases in the money stock can be counted on to have a powerful impact on nominal spending if they enter circulation through a fiscal policy action, but not if they enter circulation via other means.[118]

The Monetization Rule

With the vision of policy transmission underlying Friedman's 1948 paper thus sketched out, let us now consider some features of the policy rule advanced in the same article. One aspect of the rule that Friedman emphasized in 1948—100 percent reserve requirements—has already been considered in chapter 2, so the discussion that follows focuses on other aspects of the rule.

G. Smith (1982) and Bryant (1995) both noted that Friedman's advocacy of a constant-monetary-growth rule represented a volte-face from his 1948 position. Bryant (1995, 160) pithily remarked: "In 1948 Friedman said, roughly, that bonds should be held steady, and that money should bounce around with the deficit. In 1960 Friedman said money should be steady and that bonds should bounce around."[119] Smith suggested that this contrast justifies calling Friedman's 1948 proposal "bondism," as opposed to monetarism. This is not very appealing terminology, for two reasons. First, acceptance of the "bondism" terminology would amount to taking "monetarism" as synonymous with the constant-monetary-growth rule, which it is not. Second, it seems inappropriate to call the 1948 proposal "bondism" when that proposal involved making money the only government-issued asset. For the 1948 proposal actually envisioned the *abolition* of government bonds! Friedman wanted all issuance of bonds to be discontinued and the existing public debt to be retired, although he allowed for the conversion of the existing debt into consols as an interim measure.[120]

The set of arrangements that Friedman laid out in 1948 was accordingly one that would ultimately abolish government bonds and replace bond issuance with money issuance. In contrast, in Friedman's later constant-monetary-growth proposals, neither money nor securities would disappear from the list of government-issued instruments.

Friedman made what for him was a rare use of the term "monetization" in the 1948 paper, and that usage points to the terminology that might best be employed for the 1948 rule instead of "bondism." The 1948 framework involved a (deficit) "monetization" rule for monetary policy. Accordingly, when the discussion below refers to Friedman's 1948 proposals, the term "monetization rule" will be used as a shorthand.

One important respect in which Friedman's 1948 approach to monetary policy rules foreshadowed his later work lies in its rejection of policy proposals that relied on forecasts. "Every attempt . . . to forecast economic activity has to date met with failure," he wrote in a different article that year.[121] In the same spirit, the 1948 paper on rules stated that forecasters' poor record implied that "it hardly needs to be argued that it would be better to shun forecasting and rely instead on as prompt an evaluation of the current situation as possible."[122] Friedman repeated this sentiment in a 1949 radio appearance in which he stated that "any policy the consequences of which depend critically on the ability to forecast is not a policy which ought to be adopted."[123] A related trademark Friedman theme in the 1948 paper is the emphasis on lags in the effect of monetary policy. Indeed, the 1948 paper contained the famous Friedman phrase "long and variable lags."[124] And the problems that discretionary policy could face because of insufficient knowledge about lags was a point on which Friedman received considerable credit in his colleague Lloyd Mints's (1950) book on monetary theory and policy.[125]

Notwithstanding the motivation Friedman gave for it, the monetization rule was vulnerable to judgmental errors. The monetization rule required an estimate of the full-employment level of income as part of the process of ascertaining the cyclically adjusted budget balance. As Friedman later put it, the monetization rule required an estimate of the "hypothetical level of income corresponding to reasonably full employment."[126] In laying out his proposal in the 1948 paper, Friedman suggested that using a longer-term level of income as the criterion would reduce the estimation problem.[127] Around the same time, he stated that "forecasting short movements" was especially problematic.[128] Friedman therefore presumably regarded the focus on a long-term level target as what insulated his rule from the criticism he had already made of Abba Lerner's proposals to gear fiscal policy toward a full-employment target.[129]

Within a few years, however, Friedman would eschew policy proposals that were oriented on levels of actual or potential income. He would concentrate instead on arrangements that rested on estimates of long-term economic growth, such as the constant-monetary-growth rule. Neither these later proposals nor the monetization rule that he advanced in 1948 entailed a denial on Friedman's part that full employment and price stability were the appropriate goals of economic policy. These had in practice been federal government goals of long standing, and their status as goals had been formalized in the Employment Act of 1946. Rather, Friedman viewed the pursuit of these ultimate goals as best approached by policy makers within a rule-based framework—and after 1948 he added the proviso that in practice the most successful policy rules might be ones that put some distance between the policy instrument and ultimate objectives.[130]

Friedman prided himself on having, via his 1948 paper, cofounded the notion of a full-employment or structural budget surplus—but, as his changed perspective on rules indicates, his enthusiasm for basing policy decisions on this fiscal concept dwindled in later years.[131] In 1979 he would state that "a system of cyclically balanced budgets" was desirable in principle but could not serve as the basis for a legislative or constitutional directive to the fiscal authorities because it was too susceptible to loopholes.[132] In an echo of his 1948 proposal, Friedman in his monetarist years would write supportively of efforts to "*balance the budget at high employment*" (*Newsweek*, October 17, 1966, italics in original).[133] But his acquiescence to structural budget deficits, during the 1980s in particular, indicated that he no longer attached as high a priority to cyclical budget balance as he once had, at least for the short and medium run. In particular, as of the mid-1980s, a time when Modigliani (1986a, 311) stated that "a good case can be made for a so-called cyclically balanced budget," Friedman drew a distinction between achieving this balance by restraint of public spending—a path he favored—and by tax increases—an option he opposed and that he believed would ultimately give rise to increases in government spending.

A recommendation that Friedman voiced in the 1948 article and that he reaffirmed in his later discussions of fiscal policy was for stable tax schedules.[134] He would supplement this recommendation in the 1970s and 1980s with proposals for formal limitations on public spending. Friedman had originally seen spending restraint as indirectly implied by his 1948 proposal (see NBC 1950, 10), but his later proposals made this restraint an explicit edict. Notwithstanding these elements of continuity, the amount of stabilization of the US economy that Friedman regarded as achievable by fiscal policy fell drastically after 1948—a change reflected in his statement in 1979, "Personally, I do not believe that fiscal policy is a desirable instrument for economic stabilization."[135]

Part of the reason why Friedman would eventually reject fiscal policy as a key instrument for stabilization policy was that he had come to the view that, given monetary policy, deficit spending was not a powerful means of influencing aggregate demand. A measure of how distant Friedman's thinking on the topic as of the late 1940s was from where it would be in 1951–2006 is provided by his reply, in 1949, to a critique of the monetization rule. In the course of his reply, Friedman referred to the increased automatic flexibility of fiscal policy that arose from the enhanced importance of income tax and the introduction of withholding. Friedman declared that the enhanced degree to which the budget deficit automatically reacted to the state of the economy was "by far the most important change in recent years" in arrangements bearing on stabilization policy.[136] He went on to cite estimates by Musgrave and Miller (1948) to the effect that the automatic stabilizers were "likely to offset something like a quarter or a third of any change in aggregate demand"—an extraordinary evaluation when compared with Friedman's later perspective.

It is striking that Friedman invoked such large estimates of the effect of fiscal stabilizers on aggregate demand and in such an uncritical manner, and all the more striking when one considers that he gave no indication on this occasion that the size of the effects depended on the degree of monetary accommodation of fiscal deficits.[137] Also notable is Friedman's citation of a fiscal policy reform, instead of altered monetary policy arrangements (such as the onset of the bond-price pegging policy), as the leading change in stabilization policy in recent years. And he gave this assessment despite the fact that by 1949—likely reflecting his early work with Anna Schwartz—Friedman already saw monetary instability as of greater historical importance for US economic fluctuations than instability in fiscal policy.[138]

The key significance of the 1948 paper is that it fixed monetary economics as a permanent area of specialty for Friedman and tied him to advocacy of monetary policy rules. But the theoretical analysis in the paper, like that in his 1949 response to criticism of the paper, has little that is distinctively monetarist and, indeed, it has some notably nonmonetarist elements.

Friedman's 1948 paper, on this interpretation, is therefore not part of the monetarist literature. The paper did, however, certainly qualify as part of another literature, namely University of Chicago economists' support for monetary policy rules. In particular, in arguing for the desirability of policy rules, Friedman's 1948 paper was following in the tradition of Henry Simons, whom he cited multiple times in the article. As noted in chapter 2, however, Friedman did not overlap with Simons among the academic staff in the economics department at the University of Chicago. Friedman's start at the department in late August 1946 occurred a little over two months after Simons's death (*New York Times*, June 20, 1946; Hammond and Hammond 2006, 18, 27). One of the new graduate students in 1946, G. Warren Nutter, had already encountered Simons as an undergraduate and anticipated working with him. Instead, Nutter would become the first student to write a PhD dissertation under Friedman's supervision, with his thesis, "A Quantitative Study of the Extent of Enterprise Monopoly in the United States, 1899–1939," being accepted for his PhD in 1949 and appearing in book form, with an abbreviated title, in 1951 (Nutter 1951).

Friedman's Teaching and His Views on Monopoly

The subject of Nutter's dissertation serves as a reminder that Friedman's very early years at the University of Chicago were ones in which Friedman's own research interests were still heavily oriented on price theory. That orientation was reflected also in the Friedman-Savage research and in the Marshallian demand curve analysis discussed above. It was further manifested in the fact that the graduate class that Friedman taught in his first year in the economics department at the University of Chicago was Price Theory. He continued to teach the course into the mid-1960s and again for a spell in the 1970s.

Friedman's combination, once it emerged, of teaching price theory and pursuing research in monetary economics came as a surprise to students, but the reason for this surprise changed over time. In later years, Friedman's eminence in the monetary field was the reason why students were taken aback to find that he was teaching price theory. In the early years, however, the surprise was directed not at what course Friedman chose to teach but at Friedman's choice of research. Notwithstanding publications such as the 1948 paper on rules in his early years in the department, Friedman was widely associated in those years with research in price theory. For example, Gregory Chow, a graduate student at the university starting in the early 1950s, "was a little surprised" to find Friedman directing himself to monetary issues in his research. Familiar with the papers of Friedman and Savage, with both of whom he took classes at the university, Chow's perspective on Friedman was that he "considered him a price theorist" (Gregory Chow, interview, July 1, 2013).

Indeed, in his early years of participation in the monetary field, Friedman endeavored to give a significant share of his research time to price theory, an effort reflected in his continuing publications on decision theory through the mid-1950s. In the late 1940s, he even had in mind a follow-up on the Friedman-Kuznets research, proposing to Carl Christ (who became a graduate student in the economics department in the same year that Friedman joined the teaching staff) that Christ carry out an extension of the work.[139] "And I wasn't very interested in that, and that conversation didn't go anywhere" (Carl Christ, interview, May 1, 2013). In subsequent years, the monetary work would consume much of Friedman's research time, and, as he had done with mathematical statistics, he largely left the field of research in price theory.[140]

In light of this research choice, much of Friedman's imprint on price theory after the early 1950s is felt not in his research papers but in his Price Theory lecture notes. These notes are well recorded, partly owing to the fact that a version of the Price Theory lecture notes was published under Friedman's name (being revised by Friedman for publication in 1962, but largely reflecting his class as of the early 1950s).[141] In addition, the notes taken by a student (Kirk Johnson) of Friedman's first Price Theory class in 1947 have fairly recently seen publication (see M. Johnson and Samuels 2008; and K. Johnson and M. Johnson 2009).

As both these records of the class indicate, much of what Friedman taught was conventional microeconomic theory. In particular, the Price Theory course did not lay out a free-market manifesto: as Arnold Harberger, another member of the first cohort to take the class, recalled, the content of the course "wasn't *Free to Choose* in the classroom" (Arnold Harberger, interview, April 12, 2013).[142] To be sure, Friedman's enthusiasm for free markets was known to his students: "Oh yes, that was very clear," recalled Carl Christ, a member of the first Price Theory class. "I don't know when he acquired these views, but they were very obvious by 1946–1947 when I took his class" (Carl Christ, interview, May 1, 2013). But the manner in which those views were reflected in Friedman's teaching of price theory was largely through the making of points with which economists of widely differing views could agree. For example, Gregory Chow recalled that during Friedman's course teachings "he pointed out that price control does not do any good"—certainly a controversial position in 1946, as attested to by the reaction to *Roofs or Ceilings?*, but considerably less controversial by the early 1950s when Chow took the Price Theory class (Gregory Chow, interview, July 1, 2013).

This theme was also evident in Friedman's penultimate year of teaching the Price Theory course in 1974–75. As a student in that class, William Dougan, recalled (interview, September 19, 2013), the continuing US government controls on the price and distribution of oil came under Friedman's critical scrutiny in the class. But, as with the early years of Friedman's Price Theory course, these later classes were not remembered as featuring his enthusiastic free-market advocacy, which by the 1970s had become especially familiar from his *Newsweek* columns. Not only did Friedman seem disinclined to use the course as a free-market platform, but Kenneth Clements, another student in the 1974–75 Price Theory cohort, believes that the students would not have stood for a course that did not consist of straight economic analysis (see Clements 2012). Consequently, Friedman's price-theory teaching provided much economic analysis that could be accepted by economists who disagreed with each other on the appropriate role of government. Indeed, in coteaching graduate microeconomics at the London School of Economics in the 1970s, Richard Layard and Alan Walters, who did not agree with one another on the merits of Friedman's free-market views, both relied heavily on Friedman's *Price Theory* text in their lectures and cited it extensively in the book that sprang from their course (Layard and Walters 1978; Lord [Richard] Layard, interview, February 7, 2014).

Carl Christ recalled of Friedman's first year of teaching the Price Theory class: "It was a lecture class, and there was not a whole lot of discussion, although you could ask questions, and you would get a response" (Carl Christ, interview, May 1, 2013).

In later years, students' class participation increased, as Friedman developed a course-teaching format that consisted heavily of calling on class members to answer problems (Sam Peltzman, interview, March 1, 2013). In the view of Arnold Harberger, this later format made the Price Theory class a less effective showcase for Friedman's teaching: as Harberger saw it, Friedman became reliant on students' access to a printed version of his past years' lectures, and instead of going through the material himself in lectures, he used the class sessions as a way of establishing that students had absorbed the lecture notes (Arnold Harberger, interview, June 24, 2013). When he did interact with students in the early years of the class, Friedman, in line with the formalities of the time, would address the male students as "Mr." plus their surname, a practice that he continued to follow in his classes and workshop into the 1960s (Sam Peltzman, interview, March 1, 2013; William Gibson, interview, March 6, 2013). This was also the form of address that academic staff in the University of Chicago's economics department used for one another, at least in formal meetings, into the 1960s (Harry Johnson 1978a, 97).[143]

Another student of the late-1940s version of the Price Theory course, Friedman's later coauthor David Meiselman, recalled: "He was a magnificent teacher, and very effective, and I didn't find him difficult to follow in class. His exposition was simple, direct. And he had wonderful examples. It made a big impact on me. I remember he gave a midterm exam the first quarter I took the course, and he would read them [the completed exam answers] closely, and he corrected my English. I was using the word 'affect' instead of 'effect.' He was always that way in terms of writing" (David Meiselman, interview, April 30, 2013).[144]

The published versions of Friedman's Price Theory course, as well as Friedman's supervision of Nutter (1951), make clear that coverage of monopoly was part of Friedman's price-theoretical analysis, notwithstanding the fact that he was later be portrayed by critics as universally applying the assumption of perfect competition. On the *consequences* of monopoly and the appropriate policy response to monopoly, it is true that Friedman and George Stigler (who remained in close touch with Friedman over the 1946–57 period in which they were based at different universities) went through an intellectual change on the question of monopoly from their late-1940s stance. But it does not seem appropriate to view Friedman and Stigler as working out a joint position, and, consistent with this assessment, Stephen Stigler (interview, November 6, 2013) regarded the evolution in his father's views on monopoly as largely stemming from his solo-authored research rather than from interaction with Friedman. And it will be argued here that the changed perspective that Friedman adopted on monopoly in the late 1940s and early 1950s was most importantly on the *macroeconomic* implications of monopoly power. In particular, Friedman would no longer view the existence of monopolies as a sound basis for believing in cost-push views of inflation.

The upshot is that, although Cherrier (2011, 343) correctly notes that Friedman came to downplay the ramifications that monopoly power might have for the behavior of the US economy, it is not accurate to infer, as

Cherrier does, that Friedman denied the existence of monopoly. On the contrary, Friedman's continued affirmations after 1945 of the Friedman-Kuznets findings attested to his acceptance of the existence of monopoly. So too did his discussions of Nutter's (1951) work: here Friedman drew attention to Nutter's finding that the degree of monopoly in the US economy, while far from nonexistent and having risen over time by some metrics, had not shown a striking upward trend.[145] Another problem with Cherrier's account is that she leaps from the valid statement (2011, 347) that Friedman from the early 1950s indicated that he believed that the economy tends to a full-employment position, to the invalid conclusion that this belief amounted to a rejection on Friedman's part of the existence of imperfect competition. In fact, perfect competition is not a necessary condition for output to converge to its natural level in the long run. Such convergence takes place, for example, in modern New Keynesian optimizing models that feature monopolistic competition.[146] The typical result that these models produce is that the existence of firms with pricing power tends to lower full-employment output, but also that this distortion does not prevent long-run price flexibility and hence convergence of the economy to full employment. That result is, in turn, highly consistent with the perspective that Friedman took on the structure of the economy in his work from the late 1940s onward.

Putting the macroeconomic implications of monopoly aside, the main change in Friedman's position on monopoly over the years was that he came to believe that monopoly or cartel power of producers would be eroded over time by the emergence of competitors, unless the monopoly power was wittingly or unwittingly supported by the state.[147] One can see several developments that would have led Friedman to his position, including: the then-recent experience of what Cole and Ohanian (2013) call the "cartelization" of key US sectors as part of the Roosevelt administration's industrial policy; what Friedman perceived as the monopoly position of the medical profession—fortified, in his view, by the US government's support of medical licensure; and Nutter's (1951) aforementioned finding that, notwithstanding forces like this that reinforced monopolistic practices in the private sector, monopoly power had not increased appreciably, on net, in the US economy.[148]

Friedman's position that market forces would tend to erode monopolies was established by the early 1950s. But it would be exhibited most prominently much later, via his rash forecasts during the mid-1970s of an imminent collapse of the OPEC cartel, and in his subsequent contention that the US federal government's energy policy was bolstering the cartel.

Friedman's enhanced confidence in the existence of market mechanisms that could undermine monopoly did not initially lead him to abandon support for antitrust laws. Evidently, he continued to believe that these laws could facilitate the kind of behavior on the part of producers that would be helpful in undermining monopoly and other forms of firms' market power. But Friedman's overall attitude toward antitrust laws did eventually shift from favorable to unfavorable—a shift reinforced by his acceptance of regulatory-capture arguments.[149] Friedman came to believe that antitrust laws were the wrong way to hold back the creation of monopolies—and that, in the case of natural monopolies, unregulated monopoly might be preferable to regulated monopoly.[150] This shift in view was, as Friedman later noted, a gradual one.[151] It was not an evolution that was completed in the course of his late-1940s reconsideration of the macroeconomic consequences of monopolies. Rather, both in the late 1940s and early 1950s, Friedman voiced support for antitrust laws.[152] He continued to do so in the 1960s.[153] And even in the mid-1970s, by which time his posture toward antitrust laws had become much more negative, Friedman indicated that contracts that were in restraint of trade—which he considered the nub of "what's illegal under antitrust law"—should continue to have no legal standing: "I don't believe that contracts in restraint of trade ought to be enforced in the courts."[154]

An issue regarding firm behavior that pertained more to the area of theory rather than policy was that of the merits of the monopolistic-competition ideas of Chamberlin (1933). Friedman had written a critical review in 1941 of a book (Triffin 1940) on monopolistic competition, and he continued to criticize the theory in his 1947 Price Theory class and in his methodology paper of 1953.[155] Some accounts, such as Silk (1976, 74) and Laidler (2012), have presented rejection of monopolistic-competition theory as a keystone of Friedman's economic framework.[156] But the details of Friedman's critical comments reveal that his doubts centered on the claimed innovations of the theory, rather than on the basic ideas proposed in monopolistic-competition analysis. He made piecemeal criticisms of the monopolistic-competition literature, which he regarded as relying on vague definitions, but he did not deny the message of that literature that many firms in practice were typically in the continuum between the monopoly and pure-competition cases.[157]

Indeed, the vision of firms to which Friedman subscribed during his monetarist period—a vision that he articulated most prominently in his 1967 presidential address to the American Economic Association—contained key features that were inherent in the monopolistic-competition setup: multiple firms competing against one another, yet with pricing power and with the wherewithal and incentive to vary the markup of price over marginal cost in the short run.[158] Also significant is the fact that the Hotelling (1929) model—a model to which, as discussed in chapter 2, Friedman attached considerable practical importance—can be interpreted as a monopolistic-competition model (see McCloskey 1985, 411).

Both in his 1941 review and his methodology essay, Friedman did not argue for pure competition as the baseline assumption. Instead, he took the position that the economics of the firm as expounded in Marshall's *Principles* was applicable to cases beyond the pure, perfect-competition benchmark.[159]

Therefore, the fact that Friedman made critical observations about the monopolistic-competition literature did not mean that he was an advocate of the position that the perfect-competition framework provided the only valid way of analyzing a multiple-firm industry. His observations indicated a definite resistance to the notion that the preexisting body of economic analysis needed to be thrown out.[160] But they did not imply hostility to the characterization of firms as engaging in a mixture of monopolistic and competitive behavior. Indeed, looking back in the 1990s, Friedman seemed pleased at the way that ideas concerning monopolistic competition had been integrated into standard microeconomic theory.[161] And, as it happens, the way that monopolistic competition is used in *macroeconomics* deemphasizes or omits the aspects of monopolistic-competition theory about which Friedman had the greatest reservations.[162]

George Stigler had much more thoroughgoing objections when it came to monopolistic-competition theory. But, as has already been stressed, Stigler's positions on price theory in general, and his opposition to monopolistic-competition ideas in particular, should not be regarded as shared in toto by Friedman.[163]

An observation made by Walters (1987) concerning Friedman's Price Theory class provides a useful starting point in considering Friedman's other teaching activities at the University of Chicago in his early years with the department. Walters (1987, 424) referred to Friedman's teaching as being for the "graduate school of the University of Chicago." This way of putting the matter is easily liable to misinterpretation, because the "graduate school" terminology applies more naturally to the institution then known as the Graduate School of Business at the University of Chicago, rather than to the Department of Economics at which Friedman worked. The latter institution was not typically referred to as the graduate school. Indeed, Arnold Harberger observed (personal communication, June 27, 2014): "In my experience, both as a student 1946–1949 and as a faculty member 1953–1981, it was always 'the department.' I can't remember ever hearing the department referred to as the graduate school."

Friedman was not a teacher at the business school, although accounts would occasionally misidentify him as such.[164] That said, an appreciable number of business school students took Friedman's economics classes, and Friedman had close relations with many of the teachers at the business school.[165] Furthermore, this book will use the phrase "Chicago School of economics" in a manner that includes academic staff at both the economics department and the business school.[166]

The problem with his terminology notwithstanding, Walters was on the right track in conveying the notion that the teaching at the economics department was concentrated on *graduate* classes. Indeed, in Friedman's era as a member of the University of Chicago, there was a sharp distinction made between undergraduate and graduate teaching, with the part of the university assigned undergraduate students referred to as "the college" and regarded as separate from departments of the university like the Department of Economics. In particular, in the early years after Friedman's hiring, as Arnold Harberger would recall (interview, December 9, 2013), the training of undergraduates took the form of "that crazy system where we had a PhB [bachelor of philosophy] degree." The courses underlying this degree would concentrate on the teaching of great books. "And obviously," Harberger noted, "the amount of economics that kids got there was limited, and also different." Consequently, prestigious though it was to receive a degree from the university, "it was to some disadvantage to our students that they went out with [undergraduate] degrees that people didn't quite understand."

The undergraduate degree program at the university went through various reforms over the years, and in the 1970s the arrangement that undergraduate economics teaching was assigned to a specific college, whose staff did not overlap with that of the rest of the university, was basically allowed to lapse. From then on, university department members increasingly taught undergraduates. It had become clear, Harberger said, that "we were the leader that nobody was following." For the University of Chicago in the modern day, as Stephen Stigler noted (interview, November 6, 2013), the notion of "the college as a separate faculty has by now been obliterated, and almost every appointment in the university is jointly with the college."

However, the college teaching/graduate teaching distinction prevailed throughout Friedman's years as a department member at the University of Chicago.[167] One consequence of the distinction was that Friedman did very little undergraduate teaching in the course of his career.[168]

Even in Friedman's era as a University of Chicago instructor, however, the distinction between undergraduate and graduate teaching was not completely clear-cut. For one thing, some lecturers, especially assistant professors, were jointly appointed to the economics department and the college and so did both undergraduate and graduate teaching of economics.[169] For another thing—and more relevant for the case of Friedman—advanced undergraduate classes at the University of Chicago in the 1940s and 1950s were de facto graduate courses, and these advanced undergraduate courses *were* indeed taught by economics department staff, including its senior members. It was in this context that Friedman taught an undergraduate course in the late 1940s and the early 1950s in the field with which he would become so associated: money.[170]

Friedman would later convey the impression that, in years when he taught Price Theory, he taught nothing else.[171] But the situation that prevailed in the late 1940s and early 1950s shows that this dichotomy did not always hold, as he was teaching monetary theory and price theory in different parts of the academic year.

Marc Nerlove took Friedman's money-and-banking course in the early 1950s. By this point, as will be seen below, Friedman was becoming increasingly immersed in the monetary-economics field and had converged on the monetarist views that would characterize his research of the time and subsequently. Reflecting these developments, the course, Nerlove recalled, "was basically Friedmanian monetary economics. By far and away, he was the best teacher I had ever had anywhere, at any time. He was absolutely superb" (Marc Nerlove, interview, September 13, 2013).

Some years ahead of Nerlove, Kathy Axilrod (then Kathy Podolsky), an undergraduate and then graduate student at the University of Chicago between 1944 and 1950, also took Friedman's money-and-banking class.[172] She came out with a favorable impression of some of the leading members of the economics department at the University of Chicago, like Gregg Lewis and Frank Knight. But she had, and has, an extremely unfavorable impression of Friedman. In particular, she recalled Friedman as being unwilling to countenance deviations from his own position in the money-and-banking class: "He preached his line," with a sharp response from Friedman likely if "you departed from his line in any way."[173]

It is perhaps surprising that Friedman gave an impression of an uncompromising stance in his teaching of this course, because his own views on the subject of money were undergoing a major change during the second half of the 1940s.

II. Issues, 1944–50

THE EMERGING MONETARIST

Several discussions Friedman provided during the 1944–50 period showed clear signs of his transition to monetarism. His 1944 criticism of Keynesian analysis has already been noted, although that criticism did not take a form that emphasized the importance of the quantity of money. However, some other discussions in the years that followed did take this form, and they are considered in this section. The material stands as testimony against the prevalent view in the literature that Friedman's earliest monetarist work appeared in 1956 via his "restatement" of the quantity of money.[174] It also is a reflection of a point stressed repeatedly in this book: in the years spanning 1948 to 1951, Friedman's views on monetary economics underwent a dramatic shake-up, from which emerged his familiar monetarist position.

The catalogue that follows excludes Friedman's criticism of the Keynesian consumption function. An analysis of the development of Friedman's views on consumption is deferred until the next chapter. The discussion below concentrates on Friedman's work that was specifically concerned with monetary policy and inflation.

Over the 1946-50 period, Friedman explicitly argued the case for using monetary policy in the control of inflation. In an April 1946 radio discussion, Friedman called for taking "every measure which we can to prevent the present large supply of money and deposits from rising beyond its present level," adding, "Limiting the money supply is a subject which has received far less attention than it deserves."[175] In his pamphlet with Stigler the same year Friedman listed "control of the stock of money" as one of the "fundamental weapons to fight inflation," although the authors also listed heavy taxation and government spending reductions as such weapons.[176]

In a further radio appearance in December 1947, Friedman stated (NBC 1947a, 6, 11) that "the failure to get [higher] taxes meant that we financed the war by increasing the supply of money" and that the task now was "to prevent the total amount of money from rising any higher." In light of Friedman's retrospectives on the 1940s, such as that in his and Schwartz's *Monetary Trends*, the sense of urgency that he saw for action against inflation in 1946 and 1947 seems overdone, as a good deal of the high rates of measured inflation in the early postwar period likely reflected the unveiling, upon removal of official price controls, of wartime inflationary pressure. Measures of real economic activity—and most likely the true degree of inflationary pressure—registered weakness in the very early postwar years.[177] But the message that, *if* there is an inflationary problem, *then* monetary policy should be deployed does endure from Friedman's analysis in the mid-1940s—albeit in a context in which he still viewed monetary policy as one of a number of tools that could restrict aggregate demand.

By early 1948, Friedman's thinking had progressed to a clear focus on monetary policy for the control of inflation. A letter that he and several University of Chicago colleagues (including Aaron Director, Frank Knight, Gregg Lewis, Lloyd Mints, and Allen Wallis) wrote to the *New York Times* in early 1948 was titled "Control of Prices: Regulation of Money Supply to Halt Inflation Advocated" (January 11, 1948). The letter stated that "a marked increase of the general level of prices unaccompanied by a marked increase of the supply of money is a rare if not a nonexistent phenomenon."

Acceptance of the quantity theory of money underlay this proclamation, and the high regard in which Friedman now held the theory was evident in other writings and statements between 1948 and 1950. One analysis, by Silk (1976, 78), contended that not until the publication of remarks in the *Review of Economics and Statistics* in August 1951 was there evidence that Friedman "was on his way back to the quantity of theory of money."[178] This contention, however, is incorrect. Silk's analysis stands as an example of the errors of interpretation that can arise from heavy reliance on items in Friedman's book collections for establishing the chronology of Friedman's views, at the expense of considering non-reprinted Friedman items.[179] Friedman had already moved back to the quantity theory by August 1951. He was certainly a quantity theorist as of 1950.[180] This fact was confirmed by his own recollection in 1975 that, a quarter of a century earlier, he had been among a "small group of dissenters from the prevailing orthodoxy" with respect to money.[181]

Much more important is the record of Friedman's writings, actions, and statements in the years up to 1950, which confirm that his allegiance with the quantity theory of money predated 1951, let alone 1956. His teaching of a money-and-banking course in the late 1940s and early 1950s necessarily entailed attention to articles in monetary theory. Also working in this direction was his research into the views of Marshall: Friedman's paper on Marshall included praise for Marshall's approach to describing economy-wide behavior, in which the quantity theory was used to explain the price level.[182] Conversely, in a 1950 article that was not reprinted in his book collections, Friedman criticized Wesley Mitchell's early work for containing "a none-too-well-considered attack on a rigid form of the [quantity] theory."[183]

Friedman's statement at a conference at American University in May 1950 was another observation in support of the quantity theory: "Economists have known . . . for one hundred years or more . . . that by printing and spending enough money you can produce any desired level of [economic] activity."[184] Although Friedman characterized this proposition as common ground of all economists, in fact it formed one of the points of contention in what Friedman had in 1949 described as "the recent development of alternative monetary theories"—the theories being the Keynesian position on monetary policy and the older quantity-theory view.[185] The Keynesian position was that deep-depression conditions, at least, might render money creation ineffective as a means of stimulating the economy. Friedman's confident endorsement of the contrary position not only confirmed that by 1950 he had cast his lot with the quantity theorists. It also made clear that not only did he—as discussed presently—hold monetary policy largely to blame for the United States' entry into the Great Depression, but he was also confident that monetary policy by itself could have revived the economy once Depression conditions emerged.

The study of the Depression would, of course, figure heavily in the major project to which Friedman enlisted in 1948. Within a couple of months of the *New York Times* letter, Friedman joined, with his resumption of an NBER affiliation, Anna Schwartz in the bureau's research project on money. Hammond (1996, 52) established the Friedman-Schwartz correspondence that inaugurated the project as dated March 1948. Friedman, writing around mid-1948, gave an early public indication of his involvement in the project when he listed his research interests in the 1948 American Economic Association Directory of Members as consisting (solely) of "cyclical behavior of the money supply, its rate of turnover, and condition of banks" (American Economic Association 1948, 64). This wording lined up with the NBER's official description of the Friedman-headed project, as given in the annual report it published in May 1948 (Burns 1948, 22).[186]

The following year's NBER annual report (Burns 1949, 60) elaborated on Friedman's entry into the project: among "three new studies [that] were started during the year [1948] by the Business Cycle Unit" was one in which "Milton Friedman has begun a systematic investigation of the cyclical behavior of the money supply, its turnover, and associated changes in American banking since the Civil War." That account gave short shrift to Anna Schwartz, who was already working at the NBER on the subject of money when Friedman joined the project.[187] Schwartz would note: "When I got to the National Bureau [in 1941], the sector that hadn't been assigned to anybody was money, so my first assignment was to see if we could put together a series on US money."[188] Schwartz therefore took that responsibility for that area of the NBER's business cycle studies. Then, some years later, as Schwartz recalled, "[Arthur] Burns said to me, 'What would you think if Milton Friedman were to join you on the money project?' I said it would be great."[189] When the *Monetary History of the United States* finally appeared in 1963, Schwartz's pre-1948 work on the project received its due in Friedman and Schwartz's preface, which stated the "first product lineally related to the present study" was a 1947 NBER paper coauthored by Schwartz.[190]

By his own later account, part of Friedman's function in the project was to complement Schwartz's historical expertise.[191] The theoretical content of much of his research to date made him a natural choice to beef up the project's analytical side.

Anna Schwartz's collaboration with Friedman was conducted in large part through correspondence. They would, however, meet on occasions when Friedman was in New York City. Schwartz recalled: "What I always think about Milton is: Something bothers you, and you try to tell him what it is that somehow doesn't seem right to you, and he'll say: 'The question you *really* want to ask me is this.' And then you'll say [to yourself]: 'Yeah—that's really what made you feel something's wrong; he's really clarified what the problem is.' So it was always easy to talk to him and review what we had done and what we still had to do" (Anna Schwartz, interview, April 21, 2003).[192]

Friedman came to the project already rating the importance of monetary policy much more highly than he had a few years earlier. At the same time, it would not be correct to suggest, as Cherrier (2011, 353) does, that "Friedman began his study of the monetary history of the United States with a clear picture of the role of the Federal Reserve in the Great Depression already in mind." The evidence Cherrier provides for this claim is a remark Friedman made at the inaugural (1947) Mont Pelerin meeting. At this event, Friedman said: "The big error in Fed policy was that of 1931."[193] But the interpretation of the Great Contraction that would eventually arise from Friedman and Schwartz's account did *not* point to the 1931 discount-rate increase as the pivotal error. To be sure, Friedman, both in the late 1940s and subsequently, regarded the 1931 discount-rate increase as a perverse and very harmful policy action. Friedman put himself on the public record on this matter in comments in US forums in the late 1940s. An example was his 1949 observation in the *American Economic Review* that "on balance its discretionary action has been destabilizing, the most striking example being the sharp deflationary action it took in the fall of 1931."[194] In addition, in a February 1949 radio appearance Friedman cited the discount-rate increase as a reason why the Federal Reserve "must take a large share of the responsibility for making the depression as deep as it was" (NBC 1949, 10). In that same radio appearance, Friedman saw the "real trouble" of the economy as beginning not with the 1929 stock market crash but with the 1931 discount-rate increase (NBC 1949, 9).

In contrast, the eventual Friedman-Schwartz account in the *Monetary History*, although continuing to downplay the importance of the 1929 crash, would see a turning point as the Federal Reserve's decision to allow the failure of Bank of United States in December 1930. Criticism of the Federal Reserve for the 1931 discount-rate increase was commonplace at the time of the start of the Friedman-Schwartz project: see, for example, the textbook discussion in A. Hart (1948, 317).[195] The Friedman-Schwartz analysis would instead point to a widening of the Federal Reserve's culpability, with the central bank's most serious mistakes starting in 1930 and those mistakes seen as responsible for converting a recession into a depression. The discount-rate increase remained the easiest example to cite. Being an explicit policy tightening, that incident lent itself to "sound-bite"-style capsule accounts of the Federal Reserve's mistakes—and Friedman invoked the discount-rate increase in this fashion in a *Playboy* interview (February 1973, 53).[196] But in the *Monetary History*'s account, although the 1931 rise in the discount rate stood out as an occasion on which the Federal Reserve was actively deflationary, the Federal Reserve's earlier *inactivity* had been crucial in spurring a domino-like pattern of bank failures.[197]

That account was, however, only in its infancy in the late 1940s, and Friedman and Schwartz were at first mainly on a fact-finding mission, albeit in a context in which Friedman had a relevant theoretical background, was teaching a money-and-banking course at the University of Chicago, and was studying monetary thought as part of his research. What Friedman and Schwartz found, even in their early explorations, had the effect of elevating further the importance Friedman assigned to money, and he indicated in a January 1949 memorandum that their results to date seemed to suggest a "role of monetary factors in generating cyclical fluctuations" that was greater than was generally believed (Hammond 1996, 63).

Another part of the process in which Friedman's views were changing in the direction of monetarism in the late 1940s was the greater extent to which he made the price level an endogenous variable. As discussed in detail in chapter 7, even in the early 1940s, Friedman had posited, in some of his research, the existence of a continuous relationship between prices and real aggregate demand when output was below its full-employment level. This position contrasted with early Keynesian literature's treatment of prices as insensitive to aggregate demand until full employment was reached. Also, along with others in the economics profession, in the late 1940s Friedman incorporated into his analysis the notion of "overfull employment" or "overemployment."[198] Recognition of this notion implied that full-employment output did not constitute a ceiling on output. Instead, excessive aggregate demand could make itself felt both in above-normal output and in inflation.

The extension of this notion to incorporate a long-run-vertical Phillips curve would emerge in Friedman's work in the 1950s. In the meantime, however, Friedman was already moving to a rejection of cost-push factors as a source of sustained inflationary pressure. Even though it had rejected rent control as an anti-inflation measure, Friedman and Stigler's 1946 pamphlet had given credence to wage/price-spiral theories of inflation. Likewise, in his 1948 paper on rules and in a joint statement with a number of fellow economists the same year, Friedman had granted cost-push factors as an element driving up wages.[199] In remarks for a May 1950 conference, however, Friedman said: "My views about this have changed considerably in the last few years."[200] His rejection of the influence of cost-push is clear also in his repudiation—in his 1950 advocacy of flexible exchange rates (published in 1953)—of the proposition that exchange-rate depreciation could trigger a self-sustaining wage/price spiral.

This rejection of cost-push contrasted not only with Friedman's prior position but also with that of his teacher-turned-colleague, Lloyd Mints.

Mints was in the vanguard of defending the quantity theory during the 1940s, and he produced two enduring and highly readable books in this connection (that is, Mints 1945, 1950).[201] But Mints also made numerous concessions to nonmonetary views of spending and inflation determination in these writings—far greater concessions than would be granted in the later monetarist literature of Friedman and others. Such concessions included Mints's (1945, 1950) appeal to both monetary forces and cost-push factors in explaining price-level fluctuations. In contrast, Friedman's monetarism as of 1950–51 onward would stress that the influence of cost-push factors on inflation was short term in character.

As discussed in chapter 2 above and further in chapters 7 and 10, the position that Friedman reached by 1950 amounted to a view that the cost-push shock term in the price-adjustment or Phillips-curve equation should be presumed to have a zero mean. Friedman's position from the early 1950s was thus that cost-push factors had a zero mean in themselves; upward pressure on wages or prices in one sector would be "balanced by declines elsewhere in other prices and costs."[202] Any tendency for inflation to exhibit a sustained rise in the face of a positive wage or price shock reflected accommodation of that shock by the monetary authorities. Cost-push factors, in Friedman's revised view, could not alter longer-run inflationary expectations in the absence of a monetary expansion (or monetary contraction, in the case of negative cost-push forces).

The preceding discussion of the formation of Friedman's monetarist positions has focused on the development of his thinking on the structure of the economy rather than on rules. This choice has partly reflected the fact that, as noted earlier, Friedman distinguished monetarist theory from advocacy of rules—including the constant-monetary-growth rule that he would endorse from 1956 onward. It also reflects the reality that Friedman was already advocating rules (specifically, the monetization rule) before his monetarist theoretical position came to fruition. But Friedman's case for rules did rely partly on a strong theoretical motivation: in particular, the possibility that stabilization policies might give rise to destabilization of the economy.[203] In his 1947 article reviewing Abba Lerner's (1944) *The Economics of Control*, Friedman had remarked that in the absence of precise knowledge about the state of the economy and key structural relationships, "governmental attempts at counteracting cyclical fluctuations . . . may easily intensify the fluctuations rather than mitigate them."[204]

Furthermore, as was observed in the preceding section, in 1948 Friedman coined the "long and variable lags" phrase with which this argument would become associated. He formalized his argument about destabilizing stabilization policy in a paper published in French in 1951 and printed in English in 1953's *Essays in Positive Economics*.[205] This was an aspect of

Friedman's monetary policy contributions that even a severe critic like Don Patinkin would rate very highly: Patinkin (1973b, 458) had occasion to refer to "Friedman's own seminal contributions ... about the fundamental problem of lags," while Patinkin (1979, 231) specifically cited Friedman's stabilization policy paper as "one of his most important contributions to the analysis of macroeconomic policy." Another critic of Milton Friedman's, namely Benjamin Friedman, has likewise referred to "Milton Friedman's classic argument," as laid out in the stabilization policy paper (B. M. Friedman 2004, 148).

On a variety of fronts, therefore, Friedman's analysis crystallized in the late 1940s into the monetarist position with which he would be associated.

THE CRUSADE AGAINST CHEAP MONEY

The imperative of preventing excessive monetary expansion occupied Friedman in his discussions of current monetary policy between 1948 and 1950. The Federal Reserve had, since 1942, followed a policy of "cheap money," which initially involved the pegging of a set of interest rates on government debt of various maturities, but which evolved in the early postwar period into the maintenance of a ceiling of 2.5 percent on longer-term Treasury rates: see figure 4.1.[206]

In a retrospective on the cheap-money period in 1982, Friedman argued that the Federal Reserve had never articulated a theoretical rationale for the policy.[207] It is somewhat puzzling that he would make this complaint. For he and Schwartz were certainly able to use Federal Reserve public statements to ascertain the basis for the Federal Reserve policy (or Treasury/Federal Reserve policy, since the Federal Reserve had become, de facto, subordinate to the Treasury). It is possible that Friedman may have felt that the Federal Reserve did not give a systematic official statement that gave the pegging policy analytical foundations, of a kind comparable to those the Federal Reserve had provided for its economic-stabilization policy in the Federal Reserve Board's celebrated *Annual Report* for 1923.[208]

A twofold basis for the cheap-money policy was forthcoming from the nongovernmental but influential personage of Alvin Hansen (1945, 250–51). The first rationale laid out by Hansen for the policy was that private-sector spending in the postwar period was prone to be weak—partly reflecting what Hansen viewed as a secular-stagnation danger—and low long-term interest rates could make a small contribution to supporting demand. The second rationale was that rigid bond prices promoted the desirable goal of a stable market for government debt. Such stability would aid the authorities when they floated new securities and would, it was suggested, also contribute to economic stabilization by keeping key asset hold-

Percent

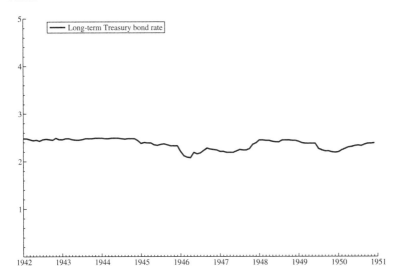

FIGURE 4.1. Long-term Treasury bond rate, January 1942–December 1950. *Source*:
Board of Governors of the Federal Reserve System (1976, table 12.12).

ings of the private sector—here comprising both commercial banks and the
nonbank private sector—from being subject to large fluctuations in valuations. Both these arguments pointed Hansen toward the conclusions that
"control [of] the cycle in the postwar years through interest rate adjustments is regarded as inadmissible" (1945, 250) and that imposition of a peg
on bond prices was preferable.

Friedman and Schwartz's account of the US government's bond-price
pegging policy recognized both these rationales as factors behind the
policy.[209] These rationales were also articulated by the Federal Reserve
officials at the time: see W. Thomas (1947, 209), for example. Of the two
rationales, the first tied in with the limited role accorded to monetary
policy by the Keynesian position. In 1933, after the United Kingdom began
its own cheap-money policy (albeit initially concentrated at the short end
of the term structure), Keynes himself recommended a bond-rate peg for
the United States in a letter to President Roosevelt.[210] Keynes repeated
his recommendation of pegging the long-term rate in the *General Theory*—
although he now qualified that recommendation with his contention that
nonpolicy forces would put a floor on the long-term rate that would limit
central banks' attempts to lower it.[211]

Indeed, notwithstanding his complaint about the absence of an official
US justification for the pegging of bond prices, Friedman on many occasions described the postwar cheap-money policy as arising from Keynesian

theory: he noted, for example, that the policy arose "partly under the influence of the ideas derived from Keynes."[212] Furthermore, the fact that the Federal Reserve, under Chairman Marriner Eccles, in effect followed Keynes's recommendations in the 1940s likely figured behind Friedman's later comment: "I believe [Eccles] played a far greater role in the development of what came later to be called Keynesian policies than did Keynes or any of his disciples."[213] But it would appear that the second, less inherently Keynesian, rationale for the cheap-money policy—that based on debt-management considerations—was an important reason why Eccles backed the cheap-money policy in the initial postwar period, to judge from the internal materials quoted in Meltzer (2003, 634, 637). The desire to provide an environment conducive to debt refinancing also figured prominently in the Federal Reserve's public statements describing its policy.[214]

If Friedman was dissatisfied with the absence of a clear-cut official articulation of the thinking behind the cheap-money policy, he could not complain about a shortage of material when it came to authoritative statements that the policy would be maintained indefinitely. "I have a favorite quotation which I did not bring with me," Friedman remarked in a talk in Florida in February 1970. "Emmanuel Goldenweiser, who was head of the research division of the Federal Reserve Board, gave a lecture in 1944, which now sounds very strange, about how the days of high interest rates were over and we were going to have to reconcile ourselves to 2½ percent money for as long as anybody could see."[215] That speech (Goldenweiser 1945), given in November 1944, was one Friedman would cite repeatedly, including in the *Monetary History* and in his 1967 American Economic Association presidential address, as an example of how deeply entrenched the cheap-money mindset had become.[216]

One of the ironies of Friedman's career is that the point at which he began a concerted study of money-stock behavior was during a period— the late 1940s—in which the distinction between money and nonmonetary assets was more blurred than usual, thanks to the bond-rate pegging policy. Indeed, Friedman and Schwartz summarized the effect of the cheap-money policy, at least when it was applied to the whole term structure, as follows: "The support program converted all securities into the equivalent of money."[217] In the same vein, in an April 1960 memorandum, Friedman acknowledged that the interpretation of monetary growth in the late 1940s was complicated by the fact of the policy of pegging the bond rate.[218]

However, the *Monetary History*, treated the money stock—an M2-type aggregate in Friedman and Schwartz's case—rather than a sum of money and bonds, as the relevant total in analyzing monetary conditions. This may have reflected a judgment that the peg made bonds equivalent to money in some respects but not in others. However, the context in which Friedman and Schwartz described the peg as making bonds equivalent to money was in a discussion of what commercial banks treated as their reserve base.[219] For businesses and households—the nonbank agents for whom Friedman and Schwartz's M2 series was intended as a measure of money balances—the complete equivalence of money and bonds was less clear, and Friedman and Schwartz in the *Monetary History* treated M2, rather than M2 plus bonds, as the appropriate monetary aggregate, even during the pegging period.

There certainly was some instability in the relationship between money and the economy over the period of the peg: for example, Hamburger (1971, 295) referred to the "poor showing of the money variables in the 1948-52 period" in explaining changes in nominal income; Robert Gordon (1982, 1107, 1112) provided evidence that the relationship between monetary growth and real output growth was weak in samples covering the period to 1954; and Friedman himself noted in 1984 that the Korean War period was associated with "unusually wide movements in velocity."[220] There were evidently other factors alongside the bond-price peg that loosened the relationship between money and the economy during the 1940s and early 1950s and that appear to have been, in fact, more quantitatively important on this score than the peg. For example, the inception of the bond-rate peg in 1942 should, by itself, have tended to drive velocity upward, as the peg conferred an increased amount of money-like qualities on key assets that were not part of M2.[221] Instead, as Friedman observed, M2 velocity "decline[d] drastically during and just after World War II," ahead of a sharp revival later in the decade.[222] See figure 4.2.

The onset of the Korean War in 1950 provided another example of aberrant velocity behavior that could not be directly attributed to the policy of pegging the bond price. Monetary aggregates behaved in a quiescent manner in the early Korean War period. See, for example, Balbach and Karnosky (1975, 15), as well as figure 4.3. But, with panic purchases by consumers providing a source of upward pressure on goods prices, nominal income had a brief surge. Friedman and Schwartz and other monetarists interpreted the accompanying upward shift in velocity as reflecting anticipations of future inflation and wartime shortages.[223]

Friedman had occasion to consider this episode further in the 1970s, and when, in 1975, one of the articles in which he had given his statement that "inflation is always and everywhere a monetary phenomenon" was reprinted, Friedman added a footnote to the article acknowledging the beginning of the Korean War as an exception.[224] In the late 1980s, he returned to the episode once more, characterizing the Korean War as "the only major inflationary episode that I know of that was not preceded by more rapid monetary growth and hence can be regarded as the result, initially at least,

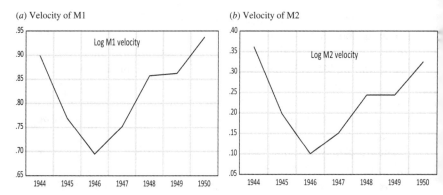

FIGURE 4.2. Monetary velocity, 1944–50. *Source*: Computed from the annual-data tables in Balke and Gordon (1986).

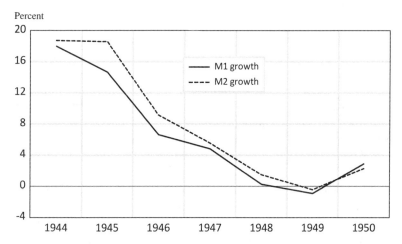

FIGURE 4.3. Monetary growth, 1944–50. *Source*: Computed from the annual-data tables in Balke and Gordon (1986).

of an autonomous increase in velocity."[225] But the velocity increase in this period was better viewed, Friedman contended, as an attempt by money holders to shift into *goods* (*Wall Street Journal*, July 5, 1989). The velocity rise of 1950 did not, therefore, reflect the shift on the part of money holders into *bonds* that was a predicted consequence of the bond-price-pegging policy. As was the case with World War II, the onset of the Korean War provided an instance in which the money/nominal income relationship had become more complicated than usual, but not primarily because of the pegging policy per se.

The outbreak of the Korean War did, however, make it easier to predict the consequences of a continuation of the policy of pegging the bond rate. In the years from 1946 to 1950, the Federal Reserve's adherence to the pegging policy did not imply a state of constant excess demand. On the whole, nominal and real income rose substantially during the initial postwar period, and in 1950 Friedman characterized the "essential feature" of US economic developments between 1945 and 1949 as one of "sizable inflationary pressure" arising from strong nominal aggregate demand.[226] In particular, private-sector spending displayed considerable resilience after the war—to such a degree that Friedman wrote in 1948, "I do not put much credence in the doctrine of secular stagnation or economic maturity that is now so widely held."[227] As Friedman wrote these words, the negative evaluation of the secular-stagnation thesis was becoming widespread; his reckoning that the stagnation thesis enjoyed a wide degree of adherence was rapidly being rendered obsolete. In the late 1940s, secular stagnation would be one of the first Keynesian ideas to be abandoned by economists—at least as a characterization of conditions that major economies were likely to face.[228]

The overall growth in the economy notwithstanding, the early postwar years were—as Friedman and Schwartz were later to note—marked by occasional interruptions to the strong upward pressure on aggregate demand.[229] And monetary policy played a role in reinforcing the downward pressure. Policy makers, as Friedman and Schwartz put it, surrendered control of the money stock throughout the pegging period.[230] But the implications for economic conditions of this accommodative policy varied over time, as figure 4.4 (which displays real and nominal GNP growth) and figure 4.5 (which shows CPI inflation) indicate. In the initial post–World War II years, the fixed-bond-rate policy implied that policy makers accommodated successive periods of upward and downward pressure on aggregate demand and inflation. At times, the peg implied a restrictive monetary policy, delivering low or negative monetary growth. In particular, both nominal income and M2 fell in 1949.[231]

As noted, however, the Korean War's eruption changed the situation. War activities amounted to an ongoing source of upward pressure on interest rates. Therefore, with the return to wartime conditions in 1950, a situation arose, as Friedman later put it, in which policy makers were going to have to allow money to grow indefinitely at inflationary rates for as long as they kept the bond-rate peg.[232] Abandonment of the peg, Friedman implored in a February 1951 appearance, was needed to "restore control over the supply of money" (NBC 1951a, 9).

An early occasion when Friedman spoke out against the cheap-money policy was in 1948, when in their aforementioned letter of January 11 to the *New York Times* he and his colleagues called for the Federal Reserve and

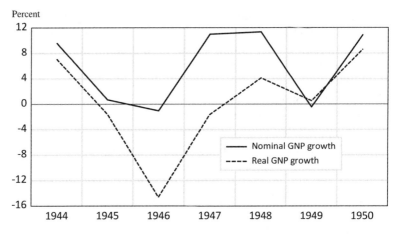

FIGURE 4.4. Growth in nominal and real US national income, 1944–50. *Source*: Computed from the annual-data tables in Balke and Gordon (1986).

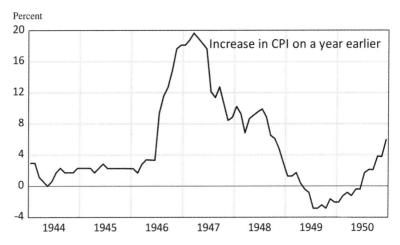

FIGURE 4.5. CPI inflation (twelve-month rate), January 1944–December 1950. *Source*: Computed from CPI series (not seasonally adjusted) in Federal Reserve Bank of St. Louis's FRED portal.

the Treasury to reassert control over the stock of money for the "highly desirable control of the general price level." Events during 1948 seemed to remove some of the urgency of the argument for abolishing the peg, as inflation fell off during the year (see Meltzer 2003, 631–32 and 657; as well as figure 4.5), at the same time as when growth in money was turning negative.[233] With the onset of the Korean War, it once again became the case that both inflation and high monetary growth were implications of the pegging policy.

Against this backdrop, Friedman and a set of University of Chicago colleagues published a manifesto in January 1951, "The Failure of the Present Monetary Policy," renewing their call for the abolition of the bond-price peg.[234] The manifesto's authors acknowledged that the Federal Reserve had taken actions, such as increases in reserve requirements, that ostensibly were aimed at restraining monetary growth.[235] But, as the authors pointed out, more onerous reserve requirements would prove ineffective in delivering lower growth in the money stock: the continuing interest-rate peg obliged the Federal Reserve to provide commercial banks with enough extra reserves to offset the impact on banks' liquidity position of a reserve-requirement increase.[236] By concentrating on the stability of one securities-market price, Friedman and his colleagues argued, monetary policy was sacrificing stability of the overall level of prices of US goods and services. This was a conclusion that key figures within the Federal Reserve System had also reached, and the battle over the bond-rate peg was approaching its endgame.

III. Personalities, 1944–50

PAUL SAMUELSON

Paul Samuelson had already made his reputation in the economics profession sufficiently by late 1946 that the University of Chicago advanced him an offer to be a professor in the Department of Economics (see Hammond and Hammond 2006, 46). The offer was made over Friedman's opposition. By 1946, it was already clear that Friedman and Samuelson, although they had been what Samuelson later described as "good friends" ever since the mid-1930s—a time when Samuelson was a noted undergraduate student at the University of Chicago (G. Stigler 1988, 25)—were already at odds with one another on many issues.[237]

The views held by each of them would continue to evolve beyond 1946, but not in ways that fostered agreement between them. In a joint television appearance with Friedman in 1962, Samuelson remarked that "we certainly were trained at the same university, we sat at the knees of the same professors, we're old friends," and that there were "thousands of things . . . that we could talk about here in which we would be in agreement," but he added that "we've not come out with exactly the same opinions."[238] Friedman would underscore the last point when, late in his life, he referred to "the key features that distinguish Paul's and my interpretation of the economic world."[239]

The preceding quotation indicates how Friedman saw himself in relation to Samuelson: they had sharply different worldviews. The present author is not, however, sympathetic to the notion that Samuelson and Friedman were the main representatives in the profession of the Keynesian and monetarist points of view. They may well have held those roles in popular debate. But Samuelson's degree of involvement in the academic Keynesian-monetarist debates was simply too peripheral for him to be regarded as Friedman's main Keynesian opponent. That said, it remains true that because Samuelson came to be regarded as the premier economist of MIT and Friedman the premier economist of the University of Chicago, and both were of the same generation, comparisons between the two were often made. It is not inaccurate to suggest that much of the economics profession took sides on the question of who was the best economist— Friedman or Samuelson. Indeed, Alan Blinder, who was a graduate student at MIT in the late 1960s and early 1970s, recalled: "There was a substantial intellectual rivalry between, you might say, Chicago and MIT, but very more specifically, Milton Friedman and Paul Samuelson. So, you know, the issue on everybody's mind was: who was the greatest living American economist. . . . [And] if you ask me the question: . . . who was the greatest American economist of, say, the second half of the twentieth century, I don't hesitate for a millisecond to say Paul Samuelson" (Alan Blinder, interview, December 6, 2013).

The generation of researchers that followed Friedman and Samuelson would be able to synthesize parts of the contributions of each and arrive at a compromise position. This would be true of Blinder: although far closer to Samuelson than Friedman on many issues, Blinder would switch from allegiance from a Samuelson-Solow (1960) permanently-downward-sloped Phillips curve to a long-run-vertical Phillips curve of the Friedman-Phelps variety.[240] And some economists of Blinder's generation would have extensive and amicable interaction with both Friedman and Samuelson. Robert Hall observed (interview, May 31, 2013) that of the "five giants" in macroeconomics of the generation ahead of him—Samuelson, Modigliani, Solow, Tobin, and Friedman—"I knew them all personally pretty well, well before I got my [PhD] degree."

In the same spirit, Jeremy Siegel (interview, September 17, 2013) recalled that his dedication in Siegel (2005) read: "To Paul Samuelson, my teacher, and Milton Friedman, my mentor, colleague, and friend." Siegel added: "Both of them were very influential in my life, and I have tremendous respect for Samuelson as an intellect—he's incredible. But in terms of someone to whom I felt more connected and who impacted my life, it was clearly Milton Friedman. And so I think that [dedication] really summarized it."

In the heyday of their activities, however—from the 1940s through the early 1980s—it was more typical for Friedman and Samuelson to be regarded as members of opposing camps.

Ebenstein (2007, 155–56), in noting the perceived rivalry between Friedman and Samuelson, makes the valid point that the majority of the economics profession probably ranked Paul Samuelson more highly than Friedman. Unfortunately, Ebenstein also makes guesses—which Ebenstein treats as certain knowledge—about the inner thoughts of both Friedman and Samuelson, in asserting that each undoubtedly considered himself the best economist of his generation. It seems most unlikely that Friedman regarded himself as a better economist than Samuelson. Samuelson made a diverse range of fundamental contributions that qualified him as the father of the economics profession in a way that Friedman could not claim to be. Mark Gertler (interview, September 26, 2014) recalled that during his time a graduate student at Stanford University from 1973 to 1978, the perception of students was that Samuelson and Arrow had, between them, built modern economics. That perception reflected the reality that, formidable though Friedman's contributions to economics had been, they had not been as wide ranging as Samuelson's.

In light of this reality, it is likely that Friedman shared the widespread judgment that Samuelson was the finest economist of their generation. Where Friedman might have regarded himself as having edged out Samuelson was with regard to a different criterion. The writings of each of them brought out clear but distinct models of the economy.[241] In the present author's estimation, Friedman was satisfied to have a state of affairs in which Samuelson held the title of the finest economist but in which Friedman was regarded as having a *better model of the economy* than Samuelson.

Friedman's and Samuelson's clashing models of the economy, in turn, reflected the different judgments that each reached—differences that, as noted, already existed in 1946 but that would multiply after 1946 as their perspectives diverged on several fronts. Friedman in the late 1940s and early 1950s was exiting the mathematical-rigor door just as the profession—partly because of the fillip provided by Samuelson's (1947) highly influential *Foundations of Economic Analysis*—was entering it en masse. Both Friedman and Samuelson, in the course of the 1940s, marked up the power they associated with monetary policy, but Friedman did so vastly more, and more rapidly. The division between Friedman and Samuelson over the role of markets also became clear at an early stage.

As Friedman had occasion to remark later, the first (1948) edition of Samuelson's textbook *Economics: An Introductory Analysis* was decidedly downbeat in its assessment of the effectiveness of monetary policy.[242] The Depression experience had, according to Samuelson, disappointed "those who thought recovery could be ensured by increasing the quantity of money" (Samuelson 1948, 294). A section titled "The Inadequacies of Monetary Control of the Business Cycle" opened with the statement: "Today few economists regard Federal Reserve monetary policy as a panacea for controlling the business cycle."[243] To begin the discussion in this way was unexceptionable. In particular, this opening statement was not one from which Friedman, even once he became a monetarist, would have dissented. Indeed, Friedman himself would write: "Monetary policy is not a panacea for all our ills" (*Newsweek*, February 19, 1968).[244] But Samuelson's discussion then went on to cast doubt not only on monetary policy's ability to lower interest rates, but on what could be achieved if interest rates were lowered, stating that "*investment is likely to be inelastic with respect to the interest rate*," especially in depressions (1948, 353; emphasis in original). The ineffectiveness of monetary policy was then extended on the following page to boom conditions.

These were views not greatly different from those Friedman had expressed earlier in the 1940s about monetary policy. Friedman's outlook toward monetary policy had, however, evolved since the early 1940s, as discussed at earlier points in this chapter. A contrast with Samuelson's position had consequently emerged. In correspondence in 1946, Friedman was already setting himself apart from "Keynesians" like Samuelson.[245] And Samuelson's statements, circa April 1948, about monetary policy in the first edition of his text contrasted with those in Friedman's *New York Times* letter to the editor of the previous January.[246]

Samuelson's views concerning monetary policy underwent considerable evolution beyond 1948—an evolution reflected not only in modifications of his textbook but also in candid acknowledgments of his change of position. Reflecting on the late 1930s and 1940s, Samuelson would observe, "As one who lived through those times, I can testify how money got lost by economists," so that "economists of my generation have had to unlearn a lot in the sphere of monetary policy."[247]

In remarks written in 1962 and published the following year, Samuelson put distance between his current position and that expressed in his earlier writings, stating: "Contrary to the opinions of many contemporary economists (and to some of my own earlier views), I believe that monetary and credit policies have great potency to stimulate, stabilize, or depress a modern economy."[248] By this stage, Samuelson's textbook featured a discussion of how "monetary policy does have an important influence on the total of spending."[249] Samuelson's respect for the power of monetary policy still left a considerable discrepancy between himself and Friedman—a discrepancy reflected in Samuelson's observation in 1984: "The day I become a monetarist is the day I have lost my marbles" (*Wall Street Journal*, December 10, 1984, 10).

By 1950, the degree of solidarity Friedman and Samuelson had on monetary matters was sufficient for them both to sign an economists' statement on the role of monetary policy (Despres et al. 1950).[250] One of the reasons they were both able to sign the statement was that Friedman was still an advocate of his 1948 rule at this stage and so was able to associate himself with sentiments that he would later be hesitant to endorse, such as that "fiscal and monetary policy . . . are in fact closely related and decisions about one will inevitably affect the other" (Despres et al. 1950, 531). Later on, Friedman would grant that debt management and monetary policy had close links, but he would insist that, extreme cases aside, fiscal and monetary policy need not be closely tied.[251]

Samuelson was, in fact, a critic of Friedman's 1948 rule. But the focus of Samuelson's criticism was on the rigidity that the rule implied for fiscal policy. Friedman's suggestion that tax revenues and transfers be allowed to vary automatically in response to the business cycle, with movements in government purchases in response to the cycle taken off the table, struck Samuelson as suboptimal and not rigorously argued; and in congressional testimony in 1967, Samuelson would applaud the fact that Friedman's proposal that purchases not be varied cyclically, although once prominent, "has since blissfully passed out of notice."[252] In contrast, the notion that monetary and fiscal policy should be coordinated was an aspect of Friedman's 1948 rule that Samuelson found congenial.

Another reason why both Friedman and Samuelson were able to endorse the 1950 statement on monetary policy was that, although it saw the bond-price pegging policy as having promoted inflation during the 1940s, it did not make a firm recommendation to abolish the peg.[253] The statement's endorsement of the notion of cost-push inflation was, however, too much for Friedman, who, as we have seen, had rejected that concept by 1950.[254] Friedman entered a dissent, of which the highlight was: "If fiscal and monetary policy prevent total money demand from falling or rising sharply, they will thereby prevent any general decline or rise in wages and prices from developing into a spiral and becoming cumulative."[255] Friedman likewise broke with the other economists when they recommended government interventions in labor and product markets for the purpose of inflation control. Disagreement on the issue of incomes policy would be a recurring feature of Friedman and Samuelson's disagreements over policy for the next three decades.

Samuelson turned down the University of Chicago offer of 1946, and allegedly part of the reason for his decision was that he wanted to avoid spending a lot of his time sparring with Friedman.[256] As things turned out, staying at the Massachusetts Institute of Technology did spare Samuelson from debating Friedman on a day-to-day basis, but going head to head with Friedman nevertheless formed a considerable part of Samuelson's activities. "They were forever being put in a debating position," recalled Robert Solow (interview, December 2, 2013).

At the same time, as stressed above, it would be incorrect to portray Samuelson as Friedman's principal antagonist in the economics profession. A number of economists could have laid a greater claim than could Samuelson to that status, as they were more involved in the debates, during the 1960s and 1970s, in the research areas in which Friedman specialized. In particular, James Tobin and Franco Modigliani were the Keynesian counterparts to Friedman in these debates. So, to a far lesser extent, was Walter Heller.[257]

But Samuelson, who set the tone for his exchanges with Friedman with his observation in *Foundations* that "Mr. Friedman's statement seems to be incorrect," did take the fight to Friedman in a variety of forums.[258] Friedman and Samuelson appeared together before congressional committees on monetary policy in 1952 and 1975, debated each other on television on several occasions starting in 1962 and stretching into the 1990s, and were both regular commentators from 1968 to 1977 in a series of audiotaped discussions of economic events.[259] In addition, they faced each other as a two-man road show visiting university campuses in the 1960s, and a similar format was the basis for a 1980 book, *Milton Friedman and Paul A. Samuelson Discuss the Economic Responsibility of Government*.[260]

Most of all, the fact that the two overlapped as *Newsweek* economics columnists from 1966 to 1981 cast them in the public eye as opposite numbers on economic matters, and it was in a *Newsweek* column that Friedman observed in 1970 that "Paul Samuelson and I disagree frequently, strongly and publicly on matters of public policy" (*Newsweek*, November 9, 1970).[261]

"I think their relationship was fairly constant," observed Robert Solow (interview, December 2, 2013). "They were wary of each other and determined, both, to observe the academic politenesses. And they did." Along similar lines, Francis Bator observed of the Friedman/Samuelson relationship that "there was a lot of senatorial courtesy on the surface" (Francis Bator, interview, January 6, 2015).

William Baumol remarked (interview, January 23, 2014): "I think that Samuelson was really very unsympathetic to anything Friedman was doing. But he did not want to get into any quarrels on the subject, so whenever he expressed to me any critical views about Friedman, he would say, 'But keep it to yourself.'"[262] Inevitably, however, Samuelson critiqued Friedman publicly on many occasions, including in the forums mentioned above.

Samuelson was, furthermore, an avid reader of Friedman's work. Indeed, in an interview given late in his life, Samuelson made the bold claim, "I don't think anybody has read every item of Milton Friedman's work in the world except me."[263] This contention is very difficult to accept at face value, once one considers the fact that Friedman's writings were extremely numerous and very widely dispersed across different outlets.[264] The present author's conjecture is that Samuelson did largely keep up with Friedman's writings during Friedman's University of Chicago years—a period that Samuelson characterized as one in which the two of them "exchanged reprints and research memoranda"—but had a less comprehensive familiarity with Friedman's post-1977 publications.[265] Asked about Samuelson's claim, Robert Solow (interview, December 31, 2013) suggested that Samuelson probably did not go out of his way to track down every item in the Friedman canon.

Another Samuelson remark in the latter-day interview, however, was even more disputable: Samuelson claimed that Friedman had never acknowledged "a mistake in his whole life." Friedman's statements over the years—including some easily accessible Friedman writings on the public record—contradict this claim, as the following sampling of quotations shows:[266]

1945: "Our initial analysis of these samples was later judged erroneous."[267]

1963: "The stated conclusions [in a passage of *A Theory of the Consumption Function*] are wrong, deriving indirectly from a confusion of stocks and flows."[268]

1964: "I am grateful to Rieber for setting me straight on these matters."[269]

1969: "As David Laidler pointed out to me after this was published, this paragraph [in a 1959 Friedman article] contains an error, the common one of confusing a function and its derivative."[270]

1973: "And I have decided that what I said last time was to some extent misleading and that I really ought to backtrack and take back some of the things I said then."[271]

1974: "I accept the criticism implicit in the comment."[272]

1974: "It appears that apparently what I thought was true is not true."[273]

1975: "My analysis was incomplete and my final conclusion wrong."[274]

1975: "Let me start by making a confession of past error."[275]

1977: "I was wrong in that statement."[276]

1982: "I goofed."[277]

1983: "Milton Friedman regrets an error in his article in the Sept. 1 *Journal*" (*Wall Street Journal*, September 7, 1983).

1984: "Now I was wrong, absolutely wrong [in a GNP prediction]. And I have no good explanation as to why I was wrong."[278]

1991: "First, I must plead guilty to the contradiction incorporated in your point 1."[279]

1998: "My implicit forecast . . . was radically wrong."[280]

2006: "You are right and I was wrong."[281]

The above sampling covers every decade from the 1940s to the 2000s except the 1950s. But the 1950s featured a confession of error on Friedman's part that Samuelson certainly was familiar with. In their December 1952 follow-up article on their work on utility, Friedman and Savage admitted that "there is a mistake . . . in our earlier paper."[282] Indeed, when their original 1948 paper was printed in the American Economic Association's *Readings in Price Theory* in April 1952, the article was amended to correct the description of the properties of the preference specification implied by their hypothesis. A footnote to the corrected description read: "In this reprint, the authors have revised point 2. . . . We are grateful to Paul A. Samuelson for having called our attention to the fact that the original point 2 was inadequate."[283]

It can therefore be seen that Friedman—contrary to Samuelson's account—acknowledged a substantial number of errors during his career; it is also the case that one of Friedman's first public acknowledgments of error credited Paul Samuelson himself with finding the mistake!

Why, then, was Samuelson left with the impression from his long study of Friedman that Friedman never acknowledged mistakes? Some clue to the answer may be provided by the observation of Ann-Marie Meulendyke, whose work with Fred Levin yielded the 1982 admission of error from Friedman quoted above. "To admit he was wrong was not something that he wouldn't do," Meulendyke observed of Friedman, from whom she had taken classes during the 1960s. "I think he'd have had a great deal of trouble saying he was wrong about his general philosophy. But to say he was wrong about a certain piece of analysis: he would [do that], yes" (Ann-Marie Meulendyke, interview, April 29, 2013). Samuelson may have been unhappy that Friedman's acknowledgments of specific errors were often accompanied by an affirmation from Friedman of his broader lines of argument, instead of leading to a reconsideration of his basic economic framework.

OSKAR LANGE

As a member of the University of Chicago's economics department, Oskar Lange had been coeditor of the volume in which one of Friedman's early publications appeared.[284] However, Lange was at the University of Chicago in a period that overlapped only slightly with Friedman's student years there, and, having left in 1945, he was gone before Friedman himself joined the department's staff. Correspondingly, Friedman would indicate that he knew Lange only slightly.[285]

Nevertheless, Friedman's name would be enduringly linked with that of Lange, as Friedman has come to be known as a leading critic of Lange's analysis (see, for example, Summers 1991, 143). This reputation largely stemmed from two book reviews that Friedman published in the latter half of the 1940s. By that time, Lange had departed the world of economic research, but he had left an imprint on it both as a developer of Keynesian economics and as an economist interested in putting socialism on a firmer theoretical footing. Of Friedman's two reviews, one took issue with Lange's development of Keynesian economics, and one challenged Lange on socialism.

The first of these reviews, appearing in 1946, consisted of a "methodological criticism" of Lange's 1944 book *Price Flexibility and Employment*.[286] Lange's work in the late 1930s and in the 1940s has been widely credited with helping formalize the *General Theory*'s ideas and derive a usable system of equations from it (for example, Samuelson 1946, 188; A. Hart 1948, 187; Bailey 1962, vii; Eisner 1963, 153; Samuelson 1971, 11; Nobay and Johnson 1977, 476). The book that Friedman reviewed was part of this work, although, consistent with his review's focus on methodology, it was not Keynesianism per se on which Friedman concentrated his fire.[287]

The economic points that Friedman made in the review overlapped to some degree with those he would repeat after his views on monetary matters crystallized later in the decade. For example, Friedman challenged Lange's implication that a theoretically optimal monetary policy rule could be carried out in practice, as Friedman stressed the lack of knowledge about the structure of the economy.[288] In addition, the review's negative perspective on general equilibrium analysis has been seen by many, including Robert Solow (interview, December 31, 2013), as articulating the outlook on economic modeling that Friedman would elaborate on in later decades.

However, in other criticisms that Friedman made of Lange on key economic matters, Friedman made points that now seem uncharacteristic of him and that he evidently came to view as of lower-order importance as his research program progressed. In particular, Friedman criticized Lange's analysis for using single-valued expectations, but Friedman's own work would of necessity take this tack as well. Allowing expectations for a single date to be a vector was hardly consistent with Friedman's later credo that one should focus on only a few key variables.[289] Indeed, Friedman's research during the 1950s not only used single-valued expectations but reexpressed the expectational terms in terms of observable data.[290]

Most jarringly, Friedman criticized Lange for not modeling the money-supply reaction function in his analysis.[291] But Friedman's later work with Anna Schwartz would, in effect, side with Lange on this matter. Friedman and Schwartz would conclude that monetary arrangements and the monetary policy reaction function had changed so much over time that the money/income regularities that endured in the data arose largely from the presence of the demand-for-money relationship, rather than the money-supply process, and that a concentration on money demand in their work was accordingly justified.[292]

Friedman's methodological criticism of Lange has been interpreted as a challenge to Lange's reliance on formal theorizing—rather than empirical evidence—for reaching conclusions concerning the structure of the economy and the form that policy measures should take (see Summers 1991, 143). That interpretation does not quite encapsulate Friedman's critique of Lange, however. For Friedman accepted that Lange had not been interested in theory for its own sake and was interested in real-world applications. The key weakness Friedman saw in Lange's work was that Lange had not compared his model with a set of empirical regularities. Instead, Lange had, as Friedman saw it, obtained abstract theoretical results and used only a sliver of empirical evidence as the basis for establishing the relevance of those results.[293] Friedman attached a term to this practice that stuck: "casual empiricism."[294] This expression has transcended Friedman's critique of Lange. Friedman reused the expression in his later research and popular writings.[295] But, also, many economists of Friedman's and later generations—including Franco Modigliani, George Stigler, Paul Krugman, Douglas Gale, Charles Bean, Michael Parkin, Robert Hall, and Robert Shimer—would deploy it in their own work.[296] So too did a vast number of writers outside the economics profession, and as of August 2018 "casual empiricism" registered over eleven thousand hits in the Google books database—the overwhelming majority of them being discussions that had no mention of Friedman, let alone Lange.

Perhaps the best example of the casual empiricism in Lange's research was not to be found in the book that Friedman reviewed, but rather in a 1939 article that drew the ire of Mints (1950, 44). Mints took Lange (1939) to task for pointing to the Great Depression and its aftermath as evidence for the secular-stagnation thesis. That critique surely resonated very deeply with Friedman who, like Mints, was by 1950 dismissive of the secular-stagnation notion and particularly ill disposed toward the notion that the 1930s was a piece of evidence in favor of the hypothesis. Rather, both Friedman and Mints were already inclined to give monetary policy a large share of the responsibility for the Depression.

A major branch of Lange's research that was largely separate from his work on Keynesian economics provided the main occasion for Friedman to refer to Lange in later years. Lange had advanced a theoretical basis for socialist economics in a pair of articles (Lange 1936, 1937) that were later printed in revised form in a book titled *On the Economic Theory of Socialism*.[297] Friedman cited that book in a review he published in 1947 of a book by Abba Lerner (1944), *The Economics of Control*. To a considerable extent, Lange and Lerner were covering the same ground and reaching the same conclusions—so much so that Friedman frequently later referred to the "Lange-Lerner" model for operating a socialist economy.[298] On one occasion, he even misremembered them as having coauthored a single book on the subject.[299]

Although Friedman concentrated on Lerner in his 1947 review and mentioned Lange only fleetingly, his critique applied to both of their analyses. As Friedman saw it, Lange and Lerner were proposing that the production and resource-allocation goals sought by a socialist policy maker could best be achieved by a policy of decentralization and of adopting many aspects of a market economy. In particular, the proposed Lange-Lerner arrangements involved assigning a profit-maximization goal to firms and allowing commodities to have their prices determined by a freely operating price system. The firms (or their shareholders) would, however, not be permitted to keep their profits, which would instead be redistributed. Friedman considered this proposal as one "essentially to have a socialist state play at capitalism."[300]

In his 1947 review, Friedman—making a point that would be repeated in *Free to Choose* in 1980—judged this proposal unworkable because of its removal of incentives. Prices, he emphasized, served multiple functions in a market economy: to transmit information, to allocate resources, and to distribute income.[301] As Friedman saw it, the Lange-Lerner template was one in which the state overrode the income distribution that the price system would usually generate but attempted to permit the price system to continue to carry out its other traditional functions. But such a separation would not succeed, in Friedman's view, because agents' motivation to supply productive resources, for the creation of goods and services, would be removed if prices were stripped of their income-distribution function. Just as he had in his expenditure tax proposal in 1943, Friedman emphasized that incentives to work and take risks would be lost if the state took major steps to preempt the income distribution implied by a market-based mechanism.

Throughout his career, Friedman always favored the pursuit of *some* redistributive policies by government.[302] Indeed, in the 1940s and 1950s he was still in favor of a progressive income tax-rate schedule (partly because, as we have seen, he rated more highly than he did later the importance of automatic fiscal stabilizers).[303] But, even then, he was concerned that state intervention in the area of incomes could reach such a scale that there was severe discouragement of effort: policy programs of this kind, he would later warn, amounted to "plans that would involve enormous redistribution of income and a drastic reduction in the incentive for people to work" (*Newsweek*, September 16, 1968).[304] The Lange-Lerner proposal exemplified such plans in an extreme form.

By the time of the appearance of Friedman's review of the Lange and Lerner works, Lange was an official in the Polish government.[305] That government eventually gave Poland the official name of the "Polish People's Republic"—the kind of formulation that, as was once remarked in one of Friedman's favorite television programs, *Yes, Prime Minister*, is a dead give-away that the country is a Communist dictatorship.[306] Lange's seniority in Poland and his eminence in socialist thought made his ideas influential in several countries of the Eastern bloc, although Layard and Walters (1978, 28) noted that, even in those nations, Lange's proposed arrangements were only "adopted in a very limited form."

Subject to that caveat, the results appeared to vindicate Friedman's skepticism about the notion that a system with market-based elements could succeed under the constraints that Lange sought to impose on its operation. Furthermore, the socialist economies, whether they adopted Lange's suggestions or not, validated another point Friedman made: that a static economy was more susceptible to planning than a dynamic economy (which was the kind of economy that was inevitable in practice).[307] As Friedman observed, a situation of constant change in the shares of output produced by individual sectors characterized "a dynamic society responsive to market conditions."[308] But, in his judgment, a system that relied on planning and that was "not going to use a capitalist system as a method of deciding who got what" was precisely one that would not deliver a dynamic and growing economy.[309]

*   *   *

In 1951, Friedman won the John Bates Clark Medal, the award given by the American Economic Association to economists under age forty for an outstanding contribution to economic research. Friedman had now reached the heights of the profession. Only someone who had kept an exceptionally close watch on his activities and public statements in the preceding couple of years could have had an inkling of how rapidly and how spectacularly his standing in the profession was about to crash.

The Clark award was received largely on the theory-oriented work Friedman had published, most recently and notably the joint work with Savage. That work, together with his position at the University of Chicago, had also made Friedman eminent enough to have an entry for himself in the 1950/1951 edition of *Who's Who in America* (Marquis Who's Who 1950, 937).

Within just a few years of these milestones, however, Frank Hahn would judge that Friedman's *Essays in Positive Economics* failed to meet either "the high standard of the deservedly famous Friedman-Savage articles on utility" or the "high standard we associate with his [Friedman's] name."[310] Those judgments capture the shift in the view toward Friedman that took place in both UK and US academia over the course of the 1950s. The assessment that Friedman was "treated as though he were some kind of nut" (in the words of Robert Lucas) is accurate in describing the reception given Friedman in the 1950s and the early 1960s.[311] Yet it is an assessment that seems jarring when one considers the prestige that Friedman had acquired among economists by the early 1950s—so jarring, in fact, that those outside the field of economic research have erroneously cited the fact that Friedman received the Clark medal as evidence that he could not have been an outcast among the economics profession over the 1950s.[312]

The change in the profession's outlook toward Friedman reflected increasing reservations about his choices on what subjects to tackle and how to tackle them. With respect to *how*, Friedman was moving away from mathematical rigor in his economic research. Robert Solow would see Friedman's 1946 review of Lange as a signal of this pattern, and he observed that "it is certainly true that Milton lost quite a lot of contact with younger members of the profession by being so averse" to formal modeling, especially in macroeconomic and general equilibrium contexts.[313]

As already discussed in chapter 3, in 1952 Friedman would refer to "mathematical economics" in a way that indicated that he did not consider his own research part of it.[314] And in 1970, Friedman would give "mathematical economist" as a label appropriate for Samuelson but not himself.[315] With respect to choice of subject matter, Friedman's research would change so much that the articles that won Friedman the Clark medal would come to be seen as unrepresentative of his body of work. Indeed, Friedman is a rare case of an individual who won both a Clark prize and a Nobel Prize but whose Nobel Prize was essentially for a separate body of work from that underlying his Clark prize. Friedman essentially rose to the top of the economics profession twice, once mainly in the 1940s and again beginning in 1963.[316] By the time of his Nobel award, Friedman's Clark-prize-winning work had receded so much in importance that his 1957 book on consumption was described in one profile as his "early work" and as his "first major study."[317]

The consumption-function work was not, however, the development that led to his peers' perception that Friedman had gone off the rails. On the contrary, it was perceived as the valuable portion of his 1950s pursuits. The aspect perceived as not valuable and prompting a negative judgment on Friedman was his focus during the 1950s on forming a critique of Keynesian economics, together with his attempt to build an alternative framework with monetary policy at its center. The Friedman that the profession faced after 1951, famously characterized by Robert Solow as having reached a state in which "everything reminds Milton of the money supply," was seen as an altogether different proposition from the twenty- and thirty-something probability-oriented microeconomist of the 1930s and 1940s.[318] In time, Friedman would regain the prestige he had obtained at the start of the 1950s. But he would first have to trawl through many years of being something of a persona non grata.

Friedman gave some intimation that his new research activities would likely generate a backlash when William R. Allen—a graduate student in economics at Duke University who attended classes at the University of Chicago in the 1950–51 academic year as part of a visiting fellowship—saw Friedman in his office. "I recall wondering if my dissertation subject was virgin territory [only] because it was not very important; he insisted that one should always pursue topics of personal interest regardless of their conspicuousness and concern oneself only with doing a good job" (William R. Allen, interview, March 14, 2014). It was a piece of advice Friedman repeated right to the end of his years at the university. Benjamin Eden, a graduate student in the department in the early and mid-1970s recalled (interview, March 14, 2014) that Friedman's view was that one should find a problem "and work on it, and don't worry about whether other people are interested in it. . . . That was my impression of him as a student." This attitude also served Friedman well during his own wilderness years in the economics profession.

The trajectory of Friedman's career, with its twin peaks of the Clark prize and Nobel Prize separated by a deep recess, has a curious counterpart with that of actress Ingrid Bergman. Bergman won Academy Awards in both the 1940s and the 1950s but, in the intervening period, experienced an estrangement from the motion-picture industry after she was involved in an extramarital affair. Long after her rehabilitation into the film world, Bergman had cause to reflect, "Thank goodness there was a period in my life when everyone was against me."[319] Friedman's own period of estrangement from his profession appears to have instilled in him a similar attitude, as at age seventy-three he would observe, "I am much more uneasy when I am in the majority than when I am in the minority" (*American Banker*, April 30, 1986, 20). From the early 1950s, both Bergman and Friedman would find themselves suddenly out of favor. In the case of Bergman this situation arose because of love; in Friedman's case, one could say it was because of money.

PART 2

Friedman's Framework

CHAPTER 5

Friedman's Aggregate-Demand Framework: Consumption and Investment

I. Backdrop for the Discussion

A key premise of this book, already expounded in the preceding four chapters, is that Milton Friedman's perspective on the structure of the economy—especially in the areas of the short- and long-run determination of aggregate output and prices—underwent considerable change during the 1940s, but that by the early 1950s it had largely crystallized into a state to which he would adhere for the rest of his life.

The narrative of this book has now come to that period of the early 1950s. Consequently, a convenient point has been reached at which to lay out systematically the basic view of the economy that Friedman articulated during his monetarist years—that is, from approximately 1951 onward.

With that aim in mind, in this chapter and the following four chapters the chronological account of this book is interrupted in favor of an exposition and analysis of the economic framework to which Friedman subscribed during his monetarist period. The current and next two chapters cover his views about macroeconomic structure, with the discussion considering in turn aggregate-demand determination (in this chapter and chapter 6) and aggregate-supply determination (in chapter 7). Chapter 8 discusses Friedman's views on policy rules—which, while still in flux in the early 1950s, had largely settled down by 1956. Chapter 9 considers aspects of Friedman's views regarding market mechanisms that were not covered by the prior chapters' macroeconomic discussion. That chapter also discusses how Friedman's position on economic-research methodology cast light on, and interacted with, his position on how the economy works.

The views expressed in this study are those of the author alone and should not be interpreted as those of the Federal Reserve Board or the Federal Reserve System. The author is grateful to David Laidler and Gerald O'Driscoll for comments on an earlier version of this chapter. See the introduction for a full list of acknowledgments for this book. The author regrets to note that, in the period since the research for this chapter was begun, Gary Becker, whose interview with the author is quoted in this chapter, has passed away.

In the present chapter, the outline of Friedman's aggregate-demand framework is preceded by a consideration, in section II, of the basic question of whether Friedman could be considered to have his own, distinct and cohesive, model of the economy. The analysis in that section suggests an affirmative answer to the question. Section III then lays out some ground rules that will be used in the analysis of Friedman's economic framework in chapters 5 through 9, and sections IV and V consider Friedman's conception of the determination of the consumption and investment components of aggregate demand, and the implied IS equation. An appendix to the chapter considers a possible representation of Friedman's views on aggregate demand that is not embraced in this book's analysis.

II. Did Friedman Have His Own Economic Model?

Much of the account in this book, but especially that in this and the next chapter, flows from and documents the contention that Friedman had an internally consistent and publicly articulated theoretical economic framework.[1] Consequently, it is useful to proceed by first considering two widely stated counterpositions. The first counterposition is that Friedman did not have a model. The second counterposition—which is an alternative rather than a complement to the first—is that there *was* a model implied by Friedman's positions, but that that model simply coincided with that of his Keynesian opponents. Each of these positions will be considered in turn.

Allan Meltzer once stated that Friedman "never developed a model. It was clear he's a brilliant man and had ideas that influenced not just me but many other people, but you never could find or write down the model." However, Meltzer immediately added that, in Meltzer (1965), he "tried to write down what I thought was the model they [Friedman and Schwartz] had in mind"—thereby conceding that Friedman had an *implicit* model in the empirical and narrative work.[2] Although the model that Meltzer (1965) proposed as representing Friedman's views is not the one used here, the basic notion underlying Meltzer's 1965 article that Friedman had an implicit model is also the position taken in this book.[3]

True, Friedman published much analysis, particularly in the area of monetary economics, that lacked a fully specified structural model. Furthermore, what detailed theoretical work he did pursue was revealing about some aspects of the economic framework underlying his monetary research, but it frequently suppressed other aspects. For example, Friedman's consumption-function book of 1957 (discussed in section IV of this chapter) shed light on his position on consumption/income relationships but less on the responses of both consumption and income to monetary policy, although it did contain some information on these items. And his

"Theoretical Framework for Monetary Analysis" of 1970 proved to be a misnomer, because its main focus was on aggregate-supply relationships rather than on the aggregate-demand area in which much of the Keynesian-monetarist debate on the monetary transmission mechanism took place.[4]

But Friedman's body of writings does provide—once its purely verbal and its formal portions are taken together—a more comprehensive perspective on his position about the determination of aggregate demand and supply than did the aforementioned specific contributions. The sentiment expressed in the first Allan Meltzer quotation above would, therefore, be more accurate (and more consistent with Meltzer's 1965 article) if rephrased as "*you never could find Friedman writing down his complete model explicitly.*"

The notion that, even in his largely verbal presentations, Friedman *did* rest his analysis on an implicit model has been endorsed by many other commentators—including those accustomed to working with formal models in their own research. For example, Robert Lucas and Sam Peltzman found that Friedman's Price Theory class, which both of them took as graduate students during the early 1960s, implicitly or explicitly used models and encouraged class members to think in terms of a modeling framework.[5] And with regard to Friedman's macroeconomics, Thomas Sargent has observed, "It's clear that there are models that underlie his thinking."[6]

Most important is the testimony of Friedman himself. What Friedman and Meiselman observed of their joint-authored work was true also of Friedman-Schwartz's monetary research and most of Friedman's solo-authored materials: that they "left our broader model implicit."[7] But, as this quotation implies, the absence of an *explicit* model did not mean that Friedman did not deploy an *implicit* model. In fact, he was emphatic that his less explicitly model-oriented work did rely on an implicit model. For example, in the context of their monetary project (which primarily encompassed narrative analysis and reduced-form data analysis), Friedman and Schwartz observed that "every empirical study rests on a theoretical framework."[8] On another occasion, Friedman included his *Newsweek* columns and the predictions contained therein as examples of writings of his that reflected an implicit model, and he observed in this connection that there is always a "general economic model which each of us must have, underlying our specific temporal predictions" (Milton Friedman, interview, January 22, 1992; also quoted in E. Nelson 2007, 174).

It also deserves emphasis that Friedman's underlying economic model was not a reduced-form model, but a structural one. He affirmed that a "fully developed theory is much to be desired" even while himself eschewing the practice of writing down that theory formally.[9] And he affirmed the need for verbal analysis to be internally consistent in a way that paralleled mathematical analysis.[10] Notwithstanding, therefore, the benefits that Friedman saw in reduced-form empirical work, he viewed a principal goal of research undertaken by institutions like the NBER, including his monetary work for that organization, as to obtain empirical findings that would point to the appropriate specification of structural equations in a formal economic model. Armed with this evidence, the task for economic researchers then became that of "putting together the structural equations" to form a complete structural model.[11]

What about the second counterposition mentioned above: that Friedman did have a model, but that it coincided with that of his Keynesian opponents? This position, like the claim that Friedman lacked a model, must be rejected.[12] The pervasiveness of this position is, however, understandable. Three main factors account for its prevalence. The first is Friedman's reluctance to write down a complete model—which left him open to the charge that he did not have a model of his own to offer. The second is the fact that Friedman's 1970 "Theoretical Framework" analysis seemingly ratified the preexisting IS-LM framework and therefore cast doubt on whether there existed theoretical differences between Friedman and Keynesians with regard to the specification of the determination of aggregate demand. The third is Friedman's much-quoted observation in 1976: "I continue to believe . . . that the fundamental differences among us are empirical, not theoretical."[13]

On closer inspection, however, none of these three factors justifies the conclusion that Friedman's and the Keynesians' models coincided. With regard to the first factor, as already indicated, Friedman had an implicit model in his analysis. This book's analysis, especially that in this and the following two chapters, brings out respects in which Friedman's implicit model departed from that adhered to by his Keynesian contemporaries.

With regard to Friedman's 1970 "Theoretical Framework," it was stressed in chapter 1 and again in the preceding discussion that the "Framework" did not convey some of the key aspects of the economic framework that was embedded in his overall body of writings. Rather, as will be detailed in chapter 14, Friedman focused his 1970 analysis on differences between himself and Keynesians on the specification of price adjustment.[14] In so doing, he played down or elided important distinctions between his own framework and that of the Keynesians in the area of the specification of aggregate demand. In particular, as discussed later in this chapter as well as in chapter 6, Friedman's overall framework did not imply an endorsement of the basic IS-LM specification of aggregate demand. The former framework instead contained a multiple-interest-rate setting, which collapsed to the IS-LM benchmark only under special conditions.

With regard to Friedman's observation that the fundamental differences between himself and his Keynesian critics were empirical, not theoretical, it is important to make a few observations, which are presented in itemized form below.

(*i*) The observation should be read in conjunction with his statement, in the immediately following sentence in the same set of remarks, "But this does not mean that we all use the same theory."[15] Therefore, even when stressing the existence of empirical differences between himself and his critics, Friedman did not concede that such empirical aspects constituted the only differences between his own and Keynesians' economic frameworks.

(*ii*) Friedman's remark was made in the context of a reply to a theoretical analysis by Tobin and Buiter (1976) in which propositions associated with Friedman were shown to hold only in very special cases. In challenging this characterization, Friedman was pressing the point that the monetary views associated with himself could not usually be overturned by a priori arguments or by showing that those views applied in the model precisely under highly restrictive parameter restrictions. Rather, his position on monetary matters might be defended as arising from a model in which certain key results and propositions did not emerge as exactly correct but were nevertheless approximately valid.

(*iii*) Although Friedman conceded that Keynesian and monetarist positions could likely be nested within a general model, he did not regard this situation as establishing a lack of difference between the Keynesian and monetarist theoretical frameworks. Nor, for that matter, did he regard subsuming the two frameworks within a common model as necessarily the most attractive way to proceed.[16] Friedman had very mixed feelings about the usefulness of distinguishing between rival theories in this way. He expressed skepticism about approaches in which variables associated with one theory and variables associated with another theory were put into the same general equation.[17] Rather, especially in empirical work, his preference was to view the theories as separate, with each theory associated with an emphasis on different variables, and with each theoretical model to be estimated individually and their predictions then compared.[18] And even when two competing viewpoints *did* agree on the set of variables that should appear in an equation or model, it did not follow that the two viewpoints corresponded to the same theory. On the contrary, the predicted economic behavior under different parameter values might diverge so materially that the imposition of alternative parameter settings amounted, in effect, to different specifications of the structure of the economy—and hence the settings were appropriately regarded as associated with alternative theories.

Two examples bring out the last point embedded in (*iii*) above. Consider the Phillips curve of the form $\pi_t = b\pi_t^e + \alpha(y_t - y_t^*) + u_t$, where $0 \leq b \leq 1.0$, π_t^e is an expected-inflation term, $y_t - y_t^*$ is the output gap, and u_t is a cost-push term. A value of $b = 1$ is formally a limiting case of this curve, but that limiting case implies a fundamentally different view of the world from that associated with the $b < 1.0$ setting. For $b < 1.0$ permits a long run in which—even when inflation and expected inflation coincide—different settings of the inflation rate imply different, and generally nonzero, values of the output gap.[19] This outcome contrasts with the zero long-run output gap that, under the $b = 1$ setting, would occur irrespective of the value of the long-run inflation rate. Another key divergence comes from the fact that the parameter setting $\alpha = 0$ implies very different behavior of inflation from neighboring values of low but positive α. In the former parameterization, inflation is exogenous. In the latter, it is endogenous and in particular is responsive to policies that affect the output gap.[20] Thus, even though the permanently nonvertical Phillips curve and the pure cost-push view of inflation can, in principle, be easily subsumed as special cases of a Phillips curve that also includes Friedman's specification ($b = 1$, $\alpha > 0$) as another special case, they are best regarded as separate theories of inflation. The special cases can each be obtained by choosing particular parameter values in a continuous parameter space; but the *discontinuities* in economic *behavior* that occur as a result of moving away from Friedman's version of the Phillips curve highlight the fact that the different parameter values correspond to different choices of theories. And the different theories would be associated with different policy prescriptions—a result that illustrates Friedman's observation that disagreement on policy can arise from reliance on different quantitative estimates of parameters.[21]

Another example in which different parameter configurations implied different theories or a discontinuity in economic behavior was brought up by Friedman in his advocacy of the negative income tax.[22] In the course of this discussion, Friedman had occasion to observe that a "positive income tax levied at a 100 percent rate differs radically from one levied at a fractional rate less than 100 percent," his grounds being that the latter tax rate would provide no incentive at all to contribute labor to the production process.[23] Again, in this example, variation in a parameter (in this case a policy parameter, the tax rate) leads to a discontinuity, in the sense that a 100-percent-taxed economy either yields no national output or—if it is associated with positive national output—is driven by labor-supply decisions that are not susceptible to standard economic analysis.

Taking the above considerations together, it is evident that Friedman's economic analysis was based on a structural model, that the model was distinct from the models typically underlying Keynesian analysis, and that the fact that the Friedman and Keynesian models could in principle be treated as special cases of a broader system in no way implied that the two models were based on the same theory or that they had the same policy implications.

With the proposition that there is a distinct Friedman model now established, the task of the remainder of this chapter is to lay out the aggregate-demand portion of that model. The challenge involved in this task was already discussed in chapter 1, but it is perhaps worth underscoring the scale of that challenge by considering remarks that appeared in three contributions to the J. Stein (1976a) conference volume on monetarism. In one of these contributions, Anna Schwartz (1976, 43) referred to "the analytical framework that Milton has developed," a remark consistent with the existence of a concrete Friedman framework. But Fischer's (1976) contribution made the valid observation that Friedman's outline of his framework was scattered across many writings. Fischer also voiced the view that the implied Friedman framework was not only vague but also might still be shifting.[24] Friedman's own contribution to the volume, mentioned earlier in this section, could have been an impetus for the last remark, for Friedman made observations in his comments that some observers interpreted as a conversion to the view that a horizontal IS curve—that is, an infinitely interest-elastic demand for real output—best described the behavior of aggregate demand.[25]

That Friedman scattered, across many publications and public statements, the remarks that elucidated his framework is not in doubt. And it is also true that the clarification of his framework occurred gradually, as new writings of his entered the public record. But notwithstanding the fact that this clarification occurred via a drip-feed of information—with his participation in a succession of different forums leading him to be drawn out on particular aspects of his thinking—it is the contention of this book that the framework that Friedman articulated was not vague, nor was it subject to major revisions in the 1960s and 1970s. Correspondingly, for reasons outlined in section IV, Friedman's mid-1970s statements concerning the horizontal IS curve did not constitute an endorsement of that specification, and still less did they signify a change in his economic viewpoint from that he had offered in his previous writings. Friedman's specification of aggregate demand had already been largely revealed in his writings of the 1950s. And as the 1960s and 1970s unfolded, occasions arose on which he elaborated further on his viewpoint on aggregate demand determination. On these occasions, he fleshed out his views, but the implied framework was essentially consistent with what he had outlined during the 1950s.

The discussion will shortly turn, as the first component of aggregate demand to be considered, to consumption spending—a topic on which Friedman made his most celebrated contribution of the 1950s and, perhaps, of any decade. As a preliminary matter, however, it is useful to state some ground rules for the analysis in this and the following three chapters.

III. Ground Rules for the Analysis

The accusation that Milton Friedman did not provide a single, self-contained, and comprehensive presentation of his views on the behavior of aggregate demand is certainly accurate. But the absence of such a single source can be overcome by considering a large body of his writings and statements, and then formalizing, via representation in specific equations, the picture of aggregate demand that emerges from that consideration. That is the task of this and the next chapter.

In endeavoring to work out key aspects of the formal model underlying Friedman's contributions, the present chapter is undertaking an enterprise not unlike that Friedman himself engaged in when, in a 1950 paper, he inferred the theory underlying Wesley Mitchell's (largely empirical) writings.[26] And, as with Friedman's work on Alfred Marshall (which was discussed in the previous chapter), the interpretation of Friedman's writings offered here is one that in large part reconciles different statements and emphasizes their consistency with one another.

In this enterprise, several ground rules are followed.

(1) *Rational expectations will be used, and adaptive expectations will not be regarded as integral to Friedman's theory.* Some of Friedman's writings used adaptive expectations in the derivation of certain equations that described private-sector behavior. But that approach to specifying the behavior of expectations was the state of the art when he first employed it. Consequently, his deployment of adaptive expectations should not be regarded as a case of resisting rational expectations. The application of rational expectations to dynamic macroeconomic models was a technology not available to Friedman for much of his research career. That technology was not available until the appearance of Muth (1960, 1961) and the 1970s monetary research of Lucas, Sargent, and others. In fact, even before this development, Friedman did essentially employ rational expectations in several of his writings in the 1940s and 1950s, especially in his microeconomic and cross-sectional work. And after the rational expectations revolution occurred, he had many favorable things to say about the spread of rational expectations to dynamic analysis in monetary research—while protesting that the rational expectations concept had actually been around prior to this new literature.[27]

In light of the preceding considerations, those equations that are employed below to represent Friedman's views will use rational expectations whenever expected values of variables appear. This approach rests on the contention not only that adaptive expectations or other types of non-rational expectations were not vital to Friedman's analysis, but also that, in key respects, deviations from rationality were inimical to Friedman's perspective on the private sector's consumption, pricing, and other decisions.[28] And in representing an economist's views via the use of a rational-expectations framework, even when that economist's research largely or wholly predated the rational expectations revolution, the posture taken here on Friedman's monetary analysis is similar to the approach that Sargent (1973b), McCallum (1986b), and Woodford (2003) used to describe Knut Wicksell's (1935) monetary analysis.

To be sure, this approach implies that the equations offered below do *not* correspond to what Friedman would have written down in the 1950s, on the basis of 1950s-vintage technology regarding the specification of dynamic models, had he been compelled to lay out his economic model explicitly. But the equations represent an attempt to capture what Friedman's framework implies for the specification of a modern macroeconomic model, as well as an effort to highlight the major differences between Friedman's framework and the modern New Keynesian benchmark model.

(2) *The assets considered in spending and portfolio choices other than money and short-term securities will be limited to a single long-term, fixed-interest nominal security.* Friedman's money-demand function of 1956 had two nominal yields as opportunity-cost variables: a return on fixed-interest securities, and a return on physical assets.[29] In this book's outline of Friedman's view of the transmission mechanism, however, the alternatives to money will consist of interest-bearing nominal securities alone, and these will, in turn, be broken into two types of assets, a short-term security and a fixed-interest long-term security. As discussed presently, the explicit allowance for two interest-bearing securities, rather than only one, is consistent with a good deal of Friedman's work. At the same time, physical assets are omitted from this book's presentation of the assets in households' portfolio decisions. This choice is consistent with the notion that it is desirable to cut through to the *essential* equations that highlight the main differences between Friedman's analysis and the New Keynesian benchmark and, in focusing on those differences, to make the equations as parsimonious in parameters and variables as possible.

The approach also has similarities with Brunner and Meltzer's (1973) attempt to formalize the differences between monetarist and IS-LM analysis by considering three assets. In Brunner and Meltzer's analysis, however, the third asset considered was the stock of physical productive capital. Inclusion of the return on a physical asset might be argued to be more consistent with Friedman's monetary analysis than the exclusion here of claims on physical capital (and the inclusion here of more than one interest-bearing security). Consequently, some more words in defense of the choice made here are needed.

Friedman's 1956 analysis in essence suggested that expected inflation was an argument in the money-demand function that appeared alongside the return on nominal securities. The rationale given for the presence of the expected-inflation term was that storable physical goods (such as productive capital or consumer durables) provided an alternative form in which to hold wealth and that the return on these goods should therefore be treated as one of the opportunity costs of holding money. At one stage, various commentators regarded the most significant contribution of Friedman's 1956 analysis to be the addition of expected inflation as an argument in the money-demand function (see, for example, Patinkin 1972a, 884). Interestingly, however, this was one area in which Friedman did not see his theoretical work on the money-demand function as particularly innovative, and he suggested that Keynes (1923) had already provided a treatment of the subject.[30]

Although some post-1956 research affirmed that the inclusion of the return on physical goods as an argument in the money-demand function has theoretical appeal (see, for example, Abel, Dornbusch, Huizinga, and Marcus 1979, 98), a specification along these lines has little justification from the perspective of models based on optimizing behavior.[31] The notion that money is a durable good may well be a reason for treating money-demand decisions as having a long horizon. But this notion can be seen as turning the variables that appear in the money-demand function into long averages of series—so that, in a forward-looking model, forward-looking averages of income and securities interest rates would appear in the function. In itself, the notion that money is a durable good does not imply that the returns on durable consumer goods or on physical-capital variables appear (for given interest rates on nominal securities) in the money-demand equation. Perhaps it will be found in the future that—in a very elaborate and comprehensive treatment of the private sector's portfolio problem—the rate of return on physical goods can be rigorously justified as an argument in the money-demand function. But whether or not this proves to be the case, it is clear that such a model property is not the obvious corollary of money being a durable good that Friedman took it to be.

Nor is there compelling empirical evidence in favor of putting the return on physical goods as an argument in the demand-for-money function. Cagan (1956) motivated his money-demand function, in which expected inflation appeared as the opportunity-cost variable, by appeal to Friedman's 1956 specification of the portfolio decision problem. However, the Cagan specification can be obtained from a standard money-demand function in which nominal securities, but not physical goods, represent the alternative to money—provided that one assumes that variations in the real interest rate are only a minor contributor to variations in the opportunity cost of money (see Sargent 1987a, 37).[32] Furthermore, in their *Monetary History*, Friedman and Schwartz acknowledged the lack of success in empirical studies in finding a significant role for expected inflation as a distinct opportunity-cost variable in the US money demand function.[33] In 1982's *Monetary Trends*, they instead primarily relied on nominal income growth, rather than inflation, to stand in as the measure of the nominal return on real assets. Although this variable entered their estimated money-demand function for the United States with a negative sign and significantly, it had a low estimated slope, both in absolute terms and compared with the estimated nominal interest-rate semielasticity.

Friedman's 1956 money-demand function also included a return on equity among the opportunity-cost terms.[34] But, once his other work is considered, it becomes clear that there is even less of a case for including that variable in a representation of his monetary analysis than there is for a direct expected-inflation term. Friedman became very skeptical of the connections between the stock market and the economy.[35] Much of this skepticism reflected doubts that equity-market-related variables appeared in the IS curve. But he also downplayed, after 1956, their importance in the money-demand equation. In *Monetary Trends*, after considering the variable, Friedman and Schwartz opted not to put an equity-return term in their money-demand equation, and later, when Friedman added a couple of equity-market-related variables to an estimated US money demand function, he found that they were present only to a minor extent in a quarterly money demand equation and that they essentially disappeared when put into a money-demand function that was estimated on annual data.[36]

In contrast, the relationship between the demand for longer-term securities and the demand for money was an issue to which Friedman directed increased attention in the 1970s and the 1980s. And even his 1956 analysis took for granted that fixed-interest longer-term securities mattered for portfolio decisions, with his later theoretical and empirical work making explicit that short-term securities certainly mattered too. Therefore, the three-asset framework used in the analysis below will include money, short-term nominal securities, and longer-term nominal securities.

(3) *Lags from monetary policy to real GDP and inflation will not be modeled*. In an analysis of the interaction between the economy and the financial system, Svensson (2015, 5) notes as an aside that he is assuming same-period reactions of real economic activity, when these "in reality [do] not occur within the quarter but over the next few quarters." Svensson justifies the assumption on the grounds of simplicity.

Much the same approach is taken here. Friedman's emphasis on lags in the reaction of the economy to monetary policy actions was an important part of his messages about both economic structure and the appropriate form of the monetary policy rule, and the absorption of those messages by policy makers and the economics profession is discussed in chapters 8, 10, 11, and 15 below. But representing such lags in a formal model is beyond the scope of this chapter. Consequently, the lag of economic activity behind monetary policy actions is not embedded into the equations used below.[37]

IV. Consumption

This and the next section discuss Friedman's consumption and investment functions, as a prelude to laying out an aggregate IS equation that captures Friedman's views on spending determination. Two points should be made at the outset.

First, the IS equation, like the consumption and investment functions that are used to motivate it, is cast in real terms. This might seem at variance with Friedman's own statements, such as when he partially endorsed Meltzer's (1965) description of himself and Schwartz as having a monetary theory of nominal income. Could one instead view Friedman as believing that nominal income is determined by one set of forces, with (for example) the Phillips curve then determining the split of nominal income between prices and output? The answer, offered in the appendix of this chapter, is that this way of viewing matters does *not* lead to an appropriate representation of Friedman's views and that Friedman did *not*, in fact, believe that the output/prices split was determined wholly separately from the forces determining nominal income. That answer is consistent with McCallum and Nelson's (1998, 3) position that the notion, present in the writings of Friedman and others, that "nominal spending growth is fundamental and [its determination] relatively well understood" is distinct from any presumption that nominal income growth is determined ahead of, or separately from, its components. An example that brings out this distinction is one in which the growth rates of nominal income and nominal money continue to be well correlated with one another in the face of a change in inflation expectations that alters the output-growth/inflation split of nominal income growth. Such a situation might well lend valid support to data analyses and policy rules that emphasized nominal income. It would not, however, follow that the reduced-form relationship between monetary growth and nominal income growth was a structural relationship or that the IS and Phillips curves were not structural.

Second, and relatedly, in building up from consumption and investment functions to an IS equation, the approach in this chapter may seem inconsistent with Friedman's endorsement of "top-down" (that is: start with a prediction of aggregate expenditure, and only then decompose the forecast into spending components) as opposed to "bottom-up" (that is: start with predictions for individual spending categories, and aggregate these predictions to obtain a forecast of aggregate expenditure) approaches to viewing aggregate economic behavior.[38] His endorsement of top-down analysis is, however, best understood as a reflection of his preference for reduced-form instead of structural empirical models of spending determination, and not as a denial that, when one *is* writing down a structural model, a bottom-up approach is valid and appropriate.

Friedman certainly did not view top-down and bottom-up approaches as inherently inconsistent with one another, and in an interview with the present author (January 22, 1992), he named Alan Greenspan as someone who was known to arrive at a forecast by using and reconciling the two approaches. Furthermore, Friedman certainly regarded it as legitimate to talk in terms of structural relationships that were labeled "the consumption function" and "the investment function." Indeed, one of his most celebrated research contributions was on the consumption function, and it is to that research that the present discussion now turns.

THE RELATIONSHIP BETWEEN
CONSUMPTION AND INCOME:
THE PERMANENT INCOME HYPOTHESIS

The central element of Friedman's view of consumption determination is of course his permanent income hypothesis, as advanced primarily in the 1957 monograph *A Theory of the Consumption Function*. There is much discussion of various aspects of this hypothesis, and the *Theory of the Consumption Function* study, in other chapters of the present book. In light of this, a key aim of this chapter's coverage of the permanent income hypothesis is to cover those aspects of the hypothesis that do not receive great attention elsewhere in the book. To that end—and in the tradition of the "miscellany" chapter of Friedman's book—the discussion of the permanent income hypothesis that follows will be broken down into a number of topics.[39]

(*a*) *Friedman's development of the permanent income hypothesis.* As has been indicated in the previous two chapters, Friedman provided inklings of the permanent income hypothesis in a number of his writings during the 1940s. Notable among these inklings was the remark in his 1943 article on the expenditure tax that households smooth their spending by saving some of the receipts acquired in high-income years.[40] That article also essentially presented a permanent-income argument because Friedman's postulate in the analysis was that consumption depended on wealth rather than income. And, as discussed in chapter 2, the Friedman-Kuznets *Income* book of 1945 explicitly used a permanent-income/transitory-income distinction, albeit not in the context of consumer theory.[41]

When, in *A Theory of the Consumption Function*, Friedman did apply in earnest his permanent-income ideas to the behavior of consumer spending, he presented it as the culmination of his research on consumption that had begun during his work in the 1930s for the US government. However, as has already been suggested in previous chapters, it would be a mistake to see Friedman as settling on the permanent income hypothesis at an early stage and sticking to it resolutely. On the contrary, his discussions in the late 1930s and very early 1940s used the Keynesian consumption function, in which households' spending depended on current income and in which the marginal propensity to consume declined as income rose. And, as was discussed in chapter 3, even his 1943 statement of permanent-income ideas, in his expenditure tax article, was followed by some backtracking later in the 1940s.[42]

Furthermore, Friedman's work on consumption in the early and mid-1950s came after a number of years in which the consumption function was not a major area of research for him and in which he made little in the way of criticism of the Keynesian consumption function.[43] To see this, consider the fact that Carl Christ (1966, 6) admonished himself for having used the traditional Keynesian consumption function (that is, $C_t = \alpha + by_t + u_t$ with $b < 1$) in his econometric model of the United States (Christ 1951).[44] In that 1966 retrospective, Christ indicated that he should have used a permanent-income specification. However, Friedman, who was the assigned discussant of the 1951 Christ study when it was presented at a 1949 NBER conference, did not include in his published comments any criticism of Christ's use of the Keynesian consumption function.[45]

However, what Christ (1966, 6) referred to as a situation in which all econometric studies using the Keynesian function "vastly underestimated the level of consumption in the United States after World War II" likely played a role in leading Friedman to direct more attention to the consumption function. Friedman would cite notes dated June 8, 1951, as the earliest document that he could locate in which he wrote down the permanent income hypothesis.[46]

Friedman would name a number of individuals as having aided his thinking about the consumption function. These included those who had been his fellow workers on US consumption data during the 1930s, but also his wife, Rose. As discussed in chapter 2, Rose Friedman had coauthored a highly influential study of saving and income, Brady and Friedman (1947). And Friedman indicated that discussions with both Brady and Rose Friedman had helped him develop and refine the theory he outlined in his book.[47]

Friedman further indicated that Margaret Reid, who became a member of the University of Chicago's Department of Economics in 1951, subsequently joined the discussions of the consumption function that he, Brady, and Rose Friedman were having.[48] Friedman cited Reid's (1952) work prominently in his book. An earlier empirical study by Reid, namely her 1934 book *The Economics of Household Production*, although not cited in Friedman's book, is widely viewed as anticipating aspects of Friedman's hypothesis, and McCloskey's (2000, 62) remark that Reid "invented permanent income" may have been a reference to her book.[49] Both Milton and Rose Friedman pointed to Reid as the key figure who urged Friedman to write up his theory of consumption.[50] And Friedman went so far as to say that his book, although solely by his own hand, was the "joint product" of the discussions among Reid, Brady, and the Friedmans.[51]

Friedman described his permanent-income setup as being derived from "the pure theory of consumer behavior" and on that score being different from Keynesian macroeconomic theories of consumption.[52] However, there was an important respect in which his permanent income theory, as well as the life cycle theory of consumption that appeared approximately concurrently, parted ways with traditional microeconomic theories regarding the consumption/saving split. As Merton (1987, 148) would note, although they were based on optimizing behavior, "the micro theories of saving at that time were purely static models, with saving treated as just one of the many goods the consumer could purchase from current income." A passage of a 1955 *American Economic Review* article by Friedman, "Leon Walras and His Economic System," had applied this criticism to Walras's writings. Walras, Friedman remarked, had "yielded to the temptation, which has claimed so many lesser men, of treating 'savings' like a consumer good and simply carrying over mechanically the formal analysis applicable to consumer goods."[53] Articulating a position that lined up with that advocated in his then-current work on consumption, Friedman went on to argue that saving, instead of being treated as a good that was desired for its own sake, should be regarded as a variable that helped deliver future consumption streams.[54] When taken in conjunction with households' desire that consumption keep pace with permanent income, this motivation meant that—as Friedman would put it in his 1957 book—the volume of saving was a "residual" whose movements arose largely from fluctuations in the transitory portion of households' income.[55]

(b) *The hypothesis in its original form.* Friedman's *Theory of the Consumption Function* decomposed a household's consumption spending C and its income y into transitory and long-term (or "permanent") components: $C_t = C_{TR,t} + C_{P,t}$ and $y_t = y_{TR,t} + y_{P,t}$. Friedman further postulated that $C_{P,t}$ is driven by the equation $C_{P,t} = k(r_t, w_t, u_{CP,t}) \cdot y_{P,t}$.[56] That is, permanent consumption was hypothesized to depend proportionately on permanent income, but with the proportional relationship subject to shifts arising from variations in the interest rate, problems accessing that part of permanent income that reflects future income from human capital, and a residual $u_{CP,t}$.

This specification would appear to yield an equation for only the unobservable variable $C_{P,t}$, not observed consumption C_t. But because Friedman postulated further that transitory consumption varied randomly and was not linked to transitory income, the equation for $C_{P,t}$ became, upon redefinition of the residual term, a stochastic equation for C_t, of the form $C_t = k(r_t, w_t, u_{C,t}) \cdot y_{P,t}$. Treating r_t as a vector of real interest rates, and suppressing the w_t term, this condition implies the loglinearized equation $\log C_t = \log E[k] + \log y_{P,t} - \tilde{b}'r_t + u_{C,t}$, where $\tilde{b}$ is a coefficient vector.

As discussed below, however, theoretical developments due to later authors carried the implication that $C_t = f(y_{P,t}, \cdot)$ is not the ideal form in which to represent the permanent income hypothesis in a modern economic model. Nor is the method that Friedman proposed to derive $y_{P,t}$ from observed time series on actual income typically the appropriate way to measure permanent income in a modern model.

(c) *Empirical evidence.* The text on the dust jacket of *A Theory of the Consumption Function* stated with respect to Friedman and the permanent income hypothesis that he "tests it against extensive statistical material." Friedman, by his own admission, did not rely heavily on formal statistical tests in the empirical analysis in his book.[57] And the statistical work in the book made considerable use of a technique (namely, reverse regression) that was neither widely used nor widely valued in mainstream econometric work by the 1960s. But that the implications of the permanent income hypothesis were indeed judged against a wide range of empirical evidence in Friedman's book is clear from the extensive cross-sectional and time-series work documented in the book.

The hostile retrospective of Mäki (1985, 64–67) portrayed Friedman as glossing over evidence that was contrary to the permanent income hypothesis. This interpretation of the way Friedman laid out his findings was, in fact, voiced in some of the more visceral early reactions to *A Theory of the Consumption Function.*[58] However, a more balanced and enduring view (and one widely held among economists who, unlike Mäki, have worked primarily in the area of macroeconomic research) is that Friedman's book provided extensive evidence for his hypothesis, that his outline of the evidence was done in a manner that permitted considerable scrutiny by other researchers, and that his own assessment of the empirical evidence was largely confirmed. On the issue of scrutiny, Walters (1987, 423) emphasized that Friedman's investigation included an attempt to find evidence against his hypothesis, as well as suggestions for how subsequent researchers might try to do so. Furthermore, Friedman himself—far more than in the case of the Friedman-Schwartz *Monetary History*—submitted his consumption-function work to extensive vetting by the profession prior to its publication, and he answered challenges to his findings. In particular, Friedman gave prepublication presentations of the consumption-function work at seminars and other forums and, simultaneously with and subsequent to the publication of the book, he participated in multiple debates in print regarding his findings.[59] These exchanges included an occasion in 1955 when James Tobin received a draft of a chapter and provided comments and corrections, as part of an exchange in which Tobin served as a discussant when Friedman presented a condensed version of his argument.[60]

From these exchanges and other examinations of Friedman's work, the majority judgment was that—of the competing hypotheses available—the permanent income hypothesis gave the most plausible explanation for the consumption/income patterns in the data.[61] This was a judgment reflected not only in comments by those who had been Friedman's colleagues or students—such as Robert Lucas, who observed that among the reasons he regarded *A Theory of the Consumption Function* as "just such a beautiful book" were his assessment that its "results were amazing and [Friedman] even made predictions that were verified later on—a pretty exciting thing for an economist" (Robert Lucas, interview, March 12, 2013).[62] It was also a judgment voiced by observers who had close ties to the MIT side of the macroeconomic debates with Friedman. Dornbusch and Fischer (1981, 164), for example, noted of permanent-income behavior: "Friedman shows that this implication is borne out by the facts." Furthermore, Paul Samuelson, who had earlier written of "my admiration of Dr. Friedman in the area of permanent income analysis" (Samuelson 1975, 75), observed in *Newsweek* in 1976 that the permanent income hypothesis "stood up so well to adversary attack," and this outcome, Samuelson contended, provided a reason that Friedman deserved to receive the Nobel in economics (*Newsweek*, October 25, 1976a).

Samuelson's glowing remarks bore testament to the reaction that *Theory of the Consumption Function* received among many leading Keynesians. Although, as will be discussed in item (*f*) of this subsection, some early interpretations treated his book as a critique of Keynesian economics, the book did not really fall unambiguously into the category of a critique. It could instead be regarded as a contribution to the Keynesian literature and as a proposal to improve the specification of Keynesian models. Consistent with this perspective, the permanent-income idea, although provocative at first, was absorbed rapidly into mainstream Keynesian thinking.

In particular, Friedman's book was well received among figures who were and remained hostile to his work on money. Indeed, Gary Becker, who worked closely with Friedman during the 1950s as a graduate student at the University of Chicago, viewed Friedman's consumption-function research as helping to dig Friedman out of the trough in prestige in which he found himself after 1951, in light of what his peers perceived as an excessive emphasis on the role of money. Friedman's reputation started to come out of the doldrums, Becker observed, "particularly after the consumption function work came out." *A Theory of the Consumption Function*, Becker added, "is such a powerful book. I think that raised his standing" (Gary Becker, interview, December 13, 2013).

The restoration was, however, only partial. Friedman's critics often took him to be a Jekyll-and-Hyde figure, whose work on monetary relations had vastly less merit than his research on consumption.[63] This was particularly so before the appearance in 1963 of the Friedman-Schwartz *Monetary History*, which established that Friedman's positions on money reflected more research and had more documentary foundation than previously believed. Even subsequent to the *Monetary History*'s publication, however, Friedman's research activities in the area of money, as well as his writings on the market system, often gave rise to a very different attitude from that generated by his consumption research. Robert Hall observed during his years as a graduate student at MIT in the mid-1960s that "there was a tendency to say: There's two Friedmans. There's the kind of free-market crusader who's treated suspiciously at MIT, and then there's the guy who wrote the consumption book which is greatly admired" (Robert Hall, interview, May 31, 2013).

For his part, Friedman regarded *Theory of the Consumption Function* as his best single piece of research.[64] But, unlike his critics, he did not perceive the order-of-magnitude difference in quality between his consumption research and his monetary research. He granted that the consumption-function research was a separate project from the monetary investigations.[65] But Friedman's citation of the consumption book in his monetary writings, and his use of the permanent-income concept in the latter, showed that he did not accept the degree of separation between the research endeavors that some Keynesians implied.[66]

In sum, Friedman succeeded in persuading the profession of the validity of the permanent income hypothesis; and this success partly reflected the fact that the evidence that he advanced stood up to criticism in the 1950s.

That said, much of the evidence that Friedman put forward in favor of the permanent income hypothesis would not qualify as a valid part of the evidence for the modern equivalent of the permanent income hypothesis. Some of the simpler pieces of evidence might still be applicable: for example, the fact that the consumption/income ratio was stable in the long-term US data instead of exhibiting a decline—a prominent motivation for

Friedman's work—was affirmed by Cochrane (1994, 242) as a point in favor of the permanent income hypothesis. But the time-series regression work in Friedman's book must be judged to be outside the body of valid evidence for the permanent income hypothesis. Why? Because that work employed the assumption of adaptive expectations. Therefore, households, although viewed in the hypothesis as concerned with the future, were modeled as making their estimate of longer-term income by using a fixed-weight sum of recent years' income. The ostensibly forward-looking consumption function therefore became a backward-looking function in practice.

The latter specification did not *necessarily* violate rational expectations, as Muth (1960) showed and as will be discussed in chapter 15. It did not do so, provided that the backward-looking function corresponded to an optimal forecast based on the time-series processes driving permanent income. But for most economic environments, the backward-looking (approximately three-year) univariate equation on which Friedman relied to generate his permanent-income series would not be consistent with the assumption of rational expectations. And, in putting the consumption function into a macroeconomic model, one would not, in any event, impose that expectations function a priori (as Friedman essentially did). Instead, one would permit it to emerge from the rational expectations solution of the model.

It is true that some empirical modelers, even in the era of rational expectations, have actually adhered to something along the lines of Friedman's original specification for the calculation of permanent income, on the grounds that the resulting consumption function embeds properties that work well empirically. For example, Carroll and Summers (1991), Juster, Lupton, Smith, and Stafford (2004, 10), and Engen, Laubach, and Reifschneider (2015, 16) have appealed to Friedman's work when advocating specifications in which households do not act in a fully forward-looking manner.[67] For the most part, however, the criterion of rational expectations has reigned as best practice in macroeconomic modeling. That situation means that, from the perspective of modern research, Friedman's backward-looking formula for calculating permanent income would not be regarded as appropriate. As a corollary, Friedman's time-series evidence for the permanent income hypothesis that rested on that formula cannot be considered lasting evidence in favor of his consumption theory.

As discussed in chapter 15, some of Friedman's work on the permanent income hypothesis using cross-sectional data did, in effect, use rational expectations. Consequently, that part of his evidence in favor of the hypothesis was exempt from some of the criticisms that would be applied to his time-series work. But even Friedman's cross-sectional evidence cannot be considered enduring evidence in favor of using the permanent income hypothesis. The reason for this judgment lies in the problematic manner in which Friedman offered his $C_p = ky_p$ equation—that is, the equation that he regarded as the structural relationship describing the permanent income hypothesis. For, entirely leaving aside his treatment of expectations, an important reason why Friedman's case for the permanent income hypothesis could not be regarded as directly applicable to modern economic analysis is that he used high-level assumptions in specifying the determination of household spending. In particular, in interviews for this book, both Kenneth Arrow (December 7, 2013) and Laurence Kotlikoff (May 26, 2015) emphasized the point that—in contrast to Modigliani in his work on the life cycle theory—Friedman did not derive his proposed consumption function from a utility-maximization problem.[68] Instead, Friedman's consumption research took a consumption/income relationship as the primitive component of the theory, instead of deriving that relationship from an optimization problem.

Notwithstanding, therefore, Friedman's modification of the original Keynesian consumption function, his work was subject to the criticism that Dixit (1976, 243) leveled at many variants of traditional Keynesian consumption analysis: it was "an *ad hoc* modification, not based on any rigorous formulation," implying that a "more rigorous formulation is clearly necessary." It follows that the empirical evidence that Friedman adduced for the permanent income hypothesis amounted to evidence in favor of an ad hoc equation, albeit one that was heavily motivated by theoretical arguments. Because modern best practice in macroeconomics is to derive the equations describing private-sector behavior from formal optimizing analysis, Friedman's original permanent-income specification cannot be accepted, and the evidence he advanced in its favor is correspondingly rendered moot. However, the basic ideas underlying Friedman's consumption specification did seem to be amenable to a rigorous justification in terms of optimizing analysis. The fact that Friedman's book had advanced appealing ideas about consumption behavior yet had provided only a partially rigorous implementation of these ideas left a gap to be filled. It was against this background that the modern optimization-based version of the permanent income hypothesis materialized.

(*d*) *The modern forward-looking version.* Robert Hall (1978), on the basis of an analysis of a utility-maximizing household in an infinite-horizon model, derived a condition in which the household's consumption purchases depend on the next-period expected value of those purchases, with a coefficient of unity. In its logarithmic form, this first-order condition—the Euler equation for consumption—has provided a building block for the equation describing the behavior of real aggregate spending in the benchmark New Keynesian model. Indeed, when variations in the real interest rate are permitted (which they were not in Hall's analysis), this Euler equation essentially corresponds, up to shock terms, to the optimizing IS equation used in New Keynesian models without capital.[69]

Hall explicitly presented this equation as an application of the permanent income hypothesis to a stochastic environment. However, the title and text of his paper indicated he was drawing a lineage between his work and the consumption theories of *both* Friedman and Ando-Modigliani-Brumberg. Others, however, have been more categorical. These authors have linked the Hall Euler equation for consumption *specifically* with the Friedman permanent-income theory and not with both of the 1950s consumption theories. For example, Robert King (1991, 290) cited Friedman's consumption-function work when discussing the behavior of optimizing consumers in a real business cycle model, while Barro and King (1984, 835) observed that Robert Hall (1978) "made explicit" Friedman's permanent income hypothesis.

As indicated above, the form of the consumption function in Hall's analysis was one in which $\log C_t$ depended on its expected future value $E_t \log C_{t+1}$ (as well as on other variables). In this approach, the link between consumption and longer-term expected income streams was embedded in the budget constraint in the consumer's optimization problem instead of appearing explicitly in the equation that came out of that optimization, and the smoothness of consumption was encapsulated in the result that, under certain restrictions, the expected percentage change in consumption was constant, rather than (as in Friedman's equation) in a structural relationship linking consumption to a smoothly changing variable.

There is some dispute over whether the Euler equation that Hall derived should truly be regarded as a legacy of Friedman's work on consumption function. In an interview for this book (May 26, 2015), Laurence Kotlikoff suggested that the link between Robert Hall (1978) and Friedman's work was tenuous and that Hall should have stressed that he was deriving the behavior of consumption implied by the Ramsey (1927) model.[70] A contrary view, however, has been expressed by many other researchers, including Robert Barro and Robert King in the references given above. One of the most emphatic statements about the connection between the Hall and Friedman specifications of consumption behavior was Sargent's (1986, 6) remark that "Hall's model precisely represents the consumption-smoothing idea present in Friedman's original work on the consumption function."[71] Still other researchers have drawn attention to the congruence between the Friedman and Hall approaches not by referring to Friedman specifically but by using the "permanent income" terminology when discussing the behavior of consumption in an infinite-horizon model. Examples of this practice include Krusell and Smith's (2015, 734) description of the consumption decision in their infinite-horizon optimizing model as "classic 'permanent-income' behavior." Furthermore, both Krusell and Smith (2015, 735) and Cochrane (1994, 242) have referred to the equation system that embeds this consumption behavior as the "permanent income model."

That there is a strong link between Friedman's permanent-income theory and consumption behavior in the modern optimizing model is also the position taken here. The permanent-income consumption *equation* in Friedman's 1950s research has not been validated by modern modeling, but the permanent income hypothesis has received such validation. The Euler equation is an authentic representation of Friedman's permanent-income idea, because the equation describes a representative household whose intertemporal behavior leads to a smooth expected consumption profile (for a given path of real interest rates).[72] In addition, in both the Friedman and Robert Hall conceptions of consumption behavior, permanent movements in the household's long-term income, and *not* the rearrangement of the income profile across periods, provide the source on the income side of movements in the level of consumption. Friedman's remark, in describing his theory, that movements in saving act "to 'straighten out' the stream of expenditures," carries over directly to the modern theory of consumption.[73]

If, as argued above, the Euler equation is indeed the appropriate vehicle with which to bring the permanent income hypothesis into a modern framework, the relevant empirical evidence for the hypothesis must be considered to be that for the Euler equation, rather than the evidence for and against Friedman's original equation. What is the verdict on the Euler equation for consumption? With respect to aggregate US data, the verdict would appear to be that the equation seems to do well and serves as a useful benchmark.

An investigation that gave some of the most negative findings regarding the performance of the Euler equation was that of Campbell and Mankiw (1990). These authors argued that, of US households, approximately half do not adhere to behavior consistent with the permanent income hypothesis. Other researchers have, however, argued that the empirical deviations from the consumption behavior implied by the permanent income hypothesis have been more minor in magnitude than Campbell and Mankiw's (1990) assessment suggested. According to this alternative view, the permanent income hypothesis is often an acceptable approximation even though not strictly accepted empirically, and a specification (like that Campbell and Mankiw preferred) in which household spending decisions are disproportionately sensitive to current income is unnecessary in many contexts. Caballero (1994, 107) has summed up this view by noting that the permanent income hypothesis "does not hold in the [US] data. . . . But it almost holds!"[74] Caballero's statement, it should be noted, pertained to consumer-spending series that excluded expenditure on durable goods. But this qualification underscores the lineage between the Euler equation approach and Friedman's work, for the exclusion of durables expenditures was a key part of Friedman's exposition of the permanent income hypothesis (see the next subsection).

Not only does the optimizing version of the permanent income hypothesis put the hypothesis on a sounder theoretical footing, but also, once the hypothesis is put in this form, it makes for a stronger contrast in the time-series context with the traditional Keynesian function. Arrow and Kurz (1970, 118) had occasion to note that "when Friedman makes explicit use of time series analysis, 'permanent income' turns out [just] to be an average of about three or four years' previous income."[75] This is (typically) no longer the case when the explicitly forward-looking version of the permanent income hypothesis is used. The forward-looking version also has the attractive feature that it implies patterns of consumer behavior that might help account for evidence that could be inconsistent with the 1957 version of the permanent income hypothesis. For example, Dynan, Skinner, and Zeldes (2004) found that wealthy US households had higher saving rates than poorer households—a result that would likely be inconsistent with the permanent income hypothesis when permanent income is measured as a backward-looking average of income. But, as Dynan, Skinner, and Zeldes (2004, 407) acknowledged, their finding was potentially reconcilable with the permanent income hypothesis in optimizing models, as the higher saving rate may represent a bequest motive. That issue is in turn related to the question of what horizon underlies the permanent income hypothesis. This question is now considered.

(*e*) *Consumers' planning horizon and comparison with the life cycle model.* Although Robert Hall (1978) derived his consumption equation in a context in which households had infinite horizons, differences of opinion exist about whether the same can be said of Friedman's formulation of the permanent income hypothesis. For example, Meghir's (2004, F296) retrospective on the permanent income hypothesis took Friedman as not taking a clear stand on the horizon to which the consumer's decision applied.

It will, however, be argued in what follows that, although Friedman did not use an *explicit* infinite-horizon model, it would not be correct to suggest that his analysis left the issue of horizon unresolved. Walters (1968, 253), Thygesen (1977, 61), and Parkin (1984a, 213) all characterized Friedman as assigning infinite horizons to consumers. These interpretations of Friedman's consumption framework are appropriate, for reasons given below.

In the aforementioned discussion, Thygesen contrasted the infinite-horizon character of Friedman's theory with that of the Modigliani-Brumberg (1954)/Modigliani-Ando (1957) life cycle theory of consumption. The latter theory is often mentioned in the same breath as Friedman's and is frequently characterized as interchangeable with it.[76] In this connection, Phillip Cooper, a graduate student at MIT in the late 1960s who worked with Modigliani (see Modigliani, Rasche, and Cooper 1970), recalled of his student days: "I always wondered:... 'What is the real distinction between what he [Modigliani] was talking about . . . and the consumption/income approach of Friedman?' But it certainly would have been, at that location, heresy for you to say, 'Well, gee, aren't these two [approaches] very much alike?'" (J. Phillip Cooper, interview, September 17, 2015).

As the quotation from Cooper suggests, Modigliani took umbrage at the suggestion that his and Friedman's theory of consumption coincided. He acknowledged that the two theories had "many affinities" with one another (Modigliani 1975a, 6), but he was also at pains to make distinctions between them. Some of the distinctions that Modigliani claimed between the two theories—such as their predictions about the relationship between the steady-state saving ratios and steady-state growth rates—were questionable.[77] But the time horizon of consumers is indeed an important matter on which the two theories differ. This contrast between the theories was given prominent and legitimate emphasis by Modigliani himself soon after Friedman first stated the permanent income hypothesis (see, for example, Modigliani and Ando 1960), and it was a difference that Modigliani continued to stress in later expositions (see, for example, Modigliani 1986a).[78] Thus, Modigliani (1986c, 224) observed that the "life-cycle model . . . implies finite life," while Modigliani (1975a, 6) noted that a feature of Friedman's framework was that "in his approximation the length of life is treated as infinite."

That Friedman used an infinite-horizon framework in his specification of consumer behavior is something that can be inferred rather than obtained directly from his writings on the consumer's problem.[79] Friedman indicated early on that he would not be wedded to a finite horizon simply because lives in practice were finite. He observed that "intuitive plausibility gives little guidance to . . . length of horizon."[80] And even this observation must be qualified by the fact that Friedman's usage of the term "horizon" referred to the period within which transitory-income fluctuations occurred, whereas the debate in macroeconomics over "infinite-horizon" versus "finite-horizon" models instead uses "horizon" to refer to the assumed length of the representative agent's life.[81] Friedman's assumption of infinite horizons (in the macroeconomic sense of that term) can be gleaned from a number of his statements, including his observation that "consumption is determined by rather long-term considerations" and his remark that his theory was designed to allow for cases in which the permanent-income calculation included expectations of receipts that would accrue "at some indefinite future time."[82]

Most importantly, the fact that Friedman modeled the household as adhering to the *same* consumption decision rule *every* period—instead of following a time-varying expenditure function whose form changed as the expected time of retirement or death approached—meant that he was taking households as infinitely lived. Friedman acknowledged in response to early feedback on his theory that the theory did not allow the ratio of permanent consumption to permanent income to vary with age. Instead, variation in the measured saving ratio by age group was primarily attributed to deviations of measured income from permanent income.[83] In his book, he indicated that he had deliberately specified his consumption function so that it could "be regarded as applying to an indefinitely long horizon."[84]

Thus, even though Robert Hall (1978) saw his consumption equation as descended from both the Friedman and Modigliani theories of consumption, the fact that the Friedman theory is open to an infinite-horizon interpretation provides one reason for seeing it as having a closer resemblance to Hall's theory than does the life cycle theory. The treatment of Friedman's theory as pertaining to an infinite-horizon household is also consistent with Paul Evans's (1983, 207) citation of *A Theory of the Consumption Function* when discussing Ricardian equivalence, whose validity depends on households having infinite horizons.

Should the property that Friedman's consumer was infinite-horizon, while Modigliani's was not, be regarded as an advantage of Friedman's approach? Some discussions that took place ahead of the modern literature on consumption suggested that it was not actually an advantage. For example, Harry Johnson (1971b, 35) argued that "the Ando-Modigliani model makes more sense than Friedman's" on the grounds that the former model was finite-horizon in character. Johnson's statement, however, preceded the truly widespread use, for the analysis of monetary policy and other macroeconomic problems, of models featuring infinite-horizon agents. Friedman's approach to consumption can be regarded as a more direct antecedent to these models, including those used in modern New Keynesian analysis, than was the life cycle theory.[85] His use of an infinite-horizon framework can therefore be viewed as a strength of his analysis. At the same time, it should be stressed that there exists a significant body of researchers who favor finite-horizon models for macroeconomic analysis. One of these, Lawrence Kotlikoff, coauthored a macroeconomics text that used the life cycle model (Auerbach and Kotlikoff 1995), and, in an interview for this book (May 26, 2015), Kotlikoff reaffirmed his preference for the Ando-Brumberg-Modigliani approach to consumer behavior.

It should also be mentioned that finite-horizon models continue to be favored as an approach to analyzing saving decisions in contexts outside monetary analysis. In this connection, Andrew Abel observed: "What the life-cycle model has, in addition to the permanent-income theory, is the notion that there's retirement and people save for retirement. And you can go a step beyond it, to think about bequests and intergenerational transfers. . . . This is useful for thinking about things like Social Security" (Andrew Abel, interview, October 14, 2014). Indeed, as discussed in chapter 13, an understanding of the differences between Friedman and others on Social Security policy is aided if one views Friedman as taking an infinite-horizon consumer as his benchmark.

That said, it is the case that, as discussed in later chapters, it seemed to take Friedman a while to be comfortable with *all* the major implications of the assumption of infinite-horizon consumers. For example, during the 1960s he was very inclined to invoke crowding-out arguments, instead of Ricardian equivalence, as the main basis for believing that fiscal deficits and aggregate demand would be loosely connected. In the course of the 1970s, Ricardian equivalence figured more heavily in his analysis of fiscal policy, before becoming central to that analysis from the 1980s onward.

(*f*) *Was the permanent income hypothesis anti-Keynesian?* In some presentations, Friedman's research on the consumption function has been depicted as strongly anti-Keynesian. Nobay and Johnson (1977, 478), for example, contended that Friedman's respecification of the consumption function to include permanent, as opposed to current, income, had "implications for the multiplier, [which] disposed of one strand in Keynesian policy thinking." The sharp initial reactions to the permanent income hypothesis by commentators such as Lydall (1958) and econometrician Jack Johnston were testimony to the early perception in some quarters that Friedman's study amounted to a fundamental challenge to Keynesian theory.[86] In a sense the study indeed had that status, as it modified one of Keynes's original equations. But the warm reception, already noted, that Friedman's consumption work got from a large number of Keynesians points to the need for a more nuanced interpretation of the import of the permanent income hypothesis.

The one respect in which Friedman's consumption function could be really considered strongly contrary to prior Keynesian positions lay in the fact that his work contradicted the notion that the share of income spent on consumption declined as income rose. This aspect of his analysis, although brought out strongly in his book's text and conclusions, was somewhat obscured in Friedman's algebraic presentation of the theory using linear equations.[87] Putting the hypothesis in loglinear form would have highlighted the fact that his theory did—and preexisting Keynesian theory did not—imply a unitary coefficient on the log income term in the consumption function: that is, it implied an income elasticity of consumption of unity.[88]

Under this parameter restriction, households' own behavior—even in the absence of stabilization policies—would keep their consumption in step with income as the latter rose over long periods, and the "secular stagnation" danger that Keynes, Hansen, and others had suggested on the basis of the original Keynesian consumption function would not arise. In his conclusions, Friedman himself highlighted the adverse result for the secular-stagnation hypothesis implied by his consumption specification. It should be remembered, however, that the economics profession had already largely—in light of the early postwar empirical evidence—abandoned the secular-stagnation position by the time of the appearance of Friedman's book.

In his book Friedman noted, too, that secular stagnation had been used to justify fiscal policy activism, including measures aimed to redistribute income from high-income households who, according to the original Keynesian consumption function, had a lower marginal propensity to consume.[89] Friedman remarked that his modification of the consumption function removed this justification for income-redistribution policies. But he was careful to note also that a policy of income redistribution could well be justified on grounds other than management of aggregate demand.[90] Indeed, as the discussion of the negative income tax in chapter 13 below will indicate, Friedman continued after the 1950s to be a supporter of a certain amount of income redistribution by government, to be effected principally via the negative income tax.

One area in which Friedman might be perceived as having been critical of Keynesianism in his book pertained to his discussion of prior empirical findings. Friedman made a statistical criticism of existing empirical consumption-function estimates. He argued that previous econometric work had spuriously obtained a finding of a declining marginal propensity to consume on the part of households. His reasoning was that, as the scale variable in the consumption function should be permanent (and not measured) income, the use of the measured-income series in estimated consumption functions meant the inclusion of a transitory-income component that mattered little for spending decisions. This component, he believed, imparted to the estimated equations an errors-in-variables factor, whose presence tended to lower the estimated slope on income.[91]

More formal econometric work initially seemed to provide confirmation of this criticism by establishing that measurement error of the kind that Friedman highlighted would lead to an inconsistent estimate of the marginal propensity to consume.[92] However, this result turned out to be inapplicable to actual US output and consumption data, as it was predicated on these two series being stationary in levels (or log levels), when, in practice, it was more appropriate to view these series as exhibiting stochastic growth. The upshot, as demonstrated by Stock (1988), was that, when the permanent income hypothesis prevailed, a unitary long-run relationship between logs of consumption and income *would* come out of ordinary-least-squares regressions estimated on large samples—even when measured income, rather than an estimate of permanent income, was used in the regressions.[93] The consistency of ordinary-least-squares estimation in this context came from the existence of a common trend, or cointegration (Engle and Granger 1987), linking log income and log consumption. This cointegration property would overwhelm the errors-in-variables factor as an influence on the estimated income elasticity of consumption.[94]

Stock did, however, endorse a form of the critique that Friedman had advanced, for Stock suggested that a below-unit income elasticity might emerge from estimation of the consumption function on small samples. In particular, log-consumption-on-log-income regressions would produce consistent estimates of the income elasticity, but the estimates obtained on finite samples would be biased downward.[95] However, whether in its original form or as revised and formalized by Stock, the Friedman critique of estimated consumption functions did not constitute a criticism of Keynesian economic *theory*—except in the sense that it buttressed the message of the permanent income hypothesis that the marginal propensity to consume was unlikely to decrease with rising income.

We come now to the aforementioned implications of the permanent income hypothesis for the magnitude and reliability of the fiscal multiplier. In a discussion of Keynesian theory in the concluding chapter of *A Theory of the Consumption Function*, Friedman indicated that "I do not myself accept this income-expenditure theory" (that is to say, Keynesian theory) as valid empirically.[96] Friedman granted nevertheless that the theory of cyclical fluctuations underlying Keynesian analysis could well prevail even with his modification of the consumption function. One qualification to this that he noted was that, under the moving-average approach he had taken to measure permanent income in time series, estimates of the multiplier effect of fiscal policy actions would be lower than those implied by traditional consumption functions. The reason for this was that the impact of a year-t fiscal action on the permanent-income measure was necessarily limited by the fact that this income series had measured income in years prior to t as a large component. But, in a prescient passage, Friedman accepted that this result was tied to his method of measuring permanent income and was not implied by the permanent income hypothesis per se.[97] And, as indicated below, once rational expectations are used for dynamic analysis of the fiscal multiplier, the use of the permanent income hypothesis does not invariably imply a lower spending multiplier than that associated with the traditional Keynesian consumption function.

In the year in which his consumption study was published, Friedman made, with Gary Becker, a more overt critique of Keynesian economics—a critique that also involved the consumption function.[98] Friedman and Becker's position was that the empirical fit of consumption functions was often cited as part of the evidence of the success of Keynesian theory of the business cycle. But much of this fit, they contended, was not surprising because consumption was a large part of income and, frequently, the two series also varied together. If the consumption portion of income was excluded, the resulting regressor did not give an account of consumption behavior that was impressive when judged against such benchmarks as random-walk and random-walk-with-drift representations of consumption.[99] Invalid inferences from the fit of consumption functions had led economists, Friedman and Becker concluded, "to accept a specification of the character of the economic structure that our data do not support."[100]

The Friedman-Becker study, Gary Becker recalled, "really upset a lot of Keynesian economists at the time; I mean, Larry Klein published a long—and pretty poor—response to it" (Gary Becker, interview, December 13, 2013). Friedman and Becker's reply to Klein (1958) has importance for our present purpose because the former authors emphasized that their critique did not rely crucially on the permanent income hypothesis but instead amounted to a call to look at the evidence in favor of Keynesian models more critically.[101] In taking this stand, they paved the way for the later Friedman-Meiselman questioning of the empirical evidence for the Keynesian multiplier.[102] But neither the Friedman-Becker nor the Friedman-Meiselman criticisms of the multiplier were very closely dependent on the permanent income hypothesis. The existence of those critiques does not, therefore, provide a valid basis for viewing the permanent income hypothesis as anti-Keynesian.

What does the permanent income hypothesis itself, as opposed to other contributions of Friedman regarding fiscal and monetary policy, imply for the fiscal multiplier? Some conclusions contrary to older Keynesian intuition do pertain if consumption depends on permanent income instead of current income.[103] As already noted, one implication of the permanent income hypothesis in a forward-looking setting is Ricardian equivalence: for an infinite-horizon household, a rearrangement of the timing of taxes between now and the future does not affect the spending decision. A related implication—which became accepted as important well before widespread professional discussion of Ricardian equivalence—was that temporary tax increases should have little braking effect on consumption. The experience of the federal income tax surcharge imposed in the United States in 1968 seemed to validate this implication of the permanent income hypothesis.[104] Another instance in which the permanent income hypothesis has the effect of disconnecting fiscal policy actions from aggregate spending is in the case of a permanent increase in government purchases. In certain circumstances, such an increase prompts an expectation of permanently higher taxes and therefore lowers consumption, leaving aggregate demand unchanged (Barro 1981).

At a deeper level, however, the permanent income hypothesis should not be regarded as having invalidated the concept of the fiscal multiplier. Rather, the hypothesis allows a spelling out of the circumstances in which the multiplier will be nonzero, and it therefore helps shed light on what types of fiscal policy actions are most likely to have an effect on aggregate spending. Robert King (1991, 290–303), for example, found, like Barro (1981), that temporary government purchases can boost real aggregate demand. King also modified the Barro (1981) result concerning permanent government spending by showing that permanent changes in government spending can boost aggregate output and real spending in a flexible-price model because labor supply might respond to the purchases.

And once sticky prices and unused resources are admitted into the analysis, the scope in a permanent-income setting for an increase in government spending to raise output is further enhanced. In this connection, Tobin (1980, 61) noted that if the economy started from a position in which output was below potential, the multiplier associated with a new government-purchase program would be boosted in a forward-looking environment because of the reaction of current income to higher expected future income. Perhaps drawing on Tobin's analysis, the *Economist* (October 27, 1984, 71) correctly observed that the application of rational expectations instead of adaptive expectations to the "basic Friedman model" of consumption would lead to a greater fiscal multiplier, as rational expectations enhanced the scope for a fiscal action to be associated with a revision to estimates of permanent income.

In sum, the permanent income hypothesis was not inherently anti-Keynesian. Keynesians who recognized this point at an early stage included economists at MIT, as already noted, but also a Keynesian whose work will be considered further in chapters 13 and 15 below: Robert Eisner. Eisner, of Northwestern University, penned an early defense of Friedman's consumption theory (Eisner 1958) and, as discussed in later chapters, would apply that theory to an analysis of the aforementioned 1968 US federal income tax surcharge.[105] Eisner (1986, 64) credited Friedman's consumption-function work with having "contributed significantly to the Keynesian theory of aggregate demand," and this assessment was a sound one.[106] Friedman accepted the notion of a consumption function and related concepts and developed them.[107] As Friedman himself would note (see Taylor 2001, 118), the permanent income hypothesis was not anti-Keynesian in the way that much of his monetary work was.[108] Rather, it was a hypothesis that could be absorbed into both Keynesian and monetarist thinking.[109]

(*g*) *Permanent income and wealth.* Harry Johnson (1971a, 9) contended that, in developing his theory of the consumption function, Friedman was simply relabeling what was usually called "wealth" as "permanent income." As Johnson offered this observation as part of a highly critical perspective on Friedman, the contention was intended as a criticism. Indeed, Johnson's discussion suggested that the use of the "permanent income" term was specifically designed to promote confusion and to conceal Friedman's reliance on the concept of wealth.[110] Johnson was presumably implying either that wealth was already widely understood to be an argument in the original Keynesian consumption function (so that Friedman's consumption function was simply the old Keynesian function), or that "permanent income" did not amount to a useful new concept.

The notion that the pre-1950s Keynesian consumption function already had wealth as an argument does not seem to have much merit. Tobin (1981a, 206) noted "Keynes's omission of wealth, in distinction from capital gains, as a determinant of consumption," and econometric modelers such as Christ (1951) accordingly represented the Keynesian consumption function as one in which current income was the sole scale variable. Friedman acknowledged that some passages of Keynes's *General Theory* were consistent with a role for wealth in households' spending decisions, but he stressed that Keynes did not integrate this role into the core theory advanced in the book, which featured a current-income consumption function.[111]

With respect to whether the concepts of wealth and permanent income coincided, Friedman granted readily, from the very beginning, that the concepts were almost interchangeable. Indeed, the motivation he offered for his consumption theory, in the opening pages of *A Theory of the Consumption Function*, had wealth as the scale variable.[112] When Friedman introduced the permanent-income concept into consumption analysis, he indicated that this income series should have a proportional relationship with wealth.[113] Furthermore, consistent with Meltzer's (1963, 235) observation that "Friedman at times refers to [permanent income] as wealth," on numerous occasions Friedman used the terms "wealth" and "permanent income" synonymously.[114]

Nevertheless, the concept of permanent income had, and has, a usefulness distinct from that of the concept of wealth. The reason for this lies in Friedman's observation that the permanent income hypothesis suggested that the key variable for consumption was "the discounted value of anticipated future receipts."[115] This concept might coincide with measures of wealth—but it need not. Standard measures of aggregate wealth—as used in Modigliani's (1971) consumption work, for example—typically rely heavily on the market values of stocks of such assets as bonds and equities. But, with regard to bonds, the permanent income hypothesis would eventually be used (by Barro 1974) to cast doubt on their routine use in wealth aggregates, as the Ricardian equivalence that Barro highlighted had the implication that government bonds were not net wealth.[116] Equity valuations, on the other hand, are rendered suspect in wealth calculations by the fact that equity prices may well be prone to be driven by bubbles. If, as suggested by Bernanke and Gertler (2001, 257), private-sector spending becomes less sensitive to asset prices when these prices are elevated by a bubble, consumption functions based on wealth as calculated by market valuations may be unreliable.

Friedman, in contrast, offered a concept—permanent income—that, although theoretically isomorphic to wealth, might well offer a more reliable guide to consumption behavior than did standard empirical measures of wealth. By his own admission, Friedman did not look in detail at asset-based wealth aggregates in his research on consumer spending.[117] Instead, he endeavored to compute a permanent-income series directly from income data. Although Friedman's particular approach to doing so (based on adaptive expectations) has been superseded, it remains true that macroeconomic models offer a way of computing the expected stream of future income. Thus, the concept of permanent income complements the concept of wealth by calling into question estimates of wealth based on asset valuations and by suggesting that these measures be cross-checked against a more direct estimate of expected longer-term income.[118]

(h) *Relationship with Irving Fisher's work.* The opening page of chapter 2 of Friedman's book indicated that the consumer's decision problem under certainty had been worked out by Irving Fisher (1907, 1930). Friedman went on to start with a two-period example that was "essentially identical with that given by Fisher [1907]."[119] From this starting point, Friedman went on to describe the multiperiod stochastic generalization of the problem Fisher had studied. The layout of Friedman's chapters 2 and 3 was recalled by Robert Lucas: "there's some real nice theory in there, with Irving Fisher: you know, it's all there. Then there's this transition into [the treatment of] stochastic, statistical models—which I think is an incredibly sophisticated discussion of how the two relate" (Robert Lucas, interview, March 12, 2013).

This layout of Friedman's book no doubt partly shaped Fama and Miller's (1972, 41) characterization of both Modigliani and Brumberg (1954) and *A Theory of the Consumption Function* as having provided deeper foundations for the already-sophisticated analysis of consumer behavior in Irving Fisher (1930).[120] Friedman's debt to Fisher and his continuation of Fisher's approach were also brought out in Don Patinkin's description of the opening of Friedman's chapter 2: "When Friedman presents this hypothesis in the first [*sic*] chapter of his *Theory of the Consumption Function* (1957), he says it's all in Irving Fisher."[121]

Despite the fact that the connections between Fisher's and Friedman's writings on consumption were acknowledged by Friedman and noted by many others subsequently, some more recent commentaries, such as that of Laidler (2013a), have cast doubt on whether there was much of a linkage. However, the position taken in these later commentaries may have reflected the evidence available at the time from the research literature. That literature has seriously understated the amount of evidence that shows that Friedman, during the quarter century to 1957, was exposed to Fisher's work.[122] Friedman's immersion in Fisher's writings during those years reinforces the evidence from the opening of chapter 2 of *A Theory of the Consumption Function* that Fisher's writings were a direct influence on Friedman's book.[123]

CLASSIFYING CONSUMER SPENDING
ON DURABLE GOODS

Although Friedman's *Theory of the Consumption Function* did not devote a great deal of discussion to households' spending on durable goods, what it did say about the matter left a lasting imprint on the consumption and investment literatures alike. His message about durables spending was encapsulated in the index entry for the book: "Durable goods purchases, treatment as capital expenditures." Friedman's study proposed that the consumption function refer to spending on nondurable goods. In this approach, spending on consumer durables would not be counted as consumption spending. Ideally, in the construction of a consumption aggregate, spending on durables would be subtracted from standard measures of aggregate consumption, and consumer durables would enter consumption spending only in the form of the "use value," or flow of services, derived from the outstanding stock of consumer durables.[124]

If purchases of durables should not be counted as consumption, what should they be counted as? Friedman's statement that "our theoretical analysis calls for treating the purchase of such goods as a capital transaction" left some ambiguity about whether he proposed to count these purchases as saving, investment, or both.[125] Other passages in the book clarified the matter. Friedman certainly affirmed that he believed that consumer durables should be counted as saving.[126] Several subsequent analyses have either endorsed the notion that consumer durables spending are a form of saving or at least taken Friedman's analyses as so implying.[127] But other discussions, such as K. Wallis (1980, 19), have taken Friedman's analysis as implying that consumer durables expenditures should be classified as part of *investment* expenditures.

Both interpretations are, in fact, correct. Adding spending on consumer durables to saving but not to investment expenditures would have meant that aggregate spending in the economy did not add up to current aggregate income. But, as discussed in chapter 2 above, Friedman's quantity-theory approach, just as much as Keynesian analysis, required that such equalities be preserved. Thus, Friedman's proposal regarding the classification of consumer durables spending amounted to a suggestion that this spending series be added to both saving and investment. That is to say, households, in purchasing consumer durables, were regarded as forgoing consumption and adding to the supply of saving, but—in devoting all those saved funds to their own durables purchases—households simultaneously added to investment by the same amount as their addition to saving. This way of viewing the matter was consistent with Friedman's observation that "the monetarist view is that 'saving' and 'investment' have to be interpreted much more broadly."[128]

Friedman's classification of consumer durables became widely adopted among both nonmonetarists and monetarists. Examples of this high degree of acceptance include David and Scadding's (1974, 226) observation that "the theory of consumer durables expenditure is a part of modern investment theory"; Kydland and Prescott's (1988, 351) statement that "consumer durables are considered part of the capital stock"; and Abel and Bernanke's (1992, 172) remark that, "in an economic sense," expenditure on durable goods helped contribute to future consumption, even though the rules of national income accounting classified that expenditure as wholly current consumption. Conversely, Dornbusch and Reynoso (1989, 205) endorsed the notion that consumer durables purchases were a means by which households added to their saving.

The treatment of consumer durables purchases as conceptually different from households' nondurables consumption allowed Friedman to account for a feature of the data that might otherwise be regarded as inconsistent with the permanent income hypothesis: the fact that windfalls to households' income tended to produce spikes in their current spending, instead of being smoothly spent over current and future periods. Friedman was able to point out that income windfalls often led to expenditure that was concentrated in durables purchases and that such a pattern did not contradict his permanent-income theory.[129] A similar observation applies to the modern version of the permanent income hypothesis. In optimizing models that make a durables/nondurables distinction, the Euler equation applies to nondurable-goods consumption. In contrast, the optimality condition for durables spending typically closely resembles that for firms' investment purchases (see, for example, Erceg and Levin 2006).[130]

Freedman, Harcourt, Kriesler, and Nevile (2013) view Friedman's proposal to exclude consumer durables spending from consumption as part of an anti-Keynes agenda on Friedman's part. This interpretation obscures the fact that Friedman's proposal was an analytical point that has been taken on board by the subsequent literature.[131] In this connection, Edey and Britten-Jones (1990, 87), although somewhat skeptical of counting durables spending as investment, acknowledged that the argument was "undoubtedly valid in principle," and they noted that some of the most forceful cases for viewing durables spending as investment—such as Shiller (1982)—came from the modern Keynesian literature.[132] In addition, it deserves emphasis that much of Friedman's testing of the permanent income hypothesis examined evidence that was based on the standard definition of aggregate consumption—that is, *including* spending on durables—even though it was accompanied by statements that durables consumption should in principle be treated differently.[133]

INTEREST ELASTICITY OF SPENDING
ON CONSUMER NONDURABLES

In addition to making permanent income the scale variable in the consumption function, and excluding durables expenditure from the spending to which the consumption function pertained, Friedman's specification of the consumption function differed from much Keynesian analysis in another respect. This difference arose from his position that households' nondurables spending was notably interest elastic.

The Keynesian position on the interest elasticity of nondurables consumer spending was articulated by Keynes (1939b, 634) when he stated that measures that operated on the rate of interest were "only relevant to those factors which are sensitive to moderate changes in interest rates (which a man's desire for a glass of beer is not)." Early Keynesians tended not to quarrel greatly with Keynes's position on this matter. Indeed, two decades after Keynes wrote, John Kenneth Galbraith felt confident enough about professional thinking on the issue to state (Galbraith 1958, 190) that the possibility of an influence of interest rates on the division of household current income between saving and spending "though once suggested, is no longer seriously urged even by the most convinced supporters of monetary policy." According to this view, insofar as monetary policy affected consumption, it did so because household spending flows were induced by flows of investment spending, and the latter flows might be interest elastic.[134]

Dennis (1981, 120) and Modigliani (1986b, 14) both credited monetarist analysis with making consumer spending interest elastic, in contrast to the preexisting Keynesian specification.[135] As already indicated, this was indeed a feature of Friedman's monetarism. Furthermore, this perspective on consumer behavior represents a case in which Friedman's position, rather than that taken in the early Keynesian literature, prevails in New Keynesian models today. The optimizing IS equation in New Keynesian analysis is derived from equations that include an interest-elastic function describing the determination of household spending on nondurable goods.

In light of this lineage between modern macroeconomic models and Friedman's work, it may come as a surprise that in Friedman's writings—despite his belief in the interest sensitivity of nondurables consumer spending—he did not play up this difference between himself and many of his contemporaries as prominently and explicitly as one might expect. When he referred to interest-elastic private spending, he often instead highlighted investment spending and households' expenditure on durable goods. For example, a discussion of crowding out in a 1977 Friedman *Newsweek* column referred to a scenario in which, when the government ran deficits, "the government gets funds that would otherwise be available for building houses or factories or machines."[136]

Nevertheless, Friedman's position that consumption was interest elastic was of long standing. His conversion to that position appears to have occurred at an early point during the years in which he transitioned to monetarism. A PhD dissertation at the University of Chicago that was completed in September 1948 attributed to Friedman the position that the interest rate was a variable to which saving and investment adjusted and that helped equilibrate the two series.[137] Even in 1952, however, Friedman, although affirming that a "rise in interest rates produced by credit policies will tend to increase the fraction of income saved by consumers," played down this channel, stating: "My own guess is that the fraction of income saved is only slightly responsive to a rise in interest rates, that business plant expenditure programs and inventory policy are much more responsive."[138] In later years, he did not depart from the (standard) view that investment expenditure was "much more responsive" to interest rates than was consumption, but he indicated that the interest elasticity of consumer nondurables spending, while not strong when judged in relation to that of investment, might be sizable in absolute terms.

In his own writings and other public statements, however, instead of dwelling at length and explicitly on his position that nondurables consumer spending was interest elastic, Friedman largely let that position emerge implicitly. It did so, for example, from his observation that interest rates were relevant for all spending that was facilitated by borrowing—provided that this observation was taken in conjunction with his intertemporal view of consumer spending, in which households' access to credit markets provided a means of smoothing their consumption.[139] In addition, the vision of interest-elastic nondurables consumption followed from the fact that Friedman saw the quantity theory of money as implying that monetary policy affected consumer spending just as it did other categories of private spending.[140]

Occasionally, however, Friedman did make explicit his view that consumption (and saving) were more interest elastic than commonly believed. Among the insertions Friedman made in his 1953 revamp of his 1942 paper on the inflationary gap was an indication that saving was interest elastic.[141] This perspective was also reflected in the appearance of an interest-rate term in the full theoretical expression for the consumption function in Friedman's *Theory of the Consumption Function*.[142] Furthermore, in the textual discussion in the book, Friedman stated that one piece of evidence examined was best explained if "the rate of interest that can be earned on savings is an important determinant of the average ratio of savings to income, a conclusion that is entirely consistent with our earlier theoretical analysis but that runs counter to widely prevailing opinions about the effect of the interest rate on savings."[143] A few years later, he and Meiselman, after outlining the monetarist view of the transmission mechanism, observed that that outline was tantamount to a statement that "savings and investment may be highly interest elastic."[144]

The reason for the scarcity of explicit Friedman discussions of the interest elasticity of consumer spending, notwithstanding his belief in a sizable value for that elasticity, was likely twofold. First, as already suggested, Friedman was a subscriber to the standard view that investment spending was more interest sensitive than consumer nondurable spending. Second, he was reluctant to talk about "the" interest elasticity or "the" interest rate because he believed that a spectrum of interest rates was relevant for the spending decisions of both households and firms. It is this multiple-interest-rate view of aggregate demand determination to which the discussion now turns.

THE MULTIPLE-YIELD CHANNEL

Milton Friedman was often accused, in his discussions of the links between monetary authorities' actions and aggregate spending in the economy, of avoiding mention of interest rates. Stephen Axilrod, who went from being a graduate student of Friedman's in the early 1950s to long service as a

Federal Reserve official—in which capacity he was often at odds with his former teacher—was known to joke that, for Friedman, the interest-rate channel was the transmission mechanism that dare not speak its name (Stephen Axilrod, interview, April 24, 2013).[145]

It was against this background that David Laidler wrote in 1982 that Friedman and Schwartz "have so often been accused of understating the importance of interest rates in their monetary analysis."[146] However, as Laidler noted, the item that appeared in 1982 and that he was reviewing—Friedman and Schwartz's final book, *Monetary Trends*—helped dispel this notion. The text of *Monetary Trends* included Friedman and Schwartz's remark that "interest rates are a pervasive and crucial phenomenon entering into every aspect of economic activity."[147] As it happened, this message of the Friedman-Schwartz book was reinforced by remarks that Friedman gave during 1982 in the course of his current economic commentary. In particular, early in 1982 Friedman observed: "What accounts for this unprecedentedly erratic behavior of the U.S. economy? The answer that leaps to mind is the correspondingly erratic behavior of interest rates" (*Newsweek*, February 15, 1982).

These comments reflected Friedman's long-standing positions.[148] Nevertheless, Friedman's emphasis on the quantity of money, together with the perception that Friedman eschewed analyses in which interest rates entered prominently, led many commentators to attribute to him a belief in a structural equation for real aggregate spending (that is, an IS equation) in which money entered directly. Indeed, some commentators even attributed to Friedman an exclusive reliance on a money-to-spending link and a belief that aggregate spending was wholly inelastic with respect to interest rates.[149]

As the discussion in this chapter has already indicated, these attributions were not well founded. With respect to the interest sensitivity of aggregate expenditures, some of the occasions on which Friedman explicitly laid out his belief in its existence were when discussing crowding out of investment. These occasions were numerous. They included some quoted above and also his 1975 observation that "higher interest rates cut off . . . demand" (Instructional Dynamics Economics Cassette Tape 161, January 1, 1975).[150] By the same token, Friedman also believed that the lowering of interest rates, associated with monetary expansion, "encourages spending" on goods and services.[151]

Another frequent context in which Friedman affirmed his belief in the interest sensitivity of aggregate spending consisted of his critical discussions of the variant of early, hard-line Keynesian views to the effect that aggregate demand was totally interest inelastic.[152] Friedman juxtaposed this extreme position against that held by others—among whom he numbered himself—that "interest rates depend on and influence real magnitudes," with the influence in question including the impact of interest rates on decisions to spend in "the real sector through either investment or consumption."[153]

With regard to whether money itself appeared directly in the IS equation, Friedman's position was that it did not. Rather, the monetary-policy-related variables in the equation were asset prices and yields, not the money stock or its growth rate. Thus, as already stressed in chapter 2 and as developed below, Friedman did not, in his monetarist period, subscribe to a belief in direct influences of money on spending.[154] Just prior to becoming a monetarist, however, he had attached considerable importance to real balance effects on wealth and hence the determination of aggregate demand. This was particularly the case in his 1948 advocacy of the monetization rule.[155] But Friedman's shift to monetarism from 1948 to 1951 saw him move to a belief in substitution effects arising from monetary policy actions and a depreciation of the importance of wealth effects. Thereafter, on numerous occasions Friedman stated that he did not believe that the real balance effect was important for output fluctuations.[156] The early literature on the real balance effect had, he granted, contributed to the revival of interest in money in the postwar period. But that literature did not provide, in Friedman's view, an important insight into the relationship between money and business cycles.[157] In 1959, Friedman stated that it was "analytically possible to treat all effects of changes in the quantity of money as taking place via changes in interest rates and their effects in turn on flows of spending."[158]

The fact that Friedman believed in an interest-elastic spending function, with no explicit term involving money appearing in that function, made him receptive to theoretical descriptions of how monetary policy exerted effects on spending that were given in terms of an asset-price or interest-rate channel. For example, in 1967 he stated: "I have no quarrel whatsoever with the view that monetary policy can always, if you wish, be regarded as operating through the medium of interest rates."[159] Indeed, he articulated matters in these terms on multiple occasions, including in lectures given in 1959, as noted above.[160] More specifically, Friedman acknowledged that the effects of monetary policy on the economy at the aggregate level could be thought of as arising from the central bank's influence—operating via its influence on monetary quantities—on nominal interest rates. What came with this influence was a temporary ability to affect real interest rates and thereby generate responses of output and other real magnitudes.[161] In the same vein, Friedman accepted as valid at an abstract level the Wicksellian analysis in which deviations of output from a baseline value, as well as variations in inflation, could be traced to deviations between a market interest rate and a natural interest rate.[162] The "one wrinkle to Wicksell" that he insisted be part of this abstract analysis was that the market and natural interest rates be specifically identified as real, not nominal interest rates.[163]

Even with the real/nominal interest-rate distinction fully taken into account, however, Friedman was very disinclined to view the interest-rate mechanism as a useful way to proceed in empirical work and in analysis of monetary developments. For Friedman regarded it as difficult to consolidate the rates that mattered for aggregate-demand variations into a single interest rate—a position reflected in his repeated use of quotation marks in the phrase "'the' rate of interest."[164] His perspective was that many real interest rates mattered for spending, with these different interest rates tending to deviate substantially from one another in the short run, although they became closer to equality with one another over longer periods.[165]

Furthermore, Friedman was concerned that organized financial markets recorded the values of only a subset of the interest rates that mattered for spending decisions. A considerable amount of the asset-price adjustment that connected open market operations to reactions of consumption and investment spending took place, he felt, in markets for durable goods for which there did not always exist a formal and centralized exchange market that recorded the relevant asset-price variations.[166] It followed that, as he and Schwartz argued in 1963, corresponding to the broad range of assets, "it is necessary to make [the] 'rate of interest' an equally broad construct, covering explicit or implicit rates on the whole spectrum of assets."[167]

The present chapter, in representing Friedman's views, does not consider the case in which the asset prices that matter for aggregate spending include unobserved prices. Instead, as already indicated, the assets considered in the equations used to represent Friedman's views are limited to money and two interest-bearing instruments: a short-term security and a long-term security. This restriction necessarily means that some aspects of Friedman's aggregate-demand framework are not being represented here. But, by the same token, the present analysis respects Friedman's edict that an exposition of the monetarist transmission mechanism requires having a minimum of three assets in the analysis.[168]

The reason for specifying two interest-bearing assets, instead of one interest-bearing asset and one physical asset, as the nonmonetary assets has already been partially outlined in section III above. That discussion explained why a physical asset was excluded. Here it is worth adding some words in defense of the use, in the analysis of this chapter, of bonds of two distinct maturities. True, Friedman's 1956 outline of the money-demand function included only one bond: a long-term security. In later years, however, he increasingly emphasized the need to consider more than one interest-bearing security. In 1959, in proposing reforms to the monetary system, Friedman indicated that, while he believed that there should be a great cutback in the number of maturities of government security on offer, he wanted two government securities to continue to be issued: one short-term, one long-term.[169] In discussions of the modeling of aggregate spending determination, he noted that it might well be worth considering more than one nominal security.[170] Friedman further acknowledged that the short-term interest rate was the interest rate most susceptible to policy influence.[171] That rate was also the most useful for much of his monetary analysis, for it was the study of the behavior of the short-term interest rate that was most amenable to treatments in which the liquidity effect and Fisher effect of monetary injections were viewed as occurring at different time horizons.

Most importantly, in representing the multiple-interest-rate channel by an IS equation in which both the real short-term interest rate and the real long-term interest rate appear, the present chapter is including rates to which Friedman assigned significance in the determination of aggregate demand. With regard to the long-term interest rate, Friedman remarked that "the interest rates that are important for housing and investment are long-term rates."[172] He clearly regarded the short-term interest rate as less important than the long-term interest rate for spending decisions. But he viewed the private sector as drawing on both short-term and long-term securities markets when making and implementing its decisions concerning saving and spending. As a result of this, the short-term interest rate and not just the long-term interest rate mattered for aggregate expenditure.[173]

The specific multiple-interest-rate IS equation proposed here as a means of representing Friedman's views will be given below after a discussion of Friedman's views on investment spending. At this stage, two further points are worth recording.

First, an analysis in which short-term interest rates and longer-term interest rates appear in the IS equation does not by itself invalidate the use of a single interest rate to measure monetary policy stance. In particular, it might be contended that the path of the current and expected short-term interest rate summarizes monetary policy's influence on aggregate demand, on the grounds that it is solely by affecting this path that monetary policy exerts effects on the yields that appear in the IS equation. Friedman, however, rejected this contention. His belief was instead that monetary injections affected both the short-term interest rate and the long-term interest rate, and that the effect of monetary policy on the latter rate took the form of both changes in the expected path of short-term rates and portfolio-balance effects on the term premium.[174]

Second, the multiple-yield channel by itself does not convey significance to the money stock as an indicator. But, in part because of the portfolio-balance effects in which Friedman believed, his contention was that the multiple-yield channel helped make the money stock or monetary growth the best indicator of monetary policy, even though the money stock did not appear directly in the IS equation. See the discussion under "Money as a Summary of Monetary Policy" in the next chapter.

V. Investment

Few topics relevant to the analysis of business cycles and monetary policy received less attention from Friedman in his research work and teaching than did that of firms' investment in physical capital.

This state of affairs likely reflected in part the division of labor within the National Bureau of Economic Research. Arthur Burns, in the year in which he assigned Friedman the directions of the NBER's research on money, listed his own research area as solely comprising "Cyclical behavior of investment."[175] Paul Samuelson (1980, 666) would recall Burns's remit for NBER personnel as "respect for the facts." Friedman's assigned fact-finding role pertained to the money stock and, in a separate strand of research, consumption. It was not his assignment to study investment. This lay instead in the hands of Burns and others. Nor did Friedman really diversify his research interests in subsequent years to include investment.

For his part, Friedman did regard himself as having done some appreciable analysis of the theory of investment. In 1982's *Monetary Trends*, for example, readers were referred to the forty-page chapter 17 of the second edition of Friedman's *Price Theory* text for "a full analysis" of the demand for and supply of physical capital.[176] But in so citing this material, Friedman was flattering himself. In the area of the demand for capital, the cited chapter of *Price Theory* was not a full analysis at all. It was heavily concerned with the supply side of the capital market and with defining concepts that were connected with capital theory. Much of the remaining analysis in the chapter was centered on the market for housing rather than for firms' capital stock.

The *Price Theory* discussion was helpful in clarifying how Friedman viewed the determination of investment in one important respect. In writing down the investment function, Friedman specified the arguments as consisting of wealth and a representative interest rate.[177] These were, of course, the same arguments as in Friedman's consumption function, once one recognizes that, for Friedman, "wealth" corresponded to expected future income streams and was ideally not to be measured by assessing the value of outstanding asset stocks. Over the years, a number of economists have conjectured that Friedman's permanent income hypothesis for consumption can be carried over to business investment, and that therefore many propositions associated with the permanent income hypothesis (for example, that the private sector's decisions will likely be insensitive to temporary tax changes) apply to investment and not just to consumption.[178] Friedman's specification of the investment function made it clear that he was also of this view. There is, therefore, a solid basis for Robert King and Alexander Wolman's (1996, 84) statement that "a central emphasis on expectations in . . . investment decisions" was part of Friedman's framework.[179] Also consistent with this characterization were Friedman's numerous statements that businesses' decisions took into account conditions expected to prevail many years in the future.[180]

The position that expectations of future economic activity mattered for today's investment decisions was basically in harmony with sophisticated Keynesian positions on investment. Partly for this reason, the specification of investment behavior did not become a major area of combat between Friedman and his Keynesian opponents. Friedman was heavily critical of the most primitive Keynesian theories of investment—in which that spending category was autonomous. He was also skeptical about the Keynesian position that volatility of total investment or of spending categories within investment presented a case for activist stabilization policies. Volatility, even when not triggered or reinforced by monetary instability, might, in Friedman's view, reflect the appropriate private-sector adjustment to real shocks.[181] But he was not in great theoretical conflict with other economists on the specification of the scale variable in the investment function. For one thing, he largely accepted the terminology of the Keynesian literature in the area of investment.[182] For another thing, to a large extent Friedman accepted the theoretical and empirical work by others on investment, and he did not mark out a distinct position of his own on the matter.[183]

One point on which Friedman did register a dissenting opinion at an early stage on the determination of investment concerned the importance of interest rates. As has been noted in chapter 3, the early development of Keynesianism was associated with a generalization of the position that monetary policy was ineffective in Depression conditions, to the postulate that it was ineffective under much wider circumstances.[184] Part of the impetus for this conclusion had come from researchers' analyses of questionnaires, filled out by business managers, about the factors entering their investment decisions. Friedman staked out from an early point in his monetarist period a caustically skeptical attitude to such questionnaire evidence and a firm opposition to the position that investment spending was interest inelastic.[185] As already indicated, in 1952 Friedman affirmed that investment responded sizably to interest-rate changes, and with a greater elasticity than that of consumption. That continued to be his position in later years.[186]

As noted in section I, some commentators have attributed to Friedman an extreme version of this position—that investment is infinitely interest elastic. In particular, Purvis (1980, 101) concluded, on the basis of a comment that Friedman made in the mid-1970s, that Friedman may have become, or had long been, a believer in an infinitely interest-elastic investment schedule.[187] However, the item in question does not, on inspection, justify the attribution to Friedman that Purvis and others made. In the comment, Friedman pointed to the horizontal IS curve, not as corresponding to a setting that captured his own view, but instead as conveying Frank Knight's theory of capital. Friedman also made the (correct) observation that the horizontal IS curve, like the vertical LM curve, corresponded to a setting in which nonmonetized government purchases had no effect on nominal and real aggregate spending.[188] Friedman did not, here or on other occasions, endorse the horizontal IS curve.

Indeed, both before and after this comment, Friedman made many analytical and empirical observations that indicated that he did *not* believe in infinitely elastic investment expenditures. In particular, as real interest-rate variations with a horizontal IS curve would send investment toward zero or infinity, the only circumstance in which a horizontal IS curve would not imply fluctuations in investment and in its share of output that would be grossly contrary to empirical evidence would be if the real interest rate were constant (or, perhaps, if its movements always corresponded exactly to movements in the natural real rate of interest). But, on the contrary, Friedman believed that in both theory and practice the monetary authorities were able to move the real interest rate in the short run (as well as change its value in relation to the natural rate), on account of their temporary ability to alter the real money stock and thereby vary the nominal interest rate.[189] Furthermore, his contention that a gradualist monetary restriction could limit the real-output costs of a disinflation—a contention he voiced on the many occasions during the 1970s when he set out the appropriate policy for transitioning from high inflation to price stability—was at variance with the existence of a horizontal IS curve. For the belief that the real-output costs of monetary restraint could be contained entailed a position that reductions in real spending were smaller, the gentler the rise in real interest rates associated with a monetary tightening.

Friedman, therefore, rejected the horizontal IS curve. But he did believe that investment was highly interest elastic.[190] Variations in the real interest rate, he stated, played a central role in understanding fluctuations in investment.[191] Friedman pointed to the fact that the real interest rate had varied over a fairly small range in the historical data as evidence that substantial changes in investment spending could be triggered by modest variations in real interest rates.[192]

As already indicated, Friedman seemed largely oblivious to the developments in the research literature on investment after the mid-1960s. A major exception was the case of James Tobin and William Brainard's work on the q-theory of investment. Friedman could hardly ignore that work, as one use to which Tobin put the q-theory was as a critique of the notion that the money stock summarized monetary conditions well.[193] Tobin offered q as a useful summary of the cost to firms of raising funds for investment. Indeed, in one treatment, Tobin and Brainard (1977) presented an analysis in which all the interest rates that mattered for aggregate demand could be summarized by q.[194] Tobin's (1969a, 29) position was that "the principal way in which financial policies and events affect aggregate demand is by changing the valuations of physical assets relative to their replacement costs," and he specifically contrasted this finding with analyses that emphasized the money stock as a summary of monetary policy's implications for economic activity.

For his part, Friedman expressed some interest in the concept of q and acknowledged that it should in principle figure into firms' investment decisions.[195] But he was not favorably inclined to Tobin's use of a priori theoretical arguments in favor of q over money as an indicator.[196] And the deep skepticism that Friedman developed from around the mid-1960s onward about the connections between the stock market and the economy necessarily hardened his doubts about the usefulness of Tobin's q—which was calculated from the stock market's valuations of firms—both as an indicator of monetary policy and as a factor in the determination of investment.[197]

One final aspect of the specification of investment behavior in Friedman's framework that needs clarification is his view of investment dynamics. Clearly, the arguments that he put into his specified investment function—wealth and the interest rate—were time-related variables, but investment is usually regarded as subject to further intrinsic dynamics, such as would emerge from capital adjustment costs or from related phenomena such as time-to-build.

Although Friedman largely abstained from commentary on, still less participation in, the literature on investment dynamics, he was a close follower of the NBER studies of the business cycle, including research on output dynamics. Partly on the basis of his absorption of this research, he accepted that there existed US output dynamics of a kind that could not be attributed simply to the dynamics of aggregate-demand policies. In particular, he viewed a rise or fall in output as having some inherent momentum or dependence on its previous behavior (Instructional Dynamics Economics Cassette Tape 181, November 1975, part 2; see also *Newsweek*,

November 8, 1971). There was, he said, an "enormous amount of inertia" in output patterns (Instructional Dynamics Economics Cassette Tape 189, April 1976, part 1).[198] It would be very difficult to attribute such serial correlation solely to the behavior of consumption, so in effect this position on business cycle dynamics amounted to a belief that investment had some inherent persistence. Friedman's commentary on output dynamics would therefore appear to imply that some form of capital adjustment costs was part of his aggregate-demand framework. This inference is also supported by Friedman's occasional remarks on investment, such as when he indicated that many businesses, once they have started a capital-expenditure project in a particular period, will feel obliged in subsequent periods to proceed with the investment expenditures associated with that project even if the economic climate has changed.[199]

AGGREGATE-SPENDING EQUATION

The preceding portrayal of Friedman's stand on the structural relationships underlying the determination of private expenditure can now be summarized. This is done with a sketch of the implied equations as well as the associated overall IS, or total real spending, equation. As indicated earlier, the Euler equation for consumption,

$$\log C_t = E_t \log C_{t+1} - b \cdot r_t + e_{C,t},$$

where r_t is the real short-term interest rate, provides a good representation of Friedman's views with regard to consumption behavior. One major qualification, already stressed above, is that his position was that the equation should include a *vector* of interest rates, rather than a single real short-term interest rate.[200] In the present chapter's analysis, this vector is limited to a short-term and long-term interest rate. Work on putting these two interest rates into the IS equation suggests that their joint presence has the effect of changing the coefficient on the expected future consumption term from 1.0 to below 1.0.[201] That being the case, the equation becomes:

$$\log C_t = a_1 E_t \log C_{t+1} - b_1 r_t - b_2 r l_t + e_{C,t},$$

where $0 < a_1 < 1.0$, rl_t is the real long-term interest rate, and b_1 and b_2 are positive constants.

It was argued above that, in Friedman's framework, investment has much the same driving forces as consumption. We can therefore use the preceding consumption equation to describe the behavior of aggregate log real spending, $\log y_t$, provided that we interpret the interest elasticities differently—specifically, as being higher for aggregate output than for consumption, owing to the greater interest elasticity of investment (including durable goods purchases) than of consumption.[202] It was also suggested above that Friedman likely saw intrinsic dynamics as a factor that justified a lagged-dependent-variable term in the equation driving output.[203] This leads to:

$$\log y_t = a_1' \, E_t \log y_{t+1} + a_2 \log y_{t-1} - b_1' r_t - b_2' r l_t + e_{y,t} \tag{1}$$

where $0 < a_1' < 1.0$, $0 < a_2 < 1.0$, and $e_{y,t}$ is a shock incorporating exogenous disturbances to consumption, investment, and other components of spending.[204] Equation (1) is the IS equation proposed here as a summary of Friedman's view of the determination of real aggregate demand.

Appendix. The Determination of Nominal Spending in Friedman's Framework

In his review of Friedman and Schwartz's book *Monetary Trends*, Charles Goodhart (1982, 1541) took exception to the procedure that the authors followed in adjusting historical price-level data for the effects of price controls. He noted that Friedman and Schwartz's adjustment procedure rested on the assumption that the course of nominal income observed in the data was the same as what would have emerged from a policy regime in which monetary developments had been identical to that observed historically but controls had not been imposed.[205] That is to say, the price controls were taken as affecting the *mix* of nominal income between output and prices, but not the course of total nominal income. Goodhart asked: "Would anyone not already convinced that nominal incomes are held in a monetary straitjacket have made such calculations?"

The aim of this appendix is to establish that Friedman's aggregate-demand framework did not actually reflect literal adherence to the view that "nominal incomes are held in a monetary straitjacket." It is consequently appropriate to regard Friedman as viewing output and prices as having their own structural equations. Accordingly, these structural equations are described in separate chapters of this book: that for output in this chapter, and that for prices in chapter 7.

Certainly, as noted in the main text of the present chapter, Friedman regarded nominal income as a key economic magnitude.[206] And the notion that he regarded nominal income as determined by monetary forces, and its split as determined by aggregate-supply forces, would appear to have support not only from the Friedman-Schwartz practice that Goodhart highlighted but also from Friedman's repeated use of equations for nominal income (or for some other nominal spending aggregate) in which the money stock appeared as a regressor.[207]

But Friedman's use of these nominal income equations did not in fact imply that he regarded it as inappropriate to use an IS or real-spending equation to describe output variations in a structural model. For the nominal income equations were unabashedly reduced-form equations, not structural equations. That this was so is clear from the fact that Friedman and Meiselman's 1963 study, having modeled nominal spending as a function of nominal money in its empirical sections, went on to describe the theoretical rationale for such relations in terms of the response of real spending to changes in asset prices.[208] Correspondingly, the practice that Friedman and Schwartz followed in *Monetary Trends* of treating the price/output combination as determined separately from total nominal income was, they acknowledged, only an approximation, and the relationship between log prices, log output, and their sum did not, they granted, really adhere to the recursive pattern involved in this approximation.[209]

CHAPTER 6

Friedman's Aggregate-Demand Framework: Money and Securities

Friedman's view of the role of money is the main subject of this chapter, especially section I. In light of the prominence of this subject in Friedman's work, however, what is said below should be taken in conjunction with the analysis provided in other chapters of this book.

I. The Role of Money

The discussion that follows begins with a consideration of the connection between the quantity theory of money and the demand for money.

THE QUANTITY THEORY OF MONEY
AND THE DEMAND FOR MONEY

Friedman's definition of the quantity theory of money in his 1956 article "The Quantity Theory of Money—a Restatement" as "in the first instance a theory of the *demand* for money" received a strongly negative reaction both as an analytical statement and as a description of the views of previous generations of quantity theorists.[1] It can, as it happens, be defended on both counts. But the fact remains that demand-for-money theory does not constitute the entirety of the quantity theory of money, including in Friedman's writings—not in his pre- or post-1956 writings on the matter or indeed in later portions of the 1956 paper. The defense of Friedman's 1956 definition of the quantity theory of money given below is therefore only partial.

Let us first consider the validity, as an analytical statement, of the con-

The views expressed in this study are those of the author alone and should not be taken as those of the Federal Reserve Board or the Federal Reserve System. The author is grateful to David Laidler and Gerald O'Driscoll for comments on an earlier version of this chapter. See the introduction for a full list of acknowledgments for this book.

tention that the quantity theory of money is a theory of the demand for money. The main consideration that gives validity to defining the quantity theory of money in terms of a proposition about the demand for money and about the stability of some of the function's key parameters is that the quantity theory of money certainly does impose restrictions on the specification of the demand for money. In particular, price-level homogeneity of the demand for money balances—a condition that implies that the long-run form of the function may be written as one for real balances (M/P) and not for (M/aP), where $a \neq 1.0$—and noninfinite values for the interest-rate elasticity (or elasticities) of money demand are vital preconditions for the validity of propositions associated with the quantity theory of money. Long-run proportionality in the response of the price level to a policy-induced injection of money—which is argued by McCallum and Nelson (2011, 99) to be a common thread across different expositions of the quantity theory—does require these two parameter restrictions on the demand function for money. For if there was not price-level homogeneity of money demand, there would be no presumption that aggregate prices would move by the same percentage as money in the aforementioned thought experiment. And if there was an infinitely interest-elastic money demand function, policy-induced injections of nominal money could lead to one-for-one permanent increases in the private sector's holdings of real money balances—without any other variable, including real income and prices, reacting.

Authors such as Patinkin (1972a) and Niehans (1978, 7) have presented the long-run monetary-neutrality property (that is, the money-price proportionality just described) as central to the quantity theory of money and as grounds for rejecting Friedman's framing of the theory as one in which the demand for money is crucial. However, the difference between them and Friedman on this matter is more apparent than real. For the monetary-neutrality result requires, as already indicated, both the property that the private sector's demand for money is a demand for real balances, and the feature that the demand function has finite interest elasticity; and these were both elements that Friedman explicitly insisted were part of the quantity theory of money, including in his 1956 exposition.[2]

In light of the close connection between the specification of the demand for money and the results typically associated with the quantity theory of money, it should not be surprising that many observers have characterized the quantity theory of money as entailing a theory of money demand and have thereby, in effect, provided backing for Friedman's definition of the quantity theory. For example, Ruffin (1979, 288) indicated that Samuelson's (1968) exposition of classical and neoclassical monetary theory put Samuelson among the "authors [who] have implicitly or explicitly written the demand function for money" as having as its "primary characteristic . . .

the absence of money illusion," while Laidler and Nobay (1976, 297) stated: "The focal point of the quantity theory regarded as a theory of the level of prices or the rate of inflation is the interaction of a demand for real balances function with a nominal stock of money."

It is true that Friedman's 1956 definition of the quantity theory of money went beyond the two properties of the demand-for-money function noted above and pointed also to the stability of other parameters in the function. Here he could have been construed as being overly restrictive in his definition. For a lack of constancy in some parameters in the money-demand function can still be consistent with essentially unitary long-run relationships between log money and log prices (or their first differences). To see this, consider a money-demand function $(M/P) = f(y, R, e)$ in which R is an opportunity-cost variable, e is a money-demand shock, and the partial derivative f_2 governs the interest elasticity of money demand (which is assumed to be finite). Provided that R is a stationary series, M may be proportional to P (conditional on real income y) even in the face of once-and-for-all changes in the parameter f_2. Furthermore, e may undergo permanent shifts, and in that respect the money-demand function may be "unstable"—but such instability could well be consistent with monetary growth and inflation having a close relationship over long periods and perhaps shorter periods as well.[3]

Thus, the close relationship over long horizons between money and prices (or their growth rates) that is associated with the quantity theory of money does not rest on or require perfect constancy of all the parameters in the money-demand function. Friedman's definition in 1956 of the quantity theory of money can therefore be judged to have been overly restrictive. In mitigation, however, two points should be made. First, Friedman's 1956 definition did not actually insist on full numerical stability of the money-demand function. An adequate criterion, he indicated, would be that it was relatively stable when judged against other functions advanced as useful for the study of aggregate economic behavior, such as the Keynesian consumption function. Second, implicitly in his 1956 definition and explicitly elsewhere, Friedman indicated that he did not believe that short-run money-demand functions would necessarily be stable. Rather, the stability in which he strongly believed pertained to the long-run money-demand function.[4]

One feature of Friedman's definition of the quantity theory of money that did apparently jar with prior definitions was his statement (made in support of his emphasis on the demand for money) that a specification of the supply function for money was not an inherent part of the theory. This statement was consistent with his later expositions of monetary history, in the sense that Friedman repeatedly expressed the view that the factors altering the money stock (both the monetary base and the money multiplier) were subject to change over time owing to variations in the policy-reaction function and evolutions in institutional arrangements. He viewed money/spending and money/prices relationships as largely resilient in the face of these changes in the supply function for money.[5] But the 1956 remark seemed to go beyond this, as it could be taken as suggesting that the central bank's influence on the nominal stock of money was not intrinsically part of the quantity theory of money.

One possible reconciliation is that, in his 1956 definition, Friedman may have been endeavoring to allow for the case in which money, prices, and aggregate nominal spending moved together—and in this respect the quantity theory of money's predictions about aggregate economic patterns were upheld—but in which money "did not matter." In such an environment, monetary *policy* was powerless because no action by the central bank could make a difference to the amount of aggregate nominal money created, and monetary *factors* were not important in determining output and price outcomes at any horizon, as the private sector's spending decisions would have been the same even if it had not been the case that the money stock had risen and fallen with nominal spending. This setting would correspond to an extreme one-way nominal-income-to-money causation of the kind that Tobin (1970a) raised as a theoretical possibility and that Kaldor (1970) advanced as empirically realistic, and which Friedman and Schwartz would label the "adaptive supply" case.[6] Friedman was long aware of reverse-causation arguments, and he likely encountered them early, including from NBER colleagues, in the period of his research on money.[7] He may therefore have been trying, in his 1956 exposition of the quantity theory of money, to provide a definition that encompassed the adaptive-supply extreme case.

Nevertheless, even in 1956 Friedman was explicit on the point that an advocate of the use of the quantity theory of money did need to take a stand on the supply function of money. If the central bank lacked any wherewithal to alter the nominal stock of money, and if factors that made for variations in the nominal quantity of money had no bearing on the private sector's spending decisions, a well-behaved demand-for-money function was of little interest. Friedman in essence recognized this point later in his 1956 paper when he stated that a quantity theorist had to insist that there existed a supply function for money distinct from the demand function for money. When that insistence was combined with the notion—pervasive in Friedman's writings—that the central bank's actions could alter the nominal stock of money, it followed that monetary policy actions gave rise not only to movements in the nominal money stock but also in interest rates and in spending aggregates. Thus, even in his 1956 restatement, Friedman indicated that an operationally useful version of the quantity theory of money had to go beyond the specification of the money-demand function and impose restrictions that allowed the central bank's behavior to matter in money-stock determination and for different monetary policies to imply different outcomes for economic magnitudes like output, prices, and nominal income.[8]

A similar judgment applies to Friedman's accompanying remark early in his 1956 restatement that the quantity theory of money "is not a theory of output, or of money income, or of the price level."[9] O'Driscoll (1977, 36) observed that "Friedman's restatement yields a theory of the equilibrium level of money income despite his original disclaimer," and in support of this contention O'Driscoll (1977, 57) noted a 1970 Friedman remark that in "monetary theory, the key question is the process of adjustment to a discrepancy between the nominal quantity of money demanded and the nominal quantity supplied."[10] O'Driscoll's framing of the matter is important because it captures the point stressed above that the quantity theory of money does entail important restrictions on the money-demand function, just as Friedman suggested, but also that this money-demand-function specification does not constitute the whole of the quantity theory of money—including the version of that theory used by Friedman in his own work.

Statements along the lines of the 1970 quotation that O'Driscoll highlighted had been made by Friedman previously, even in his earliest monetarist writings. For example, in 1953 Friedman stated that "static monetary theory . . . is designed to explain the structural or secular level of absolute prices, aggregate output, and other variables for the economy as a whole."[11] These statements were consistent with Friedman's emphasis on the demand for money in 1956 but also reflected his further condition, specified later in the 1956 essay and just discussed, that the supply of nominal money was a variable susceptible to central-bank influence. These statements also lined up with the additional remark in his 1956 article that the quantity theory of money should be used as a basis "for the analysis of the economy as a whole, such as the level of money income or of prices," as well as his remark on the first page of the article that the quantity theory of money had a pedigree as a "sensitive tool for interpreting movements in aggregate economic activity."[12]

Thus, Friedman's conception of the quantity theory of money comprised not only a specification of the demand-for-money function but also an insistence that it was realistic and appropriate to specify the supply function in a manner that allowed the quantity theory to be used to study the determination of real spending, nominal income, and prices. This was a major use to which he put the theory in his empirical work from the 1950s through the 2000s.[13] His view of the price-adjustment process, discussed in the next chapter, allowed him to view the quantity theory of money as making predictions for output at the business cycle frequency.[14] And his position that prices were fully flexible in the long run allowed him to view the theory as pertaining to the long-horizon behavior of prices and other nominal series but not of output—a position reflected in his statement that the quantity theory entailed an "emphasis on nominal magnitudes."[15]

Let us now turn briefly to the issue of whether it was valid for Friedman in 1956 to imply that prior writers in the quantity-theory tradition were, like him, forming theories about the demand for money. As noted above, this position appears defensible, on the grounds that pre-1956 quantity theorists did rely on the price-homogeneity and finite-interest-elasticity properties of money demand on which Friedman placed so much emphasis in his restatement. That reliance was, to be sure, largely implicit, and numerous quantity theorists did not speak in terms of the money-demand function. But the fact that their references to the demand for money were implicit does not render illegitimate an interpretation of their views that is cast in demand-for-money terms. A parallel to Friedman's characterization of pre-1956 quantity theorists as theorists about money demand exists in Lettau and Ludvigson's (2004, 288) interpretation of Modigliani's (1971) study of consumer spending as seeking "estimates of the cointegrating coefficients for consumption, wealth, and income." This interpretation described Modigliani's specification using terminology that was not present at the time of Modigliani's study, and using concepts (that is, those related to cointegration) that were largely implicit rather than explicit in the research literature prior to the 1980s.[16]

Nor was it the case that Friedman in 1956 was imposing, in his interpretation of the prior literature, a terminology that it had never employed. One example of a pre-1956 account of the quantity theory of money that cast matters in demand-for-money terms was provided in an 1896 paper by Wesley Mitchell that Friedman had cited in print in 1950. Mitchell had quoted F. Walker (1893, 74) stating that when the concept of money was expanded to cover bank deposits as well as currency, "it still remains true that the demand for money, whatever that may be, does, taken in connection with supply, determine prices."[17]

Let us now consider several aspects of Friedman's specification of the demand for money.

ASSET DEMAND FOR MONEY:
MONEY AS A CONSUMER DURABLE

As discussed in the previous chapter, Friedman's specification of the demand for money was one in which more arguments appeared than was standard in other work of the time, such as Baumol (1952) and Tobin (1956).[18] As noted in chapter 5, Friedman's suggestion that the expected inflation rate and the return on equity might enter the money-demand function will not be pursued in this book. But the discussion below considers other ways in which Friedman's specification of money demand was broader than that many of his contemporaries favored. As a starting point, in this subsection Friedman's specification of the scale variable of the money-demand function as being permanent income—as opposed to current income—will be considered.

As already suggested, Friedman, when discussing the properties of the demand for money, focused largely on the long-run form of the function and not on its precise dynamic specification.[19] Nevertheless, Friedman's view of money-demand dynamics must be considered here. For he argued from the late 1950s onward that permanent income (that is, a series conveying the path of current and expected future real income) should be the scale variable in the money-demand function.[20] In advancing this position, Friedman was essentially taking the stand that the decision problem for the holding of money had more dynamic aspects to it than was entailed in a standard analysis in which the scale variable was current measured income.

It is true that Lucas (1988b) was able to describe his own money-demand framework as respecting Friedman's emphasis on permanent income, even though Lucas's specification did not use permanent income as the scale variable in the function. Lucas's reasoning was that the optimization-based theory that he used pointed to consumption as the scale variable in the money-demand function. And, of course, Friedman hypothesized that consumption and permanent income were closely linked. But Friedman's own belief that permanent income appeared in the money-demand function did *not* arise from a position that consumption was the true scale variable for the demand for money. On the contrary, Friedman insisted that the money-demand function should have "some measure of real wealth or real income as a scale variable."[21]

In Friedman's conception, real money balances were demanded not only for use in current transactions but also because they provided services as a reserve against emergencies that might arise in the present or subsequent periods.[22] Real money holdings were a durable good and therefore were not a product whose services could be written as a static function of current conditions. This perspective led Friedman to emphasize that the most important feature of money was that it was held rather than that it was spent. He thus firmly put himself in the camp of those who stressed the status of money as an asset—or as Friedman preferred to put it, "a temporary abode of purchasing power."[23]

As Friedman's preferred phrase for the asset demand for money implied, the medium-of-exchange property of money did contribute, in his view, to the utility derived from real money balances—and it was a money-in-the-utility function specification, he believed, from which the private sector's demand for money emerged.[24] But the medium-of-exchange property was not, in his view, the sole source of utility generated by the holding of money balances. For because it implied that money holding was partly a function of expected future conditions, Friedman's perspective differed from transactions specifications of money demand (including those formalized in a dynamic general equilibrium context by McCallum and Goodfriend 1987, and Lucas 1988b) in which the services from money arose purely from effecting current transactions.[25] Furthermore, Friedman believed that every dollar of money was demanded to provide both current-transactions services and reserve-against-contingencies services. He therefore departed from Keynes's (1936) position that one portion of money balances was demanded for use in current transactions and that a separate portion constituted an asset stock held for speculative purposes.[26]

The idea that real money balances serve, in part, as a reserve against contingencies fits in well with the notion that the stream of current and expected real income, rather than current income, is the scale variable in money demand. For the utility from real money balances that arises from their status as an emergency reserve might well be enhanced if real money balances tend to be stable over time, other things equal.[27] But the implied aversion to instability in real money balances provides one basis for making the change in real money balances, in addition to their level, an argument in households' utility function. Evidence in favor of such a preference structure was noted in the course of Friedman and Schwartz's examination, in *Monetary Trends*, of the pattern of real money balances, in relation to the long-run factors that entered the money-demand function, in key historical episodes. That examination led them to conjecture that "there may be a fairly constant maximum *rate* at which money holders are willing . . . to readjust their money holdings from one desired *level* to another."[28] Although their emphasis on the long run in *Monetary Trends* meant that Friedman and Schwartz did not pursue the implications of this finding, the passage echoed observations Friedman had made in earlier decades, such as his remark in 1968 that "it takes time for people to readjust their money balances" to the level implied by the long-run arguments of the money-demand function.[29]

Furthermore, the perception of real money balances as being subject to a dynamic adjustment process, instead of exhibiting complete and instantaneous adjustment, to these basic drivers of the demand for money lined up well with the notion, articulated by Friedman and Schwartz in their *Monetary History*, that households and firms "look forward" when deciding how much they want to hold today in the form of real money balances.[30] For it follows from the formal analysis of dynamic optimization that, if the private sector faces adjustment costs in connection with its decisions about real money balances (or, alternatively, it has an intrinsic desire to minimize fluctuations in real money balances, other things equal), then the resulting dynamic money-demand function will feature not only the prior level of real money balances but also the expected next-period level.[31] And the latter expectational term can be rewritten as a term involving the current and expected future streams of real income (that is, essentially a permanent-income term) as well as terms in expected future values of interest rates and of the other arguments of the long-run money-demand function.

ALTERNATIVES TO HOLDING MONEY

Friedman's "Restatement" in 1956 is known for having placed a multiplicity of opportunity-cost variables in the demand function for real money balances. In terms of the three-asset framework to which we are confining ourselves here, and provided that we ignore shocks to money demand as well as the dynamics of money demand that have just been discussed, the long-run money-demand function implied by Friedman's 1956 analysis might appear to be something along the lines of:

$$\log(M/P)_t = c_1 \log y_t - c_2 R_t - c_3 RL_t, \tag{1}$$

where R_t is the nominal short-term interest rate, RL_t is the nominal long-term interest rate, and c_1, c_2, and c_3 are positive constants.[32]

Three problems immediately present themselves, however. Their joint effect is to make the money-demand function given above unattractive for use in monetary analysis and also to render it unhelpful for representing Friedman's views.

First, as Friedman himself acknowledged, the return on a long-term security could not be regarded as adequately encapsulated by the long-term nominal interest rate RL_t, because the return should also include the capital gain or loss on the security.[33]

Second, it is much harder to justify rigorously the presence of a long-term return (whether or not inclusive of capital loss) in the money-demand function than it is to rationalize the appearance of a short-term yield in that function. Friedman's 1956 analysis, like earlier treatments including Keynes (1936), employed the high-level assumption that the long-term interest rate did matter for the demand for money. But the present author is not aware of any optimization-based justification for such a specification. And, indeed, Friedman's return to the issue of the relationship between the term structure and money demand in research he conducted during the 1970s may have amounted to an implicit acknowledgment that getting long-term rates to appear as an opportunity cost in the money-demand function required a more elaborate theoretical analysis than he had reckoned in 1956.[34]

Third, even if the long-term rate could be established as an opportunity cost of holding money, that result would not imply that money injections matter for the determination of long-term interest rates. One of Friedman's major points of departure from early Keynesian analysis lay in his belief, already alluded to, that increases in the money stock could put downward pressure on longer-term interest rates in Depression conditions.[35] But putting the long-term interest rate into the money-demand function does not, in itself, make real money balances matter (for a given path of the expected path of short-term interest rates) for the determination of the longer-term interest rates. See, for example, Woodford (2012, 236).

Adding opportunity-cost variables to the money-demand function does not, therefore, seem to be a particularly promising procedure for the purpose of understanding how Friedman's work might be used to augment modern economic models, or indeed for understanding the transmission mechanism that underlay Friedman's analyses of the relationship between money and business cycles.

However, one can still draw on Friedman's 1956 analysis of money demand to enrich the transmission mechanism of monetary policy—and do so in a way that respects his and Schwartz's observation that "the range of substitutes for money is broad."[36] In particular, an equation in Friedman's "Restatement" separate from his specified money-demand function has been highlighted, accurately, by Meltzer (1977) as a key contribution to a broader view of the transmission mechanism of monetary policy. In contrasting Friedman with Keynesian theorists who claimed, as Meltzer put it, that "changes in the stock of money are adequately summarized by the response of short-term interest rates," Meltzer pointed to Friedman's equation (9), in which there is a spread between the real yields on bonds and equities.[37] Friedman's surrounding discussion, Meltzer noted, indicated that his framework was one in which interest rates "cannot be reduced to a single rate of return."[38]

By envisioning two asset yields as differing systematically from one another, instead of moving in sync according to a straightforward arbitrage condition, Friedman's 1956 analysis allowed for imperfect substitution between different types of nonmonetary assets. As discussed presently, imperfect asset substitution helps lay the groundwork for increases in the money stock to influence many interest rates—and, also, for a situation in which no single interest rate summarizes these responses of interest rates. Friedman's position can consistently be described as one in which there are many substitutes for money and in which nonmonetary assets are imperfect substitutes for one another.[39] The two characterizations are consistent with one another because in Friedman's framework the choice between two nonmonetary assets—in his 1956 exposition, equity and bonds; in the present chapter's analysis, bills and long-term bonds—depends not only on their respective returns but on the risk of the two assets. A risk premium therefore exists, whose presence implies that the yields are usually not equal. And that risk premium depends in Friedman's framework on the amount of real money balances outstanding. Accordingly, one could say that money substitutes, not just for short-term securities, but also for assets other than short-term securities.

As discussed in E. Nelson (2013a, 67–68, 78–79), one can be more specific about how Friedman perceived the imperfect substitution of assets in the case of short- and long-term securities. Friedman repeatedly emphasized that short-term securities were a better substitute for money than longer-term securities.[40] In particular, a large amount of the private sector regarded the fact that the secondary price of long-term securities could vary as a source of risk in those securities.[41] In the face of this perceived risk, these agents were more willing to hold a larger stock of long-term assets if they simultaneously could add to their stock of short-term assets.[42] In effect, the private sector had something analogous to a "desired reserve ratio" when it came to their holding of risky assets, with the reserves consisting of a weighted combination of money and Treasury bills. There were, however, some private-sector agents for which this perceived risk featured less prominently, on account of their strong inclination to hold securities through to maturity.[43] The net outcome of these considerations, according to Friedman, was that "in the real world" there was "non-risk neutrality leading to liquidity premiums" in long-term interest rates, and some of these liquidity or risk premiums were a function of real money balances.[44] That is,

$$RL_t = \{(1/T)\mathrm{E}_t[\sum_{i=0}^{T-1}R_{t+i}]\}$$

$$+ \, \xi \log([M_t/P_t + \omega\,BILLS_t]/[BONDS_t]) + t.i.p., \qquad (2)$$

where T is the maturity of the long-term security, $\xi < 0$, $\omega > 0$, $BILLS$ is the private sector's real stock of Treasury bills and other liquid short-term securities, and $BONDS$ is its real stock of long-term Treasury securities (as well as other low-default-risk bonds). Following Woodford (2003), "$t.i.p.$" denotes terms assumed to be independent of monetary policy.

A corollary of this setup was that $BONDS$ entered the money-demand function with a positive coefficient. Therefore, a simplified version of the long-run form of the money-demand function implied by Friedman's framework would be:

$$\log(M/P)_t = c_1 \log y_t - c_2 R_t + c_4 \log BONDS_t, \qquad (3)$$

where $c_4 > 0$. As already indicated, variations in real money balances could also arise because of the positive dependence on $\log(M/P)_t$ on $\log(M/P)_{t-1}$, $E_t \log(M/P)_{t+1}$, and a money demand shock, and these would appear in a dynamic version of equation (3).

But it is the appearance of real money balances (M/P) in the term-structure equation (2), not of $BONDS$ in the money demand function (3), that brings with it the implication that monetary injections can alter term premiums. And with monetary injections having such an effect, the reaction of the path of the short-term interest rate to monetary policy would no longer fully summarize the effect of monetary policy on the longer-term interest rate.[45]

Friedman's views as described above plainly have strong similarities to the positions on term-structure determination that were outlined—with considerably more detail and rigor than Friedman provided—by Tobin (1961, 1963a) and Modigliani and Sutch (1966). Tobin (1974b) stressed that the multiple-yield view of monetary policy transmission, and the position that monetary policy could alter the premiums that produced variations across those yields, were held by himself and were not special to Friedman or to monetarism.[46] To judge by his favorable citation of Tobin (1961) in his 1987 New Palgrave dictionary entry on the quantity theory of money, Friedman did not disagree.[47] Nonetheless, at the practical level Friedman's position differed from Tobin's. Friedman did not regard a dollar of Treasury bills (nor of other short-term instruments such as commercial paper) as providing nonpecuniary services that were comparable to those provided by a dollar of money. This would imply that ω was well below 1.0 in the long-term-rate expression above.[48] In contrast, in a good deal of his work, including Tobin (1958a), Tobin elided the distinction between money and bills, treating them as a single aggregate labeled "cash" (or even reserving this last term for bills).[49] This difference in perspectives led, in turn, to a much greater emphasis on the stock of money in Friedman's work than in Tobin's.[50]

MONEY AND CREDIT

In Friedman's assessment shortly after publication, "a key finding in our *Monetary History* is that the confusion of money and credit has been a primary source of difficulty in monetary policy."[51] Friedman would continue to give prominence to the distinction between money and credit in post-*Monetary History* writings, leading Tobin (1976b, 335) to criticize the repeated invocation of "Friedman's favorite money-credit dichotomy."

Friedman's interest in this dichotomy arose from four main sources.[52] First, money and credit did not necessarily move together as a matter of principle. As Friedman put it: "There is no necessary connection between a change in the quantity of money and in the volume of outstanding debts."[53]

Second, money and credit diverged from each other in practice. In the United States and many other countries, a large fraction of the volume of government securities outstanding (that is, of credit to the government sector) was held by the nonbank private sector. Furthermore, and particularly for the United States, much of the provision of credit to the nonbank private sector was not intermediated through the commercial banking system. And even the connection between bank deposits and bank credit was subject to slippages. True, for the commercial banking system as a whole, deposit creation typically came as a by-product of credit creation.[54] Even so, an increase in bank deposits did not imply that total credit in the economy had gone up; bank deposits could rise for a given volume of total credit, as banks might expand their business by intermediating a larger fraction of an economy's unchanged total volume of total credit.

Examples of factors that Friedman gave in 1972 as sources of divergence between money and credit were the existence of a large corporate bond market and the presence of a substantial nonbank mortgage lending market.[55] At the time of these remarks, savings and loan institutions and mutual savings banks were leading housing lenders whose deposit liabilities were excluded from the official US definition of M2. These liabilities were later (in 1980) incorporated into that aggregate. But it remained true even after 1980 that a very large amount of US mortgage lending was not associated with deposit creation, owing to the mortgage financing facilitated by US federal housing agencies and by the advent of large-scale securitization. Furthermore, the relationship between commercial bank credit creation and deposit creation was much looser after the 1960s than previously, on account of banks' increased tendency to finance ("fund") their loans and investments through issuance of nondeposit liabilities, including debentures and various wholesale liabilities.[56] And, as Friedman indicated, corporations' ability to raise funds through means other than taking out bank loans created a major source of discrepancy between money and credit—a discrepancy that took the form not only of firms' issuance of bonds, but also of equity. Friedman regarded funds raised by equity issuance as part of an appropriate definition of credit—because, in common with borrowing by firms, firms' equity issuance augmented their available funds while also increasing their liabilities (Instructional Dynamics Economics Cassette Tape 19, March 1969).[57]

Third, Friedman did not think that credit was susceptible to the same degree of central-bank control as was the money stock.[58] Monetary policy actions affected a spectrum of interest rates, but this spectrum did not necessarily encompass all the interest rates that mattered for the demand for credit.[59] When one takes into account both Friedman's inclusion of funds raised via the stock market as part of credit, and his growing doubts from the second half of the 1960s onward about the connection between the stock market and economic aggregates, it is clear that Friedman's skepticism about the controllability of credit (particularly over short periods) hardened over time.[60]

Fourth, Friedman came to believe that the observed connection between money and the economy did not importantly arise either from credit channels of monetary policy or from a close link between credit aggregates and the economy.[61] At an early stage of his work with Schwartz, he entertained the possibility that the most important implications for economic activity of commercial banks' operations were keyed to their lending and investing.[62] The Friedman-Schwartz research would turn Friedman away from this interpretation, in favor of a view that the money/output and money/prices relationships observed in US data reflected the combination of a fairly stable money demand function and powerful effects of monetary policy actions on total spending. In contrast, Friedman regarded the demand function for total credit as very unstable and not well understood.[63] Even in the face of instabilities in the demand for and supply of credit, the central bank could, Friedman believed, set the nominal stock of money at a level of its choosing; and stabilization of the money stock would do much to provide economic stability even if the monetary stabilization did not secure stable behavior of aggregate credit.[64] Conversely, if, as occurred in the early 1930s, the authorities allowed the nominal money stock to contract in the wake of credit-market disruptions, the effects of the credit-market developments on economic activity would be greatly magnified.

DEFINING MONEY

The Friedman-Schwartz monetary project used an M2-type aggregate (that is, a total that included the nonbank private sector's holdings of currency, demand deposits, and time deposits) to define money instead of an M1-type aggregate (that is, an aggregate that consisted of M2 minus time deposits). The late Phillip Cagan, who was closely involved in this project during the 1950s and 1960s, emphasized to the present author that this choice was dictated by the data limitations that the authors faced. In the US historical data, "there was no way to separate demand and time deposits. That's why Friedman and Schwartz just used M2 without thinking twice about it" (Phillip Cagan, interview, January 13, 1992).[65]

Superficially this characterization—which implied that it was data availability, rather than theoretical reasons, that dictated the NBER monetary project's use of an M2-type monetary aggregate instead of an M1-type money-stock series—would appear to be broadly harmonious with the well-known position of Friedman and Schwartz on the definition of money. In what they called a "strictly pragmatic" approach, they wrote in *Monetary Statistics* that "the definition of money is an issue to be decided not on grounds of principle as in the a priori approach, but on grounds of usefulness in organizing our knowledge of economic relationships. There is no hard and fast formula for deciding what total to call 'money.'"[66] This attitude was reaffirmed by Friedman in 1992: "I don't believe the issue [of defining money] is one you should have any principles about. Because they're all empirical approximations to an ideal construct that you can't conceivably identify precisely" (Milton Friedman, interview, January 22, 1992).

At a deeper level, however, Cagan's position was in conflict with that of Friedman and Schwartz. For the latter two authors acquired a degree of attachment to an M2 concept of money for theoretical and not just empirical reasons. At least from the early 1970s onward, Cagan regarded M1 as a superior measure of money on a priori grounds. He viewed it as inappropriate to include time deposits, on which it was typically not possible to draw checks, in the definition of money. In contrast, Friedman and Schwartz, although they emphasized empirical evidence as the key criterion for deciding on a particular monetary aggregate, devoted a long discussion in their *Monetary Statistics* to the very position of which Cagan became a champion, that is, that the medium-of-exchange property should be an overriding criterion in defining money. They concluded very negatively with regard to this approach.[67]

In light of this background, Friedman's statement that there should not be principles employed when choosing a definition of money should not be taken as implying that Friedman took a wholly theory-free attitude toward defining money. Instead, it can be viewed as mainly reflecting his position that one should not insist on a definition of money that was based purely on the medium-of-exchange concept. In an important sense, Friedman and Schwartz *were* attached to the notion that the choice of monetary aggregate should be based partly on theoretical considerations. Specifically, they sought an aggregate that corresponded to those money balances from which households received utility and so an aggregate that could plausibly be regarded as having a well-defined demand function.[68] The demand-for-money notion should therefore, they believed, guide the definition of money. But that criterion did not imply that the medium-of-exchange property was the overriding consideration in arriving at the choice of monetary aggregate.

Friedman had become disillusioned from an early stage with the purist position that money should correspond closely and exclusively to a medium-of-exchange concept. Some of his very early writings seemed to take it for granted that an M1-style definition of money was appropriate.[69] But his disaffection with transactions-based approaches to monetary analysis soon set in. It was evident in a highly critical discussion Friedman gave in 1952 of the $MV = PT$ (as opposed to the $MV = Py$) version of the quantity equation.[70] This attitude was further manifested in the emphasis on money as an asset in his 1956 "Restatement" and his subsequent work. Friedman believed that the champions of the medium-of-exchange concept were wrong on several dimensions: they neglected services provided by money balances other than the facilitation of current-period transactions; they overstated the degree of difficulty faced in practice by deposit holders in moving between M1 and the non-M1 funds included in M2; and they neglected ambiguity in the "medium of exchange" concept.[71]

Furthermore, as discussed in chapter 14, Friedman's criteria for defining money hardened over time. The emergence of large wholesale deposit liabilities by banks persuaded him that a currency-plus-retail-deposits aggregate that excluded these items was more appropriate, and more justifiable in terms of a theory of money demand based on household optimization.[72]

MONEY AS A SUMMARY OF MONETARY POLICY

As has already been indicated, Friedman's multiple-yield view of monetary policy transmission coexisted with his interest in the money stock. He noted this himself when, in 1967, he observed: "The fact that monetary policy may be regarded as exerting its influence through interest rates does not contradict my view that what is happening to the size of one or another monetary total is a more useful and meaningful criterion for monetary policy than interest rates are."[73]

One way of characterizing Friedman's position is by stating that, although it is interest rates and not money that appear in the IS equation, the money stock provides a convenient summary, or sufficient statistic, concerning these yields.[74] For the analysis of monetary growth and inflation, the growth of nominal money (perhaps expressed in per-unit-of-output terms) would likely be the relevant measure. For analysis of output fluctuations, however, the real money stock might be the appropriate money measure, provided that it is kept in mind that the central bank's influence over the real money stock is short-term in nature. For example, Meltzer (2001b) focused on the indicator properties of real money, and, as noted in chapter 2, Friedman also occasionally used real instead of nominal money in his analysis of cycles.

There are several interrelated reasons why the real money stock or its growth rate might give signals about monetary conditions and economic prospects not contained in the current short-term interest rate on riskless assets.[75] (1) Insofar as money demand depends on real permanent income, money balances can be informative about the (expected) future behavior of real income. (2) For given short-term interest rates, high real money balances might exert downward short-term pressure on other interest rates in the economy, via a portfolio-balance channel.[76] (3) The demand for money might depend negatively on expected future (nominal) short-term interest rates as well as current rates, and these interest rates might (in real terms) matter for current and future income. The strong short-term positive correlation between real and nominal yields would then confer on money a role as an indicator of the path of income. (4) Insofar as money demand depends negatively on a multiplicity of nominal yields, whose corresponding real yields appear negatively in the IS equation, money balances or monetary growth might index the variation in these yields.

All four of the above features can be regarded as present in Friedman's framework, as well as in other monetarist analysis such as that of Brunner and Meltzer (1973). The framework in this chapter, by allowing for portfolio-balance effects and for forward-looking terms in the money-demand function, has provided a basis for the first three features. As already noted, the fourth feature is more difficult to rationalize in optimizing models.

II. Securities Markets

In this section, two key aspects of Friedman's characterization of the behavior of rates on fixed-interest securities are discussed: those involving the liquidity effect and the Fisher effect. As Friedman's views on the determination of the term structure of interest rates have already been covered extensively in this and the preceding chapter, no separate subsection is devoted to this topic.

THE LIQUIDITY EFFECT

Friedman used the term "liquidity effect" to describe the downward pressure on short-term nominal interest rates induced by an increase in the nominal money stock.[77] His expositions, largely given in the 1960s, gave rise to a moderately sized literature in the 1960s and 1970s and then to a vast literature—one that mostly lies beyond the scope of this book—in the late 1980s and throughout the 1990s.[78] Friedman employed the term to cover pressure that arose both from open-market purchases and from other monetary injections, and he even used the term "first-round loanable funds effect" to distinguish the class of liquidity effect associated with open market operations.[79] However, the modern literature has largely taken the liquidity effect as pertaining to the open-market-operation case.[80]

The 1990s witnessed an explosion of research that emphasized that central banks in practice centered their decisions on the values of short-term interest rates, and not on reserves totals or monetary aggregates. In light of this fact, it may seem surprising that the liquidity-effect concept, which is closely tied to the notion that interest rates react to central-bank actions on monetary totals, received such attention in the same decade. However, in the context of an interest-rate-based operating procedure, one can regard the liquidity effect as describing the monetary-growth pattern that is consistent with securing a decline in the nominal interest rate in the short run (see, for example, Bernanke and Mihov 1998).[81] Therefore, the reality that central banks use a short-term interest-rate instrument does not invalidate the concept of the liquidity effect.[82]

The fact that Friedman's name became nearly synonymous with the liquidity effect is ironic for two reasons. First, in concerning himself with the liquidity effect, he was primarily aiming to describe how Keynes and his successors viewed the determination of securities-market interest rates.[83] Friedman regarded the Keynesian analysis as contending that central-bank influence over the nominal money stock translated reliably into the ability of the authorities to manipulate the real money stock. Control over the latter quantity did, he granted, imbue central banks with the ability to lower interest rates (both nominal and real) through monetary injections. But Friedman's own assessment was that the central bank's control over the real money stock wore off beyond the short run. Price adjustment, in his view, meant that the nominal money stock and the real money stock would depend on different forces over longer periods.[84] This separation of the real money stock from the nominal money stock at low frequencies provided the basis for Friedman's statement that the central bank "can only control interest rates in the very short run" (Instructional Dynamics Economics Cassette Tape 190, May 1976, part 1).[85] All that said, Friedman did accept that the liquidity effect was indeed a key part of the short-run nominal-money/nominal-interest-rate relationship.[86]

The second reason for viewing the association of Friedman with the liquidity effect as ironic is that even though his own work highlighted the relationship, he asked policy makers to put it to one side when making policy. They should "forget about interest rates," he argued (Instructional Dynamics Economics Cassette Tape 190, May 1976, part 1); in so doing, policy makers would act more in accord with Friedman's position that "monetary policy is not about interest rates; monetary policy is about the rate of growth of the quantity of money" (*Meet the Press*, NBC, October 24, 1976, p. 7 of transcript). Part of his basis for holding this position was that even in short periods, the liquidity-effect relationship might well be swamped by other factors—including what Friedman (but few others) called the "intermediate income effect," under which expectations of future income flows put upward pressure on interest rates at much the same time as when higher real money put downward pressure.[87] It was "contrary to what passes for conventional wisdom, but very much in line with a more sophisticated view," Friedman said, that nominal interest rates and nominal money might move in the same, not different, directions (*Newsweek*, August 23, 1982).

Friedman's analysis went beyond this when he considered the case of monetary injections that heralded a permanent shift upward in the rate of monetary growth. In these cases, there existed strong grounds for believing that the relationship between monetary growth and nominal interest rates would be *positive*, especially over medium to long horizons. These grounds came not from the intermediate income effect, but from the Fisher relationship between interest rates and inflation.

THE FISHER EFFECT

In 1972, Friedman had occasion to note that "Fisher's distinction between nominal and real interest rates, which dates back to some of his earliest writing, remains a seminal and penetrating insight."[88] This observation reflected the importance of the Fisher effect in Friedman's monetary framework. It also attested to the extensive familiarity that Friedman had, over the previous four decades, acquired with Irving Fisher's writings.

Fisher's writings played an important role in Friedman's education. Work of Fisher's was included in the assigned readings in the University of Chicago's fall quarter 1932 graduate course on money taught by Lloyd Mints, which Friedman took.[89] In 1972, Friedman wrote in correspondence that Mints's course had "paid a great deal of attention to Irving Fisher's work" and that Friedman's student years at the University of Chicago in the 1930s had left him "with a definite opinion that Fisher was one of the great men of the time and one of the great contributors to monetary analysis."[90] In the immediate aftermath of those years, Fisher's work was mentioned in both of the chapters of Henry Schultz's *The Theory and Measurement of Demand* for which Friedman was a credited coauthor—the specific item they discussed being Fisher's (1892) "Mathematical Investigations in the Theory of Value and Prices."[91]

That 1892 Fisher study, which was his doctoral dissertation, was described by Friedman and Schultz as one that aimed at a "general theory of the pricing process" (H. Schultz 1938, 607). In practice, however, Friedman and Schultz drew on Irving Fisher (1892) primarily for its insights concerning microeconomics. The monetary economics of Fisher that Friedman had absorbed as a student would, nevertheless, show up soon enough in Friedman's approach to issues—including in his negative reaction during World War II to the US Treasury's issuance of savings bonds at coupon rates that were manifestly below the prospective inflation rate.[92]

Irving Fisher's work also featured prominently in Friedman's teachings at the University of Chicago from the mid-1940s to the mid-1970s.[93] Marc Nerlove, a student in Friedman's undergraduate class on money in the late 1940s, had this reply to the question of whether Fisher figured in the teaching of the course: "Very much so. Fisher was very important in that course" (Marc Nerlove, interview, September 18, 2013). David Meiselman, a graduate student at the University of Chicago sporadically from the late 1940s to the early 1960s, and a coauthor of Friedman's, observed: "Milton had a very high regard for Irving Fisher" (David Meiselman, interview, July 16, 2014). In 1985, in describing his own monetary framework, Friedman declared himself to be "much closer in detail" to Fisher than to other monetary economists of Fisher's era, including those who had been located at Cambridge University.[94]

The connections between Friedman's framework and Irving Fisher's body of writings were indeed close. And they were substantially greater, and felt earlier in Friedman's writings, than both Laidler (2013a) and Bordo and Rockoff (2011, 2013b) suggest. In particular, although Bordo and Rockoff (2011, 2013b) illustrate several aspects of the influence of Fisher on Friedman's work, even their discussion constitutes a major understatement of the degree to which Friedman's writings and public statements were linked to Fisher's contributions. This point is brought out by the fact that Bordo and Rockoff's (2011, table 1) list "Milton Friedman's References to the Works of Irving Fisher" is not the exhaustive catalogue that it was intended to be. On the basis of their examination of books and articles by Friedman, Bordo and Rockoff give Friedman's mentions of Fisher in print as spanning from 1943 to 1991. But a more intensive examination of Friedman's books implies that this span of years can be validly expanded to the period from 1938 to 1998.[95] As for articles, Bordo and Rockoff's list is also incomplete, and among its omissions is the one instance in which Fisher's name appeared in the title of a Friedman paper.[96] And Bordo and Rockoff do not consider interviews and commentaries given by Friedman. Partly as a consequence, they give Friedman as not naming Fisher as the greatest-ever American economist until the 1990s, when in fact Friedman made this observation on the record as far back as the 1960s.[97]

Friedman could not claim any patent on the observation that Fisher was the greatest American economist. Paul Samuelson and James Tobin were among others who shared that view.[98] In addition, both Samuelson and Tobin were contributors to a 1967 volume, *Ten Economic Studies in the Tradition of Irving Fisher*, in which Friedman had no involvement.[99] Nor could Friedman's background give him any particular claim to have had the torch passed to him from Fisher. He never met Fisher, who died in 1947. Yale University's James Tobin could, unlike Friedman, claim a shared institutional background with Fisher, and in 1987 it was Tobin, not Friedman, who authored the *New Palgrave* economics dictionary entry on Fisher.[100]

Nevertheless, Friedman very much regarded Fisher as someone in whose tradition he was working, and with whom he had an affinity. In the early 1950s, at a time when Fisher's reputation in the economics profession was still early in its recovery phase, Friedman named Fisher as among those who had shaped the quantity theory of money and implied that this theory remained applicable.[101] Furthermore, Friedman felt sufficiently steeped in Fisher's work that he adopted the habit of describing what Fisher had been thinking when writing on a subject.[102] And when answering a question, Friedman was liable to state, also, how *Fisher* would have answered the question. Thus, to a question posed by the present author, Friedman gave a qualified answer to a question in place of responding "Yes" or "No," but then added: "Of course, Irving Fisher would have said 'Yes' right away" (Milton Friedman, interview, January 22, 1992).[103]

Among the features of Fisher's work that Friedman embraced and developed were those pertaining to the quantity theory of money and to the Phillips curve. But, in addition, and as already indicated, the appeal to the Fisher relationship regarding interest rates was a fundamental part of Friedman's monetarist framework. The Fisher relationship had two key implications. First, the private sector's spending decisions depended on real interest rates, not nominal interest rates.[104] Second, the process by which financial markets priced interest-bearing nominal securities would see an expected-inflation term embedded into nominal interest rates. Higher expected inflation would therefore lead to upward pressure on nominal interest rates, which the monetary authorities were unlikely to be able to offset except in the short run.

The Fisher effect was a phenomenon that Friedman invoked as empirically relevant very early in his monetarist period. In a 1951 radio appearance, Friedman stated that prospective bond purchasers would not buy securities issued by the US Treasury if they faced the likelihood that the bonds would be redeemed in dollars that had less purchasing power than the original investment. It was, Friedman said, therefore "extremely short-sighted" for the US authorities to hold down bond rates, as the inflation resulting from such a policy would lead the general public to require higher interest rates on Treasury securities in the future.[105] In 1956, the Fisher relation featured in Friedman's restatement of the quantity theory of money, as he showed how expected-inflation terms could be used to decompose the nominal return on securities.[106] In 1958, in a written submission to Congress, Friedman noted that, once inflation came to be expected, "interest rates will rise to allow for the price rise."[107] In congressional testimony in May 1959, Friedman voiced the judgment that the Fisher effect had been in operation in the United States in recent times: "Expectations of inflation have become more and more widespread and, partly for that reason, interest rates have risen."[108]

These references to the Fisher effect marked Friedman out from many contemporaneous commentators during the 1950s. Temin (1976, 163) contended: "Economists routinely make the distinction between nominal and real interest rates, but it is hard to find even a mention of this distinction outside the professional literature." Temin's statement was ten years out of date when he made it in 1976. Discussions of the real/nominal interest rate distinction had been pervasive in the financial press in the United States starting in the mid-1960s and in the United Kingdom starting a little later.[109] But his statement was accurate enough with respect to much of the economic discourse in the United States and other major countries in the 1951–64 period.

To be sure, there was some discussion of the Fisher relationship over this period. And, as it happened, *policy officials* in the initial years following the Federal Reserve/Treasury Accord *did* pay a certain amount of attention to the Fisher distinction between real and nominal interest rates. For example, William McChesney Martin, the chairman of the Federal Reserve Board, and other Federal Reserve officials recognized the distinction (see E. Nelson 2012b, 248–49), while in 1957 the Bank for International Settlements carried out an analysis of international behavior of real interest rates (*Financial Times*, June 6, 1957). International evidence was indeed highly germane, for the Fisher effect could, to some extent, be discerned from the data during the 1950s by comparing the experience across industrial countries, with the *First National City Bank of New York Monthly Economic Newsletter* (October 1956) noting (p. 114): "Rates are highest where inflation has been worst." The December 1956 issue of the newsletter presented a sixteen-country comparison that suggested a connection between inflation and interest rates (p. 143), while the April 1957 issue observed (p. 45): "More and more people the world over measure interest rates against experienced annual increases in the cost of living."

Alongside the First National City Bank of New York, some other participants in US financial markets, such as Alan Greenspan (1959), also emphasized the Fisher relationship. But, broadly speaking, Temin's generalization that the Fisher relationship was not widely discussed holds true for the United States in the 1950s through the mid-1960s. In fact, a notable share of the discussions of the Fisher effect that were published in the first half of the 1960s comprised either research done at the University of Chicago, or work by authors who had a connection to Friedman. The latter group of papers included Burns (1960, 18), as well as Axilrod and Young (1962, 1117) and Wallich and Axilrod (1964, 127)—Stephen Axilrod being, as noted in chapter 5, a former student of Friedman's.

This period of scarce references on the part of most economists and economic commentators to the Fisher effect was the calm before the storm, and Benjamin Friedman (1988, 444) has referred to "the enormous attention subsequently devoted to the distinction between nominal and real interest rates." The nominal/real interest-rate distinction has become second nature in both macroeconomic models and policy discussions. In light of that, it may seem peculiar to attribute recognition of its importance to only one side of the earlier Keynesian-monetarist debates. But such an attribution would indeed be appropriate—especially in view of the fact that even Keynesians who gave a strong weight to monetary policy, like James Tobin, played down the importance of the nominal/real-interest rate distinction in the discussions they provided during the 1960s and 1970s of US economic developments.[110]

Accordingly, an emphasis on the nominal/real interest-rate distinction has been put forward as a feature that distinguished monetarism from the Keynesianism of the time, both in contemporary accounts such as those of Harry Johnson (*Economist*, October 23, 1976b) and Makinen (1977, 377–78) and in retrospectives such as McCallum (2008), E. Nelson and Schwartz (2008a, 844–45), and Woodford (2008, 1563). It was also recognized by policy makers during the 1970s as a contribution of monetarism. For example, during his tenure as president of the Federal Reserve Bank of New York, Paul Volcker observed that "monetarism has also helped clear up a good deal of confusion" by creating a greater awareness of "the difference between rates of interest as observed in the marketplace and the 'real' rate of interest. . . . We have learned that lenders and borrowers have come to anticipate inflation and that they are sensitive to policies they interpret as contributing to inflation."[111]

One of the most clear-cut acknowledgments of the Fisher effect as part of the monetarist counterrevolution was that of Dornbusch and Fischer (1979, 5): "The recognition of a relationship between interest rates and inflation is quite new for the U.S. economy. Only toward the end of the 1960's, as the inflation rate increased, did monetarists draw public attention to the distinction between nominal and real interest rates, and argue that increased inflation would raise the nominal interest rate." Although the documentation of Friedman's statements given above does not support Dornbusch and Fischer's notion that he (or other monetarists) drew attention to the Fisher effect *only* starting in the 1960s, it is true that the references to the Fisher effect in Friedman's work did proliferate starting in 1965.[112] And these discussions triggered wider attention to the phenomenon, with Sargent (1973a, 429) observing: "The interaction of expected inflation and nominal rates of interest is a topic that has received its share of attention since Milton Friedman gave Irving Fisher's theory a prominent role in his presidential address to the American Economic Association in 1967."[113]

A key reason why the period starting in the mid-1960s saw more frequent references by Friedman to the Fisher effect, and strong attention by economists and the general public to those references, was that the Fisher effect was making itself felt in US interest-rate behavior. In contrast to his position in the 1950s that the Fisher effect was already visible in the US data, Friedman would later conclude that—at least in the case of short-term US interest rates—the Fisher relation became clear from the mid-1960s onward. He would adopt an interpretation in which the post-1960 US monetary regime was associated with a time-series process for inflation that promoted higher and more persistent inflation rates—a state of affairs that in turn made the link between nominal interest rates and inflation more obvious in the data.[114] In linking the behavior of inflation expectations closely to the policy regime, Friedman's interpretation contrasted with Fisher's own empirical work, in which adjustment of interest rates to the patterns in inflation was very slow and spread over decades. Thus, even though Friedman's name was associated with adaptive expectations (thanks to his deployment of it in some of his empirical work), he did not deny that expectations were in practice regime dependent and were capable of adjusting rapidly. Indeed, he made these points even before the rational-expectations revolution put them on a formal basis.[115]

Until the early 1970s, however, Friedman gave serious weight to the possibility that the US price level in the postwar period was trend stationary. Partly because of this, and notwithstanding his long-standing emphasis on the Fisher effect, in 1969 Friedman expressed surprise at the extent to which the behavior of nominal interest rates had reflected that of actual recent inflation (Instructional Dynamics Economics Cassette Tape 31, July 24, 1969). The following year, however, he contemplated the possibility that a new monetary regime, associated with secular inflation, had started around 1960 and that the behavior of US nominal interest rates reflected that situation.[116]

In sum, Friedman's position that expected inflation was embedded in nominal interest rates was of long standing, but it took him time—perhaps less than it did US financial markets—to perceive the basic character of the post-Accord monetary regime, as well as the scale of the shift in the US monetary policy regime that had taken place between the 1950s and the 1960s.[117] This delayed realization meant that the magnitude of the implications of the new monetary regime for the behavior of expected inflation was not brought home to Friedman until the 1970s.

The most fundamental point, however, is that Friedman's framework allowed for a nominal/real interest-rate distinction, with real rates mattering for the private sector's spending decisions and the expected-inflation component of the nominal interest rate an endogenous series that did not depend mechanically on the past behavior of inflation.

Friedman's Aggregate-Supply Framework

I. The Development of Friedman's Thinking on Inflation, 1941–51

In the early 1960s, during a visit to the United Kingdom, Friedman was wandering through the offices of the London School of Economics in search of a University of Chicago graduate, Ezra Mishan, who was among the LSE's economists. Upon reaching Mishan's office, however, Friedman found that Mishan was on leave and that another LSE economist, Max Steuer, was using the office in Mishan's absence. Friedman asked Steuer what he was working on. Steuer replied that he was writing a paper with an LSE colleague, Richard Lipsey, on the Phillips curve. Friedman's reply stunned Steuer: "What's a Phillips curve?"

But once Steuer had relayed to Friedman what was meant by the phrase, it became clear to Steuer that, notwithstanding Friedman's unfamiliarity with the specific "Phillips curve" terminology, he had thought deeply about the Phillips-curve regularity and its implications. Friedman turned to the blackboard in the office and elaborated on his views regarding the unemployment/inflation relationship (Max Steuer, personal communication, October 15, 2015).

This meeting was one of a number of occasions during his LSE visit on which Friedman provided an exposition of elements of what later became known as the natural-rate hypothesis. He would, of course, articulate this hypothesis more definitively and in print later in the 1960s—most notably in the published version of his presidential address to the American Economic Association.[1]

The aforementioned LSE discussions were among many foreshadowings of his theory of the Phillips curve that Friedman gave over the course

The views expressed in this study are those of the author alone and should not be interpreted as those of the Federal Reserve Board or the Federal Reserve System. The author is grateful to David Laidler for comments on an earlier draft of this chapter. See the introduction for a full list of acknowledgments for this book.

of the 1950s and during the first half of the 1960s. Several of these fore-shadowings were made on the record and are described in this chapter, as well as in E. Nelson (2009a, 478–79) and chapter 10 below. That Fried-man was conscious of the fact that his presidential address of 1967 did not amount to his staking out of an altogether new position, but instead con-stituted an elaboration (and presentation in consolidated form) of views he had held over his whole monetarist period, was evident in a remark he made a year or so after the presidential address. This remark consisted of his observation—given in an introduction to a selection of his writings since 1951—that the papers (which included his presidential address) "embody a single view of monetary theory."[2]

The manner in which Friedman arrived at the view of the determination of the inflation process that he would hold during his monetarist period is best understood as taking place in three stages. The movement from the first stage to the second stage, and then from the second stage to the third stage, occurred from the early 1940s to the early 1950s. That evolution is described in this section. Then section II considers Friedman's views con-cerning the precise sources of nominal rigidity in the US economy. Section III discusses further the matter of the interaction between real and nomi-nal variables in Friedman's framework, while section IV turns to some im-plications of the notion that inflation is a monetary phenomenon. Finally, section V deals with the concepts of the natural rate of unemployment and the natural level of output.

The first principal phase of Friedman's thinking about the connection between inflation and excess demand (and excess supply) is contained in his writings and statements from 1941 through 1947. As was discussed in chapter 3, his analysis during this period owed much to Keynes's (1940) analysis of the inflationary gap, in which increases in nominal spending tend to be associated with commensurate increases in real spending, until output reaches a maximum value that also corresponds to full-employment or potential output.

Even during this phase, however, Friedman's analysis of inflation in-cluded some features that represented a departure from the standard Keynesian position of the time.[3] These features went in the direction of specifying inflation as a function of excess demand (that is, of output in relation to potential: in percentage terms, the output gap) even before the point at which full employment was reached. In the baseline Keynesian analysis of the 1940s, the link between inflation and real variables in below-full-employment conditions was confined to a dependence of inflation on the *change* in the output gap or in the unemployment gap (see, for example, Phelps 1968b, 679). In contrast, with regard to nominal and real variables' interaction before full employment was reached, Friedman's position during this era was closer to the permanently nonvertical Phillips curve that would later predominate in the research literature. For Friedman in the 1940s had a framework in which the levels of inflation and the deviation of output from potential tended to be positively related.[4]

In his expositions during this first phase, Friedman tended to emphasize the notion that higher inflation would induce a larger response of quantities supplied: that is, as inflation rose, one could expect output to get closer to potential output. For example, in 1941 he and his Treasury colleagues referred to the fact that prices and output had risen together and stated that this "suggests though it by no means proves that the price rises may have been responsible for part of the increase in physical output."[5] Friedman's stress on a connection between inflation and equilibrium quantities supplied to the market would continue in his discussions in later years of the inflation process, and it would be reflected in the expectational Phillips curve that he espoused in the third and final phase of his thinking—that of his monetarist period.[6] In this final phase, the supply response would be offered in conjunction with the existence of the demand-pressure-generated response of inflation to the output gap as the reasons for the connection between inflation and the gap.[7] In addition, Friedman would become more insistent and explicit in this final phase that it was the unexpected component of inflation, and not inflation per se, that should be expected to be related to the output gap.

In Friedman's first phase of thinking about inflation, the connection between inflation and real output was regarded as ceasing once output reached its potential value. In common with the mainstream Keynesian thought of the time, Friedman in this era viewed potential output as synonymous with the maximum feasible level of output. That being so, increases in nominal aggregate demand would, once the economy reached full employment, translate into equal increases in the price level, with no accompanying response of output or employment. A late occasion on which Friedman voiced this view of the world was in December 1947, when he stated: "We have gotten what good we could get out of inflation already."[8]

By this date, however, Friedman was already starting to incorporate into his analysis of real/nominal interaction a modification of Keynesian economics that became widely accepted by UK and US economists from early in the postwar period (see, for example, Pigou 1950, 6). This was the notion that periods of excessive demand can be associated both with inflation and with above-normal output. That is, potential output was now seen as distinct from maximum feasible output, and a buoyant economy was viewed as associated with a situation in which actual output exceeded potential output by a sizable percentage and on a prolonged basis. An early instance, noted previously, in which Friedman recognized this point consisted of his reference in 1948 to "overemployment."[9]

Friedman thus entered the second phase of his thinking about inflation—a phase lasting roughly from 1948 to 1950-51. His acceptance over this period of both the notion that output could overshoot potential and that inflation was continuously related (for given potential output) to output meant that this period corresponded with that of Friedman's greatest degree of adherence to the notion of a downward-sloping, permanently nonvertical Phillips curve.[10] However, his advocacy of this view over this period was not always apparent, for in public statements during 1950 and into early 1951 Friedman gave the impression (once again) that potential output was the same as maximum output.[11] This inconsistency may reflect the fact stressed in previous chapters that the period from 1948 to 1951 was one of a profound shake-up of Friedman's views. What is clear is that he emerged from the shake-up with a reaffirmation that there was a ceiling or maximum level of output.[12] But he was explicit that this maximum feasible level of output was distinct from, and likely well above, potential output.[13]

As already indicated, this post-shake-up period in Friedman's thinking corresponded to the third and final phase of Friedman's outlook on inflation: that associated with his monetarist period. An important additional element in his thinking about inflation in this conclusive phase was the position that ultimately households and firms will bargain in real terms. In such circumstances, it is not appropriate to regard output (or unemployment) and inflation (or nominal wage growth) as enjoying a structural, bivariate link over long periods. Conditional on expected inflation, the two series could still be regarded as linked. But the addition of expected inflation—with unitary coefficient—made an enormous difference to the specification of the behavior of inflation. For now there was *no* long-run relationship between the levels of real output (or the output gap) and inflation (nor between the unemployment gap and inflation or nominal wage growth). Friedman's discomfort with the notion of a long-run connection between the inflation rate and real gaps was manifested in a remark he made to Paul Samuelson when both participated in the May 1950 conference on the impact of labor unions: "I don't know what you mean by saying unemployment will police inflation."[14] In congressional testimony in 1952, Friedman added: "Rather than regarding the objectives of high employment and of price stability as inconsistent, I think that fundamentally price stability will promote a high level of output by avoiding a good many of the interruptions to output that we have had in the past, by giving people stable expectations, and so on."[15]

The rest of the 1950s would see no detailed explanation of this point appear in Friedman's writings. This absence, together with the fact that even the version of the theory presented in Friedman's presidential address underwent revision in the months ahead of its delivery, bears testimony to the likelihood that, through the end of 1967, Friedman was still refining and tightening his basic argument that the long-run Phillips curve should be vertical. But the fundamental elements of this reasoning were present in his pre-1967 statements—including the early-1950s items just noted and several more that are discussed in later chapters. It was in this context that Friedman wrote in a 1966 memorandum to the Federal Reserve Board: "In my opinion, there is no perpetual tradeoff between inflation and unemployment."[16]

Another area in which Friedman's treatment of inflation in his monetarist phase differed from that in his prior two phases was that of his position on cost-push inflationary pressure. He had formerly subscribed to the position—embedded in the writings of Keynes, but also endorsed by Lloyd Mints in some of his later work—that there existed upward pressure on costs and prices, arising from the market power of firms and workers, that was separate from whatever pressure (up or down) that was coming from the state of demand. By 1951, he had abandoned this cost-push view in favor of the position that cost-push pressures might exert transitory effects on inflation but could not do so, on net, over longer periods, by themselves. That is, cost-push shocks had a zero mean.[17] Cost-push pressures could trigger inflation on an ongoing basis (for given potential output) only if policy makers accommodated positive cost-push shocks. Friedman's rejection of cost-push views of inflation, once he became a monetarist, has already been discussed in chapter 4 and will be considered further in chapters 10 and 15 below. It is therefore touched on only sparingly in this chapter.[18] Friedman's opposition to cost-push theories should nevertheless be kept in mind as a crucial part of Friedman's outlook toward the determination of inflation.

II. Sources of Nominal Rigidity

A regularity in the US data to which Friedman repeatedly drew attention was that—at the business cycle frequency—the nominal and real values of aggregate national income typically moved in the same direction.[19] Evidently, prices did not behave in a manner that allowed for the complete separation at the business cycle frequency of the determination of nominal and real variables. In particular, in Friedman's monetarist analysis, as in Keynesian analysis, output was in large part determined by aggregate demand in the short run, in the sense that changes in nominal aggregate demand were likely to give rise to output responses in the same direction.[20]

However, another cyclical regularity cited by Friedman was that, over the business cycle, the aggregate price level moved in the same direction as output.[21] Friedman's detailed study during the 1970s of behavior in monthly and quarterly data would lead him to add the qualification that there was a distinct lag of prices behind output. But the result that price changes and output were positively correlated in most business cycles remained.[22]

The fact that inflation exhibited a relationship with real economic activity contradicted the early Keynesian models in which, below full employment, the nominal price level was constant or its movements reflected only cost-push factors. As we have seen, Friedman himself moved away at an early stage from the *L*-shaped aggregate-supply curve of early Keynesian economics. Consistent with this posture and with his view of the data, Friedman called for the assumption of total price rigidity to be replaced by specifications in which some of the cyclical change in nominal spending was absorbed by price change.[23] Correspondingly, although he would emerge as a very prominent critic of the Phillips curve as specified by the Keynesian literature in the 1950s and 1960s, Friedman recognized that that literature had advanced on early Keynesian modeling by allowing for a short-run response of prices to economic conditions.[24]

A nonzero response of prices and inflation to economic conditions was not, however, the same thing as the absence of any nominal price rigidity. Although Friedman testified in 1952 that "I believe that prices are flexible," he was here referring to his belief that the price level was endogenous rather than endorsing the position that all prices were perfectly flexible.[25] This distinction was later highlighted when Friedman and Schwartz stated that they "regarded prices as flexible, though not 'perfectly' flexible."[26] They went on to remark that "prices tend to move rather sluggishly."[27] Indeed, it was because Friedman believed that the short run consisted of an intermediate case between no price-level adjustment and the full price flexibility observed in the long run that, at roughly the same point in the 1950s at which he articulated his belief that prices were flexible, he also said that prices were inflexible.[28] In 1966, Friedman spelled out the reconciliation between the two descriptions of price adjustment when he observed: "Price inflexibility need not mean complete rigidity, but rather slow adjustment."[29]

It was, in fact, evident from the point in the late 1940s when Friedman began writing regularly on monetary matters that the existence of nominal price rigidity—rigidity that mattered significantly for the course of cyclical fluctuations and for the construction of appropriate stabilization policy—figured heavily in his thinking about the economy. His 1948 paper proposing the monetization rule had stated: "Our economy is characterized . . . by price rigidities."[30] The premise of nominal price stickiness figured crucially in the argument Friedman advanced in his celebrated paper "The Case for Flexible Exchange Rates" (published in 1953, but initially drafted three years earlier). In this paper, nominal exchange-rate adjustment was advocated as a mechanism of balance-of-payments adjustment—a mechanism that, Friedman argued, was speedier, and less likely to be associated with costly output fluctuations, than the alternative of aggregate price-level adjustment. Although Krugman (1990, 164) claimed without justification that Friedman's 1953 paper was based on the assumption of a high degree of price-level flexibility, the overwhelming majority of commentators, including McCallum (1989b, 294–95) and Dornbusch and Giovanni (1990, 1272), have treated Friedman's case for floating exchange rates as resting on the existence of a large amount of short-run price stickiness. This interpretation is supported by Friedman's own words in the article: "At least in the modern world, internal prices are highly inflexible. They are more flexible upward than downward, but even on the upswing all prices are not equally flexible."[31]

It was, in fact, historical experience with regimes that blocked exchange-rate flexibility that helped impress on Friedman the importance, for the analysis of output behavior, of nominal rigidities. He and Schwartz would cite the United Kingdom's experience in the 1925–31 period, when an extremely tight monetary policy was used to enforce the fixed external value of the pound sterling, as providing a case in which nominal rigidities "prevented the deflationary pressure from reducing internal prices sufficiently, producing instead generally depressed conditions."[32] Friedman warned that a similar outcome would be the result observed in the short run if the United States were to pursue policies that sought to deflate the price level: "It would be difficult or impossible to force down prices appreciably without producing a recession and considerable unemployment."[33] The existence of some nominal rigidity struck Friedman as a phenomenon that recurred across countries and over time—a situation that would lead him and his wife to state that they knew of no instance in history in which inflation had been eliminated without interim costs in lost output and employment.[34] But in the United States in the postwar period, it seemed to Friedman that nominal stickiness was of greater importance than in prior eras: "there is no doubt that there have been greater rigidities in wages and prices" in recent decades than earlier, he noted in 1971.[35]

Note that, in the statement just quoted, Friedman cited *both* wage and price rigidity. The same is true of many other statements that he made. This raises the issue of the relative importance that Friedman attached to each of these two types of nominal rigidity for the analysis of postwar US economic behavior. It is to this issue that the discussion now turns.[36]

WAGE STICKINESS VERSUS PRICE STICKINESS

Friedman often referred to wage and price stickiness as operating in tandem; alternatively, he wrote as though postulating nominal wage stickiness had the effect of conferring stickiness on prices as well.[37] Nor did he devote great attention to the issue of whether the outstanding nominal rigidity in the US economy was wage stickiness or, instead, price stickiness.

This lack of great interest in the wage/price nexus was reflected in Friedman's generally conciliatory statements about Keynesians' treatment of markup behavior. He had sharp differences with Keynesians on the issue of what factors determined nominal wage growth, but he regarded these differences as largely the same as those on the issue of what factors drove price inflation. He did not see views on how wages behaved in relation to prices (or nominal wage growth in relation to inflation) as a principal area of combat between himself and Keynesians.[38] When he delivered his Nobel address on the Phillips curve, he indicated that he would be following convention in assuming a "roughly constant markup factor" in much of his analysis, and so would be taking propositions about the nominal wage growth/unemployment relationship to be propositions about the inflation/unemployment relationship.[39] Likewise, when writing about the *General Theory*'s analysis, Friedman stated that while he disagreed with the postulate that nominal wages and prices could be taken as totally rigid, he accepted that one of the suggestions Keynes had made in justifying that postulate—that is, Keynes's suggestion that prices and wages, when they do move, move by commensurate amounts—was "not a bad empirical approximation."[40] Although Friedman recognized that some of Keynes's discussion contemplated variations of prices in relation to costs, he did not consider such variations to be crucial to Keynes's *General Theory* analysis.[41]

There is, however, one important respect in which Friedman's theory of real/nominal interaction imposed a specific restriction on how nominal wages behaved in relation to the price level. Friedman's theory of the Phillips curve was one in which nominal wages are predetermined and prices are not. In Friedman's presidential address to the American Economic Association, the idea was advanced that in an inflationary period prices temporarily rise in relation to nominal wages; and the associated decline in the real wage was offered as a reason why firms increase their hiring in the early stages of inflation.[42] The behavior of the real wage was therefore an element of Friedman's explanation for the short-run positive relationship between inflation and the output gap. The proposition that wages tend to lag prices was one that Friedman reaffirmed in the years after his presidential address.[43] This proposition was likely one that Friedman had instilled in him by his teachers. For University of Chicago figures such as

Jacob Viner and Lloyd Mints were exponents of the notion that costs lag prices (Patinkin 1969, 57; Tavlas 1977a, 54). Friedman would also quote Irving Fisher as a source on this matter.[44]

Friedman suggested that there existed elements of wage rigidity other than wages being set a period in advance. For example, in 1962 he named the existence of "long-range wage contracts" as one reason wages were sticky.[45] It will be argued here, however, that such deeper nominal wage stickiness is not vital to Friedman's theory, and that on the whole he regarded wages as more flexible than prices over periods longer than the very short run.

The key basis for viewing Friedman as regarding wages as fairly flexible over periods longer than a quarter lies in his statements about labor supply. He was a subscriber to the position that a "rise in real wages . . . call[s] forth an increased [labor] supply," not only at low frequencies but on a period-by-period basis.[46] This position was consistent with the notion that nominal wages were predetermined one quarter ahead because he specified that, under the latter conditions, workers supplied labor on the basis of their *expected* real wage.[47] However, Friedman's other discussions of the labor market made it clear that he believed that year-to-year variations in labor-supply decisions likely reflected responses to the *actual* real wage and not merely its expectation. Most notably, his explanation of the boost to labor supply in the United States during the Second World War rested in part on the presence of temporarily higher real wages.[48] A situation in which workers are on their supply curve over a particular horizon has tensions with the notion that nominal wages are set in advance over much of that horizon. For wage-contract models often make the assumption that, once the setting of the nominal wage has been fixed by the contract, workers forfeit the decision concerning the amount of hours of work to supply in any particular period and simply allow the amount supplied to equal the quantity of labor hours demanded by employers.[49]

In Friedman's vision, therefore, nominal wages were predetermined and prices were not; but the business cycle was characterized by a situation in which laborers were on their supply curve. And Friedman regarded prices, while not predetermined, as being sticky. The setup that appears most consistent with all these features is one in which there is considerable flexibility in nominal wages for periods between a quarter and a few years, and in which persistent effects on real variables of monetary actions arise primarily from price stickiness, not wage stickiness. Accordingly, it is the former type of stickiness that will be used here when representing Friedman's Phillips-curve specification. The wage stickiness contemplated will be limited to the one-period-ahead predetermination of nominal wages. It will be assumed that the one-period contract that specifies the value of the nominal wage in period t does so by setting it at what period $(t-1)$ information suggests will be the market-clearing value of the wage in period t. This assumption is in line with Fischer (1977) as well as Friedman's presidential address.

NATURE AND SOURCES OF PRICE STICKINESS

In an unpublished 1966 draft of their sequel to *A Monetary History of the United States*, Friedman and Schwartz observed:

> Prices, wages, etc., are frequently negotiated for some period ahead and not renegotiated continually; they therefore depend not only on current conditions of demand and supply but on the conditions that are anticipated for some years to come; and such prices probably cover the bulk of the income flow. When prices have been rising, and sellers anticipate a further rise, it will take a much more unfavorable temporary situation to produce a price decline than when prices have been falling.[50]

This quotation—which lines up with Friedman's views as revealed in public statements both before and after 1966—brings out several key points.

First, as most prices are sticky, the assumption of price stickiness rather than full price flexibility is the appropriate basis on which to proceed for cyclical analysis and, in particular, for the analysis of US economic behavior at the business cycle frequency.

Second, the setting of goods prices is something that is at least partially the prerogative of sellers. The prices of firms' products are a choice variable rather than being taken parametrically by them as the outcome of market forces in which their own actions matter only trivially. As will become clear below, Friedman did not see this market power on the part of firms as corresponding to complete monopoly power; from consumers' perspective, the goods produced by different firms were partly substitutable for each other. Thus, as has been indicated in chapter 4, although he offered criticisms of the theoretical contribution of the monopolistic-competition literature, Friedman concurred with one basic idea of that literature: that an environment of considerable competition between a large amount of firms need not preclude a situation in which each firm can treat prices as a choice variable.[51] He had already signaled this position in his pre-monetarist period in a reference to the inflationary process as one in which "dealers find that they can raise their selling prices."[52] In the same vein, in 1970 Friedman described the process of the emergence of inflation in the United States as including a step in which "retailers . . . reluctantly raise their prices" (*Newsweek*, September 28, 1970).[53]

Third, neither the presence of price stickiness nor the fact that sellers influenced their products' prices implied that prices did not respond to market conditions. For demand and supply conditions determined the price that sellers charged. Prices were a choice variable for sellers, but prices nevertheless responded to fundamental shocks, because sellers' optimizing behavior would make prices an endogenous function of these shocks and of other elements of the state vector.

Fourth, not only current conditions but expected future demand and supply conditions mattered for today's price-setting decisions. Inflation consequently had a forward-looking element—as discussed further in this and the next section.

Fifth, the fact that aggregate prices responded somewhat to current conditions implied that inflation was not a predetermined variable in the current period. The notion that the aggregate price level was not predetermined formed, as already indicated, a key part of Friedman's theory of the Phillips curve. That theory had prices become elevated in relation to nominal wages in the early stages of a scenario of rising aggregate demand.

With these five points taken into account, let us consider the precise specification of the Phillips curve that might be consistent with Friedman's view of price setting. A useful basis for the discussion is the New Keynesian Phillips curve:

$$\pi_t = \beta E_t \pi_{t+1} + \alpha(y_t - y_t^*) + u_t. \tag{1}$$

In equation (1), π_t is inflation in period t, y_t is log real output in period t, y_t^* is log potential real output in period t, β is at or near unity, α is strictly positive, and u_t is a white-noise, mean-zero "cost-push" shock.

This specification captures many of the features of Friedman's framework: that prices are sticky and set by firms; that price changes, when they occur, are set in a forward-looking manner in response to current and prospective conditions; and (in the Calvo 1983 justification of the New Keynesian Phillips curve) that many prices are predetermined by contracts but some are adjusted in period t, so that aggregate inflation is not predetermined. The fact that β is typically set to somewhat less than 1.0 in empirical and theoretical work on the Phillips curve does differ from Friedman's Phillips-curve restriction of $\beta = 1$. But the theoretical justification for equation (1) suggests that β take a value close to 1.0. On the basis of the similarities between the New Keynesian Phillips curve and Friedman's perspective on the Phillips curve, the former was used in chapter 2 above to represent the monetarist view of inflation.

Two differences between Friedman's perspective on inflation and that implied by the New Keynesian Phillips curve (1) should, however, be noted here. As discussed in E. Nelson (2008a) and in chapter 15 below, there are some indications that, when he contended that the expectation of the future inflation rate mattered for the behavior of current inflation, Friedman regarded the relevant expectation as partly formed in period (t−1) or as formed at a *variety* of vantage points ranging from the current period to various dates in the past. Friedman's many references to the persistence of inflationary expectations, and to the idea that expectations of inflation would endure even once demand restriction has been introduced, are consistent with this perspective.[54]

Thus, it would appear that an accurate representation of Friedman's views would involve including weighted terms in $E_{t-k}\pi_{t+1}$, $E_{t-k+1}\pi_{t+1}$, ..., $E_{t-1}\pi_{t+1}$, and $E_t\pi_{t+1}$ in the Phillips curve. The present exposition of Friedman's views abstracts from this complication. Consequently, the representations in equation form of Friedman's views on inflation used here will limit all expectations of future inflation in the Phillips curve to the single term $E_t\pi_{t+1}$.[55]

The second difference between the Friedman specification and the New Keynesian Phillips curve pertains to the timing associated with the forcing process. Friedman's position that costs are predetermined in period t provides grounds for believing that his views are best represented by a specification in which it is not the actual current output gap that appears in the Phillips curve but, instead, the period (t−1) expectation of the gap.[56] This might be the case if, as in New Keynesian analysis, the output-gap term appears in the Phillips-curve expression because of the relationship between the gap and real marginal cost.[57] Therefore, although there are some specific further modifications considered below, a Phillips curve that captures much of Friedman's views on price setting would be:

$$\pi_t = \beta E_t\pi_{t+1} + \alpha E_{t-1}(y_t - y_t^*) + u_t. \tag{2}$$

Note that this equation, notwithstanding the use of the lagged expectation of the output gap, allows for inflation to respond to period-t news concerning the current and future gap, because such information enters the calculation of $E_t\pi_{t+1}$.

The discussion has so far considered Friedman's belief in price stickiness but has had little to say about the basic factors that lead the economy to feature price stickiness. That is a matter that is considered in the rest of this section.

Stanley Fischer recalled an occasion in the early 1970s on which he and some colleagues attempted to draw Friedman out on the matter of price setting. "I remember once we young guys, which included Buz Brock—you know, W. A. Brock, who was an assistant professor there and is very, very intelligent indeed—we decided we needed to sort of beard the lion in his den and draw on his wisdom—or whatever metaphors you want to use. So I remember we did take him [Friedman] to lunch one day to discuss the microfoundations of the Phillips curve. And I remember Milton saying, 'I really don't see *what* difference it makes who sets prices and so forth. And all this stuff you're busy talking with me about, I'm not sure that it's very important at all.' We were discussing Phelps, and Lucas, and those models. I think he knew there was a [short-run] trade-off, and that was enough for him" (Stanley Fischer, interview, August 30, 2013).

Friedman's remarks surely came as a letdown to his younger colleagues. But those remarks may not have actually reflected of a total lack of interest on his part in the topic of the microfoundations of the Phillips curve. Rather, to some extent Friedman's reaction likely reflected his belief that price stickiness could emerge in a variety of situations and might reflect factors that went beyond either particular institutional rigidities or market power of the seller. A basis for interpreting Friedman's response in this way comes from a number of comments Friedman made on other occasions. One important item among these comments was his observation, "I think prices can be sticky without being administered."[58] In elaborating on this remark, Friedman restated not only his familiar position that price changes were endogenous even when the seller had market power, but also his conviction that deviations from price flexibility might reflect mutual wishes of both customers and retailers. He gave the example of the rental market as an instance in which many buyers and sellers existed, and no agent could defy market forces, yet the equilibrium outcome was a situation of price stickiness, associated with long-term contracts.[59] This outcome, he suggested, reflected a judgment on the part of both buyers and sellers that "the cost of price flexibility is high."[60]

These observations clearly affirmed the prevalence of nominal price contracts, and Friedman would later note: "Many prices are set for a considerable time in advance."[61] But Friedman also regarded nominal stickiness as likely to prevail even in the absence of contracts: "Even when prices and wages are not fixed explicitly, it is often undesirable to change them frequently" (*Newsweek*, November 12, 1979). Retailers, he pointed out, did not engage in one-time transactions with customers but instead sought an ongoing relationship with the customer, and their behavior should be interpreted in that light.[62] This aspect of the retailer/customer relationship would suggest that if consumers disliked price changes, firms might respond by abstaining from frequent price adjustment.

The preceding considerations clearly overlap closely with the rationale that Rotemberg (1982) provided for the existence of price stickiness.[63] Rotemberg's (1982) menu-cost specification happens to imply predictions for aggregate price-level behavior that are largely equivalent to those of the

Calvo (1983) contracts-based specification of price stickiness (see Rotemberg 1987). In particular, each of them implies a New Keynesian Phillips curve like equation (1) above (see J. Roberts 1995).

Although the precise source of price stickiness was not one of Friedman's main concerns, his views on the matter evidently had elements in common with both the Rotemberg and the Calvo visions. Like Rotemberg (1982), he saw price stickiness as emerging in part from the mutual interests, and implicit agreement, of firms and customers; like Calvo (1983) and Taylor (1980), he saw price stickiness as partly taking the form of multiple-period, explicit nominal price contracts.[64]

III. Real and Nominal Interaction: Short Run

"I do not believe there is any way to avoid paying some costs of slowing down inflation." With these words, and similar statements given on other occasions, Friedman categorically associated himself with the idea that substantial interaction of real and nominal variables was a fact of life.[65] He would repeatedly indicate that, in countries like the United States, prices did respond somewhat initially once excess demand or excess supply emerged, but it could be three or five to ten years before the output response to monetary policy actions was essentially gone and those actions were almost fully reflected in prices.[66]

The present section will not consider what precise specification of price adjustment would, in conjunction with other aspects of model specification, deliver these numerical predictions. Instead, it will pursue the less ambitious goal of fleshing out some qualitative aspects of Friedman's views on real/nominal interactions. As a first step, an effort will be made to document further the connection between Friedman's views and the output-gap/inflation relationship associated with the New Keynesian Phillips curve.

FORWARD-LOOKING PRICE SETTING

The notion that the adjustment of inflation to monetary policy was spread over time was not, in Friedman's view, inconsistent with the idea that inflation exhibited a considerable degree of response to current conditions. "Inflation can reverse itself very rapidly," he granted in 1974 (Instructional Dynamics Economics Cassette Tape 156, October 23, 1974), and it has already been indicated that Friedman regarded some components of the goods-price index as jump variables. It was argued above that the presence in the Phillips curve of the period-t expectation of future inflation provides a means of capturing this aspect of Friedman's views.

More direct evidence of Friedman's belief in the existence of forward-looking inflation behavior comes from his numerous statements to the effect that expected future inflation mattered for current inflation outcomes. For example, in 1984 he stated: "Inflation is affected by many other forces, especially the public's perceptions about future inflation" (*New York Times*, April 3, 1984). Along similar lines, in a 1970 television appearance Friedman observed that "one of the problems of bringing inflation under control is to make people recognize that inflation is not the way of the future, to make people realize that it is possible to have a period of relatively stable prices."[67]

Further evidence of Friedman's belief that expected future inflation mattered for current inflation—and that such expectations were not a mechanical function of past data—included his observation in 1976 that inflation could resume prior to the output gap being closed because expectations of future buoyant conditions could boost near-term inflation (Instructional Dynamics Economics Cassette Tape 202, November 1976, part 1, and Tape 203, November 1976, part 2). In 1980, he and Rose Friedman noted the dependence of inflation expectations on signals about future monetary policy.[68] Other links between Friedman's economic framework and the postulate of forward-looking behavior are discussed in chapters 8 and 15 below.

INFLATION INERTIA

Friedman referred repeatedly to inertia in inflation. One formulation that he used on multiple occasions was that inflation had an "inertia of its own" (*Newsweek*, June 3, 1968; *Newsweek*, August 18, 1969). In a similar vein, Friedman once noted: "Inflation has a momentum of its own. It cannot be turned off like a water tap" (*Banker*, January 1967, 69). Indeed, he would go so far as to refer to the "enormous inertia" in price inflation (Instructional Dynamics Economics Cassette Tape 56, August 6, 1970).[69]

No doubt, many of these descriptions were consistent with an environment of essentially fully forward-looking price setting. Some of the descriptions, for example, might be accommodated by the notion that it is the rational expectation of π_{t+1} that matters for inflation but that some of the expectations relevant for price setting were formed at some date in the past.[70] In addition, it is plausible that inertia in inflation can arise in a forward-looking environment from doubts that a disinflationary policy would continue.[71]

But a prominent manner in which inertia in inflation is often captured in the research literature is by including π_{t-1} alongside $E_t \pi_{t+1}$ in the Phillips curve (see, for example, Fuhrer and Moore 1995a). And a few of Friedman's statements seemed most amenable to the notion that lagged inflation did appear in the Phillips curve: for example, his suggestion (*Newsweek*,

November 4, 1974) that commodity price shocks, which had raised actual inflation, had the effect of stimulating inflationary expectations.

A lagged-inflation term in the Phillips curve is sometimes motivated by appeal to adaptive expectations. But, as discussed in chapters 5 and 15 of this book, Friedman's use of the adaptive-expectations assumption was far less dogmatic than is often supposed, and many of his remarks—including those made in the study of inflation behavior—were inconsistent with adaptive expectations.

The presence of a lagged-inflation term in the Phillips curve has been given an alternative justification by Christiano, Eichenbaum, and Evans (2005), who, in a model based on rational expectations and optimizing behavior, postulated the existence of some indexation of nominal price contracts to past inflation. Woodford (2003, 348) and Giannoni and Woodford (2005, 102) have provided a formal derivation of the New Keynesian Phillips curve in the presence of such price indexation. If we interpret Friedman's references to lagged inflation in the same vein, and try to modify equation (2) to accommodate the presence of indexation, then the literature just cited suggests that the resulting Phillips curve might be something along the lines of:

$$\pi_t - \varphi\pi_{t-1} = \beta E_t(\pi_{t+1} - \varphi\pi_t) + \alpha E_{t-1}(y_t - y_t^*) + u_t, \qquad (3)$$

where $0 < \varphi \leq 1.0$. Equation (3) will be taken to be the closest representation, of the equations considered in this chapter, of Friedman's view of the Phillips curve.

Although the coefficient φ can in principle be 1.0—a value that would correspond to universal and complete indexation—it is unlikely that Friedman's own position was that price indexation was as pervasive as this parameter setting would imply. On the contrary, he strongly believed that widespread lack of indexation was a reason why movements in inflation in the United States tended to create severe distortions in the relative-price structure. It is Friedman's perspective on inflation and relative-price behavior to which the discussion now turns.

INFLATION AND THE BEHAVIOR
OF RELATIVE PRICES

Robert Hall (1981, 432) observed that "one of the central arguments" for price stability is that "by distorting relative prices, inflation interferes with efficient resource allocation." This central argument was one that featured heavily both in Friedman's description of the repercussions of inflation and in his prescription of a monetary policy designed to stabilize the price level.

Friedman remarked in a 1974 television interview: "Much of the harm which is done by inflation is because it alters unintentionally and without people knowing it the relative prices of different goods and services."[72] In this statement, Friedman really should have said something like "consciously deciding on it" instead of "knowing it." The former wording would have clarified that agents *did* know the relative-price structure and reacted to it. Indeed, it was the very fact that agents responded to the relative-price configuration that emerged in the wake of an inflationary situation that produced a distortion to resource allocation. For, as Friedman put it on another occasion, inflation tended to give rise to arbitrary relative-price changes in the short run and thereby produced "static" in the signals sent to consumers and businesses.[73] These agents tended to react to relative-price movements irrespective of their source. But when relative-price changes were due to inflation, the private-sector responses to these changes would likely generate deviations of the economy from its flexible-price level.

The relative-price distortion engendered by inflation was something Friedman cited as a reason for believing that inflation made it "more difficult to maintain the appropriate structure of relative prices, since individual prices have to change in order to stay the same relative to others."[74] Relative-price changes, he stressed, would tend to occur under full price flexibility, because changes in technology and consumer tastes would alter the composition of the flexible-price level of output.[75] But in a sticky-price environment—and, in particular, one in which not all prices had equal freedom to adjust in any particular period—monetary policy became another factor creating movements in relative prices, and so tending to produce an inefficient allocation of resources as well as deviations of output from its potential value.

The interaction of inflation and relative-price distortions was an issue that Friedman highlighted in the 1970s, both in his campaign for indexation and in his Nobel lecture.[76] Partly reflecting this impetus, the literature on nominal price contracts in the late 1970s and early 1980s—a literature that helped lay the foundations for New Keynesian economics—put great emphasis on the link between inflation (especially variable inflation) and relative-price distortion—or, in the terminology of that literature, relative-price dispersion (see, for example, Taylor 1981, 68, 72).[77] Formal derivations of the welfare costs associated with relative-price dispersion and the inefficient economic fluctuations associated with it were developed by Rotemberg and Woodford (1997) and Woodford (2003). This literature has made rigorous the connection between (monetary-policy-induced) relative-price variability and deviations of output from its natural value.

THE CODEPENDENCE OF INFLATION
AND REAL VARIABLES

Although this book is concerned with Friedman's role in US economic debate up to 1972, it is a key contention of this volume that Friedman's specifications of aggregate-demand and aggregate-supply relationships were largely formed by the early 1950s and that these specifications described his views not only through 1972 but until his death in 2006. It is therefore important to address an alternative interpretation in the literature—which is that Friedman's perspective on the Phillips curve changed radically in the mid-1970s. According to this view—advocated especially by David Laidler (see, for example, Laidler 1976, 57, 65; 1990, 55; 1995)—Friedman's outlook toward the Phillips curve switched, in the mid-1970s, from one founded principally on sticky prices to one that was—like that of the new classical economics movement of the 1970s—founded principally on flexible prices.

Some commentators dated Friedman's alleged conversion to a flexible-price-based analysis of economic dynamics back further. In particular, Modigliani (1977, 5) interpreted the model embedded in Friedman's American Economic Association presidential address as being a flexible-price one.[78] But Friedman strongly disputed Modigliani's interpretation even before Modigliani's article saw print.[79] That Friedman reaffirmed price stickiness in 1977 points to the conclusion that, not only was his presidential address published in 1968 consistent with price stickiness, but so too were his later expositions of the Phillips-curve process. And this indeed appears to be the appropriate conclusion. For, as discussed in the following paragraphs, the items in Friedman's statements (whether those published in 1968 or later) that have been cited as establishing Friedman's discarding of the sticky-price interpretation of the Phillips curve can, in fact, be reconciled with a sticky-price interpretation.[80]

The first item that has been treated as a case of Friedman casting his lot with new classical economists on the matter of nominal/real interaction is his acceptance of the point—in the 1976 version of *Price Theory* and in related expositions—that suppliers of goods respond to price signals and increase output when they perceive that their real income (per good produced) has risen.[81] This was actually a point that was part of Friedman's 1968 exposition of the Phillips curve, as Laidler (1995, 336–37) acknowledged. This point was therefore not novel to Friedman's discussions during the 1970s of the inflation/unemployment relationship.[82] The key issue is, consequently, whether Friedman's statements of that point implied an inconsistency with (or repudiation of) Friedman's various other statements (including in the American Economic Association presidential address) that prices were inherently sticky in the short run.

There is in fact no necessary inconsistency between the two sets of statements, and so no change in Friedman's views needs to be inferred. As discussed in chapter 4, in his discussions of the fundamental properties of the market system, Friedman noted that prices served multiple functions, of which the signal to producers was only one. In a similar vein, in a macroeconomic model one can view a Phillips-curve relationship that links output and prices as performing multiple functions (when put in a simultaneous-equation system). It is perfectly possible for a Phillips curve for price inflation to describe incomplete adjustment of prices to excess demand (with the latter in turn traceable to monetary policy and other factors), and for the relative-price configuration that results from that incomplete price adjustment to matter for the decisions made by goods' suppliers about the equilibrium quantities to be produced.[83] Put differently, the acceptance of the notion that suppliers respond to price signals is not the same as the assumption of price flexibility, and Friedman's belief in price-elastic supply did not imply an endorsement of the assumption of perfectly flexible prices.[84] Indeed, Friedman explicitly separated himself, in both the 1970s and the 1980s, from the price-flexibility aspects of the new classical macroeconomics: see chapter 15.

Friedman regarded the dependence of quantities supplied on price signals as contributing to the understanding of both short- and long-run movements of the economy. He did not consider this dependence to be a condition automatically ruled out by the fact of incomplete price flexibility. The two situations are in fact compatible. Consistent with their compatibility, an analysis of Friedman's pre-1970s statements points to the conclusion that his emphasis during the 1970s on the dependence of supply (both in the short and long run) on the price received by the seller did not signify the embrace of a new position. His discussion of Lange's work (see chapter 4) had taken this line; so had his 1946 case with Stigler for decontrol of rents; and so had his 1958 remark, already noted, on the interaction of inflation and relative prices. Furthermore, in 1969 Friedman observed that the "only technique that [induces higher output] in any society I know of" was to have product prices rise in relation to costs (Instructional Dynamics Economics Cassette Tape 37, November 5, 1969).[85]

Two sets of remarks that Friedman gave during 1982 point to his conviction that the price responsiveness of supply decisions was compatible with the existence of price stickiness. Friedman stated in his magazine column that "prices are sticky" (*Newsweek*, July 12, 1982) within months of giving a speech at the Federal Reserve Bank of Atlanta on supply-side economics. In that speech, Friedman had implied that it was "bad economics" to fail to recognize that the quantities of goods and labor supplied to the market depended on the prices received for those supplies.[86]

It can therefore be concluded that Friedman's emphasis on the price elasticity of aggregate supply was a feature of his framework throughout his monetarist period and that his mid-1970s references to the response of suppliers to prices was not tantamount to a denial of price stickiness.

Let us turn, therefore, to the *second* item in Friedman's mid-1970s writings that has been cited as signifying a change in his position and as implying an endorsement of flexible-price models. This item consists of his favorable remarks concerning the idea that the Phillips-curve relationship reflected inflation (or prices) driving real variables and not the reverse. The most prominent item among these remarks was a passage in the 1976 edition of *Price Theory* comparing Irving Fisher's (1926) and A. W. Phillips's (1958) studies of the inflation/unemployment relationship. In that discussion, Friedman stated: "There was, however, a crucial difference between Fisher's analysis and Phillips's, between the truth of 1926 and the error of 1958, which had to do with the direction of causation. Fisher took *the rate of change of prices* to be the independent variable that set the process going."[87]

But Friedman was also clear that both inflation and unemployment were endogenous variables.[88] That being the case, neither a story based on causation from unemployment to inflation nor a story based on causation from inflation to unemployment can be accepted as a comprehensive description of the Phillips-curve relationship.[89] A fully accurate account would have to recognize the fact that the two series are simultaneously determined. In light of this, how might one interpret Friedman's statements about Phillips being in error, and Fisher being right, in interpreting real/nominal interactions?

The answer offered here is that Friedman's perspective was that, although inflation and output were jointly determined, the former variable could in large measure be usefully regarded as the driver of the relationship because inflation is a nominal variable and hence ultimately policy determined. Fluctuations in output (in relation to potential) would not occur if the private sector's expectations of nominal variables corresponded continuously to the actual paths. In emphasizing the reaction of real variables to nominal variables, Friedman evidently wanted to convey the point that ultimately the central bank controls nominal variables and not real ones—an element of his thinking that is discussed further in the next subsection. The effects of monetary policy on real variables can then be viewed as a temporary by-product of the central bank's influence on nominal variables. The central bank can create shifts in these nominal variables away from their expected values and thereby promote fluctuations in the output gap.[90]

The interpretation just given of Friedman' position is consistent with the 1976 *Price Theory* discussion of the Phillips curve from which the preceding quotation was taken. In that discussion, Friedman was critical of a number of Phillips-curve estimates that had appeared in the research literature. But the specific grounds he cited in his criticisms pertained to the difficulties of measuring expected inflation and what he saw (correctly) as the illegitimate procedure of testing the natural-rate hypothesis using equations that included costs alongside real activity and expected inflation as an explanatory variable.[91] By this point in his *Price Theory* discussion, Friedman had already mentioned Fisher's work on inflation and unemployment. If Friedman's position was really that putting inflation on the left-hand side of a regression and the real variable on the right-hand side (and estimating by ordinary least squares) by itself made an estimated Phillips curve misspecified, he would not need to voice the specific criticisms just mentioned. He would instead be able to reject equations that used inflation as the lefthand-side variable out of hand. Yet Friedman's *Price Theory* discussion did not reject these equations out of hand but instead made specific criticisms related to the measurement and choice of variables in the estimated Phillips curves.

Also consistent with the preceding interpretation is Friedman's description—again, one given in his aforementioned mid-1970s exposition of the Phillips curve—of unemployment/inflation interaction as "a *dynamic* process arising out of fluctuations in the rate of spending about some average trend or norm."[92] This statement can be regarded as affirming that both inflation and real variables are endogenous. Under these circumstances, the sense in which nominal variables drive real series lies in Friedman's belief that a key initiating factor for unemployment/inflation fluctuations was often monetary-policy-induced variation in nominal variables.[93] This way of viewing the inflation/unemployment process also highlights a reason for Friedman's preference for Fisher's discussion of the relationship over the corresponding discussion in A. W. Phillips (1958). Fisher, as Friedman saw it, better recognized the idea that nominal variables mattered for real variables in a transitory manner that was linked to the degree to which inflation was unanticipated.[94]

The above interpretation suggests, once again, that Friedman's belief in the dependence of prices (or inflation) on output (or unemployment) was not to the exclusion of a belief in the dependence of output (or unemployment) on prices (or inflation).[95] He believed that both elements of the relationship were present in the short run; and that both were absent in the long run, when the determination of the relative prices that mattered for real decisions became wholly separate from the determination of the aggregate nominal price level.[96]

Cripps (1979) was an early discussion that reached the same bottom line as that given above. Cripps argued that Friedman's belief in prices-to-real-variables connections did not come at the expense of a belief in the dependence of inflation on the output gap or unemployment gap. Cripps based his argument largely on Friedman's Nobel lecture. But other items could be cited in which Friedman was explicit about the response of inflation to real economic activity. In a 1966 contribution, for example, Friedman described the adjustment of the overall price level to monetary policy actions—in a situation in which there is a subset of prices that might not respond to monetary actions—as involving a process in which "high unemployment put downward pressure on other prices."[97] This description—in the same volume that contained an early Friedman sketch of the natural-rate hypothesis—was a specific case in which he characterized the adjustment of prices to unemployment, and not just the reverse, as part of the dynamics of real/nominal interaction.[98] Other cases can be found in later Friedman writings, including items published in the 1980s.[99]

IV. Inflation as a Monetary Phenomenon

MONETARY GROWTH AND INFLATION

Friedman's proposition that "inflation is always and everywhere a monetary phenomenon" has been analyzed at length in Barro (1982), Mishkin (1989, 572–83), McCallum (1990c, 965–66), E. Nelson (2003), and McCallum and Nelson (2011), with the last two of these references specifically considering the sense in which the proposition holds in New Keynesian models.[100] In light of these previous discussions, only brief coverage of Friedman's proposition is needed here.[101]

The proposition that inflation is always and everywhere a monetary phenomenon amounts to a contention that higher inflation can occur on a sustained basis only if there is a sustained rise in monetary growth in relation to the growth rate of potential output. The rate of monetary growth that is consistent with long-term price stability will depend on the growth rate of potential output and on the trend rate at which private-sector agents reduce or increase their holdings of money. But, conditional on these trends, monetary growth and inflation will have a unitary relationship with one another in the long term. Furthermore, a central bank's actions can affect monetary growth. It follows that monetary policy is a necessary and sufficient means through which to control inflation.

Several points should be made in connection with the proposition that inflation is always and everywhere a monetary phenomenon. First, the contention of Patinkin (1981c, 31) and Mervyn King (1994, 261), to the effect that Friedman's statement is a trivial definition of inflation that sheds no light on its causes, is not valid. These authors suggested that, because inflation is by definition a decline in the value of money, Friedman's statement

that inflation is a monetary phenomenon is a truism that lacks policy implications.[102] This criticism is invalid because Friedman's proposition did *not*
coincide with the truism that inflation is a decline in the value of money.
Instead, his proposition ruled out as causes of sustained inflation anything
that did not affect monetary growth (in relation to output growth). In so
doing, Friedman's proposition specifically attributed inflation to monetary
policy.[103]

Second, the proposition that inflation is a monetary phenomenon does
apply to inflation dynamics (at least, those prevailing beyond the very short
run) and not simply to the steady-state behavior of inflation. But it should
not be seen a proposition that was presented as a rival or alternative, in the
construction of structural economic models, to the Phillips curve's descriptions of inflation dynamics. Instead, the two perspectives are consistent
with one another. Monetary policy can be regarded as the only tool available to policy makers that affects—at the cyclical frequency, and in a systematic manner—the output-gap term in the Phillips curve (as well as expected future output gaps, whose behavior bears on expected inflation).[104]
E. Nelson (2002a, 2003) has provided detailed discussions of the compatibility of monetarism with the Phillips-curve relationship.[105]

This compatibility should, in any event, come as no surprise. For Friedman's criticisms of the Phillips curve did not suggest jettisoning it outright
as a structural equation in macroeconomic modeling, but instead modify-
ing it with "the introduction of inflation expectations, as a variable shifting the short-run Phillips curve."[106] The Phillips-curve and monetarist perspectives also give the same message that inflation is endogenous and, in
particular, is not a pure cost-push process.[107]

It is true that Friedman and Schwartz's *Monetary Trends* did report
some regressions that might be taken to be "horse races" between monetary growth and the output gap in accounting for the observed variation in
inflation.[108] But there is a twofold basis for concluding that their analysis
should not be regarded as having treated monetary growth and the output gap as distinct sources of inflation. (*i*) Friedman and Schwartz's regressions were on heavily time-averaged data. Therefore, their results could be
viewed as the outcome of an investigation of whether longer-run inflation
behavior was susceptible to being described by the Phillips curve—which
ordinarily describes only inflation dynamics—or whether, instead, the
measured inflation fluctuations occurred on a horizon at which most connections between nominal and real variables had faded away.[109] (*ii*) The
monetary-growth term in the regression could be regarded as partly a
proxy for expected inflation. The authors found that this monetary-growth
term entered more sizably and significantly than the output gap.[110] Such
a finding might imply that the coefficient on expected inflation was larger

and more precisely estimated than that associated with the output gap, and that fluctuations in the current output gap accounted for a smaller fraction of variations in current inflation than did fluctuations in expected inflation.[111] But an outcome of this kind would not imply that the output-gap term should be excluded from (that is, its coefficient should be set to zero in) the inflation equation. Indeed, elsewhere in *Monetary Trends* Friedman and Schwartz emphasized that a sizable, positive coefficient on the output-gap term in the Phillips curve was certainly an implication of the monetarist view.[112]

The third point to make about the proposition that inflation is always and everywhere a monetary phenomenon is that it is compatible with, but does *not* require, Friedman's particular expectational version of the Phillips curve. Braun (1986, 136) claimed that the Phillips curve is consistent with inflation being a monetary phenomenon only if the unitary restriction on expected inflation is imposed in the Phillips-curve equation. However, as discussed in E. Nelson (2002a, 145) and Woodford (2008, 1594), this claim is not accurate. A Phillips-curve specification can imply that a long-run nonzero level for the output gap is attainable; yet the same Phillips-curve relationship can also be perfectly consistent with outcomes in which monetary growth and inflation enjoy a tight, unitary relationship with each other. That the natural-rate hypothesis was *not* required for the central monetarist prediction concerning the monetary growth/inflation relationship was a point that Friedman himself acknowledged (*The Times*, March 3, 1980).[113]

Fourth, Friedman's proposition regarding inflation's character has been challenged on the grounds that it is not deep enough, as it does not explain the factors that create monetary growth.[114] Friedman himself readily granted on numerous occasions that an understanding of *why* excessive monetary growth occurred was vital.[115] But Friedman's proposition is nevertheless useful as a component of positive economics—one whose specific role is to provide a description of the private sector's reaction to government-generated monetary growth. The content of his proposition does, to be sure, require that central banks can control the money stock and that—irrespective of whether they consciously aim to control monetary aggregates—their monetary policy actions have systematic effects on monetary growth.[116] Friedman, of course, firmly believed that these requirements were satisfied in practice. But he was not alone in holding this view. As discussed in E. Nelson (2003) and in other chapters of this book, the fact that central banks have typically not used a monetary-aggregate or commercial-bank-reserves instrument does not invalidate the interpretation of these monetary series' behavior as the result of central banks' actions.

Fifth, the proposition also applies to deflation. Deflation can be regarded as reflecting deficient monetary growth. Consistent with this viewpoint is Bernanke's (2011, 19) observation: "a determined central bank can always do something about deflation. After all, inflation is a monetary phenomenon, a central bank can always create money, and so on."

The Bernanke statement, although it indicates that monetary policy can prevent deflation, does not strictly imply that deflations are monetary in character. Friedman, however, would conclude that deflation was a monetary phenomenon, and that monetary measures both produced and could prevent deflations. This was a conclusion he reached as his monetary studies progressed. A very early affirmation that Friedman gave of the monetary growth/inflation relationship, in the *New York Times* of January 11, 1948, stated that the relationship held especially for "upward movements of the price level," with cases in which a "marked increase" in prices was not associated with a marked increase in money being characterized as rare or nonexistent. This characterization, like Bernanke's of 2011, left open the possibility that price deflations did not reflect monetary restriction. But, as will be discussed in chapter 8, after 1948 Friedman concluded that major deflations—such as in the United States in the 1930s—to which declines in velocity made a major contribution had actually originated in declines in the money stock, with monetary contractions tending to promote a velocity contraction. Deflation should therefore be regarded as being a monetary phenomenon.

LONG-RUN SEPARATION OF REAL AND NOMINAL VARIABLES

Let us now consider the behavior of nominal and real variables in the long run and the implications that this behavior has for Friedman's dictum that inflation is a monetary phenomenon.

The discussion that follows will use the terms "long run" and "steady state" interchangeably. This follows Friedman's own practice.[117] The analysis will be particularly concerned with the steady-state behavior of inflation. The relationship that the inflation rate has to other variables in the steady state will be taken as indicative of how the economy behaves at low time frequencies.

The analysis will take advantage of the fact that, provided that the natural-rate hypothesis holds, an economy whose prices exhibit gradual adjustment converges to the long-run equilibrium associated with the corresponding flexible-price economy. This means that many of the properties of flexible-price models, including these models' results concerning the determination of nominal and real variables, are shared by the steady state of a sticky-price model. Consequently, the discussion below can draw on results in the literature both on flexible-price models and on the steady-state or low-frequency behavior of a sticky-price model, with both sets of results treated as pertinent to the long-run behavior of inflation and real variables.

With respect to the steady state for real variables, Friedman's description of long-run conditions was: "The same real situation is consistent with any absolute level of prices or of price change."[118] This result is one that emerges frequently in textbook models. For example, Dornbusch and Fischer (1994, 230) noted: "In the long run, once wages and prices have had time to adjust fully, the model has the same predictions as the classical case. . . . An increase in the money stock has no real effects." It is also a result established in early attempts, such as that of Gertler (1979), to put sticky-price models on a more rigorous footing. Gertler (1979, 228) observed of his model: "in the steady state, the real variables are independent of monetary factors." Finally, this is also a result that has been verified as holding in the long run of infinite-horizon optimizing models, as discussed in McCallum (1990c).

McCallum (1990c, 972) acknowledged that one qualification to this result pertained to the relationship between real variables and the inflation rate or the monetary-growth rate (as opposed to the *levels* of the corresponding nominal series). Because the demand for money is interest elastic and expected inflation matters for the nominal interest rate, different steady-state inflation rates will imply different long-run values for the level of real money balances. This was a qualification that Friedman himself voiced in his own discussion of long-run interaction between nominal and real variables.[119] As will be discussed in the next section, Friedman also allowed for an influence of inflation on productive efficiency and hence on the long-run level, and perhaps also the long-run growth rate, of output. For these reasons, money was not superneutral. But these violations of superneutrality implied no relationship between *levels* of nominal and real series, and no *positive* long-run relationship between monetary growth and the growth rates of key real variables like the level of real money balances and the real volume of output. It therefore remained the case that neither monetary injections nor increases in the growth rate of nominal money could stimulate real economic activity in the long run.

The preceding results about the long-run independence of real and nominal variables were usually given in the literature on the basis of models in which the central bank was treated as using the nominal money stock as its instrument. An analogous result holds, however, if the central bank is regarded as having as its instrument a nominal interest rate. Cochrane (2013, 3), for example, observed: "When prices are flexible, the Fed loses its power to affect real interest rates and the output gap. Since r_t [the real interest rate] is given, by changing nominal rates [on securities], the Fed changes (expected) inflation, period."

Cochrane's description of real/nominal interactions in a flexible-price model holds, as already noted, also in the long run of sticky-price models, as the latter models have a flexible-price steady state. Because the analysis of flexible-price models is so relevant for the understanding of long-run patterns of nominal/real interaction in a sticky-price model, it is worth pausing to consider how the central bank controls the nominal interest rate in a flexible-price model. Cochrane takes such control for granted. However, central banks' control of nominal interest rates in a flexible-price environment turns out to be fundamentally different from interest-rate control in a sticky-price environment.

Central-bank control of interest rates is indeed possible under flexible prices. But the way in which such control is achieved sheds light on how to interpret the central bank's ability to affect steady-state behavior—and, in particular, on how the central bank can determine the long-run behavior of nominal interest rates and inflation. Examination of this steady-state behavior will reveal that it is accurate to apply even to models in which the central bank follows an interest-rate policy the description that Gertler (1979, 228) used for a model in which the central bank has a money-stock instrument: "The money growth rate uniquely determines the inflation rate."

To arrive at this conclusion, let us first return to the dynamic behavior in a sticky-price model when the central bank follows a short-term nominal-interest-rate rule (for example, a rule for a riskless short-term interest rate). If such a rate is a market rate, the central bank's means of controlling the rate arises from the combination of three factors: its monopoly power on the monetary base, the interest sensitivity of the demand for real money balances, and the existence of sticky prices. The monopoly power on the monetary base, in combination with the connection between base creation and money stock creation, gives the central bank the wherewithal to influence the volume of nominal money balances. The existence of price stickiness means that movements in nominal money balances typically translate, in the short run, into movements of real money balances in the same direction. The interest sensitivity of the demand for real money balances means that nominal interest rates have an inverse relationship (conditional on other factors) with the stock of real money balances, so that an augmentation of the volume of real balances will put downward pressure on nominal interest rates, and a reduction in real balances will tend to raise interest rates.

The above connections led Friedman and Schwartz to regard the inverse relationship between money and nominal interest rates in Keynes's (1936) analysis as reflecting Keynes's assumption that the nominal price level was rigid.[120] In the presence of complete price rigidity, central-bank control of the nominal money stock led to control of the real money stock, even over long horizons, and correspondingly there would be an inverse relationship (conditional on real income) between the nominal money stock and the nominal interest rate in both the short run and the long run.

Friedman rejected Keynes's characterization of the money/interest rate relationship as a description of long-run behavior. But, by the same token, he accepted its validity as a description of short-term patterns. Friedman's acknowledgment that there was *short-run* price stickiness led him to accept that the central bank could, in the short run, use its influence on the nominal money stock to move the real money stock in a way that generated a desired nominal interest rate. This point underlined Friedman's view of the liquidity effect, which was discussed in chapter 6.

Nor are the above characterizations of the central bank's short-run powers—that its influence on real money balances comes from price stickiness, and this influence confers on it the power to influence the nominal interest rate—at all idiosyncratic or exclusive to Friedman. On the contrary, Paul Evans (1986, 233) observed: "Conventional macroeconomic theory treats the price level as if it were sticky and hence treats the real money supply as if it were under the control of the monetary authorities for periods as short as a quarter." And in connection with interest-rate control, Bernanke, Gertler, and Watson (2004, 288) stated: "In our view, given a plausible degree of nominal price rigidity and the Fed's monopoly of the supply of bank reserves, the Fed could certainly alter the path of the nominal funds rate by the amount required by our counterfactuals."[121]

What the preceding points imply for the analysis of the steady state is that, in the long run, the central bank *loses* its ability to influence the stock of real money balances by altering the stock of nominal money balances in the same direction. It was this situation that led Friedman to observe: "This is really the basic problem of monetary policy—that what the Fed can do in the short run, it cannot do in the long run" (Instructional Dynamics Economics Cassette Tape 140, February 20, 1974). He would also observe that the distinction between the real and nominal stocks of money was the "keystone" of the quantity theory of money (*Newsweek*, July 12, 1982). The nominal stock of money could be influenced by the central bank at all time horizons. In contrast, the long-run flexibility and endogeneity of prices meant that the real stock of money was decoupled, at low frequencies, from the nominal stock of money.

Real money balances and nominal interest rates remain inversely related at low frequencies; but when attention is focused on those low frequencies, it is no longer the case that open-market purchases, which raise the nominal monetary base and tend to raise the nominal money stock, provide a means of expanding the *real* money stock. Long-run price flexibility means that the central bank can no longer expect an expansion of nominal money (or a rise in its growth rate) to lead to a movement of real money in the same direction. Furthermore, the real-interest-rate component of the nominal interest rate, which usually moves in the same direction as the nominal interest rate in the short run, is insensitive to monetary policy in the long run.

How, therefore, can the central bank influence the nominal interest rate over the long run? In public remarks in 1970, Friedman provided the answer: it can do so via the long-run Fisher relationship. With regard to behavior of the system "over a long period," Friedman observed: "The central bank cannot determine interest rates except by producing inflation" (*Sunday Times*, September 20, 1970). This remark echoed sentiments Friedman had given in a memorandum the following year to the Federal Reserve Board: "Over long periods, it [the central bank] can control nominal [interest] rates by controlling the rate of inflation."[122]

Again, this position—that price stickiness and so the liquidity effect were absent over long horizons, in which case the central bank's influence on nominal interest rates over such horizons arose from the Fisher effect—was not unique to Friedman, although he played a key role in expounding it. It was, for example, the same position as that taken by Dornbusch and Fischer (1979), who qualified their observation that "the Fed cannot, in the long run, control the rate of interest" with the statement that "the Fed cannot control the interest rate except by varying the expected rate of inflation. In the long run the nominal interest rate is determined by productivity and thrift which determine the real rate, and by the rate of inflation."[123]

The Friedman and Dornbusch-Fischer remarks provide a way of interpreting not only the steady state of sticky-price models but also how interest-rate rules could be pursued in a flexible-price model. Under flexible prices, and in the long run of a sticky-price model, neither the liquidity effect (which links money balances M to real money balances M/P and thence to the nominal interest rate R), nor a link between R and the real interest rate r, is operative. It can then be seen that, in the long run of a sticky-price model, the influence the central bank exerts on R is purely by its influence on the long-run value of (actual and expected) inflation. But to state the matter in this way is merely to raise the question: How does the central bank control the inflation rate in the long run?

Answering this question by simply postulating that the central bank can treat the long-run inflation rate as a choice variable is unsatisfactory for two reasons. First, the inflation rate reflects the aggregate of individual price-setting measures by the private sector and is therefore not literally a central-bank choice variable.[124] Second, the vehicle through which the central bank primarily influences inflation in the short run—the Phillips-curve relationship—is not available in the long run because, when the natural-rate hypothesis holds, the Phillips-curve linkage between inflation and real variables disappears in the long run.[125]

An insight into how the central bank can nevertheless control inflation in the long run is provided by the discussion in Robert Hall and John Taylor (1997). Much like the analyses noted above, these authors observed: "In the long-run growth model, monetary policy is a very simple matter. . . . The money supply has no influence on output or the interest rate."[126] With regard to conditions prevailing in this long run, the authors stated: "The Fed can choose whatever rate of inflation it wants."[127] Elaborating on this last point, Hall and Taylor concluded: "The Fed chooses the long-run rate of inflation by choosing the rate of money growth."[128]

The sentence just quoted gets to the nub of the matter.[129] Real interest rates are not subject to influence by the central bank in the long run. The long-run Fisher relationship implies that any influence that the central bank has on the nominal interest rate in the long run is due to the central bank's influence on the long-run inflation rate. Yet to take the long-run inflation rate as a choice variable for the central bank is to make a high-level assumption that overlooks the fact that inflation reflects decisions by the private sector. In contrast, central-bank actions affect nominal monetary growth irrespective of whether one is considering the short run or the long run. One can regard monetary growth as the variable the central bank can determine in the long run, even though its usual basis for influencing real and nominal interest rates has faded away at that horizon. The central bank's determination of long-run monetary growth can be viewed as the factor that pins down the long-run inflation rate and hence secures the central bank's influence over nominal interest rates at low frequencies.

The central-bank actions that determine the steady-state monetary-growth rate can consequently be regarded as setting the steady-state inflation rate. This is the long-horizon aspect of Friedman's dictum that inflation is always and everywhere a monetary phenomenon. As he put it, "no measures are likely to produce long-continued inflation or to cure long-continued inflation unless they affect the long-term rate of monetary growth."[130]

In addition, monetary theory suggests that steady-state monetary growth and steady-state inflation will have a unitary relationship with one another. In the absence of a trend in the opportunity cost of holding real money balances, the long-run form of the first difference of the money demand equation will be $E[\Delta \log M_t] - E[\pi_t] = c_1 g_{y*} + g_\eta$, where c_1 is the real income elasticity of money demand, g_{y*} is the long-run rate of growth of potential output, and g_η is the trend rate of growth of exogenous shifts in money demand. The unitary relationship between the long-run rates of increase in money and prices flows from the price-homogeneity restriction in the original, levels form of the money-demand equation. As was discussed in chapter 6, this price-homogeneity restriction is a vital component of the quantity theory of money.

V. The Natural Level of Output and the Natural Rate of Unemployment

THE NATURAL RATE OF UNEMPLOYMENT

In his American Economic Association address of 1967, Friedman observed that Wicksell's natural-rate-of-interest concept had a "close counterpart in the employment market. . . . The 'natural rate of unemployment,' in other words, is the level that would be ground out by the Walrasian system of general equilibrium equations, provided there is imbedded in them the actual structural characteristics of the labor and commodity markets, including market imperfections, stochastic variability in demands and supplies, the cost of gathering information about job vacancies and labor availabilities, the costs of mobility, and so on."[131]

After this presidential address, Friedman's explicit references to the natural rate of unemployment were infrequent.[132] As it turned out, however, he did not need to undertake a large personal effort to make his terminology well known. For the economics profession used "the natural rate of unemployment" terminology profusely in the 1970s, and the phrase would subsequently become widely employed in the financial press.

As a concept, too, the "natural rate of unemployment" became a cornerstone of both labor economics and monetary economics. By 1979, it had already done so to such an extent that Robert Hall could observe that "the basic notion that there *is* a natural rate has become reasonably well established."[133] Hall was nevertheless critical of the definition as laid out by Friedman in the quotation above—judging it "hardly more than a list of things to think about in creating a theory of the natural rate."

There is considerable validity in Hall's remark. Friedman's verbal sketch helped point the way to the appropriate basis for a definition of the natural rate of unemployment and related real variables in a dynamic macroeconomic model. But it did not provide a very detailed blueprint for a definition. And in both theoretical and empirical work, the appropriate procedure by which to achieve a formal definition of the natural values of real variables is by no means always clear-cut. The ambiguities involved are underscored in the case (discussed later in this section) of formally defining the natural level of output in the presence of capital. But ambiguities are present also when considering specifically the definition of the natural rate of unemployment.

There are, nevertheless, two very concrete components of Friedman's verbal definition that have left their mark on formal definitions of the natural rate of unemployment.

The first component stems from the fact that Friedman defined the natural rate as the value of the variable that would prevail in the equilibrium of the flexible-wage, flexible-price counterpart to an economy—the value "ground out by the Walrasian system of general equilibrium equations," in Friedman's words. Friedman's definition of the natural rate of unemployment built on the distinction—already widely used in the economic-research literature for two decades by 1967—between the maximum and full-employment levels of economic activity. Friedman's natural-rate definition underscored the point that the amount of labor input supplied under flexible prices not only did not correspond to some feasible maximum, but it was also an endogenous variable that depended on the stochastic real conditions prevailing in any period.[134] The implication was that the level of flexible-price output depended not only on features that had a fairly clear physical dimension (such as weather, demographics, and technology) but also on variations in other, less clearly physical, phenomena (such as household preferences and tax-and-transfer arrangements) that affected the optimal amount of labor supplied in the flexible-price economy.

It has sometimes been suggested that this point of Friedman's may be taken as implying that the full-employment level of output should be defined as the level of output associated with profit maximization in the face of existing real input prices (see, for example, Karnosky 1974b, 17; R. J. Ball 1985, 4). However, this proposed definition, while acceptable in characterizing Friedman's description of the *actual* level of real output produced in equilibrium, is inadmissible as a definition of the natural output level. For, as we have seen, it is precisely the observed structure of relative prices (including input prices) to which Friedman believed *actual* production responded, and deviations of these relative prices from their behavior under full wage and price flexibility were a sign that monetary policy was being nonneutral.[135] The natural rate of output, in contrast, was the level of output resulting from profit maximization in an economy in which instantaneous price adjustment insulated relative prices from monetary policy. It would therefore appear important to define the natural rates of output and employment in a manner that does not refer to *actual* relative prices observed in the economy—and Friedman's definition adhered to this practice, as he defined it in terms of the equilibrium of a *parallel* (flexible-price) economy rather than the *actual* (sticky-price) economy.

The second concrete component of Friedman's definition of the natural rate of unemployment was given in his presidential address a couple of paragraphs after the passage quoted above. In this later passage, he indicated that, notwithstanding the word "natural," the natural rate of unemployment could reflect distortions to ordinary market forces. In particular, the value of the natural rate would depend in part on the extent to which the economy deviated from conditions of perfect competition. Friedman specifically cited government-imposed minimum-wage rates and other competition-reducing labor laws as making the natural rate of unemployment higher than it would otherwise be.[136] He also stressed that improved information for labor market participants would likely lower the natural rate of unemployment. Friedman did, however, caution—for example, in his Nobel lecture—that a low natural rate of unemployment did not automatically signify an efficient economy. On the contrary, such a low rate could be a symptom of a static economy—perhaps one in which labor mobility across sectors, and the role of consumer tastes in governing the division of output across sectors, had been stifled by public-sector intervention and regulation.[137]

The latter point reflected the idea that, just as labor input under flexible prices was not simply a constant in Friedman's view, neither was the efficiency with which labor and other inputs were employed. Although it was not a focus of his monetary analysis, in many other writings Friedman emphasized the influence of nonmonetary government policy on the productive efficiency of the economy. For example, in 1970 he expressed the judgment that Regulation Q on commercial banks had the effect of lowering potential output.[138] Certain external disturbances could also reduce the productive efficiency of the US economy. In this vein, Friedman and Schwartz would grant the first OPEC oil shock of 1973–74 as a factor that reduced US potential output.[139] This acknowledgment continued a theme of Friedman's early writings, according to which tariff protection, farm price supports, and monopoly power all distorted the economy's relative-price structure and, partly as a result, lowered the efficiency of the economy (*New York Times*, January 11, 1948).[140]

That economic distortions can factor into the determination of both the mean and fluctuations of the natural rate of unemployment is a point that has been embedded in rigorous definitions of the concept. As just indicated, Friedman also believed that distortions were important for the behavior of the natural level of *output*.[141] The notion that monopoly power reduces the natural level of output has been used in formal definitions of that concept (see, for example, Mervyn King 1997c, 86). Other aspects of the natural-output concept are considered in the next section.

THE NATURAL LEVEL OF OUTPUT

In the aforementioned discussion of Friedman's natural-rate-of-unemployment concept, Robert Hall (1979, 154) referred to "economists who resisted the idea at first and who now accept the principle but give it another name." Hall may have had in mind those economists who followed Modigliani and Papademos (1976, 24-25) and Baily and Tobin (1977, 511–12) in referring to the "nonaccelerating-inflation rate of unemployment" (NAIRU) instead of the natural rate of unemployment. Friedman rejected this alternative terminology.[142] The NAIRU term is, in any event, an unsound alternative to the natural-rate terminology. Compared with Friedman's, the NAIRU terminology actually involves a substantial loss of generality in the definition of the baseline-unemployment concept. It ties the baseline-unemployment concept not to the behavior of the flexible-price economy but to a Phillips-curve specification that imposes the highly restrictive assumption that expected inflation and lagged inflation are identical.[143]

In view of the lack of generality of the NAIRU idea and especially its inconsistency, in general, with rational expectations, the modern monetary policy literature that uses dynamic stochastic general equilibrium (DSGE) models has rejected the NAIRU terminology and embraced the term "natural rate" to describe the reference values of real variables.[144] Usually, however, the models in this literature feature a representative household, or households that are alike on many dimensions. Consequently, it is often the case that these models have no laborers who are literally unemployed, either in the flexible-price economy or the sticky-price economy—even when there is economic slack in the latter economy. The baseline value for real economic activity in these models therefore tends to be defined in terms of the natural level of output rather than in terms of the natural rate of unemployment.

The concept of the natural level of output was a logical corollary of Friedman's natural-rate-of-unemployment idea. Accordingly, many authors have attributed the former concept to Friedman. For example, John Roberts (1993, 924) stated that "Milton Friedman (1968[b]) introduced the idea of the 'natural' level of economic activity"; Paul Evans (1983, 217) referred to the conditions in which "there is a 'natural' level of output, as Friedman (1968[b]) has argued"; and Woodford (2003, 152) observed that he would refer to the flexible-price level of output as "the *natural rate of output*[,] following Friedman (1968[b])."[145]

Friedman did not, in fact, specifically invoke the natural-level-of-output concept in his American Economic Association presidential address of 1967. But several other writers used it explicitly during the late 1960s and early 1970s, in the immediate wake of Friedman's address.[146] And Friedman himself used the concept in print in 1975.[147]

It turns out that the concept of the natural level of output was actually more relevant to the analysis in Friedman's presidential address than was the corresponding unemployment concept. The reason is that the verbal model in that address was—in common with much modern DSGE analysis—best interpreted as having an intensive margin (variation in hours worked) but not an extensive margin (variation in number of workers hired) with regard to labor input.[148]

Friedman's emphasis on aggregate relationships and on the effects of monetary policy meant that he did not pay a great deal of attention to the relationship between output and unemployment. For the most part, he regarded these two real series as capable of being used interchangeably as measures of real activity, especially in analytical work. Friedman had deep suspicions about the reliability of empirical measures of the US unemployment rate.[149] But he largely took for granted the existence of some kind of Okun's-law relationship between output and unemployment.[150] This attitude implied that, in considering a flexible-price economy, Friedman took there to be a natural level of output corresponding to the natural rate of unemployment.

Friedman also embraced the terminology that Okun used for the baseline output level. Much more than he used "the natural level of output," Friedman deployed the term "potential output" to describe this baseline level.[151] "Capacity output" was also a term Friedman used on multiple occasions.[152] It was clear, however, that Friedman was using these terms as synonyms for the natural level of output.[153] His treatment of the various terms as interchangeable underscores the fact that Friedman's concepts of natural values of output and unemployment were intended to put the Keynesian idea of a normal achievable level of economic activity on a more formal footing, rather than being offered as a challenge to this idea.

Consistent with the harmony between the Keynesian and Friedman concepts of a baseline output level, many authors have taken the term "full employment" or "full-employment output" to be another synonym for the natural level of output.[154] Their interpretation has received support from the fact that Friedman himself—both before and after his presidential address—used the term "full employment" in his own analysis when describing the baseline or flexible-price level of output or employment.[155] In addition, Friedman once noted that his natural-rate-of-unemployment concept was consistent with Keynes's (1936) definition of full employment.[156]

That Friedman was congenial, as an analytical matter, to the concept of full employment, and fleshed out that concept in his discussion of the natural rate in the presidential address, did not mean that he was interested in using that concept in either his empirical work or his policy prescriptions. On the contrary, as Brittan (2005, 204) observed, Friedman "consistently refused to give any estimate either of its size [that is, of the natural rate of unemployment] or that of the output gap and has preferred to keep them as conceptual tools."[157] As discussed in the next chapter, the model uncertainty that Friedman regarded as pervasive in macroeconomics led him to eschew structural empirical analysis of inflation—even when that analysis embedded the natural-rate hypothesis—and to discourage policy makers from trying to target the natural rate of *any* real variable. The imprecision of economists' knowledge about model specification and parameter values therefore formed a major basis for his opposition to activist demand-management policies that were designed to achieve full employment. "Full employment is a very difficult term to define," Friedman noted in 1980.[158]

Friedman himself struggled, in the years leading up to his 1967 address, to provide a conceptually sound definition of full employment. Some insight into this struggle is provided by considering his evolving view of the relationship between the stock of capital and potential output.

THE CAPITAL STOCK AND THE
NATURAL LEVEL OF OUTPUT

In 1982's *Monetary Trends*, Friedman and Schwartz had occasion to note the dependence of potential output on the stock of productive capital—which, properly conceived, should consist of both physical capital, such as machinery, and human capital.[159] This observation was among many statements that Friedman made indicating that an environment conducive to private-sector capital accumulation would tend to add to potential output—both by adding to the quantity of the capital input and by boosting the productivity of the labor input.[160] The conditions for greater capital formation included improvements in the incentive for households to save, as a greater savings pool promotes higher investment and so "adds to productive capacity" (*Newsweek*, July 27, 1981).[161]

But the views that Friedman expressed about how the capital stock should be treated in the analysis of potential output are also revealing about the *problems* involved in defining the natural level of output rigorously. Highly relevant here is a verbal exchange—which likely occurred around the early 1960s—that Robert Solow recalled having with Friedman: "I'm sure that that must have been in Milton's [money-and-banking] workshop, because I remember Milton was an active participant." In the exchange, "we had an argument about how to deal with measuring the effective stock of capital. And Milton's argument was that [even if] there was [varying] capacity utilization, that you should always be using the total available stock of capital. I wanted to use only, in this context, whatever was in use. And Milton refused to believe that such a thing was possible. It [the stock] was there, he said. And I said, 'Milton, imagine a machine [that is part of the total capital stock], and on it there is a switch with an "off" position and an "on" position. Well, [in the case of lower capital utilization] I want to imagine it in the "off" position.' That left him very unhappy" (Robert Solow, interview, December 2, 2013).

Judged in light of the natural-level-of-output concept that Friedman would eventually inspire, neither Solow's position nor that Friedman expressed in this exchange was wholly correct. In the presence of capital utilization, the amount of services contributed by the installed stock of capital can vary. A rigorous definition of how output behaves in a flexible-price economy should allow for this property, and variation in capital utilization can then be treated as one mechanism underlying the equilibrium response of flexible-price output to movements in real shocks (see Kydland and Prescott 1988). Solow's proposal to allow for varying utilization in defining capital would therefore appear to have validity (and Friedman's suggestion of ignoring such variation would be inappropriate). However, if the economy under study is believed to have price stickiness, Solow's proposal would not be appropriate for the specification of the behavior of potential output. For his proposal has the flaw that it incorporates in the definition of the effective stock of capital those movements in capital utilization that occur only as a result of the presence of price stickiness. For that reason, Solow's procedure would not be a viable element of a definition of flexible-price output. The upshot is that neither Solow's position on defining the effective capital stock nor Friedman's counterposition provides a reliable foundation for a construction of a measure of the natural level of output. To obtain such a measure, one would have to conduct an analysis closer to that of Kydland and Prescott (1988): that is, specify an economy with varying capital utilization and evaluate that economy's behavior in a flexible-price environment. Such a procedure would be in the spirit of Friedman's 1967 definition of the natural rate of unemployment.

Friedman's remarks to Solow at the workshop exchange reflected a pre-1967 stage of Friedman's thinking about potential output. His position during this stage had strong similarities to that he would express in 1967. But it was less rigorous, for he had not yet converged on a tenable definition of potential output. One manifestation in print of this earlier stage of Friedman's thinking came in 1963, when he ventured to offer a definition of capacity (that is, potential or natural) output.[162] A key aspect of this 1963 definition was one he would reaffirm in 1967: that the effects of monopoly power should be *included* in the definition of potential output, so that, by itself, monopoly power reduced potential output but did not make output low in relation to potential. But Friedman also included in his 1963 remarks the following statement: "A useful concept of 'capacity' should be a technical, production concept, dependent of course on factor prices but not on the state of demand."[163]

This statement could be reconciled with his later concept of the natural level of output, but only if specific constructions were put on the phrases "factor prices" and "state of demand." "Demand" in the latter phrase had to be interpreted as *nominal* demand and not real demand. It was to the former variable but not the latter variable that the natural level of output is necessarily insensitive. In a flexible-price economy, an increase in real aggregate demand can add to aggregate output if it gives rise to a higher amount of capital and labor supplied to the market. Friedman's example (discussed earlier in this chapter) of the demand for labor during World War II is an example of a change in real aggregate demand that would tend to raise the natural level of output (and not simply the actual level of output). In contrast, changes in nominal aggregate demand that affected real aggregate demand only because of price stickiness would raise output but not potential output.[164]

Friedman's suggestion that potential output was "dependent of course on factor prices" also needs to be qualified. As discussed earlier in this section, the natural level of output should indeed depend on factor prices, but, because this output concept is the equilibrium value of output in a *flexible-price* economy, the factor prices relevant for potential output are the prices prevailing in the flexible-price economy, not the *actual* factor prices observed in the sticky-price economy.

Friedman's 1963 formulation, with its references to demand and to prices, was evidently intended to capture elements that would be part of his ultimate natural-rate concept: that the baseline real series in question should "continually change"—reflecting responses to real shocks—yet should "exclude the effect of monetary policy" that was recorded in observed data on real variables.[165] Friedman's 1963 definition of capacity output cannot, however, be considered a success because—viewed from the perspective of later natural-rate definitions—it is a valid definition only under very specific interpretations of his wording. He had attempted to give a tight definition of potential output, and this attempt foundered in the face of the problems involved in this exercise. Little wonder that, around the time the 1963 remarks went into print, Friedman lamented that "it is almost impossible to define full employment in a way that is logically precise, and yet corresponds to what we have loosely in mind."[166]

It is against this background that Friedman's 1967 definition of the natural rate, which focused on the behavior of a reference flexible-price economy and did not attempt to define the natural rate in terms of observed variables such as actual prices, can be seen as a breakthrough that allowed for a definition of potential output that was logically rigorous and that embedded optimizing behavior on the part of the private sector.

Even with potential output defined as the level prevailing under flexible prices, an ambiguity remains in that definition—and the ambiguity has to do with the treatment of the capital stock. In the case of constant capital utilization, the capital stock is a predetermined variable that will appear—alongside exogenous real shocks—in the expression for potential output.

The issue that then arises is whether the capital stock used in the potential-output expression should be the economy's *observed* capital stock—even if, as will usually be the case, the behavior of that capital stock reflects effects of nominal stickiness and monetary policy in prior periods. This issue has come to the fore in discussions of the expression for the natural rate of output in dynamic optimizing models—with Woodford (2003, 372–73) arguing for conditioning the expression on the *actual* capital stock outstanding, and Neiss and Nelson (2001, 2003, 2005) alternatively suggesting that potential output should be a function of the *flexible-price* stock of capital. The choice between the two definitions involves taking a stand on whether the economy with which the sticky-price economy is compared is one that has *always* had price flexibility or instead if it is one that becomes a flexible-price economy only from period t onward.[167] Friedman did not appear to enter a clear-cut judgment concerning this choice. But he did state (in Instructional Dynamics Economics Cassette Tape 60, November 4, 1970) that a recent slowing in US firms' investment expenditures meant that US potential output would grow more slowly. This statement suggested that Friedman was comfortable with conditioning on the actual capital stock when defining the natural level of output.

THE NATURAL LEVEL OF OUTPUT
AND NOMINAL VARIABLES

The preceding analysis has taken the natural level of output as determined purely by real variables and as insensitive to monetary policy. This practice was obviously in keeping with the message that Friedman gave when extending Wicksell's natural-rate concept to measures of real economic activity. It is also a practice that has received considerable support from empirical studies. For example, Watson (1993, 1023) found that the real business cycle model "does a remarkably good job matching the very low frequency movements in output," while Crowder, Hoffman, and Rasche (1999, 117) found that real shocks accounted for over 90 percent of the forecast error variance of US real output at a sixty-quarter horizon. Because the natural-rate hypothesis suggests that output equals its natural rate at low frequencies, these findings are supportive of Friedman's notion that fluctuations in the natural rate of output are driven overwhelmingly by real factors.

Friedman did, nevertheless, spell out some ways in which monetary factors *did* affect the behavior of the natural level of output. One of the most obvious of these arose from the transactions and other services provided by money. Friedman stated that a money economy would tend to have a far greater level of productivity than an economy that ran on barter.[168] The services provided to the economy by money came from real money balances and not nominal money balances, and we have seen that the stocks of these two variables are determined by distinct sets of factors over long periods. But, as was also noted above, monetary policy has an influence on real money balances in the long run because the steady-state value of real money balances depends—negatively—on the steady-state inflation rate, which monetary policy determines. The dependence of productivity on the stock of real money balances therefore implies an inverse relationship between steady-state inflation and the steady-state level of productivity.[169]

Friedman emphasized, however, that the provision of money was only a stepping stone for an economy to achieve high productivity, as productivity also depended heavily on many real phenomena. "At most," Friedman observed, "money is a lubricator that can make it easier for those fundamental forces [initiative, thrift, and capacities for work] to manifest themselves."[170]

Friedman also regarded the existence of a market for credit as an important positive contributor to potential output. If the credit market were to close down or severely contract, the Friedman-Schwartz view was, as noted, that this "would probably greatly reduce the economy's productivity and efficiency."[171] Friedman further viewed "the ability to borrow capital" as important for productivity growth (*Dallas Morning News*, October 17, 1975). It is tempting to infer from Friedman's belief in credit/potential-output connections that the link between deposit and credit creation is another reason why real money balances matter for the behavior of potential output in his framework. As was discussed in chapter 6, however, such an inference would not be appropriate, for he stressed the *lack* of a reliable connection between aggregate credit and the stock of money, even under a fractional-reserves commercial banking system.

Friedman nevertheless believed that monetary policy could affect the credit market. For he believed that the presence of substantial inflation—certainly of rates that entered double digits—was disruptive for various markets for capital (*Newsweek*, December 27, 1976). Some of this disruption, he indicated, was due to the interaction of inflation with government regulations on the credit market—but inflation would corrode credit-market functioning even in the absence of such regulations.[172] Such credit disruption was one of various mechanisms through which Friedman believed that inflation of double digits could lower the productivity of countries like the United States and the United Kingdom, many of whose institutions were poorly positioned to adjust efficiently to expected inflation, even over long periods. He highlighted, for example, the lack of complete indexation of the tax system to inflation.[173] Friedman was also convinced that once inflation rose to moderate levels, it also became more variable.[174]

Partly for this reason, he believed that inflation—even when the stickiness of prices was put to one side—tended to distort the allocation of resources and to lower productive investment.[175] Some of these superneutrality violations could, he conjectured, matter for the *growth rate* of productivity and not just its level, and he accordingly suggested that "a slower rate of inflation may have favorable effects on output growth."[176]

Friedman regarded inflation in practice as likely to trigger policy actions such as wage and price controls that prevented the market system from operating and that thereby lowered productivity.[177] He also regarded inflation as likely to boost the ratio of tax revenue to output and consequently, he believed, to raise the share of government spending in aggregate expenditure.[178] Such a development would, Friedman contended, lower potential output.[179] But his descriptions of the links between higher inflation and higher levels of regulation, taxes, or public spending should primarily be regarded as predictions about the *policy reaction* to inflation rather than as accounts of the basic economic channels linking inflation and the natural level of output.

In contrast, a definite economic channel linking inflation to real behavior—and one prominent in Friedman's accounts of inflation—lay in the fact that deviations from price stability also encouraged the private sector to reduce its holdings of real money balances. In principle, this process could unwind the boost to productivity associated with the spread of money in an economy. Although Friedman did not regard the reduction in productivity arising from the private sector's flight from money as very important as long as inflation remained in single or low double digits, he nevertheless viewed agents' attempts to economize on money as amounting to a waste of resources.[180]

In cases of extreme inflation, especially hyperinflation, Friedman viewed the negative effect of monetary policy on potential output as extremely severe. Hyperinflation led to "a complete breakdown in the medium of exchange" and to a degree of economic turmoil that mandated a comprehensive monetary reform.[181] Thus Friedman endorsed the maxim (which, like many others, he sometimes erroneously attributed to Lenin) that the destruction of the value of money was destructive of society.[182] Friedman's own variant of this maxim was that the "cost if we let it [inflation] run unchecked will be a destruction of our system of society and government."[183] Friedman's reference to "unchecked" inflation was an important qualification. It implies that, provided inflation is kept to moderate levels, variations in the natural level of output tend to be dominated by nonmonetary factors.

CHAPTER 8

Friedman's Framework: Policy Rules

I. Friedman's Prescription of Constant Monetary Growth

In this chapter, the policy-rules aspect of Friedman's economic framework is analyzed. The analysis will cover, in section II, Friedman's perspective on the US monetary policy reaction function as observed in practice. In addition, in section III, Friedman's outlook toward optimal monetary policy will be discussed. That treatment will cover both stochastic optimal control and the place of the 1969 "Optimum Quantity of Money" analysis in Friedman's body of work. To begin with, however, the present chapter considers, in this first section, Friedman's well-known prescription of constant monetary growth.

How did Friedman arrive at that prescription? Chapter 3 discussed the fact that, in a 1948 paper, he advocated the monetization rule—an arrangement under which the federal government would run a cyclically balanced budget and would allow the deficits and surpluses that were associated with this fiscal policy to be monetized. It was argued that Friedman's rationale for the monetization rule rested partly on theoretical positions that he would dispense with when, over the period from 1948 to 1951, he became a monetarist.

It would be a mistake, however, to believe that Friedman's embrace of the quantity theory of money led automatically and immediately to his jettisoning of the monetization rule. On the contrary, in congressional testimony and other talks given during the 1951–54 period he continued to advocate that rule. Furthermore, as mentioned in chapter 4 and documented further below, he spoke favorably of the monetization rule even after he had become an advocate of the constant-monetary-growth rule.

The views expressed in this study are those of the author alone and should not be taken as those of the Federal Reserve Board or the Federal Reserve System. The author is grateful to David Laidler for comments on an earlier draft of this chapter and Gerald O'Driscoll for discussion of some of the issues covered herein. See the introduction for a full list of acknowledgments for this book.

That Friedman's becoming a monetarist did not coincide with his conversion to the cause of the constant-monetary-growth rule is testament to a dictum that he voiced on a number of occasions: that adoption of a monetarist theoretical framework did not go hand in hand with advocacy of a nonactivist monetary policy. In 1984, Friedman put the matter in these terms: "A believer in monetarist theory still can favor an activist monetary policy as a way to offset other changes in the economy."[1] Similarly, he stated on a number of occasions: "A monetarist no less than a Keynesian interpretation of economic fluctuations can lead to a fine-tuning approach to economic policy."[2]

The process by which Friedman became an advocate of a constant-monetary-growth rule is, consequently, distinct from the process by which his theoretical framework became monetarist. The latter process has been discussed in chapters 4 to 7. Friedman's shift to the constant-monetary-growth rule is the subject of the discussion that immediately follows.

From the Monetization Rule to Constant Monetary Growth

Prior to the 1950s, Friedman had considerable exposure to the constant-monetary-growth proposal—including via the writings of Clark Warburton and Lloyd Mints. The latter, in Mints (1950, 167, 172), specifically portrayed Friedman (who was by this point Mints's colleague) as a critic of the constant-monetary-growth rule and as having stressed its shortcomings in comparison with the monetization rule. During the early period of his monetarism, Friedman's rationale for the monetization rule shifted even as he continued to champion the rule. In 1948 he had regarded both fiscal policy and monetary policy as powerful. From this perspective, monetization of deficit spending magnified the already-large fiscal multipliers associated with such spending. By the early 1950s, however, Friedman's rating of the effects of fiscal policy was much diminished. He now saw deficit spending per se as not exerting a great influence on aggregate demand. But he was redoubled in his conviction that monetary policy had strong effects.

Against that background, automatically monetized fiscal deficits and surpluses, together with a rule for a balanced budget over the cycle, could be viewed as providing a convenient way of implementing stabilization policy, as these would generate a countercyclical pattern of monetary growth. Thus, Friedman reaffirmed in the 1950s his belief in the aggregate-demand-stabilizing effects of factors such as the progressive income tax structure, which helped produce an automatic reaction of the fiscal position to the business cycle.[3] Although he no longer contended that the response of tax revenues on the state of the national economy was in itself a very powerful stabilizing force, Friedman believed that it could be made into one if the associated fiscal imbalances gave rise to money creation.

In 1956, Friedman became an advocate of a policy of constant growth in the money stock. The first article in which he voiced a clear-cut preference for that rule over any other was one prepared for a conference at the Federal Reserve Board held on October 12–13, 1956; this article was published in March 1957.[4] Friedman had already signaled that he was moving in the direction of preferring the constant-monetary-growth rule when, in an unpublished talk in June 1956, he had observed with regard to arrangements for the conduct of monetary policy, "I must confess that I am myself somewhat in a state of flux about the best answer." On that occasion, he continued to speak highly of the 1948 rule but indicated that he was becoming convinced that "a much simpler, I might say simple-minded, system would do the job nearly as well," and he specified the constant-monetary-growth rule—at 4 percent per year—as that simpler alternative.[5]

But it was the October 1956 piece that represented the point at which Friedman formally shifted to advocacy of the constant-monetary-growth rule. Research he had done since his 1948 article, Friedman observed, "leads me to go even farther than I did in that paper." He explained that he had moved away from advocating the monetization rule after reaching the judgment that "a much less sophisticated monetary policy—namely, simply providing for a steady increase in the stock of money year by year—would be consistent with a high degree of stability and might therefore be preferable."[6]

In the October 1956 presentation, as in June, Friedman cited the fact that his change in viewpoint had been motivated by "research on monetary experience"—specifically, the study of the historical relationship between money and the economy in the United States.[7] The subsequent discussion in Friedman's article included a catalogue of some of the main historical findings that he and Schwartz had obtained concerning monetary policy in key historical episodes. In this overview, Friedman considered the Great Depression in detail but also cited other episodes of procyclical monetary policy: in World War I, the early 1920s, and the 1942-51 period.[8] And, by the same token, he pointed to the 1921-28 period as one in which the Federal Reserve's behavior did not add to economic fluctuations, and to the greater stability of monetary growth from 1951 as a factor that had promoted stabilization of the economy during the 1950s.[9] Furthermore, at this stage of Friedman's thinking, the Federal Reserve could be criticized for having taken actions, notably in 1931, whose effect "was to prolong and intensify the depression," but he had not yet reached the point of blaming the Federal Reserve for converting a recession into a depression by its inaction in 1930.[10]

It is therefore the case that, although the study of the 1930s played an important role in Friedman's reassessment of the historical record, that period's experience was not the exclusive part in this reassessment; it was one of several factors moving him in the direction of becoming a proponent of constant monetary growth. His criticism of the conduct of Federal Reserve policy during the 1930s was of long standing, and it continued to develop right through to the final version of *A Monetary History* in 1963. As was discussed in chapter 4, in the late 1940s Friedman voiced criticisms of US monetary policy as practiced during the Depression years. A critical attitude to Depression-era Federal Reserve policy was therefore part of Friedman's perspective on monetary policy well before his 1956 adoption of the constant-monetary-growth rule. As was also noted, the full Friedman-Schwartz indictment of the Federal Reserve from 1929 to 1933, particularly with regard to its conduct during 1930 and its acquiescence in the failure of the Bank of United States, did not crystallize until well after Friedman had become a proponent of the constant-monetary-growth rule.

On the basis of the historical record, Friedman in 1956 concluded that the really imperative break that the US monetary system needed to make from its past practice consisted of a move to arrangements that avoided procyclical variations in monetary growth. This conclusion contrasted with the reasoning underlying the monetization rule. That rule had sought countercyclical, not acyclical, monetary growth, by providing what Friedman called the "automatic stabilization" of deficit-generated countercyclical variations in monetary growth.[11]

Despite this prominent conversion to a different policy rule, Friedman continued to speak favorably from time to time about the monetization rule. His October 1956 discussion affirmed that, even though his research findings had turned him against the rule that he had proposed in his 1948 paper, the same research had "strengthened my confidence in the efficacy of the policies there proposed."[12] This theme continued in his later writings. He did not wholly repudiate the 1948 rule, and Friedman wrote flippantly in 1961 that his parentage of the monetization rule made him "loath to disinherit" it.[13] In his 1960 book *A Program for Monetary Stability*—which was adapted from lectures Friedman gave in 1959 and became one of the standard references on Friedman's case for the constant-monetary-growth rule—he prefaced his argument for constant monetary growth by affirming with regard to the monetization rule that he still had "no doubt that it would work well."[14]

By the time of the appearance of that book, Friedman had made the case for constant monetary growth in a number of congressional forums: in a 1958 submission to Congress and in two rounds of congressional testimony during 1959.[15] It was, however, *A Program for Monetary Stability* that contained an extended discussion of his reasons for dropping the monetization rule in favor of a policy of fixed monetary growth. Of these, one reason—noted above as having flowed from the historical review associated with the Friedman-Schwartz project—was that he was not convinced that constant monetary growth could be improved on (when judged against specific alternatives) in terms of the economic outcomes it delivered.[16] Another reason given was that a constant-monetary-growth rule had the attractive feature of simplicity, and public support for the rule would be fostered by the rule being easy to understand.[17] A third reason was that the new rule was solely a monetary policy rule, as opposed to a combined monetary/fiscal policy rule, and therefore its implementation in the United States would require fewer changes to institutional arrangements than would the proposals Friedman had advanced in 1948.[18]

The proposed monetary rule did indeed require fewer sweeping changes to policy arrangements than had the earlier proposal. But in citing this consideration as a factor underlying his decision to focus on monetary-growth rules, Friedman obscured the fact that his own model of the economy—specifically, his theory of economic fluctuations—had changed since 1948 in a way that also promoted a focus on exclusively monetary rules. Although Friedman in the early 1950s had, as discussed above, recast in monetarist terms his support for the 1948 rule, the original rationale offered for it had been one in which both fiscal and monetary policy each had a major potential role to play in providing countercyclical measures. The "economic stability" that Friedman believed would be associated with the monetization rule would come from both countercyclical movements in velocity—driven by the fiscal deficits and surpluses—and countercyclical movements in the money stock—provided by the monetization of the deficits and surpluses. According to this view, the private sector was a major source of destabilizing, autonomous movements in velocity, while the government was potentially a source of procyclical movements in money. The monetization rule, on this reasoning, would forestall the possibility of procyclical money movements and would instead provide countercyclical movements; in addition, the rule would be a source of countercyclical velocity movements that would offset the velocity fluctuations originating in the private sector.

In contrast, Friedman's subsequent belief in the constant-monetary-growth rule stemmed in part from his revised view that not only were private-sector-originated velocity movements difficult to offset (as discussed presently) but also that the larger velocity movements tended to come as a *result* of monetary instability.[19] The separation of monetary and fiscal policy embedded in Friedman's constant-monetary-growth-rule proposal therefore flowed naturally from his new conclusion that a policy aimed at delivering countercyclical monetary growth was unlikely to deliver much improvement—in terms of aggregate income variability—on the nonactivist monetary posture associated with constant monetary growth. For that new conclusion reflected Friedman's abandonment of his earlier attribution of major business cycle fluctuations to autonomous shifts in velocity.

Several of Friedman's discussions in policy forums highlighted a further major consideration that underlay his ultimate preference for the constant monetary growth. As was already indicated in chapter 4, the monetization rule could be criticized for the fact that its implementation required a high degree of knowledge on the part of policy makers, specifically of full-employment output. A remark Friedman made in *A Program for Monetary Stability*—that countercyclical variation in the stock of money did not correspond to a concept that could be measured unambiguously—could be viewed as an indictment of the monetization rule.[20] The 1948 rule had tensions with Friedman's skepticism, already voiced in the 1940s, about the degree of policy makers' knowledge of the economic structure. As will now be discussed, this skeptical outlook was further manifested in Friedman's writings during the 1950s on model uncertainty and on the possibility of destabilizing stabilization policy. These considerations helped sway him toward the constant-monetary-growth rule.

MODEL UNCERTAINTY

Brunner (1980c, 32) observed: "Milton Friedman made his famous case for a nonactivist strategy of a constant monetary growth (CMG) [rule] thirty years ago precisely on the basis of diffuse and uncertain structural information." Brunner then cited Friedman's paper "The Effects of a Full-Employment Policy on Economic Stability: A Formal Analysis"—published in French in 1951, but unveiled to the English-speaking world in a revised form in Friedman's collection *Essays in Positive Economics* in 1953.[21] Brunner's suggestion that Friedman advocated the constant-monetary-growth rule in 1951 (or in 1953) was definitely incorrect.[22] But Brunner was accurate in his accompanying indication that model uncertainty—the subject of the "Full-Employment Policy" paper—was an important consideration in leading Friedman to the constant-monetary-growth rule.[23]

Friedman's position was that price theory (that is, microeconomics) was a well-established, and in large part settled, body of knowledge. For him, what remained to be done in that field largely consisted of applying it to a greater range of private-sector decisions (such as gambling, as in Friedman and Savage's analysis). In contrast, Friedman believed that the specification of *macroeconomic* theory—together with the reconciliation of that theory with empirical evidence—was far from complete. This was partly because macroeconomic modeling, to a much greater extent than was the case with microeconomics, was intertwined with the matter of appropriate dynamic specification.[24] Consequently, Friedman was skeptical about formal structural macroeconomic models—an attitude that hardened in the later 1940s as he turned away from the majority Keynesian position. John Taylor observed that "his teaching and his thinking about micro stuff was very much model related . . . just basic, good old-fashioned price theory." But "he just felt that we had a long way to go with macro models" (John Taylor, interview, July 2, 2013). This attitude, although voiced by Friedman to Taylor in the last few decades of the former's life, was also evident much earlier—including in Friedman's remark in *Newsweek* in 1956 that economists' forecasts concerning the prospects for an individual firm or industry were more reliable than economists' aggregate forecasts (*Newsweek*, January 30, 1956).[25] As we have seen in chapters 1 and 4 above, the problem with setting policy in a manner that relied on forecasts was stressed by Friedman in his design of the monetization rule and, even before that, when he advised on tax policy during World War II.

As its subtitle suggested, Friedman's "Full-Employment Policy" paper represented a formalization of a number of the concerns that he had developed about stabilization policy. In what would be increasingly unusual in his monetary analysis, Friedman wrote down a formal model—a situation that would lead Okun (1972b, 134) to label the paper the "pioneer analytical article" on stabilization policy. Friedman used what he described as a "simple model implicitly accepted by most proponents of full-employment policy."[26] This consisted of a division of national income (either nominal or real) between a component consisting of its value in the absence of a stabilization policy and the component contributed by stabilization policy. Friedman used as the criterion for successful policy the minimization of the variance of income. Friedman showed that stabilization policy might add to the variance of income even if the policy responses tended, on average, to be in the right direction. The stabilization policy would truly succeed in reducing the variance of income only if the two components of income had a correlation in the −0.5 to −1.0 range.[27] The formal framework did not incorporate explicit lags in the effect of policy actions. But Friedman suggested that the presence of factors such as lags would make it more likely that the situation of destabilizing stabilization policy would prevail.[28] The model was too abstract to point toward a specific policy rule, but Friedman inferred from the results that it was prudent to rely on policies that aimed at being at most modestly countercyclical.[29]

The notion that model uncertainty should figure into the choice of policy strategy was subsequently further formalized by Brainard (1967). As president-elect of the American Economic Association, Friedman likely had a formal role in putting Brainard's paper on the program of the December 1966 American Economic Association meetings. But, although Friedman attended the session that included Brainard's presentation, Friedman made little comment on Brainard's paper (William Brainard, interview, March 5, 2014). Furthermore, Brainard's paper did not cite Friedman's work. It was therefore largely left to others to make the connections between Friedman "Full-Employment Policy" paper and Brainard's 1967 article.[30] Early discussions that did so included Okun (1971, 66; 1972b, 136), while more recent instances have included Lars Hansen and Thomas Sargent (2000, 2011).

The Hansen-Sargent research just cited was an important part of a revival of interest in the formal analysis of model uncertainty—a revival that encompassed both approaches that were in Brainard's tradition and the robust-control approach that Lars Hansen and Thomas Sargent advocated.[31] It is, however, not straightforward to judge whether this modern literature points in the direction of Friedman's constant-monetary-growth proposal. The reason for this is that the messages of the literature are very sensitive to what is treated as the monetary authority's instrument. For example, the Brainard (1967) tradition is seen as pointing to the conclusion that model uncertainty means it is desirable to lower policy responses to the state of the economy. But if the policy instrument is the nominal interest rate, less strong policy responses would imply a *greater* responsiveness of monetary growth to the state of the economy and so a more activist response when policy is judged in terms of money. That is, model uncertainty justifies a policy that is further from constant monetary growth than is the case without model uncertainty. Conversely, Lars Hansen and Thomas Sargent's (2011) suggestion that model uncertainty might, in an environment of model uncertainty, justify larger responses of the interest rate to the state of the economy might well imply a *reduced* responsiveness of monetary growth to the state of the economy, and so a less activist response when policy is judged in terms of a monetary aggregate. That is, in line with Friedman's intuition, model uncertainty in this case would appear to justify a policy that is closer to constant monetary growth than would be the case without model uncertainty.[32]

Irrespective of one's views about the implications of the modern literature on monetary policy under model uncertainty, the size of that literature leaves no doubt that the topic has become a source of great attention. It deserves emphasis that this topic was a consistent theme in Friedman's discussion. A contrary impression was left by Budd (1979, 205), who suggested that policy makers' lack of knowledge about economic structure "can be described as the 'early-Friedman' view" and that Friedman's case for monetary rules dropped the model-uncertainty argument after the early 1950s.[33]

But Friedman's articulations of the case for a monetary rule in the 1960s and 1970s actually continued to underline the importance of model uncertainty. For example, his 1972 *Newsweek* column "The Case for a Monetary Rule" included among the reasons for the rule the item, "The Limitations of Our Knowledge" (*Newsweek*, February 7, 1972). The same column quoted from Friedman's AEA presidential address of four years earlier, including the address's references to the limited "present stage of knowledge."

The AEA presidential address highlighted a particularly important feature of Friedman's emphasis on model uncertainty—one that had been present even in his earliest writings on the subject in the 1940s. This feature concerned the response by policy makers to the levels of real variables. Because policy makers' objectives for aggregate real variables involved the full-employment values of these series, and the latter were unobservable and their empirical estimates model dependent, stabilization policy was prone to make errors if it relied heavily on estimates of the series. As discussed in chapter 4, Friedman's doubts about the feasibility of obtaining accurate information about full-employment output formed part of his objections to Lerner's (1944) policy proposals.[34] These doubts included Friedman's specific objection: "To make this into a prescription to 'produce full employment,' Lerner must tell us how to know when there is 'insufficient total demand.'"[35] In view of these doubts, and the prominence Friedman gave them in his subsequent research, his own move away from the monetization rule—a rule that, as noted, required an estimate of the full-employment fiscal position—was a logical development.

Friedman also voiced from an early stage concerns about relying on the concept of the natural real rate of interest. In 1942 his paper with Allen Wallis had stressed the unobservable nature of this concept.[36] And his 1967 presidential address, while accepting the concept of the natural rate of interest and using it as the basis for a definition of the natural rate of unemployment, came out against monetary policy strategies that relied directly on estimates of either of these natural-rate series.[37] He had, of course, the same attitude when it came to policies that responded to estimates of the output gap.[38]

Friedman's appeal to model uncertainty as a basis for opposing policy activism was, as Brunner and Meltzer (1983, 87) put it, largely "independent of any specific hypothesis about money." A development that bears out this remark is the work of Athanasios Orphanides, which was partially inspired by Friedman's emphasis on model uncertainty but did not use monetary-growth rules. This line of research (see, for example, Orphanides 2003; and Orphanides and Williams 2013) stressed nominal interest-rate reaction functions that were expressed in first-difference form. Specifically, the first difference of the nominal interest rate would respond to the level of inflation and to the rate of growth of real series—a specification that avoided reliance on estimates of the levels of the output gap or the real rate of interest.[39]

This notion—that to recommend monetary policy strategies that use first differences instead of levels of real series is to be in the tradition of Milton Friedman's work on policy rules—has been vigorously challenged by Benjamin Friedman (2013). However, Milton Friedman's writings and public statements contained a multitude of warnings against relying on real levels series.[40] In the early 1960s, for example, he criticized the Kennedy administration's use of unemployment-rate targets.[41] In the early 1970s, he observed, "I believe that use of the level of employment as the primary or exclusive objective of policy would be a serious mistake."[42] And in a *Wall Street Journal* interview in 1995, Friedman remarked: "I don't know what the natural rate is, neither do you, and neither does anyone else" (*Wall Street Journal*, January 24, 1995, A8).

Conversely, Friedman was more optimistic about monetary policy strategies that were geared toward growth rates of series. For example, among the candidates that might serve as an appropriate basis on which to carry out monetary policy, he nominated stabilization of "the rate of change of nominal income."[43] During the 1970s, Friedman underscored a point that Orphanides (2003) would stress in his later study of that decade: that the growth rate of real output was much less sensitive than was the level to official revisions to national accounts data, and so the former series could be used more safely in policy making.[44] On another occasion during the 1970s, when asked if a national government should have a full-employment policy, Friedman replied, "No; of course not. It should have a policy of stable employment." The attraction of the latter policy, he explained, was that it avoided sharp economic surges and declines, while not aiming to offset minor fluctuations. The policy of stable employment that Friedman invoked on this occasion can be viewed as a policy that aims for rough stabilization of the growth rate of employment. It may be contrasted with a delicate fine-tuning policy that aimed to correct every little actual or incipient deviation in the level of employment from a target level. It is significant that only *after* elaborating on the general form that a stable policy should take did Friedman get to the specifics of his preferred version of this policy, that is, constant monetary growth.[45]

Furthermore, Friedman viewed the interest-rate pattern most consistent with economic stabilization as one in which interest rates were positively related to real output growth. Thus, although opposed to the use of the federal funds rate as a policy instrument, he suggested that, if it was going to be used, the most appropriate path for that instrument was one that was allowed to respond positively to output growth.[46] In this respect, too, Friedman's policy prescriptions were consistent with first-difference rules for a short-term interest rate.

In his normative work, Friedman sought to liberate the setting of monetary policy from a specific model of the economy. Nevertheless, his policy prescriptions *did* embed some theory. The choice of the growth rate in his constant-monetary-growth-rule prescription was informed by Friedman's assessment of the long-run relationship between monetary growth and nominal income growth, as well as his confidence in monetary analysis that suggested that the long-run real output growth rate was independent of monetary policy. Friedman's prescription therefore embedded a quantity-theory relationship between the long-run mean growth rates of output, prices, and money. In using this model-based information, Friedman was utilizing not only the quantity theory of money but also his oft-stated contention that economists knew more about long-run relations than about the short-run connections between series.[47] This perspective, together with the low rate at which he discounted the future, led him to focus on the long-run consequences of following a particular monetary policy rule and to motivate the constant-monetary-growth rule in that light.

Friedman's proposed manner for introducing the constant-monetary-growth rule—when the economy was starting from an inflationary situation—was via a gradual, multiyear step-down in monetary growth. This recommendation, too, reflected the use of theory—namely the view that there were interim real-output costs of disinflation that it was desirable to contain. "A firm committed policy," he wrote in 1978, "would provide an effective gradual transition to a lower rate of inflation without serious disruption."[48] But even this recommendation did not incorporate *detailed* information concerning the dynamics and parameters of the Phillips-curve relationship—and Friedman was perennially doubtful about the extent of the economics profession's command of this information.

His skepticism about knowledge of economic dynamics notwithstanding, Friedman did venture to suggest some ways in which constant monetary growth, once instituted, would promote stability. As already mentioned, one consequence of his rule that he noted was that it would mean that procyclical monetary growth would be removed as a factor magnifying the effect of nonmonetary disturbances.[49] But he went further, suggesting that constant monetary growth would give "a pretty good basis for a stable society" (Instructional Dynamics Economics Cassette Tape 64, December 31, 1970). Indeed, as McCallum (1989b, 243–44; 1999a, 1488) observed, Friedman clearly anticipated the rational expectations literature in suggesting that a rule would be stabilizing via its effect on expectations.[50] McCallum pointed in particular to Friedman's 1962 piece "Should There Be an Independent Monetary Authority?" as being explicit on this point.[51]

Friedman had made similar points as far back as the late 1940s, when articulating the case for his monetization rule.[52] Such points also featured in his popular expositions of the case for the constant-monetary-growth rule. For example, in *Newsweek* (February 7, 1972), he stressed that a policy of steady monetary growth announced in advance and then delivered would be more stabilizing than would a discretionary (that is, judgment-driven) policy even if the latter policy delivered, ex post, the same pattern of monetary growth as the rule.[53]

ROLE OF THE FEDERAL RESERVE

"As a matter of long-run reform, I would like to see the Federal Reserve System in its present form abolished and replaced by a ... system in which there was no monetary authority possessing discretionary powers over the quantity of money."[54] These words were written by Milton Friedman in 1951. The "system" to which he referred amounted to the monetization rule that he then favored. But the just-quoted description of the new system would also apply to the constant-monetary-growth rule that Friedman advocated from 1956 onward. And the situations prevailing under both the constant-monetary-growth rule and the monetization rule could both be accurately encapsulated by Hicks's (1963, 319) observation about the former rule: "there is still to be a Monetary Authority."

Under Friedman's policy proposals, therefore, there would still be a monetary authority providing the monetary base. In addition, in the case in which there are not 100 percent reserve requirements and the monetary-growth rule applies to a money stock measure, the monetary authority would monitor variations in the money multiplier and then make adjustments to open market operations in a manner best designed to achieve the monetary-growth target.[55] The monetary system in Friedman's vision therefore differed sharply from the arrangement urged by Hayek (1976) in which the private sector, and not the public sector, would issue base money.

It is in light of Friedman's specific prescription for a new system that his references to the desirability of abolishing the Federal Reserve should be interpreted. All Friedman's major monetary proposals from 1948 onward entailed the abolition of the Federal Reserve in the sense that that institution would cease to have prerogatives in the setting of monetary policy. As George Stigler would put it in May 1964: "My colleague, Milton Friedman, on occasion recommends the abolition of the Federal Reserve System."[56] The contrary suggestion—that Friedman proposed abolition of the Federal Reserve only in his statements from the mid-1980s onward—is incorrect.[57] Friedman himself put it this way in 1981: "I have been in favor of abolishing the Federal Reserve System for as long as I can remember" (*Human Events*, December 5, 1981, 6).

The specific institutional change that Friedman envisioned as part of the implementation of his constant-monetary-growth rule would involve the Federal Reserve ceasing to be an entity separate from the US Department of the Treasury.[58] Under this alteration in arrangements, he suggested, there would be "a single locus of authority that could be held responsible" for monetary policy.[59] Within the Treasury, Friedman recommended, a board of three persons, with a support staff working on matters of research and operations, should be given responsibility for organizing the open market operations needed to achieve the monetary-growth target.[60]

In the mid-1990s, the combination of unusual patterns in M2 velocity behavior and US economic stability prompted a changed perspective on Friedman's part. He became more optimistic than he had been for many decades about the feasibility and desirability of the direct pursuit by the Federal Reserve of a price-stability goal.[61] As between this policy and a constant-monetary-growth rule, however, Friedman remained on balance in favor of the latter arrangement. He explained that this preference was based on the fact that a constant-monetary-growth rule would, and an inflation-targeting arrangement would not, allow the Federal Reserve System to be abolished (see E. Nelson 2007, 171–72).

COMMODITY STANDARDS

Friedman parted ways with many critics of US monetary policy not only in his view that a monetary authority should be retained, but in his opposition to linking monetary policy to the price of gold or other commodities.

Neil Wallace and Ben Bernanke have both had occasion to draw attention to the same Friedman statement concerning commodity-based monetary standards:

> As regards . . . the inefficiency of commodity money, it is helpful to recall Friedman's remark which, paraphrasing slightly, is as follows: why expend resources to dig up gold simply in order to put it in a bank vault? (Wallace 1988, 30)

> Now, unfortunately, gold standards are far from perfect monetary systems. One small problem . . . is that there's an awful big waste of resources. . . . Milton Friedman used to emphasize that that was a very serious cost of a gold standard; that all this gold was being dug up and then put back into another hole. (Bernanke 2012b, 13)

Both these statements are references to Friedman's remark about the "business of digging up gold in one part of the world to bury it in another," in his 1951 paper "Commodity-Reserve Currency."[62] The references point up the fact that, from the start of his monetarist period, Friedman parted company with many quantity theorists in the negative view he took about commodity-based monetary systems, the gold standard included.[63]

And while some "hard money" advocates during the Bretton Woods era pressed for the system to become one more genuinely linked to the gold price, Friedman's own critique of Bretton Woods was along substantially different lines. It was a good thing, he believed, that the value of the US dollar and the exchange value of other currencies were not linked to gold; it would be better for the severance of the monetary system from gold to be brought out into the open, through the abandonment of the United States of its pegging of the gold price; and it would be better still if this change were accompanied by a move to a system of floating exchange rates. For Friedman, the most desirable arrangement was a fiat monetary system accompanied by a monetary policy rule directed at the national economy. In advocating that monetary policy be oriented on a domestic aggregate (in his proposal, the nominal money stock—albeit with price stability as an ultimate goal), Friedman was departing from widely held contemporaneous views. But he was following in the footsteps of some key monetary economists, including Wicksell, Fisher, and (in his pre-1936 writings) Keynes, as well as Henry Simons.[64]

When confronted with advocates of a return to the gold standard, Friedman would defend his preferred system by citing the economic instability observed under the gold standard prior to World War I (see, in particular, *Wall Street Journal*, March 4, 1988).[65] Accounts written by monetarists other than by Friedman (for example, Bordo 1981, and Meltzer and Robinson 1989) have provided more detailed indictments of US economic performance under the gold standard. They have noted that the operation of the gold standard tended to promote procyclical variation in the money stock. As we have seen, procyclical behavior of money was something Friedman saw as a recurrent aspect of US monetary behavior in the first four decades of the Federal Reserve System's existence. But this grievance regarding the US monetary system was necessarily separate from Friedman's critique of commodity-based standards.[66] For it has already been discussed (in chapter 2) that Friedman's position was that ever since 1914, the United States had *not* been beholden to the gold standard or to other international obligations in its setting of monetary policy. In Friedman's view, therefore, Federal Reserve policy, not the international monetary system, was the major source of the procyclical behavior of the money stock as observed since 1914. Friedman's perspective on Federal Reserve policy in practice is, accordingly, now considered.

II. Friedman's Views on Modeling
Monetary Policy in Practice

The constant-monetary-growth arrangement that Friedman advocated was often contrasted with the conduct of US monetary policy in practice—with the former seen as a rule and the latter as not rule-like at all. In actuality, however, US monetary policy in the postwar period did have systematic elements and, to that extent, could be regarded as partially adhering to a "rule." Although, as we shall see, the use of the term "rule" to describe actual US monetary policy was rare until Robert Lucas employed it for this purpose, Friedman frequently acknowledged that there *did* exist a systematic aspect of US monetary policy reactions during the 1950s, 1960s, and 1970s. It is therefore his view on the *actual* US monetary policy reaction function over this period with which the present section is primarily concerned. Friedman's position on monetary/fiscal policy interaction is also considered, while the section concludes with a discussion of Friedman's embrace—in many of his later commentaries—of the "public choice" view of policy agencies' behavior.

THE REACTION FUNCTION

Friedman's discussions of monetary policy as practiced in the United States in the 1950s through the 1980s put considerable emphasis on the unpredictability associated with Federal Reserve policy. The record, he remarked, was one in which "the Federal Reserve swing[s] so erratically from side to side" (*Newsweek*, July 5, 1971). He suggested that this erratic pattern made it difficult to predict future monetary developments: "My longtime record in predicting . . . what the Fed will do [is] abominable" (*Wall Street Journal*, July 5, 1989).

In contrast, Paul Samuelson, in an audio commentary in 1968, observed:

> I think that I can pretty well predict what the Federal Reserve will try to do. . . . Some people regard the behavior of officials in Washington as a great mystery: as inscrutable as the Sphinx. I must say I haven't found that to be the actual experience. I sit down on my couch and I think, "If . . . I were confronted with the present situation, what would I be tempted to do?" And it's remarkable how often, by that simple test, I can figure out in advance what Washington is likely to do. So it is with the Federal Reserve. (Instructional Dynamics Economics Cassette Tape 6 [Paul Samuelson series], December 1968)

Unlikely as it may seem, Friedman's and Samuelson's remarks on Federal Reserve policy are compatible. Samuelson's emphasis on the predictability of Federal Reserve policy arose from the fact that the authorities followed an *interest-rate* reaction function that implied systematic responses of the policy rate to the state of the economy. Friedman's complaint about the erratic and unpredictable character of monetary policy essentially arose from the behavior of *monetary growth* associated with that interest-rate policy. A key fault associated with the Federal Reserve's reaction function, he remarked, was how difficult it was "to predict what monetary growth the Fed will produce."[67]

Before elaborating on Friedman's view of the monetary policy reaction function, it is worth indicating why it is *not* appropriate to attribute to him the following position: that the Federal Reserve in practice *consciously* chose the rate of monetary growth and made that rate follow a univariate exogenous process. Although, for those familiar with Friedman's research and commentary on US monetary policy, this is surely a surprising attribution to make to him, it is one that has been surprisingly pervasive in the research literature.[68]

Characterizations of Friedman's views that go along the lines sketched in the preceding paragraph seem to result from a syllogism. From two positions that *were* indeed integral to his thinking—(1) that the Federal Reserve's actions were crucial for the course of monetary growth (including the growth of aggregates that included demand and time deposits), and (2) that US monetary growth was volatile in practice—the invalid inference has been made that Friedman believed that the Federal Reserve *deliberately* made monetary growth follow a univariate exogenous process, endowing this exogenous path with large shocks of its own making.

The text of the *Monetary History* alone repudiates this inference about Friedman's views on US monetary policy in practice. That narrative provided ample documentation of an observation subsequently made by Samuel Brittan: "In none of the periods covered by Friedman and Anna Schwartz in their *Monetary History of the United States* was there a conscious money supply policy" (*Financial Times*, February 15, 1988, 41).[69]

It was, therefore, in light of the historical record of the United States and other countries that Friedman remarked: "Monetary authorities have more frequently than not . . . paid little or no attention to the stock of money *per se*."[70] Furthermore, even in periods—such as 1951 to 1960—for which Friedman perceived the US authorities as using money-stock behavior as an indicator, the Federal Reserve responded to other variables too.[71] It followed that the behavior of the money stock during the Federal Reserve's existence was, Friedman remarked in 1969, "an incidental consequence of the other things it's doing" (Instructional Dynamics Economics Cassette Tape 40, December 17, 1969).[72] Even in 1982—by which time the Federal Reserve had elevated, once again, the status of monetary aggregates in its policy decisions—Friedman cautioned against the assumption that "observed monetary fluctuations result from explicit Federal Reserve policy," especially when that assumption was used to analyze monthly or quarterly variations in the stock of money (*Newsweek*, December 27, 1982).

Friedman further recognized that the Federal Reserve had concerned itself heavily with managing market interest rates—not merely during the pegging policy of the 1940s, but ever since the beginning of the Federal Reserve System in 1914.[73] Once the Federal Reserve resumed an active monetary policy in the early 1950s, Friedman perceived correctly that it was the level of short-term market interest rates—and not the monetary base, the money stock, or their rates of growth—that the authorities sought to steer with their tools of discount-rate policy and open market operations.[74] Chapters 10–13 and 15 below analyze Friedman's views on US monetary policy in the period from the 1950s to the 1970s. That analysis confirms Goodhart's (1989a, 331) characterization that, with regard to short-term-interest rates, Friedman "had no doubts that these were normally determined by the authorities, and could be changed by them, and were not freely determined in the market." Friedman was, in addition, of the view that, in those periods when the Federal Reserve was permitted to vary interest rates, it did so with the aim of meeting economic-stabilization goals.[75]

In light of the fact that Friedman recognized that the Federal Reserve had developed a systematic response to the economy from an early stage of its existence, and that it reverted to a systematic reaction function from 1951 onward, how did it follow that—both in the 1950s and in subsequent decades—he saw US monetary policy as volatile and often leading to unpredictable consequences for monetary growth? There are two principal reasons.

First, although Friedman's work on the liquidity effect (see chapter 6) implied a recognition of a short-run inverse relationship between market interest rates and monetary growth, he regarded the precise timing and quantitative aspects of the relationship as subject to considerable looseness, so that "many movements in interest rates . . . cannot readily be connected with movements in the quantity of money."[76] It followed that a predictable interest-rate policy did not invariably translate over short periods into predictable movements in the monetary base and money.[77]

Friedman granted, however, that a monetary policy tightening or loosening initiated by the central bank via changes in interest rates *would* in time translate into an altered path for monetary growth.[78] The systematic interest-rate reaction function therefore did imply a systematic money-supply reaction function—an implication brought out in Friedman's references to the "reaction mechanism of the Fed" (Instructional Dynamics Economics Cassette Tape 183, January 1976, part 1).

But it is the behavior of the stock of money generated by this mechanism that underlay Friedman's second reason for seeing US monetary policy in the three decades after the 1951 Federal Reserve/Treasury Accord as erratic. For, as already noted, he was critical of what the Federal Reserve's systematic policy reaction function implied for monetary growth. He believed that the implied monetary-growth pattern helped confirm that monetary policy had been destabilizing for the economy in practice, both on the dimension of output and on the dimension of prices.

Output's Role in the Monetary Policy Reaction Function

With regard to output stabilization, Friedman believed that postwar Federal Reserve policy had been counterproductive because the systematic reactions to the state of the economy had not been appropriate, by the criterion of the unconditional variance of output. Because of nominal rigidity (wage and/or price stickiness), the operation of the private economy need not imply that the output gap would be nonzero in the face of nonmonetary shocks.[79] As Friedman put it, "The 'market' rate will vary from the natural rate for all sorts of reasons other than monetary policy."[80] Under these conditions, central-bank action could be a stabilizing force by offsetting the effect of nominal rigidity and reacting to the nonmonetary shocks in a manner that made the responses of real variables to those shocks coincide with the responses of the natural values of the real variables to the same shocks. But monetary policy could also act as a force that destabilized both output and the output gap.[81] And in Friedman's view, it was the case that, on the whole, when the output-stabilizing reaction of monetary policy to a shock would have implied a certain nonzero response of monetary growth to that shock, the actual response of monetary growth had been wrongly signed, or of the right sign but too large.[82] Friedman in particular characterized monetary policy as featuring responses that were too late and too great in magnitude (see, for example, *Newsweek*, October 30, 1967). Too-late responses might be avoided by a forward-looking policy, and Friedman acknowledged that Federal Reserve policy was intended to be forward looking. But he regarded its aims at being preemptive as also being destabilizing in practice, in part because of its dependence on unreliable forecasts.[83]

US monetary policy was, on this view, destabilizing in the postwar historical record (see, for example, *Newsweek*, February 7, 1972). Friedman did not ascribe to the US authorities an *intentional* policy of increasing economic fluctuations. But he concluded that for most of the period since 1914, including in the post-1951 period, the Federal Reserve had unwittingly increased instability instead of achieving its intended aim of offsetting sources of economic instability.[84]

The preceding description of Friedman's views on monetary policy and output fluctuations contrasts with the portrayal of his views given in some of the vector autoregression (VAR) literature of the 1980s and 1990s. In that vintage of the VAR literature, Friedman's view that money mattered for output fluctuations was represented as a view that monetary policy shocks accounted for a large portion of real output variations.[85] As monetary policy innovations have rarely been found to account for a large share of the forecast error variance of either monetary policy instruments or US real output, these discussions have portrayed Friedman's view of the business cycle as having been rejected by VAR studies.[86]

But it is really the VAR literature's interpretation of Friedman, and its related inference that VAR findings contradict his theory of the business cycle, that should be rejected. The portrayal of Friedman's views in the paragraphs above has *not* relied on the existence of monetary policy shocks. Any contribution that those shocks make to output fluctuations is in addition to the fluctuations that would arise from the systematic monetary policy actions that were central in Friedman's account of money/output interaction. Friedman and Schwartz explicitly rejected the notion that the monetary variable that they considered significant for output variation consisted solely of the statistical innovation in money. They insisted instead that it was the "longer-term systematic movements" of monetary variables that mattered crucially for the course of aggregate spending.[87]

Friedman in turn traced much of the systematic variation in money to Federal Reserve reactions to economic developments (see E. Nelson 2004b; and chapters 10–13 and 15 below). It was his explicit view that cyclical fluctuations were, in practice, amplified by the Federal Reserve's reaction. Friedman and Schwartz regarded money as the "channel through which other disturbances are transmitted."[88] In particular, economic downturns in the historical record that were severe acquired this status because the Federal Reserve allowed the money stock to contract; but the Federal Reserve had not necessarily produced the initial economic downturn.[89] This regularity about large downturns also held true for longer-term movements in nominal income: "disturbances, wherever they originate, have diffused effects if and only if they trigger changes" in the quantity of money.[90] For less long-lasting and severe movements, money had a qualitatively similar role. In particular, the Federal Reserve in the postwar period had, Friedman said, "deepened recessions" through its systematic policy responses (*Newsweek*, March 10, 1980).

All in all, the Friedman emphasis on the point that US monetary policy engendered a procyclical behavior of the money stock, and his suggestion that this was testimony to a destabilizing Federal Reserve response to non-monetary developments, were very incompatible with interpretations that attributed to him the view that monetary policy innovations dominated the business cycle. Woodford (1998, 393) has been notably critical of the VAR literature's practice of associating Friedman with the primacy of monetary shocks.[91] The preceding consideration of Friedman's interpretation of the reaction function indicates that this criticism of the VAR literature is justified.

THE ROLE OF INFLATION IN THE MONETARY POLICY REACTION FUNCTION

With regard to the behavior of inflation, Friedman's criticism of the postwar monetary reaction function took a somewhat different tack. Certainly, the factors making for output variability were likely also to promote variation in inflation; but a tendency for monetary policy to be variable does not in itself imply that inflation will tend to be high and rising—as it was over much of the later 1960s and in the 1970s. As will be discussed in chapter 10, Friedman anticipated this pattern of inflation in the United States in a talk he gave in 1954 about the likely form that the monetary authorities' reaction function would take in the years ahead. As Friedman put it in a later summary of the argument, tendencies for the US authorities to inflate "arise ... from the asymmetrical attitude of policymakers toward contractions in output and expansions in output so that, in case of doubt, there has been a bias in the direction of inflation."[92] The asymmetry in question did not arise from any conscious desire to boost output above potential. It stemmed rather from the tendency for inflation that emerged from excessive demand to be attributed, in part, to nonmonetary causes—a misplaced diagnosis that would act to inhibit an adequate reaction of monetary policy to higher inflation.[93]

Friedman believed that if the authorities could be persuaded that his constant-monetary-growth rule could improve economic performance, when that performance was judged on the basis of economic outcomes prevailing over long horizons, they would be willing to adopt the rule.[94] In practice, part of that process of persuasion involved establishing that, in the past, constant monetary growth might well have been a better policy than actual Federal Reserve conduct. Friedman therefore welcomed evidence that Paul Samuelson shared some of his negative views about the Federal Reserve's postwar monetary policy record. Samuelson, as already noted, deprecated the notion that the Federal Reserve's monetary policy reactions were unpredictable. But—just as Friedman's own acknowledgment of systematic Federal Reserve reactions did not turn him away from the conclusion that monetary policy was erratic and destabilizing—Samuelson would come round to the view that US monetary policy responses had, on net, created a procyclical pattern in monetary growth that was undesirable and that could have been avoided (Samuelson 1973a, 227). Friedman seized on this aspect of Samuelson's analysis when both of them appeared in Washington, DC, at a congressional committee hearing on monetary policy held in November 1975, with Friedman remarking that he was "delighted to welcome Paul into the company of monetarists."[95] Samuelson responded sharply that his own criticisms of the Federal Reserve's record did not imply that he endorsed the constant-monetary-growth rule. Instead, Samuelson suggested that the Federal Reserve adopt a rule derived from stochastic optimal control (Samuelson 1975, 74).

But regardless of the alternative favored to actual US monetary policy practice, there was wide agreement by the mid-1970s, including between Friedman and Samuelson, that the Federal Reserve's historical policy actions could be understood in terms of a systematic reaction function and that they did not consist of wholly unpredictable and unsystematic judgmental adjustments of monetary policy instruments. This was an important area of agreement, as unsystematic judgmental adjustments had, in earlier debates on monetary policy, often been the standard description of actual policy decisions. In particular, such adjustments were what the previous generation's advocates of policy rules, such as Henry Simons, had tended to label as "discretion" or as policy making by "authorities."[96]

The rational expectations literature on monetary policy reinforced the tendency to view both actual and hypothetical monetary policies as policy rules, since, as Sargent (1996, 543) noted, that literature promoted a mindset in which different monetary policy options were classified as alternative rules. It was therefore from a rule-based perspective that Robert Lucas (1976a) wrote about actual Federal Open Market Committee policy:

the release of [FOMC] minutes will substantially help researchers who are attempting to discover the implicit *rules* which govern the way monetary policy reacts to the state of the economy. Assuming FOMC decisions are not entirely capricious, such rules must exist. Yet traditionally, the FOMC has been reluctant to describe its behavior in these terms. This unfortunate practice leaves the important task of spelling out exactly what monetary policy *is* (that is, what rules are being implicitly followed) to economists and others outside the Federal Reserve System. Any information releases, certainly including minutes of FOMC meetings, which help in this task should be encouraged and, where possible, required.

A few years later, McCallum (1980, 725) called for Keynesian-monetarist disputes on appropriate monetary policy to be cast in terms of a discussion of alternative policy rules. McCallum contended that it was "quite clear that debates between economists—for example, Milton Friedman and

James Tobin—are about the desirability of different policy rules."[97] McCallum went on to represent Tobin as favoring a money rule that responded to output with a nonzero coefficient and Friedman as favoring a zero coefficient.

The Choice of Instrument

Although it was formally valid, McCallum's way of characterizing the different positions on rules taken by Friedman and Tobin obscured an important area of difference between them: their choice of policy instrument. As discussed in chapter 5 above, and further in chapters 12 and 13 below, Tobin tended to put much less emphasis on money in his descriptions of how monetary policy worked than did Friedman. Indeed, in describing his research agenda in the mid-1960s, Tobin remarked that a theme of his work was the dethroning of money from its existing position in monetary analysis.[98] But Tobin's disagreement with Friedman pertained not only to the modeling of the structure of the economy but also to the appropriate instrument of monetary policy. In 1960, Friedman stated: "The stock of money therefore seems to me the relevant magnitude in terms of which to formulate monetary rules."[99] In contrast, in the same year Tobin (1960) called for the Federal Reserve to institutionalize its use of a short-term interest rate by paying interest on reserves and using the interest rate on reserves as the instrument with which it managed short-term market rates and carried out stabilization policy.[100]

Opinion among monetary economists since the 1980s has overwhelmingly shifted in favor of the short-term nominal interest rate, rather than money or a reserves aggregate, as the normal policy instrument. This shift has occurred partly for the reason emphasized in Poole (1970): allowing monetary quantities to adjust, and the nominal interest rate to be unchanged, in the face of an exogenous shock to the demand for money allows nominal and real income to be insulated from money demand shocks. Woodford (2003, 111, 298) has argued that the case for an interest-rate instrument goes considerably further. As well as shielding the economy from money demand shocks, an appropriately formulated interest-rate rule can be as stabilizing as any quantity rule in the response to other types of shocks, with the implication that an interest-rate rule is "unambiguously superior" to a fixed-monetary-growth rule (Woodford 2003, 111).

Friedman encountered arguments similar to these during his own period of activity in monetary economics. He granted that, in principle, it was desirable to accommodate money demand shocks. But he was concerned that a monetary policy that accommodated these shocks might also feature undesirable responses to other shocks, including accommodation of shocks that "should not be accommodated."[101] This position reflected his concern that policy makers who used an interest-rate instrument would not adjust it adequately when adjustments were required—partly because shocks were inherently difficult to ascertain, and partly because policy makers might work in an environment in which there was pressure to keep interest rates more stable than economic conditions justified.[102]

In fact, just as Friedman's view of the transmission mechanism can be described in terms of interest rates (even though he regarded money as a very useful summary of monetary policy transmission), his case for fixed monetary growth can be cast in terms of the implied behavior of interest rates. Friedman's description of constant monetary growth as an "essentially automatic stabilizing monetary policy" can be viewed as reflecting his belief that the rule would entail an appropriate relationship between the short-term interest rate and the state of the economy.[103] As just noted, Friedman was concerned that a regime in which the short-term interest rate was the monetary policy instrument would recurrently feature periods in which the policy-rate target was inappropriately held constant, or adjusted too slowly, in the face of disturbances. This pattern of policy behavior would allow the effect on the economy of the shocks in question to cumulate—a situation that would promote instability in both interest rates and economic activity over longer periods.[104] In particular, it has already been observed that Friedman was critical of the US authorities in the 1970s for not allowing the federal funds rate to respond quickly enough (and sufficiently) to changes in real output growth. A corollary is that a fixed-monetary-growth rule can be viewed as having the desirable feature that aggregate-demand pressures will automatically generate a change in market interest rates.[105]

With regard to the interest-rate response to inflation implied by a fixed-monetary-growth rule, the discussion in Woodford (2003, 131) has indicated the likelihood that the response satisfies the Taylor principle, and Friedman himself expressed a rudimentary version of the Taylor principle when in 1971 he observed that "if it [the Federal Reserve] wants to lower [interest] rates it must first move to raise them" and that the rise would need to be of a magnitude that raised real and not just nominal interest rates.[106] Friedman's position on monetary policy's response to inflation must also be acknowledged as an important distinction between his and Tobin's perspective on monetary policy rules. As will be indicated in later chapters, Tobin was skeptical not only about monetary growth as an indicator but also about the notion that low nominal interest rates in relation to inflation suggested that monetary policy needed to be tightened. He was frequently very critical, in the 1960s and 1970s, of using monetary policy to fight inflation and favored incomes policy as a separate instrument against inflation. Consequently, Tobin's and Friedman's differences with regard to appropriate macroeconomic policy went beyond both the activist-versus-nonactivist monetary policy rule issue and the quantity-versus-interest-rate policy-instrument issue.

Implications for Money/Income Relationships

The preceding discussion of policy rules in practice is closely related to a matter on which many Keynesians criticized Friedman's monetary work. Samuelson (1970c, 152; 1971, 19) and Tobin (in Tobin 1969b, 22–23; 1969c, 170; and *Economist*, October 23, 1976a, 95), for example, contended that Friedman did not reconcile his own complaints about US monetary policy in practice with his inferences from the empirical evidence on money/real output relationships. Surely, they suggested, Friedman was not being consistent when he complained about the fact that policy makers in practice made money procyclical, and yet also took the observed positive correlation between money and output as evidence of the importance of money?[107] This issue is considered in the discussion, in chapter 15, of the debate on Tobin's (1970a) "Money and Income: Post Hoc Ergo Propter Hoc?" paper. For the present, however, three points may be noted.

First, Friedman and Schwartz pointed to the resilience of the money/income relationship in the face of "radical changes in monetary arrangements" in the United States as evidence that the relationship reflected in large part the effects of monetary policy.[108] Admittedly, this point suffers from the defect that most post-1914 US domestic monetary policy regimes have been similar to one another in the sense that they involved interest-rate setting by the central bank.[109] Consequently, subject to the chosen policy rate, under essentially all US policy regimes the creation of base money (and to a large extent the creation of commercial bank deposits) has been at the option of the private sector. But it deserves underlining that be-cause—across US monetary policy regimes—the interest-rate instrument was typically varied over horizons beyond the short run, the money-supply curve was not purely horizontal over horizons longer than daily or weekly. And the curvature of the supply response may have differed across various US regimes, thereby imparting the instability to the money-supply function across different sample periods that Friedman and Schwartz viewed as a characteristic of that function. Even for the stretch of interest-rate pegging in the 1940s through 1951, variations in the natural real rate of interest and the expected rate of inflation meant that what seemed to be an unchanged policy when cast in terms of nominal interest rates could well imply a *shifting* policy when cast in terms of the money stock.

Too much, it would seem, was made of the fact that interest rates were set by central banks in practice. Certainly, that situation by no means implied that causation could be imputed as running strictly from aggregate spending to monetary policy. Nor did it imply that the supply curve for money should be treated as either fixed or horizontal for periods other than the very short run.

Second, and relatedly, a regime that is characterized by an accommodative monetary policy does not imply a situation in which monetary policy does not matter for economic behavior or that money is an invalid indicator of monetary policy stance. A decision to hold interest rates down in the face of upward pressure on aggregate demand will lead money and output to move together. But the central bank could have prevented the rise in money, had its policy been different, and that non-accommodative policy would have been associated with less buoyant behavior of output. Under both the accommodative and non-accommodative policy, the stock of money can therefore be viewed as accurately conveying the monetary policy stance in place.[110]

Third, as emphasized by Romer and Romer (1989), Friedman and Schwartz's narrative approach in the *Monetary History* isolated cases in which it was implausible to view the behavior of money as stemming automatically from feedback from income to money. Even Tobin (1965a, 481) acknowledged that Friedman and Schwartz had recovered "some convincing examples of monetary changes that were clearly independent of contemporary or immediately preceding economic events." In the same vein, Christopher Sims—who was critical of much of Friedman's statistical evidence concerning money and output—referred in a 1971 memorandum to "the Friedman-Schwartz historical analysis of causal priority in major slumps, which I regard as the most convincing evidence they put forward."[111]

MONETARY POLICY/FISCAL POLICY INTERACTION IN PRACTICE

Leeper (2010, 362–63) observed: "We have known at least since Friedman (1948[a]) that monetary and fiscal policies are intricately intertwined and their distinct impacts are difficult to disentangle." What this characterization leaves out is the fact that, in his later work, Friedman largely repudiated the positions that Leeper attributes to Friedman's 1948 article.

As has already been indicated, after 1948 Friedman became skeptical about the idea that fiscal policy actually had much of a distinct impact on aggregate demand. The empirical basis for this skepticism began to see print even in the 1950s, with Friedman's 1952 article on wartime monetary relations a particularly notable example. But the empirical documentation took its most extensive form in the Friedman-Meiselman study of 1963, which is discussed in chapter 12 below.

True, well after the appearance of the Friedman-Meiselman study, Friedman still acknowledged: "Ordinarily of course monetary policy and fiscal policy are both being conducted simultaneously and it is hard to distinguish which is doing what."[112] But in other work of around the same period, he indicated that—hard though it was to distinguish the effects of fiscal and monetary policies—it was possible to achieve such a distinction. His verdict was, once more, that fiscal deficits mattered for aggregate demand primarily because they were monetized—and not in their own right.[113] Part of the basis for this conclusion came from the evidence from episodes in which fiscal and monetary policy *did* move in opposite directions. In a 1970 discussion, for example, Friedman suggested that six such episodes existed in the prior half century of US data, and that monetary policy proved to be the clearly more important influence on aggregate economic behavior in each instance.[114] That bottom line was reaffirmed by Friedman in 1999 in a piece he wrote for the *Wall Street Journal* titled "Monetary Policy Dominates." In this discussion, Friedman recalled an occasion when he attempted to "collect all the episodes I could find in which monetary policy and fiscal policy went in opposite direction[s]." He reported that his inspection of these episodes, and of more recent evidence from the United States and Japan, had suggested that "monetary policy uniformly dominated fiscal policies."[115]

The result that fiscal policy and monetary policy were hard to distinguish arose, in Friedman's view, not from any status of fiscal policy as a powerful influence on aggregate demand, but from the fact that fiscal ease often triggered money creation by the central bank. He contended nevertheless that this correlation between monetary policy and fiscal policy was not inevitable. Friedman was emphatic that there was no need for the monetary authorities to accommodate fiscal deficits—a judgment on which he repeatedly found himself at odds with the Federal Reserve chairs from the early 1950s through the 1970s.[116] He further maintained that, provided that the Federal Reserve did not accommodate fiscal policy, inflation and output fluctuations need not result from substantial and variable fiscal deficits.

The notion that monetary policy could be insulated from variations in fiscal policy was enshrined in Friedman's constant-monetary-growth prescription and was in marked contrast to his 1948 piece. Not surprisingly, therefore, the celebrated study of Sargent and Wallace (1981) contended that Friedman's 1948 rule was more feasible and desirable than his constant-monetary-growth rule—as the former rule implied coordination of fiscal policy and monetary policy, something they regarded as essential.[117] A full discussion of the Sargent-Wallace work is beyond the scope of this book. But it should be mentioned here that Friedman was not persuaded by the Sargent-Wallace reasoning and that he suggested that relaxation of some of the authors' key assumptions restored the notion that monetary and fiscal policy could be separated.[118]

Nevertheless, Leeper (2010, 373, 423) attributed to the *post*-1948 writings of Friedman the perspective that if monetary policy was "to successfully control inflation, fiscal policy must behave in a particular, circumscribed manner," claiming that Friedman was "explicit about this necessity in his *A Program for Monetary Stability*." However, Leeper provided no page references in documenting the latter claim. And an examination of the writings of Friedman and other key monetarists reveals that, both empirically and as a matter of theory, they regarded monetary policy as crucial for inflation outcomes, and the conduct of monetary policy as capable of being insulated from developments in fiscal policy even in the case of very sizable variations in budgetary settings.[119]

What Friedman insisted on in *A Program for Monetary Stability* was instead that *debt management* and monetary policy were intimately connected.[120] Debt management did not fall into Friedman's definition of fiscal policy, which he defined as pertaining to "changes in government expenditures and tax receipts."[121] Control of the money stock was infeasible if the central bank was compelled to purchase government debt on an unlimited basis or if it felt obliged to see to it that the secondary price of that debt traded in a limited range. From this perspective came Friedman's observation in 1980 that "*debt policy* (as distinguished from the 'public expenditure and tax policy' that [is regarded as] ... 'fiscal policy') does play a critical role in controlling monetary aggregates."[122] It was therefore internally consistent for Friedman to contend, as he did in his post-1948 writings, that price stability, which rested on monetary control, required monetary policy/debt policy coordination but not fiscal policy/monetary policy coordination.

MONETARY POLICY AND THE THEORY OF PUBLIC CHOICE

Friedman's articles and statements concerning monetary policy from the mid-1970s onward heavily reflected his admiration for, and acceptance of, the analysis of the decisions of the political system and bureaucracies contained in the "public-choice" economic-research literature.

The analysis of policy making was, Friedman observed in early 1977, "a subject on which I must say I've changed my views over the years."[123] In 1951, he had declared: "The role of the economist in discussions of public policy seems to me to be to prescribe what should be done in the light of what can be done, politics aside, not to predict what is 'politically feasible.'"[124] He did find economic models, including one in the writings of Harold Hotelling, useful for the analysis of specifically political questions, such as the behavior of rival parties in the electoral system.[125] But he continued to call for a separation of discussion of monetary policy from consideration of the political context. For example, as late as mid-1973, Friedman observed in congressional testimony: "This is a question—and I do not really think we should discuss it here—it is a question of politics."[126]

Matters had changed greatly a little over six years later when the Friedmans observed in the preface to *Free to Choose* that "this book is influenced by a fresh approach to political science that has come mainly from economists—Anthony Downs, James M. Buchanan, Gordon Tullock, George J. Stigler, and Gary S. Becker, who, along with many others, have been doing exciting work in the economic analysis of politics."[127]

The main manifestation of the public-choice perspective in *Free to Choose*'s discussion of monetary matters lay in the Friedmans' recommendation that a constitutional amendment should be the means through which the constant-monetary-growth rule be implemented.[128] The influence of the public-choice literature on Friedman's perspective on the conduct of monetary policy was, however, more pervasive than an examination of the monetary analysis in *Free to Choose* would suggest. In his other writings and statements in the 1975–99 period, Friedman made it clear that the public-choice viewpoint had led him to take an even more negative perspective than previously when it came to US monetary policy as conducted in practice.

The contrast with Friedman's earlier work, including the materials considered earlier in this chapter, was underscored by the change in the tenor of his remarks concerning Federal Reserve officials. In 1956, even while criticizing the Federal Reserve's performance, Friedman had stated that "this sorry record is not an indictment of either the competence or integrity of the men who were in charge of monetary policy during this period—they seem to me an unusually able and public-spirited group."[129] A few months later, and in the same vein, he added, "the failures that I have documented do not reflect either lack of ability or public interest but indicate the enormous difficulties of the task involved in an attempt through discretionary action of individuals to steer the economy as a whole."[130] But in an assessment given in 1987—when Friedman wrote to Stanley Fischer and criticized the latter's analysis for neglecting "the public choice perspective"—Friedman was far less generous to the Federal Reserve. Friedman remarked to Fischer, "you talk about a loss function for 'the policymaker' that includes solely inflation and the deviation of real output from a target level. . . . [But] these are likely to be only very indirectly related to the real objectives of the actual policymakers. From revealed preference, I suspect that by far and away the two most important variables in their loss function are avoiding accountability on the one hand and achieving public prestige on the other. A loss function that contains those two elements as its main argument[s] will I believe come far closer to rationalizing the behavior of the Federal Reserve over the past 73 years."[131]

At times, Friedman suggested that the Federal Reserve chair and other senior policy makers themselves operated according to these prestige-seeking and accountability-avoiding objectives (see, for example, *Wall Street Journal*, December 10, 1984, 16).[132] On other occasions, he implied that it was the staff of the Federal Reserve who had these objectives: in the presence of the "able and public-spirited men who run the [Federal Reserve] system" (*Newsweek*, April 24, 1978), he suggested, an obstacle to better monetary policy was "bureaucratic inertia and the preservation of bureaucratic power and status."[133] When he emphasized the role of the bureaucracy, Friedman also suggested that the identity of the Federal Reserve chair made little difference to the conduct and objectives of US monetary policy, Friedman's grounds being his postulate that the chair would be brought round to the positions taken by the staff.[134]

But whether centering his critique on the Federal Reserve chair or on the Federal Reserve's (and primarily the Federal Reserve Board's) staff, it was clear that in Friedman's later analyses, he deviated greatly from his and Schwartz's analysis in *Monetary History* and the complementary analysis that had appeared in many of his solo-authored accounts. In that body of work, the narratives had focused heavily on flaws in the Federal Reserve's analytical framework as a source of historical policy errors: as Friedman put it in the early 1970s, "erratic and destabilizing monetary policy has largely resulted from the acceptance of erroneous economic theories."[135] Now he was largely dropping that perspective and instead attributing to himself and the Federal Reserve a largely *common* conceptual framework. Destabilizing monetary policy actions, instead of being attributed to conceptual errors, were, in this revised interpretation, ascribed to parochial motives on the part of policy officials.[136] This was an undesirable shift on Friedman's part. It had little grounding in the historical record, and Friedman's change in position suggested that he was overimpressed by the public-choice literature.

Friedman's shift to a public-choice perspective came at a particularly inopportune time. In the 1970s, the Federal Reserve embraced a cost-push view of inflation, and many of its policy mistakes of that decade can be interpreted as consequences of that embrace. As a strong advocate of a monetary view of inflation, Friedman was well situated to articulate a critique of the cost-push position. Indeed, he did so eloquently on many occasions in the early 1970s.[137] But, in the second half of the 1970s, the Federal Reserve continued to subscribe to a nonmonetary view of inflation, but Friedman's critiques of that view became rare because he did not seem capable of accepting that the Federal Reserve really believed what it was saying about the causes of inflation.

Once converted to the public-choice perspective, Friedman even suggested that the analysis of the *Monetary History* might need to be overhauled.[138] Fortunately, he did not pursue this idea. It would not have been a productive enterprise, for Friedman's application of the public-choice perspective to monetary policy was flawed. It jarred with overwhelming evidence, including that in the *Monetary History*, that US monetary policy decisions are best understood by reference to policy makers' conceptual framework. The public-choice perspective also shed little light on the reason for the inflation of the 1970s, because (in seeing the inflation as a conscious policy decision) it attributed to policy makers of the 1970s a view of the inflation process that they did not have.[139] And the view that economic policy decisions should be regarded as driven by political and bureaucratic considerations would appear far better suited to the analysis of other US policy processes—including fiscal policy decisions—than to the analysis of monetary policy.[140] Friedman seems to have accepted the last point very late in life. After 1999, he returned to viewing postwar US inflation behavior as reflecting changes in the Federal Reserve's views on the causes of inflation (see E. Nelson 2007, 172).[141]

One major message of the public-choice literature that Friedman never really accepted was that described by Dixit (1992, 969): its nihilistic attitude toward normative analysis of economic policy. The public-choice literature suggested that, constitutional change aside, insights obtained from economic analysis could have little bearing on policy choices, which would instead reflect the aforementioned political and bureaucratic machinations. Even in his years of greatest enthusiasm about the public-choice perspective, Friedman confirmed that he still regarded analysis of alternative monetary policies as valuable.[142] He continued to advocate a simple monetary-growth rule and to contemplate how economic performance would have been if the Federal Reserve had followed policies closer to his prescriptions. And, although he himself did not favor the approach, he commented sporadically about results arising from optimal-control analyses of monetary policy. This last point will be brought out in the next section, which considers Friedman's attitude toward optimal monetary policy.

III. Friedman and Optimal Monetary Policy

The final section of this chapter is concerned with the relationship between Friedman's views on monetary policy and the optimal-control and welfare-maximizing perspectives on appropriate monetary conduct. The discussion below covers first, the specification of the objective function; second, optimal stabilization policy; and third, the optimum quantity of money.

SPECIFICATION OF THE OBJECTIVE FUNCTION

Friedman's perspective on the appropriate specification of the objective function is discussed in E. Nelson (2008a, 97), in which further documentation of the points that follow are provided.

Friedman's belief was that long-run price stability was the appropriate objective of monetary policy. However, subject to that stipulation, he was agreeable to policies that achieved price stability in a manner that minimized real costs. For full employment was a desirable objective, in his view. But—in keeping with Friedman's natural-rate hypothesis—for makers of monetary policy the full-employment objective should be taken in conjunction with the realization that monetary policy could not affect real variables in the long run. Under such circumstances, the contribution to economic performance with respect to real variables that monetary policy could make amounted to keeping down variations in the output gap, that is, the percentage deviation of real output from its natural value.[143] The goals of stabilization policy should therefore be "a reasonably stable economy in the short run and a reasonably stable price level in the long run."[144] Indeed, as we have seen, one of the reasons for Friedman's advocacy of a constant-monetary-growth rule was his view that the rule would be supportive of *both* price stability and output-gap stabilization. Conversely, Friedman was critical of cases in practice—such as in the United States in the early 1980s—when, he believed, a disinflationary policy had been disorderly and had produced undesirably large costs in terms of a deep (though temporary) output gap.

To judge by his use of the variance of income as the criterion function in his "Full-Employment Policy" article of 1953, Friedman was not averse to a specification of the objective function that was quadratic in the objectives—a specification that has now long been standard in studies of monetary policy.[145] In addition, Friedman confirmed that he did not disagree with the weights on the inflation and the output-gap terms used in the specification of the authorities' objective function in Keynesian work on macroeconomic policy.[146]

Friedman maintained that the objectives of full employment (that is, a zero output gap) and price stability would not be in conflict in the long run. He acknowledged, however, that a conflict between the two objectives could arise in the short run.[147] Even in the presence of this short-run trade-off, however, he contended that it was "wise to determine monetary policy by long-term considerations."[148] As has already been indicated, Friedman's position was that full employment was a desirable objective for the managers of aggregate demand, but that an explicit full-employment policy was not.[149] The short-term objective of real stabilization, on this view, should not be achieved by policies that responded directly to real levels of series or to estimates of output gaps. Instead, it should be allowed for by the use of policy rules, such as the constant-monetary-growth-rule, that incorporated the stabilization goal indirectly.

FRIEDMAN'S VIEW OF OPTIMAL CONTROL THEORY

In the aforementioned policy debate with Friedman, Samuelson (1975, 74) distinguished his own position from Friedman's by noting that the fixed-monetary-growth proposal contrasted with "my own 'lean against the wind' optimal-stochastic-control strategy." For his part, Friedman's preference for simple rules over optimal control was indeed an important part of his perspective on appropriate monetary policy. But Friedman was not completely poorly disposed toward optimal-control approaches, as will become clear in the discussion that follows.

Friedman acknowledged that a fixed-monetary-growth rule could in principle be improved on and therefore did not correspond to optimal monetary policy.[150] What is more, and notwithstanding his skepticism about the feasibility (in practice) of a successful activist stabilization policy, he remained receptive to possible improvements on his preferred rule. This attitude partly stemmed from the very fact that model uncertainty had motivated his preference for constant monetary growth. Friedman believed that economic research and experience could well improve economists' and policy makers' knowledge and reduce model uncertainty. As Friedman put it to the present author: "In my original support for a straight money target, I always emphasized that it was partly a case based on ignorance, based on the fact that we really did not understand sufficiently well the detailed relationship between money, income, interest rates, and the like to be able to fine-tune, that our goal should be to develop a detailed enough understanding so that we could do better than a simple constant monetary growth target."[151] Along similar lines, in 1973 Friedman stated his position in the following terms: "I'm not trying to put something down in tablets of gold that shall never be changed for all time. I want us to learn from experience."[152] Earlier in the 1970s, Friedman had noted that the case for "more sophisticated rules" than his fixed rule might become compelling as economists acquired more knowledge about economic relationships.[153]

Against this backdrop, two younger colleagues of Friedman's at the University of Chicago, Stanley Fischer (from the Department of Economics) and J. Phillip Cooper (from the business school), worked on optimal-control methods in a variety of empirical macroeconomic models (Cooper and Fischer 1972, 1973, 1974). The models that the authors considered were numerous, but they included the large-scale Federal Reserve Board–MIT–University of Pennsylvania macroeconometric model. It might be thought that Friedman would have been hostile to this line of research, involving as did both large-scale models and monetary policies different from the simple rule he favored. It is true that the reception given to one of the Cooper-Fischer papers at the money workshop was stormy, partly because the paper was in a preliminary state and the authors were consequently vulnerable to attack (Stanley Fischer, interview, August 30, 2013). But Friedman's own response to the Cooper-Fischer research agenda was far from dismissive. On the contrary, he offered the authors extensive feedback and encouragement on their work.

Phillip Cooper recalled: "In my research with Stanley Fischer, our work was on stabilization policy. Milton Friedman was, by far, our best 'faculty adviser.' He was always helpful. . . . He could look at our work and say: 'Look, we don't really have disagreement; I just chose a *simple* monetary rule, a constant growth rate, [while] you people have used *another* mechanical rule. You can call it servomechanism theory or stochastic control theory—but the point is that it doesn't involve humans making decisions. And, on that, we can fully agree.' And he felt quite comfortable in buttressing our arguments. It [the dialogue with Friedman] wasn't on a continuous basis, but it came up from time to time as we produced new papers. We got quick response and advice from Milton—and not really a lot from other people in the faculty" (J. Phillip Cooper, interview, September 17, 2015).

As Cooper's recollection indicates, the key element of optimal control that found favor with Friedman was that it did correspond to a *policy rule*. He liked the automatic aspect of optimal control: the fact that it required monetary policy to follow a systematic pattern, in so doing removing the prerogatives that policy makers would otherwise have. Optimal control was also, like his constant-monetary-growth proposal, aimed at achieving a stabilizing rule, whereas Friedman believed that US monetary policy in practice had not been stabilizing in the Federal Reserve's first sixty years of existence.[154]

None of this is to suggest that Friedman was won over by the argument for optimal control. Much of his case against activist policy still applied. He disliked the fact that the optimal control rule was intrinsically model dependent and involved responses to a large number of variables and to estimates of unobserved series. The upshot was that, despite the collegial exchanges with Cooper and Fischer and his respect for their work, Friedman was an opponent of the adoption of optimal control in stabilization policy. Toward the end of the period in which Cooper and Fischer were his colleagues, Friedman remarked that "control theory . . . requires delicate fine-tuning for which the Fed has neither the knowledge nor the demonstrated capacity."[155] Around the same time, after Cooper and Fischer's research received attention in a local press report, a Chicago television station offered to arrange and broadcast a debate in which Cooper and Fischer would cross swords with Friedman on the merits of optimal-control policy and of using structural macroeconometric models. It can be safely assumed that Friedman—who was appearing frequently on local and national television by this point—readily agreed to participate. Cooper and Fischer, however, declined the invitation, partly because they did not see Friedman as an adversary, but especially because they had no doubt that Friedman's mastery of debate would lead him to emerge victorious in a televised exchange (J. Phillip Cooper, interview, September 17, 2015).[156] "He was a very, very good debater," Fischer observed of Friedman. "That much was clear" (Stanley Fischer, interview, August 30, 2013).

A postscript to Friedman's attitude to optimal-control policy came in 1980 when a UK parliamentary committee sent a questionnaire concerning monetary policy issues to many monetary experts around the world. One of the committee's questions was: "Do you believe that formal or explicit policy optimization using a range of econometric models can be an aid in the design of macroeconomic policy?"[157] Many respondents provided a detailed, and largely affirmative, answer to this question. In contrast, Friedman's reply to the question consisted of one word: "No."[158]

FRIEDMAN'S WORK ON THE OPTIMUM QUANTITY OF MONEY

To many researchers today, "the Friedman rule" means only one thing— and it does *not* mean a prescription of constant monetary growth. Instead, it refers to the instruction to manage monetary policy in a manner such that, in the steady state, prices fall at a rate sufficient to make the nominal rate of interest zero. Instead of being a rule that fixes the rate of growth of the money stock at a value consistent with long-run price stability, the Friedman rule is—to these researchers—a rule that makes the steady-state expected rate of inflation equal to the negative of the steady-state real rate of interest.[159]

The attribution to Friedman of the deflation rule—which is what the rule will be called here—arises from his 1969 article "The Optimum Quantity of Money," which appeared in Friedman's book of the same title.[160] The present book's discussion of Friedman's monetary analysis does not focus on that article. The 1969 analysis is, to a considerable degree, unrepresentative of Friedman's monetary framework. The monetary theory in the 1969 article did, it is true, pick up some earlier themes of Friedman's writings. But in developing these themes, the article made several breaks with the monetary analysis of most of Friedman's other works. Consequently, "The Optimum Quantity of Money" is really a breed apart from Friedman's main line of monetary research and is certainly not an integral component of it. Furthermore, as will be discussed at the end of this section, the deflation rule was *not* Friedman's rule: he explicitly recommended against a policy of deflation; and he did so before, in, and after his 1969 paper.

A documentation of the above points will occupy much of the rest of this chapter. Ahead of that discussion, it is worth considering another important basis for believing that the deflation rule should not be associated specifically with Friedman: the derivation of that rule had appeared in others' articles and not just his own. Indeed, a number of the derivations had appeared in print prior to the publication of Friedman's article. Phelps (1989, 90) recalled that he and Paul Samuelson worked on the topic of optimum monetary growth during the 1960s and that each of them derived the deflation rule: Phelps in Phelps (1965) and Samuelson in Samuelson (1969b) (after an informal analysis in Samuelson 1963a).[161] Phelps (1989, 90) went on to observe: "Oddly enough, however, a somewhat crude reformulation by Milton Friedman several years later became the standard reference and now receives the credit."

That Friedman is, to an overwhelming degree, portrayed as the primary author of the deflation rule is brought out not only by the prevalence of the "Friedman rule" usage but also by the literature discussions provided by many writers in the field of optimal monetary policy. For example, Barro and Fischer (1976, 144) stated: "The question posed as the optimum quantity of money is what steady-state rate of inflation maximizes steady-state welfare (minimizes the welfare cost of inflation). The answer, provided explicitly by Friedman (1969[a]) and implicitly by Bailey (1956), is that rate of inflation which makes the nominal interest rate (the private cost of holding money) equal to zero." Feldstein (1979, 752) and Lucas and Stokey (1983, 56) made attributions similar to those given by Barro and Fischer.[162] Some authors have gone somewhat further in the credit given to Friedman. For example, Robert King and Alexander Wolman (1996, 91) wrote of the "prescription for long-run deflation policy that was first made by Milton Friedman (1969[a])"; and Giannoni (2001, 10) referred to the "welfare costs of transactions first mentioned by Friedman (1969[a])"; while Abel (1987, 446) referred to "Friedman's 'full liquidity' rule," even though the "full liquidity" terminology for the deflation rule was due not to Friedman but to Phelps (whose work was not cited in Abel's article).[163] And Hahn (1971, 1990), although deeply critical of Friedman's analysis, essentially attributed the origination of the deflation-rule finding to Friedman's 1969 article.

One reason for the widespread lack of citation of the relevant pre-1969 literature in this area is surely the fact that Friedman's own 1969 article cited so little of that literature. In particular, the absence from his article of a citation of Phelps (1965) was jarring, including to Phelps (Edmund Phelps, interview, May 16, 2013).[164]

Why, then, did Friedman not cite Phelps (1965) and other prior work on the deflation rule? Part of the answer must lie in Friedman's hit-and-miss citation practice. He was better at pointing out missing bibliographical references in others' papers than in covering the relevant prior literature in his own writing on a topic. For aid in fleshing out his papers' bibliographical references, he was often reliant on suggestions that he received from readers of early drafts.

Another reason, however, may be that Friedman may have felt that he had comprehended the essence of the deflation rule much earlier than 1969 and that he saw his 1969 paper as a writing up and partial formalization of his earlier intuition. That perspective may have led him to be less than thorough in considering recent years' literature.

The main basis for the preceding conjecture lies in the fact that the essential idea that the opportunity cost of holding money may be eliminated by policies that make the nominal interest rate zero was something that Friedman articulated explicitly (albeit wholly verbally) in *A Program for Monetary Stability* in 1960.[165]

What is the position of the 1969 "Optimum Quantity of Money" analysis in Friedman's monetary framework? It will be argued that the 1969 analysis was quite discordant with his other monetary writings.

The major basis for arguing the contrary—for claiming that Friedman's "Optimum Quantity of Money" analysis was in harmony with his earlier (and later) monetary work—lies in the 1969 paper's emphasis on inflation as a tax on holding real money balances. The notion that money creation (even if it did not generate inflation) constituted an implicit tax on holders of non-interest-bearing money was not original to Friedman, but it was one that he emphasized repeatedly from the start of his monetarist period.[166] He had done so in his undergraduate money class of the late 1940s and early 1950s (Marc Nerlove, interview, September 13, 2013) and in several articles and public statements from that period onward.[167] Indeed, Bailey (1992, xix) indicated that his own (1956) analysis, which was concerned with the inefficiencies associated with the economizing on transactions-facilitating money that occurs when inflation is positive, had drawn on Friedman's analysis of the issue in his 1953 expansion of his "Inflationary Gap" paper.[168] And Phelps (1979, 121) in turn indicated that the research that led to his own derivation of the deflation rule began in 1963 when he had been stimulated by "the writings of Martin J. Bailey and Milton Friedman."

But, the 1969 paper aside, Friedman's recommended manner of minimizing the opportunity cost of holding money was not to induce nominal interest rates to fall to zero but to encourage the payment of interest on money.[169] His repeated urges for abolition of restrictions on interest payments on commercial banks' deposit liabilities, and for payment of interest on commercial bank reserves, both went in this direction.[170]

In other important respects, Friedman's 1969 analysis jarred with his other monetary work. These discrepancies are now enumerated.

First, Friedman's analysis used the criterion of maximizing the utility of a representative household. Friedman's steady-state analysis therefore embraced the Ramsey (1927) criterion for optimality. Indeed, Calvo (1978a, 1411)—using terminology that did not catch on—referred to a policy that maximized household utility as the "Ramsey-Friedman optimal policy."[171] The use of household utility maximization (albeit in a steady-state context) as a basis for establishing optimal monetary policy was a prescient element of Friedman's 1969 analysis, but it is one that has very little counterpart in his other writings on monetary policy. In the latter body of work, the criterion for success of monetary policy was the achievement of stability of the output gap and inflation, as well as of low inflation.[172]

Second, and relatedly, Friedman's 1969 analysis basically abstracted from the costs that the existence of nominal rigidity would imply for a policy of deflation, whereas, as discussed in chapter 2, his other statements abounded with warnings about the costs associated with policies that produced deflation.

Third, Friedman's treatment of money demand was very different, and much simplified, from that in his other work. In the latter set of writings, he stressed that the asset demand for money arising from money's status as a "temporary abode of purchasing power" provided a reason for believing that there were arguments in the demand-for-money function other than real income and a single interest rate; he also suggested that this asset demand for money pointed to the likelihood that the appropriate definition of money was M2 rather than M1.[173] In contrast, the "Optimum Quantity of Money" analysis invoked the notion that money served as a "temporary abode of purchasing power" but proceeded as though, even when money had this additional function (that is, one that was over and above the role money provided in facilitating current-period transactions), it remained the case that the only arguments in the demand-for-money function should be real income and a single interest rate. In addition, the 1969 analysis suggested that M1 might well be the appropriate definition of money.

Fourth, whereas in his other monetary writings Friedman emphasized that it was difficult to represent (even at low time frequencies) all the interest rates relevant for economic behavior with a single market interest rate, in his 1969 analysis he did so.

All in all, then, Friedman's 1969 monetary analysis was definitely a breed apart from his standard monetary framework, and it is the latter with which this book is predominantly concerned.

No doubt partly because of the differences between his 1969 analysis and his standard framework, Friedman distanced himself from the 1969 analysis as soon as he had laid it out. At the end of his "Optimum Quantity of Money" paper, he declared that he considered that the theoretical case for the deflation rule was too fragile for him to endorse that rule.[174] Instead, he reaffirmed his support for a constant-monetary-growth rule designed to achieve long-run price stability and some degree of economic stabilization, instead of the deflation rule, which would eschew the price-stability and economic-stabilization goals in favor of an attempt to remove the opportunity cost of holding money.

Some authors have interpreted Friedman as actually endorsing the notion that policy makers in practice should adhere to the deflation rule. These authors have suggested either that in 1969 the deflation rule became his preferred rule (see, for example, Pesek 1988, 31; *Financial Times*, June 14, 2002) or that Friedman continued to recommend a constant-monetary-growth rule to achieve a target inflation rate, but that the 1969 analysis allowed him to be specific about what the target inflation (or rather deflation) rate should be (see, for example, Cripps 1977, 105). But these interpretations are entirely inappropriate. They are refuted by the aforementioned closing passage of "The Optimum Quantity of Money." They are also contradicted by Friedman's continuing recommendation, both during 1969 and over subsequent years, of policies consistent with zero—not negative—inflation.[175] In *A Program for Monetary Stability*, he had stated that he wanted zero inflation.[176] That position did not change after 1969. For example, in 1984, Friedman indicated that a monetary policy consistent with "zero inflation . . . should be our objective."[177] And in 1989, he remarked: "I strongly favor a zero-inflation monetary policy" (*Wall Street Journal*, July 5, 1989).

Nor—as will be detailed in chapter 10—did Friedman regard an inflation rate of 1 or 2 percent as being either harmful or as really very different from price stability. In June 1969, at roughly the time when *The Optimum Quantity of Money* saw print, Friedman went against the grain of the analysis in the lead essay of that book when he noted that inflation that is anticipated does some harm "but not a great deal of harm, so long as the inflation is within moderate bounds" (Instructional Dynamics Economics Cassette Tape 28, June 12, 1969).

In 1987, in one of his rare retrospectives on the analysis in "The Optimum Quantity of Money," Friedman put, if anything, more distance between himself and the deflation rule. The use of the efficiency of the steady state as the criterion for determining appropriate monetary policy meant, he observed, being concerned with "a highly abstract long-run proposition" that was bound to be downgraded in importance in monetary policy discussions, compared with analyses that were more firmly addressed to economic stabilization.[178] The deflation rule, he noted, had suffered this fate: "despite its great theoretical interest," it had not affected actual monetary policy appreciably. Friedman even implied that the deflation-rule result had not been obtained in his own 1969 analysis but had instead been put forward by *other* authors writing in the wake of his article.[179] With this remark, Friedman's rejection of the so-called Friedman rule was complete.

CHAPTER 9

Friedman's Framework: Market Economics and Research Methodology

I. Friedman's Market Economics

The elucidation of Friedman's economic framework in the preceding four chapters concentrated on what that framework implied for the specification of a macroeconomic model. Chapters 5 and 6 concerned the specification of the IS, LM, and term-structure equations; chapter 7, the Phillips curve; and chapter 8, monetary policy rules (both the rule describing actual US practice and the rule that would prevail under Friedman's preferred monetary arrangements). In this chapter, in contrast, the focus is largely on Friedman's microeconomics.

A number of normative and positive aspects of Friedman's microeconomic framework will be considered in the course of this chapter's discussion. This section considers Friedman's advocacy of free-market economics. Sections II and III are concerned with positive economics. Section II looks at Friedman's approach to microeconomic analysis; it will include a discussion of the relationship—which is far from as close as other accounts have suggested—between Friedman's perspective on microeconomics and that of some of his colleagues at the University of Chicago. Section III considers Friedman's approach to economic-research methodology. His 1953 article on that subject will be discussed, as will be the methodological approach revealed by his research. Section IV—continuing a theme explored at the end of chapter 4—analyzes Friedman's perspective on mathematically intensive technical economics.

In his own description, Friedman was "a strong proponent of free mar-

The views expressed in this study are those of the author alone and should not be interpreted as those of the Federal Reserve Board or the Federal Reserve System. The author is grateful to David Laidler for his comments on an earlier version of this chapter. See the introduction for a full list of acknowledgments for this book. The author regrets to note that in the period since the research for this study was conducted, five of the individuals whose interviews with the author are drawn on in this chapter—Kenneth Arrow, Gary Becker, Lyle Gramley, David Meiselman, and Richard Muth—have passed away.

kets" (*Newsweek*, January 12, 1981). As has been indicated in chapters 2 and 3, this was a posture to which Friedman had adhered continuously since the early 1940s, after having already been exposed to ideas conducive to support for free markets during his years of university education, particularly the period of the mid-1930s in which he took graduate studies at the University of Chicago.

Friedman's support for market-based solutions was closely linked to his conviction that, in their participation in market activity, people behaved in a self-interested manner. He argued in a 1952 radio appearance that "we must depend largely upon the selfish interests of people and not upon their unselfish interests."[1] A quarter century later, Friedman reaffirmed that "the way in which the world runs is mostly by people seeking to pursue their self-interest," adding, "and there's nothing wrong with that."[2] Statements along the lines of the one just quoted would lead Friedman to be portrayed as an apologist for greed. But, as Friedman saw it, he was simply recognizing an unavoidable facet of human nature, and his advocacy of free markets sprang from a desire to convert that facet into something that added to economic welfare. "See, I think the problem of any society is how you keep greed in check," Friedman observed in a 1976 television interview. He suggested that "the only effective way I know to keep greed in check is by setting greed against greed" by encouraging a market system based on private property and voluntary exchange.[3] Communist and capitalist systems both operated on greed, he argued.[4] But the voluntary aspect of exchanges in a capitalist system helped facilitate "the kind of world in which greedy people can do the least harm to their fellow men," as it contrasted with a centrally planned system in which resource allocation was largely effected through overt direction of resources.[5] In addition, the capitalist system was one in which greed was directed in a way that benefited society, for, Friedman believed, in a market based on voluntary exchange "private greed is converted [in]to public service."[6]

The last point was what that Friedman took to be a key message of Adam Smith's *The Wealth of Nations*—a book that Friedman would recall first having read when he was an undergraduate.[7] Friedman alluded to Adam Smith when he stated in a 1958 talk: "If each individual enterprise separately seeks to make as much money as it can, it will, as if moved by an invisible hand, also serve the social interest. This is the fundamental justification of the free-enterprise system and of private property."[8] Friedman further stressed that *The Wealth of Nations* had established that self-interest boosts the interests of society because mutual benefits arose from market exchange—which accordingly did not correspond to a zero-sum game.[9]

There is considerable debate in the research literature about the degree to which this point was at the heart of Smith's arguments, especially when

Smith's writings other than *The Wealth of Nations* are considered.[10] But it is noteworthy that what Friedman took to be Smith's message about markets is similar to that of Baumol (1978), even though Baumol by no means shared Friedman's perspective on market economics.

Baumol (1978, 111) also observed that Smith's *Wealth of Nations* was not a work that "dedicate[d] itself to the praise of virtuous intentions and high moral standards of the capitalists." A similar observation applies to Friedman's arguments for a free-enterprise system. Friedman liked to stress that he was pro-free enterprise, not pro-business.[11] His deployment, on many occasions, of an analogy between businesses and thieves bears this out.[12] So do many of his specific comments, including his frequently stated suspicion that firms were naturally inclined to support arrangements that would make their industries less competitive and would reduce consumer welfare.[13] Friedman stated that his own conception of economic welfare was centered on the maximization of consumer utility—one in which "I want to make the citizen happy, I want to make the customer happy" (*Donahue*, NBC, September 6, 1979).

A key part of the market system was, of course, the price system. It has already been discussed (in chapters 4 and 7) that Friedman saw prices in a market system as serving multiple functions and that proposals—such as those advanced by Oskar Lange—to modify the market system to remove one of the functions (in Lange's case, that of distributing income) would severely hamper the efficiency of the economy. Furthermore, measures such as official wage or price controls would obstruct the operation of all the functions of the price system, and Friedman was an outspoken critic of such controls (either applied generally or to specific markets) from the 1940s onward.[14]

But Friedman also looked at the market system in another way—as a profit-and-loss system.[15] Critics of the market system put much emphasis on its profit-generating aspect, but Friedman laid stress on the fact that firms could make losses as well as profits. The "loss" component of the system was, he repeatedly said, as important as the "profit" component of the system, as it curtailed unproductive ventures.[16] "The enterprise that engages in an unsuccessful experiment loses money, and, whatever it may want to do, it has no choice to call a halt," he stated in 1964.[17] Friedman contrasted this state of affairs with that pertaining to a government-owned enterprise, for which the advent of losses would not mean closure but instead an infusion of taxpayer funds (*Newsweek*, August 22, 1977).

It is tempting to suggest, in light of Friedman's use of the above contrast, that the leading concerns that he had with regard to government-owned enterprises were that they put taxpayer funds at risk and they pursued economically unviable projects. These concerns certainly did play some role in Friedman's thinking, and they also underlay his hostility to government guarantees of loans to private-sector corporations and to direct governmental subsidies of firms' business ventures.[18] His position was that if the projects in question were likely to be profitable, the projects would proceed without the public sector's help.

But the main reservations that Friedman expressed about government-owned enterprises were somewhat different from the concerns just described. He granted that, for the management of state-owned enterprises, there was a stigma associated with incurring losses. Conversely, while a risky venture that became profitable would typically give high pecuniary rewards when a private entrepreneur undertook it, there might not be such a close link between firm profits and remuneration for a public-sector enterprise executive. In these circumstances, Friedman contended, the manager of a governmental enterprise might well adopt a play-safe strategy in which low-risk projects were favored.[19] The economic advances that arose from incentives to take risks would therefore be diluted in a system characterized by heavy government ownership of firms.[20]

These analytical arguments combined with Friedman's assessment of the empirical record under various economic arrangements to lead him to the conclusion that the free-market system produced the most efficient set of economic arrangements.[21] Such a system was "the most effective machine yet developed for eliminating poverty and raising the standard of life of the masses" (*Newsweek*, October 28, 1968). In this connection, Friedman would cite the growth of the UK and US economies in the late nineteenth century under relatively laissez-faire arrangements. He would also point to the economic growth in the post–World War II period of many market economies as testament to the success of the capitalist system. Among these successes he included that of the US economy, for which the postwar growth in living standards had occurred largely in spite of greater government intervention, in Friedman's view.[22] In contrast, Friedman observed, while many market economies had produced prolonged growth in living standards, "no country has succeeded in doing so via central planning!"[23]

The interwar period, which had seen a long economic slump in the United Kingdom and the Great Depression in the United States, was often cited as testifying to the failure of the market system. But to Friedman this was a misinterpretation of the historical record. His and Schwartz's account of the US experience from 1929 to 1933 in their *Monetary History* was not supportive of a purely laissez-faire system, as it took there to be public-sector responsibility for monetary management, which should include vigorous policy measures to offset private-sector forces that made for contraction in the money stock.[24] But their account contradicted the common interpretation of the Great Depression in which the nonfinancial private-market system had defects that made it prone, left to itself, to generate low levels of output and employment.[25]

Into the 1970s, Friedman found himself in a decided minority in advocating a reduction in the role of government and a greater role for markets. In a 1988 retrospective, he and his wife would date the shift in public opinion in favor of markets as having occurred in the United States around 1970.[26] But even this date seems too early when one considers the fact that 1971 saw the introduction in the United States of wage and price controls—a move that was greeted with support from the general public. These controls remained widely popular in 1972. Consequently, it is appropriate to infer that, for the whole period covered in this book, public attitudes in the United States were inclined against market-centered solutions.

Although, as indicated below and in chapter 15, Friedman accepted that the increase in government intervention in the US economy had had popular consent, he saw much of the impetus for such intervention as having come from intellectuals. In the mid-1970s, he stated: "I believe that the demand that the system be changed [from the nineteenth-century model] was instituted and spread by intellectuals and not by ordinary people."[27] In making this remark, Friedman was repeating a sentiment he had expressed on numerous occasions in prior decades, including in *Capitalism and Freedom* in 1962.[28] Part of the reason for intellectuals' support for interventionist economic policies was, Friedman believed, a widespread lack of understanding among non-economist academics of the economic case for the free market. Because this case relied on the aggregate consequences of individuals' decentralized behavior, it was, Friedman contended, an argument that non-economists found counterintuitive.[29] Economists, in contrast, were steeped in the argument; consequently, Friedman maintained, they were prone "to be far more sympathetic to the use of the market than are most other groups."[30]

But Friedman also found fault with fellow economists on these matters. As he saw it, economic analysis argued primarily for a free-market system, but economists often failed to see the forest for the trees and therefore overemphasized those aspects of economic analysis that suggested the need for government intervention in the economy. He partly regarded economists' misinterpretation of the Great Depression as making them favorably disposed toward a greater role for the government in nonfinancial economic activity. Friedman also noted, however, that, even ahead of the Depression, economists had been among the advocates of greater government intervention. In this connection he observed that the American Economic Association was founded in the 1880s by young economists who were impressed by state action in Germany and who wanted more government intervention in the US economy (*Forbes*, December 12, 1988, 162).[31]

To Friedman, Germany's economic success did not reflect state intervention, and the critics of the economic arrangements that prevailed in the United States during the nineteenth century did not sufficiently appreciate the strides in economic performance that had been achieved in that period.

With regard to government intervention at the microeconomic level—in specific markets—Friedman also believed that economists often voiced policy views that were different from the main messages of price theory. He complained in 1976: "The economist is schizophrenic. His discipline leads him to favor free markets but his self-interest leads him to favor government intervention" (*Wall Street Journal*, August 23, 1976).[32] Economists, Friedman believed, were adept at pointing to externalities in the economic system that justified government intervention. But he contended that the instances in which government intervention was actually likely to be welfare improving were far fewer than was commonly believed, and this absence of an overall improvement was especially likely to prevail when the possible by-products of such intervention were properly taken into account.[33]

All that said, Friedman was not a believer in no public sector or no intervention in the economy by the public sector. "I'm not an anarchist" was a remark that Friedman made repeatedly.[34] On the contrary, as he put it in 1977, "there is real room for government; we need government."[35] In 1991, he reaffirmed: "I am not a zero government person. I think there is a real role for government."[36]

What precise role for the public sector did Friedman envision? Friedman indicated that "the only things I would not denationalize are the armed forces, the courts, and some . . . roads and highways."[37] It is also clear that he saw a role for government in managing the monetary system. Government provision of both a court system and monetary management could, Friedman believed, provide a sound framework in which the free market could operate. The courts' activities that could aid this process included the enforcement of contracts and property rights, as well as verification that market exchanges were truly voluntary.[38] A well-functioning monetary system, on the other hand, would provide a stable background against which private-sector economic activity could proceed.[39]

Friedman's policy proposals also involved a considerable amount of transfer spending on the part of the government. Two of these proposals deserve specific mention here. First is his plan for vouchers for elementary and high school education.[40] Although this plan was portrayed by Friedman as amounting to a privatization of the education system, it could alternatively be validly described, as in Reder (1982, 25), as "substitution of publicly subsidized private schools for public schools." This way of describing the voucher plan underlines the fact that the plan entailed a substantial commitment of public spending.[41]

The second proposal consists of Friedman's idea that, via the negative income tax, government transfer spending should furnish US households with a minimum income. Friedman pointed to the market system as one that, in contrast to feudal and Communist economic systems, gave substantial opportunities for those who started with low incomes to experience a move up the income scale. He also regarded the market system as "just" in the sense that incomes received were related to marginal product. But he granted that the initial distribution of income in a market system could not be regarded as just.[42] Against this background, Friedman favored government transfers that boosted the receipts of those at the lower end of the income scale above those that the free market would generate. He was extremely critical of welfare programs in the United States in practice, arguing that they had damaged incentives and gave too little decision-making power to the welfare recipients.[43] Friedman's criticisms intensified over time: in *Capitalism and Freedom*, he suggested that welfare measures were instituted by "men of good intentions and good will," but by the late 1970s he was attributing a more self-interested motive to the modern administrators of the welfare programs.[44] But even in this later period and subsequently, Friedman was a proponent of his own form of transfer-based income support, namely, the negative income tax.

Friedman was also receptive to government intervention in response to what he perceived as major externalities. In particular, although Friedman was opposed to regulations that placed outright ceilings on economic activity that generated pollution, he was supportive of Pigovian taxes to limit pollution.[45] He described his own perspective on pollution control as being from "a rational—or economic—point of view" (*Chicago Tribune*, April 12, 1970, 67). His vantage point therefore contrasted with both non-Pigovian regulatory approaches and the libertarian no-regulation position.

Friedman saw merit, too, in measures by the government that reduced monopoly power. In 1952, upon noting that about a quarter of US private-sector output came from industries that "can be regarded as monopolistic, however liberal an interpretation of that term" was used, Friedman affirmed that he "very much wish[ed] the fraction were lower, and hope[d] that it [would] in the course of time be reduced drastically."[46] At the end of the 1970s, he indicated that the hoped-for reduction had not occurred as much as he had wished: "I would rather have a world in which there were a larger number of small companies" (*Donahue*, NBC, September 6, 1979). In the period between 1952 and 1979, Friedman had become considerably disillusioned with antitrust laws as a device to achieve the desired reduction in monopolistic power. Even so, as indicated in chapter 4, even in the 1970s he continued to favor some central planks of antitrust law for this purpose. As was also noted in chapter 4, a consistent theme of Friedman's in the postwar period was the notion that government actions actually supported key monopolies and that, in the absence of that support, monopoly power would be eroded. He further believed that federal government actions favored the emergence of large firms. Friedman's reasoning was that the corporate income tax created incentives for firms to use their profits to purchase other companies, instead of ceding these profits to shareholders.[47]

One area that Friedman regarded as being "in a different class from the other governmentally supported monopolies" was that of patents and copyrights.[48] Although Friedman struggled with the issue—a struggle reflected in his remark that the "problem of patents does raise very real problems"—his conclusion, in both *Capitalism and Freedom* and subsequently, was that patents and copyrights should be legally binding, as this arrangement would help channel the rewards for an invention toward the inventor and would thereby promote innovation.[49] In taking this position, Friedman was specifying one way in which his view that "we need government to enforce the rules of the game" should be executed in practice.[50] Friedman's endorsement of patents aligned him with the majority view of the economics profession on the issue, including the one that would be taken in the "new growth" literature (see Paul Romer 1990).[51]

Even with this concession in the direction of a role for government, however, the fact remained that Friedman was opposed to much government intervention and to the importance that the public sector had acquired in the operation of the US economy in the 1970s. As already indicated, however, he accepted that this increased role for government largely reflected the wishes of the voters. In 1975, Friedman observed: "I believe that, while there are many things wrong in Washington, fundamentally this is a representative society in which the people do have their way." The expansion of the public sector had occurred "not because some miserable, nasty, corrupt people have gotten by devious means into positions of power, but because the public at large in the United States—you and me—have been trying to follow wrong policies." Faced with this situation, Friedman said, "I regard myself as a member of the society" who was obliged to accept the laws and arrangements introduced by actual government policies (*Donahue*, NBC, September 30, 1975).

Friedman, in addition, set out his task as "trying to persuade the public that it is not in their own interest to make the kind of assignments [to government] they've been making."[52] On other occasions, however, Friedman was more limited in his vision of his own role in influencing public opinion. On these occasions, he implied that his function was to provide ideas that others more directly involved in public discourse, such as politicians, could draw on (see E. Nelson 2009a, 494). Part of the difference between these two descriptions by Friedman of his own contribution surely reflects Friedman's higher profile in popular debate from the late 1960s onward and the enhanced role in the process of public persuasion that he consequently saw as possible for himself.[53]

Friedman's basis for believing that the public could be persuaded of the merits of smaller government drew on his conviction that, although the expansion of the public sector had reflected the voters' will, that expansion had occurred through a variety of individual legislative and regulatory initiatives rather than as the outcome of a direct choice between a small and a larger public sector. Any one government initiative might have obvious benefits, and if the potential beneficiaries were a concentrated group, this group would have an incentive to see that the initiative was enacted. The costs of the initiative, in contrast, would be dispersed, so there would be little incentive for substantial opposition to the passing of the legislation enacting the initiative.[54] And even if an initiative that expanded the size of government was widely popular, that popularity might reflect the failure of the populace to recognize adverse effects that the initiative had on the economy's aggregate-supply potential—such adverse effects occurring via higher taxes and other measures. These considerations led Friedman to express frustration at a policy-making system that launched a multiplicity of government initiatives but "never gets the citizen to look at the totality of it."[55] In the 1970s, this frustration helped lead Friedman to increased advocacy of constitutional restrictions on the role of government, including limits on public spending (in relation to the economy). However, Friedman was also conscious that even the US system relied heavily on an unwritten component of the constitution.[56] This fact limited the degree to which formal constitutional change could be the route to restricting the economic role of the public sector.

As already indicated, Friedman's belief in the free-market system arose from analytical considerations and his review of historical evidence. But he was also philosophically well disposed toward the free-market system. Indeed, he gave the philosophical justification precedence over the economic justification—a priority reflected in his statement in 1990 that "the free market system's main justification is, in my opinion, its moral strength."[57]

What Friedman saw as the moral aspect of the market system did not arise from the behavior of the participants in the system but from the system itself. Unlike feudalism and Communism, the market system rested on voluntary transactions: as Friedman put it, "the essential character of a capitalist system is that it relies on voluntary exchange."[58] The voluntary character of the system was, Friedman indicated, why he would prefer a market system over a centrally planned system as the economic arrangement even if the latter turned out to be more efficient. "I stand for the values of freedom, not just the practical benefits. I've said that even if free market economics was not the most efficient system, I'd still be in favor of it, because of the human values it represents of choice, challenge, and risk. I see economics as a means to an end, not an end in itself" (*Independent on Sunday*, July 26, 1992). The hierarchical ordering of freedom above the choice of economic system was also evident in Friedman's remark, "My objective—my 'god,' if you want—is freedom."[59]

Furthermore, Friedman believed that a market system was conducive to the furtherance of democratic values. This belief was reflected in his statement: "I know of no example of a country with a large degree of political freedom which has not relied in the main on private markets and private arrangements for organizing its economic activity."[60]

Of course, and as already noted, Friedman's judgment was that the criterion of economic efficiency *also* pointed toward favoring a market system, so that, in practice, the economic freedom achieved under that system did not come at the expense of economic performance. The judgment about economic efficiency flowed from Friedman's positive economic analysis, which underpinned references like that he made in 1973 to "the enormous efficiency of a market-price system to adapt changing demands to changing supplies" (*Newsweek*, December 31, 1973).

Hahn (1954, 400) raised doubts about whether Friedman had in fact carried out the relevant efficiency analysis. Specifically, Hahn remarked: "Professor Friedman's dislike of the Walrasian system is inexplicable in one who puts such faith in the price mechanism." Hahn (1988a, 108) later elaborated his view that, although Adam Smith had made the case for the market in 1776, it was only the modern research literature—mostly that appearing after the 1930s—that had "given the proposition sufficient precision to allow it to be discussed." Implicit in this remark was the judgment that the pre-1930 economic literature, particularly that produced by Alfred Marshall, had not, by and large, provided rigorous tools for evaluating the efficiency of the market mechanism's allocation of resources. This was a judgment from which Friedman, whose analysis of market behavior owed much to Marshall, dissented. As discussed in section IV below, Friedman did not reject Walrasian analysis out of hand.[61] But he did not regard Walrasian or other general equilibrium analysis as the be-all and end-all for evaluating the efficiency of the market system. In particular, the virtues of the price mechanism and of free trade could, as he saw it, be demonstrated using the tools of Marshall, Ricardo, Smith, and others.

Friedman was not favorably disposed toward the notion that the market system should be judged efficient only if it replicated the optimal allocation of a central planner's problem. He did not view the latter concept as providing a realistic baseline, for the task of designing a workable non-market-based allocation system involved a "million and one" decisions for which "I am not enough of an expert—no one is" (*Newsweek*, December 31, 1973).[62] Thus, part of Friedman's belief in the price system arose from model uncertainty. The price system provided a means of allocating resources that did not require a heavy degree of knowledge on the part of policymakers, and it facilitated cooperation between agents even when decisions concerning consumption and production were not centralized or consciously coordinated.[63]

II. Friedman's Microeconomics

Much of Friedman's approach to microeconomics is covered in chapters 4 and 11 of this book, which consider his Price Theory graduate class and the text that came out of that class. In light of that coverage, only some brief observations are warranted here.

First, it was noted in chapter 4 that Friedman's price-theoretical analysis could be appreciated and used for microeconomics teaching even by those who rejected Friedman's advocacy of the free market. Friedman, for his part, regarded that advocacy as consistent with what he taught but viewed the two as separate, consistent with the distinction between positive and normative economics. A parallel demarcation applies to Friedman's price theory and his monetary theory. Again, Friedman regarded these as consistent with one another but as largely separable.[64] Others took the same perspective. For example, Boris Pesek, a PhD graduate of the University of Chicago who would become fervently critical of Friedman's monetary writings, praised the "superlative microeconomic rigor of Milton Friedman" that had been in evidence in the Price Theory class (Pesek 1988, viii).

Second, Friedman's microeconomics used explicit utility maximization much more than was typical in his macroeconomic writings (both those on aggregate consumption and those on money). The contents of Friedman's *Price Theory* text bear this out. So does the fact that, in the exam for the 1973–74 Price Theory class, Friedman included a question in which students were required to derive a demand function from a constrained utility-maximization problem (Charles Plosser, interview, April 2, 2015).[65]

Third, although Friedman recognized that utility functions, production functions, and constraints were the primitives in microeconomics, he saw great value in analyzing markets using demand and supply functions. A "key proposition of economics," he contended, was that price movements reflected either a change in the quantity demanded or a change in the quantity supplied.[66] Furthermore, the distinction between demand and supply in a market gained legitimacy if the arguments of the demand and supply functions did not wholly overlap, and in Friedman's view it was an "empirical generalization" that there was indeed considerable *lack* of overlap in the arguments of the functions.[67] A further property that would aid in constructing and estimating the demand function would hold if not only the supply function had arguments different from those in the demand function, but also the parameters of the supply function changed over time. Friedman raised this possibility in his microeconomic discussions.[68] But it was a possibility that gained greater prominence in his monetary analysis, as it was part of the basis for his emphasis on the demand function for money.[69]

ECONOMIC TERMINOLOGY

Friedman used the occasion of his 1976 revision to the *Price Theory* text to give vent to his dissatisfaction with the "unfortunate" terms "microeconomics" and "macroeconomics."[70] That 1976 discussion stressed the extent to which microeconomic issues trespassed on macroeconomics and vice versa. But, as already noted, Friedman did acknowledge the validity of a basic distinction between microeconomics and macroeconomics. In keeping with this distinction, the 1976 discussion of terminology was immediately followed by the statement: "This book deals entirely with price theory."[71]

What Friedman really disliked was the introduction of new labels. For him, microeconomics and macroeconomics already had acceptable names, namely "price theory" and "monetary theory," respectively.[72] After he had finished teaching at the University of Chicago, Friedman would recall having succeeded in preventing the university's graduate class Money (monetary theory) being renamed "Macroeconomics" (*Margin*, January 1986, 4). Such a victory must be considered pyrrhic, however, for the University of Chicago's Department of Economics created a graduate macroeconomics class distinct from the monetary-theory class, with the macroeconomics class subsequently becoming the basis for Bailey's (1962) text. Furthermore, Becker (1991a, 140) referred to Friedman as "Mr. Macro" and implied that this term, together with the corresponding label "Mr. Micro" for George Stigler, was prevalent at the University of Chicago.[73] Becker later recalled that "those were the names that were given to them because the terms 'macro' and 'micro,' whether they liked them or not, became, you know, [in] pretty general [use], even at Chicago, and certainly outside of Chicago" (Gary Becker, interview, December 13, 2013).[74]

Notwithstanding his outspokenness on the "microeconomics"/"macroeconomics" labeling, the area of terminology was not one in which Friedman was often conciliatory and willing to fall in line with the professional consensus. He did insist that "money" be used in a way that did not make it a label for income, wealth, or credit, but here he was simply calling for a degree of terminological precision that was necessary in order for monetary analysis to proceed. He disliked the term "monetarism," but in practice he ended up using the term frequently.[75] And as was discussed in chapter 5, Friedman largely accepted the concepts and terminology of Keynes's work on the consumption function. What is more, he praised Keynes for having "developed a terminology that has turned out to be very useful to people like myself."[76]

Indeed, Friedman was, if anything, *too* willing to try to concede on terminological matters and to be overconfident about the extent to which differences among economists on matters of substance could be bridged by changing his terminology. For example, Baumol (1951, 65) indicated that Friedman in correspondence had suggested that he was leaning toward using the term "choice-generating function" instead of "utility function."[77] Needless to say, Friedman ultimately retained the "utility function" terminology. Another example came when Friedman replied to early reaction to *A Theory of the Consumption Function*. In his draft reply, Friedman stated: "I have become increasingly impressed with the deficiencies of the term 'permanent' that I adopted. 'Planned' or 'anticipated' might well have been preferable."[78] In the event, Friedman's revision for publication of this draft reply resulted in a greatly abridged piece that did not express misgivings about the "permanent income" terminology—which, of course, became a standard part of the language of economics.[79]

THE SCOPE OF MICROECONOMICS

What, in Friedman's view, defined the coverage of microeconomics or price theory, other than the fact that it excluded analysis of aggregate economic behavior? His opening remarks in the 1962 version of the *Price Theory* text suggested a broad definition: "This concept of an economic problem is a very general one and goes beyond matters ordinarily thought of as belonging to economics."[80] Friedman went on to give as an example of a nonmarket activity that was susceptible to economic analysis the choice that households made among potential activities to which they could devote scarce leisure time. Furthermore, as the Friedman-Savage analysis of gambling made clear, Friedman regarded the economist's analytical tool of utility maximization as applicable not only to the choice *between* leisure activities but to the analysis of how a household carried out its application of a *specific* leisure activity.

Friedman was therefore inclined to see utility optimization and the accompanying self-interested behavior as applicable to both market and nonmarket human activity. However, he emphasized that the inclusion of nonmarket activity within economic analysis required viewing such analysis as pertaining to the "interaction among persons pursuing their own self-interests (broadly interpreted)."[81] The broad definition of self-interest on which Friedman insisted was one in which agents engaged in actions that contributed to their utility even though these actions were not remunerative in the sense of making the agents wealthier.[82] In this connection, he cited charitable activity as arising out of self-interest.[83] This flowed from his contention that "self-interest should not be interpreted as narrow selfishness. The most high-minded people in the world are acting out of self-interest."[84] In Friedman's conception, therefore, although entrepreneurs seeking to maximize profits were more transparently self-interested in their orientation than people involved in humanitarian or scientific activities, *all* these individuals were, in fact, optimizing agents. Over the years, Friedman made this contention more concrete by naming names. "I think that an Einstein, a Newton, a Florence Nightingale were pursuing their self-interests," he observed in 1980.[85] By the early 1990s, he had updated the names he used to get this point across. "Mother Teresa is pursuing her own personal interest just as much as Donald Trump is pursuing his."[86]

For the study of market behavior, however, Friedman adhered to a more conventional conception of self-interest based on material or pecuniary considerations. In this field, he affirmed that "most people are selfish in a narrow material sense."[87] Friedman distinguished agents' behavior in organized markets from activities such as charitable giving as follows: "People are selfish and greedy in one aspect of their activity. They are unselfish and generous in another."[88] But he regarded the generosity in the latter field of activity as reflecting a form of self-interest.

It should be clear from the preceding description of Friedman's perspective on economics that he did not share Irving Fisher's (1911b, 1) dictum that it was not "within the province of economics to study all aspects of human life and welfare, but only such as are connected in some rather direct manner with wealth." In terms of his Price Theory teaching and his research agenda, however, Friedman did largely conform to Fisher's strictures. And his teaching of microeconomics, although it referred favorably to a wide definition of economics, stuck largely to conventional topics. Furthermore, Friedman's research, being overwhelmingly macroeconomic in content from the late 1940s onward, necessarily covered topics that were standard ones in economics. In particular, Friedman did not devote a great deal of research effort to the application of economic analysis to day-to-day nonmarket social activities—in great contrast to his student and later colleague Gary Becker. This fact points up the need to distinguish carefully, and sharply, between Friedman's economics and that of prominent microeconomists at the University of Chicago. It is to this distinction that the discussion now turns.

MICROECONOMISTS AT THE
UNIVERSITY OF CHICAGO

Lucas (1994a, 154) deplored retrospectives on macroeconomics that so downplayed the differences in views among key figures that "Friedman, Schwartz, Keynes, Hicks, [and] Modigliani become merely interchangeable spokesmen for a fixed set of ideas." A similar negative verdict should be cast on the practice (followed by Hammond and Hammond 2006, for example) of treating Friedman and George Stigler as contributors to a single, jointly produced "Chicago price theory."

The "Chicago price theory" label is undesirable because Friedman and Stigler did not have the same microeconomic theory. They did not, in fact, possess identical perspectives on microeconomics. It would also be inaccurate to see them as coordinating their research in order to build an analytical structure to which they both subscribed. Furthermore, as will be seen, they had different research interests, and Stigler was unfamiliar with several of Friedman's key writings.[89]

Richard Muth, who took Friedman's Price Theory class, and who subsequently was a colleague of Stigler's at the business school from 1959 to 1964, observed of the pair, "they were close friends. . . . They were also independent thinkers" (Richard Muth, interview, May 20, 2015). This independence was reflected in the different manners in which Friedman's and Stigler's research careers proceeded. Although, inter alia, they were classmates in the mid-1930s and served together at Columbia University on wartime statistical research, they were not located at the same institution for most of the years in which Friedman devoted considerable research time to microeconomics. As was discussed in chapter 4, Stigler disagreed strongly with one of Friedman's main microeconomic contributions during those years: his paper on Marshall. Friedman's interpretation of Adam Smith's economics also differed significantly from Stigler's interpretation.[90]

Accounts in which Friedman and Stigler are seen as working together intensively to obtain a common analytical framework are also contradicted by the fact that—as stressed by Reder (1982, 25)—their research interests differed after the mid-1940s. Richard Muth recalled that Stigler "was asked one time if he knew anything about macroeconomics. He said, 'No, and I thank God for that every day'" (Richard Muth, interview, May 20, 2015). In contrast, of course, macroeconomics became Friedman's main research interest. Stigler's lack of interest in macroeconomics was reflected in remarks that showed he was poorly informed about Friedman's work in that field. It is very clear that he did not follow closely either Friedman's work on consumption or Friedman's research on money.

A revealing indication of Stigler's lack of familiarity with Friedman's consumption work was a statement in G. Stigler (1966, 35) to the effect that he had come across Friedman's "permanent income" terminology only a considerable time after *A Theory of the Consumption Function* was published. Stigler's public statements likewise confirmed that he was unfamiliar with Friedman's debates with Keynesians on money.[91] In addition, a prescription that Stigler made concerning the control of inflation, in which monetary and fiscal actions would be "supplemented by antitrust remedies" (*Business Week*, September 30, 1961, 90), contrasted with Friedman's denial of an important connection between monopolistic power and inflation.

It would also be a mistake to regard Friedman as deeply engaged in a joint research agenda with another prominent microeconomist at the University of Chicago, Gary Becker. In his years as a graduate student, Becker was certainly closely involved in Friedman's *Theory of the Consumption Function* as a research assistant. In addition, he and Friedman published some joint work that was an offshoot of the consumption project: see chapter 5. Becker also attended Friedman's money workshop: "Becker was very smart, so he would be there," David Meiselman recalled. But Becker's attendance of the money workshop occurred when his research interests already lay elsewhere: "Becker was working on his stuff on discrimination" (David Meiselman, interview, April 30, 2013).[92]

After the 1950s Becker was, like Stigler, distant from Friedman's research. During that later period, Richard Posner recalled that "Gary was very, very respectful of Friedman's instruction, but he [Friedman] was basically a macroeconomist, even though he did other stuff. . . . So they didn't really overlap in their work at all" (Richard Posner, interview, October 27, 2014). Indeed, Becker told Friedman in 2002 that he did not know much about the latter's critique of Keynesian economics.[93]

This unfamiliarity reflected Becker's specialization in microeconomic research. As has already been suggested, even during his time as a graduate student, much of what Becker gained out of his interaction with Friedman was from the latter's command of microeconomics. Becker remembered the Friedman of that period as being a "superb price theorist who would attend workshops in agricultural economics, labor economics, I.O., Stigler's workshop, and the like . . . not, by any means, restricted to monetary economics." Becker's dissertation, which was purely in microeconomics, was supervised by Friedman, and Becker recalled Friedman as "very active in my dissertation committee" (Gary Becker, interview, December 13, 2013). In addition, as noted in chapter 2, Becker's subsequent work on human capital took some cues from Friedman's research.

But Becker's famed approach of applying economics to the analysis of the family and other social phenomena did not reflect a joint effort with

Friedman, who served as a consumer and admirer of Becker's research in this area rather than as collaborator. Friedman would also be an admirer of the public-choice literature, and he would name Becker and Stigler as key contributors in that field. But this literature emerged fairly late in Friedman's research career, and Friedman's own applications of the public-choice approach would predominantly appear in the form of public policy writings rather than research contributions.[94] Furthermore, Friedman had no major role in another area of microeconomics with which the University of Chicago became associated, namely the law-and-economics tradition.

All in all, then, the major microeconomists at the University of Chicago—even those who were close friends of Friedman—did not coordinate with him in any important way when carrying out their main research agendas. It would be wrong to regard Friedman's microeconomic framework as identical to, or subsumed within, that of his colleagues.

III. Friedman's Approach to Research Methodology

In this section Friedman's approach to the methodology of economic research is considered. The discussion begins with a consideration of Friedman's article concerning the methodology of positive economics. Then the roles of historical analysis and empirical evidence in his own published research are examined.

FRIEDMAN'S ARTICLE ON METHODOLOGY

In the late 1950s, Friedman was having great difficulty in getting the economics profession to give his research on money the weight and attention that he believed that it deserved. This situation would continue into the early 1960s.[95] In the midst of this inattention to this monetary research, however, an article devoted entirely to Friedman's work appeared in the *Quarterly Journal of Economics*. But the title of Rotwein's (1959) article, "On 'The Methodology of Positive Economics,'" confirmed that it was not Friedman's monetary research that was being given prominence but instead his 1953 article on economic-research methodology.[96]

The Rotwein article was part of what became a vast literature concerning Friedman's article on methodology. A great deal of that literature was authored by figures who did not work in Friedman's areas of research—either because they were writing from the vantage point of the history of economic thought, or because they were outside the world of economic research altogether. Indeed, the fact that contributors to that literature have come to refer to Friedman's article as "F53" (see Mäki 2009) attests to the great gulf between that literature and the macroeconomic literature. No one who really understood the importance of Friedman's 1953 "The Case for Flexible Exchange Rates" or his 1953 article on stabilization policy (which was alluded to in the official citation for Friedman's 1976 Nobel Prize) could feel comfortable with the "F53" label. For that portentous label is imbued with the poorly informed notion that the methodology article was the only notable Friedman paper in the year 1953.[97]

Essentially the entirety of the literature on Friedman's methodology article is outside the scope of the discussion of the present book, which focuses on debates on specific economic topics in which Friedman was engaged, rather than on methodological discourse. But it is worth considering the impact that the 1953 methodology article had on some key participants in Friedman's own research fields of monetary analysis and macroeconomics.[98]

That impact is sometimes discernible in discussions in which no explicit mention of Friedman or citation of his article appears. Kareken and Wallace (1977, 43), for example, were likely alluding to the 1953 methodology article when they wrote: "We happen to think that it is reasonable, maybe even (heaven forbid) realistic, to assume a nonreproducible factor of production." So too were Shiller and Modigliani (1979, 303) in their phrase, "under the following fairly 'realistic' assumptions." A more overt case was that of Tobin (1981d, 391), who stated that a particular procedure under discussion "cannot be justified by 'the methodology of positive economics,'" but who did not mention Friedman by name or include the methodology article in his bibliographical references.

As the Tobin example establishes, some of the prominent Keynesian and anti-monetarist economists whom Friedman faced in exchanges on macroeconomics were also critical of his methodology article. Alongside Tobin, critics in this category included Paul Samuelson and Frank Hahn. But one could be forgiven for thinking that Tobin, Samuelson, and Hahn all displayed some inconsistencies in their position on Friedman's methodological approach. Tobin once stated that "Friedman's methodology of positive economics . . . has done great damage."[99] But Tobin rated highly Friedman's *Theory of the Consumption Function*, a book that, as discussed below, Friedman regarded as an application of his methodological prescriptions. Likewise, Samuelson took to print to criticize Friedman's article on methodology. Yet, Samuelson, too, was an admirer of *Theory of the Consumption Function*, and the posture that Samuelson took in the "Cambridge-versus-Cambridge" debate on capital theory can be regarded as consistent with that espoused in Friedman's 1953 piece.

The inconsistencies are, however, most jarring in the case of Frank Hahn. In his review of the *Essays in Positive Economics* collection in which Friedman's methodology article appeared, Hahn (1954, 401) stated that "the chapter on methodology is first rate." But Hahn (1983a, 75) indicated, "I do not subscribe to Friedman's 'as if' methodology," and Hahn (1987, 322) further declared that "the whole 'as if' methodology proposed by Milton Friedman is not one which can survive a modest amount of reflection." It is possible that the intensification after 1953 of the debate between Friedman and his critics on macroeconomic matters led some of those critics to look again at his article on methodology and to reach a more negative perspective concerning that article.

One component of Friedman's article—and perhaps that which most gave rise to Hahn's initial favorable reaction to it—was the offering of a justification of existing practice. In response to criticisms of standard economic analyses that modeled households as selfish utility maximizers and firms as solving complex profit-maximization problems, Friedman offered the argument that such assumptions about behavior could be justified as a reasonable approximation of agents' behavior, even though the assumptions were not literally correct and were indeed seemingly unrealistic.[100] This argument represented a continuation, and wider application, of a theme Friedman had articulated in the late 1940s, when he had been critical of questionnaire evidence as a means of ascertaining the objectives and process of making decisions on the part of agents.[101]

It should be emphasized that the Friedman argument just summarized applied to the behavior of the private sector, not to the public sector. Friedman was not, at this stage, an advocate of the assumption that the public sector was optimizing. Furthermore, his work on monetary history with Anna Schwartz would rely heavily on documentary evidence, and not just data outcomes, to ascertain policy makers' objectives as well as their model of the economy. Consequently, the specification of the objectives of policy makers was not a matter on which Friedman was advocating that assumptions be imposed a priori.

As noted in chapter 8, at a later point in his career—that is, in the 1970s—Friedman *did* become enamored of modeling policy makers as optimizing agents. It was argued in that chapter that this shift on Friedman's part was not desirable, as the shift turned him away from the important task of ascertaining policy makers' model of the economy (and instead led Friedman to attribute to policy makers knowledge of the correct model). In any event, the fact remains that the 1953 methodology article was not concerned with modeling of policy makers' behavior.[102] And the case that he articulated in that article for the "as-if" approach to modeling private-sector decisions does not readily carry over to the modeling of policy makers' choices.[103]

Another component of Friedman's article was his argument for what should be the basis for evaluating a model, if the realism of assumptions was put aside as a criterion. On this subject Friedman offered the much-quoted judgment that "the only relevant test of the *validity* of a hypothesis is comparison of its predictions with experience. The hypothesis is rejected if its predictions are contradicted."[104] This famous dictum, which Friedman had anticipated by using related formulations in print in the lead-up to 1953, has been echoed in one form or another by many economists in later generations.[105] For example, Robert King and Charles Plosser (1981, 406) stated with regard to optimization-based models of business cycles, "from our viewpoint, the only valid ground for dismissal is that the predictions of these models are inconsistent with the facts."[106]

Another criterion that Friedman's article on methodology laid out regarding model choice sheds light on how Friedman himself approached the issue of testing a model. This criterion was that of parsimony. In 1969 Friedman, in discussing others' research, praised a modeling practice in which one "picks out the key elements of a problem [and] strips away all irrelevant complications."[107] He had foreshadowed this attitude when he declared in the 1953 methodology article: "A hypothesis is important if it 'explains' much by little."[108]

Not only is this phrase from the article quoted directly in Harvey's (1990, 5) explanation of the case for parsimony in econometric models; it also conveyed a sentiment that has been reflected in the modeling choices of many later macroeconomists when they used dynamic general equilibrium models. One of the contributors to those models, Robert Shiller, described term-structure models as based on the "assumption that the real world in some limited sense approximates such an idealized world."[109] And Thomas Sargent noted that Friedman was "a master at saying, 'OK, there's a whole bunch of details, but those are just details, and I'm going to focus on the main forces. And here's the main forces.' Sherwin Rosen used to do that [too]. He'd just cut through a bunch of details and give you the main force. And Bob Lucas does that. Lars Hansen can do it. It's a very rare thing. It requires a confidence and almost a brashness to say: 'Out of all this myriad of forces, here's what's really driving in this situation'" (Thomas Sargent, interview, January 24, 2014). Lucas (1987, 11) himself articulated his desire for parsimony as follows: "A key to success in applied science, I think, is to operate on as shallow a level as one can get by with."[110]

For Friedman specifically, the criterion of parsimony provided a basis for believing that the "test" of a model did not correspond wholly to an econometric test. He applied his "as-if" approach not only to the assumptions embedded in a model but also the parametric specification of a model intended for empirical analysis. He was amenable to imposing parametric restrictions that were not literally valid according to formal econometric tests, provided that the numerical difference between the unrestricted and restricted parameter values was not large. One example of this practice was in a 1976 comment in which, referring to parameter restrictions that would limit the power of monetary policy, Friedman stated that the "failure of these [parametric] conditions to be satisfied perfectly" did not preclude a situation in which in practice "sufficiently correct results will be obtained by treating them *as if* they were perfectly satisfied."[111] Another example was his frequent use of a unitary income elasticity of money demand even though he believed that the evidence was that the income elasticity in the United States somewhat exceeded unity.[112]

Still another example of Friedman's application of the "as-if" approach in the name of model simplification was highlighted in this context by Thygesen (1977, 57–58): Friedman's position that money could serve as a summary of the stance of monetary policy. As discussed in chapter 6, this approach in effect used the money stock, or its growth rate, as a proxy for the spectrum of interest rates that mattered for spending decisions. As the restrictions under which money *perfectly* indexed this menu of interest rates were unlikely to hold exactly, Friedman's reliance on money amounted to the adoption of an "as-if" posture. Friedman was reinforced in this perspective by his belief that model uncertainty and related measurement issues prevented economists from locating and observing all the interest rates relevant for spending determination. Model uncertainty, especially with regard to aggregate-supply relationships, also contributed to Friedman's emphasis on empirical relationships—often reduced-form in character—between nominal variables like the nominal money stock and nominal spending, even though he acknowledged that the structural macroeconomic spending relationships pertained to real and not nominal spending.

The examples given above show that, in Friedman's own research, deployment of empirical testing of hypotheses, and adherence to model parsimony—practices heavily endorsed in his methodology article—were accompanied by features that were less explicit in his article—notably his deemphasis of the results of formal statistical tests and his preference for reduced-form modeling over structural modeling. The presence of the latter elements in Friedman's research means that John Taylor's (2001, 102) statement that "Milton Friedman . . . laid out a specific methodology of positive economic research" needs to be qualified by the remark that supporters of the arguments in Friedman's methodology article did not necessarily endorse the chapter and verse of his actual empirical research. In this connection, Bennett McCallum—a strong supporter of Friedman's methodology article—pointed to "some questionable methodology" in Friedman's empirical work with David Meiselman (McCallum 1986a, 11). In particular, McCallum regarded Friedman and Meiselman (whose research is discussed in chapter 12 below) as taking the criterion of parsimony to extremes via their emphasis on simple regression analysis instead of multiple regressions. This example underlines the fact that Friedman's 1953 methodology article did not provide an exhaustive exposition of his approach to economic research.

It is nevertheless certainly true that Friedman's empirical work applied the ideas advanced in that article. Freedman's (2008, 428) assertion that "Milton Friedman never employed his own prescribed methodology" is, consequently, not appropriate. That assertion should be rejected in light of the examples given above as well as the case of *A Theory of the Consumption Function*, which Walters (1987, 423) considered the clearest instance of Friedman applying the 1953 methodological approach. Friedman himself endorsed that characterization of *A Theory of the Consumption Function*.[113] The book comprises Friedman's efforts to understand a world in which agents are heterogeneous and the capital market is imperfect using a model in which there is a representative agent with access to a perfect capital market. The model's ability to account for actual consumption behavior, not judgments about the model's inherent realism, formed the criterion for evaluating the model's success. The approach of the book was therefore closely aligned with the perspective Friedman took in his article on methodology.

Let us now turn to some of the material in the penultimate section of Friedman's article—the section titled "Some Implications for Economic Issues." The discussion in that section of a particular issue—models of imperfect competition—has been one source of the oft-repeated claim that Friedman would not countenance modeling firms' behavior using any assumption other than that of perfect competition. Yet it has already been argued (in chapter 7) that Friedman's economic model actually did feature some market power by firms, and it is worth discussing why the present author does not see the 1953 methodology article as contradicting that argument.

Paul Romer (*PaulRomer Blog*, May 18, 2015) has satirized Friedman's discussion of the matter as consisting of "a syllogism: *Major Premise*: Better theories have more unrealistic assumptions. *Minor Premise*: Perfect competition has assumptions that are more unrealistic than monopolistic competition. *Conclusion*: Perfect competition is the better theory." What this characterization misses is that Friedman was *not* advocating that the assumption of perfect competition should be applied whenever an environment containing many firms was analyzed.[114] Indeed, his 1953 discussion included the argument that the assumption of monopoly power might be appropriate in some situations to which the assumption of perfect competition was usually applied.[115] Instead of arguing for the universal applicability of perfect competition, Friedman—echoing an argument he had made in 1941—was maintaining that Marshall's analytical framework was able to accommodate a situation in which there were multiple firms. He challenged others to establish that Marshall's work could allow only for the perfect-competition case: "The reader will search long and hard—and I predict unsuccessfully—to find in Marshall any explicit assumption about perfect competition or any assertion that in a descriptive sense the world is composed of atomistic firms engaged in perfect competition."[116]

But Friedman granted that Marshall had not formalized the intermediate case between monopoly and perfect competition and that rigorous elaboration of that intermediate case was something to be wished for: "It would be highly desirable to have a more general theory."[117] What he challenged was the notion that monopolistic-competition theory as it stood in the early 1950s had succeeded in achieving this rigorous formalization.[118] Nevertheless, Friedman's macroeconomic framework, as expounded from 1951 onward, took for granted that a formalization of the intermediate case *could* be achieved. For that framework took a situation in which there were many firms as compatible with the notion that firms regarded prices as a choice variable. Indeed, Friedman's defense in his methodology article of the assumption that private-sector agents behaved optimally included a reference to firms' price-setting decisions.[119]

Friedman's use of analyses in which firms had some market power, alongside his reservations concerning existing theories of monopolistic competition, might be regarded as consistent with some of the early contributions to New Keynesian economics, like Taylor (1980), Calvo (1983), and Rotemberg (1982). In each of the latter three analyses, monopolistic competition was not specifically invoked. Yet the analyses all took it as valid to assume that there was a multiplicity of firms, each of which had pricing power.[120] Arguably, a tractable and rigorous version of the monopolistic-competition apparatus was not available until Dixit and Stiglitz (1977), whose work did not really become integrated into macroeconomic research until the mid-1980s. Be that as it may, however, Friedman's remarks in his methodology article were consistent with his remark nearly a quarter century after that article was published: "You say I assume perfect competition. . . . I don't assume anything of the kind. I assume that you have a world of the kind you have."[121]

Friedman, who did not always display an accurate memory of the chronology of his own research, repeatedly stated that he never replied to critics of his article on methodology.[122] For the most part, this characterization was correct—although Friedman did make numerous subsequent references to his original article.[123] In 1958, however, he made something of an exception to his no-replies rule when he decided to respond directly, with Gary Becker, to Lawrence Klein's (1958, 543) suggestion that the use, in recent solo and coauthored work, of in-sample fit as the criterion for the success of a model was inconsistent with his 1953 emphasis on predictive accuracy as a criterion. The reply to Klein indicated that the "predictions" of a model should be taken to include what it implied for the behavior of historical data and not just the forecasts that it generated.[124]

Friedman's conception of empirical evidence in fact went beyond in-sample fit and out-of-sample forecast performance, because his monetary project with Anna Schwartz brought with it a heavy emphasis on historical evidence. The multidimensional role of empirical evidence in Friedman's research is now considered.

HISTORICAL EVIDENCE AND EMPIRICAL TESTING

In a 1957 discussion, in which he recommended that the US authorities eschew direct controls on credit and also streamline their methods of monetary control, Friedman indicated that "this judgment is based not on some abstract notion but on an examination of our history."[125] This remark highlighted what would become one of the most remembered aspects of Friedman's approach to economic research: his emphasis on the historical record. This emphasis was evident also when, in 1963, Friedman indicated that the "whole record of history" of various countries informed his analysis of the causes and consequences of inflation.[126] And as discussed in section I of this chapter, the historical record served to inform and reinforce Friedman's advocacy, in public policy debate, of a market-based organization for economies.[127]

But it is not Friedman's writings on markets, extreme inflations, or policy rules that really linked his name to the study of history. Instead, it was his monetary project with Anna Schwartz—and especially their 1963 *Monetary History of the United States*—that did so.[128] Indeed, the Nobel Committee in 1976 indicated that Friedman's work in the field of monetary history was part of the reason for his receipt of the economics award.[129]

The *Monetary History*—which will be discussed in detail in chapter 11—was essentially a chronological account of US experience. But the impact of Friedman and Schwartz's work on professional opinion about monetary matters owed much to their extraction of what Friedman called "bits of history."[130] Friedman and Schwartz's analysis of the US historical record pointed to specific episodes in which the impact of monetary policy on real economic activity appeared particularly clear-cut. It appeared clear-cut for two reasons: (1) the episodes had featured substantial movements in US output in the same direction as, and on a magnitude comparable to, the money-stock movement; (2) the historical circumstances of the episodes provided grounds for believing that the monetary movement mainly arose from reasons other than those connected to the contemporaneous behav-

ior of real output and prices.[131] This emphasis on behavior during crucial episodes was a cornerstone of the narrative approach that Romer and
Romer (1989), in particular, associated with the *Monetary History*.

Empirical Evidence and Keynesianism versus Monetarism

A central attraction to Romer and Romer (1989) of the Friedman-Schwartz
method was that it was largely a *substitute* for statistical approaches to the
problem. By the late 1980s, statistical approaches had become very much
predominant in studies that attempted to ascertain the effects of monetary
policy on the economy. It is worth recalling, however, that in the heyday of
his own research in monetary policy, such studies were far less common. Indeed, in conjunction with his narrative analysis, Friedman was concerned
with making up for the dearth of statistical studies of the effects of monetary policy with research of his own. This work primarily took the form of
research with Schwartz other than that published in the *Monetary History*
as well as in his other publications, most notably his aforementioned 1963
study with David Meiselman, "The Relative Stability of Monetary Velocity
and the Investment Multiplier in the United States, 1897–1958."[132]

In pursuing these statistical studies, Friedman was again putting emphasis on historical evidence, as the statistical studies with Schwartz and
Meiselman used long runs of historical US data. But, much more than
the *Monetary History*, in which the mentions of Keynes and Keynesian
economics had been sparing, these statistical studies—especially the
Friedman-Meiselman piece—were engaged in directly pitting the Keynesian and quantity-theory views against one another. The absence of empirical comparisons of these theories likely underlay Friedman's remark, published in the early 1950s, that the economics profession puts "all too much
emphasis on the derivation of hypotheses and all too little on testing their
validity."[133] He and Meiselman would point to the lack of recourse to empirical evidence as a means of discriminating between Keynesian theory
and the quantity theory as testament to the "flabbiness" of the economics
profession.[134]

As discussed in chapters 2 and 12 of this book, there were, of course,
some precursors to the Friedman-Meiselman study, including the work of
Clark Warburton. But that fact did not really undercut Friedman's above-
noted criticism of the economics profession. For what work that had been
done before 1963, including Friedman's own research, had tended to favor
the quantity theory of money, and so it could not be regarded as giving empirical support for the profession's embrace of Keynesianism. The notion
that the Keynesian position had *not* been founded on an examination of
the historical data was something Friedman pressed again in 1967, when

he told the readers of the *Washington Post*: "Those of us who have been working on monetary problems have at least tried to assemble some empirical evidence to justify our assertion [about] . . . changes in the quantity of money and in national income. . . . Is it not time that the new economists [that is, the Keynesians] offered some evidence to support their [own] claims?" (*Washington Post*, November 5, 1967, H1).

If the Keynesian explanation of business cycles, with its deemphasis of monetary factors, did not fit the historical evidence, why had it become prevalent, in Friedman's view? Part of the reason was one he had cited as far back as 1944: the multiplier analysis associated with Keynesian economics had an a priori plausibility and appeal.[135] But, of course, he also regarded the misinterpretation of the Great Depression experience as crucial. Correspondingly, he viewed his and Schwartz's reexamination of the Great Depression from the perspective of the quantity theory of money, and the evidence of the effects of monetary policy accumulated from the experiences of the 1940s and 1950s, as reaffirming the validity of the quantity theory and creating conditions in which the theory would be restored in prestige.[136]

At the same time, Friedman did not hold quantity theorists blameless for the decline in the prestige of the theory that had occurred during the interwar period. As he saw it, during the 1700s David Hume had provided a sophisticated version of the quantity theory of money that had accounted for the positive relationship between money and nominal spending and had also offered an explanation of movements in velocity.[137] He contrasted Hume's sophisticated account with the expositions of the quantity theory given by some of the theory's later proponents—who, he believed, had focused excessively on the constant-velocity case.[138] This left the theory open to be criticized during episodes, such as the United States in the 1930s, in which large movements in velocity occurred. Thus Friedman remarked, "I don't think theories get discredited, I think theories get misinterpreted, and the misinterpretations appropriately get discredited" (*Evening Post*, April 27, 1981).

Just as he regarded quantity theorists as themselves partly to blame for the theory's slump in popularity, Friedman recognized that the acceptance of Keynesian theory was an understandable development. Even though economists until the 1960s did not consult the data as much as he would have liked, Friedman still believed that no hypothesis would have come to dominate professional opinion unless it was believed consistent with historical experience.[139] The Great Depression had been *perceived* to be an event that was nonmonetary in character, and therefore the *General Theory* appeared to advance a hypothesis that lined up with experience. Friedman praised Keynes for producing an internally consistent nonmonetary interpretation of the Depression. Keynes's hypothesis about the Great Depression was incorrect, in his view, but it was internally consistent and novel.[140] Keynes's contribution was productive also because it was in the tradition of constructing hypotheses, most of which would likely prove to be wrong. In Friedman's view, this process provided the basis for advances in economic knowledge.[141] Indeed, Friedman implied that the quantity theory of money, while more useful than Keynesian theory for understanding the historical record, would ultimately meet "destruction" in the sense that economists would find facts for which it could not account and it would be replaced by a broader theory that *could* explain those facts.[142]

Friedman's emphasis on the importance of historical evidence in monetary analysis would modify his own perspective toward the notion that extensive knowledge of the institutional framework was important for the analysis of economic relations. In particular, he would become far more well disposed toward this notion after the early 1950s. His article on methodology had distinguished between "descriptive accuracy and analytical relevance" when judging the merits of economic theories and had, of course, emphasized that a theory might be analytically useful even when applied to an environment that had features clearly not included in, or that were in conflict with, the theory.[143] This sentiment was certainly felt to some degree in the area of Friedman's monetary analysis. It was manifested especially in his application of the quantity theory of money to different periods and across countries, notwithstanding the differences in monetary and financial institutions over time and space. His conclusion was that "major differences among countries and periods in monetary institutions and other factors affecting the supply of money do not produce widely different relations between money and income."[144]

When one examines the details of this conclusion, however, it becomes clear that Friedman *had*, as indicated above, come to give considerable weight to institutional factors in understanding the money/income relationship.

To be sure, the just-quoted passage reflected Friedman's conviction that differences in financial institutions across countries, and the evolution of those institutions over time, had not prevented central banks from being able to exert a decisive influence on the nominal stock of money, and also that the correlation between the growth rates of nominal money and nominal income that was typically observed could be regarded as testament to the importance of monetary policy.

That conviction, however, went alongside considerable respect on Friedman's part for the importance of understanding institutions. His and Schwartz's construction of monetary data for the United States had inevitably involved extensive study of US banking institutions. One example of how institutional considerations shaped their judgment was their exclusion (see chapter 14 below) of negotiable certificates of deposit from the definition of money. This decision reflected an evaluation that those instruments differed in character from other categories of time deposits.

Friedman reconciled his belief in the generality of the quantity theory of money with his recognition of the importance of institutional differences in two principal ways. First, as already indicated, institutional detail was a factor informing Friedman and Schwartz's construction of monetary data and their choice of definition of money. Second, Friedman's contention, quoted above, that different institutional arrangements mattered little for the money/income relationship applied when the relationship was interpreted as the correlation between the growth rate of nominal money and the growth rate of nominal income. He recognized that the *absolute level* of velocity (the inverse of the money-to-income ratio) *did* depend on country-specific characteristics. In particular, Friedman and Schwartz affirmed "the importance of the financial and economic structure for the demand for money" and cited this as the explanation for the fact that the level of US M2 velocity had been much higher than the level of UK M2 velocity.[145]

Friedman went even further and recognized that the *trend growth rate* of velocity might vary across countries because of the different financial characteristics of those countries.[146] In addition, following criticism from James Tobin of their *Monetary History*, Friedman and Schwartz came to accept that the downward trend in velocity in the United States during the late nineteenth century reflected the spread of commercial banking.[147] It is notable that they simply allowed for this trend in velocity by straightforward removal of the trend prior to their money-demand analysis. This approach contrasted sharply with Friedman's ambitious goal, laid out in 1956, of trying to trace explicitly the variations in trends in payments technology to the optimizing behavior of individual households.[148]

This acceptance of the importance of institutional detail by Friedman and Schwartz still left key differences between them and some of the most prominent advocates, in the field of monetary analysis, of the importance of institutions. In particular, in the United Kingdom Richard Sayers and Nicholas Kaldor had suggested that financial developments had extinguished the concept of a well-defined demand for money.[149] In contrast, in the Friedman-Schwartz account, financial structure did help determine the level of the money/income ratio, and, to some extent, it accounted for the difference between the trend growth rates of money and income. But the demand function for money remained well-defined and was a key factor producing the positive correlation between monetary growth and nominal income growth.

This position, combined with his view of the appropriate specification of aggregate-supply relationships, made Friedman extremely hostile to accounts of the behavior of inflation that cited institutional factors.[150] The accounts in question alleged that features such as labor-union strength and firms' monopoly power were important sources of cost-push pressures. Friedman's debates with the advocates of cost-push explanations for inflation are detailed in chapters 10 and 15 below.

IV. Friedman and Technical Economics

"Most of my publications are technical, scientific, economic publications which really do not have any great interest to the public at large," Friedman observed in a 1994 interview.[151] As this remark was concerned with distinguishing Friedman's body of research work from public policy writings like his *Newsweek* columns and the Friedmans' *Free to Choose* book, it was conveying a legitimate point. Nevertheless, to those in the field of economic research Friedman's association of himself with "technical" publications surely seems somewhat jarring. For, by the standards of his contemporaries in economic research, and even more by the standards of researchers of subsequent generations, many of Friedman's key contributions were not technical.[152]

True, it remains the case that those contributions are unambiguously "directed at the specialized research worker rather than the general reader," as Friedman put it in 1958. And this is decidedly so in the case of the item to which Friedman was referring in that 1958 remark: *A Theory of the Consumption Function*.[153] But even his more explicitly model-oriented contributions were usually characterized by a considerable degree of accessibility to nontechnical readers. This was truer still of contributions like the Friedman-Schwartz *Monetary History*.

Some Friedman contributions to the research literature were so nontechnical that they could be changed into popular articles without great difficulty. It is unlikely that anyone other than Friedman has had a *Journal of Monetary Economics* publication adapted into an article for the *New York Times*.[154] And, although the *Journal of Economic Perspectives* aims for a broad audience, not all its papers are so nontechnical that they lend themselves naturally to being converted into a *Wall Street Journal* op-ed article. Yet that is what happened to Friedman's contribution to the *Journal of Economic Perspectives*.[155]

The present section will characterize Friedman's attitude to technical economics and will provide some links between Friedman's contributions and more technical writings by other economists.

MATHEMATICAL ECONOMICS AND
GENERAL EQUILIBRIUM THEORY

In recalling Friedman's Price Theory class of the early 1950s, Gary Becker noted that one criticism he had of the course was its inattention to mathematical economics and general equilibrium theory.[156] This feature of Friedman's teaching of price theory was also true of his research in monetary analysis.

By the early 1970s, Friedman was well known as being one of the least technical among leading economic researchers, when this assessment was based on the criterion of the technical difficulty of his writings. Indeed, his secretary from 1972 onward, Gloria Valentine, accepted the position as his secretary partly because of that reputation. Valentine recalled: "I was working at Continental Illinois National Bank in the Public Affairs Division, but I very much wanted to return to working at the University of Chicago where I had worked on two other separate occasions. . . . Because of having worked at the University before, I knew the administrative assistant in the Department of Economics, and she was a good friend of mine. . . . I asked the administrative assistant about secretarial openings in Econ. She told me that she was getting the positions upgraded for better pay and that she would let me know when the positions were upgraded and what openings were available. Some months later she let me know she had been successful with the upgrades and that there were two openings from which I could make a choice: Marc Nerlove or Milton Friedman. I asked which professor was the less mathematical, i.e., didn't use equations ad nauseam. She said that would be Milton Friedman, so I opted to work for him." Valentine added that, in the main, "the administrative assistant was absolutely correct. . . . I rarely got equations in subsequent papers through the years" (Gloria Valentine, personal communication, November 4, 2014).[157]

Friedman certainly granted that his research was less technical than that of the economists with whom he typically interacted. He also indicated that this state of affairs reflected a conscious decision on his part.[158] On one occasion, probably late in 1972, Friedman walked past Valentine and noticed that she was typing up a paper that, by his reckoning, contained a mass of equations. A bemused Friedman asked Valentine: "What is that? Who are you typing for?" Valentine replied that she was typing up a draft paper by Robert Barro, who at the time was a junior colleague of Friedman's in the economics department and who was, with Friedman, one of the economists for whom Valentine had been assigned secretarial duties. Friedman's reaction to this information was philosophical. "Oh," Friedman said. "He's young. He'll learn better" (Gloria Valentine, interview, April 1, 2013).

This reaction underscored the fact that Friedman's career had itself involved a shift away from mathematical rigor. In the 1990s, Friedman would observe that "individuals who have exceptional mathematical ability get early deference," and his own career through the early 1950s, in which he had won accolades in part through technical contributions to mathematical statistics and to the economics of choice, likely partly accounted for this remark.[159]

Although Friedman would be more outspoken about his rejection of his early Keynesian views than about his turning away from very technical work, the latter feature was an important component of the shake-up in Friedman's outlook toward economic analysis. His statement in Taylor (2001, 121) that there was "too much emphasis on mathematics as such and not on mathematics as a tool in understanding economic relationships" echoed what he had said for fifty years.[160] The Friedman statements on the matter after he left the University of Chicago were, it is true, more categorical in character. Indeed, on one occasion in the 1980s his critique extended to naming names, as he spoke acidly of "viewing economics as a branch of mathematics—as a game—as an intellectual game and exercise—as Debreu, Arrow and so on [do]."[161] And, in a 1981 *Newsweek* column, Friedman indicated that one possible benefit of terminating government funding of academic economic research—a measure that the column was advocating—was that it might lower the proportion of "highly mathematical research" in the publications that economists produced (*Newsweek*, May 18, 1981).

Friedman, therefore, left an abundant paper trail of acerbic comments about the degree to which highly mathematical modeling had been prioritized in economic research. The existence of this paper trail should not, however, disguise the fact that he contended that models underlay his thinking, that he viewed models as necessary, and that he believed that productive debate between economists should involve a clarification of the model being advanced by each side.

It should also not be overlooked that Friedman had a high regard for the economic analysis of several major mathematically oriented economists, including those who worked heavily in general equilibrium theory. There are many such examples, but a recurrent feature of the praise Friedman gave for the economists in question was their interest in practical problems. He cited both the work in general equilibrium theory by his University of Chicago colleague Hirofumi Uzawa, and that of his and Uzawa's student Miguel Sidrauski, as commendable in its insistence that results obtained using mathematical analysis be highlighted only if they were associated with "a meaningful economic interpretation."[162] And when recalling the work of Harold Hotelling, an economist who had trained him in his more mathematically inclined years of the 1930s, Friedman cited the fact that Hotelling's (1929) paper contained concrete economic implications even though the paper's analysis adhered to a mathematical format (Instructional Dynamics Economics Cassette Tape 18, March 1969).

Friedman extended the same type of praise to Kenneth Arrow, who was a colleague of Friedman's during the late 1940s and early 1950s.[163] Lester Telser recalled, from his interaction with Friedman from the 1950s to the 1970s, that Friedman's opinion of Arrow was very high (Lester Telser, interview, October 8, 2013). This was also the impression that Arrow received from Friedman. This impression was reinforced when Arrow heard that, in the early 1950s, Friedman had urged department head Theodore Schultz to retain Arrow when Stanford University approached Arrow with a job offer. Schultz had assumed that Friedman regarded the work of Arrow, who was part of the Cowles Commission group within the economics department, with the same misgivings that Friedman had toward the work of other key members of the foundation (see chapter 10). Instead, however, "Friedman said [to Schultz], 'No, Arrow is different.'" Arrow believed that Friedman's attitude reflected the fact that "he was impressed at least at that time with my social-choice results" (Kenneth Arrow, interview, December 7, 2013). In particular, Friedman valued Arrow's (1950) impossibility theorem highly. In Friedman's Nobel lecture, he would point to this work by Arrow (albeit without explicit bibliographical citation) as an important step in the application of economic analysis to the political process.[164]

In light of this high regard for the economic relevance of Arrow's research, Friedman's later negative statement (quoted above) about the economic relevance of the work of Arrow and Debreu may have been more directed at Debreu than at Arrow.[165] It may also have reflected Friedman's disaffection with research that was not by Arrow but that was perceived to be in the Arrow general equilibrium tradition, such as Frank Hahn's work in monetary analysis.[166]

It is clear from the above, however, that Friedman did like aspects of the work that flowed from general equilibrium analysis. Indeed, as will be seen, he invoked general equilibrium analysis in his own research. Before discussing this point, let us consider the respects in which highly mathematical economic analysis and its general equilibrium variant did not find favor with Friedman.

One reason for Friedman's outlook toward mathematical economics was that he felt it too often got economists involved in highly technical work and away from practical matters. This feeling was exemplified by Friedman's complaint that Leon Walras was not sufficiently interested in using his analysis to develop an apparatus that could be pressed into service for the analysis of concrete economic problems.[167] Even in his own model-based work, Friedman preferred to make high-level technical assumptions that established certain regularity conditions, in order that he could proceed with the analysis of the economic problem of interest. For example, in his 1948 paper with Savage, a footnote considered the case of a "kink or a jump in the utility function," but the authors indicated that the main text would abstract from such cases on the grounds that "one can always think of rounding the kink ever so slightly."[168] In contrast, an alternative, more mathematically oriented approach would justify rigorously the smoothing of the utility function and other functions. For example, Stokey, Lucas, and Prescott (1989, 101, 287) cited Blume, Easley, and O'Hara (1982) in connection with the differentiability of key functions.[169] Blume, Easley, and O'Hara (1982, 229) in turn were directed at establishing formally conditions in which one could "'smooth out' possible discontinuities in the derivatives." They were therefore concerned with studying rigorously an issue in mathematical economics of the kind that Friedman had no interest in considering in detail.

But, as this example indicates, Friedman's lack of interest in establishing formal regularity conditions did not mean that his own analysis was unrelated to those conditions. *Someone* had to study and establish those conditions, precisely in order for the kind of economic analysis in which Friedman and Savage engaged (that is, with continuous functions) to have a solid foundation. A similar example comes from Arrow-Debreu securities. As indicated in chapter 4, the main Arrow-Debreu contributions in this area came after Friedman had largely left the research area of agents' behavior under uncertainty, and Friedman had little to say specifically about these contributions. But a model in which a full set of Arrow-Debreu securities is traded is clearly an unrealistic abstraction. Indeed, Friedman and his wife themselves went on record as saying: "There is not enough fine print in the world to specify in advance every contingency that might arise and to describe precisely the obligations of the various parties to the exchange in each case."[170] The Arrow-Debreu construct does, however, provide a basis on which models that *are* concerned with practical economic problems can proceed. The postulated existence of Arrow-Debreu securities can therefore be considered among the unrealistic but useful assumptions employed in the specification of such practical models. Indeed, Blume and Easley (2006) and Cogley, Sargent, and Tsyrennikov (2014) have argued that the presence of Arrow-Debreu securities is a necessary part of the model if some of Friedman's ideas in price theory are to be rigorously justified.[171]

Friedman himself seemed to recognize the need for such infrastructure for economic models, as well as the fact that an appropriate division of labor within the economics profession required that some researchers be working on this infrastructure. For example, Friedman praised Paul Samuelson for having "helped to reshape and improve the theoretical foundations of our subject" and described how some of the material in Samuelson's *Foundations of Economic Analysis* achieved this goal (*Newsweek*, November 9, 1970).

The Role of Mathematics in Economic Analysis

When it came to other instances of the application of mathematics to economics, however, Friedman was concerned that mathematics, instead of complementing and fortifying economic analysis, could distract from the study of substantial economic issues. One long-standing complaint he had was about analyses that were so framed in mathematical terms that the economic content—although substantial—was obscured.[172] In addition, Friedman felt that a mathematical approach could lead to exercises for which an economic foundation was missing, and whose lack of value could have been discerned if the analyst had applied more economic intuition. Friedman cited Walras as someone who had occasionally followed this path and thereby produced some results that were economic "nonsense."[173]

A related criticism that Friedman advanced was that general equilibrium analysis, even when it focused on problems that had economic substance, frequently overemphasized striking results that emerged under very special conditions. Such cases might lack an empirical basis or be fragile, perhaps because of their reliance on specific parameter settings. Friedman's challenges to the work of Oskar Lange, which were discussed in chapter 4, embedded this criticism. So too did his later critique (see chapter 15) of the results in Tobin (1970a), which were obtained from a special setting of the money-demand function.[174] A feature of this criticism was Friedman's lack of interest in the study of special or degenerate cases if there was not a clear economic basis for focusing on these cases.

On the other hand, Friedman felt that approaching economic analysis from a mathematical perspective could lead economists away from some special cases that *were* relevant. For example, a mathematical criterion might lead an economist to judge that results that were associated *only* with a specific parameter value were without interest, because that value was of zero measure in the parameter space. But, from an early stage, Friedman rejected such a criterion: the measure-zero setting, he argued, sometimes corresponded to the economically relevant case.[175] Indeed, the natural-rate hypothesis that Friedman would develop was, as discussed in chapters 5 and 13, an instance in which he insisted on a specific parameterization of the Phillips curve that was of zero measure. The element common to Friedman's rejection of others' emphases on special cases and those arguments for specific parameter settings that appeared in his own work was an insistence on economic, and not mathematical, criteria as the basis for specifying an economic model.[176]

It is useful to keep in mind Friedman's focus on the deployment of economic arguments in the assignment of parameter values when one considers his outlook toward general equilibrium models. Laidler (2012, 14, 21) suggests that Friedman disliked Walrasian, or general equilibrium, analysis because he associated that analysis with models that were vacuous in the sense that they lacked predictive content, being completely general systems. It is certainly true that Friedman had disdain for setups that nested all economic theories as special cases.[177] He regarded those models as empty of content and reflecting a failure on the part of the modeler to apply economic restrictions that would produce a specification that—by generating predictions that could be contradicted by empirical evidence—could be regarded as having genuine economic substance.[178] He saw a key function of economists as that of making firm decisions about the specification of the model, and the choice of model solution, in order that a single prediction arose from a model, instead of a menu of possibilities.[179] This sentiment was obviously related to Friedman's desire for parsimony, and Lucas (2004a, 15-16) has suggested that a reaction that Friedman relayed to Don Patinkin on the latter's work reflected this sentiment.[180]

It would, however, not seem appropriate to attribute to Friedman the view that general equilibrium analysis is inherently associated with the absence of definite solutions or definite predictions. As already indicated, he saw Lange's general equilibrium analysis as leading to definite results (albeit ones with which Friedman disagreed). It seems more appropriate to regard Friedman's grievance with general equilibrium analysis as arising from the factors given above: its tendency to emphasize mathematical instead of economic criteria in arriving at the model specification and to provide results for which the economic intuition was unclear or absent. In addition, although he accepted that general equilibrium models could be used to generate definite results, his own preference was for more highly aggregated models than those typically associated with general equilibrium analysis. And, with regard to the merits of free markets, Friedman believed—as noted in section I of this chapter—that a valid economic case for the market system could be made using individual-market analysis of the type associated with Marshall, and without reliance on results obtained from multiple-market models of the kind associated with Walrasian analysis.

What Friedman Valued in General Equilibrium Analysis

But it is important also to indicate what Friedman did *not* reject in the Walrasian approach. He did not reject the notion that partial equilibrium analysis could be fallacious and that, in one way or another, general equilibrium effects needed to be taken into account.[181]

Furthermore, Friedman did not reject the need for economic theory or the requirement for an underlying economic model in order to carry out a coherent analysis of an economic problem.[182] He described himself as having a natural tendency to look at things from the point of view of economic theory.[183] However, a characteristic that Friedman believed set him apart from the bulk of the general equilibrium theorists was that he was not interested in theory for its own sake, but instead in the practical application of economic theory—a perspective that he believed he shared with Keynes (*Economist*, June 4, 1983). Along these lines, Stanley Fischer recalled of Friedman: "I don't think he was incredibly interested in macro theory, although he had [contributed] a couple of lovely things—including permanent-income theory, which was nicely done.... So, you know, he was no slouch intellectually. But I don't think he was very into the theoretical stuff.... Milton's [perspective] was very much something which I now *like*, which is: 'Here are the facts, and let's get on with the real world as it is'" (Stanley Fischer, interview, August 30, 2013).

Most important of all, Friedman's own model included material from Walrasian general equilibrium analysis. He was exposed to such analysis at an early stage, owing to his drawing on Irving Fisher's work of the 1890s.[184] Fisher's work in that decade included general equilibrium analysis; indeed Calvo (1978b, 321) referred to the "Walras-Fisher" general equilibrium framework. Friedman's later disaffection with mathematical economics went alongside his continued acceptance that formal general equilibrium analysis could be useful, including for the problems in which he was himself interested. He not only accepted that Walrasian general equilibrium analysis was capable of making definite predictions, but he also used the flexible-price equilibrium unemployment rate associated with general equilibrium analysis as his definition of the natural rate of unemployment.[185]

Furthermore, this flexible-price equilibrium—although it in the short run merely determined the natural values of series—described the behavior of the *actual* values of real variables over longer horizons. In 1970, Friedman elaborated his view that a model in which the effects of monetary policy wore off in the long run should have a long-run equilibrium in which one block of equations had nominal variables being determined by the monetary authority's actions and another block consisted of "the Walrasian equations" by whose interaction real variables were determined.[186]

As well as employing Walrasian general equilibrium analysis in his own conceptual framework, Friedman accepted the usefulness of mathematical analysis as a means of exposing flaws in economic analysis that was based on faulty verbal analysis. He contended that "it is far easier with words than with formal mathematics to be illogical."[187] In his view, mathematical formalizations of economic propositions allowed precision and could facilitate communication among economists.[188] Such formalizations were also helpful in securing the avoidance of an internally contradictory piece of economic analysis.[189] These positions were ones to which Friedman adhered right to the end. They were reflected in his remark in 2006: "I am dictating this answer to your note which is why there are no mathematics in it."[190]

Clearly, then, Friedman was appreciative of the internal logic and coherence of the work of those in the areas of general equilibrium theory and mathematical economic analysis. However, the feeling was not always mutual. Over the years, the opinion has been offered by a number of prominent economists in the areas of general equilibrium theory and mathematical economic analysis that the propositions that Friedman advanced in his monetary analysis would not stand up if they were scrutinized in a more mathematically rigorous context. One proposition to which this criticism was applied was Friedman's belief that the long-run Phillips curve was vertical. As discussed in chapters 13 and 15, however, Friedman's proposition largely stood up when examined using formal models. The same is true of several other Friedman propositions. Some examples follow of cases in which Friedman was able to intuit an answer to a modeling question and in which that answer later received verification by more mathematically rigorous researchers.

The first example is that of the natural rate of unemployment. Various economists, including Hahn (1983b), claimed that the concept of the natural rate of unemployment could not be rigorously justified, and Solow (1986, S30) stated, "I doubt that many of those who use the [natural-rate] concept would accept Friedman's definition." In particular, Solow expressed skepticism about whether a Walrasian model would be the vehicle with which macroeconomists formalized the natural-rate concept. In contrast to this assessment, Lucas and Prescott (1974) and Robert Hall (1979), among others, justified the concept of the natural rate of unemployment using flexible-price general equilibrium models, with Robert Hall (1979, 154) noting: "The spirit of Friedman's definition is preserved—unemployment is treated as a phenomenon that can be understood within a general equilibrium Walrasian model, provided the model is suitably extended." In addition, more recent contributions have shown that the concepts of the natural rates of output and unemployment remain viable when the flexible-price model has noncompetitive elements. These findings largely confirm Friedman's definition of the natural rate of unemployment. And they do not support the contentions of Fellner (1976, 55) and Hahn (1983b, 86) that the natural-rate notion was coherent only for a perfectly competitive economy.[191]

A second example pertains to the question of whether a nonzero interest elasticity of the demand for money, by itself, prevents a classical-dichotomy result in which real and nominal variables are determined separately. Friedman's position was that temporary price stickiness could deliver a situation in which real and nominal variables were (in the short run) determined jointly, but that a nonzero interest elasticity of money demand per se would not do so. His attempt to establish this contention consisted of a strategy that would not be acceptable from the viewpoint of general equilibrium theorists: a verbal examination of the behavior under flexible prices of a simple IS-LM system.[192] But this demonstration, in a 1966 Friedman paper, was subsequently fortified by the general equilibrium analysis of Fischer Black (1972), Brock (1974), and others.[193] These papers verified that in a dynamic general equilibrium model with money, monetary policy had no effects on real output if wages and prices were flexible, even when the demand for money was interest elastic. Furthermore, in *Monetary Trends* in 1982, Friedman and Schwartz cited these rigorous 1970s analyses, rather than Friedman's 1966 paper, to document the result in question.[194] This practice confirmed Friedman's willingness to accept that general equilibrium analysis could provide a more rigorous basis for points that he himself had made.

A third example consists of Friedman's reaction to Fischer Black's (1974) finding that, in a dynamic general equilibrium model with money, inflation could have explosive dynamics even in the face of a constant money stock or constant monetary growth. Friedman suggested that this result reflected "ingenious mathematical constructions, without substantive content, because they beg the question of the transmission mechanism."[195] Subsequently, results in McCallum (1983b, 151–54) provided support for Friedman's conjecture. McCallum showed that Black's result no longer held if one solved Black's model using a procedure that excluded state variables whose presence could not be justified by the structure of the model.[196] Once again, in an informal discussion Friedman had hit upon the answer that would arise from formal analysis.

FRIEDMAN AND ECONOMETRIC ANALYSIS

Longbottom and Holly (1985, 3) characterized Friedman and Schwartz as researchers who "put great emphasis on the use of econometric techniques to resolve theoretical controversy." Although this statement was made with specific reference to Friedman and Schwartz's *Monetary Trends* volume, it does have a considerable amount of applicability to Friedman's other writings. Indeed, the notion that econometric evidence should be the arbiter in judging theories might be regarded as a corollary of Friedman's stress, in his 1953 methodology article and elsewhere, on the role of empirical evidence. But running parallel with this stress in Friedman's writings were many other statements expressing misgivings about econometrics. Indeed, at roughly the same time as his methodology article, Friedman referred to "extensive statistical studies of economic phenomena" in a negative manner and implied that these went contrary to the direction in which he would like to see economic research go.[197] In light of these tensions, this chapter will conclude with some observations that are intended to shed light on Friedman's approach to econometrics.

A number of the reasons for Friedman's ambivalence toward econometrics have been brought out in discussions provided earlier in this book. One of these—his belief in the usefulness of historical and narrative information—was discussed in section III. Another—his skepticism about multiple regressions and especially his concern that they could produce fragile results—was shown in chapter 4 to have been present in Friedman's thinking by 1940.

Against this background, and notwithstanding his own deep training in and familiarity with statistics, Friedman often relied on techniques other than regression in his empirical work. For example, in a 1961 analysis that used detrended values of money, consumption, and income, Friedman stated that the "trends were fitted graphically" instead of using regression-based trend estimates.[198] Such choices very likely partly reflected computational limitations: this was an era in which, as David Meiselman recalled, both he and Phillip Cagan had to key in data and formulas into desk calculators in the course of their work with Friedman (David Meiselman, interview, April 30, 2013). But Friedman affirmed that his monetary project with Schwartz, although it involved a "great deal of statistical curve-fitting," deliberately used graphical instead of econometric techniques in obtaining some of the main numerical results, including those concerning leads and lags (Instructional Dynamics Economics Cassette Tape 101, June 14, 1972).

It nevertheless remains the case that, even prior to *Monetary Trends*, a considerable amount of Friedman's work on money involved regression analysis. Of these, his project with David Meiselman was the most prominent. As discussed in chapter 12, that project's considerable impact resulted in good part from the fact that other researchers were able to reproduce the Friedman-Meiselman econometric findings. That his own work was replicable by others was an explicit concern of Friedman's, and whether research results were replicable also formed a basis on which he took others to task.[199]

It would be tempting to add that other pervasive features of Friedman's econometric work were his use of low-frequency data (either based on annual averages, or on the still-greater degree of time aggregation associated with NBER business cycle methods) and his comprehensive rejection of short-term forecasting. However, although these features indeed characterized the bulk of his work with Schwartz and with Meiselman, in some of his monetary analysis Friedman was prepared to engage in shorter-term econometric analysis. In particular, as discussed in chapters 13 and 15 below, during the second half of the 1960s and the early 1970s Friedman estimated aggregate-income-growth regressions on monthly and quarterly US data. Furthermore, although he and Schwartz would refer witheringly to the "explosive growth of the short-term economic forecasting industry," Friedman himself would for a time use his income-growth regressions to make short-term forecasts.[200]

What this short-term analysis had in common with Friedman's main monetary research was his preference for the study of bivariate relationships, often of a reduced-form character, over multivariate or multi-equation econometric approaches. Lyle Gramley, at the time a senior adviser at the Federal Reserve Board, heard Friedman on this subject in the course of a conference at Ditchley House, United Kingdom, in September 1968.[201] Gramley recalled that "during one of the breaks I happened to walk up to a conversation that was going on between Jim Duesenberry and Milton Friedman. Duesenberry was saying, 'Well now, Milton, you have to grant that all these big models that are being produced these days find a very important role for monetary policy.' And Milton responded, 'Well, that's true, but these things are so unstable. You get one year past the period of fit, and they blow up.'" Friedman went on to suggest that simple income-on-money regressions might be more robust than these large models (Lyle Gramley, interview, June 24, 2013). Friedman's conviction that large econometric models had a chronic tendency to undergo revision in light of serious forecast errors was one he reaffirmed in 1987.[202]

Friedman's negative perspective on large-scale structural econometric models was also evident in his interaction during the late 1940s and early 1950s with the Cowles Commission. This interaction forms part of the coverage of the next chapter, which opens part 3 of this book and which resumes the chronological account of Friedman's participation in US economic debate.

Friedman's Monetarist Years, 1951 to 1972

· CHAPTER 10 ·

The Accord and
the New Regime,
1951 to 1960

I. Events and Activities, 1951–60

Chapter 11 of Friedman and Schwartz's *Monetary History* was titled "Revival of Monetary Policy, 1948–60." Their decision to trace the revival of monetary policy back to 1948 implied that their chapter encompassed the three years leading up to March 1951, a period when the Federal Reserve remained "under Treasury control," in the phrase of Meltzer (2003, 579), and in which the policy of pegging the longer-term US government bond rate remained in force. Classifying the years 1948–50 as part of the period of the revival of monetary policy did allow Friedman and Schwartz to include, as one of the elements of the revival, the loosening of the constraints on Federal Reserve policy at the *short-term* portion of the securities market—a process that began even before 1948.[1]

Furthermore, an important component of the revival of monetary policy was a change in academic opinion: from widespread support for cheap money, to heavy opposition to this policy. A counterpart to this change in policy prescription was a shift in the weight that academic economists gave to the power of monetary policy to affect aggregate demand—from the low weight that had been assigned by Alvin Hansen, Paul Samuelson, and others, to a somewhat higher weight (at least for conditions other

The views expressed in this study are those of the author alone and should not be interpreted as those of the Federal Reserve Board or the Federal Reserve System. The author thanks David Laidler and Rajat Sood for their comments on an earlier draft of this chapter. The author is also grateful to Miguel Acosta, George Fenton, and William Gamber for research assistance, and to participants in the University of California, Berkeley, Economic History seminar, including J. Bradford DeLong, Barry Eichengreen, Martha Olney, Christina Romer, and David Romer, for comments on a presentation of portions of this chapter. See the introduction for a full list of acknowledgments for this book. The author regrets to note that, in the period since the research for this chapter was conducted, four individuals whose interviews with the author are drawn on below—Carl Christ, Lyle Gramley, David Meiselman, and Charles Schultze—have passed away.

than those associated with depressions). And, as was discussed in chapter 4, Friedman himself, in the course of the second half of the 1940s, went through a major change in thinking about monetary policy. In his case, however, the change was more dramatic than that of most of his fellow economists—a situation that would lead Barro and Fischer (1976, 134) to observe that "Friedman's own transition to a belief in the potency of money summarizes the direction of change, if not the magnitude of change" of professional thinking.

In terms of actual practice, however, the important institutional change that permitted the revival of monetary policy was not anything that occurred in the years 1948–50. Rather, it was the Federal Reserve/Treasury Accord, which was released publicly on March 4, 1951 (Meltzer 2003, 712).

The Accord ended the situation that the *Financial Times* described as one in which "both the British and American governments seem to be determined not to use higher interest rates to combat inflation" (*Financial Times*, February 10, 1951). The sequence of events that led to the Accord included a dispute between the Federal Reserve and the Truman administration. Marriner Eccles, formerly Federal Reserve chairman and still seated on the Federal Reserve System's Board of Governors, played a leading part in making the dispute known to the public (see Meltzer 2003, 705–6). Ironically, as this dispute was unfolding, Eccles's own perception of the feasible degree of Federal Reserve independence was modest. In February 1951, he wrote in a letter to Friedman that it was unrealistic to expect that long-term interest rates would be completely unpegged. The most that could be hoped for, Eccles implied, was that the value of the bond-rate peg would be raised by about 50 basis points.[2]

The Accord returned autonomy regarding monetary policy decisions to the Federal Reserve and, in the process, permitted the dropping of the bond-rate pegging arrangement. The Accord therefore marked, Friedman would say, "a distinct change in the role of monetary policy and its possibility."[3] However, as Friedman's accounts would stress, and as detailed in the next section of this chapter, the Federal Reserve extricated itself from its pre-1951 arrangements only gradually. The limited degree of bond-rate flexibility that Eccles had sketched in his letter to Friedman proved to be close to the practice initially followed after the Accord, with some central-bank maintenance of prices in the US Treasury bond market lingering into about 1953.

The backdrop for the Accord was, of course, the Korean War and the reemergence of inflationary pressure in the United States. Nearly two decades after the advent of the Accord, at a conference at the University of Sheffield (United Kingdom) in September 1970, Roy Harrod would preface his comments on a paper of Friedman's with a recollection. Harrod stated that Friedman "has been a good friend of mine over many years. I think that the first time I met him was at a conference at White Sulphur Springs in West Virginia in March 1951." Harrod added that the conference participants, meeting to discuss the appropriate policy response to the Korean War inflation, were unaware that, concurrently with the conference, Federal Reserve and Treasury officials in Washington, DC, were hammering out the text of the Accord.[4]

In an important respect, however, Harrod's memory played him false. The academic conference in question was *not* concurrent with the Accord negotiations. Rather, it was convened April 5–8, 1951, a little over a month *after* the announcement of the Accord. The transcript of the conference proceedings was published later in 1951.[5] That record of the conference does, however, strongly support Harrod's recollection of the "vigorous part played by Professor Friedman" at the event.[6]

Friedman did not kick off the discussion of monetary policy—that assignment instead went to his older colleague in the Department of Economics, Lloyd Mints—but he was asked to summarize the conference's session on the topic. There had been "two major positions" expressed, Friedman observed in his summary remarks. "One position," he went on, "presented by Mr. Mints, and which, I may say, I share, is that monetary measures, given a reasonable fiscal policy, could be effective in stabilizing the level of prices."[7] Friedman characterized the appropriate monetary policy as one in which monetary growth was varied in a manner that offset the effects on the economy of changes in velocity. The problem of velocity shifts was no doubt fresh in his mind in light of the rise in velocity associated with the outbreak of the Korean War. And—in line with his perception at that time that monetary policy could readily offset velocity shocks—Friedman had said, in a radio appearance a couple of months prior to the conference, that monetary action could have prevented the inflation that had been observed since the war's outbreak (NBC 1951a, 2).

As the 1950s proceeded, however, Friedman became increasingly doubtful about the precision with which velocity shifts could be offset by policy makers—especially once account was taken of the likelihood that monetary policy measures, which in principle could deliver such offsets, exerted their effects on the economy with lags. This consideration, coupled with his conclusion that autonomous sharp year-to-year changes in velocity of the Korean War kind were infrequent, would lead him in the second half of the decade to advocacy of the constant-monetary-growth rule.

Friedman's 1951 summing up explicitly contrasted the stand taken by himself and Mints with the other major position articulated at the conference. According to the latter position, Friedman noted, "monetary policy can do some good but cannot . . . be expected to prevent completely the kind of inflation which is now occurring."[8] Harrod had taken that position at the conference, voicing his doubts "that in history we can find an example of pure monetary control preventing an inflation of the sort with which we are threatened."[9] Harrod diagnosed the United States and other countries as suffering from a spiral in costs—a spiral that was superimposed on what he conceded were demand pressures making for inflation. Reflecting his acknowledgment of a demand-pull element in current inflation, Harrod granted that policy tools to affect spending (among which he favored fiscal policy over monetary policy) could help contain some inflationary pressures. But, Harrod claimed, other tools were also imperative, particularly price and wage controls that "can stop spiral inflation."[10]

In sharp contrast, Friedman had, by 1951, rejected the idea that autonomous wage/price spirals were a factor behind inflation. He regarded the appearance of spirals in historical inflation experience as actually reflecting the lagged adjustment of inflation to aggregate-demand pressure. From that judgment flowed the conclusion that monetary actions were appropriate and sufficient measures to take against inflation.[11]

Harrod's views contrasted with Friedman's in a still further respect: physical controls such as rationing, he said, were preferable to allowing open inflation.[12] This judgment clashed not only with the philosophy underlying Friedman and Stigler's *Roofs or Ceilings?*, but also with what became a familiar Friedman dictum: that open inflation was far preferable to suppressed inflation.[13]

Interest-Rate Policy

In the half century and more after 1951, Friedman would receive a lot of criticism from monetary researchers and practitioners for his alleged neglect of interest rates and his supposed reluctance, or outright unwillingness, to describe monetary policy actions or their effects in terms of interest rates. However, it was concluded in chapter 5 that the record of Friedman's statements is more nuanced than this criticism suggests. Friedman's discussions of the transition from the pre-Accord environment reinforce this conclusion. At the 1951 conference, he welcomed the end of the cheap-money consensus, offering praise for participants' "agreement that a particular, single, rigid rate of interest derived from past history is not sacrosanct and should not be allowed to interfere with further use of monetary policy."[14] But Friedman also stated that monetary policy, once applied, could be viewed as a tool that "depends very largely on the use of the interest rate" for influencing total spending.[15] Indeed, in an article later in the year, Friedman acknowledged—making a point that is more associated with the New Keynesian literature than with monetarism—that price stability dictates what is "the necessary rise in the rate of interest" and that the money demand function then "only determines the amount by which the stock of money will have to be reduced" to secure this interest-rate rise.[16]

Of course, the absence of a direct empirical counterpart to "the" interest rate was a reason Friedman was more interested, when assessing the degree of monetary restraint or ease, in looking at measures of the stock of money than at any specific interest rate. The broad-based view of the transmission mechanism that he was developing in the early 1950s would harden this inclination, as it would underscore the unobserved and multifold nature of the channels through which monetary policy actions affected economic activity. Consequently, Friedman became much less inclined after the early 1950s to refer to "the" interest rate in his analysis of monetary matters.[17] However, Friedman did grant—both in the early 1950s and for the rest of his life—that variations in observed securities-market interest rates, such as Treasury bill and bond rates, would come about from pursuit of the monetary policy that he favored—that is, a policy whose focus was on price stability.[18] As he put it in January 31, 1952, testimony, "the rate of interest should be allowed to vary to whatever extent is required for the far more important objective of preventing inflation."[19]

Securities-market interest rates would move, Friedman said, but the degree of movement of interest rates should not be the metric used in judging the amount of tightening required. An appropriate criterion was instead the "effect on the quantity of money," with price stability as the ultimate goal.[20] In a radio broadcast in February 1951, Friedman indicated that what "the Federal Reserve System should do" is "take the position that its primary responsibilities, and its primary concern, will be with the supply of money and the price level."[21] The Federal Reserve, in this schema, would organize its actions with the conscious aim of making adjustments to the money stock, but with a view to achieving an objective for the price level. This formulation was testament to Friedman's continued desire—at this stage of his thinking—that year-to-year velocity changes be routinely offset by appropriate monetary action. But with his work with Anna Schwartz proceeding apace over this period, Friedman was already approaching the conclusion that occasions like that in 1950—when velocity dominated price-level fluctuations—were uncommon; more usually, low monetary growth would secure price stability.

Accordingly, in testifying to the Joint Committee on the Economic Report on March 25, 1952, Friedman declared, "There is scarcely a case on record in which a substantial rise in the stock of money over a short period has not been accompanied by a substantial rise in prices," and he urged that monetary policy be carried out with that relationship as a guide.[22] Friedman made no bones about the interest-rate variation that might have to be accepted as part of this policy. Paul Samuelson, who was testifying along-side Friedman, pressed him: Was Friedman prepared to see bond prices fall to levels as low as fifty or sixty? Friedman replied that if a decline of bond prices to fifty was required, then "of course, I would be prepared to see it go to 50," but whether this was necessary depended on the scale of "the inflationary pressures to be counteracted."[23]

With respect to Samuelson, Patinkin (1983, 165) stated that his "shift toward a greater emphasis on monetary factors began to take place in the mid-1950s, well before the growing influence of monetarism had manifested itself." But the fact that Samuelson interacted with Friedman at this 1952 hearing as well as in other forums around the same time, together with Samuelson's acknowledgment that he was a voracious reader of Friedman's work, casts doubt on Patinkin's implication that Samuelson's change in views on monetary policy—discussed in chapter 4 above—occurred without influence from Friedman. Patinkin's interpretation also clashes with Samuelson's own acknowledgment in 1962 that "I've studied Professor Friedman's arguments on these matters [monetary history and policy] and I've derived a great deal of benefit from them."[24]

By the time they testified together, Friedman and Samuelson had co-signed a statement titled "Monetary Policy to Combat Inflation," released publicly on January 21, 1952.[25] The statement was an outgrowth of a conference of university economists the previous October, but several conference attendees, including Alvin Hansen and Jacob Viner, refused to sign the statement. Hansen withheld his signature because he felt that fiscal policy was a more appropriate weapon to use against inflation, and because he opposed policies that implied a major increase in interest rates. For Viner, however, the statement's endorsement of monetary measures was "too weak and excessively qualified."[26] Friedman clearly felt the same way, but, instead of refusing to lend his name to the statement, he peppered it with solo-authored qualifications and dissents. In total, these dissents brought out the greater confidence that Friedman had, compared with his peers, in the capacity for monetary policy actions to secure price stability. They also confirmed that Friedman by this point already regarded open market operations as the only tool that was essential for the execution of monetary policy. In this connection, one of Friedman's dissents—that with regard to the statement's recommendation of "selective credit controls"—foreshadowed his disagreement with Samuelson in 1980 about the desirability of President Jimmy Carter's program of direct controls on credit.[27] Friedman's 1952 dissent read: "I disapprove of selective credit controls. Such controls, like other 'direct' controls, are an inequitable and inefficient means of altering resource allocation. The 'interest rate,' despite admitted deficiencies, will do a far better job."[28] He would express very much the same sentiment in 1980.

Fiscal Policy and Price Stability

In the preceding discussion, a 1951 Friedman remark was quoted in which he stated that monetary policy could deliver price stability, provided that there was a "reasonable" fiscal policy. What, specifically, did Friedman's regard as the fiscal/monetary combinations that could deliver price stability? An examination of Friedman's other statements over this period answers this question, and that examination shows that he had come to see inflation as an exclusively monetary phenomenon. Friedman had abandoned both his early-1940s position that fiscal deficits mattered for inflation in their own right (that is, even if they were not monetized), and his 1948 position that budget deficits financed by Treasury bill issuance had powerful effects on aggregate demand and inflation.

Friedman's January 1952 congressional testimony gave a position that lined up with the many discussions he provided on the subject during the 1960s and 1970s.[29] "Everything depends on how the deficit is financed," Friedman testified. If the deficit led to money creation, either directly through the process of governmental borrowing from the central bank, or indirectly via the floating of government debt at too-low interest rates, it would promote inflation.[30] But "if the deficit is financed by borrowing from the public at whatever rate of interest is required," price stability would not be jeopardized.[31] This exposition implied that Friedman's conception of a "reasonable" fiscal policy was a combination of tax-and-public-spending choices and debt-management arrangements that put no obligation on the central bank to provide high rates of money creation.

Friedman's new position—under which deficits were relevant for inflation only insofar as they had a bearing on monetary growth—was an outgrowth of his continuing work with Anna Schwartz on monetary history. The study of wartime inflations had acquired renewed topicality in light of the Korean conflict, and Friedman was already on record as believing that it was the really large variations in the data that would shed light on issues such as the size of the fiscal multiplier (see Machlup 1943, 48). Against this backdrop, in 1951 Friedman looked to the United States' experiences during the Civil War, World War I, and World War II for the information these episodes—each of them associated with very sizable variations in money and the economy—provided about the relative importance of fiscal and monetary factors for aggregate income and price fluctuations. Friedman mentioned this research at the 1951 White Sulphur Springs conference.[32] And he presented the ensuing article at the December 1951 American Economic Association meetings—a presentation that led to the article's publication in May 1952. The published paper, which Anna Schwartz has called the "first output of the [Friedman-Schwartz] project" (E. Nelson 2004a, 401), concluded that fiscal influences were "important for the problem of inflation primarily because of their effects on the stock of money per unit of output, and they are only important insofar as they have such effects."[33] This would be a position that Friedman would maintain for the rest of his life. He would reaffirm it emphatically in his statements and writings of the early twenty-first century.

Now that price stability and fiscal policy had largely been separated in Friedman's thinking, he could give greater consideration to other criteria when considering what factors should govern decisions about deficit spending. Friedman's attitude to deficit spending became more relaxed later in the 1950s as he moved from advocacy of the 1948 monetization rule to the constant-monetary-growth rule, and still further during the 1960s as he adopted the "starve-the-beast" position concerning public spending. As of the early 1950s, however, although he no longer perceived a close, inherent inflation/deficits connection, Friedman was still inclined to favor linking new spending to new tax revenue, insisting "we should make every effort to pay as we go."[34]

That said, it should be stressed that during the Korean War Friedman took a more flexible attitude toward deficit spending in emergencies than he had taken during World War II. This new flexibility was apparent at the April 1951 conference on inflation, at which Friedman stated that he saw "some positive advantage" in debt issuance over tax increases if wartime spending reached new heights.[35] In his January 1952 congressional testimony, Friedman expressed views about temporary wartime spending that have similarities to the recommendations of the modern public-finance literature:

> My own judgment is that[,] at presently expected levels of expenditures[,] we should aim for a roughly balanced cash budget; that we should do so equally for moderately higher levels of expenditures expected to be maintained more or less indefinitely, but that we should borrow to finance any temporary "hump" in expenditures as well as part of any level substantially above those now in prospect. (Joint Committee on the Economic Report 1952b, 334)

Friedman was, however, still some distance from a tax-smoothing prescription. He granted that the decision regarding whether to run deficits "depends on how much we have to push taxation [up]."[36] But he still adhered to a strong presumption that taxes should be raised if government spending looked to be "much above" present revenue.[37] Indeed, in a January 1952 statement that, in retrospect, calls attention to the changes that were still to come in his views on fiscal policy, Friedman called for a combination of tight money and "high taxation."[38] This was very different from Friedman's position from the 1960s onward. By the early 1950s, therefore, Friedman had come to the conclusion that a tight monetary policy alone could handle inflation, but he still viewed a tight fiscal policy, marked by deficit limitation, as extremely useful for facilitating the monetary restriction.

One basis for Friedman's view that tight fiscal policy had this role is that, at this point, he was strongly inclined to see bond-financed deficits as a significant source of upward pressure on interest rates. Tighter fiscal policy could, on this view, lower the interest rates that were implied by maintenance of monetary growth at noninflationary levels.[39] A further basis for Friedman's backing of tight fiscal policy lay in the fact that, although his *research* was pointing to the separability of fiscal and monetary policy, in *policy prescriptions* in the early 1950s he was still advocating his 1948 rule, under which monetary policy and fiscal policy moved in lockstep.[40] As indicated above, Friedman was taking the position that a monetary policy directed solely toward the prevention of inflation was paramount and that such a policy was feasible in the presence of sizable deficits.[41] But he continued to see the ideal arrangement as featuring fiscal/monetary policy coordination of the kind he had outlined in 1948: an arrangement in which the federal fiscal balance was varied cyclically and was routinely monetized. Friedman's policy recommendations during the Korean War were motivated by a desire to shift the direction of policy toward his 1948 rule.[42] The approximate US budget balance that was observed in practice during the Korean War was not too far from the situation of budget surplus that Friedman was, at the time of that war, indicating was appropriate in conditions of an inflationary boom.

A Depression-Proof Economy

Along with the changes in fiscal, monetary, and debt-management arrangements that it entailed, the 1948 rule proposal included, as chapter 4 above discussed, a shift to 100 percent reserve requirements. In a presentation in Sweden in April 1954 titled "Why the American Economy Is Depression-Proof," Friedman attempted to make the argument that a shift to 100 percent reserve requirements would not imply a wrenching change to the commercial banking system.[43] To this end, he noted that in the wake of the Second World War, commercial banks had about half their assets in the form of investments in government securities. Therefore, Friedman argued, the bulk of commercial banks' deposit liabilities could be considered to be, in essence, government-created money.[44]

This argument did not, however, prove to be one that he could deploy for very much longer, as a major shift in commercial banks' behavior was underway. Commercial banks would, in the course of this shift, alter the asset composition in their portfolios away from holdings of government securities in favor of loans to the private sector.[45] A footnote that Friedman added to a 1968 reprint of his 1954 talk contained the sheepish acknowledgment that the steep rise in the government-security share of banks' assets that he had highlighted in 1954 had since been completely reversed.[46]

In the 1960s through the 1990s Friedman, as was noted in chapter 2, continued to speak highly of 100 percent reserve requirements as a prospective arrangement for the United States. But he would also acknowledge that the further that the US commercial banking system moved from a government securities-oriented asset structure, the less 100 percent reserves became a likely reform.[47]

In his 1954 talk, Friedman also laid out a more general assessment of the prospects for postwar stabilization policy. Although, in his view, the economics profession still did not appreciate the key role played by monetary policy in producing the Great Depression, he was confident that enough had changed since the 1930s in institutional arrangements to avoid a recurrence of the Depression. Consequently, the United States was now "Depression-proof."

In making this case, Friedman articulated his position, already discussed in chapter 2, that the creation of the Federal Deposit Insurance Corporation had largely removed the danger of a major monetary collapse. But, in pointing to sources of greater stability, Friedman also assigned a prominent role to changes in fiscal policy, especially the development of automatic stabilizers on both the spending and revenue side. As he had done in the late 1940s, Friedman cited the progressive income tax structure and tax withholding as among the stabilizing features that had been introduced on the revenues side of the federal budget. And he went so far as to state that the automatic stabilizers "offset directly from 30 to 40 percent of any change that would otherwise take place in national income."[48] In saying this, Friedman was basically repeating estimates he had given in his premonetarist period. In these early monetarist years of the 1950s, Friedman continued to believe that elements of the federal budget structure exerted a strongly stabilizing effect on the economy. But he now saw their stabilizing influence as largely working via their impact on the stock of money.[49] He viewed budget deficits as in practice largely monetized.[50] And, according to his 1948 rule, that was the way it should be, insofar as the existence of deficits reflected the operation of automatic stabilizers.

Friedman's 1954 assessment also pointed to changes in public and professional opinion as factors making for a Depression-proof economy. As he saw it, economists' retrospectives on the 1930s, while not stressing monetary factors to an adequate extent, had properly diagnosed deficient aggregate demand as the problem of that decade. That correct diagnosis, coupled with public resistance to high unemployment, gave Friedman confidence that, in the postwar period, the automatic fiscal responses to a weakening economy would be supplemented by vigorous monetary and fiscal easing. This factor bolstered the Depression-proof character of the modern US economy, but it also led Friedman to voice a warning. Mild recessions, he stressed, were unavoidable, and Friedman was concerned that overreaction of policy makers to mild recessions might lay the groundwork for recurrent peacetime inflation. The state of public opinion made it attractive to "take precipitate and drastic action," so that the prospect for the United States was one of "recurrent bouts of inflation produced by overreaction to the temporary recessions."[51]

Stabilization Policy and Inflation

This fear—that stabilization policy in practice was liable to create inflation—had previously been voiced by Friedman in remarks delivered in 1950.[52] His 1954 talk, however, constitutes the key exposition by Friedman on this matter, for it outlined an important element of his argument that is often overlooked. The importance of this element arises because to argue that overreaction to economic developments will trigger inflation does not by itself constitute a fully coherent position. To be sure, Friedman did provide good reasons, other than political pressures, why policy makers might well overdo their policy responses. Most prominently, Friedman's parallel work during this period regarding the uncertainty about the lags in effect of monetary policy implied that policy might be unintentionally destabilizing—as lags in policy's effect would give the impression that the economy was not responding (or was deteriorating) and therefore prompt a further dose of policy actions.[53]

But it is crucial to note that a policy maker overreaction to the state of the economy—that is, an overzealous stabilization policy—is *not* in itself a basis for believing that inflation will be higher, on average. The expectation that policy would be overreactive and destabilizing, and Friedman's cogent arguments for this expectation, did not by themselves imply a prediction of high inflation. For the overreaction argument was consistent with the notion that policy makers' errors would be symmetric across periods of excessive and deficient aggregate demand.[54]

It is here that the neglected component of Friedman's 1954 account comes into play. The prediction Friedman made in 1954 of a future era of inflation did not rest on any claim that policy makers' degrees of aversion to inflation and negative output gaps were different from one another. The prediction instead rested on Friedman's contention that inflation, when it did emerge, was liable to be attributed in large part to *nonmonetary* factors.

In this connection, it should be recalled that he believed that wage/price spirals, even though they simply reflected demand pressure, were prone to be misdiagnosed as evidence in favor of cost-push views of inflation. If inflation was not perceived as reflecting an excess-demand problem, its emergence was unlikely to prompt a monetary policy tightening on a scale sufficient to restore price stability. According to Friedman's account, this misdiagnosis of the cause of inflation would be the source of an asymmetry in policy reactions—an asymmetry that implied that a regime in which there was entrenched support for a vigorous stabilization policy would be a regime associated with secular inflation.

A further reason underlying Friedman's judgment that inflation lay in the US economy's future was the emergence of a greater role for welfare provision among the federal government's responsibilities. Friedman acknowledged that this development helped in the Depression-proofing of the US economy, by leading to some additional automatic stabilizers in the form of such measures as Social Security and unemployment insurance.[55] In the longer term, however, Friedman saw the move to larger-scale social programs as likely to create calls for still further government-provided services. This development, he believed, would tend to produce chronic budget deficits that led, via monetization, to inflation. In keeping with this perspective, Friedman stated in an April 1950 radio appearance that "the strong pressure on the part of many groups for government expenditures" meant "that my own expectation is that the next twenty years will see in this country a substantial inflation."[56]

In time, Friedman would view these factors—particularly that of activist stabilization policy—promoting peacetime inflation as having made themselves strongly felt in US policy decisions. But for the moment—that is, for the rest of the 1950s—he felt that his fears had not been realized in the United States. Friedman did not regard the post–Korean War years of the 1950s as inflationary years, nor did he regard the seeds of later inflation as having been laid by a policy of ease during the 1950s. On the contrary, he regarded the price environment of those years—amounting to an average inflation rate for 1954–60 of close to 2 percent, according to both Balke and Gordon's (1986) annual data for the GNP deflator and modern annual data on the GDP deflator—as corresponding to reasonable price stability and economic policy as commendably restrained. Friedman would not have concurred with Ohanian's (1998, 101) assessment that World War II's inflation "ushered in the postwar US policy of persistent inflation that has continued over the past 50 years," nor even with the implication of David Fand—who had been a graduate student of Friedman's during the first half of the 1950s—that the United States had had unbroken inflation since about 1954.[57] Rather, Friedman came to the view that the dangers he had outlined in his 1954 talk and elsewhere had been warded off for the rest of the decade. His assessment would instead be that it was "clearly 1960" when the activist policies that he had anticipated finally gained ascendancy in the United States, with the election of John F. Kennedy.[58]

President Eisenhower and Economic Policy

The identity of the US president was, indeed, a factor that Friedman repeatedly invoked over the years in accounting for the price stability in the decade after the Korean War. The praise that Friedman gave to President Dwight D. Eisenhower for keeping inflation in check may seem jarring in view of Friedman's emphasis on inflation as a monetary phenomenon and the fact that Federal Reserve independence had been formally reestablished with the Accord, nearly two years before Eisenhower took office. But Friedman argued that a large part of the credit for the anti-inflationary monetary policy of the 1950s should go to the Eisenhower administration. He suggested that encouragement from the Eisenhower administration had helped move the Federal Reserve away from its stance of 1951–53, an interregnum in which the Federal Reserve had continued aspects of the bond-price peg.[59] Over the subsequent years of the 1950s, in Friedman's view, the administration had shown solidarity with the Federal Reserve and resisted the "temper of the time" that favored aggressive stimulation of aggregate demand (*Newsweek*, December 6, 1976).

The Eisenhower administration also earned praise from Friedman for not overreacting on the fiscal policy side. As has been indicated above, Friedman viewed monetary restraint as achievable in the face of sizable budget deficits. He would later be able to cite examples in postwar US history of just such combinations, such as in 1966, 1975, and 1981. But he did perceive fiscal restraint as a factor conducive to Federal Reserve policies that delivered moderation in monetary growth. This restraint did not amount to a change in the direction of fiscal policy, and Friedman acknowledged that the Truman administration had delivered roughly balanced budgets.[60] But fiscal restraint did continue over the rest of the 1950s under the Eisenhower administration. In his 1954 Stockholm talk, Friedman noted that the recession that had emerged in 1953 had been associated with pressure from Congress for fiscal stimulus, in the form of a major reduction in taxes. Friedman had not yet arrived at the point of viewing tax cuts in "starve-the-beast" terms, and so he had been an opponent of the 1953 tax-cut proposal. Accordingly, he supported the administration's resistance to the proposal. The administration did, however, feel obliged to propose a tax cut in response to the next recession, which began in 1957. Friedman opposed this proposal too, despite attempts by Arthur Burns (who had by then completed a period as chairman of Eisenhower's Council of Economic Advisers, but who retained close contact with the administration) to persuade Friedman of the desirability of the tax cut.[61] However, notwithstanding occasions such as this, Friedman recognized that fiscal restraint had, on the whole, continued over the second half of the 1950s.

Some commentators have put a great deal of weight on the fiscal restraint of the 1950s as an underlying source of monetary restriction. William Dewald, for example, would contend: "The very big increase in the budget surplus in 1959 certainly played a role in this very tight monetary policy."[62] And Meltzer (2009a, 48, 90) argued that the Eisenhower administration's fiscal conservatism is the key to understanding the monetary restraint of the 1950s. In contrast, Romer and Romer (2002a) contended that there was a coherent analytical basis underlying the conduct of monetary policy of the 1950s, so that the price stability over which the Federal Reserve presided was not simply a side effect of the US government's fiscal restraint. Friedman's position, as revealed by retrospectives he gave on the economic policy of the 1950s, was closer to the position of Romer and Romer than of Meltzer. Friedman did see Eisenhower's fiscal posture as helping to establish conditions favorable for monetary restraint.[63] But he also saw an enlightened Federal Reserve policy-making framework as an important factor in the success of monetary policy in the 1950s. In particular, as discussed below, he and Schwartz pointed to an enhanced appreciation by the Federal Reserve of the money stock as an element behind improvements in monetary policy conduct during the 1950s.

The Eisenhower administration nonetheless came out favorably in Friedman's account of monetary developments because of the administration's posture. Indeed, Friedman gave pride of place to the Eisenhower administration's perspective on economic policy in accounting for the course of stabilization policy during the 1950s.

The greatest praise Friedman gave to Eisenhower stemmed from what Friedman perceived as Eisenhower's status as a "nonpolitical president" (*Newsweek*, December 6, 1976). Eisenhower's electoral success was, in Friedman's view an "exceptional case of a particular personality" interrupting political and policy-making trends in the United States (Instructional Dynamics Economics Cassette Tape 18, March 1969). Friedman did not view Eisenhower, as he would Ronald Reagan, as a president making a concerted effort to change public opinion about the direction in which the country should move. Friedman therefore did not exclude Eisenhower from the generalization he gave in 1982 that all presidents in his lifetime, prior to Reagan, had assessed public opinion and followed policies in light of that assessment.[64] What distinguished Eisenhower's tenure for Friedman was not a strong desire on the president's part to defy trends in opinion. The distinguishing factor was instead President Eisenhower's *disinterest* toward those trends. The lack of a strong political antenna led Eisenhower, in the Friedman interpretation, to be less susceptible to congressional and public pressure and disinclined to adopt fashionable Keynesian views.[65] The corollary of this Eisenhower trait was that the president was more inclined to accept economic advice from his professional staff, most notably Arthur Burns—who, as already noted, was chairman of the Council of Economic Advisers in the early Eisenhower years.[66] Friedman also gave the Eisenhower administration credit for coaxing the Federal Reserve into shaking off the remnants of the bond-price peg and thereafter allowing the Federal Reserve to carry out a monetary policy that was centered on the control of inflation.

Consequently, Friedman saw Eisenhower as having helped foster conditions in which the United States experienced only "very mild creeping inflation" in the second half of the 1950s.[67] In addition, Eisenhower had, Friedman believed, permitted the pursuit of "monetary restraint . . . [that] eliminated inflation by 1960."[68] In fact, as we shall see below, Friedman in the late 1950s and 1960s was so convinced that inflation had been avoided that he gave credence to the notion that the US price level might be stationary or mildly trend stationary in the post-Korean War period.

The disciplined economic policy of the 1950s also left an imprint, Friedman suggested, on the first half of the 1960s, as the economic expansion of 1961 to 1964 could take place against a background of quiescent inflationary expectations.[69] In the memoir volumes covering his presidency, Eisenhower observed that his tenure had seen "remarkably steady" price behavior, but he argued that this outcome was achieved only because policy makers confronted and extinguished an inflationary mindset prevailing in the community (Eisenhower 1963, 126; see also Eisenhower 1965, 461–63). Friedman credited the president and other policy makers of the time with having successfully warded off the threat of inflation. The burying of inflationary expectations by the early 1960s, Friedman contended, resulted from "the [economic] slowdown that Mr. Eisenhower was willing to accept at the end of the 1950s."[70] As we shall see at the end of this chapter, however, Friedman believed that this slowdown could have been implemented more smoothly over the course of the 1950s, and he contended that, at the close of the decade, the course of monetary restraint went too far.

The lack of interest on Eisenhower's part in keeping up with trends in political opinion was also felt, to some extent, in the lack of a major *extension* of the role of government. To be sure, Eisenhower did not roll back the welfare-expanding aspects of the New Deal, and government spending for nondefense purposes rose robustly during Eisenhower's tenure. The share of aggregate public spending in national income (GDP, by today's measure) was little changed in fiscal year 1961 from fiscal year 1954—but this near-constancy reflected the fact that the decline in defense spending's share of national income, by about 4 percent of GDP, offset the corresponding rise in the ratio of nondefense outlays to GDP.[71]

In addition to being dissatisfied with this growth in federal spending, Friedman also would find fault with the Eisenhower administration for not abolishing the New Deal agricultural programs.[72] Furthermore, he would cite Eisenhower's introduction of oil import quotas both as a blow to free trade and as a step that laid the foundation for later federal controls on energy pricing and allocation.[73] But, by the same token, Eisenhower did not launch new domestic government programs on a scale comparable to the Great Society measures introduced in the 1960s; and so Friedman would later judge that the trend toward bigger government continued under Eisenhower, albeit at a slower pace.[74]

Even before the post-Eisenhower years could be used as a reference point, Friedman's evaluation was that Eisenhower was turning out well as president, and in private conversation around early 1954 he endorsed a letter that he had received from Arthur Burns expressing that sentiment (Brittan 2005, 294). Friedman was, in addition, delighted with Burns's tenure as chair of the Council of Economic Advisers in Eisenhower's first term, later stating that Burns had done "a rather excellent job" as CEA chair and helped confer on it the image of a nonpolitical, expert body.[75] Friedman contrasted the CEA under Burns with the council's status in the Truman years when it was chaired by Leon Keyserling—an individual about whom Friedman could be trenchantly critical.[76]

The upshot was that, during the 1950s, Friedman's critique of the role of government was often directed at intellectual trends rather than at recent expansions of public-sector activity. For example, both his *Collier's Year Book* entry in 1955 titled "Liberalism, Old Style" and a conference paper Friedman produced in 1956 titled "Capitalism and Freedom"—whose published version in 1958 was a prototype for part of the 1962 book of the same title—considered the relationship between economic and political freedom.[77] When they were applied to actual government initiatives, Friedman's discussions during the 1950s largely pertained to measures that were already in place by the beginning of the decade. His oft-discussed vouchers proposal, designed as he saw it to reduce the role of government in education, was one example.[78] Another example was antitrust. Although, as noted in chapter 4, Friedman remained basically very supportive of antitrust laws into the late 1960s, by the mid-1950s he was starting to voice some reservations. In particular, in his 1955 *Collier's* entry, Friedman noted that "the claim of natural monopoly is more often an excuse for intervention . . . than a valid justification."[79] Friedman made it clear in the *Col-*

lier's piece that he did not agree with Henry Simons's position that nationalization was an appropriate policy response when a situation of natural monopoly was encountered.[80] Friedman also expressed doubt regarding whether regulation of private monopoly had improved matters compared with a situation of unregulated monopoly—a sentiment that foreshadowed Friedman's later verdict against such regulation.

During the 1950s Friedman appeared in a number of popular or semipopular forums to advocate free-market-oriented solutions to problems of public policy. A prominent forum that Friedman used for this purpose was the *University of Chicago Round Table*, on which Friedman continued to appear frequently as a panelist until the series terminated in 1955. Transcripts of these radio appearances were also published regularly.[81] In one panel debate, a wide-ranging discussion in mid-1952, Friedman advocated a return to a more limited role for government, namely "as an umpire . . . trying to promote competition in a free market place" (NBC 1952c, 4). Turning to monetary policy, he said that it could offer the possibility, by delivering an environment of price stability, of providing "a favorable framework for [output] expansion" in which "we can maintain our economic and political freedoms" (NBC 1952c, 11).

The last observation, in which Friedman linked up his position on monetary policy with his perspective on market economics, underscores the fact that, for all his enthusiasm about the advocacy of free markets, this advocacy was not Friedman's main area of intellectual activity during the 1950s. That consisted instead of his research, including his work on consumption—discussed in chapter 5—and on money. Friedman's monetary research proceeded along two tracks during the 1950s: his work with graduate students at the University of Chicago, and his ongoing project with Anna Schwartz. That these were two distinct enterprises—albeit with Friedman coordinating the research undertaken in each of them—is brought out by noting that Schwartz was based in New York City (at the time, the principal location for the National Bureau of Economic Research). She rarely, if ever, visited the University of Chicago's premises during Friedman's years at the institution.[82]

The Cowles Commission

The fact that Friedman was deeply involved in an NBER project tended to put him in an adversarial posture against a particular colleague at the University of Chicago in the late 1940s and early 1950s. Tjalling Koopmans was a prominent member of the Cowles Commission, which at that time was connected to the University of Chicago's economics department, and Koopmans had been sharply critical of the Burns-Mitchell NBER procedures in Koopmans (1947). In the brief discussion that he provided in his memoirs of the Cowles Commission and of its relocation (in the mid-1950s) from the University of Chicago to Yale University, Friedman expressed regret about the move and downplayed his own antipathy toward the commission.[83] In other contexts, however—such as in his remarks in Hammond (1992)—Friedman was more candid about his disagreement with Cowles Commission members and their research agenda, and Friedman's correspondence, the recollections of others in interviews, and, indeed, Friedman's own published remarks on the Cowles Commission are all testament to his disdain for the commission's approach.[84]

That this was Friedman's attitude is not surprising: the Cowles Commission was focused on large-scale econometric models. In contrast, Friedman—having already voiced doubts about ambitious multi-equation modeling of the economy in his reviews of the work of Tinbergen and Lange—had become even less well disposed toward such modeling in his early years at the University of Chicago. The monetary project with Schwartz had steered Friedman toward an emphasis on the value of bivariate statistical analyses and of concentration on qualitative evidence.

When it was suggested to Kenneth Arrow—a member of the Cowles Commission whose work Friedman *did* rate highly—that Friedman was unsympathetic to the Cowles Commission, Arrow responded: "That is a gross understatement. He was extremely antagonistic, making fun of them, deriding them. . . . And it was pretty clear he had a very low opinion of both Marschak and Koopmans—and didn't conceal it." Arrow noted that Friedman's criticism included the contention that Cowles's "whole statistical program, based on the idea of identification, was completely wrong" (Kenneth Arrow, interview, December 7, 2013). David Meiselman recalled that the Cowles Commission "had their own seminar once a week, and I couldn't follow what the hell they were talking about. But it was top-grade stuff." On Friedman's presence at the seminars, Meiselman remarked: "He would sit by himself, and they would go their way, and he would go his way. And they would fight. This was an ongoing fight. He said they were not scientific. . . . But he would drive them crazy" (David Meiselman, interview, July 7, 2014).

Some of Friedman's ideas about identification (that is, the practice of isolating, using data, a relationship, parameter, or response of interest) have continuing appeal. These included those stemming from his and Schwartz's emphasis on key historical episodes. This approach was evident in Friedman's 1952 paper on wartime episodes and permeated the subsequent Friedman-Schwartz *Monetary History*. The approach can, as Romer and Romer (1989) and Miron (1994) stressed, deliver a form of identification.[85] But Friedman also had some peculiar ideas about identification that arose from his idiosyncratic statistical training and that neither econometricians of the 1950s nor those of today would usually regard as valid.[86] Indeed, Friedman and Schwartz's later polite citation of Koopmans's work on identification may have been a sign that Friedman was no longer willing to press his criticism of the Cowles Commission agenda as hard as he once had.[87] And Friedman's own strictures about modeling did not, in any case, all necessarily point in the same direction. He stressed that empirical evidence should figure heavily in model choice, but he was also an advocate of using economic theory to impose tight a priori restrictions on models. In any event, Friedman's strong opinions, of varying merit, about identification put him at odds with the econometric approach of Koopmans and others in the Cowles Commission.

Hildreth's (1986) account of the Cowles Commission's years at the University of Chicago contained only fleeting mentions of Friedman. Indeed, Hildreth did not even cite explicitly the brief discussions of the Cowles Commission that Friedman made in print during the 1950s.[88] It is possible that the brevity of Hildreth's references to Friedman represented an attempt to play down the controversy involving Friedman and the commission.[89] Another possibility, however, is that the Friedman/Cowles Commission conflict were not as important an element of the Cowles Commission's period at the University of Chicago as some have suggested. Under this scenario, the heavy, and likely excessive, weight that the conflict between Friedman and the members of the Cowles Commission received in some retrospectives arose partly from the fame that Friedman acquired from other, later debates that did not involve the Cowles Commission.

Consistent with this possibility is the recollection of Carl Christ. When he was a graduate student in the University of Chicago's economics department in the late 1940s, Christ worked on econometric modeling of the US economy, and he was affiliated with the Cowles Commission (see Christ 1951, 1994). His close relationship with the commission would continue in the 1950s and 1960s, and his econometrics textbook—which was copyrighted by the commission—opened with the dedication: "To T.C.K. and J.M." (Christ 1966, v).[90] Carl Christ recalled that, at the time he was working at the Cowles Commission and was producing the dissertation work on econometric modeling that became Christ (1951), he was not strongly aware of conflict between Friedman and the leading members of the commission. In particular, he found that Friedman and Jacob Marschak had cordial relations with one another as members of Christ's dissertation committee. And Christ did not perceive Friedman's comments on his (1951) work, skeptical though they were, as reflecting a wholly hostile attitude toward the Cowles Commission (Carl Christ, interview, August 15, 2015).

Marc Nerlove, who would work in the Cowles Commission both at the University of Chicago and at Yale University, would over the years learn from discussions with Friedman and others about the circumstances of the commission's move. Friedman's attitude toward the commission—which comprised not only his negative views on its methodology but also his reservations about giving the commission a greater role in the economics department's hiring decisions—was, Nerlove ascertained, "a major factor in forcing them out." However, Nerlove added that the Cowles Commission's transfer from the University of Chicago to Yale University was a voluntary decision rather than a mandatory ejection (Marc Nerlove, interview, September 18, 2013).

Indeed, not only did the Cowles Commission leave voluntarily, but also it was out of Friedman's power to decide whether the University of Chicago would have an affiliation with the commission. It should always be kept in mind that, although he was a senior and vocal member of the Department of Economics, Friedman was a salaried employee who did not have the unilateral authority to hire or fire colleagues. The limits to his formal role in these matters was shown by the fact that he did not hold the position of the head of the economics department. He was, therefore, not the department member with the greatest involvement in deliberating on such issues as the relationship between the university and the Cowles Commission. And the long-standing head of the department, Theodore Schultz, was not beholden to Friedman. This point was made forcefully by Dudley Wallace— who was a graduate student in the department shortly after Cowles's departure, and who later got to know Tjalling Koopmans—when he reflected on the commission's relationship with the University of Chicago. With respect to Friedman's attitude to the commission's departure, and whether Friedman instigated that departure, Dudley observed: "I don't think he would have felt any great loss, but, no, I don't think he had that much political power at Chicago. You know, we're talking about some pretty tough guys here. Ted Schultz [later] won the Nobel Prize. He was nobody's flunky" (T. Dudley Wallace, interview, July 20, 2015).

It is also notable that, with Friedman's enthusiastic support, the University of Chicago's economics department would later recruit former members of the Cowles Commission, including Nerlove and Carl Christ, while also unsuccessfully trying (again on Friedman's urging) to rehire Kenneth Arrow some years after he had left the department in 1951 (Kenneth Arrow, interview, December 7, 2013). But that Friedman had differences of opinion with the leaders of the Cowles Commission on the best approach to economic research is not in question.

Benchmarking Models

Mention should be made of a constructive element of Friedman's critique of econometric models, one that emerged in the course of his discussion of the Cowles Commission agenda. This constructive element was his suggestion, in the early 1950s, of a random-walk or constant-change forecast as a benchmark against which forecasts that arose from structural econometric models should be judged.[91] David Meiselman observed of Friedman, "he proposed alternative tests of the data, a pair of tests: [1] today is the same as yesterday; or [2] tomorrow is the same as today, except a little bit more" (David Meiselman, interview, July 16, 2014). The first of these benchmarks, which Christ (1951, 56) labeled "Naïve Model I," resembles the random-walk benchmark. The second, Christ's "Naïve Model II," is closely related to the random-walk-with-drift (or constant-change) benchmark.[92] These benchmarks often did well when pitted against the forecasts from early econometric models, such as the Lawrence Klein (1950) model with which Carl Christ was concerned.

The instigation of these benchmarks was not wholly due to Friedman. In particular, as emphasized by Carl Christ both in Christ (1951, 35, 56–57) and in an interview for this book (August 15, 2015), the two benchmarks, as well as their "Naïve Model" labels, had been advanced by Andrew Marshall in a master's thesis written at the University of Chicago around 1948. However, Christ (1951, 57) indicated that Friedman, too, had put forward these benchmarks (albeit using different labels for them), and Christ further suggested (interview, August 15, 2015) that Friedman could well have been involved in the advice for Marshall's thesis work that led to Marshall's use of the naïve tests. Friedman's proposal also had an antecedent in his emphasis in Friedman (1940) on out-of-sample predictions as a test of econometric models, and Christ (1994, 33, 46) highlighted the continuity between the content of this 1940 book review and Friedman's discussions of econometrics during the 1950s.

As Samuelson (1956, 132) anticipated in an early discussion of Friedman's proposed criterion, the creditable predictive performance of the random-walk baseline did not lead to the abandonment of structural econometric modeling. Instead, it provided a minimal measure of forecasting performance that structural models, in order to be tenable, would have to surpass. In this spirit, the random walk, or generalizations of it in the form of the autoregressive integrated moving-average (ARIMA) process, would become an enduring benchmark against which structural econometric models have been judged (see, for example, C. R. Nelson 1972; Cooper and C. R. Nelson 1975; and Atkeson and Ohanian 2001).[93]

The Workshop on Money and Banking

Friedman's largest impact on the specification of large-scale econometric models would not come from his suggestions regarding the identification and testing of those models. Instead, it would arise from the impact his research produced in forcing econometric modelers to upgrade the importance they attached to monetary policy. Part of Friedman's research program on money was, as already noted, carried out via his work on the NBER project with Schwartz. Less significant than his work with Schwartz, but still an important aspect of Friedman's monetary-research activities, was his creation and oversight of the University of Chicago's Workshop on Money and Banking.[94] The workshop (i.e., seminar series) was regularized in 1953 after Friedman had run a version of it at the university starting in 1951.[95] The series primarily consisted of presentations by the University of Chicago's graduate students in economics, some of whose PhD dissertations would emerge in print in 1956 in the Friedman-edited *Studies in the Quantity Theory of Money*.[96] Talks in the workshop by external presenters (that is, those not from the University of Chicago) were common in the series by the mid-1960s.[97] Indeed, they may have been part of the workshop roster from the beginning, as Harrod (1971, 58) recalled being invited to speak at Friedman's seminar in April 1951 for a discussion of monetary velocity.[98]

Especially in its early years, the workshop typically had only a small number of core attendees. George Macesich, a graduate student attending the workshop in 1955–56, recalled: "We had about four or five of us down there, that was about it . . . in a basement" (George Macesich, interview, May 28, 2013).[99] Of the students, only those intending to write a dissertation in the area of monetary policy typically attended. Furthermore, a quid pro quo for students' attendance was that the attendee had to present a paper in the workshop at some point. Paul Evans, a workshop member in the early and mid-1970s, observed (interview, February 26, 2013) that Friedman "would tell people that in his workshop there was 'no representation without taxation,' meaning that you had to present, and if you weren't going to present at a workshop and you weren't going to do the work associated with [attending] a workshop, then he was going to disinvite you." This requirement was instituted only sporadically, however. David Laidler (in the 1961–62 academic year) and Robert Hodrick (in the period 1974–76) were examples of graduate students who attended the money workshop without having to present a paper (David Laidler, personal communication, September 23, 2015; Robert Hodrick, interview, January 23, 2016).

Furthermore, the requirement to present did not apply at all to teachers at the University of Chicago, so other academic staff members—from the economics department, the business school, or elsewhere—would sporadically attend the workshop alongside Friedman.[100] On one occasion in the 1950s, Friedman asked his graduate student David Meiselman to encourage Friedrich Hayek to attend the workshop. Meiselman recalled:

Somebody gave a paper [in which] there was some complicated discussion about the money-supply process in the UK. And it seemed that Hayek did not have any interest [in that] at all. For people who were working in that area, it was fine. But for Hayek, it must have been very boring. He sat there quietly for two hours and then he left. . . . And the next week, he didn't come back [to the workshop]. He never came back. (David Meiselman, interview, April 30, 2013)

Meiselman's observation points up the fact that it would be a mistake to regard Friedman and Hayek during this period as in close touch and regularly comparing notes on each other's work. They were both in the same building on the University of Chicago campus in the 1950s, and this, together with their advocacy of free markets and their association with the Mont Pelerin Society, seems to have motivated non-economists such as Burgin (2012) and D. Jones (2012) to treat them together.[101] But in the years in which Hayek was among the academic staff of the University of Chicago, he was not a member of the economics department. Furthermore, he had largely left the world of monetary economics.

Arnold Harberger emphasized the economics department's arm's-length relationship with Hayek in the 1950s, notwithstanding Hayek's close physical proximity to the department: "He was appointed in the Committee on Social Thought, which was on the fifth floor when we were on the fourth floor. So we rode with him in the elevator up several times a week, you know. But he was working on *The Constitution of Liberty* [Hayek 1960], and he thought of himself more as a philosopher than as a technical economist" (Arnold Harberger, interview, May 2, 2013). And in the early 1960s, Hayek departed the University of Chicago altogether.

Further discussion of the money workshop is deferred until later chapters. Likewise, because the *Monetary History* appeared in print in 1963, the development of his and Schwartz's monetary work is considered in more detail in the next chapter.

Although the standing in which monetary policy was held had risen considerably since the war, Friedman remained dissatisfied with the economics profession's consensus on this issue. In his 1954 lecture in Sweden, Friedman contended that the reemphasis on monetary policy among economic experts had "not yet gone far enough."[102] In 1955 he wrote that the "derogation of the significance of monetary factors" was a feature not only of "the recent past" but of the present, and that more stress needed to be put on monetary growth when interpreting historical fluctuations of the US economy.[103] Friedman would retrospectively date the revival of interest in money to about 1954.[104] And he would give the years of the dearth of a discussion of money as roughly spanning the years from 1935 to 1955.[105] But he remained unhappy even at the end of the 1950s with the weight given by economists and policy makers to monetary policy, especially in relation to fiscal policy. This attitude was reflected in the *Monetary History*'s account, which described the revival of monetary policy as one in which confidence in the effectiveness of monetary policy had been only "somewhat restored."[106]

In emphasizing the strength of monetary policy's effects, on both output and prices, Friedman was a maverick during the 1950s. His advocacy of money's role earned him the designation from *Fortune* magazine as "one of the leading orthodox economists"—orthodox here not meaning "mainstream," but, instead, pre-Keynesian.[107] And Friedman would find himself at odds even with his fellow "orthodox" economist Arthur Burns, when the latter discussed monetary policy in his 1957 Millar lectures at Fordham University (a lecture series to which Friedman himself would contribute in 1959 with his "Program for Monetary Stability").[108] Burns took what Friedman saw as a too-narrow view of monetary policy transmission—one in which only investment spending was sensitive to interest rates and the relevant interest rates were exclusively those generated by organized securities markets.[109] David Meiselman, who was working with Friedman during this period, had a powerful recollection of Friedman's reaction to Burns's draft monograph: "he hated it." Friedman defended Burns to some extent in conversation with Meiselman, who was agitated and angry about the content of Burns's lectures. Nevertheless, as Meiselman recalled, Friedman "wrote a long letter to Arthur Burns. . . . I never saw the letter, but I understand it's pretty harsh" (David Meiselman, interview, April 30, 2013).[110]

In sum, although the 1950s witnessed a revival of monetary policy, for Friedman it was a decidedly incomplete revival. His dissatisfaction on this score was reflected not only in his reaction to colleagues' views about monetary policy, but in his evaluation of the conduct of US monetary policy in the years after the Accord. It is to the latter subject that the discussion now turns.

II. Issues, 1951–60

THE INCOMPLETE REVIVAL OF MONETARY POLICY

In late 1962, the London *Financial Times* referred to "Americans' surprising addiction to pre-Keynesian economics" (*Financial Times*, December 29, 1962), a remark undoubtedly prompted by the US economic policy record of the 1950s.[111] To be sure, members of US policy circles in the 1950s were not pre-Keynesian in the sense of seeing output as determined by supply forces in the short run. On the contrary, as Arthur Burns observed in 1968, on account of the acceptance that "aggregate demand is the proximate determinant of a nation's overall economic activity," it was the case in the postwar environment that "every administration in Washington, whether it has explicitly recognized it or not, has been guided by the theory of the new economics."[112] But such an acceptance was common ground between Keynesian economics ("the new economics," in the terminology of US economists) and many pre-Keynesian versions of the quantity theory of money.[113]

Furthermore, the existence of that common ground left considerable scope for differences in judgment about the vigor with which aggregate demand policies should be used for short-run output stabilization, and about the prominence that should be given to inflation control in the conduct of monetary and fiscal policy. It is in these areas that the economic policy in the United States during the 1950s was perceived as "pre-Keynesian." Not only was fiscal policy generally conservative, but, as already indicated, monetary policy exhibited considerable restraint in the wake of the Accord. Indeed, Romer and Romer (2002a) provided evidence, based on documentary material and policy-rule estimates, that US monetary policy over this period had a modern inflation-oriented outlook—an orientation earlier acknowledged, albeit pejoratively, by Paul Samuelson when he referred to the Federal Reserve's "anti-inflation paranoia of the 1950s" (*Financial Times*, December 31, 1965).

Romer and Romer (2002a, 121) contended that Milton Friedman did not judge 1950s monetary policy favorably. This characterization has some validity. As discussed presently, there are several counts on which Friedman found fault with 1950s policy. However, the characterization does not capture the considerable amount of praise that Friedman advanced for monetary policy, both during the 1950s and subsequently.

On performance with respect to price-level behavior, Friedman was, as already indicated, nearly unqualified in his praise. From 1954 to 1960—that is, in the post-Korean War portion of the decade—inflation had been low, low enough for Friedman to characterize the period as featuring "rough stability" in prices (*Wall Street Journal*, November 17, 1989). Furthermore, as noted in section I above, Friedman viewed inflation expectations as having been squeezed out of the US economic environment at the end of the decade.

On output stability during the 1950s, Friedman drew a sharp distinction between comparison *with historical performance* and comparison with a simple benchmark policy, specifically the constant-monetary-growth rule that he advocated from 1956–57 onward.

In comparisons he made with the prior Federal Reserve record, Friedman cited actual policy during the 1950s as a distinct improvement. In a paper for a conference in October 1956, for example, Friedman noted the achievement of a greater degree of economic stability, and he argued that monetary policy of late had magnified US cyclical fluctuations to a lesser degree than had been the case in previous decades. On a related point, he referred to the stability of both monetary growth and the economy in the preceding five years.[114] A few months later Friedman declared that, with the Accord, the United States had "entered a period in which on the whole the Federal Reserve['s] policy has been commendable and has been associated with a great deal of stability."[115]

Admittedly, when Friedman made these observations, the United States had experienced only one of the three Eisenhower-era recessions. But the single recession that had occurred—that of 1953–54—was one Friedman had described in a 1955 radio appearance as an "extremely mild" recession.[116] And neither of the two subsequent recessions (that is, those of 1957–58 and 1960–61) would qualify as what Friedman would later term a "really major recession," which he defined as a recession in which real output declined by 4 to 6 percent.[117]

Friedman's predecessor in the advocacy of monetarism Clark Warburton was still making occasional interventions in monetary economics discussions during the 1950s. Warburton, too, found much to admire in the monetary policy of the 1950s, particularly when judged by the criterion of stability in aggregate US output. For a conference in December 1958, Warburton wrote:

> As a matter of fact, analysis of statistical data regarding central bank operations and the money supply indicate that for the past ten years monetary policy in the United States has been substantially more stable than in any other period since the Federal Reserve System was established, except from 1922 to early 1929. This comparative stability of monetary policy is, to my mind, undoubtedly causally associated with the comparative stability of the economy as a whole, for which again the only precedent since establishment of the Federal Reserve System is the period from 1922 to 1929. (Warburton 1958, 211)[118]

It was not just the scale of the output declines during the 1950s recessions that contrasted favorably with most pre–World War II contractions. It was also the brevity of the recessions: the longest of the three recessions over the years from 1951 to 1960—that of 1953–54—lasted about a year, shorter than most of the downturns in the 1919–38 period.[119] In addition, the recoveries from the 1953–54 and 1957–58 recessions conformed to the rapid V-shaped pattern that Friedman would come to see as typical of economic recoveries after pronounced downturns.[120] The flipside, however, of the presence of these V's in the data was that real GNP variability was high in comparison with later postwar patterns. Consequently, Fuhrer, Olivei, and Tootell (2012, 86) characterize the ten years of data starting in 1954:Q1 as featuring relatively large output fluctuations, and Friedman himself endorsed the judgment that the period from 1953 to 1957 featured "highly unstable economic activity."[121]

A constant-monetary-growth rule could, Friedman would judge, have delivered a more stable economic performance over the 1950s than what actually occurred.[122] Although he applauded the price stability that monetary policy had delivered, Friedman felt that a steadier policy, one involving less pronounced fluctuations of monetary growth around its downward trend, could have generated the same result. Actual policy, he believed, had worsened business cycle fluctuations by engaging in ill-timed finetuning. In addition, as discussed later in this chapter, Friedman felt that by 1960 the Federal Reserve—instead of achieving conditions consistent with long-run price stability—had shifted to a policy setting that, if it had been maintained, would have produced deflation. This last judgment has since been buttressed by Romer and Romer's (2002a) appraisal of the monetary policy decisions that took place at the end of the 1950s.

The decade of the 1950s was, accordingly, included in a number of negative evaluations that Friedman gave of postwar monetary policy performance, among them: (*i*) His generalization in 1967 that "throughout the post-war period . . . the Fed has tended first to delay action and then, when it did act, to go too far" (*Newsweek*, October 30, 1967). (*ii*) His statement in 1964 that "we ought . . . to convert monetary policy from being a destabilizing force into at least being a neutral factor."[123] (*iii*) His assessment in 1973 that the United States had had fifty years of "stop-go-stop" policies.[124]

These were retrospective judgments, given in the 1960s and 1970s. But Friedman had made similar criticisms of US monetary policy as the 1950s were unfolding. In a television appearance in early 1958, he praised the use of tight monetary policy to counter inflation, pointing to the appropriate match between the monetary policy weapon and the price-stability objective. But he added that the tightening had been carried too far and had produced the 1957–58 recession.[125] Subsequently, Friedman contended, that recession had then led the Federal Reserve to overreact with an "extremely easy money policy."[126] Postwar monetary policy, he stated in lectures given near the end of the 1950s, had delivered monetary behavior more closely approaching that implied by a constant-monetary-growth rule than had policy of prior eras.[127] But he insisted that had a constant-monetary-growth rule actually been followed literally, US output would have followed a more stable course during the 1950s.[128]

Indeed, the Friedman-Schwartz *Monetary History* would point to monetary policy as a factor behind the timing and severity of all three of the Eisenhower-era recessions. Other monetarists would reach the same conclusion.[129] For example, R. Weintraub (1969, 312) judged that the Federal Reserve had followed policies that permitted three appreciable downturns in monetary growth during the 1950s, "thereby inducing three economic recessions," and Brunner (1971b, 48) pointed to the fact that monetary growth "declined substantially and persistently many months" before the first, and possibly most severe, of these recessions began in mid-1953. The experience of the decade of the 1950s reinforced the conclusions that Friedman and Schwartz were reaching from their research into US historical evidence of prior decades. The gathering of this evidence led Friedman to note in 1968 that he had become persuaded that the link between monetary and economic fluctuations was even closer than he had believed at the time of his 1954 talk on the depression-proof American economy.[130]

All told, and notwithstanding the improvements over historical performance that he perceived, Friedman found that US monetary policy performance was still wanting during the 1950s. The unfavorable verdict that Friedman reached on the monetary policy of the 1950s, when comparing that policy with the constant-monetary-growth rule, was linked to his criticism of Federal Reserve doctrine of that decade. From that criticism of doctrine flowed another key Friedman objection to the practice of monetary policy: his disagreement with the Federal Reserve's operating procedures. Both of these criticisms are considered in the discussion below.

With regard to Federal Reserve doctrine, Friedman's criticism was—like his discussion of monetary policy performance—tempered by his recognition of the improvement registered during the 1950s over the record of past decades. The *Monetary History* had praised the "near-revolutionary change" in official statements in between 1952 and 1954 toward acknowledging the importance of the money supply.[131] Federal Reserve statements referring to the money supply included several from Chairman William McChesney Martin as well as those of other policy makers and of senior Federal Reserve Board staff.[132] Friedman contrasted this situation with the 1930s, when "the Federal Reserve System was never concerned with the quantity of money."[133]

The official acceptance of the money stock as an input into policy decisions had, Friedman contended, had a counterpart in the material improvement in monetary policy performance. In particular, although—as will be discussed the end of this chapter—Friedman was critical of the Federal Reserve for allowing the 1960 economic downturn (and the prior monetary weakness) to emerge, he also suggested that the Federal Reserve's attention to money-supply data during 1959–60 helped stop the recession of 1960–61 from being worse.[134]

In fact, the 1960 easing was the second of two important instances during the 1951–60 period in which Friedman exempted the Federal Reserve from his generalization that it reacted too late to events (and the corollary that it failed to incorporate the lags in effect of monetary policy into its decisions). The first of these instances pertained to the Federal Reserve's behavior—specifically, its easing—ahead of the 1953-54 recession. As the Brunner quotation given above indicates, monetary growth declined substantially prior to that recession. This pattern, along with the narrative evidence of Romer and Romer (1989) and the interest-rate evidence of R. Weintraub (1967), points toward a role played by monetary policy in producing the 1953-54 recession or making it worse. But the fact that, subsequently, monetary growth started being moved *up* before the recession began struck Friedman as an "an absolutely unprecedented event."[135] In 1955, the Federal Reserve drew praise from Friedman, both publicly (in a radio appearance) and privately (in a memorandum Friedman wrote to the Federal Reserve Board) for its preemptive reaction to the most recent recession.[136] The *Monetary History*'s account of the 1950s expressed a similar judgment. As Tobin (1965a, 485) observed, Friedman and Schwartz's history "praise[d] the shifts to ease that occurred before the cyclical peaks of 1953 and 1960."[137] The former easing likely played a part in Romer and Romer's (2002a, 125) finding that monetary policy in the 1950s, as represented by an estimated federal funds rate policy rule for 1952:Q1-1958:Q4, responded in a stabilizing manner to expected future inflation.

On other occasions during the 1950s, however, the Federal Reserve had not apparently acted in such an obviously stabilizing manner. Both M1 growth and M2 growth displayed considerable swings during the 1950s: see figure 10.1. Furthermore, it is hard to make the case that these fluctuations simply amounted to Federal Reserve accommodation of money-demand shocks, because the variability in monetary growth is largely associated with corresponding fluctuations in the growth rates of nominal income and real output: see the GDP data in figures 10.2 and 10.3.[138]

Granted, the monetary regime in force during the 1950s can be regarded as curbing *longer*-term fluctuations in nominal income growth. In this connection, C. R. Nelson (1981, 9) characterized "the [US] monetary environment of the 1954-1960 period" as one of "strongly mean-reverting" nominal income growth, with an autoregressive coefficient of 0.36. In terms of figure 10.2, this description is borne out by the fact that nominal income growth has a noninflationary mean and its fluctuations, although fairly wide, are short-lived. These features, in turn, helped ensure that inflation, too, exhibited little persistence over the 1950s (McCallum 1994a, table 1, p. 235; Erceg and Levin 2003, 917). Indeed, inflation not only lacked persistence during the 1950s, but, in contrast to nominal income growth, it varied only mildly (Romer and Romer 2002a, 121, 124).

This stability of the inflation rate implied that the sharp movements in

Percent change on year earlier

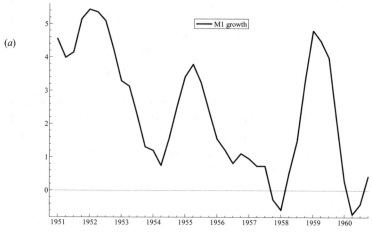

Percent change on year earlier

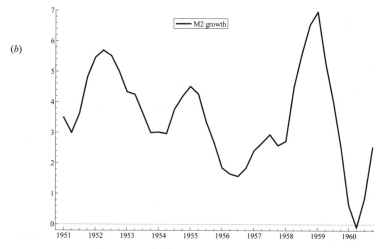

FIGURE 10.1. Monetary growth (four-quarter), 1951:Q1–1960:Q4: (*a*); M1; (*b*) M2.
Source: Lothian, Cassese, and Nowak (1983) data on old (pre-1980) M1 and M2 series.

nominal income growth in figure 10.2 were reflected in sharp movements
in real output growth. The main thrust of Friedman's critique of monetary
policy in the 1950s was that much of this income variation was unnecessary; a monetary policy that delivered monetary growth of the same mean,
but with *less variability* in monetary growth, would have secured benefits
similar to those achieved in terms of low and stable inflation but would also
have delivered a more stable pattern of output behavior. Although interest-
rate policy was far more flexible after 1951 than previously, it was still not,

Percent change on year earlier

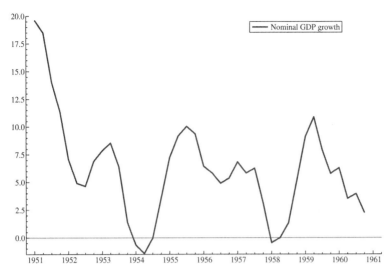

FIGURE 10.2. Nominal GDP growth (four-quarter), 1951:Q1–1960:Q4. *Source*: Federal Reserve Bank of St. Louis's FRED portal.

Percent change on year earlier

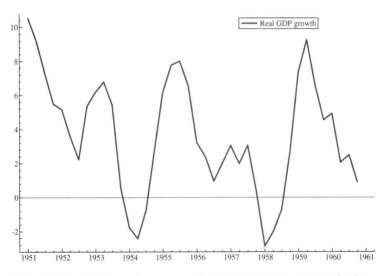

FIGURE 10.3. Real GDP growth (four-quarter), 1951:Q1–1960:Q4. *Source*: Federal Reserve Bank of St. Louis's FRED portal.

in Friedman's view, flexible enough, and the consequence of this was undesirable variation in monetary growth. The possibility that monetary policy magnified cyclical fluctuations in the 1950s by inducing too much interest-rate stability was also raised by Gordon (1976a, 62). In Wicksellian terms, this diagnosis suggests that fluctuations in the natural real rate of interest were high in relation to those of actual nominal and real short-term interest rates—a situation that generated procyclical fluctuations in monetary growth.

Why was monetary growth not more stable during the 1950s? As indicated above, one reason Friedman cited, and something he stressed in his 1955 memorandum to the Federal Reserve Board, was that that the Federal Reserve put too much emphasis on interest rates as a criterion for policy. In particular, Friedman saw policy makers as taking a rise in short-term interest rates in the second half of 1952 (of about 50 basis points) as a tightening of monetary policy.[139]

Friedman's criticism of Federal Reserve interest-rate policy did not rest, in this instance, on the real/nominal interest rate distinction. A criticism based on that distinction would in fact have been somewhat misplaced, as Federal Reserve officials during the 1950s voiced their *awareness* of the real/nominal rate distinction.[140] And, in any event, as Romer and Romer (2002a) stressed, nominal and real short-term interest rates likely had similar movements over much of the 1950s, owing to the stability of inflation. In the 1950s, Friedman's criticism of the interest-rate criterion took a different tack—one in which he concentrated on the different signals coming from monetary growth and interest rates. Friedman noted the contrast between what data on monetary growth suggested about monetary policy stance and what might be inferred from the behavior of short-term interest rates. For example, monetary growth (by the M2 measure) was higher in 1952 than in 1951—which suggested that policy makers might have been mistaken in their belief that they had tightened appreciably during 1952. The robustness of monetary growth during 1952 can, in Friedman's framework, be seen as an indication that the broad set of interest rates relevant for aggregate demand had not, in fact, risen by a great overall amount, in which case the increase in the average value of the short-term interest rate was providing a misleading indication of the magnitude of tightening.

Some other evidence in support of the Friedman notion that yields, broadly defined, did not rise much during 1952 is provided by the behavior of the long-term Treasury rate. In December 1952, this rate was only 5 basis points above its level of a year earlier (Meltzer 2009a, 95). This was perhaps only around half the increase that one would normally expect in view of the 37 basis point rise in short-term rates over the same period.[141] For his part, Friedman would see the true dismantling of the official peg of US bond prices as a protracted process, occurring over a couple of years, with the "explicit abandonment of the support policy" taking place only with the switch by the Federal Reserve in 1953 to its bills-only policy for open market operations.[142]

On top of the fact that the Federal Reserve withdrew only slowly from the long-term securities market was the behavior of the US Treasury. The Treasury was hesitant in the new bond market environment, waiting until well into 1952 to make a major issuance of higher-yielding long-term instruments (Meltzer 2009a, 59, 99). Indeed, one commentary in the 1950s judged that the long-term securities market was not really reopened until 1953, when the Treasury launched an issuance of a thirty-year bond with a 3¼ percent coupon (*First National City Bank Monthly Letter: Business and Economic Conditions*, July 1958, 79; see also *Ada Evening News*, April 24, 1953).

The transition from the pegging era was therefore considerably drawn out. And in this early post-Accord period, short-term interest rates may not have provided a very reliable guide to overall monetary conditions. Certainly, the factors in play during this transition period also implied that monetary growth had imperfections as an indicator, and in 1977 Friedman noted that the move in 1953 to a truly decontrolled bond market "demonetized a large volume of assets" and meant that the decline in M2 growth that year understated the decline in the properly measured volume of money.[143] Nonetheless, in registering ease and then tightening in 1952–53, monetary growth, as Friedman saw it, had shown itself to be a more accurate indicator of monetary conditions than short-term interest rates had been, and the considerable weight that policy makers had attached to the latter series had misled them in their decision making.

Friedman's objection to the use of the interest-rate criterion in the evaluation of monetary policy—although voiced in regard to the immediate aftermath of the Accord—applied to the remainder of the 1950s as well. In these later years of the decade, however, Friedman's critique acquired a somewhat different emphasis. For it was not the case during the mid- to late 1950s that there was a great conflict between short-term interest rates and monetary growth as signals of monetary conditions. Friedman would acknowledge in a 1966 memorandum to the Federal Reserve Board that movements in the two series had enjoyed a significant (inverse) relationship with one another over the preceding decade.[144] Consistent with this characterization, the episode-by-episode study of this period by R. Weintraub (1967) found that sizable interest-rate increases were associated with declines in monetary growth.

And it deserves emphasis that a regime in which the short-term interest rate was the policy instrument was indeed the post-1951 Federal Reserve setting. In a pattern that would be repeated from 1982 to 1994, Federal Reserve officials during the 1950s were, in public, reticent when it came to describing their monetary policy decisions as actions on short-term interest rates. They often preferred to characterize policy changes in terms of actions on commercial bank reserves—typically the "free reserves" total discussed further below. But, as Meltzer (2009a, 6) noted, casting its monetary policy actions in these terms allowed the Federal Reserve "to mask its role in affecting interest rates." This feature of Federal Reserve monetary policy in the 1950s was earlier noted by Duesenberry (1983, 133), who made the further observation that the Federal Reserve Board tended to present its discount-rate decisions as responses to movements in market rates—when, in fact, the latter movements had been set in train by monetary policy and were being reinforced by the discount-rate actions. This last feature of Federal Reserve policy in the 1950s was not lost at the time on Friedman, who numbered discount-rate adjustments among the measures that the authorities used to influence market interest rates.[145] It was, in fact, common knowledge among informed monetary policy watchers in academia, financial markets, and the financial press in the 1950s that the Federal Reserve was, in effect, centering its policy decisions on an adjustable target for short-term market interest rates.[146]

On the basis of the preceding discussion, Friedman's critique of US monetary policy in the decade after the Accord can be distilled into two contentions. (1) The Federal Reserve was too willing to take movements in short-term interest rates as the metric for the direction in which monetary conditions were moving, even when that movement was not confirmed by monetary growth.[147] (2) On other occasions, when monetary growth and interest rates were *not* sending different signals, monetary policy actions were delayed and too violent. Both of these contentions pointed to the conclusion that too much procyclicality was permitted in monetary growth, with monetary policy contributing to, instead of stabilizing, fluctuations in output.

How does one square Friedman's notion that the policy regime of the 1950s gave rise to considerable economic fluctuations with Romer and Romer's (2002a) evidence that the policy behavior underlying federal funds rate movements in the 1952:Q1–1958:Q4 period resembled that observed in the Volcker-Greenspan era—a period that covered much of the Great Moderation, and that is considered by many to be an era of a highly stabilizing monetary regime? There are several reasons for believing that the Friedman and Romer-Romer positions may not be in conflict.

First, Friedman did grant that 1950s monetary policy was firmly oriented toward low inflation—a property that is also evident in Romer and Romer's estimate of a federal funds rate response of 1.18 to inflation and in the low target rate of inflation implicit in their estimated interest-rate rule.

Second, some of the procyclical monetary growth of which Friedman complained may, in fact, be implied by Romer and Romer's estimates. Romer and Romer found little evidence of any direct response of the federal funds rate to real economic activity. Friedman emphasized that interest rates have a natural procyclical tendency. Attempts by the monetary authorities to suppress this procyclicality in interest rates might invite more intense fluctuations in money and output. Against this background, the failure of the federal funds rate to register much response to a real variable—such as Romer and Romer's real-activity variable (output in relation to trend) or output growth (the variable Friedman tended to stress when referring to the procyclicality of interest rates)—may be seen as one feature of the estimated interest-rate rule that tended to promote swings in output in the 1950s. This characteristic of the estimated reaction function may seem at odds with Friedman's position that monetary policy was characterized by overreaction and by ill-timed fine-tuning. But it must be recalled that Friedman was thinking in terms of the *money-stock behavior* implied by monetary policy decisions; and Friedman believed that a policy that implied a muted and delayed response of the short-term interest rate to economic activity would lead to sizable and procyclical swings in monetary growth and to a magnification of business cycle variations.

The third element that reconciles the Friedman and Romer-Romer findings regarding monetary policy in the 1950s is that there are considerable deviations of the actual federal funds rate from Romer and Romer's (2002a) estimated rule for that decade. These deviations include not only the in-sample residuals of their rule but also the out-of-sample observations for 1959, at which point the rise in the federal funds rate greatly exceeds the increase predicted by the estimated rule. And the tightening in 1959 was, as will be discussed at the end of this chapter, one of Friedman's examples of an excessive policy firming—and one whose severity could, he believed, have been avoided if monetary growth had had a more central place in policy makers' evaluation of the stance of monetary policy.

If, as Friedman had recommended, stability in monetary growth had been a more prominent consideration in monetary policy during the 1950s, would this have been at the cost of some of the desirable properties of the actual monetary policy reaction to the economy during the decade? In particular, would the preemptive response to inflation reported by Romer and Romer (2002a) have been absent, had a constant-monetary-growth rule been followed? To some extent, some of the preemptive aspects of policy would indeed likely have been lost if policy makers had gone for a constant-monetary-growth rule. As noted above, Friedman and Schwartz praised the Federal Reserve's achievement in producing preemptive policy moves that generated stabilizing movements in monetary growth at certain critical points during the 1951–60 period—specifically in its loosening of policy even before recession conditions emerged in 1953 and 1960. A constant-monetary-growth rule would not have been able to replicate this characteristic of actual Federal Reserve policy. The rule would necessarily have avoided outcomes in which monetary growth was procyclical and thereby contributed to fluctuations. But constant monetary growth would also have meant that the money stock could not be varied to offset nonmonetary factors making for recessions.

Nonetheless, a rule oriented on monetary growth can be regarded as one type of a preemptive, forward-looking monetary policy. As Mervyn King (1997b, 435) stressed, a monetary-growth-based policy concentrates on a variable that reacts to monetary policy actions earlier than does inflation. In that respect, the policy is preemptive. Furthermore, a constant-monetary-growth rule avoids problems that might arise from policies that respond to short-term variations in measured inflation. In addition, a focus during the 1950s on monetary growth would likely have helped on the dimension of real economic stabilization, because of the automatic adjustments that a monetary-growth-stabilizing policy implies for interest rates. As was discussed in chapter 6, constant monetary growth, in a situation in which nonmonetary factors are producing upward pressure on aggregate demand, tends to lead to interest-rate increases. Conversely, the policy leads to interest-rate reductions in instances of downward pressure on aggregate demand.

An advantage, as Friedman saw it, of the constant-monetary-growth rule was that it built in preemptive responses, such as those just described, in an automatic fashion, without requiring reliance by policy makers on forecasts. His position about the undesirability of embedding explicit forecasts into policy making contrasted with the view taken in policy circles on the matter during the 1950s (and, for that matter, in later decades). Ralph Young, at the time the director of the Federal Reserve Board's Division of Research and Statistics, stated in 1958: "The forward-looking nature of monetary policy forces the central banking statistician to forecast, no matter how inadequate the tools for doing so."[148] In contrast, Friedman's reservations about reliance on forecasts, already voiced in the 1940s, continued in the 1950s.[149] He articulated his doubts in remarks in an interview with *Newsweek* (January 30, 1956, 79): "General forecasts are a dime a dozen—and they aren't worth the dime. . . . I think we can solve the problem of short-term forecasts, but we haven't done it yet."[150] Although his remarks in the interview foreshadowed a time when economists *would* master economic forecasting, nearly forty years later he declared that this problem remained unsolved. "I don't try to forecast short-term changes in the economy," Friedman stated in 1995. "The record of economists in doing that justifies only humility" (*Wall Street Journal*, January 24, 1995, A8).[151]

The relevance of this point for the analysis of developments during the 1950s is brought out by the analysis of Romer and Romer (2002a, 126). As they discussed, flawed forecasts of inflation seem to have played an important role in monetary policy developments during the 1950s. They suggested that policy makers' expectations of inflation rose around 1958, and they noted that Livingston survey measures of expected inflation increased from mid-1958 through the end of 1959. Along similar lines, Burns (1960, 18) argued that the behavior of US bond and stock prices from mid-1958 reflected a rise in inflation expectations. The rise in inflation expectations, although it did not seem to be soundly based on macroeconomic developments, evidently encouraged a sharp monetary policy tightening late in the decade—a tightening that, as discussed at the end of this chapter, formed the basis for Friedman's main indictment of monetary policy in this period.

It seems appropriate, therefore, to judge that stabilization of monetary growth would indeed have improved on actual monetary policy in the 1950s in terms of the stability achieved in nominal and real income growth. A policy more heavily directed toward constant monetary growth would likely have triggered interest-rate adjustments in a prompt manner and in a way that did not call on policy makers to rely on forecasts, while also avoiding the excessive shifts in monetary policy that seem to have been an important source of the economic fluctuations observed in the United States during the 1950s. By abstaining from using monetary growth to offset other forces, policy makers would have prevented themselves from carrying out the theoretically optimal monetary policy; but if they had delivered a smooth path for monetary growth, policy makers likely would have generated a more stable pattern for economic activity than that actually observed in the 1950s.

In addition to his critique of the Federal Reserve's use during the 1950s of interest rates as an instrument and a criterion, Friedman questioned policy makers' conduct on another ground. He disagreed with the attention they gave to free reserves in setting policy. Free reserves consisted of the reserve balances of commercial banks (that is, their deposits with the Federal Reserve) that were member banks of the Federal Reserve System, minus the sum of their required and borrowed reserves. The monetarist literature of the 1950s and 1960s devoted a great deal of critical analysis to the Federal Reserve's invocation of free reserves as its metric for policy tightness or ease. Brunner and Meltzer (1964b) wrote a lengthy historical study of the subject, while Dewald (1963) published a shorter critique focusing on the 1959-61 episode. And Friedman supervised a PhD dissertation in the area, and it was subsequently published as Meigs (1962).[152] Friedman himself judged that "the level of free reserves . . . may be a misleading indicator of the degree of ease or tightness of monetary policy." But he wrote only sparingly on the subject. The two critiques of the concept he wrote in 1960-61 amounted to a couple of pages apiece.[153]

As both Romer and Romer (2002a, 123-24) and Meltzer (2009a, 6, 82, 113) have stressed, the fact that in practice the Federal Reserve was setting short-term interest rates in the 1950s puts the Federal Reserve's repeated public emphasis on free reserves in a particular light. The Federal Reserve evidently perceived free reserves as an important criterion, but the usefulness of this criterion evidently resulted from two properties: (*i*) free reserves typically had a close relationship to short-term interest rates; (*ii*) expressing policy changes in terms of the behavior of free reserves allowed policy makers to appear to have an arm's-length relationship with the setting of interest rates. In the face of this reality, were monetarists misguided in spending so much time analyzing "the Federal Reserve's attachment to the free reserve concept," to use the title of Brunner and Meltzer's (1964b) study?

The answer seems to be no. Monetarists studying the free-reserves concept were well aware that the policy makers of the 1950s and 1960s were, essentially, using a short-term interest-rate instrument. Indeed, Meigs was an official at the Federal Reserve Bank of St. Louis while working on his monograph on free reserves, and he attended several FOMC meetings from 1957 to 1960. Monetarists scrutinized the free-reserves aggregate principally because the Federal Reserve had, as already indicated, expressed some interest during the 1950s in the money stock as a criterion of policy. In this connection, some Federal Reserve statements had given the impression that free reserves provided a good indication of the impact of policy actions on the money stock. The monetarist critics of this official view argued that the free-reserves series should not have been so used, that the stock of total commercial bank reserves was a far better guide to the impact of monetary policy actions on the money stock than was the volume of free reserves. The monetarist critique of the free-reserves concept can, therefore, be viewed as a questioning of free reserves' merits as a measure of overall reserve pressure—and so of the implications of monetary policy measures for money-stock behavior. In addition, on account of the acknowledged connection between free reserves and short-term interest rates, the critique of free reserves supplemented the criticisms that monetarists, including Friedman, advanced regarding short-term interest rates as measures of policy stance.

For all his catalogue of complaints about monetary policy over the 1950s, however, it deserves restating that Friedman looked favorably on many aspects of monetary policy conduct in that period and that he voiced this judgment both at the time and subsequently.

It should also be mentioned that monetary policy in the 1950s had two particular features in common with Friedman's proposed constant-monetary-growth rule. First, monetary policy in the 1950s was largely concerned with domestic objectives and not with US international commitments. This feature was far from unprecedented, in Friedman's view. The

United States' adherence to gold standard rules before 1933 had been loose and sporadic, with routine sterilization of gold movements in the 1920s, and the post-1933 arrangements had been even looser.[154] The tendency toward US monetary policy autonomy was fortified by the 1933–34 changes in US policy on the exchange rate and gold, and the Bretton Woods system introduced in 1944 essentially institutionalized that autonomy. Notwithstanding the central role that the United States had in the Bretton Woods arrangements, the US authorities had, as Friedman saw it, been able to choose a course for monetary policy that was centered on domestic economic considerations.

This state of affairs arose in part because of the United States' dominant status as an economy—which implied that so much of the adjustment of balance-of-payments positions was borne by other countries. But it also arose in part because of a number of nonmonetary devices (including restrictions on US residents' gold holding and various barriers to the movement of capital and goods) that disconnected US monetary growth from the United States' international monetary obligations. Friedman disapproved of these controls as a matter of principle, but they did help decouple US domestic and international economic policy. Friedman saw foreign exchange controls as bound to be the instrument of choice of policy makers, in the United States and elsewhere, for reconciling international and domestic economic policy goals—so long as exchange rates remained fixed. The reason for this judgment was that he could not see any country in the modern era as being prepared for very long to subordinate aggregate-demand management to the country's external obligations.[155] From this flowed Friedman's dictum that, in the era in which governments had accepted responsibility for stabilization of their domestic economies, support for fixed exchange rates implicitly amounted to support for foreign exchange control.[156]

A second major desirable feature of the monetary policy regime that emerged in the 1950s, from the perspective of Friedman's views on appropriate monetary policy, was that it aimed for low inflation—*not* a stationary price level. It was clear that postwar US policy makers were taking a tolerant attitude regarding a gently rising trend in the price level. As one financial columnist put it in 1966, although 3 percent price rises were "over the borderline and into the area of inflation," the same was not true of a 2 percent inflation rate: rather, "modern history indicates that it [2 percent inflation] is close to the equivalent of price stability" (*Detroit Free Press*, February 24, 1966). It is true that even low single-digit inflation was nearly squeezed out of the United States in the wake of the monetary tightening of late 1950s. But it is doubtful that policy makers intended policy to be so tight in this period. And, for his part, Friedman, as detailed at the end of this chapter, judged this late-decade disinflationary policy to be overkill, in addition to being far too rapidly executed.

Thus, the policy in force for the bulk of the 1950s was—in common with Friedman's constant-monetary-growth rule—an inflation-oriented rather than price-level-oriented regime, in the sense that it was not the intention or practice of policy makers to try to claw back past increases in the price level. For example, as Brunner and Meltzer (1964c, 65) observed, the Federal Reserve did not "attempt to 'roll back' prices" after the Korean War's price-level surge. Figures 10.4 and 10.5 plot the price level and inflation, respectively, for January 1950 to December 1965, using the CPI. These figures confirm that, although deflation was registered in the mid-1950s, it was small in relation to the prior Korean War inflation and was followed by a period in which price rises exceeded 3 percent.

In Friedman's view, it took some time for the private sector to digest the fact that the post-Accord regime was not delivering a stationary price level. His Nobel lecture of December 1976 would state, with respect to the United States and the United Kingdom in the postwar period: "The concept of a 'normal' price level was deeply imbedded in the financial and other institutions of the two countries and in the habits and attitudes of their citizens."[157] In the same vein, the Friedman-Schwartz *Monetary History* characterized the early post–World War II period in the United States as a time during which the community was surprised to find that the wartime increase in the price index was not wound back.[158]

It took quite some time for Friedman himself to accept completely that stationarity of the price level was a thing of the past. Many of the ingredients required for an acceptance of the price-level nonstationarity were present in his writings. As noted, he himself did not advocate rules that implied a mean-reverting (as opposed to a driftless or mildly drifting) price level, as he preferred to let past price-level reductions and increases be bygones. And his own view that the economy was Depression-proof partly reflected his judgment that substantial deflations would be avoided henceforth. Furthermore, as already suggested, he cited the World War II inflation as a price-level increase that was not clawed back.[159] Yet, in the twenty years to the end of the 1960s, Friedman gave many signs of believing that monetary policy had not changed so drastically that one could claim that deflationary episodes were wholly a thing of the past for the United States. For example, in a radio appearance in early 1949, he stated, "We have had them [deflations] on and off for centuries."[160]

Although Friedman did rule out the future occurrence of severe deflations, Friedman still saw regular business cycles as the way of the future—and, as a corollary, he believed that recessions could feature mild declines in the absolute price level, as opposed to merely dips in inflation. Thus in

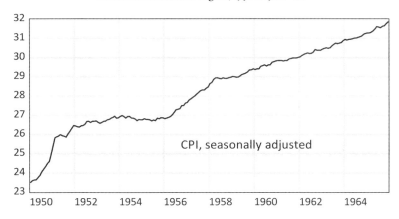

FIGURE 10.4. Consumer price index, seasonally adjusted, January 1950–December 1965. *Source*: Federal Reserve Bank of St. Louis's FRED portal.

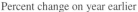

FIGURE 10.5. Twelve-month percent change in CPI, January 1950–December 1965. *Source*: Computed from seasonally adjusted CPI in Federal Reserve Bank of St. Louis's FRED portal.

1959 he resisted referring to the United States' mid-1950s price rise as "inflation." He chose, instead, to regard it as a cyclical spike in prices that might be reversed in future recessions.[161] Furthermore, Friedman's empirical research in the 1950s on the demand for money—encapsulated in his 1959 paper "The Demand for Money: Some Theoretical and Empirical Results"—used, as an argument in the money-demand function, a "permanent prices" concept.[162] The series was generated empirically as a dynamically stable, autoregressive forecast of the price level. The series' construction therefore rested on the assumption of a stationary price level.[163]

As late as July 1969, Friedman attached significance to the notion that the 1930s price level was "low" and the 1960s price level was "high," and he considered those decades a demonstration of the validity of the Gibson Paradox (Instructional Dynamics Economics Cassette Tape 31, July 24, 1969). In contrast, a mindset that sees the price level as nonstationary is likely to regard the prevailing value of the absolute price index as of little interest, and to concentrate attention instead on inflation.

It was only in the 1970s that Friedman wholly accepted the reality that the modern US economy had a nonstationary price level. By then, he had had a chance to absorb more of the postwar experience as well as studies of that experience by his former student Benjamin Klein. In an effort to teach himself time-series methods, Klein had embarked on a study of the postwar monetary policy regime, as reflected in US price-level behavior.[164] Klein's conclusion was that there was clearly a unit root in the price level under what he called "our new monetary standard" (B. Klein 1975a). Indeed, as additional data for the 1970s accumulated, researchers would find not only that the US price level was nonstationary but that even its first derivative—the inflation rate—was coming perilously close to exhibiting a unit root. Friedman's "permanent prices" estimates, with their presumption of a stationary price level, were clearly no longer viable, in light of the cumulative postwar evidence from US data. As Benjamin Klein (1977, 702) put it: "Friedman's series, which is merely a weighted average of past measured price levels with no adjustment made for trend, cannot be meaningfully extended through the 1960s."[165]

Friedman incorporated the lessons of Klein's research on price-level behavior into his later work. He and Schwartz copiously cited Klein's writings in their 1982 *Monetary Trends* and interpreted economic events in light of the reality of a nonstationary price level in the postwar period.[166]

The experience of the 1960s and 1970s, in conjunction with research like Klein's, clearly put paid to any lingering notion on Friedman's part that the price level was still stationary. But there could still be a world of difference between various alternative monetary policy regimes, even if they had in common the property that they delivered a nonstationary price level. A nonstationary price level could be consistent with a disciplined monetary policy regime, as was the case during the 1950s. It could also be consistent with regimes that featured a high level of uncertainty and indiscipline, as was the case with US monetary policy in the 1970s.

One by-product of the monetary policy regime in force in the 1950s, in which inflationary expectations but not the long-run price level was anchored, was that inflation was close to a white-noise process. This characterization of inflation behavior during the 1950s, which was found in a number of studies cited earlier, is in contrast with the contention of the 1961 Stigler Committee.[167] The picture painted by George Stigler's report was that, in the period since the Korean War, the price level may have been basically constant, with the measured inflation rates actually reflecting quality changes, rather than bona fide upward pressure on consumer prices.

Friedman made sympathetic remarks about the Stigler Committee over the years.[168] Friedman's favorable disposition toward the committee's work, however, may well have largely reflected his high regard for Stigler, as well as agreement with its theme of the pervasiveness of measurement difficulties in economics. It is far less likely that he wholeheartedly accepted the committee's skepticism regarding the existence of inflationary pressure in the postwar period. Robert Gordon has argued that Friedman did not incorporate the Stigler Committee's finding into his own work.[169]

Consistent with Gordon's contention, many of the key empirical regularities on which Friedman focused clashed with the idea that the price level was constant in the period from the end of the Korean War through the mid-1960s. For example, M2 velocity was stationary in the four decades after the Accord.[170] The stationarity of velocity, after an initial postwar rise, underlay much of Friedman's solo- and coauthored discussions of money demand behavior.[171] The posture taken in these discussions amounted to a rejection of Stigler's suggestion that the upward trend in the price data in the 1950s was spurious.[172]

Another example of the discord between the Stigler Committee's finding and the work of Friedman (and of many others) comes from US inflation/unemployment patterns. Actual inflation data from 1954 to the end of the 1960s fit into a well-behaved downward-sloping Phillips-curve pattern, as the Council of Economic Advisers (1969, chart 8, 95) showed, and as was also plotted in Boskin (1987, 16); McCallum (1989b, 180); and Fuhrer, Olivei, and Tootell (2012, 87).[173] Part of Friedman's basic story concerning the Phillips curve rested on an acceptance that the fluctuations in measured inflation shown in these figures corresponded to bona fide variation in inflation. Also consistent with Friedman's taking the US inflation data at face value was his 1962 observation that a more stable pattern of monetary growth during the 1950s would have removed some of the observed wage and price fluctuations of that decade.[174] In a similar vein, Friedman's basic account of the behavior of inflation during the Eisenhower years, discussed previously, essentially took the recorded inflation series at face value, as that account referred to the elimination under the Eisenhower administration of creeping inflation. Indeed, in 1977 Friedman credited the restraint of the Eisenhower years with bringing inflation down from the 3–3½ percent range to around zero.[175] In 1980, he specifically indicated that US postwar inflation "started in the 1950s," only to be interrupted by the weight of the 1957–58 and 1960–61 recessions, which brought inflation "close to zero."[176]

In view of the fact that measured inflation in the early 1960s was around

1 percent rather than zero, it would appear that Friedman viewed recorded rates of inflation following the Korean War as perhaps overstating actual inflation by around 1 percentage point on average—a degree of overstatement that would still leave a notable amount of genuine inflation occurring in the mid- to late 1950s.[177] Further testament to the fact that Friedman viewed recorded inflation in the 1950s as largely accurate is the existence of another, later presentation (in *Wall Street Journal*, April 15, 1988), in which Friedman took the 2.3 percent average rate of inflation for the decade to 1962 at face value and then used it to infer how much lower monetary growth would have needed to have been to deliver zero inflation.

In contrast, the "Stigler adjustment" to price-level trends would have produced a different picture by removing much of the price-level movement recorded in the United States during the 1950s. On the whole, therefore, Friedman's accounts, taken together with much other evidence, support the notion that, during the 1950s, inflation behaved in much the way the official data said it did: fluctuating mildly, but distinctly, around a low, but nonzero, rate.

COST-PUSH DEBATES

As discussed in chapters 4 and 7, Friedman over the years 1948 to 1951 shook off the cost-push views of inflation to which he had adhered over much of the 1940s. In terms of a New Keynesian Phillips curve like that in chapter 2,

$$\pi_t = \beta E_t \pi_{t+1} + \alpha(y_t - y_t^*) + u_t, \tag{1}$$

the evolution of Friedman's position can be seen as having proceeded in stages. Prior to the start of the evolution—that is, before 1943—he largely endorsed the notion of an L-shaped aggregate-supply function, in which there was no connection between inflation and demand pressure when the economy was operating below full employment. That is, for this region, he subscribed to an inflation equation of the form:

$$\pi_t = \beta E_t \pi_{t+1} + u_t \quad \text{for } y_t < y_t^*, \tag{2}$$

and he believed that, beyond the point of full employment, $\alpha = \infty$ was a good approximation, so that maximum and full employment coincided, with excess-demand pressure manifested only in inflation and with cost-push factors (u_t) superimposing inflation on the demand-pull inflation.

In the next stage of Friedman's thinking—that is, from the mid-1940s to the late 1940s—he saw an expectational Phillips curve, much like equation (1), as a good approximation for the slack-economy range of $y_t < y_t^*$. But he continued to view the full-employment level of output as the maximum feasible level of output. Furthermore, in both the first two stages of his thinking about the forces driving inflation dynamics, Friedman essentially regarded cost-push forces, as represented in the u_t term, as persistent with a positive mean.

The third stage of Friedman's thinking about inflation—clearly apparent during the early 1950s—signified his adoption of a modern, expectational Phillips-curve approach. In terms of equation (1), this approach implied: (*a*) the position that β is well approximated as being unity, (*b*) the requirement that the value of α, the key parameter governing the response of inflation to the output gap, is finite but nonzero, and (*c*) the stipulation that u_t is mean zero and is approximately white noise.[178]

Discussions of Friedman's views on the Phillips curve have predominantly focused on the first of these restrictions—that is, restriction (*a*). This restriction is the one familiar from his most well known research contributions. It corresponds to the insistence that the expectational term is important enough that the Phillips curve in the long run is essentially of a vertical shape, and that the structural Phillips-curve relationship is one linking the deviation of inflation from its expectation to the output gap, as opposed to one linking the levels of inflation and the output gap.

But important though this contention was in Friedman's discussions, it is also true that a great deal of Friedman's energies from the 1950s to the 1970s—particularly in the context of policy debates—was devoted to pressing the case for the *second* and *third* restrictions on the Phillips curve rather than the first. In particular, it was these last two restrictions, (*b*) and (*c*), that were at the heart of the debate on cost-push inflation.

The believers in cost-push inflation whom Friedman confronted took the position that u_t was persistent and had a positive mean. The more extreme of them further believed that α was zero below full employment. This extreme cost-push view of inflation, under which negative output gaps exerted no downward pressure on inflation, was pervasive in the United Kingdom in the first few postwar decades.[179] In the United States, it would not be until the 1970s that this extreme view gripped policy making—as will be discussed in chapter 15. In the 1950s, in contrast, that purist variant of the cost-push position was not particularly influential in the United States. It was associated principally with John Kenneth Galbraith, whose 1952 book *A Theory of Price Control* had been predicated on the notion that inflation was not amenable to control via demand-management tools.

Friedman, while disagreeing with the argument made in the book, would give Galbraith his due for seeking to articulate a coherent case for price controls as a permanent anti-inflation weapon.[180] The lack of influence of Galbraith's book among academic economists, however, played a role in his decision to concentrate on popular writing in economics.[181]

Much of Galbraith's later output was, as Friedman would note, only peripherally related to inflation and concentrated on industrial-organization issues.[182] But Galbraith achieved an image in the public mind as a leading economist, and this image made him difficult to ignore for those economists, like Friedman, who kept a hand in public policy debates. One of many face-to-face debates that Friedman would have with Galbraith occurred in 1953, when the two participated in a radio panel discussion. The debate had a macroeconomic focus, and in the course of the debate, Friedman made it clear that he did not accept Galbraith's cost-push diagnosis. "I think you tend to overrate the importance and significance of monopoly," he told Galbraith, adding: "I think that you grossly overrate the influence which the organization of the union had on wage rates and conditions in these areas."[183] The same topic came up during the many discussions Friedman and Robert Solow had when both visited Stanford University's Center for Advanced Study during the 1957–58 academic year. "We talked about policy, and markets, and should you regard markets as perfect with a few imperfect blemishes, or as imperfect with a few occasional perfect spots," Solow recalled (interview, December 2, 2013).

In taking on pure cost-push views, Friedman was drawing on his own research regarding the effect of labor unions.[184] As might be expected, Friedman noted that labor unions were much less important in the United States than in some other major countries.[185] But he granted that market power existed for suppliers of labor in certain sectors—indeed, that had been a point of his *Income* work with Kuznets—and in 1980 the Friedmans affirmed that unions had "considerable strength" in the United States.[186] But Friedman rejected the practice of applying this conclusion about union power to the economy as a whole. Restrictions on labor supply in a particular sector of the economy could push up wages in that sector, but, with total money spending in the economy fixed by aggregate-demand policies, the nonunionized or weakly unionized sectors would experience downward pressure on wages that offset—possibly with a lag—the impact on aggregate costs of the union-driven wage boosts.[187] A similar line of argument applied to upward pressure on prices in certain sectors arising from *firms'* monopoly power. These considerations underlay the restriction on inflation dynamics in the framework that Friedman had settled on by 1951. In that framework, cost-push forces had a zero average effect on inflation. In terms of a Phillips curve like equation (1), α was positive (in which case lack of monetary accommodation of a certain price rise would set in motion downward pressure on other prices).

In sum, although Friedman regarded unions as a source of certain economic inefficiencies, he did not see them as a source of inflation.[188] As he put it in December 1958, although he was unaccustomed to defending trade unions, his economic analysis drove him to do so on the matter of the causes of inflation.[189]

Furthermore, in Friedman's view, the perception of the influence that unions had on wage increases in their own sector was exaggerated by the fact that much of the increase in wages observed in unionized sectors reflected the influence of demand pressures and did not signify bona fide cost-push forces. That is to say, wage and price increases arising in monopolistic sectors were very typically a response to positive demand forces and were *not* an exercise of market power on the part of wage setters and price setters. Indeed, one feature that Friedman stressed was the similarity, across conditions of perfect and imperfect competition, of the forces producing fluctuations in prices (both of goods and of factors of production). Friedman was confident that many of the results prevailing under perfect competition carried through to an economy with market power. This perspective had already been reflected in the contention he voiced in the 1940s that Marshallian analysis was highly general. It also featured prominently in his 1953 methodology article.

Friedman's research during the early 1950s on economic outcomes in the presence of labor unions likely bolstered his confidence on this matter. This likelihood is brought out by considering that in the late 1930s he had suggested that the payment of marginal product for a factor service was a feature of a "*laissez-faire* economy."[190] In contrast, in 1962 he regarded such a condition as a good approximation when describing the situation for the "capitalist system"—a term he used to encompass systems that included imperfectly competitive elements.[191]

Market power did, Friedman conceded, produce some differences in outcomes: it lowered the overall efficiency of the economy; and sectors in which market power existed had high prices. But absent an *increase* in market power, market power in itself did not constitute a source of *rising* prices in those sectors. Nor did it make pricing behavior in those sectors immune to the influence of demand and supply.[192] This argument applied both to cost increases that seemingly occurred at the initiative of labor unions and to price increases that were proximately imposed by powerful firms. In terms of equation (1), the implication was that the cost-push term u_t had a zero mean and this term was, therefore, not a systematic source of upward pressure on inflation.[193]

As noted above, Friedman faced few advocates of *pure* cost-push inflation theories in the United States during the 1950s other than Galbraith. What Friedman instead had to counter was the increasing advocacy of hybrid cost-push/demand-pull views of inflation. Proponents of this hybrid position, which might be called "partial cost-push," granted that $\alpha > 0$ in an equation like (1)—so that policy makers' restriction on aggregate demand could in principle block a particular price increase from showing up in the ongoing inflation rate. But the hybrid position also maintained that u_t was positive in mean as well as persistent—so that in the face of these cost-push shocks, demand restriction could maintain price stability only at the cost of excessive unemployment (i.e., a permanently negative output gap).[194]

It was this disagreement about the nature of cost-push forces—a zero mean versus a positive mean of u_t—that was crucial to the debate over the existence of a long-run trade-off between inflation and unemployment. Friedman's position that the long-run Phillips curve was vertical at the natural rate of unemployment required the condition that $E[u_t] = 0$ to hold. His and Edmund Phelps's proposal that β be restricted to unity, a proposal that is a much more celebrated part of the Phillips-curve debate (and which is considered in chapter 13), does not deliver a long-run curve at the natural rate unless the condition that $E[u_t] = 0$ is also satisfied.[195]

An early occasion on which Friedman found his views about inflation juxtaposed with that of the emerging "partial cost-push" alternative—that is, the view that amounted to setting $\alpha > 0$, $E[u_t] = 0$ in equation (1)—occurred with the publication in 1958 of a Joint Economic Committee collection of invited submissions, *Relationship of Prices to Economic Stability and Growth*.[196] Friedman's chapter, "The Supply of Money and Changes in Prices and Output," was concerned principally with outlining the findings of his monetary research with Schwartz and with advocating his constant-monetary-growth rule, rather than with taking on the cost-push argument. Friedman nevertheless included in his piece a skeptical account of the position that "costs . . . have a tendency to be pushed up with little reference to the state of demand as a result of strong trade unions."[197]

Immediately following Friedman's chapter, however, was Abba Lerner's chapter, which endorsed the existence of cost-push inflation (or, as Lerner preferred to call it, "sellers' inflation").[198] "A sellers' inflation could just as well be started by an increase not in the wage asked, but in the percentage of markup of price above cost," Lerner (1958, 259) asserted. Lerner granted that monetary accommodation could stop cost-push forces from being transmitted to inflation—"an increase in the supply of money . . . [is] one of the necessary conditions for an inflationary process to be able to continue" (257). But he argued that this option could be exercised only at the cost of permanent unemployment:

> If there is no increase in expenditure[,] the number of units of goods bought must fall in the same proportion as the price per unit is raised by the sellers. A 10 percent increase in prices would thus result in a fall in

output of about 10 percent. . . . By reducing total expenditure, or perhaps by merely refusing to permit the increase in total expenditure needed to accommodate the increased prices, the authorities would bring about depression and unemployment. This would stop the sellers from increasing prices. (Lerner 1958, 260)

The battle lines were thus being drawn between Friedman's view that ongoing inflation was a monetary phenomenon and that maintenance of price stability did not require a persistently negative output gap, and others' position that there were major nonmonetary factors in the inflation process—factors whose impact on overall inflation could be offset by monetary policy only at the expense of permanent unemployment. Friedman could at least be grateful that his main opponents in this debate were believers in *partial* cost-push views of inflation: they did concede that monetary policy *could* stop inflation, albeit at a permanent real cost. Even that concession would not be granted in the extreme variant of cost-push views, which was, as noted, already prevalent in UK academic and policy circles in the 1950s, but which would not gain a large following among the corresponding US bodies until the 1970s (see chapter 15).

Two prominent articles appearing in 1959–60 gave further impetus to the notion that cost-push elements were a major element of inflation. The study by Samuelson and Solow (1960), delivered at the American Economic Association in December 1959 and published in May 1960, is best known for its presentation of an empirical downward-sloping Phillips curve for the United States. Samuelson and Solow's analysis was important in helping to provide an intermediate step between the *L*-shaped aggregate-supply function of early Keynesian theory and the augmented, long-run-vertical Phillips curve of Friedman and Phelps. It is clear, therefore, that Samuelson and Solow made a contribution to the inflation literature that endures as part of the modern consensus.[199] Friedman himself would acknowledge that the Phillips-curve literature, by making inflation an endogenous variable at all levels of employment, helped "bring the determination of prices back into the body of economic analysis."[200]

A great deal of Samuelson and Solow's discussion was, however, devoted to a further innovation—one that is, by and large, not accepted today. This innovation was their advocacy of a framework in which systematic cost-push and demand-pull pressures on inflation could both be contemplated. In effect, Samuelson and Solow formalized the partial cost-push view of inflation described above. In particular, reflecting their position that an "element of validity would have to be conceded to both views" (Samuelson and Solow 1960, 191), the Samuelson-Solow proposal entailed incorporating both a continuous relationship between inflation and the output gap ($\alpha > 0$) and systematic upward pressure on inflation from cost-push forces

$(E[u_t] > 0$ and u_t persistent). The latter element, supplemented by the authors' position that the Phillips curve was nonvertical (i.e., $\beta < 1$), underlay the Samuelson-Solow contention that there was a permanent trade-off between inflation and unemployment.

Solow and, especially, Samuelson, would repeatedly voice a belief in this trade-off in statements during the 1960s and 1970s. They did so even at the conclusion of their 1960 paper with their reference to "the disharmony between full employment and price stability."[201] Samuelson elaborated on this point in a joint television appearance with Friedman in 1962. On the program, after Friedman had observed that "it seems to me there is no fundamental incompatibility" between high employment and price stability, Samuelson replied: "Now this is what worries me: How many times in the last 30 years and for how many months—I won't even say 'years'— have we enjoyed . . . 4 percent unemployment, as we measure it, and stability of the consumers' price index? Going abroad . . . [for] how many countries and in how many months can you point out [cases in which] there was high employment, as they measure their employment, and price stability? . . . I looked over the record. I was shockingly disappointed at how few such occasions [there] are, and so that's why I'm alerted to the possibility of having to worry about this problem."[202]

The position that price stability and high employment had a tendency to be incompatible would be influential in US academic circles. One example of the influence came in the position taken by Harvard University's James Duesenberry. At a 1959 conference, Duesenberry had stated that "there is no necessary conflict between full employment and price stability" (Duesenberry 1962, 145). By the early 1970s, however, Duesenberry's position had become: "A fiscal and monetary policy aimed at price stability will lead to too much unemployment" (Duesenberry 1972, 127). As with the statements by Samuelson and Solow, Duesenberry's formulation left the possibility open that the two goals might be reconcilable if an incomes policy was used to suppress cost-push forces.

The second prominent article from the late 1950s that considered the matter of cost-push—and a study that was cited by Samuelson and Solow— was Charles Schultze's monograph *Recent Inflation in the United States*, a study commissioned by the Joint Economic Committee and released in September 1959 (Schultze 1959). This study, Schultze would recall, received considerable press coverage (Charles Schultze, interview, July 9, 2013). It would also become a standard reading on cost-push inflation for US graduate classes in the 1960s.[203] The Schultze analysis took a position like the hybrid view just exposited: that there was "an upward bias imparted to the price level by the nature of our price- and wage-setting mechanisms" (133) even in the absence of excess demand and that monetary policy could offset this pressure only at the cost of major unemployment (5, 133). Keeping the output gap at zero would, on this view, not suffice to prevent cost-push pressures showing up in the inflation rate.[204] Consequently, concluded Schultze (1959, 134): "By using monetary and fiscal policy to prevent excess aggregate demand from emerging[,] we can control [only] one type of inflation."

In contrast to the Lerner and Samuelson-Solow articles, neither of which mentioned Friedman, Schultze (1959, 4) acknowledged Friedman as a representative of "the demand-pull theorists," citing (38) the paper Friedman had written for the 1950 conference on labor unions.[205] For his part, Friedman distinguished sharply between price stickiness, which he found plausible, and a tendency for market power to steepen the upward trend in the price level, which he did not find plausible. Indeed—on a drive with Friedman that took place sometime around the 1959–60 academic year, in the aftermath of a talk Friedman had given at Indiana University—Schultze discussed his study briefly with Friedman.[206] Friedman suggested to Schultze that while he concurred with the notion that prices in certain sectors exhibited rigidity downward, he saw this tendency as likely to wear off over time (Charles Schultze, interview, July 9, 2013).

The skirmishes between Friedman and various proponents of cost-push theories would continue in the 1960s and 1970s, when the adherents to the cost-push position would see their beliefs translated into the deployment of nonmonetary tools against inflation by the US government, including the wage/price guideposts of the 1960s, the Nixon wage/price controls, and the various nonmonetary measures taken against inflation by the Carter administration (in which Schultze served as chairman of the Council of Economic Advisers). Samuelson and Solow (1960, 194) foreshadowed this debate on policy tools with their reference to the "important question of what feasible institutional reforms might be introduced," naming "direct price and wage controls" among possible measures "to move the American Phillips curves downward and to the left." In contrast, Friedman told a meeting of the American Petroleum Institute in November 1958 that wage and price controls were useless for fighting inflation and that their imposition would jeopardize the foundations of a free society.[207]

The previous July, speaking at the Stanford Business Conference, Friedman had suggested that the shortages that would result if wage/price controls were imposed would ultimately lead to the government stepping in to direct the allocation of labor and other factors of production. On the same occasion, Friedman had criticized the concessions that the Eisenhower administration had made to cost-push ideas, in particular, the public appeals that President Eisenhower had voiced for restraint in wage and price setting (*Austin American*, July 22, 1958).[208]

Friedman was, however, relieved that the Eisenhower administration held the line against pressure to introduce wage/price controls. Indeed, notwithstanding the minor degree of backtracking in which he engaged during his second term, President Eisenhower had set the tone of economic policy for the whole of his presidency when, in his first State of the Union address, he stated: "Direct controls, except those on credit, deal not with the real causes of inflation but only with its symptoms."[209]

Friedman gave Arthur Burns kudos for prevailing on Eisenhower not to seek wage/price controls.[210] Although, as already indicated, Friedman did take issue with some of the statements about monetary policy in Burns's (1957) lecture series, Burns's lectures gave a negative verdict on incomes policies and, in this respect, the lectures met with Friedman's approval. Throughout the 1960s, Friedman and Burns would remain in accord regarding incomes policy. Their parting of ways on the issue would not occur until 1970.

III. Personalities, 1951–60

SENATORS PAUL DOUGLAS AND PRESCOTT BUSH

From the vantage point of the early 1980s, Friedman declared Paul H. Douglas, University of Chicago economics professor turned US senator, to be "the first recent example of the influence of the Chicago school on monetary policy."[211] Friedman was referring to the impact that Senator Douglas created as chairman of the Subcommittee on Monetary, Credit, and Fiscal Policy of the Joint Committee on the Economic Report during the subcommittee's hearings in between September and December 1949. Friedman did not participate in the hearings, but he and Schwartz cited them, as well as the resulting report, under the heading "Revival of Monetary Policy" in the *Monetary History*.[212] "Throughout those hearings, [Douglas] kept hammering away on the undesirability of pegging bond prices," Friedman assessed from reading the hearings. "I have very little doubt that his pressure played a critical role in finally producing the Federal Reserve/Treasury Accord."[213]

From a vast amount of testimony and submissions on the subject of the bond-price peg, Douglas's subcommittee was able to produce a report in January 1950 that was a concise fifty-one pages. A key recommendation concerning monetary policy appeared on page 17: "The vigorous use of a restrictive monetary policy as an anti-inflation measure has been inhibited since the war. . . . But we believe that the advantages of avoiding inflation are so great and that a restrictive monetary policy can contribute so much to this end that the freedom of the Federal Reserve to restrict credit and raise interest rates for general stabilization purposes should be restored."[214]

The way in which this recommendation was framed sheds light on the objectives of economic policy as they were perceived in the 1950s. Page 1 of Douglas's report indicated that the monetary policy recommendation was being made for "achieving the purposes of the Employment Act."[215] It is sometimes argued that the Employment Act of 1946 assigned only real (i.e., production and employment) goals to the federal government (including the Federal Reserve) and that the interpretation of the act's "maximum ... purchasing power" goal as a price-stability goal was an ex post construction put on the act's wording.[216] For example, Fellner (1956, 87) acknowledged that the act "defines maximum purchasing power as a desirable objective." However, he then immediately asserted: "But purchasing power is here presumably used in the sense of 'effective demand,' not in the sense of 'value of the dollar.'"

President Eisenhower in effect gave credence to analyses like Fellner's by calling in his January 1959 State of the Union message for an amendment to the employment act to include a price-stability mandate, and Friedman expressed support for such an amendment when testifying before Congress a few months later.[217] The legislative history for the employment act, however, supports the notion that the purchasing-power responsibility described in the act was always envisioned as a price-stability mandate.[218] And, as has been seen, Douglas's subcommittee in the late 1940s clearly took that position when conducting its investigation into Federal Reserve policy. Furthermore, the Federal Reserve during the 1950s took the employment act as including a price-stability assignment, and Friedman (in *New York Times*, October 11, 1964, 134) acknowledged that the employment act had been interpreted as including a price-stability mandate.[219]

The Douglas subcommittee's report characterized appropriate monetary policy as featuring "timely flexibility toward easy credit at some times and credit restriction at other times."[220] This might appear to conflict with the constant-monetary-growth rule that Friedman was advocating from the second half of the 1950s. But in fact, there need not be any conflict: as indicated earlier, a monetary-growth rule would generate upward interest-rate pressure (or "credit restriction") in expansions and downward pressure (or "easy credit") in recessions.[221] In particular, as Douglas put it during the subcommittee hearings, "in periods of inflation the interest rate will be increased."[222]

Friedman and Douglas concurred during the 1949–51 period on the need to drop the bond-price peg and let interest rates rise. But, once the peg was dropped, they would frequently find themselves at odds with each other regarding monetary policy. Whereas Friedman would take the position that 1953–59 monetary policy was too variable but on average was about right, Douglas (as a Democratic member of the Joint Economic Committee, which he also intermittently chaired) would at the end of the 1950s criticize post-Accord monetary policy for being too tight Ahearn 1963, 1; Meltzer 2009a, 68).[223] In addition, Douglas would give considerable credence to cost-push views of inflation.

The Joint Economic Committee would, however, also provide a venue in which Friedman could express a view different from Douglas's own and also make the case for a policy rule of constant monetary growth. Ironically, this was a rule that Douglas had advocated when, back in the late 1920s and early 1930s, he had been commenting on economic developments from his then-base of the University of Chicago.[224] Friedman testified in favor of the constant-monetary-growth rule in presentations to the Joint Economic Committee in both May and October 1959.

The first of these occasions would provide a poignant exchange between Friedman and the Republican senator Prescott Bush, of Texas. Friedman would know three generations of Bush politicians: in the 1980s he would work with Prescott Bush's son, Vice President George H. W. Bush, on the President's Economic Policy Advisory Board, and in 2002 President George W. Bush would host an event at the White House in Friedman's honor. However, the May 1959 back-and-forth between Prescott Bush and Friedman did not really foreshadow the economic debates of the 1980s and subsequently. Instead, a specific exchange between the two of them gave a foretaste of issues that would figure prominently in the more immediate future—that is, in the 1960s and 1970s. Senator Bush asked Friedman: "One of the principal objectives of this committee's work this year is to try to find out the relationship between the maintenance of employment and price stability. I would like you to comment on that. Do you think those are mutually conflicting or not? How do you feel about that?" Friedman answered: "I do not believe they are mutually conflicting."[225]

WILLIAM MCCHESNEY MARTIN

As noted in section I of this chapter, Friedman during the first half of the 1950s regarded the direction in which stabilization policies were proceeding as prone ultimately to produce a major inflation. He reiterated this concern in the late 1950s, arguing that the likelihood of inflation "arises from widespread acceptance of 'full employment' as a major governmental responsibility."[226] But although Friedman regarded policy as likely to be, on average, too loose, the possibility that policy actions could be too sharp in both directions also featured in Friedman's message, and in 1958 he underscored this by noting the danger of overreacting "in the face of ... relatively mild price rises."[227] He feared that policy makers would too rarely make the accurate diagnosis that inflation was demand-pull in character; but he also worried that, when they did so diagnose inflation, they might overreact with an excessive tightening of monetary policy.

The monetary policy sequence that followed in 1959–60 was one that Friedman would regard as a prime example of such an overreaction. In its wake would occur the third recession of the Eisenhower years, that of 1960–61, and one that Friedman would consider unnecessary.[228]

The extent of the monetary policy tightening that took place between 1958 and 1960 is evident in the twelve-month percentage changes of M1 and M2 (calculated from data on these series that Friedman and Schwartz published in their *Monetary Statistics*).[229] Twelve-month M1 growth fell from 3.8 percent in December 1958 to –2.6 percent in July 1960; twelve-month M2 growth fell from 6.8 percent to –1 percent over the same period. M1 (but not M2) had been allowed to undergo an absolute decline in late 1957 and early 1958, too (see again figure 10.1). The fact that the Federal Reserve permitted these declines appears puzzling in light of the fact that Friedman highlighted the 1950s as the first decade in which the Federal Reserve had indicated that the behavior of the money supply was a criterion on which monetary policy decisions should be made. It may seem doubly puzzling that M1 declined when one considers that the Federal Reserve referred to this concept, and not to the M2 total that Friedman was emphasizing, as the "money supply."[230]

A large part of the resolution of this puzzle lies in the fact that the Federal Reserve viewed monetary aggregates as one of *many* criteria for use in policy making. In the late 1950s, some of these other criteria clashed with monetary aggregates in the signals they provided about financial conditions. This conflict likely tempered policy makers' inclination to regard the weakness of monetary growth as worrying. And the Federal Reserve System generally, although aware during the 1950s of Friedman's research, was unconvinced by his strong emphasis on the stock of money.[231]

Indeed, the Federal Reserve System viewed his work with great skepticism. Some of this skepticism was clear enough in the public record, as when the Federal Reserve Bank of Chicago published an unsigned article in 1958 noting the recent decline in the money supply. The article acknowledged that this decline might appear "of critical importance" to "those who regard money supply as a 'lead indicator' of business activity."[232] (Friedman was not named in the article, even though Chicago was his home town.)[233] But the article went on to play down the importance of the decline in the money stock. Rather, it contended that velocity was highly variable, so that implications for the economy of the behavior of monetary aggregates could not easily be drawn.

Other elements of the Federal Reserve's reaction to Friedman's work during the 1950s are better described as outright suspicion than as mere skepticism. A Federal Reserve Board internal report on monetary statistics in October 1959 contained an article by staff member Robert Einzig that stated: "Given the change in M which may occur, we know little about the relation between such a change and the change in the real magnitudes in the economy. The studies which have been made, mainly at the University of Chicago, are ordinarily aggregative in character, do not break out separate economic sectors, and may also suffer in their explanations of relationships from the defect of being committed to establish a convincing relationship between M and business activity before the data are consulted."[234]

It is just as well that this discussion of Friedman's work was kept internal. He would not have taken kindly either to the convoluted wording used to describe his work or to the implication about his research agenda. Few things were more guaranteed to cause Friedman to erupt than evaluations of his work that suggested that he had a predetermined conclusion ahead of carrying out an analysis. Friedman's 1957 study of consumer credit control proposal had been accompanied by a discussant's comment who took such a line. The discussant, who favored direct credit controls, claimed that Friedman's "conclusions are all but predetermined."[235] Later, in 1964, one of Friedman's academic critics, John Culbertson, put a sting in the tail of his seemingly heavily complimentary review of the *Monetary History*, by suggesting that Friedman's a priori views were driving the Friedman-Schwartz conclusions. Friedman considered bringing suit against Culbertson, before thinking better of it.[236]

Friedman regarded judgments such as those quoted above as impugning his motives as well as his integrity as a researcher. Some perspective on these accusations is given by remarks of Lyle Gramley, who served on the Federal Reserve Bank of Kansas City research staff from 1955 and subsequently moved to the Federal Reserve Board. Gramley observed that the Federal Reserve was, in retrospect, much too skeptical about Friedman's work: "we were pretty much all Keynesians at that time. We didn't have a lot of sympathy with it—less probably than we should have. So we were aware of what was going on [at the University of Chicago], but not paying an awful lot of close attention to it" (Lyle Gramley, interview, April 2, 2013). Gramley went on to date the main shift of views on money at the Federal Reserve Board to the mid- to late 1970s. As early as 1969, however, Gramley—in a talk given when he served on the Federal Reserve Board's senior staff—stated publicly that "the fields of monetary economics and stabilization policy, in my judgment, owe an enormous debt to Professor Friedman for insisting that the role of money as a determinant of national income be given more careful consideration than it was from the period of roughly 1935 to 1965."[237]

The monetary policy developments of the late 1950s would lead Friedman to view the Federal Reserve as having backtracked on its reemphasis on monetary aggregates. They would also lead him to intensify his complaint—which he had already voiced in the earliest years of post-Accord policy—that the Federal Reserve largely restricted its attention to observed interest rates in evaluating monetary conditions. Indeed, Friedman would complain at the close of the 1950s that both within and outside the Federal Reserve System the interest-rate-based approach to analyzing monetary policy held sway, with "complete neglect" of monetary growth.[238]

At this point in its history, the Federal Reserve was taking much criticism for the lack of clarity about the basis for monetary policy decisions. Critics on this score included Friedman as well as Clark Warburton (1958, 211), who expressed the wish that Federal Reserve Board officials "would tell us how the mass of data available to the Federal Reserve System is used in the formation of policy." Alluding to such criticisms, a Federal Reserve official had written in the aforementioned 1959 internal report, "let me point out that the Federal Reserve has explained in detail how it operates and the kinds of effects its actions have on the economy in numerous publications and public statements. For example: the article in the *Federal Reserve Bulletin*, March 1953, entitled 'Influence of Credit and Monetary Measures on Economic Stability,' and Ralph Young's [1958b] 'Tools and Processes of Monetary Policy,' published in *United States Monetary Policy*."[239]

In retrospect, it is clear that there is considerable merit in the view that during the 1950s the Federal Reserve put on the public record much information regarding its views of strategy and policy transmission. Apart from the items listed in the preceding quotation, official statements shedding light on policy strategy included the Federal Reserve Board's *Annual Report* (with its capsule summaries of the year's FOMC meetings) and speeches and testimony by senior staff and policy makers—most notably William McChesney Martin, who served as Federal Reserve chairman for almost nineteen years beginning on April 2, 1951.

The principal item that was notably absent from the public record during the 1950s was the text of the "Minutes" of FOMC meetings. In the 1950s, the "Minutes" were written in the form of a near-transcript.[240] At the time, they were intended to be permanently confidential (Romer and Romer 2002b, 16). For their *Monetary History*, Friedman and Schwartz wrote the account of developments in the 1950s without the benefit of access to the FOMC Minutes, for which the practice of public release (after a lag) began only in the mid-1960s (*Wall Street Journal*, December 20, 1993).

Warburton's 1958 discussion had conceded that the Federal Reserve had put onto the public record some relevant material about monetary policy strategy. He had singled out not the articles listed above but instead a Federal Reserve Bank of New York booklet, Roosa (1956). Warburton (1958, 211) regarded this book as providing to provide a "tantalizing clue" about the formation of monetary policy. That booklet was, in fact, concerned with tactical and operational aspects of Federal Reserve actions rather than the strategic considerations underlying monetary policy. An aside in the book, however, indicated that the financial aggregate with which the Federal Reserve was most concerned was bank credit, and that decisions about monetary policy boiled down to the question of what growth rate in bank credit policy makers were going to permit over a certain period.[241]

The notion that the Federal Reserve in the 1950s and 1960s attached more significance to bank credit than money-supply series accords with other evidence, including that in Rotemberg (2014), and also matches Friedman's later conclusion that, although they increased the coverage given to money in their statements, Federal Reserve officials in the 1950s and 1960s put more emphasis on credit series than on monetary aggregates.[242]

However, policy makers' focus on bank credit gives little insight into why money was allowed to decline in 1959–60. The 1950s were an era that preceded the advent of a major wholesale deposit market and the revival of a bank debenture market. Retail deposits (which formed the dominant, noncurrency, component of Friedman and Schwartz's M2 concept) were the overwhelming means by which commercial banks financed their loans and investments. Consequently, the growth rates of bank credit and (old) M2 largely moved together during the 1950s.

For Friedman, the reason the money stock was allowed to decline was to be found elsewhere, in a factor encapsulated in an observation Friedman made in 1968: "Mr. Martin is likely to think as much in terms of interest rates as in terms of the quantity of money" (*Dun's Review*, February 1968, 94). The fact that the post-Accord Federal Reserve, under Chairman Martin, used a short-term interest rate instrument led it, Friedman believed, to misjudge monetary policy stance between 1958 and 1960, and to neglect the more dependable metric of M2 growth.

In the late 1950s, the federal funds rate—which, after a long lull, was from the mid-1950s regaining its status as a key short-term interest rate in US financial markets—rose in total by about 300 basis points, from well below 1 percent in July 1958 to 4 percent in December 1959, before leveling off in the first quarter of 1960. Yet this 300 basis point rise was associated with a sequence of different patterns of (old) M2 growth: twelve-month M2 growth continued to increase until the start of 1959, by which time about half the 300 basis point funds rate increase had been completed, then it experienced a roughly 8 percentage point decline to mid-1960, continuing to fall after the federal funds rate had peaked.[243]

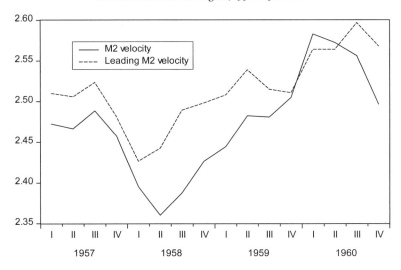

FIGURE 10.6. Velocity of M2 and leading velocity of M2, 1957:Q1–1960:Q4. *Sources*: Lothian, Cassese, and Nowak (1983) for data on old (pre-1980) M2; Federal Reserve Bank of St. Louis's FRED portal for data on nominal GDP.

Meltzer (2009a, 196) noted declining M1 growth in 1959 but suggested that this decline had little in the way of repercussions for economic activity, as Meltzer observed that velocity growth rose markedly in the same period. This account is largely accurate as a description of the arithmetic contributions of monetary growth and velocity growth to nominal income behavior. But it surely understates the significance of the change in monetary conditions associated with the decline in monetary growth. The reason is that—as Friedman would repeatedly emphasize during the 1970s and 1980s—contemporaneous velocity growth is misleading when there is a lag between changes in monetary growth and changes in nominal income growth.[244] On the interpretation of developments between 1959 and 1961 given in the *Monetary History* (along with that in other studies, such as Meigs 1972, 28, 105), the decline in monetary growth (whether measured by M1 or M2) in 1959 amounted to a monetary tightening that gave rise to the sharp downturns in nominal and real income growth in 1960 (declines brought out in figures 10.2 and 10.3). On this interpretation, too, the rise in velocity in 1959 was largely an artifact of the lag between movements in money and in nominal income. This conjecture is borne out by the fact that, as figure 10.6 shows, the rise in velocity is less marked when the velocity concept used is "leading velocity." Leading velocity (to use the terminology Friedman employed in *Wall Street Journal*, September 1, 1983) is defined as nominal income divided by a prior quarter's money stock, and in figure 10.8 this concept of velocity is defined as nominal GDP divided by the value two quarters earlier of M2 (old definition).[245] The two-quarter discontinuity between the numerator and denominator is meant to capture the average lag of nominal income behind money.

On Friedman's interpretation, therefore, the decline in monetary growth in 1959 that continued in 1960 reflected a sharp tightening in monetary conditions, in excess of the tightening the Federal Reserve had intended.[246] Friedman, according to an interview later given by his University of Chicago colleague Allen Wallis, made a prediction around April 1959 that there would be a recession in about a year's time, on the basis of the monetary contraction that was in process (*U.S. News and World Report*, February 13, 1961, 62).

In November and December 1959, according to Friedman's recollection in 1970, he was writing letters to friends "in high places" about the matter, including Arthur Burns, who had been out of government since 1956 but who kept in close touch with the administration.[247] By early 1960, Friedman and Burns shared a concern about the likelihood of recession. Both of them, Friedman later recalled, were worried about the extent to which the slowdown in monetary growth in 1959 might be making likely a recession for 1960 "which would be adverse both to the economic interests of the country and to Mr. Nixon's prospects for election."[248] In March 1960, Burns took the matter to Vice-President Richard Nixon, who was seeking the Republican Party's nomination for president.[249] Burns specifically highlighted to Nixon the weakness of M1 growth.[250] In April, Friedman visited Washington, DC, at the arrangement of Burns and other Nixon associates, in order to discuss the monetary situation in separate meetings with Secretary of the Treasury Robert Anderson and Chairman Martin.[251]

What Friedman recalled as "a long and very friendly talk with Bill Martin" concentrated on the fact that the money stock was falling. Martin told Friedman that the authorities did not intend for the quantity of money to be falling, but the chairman contended that the Federal Reserve's instruments gave them little scope to boost the money stock. To Friedman's dismay, Martin invoked the familiar aphorism about being able to lead a horse to water but not to make it drink. Martin challenged Friedman: "What do you want us to do—lower the discount rate?"[252] These were fighting words to Friedman. He had recently given a lecture series at Fordham University, which would see print in 1960 as what Friedman called "my little book, *A Program for Monetary Stability*."[253] That book had contained a long section titled "The Sufficiency of Open Market Operations."[254] Friedman recognized the reality that in practice central banks used both the discount window and open market operations as a means of supplying reserves to commercial banks, so that the two were tools operated in tandem—like two blades of scissors.[255] Martin saw that state of affairs as the natural one; in

June 1956, Martin had testified that "discount policy is closely interwoven with open-market policy."[256] But Friedman wanted to institute arrangements under which discounting's status as a method of routinely supplying reserves was brought to heel.

Consequently, Martin's question provoked a sharp reaction from Friedman, which the latter remembered as, "Oh no, Mr. Martin, why don't you raise the discount rate to 10 percent and get it out of the way, so that we can get rid of the disturbances that discounting brings into the system. What you should do is to go out and buy [securities] in the open market. If you just buy enough in the open market, you don't have to worry—the horses will drink."[257] The 10 percent rate value for the discount rate given by Friedman in this reply was probably offered facetiously, but he certainly did believe that, in a regime that had a discount-window function for the central bank, the discount rate should ordinarily be a penalty rate compared with market rates.[258] And, in retrospect, the 1950s through the 1980s appear to be a period in which the monetary base was reliably linked to both M1 and M2.[259] Consequently, Friedman's confidence that actions on total reserves would have been able to jump-start growth in bank deposits seems to have been justified. From his perspective, the authorities had produced the excessive tightening of monetary policy by relying on short-term interest rates rather than monetary aggregates to determine the appropriate degree of policy firming; and, once the monetary contraction occurred, the authorities did not appreciate how readily they could boost monetary growth with the tools at their disposal.

Friedman put his concerns about recent patterns in monetary growth in written form, in an April 1960 memorandum to Secretary Anderson. In this analysis, Friedman highlighted the fact that two key monetary aggregates had fallen from July 1959 to March 1960. In fact, he designated the two aggregates M1 and M2, making the memorandum one of the first occasions on which he used these labels for the aggregates.[260] Friedman's analysis stated that this was only the second episode in the postwar period in which M2 had fallen, and that this decline had troubling implications for the economy.[261]

At its meeting of April 1960, the Federal Open Market Committee discussed the money supply at length, and Chairman Martin expressed views at the meeting much like those he had given to Friedman. That is, Martin agreed that a higher money stock was desirable but expressed doubt that monetary policy tools could achieve this outcome.[262] The committee nevertheless resolved to take action to stimulate the money stock. In particular, open-market purchases, whose commencement Friedman and Schwartz would date to March 1960, proceeded over much of the rest of the year.[263]

Friedman's verdict on Federal Reserve policy in this episode was mixed.

On the one hand, he would cite the early-1960 period as one in which Federal Reserve actions intensified the decline in monetary growth.[264] In this connection, he would bluntly refer, a couple of years after the episode, to the "exceedingly inept monetary management at the end of 1959 and early 1960."[265] On the other hand, he and Schwartz would take "the sharp reversal of monetary policy in March 1960" as an event that eventually arrested the decline in the money stock.[266] The Federal Reserve Bank of St. Louis's adjusted monetary base series (seasonally adjusted) registers a decline in the early months of 1960, and its twelve-month growth rate troughs in May 1960. This weakness is then followed by a slow pickup in the series. Over the same period, the federal funds rate underwent a major decline. As noted earlier, M2 growth also turned around during 1960. So did the growth of M1—whose negative growth rates had received attention in the press in the middle of the year.[267]

The recession that Friedman had predicted as a result of the prior monetary tightening did come to pass. It is dated by the NBER as taking place following an April 1960 cyclical peak and culminating in a January 1961 cyclical trough. The recession was described by Friedman and Schwartz as "extremely brief and mild."[268] Indeed, on modern real GDP data, the decline in output in the course of the recession was a little over 1 percent.[269]

Its mildness notwithstanding, the recession was, in Friedman's evaluation, a sufficiently adverse event to be decisive for the result of the US presidential election. Friedman stressed that many events, including a predominantly poorly received presentation by Richard Nixon in his television debate with John F. Kennedy, had played a role in affecting the election result, and that, in view of Kennedy's narrow margin of victory, an alternative outcome for any one of these events could have tipped the scales. But the recession, together with the tight monetary policy that precipitated it, was one of the factors that Friedman saw as making a difference to the election result. The economic recovery of the late 1950s had been "choked to death early" because "money was tightened up unduly early," Friedman later judged.[270] The recession that began in 1960 underlay Friedman's remark, "I've often said that there is little doubt that it was William McChesney Martin who elected John F. Kennedy President of the United States."[271]

Notes

Introduction

1. This study comprises two volumes, volume 1 and volume 2. However, references to "this book" in what follows are to volume 1 and volume 2 combined.

2. Even the literature considered in this book is mainly confined to items written before 2013.

3. In the meantime, extensive analysis and discussions of Friedman's participation in 1973–2006 US economic debate are available in E. Nelson (2007, 2008a, 2016).

4. Similar reasoning led to the omission from this book of coverage of Friedman's views on the role of foreign aid for economic development (Friedman 1958f, 1961e).

5. Along similar lines, Friedman's "starve the beast" perspective on fiscal policy receive only incidental coverage in this book. The evolution of Friedman's perspective was covered in some detail in E. Nelson (2009b). Furthermore, Friedman's support for indexation of contracts, although voiced by him early on, achieved its greatest prominence after 1972 and so is not given a detailed treatment in this book. It is covered in E. Nelson (2018). Coverage of Friedman's various proposals regarding the marketing of government debt is also deferred to a later study.

Conventions Used in This Book

1. Throughout this book, "Romer and Romer" refers to Christina Romer and David Romer, unless otherwise indicated.

2. An exception is made in the small number of cases, which include Friedman (1973c), in which there was no credited interviewer and in which Friedman was listed in the publication as the article's author, even though the article was published in question-and-answer format.

Chapter One

1. The published record of the hearing gave only five individuals on the witness list, but that list omitted the Treasury general counsel, Randolph Paul, who participated heavily in the proceeding.

2. The *New York Times* report on the hearing gave Ruml's position only as "chairman of the New York Federal Reserve Bank" (*New York Times*, August 20, 1942), while Jim Powell (2003, 246) described him as "Federal Reserve Bank chairman" and gave the Macy's affiliation as a subsidiary position. In contrast, the witness list for the published version of the hearing (Committee on Finance 1942a) gave Ruml the sole affiliation of "R. H. Macy,

Co., Inc." This convention seems preferable, as the references to a job title that includes the words "Federal Reserve" and "chairman" could easily be misinterpreted as implying that Ruml was a monetary policy decision maker and sat on the Federal Open Market Committee, which he did not. The position of chair of the Federal Reserve Bank of New York is not a monetary policy–making position. The Reserve Banks, being quasi-private institutions, have a board of directors, including a chair, whose members' main occupations are typically in the private sector. The position of the Reserve Bank chair is accordingly very dissimilar to that of the Reserve Bank president, who sits on the Federal Open Market Committee.

3. From Friedman's remarks in Instructional Dynamics Economics Cassette Tape 69 (March 12, 1971). Chapter 6 below discusses in detail Friedman's perspective on the Fisher relationship between nominal interest rates and inflation.

4. From Friedman's remarks of April 8, 1981, in Friedman, Porter, Gruen, and Stammer (1981, 8). For similar remarks, see his answer (during a February 6, 1978, appearance) recorded in the video series *Milton Friedman Speaks* (episode 7, "Is Tax Reform Possible?," p. 26 of transcript); his *Newsweek* column of July 24, 1978; Friedman and Friedman (1985, 53); O'Driscoll et al. (1997, 8); and the quotation from Friedman in *New York Times*, November 17, 2006, B10.

5. Committee on Finance (1942a, 15). Friedman's initial interjection is on p. 13.

6. Committee on Finance (1942a, 56).

7. Committee on Finance (1942a, 56).

8. Committee on Finance (1942a, 56–57).

9. Joint Economic Committee (1995, 54).

10. Joint Economic Committee (1995, 54).

11. Joint Economic Committee (1995, 54–55).

12. Joint Economic Committee (1995, 55).

13. Joint Economic Committee (1995, 70).

14. Friedman (1958a, 24).

15. From the end of 1992, Friedman can be regarded as largely outside the research world (after tapering off his research activity over the prior two decades), and it is also from around this time that he ceased being a close observer of monetary developments.

16. Newman (1954) provides a convenient snapshot of the profession's perception of Friedman at this time.

17. Friedman (1957a). This work is discussed in chapter 5.

18. The quotation is from American Economic Association (1952, 710).

19. Friedman (1962a) and Friedman and Schwartz (1963a). A strong case can be made that the early 1960s saw not two but three contributions from Friedman that commanded the profession's attention, as Friedman and Meiselman (1963) provoked considerable commentary and debate on publication. See chapter 12.

20. *Time*, December 19, 1969. The momentous occasion on which Friedman "made the cover of *Time*" was noted in Dornbusch and Fischer (1978, 513); but it is not accurately recorded in a 2007 biography of Friedman, which incorrectly gives the *Time* cover story on Friedman as having appeared in *Fortune* magazine (see Ebenstein 2007, 180, 274).

21. This statement is based on an accounting by the present author that counts a book as authored by Friedman if it was in English and if his name appeared on the cover, and after excluding cases in which he only contributed a foreword or introduction. Friedman and Schwartz's (1965) *The Great Contraction* is treated as a distinct book from the *Monetary History* (despite being primarily a reprint of the *Monetary History's* chapter 7) because

of its additions of an authors' introduction and glossary. Pamphlets that were retailed as books (for example, in being assigned an ISBN number, being offered for sale, and being kept in print via new impressions), such as Friedman (1970a), are regarded as books in this accounting. Second or later impressions of a book are not counted as new books, but Friedman (1976a) and Friedman and Friedman (1985) are treated as distinct from Friedman (1962b) and Friedman and Friedman (1984), respectively, on the grounds that, in both cases, the new version of the book included a slight change in title and the inclusion of new content in the text. Finally, for the purpose of this count, Friedman and Friedman (1980) is classified as a 1979 book: although the hardback edition of this book is conventionally cited as published in 1980, its copyright page lists both the years 1979 and 1980, and the book reached US bookstores before the end of 1979.

22. Brunie (2007); also Charles H. Brunie interview, July 15, 2013.

23. See Friedman (1962b, 1976a).

24. As Brittan (2005, 292) perceptively observed, "there is no systematic treatise—only some written-up lecture notes—outlining Friedmanite economics or even Friedmanite monetary theory." And, as noted, even the lecture notes that Brittan alluded to (that is, Friedman 1962b, 1976a) pertained only to price theory.

25. The absence of a laid-out theoretical framework from the *Monetary History* has been noted often over the years, including by Meltzer (1965) and Romer and Romer (2013a). Bordo and Rockoff (2013a, 61) indicate that Friedman (1956a) provided the theoretical framework for the *Monetary History*. But one of the main concerns of Friedman and Schwartz (1963a), as noted by Friedman and Schwartz (1982a, 407), was with the dynamic interaction between money and real output. Friedman (1956a) cannot be considered to have provided an adequate theoretical basis regarding this concern because that study developed a theory for the demand for money in an environment that was valid under different assumptions about price adjustment (and so might be consistent with no effect of money on output at any horizon). As shown in the chapters that follow, it would be more accurate to state that a theoretical framework for Friedman and Schwartz (1963a) was provided by Friedman's 1950s writings as a whole, of which the money-demand material in Friedman (1956a) was only part. The fact that Friedman's (1956a) money-demand equation can be considered only part of a theory necessary to study money/income relations was also stressed by Benjamin Friedman (1986, 454).

26. Among the familiar aspects of Friedman's monetarism that are not to be found in the Friedman (1969b) collection are the use of the dictum (discussed in chapter 7 below) "inflation is always and everywhere a monetary phenomenon"; any explicit presentation of the equation of exchange; the rule of thumb that the lag in response of economic activity to monetary policy actions is about six to nine months; and his 1960s contributions to the debate about the comparative effectiveness of monetary policy and fiscal policy.

27. See Friedman (1970b) and R. Gordon (1974a). For a detailed discussion, see chapter 14 below.

28. See Friedman (1970a).

29. Friedman (1973a, 4). At the time Friedman wrote, he was speculating about the likely contents of the ninth edition of Samuelson's text, the eighth edition (Samuelson 1970a) being the most recent to have appeared. Friedman and Schwartz (1963b, 32) had earlier quoted the third edition (Samuelson 1955, 224) to provide a representation of a nonmonetary view of cyclical fluctuations. See also E. Nelson (2005a) and chapter 4 below for analysis of Samuelson's evolving views on monetary issues.

Ebenstein (2007, 156–57) notes the increased role given to monetary policy in successive editions of Samuelson's text. Ebenstein does not, however, acknowledge Friedman's own commentary on those changes to Samuelson's treatment, and Ebenstein incorrectly states that Samuelson made no reference to Friedman's work when altering his text's coverage of monetary matters. Furthermore, Ebenstein gives the wrong flavor of the contrast between the Friedman and Samuelson positions by implying that Friedman would have dissented from the notion that monetary policy is no panacea for economic stabilization, and by failing to consider the treatment given in Samuelson's textbook to the topic of inflation.

30. Dornbusch and Fischer (1978, 520).

31. As Samuelson's was a principles text and Dornbusch and Fischer's a macroeconomics text, the preceding juxtaposition of the two books might be challenged. However, Dornbusch and Fischer did produce a principles text (Fischer and Dornbusch 1983). That textbook featured the same contrast in its coverage of Friedman and Samuelson: an eleven-line index entry for Friedman, and a single page reference for Samuelson's index entry.

32. Blanchard and Summers (1986, 15).

33. At the end of the 1980s, another paper appeared in *NBER Macroeconomics Annual* that was to become very well known; in this case, the authors not only explicitly cited Friedman but referred to him and Schwartz in the paper's title. See Romer and Romer (1989).

34. Bernanke (1986, 49).

35. Friedman (1953a).

36. Friedman (1955a, 402). Likewise, in Instructional Dynamics Economics Cassette Tape 182 (December 1975), Friedman remarked of labor economics, "I'm no expert in this field."

37. Shimer (2010, ix) notes: "Lucas and Rapping's (1969) theory of intertemporal substitution in labor supply is the starting point for any modern analysis of employment fluctuations, including the Real Business Cycle (RBC) model and the New Keynesian model." In light of this observation, it is noteworthy that Lucas and Rapping (1969, 729) observed: "To the best of our knowledge, Friedman [1962b] was the first to suggest the empirical usefulness of the permanent-transitory wage-rate distinction when studying the supply of labor." K. Clark and Summers (1982, 828) likewise credited Friedman with "perhaps the first statement of the timing hypothesis," and they quoted the relevant passage (from Friedman 1962b, 205).

38. It was in the context of a discussion of the natural rate of unemployment that Friedman was the first name mentioned in chapter 1 of Shimer (1996), a dissertation in the area of labor economics. See Shimer (1996, 8).

39. Schwartz (1998, 5).

40. See Walters (1987, 426–27).

41. *Car and Driver*, September 1981, 83; *Professional Engineer*, June 1982, 9. For the references to Friedman in the books just mentioned, see Dormen and Zussman (1984, 66) and Swenson (1981, 100), respectively.

42. *Playboy*, February 1973; *People Weekly*, April 5, 1976; *Penthouse*, January 1987.

43. See *Los Angeles Times*, November 7, 1977; see also the AP wire joint photo of the three in *Irish Times*, November 9, 1977.

44. This episode, along with Friedman's role in the story line, was discussed in Stallings (1991, 108).

45. See also E. Nelson (2009a, 2009b) for a consideration of Friedman's celebrity status in the United Kingdom.

46. This was an impression that Friedman's memoirs with his wife, *Two Lucky People* (Friedman and Friedman 1998), did not altogether dispel, since, in the view of Anna Schwartz and others (including the present author), those memoirs had far too much travelogue content (with extremely detailed accounts of the Friedmans' journeys around the world) and too little coverage of economic research and economic policy. The country-specific books mentioned in the text are Friedman (1975i, 1990a) and Feldberg, Jowell, and Mulholland (1976).

47. See E. Nelson (2007) for a detailed discussion.

48. See Taylor (2001, 102) and Paul Samuelson's remarks in *Newsweek*, October 25, 1976a. Much earlier, the "economist's economist" label had been applied to Friedman by the *Economist* (May 8, 1954), in reviewing Friedman (1953b).

49. In *Newsweek*, September 21, 1981.

50. The quotation is from Friedman (1993, 171).

51. A consideration of more technical aspects of Friedman's work gives rise to further seeming paradoxes. He was an innovator in the area of developing test statistics, yet he came to shun formal statistical testing in empirical work. He was one of the developers of adaptive expectations, yet he was distrustful of the use of lagged dependent variables in empirical studies.

52. Instructional Dynamics Economics Cassette Tape 193 (June 1976, part 2).

53. For further discussion, see chapter 8, including the quotation from John Taylor given in that chapter.

54. For a treatment that, in contrast, puts more emphasis on Friedman's status as a critic of the theory of imperfect competition, see Laidler (2012). Chapters 4 and 7 below explain why the present author regards Friedman as accepting key elements of monopolistic-competition theory and adopting a version of the theory in his own work.

55. See Taylor (2001, 120); and E. Nelson and Schwartz (2008a, 2008b).

Chapter Two

1. *Donahue*, NBC, April 25, 1984.

2. See Friedman and Friedman (1998, 25).

3. Leube (1987, xiii) described the degree Friedman received from Rutgers University as "a bachelor's degree in mathematics and economics," while Ebenstein (2007, 19) claimed it was a "bachelor's degree in economics," but neither of these was the title of the bachelor's degree conferred on Friedman. Both contemporary accounts and Friedman's later biographical data established that the formal name of the degree was a bachelor of arts, or AB (*New York Times*, June 11, 1932; Who's Who, Inc. 1976, 1080).

4. See CSPAN, November 20, 1994 (p. 6 of hard-copy transcript); Friedman and Friedman (1998, 29); and Parkin (1990, 97). Although Friedman described himself in Snowdon and Vane (1997, 193) as having been a joint major in mathematics and economics, in Friedman and Friedman (1998, 29) he gave the impression that his move to economics entailed dropping the mathematics major. The fact that, at his graduation ceremony, Friedman received awards for both economics and mathematics—see below—indicates that the latter impression was an incorrect one.

5. Idea Channel (1987). In Friedman (1976b, 434), however, he noted two non-economics career paths that he was considering during his Rutgers University years, namely actuarial studies and mathematics.

6. The teaching job was so temporary, in fact, that Jones did not list the Rutgers Univer-

sity position as prior employment in his 1970 and 1981 entries in the American Economic Association directory of members (American Economic Association 1970, 218; American Economic Association 1981, 216).

7. Friedman credited Burns and Jones with focusing him on economics on a number of occasions, including in Friedman (1976b, 434); G. Martin (1983, 52); and Friedman and Friedman (1998, xi, 33). Friedman indicated that he took "several" courses with Jones in G. Martin (1983, 52).

8. Jones completed his University of Chicago PhD only in 1949 (American Economic Association 1970, 218), after Friedman had joined the Department of Economics. As Jerry Jordan remarked in an interview for this book, "when Milton was at Chicago, Homer wrote his own dissertation under his former student. And years after that, Homer's wife, Alice, also wrote her dissertation under Friedman in Chicago. So they were very close, longtime friends, going back to when Milton was an undergraduate" (Jerry Jordan, interview, June 5, 2013). Indeed, one of the unusual aspects of Friedman's early years in the University of Chicago is that he was, in effect, in a teacher/adviser role in relation to one former teacher of his (Jones) while, once Friedman became a full professor in the department in 1948, the colleagues whom Friedman outranked included Lloyd Mints, who had taught the monetary-economics course Friedman had taken in the 1930s and who did not reach the position of full professor.

9. See Friedman (1976b, 434); G. Martin (1983, 53); and Friedman and Friedman (1998, xi, 33).

10. Jones's years as director of the Federal Reserve Bank of St. Louis's research department were given in American Economic Association (1981, 216). It also deserves note that when Homer Jones served as a chief in the Federal Deposit Insurance Corporation, he encouraged and authorized the research of Clark Warburton on money, discussed in the next chapter. (Warburton acknowledged Jones's encouragement of his research in a January 7, 1974, letter to Leland Yeager, held at the Clark Warburton papers, George Mason University. In addition, Warburton's son, the late Peter Warburton, wrote to the present author in a letter dated May 27, 2007: "Clark was always pleased that his former FDIC boss Homer Jones carried Clark's research to St. Louis.")

11. Friedman and Friedman (1998, xi). In an October 1999 interview (quoted in J. Martin 2001, 30), Friedman qualified this description somewhat by saying that Burns was "almost a surrogate father." Friedman (1976b, 433) would remark on the oddity that during his undergraduate schooling he regarded Homer Jones (1906-86) as much more senior than himself when Jones was only twenty-four. As Friedman essentially acknowledged in Friedman (1987c) and Friedman and Friedman (1998, 29-30), a similar observation applies to Burns (1904-87), who was not yet out of his twenties when Friedman completed his undergraduate studies.

12. See chapters 3 and 4 below for a detailed discussion.

13. Friedman (1967a, 1).

14. In addition to being a dubious way of proceeding, Breit and Ransom's (1971, 226) attempt to map between Friedman's own attributes and those of his specific teachers is further marred by their incorrect suggestion (not adequately corrected in later editions) that Friedman did not take classes from Wesley Mitchell.

15. Friedman (1972a, 937).

16. Friedman (1972a, 937).

17. Friedman (1972a, 941).

18. See, for example, Friedman (1984a, 10).

19. See, for example, Friedman (1976c, 1977a) and Instructional Dynamics Economics Cassette Tape 122 (June 6, 1973). Friedman's discussion of Smith's views focused predominantly on Adam Smith's (1776) *The Wealth of Nations*.

20. Groenewegen (2003, 22) interpreted Viner's (1927) paper on Adam Smith as a study that showed Smith's belief in "fairly extensive" state intervention in the economy. In contrast, it is difficult to believe that many would see Friedman's own analyses of Smith as doing so. Also worthy of note in this connection is a book-length study of Smith's views by Donald Winch. Winch's (1978) interpretation of Smith has been contrasted with Friedman's own interpretation on a number of occasions (for example, in Teichgraeber 1979, 567; and in the *Listener*, March 6, 1980). Winch—a student of Viner's during the latter's years at Princeton University (see Winch 1981, 1983)—cited Viner (1927) as a study that, like Winch's, challenged "the conventional portrait of Smith as an advocate of strictly limited or minimal government" (Winch 1978, 14).

21. CSPAN, November 20, 1994 (p. 7 of hard-copy transcript). Likewise, in Friedman and Friedman (1998, 24) Friedman observed that reading "played as important a role in my education as the schools that I attended." Although these words were written with reference to Friedman's high school years, they also constitute a plausible description of his later education.

22. Friedman (1936, 532). On the fact that Friedman never met Pigou, even when Friedman visited Cambridge University during the 1953–54 academic year, see Friedman and Friedman (1998, 53).

23. Friedman (1976b, 434).

24. Quoted in Breit and Ransom (1971, 226), who sourced it to a letter they received from Friedman dated June 22, 1967. Friedman made similar remarks in Friedman (1971a, 247), in an obituary for Viner (unsigned, but confirmed in R. D. Friedman 1976a, 29, as penned by Friedman). Friedman also paid tribute to Viner's class in the acknowledgments of Friedman (1949a, 463), in which, however, he was more specific about ideas he had picked up from that class, while Friedman (1986a, 83) credited Viner with providing a more unified framework for economic analysis than Friedman had hitherto been exposed to.

25. Schwartz (1998, 5).

26. See Friedman's remarks in Friedman (1976b, 434) and G. Martin (1983, 53).

27. See Friedman (1986a, 82) and also Friedman's remarks in Hammond (1989, 6).

28. See Friedman (1976b, 433–34) and Friedman and Friedman (1998, 31).

29. Joseph Burns noted that his father's copy of Marshall's *Principles*, still in Joseph Burns's possession, had page-by-page annotations made by Arthur Burns (Joseph Burns, personal communication, December 18, 2014). Friedman in Friedman and Friedman (1998, 30) credited Arthur Burns with introducing him to Marshall's *Principles*.

30. Parkin (1990, 97). See also Friedman (1987c) and Friedman and Friedman (1998, 30). According to R. D. Friedman (1976a, 29), Burns's seminar class had only three students in it; and according to Friedman and Friedman (1998, 30), the class ended up consisting of only Friedman and one other student. Although the dissertation work was presented as a learning tool, Friedman (1986a, 81) noted that Burns was actually still finalizing his dissertation during this period. The dissertation was later published as Burns (1934), and the book version was cited by Friedman and Schwartz (1963a, 38, 43; 1982a, 588).

31. See Burns (1929, 562). For Friedman's own identification of Keynes as a quantity theorist, up to and perhaps beyond 1936, see, for example, Friedman (1972a, 933) and *Wall Street Journal*, August 31, 1984.

32. Friedman made this observation in the 1960s. See Friedman (1968d, 15) and his letter in *Time* magazine (February 4, 1966). See also chapter 12 below.

33. For example, Burns (1965, 58, 59), like many other pieces written by Burns, used "to be sure" as a synonym for "certainly." Friedman seldom used "to be sure" in this sense, except when quoting others (as, for example, in Instructional Dynamics Economics Cassette Tape 127, August 15, 1973; and in Friedman 1976a, 349). One rare instance in which Friedman used the phrase himself was in *Newsweek*, April 11, 1977.

34. In the case of Burns, the characterization became famous via Koopmans's (1947) review, "Measurement without Theory," of the Burns-Mitchell business cycles study. In the case of Friedman, see, for example, Allan Meltzer's statement that Friedman "never developed a model" (in McCallum 1998, 250). Insofar as Meltzer's position was that Friedman did not consolidate his various economic positions into a formal model, the present author would not dispute Meltzer's statement. But, as argued in this book, and as Friedman himself observed, a detailed implicit model underlay his work during his monetarist period.

35. See chapter 5.

36. See, in particular, Friedman (1976d). Among the many places in which Burns emphasized the longer-term interest rate was Burns (1977a, 724).

37. For more on Friedman and religion, see the next chapter. Burns's religious faith was noted in profiles that appeared in the press while he was Federal Reserve chairman (for example, in *Time*, December 26, 1977). Burns's son Joseph recalled of his father: "He was religious in the sense that he read and knew the Bible quite well. He read it, I think, nightly. He didn't go to the synagogue often. He went on the high holidays and maybe gave a lecture or two during the year. But I would say that he was religious in his own way, a very personal way" (Joseph Burns, interview, September 12, 2013).

38. See, for example, G. Martin (1983, 53); CSPAN, November 20, 1994 (p. 7 of hard-copy transcript); and Friedman and Friedman (1998, 33). In the last of these references, Brown University's offer was clarified as pertaining to study in applied mathematics.

39. See, respectively, Friedman (1986a, 82) and Friedman and Friedman (1998, 33).

40. On the fact that Great Depression was a factor motivating Friedman's study of economics, see, for example, R. D. Friedman (1976a, 28–29); Friedman (1986a, 82–83); and Milton Friedman's remarks in CSPAN, November 20, 1994 (p. 7 of hard-copy transcript). In Parkin (1990, 97), in contrast, Friedman attributed even his initial taking up of economics study at the undergraduate level in 1930 to a desire to understand the emerging economic downturn.

41. The designation of the master's degree as AM rather than MA is a University of Chicago convention; indeed the alumni periodical *University of Chicago Magazine* routinely referred to Friedman over the years as "Milton Friedman, AM '33" (see, for example, the issue for January/February 2007). Friedman sometimes used the more conventional "MA" terminology for his degree: for example, in his entry for the 1970 American Economic Association directory and elsewhere (Friedman 1968h, 202; American Economic Association 1970, 143; see also R. D. Friedman 1976a, 31). However, in some other autobiographical profiles that he supplied, Friedman used the "AM" designation (for example, Marquis Who's Who 1976, 1080). Notwithstanding the difference in abbreviation, the University of Chicago's full name for the degree was the same as that used in other institutions: master of arts (see, for example, Friedman 1933).

42. One account that did state the chronology correctly was Rose Friedman's profile of

her husband in the little-known (and archaically titled) periodical the *Oriental Economist* (R. D. Friedman 1976a, 31). (At the start of 1986, the *Oriental Economist* changed its name to *Tokyo Business Today*.)

43. In the same spirit, Heukelom (2014, 40), in describing Friedman's position as of 1950, asserts that he had been "at the University of Chicago since the 1930s."

44. This is also true of the biographical sketches in G. Martin (1983, 49); and Leube (1987, xiv). The latter reference also erroneously gave Friedman's year of classes at Columbia University as calendar 1934 rather than academic year 1933-34.

45. Marquis Who's Who (1976, 1080). This could be a typographical error, but, if so, confusion arising from the error could have been avoided if the entry had provided a more detailed accounting of Friedman's other 1930s activities.

46. American Economic Association (1970, 143) and Blaug (1986, 291).

47. Walters (1987) presented this information after Anna Schwartz (in a letter to Walters dated June 10, 1985) corrected Walters's initial draft, which had given Friedman as being at the University of Chicago in 1932-35 and had omitted Friedman's 1933-34 year at Columbia University (see Anna Schwartz papers, Duke University). Even in the published version, Walters (1987, 422) pointed readers in the wrong direction by suggesting that Friedman's status as a Columbia University student was limited to the 1933-34 academic year; in so characterizing Friedman's activities, Walters neglected the years 1937-40, during which Friedman had a Columbia University affiliation and was carrying out the work that culminated in his Columbia University PhD in 1946. In fairness to Walters, however, it might be noted that Rose Friedman objected strongly in Friedman and Friedman (1998, 101) to the notion that Friedman should be categorized as a Columbia University student beyond the 1933-34 academic year. She may not have been counting the 1937-40 period on the grounds that (according to American Economic Association 1970, 246), Friedman's PhD supervisor, Simon Kuznets, had an NBER affiliation in those years but not a formal Columbia University affiliation. Another possibility is that Rose Friedman was drawing a distinction similar to that Friedman made on occasion (for example, in *California*, October 1984, 77; see also the *Margin*, January 1986, 4) between "graduate work" (by which Friedman apparently meant coursework and the taking of PhD preliminary examinations) and dissertation work, with only the former activity apparently corresponding to being a "student." In addition, Friedman may have not regarded himself as having been a student between 1937 and 1940 because he was paid a salary for the work with Kuznets in the late 1930s (*Margin*, January 1986, 4).

In the view of the present author, however, ordinary terminological convention demands that Friedman be regarded as a Columbia University student for the whole of the time he was completing his Columbia University PhD dissertation, and certainly for his on- or nearby-campus years up to 1940. Consequently, Becker's (1991a, 138) characterization that one element of Friedman's activities between the mid-1930s and the mid-1940s was that he "completed his studies at Columbia" seems an accurate one to the present author, even though it apparently constituted the sort of statement to which Rose Friedman took exception.

48. Friedman, Jones, Stigler, and Wallis (1935). The fact of Friedman's coeditor credit was sufficient for Congdon (1978, 15) to contend that Friedman was "well known at Chicago in the 1930s," an assessment that seems to be overstating the matter somewhat.

49. Friedman and Friedman (1998, 51). R. D. Friedman (1976a, 31) also provided this information in her little-circulated piece. Although the account in the Friedmans' memoirs clarified Friedman's activities in the 1930s in several respects, it did add confusion

on one matter, as Rose Friedman in Friedman and Friedman (1998, 50) stated that Milton Friedman returned to the University of Chicago from his Columbia University studies in "the fall of 1935." This should be 1934.

50. Although it did include some PhD studies at the University of Chicago, Friedman's Chicago credentials are certainly less straightforward than those of Patinkin, whose *Who's Who in Economics* 1986 entry (Blaug 1986, 665) read: "Born 1922, Chicago, IL, U.SA. . . . Degrees: B.A., M.A., Ph.D. [from] Univ. Chicago 1943, 1945, 1947."

51. In this connection, it is notable that Patinkin (1981a, 3) made a point both of stating that Friedman's University of Chicago qualification consisted of his 1933 master's degree and of (erroneously) indicating that Friedman's "return" to the university did not occur until Friedman became a member of the economics department in 1946.

52. Rose Friedman did not return to graduate studies, although Friedman and Friedman (1998, 572) noted that she later received an honorary doctorate from Pepperdine University. Rose Friedman's work would be important in putting Friedman (1962a) into publishable form; she also coauthored the later popular books with Friedman and made uncredited contributions to his other public policy writings (as acknowledged by him in Friedman and Friedman 1998, xii). In addition, she kept up with and shared his activities on such issues as education reform. The evidence suggests, however, that Rose Friedman did not keep close tabs on Friedman's economic research. For example, a characterization she gave of Friedman's research—that it applied mathematics and statistics to economic problems—was not accurate by the time Rose Friedman voiced it in 1976, being fifteen or more years out of date (Rose D. Friedman 1976a, 28; see also Walters 1987, 423, in which it was accurately noted that, in his research career beyond the 1940s, Friedman did *not* focus on the application of statistics to economics). Her questions to Friedman about his monetary views of inflation in Instructional Dynamics Economics Cassette Tape 127 (August 15, 1973), while incisive and appropriate for the interview format, were elementary. And her claim (accepted uncritically by Ebenstein 2007, 156) that Paul Samuelson was Friedman's major opposite number in the economics profession seems inappropriate in view of Samuelson's absence from much of the key Keynesian-monetarist debates in the research literature in the 1960s and 1970s. For Friedman's monetary work, the constant presence and source of collaboration (although she was living in another city—see chapter 4) was instead, of course, Anna Schwartz.

The preceding characterization, although based on other sources, seems to the present author consistent with Friedman's brief description of his collaboration with his wife in Friedman and Friedman (1998, xii). For further discussion, see chapter 11 below.

53. Friedman's *Who's Who in Economics* entry for 1986 (Blaug 1986, 291) gave his employment in 1937 to 1940 as consisting both of an NBER position and a post of part-time lecturer at Columbia University. Likewise, the biographical information on Friedman in NBC (1947a, i) listed him as having been "a part-time lecturer at Columbia University." See also Friedman (1970g, 434; 1971f, i; 1977b, 11; 1986a, 92).

This information means that discussions of Friedman's teaching career in some published profiles of Friedman are incorrect. The suggestion in a *New York Times* profile (January 25, 1970, 80) that Friedman did no teaching until he took up a position at the University of Wisconsin in 1940 was not accurate. Likewise, Medema's (2007, vii) statement that Friedman spent "much of the period from 1935 to 1946" outside academia apparently rests on counting the periods 1937-40 and 1943-46 as nonacademic employment when, in fact, Friedman had a Columbia University affiliation in both of these periods. (To this must be added the fact that the NBER had, during Friedman's period of early bureau employment, strong connections to Columbia University—as Laidler 2012, notes—not least via the presence of Arthur Burns and Wesley Mitchell at both institutions.) All told, then, Friedman had a teaching or other affiliation with universities for seven or eight of the twelve years from 1935 through 1946. Silk (1976, 54) was therefore correct to categorize Friedman's 1935 move as only a "brief leave from academia."

54. The quotation is from *Reason*, August 1977, 29. Likewise, in 1982, Friedman observed that "people seldom change their ideas after they get to the age of 25" (Friedman 1982a, 12)—although on another occasion he gave the cutoff age as "25 or 30" (*Open Mind*, PBS, May 31, 1977, p. 3 of transcript). There is something of a parallel between this rule of thumb and Mankiw's (1986, 141) observation that few people alter their views about the effects of monetary policy after age twenty-six. (Mankiw—presumably overgeneralizing somewhat from his own experience—took this age as corresponding to when one finishes graduate school. For Friedman, completion of graduate school took place closer to age twenty-eight, while the firming of his views on money took place at about age thirty-eight.)

55. Letter from Milton Friedman to the author, July 16, 1991.

56. *Meet the Press*, NBC, June 28, 1970, p. 3 of transcript.

57. See Friedman (1976e, xxi). See also Friedman's remarks in the *Margin*, January 1986, 4.

58. See Rose Friedman's remarks in Friedman and Friedman (1998, 38). For details on the monetary-theory course that Milton Friedman and Rose Director took, see Leeson (2003a) and Steindl (2004). (Although Steindl's paper had the sweeping title "Friedman and Money in the 1930s," it concerned mainly Friedman's University of Chicago education in monetary matters, rather than Friedman's own contemporaneous views on 1930s monetary developments.)

59. See Kneeland et al. (1939). Friedman had left the Study of Consumer Purchases project in 1937, and he later indicated that he did not participate in any of the data work after that date (Friedman 1957a, ix). Furthermore, Friedman did not purchase a copy of the *General Theory* until 1938 (see Snowdon and Vane 1997, 194). The extent to which the final 1939 report on consumer expenditures reflected Friedman's views is therefore unclear. But Friedman felt sufficiently comfortable with the published 1939 version to cite it in a 1941 Treasury staff memorandum (Shoup, Friedman, and Mack 1941, 31) and to list it, in the postwar years, in his official bibliography.

60. See, for example, Patinkin (1973a) and Rayack (1987, 108-9).

61. See Friedman (1976b, 434) and Friedman and Friedman (1998, 32).

62. See chapter 4.

63. This is what Friedman emphasized in his retrospective accounts, such as Friedman (1972a, 937).

64. See especially Friedman (1970a, 1970b, 1972a). Friedman therefore distinguished between the emphasis that Keynes, in analyzing slumps, placed on deficient demand—an emphasis that Friedman felt was valid but not special to Keynes—and the arguments that Keynes advanced about the ineffectiveness of monetary policy, which Friedman regarded as special contributions on Keynes's part, but which Friedman did not regard as empirically valid.

65. On the impression that Fisher's work left on Friedman, see the discussion in chapter 6.

66. Long as Friedman's career in publishing research was, some sources have incorrectly stretched it back even further. Walters (1987, 422) gave Friedman (1935a) as published in 1934, and so did the official Friedman bibliography as printed in the 1987 volume *The Essence of Friedman* (Valentine 1987, 529). Correspondingly, it is unlikely that

Friedman was twenty-one when he drafted the challenge to Pigou, as one profile (*New York Times*, January 25, 1970, 23) claimed. Friedman dated the drafting of the critique to the 1934–35 academic year (Friedman and Friedman 1998, 52), which would put his likely age at twenty-two during its composition.

67. See *New York Times*, January 25, 1970, 23; and G. Stigler (1988, 24).

68. Accordingly, Friedman signed off the article with a University of Chicago affiliation (Friedman 1935a, 163). Page 159 of this article indicated that his work for what became H. Schultz (1938) led to his critique of Pigou.

69. As Friedman (1935a, 151) indicated, he focused his critique on a revised version of the Pigou article that appeared in Pigou (1932).

70. Friedman (1935a, 153).

71. *Firing Line*, syndicated January 8, 1968, p. 2 of transcript. Friedman (1961a, 259) had made the same distinction.

72. Patinkin (1965a, 114). Markowitz (1952, 151) is also an early reference that indicated an explicit preference for the terminology "utility of wealth" over both "utility of money" and "utility of income." The drift away from the Marshallian terminology was also manifested in the work of Arnold Harberger, who took Friedman's Price Theory course in 1947 and who later regularly taught price theory himself when, as a member of the University of Chicago's economics department, he offered a price-theory course in a different part of the year from Friedman's course. Harberger (1954, 82) used the Marshallian "marginal utility of money" terminology, but during the next quarter century Harberger switched to "marginal utility of wealth or income" (Harberger 1978, S111).

73. See B. Klein (1974, 933). Klein had made a similar admonition in the dissertation proper (B. Klein 1970, 10).

74. See, for example, Friedman and Savage (1948, 280, 283, 294); Friedman (1949a, 477); the February 27, 1950, letter from Friedman to George Stigler in Hammond and Hammond (2006, 109, 110, 111); and Friedman (1962b, 68).

75. Friedman (1976a, 38). Page 15 of this version of *Price Theory* did employ the old terminology while noting that it was Marshall's usage. Page 75, however, used the old terminology without a caveat.

76. A similar defense of Pigou's method was advanced by A. Brown and Deaton (1972, 1205).

77. H. Schultz (1938, 569). These chapters were, however, mostly written in the first-person singular (see, for example, pp. 602 and 603), and Friedman received no formal coauthor credit on the title page of the book. Although acknowledged, Friedman's contribution to the volume was evidently not set out clearly enough, for a 1966 text that was written by a former student in the University of Chicago Price Theory course and that went out of its way to draw on and cite Friedman's work in the area of price theory discussed H. Schultz's (1938) "pioneer research" without mentioning Friedman (Gisser 1966, 69).

For his part, Friedman's participation in the making of the Schultz book did not restrain him from referring a few years later to Schultz's "brilliant presentation of indifference analysis in *The Theory and Measurement of Demand*" (see W. A. Wallis and Friedman 1942, 175).

78. Kenneth Arrow, interview, December 7, 2013. As Arrow's remarks implied, Friedman was not very impressed by Schultz's command of technical matters. In conversations in the postwar decades with Marc Nerlove, whose father had known Schultz well, Friedman would recall working with Schultz. Nerlove recalled (personal communication, September 9, 2014): "Schultz, he said, kept getting things wrong as he, Schultz, was working

on his monumental *Theory and Measurement of Demand*. Friedman described himself as a brash kid … and was rather abrasive in telling Schultz off, but Schultz was a glutton for the truth. Friedman said that although, at the time, he rather despised Schultz, in later life he came to admire him for his stubborn quest to get things right. He, Friedman, would consider every question and any idea, no matter how dumb, carefully without dismissing it out of hand. He learned that from Schultz."

An early instance in which the negative aspects of Friedman's assessment of Schultz reached print was Reder (1982, 4), whose discussion communicated Friedman's low rating for Schultz's technical abilities. Friedman himself later publicly stated (in Hammond 1992, 98) his view that Schultz was not "very smart." See also Friedman's related remarks on the aforementioned matters in Hammond (1989, 14-15).

79. In particular, Schultz's discussion of Friedman's 1935 critique used (on p. 111) the word "rationale," a word Friedman himself very seldom employed (the rare cases of his doing so including his *Newsweek* column of May 5, 1969). Furthermore, Hendry and Morgan (1995, 34) noted, on the basis of Schultz's pre-1938 work, that "Schultz is not statistically sophisticated," citing in particular Schultz's tendency to regard estimated relationships as holding exactly in the absence of measurement error. The 1938 monograph contains a couple of remarks to this effect, further raising the likelihood that the book's text is—the explicitly coauthored chapters aside—solely from Schultz's hand.

80. H. Schultz (1938) was published in July 1938; Friedman turned twenty-six at the very end of that month.

81. Likewise, A. Powell (1966, 668) characterized Friedman (1935a) as concerned with "the exact implications" of Pigou's procedure.

82. See, for example, Friedman (1970c).

83. In particular, P. Phillips (1991, 458) observed: "Approximations are often said to be the soul of science."

84. See, for example, Friedman and Schwartz (1982a, 210, 214-15, 354), and Friedman (1988a, 225).

85. See H. Schultz (1938, 614) as well as the subsequent discussion (614-19). This solo-authored 1934 paper is not to be confused with the later—basically wholly verbal—analysis of indifference curves in W. A. Wallis and Friedman (1942).

86. Likewise, Becker's (2007, 183) appraisal—even though explicitly focused on Friedman's contributions to microeconomics—skipped Friedman's 1935-36 publications and described Friedman (1937a) as "his first important article."

87. Ekelund, Furubotn, and Gramm (1972a). This collection also included a bibliography (95-106) that cited (on p. 98) Friedman (1949a, 1957a, 1962b) and Friedman and Savage (1948), but not the 1935-36 Friedman papers.

88. Lucas (2001, 8) pointed to Samuelson's discussion as a case in which Samuelson took issue with Friedman. But, in putting forward the *Foundations* passage as one in which Samuelson challenged University of Chicago positions, Lucas may have been taking a somewhat ironical perspective. In particular, Lucas's discussion may have been intended to underscore the notion that very early discussions provided by Samuelson's of Friedman's work become more notable when their subsequent activities in the profession (especially the reputation they acquired as sparring partners) are considered. At the time when Samuelson likely was writing *Foundations*, Friedman was not a University of Chicago economics department teacher, and Samuelson had spent more years at the University of Chicago (as a student) than Friedman. (Friedman emphasized Samuelson's longer exposure to University of Chicago classes when he observed in 1969: "Both Profes-

sor Samuelson and I have degrees from the University of Chicago. Indeed, he has two, and I only have one" [from *The Great Economics Debate*, PBS, WGBH Boston, May 22, 1969]. Friedman here may have been taking Samuelson as having picked up the master's degree that, as noted in chapter 4 below, advanced undergraduate students at the University of Chicago often proceeded toward in this era. Alternatively, he may have been including Samuelson's honorary doctorate in law from the University of Chicago, which Samuelson received on May 4, 1961: see https://convocation.uchicago.edu/traditions/honorary -degree-recipients/past-honorary-degree-recipients/.) These considerations imply that Samuelson was therefore unlikely, at the time of writing *Foundations*, to be inclined to view Friedman as a prominent voice of the Chicago School.

Ebenstein (2007, 138), in quoting Lucas's discussion, takes for granted that Friedman would have stood by his 1935 paper, a presumption that is contrary both to Friedman's post-1936 statements on the matter and to the interpretation given here.

89. Friedman and Friedman (1998, 53), quoting Friedman's correspondence with Pigou during Friedman's 1953–54 visit to Cambridge University.

90. Georgescu-Roegen (1988, 27). This event likely took place in the late 1960s, as, from Georgescu-Roegen's description, it would appear that he was presenting a version of Georgescu-Roegen (1970).

Friedman's second thoughts about his early work did not, however, prevent him from making it known to later researchers working in related research areas. In citing Friedman (1935a), A. Powell (1966, 668) thanked Friedman for drawing his attention to the 1935 article.

91. Friedman (1933). This dissertation was a revision of material Friedman had written as an undergraduate (R. D. Friedman 1976a, 31).

92. Friedman and Schwartz (1963a, 411) and Friedman (1962c, 20) criticized the economic-research literature of the early 1930s for being preoccupied with problems other than the economic and financial crises that were in process. And in *Fortune* (June 1, 1967, 148), Friedman would praise the example of Friedrich Hayek, who suspended his work on capital theory to write the more immediately policy-relevant *The Road to Serfdom* (Hayek 1944).

93. The culmination of Friedman's studies of spurious results was Friedman (1992a), a paper that has a good claim to being Friedman's last attempt to make a real contribution to the research literature. That 1992 paper highlighted a case in which a statistical property of least-squares estimation, and not economic phenomena, likely lay behind reported findings in the literature on cross-country economic growth. In effect, the paper highlighted a more recent case of the "regression fallacy" in operation than the example provided by Hotelling (1933), a paper to which Friedman's 1992 article paid homage. See S. Stigler (1996) for a discussion of Hotelling's paper and its demonstration of the regression fallacy.

On the other hand, Friedman's 1938 criticism of taking moving averages of the data sits uncomfortably with his later practice of doing so as part of implementing NBER statistical procedures.

94. Friedman (1938a, 454).

95. Friedman (1986c, 8).

96. See Friedman and Friedman (1998, 60–61) for Friedman's discussion of this period.

97. This was the affiliation given in Kneeland, Schoenberg, and Friedman (1936, 140). In Kneeland et al. (1939, iv), he was listed as being among the NRC's "Technical staff," with Kneeland in charge.

98. Kneeland et al. (1939).

99. See, for example, Friedman's preamble in Friedman (1952a, 9).

100. Kneeland, Schoenberg, and Friedman (1936).

101. Samuelson (1941, 250).

102. See, for example, Friedman (1957a, 4), as well as Modigliani's (1986a, 298) reference to the "path-breaking contribution of Dorothy Brady and R. D. Friedman (1947)."

103. See the discussion in Friedman (1952a, 11), indicated (on p. 9 of the article) as written in 1935.

104. Lunch conversation with Anna Schwartz at City University of New York, October 14, 2010.

105. Friedman (1965, 9). More than a decade later, by which time the community's views on women in the workplace had moved much closer to his own long-standing position, Friedman affirmed, "I think women ought to be able to compete on a fair and even basis with anybody else" (*Dinah!*, March 30, 1977).

106. For discussion of the second of these books, see the next chapter.

107. Friedman (1986a, 85). See also Friedman's remarks in Friedman and Friedman (1998, 48), and for a similar observation see R. D. Friedman (1976a, 31).

108. See Friedman and Friedman (1998, 44–45) on Mitchell's classes. For Friedman's study of Mitchell's underlying theoretical framework, see Friedman (1950a).

109. In Friedman and Friedman (1998, 44, 46), Friedman credited Hotelling with influencing him more than any of his other teachers at Columbia University.

110. For example, in *Milton Friedman Speaks*, episode 9, "The Energy Crisis: A Humane Solution," taped February 9, 1978.

111. See *Milton Friedman Speaks*, episode 9, "The Energy Crisis: A Humane Solution," taped February 10, 1978, p. 8 of transcript, as well as R. D. Friedman (1976a, 31). A later Friedman discussion of Hotelling (1931) was in Friedman and Friedman (1998, 44), by which time the 1931 Hotelling paper had also been referenced in the major study by Stokey, Lucas, and Prescott (1989, 7). See also Silk (1976, 53).

112. Friedman discussed this analysis (Hotelling 1929) at length in Instructional Dynamics Economics Cassette Tape 18 (March 1969) and Instructional Dynamics Economics Cassette Tape 103 (July 12, 1972). For a more recent discussion of Hotelling's theory of political parties' behavior, see Mirrlees (1989, 87), and see McCloskey (1985, 411–14) for an exposition of the Hotelling (1929) model.

113. Friedman and Friedman (1998, 69). Friedman noted in that discussion that he discovered "a few years ago" that the Friedman test was embedded in statistical packages' routine output. He may have learned this from the December 1986 *Los Angeles Times* article just mentioned.

114. For one exception, see G. Reid (1990).

115. Although it was a New Deal measure, Social Security was something that Friedman analyzed mainly in the context of the postwar economic situation rather than in his accounts of the 1930s. Consequently, a discussion of Friedman's views regarding Social Security is reserved for a later chapter (chapter 13).

116. Friedman and Friedman (1980, 93). See also Friedman's letter of May 12, 1977, to William E. Simon (Sr.), in the Simon papers in the Lafayette College Special Collections.

117. *Donahue*, NBC, September 6, 1979. See also Friedman and Friedman's (1985, 70) observation that, in scaling down the role of government, it would be undesirable to wind back the clock to 1920.

118. Writers who are inclined to attribute to Friedman blanket opposition to New Deal

measures fail to make this distinction. For example, D. Jones (2012, 202) attributes to Friedman and Schwartz the view that the Roosevelt administration "made worse" the Depression by "economic regulations and price controls"—a characterization that fails to distinguish between monetary and supply-side measures among the "economic regulations." As will be seen, in the Friedman-Schwartz account, the advent of deposit insurance unambiguously improved matters.

119. Friedman and Friedman (1998, 59).

120. It is thus not correct to suggest, as in Ruger (2011, 15), that Friedman retracted his initial view that the government should step in. See also the acknowledgment in Friedman and Friedman (1980, 94) of the success of the Roosevelt administration in stabilizing the situation.

121. See Friedman and Schwartz (1963a, 331) and Meltzer (2003, 368).

122. Friedman and Schwartz (1963a, 434).

123. See, for example, Friedman (1957b, 75-76; 1960a, 21; 1962c, 23) and Friedman and Schwartz (1963a, 442). This contention on Friedman's part was also reported in press articles, such as those in the March 1955 issue of *Fortune* (194) (see Mulcahy 1957, 92) and *San Jose Mercury News*, February 12, 1979.

124. From Friedman's remarks in *The American Economy, Lesson 48: Can We Have Full Employment without Inflation?*, CBS College of the Air, filmed circa June 5, 1962.

125. Friedman and Schwartz (1963a, 346).

126. Friedman and Schwartz (1963a, 441).

127. See Friedman and Schwartz (1963a, 420).

128. Friedman and Schwartz (1963a, 443-44). See also Friedman (1970d, 18), a discussion in which Friedman noted post-1963 studies that supported the skepticism expressed by Friedman and Schwartz, including Cox (1966).

129. See Friedman's comments in Instructional Dynamics Economics Cassette Tape 4 (November 1968) and Friedman (1970d, 15-16). The time deposit ceiling rates were fixed from January 1, 1936, and the only pre-1962 increase in the ceilings was on January 1, 1957 (McKinney 1967, table 1, p. 74); see also Friedman (1962c, 26).

130. See Friedman (1969a, 42) and Friedman and Schwartz (1963a, 444-45; 1982a, 259-71). In his discussions of this matter from 1969 onward, Friedman was partly drawing on the dissertation work of B. Klein (1970, 1974) that he had supervised.

131. The discussion in Friedman and Schwartz (1963a, 445) indicated that this was so.

132. See Friedman and Schwartz (1963a, 462-65, 469, 699).

133. See also Friedman (1957b, 98); Cagan (1965, 254-55); and Bordo, Choudhri, and Schwartz (1995, 486-87).

134. From Friedman's remarks in *The American Economy, Lesson 41: How Important Is Money?*, CBS College of the Air, filmed June 4, 1962.

135. See, for example, Friedman and Schwartz (1963a, 360, 396). See also Meltzer (2003, for example, 277, 504). It is beyond the scope of this book to provide a detailed discussion of this issue. Eichengreen (1992) became a major statement of the position that pre-1933 international obligations had more binding effects on US monetary policy than Friedman and Schwartz suggested.

136. See, for example, Friedman and Schwartz (1963a, 699); Friedman (1960a, 41; 1966a, 22, p. 102 of 1968 reprint); and C. Romer (1992, 759, 773; 1993, 35).

137. See Friedman (1960a, 81; 1961h, 74; 1962a, 58) and Friedman and Schwartz (1963a, 472, 487).

138. See, respectively, Friedman and Schwartz (1963a, 469) and Friedman (1984b).

139. See Friedman's May 25, 1959, testimony, in Joint Economic Committee (1959a, 619). This indication was consistent with, but more specific than, Friedman's statement around the same time in Friedman (1958b, 256; p. 187 of 1969 reprint) that his opposition to an attempt at a very precise stabilization policy did not amount to call "for irresponsibility in the face of major problems or for failure to correct past mistakes."

140. Friedman (1972a, 913). Friedman's articulation of this aspect of his constant-monetary-growth rule was rarely noted by others, one exception being Keller (1977, 151).

141. See also Friedman (1973b). Note that this position of Friedman's did not signify an endorsement of arrangements in which monetary policy actions are geared to estimated levels of the output gap; as implied by Friedman's (1972a) discussion and as stressed by Orphanides and Williams (2013), growth-rate-based policy rules can also be attuned to the existence of initial conditions in which slack exists.

142. On this, see chapters 7 and 13 below, as well as the discussion in the next subsection.

143. Friedman (1976a, 237).

144. The quotation from Friedman is from *Speaking Freely*, WNBC, May 4, 1969, p. 17 of transcript. Friedman (1966a, 22) was a written account that also conveyed this message. See also Friedman (1968d, 12). Hausman (2016, 1103) claims that Friedman and Schwartz did not attribute the post-1932 recovery to monetary expansion; instead, he names C. Romer (1992) as the first exponent of that position. But Hausman's interpretation is directly contradicted by the textual evidence in the *Monetary History*, and in particular by the judgments expressed in Friedman and Schwartz (1963a, 544). As that discussion made clear, Friedman and Schwartz saw rapid monetary growth in the three years from June 1933 to June 1936 as underpinning the economic expansion over those years. However, while they emphasized the end of monetary contraction as a factor behind the end of the economic contraction, they conceded that the vigor of the expansion in the *immediate* aftermath of the economic contraction—i.e., the initial months of recovery from March 1933—largely reflected an uptick in velocity: see Friedman and Schwartz (1963a, 433-34). As discussed in the coverage of Henry Simons in the next section, Friedman and Schwartz attributed this upward shift in velocity to the enhanced confidence in the US banking system induced by the New Deal reforms.

145. Friedman and Schwartz (1963a, 678).

146. Friedman and Schwartz (1963a, 465, 498).

147. See, for example, Roose (1954, 61, 144); Weinstein (1980); Hanes (2013); and Cole and Ohanian (2013, 4). In addition, Friedman and Friedman (1985, 12) were among those looking back on the 1930s who made note of the fact that New Deal measures declared void were revived in a different form.

148. Friedman and Friedman (1998, 59).

149. Friedman (1970o, 87).

150. For background and derivations, see John Roberts (1995); Clarida, Galí, and Gertler (1999); Woodford (2003); and Walsh (2003).

151. A concise expression of Friedman's position is the one that he gave in *Newsweek*, September 28, 1970.

152. See, for example, his remarks in Ketchum and Kendall (1962, 52) and *The Times* (August 29, 1973), as well as the discussions in Friedman and Schwartz (1963a, 498) and Friedman (1966a, 22; p. 102 of 1968 reprint).

153. See, among other references, Friedman and Schwartz (1982a, 57). In a number of Friedman's empirical studies, this point was conveyed by using money/prices or mone-

tary growth/inflation comparisons in which the money series was expressed in terms of money per unit of output. For early examples of this practice on Friedman's part, see Friedman (1958b, 247; p. 177 of 1969 reprint) and his presentation in *The American Economy, Lesson 41: How Important Is Money?*, CBS College of the Air, filmed June 4, 1962.

154. The notion that expectations of inflation were helpful for output in the period 1933–37 was also expressed by old-style Keynesian Abba Lerner in debate with Friedman in Ketchum and Kendall (1962, 57). In addition, Tobin (1981a) suggested that boosting inflation expectations was missing from Keynes's suggestions regarding how to stimulate the economy when nominal interest rates were low. See also the 1989 Tobin quotation given at the end of this section.

155. The fact that nominal income growth in fact exceeded monetary growth will be taken up in the discussion of Henry Simons in the next section.

156. See especially Friedman (1966a).

157. Kindleberger (1986, 200) stated: "The National Industrial Recovery Act has come to be regarded by 1980s monetarists as a major part of the explanation why the expansion of the money supply after 1933 produced increases in prices and wages rather than a far-reaching reduction in unemployment." In this connection, Kindleberger cited a number of 1980s references, and no items by Friedman or Schwartz. But, as discussed here, the "1980s monetarist" explanation of 1930s economic developments was already part of the accounts laid out in Friedman and Schwartz (1963a) and Friedman (1966a).

The view that the Roosevelt administration's industrial reforms were damaging to output was also voiced in the 1930s by Keynes, whose objections differed in detail from those in the subsequent monetarist account but shared with it the concern that the reforms would lower rather than raise real aggregate demand. See Winch (1969, 233–34) and Skidelsky (1992, 493).

158. The quotation is from Friedman's endorsement of Jim Powell (2003), an endorsement that appeared on the back cover of that book.

159. Ohanian recalled (interview, September 26, 2013): "I think it did fit in with the themes he was talking about, because anybody who looks at that period sees there was a remarkable expansion in most measures of the money supply, but labor input at least doesn't come back very much. So, yeah, he did find it somewhat appealing. He was very engaged. He asked a lot of detailed questions [such as]: Where do you get these wage data? Where do you get these price data?"

160. Evidence that New Deal era monetary actions did lower term premiums is provided by Hanes (2013).

161. In particular, in Friedman and Schwartz (1963b, 1982a).

162. In addition to the discussion that follows, see the related coverage in chapters 3 and 8 below.

163. Friedman and Schwartz (1963a, 91). (The same portion of US experience evidently underlay Friedman's remark about mild deflation in Friedman 1958b, 253 [pp. 183–84 of 1969 reprint]). See also Snowdon and Vane (1997, 200), in which Friedman assessed US performance in the periods 1879–96 and 1896–1913.

164. See Friedman and Schwartz (1963a, 139) and, on the second point, their pp. 91 and 93.

165. Friedman and Schwartz (1963a, 92).

166. See Friedman and Schwartz (1963a, 92–93; quotation from p. 93). See also Friedman and Schwartz (1963a, 104) on the "the disturbed years from 1891 to 1897," a phrase Friedman would underscore by quoting it in Friedman (1990b, 1175; 1992c, 76).

Friedman and Schwartz (1982a, 629) treated the 1890s up to 1896 as featuring expectations that, on balance, tilted toward positive inflation. Insofar as this state of affairs prevailed, it presumably helped real output to advance, on net, over that period, notwithstanding the contractions of 1893-94 and 1896.

167. Bordo and Redish (2004) stressed that the late nineteenth-century US deflation cannot be regarded as being "good" for economic activity, even though that deflation coincided with stretches of positive economic growth.

168. See Friedman (1990b, 1175-76; 1992c, 76).

169. Specifically, both sets of authors pointed to the role of the deflation in pushing up real interest rates. See also Bordo and Landon Lane (2010, 39).

170. Following Barro (1977), Bernanke (1982, 146) actually measured the monetary terms not by M1 growth but by "money shocks," defined as the residual from a regression of monetary growth on lags of itself, inflation, and industrial production. Bordo, Choudhri, and Schwartz (1995) found, however, that monetary growth (measured using M2) in the interwar period is not well accounted for by prior price and output behavior. This finding, alongside the fact that M1 and M2 exhibited similar movements in the interwar years, suggests that Bernanke's results would have been similar had he simply used M1 growth as a regressor.

171. Nor is it plausible to suggest that the monetary authorities in the 1930s could have influenced only the monetary base and not aggregates like M1 or M2. The reforms to international arrangements in 1933 have already been indicated as a case in which policy changes secured increases in both US commercial bank reserves and deposit-inclusive US monetary aggregates such as M1 and M2. The banking panics during the early 1930s, and the related phenomenon that the monetary base and commercial bank reserves went in opposite directions, imply that there is a low simple correlation between the growth in the monetary base and growth in deposit-inclusive monetary aggregates when the decade is considered as a whole. But McCallum (1990b) showed that a significant relationship between base growth and M1 growth in the 1930s reemerged upon inclusion of a variable that proxies for the panics.

172. Friedman and Schwartz's (1970a, 29) M1 and M2 series, as well as an M3 total that includes deposits held at thrift institutions, all exhibit a trough in April 1933 and a gentle rise over the rest of 1933, ahead of more rapid growth the following year. The *Monetary History* used employed an aggregation of the money total that differed somewhat from that applied to the M2 series settled on by Friedman and Schwartz (1970a); for the *Monetary History*'s monetary total, the rise after April 1933 and through December 1933 exceeds that in Friedman and Schwartz's (1970a) M2 series. See Friedman and Schwartz (1963a, 429, 432-33, 714).

173. See, for example, Friedman and Schwartz (1982a, 343). For reduced-form evidence to the effect that this approximation may well be useful in understanding 1930s economic fluctuations, see the McCallum (1990b) study.

174. From Tobin's November 9, 1989, testimony, in Committee on Banking, Finance and Urban Affairs (1990, 44).

175. Friedman (1967a, 2). In contrast, Van Overtveldt (2007, 161) sees in Rose Friedman's praise for Lloyd Mints's teaching (in Friedman and Friedman 1998, 38) a latter-day downgrading on Milton Friedman's part of the significance of Simons's contribution to monetary thought at the University of Chicago. But it seems misguided to see significance in the absence from *Two Lucky People* of praise for Simons's teaching, when Simons was not Milton Friedman's teacher for monetary theory. Nor did Simons figure at all among Friedman's course teachers in the 1932-33 academic year, the two instead getting to know each other via other means, including Simons's direct interaction with the uni-

versity's graduate students (see Friedman's remarks in Hammond 1989, 6; and Taylor 2001, 111). Van Overtveldt's inference that Friedman in later life did not rate Simons's monetary work highly is further invalidated by the discussions in Friedman items that Van Overtveldt does not cite. These include Friedman's January 1976 submission in Committee on Banking, Currency and Housing (1976a, 2157), which noted Simons as a predecessor in advocacy of 100 percent reserve arrangements; Friedman's (1982b, 100) observation that Simons identified the "fundamental issue" of monetary policy rules; and Friedman's (1975a, 177-78) description of himself as one of Simons's followers, together with his acknowledgment of Simons as a crusader for central-bank transparency. Friedman also praised Simons during the 1970s on his cassette commentary series, including in Instructional Dynamics Economics Cassette Tape 110 (November 1, 1972) and Instructional Dynamics Economics Cassette Tape 146 (May 20, 1974); and in the 1980s in Friedman (1985e, 17; 1986b, 54). In addition, Friedman emphasized the importance of Simons's work in commenting on others' research, such as he did in a June 23, 1981, letter to Robert Hall when giving reactions to a manuscript of Hall's (information provided by Robert Hall).

176. Friedman (1967a, 1). Friedman did not include "colleague" in his description of Simons because Simons's death in 1946 shortly predated Friedman's arrival at the staff of the economics department. See chapter 4 below.

On the other hand, it is notable that Friedman included "teacher" in his description of Simons's connection to himself, notwithstanding the dearth of formal classes taken from Simons; Friedman's use of this label was testimony to Simons's conviviality with the student body. Simons's premature death and Friedman's later fame would mean that the Simons-Friedman interaction would be one of the most noted aspects of Simons's career—as was demonstrated in 1979 when a newspaper discussing Simons's views on the labor market identified Simons as "the teacher of Milton Friedman" (*Daily Telegraph*, February 12, 1979).

Another student of Simons's, George Stigler, would pay tribute to Simons when Stigler, in the early 1960s, produced a set of postcards depicting major economists. Simons was used as the University of Chicago's representative in the series, which also included portraits of Marshall, Ricardo, and Mill (Stephen Stigler, interview, November 6, 2013).

177. Van Overtveldt (2007, 161) incorrectly claims that the Friedmans' 1998 memoirs contained no reference to Simons in the context of monetary thinking at the University of Chicago in the 1930s. Milton Friedman in fact did refer to Simons in this context on p. 41 of those memoirs (a reference to Simons that does not appear in the memoirs' index entry for Simons). See also the preceding discussion.

178. Friedman (1967a, 2).

179. Friedman (1977b, 33), also in Friedman (1978a, 65).

180. Simons et al. (1933), cited in Chapin (1959) and also referred to in Friedman (1967a, 2).

181. For example, in Friedman (1960a, 66).

182. See Friedman (1948a). Reflecting this connection, the American Economic Association reprinted Simons (1936) and Friedman (1948a) back-to-back in a book collection (Lutz and Mints 1951).

183. Friedman (1967a, 5, 8).

184. See Friedman (1967a, 3).

185. Although Friedman in 1948, as Simons had before him, saw consols as a nonmonetary instrument, Friedman wanted them ultimately eliminated too, allowing base money to become the sole form of government debt.

186. The criticisms of 100 percent reserve banking given by Williamson and Wright (2011), while largely valid, are not new and did not originate in the literature that they cite. Essentially the same criticisms have been part of textbook discussions for over thirty years (see Mishkin 1989, 383).

187. An early example is Friedman (1968b). A later one is Friedman (1982b, 117), in which he advocated that the Federal Reserve hit a specified M2 target by estimating the amount of open-market purchases required to deliver the target and then carrying out those purchases.

188. See Friedman (1967a, 3–4). Likewise, Lucas (1980a, 200), in interpreting Friedman's constant-monetary-growth rule, took it to be the variant that did not impose 100 percent reserve requirements.

189. Friedman (1960a, 68).

190. See, for example, Friedman and Schwartz (1963a, 294 and chapter 7), and Friedman (1974a, 22). An early statement in this connection was Friedman's remark in Joint Committee on the Economic Report (1952d, 1300) that the "Federal Reserve already has ample power to control the volume of money through open market operations."

191. See Friedman (1974a, 1982b).

192. *Newsweek*, January 8, 1979. Similar judgments expressed in Meltzer (2001a, 25; 2009a, 170, 199, 566; 2009b, 897). These characterizations referred to postwar practice. An instance in which it was emphatically not the case that the Federal Reserve offset the effect of reserve-requirement changes was the 1936–37 increase in reserve requirements, discussed presently.

193. Friedman (1974a, 23).

194. See Friedman (1960a, 108) and, for the presentation of the extremes as two desirable alternatives, Friedman (1978b). The favorable discussion of zero reserve requirements in Friedman (1960a) was rarely noted in the subsequent literature; an exception was White (1987, 342). (For more recent references to the passage, see E. Nelson 2011, 10; and Sargent 2014, 148.) Friedman's discussion credited Gary Becker with pressing on him the merits of this arrangement. Around the time of these discussions, Becker wrote a paper on the matter, cited as Becker (1957a) in Rockoff (1975), that finally appeared in print (see Becker 1993) in a volume that White edited. See also John B. Taylor's remarks in his economicsone blog (September 2, 2014) for a discussion of Becker's paper. The Federal Reserve Board made reserve requirements zero in March 2020.

One problem with Friedman's 1960 discussion, as opposed to his later treatments of zero reserve-requirement arrangements, is that the 1960 discussion treats zero-requirement proposals as part of a package that would include the (logically separate) proposals to remove bank supervision and deposit insurance.

195. In Instructional Dynamics Economics Cassette Tape 188 (March 1976, part 2), for example, Friedman cited the fact that the instruments had a fluctuating market value as a basis for distinguishing both Treasury bills and commercial paper from money.

196. Simons (1936, 16–17), reprinted in Simons (1948, 171).

197. See Director (1948, v). Perhaps not wishing to appear parochial, Director referred to Simons as the emerging "head of a 'school'" of liberal economics, rather than of the "Chicago School" per se. The individual whom Director saw Simons succeeding as head of the Chicago School was presumably Frank Knight. (Knight was identified as the leader of the Chicago School in the 1940s by Paul Samuelson in *Newsweek*, July 31, 1972; in *Newsweek*, October 25, 1976a, Samuelson added that Knight should be considered the founder of the Chicago School.)

198. As the emphasis on laissez-faire in Friedman's (1967a) discussion of Simons's

views indicates, both Simons and Friedman advocated free-market arrangements for the nonfinancial economy—with those arrangements meaning a system as competitive as possible. It is therefore not correct for Cherrier (2011, 345) to infer that, because Simons spoke out against monopolistic behavior on the part of firms and labor, Friedman was mistaken in attributing to Simons a strongly free-market position. On the contrary, although Friedman—as noted in this book—became disenchanted with antitrust measures as a means of discouraging monopolistic practices, he and Simons had in common the belief that monopolistic behavior was undesirable, and their conception of the free market corresponded to an environment in which such behavior was absent. (Friedman's position vis-à-vis Simons's on the case of natural monopoly, in which monopolistic behavior becomes unavoidable, is discussed in chapter 4 below.)

199. The quotation is from Friedman (1980a, 61; also p. 61 of 1991 reprint).

200. See, for example, Friedman (1978a, 3) and Friedman and Friedman (1980, 66). In *Milton Friedman Speaks*, episode 15 ("The Future of Our Free Society," taped February 21, 1978, p. 4 of transcript), Friedman suggested that such a reduction in regulation would make it easier for small corporations to issue securities.

201. Friedman and Schwartz (1963a, 247).

202. See Friedman (1967a, 4); see also Friedman (1995, 167–68). The main qualification to this position that Friedman voiced in later years was that he saw merit in a capital requirement on commercial banks. See E. Nelson (2013a).

203. See chapter 6 and E. Nelson (2013a).

204. See, for example, Friedman (1948a, 247).

205. Among US economists, a very prominent prior advocate of using monetary policy to stabilize the country's price level was Irving Fisher (1911a). Pigou (1917, 57), in an article to which Friedman was exposed at an early stage (see the next subsection), had highlighted the fact that Fisher set himself apart from many others in proposing price-level stabilization rather than exchange-rate stabilization as the goal of monetary policy. The emphasis on a domestic aggregate rather than the exchange rate as the appropriate goal for monetary policy was an element of Fisher's approach to which both Simons and Friedman would adhere.

206. Friedman quoted this phrase twice in his lecture on Simons (Friedman 1967a, 7, 12). For an example in which critics of monetarism used the Simons quotation, see Miles (1984, 107).

207. Friedman and Schwartz (1963a, 352). See R. G. Anderson, Bordo, and Duca (2016) for an examination of the behavior of US M2 velocity in economic downturns and financial crises since 1929.

208. This interpretation was also a reflection of the fact, noted above, that Friedman saw deflation as a factor likely in practice to be a hindrance to economic stability.

209. A somewhat different example was also provided by Friedman and Schwartz (1982a, 159, 168, 609) for the United Kingdom. The United Kingdom neither had a US-style near financial collapse in the 1930s nor an economic collapse on a US scale. Consistent with this and with Friedman and Schwartz's interpretation of Canada and US money/velocity developments, velocity fell less in the United Kingdom in the early 1930s than in either the United States or Canada.

210. Friedman and Schwartz (1963a, 352).

211. Friedman (1964a, 1222). See also Friedman (1967a, 12).

212. The rise in velocity in this period also features prominently in the analysis of Jalil and Rua (2015). Although to a considerable degree their account is, as they note, consistent with "the quantity-theory interpretation of events" (Jalil and Rua 2015, 41), these

authors stress the difference in their account from that in the *Monetary History* arising from the fact that Jalil and Rua point to price rises, rather than banking reform and the reduction in uncertainty engendered by that reform, as the factor driving the 1933 surge in velocity. However, Jalil and Rua (2015, 40) acknowledge that price rises did not, in fact, figure particularly heavily in the rise in nominal income that accompanied the 1933 step-up in velocity.

213. Friedman and Schwartz (1982a, 19, 342). There is another channel through which monetary expansion might set in train a velocity expansion, although it is not one that is very important for studying US monetary relationships in the 1930s. This is the tendency for a positive monetary-growth trend to induce a trend in velocity by producing inflation and therefore a Fisher effect on interest rates.

214. The 1930s illustrate the problem of making any general statement about the relationship between nominal and real money balances in business cycles. A movement in nominal money has implications for the short-run behavior of real interest rates and real output precisely because real money balances tend to move in the same direction as nominal balances in the short run. It was probably in light of this consideration that Friedman used the real money stock in some of his later work when examining the relationship between money and output (see Taylor 2001, 103). Real money balances have also been used as an index of short-run monetary conditions by Meltzer (2001b, 2003) and others. (Note that this practice does not in any way imply acceptance of important Pigou-Patinkin real money balance effects. Instead, the practice is consistent with the notion that a changed volume of real money balances has repercussions for output solely via the reaction of interest rates.)

Another aspect of the short-run relationship between real money balances and nominal money balances is, however, that discussed in the text: real money demand depends on precautionary factors, and a contraction of nominal money can produce economic dislocation that in turn triggers an increase in desired real balances. Even in the face of a contracting nominal money stock, higher real money balances can be obtained over time via downward pressure on the price level.

Consequently, the nonneutrality of monetary policy implies two different aspects are prominent in the relationship between nominal and real money balances—leading to a complicated interpretation of the latter series. In light of this consideration, the practice of expressing money stock behavior in terms of real money balances as an indicator was criticized by Karnosky (1974a), Schwartz (1981), and Friedman (for example, in Instructional Dynamics Economics Cassette Tape 56, August 6, 1970, and Tape 140, February 20, 1974; and in *The Times*, May 2, 1977). This consideration implies that focusing, as in Eggertsson (2008), on the behavior of real M2 as evidence against the monetarist interpretation of the 1930s is inappropriate.

215. A number of these authors took, in their other work, monetarist positions regarding the transmission mechanism and monetary policy. This fact underscores the point that advocacy of 100 percent reserves is separable from monetarism.

216. See Friedman (1971b, 17) on reserve requirements, and Friedman (1957b, 86–87, 102) on the incentives for financial institutions to avoid controls more generally.

217. See Friedman (1981a, 10) and Friedman (1992b, x–xii). Roughly between these two statements, Friedman also reaffirmed his support for a 100 percent reserve system in a February 3, 1986, letter to John Hotson (in response to Hotson 1985) that has been quoted at length in both R. Phillips (1995, 174) and Hellyer (2010, 180).

218. Hirsch and de Marchi (1990, 234) characterized the increase in high-powered money (i.e., the unadjusted base) after the reserve-requirement increase as evidence

against the *Monetary History*'s interpretation that the reserve-requirement increases amounted to a policy tightening. But this characterization betrays a misunderstanding of reserve-requirement increases. An increase in total commercial bank reserves in the wake of an increase in reserve requirements can be consistent with the latter being a genuine policy tightening if the rise in bank reserves is small in relation to the rise in reserve requirements. And, indeed, this condition was met in 1937, as the adjusted monetary base declined even though high-powered money (the unadjusted base) rose. (Hirsch and de Marchi 1990, 234, also described the notion that "excess reserves were accumulated deliberately by banks" in the 1930s as a "conviction" on the part of Friedman and Schwartz—but it is actually a truism, embedded in the definition of excess reserves, and no "conviction" is required to accept it. What is at issue is, instead, what motivated the deliberate accumulation of reserves.)

That the reserve-requirement increases produced balance-sheet contraction on the part of the commercial banks was verified in the analyses by Telser (2001) and Cargill and Mayer (2006) of the behavior in 1936-37 of commercial banks that were Federal Reserve System member banks. The first of these studies interpreted his result as inconsistent with Friedman and Schwartz's (1963a) position that the reserve-requirement increases had a contractionary effect on the economy. But Telser's basis for reaching this judgment was the absence of a contraction of bank lending in the wake of the reserve-requirement increases. The Friedman-Schwartz view of fluctuations was, however, grounded on the link between money and the economy, not on the link between bank loans and the economy. For reserve-requirement increases to generate monetary contraction, it is not required that bank loans contract; rather, it is required only that total bank assets do so (a contraction that would in turn put downward pressure on bank deposits). Telser's analysis confirmed that bank assets contracted in response to the reserve-requirement increase, as he reported that member banks ran down their holdings of Treasury bills.

In addition, it should be pointed out that the contention of Calomiris, Mason, and Wheelock (2011) that the reserve-requirement increase still left required reserves short of commercial banks' total demand for reserves does not have the implication that they claim for their finding—that claimed implication being that the reserve-requirement increase was not contractionary for the money stock. For the reserve-requirement increase to have had a contractionary effect on commercial bank deposits, all that is required is that the increase in reserve requirements left commercial banks with a smaller buffer of precautionary reserves than they desired to hold, in relation to their required reserves. This crucial point underlay the discussions in Friedman (1960a, 46; 1961c, 181) and Friedman and Schwartz (1963a, 348, 461, 532).

219. For Friedman's attachment of significance to the gold operations, see, for example, Friedman and Schwartz (1963a, 510, 544-45; 1963b, 52) and Friedman (1960a, 20; 1984c, 25).

220. As well as the examples that follow, see that in the *Listener* (London), January 5, 1978.

221. See Conference on Research in National Income and Wealth (1937, 1938, 1939) and Warburton (1958, 212). Another item of this vintage that Warburton could have cited (but did not) is Kuznets's (1937) *National Income and Capital Formation, 1919–1935*. In addition, Patinkin (1982, 130, 235, 244) pointed to Kuznets (1934), a joint NBER/governmental product, as an earlier source of preliminary national accounts estimates, an item that Friedman himself highlighted in Friedman and Friedman (1998, 68). With respect to the United Kingdom, Patinkin (1982, 244-45, 251-60) stressed that research on national accounts proceeded during the interwar period ahead of the *General Theory*. However,

Patinkin also credited the Keynesian revolution and, especially, the demands on economic policy created by World War II with setting in motion the publication in the United Kingdom, from 1941 onward, of official estimates of national income.

222. Friedman (1961b, 269). In the same vein, Otto Eckstein balanced the contributions of Keynes and Kuznets by stating (in the *Wall Street Journal*, August 27, 1979) that it was because of the collective of "Kuznets-Keynes-Tinbergen" that the "income-expenditure approach" was introduced into econometric models. This formulation on Eckstein's part was evidently a means of giving Kuznets credit for introducing national income accounts. However, the term "income-expenditure approach" was one that Friedman, for one, came to associate specifically with Keynesian economic analysis rather than with the use of national income accounts per se.

223. See Conference on Research in National Income and Wealth (1937, 1938, 1939). Friedman mentioned his role as editor of the early NBER publications on national accounts in both Hammond (1992, 106) and Friedman and Friedman (1998, 70, 619). The text of the introduction to the 1939 volume confirms Friedman as the editor, although the title page did not give him an official "Edited by" credit. (Silk 1976, 55, gave Friedman as editing only the latter two volumes, but the foreword to the first volume stated, on p. xviii, "The editing of the reports and the discussion was done by Milton Friedman." Note also that "editor," whether credited or not, is not the same as "author," so it seems inappropriate to give Friedman the grand title of "coauthor of *Studies in Income and Wealth*," as in Ebenstein 2007, 283. Friedman's official bibliography more accurately described him as an "editor and minor contributor" for the 1937-39 volumes of the series. Friedman's contribution to the first volume as a credited author is only about three pages—see Friedman 1937b.)

224. Friedman (1935b).

225. Friedman and Friedman (1998, 68).

226. As already noted, the Friedmans' later accounts emphasized Friedman's status as an employed researcher in the period 1937-40, and Friedman's (1986a, 85) description of the situation was that he was hired by Kuznets to work on Kuznets's project. Friedman was, however, essentially working on a PhD dissertation in conducting this work.

227. In addition, an early study of US fiscal policy (A. Hart and Allen 1941, v) thanked Friedman for advice "on the use of national income data in tax estimation." Because of this mention of Friedman, Friedman's name appears in the book's index—on the same page (274) as the index entry for Keynes. Another early case in which the names of Keynes and Friedman appeared on the same page in print was a passage of Machlup's (1943, ix) foreword, which acknowledged the inspiration that Keynes's work provided and thanked Friedman for specific comments that Friedman had given Machlup during the latter's drafting process.

228. See, for example, Friedman and Schwartz (1982a, 21-22). The income version of the equation of exchange (as opposed to the transactions form, $MV = PT$) was advanced by Pigou (1917)—a paper that Friedman had studied as part of the monetary theory course he took at the University of Chicago in the 1932-33 academic year (see Leeson 2003a, 509).

229. Patinkin (1982, 77), for example, noted that the *General Theory* was marked by "concentration on national-income magnitudes and functional relationships among them."

230. Friedman stressed Kuznets's finding at the very start of his book on the consumption function (Friedman 1957a, 3-4), citing a latter-day summary by Kuznets of his finding (Kuznets 1952). The more standard reference on this point (see, for example, Blaug 1990, 36) is, however, Kuznets (1946), while Modigliani (1975a, 3) cited Kuznets (1942) in the same connection. As early as 1950, a textbook presentation, likely informed by Kuznets's

results, suggested that Keynes had been overconfident about the empirical validity of the consumption/income link that had been hypothesized in the *General Theory* (Shaw 1950, 363). As we shall see, the way out that Friedman would offer in the 1950s was a reformulation in which the notion of a stable relationship between consumption and income was affirmed but with the vital qualification that the income concept had to be redefined.

231. Through this interaction, Friedman would strike up a rapport with Taft, a prominent Republican senator. However, during their 1940-41 interactions they would be at odds regarding the case for the United States joining World War II. Friedman would recall about thirty years after the event, "I personally happened at that time to be an interventionist. I disagreed with Bob Taft" (*NET Journal Presents Conservative Viewpoint*, PBS, May 4, 1970).

232. The arrival date of September 1937 was given in Friedman and Friedman (1998, 69). Some idea of the vast span of years over which Friedman was a member of the economics profession is given by the following facts: (*i*) Friedman's most famous NBER study, Friedman and Schwartz (1963a), did not see print until more than twenty-five years after he first joined the bureau; (*ii*) Friedman lived to see, and comment on via correspondence, thirty-year retrospectives on Friedman and Schwartz (1963a) that appeared in the *Journal of Monetary Economics*; (*iii*) one of these reviews, Lucas (1994b), was by Robert Lucas—who was *born* in September 1937, the month that Friedman first arrived at the NBER.

233. See, for example, Friedman (2001).

234. Kuznets and Friedman (1939).

235. This was not the first time Friedman had received coverage in that newspaper. Friedman had first been mentioned by the *New York Times* at age nineteen when he had come in second in an examination taken by Rutgers University honors students in a contest for the Jacob Cooper Logic Prize, a $200 award offered at the university (*New York Times*, April 25, 1932).

236. Friedman (1939, 136).

237. Some of Friedman's own biographical listings (for example, NBC 1946a, i) incorrectly kept the plural form in citing the 1945 full-length book version. On the other hand, Mayer (1972, 82) added a plural "s" to both "Income" and "Practice" when referring to the "famous study" by Friedman and Kuznets.

238. Friedman and Friedman (1998, 71).

239. In E. Nelson (2004a, 399). See, however, Weyl (2012) for an argument that elements of Kuznets's background would have led him, too, to support the critical perspective on entry into the medical profession that underlay Friedman and Kuznets (1945).

240. Friedman and Kuznets (1945).

241. See All Participants (1951, 251) and Friedman (1949c, 198-99; 1952c, 457; 1953c, 31). See also Friedman's remarks, given in 1979, in M. Anderson (1982, 201-2), and those in *Nightline*, ABC, November 6, 1987, p. 34 of transcript.

242. This aspect of Friedman's posture toward questionnaires was stressed by David Laidler in personal communication (November 6, 2014).

243. Friedman (1943a, 58).

244. See Friedman and Friedman (1998, 71). Friedman would, however, also grant that the treatment offered in Friedman and Kuznets (1945) had been superseded by the later human-capital literature: in redrafting a portion of Friedman (1955b) for a discussion in *Capitalism and Freedom*, Friedman (1962a, 101-2) replaced a reference to Friedman and Kuznets's (1945) estimates with citations of Becker (1960) and T. Schultz (1961).

245. Likewise, Patinkin (1973a, 794) named these two authors as the Chicago School contributors to the theory of human capital (in a passage that, curiously, seemed also to attribute origination of the "human capital" terminology to Becker and Schultz).

246. In addition, Becker (1964, 7; 1975, 15) acknowledged that the Friedman-Kuznets study "greatly influenced my own thinking."

247. See Wallechinsky, Wallace, and Wallace (1981, 417–18).

248. Friedman was making this point at a time when a tax on wealth was being prominently proposed in UK discussions of tax policy. At a later stage of this UK debate, Kay and King (1978, 74) argued that a tax on wealth would be impracticable, making use of much the same objection as Friedman had raised.

249. See also Manuelli and Seshadri (2014) for a recent construction of estimates of human capital stocks for different countries.

250. *Newsweek*, October 25, 1976b, 89.

251. Friedman and Friedman (1998, 71). Likewise, R. D. Friedman (1976b, 19) stated that the "study was completed by 1941," and Silk (1976, 59) made a similar but slightly stronger claim. More accurately, Friedman and Kuznets (1945, x) indicated that the analysis for the book was completed in 1941 and the draft revised thereafter. In the *Margin* (January 1986, 4), Friedman stated he had really completed the work in the late 1930s. This observation may, however, have been a reference to the February 1939 release of the summary of the research rather than a claim that a full version of the Friedman-Kuznets manuscript was completed in 1939.

252. See Friedman and Friedman (1998, 74–75). In a previous account, R. D. Friedman (1976b, 19) had not referred to this controversy in detail; instead, she had simply attributed the delay in publication to the war.

253. After noting Friedman's 1946 PhD, Breit and Ransom (1971, 226) stated that an "expanded version was later published with Simon Kuznets" in book form in 1954. This claim reflects a number of confusions. First, the book was published before the dissertation; indeed, as noted here, publication was a condition for the granting of Friedman's dissertation. Second, the work in question was always coauthored with Kuznets (whose input into the draft diminished over time). Third, the 1954 book was a reprint of the 1945 version. (The fact of the 1954 reprint also accounts for Friedman and Kuznets 1945 being listed as a 1954 publication on the NBER's website for many years.)

For his part, in the entries he supplied for *Who's Who in the Midwest 1972/1973* and *Who's Who in America 1976/1977*, Friedman listed the publication date of Friedman and Kuznets (1945) as 1946, thereby confusing his degree receipt date with the year of the book's publication (Marquis Who's Who 1972, 249; 1976, 1080). A *Fortune* profile of Friedman (June 1, 1967, 132) made the same mistake.

254. In E. Nelson (2004a, 401).

255. On Friedman's remarks on Mitchell, see Friedman and Friedman (1998, 75). Mitchell stepped down as director of research at the NBER in 1945, being succeeded by Arthur Burns (Burns 1952b, 35).

256. Mitchell's reservations about the dissertation were related to the author in an interview with Joseph Burns (September 12, 2013). Joseph Burns has also deposited, in the Arthur Burns papers at Duke University Library, a letter to Burns that Mitchell wrote on August 27, 1945. In that letter, Mitchell recounted his concerns about the approach taken in Friedman's dissertation. The letter indicated that Mitchell regarded these concerns as largely confirmed by C. Reinold Noyes's critique of Friedman-Kuznets, discussed below.

257. Friedman (1951a, 215). Likewise, in a 1969 television interview Friedman said,

"I often have fun by asking people: 'What do you suppose is the most powerful trade union in the United States?' And almost never does anybody give the right answer, which is the American Medical Association" (*Speaking Freely*, WNBC, May 4, 1969, p. 34 of transcript).

258. Friedman (1962a, 149–60); Instructional Dynamics Economics Cassette Tape 113 (January 17, 1973); *Milton Friedman Speaks*, episode 10, "The Economics of Medical Care," taped May 19, 1978; *Milton Friedman Speaks* episode 13, "Who Protects the Worker?," taped September 29, 1977, p. 11 of transcript; Friedman and Friedman (1980, 238–39 and 324). Likewise, Friedman (1986a, 85) suggested that the Friedman-Kuznets conclusions probably still held.

259. Friedman and Friedman (1998, 72).

260. See Friedman and Schwartz's (1963a, 407–19) section titled "Why Was Monetary Policy So Inept?" For the "Director's Comment" on Friedman and Schwartz (1963a), see Hettinger (1963).

261. Along with the discussion that follows, see also Hammond (1996, 56).

262. Without explicitly recommending it, Friedman and Schwartz (1963a, 252, 545) were also able to sneak favorable discussion of constant monetary growth as a policy option into the *Monetary History*. In addition, they were able to criticize reserve requirements as a monetary policy tool by expressing their reservations as technical in character (see Friedman and Schwartz 1963a, 531).

With respect to the later Friedman-Schwartz book *Monetary Trends*, Hendry's (1985, 77) observation that "Friedman and Schwartz immediately drew major policy implications from their study" prompted the sharp rebuke from Hammond (1996, 198) that this was a "misinterpretation," on the grounds that "Friedman and Schwartz drew no policy implications in the book." But Hendry's observation (which he essentially repeated in Ericsson 2004, 774) was correct. Friedman and Schwartz did not draw explicit policy implications *in* their book (although the discussion of Keynes in Friedman and Schwartz 1982a, 621–22, came close to doing so), but they did so in various writings and statements that drew on the *Trends* findings. For example, Friedman (1980a, 56, paragraph 8; p. 52 of 1991 reprint) provided monetary policy recommendations for the United Kingdom that he indicated drew "heavily" on his research findings, including those in *Trends*, and he went on to describe the material in *Trends* as "most relevant" for his support for the Thatcher government's economic strategy (1980a, 61; also p. 61 of 1991 reprint). In addition, Friedman alluded to the results in *Monetary Trends* in his endorsement, in the August 6, 1980, edition of the London *Daily Express*, of the Thatcher government's strategy. See also Schwartz (1984, 130, 136).

263. *Business Week* (May 6, 1967, 120).

264. See also Becker (1991a, 140). However, for discussions in which the reader's comment received more favorable treatment, see R. L. Anderson (1946, 400) and Arrow (1963, 955). Arrow added in an interview for this book (December 7, 2013) that he believed that the argument, "laid on pretty thick in Friedman and Kuznets," to the effect that the medical profession was monopolistic, was flawed because it neglected important institutional features special to health-care provision. "I don't think that the argument that this represents any sort of monopoly, in any simple sense, is appropriate."

265. March 17, 1938, letter from Milton Friedman to Rose Friedman, quoted in Friedman and Friedman (1998, 77).

266. In NBC (1954, 8).

Chapter Three

1. This was the title that Friedman gave for the position in his *Who's Who in America 1976/1977* entry (Marquis Who's Who 1976, 1080).

2. See, for example, Rose Friedman's account in Friedman and Friedman (1998, 100).

3. Quoted in E. Nelson (2004a, 401). Consistent with Schwartz's characterization, a review of Friedman and Kuznets (1945) that appeared in a statistics journal would take for granted readers' familiarity with Friedman's 1937 paper on ranks. See R. L. Anderson (1946, 399).

4. Neyman (1938, 101). Friedman's question was reprinted in Neyman (1952, 127).

5. In *Newsweek*, November 9, 1970; and Instructional Dynamics Economics Cassette Tape 60 (November 5, 1970).

6. Rose Friedman, whose narrative formed the bulk of chapter 6 of Friedman and Friedman's (1998) account of their University of Wisconsin experience, mentioned anti-Semitism as a factor in Friedman's departure on pp. 100–101 of her account; this passage also discussed—as does S. Stigler (2007, 8)—colleagues' resistance to Friedman's proposed changes to the teaching of statistics at the university. Friedman's encounters with anti-Semitism in this period have also been mentioned in a number of other accounts, some early (if nonspecific) discussions including those in *New York Times*, January 25, 1970, 80; Breit and Ransom (1971, 227); Silk (1976, 59); and *Los Angeles Times*, December 14, 1986, 16.

7. In Instructional Dynamics Economics Cassette Tape 215, released in 1978 but recorded in late 1977, Friedman said, "May I join in that," when his wife told subscribers, "I wish you a very, very Merry Christmas." Friedman's secretary from 1972 to 2006, Gloria Valentine, recalled, "They celebrated Christmas, very much so, and I got a Christmas gift [from the Friedmans] every year" (Gloria Valentine, interview, April 1, 2013). Anna Schwartz told the author (in a September 18, 2009, conversation) that Friedman celebrated both Christmas and Easter, and that Friedman had told her that he had stopped being interested in Judaism as a religion after age eleven. Elsewhere, Friedman gave the specific age at which he stopped being religious as about age twelve (Friedman and Friedman 1998, 23), "twelve or thirteen" (G. Martin 1983, 55), or age thirteen, having been "devoutly religious" until then (*California*, October 1984, 163). As Schwartz noted, however, Friedman's adulthood observance of Christmas was as a secular holiday, not a religious one; he was an agnostic (G. Martin 1983, 59; Friedman and Friedman 1998, 23).

8. Friedman (1972a, 936).

9. For example, in 1977, Friedman observed that "the group obviously I've been closest to are the Jews" (*Milton Friedman Speaks*, episode 1, "What Is America?," taped October 3, 1977, p. 27 of transcript).

10. Friedman talk, April 18, 1996, at Claremont McKenna College, broadcast on CSPAN on December 26, 1996.

11. Friedman and Friedman (1998, 58).

12. The Leeson sentence originally appeared in Leeson (1998, 70). Ebenstein quotes it with ellipses, omitting the "at least."

13. Friedman gave March 1, 1943, as his first day at the Statistics Research Group (Friedman and Friedman 1998, 125).

14. The way Friedman put it in Friedman (1986a, 86) was that in the first two years of the war he was employed in tax policy, and the next two years in mathematical statistics. In that statement, he seemed to be counting his whole two years at the Treasury, includ-

ing the period before December 1941, as wartime. The period before December 1941 certainly counted as wartime conditions from the US Treasury's perspective; even though actual defense spending by the United States started from a relatively subdued level in 1940 (a fact Friedman noted in *Newsweek*, April 18, 1983), US defense-spending plans turned up dramatically in 1940, leading to a sharp rise in outlays in 1941. Friedman and Schwartz (1963a, 557) would regard the shift of resources from nondefense to defense purposes as proceeding rapidly in the United States beginning in early 1940 and, consistent with this judgment, studies of US fiscal policy shocks treat the whole 1940–45 period as World War II for the United States (see Ramey 2011; and Barro and Redlick 2011; see also Seater 1993, 173, on the rise during 1941). Friedman therefore joined the Treasury after the United States' defense activity had entered war mode, but before it formally joined hostilities (a distinction that should have been made in the discussion of Friedman's Treasury years in E. Nelson 2009a, 469).

15. See Rose Friedman's remarks in Friedman and Friedman (1998, 147).

16. That is, Friedman (1944), discussed in the next chapter.

17. If the full 1939–45 World War II period is considered, additional Friedman activity in economics from 1939 to 1941 should be added to this list, including his dissertation work and teaching at both Columbia University and the University of Wisconsin; the latter teaching included a course on business cycles in 1940 (*National Review*, June 16, 1989a, 25). (Steindl 2004, 522, discussed the business cycle course but gave the impression that the only prior reference to that course in print was that in Hammond 1996, 48–50—thereby neglecting Friedman's own 1989 discussion of that course.)

18. Friedman (1942a, 1943a).

19. Wallis and Friedman (1942).

20. Shoup, Friedman, and Mack (1943), discussed below.

21. That is, Friedman and Kuznets (1945). Some sources (for example, Library of Congress 1942, 24) have also listed among Friedman's credits for this period the coauthorship of an article titled "Consumer Spending, Inflation, and the Wage Earner in the United States," which appeared in the February 1942 issue of *International Labour Review*. However, this credit is erroneous, for the article was actually coauthored by Otto Nathan and by Friedman's near-namesake, Milton Fried (Nathan and Fried 1942).

22. For the quotation, see Friedman and Friedman (1985, 53).

23. Committee on Appropriations (1943, 463). In describing his staff's background, Blough also felt it necessary to add: "Almost all of these people are married and have families."

24. *Donahue*, NBC, September 30, 1975. Friedman also said in his answer, "As it happens, I have had some business experience and so on, but that's all irrelevant." It is not clear what experience Friedman had in mind here; he may have been referring to the same boyhood work at his family's retail store that Blough had invoked in 1943. Alternatively, Friedman might have had in mind investments he had made in various business ventures during adulthood. Still another possibility was suggested by Gloria Valentine (personal communication, March 24, 2013): Friedman might have been referring to his activities as an undergraduate, which included tutoring high school students and being involved in the sale of clothing and secondhand books, as described by Friedman in Evers (1990, 50) and Friedman and Friedman (1998, 26–27). (Another source of income during Friedman's Rutgers University years—albeit one that could not easily be regarded as counting toward his business experience—came from working as a waiter at a campus restaurant, a job that he recalled in *Australian Business Monthly*, October 1993, 54. He also

served, presumably without pay, as copyeditor for the student newspaper: see, for example, *New York Times*, July 26, 1964, F13; and *Rutgers* magazine, Fall 2006, 26.)

25. In G. Martin (1983, 60).

26. On this topic, at least, Friedman's sentiments would be shared by Paul Krugman, who in a *New York Times* column of January 13, 2012, stated: "America is not, in fact, a corporation. Making good economic policy isn't at all like maximizing corporate profits." In the same vein, Krugman more recently affirmed (*New York Times*, November 3, 2014) that "success in business does not seem to convey any special insight into economic policy."

27. *Donahue*, NBC, September 6, 1979. Friedman's hesitancy to speak on this occasion probably partly reflected his lack of expertise on K-Mart's rise, but it also likely stemmed from the fact that he had not kept up his early interest in the literature on industrial organization or the theory of the firm.

28. For the quotation, see Friedman (1982c, 55).

29. See, for example, *National Review*, June 16, 1989a.

30. Some accounts classify Friedman as working for the government in 1943 to 1945 in his capacity as a member of the Statistical Research Group. This is not an appropriate classification, as discussed in the next chapter. If Friedman had been a government employee at the Statistical Research Group, he likely could not have made public statements giving his own views on policy matters (as he did in his June 1943 radio appearance).

31. See his columns in *Newsweek*, January 10, 1977; and May 31, 1982.

32. Friedman (1986a, 86).

33. In E. Nelson (2004a, 404).

34. Earlier, Friedman had remarked on the record: "I haven't had any interest or urge to run for office" (*Chicago Tribune*, November 28, 1976). See also Friedman (1965, 8).

35. Friedman (1976e, xxi). See also the previous chapter.

36. See especially Friedman and Friedman (1998, 60-61). See also *Wall Street Journal*, August 23, 1976, in which Friedman seemed to indicate that when he was a government employee from 1935 to 1937 he favored government intervention in the economy.

37. Friedman (1976e, xxi).

38. Consistent with this—although less reliable, because of Friedman's very imperfect latter-day memory, than the contemporaneous record—Friedman said (in *Rutgers* magazine, Fall 2006, 27) that by 1941 he had "already gone a long way" toward the free-market views with which he would be associated.

Burgin (2012, 170) claims that Friedman "parroted" Hayek's positions on the role of government when Friedman wrote on the matter in the early 1950s, but this pejorative characterization neglects the championing of free-market positions on Friedman's part during his Treasury years, even before Hayek (1944) appeared. (Burgin's position that Friedman as of the early 1950s offered a much more qualified advocacy of free markets than that he put forward in *Capitalism and Freedom* is also erroneous. Some pieces of textual evidence that invalidate Burgin's argument, and that cast doubt on a number of other contentions in Burgin's account, are noted in later chapters.)

39. The quotations are respectively from Friedman (1943a, 62) and Friedman and Kuznets (1945, v).

40. Friedman and Friedman (1980, 94).

41. See Friedman and Friedman (1980, 94-95; 1998, 145).

42. Ruger (2011, 202) cites this testimony as an unpublished statement available in the archive of Friedman's papers at the Hoover Institution (which today also has a version of the submission available on its website). In fact, however, the item (Friedman 1942b) was

printed in a Treasury package of submissions that has long been publicly available and is in the book holdings of several US libraries.

The Friedman item in this package was a written submission. However, Friedman (in *Newsweek*, August 30, 1971; see also Friedman and Friedman 1998, 112) indicated that he also gave a spoken presentation of the material to the same committee.

43. Friedman (1942b, 172).

44. Another item that Ruger suggests as evidence of Friedman's anti-market stance in 1942—support for high taxation—is discussed in the next section of this chapter. It can be stated with confidence that Friedman's support for high taxes in war is, contrary to Ruger's suggestion, not good evidence of a change in Friedman's views on markets between the early and late 1940s. The basis for this confidence lies in the fact that Friedman supported high taxes in the Korean War too: see the next chapter and chapter 10.

45. Friedman and Schwartz (1963a, 557) gave the imposition of general price controls in the United States as "early 1942."

46. As Friedman himself put it in the 1970s, "Anybody on the inside, and I'm not criticizing them, has to adjust what they say to what is the administration policy" (*Chicago Tribune*, November 28, 1976).

47. Friedman (1942b, 172). In the same spirit as his 1942 submission, which accepted controls as an existing policy tool but emphasized the other tools, Friedman would state later (Instructional Dynamics Economics Cassette Tape 161, January 1, 1975) that President Gerald Ford could not stop pressure to expand the budget deficit but could steer that pressure in the least dangerous direction.

48. Friedman recalled this in *Newsweek*, August 30, 1971.

49. Shoup, Friedman, and Mack (1941, 14). Silk (1976, 66–67) was inconsistent on Friedman's wartime position on controls, first stating that "Friedman was personally against controls" but then suggesting that Friedman's wartime views were unknown. As the material cited here indicates, however, Friedman did put on the record in the 1940s his opposition to controls, and this posture is consistent with Friedman's downplaying, in the statements he gave as a Treasury official, of the part that controls should play as an anti-inflation measure.

50. Friedman (1942a, 319).

51. See NBC (1943, i).

52. NBC (1943, 8, 10).

53. Around the time of the 1946 pamphlet (Friedman and Stigler 1946), Friedman also criticized controls in other popular outlets, including in a further appearance on the *University of Chicago Round Table* (NBC 1946a, 7–8).

These examples also indicate that Friedman's very latter-day claim (in *Reason*, June 1995, 34) that what took him into policy issues in earnest was the first Mont Pelerin Society meeting in 1947 should not be regarded as valid. Indeed, the 1995 claim flies in the face both of the record of Friedman's pre-1947 activities and his own 1976 observation, quoted earlier, that his Treasury employment got him involved in policy issues. Therefore, although treated as accurate in Burgin (2012, 169), the 1995 statement is a Friedman recollection that, like others he supplied from the 1970s onward (especially those made after his move to California in 1977), is testament to the haziness of his memories of his early career, particularly with respect to the chronology of events.

Another mid-1990s statement by Friedman has the effect of both further undermining his June 1995 *Reason* statement and reinforcing doubt about the precision of his latter-day recollections. In *Hoover Digest* (no. 2 [1996] 133), Friedman strongly agreed with a statement that he was a "policymaker" at the US Treasury—which he most certainly was not.

54. Breit and Ransom's (1971, 226) claim that Friedman was the "leading spokesman for the withholding tax" in the Second World War was not correct.

55. See Committee on Finance (1942a) and Friedman and Friedman (1998, 115, 121).

56. From Roy Blough's testimony of January 8, 1943, in Committee on Appropriations (1943, 457, 463).

57. See Friedman and Friedman (1985, 53) and Friedman and Friedman (1998, 119–23). In addition to the August 19, 1942, testimony discussed in chapter 1, Friedman returned to testify to the same subcommittee three days later, on August 22 (a Saturday) (Committee on Finance 1942b).

58. Friedman and Friedman (1998, 123).

59. Amity Shlaes (in *Wall Street Journal*, April 15, 1999) stated, "Later [i.e., after 1942], Mr. Friedman called for the abolition of the withholding system." Abolition of income tax withholding is implied by some of the tax reform proposals on which Friedman spoke supportively over the years—after all, one option he favored was an expenditure tax—but not by all of them, and Friedman certainly did not call for withholding's abolition in the statement in Friedman and Friedman (1998) on which Shlaes relied. Likewise, although Skousen (2001, 387) preceded an account of the introduction of withholding with the statement "Friedman makes the worst mistake of his career," that characterization was not Friedman's; indeed, Skousen's source (alongside Friedman and Friedman 1998) for relating the story was Friedman's June 1995 *Reason* interview, in which Friedman actually said that withholding was a "necessary" measure and that he was not making apologies for it (33).

It also deserves mention that both Shlaes and Skousen, when writing about economists, basically do so from a vantage point outside the economic-research world and not from within it. Consequently, they may not fully appreciate the tendency for economists who have made a mark to make lighthearted confessions, mea culpas, or apologies in talking about enduring parts of their work. For example, at research conferences that the present author has attended, John Taylor offered what he called a "confession" of suggesting the term "calibration" to Kydland and Prescott (1982), while David Hendry expressed regret for the term "error-correction mechanism" (Bank of Canada workshop, Ottawa, August 17, 2000, and Carnegie-Rochester Conference, Pittsburgh, November 1996, respectively). Friedman himself behaved in this way in 1977 when he apologized for coining the terms M1 and M2 (see chapter 10), and John Hicks on many occasions (for example, in Hicks 1980) claimed to regret producing the IS-LM framework (in Hicks 1937).

In any event, when considering Friedman's public interventions regarding US policy, the introduction of withholding is ruled out of candidacy as his greatest mistake when one considers that, at the time of its passage, Friedman opposed the Civil Rights Act of 1964. Many others on both sides of politics opposed the act at the time, and Friedman differed from many of the act's opponents in his support for the act's objectives; all the same, his opposition to the act (discussed further in chapter 12) must qualify as a clear-cut mistake on Friedman's part that put him on the wrong side of history.

60. See respectively, Friedman's August 22, 1942, testimony in Committee on Finance (1942b, 136) and the Friedmans' remarks in Friedman and Friedman (1985, 53).

61. See Friedman's June 30, 1996, remarks in O'Driscoll et al. (1997, 8).

62. Friedman (1954a; p. 84 of 1968 reprint).

63. See Friedman (1954a), and for a later affirmation that it is desirable that tax receipts be sensitive to the business cycle, see Friedman and Friedman (1985, 60).

64. Instructional Dynamics Economics Cassette Tape 103 (July 12, 1972). As the message of this commentary was that taxpayers largely brushed aside the existence of withholding in making their within-year spending decisions, it amounted to a further qualification to Friedman's view that a cyclically sensitive tax system contributed to economic stabilization. There is no basic contradiction between the two positions, however. According to the permanent income theory, consumers who look through short-term fluctuations in disposable income when deciding on spending will not similarly ignore fluctuations in permanent income, and a system of tax withholding makes revenue more sensitive to *both* transitory and permanent income.

65. Shoup, Friedman, and Mack (1941); Friedman (1942a); and Shoup, Friedman, and Mack (1943), the last of these including Friedman (1943b).

66. See *Newsweek*, July 24, 1978; and Friedman and Friedman (1985, 53).

67. Skousen (2001, 399) quoted Friedman stating in correspondence: "I was never a Keynesian in the sense of being persuaded of the virtues of government intervention as opposed to free markets." This statement does not contradict the characterization provided in the present chapter. Friedman's embrace during the 1940s of the Keynesian approach to the analysis of national economic magnitudes during the 1940s coincided with his return to a strong endorsement of the use of the price system and other market mechanisms for resource allocation; and Friedman's (1948a) subsequent advocacy of an actively countercyclical (albeit rule-based) fiscal policy in the 1940s explicitly separated this recommendation of an activist policy from any guidance about the overall level of government spending, other than the injunction that this level be kept stable. Friedman therefore did not accept the need for detailed economic planning and a large peacetime public sector—elements that some Keynesians included in their policy recommendations. As the discussion in this chapter shows, however, Friedman was a Keynesian during his Treasury years on the matters of the determination of national income and inflation. The inference drawn by Skousen that Friedman "never bought the Keynesian mindset" (399) is therefore not valid. Likewise, Cherrier's (2011, 345) claim that Friedman was "remarkably immunized" from Keynesianism in the 1940s is certainly not correct.

68. See Friedman (1940).

69. That Friedman's criticisms of Tinbergen did not in themselves amount to a critique of the Keynesian approach is underlined by the fact that some points in Friedman's review overlapped with Keynes's (1939a) own review of Tinbergen's work. The Keynes review, which would be quoted approvingly a half century after the event in Friedman (1991b, 36), became a much more well known critique of Tinbergen and of econometrics than Friedman's (1940) review. However, Patinkin (1976b) suggested that during the 1940s Keynes disavowed much of his critique of econometric model-building.

70. Around this time, in a biographical sketch that preceded one of his articles, the list of Friedman's books began only with Friedman (1953b). The existence of Shoup, Friedman, and Mack (1943) and other pre-1953 books was only alluded to, via the statement that the list was of his "most recent" books (Friedman 1964g, 162). However, the longer list of publications in Friedman's *Who's Who in America 1964/1965* entry did, as had prior years' entries, include his 1943 book with Shoup and Mack (Marquis Who's Who 1964, 695).

71. Friedman (1972b, 183), referring to Friedman (1942a).

72. In Taylor (2001, 118).

73. From Friedman's remarks in *The Great Economics Debate*, WGBH Boston, May 22, 1969.

74. CSPAN, November 20, 1994, p. 15 of hard-copy transcript. Friedman made these remarks as he was writing the early parts of his memoirs, and the published memoirs (Friedman and Friedman 1998, 112) would relate his surprise on rediscovering the "thoroughly Keynesian" character of the material that he wrote at the Treasury.

75. See Friedman (1982c, 54). Likewise, on UK television in 1980, Friedman said: "I have never argued that deficits are the cause of inflation, except if the deficits are financed by printing money" (*Free to Choose*, UK television version, "How to Cure Inflation," debate portion, BBC2, March 22, 1980, p. 14 of transcript).

76. Along with the example in the text, another prominent instance of a Friedman statement in this vein was his denial in Friedman (1972a, 947; 1976f, 317) that he had ever believed wealth effects were an empirically important part of short-run monetary policy transmission. In the late 1940s and in the first half of the 1950s, Friedman had, in fact, seemed to regard real balance effects as sizable.

77. Shoup, Friedman, and Mack (1941, 12).

78. See his August 19, 1942, statement in Committee on Finance (1942a, 63).

79. Friedman (1953f, 251, 253); Friedman also mentioned the 1953 insertions in Friedman (1972b, 183) and Friedman and Friedman (1998, 113).

80. See Friedman (1953f, 253–57) as well as the smaller insertions on subsequent pages. Other than the modified 1942 paper, the earliest paper in the Friedman (1953b) collection was his (1946) review of Lange (1944), discussed in the next chapter. Friedman (1953b) classified the 1946 paper as one of his "Comments on Method" rather than as one of the papers to be covered under "Monetary Theory and Policy." However, an American Economic Association bibliography (H. Smith 1951, 473) treated Friedman (1946) as a contribution to the monetary literature, citing in particular the paper's discussion of price rigidity.

81. Friedman (1953f, 251, 253). The footnote has been much mentioned (for example, Butler 1985, 9) and quoted (for instance, in Barro and Fischer 1976, 134; and Silk 1976, 65).

82. These authors also cited Friedman (1971c) in this connection.

83. Burmeister and Phelps (1971, 155) also referenced Friedman's inflationary-gap paper as an early contribution to the literature on optimal monetary policy, but they used the more apposite 1953 version of the article in their citation.

84. That is, Friedman (1940), discussed in the next chapter.

85. Rasche (1981, 267), in discussing the judgmental practices followed by econometric model-builders in arriving at their preferred specification, described them as "adamantly defended by the model manufacturers and strongly criticized by the statisticians." Friedman's 1940 critique of econometric modeling can be regarded as an early example of the criticism that statisticians would advance.

86. See Friedman and Schwartz (1963a, 252–53, 296); see also Mints (1945, 271). In his *Newsweek* column of February 7, 1972, Friedman dated a rudimentary stabilization goal on the part of the Federal Reserve back to 1914. In contrast, James Tobin went so far as to say of the Federal Reserve, "when it was founded in 1913, nobody at that time had any idea that there was such a thing as federal stabilization policy or demand management," and to suggest that this remained the case even as of 1935 (from Tobin's testimony of November 9, 1989, in Committee on Banking, Finance and Urban Affairs 1990, 26).

87. See Friedman (1982c, 60).

88. The author of this judgment, Henry C. Murphy, was a US Treasury economist from 1935 to 1948.

89. The quotation is from the filmed portion of episode 2, "The Tyranny of Control," of

the US (PBS) version of *Free to Choose*, January 19, 1980, p. 2 of transcript; it also appeared in the *Listener*, March 27, 1980, 393.

90. Shoup, Friedman, and Mack (1941, 1).

91. Friedman and Friedman (1980, 94).

92. These recommendations were not literally taken from the *General Theory*. For a discussion emphasizing that Keynes put out policy recommendations of this kind (such as public-works programs) primarily in venues other than the *General Theory*, see Patinkin (1982, 7).

93. Friedman and Meiselman (1959, 10).

94. Keynes (1940) originally appeared in the form of articles for *The Times*, and as such was one of many contributions Keynes made to popular or semipopular publications. This aspect of Keynes's career was one that had a counterpart in Friedman's own written output—a similarity noted by Patinkin (1984, 99).

Friedman himself would remark in G. Martin (1983, 62) that Keynes was a national celebrity and that this was one parallel between himself and Keynes. Indeed, several of the economists to whose work Friedman had been heavily exposed by the 1940s—including Keynes, Pigou, Marshall, and Irving Fisher—were deeply involved in discussions of economics in forums other than research publications (including not only popular writings but also parliamentary submissions or testimony to legislative bodies—which, of course, was an activity in which Friedman was involved at an early stage, via his Treasury position). Burgin (2012, 168) neglects these forerunners in claiming that Friedman was deviating from the practice of the profession when deciding to write material for popular audiences. (And in implying that Friedman's discussions of economics for popular audiences began with Friedman and Stigler 1946—see, for example, Burgin 2012, 174—Burgin, like others, overlooks the fact that Friedman's debut as a participant in radio discussions—another forum that Patinkin 1984 noted was used by both Friedman and Keynes—preceded 1946.)

95. See Friedman's remarks in Instructional Dynamics Economics Cassette Tape 17 (March 1969) and in Snowdon and Vane (1997, 204).

96. Friedman (1943b, 131).

97. Comstock (1942, 99). In addition, a 1941 book *Paying for Defense* (A. Hart and Allen 1941) had a chapter on the Keynes Plan. Although Friedman was not a contributor to the book, its subject matter (the interaction of fiscal policy, inflation control, and the defense effort) was identical to that he was assigned to analyze at the Treasury, and he was certainly familiar with the book (an item published by September 1941, which the Federal Reserve Board Library lists as its acquisition date). As noted in the previous chapter, the preface of the book thanked Friedman (giving his University of Wisconsin affiliation) for providing advice on the material in the book. Shoup, Friedman, and Mack (1943, vi) in turn included Hart in the acknowledgments for their book, and Friedman's contribution to the book cited A. Hart and Allen (1941) (see Friedman 1943b, 127).

98. Friedman (1943b, 131). So too had the A. Hart-Allen book on wartime fiscal policy (1941, 224).

99. See, for example, Keynes's (1940, 70) statement that in war conditions of full employment there is "a fixed maximum output."

100. See Patinkin (1976a, 104–5) for a discussion.

101. For Friedman's discussion of Keynesians' pessimism about the scope for monetary policy to affect aggregate demand, even outside Depression conditions, see Friedman (1968b, 2) and Friedman and Schwartz (1982a, 55).

102. Friedman (1943b, 121).

103. Friedman (1943b, 119).

104. This result comes out of a standard IS-LM analysis in which a peg is represented as a horizontal LM curve. Christiano, Eichenbaum, and Rebelo (2011) derive much the same result in a general equilibrium framework.

105. This is the way in which Friedman's continued emphasis during the Korean War on deficit control, notwithstanding his shift to a monetarist viewpoint, should be viewed. See the next chapter and chapter 10.

106. Friedman (1970a, 24, point 9; p. 16 of 1991 reprint).

107. In addition to the items cited in the discussion of withholding earlier in this chapter, see Friedman (1948a) for an endorsement (while still in his pre-monetarist phase) of cyclical variations in the budget deficit; and for latter-day reaffirmations of the same principle, see, for example, Friedman (1979, 412) and Friedman (1980a, 61; p. 60 of 1991 reprint). See also the next chapter.

108. See Friedman (1979, 412-13; 1982c, 62) and Friedman and Friedman (1985, 60).

109. Friedman (1979, 412).

110. The aforementioned former US Treasury official Henry C. Murphy recalled that as of 1935 the prevailing US Treasury department view was that the budget "was to be balanced as nearly as feasible in each peacetime year" (*South China Morning Post*, January 29, 1971, 1). Similarly, Alvin Hansen (1951a, 520) observed that in the 1920s fiscal policy was "limited by the tenets of so-called 'sound finance.'"

111. A proposed constitutional amendment to limit government spending, issued on January 30, 1979, that Friedman helped draft, did not explicitly cite war as grounds for an exemption. Instead it stated that if the president declared an emergency, a two-thirds vote of both houses of Congress could authorize spending above the amendment's ceiling (see Friedman and Friedman 1980, 313). But during the period when the proposed amendment was being prepared, Friedman indicated his view that war conditions did indeed justify deficit spending. He stated: "The amendment will also have to have a provision for emergencies. After all, if you get into a war or some other great emergency, you mustn't be hidebound" (*Meet the Press*, NBC, November 12, 1978, p. 6 of transcript). This reaffirmed an attitude Friedman had stated earlier, including in 1970 when he remarked: "You cannot responsibly tie the hands of the government in [the] case of an enormous emergency—if you have another World War II" (*Chicago Daily News*, July 29, 1970, 4).

The balanced-budget amendment that Friedman advocated during the 1980s did include an explicit reference to war as a situation in which deficit spending was permissible (see Friedman and Friedman 1985, 59).

112. Shoup, Friedman, and Mack (1941), writing before Pearl Harbor and conditioning on the assumption that the United States would not fully enter hostilities, had envisioned a balanced budget as feasible in the period ahead. But it is likely that, once federal spending had taken another dramatic step up with full US mobilization, Friedman recognized that some deficit spending was inevitable. Even Keynes (1940, 6), although pressing for tax increases in the war, had acknowledged that complete financing of wartime government spending by taxes was "not practically possible" in the case of the United Kingdom.

113. Barro (1986, 361) in turn traced the tax-smoothing ideas to Pigou (1928).

114. For the purpose of this discussion, the compulsory private saving (or compulsory loans to the government) recommended by Keynes (1940) are treated as taxes. Indeed, Cooley and Ohanian (1997, 444) labeled such measures "levies," thereby underscoring the tax-like character of the measures.

115. *Economist*, June 4, 1983 (37), quoting Keynes (1940, 51).

116. Friedman (1943a, 51).

117. Friedman (1966a, 39; p. 120 of 1968 reprint). See also NBC (1951b, 11), Friedman (1958a, 21–22), and Instructional Dynamics Economics Cassette Tape 28 (June 12, 1969).

118. See, for example, Friedman (1984c, 37) and Friedman's answer in Snowdon, Vane, and Wynarczyk (1994, 176).

119. Keynes too has been said to have been of the view that inflation created distortions when it exceeded 3 percent; Keynes is further reputed to have stated that 2.5 percent to 3 percent inflation was the appropriate rate (see Horne 1989, 70).

120. See his October 7, 1965, memorandum to the Federal Reserve Board, in Friedman (1968a, 139). In the same vein, Friedman (1960a, 93) indicated that it was likely desirable to permit higher monetary growth in war conditions. See also Friedman (1963c, 17; p. 38 of 1968 reprint).

121. Shoup, Friedman, and Mack (1941, 13).

122. Friedman (1943a, 57). See also the discussion of Clark Warburton's views on deflation later in this chapter.

123. *Firing Line*, PBS, January 5, 1972, p. 10 of transcript. In this television appearance, Friedman drew a parallel between households' gearing consumption to their permanent income and the government aligning its spending to longer-term tax revenue.

124. Robert Barro (personal communication with the author, June 11, 2013) has stressed that the tax-smoothing approach, while suggesting that primary reliance should be placed on deficit financing of World War II defense expenditures, is not inconsistent with a large increase in tax revenues and collections. Accordingly, Barro does not see Friedman's position in the November 1995 *Reason* letter (and Friedman's support for withholding) as out of line with the tax-smoothing perspective. As noted in the text, however, Friedman's position jars in key respects with the war-financing package offered in Ohanian's (1998) tax-smoothing-based analysis of budgetary management in World War II.

125. And even as early as 1948—at a stage of his thinking in which he perceived benefits in monetizing peacetime deficits—Friedman regarded issuance of (longer-term) government bonds to finance spending as necessary for noninflationary financing of war. See Friedman (1948a, 247, 250). This position was predicated on the absence of a policy of pegging interest rates, as such a policy would likely lead the Federal Reserve to purchase the bonds.

126. The same is true of the discussion in Friedman (1951c, 187), in which Friedman likewise expressed the view that higher inflation might be preferable to increases in certain types of explicit taxes.

127. Friedman and Schwartz (1963a, 571).

128. See Friedman and Schwartz (1982a, 102–4). Friedman and Schwartz used the net national product deflator, but for the period between 1938 and 1950 its mean growth rate is very similar to Balke and Gordon's (1986) GNP deflator series.

129. Friedman and Schwartz (1982a) assumed a static relationship between nominal income growth and inflation in adjusting prices for price-control episodes. As discussed in E. Nelson (2013b), a more realistic assumption would have been that inflation lags nominal income growth. Under that alternative assumption, the adjustment for price controls would have likely led to the peak in inflation occurring later in the war than in 1942–43.

130. Friedman (1943a, 50).

131. Friedman (1943a, 52, 60).

132. Friedman (1943a, 62).

133. Friedman (1943a, 55).

134. Friedman (1943a, 60).

135. Friedman (1943b, 120) contrasted what he perceived to be the unstable money-

and-income relationship with what he called the "considerably more regular" empirical relation between consumption and income.

136. See chapter 1.

137. In particular, Friedman may have accepted the arguments, discussed later in this chapter, that Hansen advanced in the mid-1940s (in Alvin Hansen 1947a, for example). He may have also been sympathetic at this point to modifications of the Keynesian consumption function—such as those that would be made by Duesenberry (1949) and T. Brown (1952)—that were less fundamental than that implied by the permanent income hypothesis.

138. Friedman (1943a, 61).

139. For example, many of the UK treatments of the expenditure tax that came in the wake of Kaldor (1955) did not mention Friedman's work in the area. A recent discussion that follows this practice is that of Skidelsky and Skidelsky (2013, 206), who state that the "expenditure tax had distinguished supporters before Kaldor," although they name only John Stuart Mill and Irving Fisher. In a similar vein, Kay and King's (1978, 74) list of the key figures who had advocated an expenditure tax named "Hobbes, Mill, Fisher, and, more recently Kaldor," while Mervyn King elsewhere (*New Statesman*, April 13, 1979, 508) named Kaldor (1955) as the key reference but added: "Other distinguished economists had recommended the idea before Kaldor."

Such a practice is, however, not unique to UK discussions. For example, Auerbach and Hassett (2015, 41) state that "implicit in some of the early arguments for consumption taxation (e.g., Kaldor [1955]), is the ability of consumption taxes to hit existing sources of wealth, attributable to rents, inheritances, disguised labor income, etc." This argument was, in fact, present (and *ex*plicit) in both Kaldor (1955) and Friedman (1943a), although the authors' citation of the former reference may have been helpful in underscoring the point that the argument has been advanced by economists of varying political views.

140. Friedman's advocacy of the expenditure tax also differed from the US Treasury's official wartime position, which did not see the expenditure tax replacing the income tax (Prest 1956, 36).

141. A still later occasion on which Friedman advocated a tax system that consisted principally of a flat tax on spending took place on March 31, 2005, when he appeared before the President's Advisory Panel on Federal Tax Reform (2005, 103).

142. See Friedman (1972b, 184); see also Friedman and Schwartz (1982a, 207) and Friedman and Friedman (1998, 223). Similar assessments by others include Seymour Harris's description of Hansen as "the most prominent Keynesian in the United States" (in his editor's introduction in Alvin Hansen 1953, xi); Tobin's (1987a, 95) observation that Hansen "became the leading apostle and interpreter of Keynes in America"; and Sims's (2012, 1187) reference to "the leading American Keynesian, Alvin Hansen."

143. Alvin Hansen (1932) was referenced in Friedman and Schwartz (1963a, 306, 409).

144. See Friedman's remarks in Snowdon and Vane (1997, 194–95); the quotations are from pages 195 and 194, respectively. In his interview with Snowdon and Vane, Friedman also cited Hansen's genial personality as a factor behind his influence. In an interview for this book, George Kaufman has suggested that part of Friedman's success in the postwar period reflected the same phenomenon. "My view of Friedman was he was a delightful person. He gave me a recommendation when I went to Oregon, and he treated me well. He treated everybody well. I always tell people that if he had not been such a nice person, he probably would never have had the influence that he had" (George Kaufman, interview, November 12, 2013).

All that said, both Hansen and Friedman had an acerbic side. This fact was borne out by the content of many of their published rebuttals to critics and, in Friedman's case, by Bennett McCallum's remark to the present author (in August 1994) that Friedman was indeed a nice person, but that he became less nice when you disagreed with him. See also the next chapter.

145. After making this observation, Robert Solow (interview, December 2, 2013) elaborated: "First of all, when I was an undergraduate—this was before the war—Keynesian economics was *verboten*. The official department refused to recognize it." Solow went on to observe that this remained the case in the early years after the war. "I came back in 1945 from the army, and I was in the money-and-banking course, which was the macroeconomics course and was taught with graduate students and undergraduates together. And John Williams did some of the lecturing, and Alvin Hansen did some of the lecturing, and there was very little Keynesian economics taught. There was the famous fiscal policy seminar that Hansen ran—well, Hansen and Williams when Williams was present—and apparently, graduate students—those who were advanced, older than I—were able to talk about Keynesian economics there. But apart from that seminar, I would not have described Harvard as a center of Keynesian economics at all. Lloyd Metzler was gone; Jim Tobin was gone. It was really only Hansen, and then only in that one advanced seminar, and then watered down by John Williams." (A related judgment was expressed by Samuelson 1976, 24, 26.)

In the following generation, however, Hansen's teaching of Keynesian economics would figure prominently in the university's graduate courses, and in the late 1950s Dale Jorgenson was one of the last students to take Hansen's course, which drew largely on Alvin Hansen (1953) (Dale Jorgenson, interview, September 12, 2014).

146. See Samuelson (1946, 188); Lucas (1994a, 2004), Charles Plosser's remarks in Snowdon, Vane, and Wynarczyk (1994, 285); and Bennett McCallum in Backhouse and Salanti (2000, 86) and McCallum (2014). Samuelson, and most of the others just mentioned, also credited the post-Keynes authors with providing a more internally consistent model than that available in the *General Theory*, a judgment with which Robert Solow also provided sympathy in an interview for this book (December 31, 2013). See also Friedman's favorable reaction in Snowdon and Vane (1997, 195) when given Plosser's judgment on the matter.

147. For example, Friedman and Meiselman (1963, 187) cited portions of Alvin Hansen's (1951a) *Business Cycles and National Income* as the basis of their characterization of the simple income-expenditure theory, with which they contrasted the quantity theory. Likewise, one critic of Keynes has claimed that "the income-expenditure model . . . was developed by Hansen et al. to explain Keynes" (*Listener*, January 5, 1978). A similar judgment regarding Hansen's contribution was expressed by Samuelson (1976, 25, 29).

148. For an example of Simons's criticism of Hansen in print, see Simons (1942). This article included Simons's declaration, "I come to bury Hansen—albeit respectfully and despairingly" (Simons 1942, 162)—the first part of which was later used by *Fortune* magazine (June 1, 1967, 132) to summarize Simons's position.

149. See Alvin Hansen (1947b; 1947c, 143). These two discussions considered Burns (1946), with the second discussion attributing to Burns a "number of elementary misconceptions."

150. Specifically, these were the April 1951 Sulphur Springs conference on inflation (Director 1952) discussed in chapter 10 below, and an October 1951 conference in Princeton, New Jersey, organized by the National Planning Association (see Joint Committee on the Economic Report 1952a, 1297). A Friedman entry appeared in the index for Hansen's aforementioned 1951 book, *Business Cycles and National Income*. But the entry was not for

Milton Friedman; it was for Rose Friedman, whose work on consumption with Dorothy Brady (Brady and Friedman 1947) Alvin Hansen (1951a, 168) cited. In connection with the symposium on monetary policy discussed presently, see Harris (1951); Friedman (1951c); and Alvin Hansen (1951b).

151. As discussed in the next chapter, Friedman's comments (Friedman 1951c) were written soon after his views had crystallized into the familiar monetarist positions with which he would subsequently become associated, and his article included an affirmation of the appropriateness of monetary policy actions, rather than the deployment of fiscal policy or incomes policy, against inflation. However, Friedman's discussion played down the contrast of these views concerning monetary policy with those of the Keynesian Harris, with Friedman emphasizing the parts of Harris's (1951) paper that had acknowledged both the effectiveness of monetary policy and the problems with past monetary policy, and casting Harris as regarding monetary measures against inflation as desirable but unlikely to occur.

In taking this tack, Friedman glossed over many of the differences between himself and Harris, whose views on monetary policy and on the structure of the economy coincided closely with those of Alvin Hansen. A blunter discussion of Harris's views on these matters came in a memorandum to Federal Reserve chairman William McChesney Martin in October 1963 by Ralph Young of the Federal Reserve Board's senior staff. Young wrote that Harris had long taken the position "that monetary policy was relatively unimportant and impotent," and that Harris had in the 1950s and early 1960s modified this position in a way that still left him a critic of the idea that monetary policy should focus on the control of inflation (Young 1963, 3).

152. See Friedman (1943b, 117).

153. See, for example, Friedman (1980b, 502, 511), as well as the items cited earlier.

154. See, for example, Friedman and Schwartz (1982a, 207).

155. From Friedman's May 17, 1979, testimony, in Committee on the Judiciary (1980, 149).

156. See, for example, Friedman and Heller (1969, 74). As acknowledged in Friedman (1962a, 75–76), however, the particular "secular-stagnation" thesis, advocated by Hansen and discussed presently, did establish a strong presumption in favor of government spending as the means of providing fiscal stimulus.

157. Alvin Hansen (1953, 76–77). Hansen also employed arguments to the effect that the observed stability of the consumption/income ratio over time reflected the stabilizing effect of other factors, and that, absent these factors, consumption would not keep pace with potential income (Alvin Hansen 1947c, 137; see also Hazlitt 1959, 115). In effect, this amounted to arguing that a declining-marginal-propensity consumption function was indeed the underlying structural relationship in the US data. According to this argument, the downward pressure on spending imparted by households' preferences was not detectable in US data because of the offsetting actions by the fiscal authorities.

158. See, for example, Alvin Hansen (1938a; 1938b, 72; 1939a, 4–5 and 1, 9–11; 1939b, 1) for Hansen's early discussions of secular stagnation. Another early study was Lange (1939), which was concerned with what Lange described as a "widely held" view "that the American economy has lost its momentum of expansion and reached a stage of more or less permanent stagnation" (503) and which went on to endorse that view. See *National Review*, June 16, 1989a, for Friedman's characterization of the state of professional thinking on the issue of secular stagnation as of 1940, alongside Robert Solow's response (June 16, 1989b). See also Boianovsky (2016).

Because one pillar of the stagnation hypothesis was that monetary policy was incapable of providing stimulus to demand that offsets the underconsumption, it is possible, as in Schlesinger (1956) and Wilson (1976, 106), to view the secular-stagnation position as part of Hansen's and the *General Theory*'s denial of the effectiveness of monetary policy. Furthermore, the scenarios in which Keynes pictured the liquidity trap as relevant frequently coincided with cases in which secular stagnation also prevailed: this is clear from Friedman's (1972a, 945-46) own list of Keynes's (1936) references to the liquidity trap, particularly items 6 and 13 in Friedman's list. Appropriately, therefore, in the aforementioned 1989 piece Friedman himself identified both Keynes and Hansen with the secular-stagnation thesis.

159. Friedman (1972a, 942).

160. Friedman's interpretation of Keynes occupied much of Friedman (1963a, 1970a, 1970b, 1972a). In particular, as discussed in chapter 14, it proved to be a major area of contention in Friedman's 1970-72 *Journal of Political Economy* exchange with his critics. In this connection, Littleboy's (1990) analysis is worth noting. That study carried out an extensive analysis of different interpretations of Keynes, one of Littleboy's concerns being the degree of opposition voiced in the literature to the notion that Keynes endorsed the liquidity trap. In judging that Keynes was willing to rely, "if pressed," on the trap argument in forming a case against the effectiveness of monetary policy, Littleboy (1990, 189) came out with a conclusion that closely matched Friedman's.

The conformity of Friedman's characterization of Keynes's views, both on the aggregate demand and supply side, with the interpretation offered by Keynes's biographer Roy Harrod is discussed in E. Nelson and Schwartz (2008a); see also Tavlas (1989) as well as Harrod's discussions of the *General Theory* in Harrod (1937, 1951) and in *New Statesman*, December 5, 1969. For more on Friedman's interpretation of Keynes's views, see E. Nelson (2009a, 2009b).

161. See, for example, Friedman (1964b, 1972b, 1975a), and Friedman and Schwartz (1963a, chapter 11). See also Fischer (1975) and Barro and Fischer (1976).

162. Friedman (1980b, 502, 511). Friedman and Schwartz (1970a, 101-2) earlier cited Alvin Hansen (1949) because it was a study that compiled data on the stock of money.

163. See p. ix of Seymour Harris's introduction to Alvin Hansen (1949).

164. Nor could Alvin Hansen (1953), which is the reference that Sims (2012, 1187) singles out as being dismissive of monetary policy.

165. In contrast, adjustments to, or variations in, interest rates would be an implication both of monetary-growth rules of the kind Friedman later advocated and of the interest-rate rules that arise from analyses based on Wicksellian and New Keynesian principles.

166. Friedman (1968b, 2). As already discussed, Friedman as of 1943 appeared to subscribe to the view that the IS curve was vertical, and he was therefore a believer in this second form of "damnation" of monetary policy.

167. Friedman (1968b, 4).

168. See Alvin Hansen (1945, 250-55); and Friedman (1972b, 184).

169. See Friedman and Schwartz (1963a, 624), citing Alvin Hansen (1951b).

170. Friedman and Schwartz (1982a, 207). See also Alvin Hansen (1953, 188); and Keynes (1936, 299).

171. Friedman (1964a, 1222). From the beginning, Friedman viewed his project with Schwartz as entailing a study of velocity: see the next chapter.

172. See also Modigliani (1986b, 12) for a discussion.

173. See Friedman (1968d, 11; 1970a, 13 [p. 6 of 1991 reprint]; 1980b, 502) and Friedman and Schwartz (1982a, 207).

174. See his remarks in Klamer (1983, 135).

175. An example, discussed in the previous chapter, is the case of the 1930s.

176. See Friedman (1976f, 316). From this focus on velocity sprang Friedman and Meiselman's (1963) description of the difference between the Keynesian and monetarist schools in terms of the relative stability of the multiplier and of velocity. Indeed, Friedman (1971d, 330) went so far as to describe the monetarist view as implying that "nominal variables [are determined] by velocity"—by which he meant, not that velocity swamps money as a source of variations in nominal income, but that there is structure to the behavior of velocity in a way that allows predictions of nominal income behavior using money.

177. Friedman and Schwartz (1963a, 523).

178. *Newsweek*, June 16, 1975. Samuelson (1976, 30–31) made a similar statement. In that later discussion, Samuelson indicated that Hansen adhered to this view by 1945, although Samuelson did not provide a specific reference. Samuelson likely had in mind passages like Hansen (1947a, 236) in which Hansen verbally sketched a downward-sloping Phillips curve that held in a region in which unemployment was near but above the full-employment rate. A subsequent book by Alvin Hansen (1957) was excerpted in Okun's (1972a) collection in a section Okun titled "The Unemployment-Inflation Dilemma." However, the late date of Alvin Hansen (1957) means that it cannot be the contribution to which Samuelson was referring in his 1975 retrospective. Furthermore, the discussion in Alvin Hansen (1957)—for example, pp. 43–45—was principally concerned not with the inflation/unemployment trade-off but with the possible conflict between maximum economic growth and the pursuit of zero inflation.

179. The other matters in question included the sharp distinction between money and credit, on which Friedman and Schwartz (1963a, 448) went out of their way to acknowledge Warburton as a forerunner. However, their acknowledgment of Warburton's work on this topic also underscores the absence of a discussion in the *Monetary History* of the emphasis on the money/credit distinction given by Lauchlin Currie (1934), whom Meltzer (2003, 30) argued was responsible for making the distinction an important part of the analysis of Federal Reserve policy. For a discussion of Currie, see chapter 11 below.

180. Cagan (1987, p. 196 of 1989 reprint).

181. Friedman and Schwartz (1963a, xxii). This remark came after the authors thanked Warburton for "detailed and valuable comments on several drafts" of the *Monetary History*. Warburton was also mentioned on several occasions throughout the text of the book, a fact reflected in his three-line entry in the book's index of names (an entry that was incomplete, failing to include Friedman and Schwartz's mention of Warburton in the preface). Karl Brunner and Allan Meltzer, in their historical analysis of Federal Reserve strategy, offered similar praise: "we wish to acknowledge a large debt to Clark Warburton[,] whose published descriptions of Federal Reserve policy and its consequences are in many ways unique. We were often heartened, on arriving at an interpretation of the reasons for Federal Reserve procedures, to find that he had arrived at the same interpretation much earlier" (Brunner and Meltzer 1964a, viii).

182. The discussion that follows focuses on the analysis Warburton provided during the war years and its relationship to Friedman's work. Bordo and Schwartz (1979, 1983) and Cargill (1979, 1981) provided more wide-ranging treatments of Warburton's contributions.

183. Warburton (1943a, 1943b, 1944).

184. Friedman's advocacy of this point featured especially prominently in Friedman (1952b). Warburton's analysis of this issue, like Friedman's, bears witness to the fact noted above (in the discussion of Alvin Hansen) that the quantity-theory approach makes velocity a key structural variable.

185. Although he was critical of much of their analysis, Friedman noted in a 1992 interview that Federal Reserve staff "made important contributions to monetary analysis and theory going back to the 1920s" (Levy 1992, 8). See also Friedman (1960a, 93). On other occasions, however, he emphasized that a lull occurred in the Federal Reserve's prominence in research between the 1920s and the 1960s (see, for example, Friedman 1976b, 435; and Instructional Dynamics Economics Cassette Tapes 12, January 1969, and 62, December 3, 1970; see also *Newsweek*, March 1, 1971). As of the late 1940s, the Federal Reserve Board (which also had, and still does have, a division called the Division of Research and Statistics) was considered unusual among governmental agencies in having staff for whom publication of research was a regular part of their work (see Bach 1950, 124).

186. Yeager recalled this gag order as having been issued during the Eisenhower administration—a chronology that is consistent with the 1953 date given in Leeson (2003d, 286).

187. NBC (1946a, 12). A full discussion of the evolution of Friedman's views on inflation is deferred until chapters 4 and 7. But a major reason for doubting that the 1946 broadcast remark was a recommendation for deflation is that at the time the large excess of measured inflation over monetary growth prevailing may have led Friedman to believe that a money-stock decline was needed simply to deliver price stability. (In retrospect, as figure 3.1 suggests, much of the measured difference seems to have reflected simply the removal of price controls.) In the same spirit, in a 1951 broadcast (NBC 1951a, 6) Friedman stated that the Federal Reserve should have reduced the money stock in the period since June 1950 by an amount sufficient to keep prices stable.

188. See Friedman (1949b, 954), and for the quotation, see Friedman (1951a, 233).

189. See the previous chapter.

190. For Friedman's remarks to the effect that mild deflation might be compatible with satisfactory performance of the real economy, see House Republican Research Committee (1984, 44), and for his indication that he nevertheless recommended zero inflation, see House Republican Research Committee (1984, 42, 44). These remarks were given in July 1984; in late June, Friedman had recalled, in an unfavorable manner, the steep rates of deflation of the early 1930s (see Heller et al. 1984, 47).

191. Warburton's analysis so clearly anticipated Friedman's work that it is important not to overstate Warburton's lead in years. One such overstatement appears in Yeager (1981, 280), via the claim, "I recall Warburton's mentioning to me, probably in 1953, that he had recently heard that Friedman was turning his attention to money." By no means did Friedman turn his attention to money only in 1953. By 1953, Friedman had already published early findings on monetary relations, drawing on his work with Anna Schwartz (see Friedman 1952b); had testified to Congress using quantity-theory analysis (in Joint Committee on the Economic Report 1952b, 1952c); and had urged the removal of the Federal Reserve's peg of the long-term bond rate doing so most notably (in the course of 1950 and 1951—for example, in Friedman et al. 1951). As stressed repeatedly in this book, Friedman was recognizably monetarist in his written work by 1951 after a transition period starting in 1948. Indeed, one of his earliest monetarist writings (specifically, Friedman 1951f) was cited by Warburton (1952, 500), and Warburton was corresponding with Friedman on money by that point (see, for example, Leeson 2003d, 286; Lothian and Tavlas 2018; and the Friedman/Warburton correspondence held in the Clark Warburton papers, George Mason University).

192. Specifically, Cargill (1979, 444) asserted: "Warburton used the equation-of-exchange version of the quantity theory as his framework, while present-day monetarists reject this formulation."

193. Friedman (1972a, 915).

194. Mehrling (2014, 182, 184) contended that "Samuelson took the lesson that the classical equation of exchange, $MV = PY$, presents an overly simplified view of the role of money," prior to referring to "the simplistic quantity equation that Samuelson rejects in 1947 and that Friedman resuscitates in his 1956 'Restatement.'" However, contrary to Mehrling's characterization, Friedman (1956a) did not, in fact, use the equation of exchange in his analysis. By the same token, the Cargill position that is challenged in the text of the present section—that is, that modern monetarists did not use the equation of exchange—could be defended if the Friedman (1956a) article was used as the sole representation of the monetarist position.

195. See Joint Committee on the Economic Report (1952c, 743) and Friedman (1968c, 1974b); other examples include Friedman (1970b, 1973b) and (among items that appeared after Cargill wrote his paper) Friedman and Schwartz (1982a), Friedman (1987a, 1992c), and Friedman's *Wall Street Journal* pieces of July 5, 1989, and August 19, 2003. That Friedman was well disposed toward organizing analysis in terms of the equation of exchange is also borne out by the fact that his car license plates, in a November 2005 photograph on Robert Gordon's webpage, reads "MV · PY."

196. See Friedman (1987a, 1987e). Newcomb's contribution had also been stressed in Arthur Burns's (1929) discussion of the quantity theory of money.

197. See, for example, Friedman (1973b). See also Patinkin (1995, 123) and McCallum and Nelson (2011, 99), among others, for more recent discussions of the connection between the equation of exchange and the quantity theory of money.

198. Another claimed difference between Warburton and Friedman is that the former, according to Bordo and Schwartz (1979, 51), neglected a price rise as a way in which an inflationary gap created by excess money might be closed. But this is such a fundamental point that it seems implausible that it eluded Warburton, although the passage Bordo and Schwartz apparently had in mind (in Warburton 1943a, 368) could be interpreted as containing the error they cited. Another interpretation of the passage in question, however, is that Warburton was arguing (correctly) that a one-time price level increase does not eliminate excess purchasing power if the latter was stemming from a continuous increase in the money stock.

199. Although Warburton (1946b) was reprinted in the American Economic Association's *Readings in Monetary Theory* in a section titled "Money, the Rate of Interest and Employment" (Lutz and Mints 1951, part 3), Warburton's paper was principally concerned with money and aggregate economic activity, and not with interest rates.

200. Even so, Warburton appeared, in correspondence with Friedman, to take joint credit with Friedman for the latter's ideas about the Phillips curve. See the quotations from a January 1968 letter from Warburton to Friedman in Leeson (2003d, 286). From the material quoted, however, it is not certain that Warburton was classing the Phillips-curve material in the draft of Friedman's (1968b) address as a set of views that the two of them shared. He may have been referring to other aspects of Friedman's address—such as the critique of early Keynesian views on monetary policy or the advocacy of rules for monetary growth—on which it is not controversial that Warburton anticipated Friedman. In addition, it should be noted that, in the portion of the Warburton letter that follows the passage quoted in Leeson (2003d), Warburton emphasized his and Friedman's debt to their predecessors and thus moved away from the notion that Friedman followed specifically in Warburton's footsteps (copy of letter in Clark Warburton papers, George Mason University).

201. For his part, Friedman traced the expectational-Phillips-curve idea to David Hume. See chapter 13 below.

202. That is, Friedman marked himself out via the natural-rate hypothesis, of which Friedman's most famous exposition was in Friedman (1968b).

203. See Friedman and Schwartz (1963a, 355–56) and Friedman (1970a, 16–17; pp. 9–10 of 1991 reprint) as well as Despres et al. (1950, 532). See also E. Nelson (2013a) for a discussion.

204. Warburton (1943b, 610).

205. Warburton (1951, 340; p. 414 of 1966 reprint).

206. Although Kashyap and Stein (2000) focused on the assets side of commercial banks' balance sheets, their results supported the notion that bank capital bears on the value of the money multiplier. Congdon (1994, 18; 2011, 378; 2014) has also emphasized the role of bank capital in money-supply determination. (However, Congdon's work differs from that of Friedman and Warburton because Congdon downplays the role that commercial bank reserves play in banks' decisions concerning balance-sheet size.)

207. Tavlas (1989, 237) gave a similar assessment.

208. In the same vein, a letter to *Business Week* (January 11, 1964) said of Friedman: "He has built, for example, on the very massive evidence produced by Dr. Clark Warburton prior to 1950 on the relationship of money supply and the business cycle."

Warburton also served as one of the discussants of Friedman and Schwartz (1963b) when that paper was presented at the Carnegie Institute of Technology. His brief discussion (given in 1962 with the published version appearing as Warburton 1963) was matter-of-fact in tone, accepting Friedman and Schwartz's findings but without enthusiasm. It was a seemingly jaded reaction, taking the position that Friedman and Schwartz were reporting regularities that he endorsed but that he felt should already have been widely known. This reaction was consistent with the characterization of Warburton's attitude to Friedman's research that Leland Yeager gave in the interview quotation provided above, as well as with Warburton's reaction, in conversation with Thomas Cargill, to the wide attention given to Friedman-Schwartz work (see Cargill 1981, 90).

A further hint of Warburton's disillusionment by 1963 with the effort to get his own research recognized is provided by the fact that, having been given this opportunity to appear in print again in a major journal, Warburton provided only a short (two-page) comment that cited none of his earlier work. Warburton's 1963 comment also appears to have been a rushed effort—as it at one point referred sloppily to Friedman and Schwartz (1963b) as a solo-authored Friedman article.

Chapter Four

1. Friedman's *Who's Who in America 1976/77* entry (Marquis Who's Who 1976, 1080) gave his position as associate director, Statistical Research Group, Division of War Research, Columbia University; see also Friedman and Friedman (1998, 125). The director of research at the SRG was W. Allen Wallis, Friedman's 1942 coauthor. Wallis had also been a student at the University of Chicago from 1933 to 1935 (American Economic Association 1970, 459), and so he overlapped with Friedman there in the 1934–35 year, during which they both helped edit the volume that paid tribute to Frank Knight.

2. See, for example, Walters (1987, 422–23); and Friedman and Friedman (1998, 125, 133).

3. W. A. Wallis (1947, vii) stated that the organization's operations disbanded on September 30, 1945, with the exception of work to compile the two books providing the unclassified portion of the SRG's research.

4. See Eisenhart, Hastay, and Wallis (1947) and Freeman, Friedman, Mosteller, and Wallis (1948); see also Friedman (1946, 613). Frazer's (2002, 271) statement that Friedman worked at the "U.S. government, wartime Statistical Research Group" was therefore not appropriate; nor is Ebenstein's (2007, 44) reference to the "Statistical Research Group, a wartime government research entity" altogether apposite. Similarly, as noted in chapter 2, Medema's (2007, vii) claim that Friedman was "outside of academia" for "much of the period from 1935 to 1946" gives the wrong impression (as did a statement in a *Glasgow Herald* profile of July 30, 1982, that Friedman spent ten years in government agencies). Friedman had affiliations with academic institutions for roughly two-thirds of the period from 1935 to 1946, including his Statistical Research Group affiliation of 1943–46 (which Medema erroneously takes as a post outside academia).

It is also noteworthy in this connection that the dust jacket for Friedman (1953b) named Columbia University among the institutions with which Friedman had "been associated, in various teaching and research positions." At different times, Friedman had indeed been both a teacher and a salaried researcher at the university.

5. Friedman's affiliation on the title page of Friedman and Kuznets (1945) was instead given solely as the National Bureau of Economic Research, and his name also appeared on the NBER's "Research Staff" page of the book. Although that book was an NBER product, Friedman would not have been allowed to give his affiliation as NBER if he had departed the bureau altogether: for example, in the 1982 Friedman-Schwartz NBER book *Monetary Trends*, no NBER affiliation appeared alongside Friedman's name, as he had left the NBER for good in 1981. (In Friedman and Schwartz 1986a, 199, both Friedman and Schwartz were listed as current NBER affiliates, but this was a mistake.) Friedman was able to be designated an NBER affiliate in Friedman and Kuznets (1945) because he remained officially affiliated with the NBER between 1940 and 1945, although formally on leave from the organization (Friedman 1946, 613; Europa Publications 2003, 567). This also explains why, although in *Who's Who in America 1976/77* Friedman listed his period as a member of the NBER research staff as 1937–46 and from 1948 onward, in Blaug (1986, 291), Friedman instead gave his time on the NBER research staff as limited to the years 1937–40 and 1948–81. In the latter entry, Friedman was evidently restricting the years listed to those for which he had been a remunerated employee of the NBER.

6. See Snowdon, Vane, and Wynarczyk (1994, 173).

7. Friedman (1944, 101).

8. Friedman (1970b, 207); see also Friedman and Schwartz (1982a, 43).

9. Friedman (1944, 102).

10. Friedman (1944, 102).

11. Friedman and Meiselman (1963, 169).

12. Friedman (1968d, 10) and *Wall Street Journal*, April 26, 1984. On other occasions Friedman made the similar observation that one cannot beat a candidate without a candidate (for example, in M. Anderson 1982, 202).

13. American Statistical Association (1950, 271).

14. Friedman (1946, 613).

15. See Walters (1987, 423); Olkin (1991, 125); and Friedman and Friedman (1998, 134–37). It might appear that still another dimension of Friedman's contribution to the United States' war effort was brought out by the reference in Speers (1982, 12) to "Milton Friedman, the great U.S. code-breaker of World War II." This reference, however, was simply a result of a confusion of the names of Milton Friedman and code breaker William F. Friedman.

16. From Friedman's concluding remarks in Friedman and Schwartz (1991, 48).

17. See the Friedman remarks in Friedman and Schwartz (1991, 49).

18. The quotation is from Friedman's addendum in Friedman and Schwartz (1991, 48).

19. Consider, for example, this recollection in Burman (1969, 154): "But even if we found an R^2 [for a regression] as high as 0.9, in the absence of any causal explanation we would do well to be very skeptical of its future performance. To give an example, several years ago I published a regression with 20 observations on one variable that gave a [squared] correlation of 0.995. . . . Yet in later years the prediction errors in the equation became much larger and it had to be abandoned." In addition, a time-series statistician, Oliver Anderson, observed (1976, 488): "As everyone should know, goodness of fit to the past is no measure for quality of agreement between forecasts and future outcomes." The basic message concerning regression analysis that underlay Friedman's anecdote was so familiar that Bennett McCallum, when serving as the editor for Friedman and Schwartz (1991), suggested to Friedman that he delete the anecdote from the final version of the paper, advice that was not accepted (Hammond 1996, 206; also, author's conversation with Bennett McCallum in the mid-1990s).

20. See his remarks in Friedman and Schwartz (1991, 48).

21. On that occasion, Friedman mentioned Wesley Mitchell as someone who had made similar points (Friedman 1940, 659).

22. For the quotation, see Friedman (1952a, 14). That the remarks were written in 1935 was noted in Friedman (1952a, 9).

23. The quotations are respectively from Friedman's remarks in Friedman and Schwartz (1991, 49) and from Friedman (1940, 659).

24. See Friedman (1986a, 87–88). Friedman would recount the story again in his solo-authored addendum to Friedman and Schwartz (1991), in Friedman and Friedman (1998, 142–44), and in Taylor (2001, 122).

25. Friedman and Schwartz (1991, 49). For an earlier statement along similar lines, albeit focusing on the problems of the interpretability rather than the fragility of multiple regressions, see Friedman (1960b, 191–92).

26. See, for example, Hammond (1992, 109). See also the extensive discussion in chapter 10 below.

27. W. A. Wallis (1948, ix). (Wallis, like Friedman, was on the academic staff of the University of Chicago starting in 1946: in Wallis's case, at the Graduate School of Business, to which he was initially appointed a professor of statistics and economics: see American Economic Association 1970, 459.) As noted above, a companion volume covering some other SRG research had appeared in 1947; in the latter case, the introduction was dated January 1947 (W. A. Wallis 1947, x). Friedman authored three chapters (in two cases as solo author) for the 1947 volume but, in contrast to *Sampling Inspection*, was not a credited coeditor.

28. Not just statisticians but also eminent economists have made a point of noting this connection. For example, in an interview for this book (January 24, 2014), Thomas Sargent observed that "if you read Abraham Wald's work on sequential analysis, he thanks Milton Friedman for suggesting the problem to him." Paul Samuelson also alluded to this acknowledgment in a 1976 *Newsweek* column on Friedman (October 25, 1976a).

29. See Friedman's remarks in Friedman and Friedman (1998, 145) for this judgment. The same assessment was earlier expressed, presumably on the basis of information from Friedman, in Silk (1976, 67), and by Friedman in a November 1976 letter to Stephen Stigler (quoted in S. Stigler 2007, 10).

30. The *New York Times*, led astray by Friedman's continuing publications in the statistical field, would erroneously claim (September 5, 1947) that Friedman was an associate professor of statistics at the University of Chicago.

31. In Sanderson (2012, 8).

32. Stigler joined the University of Chicago staff in 1958 (American Economic Association 1970, 424) as both a member of the economics department and the business school (G. Stigler 1988, 157). As discussed below, Stigler had missed out on the economics slot into which Friedman moved in 1946.

33. Arnold Harberger (interview, April 12, 2013), commenting on the gladiatorial reputation that the University of Chicago's economics discussions would acquire, stated, "I would say the grand gladiator of that era was Stigler, who could throw barbs in every direction." Stephen Stigler (interview, November 6, 2013) observed: "My father was incredibly quick in that department—and sometimes quicker than he really wanted to be, because sometimes this would injure people where no injury was intended." In contrast, "Milton had a sense of humor, but that was not his forte, really. His forte was that he could see to the bottom of an argument and the implications of certain premises faster than most people. And that gave him an incredible leg-up in debates and conversations of a different type."

34. On Friedman's accessibility to members of the public via correspondence, see, for example, Meltzer (2011). For a negative perspective on Friedman's accessibility, in which Friedman's nontechnical way of communicating to non-economist audiences is portrayed as condescending, see Paul Samuelson's remarks in Silk (1976, 52). An alternative perspective is that Friedman got to the heart of issues when he presented nontechnical expositions of his economic arguments. This perspective is pursued in the comparison of Friedman's and Samuelson's *Newsweek* columns in chapter 14 below.

With respect to Friedman's accessibility to students, some perspective is offered by Sam Peltzman's discussion of his experience in the early 1960s of having George Stigler as his adviser: "We got along very well, but his [Stigler's] guidance was the following type: . . . 'My job is done. I told you what the problem is; you go out and solve it.' But Friedman did offer a lot of useful suggestions. He said, 'Why don't you think about setting it up this way instead of that way,' and so on and so forth. It turned out to be very useful to me" (Sam Peltzman, interview, March 1, 2013). In the same vein, Lester Telser (personal communication, November 5, 2014) recalled that Friedman, as one of Telser's PhD thesis supervisors in the mid-1950s, would go over Telser's drafts line by line and that Friedman observed to Telser that this had been Wesley Mitchell's practice with regard to Friedman's own dissertation work.

35. Friedman and Friedman (1998, 212).

36. See, for example, Friedman (1957a, x; 1968a, iv; 1968b, 1).

37. Georgescu-Roegen (1988, 27).

38. Friedman (1944, 101).

39. Carl Christ, personal communication, July 3, 2014. Carl Christ's years at the university are sourced from American Economic Association (1981, 96) and from the author's interview with Carl Christ (May 1, 2013).

40. This profile was written by Larry Martz, a *Newsweek* associate editor whom Rose Friedman (1977b, 26) judged gave an accurate picture of her husband. A *Time* magazine profile of Friedman of the same vintage (October 25, 1976) similarly referred to Friedman's "characteristic acerbity."

41. Modigliani (in August 1982 remarks given in Klamer 1983, 120) was recalling the

Friedman-Modigliani (1977) debate. Brittan (2005, 294) reported that, as early as 1953–54, Friedman was capable of among "the best put-down remarks I have ever encountered."

42. See Hammond and Hammond (2006, 32, 41).

43. Indeed, Paul Samuelson was quoted in Silk (1976, 71) as saying that the fact that the arguments in *Roofs or Ceilings?* "outraged" economists "shows you where we were in our mentality in the immediate postwar period." In fact, at the time he spoke to Silk, Samuelson was not in an ideal position to talk about the distance the profession had traveled since 1946: Samuelson had spoken favorably about wage and price controls in the early 1970s, and he was a prominent supporter of the wage/price freeze imposed in the United States in August 1971. See chapter 15.

44. Friedman and Stigler (1946; p. 173 of 1991 reprint).

45. Friedman and Stigler (1946; p. 172 of 1991 reprint).

46. An early occasion on which Friedman referred to these exchanges was in October 1968, when he spoke at an event in honor of the editor, Leonard Read, with whom Friedman had had a reconciliation. See Friedman (1968i, 23).

47. In Vaizey (1975, 76). See also *Listener*, May 30, 1974, 690. It is important not to overstate the difference in this position from that taken by Friedman and Stigler in 1946. Their disputed passage did not call for sweeping changes in the distribution of income; and, indeed, other Friedman writings in the 1940s emphasized the economic harm (in the form of the disincentives to supply productive resources to the market) liable to arise from highly redistributive government policies. See, in particular, the Friedman (1943a) spendings tax paper discussed in the previous chapter, Friedman's (1947) critique of the Lange-Lerner proposals (covered in the final section of this chapter), and his various early discussions of high marginal tax rates (also referenced in this chapter's final section).

48. *Free to Choose* (US version), PBS, episode 5, "Created Equal," filmed portion, broadcast February 15, 1980, p. 2 of transcript. This episode's filmed portion was turned into an article for the *Listener* (April 10, 1980; see p. 457 for quotation).

49. See chapter 1 as well as Friedman's remarks on CSPAN (November 20, 1994, p. 11 of hard-copy transcript). The *New York Times* (January 25, 1970, 80) described Friedman's upbringing as "impoverished."

50. Friedman (1965a, 7).

51. See, for example, Friedman's remarks in the studio debate portion of *Free to Choose* (US version), episode 2, "The Tyranny of Control," PBS, broadcast January 19, 1980, p. 9 of transcript; and in Vaizey (1975, 72, 74) (see also *Listener*, May 30, 1974, 689, 690).

52. The quotation is from National Educational Television's *Great Decisions 1968 #7: The Dollar in Danger*, WETA, March 17, 1968, p. 9 of transcript. The *University of Chicago Round Table* radio debates, although mentioned in Friedman and Friedman (1998, 189, 622), do not appear to have been examined in the research literature until E. Nelson (2012a, 2013a). Friedman's own coverage of the program in his memoirs was vague, and he confidently but erroneously stated (p. 622) that he began participating in the series only in December 1946. Other than the instance mentioned in the text, pre-1998 references to Friedman's participations in the radio series included Holden (1984, 258) (which reprinted a profile of Friedman that appeared in the *Observer*, February 17, 1980, 35).

53. Burgin (2012) contends that there is a sharp contrast between the views on the nineteenth-century laissez-faire era that Friedman expressed in *Capitalism and Freedom* (and thereafter) with those he voiced in the early postwar years. In particular, Burgin claims that Friedman shifted from holding a highly ambivalent position regarding the laissez-faire era, to taking a stand in which his praise for the era became nearly un-

conditional. Burgin's conclusion, however, is unwarranted: the elements of Friedman's discussion of the nineteenth century that Burgin claims were absent from Friedman's subsequent coverage of that period are, in fact, present in Friedman's later statements; conversely, the praise for the laissez-faire era given in Friedman's later analyses has a counterpart in the observations he provided during the early postwar period. In particular, it is not the case that only in the earlier period did Friedman regard it as desirable for the government to provide a greater welfare safety net than that available during the nineteenth century: in the 1970s, for example, Friedman stated, "I would certainly agree with you that the nineteenth century was not Utopia. But one has to look at it in terms of its time, and not ours. . . . We are standing on the shoulders of the nineteenth century" (*The Jay Interview*, ITN, July 17, 1976). Related remarks appeared in Friedman's narration in the filmed portion of *Free to Choose* (US version), episode 1, "The Power of the Market," PBS, broadcast January 12, 1980, p. 1 of transcript; and in Friedman and Friedman 1985, 70. And Friedman's praise for the rise in living standards achieved during the nineteenth century was a recurrent element of his discussions: the 1946 remark just quoted in the text has an echo in the assessments Friedman gave in later decades (for example, in Friedman 1976j, 5–6; pp. 62–65 of 1983 reprint).

54. E. Nelson (2009b, 473) discusses recollections of this trip that Friedman would relate in the 1960s and 1970s. An extensive discussion of Friedman's activities in the United Kingdom and continental Europe, including visits made for conferences of the Mont Pelerin Society, lies outside the scope of this book.

55. This sequence of positions accounts for some discrepancies between different listings Friedman gave of his successive University of Chicago affiliations. His fuller listings (such as those in *Who's Who in America 1976/77* and *Who's Who in Economics* 1986) correctly give him associate professor between 1946 and 1948 and professor thereafter. On the other hand, Friedman's listing in the 1970 American Economic Association Directory of Members gave him as professor since 1946 without distinguishing between his spells as associate professor and professor (American Economic Association 1970, 143), while his 1981 entry (American Economic Association 1981, 153) listed him as professor at the University of Chicago from 1948 onward but without any indication that he was already a department member from 1946 to 1948. Becker (1991a, 146) similarly erroneously suggested at one point that Friedman joined the department only in 1948.

The fact that Friedman became a full professor only in 1948 also should give pause before accepting too literally Rose Friedman's (1976c, 21) characterization that Friedman's appointment in 1946 was "to replace Jacob Viner," who was, of course, a full professor when he departed the University of Chicago. Friedman taught graduate price theory, as had Viner right up to his departure (Hammond 1999, xii), but he was not taking up Viner's position in the department hierarchy.

56. W. A. Wallis and Friedman (1942, 189).

57. Morgenstern (1972, ix).

58. Friedman and Savage (1948, 1952a). At the time of the publication of the articles, Friedman and Savage were both at the University of Chicago. Their prior joint work (Friedman and Savage 1947), although published with their University of Chicago affiliations given, reflected their collaboration at the SRG.

59. See Friedman (1957a, ix).

60. In addition to Friedman and Savage (1948, 1952a), see the exposition of the Friedman-Savage work in Friedman (1962b, 68–73). Paul Samuelson's capsule summary (in *Newsweek*, October 25, 1976a) of the Friedman-Savage work was that it provided the

answer to the question: "If it pays to reduce risk by insuring, how at the same time can it pay to increase risk by backing long shots?"

61. Friedman emphasized the dissonance between the Friedman-Savage papers and the Knightian perspective in Hammond (1989, 20) and indicated in Friedman (1976a, 84, 282) that he believed that the expected-utility approach, especially as developed by Savage (1954), handled stochastic problems adequately without the need for Knight's risk/uncertainty distinction. Pelloni (1987, 1996) stressed Friedman's rejection of the risk/uncertainty distinction (an aspect of Friedman's approach already noted by other commentators, including Blatt 1983, 266); oddly, however, Pelloni (1996) did not reference any of the joint Friedman-Savage work.

62. See, for example, Telser (2007, 79); Posner (2011); and Lars Hansen, Thomas Sargent, and Thomas Tallarini (1999).

63. The aforementioned Pelloni (1987, 1996) papers stressed the similarities between Friedman's approach to probability and that of the Bayesian approach. Those similarities had, however, been noted in the literature prior to Pelloni's articles: see, for example, the remark by Robert Lucas in Klamer (1983), noted below, as well as Zellner (1984, 307).

64. In particular, although the discussion in Friedman and Schwartz (1991) had, like other Friedman writings dating back to 1940, expressed concerns about econometric practice that coincide with many of those in the Bayesian literature, Friedman (1991b, 36) acknowledged that his own use of regression analysis frequently deviated from the strictures that would be implied by his critique of standard econometric practice.

65. See Hahn (1954) and the discussion at the end of this chapter.

66. Friedman (1964c).

67. In addition, Ekelund, Furubotn, and Gramm (1972b, 82) cited Friedman and Savage (1948) as among the "leading contributions to the literature" in the wake of von Neumann and Morgenstern (1944). Also, in what amounted to a tribute to Friedman's skill as an expositor, they quoted Friedman and Savage (1948, 287–88) rather than von Neumann and Morgenstern themselves in order to provide a capsule summary of the von Neumann-Morgenstern expected-utility theory.

68. And, in particular, Friedman (1953e). See also Friedman (1955c).

69. See in particular Friedman (1976a, 82). For treatments of Savage along the same lines see Rachev, Stoyanov, and Fabozzi (2008, 140) and Sugden (2004, 726–30).

70. For example, in Klamer (1983, 40), Robert Lucas stated that Friedman was "very influenced by Savage and by this Bayesian way of thinking about probabilities. So when I talk about people 'knowing' a probability, he just can't reach that language." Likewise, B. Klein (1978, 87) reported that Friedman had urged him to look at "probability in the purely subjective (Savage) manner." For observations that corroborate these accounts of Friedman's views, see Friedman and Schwartz (1982a, 557, 629–30) and Friedman's remarks in Snowdon and Vane (1997, 199). Frazer (1988a, 135; 1988b, 798) also quoted Friedman's praise for Savage's view of probability. (Frazer did not source the quotation; it may have been from dialogue with Friedman.) Another adherent to the Savage position was Sims (1982, 317) who stated: "The personalist interpretation of probability, as exposited in the writings of L. J. Savage, is convincing to me."

It deserves note that, although Friedman was in principle sympathetic to the Savage interpretation of probability, his own preference was to conduct the analysis of fiscal and monetary issues in the context of highly aggregated models that abstracted from differences between individuals' expectations.

71. Rosen (1981, 847) cited Friedman (1953e) as the source of the hypothesis, while

Murphy and Wolfson (2013, 3) cite Friedman and Savage (1948) (although Murphy and Wolfson then immediately refer to it as the "Friedman hypothesis," presumably in light of the fact that, of the two authors, Friedman eventually exceeded Savage in name recognition).

One factor that has likely held back acceptance of the Friedman-Savage proposal is that their postulated convex region of the household utility function might well be viewed as a high-level assumption that generates "risk-loving" behavior too easily. In this respect, the reaction to the Friedman-Savage proposal has mirrored the research literature's response to Kydland and Prescott's (1982) attempt to account for inventory/output interaction by putting inventories directly into the production function. However, see Gregory (1980) and Rosen (1997, 190) for discussions of how the Friedman-Savage specification might emerge from a more fundamental analysis of consumer preferences.

72. And, even when concerned specifically with the topic of the compatibility of expected utility theory and lotteries, Arrow and Priebsch (2014) cited Savage (1954, 1972) but not the Friedman-Savage articles.

73. In Friedman's class teaching of the standard case of concave utility functions and convex indifference curves, an echo of the Friedman-Savage modification was registered on one occasion. Dudley Wallace, a student in Friedman's Price Theory class in the mid-1950s, recalled: "I remember one time in class he wanted to talk about indifference curves, and he drew a diagram on the board—and he had an indifference curve concave to the origin. And all of us looked at it and looked at each other and shook our heads. But nobody had the nerve to put up their hand. And then he finally realized he'd drawn it wrong and looked at all of us and said, 'Why didn't somebody say something?' Well, we didn't say anything because he had all of us pretty well stupefied" (T. Dudley Wallace, interview, July 20, 2015).

74. See, for example, Mankiw, Rotemberg, and Summers (1985, esp. 241) and Eichenbaum, Hansen, and Singleton (1988, 64).

Similarly, in the social-welfare and public-finance fields that lie at the intersection of microeconomics and macroeconomics, a household utility function that is globally concave has remained the benchmark. In this connection, it is significant that Arnold Harberger—no stranger to Friedman's research—observed that the "notion of a diminishing marginal utility of income pervades the classical and neoclassical economic literature" and went on to note that this notion remained overwhelmingly accepted (Harberger 1978, S110-S111; quotation from p. S110).

75. Another reference that viewed the Friedman-Savage work in terms of its mathematical contribution is Feibes (1974, 104). But for latter-day discussions of that work's contribution to utility theory, see Forbes (2009, 29) as well as the Hartley and Farrell (2002) article mentioned above.

76. In Taylor (2001, 115), Friedman made a similar observation about Savage and their joint work.

77. Arrow's positions at the University of Chicago included assistant professor in the Department of Economics in 1948-49 (according to American Economic Association 1970, 13) and research associate at the Cowles Commission in 1947-49 (according to American Economic Association 1981, 44).

78. The later work would therefore fly in the face of Hahn's statement (1954, 400): "Expectations, especially the destabilizing kind, are either ignored or discounted in everything Professor Friedman writes." Hahn was referring specifically to the papers in Friedman (1953b), but his generalization about this collection is questionable, since the lead

paper (Friedman 1953c) has in recent years been presented as propounding a line of argument to the effect that agents will converge to the rational-expectations equilibrium (see Blume and Easley 2006; and Cogley, Sargent, and Tsyrennikov 2014). See also the discussion in chapter 15 below on Friedman's connections with, and perspective on, the rational-expectations revolution.

79. See Friedman (1969a, 3) and Friedman (1972a, 923). A more standard statement would be that positive demand for money requires a friction, rather than uncertainty per se (see, for example, Wallace 1977). It is possible to derive a demand function for money formally in nonstochastic models, for example in models using money in the utility function or a shopping-time technology (see, for example, McCallum and Goodfriend 1987; Lucas 1988b; McCallum 1990c; and Walsh 2003), and these demonstrations would seem to contradict Friedman's claim. A reasonable conjecture about what Friedman's response might be in the face of such demonstrations is that the nonstochastic shopping-time technology is proxying for payments-and-receipts arrangements that contain a stochastic element. (In support of this conjecture, see especially Friedman 1977d, 409.)

80. In particular, Friedman and Schwartz (1963a, 1982a) emphasized the uncertainty associated with the Depression and war as a source of increased demand for money. The relationship between uncertainty and velocity during the 1930s was discussed in chapter 2 above. With respect to wars, Friedman pointed to the downward pressure on prices at the start of the World War I and World War II as "the most extreme evidence" that uncertainty raised the demand for money (Milton Friedman, interview, January 22, 1992; see also Friedman 1956a, 9, point 6). In addition, Friedman and Schwartz (1963a, chapter 12) saw increased confidence (that is, reduced uncertainty) as a source of increases in velocity in the United States in the immediate postwar decades. See also Friedman (1968c, 440), Friedman (1983a, 1984d), and *Newsweek*, October 16, 1972, for cases in which Friedman invoked uncertainty as a source of changes in velocity in still later postwar episodes. E. Nelson (2002b) and S. Hall, Swamy, and Tavlas (2012) have provided further discussions of Friedman's emphasis on the connection between the demand for money and the degree of uncertainty.

The fact that Friedman considered confidence to be an argument in a well-behaved demand-for-money function invalidates an attempt by Patinkin (1982, 178) to create a distinction between Friedman's view of velocity and that of the (interwar) UK Cambridge School. Patinkin noted that the Cambridge view emphasized changes in confidence as an influence on velocity; hence, Patinkin alleged, the Cambridge School "did not think of velocity . . . as a stable function." This inference on Patinkin's part does not hold if confidence or uncertainty is one of the factors entering a stable money-demand function.

81. See, for example, Baker, Bloom, and Davis (2013).

82. Friedman (1972a, 923). See also Friedman and Schwartz (1982a, 60-61), who presented an expectational Phillips curve with no explicit shock term, even though the surrounding discussion was conditioned on the notion that the equation was subject to disturbances and that expected and actual values of variables did not coincide.

83. In making this observation, Friedman (1964c) strongly disputed the notion that his paper on risk and income distribution (Friedman 1953e) should be regarded as presenting a case against the public sector's welfare support for the poor, the grounds for that case allegedly being that "poverty is simply a matter of choice" (as Seligman 1964, 12, so characterized the position of Friedman's paper). Indeed, as has been noted, Friedman's support for a government-provided guaranteed income set him apart from libertarians.

One interpretation that Friedman was prepared to accept of his (1953e) paper was that the existence of extensive government tax and transfer measures reflected a public desire to prevent results concerning the distribution of income that would otherwise flow from the operation of the market—results that the community considered unacceptable. Friedman added, however, that he felt that government intervention in the process of income distribution had gone, by 1977, "far beyond" what could be rationalized by this public desire. See *Financial Times*, January 6, 1977. See also Friedman (1962a, 163).

84. See, for example, Friedman (1976a, 2) on the wide applicability of economic analysis, and Friedman and Friedman (1980, 25–27; 1998, 210) on the need for broad definitions of self-interest and markets in applying economic analysis. Along similar lines, Friedman said in a 1976 television interview: "I do not myself like to regard 'market' as restricted to the narrow economic sphere. It has to do with any voluntary activity" (*The Jay Interview*, ITN, July 17, 1976).

85. One writer on Friedman's work (Frazer 1994, 1997) took strong exception to the notion that Friedman was an advocate of a utility-maximizing characterization of private-sector behavior. But there is abundant evidence, not least in Friedman's own words, supporting the notion that Friedman endorsed the expected-utility idea, and Frazer's convoluted attempt at an alternative interpretation is not attractive.

86. Friedman's endorsement of the public-choice literature, and his partial incorporation of its analysis into his own discussions, occurred at a fairly late stage of his career (roughly speaking, 1973 onward). See chapter 8 below.

87. Friedman and Savage (1948, 279).

88. Friedman and Savage (1952a, 474).

89. Friedman and Savage (1948, 287, 298, 303).

90. That is, that in a game of billiards or snooker, the judgments that a skilled player makes about the appropriate actions are like those that would arise from a formal optimization exercise, even though, in reaching those judgments, the player does not perform the mathematical calculations associated with formal optimization. The billiard-ball analogy appears in Friedman and Savage (1948, 298) and Friedman (1953c, 21). Friedman produced an early draft of the methodology paper in the summer of 1948 (Hammond and Hammond 2006, 9).

91. Friedman (1949a, 463–64). This remark is particularly apposite for the present book. The set of chapters that immediately follow the present one discuss Friedman's framework, and they show that a number of Friedman statements that have been claimed to show him guilty of theoretical inconsistency are conducive to a straightforward interpretation under which there is no inconsistency.

92. A terminological matter also deserves mention. The nomenclature in Friedman's (1949a) article brings out sharply the problems, discussed in chapter 2, associated with the term "marginal utility of money." Following Marshall, Friedman used this phrase to refer to what is more normally called the marginal utility of income or wealth (Friedman 1949a, 477, 479, 484, 494). But in the same article Friedman used the phrase "purchasing power of money" (for example, pp. 465, 480, 481, 483); in this instance, "money" really did refer to (nominal) money.

93. See Friedman (1949a, 463) for an acknowledgment that many readers were unconvinced by a prior draft. Hammond and Hammond (2006, 11) gave the impression that Stigler was won over by Friedman's argument by the time the paper was published, but to make this claim is to overlook the fact that, in rebutting Friedman's interpretation of Marshall, Baumol (1954, 463) thanked Stigler for providing him with textual evidence against the Friedman position.

One issue in the debate was what text to use as the definitive statement of Marshall's views. Although he quoted from the final edition (Marshall 1920) of Marshall's *Principles* in his discussion, Friedman checked the text against earlier editions (Friedman 1949a, 490) and indicated he would put less weight on Marshall's later writings, conjecturing that Marshall's thinking had become less organized (Friedman 1949a, 494). This was a point on which Alford (1956, 44) entered a dissent.

94. In asserting that Friedman (1949a) "drew little initial comment, except on the part of Roger Alford (1956)," Frazer (1994, 13) neglected the Bailey (1954) critique of the paper (which focused on the usefulness of the specification rather than its doctrinal origins), as well as the fact that a number of commentaries on the paper were embedded in reviews of Friedman (1953b), a book in which the article was reprinted. An assessment of the issue that was very different from—and vastly more authoritative than—Frazer's was that of Bailey (1992, xiv), who referred to "Friedman's well-known paper, 'The Marshallian Demand Curve'" and labeled the latter the *locus classicus* on the matter of linking up compensated-demand analysis with the theory of aggregate consumer behavior.

95. Friedman (1954b, 262).

96. Friedman (1954b, 262).

97. Friedman (1949a, 476). See also Becker (2007, 181), who emphasized this aspect of Friedman's outlook.

98. Again, see Friedman (1949a, 476).

99. Roger Alford (interview, January 23, 2014) suggested that the reason that these others, including himself in Alford (1956), went for this interpretation lay in the fact that "the whole approach of Marshall was that he was dealing with relatively tiny individual commodities, and therefore real income movements [from changes in one commodity's price] along the demand curve were negligible anyway," so that the nominal income/real income distinction seldom arose. Alford recalled that he drafted his critique of Friedman (1949a) during the 1953-54 academic year. Friedman "was visiting Cambridge [University] at the time, and I sent him a draft, and he wrote back, naturally disagreeing with it. But it [Friedman's letter] was several pages, you know, which was very thoughtful of him, given the fact that he was a distinguished visitor, and I was a very minor cog in LSE's wheel."

100. Friedman (1956a). From the perspective of money-demand theory, of course, nominal interest rates (and inflation) can be considered "real" opportunity-cost variables—that is, not measured in dollar or other nominal units.

101. See, for example, Friedman (1974c; 1977e; 1980a, 56, paragraph 4, p. 50 of 1991 reprint). Friedman had earlier referred, in a memorandum penned at the Treasury (Friedman 1942c), as well as in his published work on taxation, to the disruption of the structure of relative prices that was typically created by inflation. See also the discussion in chapter 7 below of Friedman's aggregate-supply framework.

102. "Value theory" was another term for price theory, but perhaps a less attractive alternative to "microeconomics" as far as Friedman was concerned because, while "value theory" had a long pedigree in the mainstream economic literature, it was also prevalent in the Marxist economic literature. Although Leeson (2000a, 99) named "value theory" as the term preferred over microeconomics by "many Chicago economists," that should not be regarded as Friedman's preferred label: in Taylor (2001, 111), for example, Friedman emphatically endorsed the "price theory" terminology, and "Price Theory" was and is the official name for the University of Chicago economics department's graduate microeconomics course.

Arguably, "value theory" is a broader term on the grounds that it could cover distributional issues beyond price theory, but Friedman's (1962b) price-theory coverage simply took the distributional matters under the umbrella of price theory; and, on one occasion on which he distinguished distributional issues from price theory, Friedman avoided the "value theory" terminology by referring to "price theory . . . and the allocation of resources" (G. Martin 1983, 61).

For its part, the publisher of Friedman's Price Theory described the book as a "rigorous text on value and distribution theory" (see Aldine Publishing Company's house advertisement on the dust jacket of Friedman 1969b). This description may have been adapted from a passage of Friedman's Price Theory lectures deleted from the book version. That passage stated that "price theory" encompassed value theory and distribution theory.

103. Patinkin (1973a, 794) likewise wrote favorably about the constant-real-income approach to demand analysis and, as had Friedman (1949a), saw this approach as in keeping with the price-theory teachings of Jacob Viner.

104. Friedman (1976b, 435). Similarly, Friedman (1972d, 38) stated that his "major professional interest for many years has been the role of money in the economy."

105. Prior to its publication, Friedman presented the paper at a September 17, 1947, session of the Econometric Society meetings held in Washington, DC (Econometric Society 1948, 106-7).

106. Cagan (1987, p. 195 of 1989 reprint).

107. In E. Nelson (2004a, 401), Schwartz agreed with, and expanded on, the present author's assessment that Friedman was not a monetarist as of 1948.

108. See Samuelson (1997, 155) for a similar assessment of Friedman's 1948 paper.

109. In a 1994 speech, Bernie Fraser, then governor of the Reserve Bank of Australia, stated: "The idea of giving monetary policy the *sole task* of achieving a set rate of growth of a monetary aggregate dates from the old Quantity Theory of Money, which was revived by Milton Friedman in a famous paper in 1948" (Fraser 1994, 20, emphasis in original). This statement could be taken as claiming that Friedman (1948a) was Friedman's first article in the monetarist literature, or that the 1948 paper advocated constant monetary growth. The latter claim is certainly not valid, and the present discussion will argue that the former claim is not correct either.

110. See Friedman (1983a, 2-6; 1984e). Friedman explicitly rejected treating monetarism as synonymous with a constant-monetary-growth rule and indeed did not regard that specific prescription as an integral part of monetarism. In the same vein, Samuelson (1970b, 38) recognized that Friedman's views on economic structure (especially the determination of aggregate demand) were separable from his policy prescription of constant monetary growth.

111. For example, in the same year in which an early outgrowth of his work with Schwartz appeared in the form of Friedman (1952b), Friedman also gave testimony and submissions to Congress in which he championed both the quantity theory of money and his 1948 policy rule (Joint Committee on the Economic Report 1952c, 745, in particular).

112. Once viewed in this light, the article should be categorized as one of the Keynesian contributions to the American Economic Association's Readings in Monetary Theory collection (Lutz and Mints 1951). The reprint of Warburton (1946b) in the same volume better qualifies, among the 1940s articles reprinted, as a forerunner to the monetarist literature. So too would Modigliani (1944), which also appeared in the readings and which, in Friedman's (1977c, 12) later evaluation, "certainly qualifies as a major element in the so-called monetarist structure."

113. This fiscal-multiplier-based perspective concerning how monetary policy affects total spending contrasts not just with Friedman's later work but also with the 1940s contributions by Warburton.

Another contribution that was underway during the 1940s and that, like Warburton's work, emphasized the importance of money in its own right—albeit an item that did not see print until after Friedman himself had changed his views substantially—came from Edward S. Shaw of Stanford University. The preface (dated March 1950) to Shaw's monetary text stated (1950, vii): "Unfortunately, the regulation of money has not been notably competent, and monetary disturbances have taken a heavy toll in economic instability. The monetary system that creates and retires money has a deplorable record for aggravating the ups and downs in our national level of employment and real income." Furthermore, Shaw's (1950) text contained chapters on interest-rate determination and observed (247), "It may be that the authorities underestimate the sensitivity of expenditure to interest rates and exaggerate the hazards of changing interest rates both for Treasury refinancing and for general economic stability."

Shaw thus put himself on record at the start of the 1950s as an advocate of the importance of money and monetary policy; indeed, Harry Johnson (1976a, 298) noted Shaw's unusual status during the 1950s as a monetarist who worked separately from, and often disagreed with, Friedman. By the end of the 1950s, however, Shaw had become skeptical about the effectiveness of monetary policy, to such an extent that Friedman and Schwartz (1982a, 207) listed Gurley and Shaw (1960) among those who denied the importance of money. Against this background, Shaw continued to have strong reservations about Friedman's monetary economics. When, in 1964, the economics department at Stanford University proposed to make a job offer to Friedman, Shaw told his colleagues that he would not stand in the way of the offer but that he was not very enthusiastic about Friedman's work and that he would not be willing to continue teaching monetary economics if Friedman joined the department (Marc Nerlove, interview, September 18, 2013).

The aforementioned shift on Shaw's part toward a more skeptical view about monetary aggregates may not, however, have been as thoroughgoing as Friedman and Schwartz implied. Shaw's (1964) contribution to a book on monetary policy in which Shaw, although considering a variety of views about the importance of money, seemed sympathetic toward a prescription of constant monetary growth (see especially 77, 90). See also Tobin (1963b, 410). At the same time, Shaw's ambivalence toward Friedman's work was evident in the fact that the only reference to Friedman in Shaw's article was in a footnote to a table, citing Friedman and Schwartz (1963a) as a data source (see Shaw 1964, 93).

114. Friedman (1948a, 259). It would *not* be appropriate to view Friedman's 1948 abstraction from an interest-rate channel as in line with his later emphasis on money, rather than specific interest rates, as an indicator. As discussed in chapter 6, that emphasis rested on a view that monetary policy affected the economy through its influence on a multiplicity of interest rates.

115. See Friedman (1948a, 250–51, 257).

116. It is for this reason that the present author would not go quite as far as Tavlas (1977a, 69) did in interpreting the 1948 paper as recognizing that monetized deficits are more expansionary than deficits financed by "issuing interest-bearing securities." Friedman did not in 1948 indicate categorically that monetized deficits were more expansionary than deficits financed by issues of short-term securities. However, the analysis here supports Tavlas's contention that the analysis in Friedman's 1948 article rested on a transmission mechanism different from the multiple-yield mechanism that Friedman advocated from the 1950s onward.

117. For example, the discussion in Friedman (1948a, 257) endorsed the view that deficit spending stimulates income irrespective of monetary policy and that this influence does not rely on a reaction of interest rates, while monetized deficits add to the stimulative effect of deficit spending in part because monetization creates downward pressure, or reduces upward pressure, on longer-term interest rates.

118. Thus Friedman's 1948 position conflicted with his denial, in his monetarist period, of the importance of the first-round effect (for example in Friedman 1972a, 917 and 921–23; Friedman and Schwartz 1982a, 29–31; and Friedman 1987a, 10). See also chapter 6 below.

119. Bryant was referring to Friedman (1960a). In fact, Friedman's advocacy of the constant-monetary-growth rule began earlier than 1960—specifically, in 1956. See chapter 8.

120. Sargent (1982a, 107) stated that the 1948 proposal was in essence an edict that the government refrain from issuing long-term debt. (Sargent did not provide a bibliographical citation, and throughout his discussion he referred to Friedman's recommendation as a 1949 proposal, but the proposal in the 1948 paper seems to be what Sargent was referring to.) The 1948 Friedman proposal might be more precisely regarded as a recommendation to move to a situation in which the government issued no new debt securities of any maturity (no debt issuance, that is, other than issuance of money, which was formally government debt but in Friedman's view was not so in practice—see, for example, Friedman 1974b, 352; Friedman 1980a, 58, paragraph 14; p. 54 of 1991 reprint; and Friedman 1984c, 59). As noted previously, the 1948 Friedman proposal permitted a one-time issuance by the government of some very long-term debt (consols) as a way of mopping up the outstanding amount of short- and intermediate-term debt that could not be immediately monetized without compromising stabilization goals (see Friedman 1948a, 251). This fixed amount of consol debt could then become a negligible share of nominal national income as the economy proceeded along a noninflationary growth path.

121. Friedman (1948b, 141).

122. Friedman (1948a, 255).

123. NBC (1949, 4).

124. Friedman (1948a, 254).

125. See Mints (1950, vii, 138). See also Patinkin (1969, 52) and the next section.

126. Friedman (1951f, 228).

127. Friedman (1948a, 250).

128. NBC (1949, 3).

129. For a perspective that emphasized this aspect of Friedman's (1947) criticism of Lerner's proposal, see Orphanides (2003, 636).

130. In this connection, he specified that the rule be in growth rates—an aspect of Friedman's approach stressed in Orphanides (2003) and discussed in chapter 8 below. Hammond (2011a, 643) claims that Friedman's emphasis on uncertainty as a factor motivating his policy prescriptions is "commonly overlooked" in discussions, but Hammond neglects to mention several recent monetary policy studies that have stressed precisely this aspect of Friedman's policy prescriptions, including Orphanides (2002, 2003); Orphanides and Williams (2002); Lars Hansen and Thomas Sargent (2011); and E. Nelson (2004b, 2008a).

131. See his remarks in Friedman and Heller (1969, 52, 85). On that occasion, Friedman credited the Committee for Economic Development (CED) (1947) with having independently come up with the same concept. In the same vein, Friedman (1948a, 249) noted that both the CED study and Ruml and Sonne (1944) had, like him, proposed a cyclically balanced budget.

132. Friedman (1979, 412).

133. See also Friedman's remarks in *Newsweek*, January 31, 1972 (75), excerpted in Friedman (1972d, xvi), and those in *Firing Line*, PBS, January 5, 1972, p. 10 of transcript.

134. For example, Friedman stated in 1962 that taxes should "not be changed for the purpose of countering cyclical movements, but only for the purpose of raising more funds for governmental measures" (in *The American Economy, Lesson 48: Can We Have Full Employment without Inflation?*, CBS College of the Air, filmed circa June 5, 1962).

See, in addition, Friedman's similar remarks in a 1980 memorandum on UK economic policy (Friedman 1980a, 61; p. 60 of 1991 reprint). The continuity between Friedman's 1980 remarks about fiscal policy and Friedman's 1948 views was also noted by D. Smith (1987, 13), although Smith did not explicitly cite the 1980 memorandum and he very slightly misquoted it.

135. Friedman (1979, 413).

136. Friedman (1949b, 953).

137. Friedman essentially reiterated these estimates in a talk he both delivered and published in 1954 (Friedman 1954a; p. 85 of 1968 reprint), but in a context that permitted viewing the swings in the budget deficit as exerting their stabilizing effects via their impact on the money stock.

138. Friedman (1949b, 954).

139. The proposed extension had to do with resampling the data used by Friedman and Kuznets (1945) in a way that was more clearly random than Friedman and Kuznets's sampling procedure.

140. However, some effort on Friedman's part to follow the microeconomic literature after the mid-1950s is shown by the fact that his name appeared in the acknowledgments of articles in microeconomics that were published well after he left research in price theory (see, for example, Sen 1970, 152).

141. See Friedman (1962b).

142. In the same vein, Richard Muth, who took the Price Theory class during the 1950s, observed: "I don't recall his pushing free-market ideas in the course. It was almost totally technical" (Richard Muth, interview, May 20, 2015).

143. Arnold Harberger recalled of his time as a member of the department, "we all proudly stuck to the rules of etiquette that say [that] PhDs, LLDs, JDs, and the like, should always be addressed and referred to as Mr., Mrs., Miss or [later] Ms.—never as 'Dr.' That form is reserved for medical doctors and dentists" (Arnold Harberger, personal communication, June 30, 2014).

Skousen (2001, 391), having validly noted this University of Chicago practice, went on to state with certainty that Friedman would never publish a book for which the cover listed "Dr." ahead of his name. Skousen was in error in making this claim, for the trade paperback edition of *Dollars and Deficits* (Friedman 1968e) had "By Dr. Milton Friedman" on the cover.

144. This point persisted in Friedman's comments to students right up until his final year at the University of Chicago: 1976, the year when one of his students, Jo Anna Gray, finalized her dissertation. Friedman wrote a letter to Gray praising her dissertation, but, as Gray recalled, the letter added that "the one thing he would like to insist on is that I learn the difference between 'effect' and 'affect'" (Jo Anna Gray, interview, August 8, 2013).

145. See Friedman (1952d, 13–14). In *Capitalism and Freedom*, Friedman (1962a, 122) cited both Nutter (1951) and G. Stigler (1949) on this score.

146. In particular, Blanchard and Kiyotaki (1987, 647) observed that the presence of monopolistic competition by itself (i.e., without other model features such as price stickiness) "cannot explain why changes in nominal money have real effects." Furthermore, once price stickiness *is* introduced, the presence of monopolistic competition does not prevent the effects of monetary policy on output from wearing off over time. For observations and results relevant to this point, see, among others, McCallum (1989a, 235); Rotemberg and Woodford (1999a, 72); and Woodford (2003, 152).

147. See, for example, Friedman's observations in Friedman (1951a, 214; 1962a, 125–27, 129; 1962b, 161; 1976a, 165); Friedman and Kristol (1976, 40); Ketchum and Strunk (1965, 55); *The Jay Interview*, ITN, July 17, 1976; *Milton Friedman Speaks*, episode 1, "What Is America?" (taped October 3, 1977, pp. 23–24 of transcript); *Milton Friedman Speaks*, episode 9, "The Energy Crisis: A Humane Solution" (taped February 10, 1978, p. 32 of transcript); *Newsweek*, May 5, 1980; and *Chicago Tribune*, July 20, 1980, 21.

In taking the position that private-market activity did not possess an inherent tendency toward greater monopolization, Friedman was, once again, parting company with Frank Knight. Patinkin (1973a, 799) pointed to Knight's view that market power in industries tended to become concentrated. However, Friedman's position *was* consistent with that eventually voiced by another famed University of Chicago economist of Knight's era (albeit one whose positions on markets typically differed very greatly indeed from Friedman's), Oskar Lange. For Lange (1970, 4) contended: "It is only State intervention that can create monopoly conditions for capitalist combinations."

148. Van Horn (2009, 219–20) instead suggests that Friedman's belief that market forces were a major factor undermining monopoly did not arise from empirical findings. This interpretation is inappropriate: both Friedman's own dissertation and the first doctoral thesis he supervised were empirical studies of monopoly, and they likely figured heavily in Friedman's changed position, for which he cited evidence.

149. See, for example, Friedman (1950b, 7; 1970g, 435–36, 441; 1972c, 23); *Newsweek*, August 26, 1968; *Newsweek*, December 1, 1969; *New York Times*, November 24, 1971; *Playboy* (February 1973, 56) (as reprinted in Friedman [1975e, 12–13; 1983b, 24–25]); and Friedman's remarks in *Milton Friedman Speaks*, episode 12, "Who Protects the Consumer?" (taped September 12, 1977, pp. 9, 11, and 19 of transcript).

Baran's (1963, 594) review of *Capitalism and Freedom* perceived regulatory capture as an idea covered in that book. The idea was indeed touched on there briefly—see Friedman (1962a, 128)—and was also stressed by Friedman in 1963 (*Gazette-Telegraph*, December 18, 1963; see also Friedman 1955e, 362). To the present author, however, the 1970s items cited in the preceding paragraph indicate an increased emphasis, in Friedman's later analysis, on regulatory capture.

150. With respect to the notion that natural monopoly not be regulated, see Friedman (1962a, 128) for a qualified suggestion along these lines, and more categorically, Friedman's statement in *Playboy* (February 1973, 58), as reprinted in Friedman [1975e, 14–15; 1983b, 27]). Friedman also shifted emphatically against nationalization of natural monopolies (other than in very specific areas such as that of money issuance): for while Friedman (1955e, 362) noted but did not endorse Henry Simons's position that natural monopolies should be nationalized, R. D. Friedman (1976a, 30) observed explicitly that Milton Friedman was opposed to this Simons position.

151. See Friedman's remarks in Cabral (2000, 10). A contrary interpretation, in which Friedman abandoned support for antitrust as early as 1951, is expressed by Van Horn (2009, 219–20), but Van Horn's discussion confounds Friedman's position on the macro-

economic consequences of monopoly and Friedman's views concerning the distortions to resource allocation from monopoly. In the interpretation offered in the present book, it was only the former position of Friedman's that changed sharply in the early 1950s. Van Horn's contrary interpretation is contradicted by Friedman's continuing endorsement of antitrust laws into the 1950s. In particular, Van Horn's implication that Friedman was against regulation of private monopoly by 1951 seems inconsistent with Friedman's (1950b, 7; 1952d, 16–17) endorsement of measures to eliminate monopoly.

152. See, for example, *New York Times*, January 11, 1948; and Friedman (1952d, 13). A position closely matching Friedman's—i.e., that monopolistic firms distorted resource allocation, but that pricing decisions by these firms did respond to market forces—was expressed in 1958 in congressional testimony given by Martin Bailey, who was at the time a junior colleague of Friedman's in the University of Chicago's economics department and a fellow monetary economist. In his May 13, 1958, testimony to the Joint Economic Committee, Bailey rejected cost-push views of inflation, explicitly referring to Friedman (1958b) on this score, while also affirming support for antitrust laws for the goal of microeconomic efficiency (Joint Economic Committee 1958a, 51, 53). The case for seeing Bailey and Friedman as having a common view on monopoly by the late 1950s is far stronger than is the more commonly made case that Friedman's view on monopoly by this point coincided with those of other economists at the university, such as Stigler or Aaron Director, whose work focused on industrial organization rather than macroeconomics.

153. See Friedman (1962a, 116, 132, and esp. 199). Burgin (2012, 171) claims, without providing a source, that Friedman during the 1950s "abandoned" the favorable perspective he had expressed about the Sherman antitrust law in the early 1950s, but this dating is contradicted by the favorable judgment on the Sherman legislation given in Friedman (1962a, 199). Friedman was still endorsing antitrust laws as of the late 1960s, doing so in a May 1969 television interview (*Speaking Freely*, WNBC, May 4, 1969, p. 16 of transcript) and in an appearance at the Massachusetts Institute of Technology in which Friedman stated, "I agree with Paul [Samuelson] that we ought to have vigorous enforcement of the antitrust laws" (in *The Great Economics Debate*, WGBH Boston, May 22, 1969). In the same vein, during a television panel discussion in June 1970, Friedman remarked, "I am strongly in favor of antitrust legislation" (*NET Journal Presents Conservative Viewpoint*, PBS, May 4, 1970). See also Friedman's remark in *Playboy* (February 1973, 74) endorsing the practice of government "prosecuting antitrust violations" (reprinted in Friedman 1975e, 37 [1983b, 57]). A turning point in his views is better dated to 1973-74.

154. *The Jay Interview*, ITN, July 17, 1976. Consistent with this 1976 observation, the 1976 edition of Friedman's *Price Theory* text retained from the original edition the statement that "free enterprise" should not be taken as implying the granting to firms of the prerogative of "preventing others from setting up enterprises" (Friedman 1962b, 8; 1976a, 7).

155. That is, Friedman (1953c), discussed in chapter 9 below.

156. Some authors have gone further. For example, Leeson (1996, 5) stated that "a student trained using . . . Friedman's *Price Theory* (1962[b]) would remain unaware of the monopolistic competition revolution." This statement was certainly not correct. The readings listed in Friedman (1962b, 265–66) included Chamberlin's (1933) *The Theory of Monopolistic Competition* and Robinson's (1933) *The Economics of Imperfect Competition*, as well as G. Stigler (1949) and Triffin (1940).

157. Silk (1976, 29) claimed that Friedman's criticism of monopolistic competition stemmed from a desire to impose "*laissez-faire* doctrine," but this claim is immediately refuted by the fact that Friedman's criticisms of the monopolistic-competition theory were

voiced at a time when he was a supporter of antitrust laws and also when he was suggesting that the medical profession should be treated as a monopolistic body. Indeed, Friedman and one of the architects of monopolistic-competition theory, Edward H. Chamberlin, were recorded as agreeing at the 1950 conference on labor unions that "corporate power must be subject to restraints for the public welfare" (Wright 1951, 379).

158. See chapter 7 for a discussion of these aspects of Friedman (1968b).

159. See Friedman (1941, 390; 1953c, 34).

160. Such a notion was prevalent in the 1940s. For example, Shove (1942, 319) contended that the emergence of a situation in which large firms were arrayed against one another "has done more than anything else to render [Marshall's] theoretical analysis inapplicable to the world of today."

161. See his remarks in Snowdon, Vane, and Wynarczyk (1994, 172) and Snowdon and Vane (1997, 203).

162. Consider, in particular, the following:

(*i*) Especially in the wake of the work of Dixit and Stiglitz (1977)—a microeconomic study whose analysis has been used heavily in macroeconomic modeling—the theory of monopolistic competition has, indeed, developed in such a way that it now largely consists of marginal-cost-oriented analysis, based on a representative firm, much like the analysis associated with Marshall. See, especially, the macroeconomic analysis using monopolistic competition in Rotemberg and Woodford (1999b). (It is notable that one of the authors of the Dixit-Stiglitz paper has said that Friedman's *Price Theory* text "is still highly worth reading. I got my own introduction to practically applicable microeconomic theory from it." See Dixit 2014, 119.)

(*ii*) Harcourt (1977, 137) referred to "the Marshallian notion that the economy or industry was a large-scale replica of the representative firm" as an element of microeconomics that later literature challenged, but, as implied in (*i*), modern-day applications of monopolistic competition in macroeconomics largely validate this "Marshallian notion."

(*iii*) One feature of monopolistic-competition theory that Friedman (1953c) questioned was whether product differentiation played as great a role in the theory as its proponents suggested. Consistent with this reservation, users of monopolistic competition in macroeconomics have tended to downplay product differentiation. For example, O. Hart (1982, 110) stated that "product differentiation will not be emphasized in our analysis," while in analyses based on the Calvo (1983) pricing framework, the degree of product differentiation is typically treated as superficial in character, its presence serving mainly as a means by which each firm is imbued with some market power.

163. Stigler, like Friedman, argued that Marshallian analysis was applicable to environments for which monopolistic competition had been advanced as the appropriate assumption (see Schmalensee 1983, 79, for a discussion). But even this area of general agreement between Friedman and Stigler should not be overstated: for, as indicated above, they themselves disagreed about the appropriate interpretation of Marshall.

The dearth of extended Friedman critiques of the monopolistic-competition approach is brought out indirectly by two discussions in the literature. Both of these discussions downplayed the distinction between Friedman's and Stigler's contributions. First, Leeson (1996, 5) put quotations from Friedman and Stigler on monopolistic competition in the same sentence and presented them as reflecting a single position. Second, Hammond (1996, 36-39) quoted extensively from Stigler's work—which, Hammond implied, corresponded closely to what Friedman would have said about monopolistic-competition theory, had he written more extensively on the matter.

See also chapter 9 below for a discussion of the differences in the postures of Friedman and Stigler concerning microeconomics.

164. For example, an article on the business school in the *Wall Street Journal* (May 18, 1981, 29) referred to Friedman as "a former professor at the school."

165. On the former point, the *Wall Street Journal* (October 30, 1973, 1) noted that, although Friedman's classes were provided by the Department of Economics, they "were well attended by graduate business students." Examples of such attendees included four business school graduates interviewed for this book: John Gould, John Paulus, Charles Plosser, and David Ranson. Plosser noted that the Price Theory course taught by the economics department was part of the standard program of courses required in the PhD program of the business school (Charles Plosser, interview, April 2, 2015).

166. This is consistent with standard usage. See, for example, Emmett (2011, 95).

167. Of course, in everyday US parlance, and contrary to the traditional University of Chicago terminology, "college" is often used as a term synonymous with—albeit usually less formal than—"university." Following this convention, one biographical sketch described Friedman as a "college professor" (Clark and Cohen 1963, 543). Needless to say, Friedman himself often used the word "college" in this way, as when he indicated that his main career had consisted of "college teaching" (Idea Channel, 1987) and when he himself used "college professor" to describe his own position (*Listener*, May 30, 1974, 690).

168. Friedman did, however, make some informal contributions to the economics teaching of the college. For example, in early 1957 he supplied a typescript version of an analysis that he had written of the Indian economy when the college put together a book of readings. The analysis was subsequently published in slightly revised form in the London public-affairs periodical *Encounter*. See Friedman (1957c, 1957d).

169. Among former University of Chicago economics department members interviewed for this book, examples included William Dewald and Robert Gordon, both of whom recalled teaching undergraduate courses during their time at the university.

170. This course in Friedman's early years of teaching at the university was basically not covered in Friedman's memoirs but had received a fleeting acknowledgment on an earlier occasion, in Rose Friedman's reference to "an undergraduate course in monetary theory" (R. D. Friedman 1976c, 21). The undergraduate course was also mentioned in Hammond (1999, xl) and is referred to in Ruger (2011, 29). Ruger, however, takes the paucity of Friedman's undergraduate teaching as an indication of a lack of interest in undergraduates. In drawing this inference, Ruger neglects the fact that the economics department was predominantly a graduate-teaching institution during Friedman's time.

There are also direct counterexamples that contradict Ruger's characterization of Friedman's posture with regard to undergraduate students. Thomas Campbell was an undergraduate student at the University of Chicago in the early 1970s. As he mentioned in an August 19, 2015, interview for this book, Campbell was assigned Friedman as his faculty adviser, in the expectation that Campbell would progress to graduate studies at the university after he completed his undergraduate work. In addition, the present author was an undergraduate when he first discussed monetary issues with Friedman in correspondence in 1991.

171. See especially Friedman (1976a, vii). However, Friedman (1969c, 129) did imply that he taught multiple courses in the mid-1960s (a time when he was not actually teaching Price Theory at all, instead giving, during different parts of the year, graduate courses in monetary theory and in business cycles).

Another complication was that the graduate program in Price Theory was broken into segments, each comprising one academic quarter, and the two quarters of Price Theory that Friedman typically taught could be formally characterized as two courses (and were described as such by Robert Lucas in McCallum 1999b, 281). In the 1973-74 academic year, Friedman, in the aftermath of illness, taught only the first quarter of the Price Theory course program, that in calendar 1973's fall quarter (Charles Plosser, personal communication, April 13, 2015).

172. Kathy Axilrod, interviews, April 25, 2013, and June 26, 2014.

173. Kathy Axilrod, interview, April 25, 2013.

174. See, for example, Cross (1984, 79), Eshag (1983, 65), and D. Smith (1987, 13–16) for such claims. In addition, the argument in Freedman (2008, chapter 10), itself resting on Harry Johnson (1971a) and other articles reprinted in Leeson (2003b, 2003c), that Friedman chose the tactic of relaunching the quantity theory by appeal to University of Chicago monetary traditions, is based on the false premise that Friedman's advocacy of the quantity theory began with Friedman (1956a). Arguments of this kind typically reflect an inadequate examination of the body of Friedman's published work, and, in particular, a failure (considered further below) to consider writings that did not appear in his book collections. (Even then, the arguments require overlooking Friedman 1952b—a pre-1956 affirmation of the quantity theory that was reprinted in Friedman 1969b—as well as Friedman 1953c, 42, in which Friedman characterized the quantity theory as a body of thought to which Fisher and Keynes contributed and as being a still-valid perspective on the determination of key economic magnitudes.) Some perspective on Freedman's coverage of Friedman's monetary work is provided by considering Freedman's (2008, 243) contention that Friedman "steadfastly refused to grant any significant degree of originality to Keynes and especially to his most influential work, *The General Theory*" when, in fact, the record of Friedman's statements on Keynes includes Friedman (1972a, 908): the *General Theory* provided a "new, bold, and imaginative hypothesis."

As discussed presently, Harry Johnson himself acknowledged in his later work (Nobay and Johnson 1977, 477) that Friedman's monetarist writings predated 1956.

175. NBC (1946a, 12).

176. Friedman and Stigler (1946, p. 173 of 1991 reprint).

177. Friedman and Schwartz's (1963a, 580) remark that in 1947 commentators' concerns were improperly focused on inflation rather than on the economic contraction might, therefore, have been in part intended as a criticism on Friedman's part of his own previous analysis. However, Friedman and Schwartz's (1963a, 585) position that lower monetary growth would have been preferable in 1946 and 1947 shows that they had not yet come to their position in Friedman and Schwartz (1982a) that measured inflation in those years was greatly overstated, still less to their position (one established firmly, as chapter 15 below shows, in Friedman's writings from the early 1970s onward) that inflation reacts to monetary policy with a decidedly longer lag than does nominal income growth.

178. The August 1951 article referred to was Friedman (1951c).

179. For a further discussion of the problems that typically arise from a heavy reliance on book collections of Friedman articles to glean his views, see E. Nelson (2012a). These problems should gradually diminish with the appearance of further compendiums, such as Leeson and Palm (2017), that expand the volume of Friedman's writings available in book collections.

180. This conclusion, which flows from this chapter's analysis of Friedman's statements during 1950, is also supported by the account in Brunner (1980a, 404) of Brun-

ner's discussions with Friedman in 1950. The conclusion that Friedman was a monetarist by this point is also consistent with the analysis in Tavlas (1977a, 69-70) who, unlike Silk (1976), and in line with the interpretation offered here, regarded the 1951 *Review of Economics Statistics* article as part of Friedman's body of monetarist work. The present analysis considers Friedman's statements between Friedman (1948a) and Friedman (1951c) and so tracks the development of Friedman's views over this period in more detail than did Tavlas (1977a).

Nobay and Johnson (1977, 477) dated Friedman's monetarist writings to 1952, citing Friedman (1952g), and stated that they had thereby traced 'the "beginnings" of monetarism . . . to a contribution by Friedman in a now obscure volume." The contents of that Friedman article are indeed important, but what Nobay and Johnson overlooked was that the "obscure" 1952 Friedman paper was actually a lightly edited reprint of Friedman (1950a), an article that appeared in a journal for which Johnson later served as an editor: the *Journal of Political Economy*.

Gale (1982, 7, 24) accurately dated Friedman's advocacy of the quantity theory to the early 1950s. However, Gale's conjecture that Friedman's interest in the theory was instigated by the Korean War inflation, although understandable in light of Friedman's prominent articles on money in 1951 and 1952, is not supported by the totality of the documentary evidence, which shows Friedman's view that monetary policy was key to the control of inflation was in evidence soon after World War II.

A rare instance of a textbook treatment that accurately dated Friedman's monetarist writings to the early 1950s was Amacher and Sweeney (1980, 249).

181. Friedman (1975a, 176). This observation could be regarded as a clarification of Friedman's (1972b, 187) tracing of the revival of the quantity theory of money to a "stream of theoretical literature [that] started emerging" in the mid-1950s. It is true that Friedman's theoretical work on the demand for money emerged only in the mid-1950s, but by then he had already published both analytical and empirical work supporting a monetary perspective on the forces driving aggregate spending and inflation.

182. Friedman (1949a, 475). This passage implies that it is not appropriate to conclude, as Hammond (2011a, 654) does, that reading of monetary theory did not form part of Friedman's activities when he and Schwartz began their NBER project. As already indicated, the fact that Friedman was teaching a monetary theory course during this period further argues against Hammond's contention.

183. Friedman (1950a, 474).

184. In All Participants (1951, 241). Friedman had made a similar comment during a 1949 radio appearance, in which he stated that for a century economists had known "that by printing enough money and spending enough money we can create any degree of activity or provide any rise in prices we wish" (NBC 1949, 16). On that occasion, one of Friedman's fellow panelists, Roy Blough, correctly interjected that the 1930s had produced division among economists on this point.

185. Friedman (1949a, 476).

186. See also Hammond (1989, 47).

187. The previous year's NBER *Annual Report* had also mentioned the fact that Friedman had joined the project (see Burns 1948, 22; and Abramovitz 1948, 36), again without mentioning Schwartz.

188. Anna Schwartz, interview, April 21, 2003, published as E. Nelson (2004a, 400).

189. In E. Nelson (2004a, 401).

190. Friedman and Schwartz (1963a, xxi). The authors cited Schwartz and Oliver (1947). That paper was the first that Anna Schwartz contributed to the NBER's various

working paper series and was issued as NBER Technical Paper no. 4. It is a testament to the longevity of Schwartz's career that, in her lifetime, her final contribution to these series appeared sixty-five years later, a couple of months before her death, as NBER Working Paper No. 17984 (Bordo, Humpage, and Schwartz 2012).

191. Friedman (1989, 249).

192. The same trait manifested itself, albeit in a more reproachful form, in Friedman's conference and seminar interventions over the years. Gordon and Hall (1980, 3) noted that it was a characteristic of Friedman that when "impatient at a confused comment, he interrupted to restate the point clearly."

193. Quoted in Cherrier (2011, 353).

194. Friedman (1949b, 950).

195. Similarly, A. Hart (1953, 305) stated: "It should never be forgotten that the great depression of the 1930's was marked by the greatest monetary deflation of a century—that of 1931–33." Hart then specifically distinguished between monetary policy in 1930, on whose appropriateness he indicated there remained room for debate, and "the policy of tight money adopted in 1931 [which] was simply suicidal." (Hart's paper was largely written in early 1949—see A. Hart 1953, 303.)

196. See Friedman (1975e, 5; 1983b, 14).

197. In the words of Anna Schwartz, the monetary contraction during the Depression reflected "the results of actions or inactions by the Federal Reserve" (Schwartz 1981, 31). In the same vein, Friedman (1954a; p. 81 of 1968 reprint), without mentioning the Bank of United States failure specifically, characterized Federal Reserve policy from 1929 until 1931 as "largely passive." However, a Friedman narrative given in 1956 focused on the 1931 measures of the Federal Reserve and omitted mention of the Bank of United States: see Friedman (1957b, 97). Similarly, in Friedman's (1957f, 72) summary of Federal Reserve policy between 1929 and 1933, Friedman again viewed the Federal Reserve actions as not featuring an "important failure"—in the sense of the taking of an action that was in the wrong direction—until 1931. But the theme of passivity prior to 1931 did come through in his remark that, in that earlier period, the Federal Reserve "did too little."

These descriptions reflected the phenomenon that (at least if hypothetical arrangements like 100 percent reserve requirements are ruled out) maintenance by policy makers of total commercial bank deposits will call for large-scale policy initiatives like a concerted open-market-purchase policy. This remains so even when policy makers are given an assignment (as they are in Friedman's constant-monetary-growth rule) to generate money-stock behavior that is "passive" in the sense of not being a function of the state of the economy.

198. The latter term was used in Friedman (1948a, 261). Again, see chapter 7 for further discussion.

199. See Friedman and Stigler (1946, p. 173 of 1991 reprint) and Friedman (1948a, 253).

200. Friedman (1951a, 228).

201. Mints was also continuing to teach graduate monetary theory in the period covered in this chapter, but he was not entirely successful in converting the book material into interesting classes. "His classes were sort of boring," Arnold Harberger, a graduate student at the time, recalled (interview, May 2, 2013). Harberger added that Mints's writings "were better than I think many people realize," citing in particular Mints's insights concerning open economies.

202. March 25, 1952, testimony, in Joint Committee on the Economic Report (1952c, 736). See also chapters 7, 10, and 15 below.

203. In addition to the destabilization argument, Friedman's case for the constant-

monetary-growth rule was motivated by a number of further theoretical propositions, particularly the long-run aspects of the predictions of the quantity theory of money. See chapter 8 for further discussion.

204. Friedman (1947, 414).

205. See Friedman (1953d).

206. The cheap-money policy was also followed in the United Kingdom. E. Nelson (2009a, 2009b) considers Friedman's perspective on that country's cheap money experience.

207. Friedman (1982b, 104). Friedman specifically rejected the notion that the real bills doctrine, which Friedman and Schwartz (1963a) emphasized as adhered to by Federal Reserve policy makers since the Federal Reserve System was founded, could rationalize an interest-rate peg. His interpretation of the real bills doctrine therefore differed from that of Sargent (1979, 92–95), Patrick Minford (in the *Banker*, July 1979, 30), and Humphrey (1982a, 3), who perceived interest-rate-pegging as a policy prescription that flowed from the real bills doctrine.

208. See Federal Reserve Board (1924).

209. With regard to the rationale based on supporting aggregate demand, see Friedman and Schwartz (1963a, 700); on the rationale of avoiding fluctuations in the value of the private sector's holdings of government debt, see Friedman and Schwartz (1963a, 621) as well as Friedman's remarks elsewhere, including *New York Times* (January 11, 1948).

210. See Congdon (2011, 386, 418). Keynes's support for long-term interest-rate management and for holding down the long-term rate in conditions of economic weakness permeated his *Treatise on Money* (Keynes 1930) and was also an auxiliary theme of his *General Theory*; Keynes's recommendations in this area have been discussed by Brothwell (1975, 13); Meltzer (1992, 158); P. Turner (2011); and Meiselman (1962, 38), the last of these items being a doctoral dissertation that Friedman supervised. Friedman himself mentioned Keynes's views on long-term interest-rate management in Friedman and Meiselman (1963, 168) and Friedman (1972a, 942).

211. Keynes (1936, 207). See also Friedman (1967a, 7–8) and Friedman (1972a, 942).

212. May 25, 1959, testimony, in Joint Economic Committee (1959a, 607). See also Friedman and Schwartz (1963a, 533, 626) and, inter alia, Friedman (1963a, 6; 1964e, 8 [p. 262 of 1969 reprint]; 1968a, 12; 1968b, 2; 1970a, 13–14 [pp. 7–8 of 1991 reprint]; 1972b, 185, 192; 1973b, 5; 1975a, 176). Likewise, Dacey (1947, 60), referring specifically to the UK situation, spoke of "the Keynesian analysis on which the whole cheap-money policy is based." See also Harrod (1971, 59–60) for a similar observation. In addition, Hallowell (1950, 67–68) catalogued statements by the US authorities rationalizing the cheap-money policy. On the whole, then, Friedman's (1982b) conjecture that the US policy was not officially rationalized does not seem well founded.

213. From Friedman's July 22, 1983, letter quoted in Israelsen (1985, 362). It was also the case that Eccles's views on fiscal policy had similarities to Keynes's positions (see *Fortune*, March 1955, 189, reprinted in Mulcahy 1957, 90; Friedman and Schwartz 1963a, 534; Meltzer 2003, 477). Indeed, Friedman (1970e, 12) contended that "Eccles, who was one of the chief proponents the pump-priming program, [first] made his suggestions before he read Keynes." An instance in which Eccles's positions on fiscal policy came through clearly was his account of prospective postwar conditions in a speech given in 1944. That discussion contrasted the "limited" powers of monetary policy over spending with the "far more direct and powerful" effects of fiscal policy (Eccles 1944, 233).

214. See, for example, the Federal Reserve Board's *Annual Report* for 1945, quoted in Meltzer (2003, 641).

215. Friedman (1970e, 14).

216. See Friedman and Schwartz (1963a, 626) and Friedman (1968b, 3-4). Friedman also quoted Goldenweiser's talk in Friedman (1964b, 3; p. 71 of 1969 reprint). The latter two articles were reprinted in Friedman's *Optimum Quantity of Money* collection in 1969, leading Hahn (1971, 79) to note that, in Friedman's book, "poor Mr. Goldenweiser is shown to have made some very injudicious Keynesian-sounding statements." Friedman again quoted from Goldenweiser's talk at length in a talk to the American Philosophical Society in November 1971, as a demonstration of the cheap money orthodoxy in place in the mid-1940s (see Friedman 1972b, 184), and he cited Goldenweiser once more in his 1972 Horowitz lectures (Friedman 1973a, 5).

217. Friedman and Schwartz (1963a, 563). See also Friedman (1960a, 108).

218. Friedman (1960c).

219. Bach (1950, 46) likewise focused on the implication that the pegging arrangement made banks' bond holdings equivalent to bank reserves.

220. Friedman (1984c, 34).

221. However, insofar as the onset of the peg signified a shift to a situation of lower nominal interest rates than those prevailing previously, the upward pressure on velocity arising from the enhancement of the money-like character of bonds would be offset to some extent by the downward pressure from the shift to a lower opportunity cost of holding money.

222. Friedman (1971e, 152).

223. See Friedman and Schwartz (1963a, 611) and Friedman (1973a, 24; 1973b, 8; 1982b, 104). For other monetarist accounts that offered similar interpretations, see for example, Cagan (1974, 1; 1979a, 3-4, 97), and Meltzer (2003, 632).

224. See Friedman (1975b, 115). Friedman put in this amendment after he had extensively reexamined the behavior of velocity during the Korean War era. For his discussions of this reexamination, see for example Instructional Dynamics Economics Cassette Tape 119 (April 25, 1973) and *Newsweek*, August 6, 1973. It is debatable, however, whether the "inflation is always and everywhere a monetary phenomenon" proposition actually demanded modification in light of the Korean War episode. The velocity surge in the early 1950s corresponded to a one-time price-level increase, and Friedman and other monetarists frequently distinguished one-time price-level increases from inflation. (See, for example, Friedman's observation in *Newsweek*, April 24, 1978, as well as the discussions in McCallum 1990c, 966; and Meltzer 2003, 632; and the coverage of Despres et al. 1950 in the discussion of Paul Samuelson in the next section.)

225. Friedman (1988a, 229). See also the summary of Friedman's floor remarks at the 1987 Festschrift for Anna Schwartz (in Bordo 1989a, 78).

226. Friedman (1951a, 229).

227. Friedman (1948a, 262). Another occasion when Friedman gave voice to his skepticism about secular stagnation was in Friedman (1948b, 141).

228. As noted in the previous chapter, the secular-stagnation theory, although developed by Alvin Hansen, could be found in Keynes's *General Theory*. In this connection, it is noteworthy that even in the United Kingdom, in which 1930s-vintage Keynesian views were far more pervasive in postwar theorizing and policy making than in the United States, the secular-stagnation theory was an aspect of the *General Theory* that was widely rejected even by the 1950s; the *Financial Times*, for example, referred to "Keynes' one-sided fear of over-saving" (May 23, 1955) and to "Keynes' incredibly shortsighted forecast of declining investment opportunities" (October 15, 1956).

George Stigler observed (in American Bankers Association 1963, 110): "No one has yet refurbished the stagnation theory of the late 1930s." Some fifty years after Stigler made this remark, however, the secular-stagnation thesis was indeed revived—not as a characterization of the 1940s but as a description of underlying private-sector behavior in the most recent decades—by Summers (2015). (Eggertsson and Mehrotra 2014 provide a formalization of the argument; see also, however, John Taylor's article in the *Wall Street Journal*, January 2, 2014, for a negative verdict on Summers's interpretation.)

229. See Friedman and Schwartz (1963a, 577–78). See also Friedman (1960a, 22) and Meltzer (2003, 631).

230. Friedman and Schwartz (1963a, 585). See also their discussion on p. 605.

231. Friedman and Schwartz (1982a, 125).

232. Instructional Dynamics Economics Cassette Tape 179 (October 1975, part 3).

233. In part the slowing of inflation during 1948, and certainly the decline in the four-quarter rate, reflected the fact that the removal of price controls boosted early-1948 inflation readings, as stressed in Meltzer (2003, 631) and also mentioned by Friedman in Director (1952, 176). This was somewhat contrary to the position of Friedman and Schwartz (1982a, 102–7), who treated the US price index by 1947 as free of distortions arising from controls; that treatment should perhaps be regarded as a simplification, reflecting their use of annual data.

234. Friedman et al. (1951). The statement was mentioned at a February 2, 1951, hearing of the Joint Committee on the Economic Report and appended to the record.

235. The Federal Reserve Board had done this in December 1950 (Meltzer 2003, 697).

236. That is to say, the peg implied that, in contrast with the situation associated with the 1936–37 increases in reserve requirements, the Federal Reserve increased the stock of reserves by enough to leave the adjusted monetary base (i.e., the monetary base corrected for reserve-requirement variations) unchanged by the shift in the reserve requirement.

237. The Samuelson quotation is from *Newsweek*, October 25, 1976a. Samuelson (1971, 8) specifically dated his friendship with Friedman back to 1934. In addition, Samuelson (1973b, vii; 1983a, xi) described Friedman as "an old friend," and Samuelson would also write that Friedman should be classified as the eighth or ninth wonder of the world—possibly ahead of the Grand Canyon (*Financial Times*, June 14, 1967).

238. In *The American Economy, Lesson 48: Can We Have Full Employment without Inflation?*, CBS College of the Air, filmed circa June 5, 1962.

239. Email from Milton Friedman to the present author, May 17, 2002.

240. See E. Nelson (2008b, 1793) and the discussion in chapter 13 below.

241. Hammond (2011a) instead characterizes Samuelson as not developing a concrete model of the economy and contrasts this with Friedman and Schwartz who, he argues, did so. However, Hammond cites barely more than a handful of Samuelson references—and none of Samuelson's economic commentaries in *Newsweek* and similar outlets. As in the case of Friedman, these commentaries flesh out details of Samuelson's view of the economic world, a point developed in E. Nelson (2004b, 2005a).

This judgment is consistent with the recollection of Robert Solow (personal communication, November 13, 2014): "I could not count the number of times I heard Samuelson refer precisely to 'the model in my head,' and I rather knew the model he had in mind. He would also say that the model in his head was too subtle to be stated baldly, or else that he knew when not to apply the model."

242. See chapter 1 as well as Friedman's remarks on *Firing Line*, syndicated January 8, 1968, p. 2 of transcript. Another early account of the increasing weight given to monetary policy in editions of Samuelson's textbook took place in a *New York Times* article (January

25, 1970), which noted (83) the rising weight as a mark of Friedman's influence but incorrectly implied (as does Ebenstein 2007, 156) that Samuelson did not acknowledge Friedman in his text. In fact, even at the start of the 1960s, Samuelson (1961) had two references to Friedman, both respectful, one noting Friedman's consumption work (253), and one naming him as an authority on money (315).

243. Samuelson (1948, 353). Ebenstein (2007, 156), apparently relying on secondary sources for accounts of Samuelson's textbook, gives the incorrect impression that the passage only originated in 1950s editions of Samuelson's *Economics* text.

244. Similarly, Friedman testified in May 1959 that his own constant-monetary-growth proposal "would be no panacea" (in Joint Economic Committee 1959a, 612). The implication in both Skousen (2001, 392) and Ebenstein (2007, 156) that Friedman would have disputed Samuelson's statement that monetary policy is no panacea must therefore be judged to be incorrect. The notion that monetary policy is not a panacea is not controversial and should not be regarded as equivalent to denying that monetary policy affects aggregate demand. In the same spirit as Friedman's injunction, Federal Reserve chairman Ben Bernanke observed, in a September 2012 press conference, "monetary policy, as I've said many times, is not a panacea" (Bernanke 2012a, 8).

245. Hammond and Hammond (2006, 46).

246. Samuelson (1948, vii) signed off his preface with the date of April 1948.

247. The quotations are from Samuelson (1971a, 11) and Samuelson (1960, 267), respectively.

248. Samuelson (1963a, 15). Ebenstein's (2007, 156) suggestion to the effect that Samuelson did not acknowledge that he had changed his views is thus not correct. Indeed, *Business Week* (November 23, 1963, 108) highlighted this Samuelson quotation as an explicit recantation by Samuelson of his prior views. The article also attributed the change to Friedman's influence. (See also chapter 10 below.)

249. Samuelson (1961, 315). See also Blinder (1986), Patinkin (1983), Wallich (1983), and *Wall Street Journal*, December 10, 1984, for discussions of the evolution of the treatment of monetary policy in Samuelson's textbook.

250. It is apparently this report to which Leeson (1997a, 142) was referring when he mentioned the "1950 Report of the Public Issues Committee of the AEA." Leeson, however, did not actually cite the report in question (relying instead on secondary references) and stated of it, "Paul Samuelson was a coauthor and Milton Friedman a dissenter." In fact, however, Friedman and Samuelson were *both* among the credited authors of the report, and Friedman's dissent (described below), while important, did not disassociate him from the whole report. Rather, the dissent was limited to one long footnote of section 7 of Despres et al. (1950).

251. See, for example, his remarks in Friedman (1980a, paragraphs 11 and 19, pp. 57 and 59; pp. 53 and 56 of 1991 reprint) and in Friedman (1987b). See also chapter 8 below.

252. From Samuelson's June 29, 1967, testimony, in Joint Economic Committee (1967a, 166). The reasoning behind Friedman's (1948a) proposed prohibition of cyclical variations in government purchases had earlier been criticized in Samuelson (1953, 561–62).

253. See Despres et al. (1950, 528–29).

254. The joint statement indicated (Despres et al. 1950, 536) that "inflation induced by rising costs rather than excess demand offers a very grave dilemma for fiscal and monetary policy."

255. Despres et al. (1950, 535). (Here, "money demand" meant nominal spending.) Friedman's discussion leading up to this key sentence was not quite as clear on this mat-

ter, as he conceded the argument that monopoly pressure could drive up costs and thus render aggregate-demand policy "largely ineffective" in delivering joint achievement of full employment and price stability (534). In contrast, his more familiar position (at least when not considering the special case of the United States from 1933 to 1937) was that distortions to the market might raise the natural rate of unemployment but would not render full employment (in the sense of unemployment equal to the natural rate) inconsistent with price stability. Friedman's 1950 reference to policy ineffectiveness might be a sign that his views on the long-run inflation/unemployment trade-off were still evolving. It can, however, be reconciled with his later position if we take it as a reference to an *increase* in monopoly power in a particular sector. Such an increase can, in standard monetarist analysis, be viewed as a source of price-level shocks—which even in Friedman's monetarist framework created a temporary unemployment/inflation trade-off—as distinguished from ongoing inflation (see, for example, Friedman and Schwartz 1963a, 498–99; Friedman and Friedman 1985, 83–84 and 90; L. Ball and Mankiw 1995; and the analyses of inflation in Meltzer 2009a, 2009b). For further discussion, see chapter 7 below.

256. See Silk (1976, 18). Silk gave the date of the offer to join the University of Chicago as 1948, but the correspondence in Hammond and Hammond (2006, 46) indicates that the offer took place earlier (in the 1946–47 academic year).

257. These individuals, and not Samuelson, were in the published debates on monetary and fiscal policy in Modigliani and Ando (1965), Friedman and Meiselman (1965) and Friedman and Heller (1969), and on monetarism such as the exchanges in R. Gordon (1974a). Of course, Friedman's work on the Phillips curve was essentially a challenge to Samuelson and Solow (1960), but Samuelson left the counterattack largely to others (including Solow 1969). On these matters, see also chapters 12–14 below.

Robert Gordon observed that Samuelson's minor role in the Keynesian-monetarist debates was a factor weighing against inviting him to participate in the 1972 *Journal of Political Economy* debate on Friedman's monetary framework that was later packaged as R. Gordon (1974a). See chapter 14.

Nevertheless, Samuelson made many commentaries on monetarism, which will be considered in later chapters.

258. The quotation is from Samuelson (1947, 182). Samuelson was discussing Friedman's (1935a) critique of Pigou. As discussed in chapter 2, however, it would appear that Friedman by the 1950s was no longer standing by the spirit of that critique.

259. On the 1962 joint appearance (an episode of *The American Economy* broadcast on November 30, 1962), see Coleman and Alexander (1962, 72–73) as well as the discussion of this exchange elsewhere in this book. The latter-day joint appearances included *MacNeil-Lehrer NewsHour*, PBS, August 27, 1990; and *Wall Street Week*, Maryland Public Television, February 21, 1992.

260. Friedman and Samuelson (1980). The earlier "road show" debates were recalled by William Poole in an interview for this book (March 25, 2013).

261. See also Friedman and Friedman (1998, 357).

262. Samuelson made a similar admonition to Lawrence Summers in correspondence after Friedman's death, informing Summers, "for your eyes only," that he gave a low rating to Friedman's macroeconomics (*Wall Street Journal*, September 14, 2013). As with so many of Friedman's critics in the economics profession, however, Samuelson made an exception for Friedman's permanent income hypothesis, which Samuelson regarded as a highly valuable contribution. See *Newsweek*, October 25, 1976a, and the next chapter.

263. In Horn (2009, 49).

264. Samuelson did, however, have regular access to Friedman's Instructional Dynamics recorded commentaries from 1968 to 1977. Although these tapes were available to the public by subscription, the high subscription price of, and lack of publicity for, the cassette series implied that the tapes received very limited circulation, and Samuelson (1969a, 8) noted that few economists other than himself had access to them in practice.

That Samuelson did read *a lot* of Friedman's statements and writings is not in doubt. Indeed, Samuelson's familiarity with Friedman's positions came out in Samuelson's distinction, already noted, between monetarist theory and monetarist policy recommendations, a distinction that Friedman himself emphasized. In contrast, Patinkin (1995, 127) revealed unfamiliarity with this distinction when he made the claim that monetarism was principally concerned with, and was tied to, specific policy recommendations.

265. The Samuelson quotation is from *The American Economy, Lesson 48: Can We Have Full Employment without Inflation?*, CBS College of the Air, filmed circa June 5, 1962.

266. Another manifestation of Friedman's willingness to acknowledge error was his interest in revising papers in response to comments. Anna Schwartz (in conversation with the author on October 14, 2010) pressed this point, saying that Friedman viewed a draft as always capable of being improved by rewriting. In an earlier conversation with the present author, Schwartz said: "And, working with Friedman, I could criticize what he did. There was no problem saying to him, 'This isn't clear,' or 'This doesn't follow from what you've written a couple of pages earlier.' You couldn't criticize Arthur Burns that way" (in E. Nelson 2004a, 405). This approach may also be contrasted with Samuelson's (1983b, 11) admission that "I am a prisoner of my first drafts."

267. Friedman and Kuznets (1945, 305).

268. Friedman (1963b, 12).

269. Friedman (1964d, 513).

270. In a footnote (footnote 4a, p. 119) added for the reprinting in Friedman (1969b) of Friedman (1959a).

271. Instructional Dynamics Economics Cassette Tape 120 (May 11, 1973).

272. *Long-Term Solutions to the Energy Crisis*, January 24, 1974.

273. Instructional Dynamics Economics Cassette Tape 149 (June 26, 1974).

274. *Newsweek*, June 23, 1975.

275. Instructional Dynamics Economics Cassette Tape 168 (June 1975, part 1).

276. Instructional Dynamics Economics Cassette Tape 206 (January 1977).

277. Friedman (1982d, 404).

278. July 19, 1984, interview, with William Greider, quoted in Greider (1987, 543).

279. Letter from Milton Friedman to the present author, July 16, 1991.

280. Friedman and Friedman (1998, 327).

281. Email from Milton Friedman to the present author, April 13, 2006.

282. Friedman and Savage (1952a, 467).

283. Friedman and Savage (1952b, 71). Perhaps in recognition of the fact that the reprint incorporated the correction, Becker (1964, 56) cited the reprint rather than the original 1948 version of the paper. Unfortunately, a posthumous selection of reprints of Friedman's *Journal of Political Economy* articles (Friedman 2007) used the original, incorrect, published version of Friedman and Savage (1948) as the basis for the reprint. (In mitigation, the collection also included Friedman and Savage (1952a), an article in which the authors' 1948 error was noted and corrected.)

Another important instance in which Friedman acknowledged an error in a previous paper, declaring his mistake in Friedman (1952e) to have been "a dud" and an "inexcusable blunder," was that of his response to Phipps (1952): see Friedman (1952f, 334, 335). However, prefiguring a much later occasion on which he admitted an error (in his reply in Friedman 1982d, to F. Levin and Meulendyke 1982), Friedman followed this concession with a sharp defense against Phipps's other criticisms of his paper. That said, Friedman again thanked Phipps in Friedman (1953b, 100) when he published a revised version of Friedman (1952e), and Friedman (1954b, 265) noted that the version that appeared in Friedman (1953b) was a "corrected form" of the original (1952e) article.

284. The paper in question was Wallis and Friedman (1942).

285. See Friedman and Friedman (1998, 55).

286. Friedman (1946).

287. Nor did Friedman concentrate on challenging Lange's (1944) critique of classical economics. Later work by Archibald and Lipsey (1958) did so. More recent discussions of Lange's critique are in McCallum (2001a, 151), who traced it to Lange (1942) (an article that appeared in the same collection as W. A. Wallis and Friedman 1942), and Sargent (1987a, 107–10), who provided a more modern treatment of Archibald and Lipsey's refutation.

288. Friedman (1946, 622).

289. See Friedman (1972a, 908), for example.

290. In discussing the rational-expectations literature, however, Friedman (1978c, R-185) did list incorporation of multivalued expectations as one avenue that the research literature should follow. See also Friedman (1977e, 466). Of course, it could be countered that stochastic models that embed rational expectations do allow for a form of multivalued expectations because expected values in these models correspond to the first moment of a probability distribution and this distribution is typically nondegenerate.

291. Friedman (1946, 615).

292. See especially Friedman and Schwartz (1970a, 139–40).

293. This aspect of Friedman's critique was also highlighted in Hirsch and de Marchi (1990, 150).

294. See Friedman (1946, 622–25 and 631).

295. See, for example, Friedman (1967a, 13; 1972a, 922); Friedman and Schwartz (1970a, 141; 1982a, 31); and *New York Times*, September 23, 1973 (67, 69) (pp. 279, 280 of reprint in Friedman 1975e).

296. See Modigliani (1986b, 125); G. Stigler (1960a, 719); Krugman (1980, i; 1999, 83); Gale (1982, 138); Bean (1988, 42); Parkin (1982, 69); R. Hall and Milgrom (2008, 1672); and Shimer (1996, 4).

297. Lange and Taylor (1938).

298. See, for example, Friedman (1984f, 12–13 and 21); and *Wall Street Journal*, January 8, 1991. See also Rose Friedman's reference in Friedman and Friedman (1998, 513) to the "Lange-Lerner vision of a socialist market economy."

299. Instructional Dynamics Economics Cassette Tape 132 (October 24, 1973). Friedman evidently had telescoped Lange and Taylor (1938)—which, as noted, he had cited in Friedman (1947, 415), and which reprinted and juxtaposed solo-authored articles by Lange and Fred M. Taylor—and Lerner (1944)—into a single book.

300. Instructional Dynamics Economics Cassette Tape 132 (October 24, 1973).

301. For Friedman's later restatements of this point, see Friedman (1962b, 10; 1976a, 10; 1984f, 9), *Milton Friedman Speaks*, episode 1, "What Is America?," taped October 3, 1977 (p. 16 of transcript); and *Free to Choose* (US version), filmed portion of episode 1, "The Power of the Market," PBS, broadcast January 12, 1980, p. 5 of transcript.

302. This fact underscores the limited character of Friedman's (1953e) use of Friedman-Savage preferences to interpret observed income differences. As we have seen, Friedman objected to Seligman's (1964) interpretation that the 1953 Friedman analysis amounted to an endorsement of existing income distributions. In part, this objection arose from Friedman's position that the theory used in Friedman (1953e) abstracted from various important factors that bore on the distribution of income (as well as his assessment that Seligman was, in any case, misinterpreting that theory). But another element underlying Friedman's objection was that his ability to rationalize the income differences that the private sector's utility-maximizing behavior (including its gambling activity) could generate did not amount to an opposition in principle to government policies aimed at redistributing income.

303. See for example, Friedman (1954a; pp. 84-85 of 1968 reprint) and his discussion in Joint Committee on the Economic Report (1952c, 745). Even by this stage, however, Friedman saw a highly progressive tax system as likely to discourage risky investments (Friedman and Savage 1948, 302) and regarded the marginal rates in the upper income brackets as so high as to leave little more to be taxed (NBC 1951b, 6). See also the next note.

304. Friedman had called for lower marginal income tax rates even in the 1951-52 period when he was still in favor of a progressive tax-rate schedule and in a context of explicitly advocating high taxes for containing the Korean War boom. See NBC (1951b, 1); Director (1952, 18, 96); and Friedman's January 31, 1952, testimony in Joint Committee on the Economic Report (1952b, 350).

305. Specifically, at the time (September 1946) when Friedman's review appeared in print, Lange was serving as Poland's ambassador to the United States (*New York Times*, August 18, 1946).

306. Friedman praised both *Yes Minister* and *Yes, Prime Minister* series (which were coscripted by Antony Jay, a creative consultant for the *Free to Choose* television series) in Friedman and Friedman (1998, 633). He initially encountered the *Yes Minister* series through the novelizations of the series' episodes, and on viewing the television episodes Friedman initially thought that they were adaptations of the books rather than the other way around; "I sent a copy of the [first] book to Milton," Jay recalled, "and he loved it, and he thought that the book had preceded the television series; he said how well the television series had caught the spirit of the book" (Sir Antony Jay, interview, May 29, 2013). Ironically, this was the same misconception that many had regarding the relationship between the *Free to Choose* series and book. Friedman later provided an endorsement of the *Yes Minister* books when they were collected for a US edition (Lynn and Jay 1988).

On the formal name of Poland being the "Polish People's Republic" in its period of Communist rule, see for example Szyr (1964).

307. *Forbes*, December 12, 1988, 168. See also Dolan and Lindsey (1977, 580-89) for an application of this argument to Lange's proposals.

308. Friedman (1957b, 78).

309. Instructional Dynamics Economics Cassette Tape 132 (October 24, 1973).

310. Hahn (1954, 399, 401).

311. The quotation is from Klamer (1983, 53). See also chapter 1 above.

312. See Ruger (2011, 166). Ruger is correct in implying that Friedman was not an outcast for the *whole* of the 1960s. As stressed in E. Nelson (2004a, 397) and in later chapters of this book, 1963 was a turning point in altering Friedman's standing in the profession. But, as argued here and in E. Nelson (2009a, 2009b), it is appropriate to view Friedman as experiencing a period of relative estrangement from the economics profession from 1951

to 1963, with his monetary work rated much lower than his 1940s research. The major qualification that should be made is that Friedman's (1957a) contribution on the consumption function was very well received (see the text that follows and the next chapter).

313. Robert Solow, interview, December 2, 2013. For a picture of professional opinion in the 1960s that supports Solow's assessment, see Sargent (1996, 540).

314. Friedman (1952c, 457).

315. *Newsweek*, November 9, 1970; and Instructional Dynamics Economics Cassette Tape 60 (November 5, 1970). In the same vein, in a talk he gave to University of Chicago PhD students while passing through the Chicago area in the early 1980s, Friedman said he was no mathematician (*Sydney Morning Herald*, August 12, 1993).

316. Becker (1991a, 140) took only the second of these as Friedman's rise "to the top," and Becker's interpretation is adopted uncritically in Ebenstein (2007, 138). But the achievement of winning the Clark Medal certainly qualifies as rising to the top. Likewise, Burgin's (2012, 153) reference to "a rapid personal and professional ascent" on Friedman's part, in which he "solidified" his reputation as an economist in the 1960s, begs the question of why *any* ascent was needed once Friedman had won the Clark prize. Burgin's characterization would be more defensible had he used the word "reestablished" instead of "solidified."

317. *Newsweek*, October 25, 1976b, 86.

318. The quotation is from Solow (1966b, 63).

319. *Photoplay Film Monthly* (September 1975), 21.

Chapter Five

1. Apart from the analysis in this and the next chapter, see in particular chapters 1 and 4 above.

2. The Meltzer quotations are from McCallum (1998, 250).

3. Friedman's own perspective was that he accepted much, but also disagreed with much, of what "Meltzer [1965] says about the theory underlying *A Monetary History*" (Friedman 1971d, 334).

4. However, the motivation that R. Gordon (1974b, ix) provided for Friedman's "Theoretical Framework" analysis—that a more formal and thorough statement of Friedman's view of monetary relations was needed than that provided in Friedman (1956a)—was a valid one, as has already been indicated in chapter 1 above. The same motivation drives much of the attempt in this chapter to prise out of Friedman's scattered statements on monetary matters a systematic representation of his theoretical framework.

5. See chapters 11 and 15 below for further discussion.

6. In Klamer (1983, 63).

7. Friedman and Meiselman (1964, 371).

8. Friedman and Schwartz (1982a, 16).

9. Again, see Friedman and Schwartz (1982a, 16).

10. Friedman (1961f, 1052).

11. Friedman (1951b, 114).

12. The position has been voiced not only by Keynesian critics of Friedman, but also by some observers who were more congenial to Friedman's policy views. Burton (1981), for example, applauded Friedman's perspective on free markets and on policy rules, while taking it as a fact that Friedman's theoretical framework was the same as Keynes's, except for the definition of the income variable in the consumption function. However, Burton's characterization neglected several differences between Friedman's and Keynes's

specifications of aggregate-demand behavior, particularly with regard to the number of monetary-policy-sensitive interest rates in the IS equation. Burton's analysis also proceeded from the correct premise that Friedman and Keynes agreed that prices were not fully flexible in the short run to the incorrect inference that the two economists' preferred specifications of aggregate price adjustment coincided.

13. Friedman (1976f, 315). Those who have used or paraphrased this quotation in discussing Friedman's views have included Hahn (1980, 1), whose analysis, like that of the present chapter, disputed the premise that the distinguishing aspects of monetarism were, in fact, simply confined to empirical points.

14. That he did so in an IS-LM context is testimony the fact that use of IS and LM equations does not amount to taking a stand on the degree of price flexibility (which is instead given by the Phillips-curve specification). See Patinkin (1990, 123–24) and McCallum and Nelson (1999, 298) for discussions that stressed that reliance on an IS-LM specification of aggregate-demand behavior does not involve assuming a fixed or rigid price level.

15. Friedman (1976f, 315).

16. His subsequent reservations about having, to some extent, done so himself in Friedman (1970b) underscore this point (see chapter 14 below).

17. See, in particular, Friedman and Schwartz's (1991, 39) remark.

18. See, in addition to Friedman and Meiselman (1963), Friedman (1976f).

19. This result also requires that u_t have a zero mean.

20. As discussed in chapter 10 below, the pure-cost-push setting would specify the u_t process differently from Friedman's theory, with the restrictions implied by the Friedman position including the aforementioned requirement that the process is a zero-mean white-noise process.

21. See Guillebaud and Friedman (1957, vi).

22. Friedman's advocacy of the negative income tax is detailed in chapter 13 below.

23. See Friedman (1966f, 2733; p. 112 of 1968 reprint) for the quotation. See also Friedman (1968h, 214). The point in question is, of course, one that entered prominently the discussion of supply-side economics in the United States in the 1970s and 1980s, especially debates regarding the Laffer curve.

24. See Fischer (1976, 322–24).

25. See the discussion in section IV below.

26. Friedman (1950a).

27. See chapter 15.

28. This contention, which is documented in chapter 15, is highly consistent with Friedman's (1963b, 3) observation that adaptive expectations assumption was a "supplement" to his permanent income theory rather than being inherent to that theory. See also Friedman (1957a, 143, 225–26; 1961a, 262) for related observations.

29. Friedman (1956a, 11). See also Friedman (1987a, 9). Formally, the 1956 presentation had a bond rate, a real return on physical assets (or on claims over those assets), and the expected rate of inflation, but the latter two series can conceivably be consolidated into a nominal return on physical assets, as implied by the discussion in Friedman (1956a, 9) and as implemented in Friedman and Schwartz (1982a). Therefore, the case made below against including expected inflation as an argument in the money-demand function can also be viewed as a critique of putting the nominal return on physical assets into the function.

30. See Friedman (1972a, 944).

31. As indicated below, the inclusion of the interest rate on longer-term nominal securities in the money-demand function is also difficult to reconcile with optimizing models.

It is, however, less difficult to rationalize such a term than it is to justify inclusion of the return on equity or on physical goods.

32. Cagan (1956, 31) implied that his model admitted this interpretation. Similar comments apply to other cases in which the money-demand function was specified with expected inflation as the sole argument, such as Harberger (1960). See Wachter (1976, 3) for a discussion. See also Woodford (2003, 108) for a related analysis.

Like Sargent (1987a), the analyses of McCallum (1989b, 134), and Robert King and Mark Watson (1998, 1018–19) interpreted Cagan's (1956) money-demand function as featuring the nominal interest rate as the single opportunity-cost term.

33. Friedman and Schwartz (1963a, 657). It also deserves emphasis that a good deal of what evidence there is that inflation or its expectation appears in the money-demand function may in fact reflect the absence of short-run price homogeneity in the money-demand function, and not the status of inflation as an opportunity-cost variable. See Goldfeld and Sichel (1987) for an analysis (albeit in the context of largely backward-looking money-demand functions).

34. So too did his exposition in Friedman (1970b, 204).

35. See the discussion later in this chapter and in chapter 14.

36. See Friedman (1988a, sections II and III).

37. The decision to abstract from sources of lags is consistent with Friedman's (1971d, 335–36) observations to the effect that the framework he was using on that occasion did not adequately capture the phenomenon that velocity growth and monetary growth moved in opposite directions in the very short run, and to a greater degree than could be accounted for by a standard interest-elastic money-demand function. However, as has already been indicated, the abstraction from lags was only one of many simplifications of his aggregate-demand framework that Friedman made in his (1970b, 1971d) discussion.

The "variable" aspect of Friedman's "long and variable lags" dictum has been argued by Frydman and Goldberg (2011) as grounds for believing that Friedman's specification of aggregate-demand behavior was not subsumable within a constant-probability-distribution framework, which is used here and which is standard in most macroeconomic analysis. However, it should be noted that Friedman in his empirical work was sometimes content to use constant-parameter, fixed-lag representations of the relationship between monetary growth and nominal spending growth (as when, as discussed in chapters 13 and 15 below, he employed his own version of the St. Louis equation). Although reduced-form, these representations can be regarded as resting on the assumption that it is reasonable to approximate the economic structure as being associated with a constant probability distribution.

38. See Friedman (1976f, 316) as well as his remarks in Instructional Dynamics Economics Cassette Tape 62 (December 3, 1970).

39. "A Miscellany" was the title of chapter 8 of Friedman (1957a).

40. Friedman (1943a, 56). See also Friedman (1942a, 316).

41. Friedman (1976a, 288) also referred to work in capital theory, including that of Frank Knight, as having long used the concept of permanent-income streams.

42. See the discussion in chapter 3 of Friedman (1943a) and Friedman's later statements on consumption.

43. Friedman maintained, however, that he closely monitored economic research on consumption as it emerged during these years, in part because of Dorothy Brady's and Rose Friedman's interest in the subject (Friedman 1957a, ix).

44. Here and for the remainder of this chapter, as well as in chapter 6, y_t denotes the

absolute level of aggregate real income. In the rest of this book, however, the convention followed is that y_t refers to the natural logarithm of output.

45. In fact, one can go further. Notwithstanding Friedman's role as its published discussant, the Christ (1951) research was done at the University of Chicago, and Friedman was on Christ's dissertation committee, so the Keynesian consumption function appeared in work that Friedman partly oversaw and on which Friedman provided formal input. For more discussion of Christ (1951) and its role in the debate between Friedman and members of the Cowles Commission, see chapter 10 below.

46. Friedman (1957a, ix). Other relevant activity in this period was Friedman (1951d).

47. The influence of Brady and Friedman (1947) extended also to Franco Modigliani, who described it as a "pathbreaking paper" (Modigliani 1975a, 3) and who, as already noted, subsequently cited the paper prominently in his Nobel lecture (Modigliani 1986a). Beyond the Modigliani (1975a) paper just mentioned, a further study that considered developments in the theory of consumption during the 1940s and early 1950s was Hynes (1998). Hynes's study was, however, not very germane for the understanding of Milton Friedman's contribution to the consumption literature. Although Hynes was concerned specifically with developments in the literature up to 1952, Hynes did not cite any pre-1953 publications of Friedman other than Friedman and Kuznets (1945). As the present book documents, other writings by Friedman from the 1930s through the early 1950s included many observations relevant to the study of consumption.

48. Friedman (1957a, ix). The date at which Margaret Reid became a member of the economics department was given in American Economic Association (1970, 360).

49. Alternatively, this may have been a reference to an unpublished paper on permanent income written by Margaret Reid in the 1949-50 period and mentioned by Modigliani (1975a, 4), or to M. Reid (1952). These two Reid references, however, appeared well after the appearance of Friedman and Kuznets's (1945) discussion of permanent income. Mayer (1972, 165) also noted Margaret Reid (1952) as an empirical study that anticipated "the full-scale wealth theories" of consumption (that is, those of Friedman and Modigliani-Ando-Brumberg).

50. Friedman (1957a, ix); R. D. Friedman (1976d, 27).

51. Friedman (1957a, ix). In part, however, Margaret Reid occupied the same place with respect to Friedman's work on consumption that Clark Warburton held with respect to Friedman's monetary economics. In particular, Reid was heavily thanked and acknowledged in Friedman's writings as a precursor, yet many others took little note of those acknowledgments. And, in another parallel with the case of Warburton, Reid apparently became somewhat unhappy with the degree to which the research program to which she had contributed came to be regarded as synonymous with Friedman rather than being associated with a group of researchers that included herself.

Another figure who may have felt disenchanted with the sole attribution to Friedman of the permanent-income consumption research was Friedman's graduate student of the early 1950s Phillip Cagan. In a 1971 published comment for a Federal Reserve Bank of Boston conference volume, Cagan took the unusual step of drawing attention to the fact that, as a research assistant, he had performed the time-series regressions that Friedman reported in *A Theory of the Consumption Function*. Specifically, Cagan wrote: "You can see this in the chart of the permanent-income function that I fitted for Milton Friedman in his study of the consumption function" (Cagan 1971, 225). Friedman acknowledged in Friedman (1957a, x) that both Phillip Cagan and Gary Becker had computed regressions for the book, and a very generous acknowledgment of Cagan's work on the time-series regressions also appeared on p. 145 of *A Theory of the Consumption Function*. One could be forgiven for thinking, however, on the basis of remarks in Friedman and Becker (1957, 66–67; 1958a, 546) that the regression work was done by Friedman or Becker but not by Cagan, and the wording of the Friedman-Becker discussions may have played a role in Cagan's later insistence on identifying himself as a fitter of the regressions.

52. Friedman (1963b, 3).

53. Friedman (1955g, 907).

54. Friedman (1955g, 908).

55. Friedman (1957a, 28). Similarly, Tobin and Buiter (1980, 83) observed that volatile household saving behavior was implied by Friedman's theory of consumption.

56. See, for example, Friedman (1957a, 26, 228). In his book and other expositions of the hypothesis, Friedman largely worked without explicit time subscripts, and so he was not faced with the obvious potential for conflict in notation in having t or T being a subscript meaning "transitory" when these subscripts might also well denote either a generic time period or the final period in the analysis. In view of this conflict, TR is used here to denote "transitory."

57. Friedman (1957a, ix).

58. In particular, Lydall (1958, 564) stated that Friedman found that the permanent-income approach "works well in some cases and badly in others. When it works well[,] Friedman claims support for the hypothesis; when it works badly[,] he is inclined to doubt the validity of the data."

59. On the pre-1957 presentations, see, for example, chapter 10 below. Friedman's written replies to critics of his consumption study included Friedman (1957e, 1958h, and 1963e). Friedman (1963b), which was first drafted in the late 1950s (Friedman 1963b, 4) was also a defense of the hypothesis in response to postpublication feedback, but it also corrected some errors that had been present in the original exposition.

60. See Friedman (1957a, x) and Friedman (1958h) and Tobin (1958b), the latter two articles being written versions of their 1955 exchange.

Hirsch and de Marchi (1990, 260) stated that it was "curious that Friedman allowed himself to be drawn into debate with Tobin" in the 1970s. This statement is itself curious. Friedman's debate with Tobin was not something that he was drawn into during the 1970s. As already indicated, he debated Tobin on consumption in the 1950s, and, as discussed in chapter 12 below, his debate with Tobin on monetary issues contained many rounds and began in the first half of the 1960s.

61. Mayer (1972) argued that no finding that Friedman reported in favor of his consumption function was not susceptible to some other explanation. But the position that the permanent income hypothesis and *some* other hypothesis are each capable of explaining a particular data regularity is different from the position that a *specific* alternative hypothesis concerning consumption does better in matching all the data regularities of interest than the permanent income hypothesis. Mayer's critique (on which Mäki 1985 would rely extensively) did not establish the latter position.

62. Comments of a similar nature included that of the University of Chicago business school's Arnold Zellner (1984, 30) that Friedman had spelled out multiple ways in which his theory of consumption could be tested and that in the subsequent literature "many of these tests have been performed with most of them yielding results in accord with [his] prediction." Another example was the statement by Friedman's former student John Scadding that "the permanent-income specification of the consumption function . . . is supported by a large body of other evidence" (Scadding 1979, 14).

63. This outlook toward Friedman did not go away in the case of some Keynesians, as the discussion of Friedman's research in Solow (2012, 43) brings out clearly.

64. See, for example, Friedman's remarks in the *Margin* (January 1986, 3); CSPAN, November 20, 1994 (p. 9 of hard-copy transcript); *Reason* (June 1995, 38); Friedman and Friedman (1998, 222); and Taylor (2001, 116).

65. See, for example, Friedman (1956a, 19; 1961a, 261) and Friedman and Schwartz (1982a, 38). (Both research projects were, however, part of Friedman's work with the NBER.)

In contrast, George Stigler (1988, 155) classified the consumption-function work as part of Friedman's research in "monetary economics." This reference may have been a case of the practice—which Friedman himself certainly followed—of using "monetary analysis" or "monetary economics" as a synonym for "macroeconomics." It could, however, also have been a reflection of the fact that Stigler made no claim to a strong familiarity with either the field of macroeconomics as a whole or Friedman's researches in macroeconomics in particular.

66. For Friedman's citation of Friedman (1957a) in his monetary research see, for example, Friedman and Schwartz (1982a, 173) as well as the numerous uses of the permanent-income concept in Friedman (1959a) and his later monetary studies.

67. Carroll and Summers (1991, 335) went so far as to say: "Milton Friedman explicitly rejected the idea that consumers had horizons as long as a lifetime[,] in discussing the permanent income hypothesis." Their characterization of Friedman's stance had a literal accuracy, because of Friedman's method for calculating permanent income in time-series data. But, to the present author, it would seem that Carroll and Summers's characterization confounded two different issues connected to Friedman's consumption specification: (*a*) whether the representative household's permanent income corresponds to a concept of a (possibly infinite) lifetime income, and (*b*) whether, when made operational, the permanent-income measure is generated under the assumption of rational expectations. It is argued below that Friedman subscribed to (*a*), even though his time-series work was in general inconsistent with (*b*).

68. This criticism may also have underpinned Krugman's (2007, 27) observation that Ando and Modigliani's life cycle specification (see Modigliani and Ando 1957 and Ando and Modigliani 1963; see also Modigliani and Brumberg 1954) took "even more care in thinking about rational behavior" than did Friedman's permanent-income work. As some of Friedman's work did, in fact, use rational expectations, Krugman's point would have been more clearly made if he had used the word "optimizing" instead of "rational." Although "rational" and "optimizing" are sometimes regarded as implying one another in macroeconomic discussions (see, for example, Sargent 1987a, xxi), it is useful to distinguish the two concepts when comparing the Friedman and Modigliani bodies of work on consumption. Friedman's consumption work was not optimization based but did sometimes use rational expectations, while Modigliani's life cycle work was optimization based but made less use of rational expectations than did Friedman's permanent-income research.

69. This literature on the New Keynesian IS equation appeared primarily in the 1990s. However, earlier cases in which the representative household's first-order condition for consumption was explicitly labeled an IS equation and put in an IS-LM system included Koenig (1987) and McCallum (1989b, 102–7).

70. A similar view clearly underlay Carroll and Summers's (1991) discussion of Hall's work (see especially their discussion on pp. 308, 318–19, and 336, as well as the contrast they draw between the Ramsey model and their characterization of Friedman's findings).

Some support for this position is provided by the fact that Blanchard and Fischer's (1989, 37) detailed discussion of what they called "the Ramsey infinite-horizon optimizing model" had no reference to Friedman's work. However, this discussion of the Ramsey model was in the context of considering economic growth rather than consumption. When, later in their book, Blanchard and Fischer turned to the Robert Hall (1978) specification of consumer behavior, they did mention the properties it shared with those of Friedman's consumption theory. (Although *A Theory of the Consumption Function* did not appear in Blanchard and Fischer's bibliography, they clearly intended to cite it, as their citation on p. 287 of Friedman 1956a, when discussing the permanent income hypothesis, was obviously meant to be a reference to Friedman 1957a.)

71. The common elements of the Friedman and Robert Hall approaches are also brought out by Atkeson, Chari, and Kehoe's (1999, 3) observation that it is "recent economic theory" that features "models in which the saving rate is not fixed, but is rather chosen by consumers, to maximize their utility from consumption over time."

72. This shared property of the Euler equation and Friedman's consumption theory was stressed in Sargent (1987c, 4) as well as in the aforementioned Sargent (1986) piece.

73. Friedman (1957a, 7). (Friedman 1976a, 60, instead stated that saving served to "straighten out the income stream." Here he may have meant "straighten out the response of expenditures to the income stream.")

74. See Cochrane (1994, 242) for a similar assessment.

75. Even the NBER's own summary of Friedman's book acknowledged that upon being implemented on time series, his theory became "very similar" to preexisting theories, derived from the assumption of habit formation, in which consumption depended on lagged consumption (Fabricant 1958, 3). See also Modigliani (1975a, 16).

76. The tendency for the life cycle hypothesis and the permanent income hypothesis to be considered together dated back to 1957, when Modigliani and Ando (1957) and Friedman (1957e) were published back-to-back in the same issue of the same journal, with Friedman (1957e, 125) referring to the life cycle and permanent-income frameworks as "related theories."

77. Modigliani (1975a, 11) pointed out that the life cycle hypothesis, while implying a constant saving rate for a given upward path of real income, also implied that the saving rate increases if the secular growth rate rises. He contrasted this with Friedman's permanent income hypothesis, seizing on a statement in Friedman (1957a, 234) that an upward revision in the expected path of income, for given current income, would likely reduce the saving ratio. But the Friedman passage in question did not really contradict the notion that the saving rate is increasing in the steady-state growth rate. It could instead be taken to be a description of the repercussions of a lasting intercept shift in the path of income, spread over several periods, and not a shift in the slope of the path. Indeed, Krusell and Smith (2015) emphasize that a positive saving-rate/growth-rate relationship is a prediction of the modern, optimization-based, version of the permanent income hypothesis. (None of the preceding is to deny that Modigliani worked out the implications of his theory for the saving-rate/growth-rate relationship more fully and explicitly than Friedman did for the permanent income hypothesis.)

78. Modigliani's rejection of Ricardian equivalence, both in writings such as Modigliani (1964a) that preceded the Barro (1974) formalization of that idea and in his later work (such as Modigliani and Sterling 1986, 1990), also attested to the fact that he found the permanent income hypothesis, with its infinite-horizon setting, inimical.

Others, while not specifically characterizing Friedman's permanent income theory as necessarily implying an infinite-horizon framework, have acknowledged that the theory was amenable to an infinite-horizon interpretation. See, for example, Tobin and Buiter (1980, 81, 83) and Blanchard (1985, 224).

79. It is tempting to see the appearance of infinitely spanned integrals of time in Friedman (1957a, 143-45, 229), Friedman (1963b, 21), and Friedman and Becker (1957, 67) as establishing that the assumption was being made that the household was infinitely lived. Such an inference would not be appropriate, however. For one thing, the equations were the adaptive-expectations expressions for permanent income, which, as already indicated, were not part of the permanent income hypothesis proper. For another thing, the equations were written for a continuous-time framework, and an infinite number of time periods in a continuous-time context need not imply that a discrete-time version of the same model has an infinite number of periods.

80. Friedman (1957a, 25).

81. See Friedman (1963b, 3-4) on his usage of the "horizon" term.

82. Friedman (1957a, 28) and Friedman (1963b, 6).

83. Friedman (1957e, 125).

84. Friedman (1957a, 14).

85. This is so even though the life cycle hypothesis was embedded in macroeconometric models used for monetary policy analysis during the 1960s and 1970s—a development that reflected the close involvement of Ando and Modigliani in those models' construction.

86. Johnston actually published three separate critiques of Friedman in two successive issues of the *Review of Economics and Statistics* in 1958: Johnston (1958a), commenting on Friedman and Becker (1957); Johnston (1958b), challenging Friedman's position on cost functions; and Johnston (1958c), reviewing Friedman (1957a). Friedman and Becker (1958b) replied to the first of these critiques.

87. In empirical implementation of the hypothesis, however, Friedman typically used loglinear equations, as he noted (Friedman 1957a, 223).

88. This perspective on Friedman (1957a) was clear in Liviatan's (1963, 53) observation that "Friedman's fundamental hypothesis" was a unitary elasticity of permanent consumption (and hence actual consumption) with respect to permanent income (see also Scadding 1979, 14). Barrow et al. (1997, 104) simply stated that there was a value of "unity for the income elasticity in most models of consumption." They did not name the permanent income hypothesis specifically—perhaps because the unitary aggregate income elasticity is common to the permanent-income and life cycle specifications of consumption behavior.

89. Paul Samuelson also highlighted this implication of Friedman's specification of consumption (*Newsweek*, October 25, 1976a). It was, in addition, what Friedman himself emphasized when giving an interview about the permanent income hypothesis a couple of years after the publication of Friedman (1957a). On that occasion, Friedman said: "It was argued that the lower-income groups spent a larger portion of their income than the upper-income groups and, therefore, that the thing to do in time of depression was for the government to tax away income from people in higher-income brackets and distribute it to people in lower-income brackets. It was argued that this would reduce savings and stimulate purchasing power. This argument does not hold water" (*Cleveland News*, May 25, 1959).

90. Friedman (1957a, 236-37).

91. See Friedman (1957a, 125-29, 222-23). This critique was distinct from one in which

estimated consumption functions could be criticized because income and consumption were measured using similar sources and therefore had common measurement error. Under this alternative critique, the common measurement error likely pushed up the correlation between the two series and perhaps made coefficient estimates derived from these data unreliable. As a related matter, one critique of consumption and income regressions that could be made was that the two series were simultaneously determined.

Friedman certainly had sympathy with both these alternative lines of argument. (With respect to the first one, see especially Friedman 1957a, 149; Friedman and Meiselman 1963, 175; and Friedman and Schwartz 1982a, 418.) But they were *not* ones on which his research on consumption in either Friedman (1957a) or Friedman and Becker (1957) relied heavily. In fact, both Friedman (1957a) and Friedman and Becker (1957) made considerable use of consumption-on-income regressions, and some of the resulting regression estimates were treated as valid.

Both the just-mentioned arguments were primarily associated with the study by Haavelmo (1943) (see, for example, L. Klein 1958, and Hendry 1972), and Friedman and Becker (1958a, 545) affirmed (correctly) that their own (1957) argument about the testing of Keynesian models was distinct from that advanced by Haavelmo. That Friedman's consumption-function work did not deploy the Haavelmo line of argument is perhaps best brought out by the fact that Sargent (1978) was concerned with applying the Haavelmo critique of ordinary-least-squares estimation of consumption functions to estimation of the Friedman consumption function.

One reason why Friedman may have refrained from emphasizing the simultaneous determination of consumption and income in his 1957 work was that he had an exaggerated confidence in the notion that running regressions both ways (that is, regressing consumption on income and then income on consumption) provided a means of obtaining estimates of the parameter of interest (the response of consumption to income) in an environment in which the two series were simultaneously determined. See chapter 10 below for further discussion.

92. See, for example, Goldberger (1964, 283-84); Walters (1968, 250-51); Holmes (1970, 1160); R. J. Wonnacott and T. H. Wonnacott (1979, 257-66); and K. Wallis (1980, 13-18).

93. See also Crowder, Hoffman, and Rasche (1999, 110).

94. This was a phenomenon that Friedman himself recognized as likely to occur in large samples. See Friedman (1957a, 127).

95. As econometricians have had occasion to lament (see, for example, Sims 1991, 426; Watson 1988, 408), "biased" is often misused to be a synonym for "inconsistency" in discussions of the properties of econometric estimators. In particular, textbook results labeled "errors-in-variables bias" and "simultaneous equations bias" typically pertain to results concerning inconsistency, not bias. The discussion of Friedman (1957a) by Liviatan (1963, 29, 32) featured this slippage in terminology, as he referred to Friedman's original result as a finding of bias in previous consumption-function estimates, when in fact it was a suggestion of inconsistency. This slippage may have been a blessing in disguise, in view of the fact that Stock's (1988) analysis suggested that the inconsistency that Friedman stressed was actually unlikely to be important for the data he studied, but that bias of the estimators may well have been a major factor.

The possibility of cointegration between log real consumption and log real income also provides some retrospective support for the approach that Friedman took in his book of examining the bivariate relationship between consumption and income series. Chick

(1973, 41) claimed that Friedman's analysis proceeded on the "(unreported) empirical result that the interest rate was not significant." This, however, was clearly not Friedman's position. For, as discussed below, he subscribed to the view that consumption was interest elastic. Both the opening and closing chapters of *A Theory of the Consumption Function* had interest rates in the function, and Modigliani (1975a, 5–6) accepted that a dependence of consumption on real interest rates formed part of Friedman's consumption theory. In the face of interest-sensitive consumption decisions, Friedman's concentration on bivariate consumption-income regressions in his (1957a) study can be given ex post justification from the cointegration literature. If log consumption and log income are both I (1) series and cointegrated, and real interest rates are $I(0)$, much of the theory of cointegration suggests that inclusion of real interest rates is unnecessary in ascertaining the consumption-income relationship. This theory therefore lends support to an approach to the relationship between consumption and income in which, in the words of Friedman and Schwartz (1982a, 173), attention is restricted to "the systematic element which is common to the two."

96. Friedman (1957a, 236).

97. See Friedman (1957a, 238).

98. See Friedman and Becker (1957).

99. See chapter 10 below for a discussion of Friedman's interest in these benchmarks in forecasting.

100. Friedman and Becker (1957, 74).

101. Friedman and Becker (1958a, 545–46).

102. The Friedman-Meiselman studies are discussed in chapter 12 below. The linkage between the Friedman-Becker and Friedman-Meiselman contributions was stressed by Bodkin (1995). Unlike Bodkin, however, the present author would not regard the Friedman-Becker piece as itself a contribution to the monetarist literature.

103. In what follows, it is assumed that the fiscal actions discussed are not accommodated by monetary policy.

104. See chapter 13.

105. For Friedman's favorable response to Eisner (1958), see Friedman (1958i).

106. In the same vein, Burton (1981, 57) characterized Friedman as accepting, but improving, the Keynesian concept of the consumption function.

107. This acceptance continued after 1957. For example, Friedman and Meiselman (1963, 172–73), although critical of the empirical importance of the Keynesian multiplier, used the "marginal propensity to consume" and "average propensity to consume" concepts (while emphasizing—as in Friedman 1957a—the dependence of the marginal propensity to consume on the permanence of the expected change in income). As discussed in chapter 12 below, in taking this perspective Friedman parted ways with hard-line critics of Keynesianism, such as Henry Hazlitt, who were more inclined to deny outright the validity of key Keynesian concepts and who eschewed Keynesian terminology.

108. That the monetary work *was* critical of Keynesianism (including the latter's emphasis on fiscal policy) was not something he disputed. (See, for example, the reference in Friedman 1968c, 445, to the "negative implication of the quantity theory" for the effectiveness of fiscal actions that were not accommodated by monetary policy.)

109. Once this common ground is taken into account, specifications of consumption behavior (such as those contemplated by Campbell and Mankiw 1990) in which current income has a role in household spending decisions that is out of proportion to its weight in the permanent-income calculation can be regarded as having a *distinctly* Keynesian component, as suggested by Bernanke (1981, 157).

110. A case in which the notion that permanent income was the same concept as wealth was advanced in a more matter-of-fact manner, and not as part of a criticism of Friedman, was the discussion by Eckstein (1983, 83, 92).

111. See Friedman (1970b, 206) and Friedman and Schwartz (1982a, 42, 45). In one of his other 1971 publications, Harry Johnson (1971b, 26) seemed to acknowledge that a wealth-based consumption function was not in the original version of Keynesianism, as he observed that "for both Friedman and Fisher it is wealth that is the basic determinant of consumption."

112. Friedman (1957a, 9). See also Friedman (1963b, 5) and Fama and Miller (1972, 54).

113. See Friedman (1957a, 11; 1963b, 7).

114. See, for example, Friedman and Schwartz (1982a, 258); Friedman (1964b, 5; p. 74 of 1969 reprint; 1976a, 60; 1987a, 8); and Friedman's remarks in *Cleveland News*, May 25, 1959; and *Wall Street Journal*, April 26, 1984.

115. Friedman (1963b, 7).

116. In his pre-monetarist and (largely) pre-permanent-income-hypothesis days, Friedman had routinely accepted that government bonds were net wealth. See Friedman (1948a, 259n17).

117. See Friedman (1957e, 125).

118. The notion that direct estimation of expected income streams may provide a more reliable measure than does reliance on the value of asset stocks was pursued by Abel and Blanchard (1986) in the context of studying the drivers of investment.

119. Friedman (1957a, 7).

120. See also Becker (2007, 183) for a similar assessment.

121. From Patinkin's floor discussion in Patinkin and Leith (1977, 123). Patinkin went on to note important respects in which Friedman's analysis went beyond what was in Fisher's work (124).

The link between Friedman and Fisher's work on consumption was also alluded to by the National Bureau of Economic Research shortly after *A Theory of the Consumption Function* was published. The NBER's summary of Friedman's book read, in part: "Friedman's explanation of change in consumption runs primarily in terms of consumers' expectations concerning income. . . . Naturally, expectations are influenced by developments in the past. . . . But Friedman's analysis leads us to look ahead, not backward. . . . It is evident that Friedman abandons the conception of the consumer as [enforcing] a mechanical link between current income and consumption, a notion that Keynes set forth in 1936 and that played a large role in economic thinking in the years following. Friedman returns to the older theory of consumer behavior, in which consumers' plans and decisions are influenced by the future as well as the present and the past, and his explanation is thus consistent with much that economists have learned about consumer behavior over the past century or more" (Fabricant 1958, 2–3).

122. For example, the study by Bordo and Rockoff (2013b), although it is described by Belongia and Ireland (2016, 1224) as "a comprehensive discussion of Fisher's influence on Friedman's monetary economics," is not in fact a comprehensive discussion of the matter (although it does cover some very important ground). In particular, the Bordo-Rockoff analysis omits important early Friedman discussions of Fisher's work and of the Fisher effect. See the next chapter.

123. It is also noteworthy that Friedman (1943a)—the item in Friedman's pre-1951 work that articulated a skeletal version of his permanent income theory of consumption—pointed to Fisher as a prior advocate of the expenditure tax measure espoused by Friedman in that paper (Friedman 1943a, 61).

124. See, for example, Friedman (1957a, 28, 40, 214).

125. Friedman (1957a, 214).

126. See, for example, Friedman (1957a, 91, 194).

127. See Boskin (2005) for an example of the former and Darby (1975, 123) for an example of the latter.

128. Friedman (1972a, 915). See also Friedman and Schwartz's (1982a, 262) reference to consumer durable goods as "consumer capital."

129. Friedman (1957a, 28). See also Darby (1975, 123).

130. However, the models with this feature do involve a three-way division between consumption spending, consumer durables spending, and purchases of physical capital. So too did earlier work, such as the studies collected in Harberger (1960). These approaches therefore involved a finer disaggregation of private spending than was implied by Friedman's recommendation.

131. As noted below, it was also a point that Tobin (1974b) insisted had long been absorbed into his own analysis.

132. Indeed, Edey and Britten-Jones (1990) did not cite Friedman (1957a) or attribute this specific point to Friedman.

133. See, for example, Friedman (1957a, 91, 126, 194, 214; 1958h, 466).

134. See, for example, Friedman and Meiselman (1963, 177); Friedman and Schwartz (1982a, 486); and Morgan (1969, 46). Of course, in much early Keynesian analysis, even the interest elasticity of investment was cast into doubt, particularly in Depression conditions. See chapter 3 above, as well as the discussion of investment in section V of the current chapter.

135. This contrast between the standpoints of Keynesians and of Friedman was also noted in E. Nelson and Schwartz (2008a, 847).

136. From *Newsweek*, May 17, 1977. (The phrase was largely repeated in Friedman and Friedman 1985, 19.) See also *Banker* (January 1967, 69); *Newsweek*, May 12, 1975; and Instructional Dynamics Economics Cassette Tape 181 (November 1975, part 2), all of which were discussions in which Friedman was considerably more explicit than in his 1977 commentary on the role of higher interest rates in discouraging private investment spending. After the late 1970s, Friedman's references to crowding out tapered off. As already suggested, in this later period he became persuaded that Ricardian equivalence, rather than crowding out, was the vital reason for the looseness of the relationship between aggregate demand (both nominal and real) and fiscal deficits.

137. McKean (1948, 101). See also Patinkin (1969, 57). In addition, Friedman (1942a, 319) had earlier suggested that the amount consumed out of current income could depend on "relative prices" (and hence perhaps on interest rates), but at the time he described this possibility as "of secondary importance."

James Tobin may also have been among those who were open-minded in the late 1940s about the interest elasticity of consumption, for in 1947 he granted the possibility that "either investment or the propensity to consume" might be interest sensitive (Tobin 1947, 126). It is not clear, however, whether Tobin mainly confined this interest elasticity of consumption to durables spending, which, as already indicated, he later stated was a category of household expenditure that he had always regarded as investment spending (Tobin 1974b, 89).

138. Joint Committee on the Economic Report (1952d, 1019 and 1019-20).

139. For the first observation, see Friedman and Heller (1969, 54).

140. Friedman and Meiselman (1963, 176-77). See also the remark by Friedman and Friedman (1985, 98) that "total spending by consumers and businesses" responded to

monetary actions, and Friedman and Schwartz's (1982a, 620) statement that "monetary disturbances will produce systematic patterns in the reaction of such components of output as construction, other investment, consumption, and so on."

141. Friedman (1953f, 260).

142. Friedman (1957a, 26, 222). In addition, in the *Cleveland News*, May 25, 1959, Friedman was pictured drawing on a blackboard what seems to be an interest-elastic saving function.

The same year as the release of *A Theory of the Consumption Function* saw publication of a theoretical study by Friedman's colleague Martin Bailey titled "Saving and the Rate of Interest," which judged that "for most practical purposes ... consumption almost without exception will fall when the rate of interest rises" (Bailey 1957, 305). The analysis and conclusion were Bailey's, not Friedman's; but Bailey thanked Friedman by name for comments (279), and Bailey (1992, xiv) indicated that the analysis in his 1957 paper had been influenced by Friedman's prior work on consumer demand. Friedman included the Bailey (1957) paper as a reading on the consumption function in his winter 1968 graduate course, Income, Employment and the Price Level (the last piece of information was provided to the author by Ann-Marie Meulendyke, a student in the course).

143. Friedman (1957a, 78). Having written this, Friedman immediately moved his discussion on to another topic, and, as already indicated, he did not include the interest rate in his empirical estimates of the consumption function, keeping the focus instead on bivariate consumption/income regressions.

144. Friedman and Meiselman (1963, 221). See also Friedman (1971d, 330; 1972a, 915–16) as well as Friedman's remarks in Instructional Dynamics Economics Cassette Tape 197 (mid-August 1976) and in *National Review*, June 16, 1989a, 25.

145. See also the 1965 remarks by Robert Solomon quoted in chapter 12 below.

146. Laidler (1982, 300). A latter-day observation along the lines Laidler described (albeit not naming Friedman and Schwartz specifically) was that of Mervyn King (1994, 264), who stated that "some of those for whom money is the key driving variable in the economy sometimes overlook the crucial role of interest rates in the transmission mechanism." It should be mentioned that this statement was made ahead of the period, starting in the late 1990s, when King came to be more favorably disposed toward, and likely more steeped in, the core monetarist literature of Friedman-Schwartz and Brunner-Meltzer, particularly in the area of the transmission mechanism.

147. Friedman and Schwartz (1982a, 500).

148. This fact is brought out by Allan Meltzer's comment, in his aforementioned review of Friedman and Schwartz (1963a), that "in any case it is abundantly clear to the reader of [*A Monetary History*] that Friedman and Schwartz do not deny that interest rates and relative price changes have an influence on ... real magnitudes" (Meltzer 1965, 415). Consequently, Meltzer concentrated his criticism on what he perceived as the book's understatement of the role of (nominal) interest rates in the United States' demand-for-money and money-supply functions. That criticism raised issues separate from that discussed here (which pertains instead to the specification of the IS equation), and these issues are covered in chapters 12 and 13 below.

149. See, for example, Robert Hall (1977, 61) and Laurence Harris in *Bankers' Magazine* (July 1969, 7–8). In addition, Lester Thurow (Milton Friedman's alternate as a *Newsweek* columnist after Paul Samuelson bowed out) claimed: "According to the stone tablets of monetarism, interest rates don't matter—only the rate of growth of the money supply matters" (*Newsweek*, November 16, 1981).

150. See also Friedman (1962a, 83).

151. Friedman (1970a, 25; p. 17 of 1991 reprint).

152. See, for example, Friedman (1962a, 82; 1968b, 2).

153. Friedman (1966d, 75).

154. See, in particular, Friedman and Schwartz (1970a, 126). See also E. Nelson (2002b, 2004c) for further discussion.

It should be mentioned that a passage in Lucas (1977) did lend itself to the interpretation that he, and perhaps the monetarist literature on which he built, subscribed to the position that money entered the IS equation directly. In particular, Lucas (1977, 11) stated that "econometricians from Tinbergen on discovered that monetary factors did not seem very important," and he added in a footnote: "Tinbergen [1939], as did most subsequent macroeconometricians, used the significance of interest rates to test the importance of money." The footnote might be taken as suggesting that econometricians were misguided in putting interest rates instead of money in the IS or other spending equations. However, this was not Friedman's position, which was that (various) real interest rates entered the *structural* IS equation but that in practice money typically better summarized these rates' behavior than did observed interest rates. From this perspective, the Tinbergen equations could be criticized for various specification errors, among them the reliance on a too-narrow set of interest rates and the use of nominal rather than real interest rates, but not for their exclusion of money from the spending functions.

If Lucas's (1977) statement reflected the viewpoint that money appeared explicitly in the true IS equation (or perhaps the labor-supply equation), that may have reflected intuition arising from his use in his early monetary research (most notably Lucas 1972b) of overlapping-generations models. In these models, the structural equations can include direct monetary-transfer terms, while explicit interest-rate variables need not appear (see McCallum 1984a). However, even if this was Lucas's intuition, it was not Friedman's. Overlapping-generations models differed substantially from Friedman's view of economic behavior (see chapter 13 below), and he was critical of using these models for monetary analysis (see Friedman and Schwartz 1982a, 37). It should also be noted that, from the late 1970s onward, Lucas worked primarily with infinite-horizon models, which (under additively separable utility) do not give support for the notion that money enters either IS or supply equations directly.

155. See the previous chapter. Furthermore, Patinkin (1965a, 637) saw the additional material on money in Friedman (1953f) as incorporating a recognition of the real balance effect. This was likely indeed Friedman's principal motivation for adding this material, although that material can be reconciled with his subsequent emphasis on substitution effects.

156. See especially Friedman (1972a, 947; 1976a, 321; 1976f, 317).

157. Friedman (1964b, 3–4; pp. 71–73 of 1969 reprint).

158. Friedman (1960a, 43).

159. In Friedman (1967b, 100).

160. Friedman (1960a, 43). See also Friedman and Meiselman (1963, 217).

161. See Jacobs and Pratt (1968, 43–44) and Instructional Dynamics Economics Cassette Tape 86 (November 20, 1971).

162. Leijonhufvud (1977, 290) claimed that a contrast between monetarism and prior traditions in economics was that monetarists did not "accord Wicksellian themes a prominent role." But his discussion provided no evidence for this assertion, which is directly refuted by the content of Friedman (1968b) (an article that Leijonhufvud did not cite).

163. Friedman (1968b, 8). See also the discussion of the Fisher effect in the next chapter.

164. See, for example, Friedman (1951c, 189; 1956a, 4) and Friedman and Schwartz (1963a, 646; 1982a, 481).

165. See for example Friedman (1957a, 120; 1963b, 25; 1992c, 25).

166. See, for example, Friedman (1960a, 43; 1961d, 462; 1972a, 909-11, 945) and Friedman and Schwartz (1982a, 57-58, 486).

At an early stage, Friedman indicated that part of his doubt about the scope to obtain a single representative interest-rate series arose from the fact that lenders, including banks, raised the cost of obtaining funds through nonprice methods as well as through explicit interest-rate increases (Friedman 1951c, 189). This continued to be his view of banks' method of adjusting their customers' deposit-holding and borrowing costs in the face of traditional obstacles, which included the ceilings on deposit interest rates associated with Regulation Q (see, for example, Friedman 1970d; and Friedman and Schwartz 1982a, 260) and informal arrangements not to adjust bank interest rates rapidly (as was the case with some key commercial-bank lending rates such as the prime rate—see, for example, Friedman's analysis in *Beaver County Times*, January 8, 1969). In the main, however, Friedman's emphasis from 1956 onward on the imperfect substitutability of assets altered his basis for believing that interest-rate patterns could not be encapsulated by the behavior of a single observable interest rate. The basis for this belief shifted from the existence of credit rationing to his conviction that there was a multiplicity of important asset prices.

167. Friedman and Schwartz (1963b, 61).

"A Tentative Sketch of the Mechanism Transmitting Monetary Changes" as given in Friedman and Schwartz (1963b, 59-63) is widely considered one of Friedman's most elaborate descriptions of the transmission mechanism. An exposition of the transmission mechanism in Friedman and Meiselman (1963, 217-22)—one that previously appeared in abridged form in Friedman (1961a)—complemented that in Friedman and Schwartz (1963b) (see also chapter 13 on the relationship of this position to that articulated in other monetarist work such as Brunner 1961a, 1971a). Consequently, Friedman and Meiselman (1963) is sometimes cited as a key reference on the monetarist transmission mechanism: see, for example, Friedman and Schwartz (1982a, 58-59); Meyer (2001, 4); and the glowing references to Friedman and Meiselman (1963) in Goodhart and Crockett (1970, 164) and Goodhart (1989b, 119). One reason for favoring the Friedman-Schwartz exposition over the Friedman-Meiselman discussion is that the latter pair of authors classified the single-interest-rate perspective as a "credit view" of the transmission mechanism. They thereby fostered the incorrect impression that a single-interest-rate view of monetary transmission was intrinsically linked to a belief that credit aggregates, as opposed to monetary aggregates, were crucial in analyzing monetary policy. Although Friedman was indeed at odds with economists who attached great importance to lending or credit totals, their outlook had no necessary connection to the position that a single interest rate summarized monetary transmission. Indeed, through their frequent emphasis on nonprice rationing of bank credit, these credit-oriented analysts offered a view that potentially discouraged a focus on a single, observed interest rate. See also Tobin (1965a, 466-67) Silber (1969, 82), and Chick (1973, 41) on the ambiguities entailed in associating the Keynesian view of the transmission mechanism with a stress on credit.

168. See Friedman (1963a, 11) and Friedman and Schwartz (1963a, 645-46). As has already been seen, this was also Brunner and Meltzer's position.

169. See Friedman (1960a, 63–64), as well as Friedman's October 30, 1959, testimony in Joint Economic Committee (1959b, 3024). This was one of several respects in which Friedman's *Program for Monetary Stability* proposals represented a break from his 1948 rule. See chapters 4 and 8 for further discussion.

170. See Friedman (1970b, 204; 1987a, 9) and Friedman and Schwartz (1982a, 40). Friedman (1956a, 10, point 7 [iii]; 19, point 23) had made similar observations.

171. See Friedman's March 3, 1964, testimony, in Committee on Banking and Currency (1964, 1148), and his remarks in *Wall Street Journal*, April 5, 1990.

172. Friedman (1976d, 131). This may seem to be a statement that is very specific to the conditions in the United States, and to be less applicable to countries like the United Kingdom. In the latter country, a great deal of mortgage and corporate borrowing has, since at least the 1970s, taken the form of bank loans whose interest rates tend to be linked, on a rollover-credit basis, to short-term securities-market interest rates. Against this, however, it should be acknowledged that in recent years the UK monetary authorities have paid great attention both to stimulating, and to lowering the cost of, fixed-rate long-term borrowing. And even before this development occurred, Mervyn King (1994, 263) noted with regard to the United Kingdom that "it is the entire spectrum of interest rates which affects the spending decisions of families and businesses."

173. See, for example, Friedman (1985c, 59).

174. On this matter see, in addition to the discussion of imperfect asset substitution and the maturity structure in the next chapter, the coverage of Operation Twist in chapter 11 below, as well as the remarks in Friedman's June 1966 and June 1971 memoranda to the Federal Reserve Board (respectively, Friedman 1968a, 156; 1971g, 5) and the analyses in E. Nelson (2009a, 472; 2013a). In the discussion that follows, "term premium" will be used interchangeably with "liquidity premium" and "risk premium" to describe that part of the variation in long-term interest rates that represents deviations from the expected path of short-term interest rates.

175. See American Economic Association (1948, 28).

176. Friedman and Schwartz (1982a, 485). Similarly, among the readings for "The Investment Function" for his winter 1968 course Income, Employment and the Price Level, Friedman had included pp. 244–63 of the first (1962b) edition of *Price Theory* (information from Ann-Marie Meulendyke).

177. Friedman (1976a, 312).

178. See, in particular, Eisner (1967). Another notable comment on this topic was made by Arthur Burns in congressional testimony given on February 18, 1970, shortly after taking office as Federal Reserve chairman. After remarking that a short-lived tax increase would have little effect on firms' capital expenditures, Burns remarked that this finding "has nothing to do with all kinds of controversy about what is Keynesianism or non-Keynesianism. It is simply good economic sense, or if you prefer, good Keynesianism, to take into account the time factor in the tax package" (in Joint Economic Committee 1970c, 178). This last observation could be taken as implying that Friedman's permanent income hypothesis was a contribution to Keynesian economics rather than a critique of it—a position that, as discussed above, has considerable validity. Alternatively, Burns may have been implying that the role of expectations in investment decisions was widely accepted by postwar economists even before they accepted a comparable role for expectations in consumption decisions.

179. In addition, Friedman (1970b, 222) applauded others' analyses that endeavored to put expectations into the analysis of investment, citing Koyck (1954) in this connec-

tion. That said, Friedman did not appear to keep close tabs on the more modern investment literature, as already indicated. For example, Sargent (1987a, xxi) named Jorgenson and Lucas as authors who made contributions to the theory of investment on the eve of the rational-expectations revolution, but Friedman did not include Jorgenson (1963), Lucas (1967), or similar items in the reading list on investment in the 1976 edition of *Price Theory*.

180. See, in particular, Instructional Dynamics Economics Cassette Tape 40 (December 17, 1969). See also *Milton Friedman Speaks*, episode 15, "The Future of Our Free Society" (taped February 21, 1978, pp. 10-11 of transcript); and Friedman (1984a, 1998).

181. See Friedman (1957b, 91-92) for an application of this argument to households' spending on durable goods.

182. For example, Friedman used the concept of "marginal efficiency of investment" in Friedman (1976a, 288).

183. For example, Friedman included Lerner's (1953) article on the marginal efficiency of investment in his reading list on investment behavior in Friedman (1962b, 266; 1976a, 327).

184. See also Friedman (1951c, 189; 1987a, 13) and Friedman and Meiselman (1963, 167). In addition, chapter 3 above covered this matter.

185. See, in addition to the discussion here, the analysis in chapters 2 and 4.

186. See, for example, Instructional Dynamics Economics Cassette Tape 91 (January 26, 1972) as well as the discussion below of the IS curve.

187. For similar attributions of this position to Friedman, see Hirsch and de Marchi (1990, 246); and Harrigan and McGregor (1991, 113).

188. Friedman (1976f, 311). See also Carlson and Spencer (1975, 6) for a more extended discussion, of the same vintage as Friedman's comments, that made the same two points about the horizontal IS curve: its implications for fiscal policy and its connection to Knight's views.

As the Carlson-Spencer example shows, Friedman was not, of course, alone in making statements about the *theoretical* possibility of situations in which very substantial alterations in expenditure could be set in motion by extremely slight interest-rate movements.

189. See, for example, Friedman (1968f) and Friedman and Schwartz (1982a, chapter 10, including the application to a historical episode on p. 531). See also the discussion of the liquidity effect in the next chapter.

190. See, for example, Instructional Dynamics Economics Cassette Tape 191 (May 1976, part 2) and Friedman and Schwartz (1982a, 494) as well as the discussions published in the 1950s and 1960s that were mentioned earlier. A latter-day affirmation of this view came in Friedman's observation in *Forbes* (July 9, 1990, 67) that deviations of the real interest rate from its natural value "have such very large effects."

191. Friedman (1971d, 330).

192. See Friedman (1976f, 311) and Friedman and Schwartz (1982a, 494).

193. See chapter 13 below.

194. Theoretical support for the concept of Tobin's q was also provided by subsequent studies, including Abel (1979) and Sargent (1980).

195. See Instructional Dynamics Economics Cassette Tape 149 (June 26, 1974) and Heller et al. (1984, 48).

196. See Friedman and Schwartz (1982a, 31-32).

197. Philippon (2009) suggests that a much more reliable measure of Tobin's q than those traditionally derived from stock-market valuations can be obtained from data ob-

tained from the corporate bond market. Such a conclusion might bolster the usefulness of Tobin's q concept, but it would also imply that many of the judgments Tobin made in the 1960s and 1970s about the implications of q for aggregate demand and monetary policy were likely flawed, as these judgments were made on the basis of the stock-market-based measure of q.

198. In the same cassette discussion, Friedman named Wesley Mitchell as a researcher who had documented this point.

Friedman's "plucking model" of economic fluctuations (on which see Friedman 1964e and 1993; as well as Kim and C. R. Nelson 1999; and Sinclair 2009) is not discussed here as it was a description of the univariate behavior of output and was explicitly recognized by Friedman as a reduced-form representation of output, that is, as the result of the interaction of structural and monetary policy patterns. (However, for an analysis that embeds the plucking property in a structural model, see Dupraz, Nakamura, and Steinsson, 2018.)

199. Observations by Friedman to this effect appeared in, for example, Friedman (1980c, 84; 1985c, 59) and in *Barrons*, October 25, 1982 (6). Such remarks were consistent with Friedman's reference (albeit when discussing Frank Knight's views rather than his own) to "new investment" as the variable sensitive to current interest rates (Friedman 1976f, 311). Friedman used the term "new investment" as a concept distinct from net investment (see, for example, his remarks, quoted in Hammond 1996, 75, in May 1957 NBER correspondence).

200. In standard, linearized New Keynesian models, the real long-term interest rate does not matter in its own right for spending decisions; only the component of the real long-term rate that corresponds to the expected path of short-term interest rates does so (see Rotemberg and Woodford 1999a, 61; Andrés, López-Salido, and Nelson 2004, 666). However, in Instructional Dynamics Economics Cassette Tape 149 (June 26, 1974) Friedman indicated in essence that his view was that the term-premium component of the real long-term interest rate also mattered for spending decisions. See also Rudebusch, Sack, and Swanson (2007) for an empirical finding that the term premium does matter for US aggregate-demand behavior.

201. See Andrés, López-Salido, and Nelson (2004); Chen, Cúrdia, and Ferrero (2012); Harrison (2012); Kiley (2014); and Ireland (2015).

202. Similar reasoning for moving from a consumption equation to an aggregate spending equation was offered by Rotemberg and Woodford (1997, 321–22).

203. Habit formation in consumption might be cited as another reason for this expectation, but Friedman showed little inclination to include this feature in the specification of the consumption function, while Barro and King (1984, 835) and Bodkin (1995, 57) argued that time separability of consumption preferences was a key part of Friedman's permanent income hypothesis.

204. The "lags-imply-leads" property of rational-expectations models (see, for example, Sargent 1980, 108; Robert King 2009, 339) implies that the forces making for the appearance of lagged output in the equation would also likely mean that expected future output (one or, perhaps, two periods ahead) would enter the equation. For simplicity, the expected-future-output terms are limited in the equation used here to a one-period-ahead term, and the value of its coefficient can be regarded as partly reflecting the same investment dynamics that lead to the appearance of a lagged-output term.

As indicated above, some of Friedman's remarks about output persistence were consistent with inherent persistence in the *growth rate*, not just the (detrended) log level, of output—a viewpoint that lined up with his observation that US output growth tended to be serially correlated in many different sample periods (Friedman and Schwartz 1982a, 455). A recognition of this point might imply the presence of a second lag of log output in the IS equation (1) reported in the text. Such a second lag might emerge if capital adjustment costs, instead of being centered on the change in the capital stock (as in Abel 1983, for example), pertained largely to the change in investment. On this matter, see especially Christiano, Eichenbaum, and Evans (2005).

205. See E. Nelson (2013b) for a detailed discussion of their procedure.

206. However, he used many different labels for nominal income. One of the earliest-used and most cumbersome of these was "the pecuniary volume of business" (Friedman 1950a, 485).

207. Examples of this practice included those given in the text following, as well as the nominal income equations Friedman used in his mid-1960s memoranda to the Federal Reserve Board and in forecasting nominal spending during the early 1970s. See chapters 12, 13, and 15 below.

208. Conversely, the nominal income/nominal money regressions in *Monetary Trends* were presented only after Friedman and Schwartz had, in an earlier chapter, outlined an asset-price-based view of monetary policy transmission. The nominal income equations were derived as reduced-form equations—"transformed [money] demand equations" obtained from what the authors presented as a structural demand-for-money equation (see Friedman and Schwartz 1982a, 345; see also their section 8.2 as well as Schwartz 1984, 130, 133).

209. See Friedman and Schwartz (1982a, 102, 343). See, however, E. Nelson (2013c) for an attempt to work out how one might embed into an optimizing model the property of a nominal-to-real-spending recursion.

Friedman and Schwartz were not alone in using, as an approximation, the idea that monetary policy or aggregate demand policy determines nominal income, with the split of nominal income among components being determined by private-sector forces. For other examples of this practice, see Kohn (1990, 12); Sims (1992, 979–80); and Mervyn King (1997a, 90).

Chapter Six

1. See Friedman (1956a, 4, point 1, emphasis in original) and the discussion that follows.

2. Friedman (1956a, 16–17). See also Friedman and Schwartz (1982a, 206). Niehans (1978, 202) dismissed the Friedman definition of the quantity theory of money as too weak, being a "mere homogeneity postulate" concerning the demand function. But Niehans's discussions of the quantity theory of money in Niehans (1978, 5, 202) implied that the demand for money was certainly part of his own conception of what the theory meant. And the "mere homogeneity postulate" is in fact vital for the long-run monetary-neutrality proposition on which Niehans's exposition of the quantity theory focused.

3. See McCallum (1993c, 2004) as well as the related discussion in McCallum and Nelson (2011, 99–100). The same line of argument perhaps underlay Lucas's (1980c, 1005) brief but largely negative remarks concerning Friedman's (1956a) definition of the quantity theory of money.

4. See, for example, Friedman's remarks in Darby et al. (1987, 22). Note that this position did not amount to an affirmative statement that the short-run money-demand function *was* unstable. As discussed later in this chapter, Friedman was inclined to view insta-

bility in the money-demand function reported by researchers in the 1970s as reflecting specification error rather than actual lack of constancy in demand-for-money parameters. However, he did grant that the information gleaned from the data about short-run money-demand behavior was much less reliable than the corresponding information on the long-run money-demand function (see, for example, Friedman 1980a, 58, point 14; pp. 54–55 of 1991 reprint). In line with this perspective, Friedman later said to the present author that, although he would not go so far as to say that estimates of the short-term money-demand function were not useful, "I think it's clearly difficult when you're using quarterly data and relying on these short things . . . to be sure what you've got, and that, therefore, the results are subject to a very wide margin of error and [can] change all over the place over very brief times" (Milton Friedman, interview, January 22, 1992). Note also that a belief in instability in the short-run money-demand function is not the same as a belief that the money market does not clear in the short run.

5. See, for example, Friedman and Schwartz (1963a, 686, 694; 1970a, 139; 1982a, 626) as well as the discussions in chapters 8 and 15 below.

6. See Friedman and Schwartz (1982a, 206).

7. See chapter 15.

8. Friedman (1956a, 17). Thus here Friedman spoke of "the critical importance of the supply of money," notwithstanding his initial statement that the quantity theory of money was "in the first instance a theory of the *demand* for money" (Friedman 1956a, 4, emphasis in original). For the reasons just discussed, these statements did not contradict one another. But Friedman's failure to thread them together adequately underscores Walters's (1987, 425) observation that "The Quantity Theory of Money—a Restatement" did not constitute "one of Friedman's better expositions." It also reinforces Walters's related implication that the papers by Friedman's students in the *Studies in the Quantity Theory of Money* volume (Friedman 1956b), for which Friedman's article was the curtain-raiser, were more effective in conveying the point that the demand function for money could be a foundation stone for the analysis of variations in nominal income and prices. Walters mentioned Cagan (1956) specifically in this connection. For his part, Cagan subsequently voiced the assessment that "the quantity-theory tradition [is one that] emphasizes the supply of and demand for the stock of money" (Cagan 1972a, 113).

See also the discussion of Laidler and Nobay (1976) in the note below.

9. Friedman (1956a, 4, point 1).

10. See Friedman (1970b, 225). See also Friedman and Schwartz (1982a, 62).

11. Friedman (1953c, 42).

12. Friedman (1956a, 16 and 3, respectively). See also Friedman (1956a, 17, 20–21).

13. In a related vein, Laidler and Nobay (1976, 296) observed that much of the early research in which Friedman was involved as an author or supervisor "dealt with the determination of the time path either of prices or money income." In this connection, they cited 1960s studies coauthored by Friedman as well as the Cagan (1956) study that appeared in the same volume as Friedman (1956a) and which was a revision of Cagan's doctoral dissertation, which Friedman supervised. A still earlier example is, however, available, namely Friedman (1952b).

14. Because prices were not wholly rigid at this frequency and exhibited some gradual adjustment to monetary actions, the quantity theory could also be used for the analysis of inflation at business cycle horizons.

15. Friedman (1987a, 18).

16. In later work (Modigliani and Sterling 1990) of Modigliani that Lettau and Lud-

vigson (2004) did not cite, the concept of cointegration was used explicitly. In addition, Stock (1988, 403) perceived an essential grasp of the cointegration concept in the work of Ando and Modigliani (1963).

17. Mitchell (1896, 140), quoting F. Walker (1893) (see also F. Walker 1895). Mitchell (1896) was discussed in Friedman (1950a, 474). The present discussion has not been concerned with the extent to which money-demand-oriented discussions of the quantity theory of money were present at the University of Chicago before the 1950s. As noted in chapter 2, that subject has been treated by a large number of studies and is outside the scope of this book.

18. Rockoff (2015) speculates that the work on consumer demand by Henry Schultz in the 1930s influenced Friedman's money-demand research by, in effect, persuading Friedman of the merits of narrowing the number of variables in the money-demand function to a few variables. However, this suggestion is countered by the fact that Friedman's (1956a) demand-for-money function had more variables, not fewer, than was featured in Keynes's (1936) money-demand function and in prominent work by Baumol and others in the lead-up to 1956.

19. Tavlas (1989, 248) stated: "Friedman's empirical work has always used a long-run (i.e., no lagged dependent variable) specification of the demand for money." This statement was not wholly correct. In Bach et al. (1976, 37), Friedman and his coauthors drew on results from money-demand regressions that they had commissioned and which included lagged-dependent-variable terms, and in Friedman and Schwartz (1982a, 255–56) the authors presented some money-demand equations that included a lagged dependent variable. Furthermore, shortly before Tavlas's paper appeared, Friedman (1988a, 230–32) reported an estimated velocity equation that included a lagged dependent variable, albeit not as his preferred specification.

It is true, however, that Friedman was not well disposed toward including lagged dependent variables in empirical work, both because of his aforementioned greater interest in long-run behavior and because he believed that using lagged dependent variables to model dynamics was fraught with statistical problems. Among the latter was the danger that the statistical significance of the lagged dependent variable in a regression might in part be due to the omission of relevant explanatory variables. (On this, see Friedman 1964h; and Friedman and Schwartz 1982a, 256.) Consequently, Friedman rarely used lagged-dependent-variable terms, even in instances in which his empirical work (such as that portion of the work that used adaptive expectations) suggested that inclusion of lagged dependent variables might well be a logical option.

Friedman's perspective on this matter was also brought out by the distinction that he made between bona fide instability in the demand for money and the "breakdown in the bad [money] demand functions that people fit," by which he presumably primarily meant Goldfeld (1973, 1976), whose specifications included a lagged dependent variable. (The quotation is from Friedman and Modigliani 1977, 24.)

20. See Friedman (1959a, 333; 1987a, 8, 17) and Friedman and Schwartz (1963a, 642–43; 1963b, 44, 57; 1982a, 253, 258). See also Meltzer's (1977, 153; p. 149 of 1978 reprint) retrospective on Friedman (1956a), in which Meltzer inferred that that analysis, too, used a permanent-income concept.

21. Friedman (1983a, 2).

22. See, for example, Friedman (1957a, 69, 218, 227; 1976a, 60, 203, 314) for use of the "reserve against emergencies" terminology, and Friedman and Schwartz (1982a, 262) and Friedman (1983e, 3) for deployment of similar terminology in the specific context of a discussion of the demand for money. This perspective on money demand lined up with Mints's (1945, 97) observation that "anything held in contingency reserves of ready

purchasing-power is 'employed' as money," as well as Modigliani's (1944, 51) perception that money was superior to other assets as a "reserve against contingencies." In his own work Friedman was, however, more insistent than Modigliani had been in his 1944 discussion that the asset that had this status was real money balances, not nominal balances, and Friedman further contended that this reserve-against-contingencies function pointed toward a more complex money-demand function than that Modigliani (1944) used.

23. Occasions on which Friedman used this phrase in his writings included Friedman (1963a, 10; 1987a, 9; 1992c, 16, 22) and Friedman and Schwartz (1963a, 650; 1966, section 1, 123, 151; 1970a, 125; 1982a, 24–25). (Friedman 1961a, 263, and 1961g, 41, used the phrase "temporary abode for generalized purchasing power." Friedman 1974b, 353, used the phrase "temporary store of purchasing power.")

Friedman also described money as a "temporary abode of purchasing power" in Friedman (1969a, 3), but, as stressed elsewhere in this book, this 1969 analysis was a breed apart from the bulk of his monetary work, not least in its downplaying of the distinction between asset and transactions approaches to money demand.

24. For passages in which Friedman in effect endorsed the money-in-the-utility-function approach, see, for example, Friedman (1956a, 10, point 8; 1968c, 440; 1970b, 200, 201; 1987a, 8) and Friedman and Schwartz (1963a, 644–45; 1970a, 152; 1982a, 38–40, 68, 145, 261, 413).

25. See, in particular, Friedman and Schwartz (1970a, 107–109).

26. See Friedman (1956a, 14, point 14). This aspect of Friedman's analysis was acknowledged by Patinkin (1965b, 75).

Friedman did, however, view the emphasis on money as an asset as consistent with pre-1936 work on money demand by Keynes and others at Cambridge University in the first third of the twentieth century. See, for example, the discussion in Friedman and Schwartz (1970a, 106).

27. See E. Nelson (2002b) for prior argumentation along these lines.

28. Friedman and Schwartz (1982a, 248, emphasis in original).

29. Friedman (1968c, 442). Friedman repeated this phrase in Friedman (1987a, 16).

30. Friedman and Schwartz (1963a, 673).

31. This result is a leading example of the "lags-imply-leads" principle that, as noted in chapter 5, has been stressed in work on rational-expectations models by Robert King and Thomas Sargent. The basic principle was, however, well known even before the rational-expectations literature put a spotlight on it. B. Klein (1976a, 958), for instance, observed that adjustment costs in money holding provided a basis for believing that expected future short-term interest rates appeared in the money-demand function.

32. Because this is the long-run function, no distinction between measured (or current) and permanent real income is required in the specification. Also, as usual, the intercept is suppressed.

33. See Friedman and Schwartz (1982a, 262). See also, for example, Mishkin (1983).

34. Perhaps because of the lack of a clear microeconomic foundation for Friedman's (1956a) money-demand function, Sargent (1987a, xxi) treated Tobin, Baumol, and Samuelson, but not Friedman, as providing optimization-based foundations for the demand for money.

35. See Friedman (1968b, 2).

36. Friedman and Schwartz (1982b, 201). Goodhart and Crockett (1970, 164) likewise characterized the monetarist view as one in which money substitutes "generally for all assets."

37. See Friedman (1956a, 9, in the discussion of point 7). In the analysis of this equa-

tion, equation (8), and its special case, equation (9), Friedman emphasized divergences between the dynamic paths of equity and bond yields. Although, as chapter 5 observed, he saw differences between interest rates on alternative assets as diminishing over time, his inclusion of multiple yields throughout the largely static portfolio analysis of Friedman (1956a) as well as in the long-run empirical money-demand functions in Friedman and Schwartz (1982a) indicated that he believed that discrepancies between alternative yields could remain important over long horizons.

38. The quotations are from Meltzer (1977, 154, 163; pp. 150, 159 of 1978 reprint). This aspect of Friedman's (1956a) analysis was also noted by Friedman and Schwartz (1982a, 40).

39. An early discussion that characterized Friedman's (1956a) analysis in terms of imperfect substitutability of assets was that of Hodrick (1978, 101).

40. See Joint Committee on the Economic Report (1952a, 690); Friedman (1960a, 62); and Friedman and Schwartz (1982a, 300).

41. See, in particular, Friedman and Schwartz (1970a, 132–33).

42. See Friedman's remarks in *Newsweek*, March 1, 1971; and in Friedman (1988a, 223). See also Friedman's (1972a, 922) mention of the possibility that "the demand for money depends on the structure of government liabilities." See, too, Friedman (1987a, 10).

43. See, for example, Friedman (1977d, 403) and Friedman and Schwartz (1982a, 572).

44. The quotation is from Friedman (1977d, 402). For instances in which Friedman specifically indicated that long-term interest rates could be affected by money injections, for a given path of short-term interest rates, see the discussion "The Multiple-Yield Channel" in section IV of chapter 5 above. This position also underlay his rejection, voiced many times, of the liquidity-trap notion.

45. The characterization given here of Friedman as a believer in a term premium that decreased in the face of money injections may seem at variance with the fact that he was dissertation supervisor for Meiselman (1962)—a study widely seen as supportive of a strict expectations theory of the term structure (see, for example, Nielsen 1992). It is true that Meiselman himself was very skeptical of both the wisdom and effectiveness of the US authorities' efforts to affect the term premium via bond purchases, and he had a negative view of both Operation Twist and the Federal Reserve's 2008–13 large-scale bond-purchase programs (Morris 1968, 23; David Meiselman, interview, April 30, 2013). But a good deal of Meiselman's dissertation was concerned not with the issue of whether monetary injections could affect the term premium but instead with whether the pure expectations theory shed more light on term-structure behavior than a framework in which short- and long-term securities markets were *completely* segmented. He found that it did. This finding left open the possibility that the substitution between short-term and long-term securities, while considerable, was imperfect. Consequently, Meiselman's (1962) findings could be consistent with the hypothesis that changes in relative asset stocks alter term premiums. Friedman clearly subscribed to this hypothesis, as his own writings and statements establish. See also Bernanke (2002a).

46. See also Tobin (1976b) and chapter 13's discussion of the similarities of the Tobin and of Brunner-Meltzer models.

47. Friedman (1987a, 13). See Friedman (1968c, 439).

48. See, for example, Friedman and Schwartz (1970a, 80, 90, 148) and Friedman (1963a, 9; 1963b, 9–10; 1972a, 916–17; 1976f, 314). A setting of $\omega = 0$ would be the parameterization that most justified the long-run money demand equation given previously.

49. See also Grossman (1975, 831). Similar comments apply to Keynes in his *General*

Theory analysis, which treated money and bills largely as a single total. Friedman and Schwartz (1963a), in contrast, used such terms as "liquid assets" when they were referring to a money-plus-bills aggregate. The fact of the important distinction in Friedman's analysis between money and short-term securities might also help explain the dearth of references to "liquidity" in Friedman (1956a). Patinkin (1965b, 55; 1969, 49) portrayed this tendency as an attempt on Friedman's part to play down the similarity of his analysis to Keynes's. Contrary to this interpretation, it can be noted that Friedman's distinction between money and bills (which became more prominent in writings other than Friedman 1956a) was a point of *dissimilarity* between his analysis and that of Keynes.

50. Other differences between Friedman's and Tobin's perspectives, noted elsewhere in this and other chapters of this book, reinforced their divergence on the matter of the importance of the money stock.

51. Friedman (1964e, 9; p. 263 of 1969 reprint).

52. As well as the discussion that follows, see E. Nelson (2013a, 62–64).

53. Friedman (1972a, 929).

54. See also chapter 13 for a discussion of criticisms made of the monetarist literature for neglecting this point. Even in the case in which deposits are the only commercial-bank liability, discrepancies between growth in bank credit (banks' loans and their investments in marketable Treasury securities) and in deposits can arise if bank reserve balances increase sharply as a share of bank assets, as they did in the 1930s (and again in the 2008–14 period).

55. Friedman (1972b, 192).

56. See chapters 12 and 14 below.

57. In the same vein, Mints (1950, 98) described a person who bought an equity claim on a firm as essentially being a "'lender'" to that firm. See also Friedman and Schwartz's (1970a, 113) classification of commercial bank net worth as a bank liability (as opposed to the alternative convention of seeing this magnitude as the difference between a bank's assets and its liabilities). Niehans (1978, 170) also used this convention.

58. See, in particular, Instructional Dynamics Economics Cassette Tape 19 (March 1969) and Friedman (1970d, 19-20; 1992d, 523).

59. Friedman (1962d, 237 [p. 189 of 1968 reprint]; 1980a, 58 [p. 54 of 1991 reprint]).

60. The sharp empirical divergence between deposits and (bank or total) credit is sometimes taken as a result that should discourage a focus on money (see, for example, Woodford 2010). But it is also possible, as was Friedman's practice, to emphasize this divergence and yet concentrate on money, especially if the latter series has a better relationship with economic activity than does credit. As one of Friedman's former students, John Scadding, summarized the monetarist position: "if you believe money matters . . . it's not a question of whether credit expands; it's the question of what form it [the financing of the credit] takes on the liabilities side of the [banks'] balance sheet" (John Scadding, interview, January 7, 1992).

61. See especially Friedman (1970d, 20). For a discussion of Friedman's views on the credit channel that compares them with those of Bernanke (1983), see E. Nelson (2013a).

62. See his May 3, 1949, letter to Arthur Burns, quoted in Hammond (1996, 79).

63. E. Nelson (2013a, 64), and Milton Friedman, interview, January 22, 1992.

64. One of the ways in which Friedman expressed this position was to say that he did not believe that the relationship between monetary growth and national income growth depended greatly on whether the new money was created by a commercial bank loan or by some other means. That is, the "first-round effect" of monetary expansion was not of

great importance in assessing the overall effects of monetary policy. On this point, see Friedman (1972a, 917 and 921-23; 1987a, 10); Friedman and Schwartz (1982a, 29-31); and Bordo (1972, 1975).

65. Specifically, Friedman and Schwartz (1970a, 154-55) noted the scarcity of information on the split of total bank deposits between demand and time deposits for the pre-1914 period. See also Friedman's January 1976 remarks on this matter in Committee on Banking, Currency and Housing, US House (1976, 2181). But see Meltzer (1963) and Lucas (1988b), among others, for cases in which US annual data on M1 were constructed for the period starting in 1900.

The Cagan statement just quoted seemed to support an interpretation that another former student of Friedman's, John Scadding, noted had been voiced about Friedman's use of M2. "Of course, the cynics always argued that the only reason Milton chose M2 was because he was doing the *Monetary History*. You could only get [monetary] data for a long historical period on that basis. [Data on] M1 didn't go that far back." Scadding added that, although this position had been taken by critics of Friedman, "that's not to say it isn't true. That may have been the reason for the initial choice" (John Scadding, interview, January 7, 1992).

66. Friedman and Schwartz (1970a, 1, 104). Similar sentiments had earlier been expressed in Friedman and Schwartz (1963a, 650).

67. In addition, and contrary to Cagan's characterization above, Friedman and Schwartz contended that their treatment of demand and time deposits as equivalent before 1914, although it had been influenced by data limitations, accurately captured the way in which holders of money had in practice treated the two types of deposit (Friedman and Schwartz 1970a, 155). Earlier, Friedman (1960a, 90) had stated his and Schwartz's preference for M2 as reflecting a finding that it was "the most useful concept."

68. See in particular Friedman and Schwartz's observation (1970a, 139) that they "put primary emphasis on demand" and so aimed for a money definition "that could be regarded as having as nearly as possible the same meaning to the holders of money balances over the entire period of our study."

69. Alan Walters, in an interview with the present author (April 6, 1992), contended that Friedman in his early monetary research was an advocate of an M1-type concept of money. Walters may have been referring to Friedman's (1951f, 207) reference to "circulating medium proper (currency plus demand deposits)." (In addition, during his nonmonetarist period, Friedman 1943b, 118, had used an M1-type aggregate when scrutinizing the empirical work of Angell 1941.)

70. See Friedman's March 25, 1952, comments in Joint Committee on the Economic Report (1952c, 719) as well as his written comments on p. 743 of the same volume.

71. See especially Friedman and Schwartz (1970a, chapter 3, section 1). Friedman's reliance on M1 during the period 1982-86 in part reflected his mistaken belief that the Federal Reserve Board's 1980 redefinition of M1 had made the aggregate similar to Friedman and Schwartz's M2. On this matter, see E. Nelson (2007).

72. In Friedman's analysis, firms were taken as having a money-demand function of the same form as that of households. See Friedman (1956a, 11-14, points 10-12; 1970b, 205-6) and Friedman and Schwartz (1982a, 40-41).

73. Friedman (1967b, 101).

74. To the best of this author's knowledge, the first instance in print in which the monetarist position was characterized as viewing money as a "sufficient statistic" for variation in economically important interest rates was Sheffrin (1982, 163). More recent examples

include Sims (1998, 934); E. Nelson (2002a, 151); and Mervyn King (2003, 76). Weyl (2015) indicates that there is a long tradition in work on price theory at the University of Chicago, when confronted with an analysis that involves many state variables, of approximating the information relevant for the problem with a single price, which can then serve as a sufficient statistic in the analysis. Friedman's approach to monetary analysis can be regarded as approximating the information provided by a vector of prices by a single quantity (the money stock, or its growth rate).

75. The list that follows does *not* include either the notion that money might be useful as an indicator of current income or the notion that movements in money reflect discrepancies between the outstanding money stock and the amount demanded, which will be eliminated in future periods. The reason for excluding the first of these bases for seeing money as an indicator is discussed in McCallum and Nelson (2011, 144). (In effect, that exclusion means that the criterion for money here is primarily that it be enlightening about *future* income behavior, not current economic activity.) The reason for excluding the second basis is the present author's contention that Friedman was sympathetic to, but did not himself use the framework implied by, the literature on buffer-stock money.

The list of reasons for believing that money is a sufficient or near-sufficient statistic given here is, to the best of the author's knowledge, more succinct and itemized than those that have been provided in prior discussions in the literature. However, many prior discussions have correctly gleaned the reasons for looking at money that are suggested by the monetarist position. These include the discussions of the matter provided by several key monetarists. In addition, however, two commentaries should be singled out in this connection. First is Thygesen's (1977, 58) observation that Friedman did not contend "that movements in interest rates are not an important element in the transmission process; on the contrary, he stresses their essential role . . . [but] he considers movements in the money stock a useful proxy . . . for the broad range of financial changes that would normally accompany them." Second is Rowan's (1980, 109) observation that monetarists "use the money supply (in one of its definitions) as a proxy for the whole range of rates."

76. In the present chapter's analysis, this pressure has been specialized to pressure on longer-term interest rates.

77. Early discussions that used the term "liquidity effect" included Friedman's October 1965 and June 1966 memoranda to the Federal Reserve Board (see Friedman 1968a, 137, 150, 162). On Friedman's work on the liquidity effect, see, in addition to the discussion that follows, that in chapter 12.

The Radcliffe Committee in the United Kingdom had used the term "general liquidity effect" (Committee on the Working of the Monetary System 1959, 131, paragraph 385; see also Davidson 1970, 189), but it had done so to describe the relationship between wide measures of liquidity and decisions by the private sector to spend, not the relationship between money and interest rates.

78. This literature was more focused than were Friedman's initial discussions on the reaction of the short-term interest rate as opposed to longer-maturity rates. However, Friedman and Schwartz (1982a, chapter 10) ended up concentrating on short-term interest rates. In part, this was in order to abstract from variations in interest rates due to variations in term premiums: see Friedman and Schwartz (1982a, 507). Another motivation was that concentration on a short-maturity asset allowed the liquidity effect and the Fisher effect to be treated as operating at different time horizons, rather than occurring simultaneously. The later literature shared this view (see Cochrane 1989, for example).

79. See, for example, Friedman and Schwartz (1982a, 483–85). But see Friedman

(1987a, 10) for an exposition in which this distinction was downplayed and in which Friedman associated the "important transitory effects on interest rates" of monetary expansion specifically with the expansion of the volume of loanable funds.

80. Friedman's wish to cover cases beyond those associated with open market operations likely reflected the lineage that he perceived between his work and Hume's (1752) "Of Interest." Hume, of course, lived in an era that long predated the advent of open market operations and many other central-banking tools.

81. Alternatively, one might confine attention to a category of central-bank asset or liability that is influenced by open market operations and then view the reaction of the nominal interest rate to variations in this total as an empirical regularity deserving of study—perhaps one on which the performance of theoretical models should be evaluated. Eichenbaum (1995, 1611, 1612), for example, emphasized that interest rates typically change in response to changes in the Federal Reserve's holdings of government securities or to changes in particular aggregations of bank reserves. As central banks in the future reduce their reliance on open market operations as a means of controlling short-term interest rates (in favor of practices such as altering the interest rate paid on reserves), it is likely to become difficult to isolate a liquidity effect of the kind that was the focus of Eichenbaum's discussion.

82. This perspective is sharply different from that expressed in Tim Congdon in the *Banker* (July 1983). In this contribution (which was later cited favorably by Hendry and Ericsson 1991b, 27), Congdon viewed Friedman and Schwartz's (1982a) emphasis on the liquidity effect as reflecting factual and analytical shortcomings of their work, with Congdon contending that Friedman and Schwartz overlooked the fact that central banks controlled interest rates and did not exogenously fix money or the monetary base. However, the notion of the liquidity effect does not require money to be exogenous, and the fact that central banks control short-term interest rates can be reconciled with the liquidity-effect notion by viewing the liquidity effect as the mechanism through which central banks exercise control over interest rates at business cycle horizons (see E. Nelson 2008b for further discussion).

It should also be stressed that, although Congdon interpreted the Friedman-Schwartz emphasis on the liquidity effect as a reflecting nonpractitioners' misunderstanding of what central banks do, many analysts in central-banking circles have accepted the validity of the liquidity-effect notion. For example, Philip Lowe—later the governor of the Reserve Bank of Australia—once characterized his own view of the transmission mechanism as follows: "Changes in real money balances brought about by monetary policy cause a strong liquidity effect at the short end of the yield curve. This results in changes in real output in the short/medium term which eventually get translated into changes in prices" (Lowe 1992, i.)

83. See, for example, Friedman (1967b, 101) and Friedman and Schwartz (1982a, 481, 486).

84. See the next chapter as well as E. Nelson (2008b). In stressing that the repercussions of money-supply injections for interest rates involved not only the liquidity effect but also further effects, Friedman was following previous authors, among them David Hume, as already noted, and Irving Fisher, as discussed below, but also J. S. Mill and Alfred Marshall. On the views of the latter two figures, see Laidler (1991a, 18–19, 90–91).

85. Friedman's statement on this occasion did not allow explicitly for the fact that, by exploiting the Fisher effect, central banks can control nominal interest rates over horizons in which the liquidity effect no longer operates. A more complete statement on the matter was given by Friedman in 1980: "If you hold down the rate of monetary growth, interest

rates will fall. But if you try to work that in reverse—if you induce a cut in interest rates—the only way you can temporarily maintain it is by re-stimulating inflation, and even that won't maintain it for very long" (*Scotsman*, October 20, 1980). Even this statement, however, did not encompass the hypothetical case in which a central bank lowers nominal interest rates by using the liquidity effect of a monetary expansion, then entrenches the lower level of rates by shifting permanently to a lower monetary-growth rate that is associated with lower inflationary expectations. This case was outlined in Woodford (1994, 371–72). See also McCallum (1986b, 154–55) for a related discussion.

86. He was also, as indicated in chapter 2, far more confident than was Keynes that increases in the nominal and hence real money stock could stimulate economic activity in Depression conditions, even after nominal short-term interest rates had reached a floor. The reason was that Friedman regarded increases in the real money stock as able to put downward pressure on term premiums.

87. See Friedman and Schwartz (1982a, 485–87) for an example of the use of this terminology for the effect (which in his June 1966 memorandum Friedman had simply called an "income effect": see Friedman 1968a, 162), and see also Friedman (1961d, 462; 1983a, 3) for other discussions of the effect in question. The 1982–83 analyses just cited included the suggestion that the income effect would be roughly equal to the liquidity effect in its impact on the nominal interest rate, implying that the combination of these two effects would bring the nominal interest rate back to its initial level.

88. Friedman (1972a, 935). Friedman repeated this observation in 1982's *Monetary Trends* (Friedman and Schwartz 1982a, 46). However, this reference was missing both in the index entry for Fisher in *Monetary Trends* and in Bordo and Rockoff's (2011) listing of Friedman's mentions of Fisher.

89. Friedman confirmed Fisher as a reading in the course when sending his notes on the readings to David Laidler in correspondence in June 1994 (David Laidler, personal communication, May 28, 2013). Nonetheless, Laidler (2012, 5) has questioned whether Fisher's work figured importantly in Friedman's education, stating: "Fisher's name appears in neither the Index nor the Bibliography of Friedman and Friedman (1998). It is hard, therefore, to make a case for a direct Fisherian influence on Friedman." However, the index to *Two Lucky People* turns out not to be a reliable indicator on this matter, because Fisher *was* mentioned in the book, and the reference to Fisher was one that affirmed the importance of Fisher's work as an influence on Friedman from his student days onward. See Friedman and Friedman (1998, 621).

90. From Friedman's letter to Don Patinkin of July 19, 1972, quoted in Leeson (2003a, 503–4).

91. See H. Schultz (1938, 570, 607).

92. See chapter 1.

93. This matter also bears on Bordo and Rockoff's (2011) catalogue of Friedman's references to Friedman. Their list (which is discussed below) does not include the extensive references to Irving Fisher in the second edition of Friedman's *Price Theory*. Although Fisher did not appear in the index for the book, the text of the book made references to Fisher in connection with both the Phillips curve and capital theory. The capital-theory material in the book had been taught by Friedman in class.

94. From Friedman's May 8, 1985, letter to John Presley, quoted in Presley (1986, 198).

95. This is because a truly complete list of references that Friedman made to Fisher would include the H. Schultz (1938) and Friedman and Friedman (1998) passages that have already been mentioned.

96. That is, Friedman and Schwartz (1976).

97. See *Wall Street Journal*, November 4, 1969 (1). Other instances in which Friedman made this observation included Friedman (1970a, 8 [p. 2 of 1991 reprint]; 1970e, 4; 1971h, xxii; 1985d, 214; 1992c, 37) and Friedman and Friedman (1998, 621).

98. Robert Solow observed: "If you'd asked Paul who was the greatest American economist of the early twentieth century, he would've said, without any question, it was Irving Fisher." Asked about the aspects of Fisher's work that found favor with Friedman and Samuelson, Solow remarked, "I'm not sure about Friedman, but Samuelson was not especially enamored of Fisher's macroeconomics." Instead, in Fisher's work, "Samuelson liked the theory of interest, and of capital and interest. First of all, Fisher's early understanding of general equilibrium theory, as in his PhD thesis, and then his work on intertemporal economics, were certainly what attracted Samuelson. Whereas I think Friedman may have been more interested in Fisher as a monetary economist. So, they could both be admiring of Fisher, but primarily of different aspects of Fisher" (Robert Solow, interview, July 7, 2014).

William Brainard recalled: "Jim Tobin often said he agreed with Milton (and Samuelson) that Fisher was the greatest American economist of all time. Jim often referred to something Fisher had said or done, but he was not without criticism of Fisher (or, for that matter, of Keynes)" (William Brainard, personal communication, May 23, 2014).

99. See Fellner et al. (1967).

100. See Tobin (1987b).

However, Friedman's brother-in-law, Aaron Director, had been an undergraduate student at Yale University, and Henry Manne, a student of Director's at the University of Chicago in the early postwar period, was under the impression that Director had known Fisher (Henry Manne, interview, April 30, 2014).

101. Friedman (1953c, 42). David Meiselman observed that while "of course, in Irving Fisher's late days, his general reputation took a terrible beating" owing to overoptimistic forecasts, Friedman "didn't pay much attention" to the negative reaction to Fisher and emphasized the importance of the latter's contributions to economics (David Meiselman, interview, July 16, 2014). In contrast, at an April 1951 University of Chicago conference attended by Friedman, Eugene Rostow of Yale University felt obliged to state: "Although I think I am the only speaker here from Yale, I hasten to reassure Mr. Viner that we are not still worshiping at the shrine of Irving Fisher in New Haven and do not blindly follow his oversimplified version of industrial fluctuations" (in Director 1952, 195).

102. See, for example, Friedman's (1976a, 216; 1985a, 15) references to what Fisher "had in mind."

103. In a similar vein, Friedman (1963a, 4) referred to what Fisher "would have said."

104. See, for example, Friedman (1957a, 120).

105. NBC (1951a, 7).

106. Friedman (1956a, 9). Laidler (2013a, 7) interprets this discussion by Friedman as one of *skepticism* about the Fisher effect, pointing to Friedman's words "we cannot suppose (9) to hold." But the equation (9) in question embedded not the Fisher effect alone but also the equality of the real returns on longer-term securities and on equities. It is perfectly consistent with confidence in the Fisher effect to suggest that the real returns on equity and bonds can differ from one another for lengthy periods. Indeed, as already suggested, an important part of the monetarist position is that the yields that appear in the IS and other key relationships cannot be consolidated into a yield on a single asset. As Friedman (1956a, 9) described it, such consolidation required that "bonds and equities were equivalent" in a static analysis and also that, in a dynamic analysis, there were

"no differences of opinion" that created a divergence between the expected price paths of the two assets. In the absence of these consolidation conditions, it would make sense even for a strong believer in the Fisher effect to doubt that real yields on alternative assets will coincide (in which case Friedman's equation (8), describing the equity/bond yield spread, might not hold in its own right—because that equation required the spread to converge over time to zero—and would certainly not collapse to his equation (9), in which the spread was zero every period). (A separate point, noted in Friedman 1956a, 9–10, as a further reason why equation (9) would not prevail, is that it was written as a perfect-foresight relationship and so imposed equality of actual and expected inflation.)

The interpretation just given of Friedman's (1956a, 9) discussion—that it did not deny the Fisher effect but that it questioned the equality of different yields—coincides with that of Meltzer's (1977, 163; p. 159 of 1978 reprint) examination of the same passage. It also lines up with Friedman's (1987a, 9) *New Palgrave* entry on the quantity theory of money, which provided Friedman (1956a) as a reference in support of the Fisher relation. On a related point, it deserves emphasis that although Laidler (2013a, 7) describes Friedman (1956a) as the "opening manifesto" in the monetarist counterrevolution, Friedman had in fact been advocating monetarism for more than five years prior to the appearance of Friedman (1956a), and those pre-1956 statements had included his already-noted 1951 endorsement of the Fisher effect.

107. Friedman (1958b, 252; p. 183 of 1969 reprint).

108. From Friedman's May 25, 1959, testimony, in Joint Economic Committee (1959a, 610–11).

109. On this, see chapters 12, 13, and 15 below, and for the case of the United Kingdom see Batini and Nelson (2005, 43–44).

110. See chapter 13.

111. Volcker (1977, 24). For a similar acknowledgment, see Wallich (1977, 281, 283).

112. See chapters 12 and 13 below. Among the early examples in this period were Friedman's discussions of changes in "price anticipations" (really inflation anticipations or expectations) and in interest rates in his October 1965 and June 1966 memoranda to the Federal Reserve Board (Friedman 1968a, 137, 157–64; quotation from p. 164).

113. Friedman 1968b. An acknowledgment that was similar in substance to Sargent's, but more skeptical in tone, also appeared in 1973. Chick (1973, 110) observed that economists based or trained at the University of Chicago were "well schooled in the work of Irving Fisher, [and] they have made much of his concept of the real rate of interest and the distinction between it and the money or nominal rate."

114. See chapter 13.

115. See chapter 15.

116. See chapters 10 and 15.

117. Chapter 10 is concerned with US monetary policy in the first decade after 1951's US Federal Reserve Accord/Treasury.

Chapter Seven

1. That is, in Friedman (1968b), a paper that is discussed in detail in chapter 13.

Steuer gave the date of the meeting with Friedman as 1960. In chapter 13, however, it is suggested that the Friedman visit in question (during which he also talked to Lipsey and to Phillips himself) may well have occurred during the 1962–63 academic year. A 1960 date would be consistent with the possibility that the work that Friedman and Steuer discussed was what became Lipsey and Steuer (1961). That date would, in addition, seem to be consistent with Friedman's unfamiliarity with the "Phillips curve" terminology. Even by 1962, however—although Friedman certainly knew the A.W. Phillips (1958) paper itself—his familiarity with the Samuelson-Solow (1960) paper that used the "Phillips curve" terminology was limited, if the absence of a reference to that paper from Friedman's (1962b, 284) discussion of Bowen's (1960) US application of A. W. Phillips's (1958) study is anything to go by. At the same time, it should be emphasized that—although Friedman might not by 1962-63 have been particularly familiar with the Samuelson-Solow study—he was certainly very aware of Samuelson's belief in an unemployment/inflation trade-off, having had face-to-face exchanges with Samuelson on the matter from mid-1950 to mid-1962. See the discussion that follows in the text of this chapter, as well as that in chapter 13.

2. Friedman (1969b, v). The first of the items in the collection was Friedman (1952b), an abridgement and revision of a paper that Friedman had presented in December 1951. The chronologically last item in the collection was Friedman (1969a)—a piece that, as discussed in the next chapter, actually parted company in some major respects with the monetary theory Friedman expounded in articles written both before and after that paper.

3. An exception was Friedman (1943b), whose analysis did adhere closely to the inflationary-gap analysis as developed in the United Kingdom.

4. Friedman was not alone in this era in favoring such a modification of the L-shaped aggregate-supply curve, as Phelps (1968b, 679) discussed.

5. Shoup, Friedman, and Mack (1941, 13). See also Friedman (1942a, 317; 1943a, 51).

6. For further discussion of this matter, see section III below.

7. This demand-pressure connection between the output gap and price setting was acknowledged by Friedman as a theoretical matter as early as 1946 (Friedman 1946, 615).

As discussed in section II below, the notion that the inflation/output-gap relationship reflects a link between quantities supplied and (unexpected) inflation is compatible with, rather than a substitute for, the notion that inflation pressures build as the output gap becomes more positive. Furthermore, the phrase "quantities supplied" as used here is distinct from potential output; the former denotes actual equilibrium output, the latter the natural or flexible-price value of output.

8. NBC (1947a, 4).

9. Friedman (1948a, 261). See also chapter 4 above.

10. That is, downward-sloping when inflation was plotted against the unemployment rate.

11. NBC (1950, 3, 6; 1951a, 3).

12. See, for example, Friedman (1956a, 15, point 17; 1964e, 17 [p. 274 of 1969 reprint]); Friedman and Schwartz (1982a, 164); Instructional Dynamics Economics Cassette Tape 124 (July 4, 1973); and Instructional Dynamics Economics Cassette Tape 169 (June 1975, part 2).

13. See, for example, Friedman (1973a, 35; 1976a, 233) and Instructional Dynamics Economics Cassette Tape 182 (December 1975).

14. In All Participants (1951, 243). This statement, together with those Friedman made later in the 1950s, lends support to Friedman's recollection, in Instructional Dynamics Economics Cassette Tape 205 (December 1976, part 2), that he questioned the notion of the Phillips curve "from the very outset." See also Friedman (1977e, 455).

15. From Friedman's March 25, 1952, testimony, in Joint Committee on the Economic Report (1952c, 727).

16. From his June 15, 1966, memorandum in Friedman (1968a, 159).

17. See chapter 10 below, as well as E. Nelson (2005b). Writings and statements by Friedman that had this implication or were amenable to being interpreted in this way included Friedman (1953a, 180–81; 1966a, 21–22 [pp. 101–2 of 1968 reprint]); and Friedman and Friedman (1985, 83–84), as well as Instructional Dynamics Economics Cassette Tape 139 (February 4, 1974). The basic argument was laid out as a theoretical possibility in Friedman (1946, 615), but it is Friedman's statements from the early 1950s onward that emphasized the empirical validity of the argument.

The reason for viewing cost-push shocks (u_t) as having a zero mean in Friedman's framework is the following. Friedman argued in the references just cited (and elsewhere) that, for fixed values of aggregate nominal spending and potential output, the long-run response of the aggregate price level to a 1 percent cost-push shock was zero. The basis for this result lay in his prediction that the positive impact of the cost-push shock on inflation would eventually be fully offset by the response of inflation to a negative output gap (with the latter induced by the drain on real spending associated with the initial rise in prices). This argument implied that if the cost-push shock had a nonzero unconditional mean— that is, if $E[u_t] \neq 0$—then the output gap, too, would tend to have a nonzero unconditional mean—that is, $E[y_t - y_t^*] \neq 0$. But the natural-rate hypothesis posits that $E[y_t - y_t^*] = 0$. It follows that $E[u_t] = 0$ has to hold under this hypothesis.

18. This is an appropriate way to proceed because this chapter is largely about the precise manner in which inflation, in Friedman's view, responded endogenously to aggregate-demand forces. In contrast, the pure cost-push position denied the importance (and, over a large region of values of aggregate demand, even the existence) of this endogenous response for the understanding of the behavior of inflation. Consequently, Friedman's rejection of the cost-push position underlies the whole discussion that follows—but is not the focus of it.

19. See, for example, Friedman and Schwartz (1963a, 678; 1963b, 57) and Friedman's remarks in Ketchum and Kendall (1962, 54).

20. See, for example, Friedman (1974a, 21; 1980a, 59, paragraph 21, p. 57 of 1991 reprint) and *Newsweek*, November 12, 1979.

21. See, for example, Friedman and Schwartz (1963b, 57).

22. See chapter 15 on the change in Friedman's views about the within-cycle dynamics of the relationship between inflation and output.

23. Friedman (1963a, 15). See also Friedman and Meiselman (1963, 172).

24. See, for example, Friedman (1970b, 209, 220) and Friedman and Schwartz (1982a, 47–48) as well as chapter 10 below.

25. From Friedman's March 25, 1952, testimony, in Joint Committee on the Economic Report (1952c, 729).

26. Friedman and Schwartz (1982a, 58).

27. Friedman and Schwartz (1982a, 507).

28. See the Friedman (1953a, 165) quotation discussed presently.

29. Friedman (1966d, 81).

30. Friedman (1948a, 254).

31. Friedman (1953a, 165). Much like Krugman, L. Ball and Mankiw (1995, 162) claimed: "Friedman's analysis implicitly assumes that nominal prices are perfectly flexible." The particular item they cited as the basis for this claim was Friedman's *Newsweek* column of June 24, 1974 (incorrectly given as 1975 by the authors, who also provided an incorrect title for the column). In fact, however, that column's analysis did not rest on perfect short-run price flexibility, as a reading of the complete column would establish.

32. Friedman and Schwartz (1963a, 284). See also Friedman (1974b, 354).

33. From Friedman's November 14, 1963, testimony, in Joint Economic Committee (1963a, 453–54).

34. See Friedman and Friedman (1980, 276–77). See also the discussion in section III below.

35. From Friedman's September 23, 1971, testimony, in Joint Economic Committee (1971b, 734). See also Friedman and Friedman (1985, 108). A similar view was espoused by Taylor (1986). On earlier views that opposed flexibility, see Roose (1984, 155).

It may be that Friedman's judgment was that the post-World War II experience, and perhaps the interwar years too, had tilted the US economy in a direction that made price stickiness more important than previously, in relation to wage stickiness, as a source of nominal rigidity. He was aware that Henry Simons had believed that wage stickiness was the US economy's important nominal rigidity and that views along these lines had led Simons and others to propose monetary policies that promoted a constant nominal wage index—policies that, because of productivity growth, also implied gentle price deflation (see Friedman 1958b, 252–53 [pp. 182–83 of 1969 reprint]; 1967a, 12; 1971c, 854). Simons's view had necessarily been formed largely on the basis of the pre–World War I evidence, and Friedman (1960a, 11) seemed to express very qualified agreement with that judgment when he referred to the degree to which prices proved downwardly flexible in the late nineteenth century. Too much should not be made of this possible change in perspective, however. It is clear from Friedman's discussions of nineteenth-century economic behavior, both in the 1960 reference just mentioned and Friedman and Schwartz (1963a), that he regarded the deflation observed in the later nineteenth century as often associated with poor real outcomes, and that he regarded lack of *complete* nominal price-level flexibility as a key reason for the weakness in real economic activity during much of the era. See the discussion in chapter 2 above.

36. To repeat, the discussion below will concentrate on Friedman's position with regard to postwar US conditions. In this context, "price stickiness" often meant prices rising at a faster rate or slower rate than the inflationary pressure implied by aggregate-demand policy; the aggregate US price level was rarely under great pressure to undergo an absolute decline. Partly for this reason, the notion that nominal prices and wages are particularly resistant to pressure to fall in absolute terms is not considered in what follows—even though, as Friedman's (1953a) discussion implied, it was a notion to which Friedman subscribed.

37. See, for example, Friedman (1960a, 109).

38. This is so, at least, if the cost-push versus monetarist aspect of the Keynesian-monetarist debate is put to one side.

39. Friedman (1977e, 454).

40. Friedman (1997, 16).

41. See Friedman (1971d, 324–25) and Friedman and Schwartz (1982a, 46). In particular, Friedman did not suggest that Keynes regarded a boost to prices (and the associated decline in real wages) as the means by which aggregate-demand stimulation led to higher employment. In contrast, many accounts have suggested that this was Keynes's position (see, for example, Levacic 1984; Christiano and Eichenbaum 1992, 430), and the notion that inflation can be used to stimulate employment has even been suggested as common ground between Friedman and Keynes, at least with regard to short-run economic behavior (Shiller 1978, 8). But, as discussed by Nicholas Kaldor (in *Financial Times*, June 3, 1985), Keynes's post-1936 writings tended to indicate that he did not regard movements in real wages as essential to his theory. That being the case, Friedman's

attribution to Keynes of a proportional relationship between wages and prices would appear to be acceptable.

42. See chapter 13 for a detailed discussion. This setup allows nominal wages to be bid up as the labor market tightens but requires that the wages are set before workers know the current value of the economy-wide price level.

43. See, for example, Instructional Dynamics Economics Cassette Tapes 140 (February 20, 1974) and 182 (December 1975, part 1); *Saturday Briefing*, BBC2, March 12, 1983, p. 6 of transcript; and Friedman (1984i, 44).

44. See Friedman (1975d, 12; p. 64 of 1991 reprint; 1976a, 216). He also attributed this position to Wesley Mitchell (Friedman 1950a, 491).

45. In Ketchum and Kendall (1962, 53). Friedman made similar remarks in *Newsweek*, August 18, 1969, in Friedman (1980a, 61; p. 60 of 1991 reprint), and in other places, while in Friedman (1973c, 32) he mentioned specifically that some key employment contracts pertained to periods two or three years ahead.

46. Friedman (1977e, 457). In addition, on many occasions Friedman suggested that labor supply was dependent on tax rates (for example, in *Newsweek*, August 18, 1980).

47. The fact that an elastic short-run labor supply is a feature of Friedman's model of the Phillips curve was stressed by Gertler (1985, 285-86), who noted that post-1968 theoretical developments built on this feature and linked the labor-supply response more explicitly to intertemporal substitution in hours.

48. This was the passage in Friedman's 1962 *Price Theory* cited in chapter 1. Mulligan (1998, 1036, 1042, 1050) also cited *Price Theory*, together with Lucas and Rapping (1969), on this matter. In doing so, however, Mulligan cited the 1976 revision of *Price Theory*, so he left the erroneous impression that Friedman's consideration of the issue postdated that of Lucas and Rapping.

Enders (1995, 186) noted: "Labor economists argue that 'hours supplied' is more sensitive to a temporary wage increase than a permanent increase." In fact, as has been noted, Friedman has been credited with having advanced this point in his 1962 *Price Theory* discussion well before it became a focus of attention on the part of labor economists. That said, both Lucas and Rapping (1969, 732) and Lucas (1972a, 52) pointed to Hicks (1946) as another reference that anticipated the aspects of concept of intertemporal substitution in labor.

49. See, for example, Gray (1976a, 224); Mankiw, Rotemberg, and Summers (1985, 227); and Parkin (1984b, 29).

50. Friedman and Schwartz (1966, section 2, 76).

51. In addition, as was also indicated in chapter 4 and will be further discussed in chapter 13, Friedman was amenable to monopolistic-competition ideas in the sense that he believed that neither complete monopolies, nor cartels that included all major sellers, were a durable feature of market economies, unless actions by the state entrenched the monopoly. He believed that actual monopolies were vulnerable to the emergence of competitors, that cartels were fragile and tended to break up, and that many of those firms designated as monopolies were not, in fact, monopolies. One observation Friedman made in 1981 is relevant on the last of these points: "I think your statements about multinationals are neither factually correct, nor historically correct. Multinationals in general do not have a monopoly position" (Friedman 1981a, 21).

52. Shoup, Friedman, and Mack (1943, 4). See also Friedman (1942a, 317).

53. See *Newsweek*, November 12, 1979, for another discussion in which Friedman characterized sellers as having prices as a choice variable. His depiction in that column of the decision problem faced by such a firm had parallels with one of his earliest discussions

of the situation in which a firm has some market power (Friedman 1941). It was inappropriate, he noted in that 1941 discussion, to regard such a firm as choosing the quantity produced of a good and taking the good's price as wholly externally given, for the link between the equilibrium quantity produced and the equilibrium price of the good had to be recognized. But he added that the firm could be regarded as taking a quantity decision that entailed an implied choice for the price, or a price decision for which a choice of quantity produced was implied. In the same vein, his 1979 column discussed the circumstances in which the firm would respond to the state of demand by acting on "prices rather than output" and other circumstances in which it would change "output rather than prices."

54. For example, in Instructional Dynamics Economics Cassette Tape 38 (November 19, 1969), Friedman stated that the existence of inflationary expectations was a basis for his belief that inflation would only gradually slow down in response to the disinflationary policy then in force. See also, among other discussions, those in *Newsweek*, August 18, 1969; and *Newsweek*, June 15, 1970; as well as Friedman (1974c, 95; p. 150 of 1975 reprint); and his October 6, 1969, testimony in Joint Economic Committee (1970a, 817).

55. The next section will, however, consider the case in which the lagged level of inflation appears alongside expected future inflation.

56. Under this convention, those changes in prices that occurred in period t were made on the basis of period-t information; but it happened that the period-t expectation of one relevant variable, costs, would be a function of a variable—the lagged expectation of the current output gap—that is known prior to period t.

57. See, for example, Sbordone (2002); Galí, Gertler, and López-Salido (2001); Walsh (2003, 238-39); and Woodford (2003, 152, 180). A variation, not explored here, that might more closely match Friedman's views would involve period-t wages being contracted to be a function of actual period-t employment but the wage contract being based on the period $(t-1)$ expectation of the period-t aggregate price level.

58. In Ketchum and Kendall (1962, 52).

59. In Ketchum and Kendall (1962, 52-53).

60. In Ketchum and Kendall (1962, 53).

61. Friedman (1974h, 63).

62. *Milton Friedman Speaks*, episode 12, "Who Protects the Consumer?" (taped September 12, 1977), p. 24 of transcript.

63. They also line up with other contributions to the early New Keynesian literature, as well as with Dornbusch and Fischer's (1978, 360) observation that "price changes (increases) annoy customers and lose goodwill for firms."

64. The Calvo-Taylor notion that these contracts were staggered was also something manifested in Friedman's views on the setting of prices—in particular, in his belief that a portion of prices did adjust each period and could react promptly to news. See Friedman (1974c, 95; p. 151 of 1975 reprint) as well as the discussion earlier in this section.

65. From Friedman's October 6, 1969, testimony, in Joint Economic Committee (1970a, 817).

66. See, for example, Friedman (1970a, 23, point 7 [p. 16 of 1991 reprint]; 1970i, 6; 1987a, 17, point 9; 1992c, 48). (In the 1970 references, the short run was given as being as long as five to ten years, while the later references instead referred to "three to ten years." The changed formulation may have reflected a lowering of Friedman's estimate of the average lag between monetary changes and output changes, as a result of his 1970-72 research on lags, which was noted above and is discussed in detail in chapter 15 below.

However, Friedman did use the terms "five or ten years" and "five to ten years" even in the immediate aftermath of doing this research: in Friedman 1973a, 28, and in Friedman 1974b, 355, respectively.)

In other expositions, Friedman emphasized that it would be decades before the economy *fully* adjusted itself to monetary actions (see, for example, Friedman and Schwartz 1982a, 8, 433–40). However, the notion that a complete adjustment to monetary policy actions might well take decades (and indeed, in principle, would take an infinite amount of time) tends to be implied by any model with autoregressive dynamics, and it is consistent with results (including those in Friedman and Schwartz (1982a, 438–40), in which the boost to output from monetary expansion has essentially vanished within a decade. And well before a decade had elapsed, prices would have responded very substantially, with Friedman (1975a, 178) stating that about eighteen months after US output started to exhibit appreciable responses to monetary actions, "the main effect" of those actions switched from being on output to being on prices. See also the discussion of the Phillips curve in chapter 13 below.

67. *Meet the Press*, NBC, June 28, 1970, p. 5 of transcript.

68. Friedman and Friedman (1980, 279).

69. Among other characterizations he gave were that inflation was "rather inertial" (Friedman 1983a, 3) and that it had "a great deal of inertia" (Friedman 1985c, 52).

70. It has already been discussed that Friedman was sympathetic to the notion that the inflation expectations relevant for price setting were formed at a number of dates.

71. Friedman emphasized such doubts in his discussions of the Nixon administration's disinflationary policy of 1969–71. See the *Meet the Press* quotation given above as well as the discussion in chapter 15 below.

72. *Newsday* (BBC2 television program), September 20, 1974, p. 3 of transcript.

73. Friedman (1980a, 56, paragraph 4; p. 50 of 1991 reprint). See also Friedman and Friedman (1980, 17–18).

74. Friedman (1958b, 252; p. 183 of 1969 reprint).

75. Friedman (1951b, 113; 1968b, 13). In some writings (for example, Friedman 1949b, 952), Friedman suggested that the absence of short-run price flexibility (and, by implication, the unattainability—even in a noninflationary environment—of fully efficient adjustment of relative prices in the short run) might tend to lower the average level of output. Such a position might be viewed as having some support in the New Keynesian literature (see, for example, the results and discussion in Khan, King, and Wolman 2003, 840–42). However, the possibility of a link between short-run price stickiness and the long-run level of output will not be contemplated further here. The long-run level of output will be taken as equal to the value it would attain in an economy that had continuous price flexibility. Under that convention, the long-run level of output can be regarded as sensitive to the degree of monopoly power and other real distortions in the economy, but as invariant to the degree of short-run flexibility in nominal prices or wages.

76. See Friedman (1974c, 95 [p. 151 of 1975 reprint]; 1977e, 467) and Nelson (2018).

77. See also Fischer (1981). Taylor (1981, 57–58) cited Friedman's (1977e) Nobel lecture as a motivation for his analysis.

78. Braun (1986, 136–39) articulated a similar interpretation of this line of work.

79. See Friedman (1977c, 13).

80. Similar comments apply to a still-earlier paper—Friedman (1966d)—which Tobin (1995, 41) took as endorsing the ideas of what became known as new classical economics. In addition, mention should be made of Laidler's (1995, 334–35) conjecture that the

lack of great interest displayed by Friedman in the microfoundations of the demand for money was a posture that would make him amenable to flexible-price models. In opposition to this conjecture, it can be noted that neither traditional IS-LM analysis nor a modern optimization-based approach really suggests a strong connection between the specification and microfoundations of money-demand relationships, on the one hand, and the choice between sticky-price and flexible-price setups, on the other (see, for example, McCallum and Nelson 1999, 296–300, for a discussion). It should also be recorded that Friedman's consideration of the underlying basis for the demand for money appeared in several other places beyond the Friedman (1969a) article on which Laidler concentrated; and that, for reasons discussed in chapter 8, the present author does not, in any event, regard Friedman (1969a) as very representative of Friedman's monetary analysis.

81. The principal items typically cited in this connection are Friedman (1975d, 1976a). But similar material appeared in his July 1974 *Fortune* piece (Friedman 1974c, 94 [p. 150 of 1975 reprint]; see also Friedman 1974g, 16) and Friedman (1975a, 178).

82. See also the discussion, in the preceding section, of real wages and labor supply.

83. Here "excess demand" refers to the (percentage) difference between the actual (that is, under sticky prices) and natural (that is, under flexible prices) values of output, and "equilibrium quantities" refers to the items that make up the equilibrium level of output in a period. "Equilibrium level of output" then corresponds to the actual, not natural, level of output—just as it does in standard aggregate-demand/aggregate-supply analysis.

84. For this reason, the present author would regard Laidler's (1990, 55) attribution to Friedman of "the interpretation of the Phillips curve as a reflection of an aggregate supply relationship" and as the result of rational expectations, as acceptable, but not the inference that these aspects of Friedman's interpretation meant that he subscribed (at least from the mid-1970s onward) to the flexible-price interpretation of the Phillips curve advanced by Lucas (1973). (Laidler may, however, have been, like Braun 1986, taking the term "aggregate supply relationship" as automatically entailing an assumption of flexible prices—a convention not adopted in this book.)

85. Around the same time, Friedman criticized the United States' Regulation Q deposit-interest-rate ceilings on the grounds that they were "offering too little inducement to investors" to supply funds to commercial banks (*Phoenix Gazette*, November 24, 1969). This was another indication, albeit in the context of a discussion of the credit market rather than the goods market, that Friedman believed that quantity supplied was a function of price.

86. Friedman (1982c, 54). An earlier example of the compatibility of the two perspectives was Friedman's (1953a) exchange-rate analysis, in which he assumed both price stickiness and the dependence of production on price signals.

87. See Friedman (1976a, 216, emphasis in original). This passage, like those surrounding it, was the same in all essential respects as that in Friedman (1975d, 12; p. 64 of 1991 reprint), which was in turn a record of a talk that Friedman gave in London in September 1974. See chapter 13 for a complementary discussion of the post-1968 occasions on which Friedman discussed the Phillips curve.

88. For example, in an October 31, 2002, letter to the present author, Friedman stated that as a matter of principle: "The quantity of money, the level of prices, output, and all of the other economic variables are variables in a multi-equation system of simultaneous determination."

89. Modigliani (1977, 5) also interpreted the Friedman (1968b) analysis as altering the causation in the Phillips curve from employment-to-inflation to inflation-to-employment. But he did not specifically attribute this causal interpretation to Friedman himself. Nor

did Modigliani explain why he was associating the rival Phillips-curve theories with strict one-way causation instead of contemplating the possibility that inflation and real variables were jointly determined in either or both of the theories.

90. This perspective on the Phillips curve was certainly not new to Friedman's mid-1970s expositions. For example, in Instructional Dynamics Economics Cassette Tape 37 (November 5, 1969) he stated: "What encourages additions to output and employment of more people is *not* rising prices, but prices rising *faster* than people anticipate that they will rise." See also Friedman (1968b, 11).

91. Friedman (1976a, 228-29).

92. Friedman (1976a, 216, emphasis in original).

93. If an IS equation is used, the "nominal variables" in question can be regarded as the nominal money stock, which matters for nominal and real interest rates, with real rates then bearing on the behavior of real spending. If, instead, a reduced-form approach is used in which an equation for nominal spending represents the aggregate-demand portion of the model, the "nominal variables" can be taken to be either the nominal money stock, or (as in Friedman 1977e, 454, 456, 469) nominal spending itself.

One should also keep in mind that Friedman used the terms "slower rate of inflation" and "policy of reducing inflation" synonymously when describing a restriction of aggregate nominal demand (see Friedman 1980a, 55, 56, paragraphs 2 and 5; pp. 50, 51 of 1991 reprint). Similarly, he referred to an "inflationary period" in such a way as to include the period of the initiation of a loose monetary policy, even though that period was typically associated with an upturn in nominal spending growth but with little reaction of inflation (see E. Nelson 2007, 161).

94. On this, see, in addition to Friedman's 1976 *Price Theory* discussion, that in Friedman and Schwartz (1982a, 440-41).

95. There is consequently a parallel between Friedman's discussion of the inflation/ unemployment relationship and his perspective on the relationship between a country's interest rates and the capital-account component of its balance of payments. Friedman emphasized that capital inflows put downward pressure on interest rates, and he sometimes presented this position as in competition with the view that higher domestic interest rates generated capital inflows (see, for example, Friedman and Schwartz 1963a, 70; see also 496). He nonetheless acknowledged that, in fact, the two series were determined simultaneously and that interest-rate variations triggered capital movements (see, for example, Friedman 1953a, 166; Friedman and Schwartz 1963a, 146; and 1982a, 335; and Friedman and Friedman 1985, 122-23).

There is also a parallel between Friedman's discussions of Phillips-curve causal relations and those he earlier made about the relationship between prices and nominal wages (or costs). On occasion, he presented cost increases as being a result of inflation (see Brozen and Friedman 1966, 26; *Newsweek*, September 28, 1970). These characterizations, like those he made of the unemployment/inflation relationship, underscored his view of inflation as ultimately determined by monetary policy and did not really constitute a denial that production costs and prices were simultaneously determined.

96. There is a standard but important qualification to the latter statement. The long-run value of the aggregate natural level of output does obviously matter for the value of the long-run price level, and the behavior of relative prices is relevant for the determination of the natural level of output. But, as already noted, it is being taken for granted here that distortions to the relative-price structure arising from short-run nominal price stickiness do not have any bearing on the long-run value of the natural level of output.

97. Friedman (1966a, 22; p. 102 of 1968 reprint).

98. A reader of this chapter has suggested that the fact that a number of Friedman's statements that inflation drove unemployment appeared after the reprinting (as Irving Fisher 1973) of Irving Fisher (1926) is evidence that he did change his mind (in favor of a belief in unidirectional inflation-to-unemployment causation) after absorbing the reprinted Fisher article. But this suggestion is inconsistent with the indications that Friedman long believed in two-way causation between the two variables. Evidence to this effect comes in his pre-1973 affirmations, and post-1973 reaffirmations, of a dependence of inflation on unemployment, as well as in his pre-1973 indications (for example, Friedman 1967c, 12) of a dependence of unemployment on inflation.

99. See the Friedman and Friedman (1985) passage cited earlier. Also relevant is Friedman's (1977e, 470) statement: "The natural-rate hypothesis contains the original Phillips curve hypothesis as a special case." (This special case corresponds to a setting in which expectations of inflation are stable: see, for example, Friedman 1968b, 8–9.) Furthermore, in his *Newsweek* column of November 12, 1979, Friedman affirmed that the notion that inflation responded to economic slack formed part of the correct interpretation of the inflation/unemployment relationship, and Friedman and Schwartz (1982a, 397) implied that the output gap was a factor "determining the rate of price change." (This implication lined up with their theoretical analysis on pp. 60–61, discussed below.)

100. Friedman's uses of the phrase included those in Friedman (1963c, 17; p. 39 of 1968 reprint), which Friedman (1992c, 262) regarded as the first time he used it in print. Instances in the decade after 1963 in which Friedman repeated the phrase included Friedman (1966a, 18, 25 [pp. 98, 105 of 1968 reprint; see also the conclusion of the same article]; 1968a, 18; 1970a, 24 [p. 16 of 1991 reprint]; 1970i, 6; 1973a, 28, 40); *Time,* January 10, 1969; and his *Newsweek* columns of February 2, 1970, and September 28, 1970.

101. The discussion that follows does not consider the interest elasticity of money demand in detail, but the conclusion about inflation being a monetary phenomenon is common to the cases of (finitely) interest-elastic and interest-inelastic demand functions for money. See chapter 12 for further analysis.

102. Specifically, Patinkin (1981c, 31) suggested that Friedman's statement was analogous to declaring that "the price of potatoes is everywhere and at all times a potato phenomenon" (see also Patinkin 1993, 104–5), while King deprecated Friedman's proposition along similar lines, arguing that it was no more helpful than saying that a "rise in the price of whisky is a whisky phenomenon" (M. King 1994, 261). It should be underscored that King's statement was made before his late-1990s movement to a more favorable view toward the monetarist literature (and also prior to his own direct interaction with Friedman).

103. If, in contrast, monetary policy was completely *unable* to affect inflation, Friedman's proposition would be contradicted, but the truism that inflation is a decline in the value of money would remain valid.

104. In addition, as Friedman (1966a, 18; pp. 98–99 of 1968 reprint) noted, one could believe that fiscal policy affected the output gap strongly—and reject Friedman's emphasis on money—yet share his view that inflation was related to aggregate spending via an output-gap channel, and that cost-push forces were unimportant for the understanding of inflation.

105. Two earlier discussions also deserve special note for their grasp of this point. First, Laidler (1981, 8) observed: "Although some commentators . . . treat the Phillips curve as providing an alternative theory of inflation to the monetarist approach, this is surely a mistake." Second, Meyer and Varvares (1981, 13) observed that "a monetarist reduced-form

equation for inflation, in which inflation depends directly on current and past monetary growth, is not inconsistent with the existence of a Phillips curve." However, having made this valid point, Meyer and Varvares proceeded to follow the invalid practice of treating the natural-rate restriction in the expectational Phillips curve as implying that "the sum of coefficients on the past inflation rates is not significantly different from unity" (19)—a criterion shown much earlier by Sargent (1971) to be invalid. With regard to this criterion, see also the discussion in chapters 13 and 15 below.

106. Friedman (1977e, 451). Of course, the unitary restriction on the coefficient on this expectational term was another vital implication of Friedman's modification.

107. It was therefore consistent for advocates of the pure cost-push position to be critical of both the Phillips curve and monetarism, and to regard the latter two as intertwined. In this vein, Cripps (1977, 111) made the perfectly reasonable statement: "Without the Phillips curve, the monetarist theory of inflation is not valid."

108. See their regressions and accompanying discussion in Friedman and Schwartz (1982a, 440–49).

109. See Friedman and Schwartz's (1982a, 462) acknowledgment of the possibility "that we have used too lengthy a unit of observation" to uncover Phillips-curve regularities.

110. Friedman and Schwartz (1982a, 448) highlighted this finding.

111. Friedman appeared to give an interpretation along these lines in a contribution he made to a floor discussion during the Festschrift conference held for Anna Schwartz in October 1987 (see Bordo 1989a, 78).

112. See Friedman and Schwartz (1982a, 60–61). On p. 442 of *Monetary Trends*, however, they made a major verbal slip, in their inaccurate reference to the case in which the current output gap matters for inflation, and expected inflation does not, as the "simple Keynesian hypothesis." Elsewhere in the book—including in chapter 2 and on pp. 396–97—Friedman and Schwartz's discussion of aggregate price-level behavior had appropriately reserved the "simple Keynesian" terminology for a specification in which inflation depended on the output gap only once full employment had been reached. What Friedman and Schwartz (1982a, 442) called the "simple Keynesian hypothesis" concerning inflation should have been called the simple Phillips-curve case (in which the output gap appears, but no expected-inflation term enters at all). Labeling this case the "simple Keynesian" setting obscured the point that Friedman believed, and many Keynesians of various eras did not believe, that negative output gaps put downward pressure on inflation.

113. The converse is also true. As Brittan (1983, 92) put it, the basic idea of the natural-rate hypothesis was "in no way tied to Friedman's detailed views about the role of the money supply." The separability of the two sets of ideas was a matter stressed by Edmund Phelps during the early 1970s—as will be discussed in chapter 13.

114. See, for example, Robert Gordon (1975, 807–8; 1977, 129), Brittan (1978, 161), and Parkin (1993, 63–64) for articulations of this criticism.

115. For example, Friedman (1961f, 1055) stated: "An understanding of the channels whereby changes in the stock of money may be produced is of course an essential part of the analysis of inflation." See also, among many other examples, Friedman (1952b, 619; 1963c, 23 [p. 44 of 1968 reprint]; 1970i, 13; 1975i, 12; 1980a, 55, paragraph 2, p. 49 of 1991 reprint; 1990a, 106); Friedman and Friedman (1980, 254; 1985, 85); and Friedman's remarks in *The Times*, September 13, 1976.

116. For an open economy with fixed exchange rates and full capital mobility, this

statement would need to be qualified to recognize the international sources of monetary growth. Even in this environment, however, one would still be able to describe inflation as a monetary phenomenon. See also Patinkin (1995, 121-22).

117. Friedman (1971c, 853), for example, wrote: "The preceding analysis is for the long run, for steady states."

118. Friedman (1977e, 469).

119. Again, see Friedman (1977e, 469).

120. Friedman and Schwartz (1982a, 481).

121. Similarly, Dornbusch and Fischer (1979, 19) remarked: "In the short run the Fed can use its control over the nominal money stock to affect interest rates."

122. Friedman (1971g, 5).

123. Dornbusch and Fischer (1979, 14, 15). In the same vein, Goodhart (1992, 315) noted that a central bank possessed the "ability to vary money market interest rates . . . via open market operations to alter the amount of base money available to the banking system," while adding the caveat that the time horizon over which this ability existed was "relatively short, in terms of weeks, quarters or a few years. In the long term, nominal interest rates will be determined by real (international) forces and the expected rate of inflation."

124. In some thought experiments, such as one in which the central bank sets the aggregate volume of the money stock, it would be true to say that a variable is determined in aggregate by the monetary authority even though individuals choose their own quantity of that variable (see, for example, Friedman 1961a, 259). This reasoning does not carry over to the analysis of the price level or the inflation rate when the private sector produces and sells goods. In the absence of official price controls, the aggregate behavior of inflation reflects governmental decisions only insofar as the private sector responds to variables that depend on those decisions.

125. A Phillips curve based on a price-setting relationship will, if the natural-rate hypothesis holds, be able to be written in terms of deviations of output from potential and deviations of inflation from its expected value—and both these deviations will be zero in the long run. A Phillips curve based on a wage-setting relationship may collapse in the long run into an equation expressed only in terms of real variables, such as real wage growth, that are insensitive to monetary policy in the long run. Thus, neither price-based nor wage-based Phillips curves offer a long-run equation that can be used to analyze the steady-state connection between monetary policy and inflation.

126. Robert Hall and John Taylor (1997, 113).

127. Robert Hall and John Taylor (1997, 114).

128. Robert Hall and John Taylor (1997, 116).

129. In addition to what follows, see the discussion in E. Nelson (2008b).

130. Friedman (1974g, 13). This discussion also contained the appropriate qualification that the key monetary-growth variable in this case was the growth of nominal money in relation to the growth of real output.

131. Friedman (1968b, 8).

132. For exceptions, see Friedman (1975a, 177) and the items discussed in chapter 13 below.

133. R. Hall (1979, 154). Another sign of the acceptance of the concept was the material in Prescott's (1975) paper "Efficiency of the Natural Rate," which used the natural-rate-of-unemployment concept throughout (albeit without a single mention of Friedman).

134. Of course, insofar as the flexible-price economy is driven by exogenous real shocks, the natural rate of unemployment can be written in equilibrium as a function of

those shocks and in that sense treated as exogenous. But obtaining such an expression requires solving for the equilibrium of the model and so initially treating the natural rate of unemployment as an endogenous variable.

135. That is, they indicated that nominal prices were sticky and that monetary policy was acting in a manner that did not remove the effect of price stickiness on the behavior of real variables.

136. Friedman (1968b, 9). In this discussion, he named strength in labor unions as another factor tending to raise the natural rate of unemployment. But this was a point on which Friedman was often ambivalent, and in discussions both before and after his presidential address he offered grounds for believing that the presence of unions changed the division of employment among sectors but did not necessarily raise the aggregate natural rate of unemployment. See E. Nelson (2009a, 478) and chapter 10 below.

137. Friedman (1977e, 459). Friedman had much earlier expressed a similar sentiment in these terms: "Don't take full employment too seriously. We can have full employment without prosperity, such as they have in prison or in the army. . . . We don't want full employment in the sense of long hours and back-breaking labor. We want prosperity and to work as little as possible to get it" (*Sunday Journal-Star*, January 29, 1956). See also Friedman (1963c, 18; pp. 39–40 of 1968 reprint).

138. Friedman (1970d, 31).

139. Friedman and Schwartz (1982a, 414).

140. See also Friedman (1962a, 38).

141. Friedman also believed that "small businesses are at the root of most productive change" (*Election 2004: The Economy*, WQED San Francisco, October 15, 2004). (Friedman made similar observations in *Nightline*, ABC, March 17, 1987, p. 4 of transcript; see also Friedman 1977b, 17–18.) Insofar as firms' largeness was accompanied by some monopoly power on their part, this observation carried the implication that monopoly power reduced the growth rate of the natural level of output.

142. See his remarks in R. Kuttner (2005).

143. See McCallum (1982, 8) for this critique of NAIRU terminology. It also deserves mention that the natural-rate-of-unemployment concept holds even in an environment in which the long-run Phillips curve is not vertical, while the NAIRU concept was intended to be applied only in a context in which the long-run Phillips curve is vertical.

144. An early effort to make the natural-rate concept rigorous in the context of dynamic optimization by agents was Bazdarich (1982).

145. Emphasis in original. See also Woodford (2003, 8).

146. For example, Solow (1969, 7) referred to the "natural level of output"; Phelps (1971, 38) to the "natural output level"; and Lucas (1972a, 58; 1973, 330) and Sargent (1973a, 442) to the "natural rate of output." Gramlich (1970, 96) referred to "GNP . . . at its natural level." In addition, Modigliani (1977, 15) invoked the concept of the natural rate of employment (as opposed to unemployment).

147. He referred to the "natural level" of output in Friedman (1975a, 178) (although the passage in question was somewhat ambiguous and can be criticized for lack of clarity in distinguishing levels from growth rates).

It should also be noted that the economic-growth and money-and-growth literature had established a concept of a "natural" growth rate of real output: see, for example, Tobin's (1969c, 171) reference to the "natural rate of growth of the economy." This natural-growth concept was distinct from that of the growth rate of the natural level of output: the former referred to long-run trend output growth, while the latter included short-run stochastic variation in potential output growth. The distinction between the two concepts perhaps underlay Friedman's (1984c, 33) apparent reluctance to accept the term "natural growth rate" as a label for trend output growth.

148. See Okun (1981, 77) and chapter 13 below.

149. See especially chapter 11 below.

150. See, for example, Friedman (1971i, 62). Later in the 1970s, however, Friedman put considerable emphasis on the loosening of the relationship between the unemployment rate and other aggregate variables—including measures of hiring conditions and of national economic activity. See E. Nelson (2007, 158).

151. In addition to the Friedman (1970d) reference mentioned above, see Friedman (1966a, 18 [p. 99 of 1968 reprint]; 1970a, 23, point 4 [p. 15 of 1991 reprint]; 1971i, 62; 1973a, 28); Friedman and Schwartz (1982a, 396, 397, 414, 416, 442); and Instructional Dynamics Economics Cassette Tapes 55 (July 27, 1970), 60 (November 4, 1970), and 63 (December 16, 1970).

152. See, for example, Friedman (1970i, 11) and Instructional Dynamics Economics Cassette Tape 85 (November 3, 1971).

153. He also indicated that potential output and permanent income coincided in the long run. See Friedman and Schwartz (1982a, 416) as well as Friedman (1970b, 223).

154. See, for example, Gramlich (1970, 96); Phelps (1970a, 1); Tobin (1975, 196); Modigliani (1977, 12); Volcker (1978, 337); and McCallum (1979, 240).

155. See, for example, Friedman (1951a, 226; 1957a, 236–37; 1963a, 5; 1966d, 79, 80, 83; 1967c, 42; 1970b, 206–7, 209, 223, 224, 229; 1971d, 323, 325, 327; 1972a, 913, 926–29, 936, 942–43; 1975g, 9, 12 [pp. 701, 704 of 1979 reprint]); 1976a, 315; 1997, 7, 10–15); Friedman and Meiselman (1963, 167, 172, 187, 209); and Friedman and Schwartz (1963a, 559; 1967, 37; 1982a, 41, 42, 397, 623).

156. See his remarks in Snowdon and Vane (1997, 198). Similar judgments about the compatibility of the two concepts were expressed by Brittan (1976, 259), Kaldor and Trevithick (1981, 9), and Modigliani (1977, 4; 1986b, 23), while Hutchison (1977a, 14–16) noted the presence in Keynes's post-1936 writings of a natural-rate-style definition of the target unemployment rate.

157. Brittan immediately added that, for the United Kingdom, a "sensational vindication of this reluctance has been provided by a little-known Bank of England research paper." The present author cowrote the "little-known" article in question (E. Nelson and Nikolov 2003).

158. *Free to Choose* (UK television version, debate portion), BBC2, episode "From Cradle to Grave," broadcast March 1, 1980, p. 11 of transcript.

159. Friedman and Schwartz (1982a, 414).

160. See, for example, his remarks in Friedman and Heller (1969, 47); Friedman (1970a, 24, point 7 [p. 16 of 1991 reprint]; 1976a, 285; 1980a, 57, paragraph 9 [p. 52 of 1991 reprint]); *Newsweek*, July 27, 1981; and *Donahue*, NBC, September 6, 1979; as well as Friedman's May 25, 1959, testimony, in Joint Economic Committee (1959a, 629).

Friedman was, however, often critical of using tax concessions to boost private investment spending and of government efforts to add to the capital stock through its own expenditures or by compulsory saving schemes. According to his perspective, increments in saving and investment tended to go hand in hand with expansion of potential output; but governmental attempts to force higher levels of saving and investment on the economy did not provide a path to strong economic growth. On these matters, see chapters 11 and 13 below, as well as Friedman's article in the *Wall Street Journal* of April 30, 1962.

161. At first glance, this position might seem inconsistent with Mishkin's (1986, 70)

reservation that "I have never seen a structural model that suggests that investment is a function of saving." However, Friedman's belief in an investment/saving connection stemmed from the relationship that each series had with interest rates. The belief was therefore consistent with the Mishkin statement.

162. This discussion (Friedman 1963d) was in a microeconomic context, but the principles he discussed about an individual firm's capacity output have a counterpart in a definition of the aggregate economy's productive capacity.

163. Friedman (1963d, 67).

164. The need to distinguish changes in real demand that were due simply to the effects on real variables that monetary policy had under price stickiness, from changes in real demand that would occur even if monetary policy had no such effects, was recognized explicitly by Friedman (1968b, 7) in considering the demand for money balances.

165. The quotations are from Friedman (1970b, 207) (see also Friedman and Schwartz 1982a, 42) and Friedman (1968b, 7), respectively.

166. Friedman (1963c, 18; p. 40 of 1968 reprint).

167. It would appear that the bulk of the DSGE modeling work that has occurred since 2003 that has allowed for capital accumulation and has computed the model-consistent output gap has tacitly used the Neiss-Nelson definition of the natural level of output (that is, this work has treated the flexible-price economy as having always featured price flexibility), rather than Woodford's definition. For example, the method described in A. Levin, Onatski, Williams, and Williams (2005, 265) for the computation of potential output in their model amounts to the procedure outlined in Neiss and Nelson (2001, 39). So is that in Andrade, Galí, Le Bihan, and Matheron (2018).

168. Friedman and Friedman (1985, 107). See also Friedman (1957c, 73); and Friedman and Schwartz (1982a, 145). These observations underscore the point that the flexible-price economy that Friedman used as his basis for the natural-rate definition *is* a money-using economy.

169. As Marty (1994) stressed, the dependence of productivity (as well as output and the labor input considered separately) on monetary services was one reason money could not be considered wholly superneutral in economic models, even in the long run.

170. Quoted in Feldberg, Jowell, and Mulholland (1976, 51).

171. Friedman and Schwartz (1963a, 247). Friedman pointed toward the contribution of the credit market to the size of potential output during his debate with Senator Joseph S. Clark, "The Role of Government in Our Society," at the US Chamber of Commerce, Washington, DC, May 3, 1961.

172. See, for example, Friedman and Schwartz (1982a, 496). On numerous occasions (for example, Friedman 1984c, 47–48, 59; Friedman and Friedman 1985, 100–102), Friedman proposed and endorsed certain innovations that might make the private-sector credit market's adjustment to price-level movements more automatic.

173. By the mid-1990s, however, Friedman regarded the US tax system as better approximated as indexed than as nonindexed (O'Driscoll et al. 1997, 7).

174. See, especially, Friedman (1977e, 465–66).

175. See, for example, Friedman (1958b, 252 [p. 183 of 1969 reprint]; 1977e, 466).

176. Friedman (1980a, 55, paragraph 2 [p. 50 of 1991 reprint]).

177. See chapter 15 for a discussion.

178. See chapter 13.

179. See, for example, Friedman (1980a, 1983e).

180. See, for example, Friedman (1980c, 82). See also the next chapter.

181. Friedman (1968c, 443). See also Friedman (1987a, 16).

182. Friedman (1962a, 39). When Friedman (1983e, 15-16) repeated a version of this maxim, he more correctly attributed it to Keynes.

183. From Friedman's September 5, 1974, remarks at the Economists Conference on Inflation, Washington, DC, in Council of Economic Advisers (1974, 76).

Chapter Eight

1. Friedman (1984e, 3).

2. Friedman (1985e, 15; 1986b, 52; 1997, 21). In contrast, Macfarlane (2006, 32) contended that the "term ['monetarism'] should be used to describe only ... the method of setting a quantitative target for the growth of the money supply as proposed by Milton Friedman." This contention is belied by a reference that Macfarlane himself cited—Friedman (1970a)—in which Friedman's section "Key Propositions of Monetarism" (pp. 22-26 [pp. 14-18 of 1991 reprint]) did *not* include monetary targeting or the constant-monetary-growth rule in the provided list. See E. Nelson and Schwartz (2008a, 849) for a related discussion.

3. See Friedman (1953d, 127-28) and chapter 10 below. A late example of this attitude was Friedman's reference to "the stabilizing effects of the progressive personal tax structure" in Friedman (1957a, 238).

4. See Friedman (1957b). Early and rare instances in which Friedman's switch was traced to this paper (and the occasion of the switch identified as being in 1956) were the discussion in Selden (1962, 324-25), also in Ward (1966, 323). In the modern literature on Friedman, the first contribution that dated Friedman's embrace of the constant-monetary-growth rule to 1956 was E. Nelson (2013d) (see pp. 8, 10).

5. Friedman (1956c). Lothian and Tavlas (2018) take this talk as marking the point at which Friedman became converted to the constant-monetary-growth rule. In the present author's view, however, it is Friedman (1957b) that has this status.

Irrespective of which of these 1956 discussions is regarded as marking the definitive shift on Friedman's views concerning the appropriate rule, it is certainly not the case that his "Restatement" paper on the quantity theory of money (Friedman 1956a) contained advocacy of the constant-monetary-growth rule—notwithstanding Leeson's (2003e, 18) erroneous attribution of such advocacy to the "Restatement."

6. Friedman (1957b, 76).

7. Friedman (1957b, 76).

8. See Friedman (1957b, 96-99).

9. On the 1920s, see also Friedman (1957f, 72). For Friedman's perspective on US monetary policy in the early post-Federal Reserve/Treasury Accord period, see Friedman (1957b, 99-100; 1957f, 73) as well as the discussion in chapter 10 below.

10. Friedman (1957b, 97). Similarly, and only slightly more strongly, a few months later (in February 1957) Friedman stated: "I think this depression was in part brought about by unduly tight money policies" (Friedman 1957f, 72). In 1954, he had made seemingly stronger statements—to the effect that monetary factors had been of "importance in producing depression" in the 1930s and that "no major depression" had not gone hand in hand with a US monetary collapse (Friedman 1954a; p. 79 of 1968 reprint)—but, in common with his 1957 discussions, he concentrated his criticism on Federal Reserve policy from 1931 onward rather than including 1930 in the indictment.

11. Friedman (1961d, 465).

12. Friedman (1957b, 76).

13. Friedman (1961d, 465).

14. Friedman (1960a, 90).

15. The congressional submission was Friedman (1958b), and the Friedman congressional testimony given during 1959 appeared in Joint Economic Committee (1959a, 1959b). See chapter 10.

16. Friedman (1960a, 93).

17. Friedman (1960a, 90). Understanding on the part of the general public would also be a consideration that Friedman would invoke when, much later, he was asked to comment on proposals made in the research literature to shift from rules for targeting monetary growth to rules for targeting nominal income growth. Friedman stressed that, while he was not himself opposed to such rules, he was concerned that they might encounter difficulty in being understood by the "man in the street" (Milton Friedman, interview, January 22, 1992). See also Friedman (1983a, 5).

18. The last two of these reasons were given in condensed form in Friedman's (1957b, 76) reference to the "ease of public understanding and administrative operation" associated with the constant-monetary-growth rule, when compared with the monetization rule.

19. See chapter 2 and Friedman (1967a, 12).

20. Friedman (1960a, 95).

21. Friedman (1953d).

22. In the same vein, Purvis (1980, 100) incorrectly identified Friedman (1953d) as corresponding to "Friedman's original case for a constant money growth rule." (A similar attribution was made by Kiley 2003, 393, 405.) In fact, Friedman (1953d, 127) suggested that his monetization rule was his currently preferred rule. Indeed, in *Essays in Positive Economics*, the "Full-Employment Policy" paper led immediately into a reprint of Friedman's 1948 policy proposal.

23. An earlier occasion on which Brunner stressed that Friedman's case for constant monetary growth rested on uncertainty was when he and Allan Meltzer had a letter published in the *Washington Post* (April 30, 1967). See also Brunner (1971b, 37).

24. This is not to deny that Friedman recognized that price theory had a dynamic dimension about which further knowledge was needed. See Friedman (1951b, 113–14).

25. Lars Hansen and Thomas Sargent (2011, 1104) cast the situation as being one of "Milton Friedman's ambivalence about expected utility theory," by which they mean the contrast between the use of utility maximization in Friedman and Savage (1948) and Friedman's rejection of optimal-control techniques for practical monetary policy. Although they correctly emphasize model uncertainty as the reason for the latter attitude, Hansen and Sargent do not, in the present author's view, sufficiently stress the point that, for Friedman, model uncertainty was more pervasive in macroeconomic than in microeconomic analysis.

26. Friedman (1953d, 129).

27. Friedman (1953d, 125).

28. See Friedman (1953d, 129). The discussion on this page of Friedman's article of issues involving lags has led observers (usually without citation of specific paper) to credit Friedman with the concepts of the inside and outside lags. However, in the discussion in question, Friedman used these concepts but not the terms themselves.

29. As already indicated, at this stage he saw his (1948a) rule as appropriate in this light. See Friedman (1953d, 130).

30. Earlier, Baumol (1961, 21) drew a close connection between the message of Friedman's (1953d) analysis and that of A. W. Phillips (1954). Discussion of the latter paper is outside the scope of this chapter.

31. That model uncertainty had slipped into the background of discussions of monetary policy rules is brought out by the fact that Kydland (1992, 379) maintained that in the "modern argument in favor of rules . . . lack of knowledge about the effects of policy no longer play[s] a role."

32. See also E. Nelson (2007, 170); and Kilponen and Leitemo (2008).

33. In a similar vein, Portes (1983, 161) contended that model uncertainty was part of "Friedman's early arguments" for a nonactivist rule but was not redeployed by him in his later writings.

34. As was mentioned in chapter 4, and as explored further below, this was a feature of Friedman's critique of Lerner that was highlighted by Orphanides (2003). See also Hirsch and de Marchi (1990, 193).

35. Friedman (1947, 413).

36. W. A. Wallis and Friedman (1942, 176).

37. This aspect of Friedman's address was stressed by Orphanides (2002, 116, 119). Chapter 13 below discusses Friedman's presidential address in detail.

38. Friedman's doubts about the reliability of estimates of potential output and the output gap has been highlighted over the years in textbook presentations, such as those of P. Wonnacott and R. J. Wonnacott (1979, 333–34) and Stevenson, Muscatelli, and Gregory (1988, 69). For further discussion, see chapter 11 below, as well as the account given presently of Friedman's view on the appropriate response of monetary policy to the levels of economic variables.

39. See also Beyer, Gaspar, Gerberding, and Issing (2013) for work in this vein.

40. In addition to the discussion that follows, see E. Nelson and Schwartz (2008a, 846).

41. See chapter 11 below.

42. Friedman (1972b, 194). Along the same lines, in early 1972 Friedman stated: "We should not try to set a numerical goal [for the unemployment rate]" (*Newsweek*, January 31, 1972, 74; see also Friedman 1972d, xv).

43. Friedman (1972b, 194).

44. Specifically, in May 17, 1979, congressional testimony (Committee on the Judiciary 1980, 153), Friedman defended the use of real national income growth in a proposed constitutional rule for fiscal policy with the observation that "if you look at the past revisions that have been made [to real GNP], they have much less effect on the year-to-year change than they do on the level." Friedman made a similar observation in the *Atlantic* (February 1983, 23).

45. *Monday Conference*, ABC Television (Australia), April 14, 1975, p. 16 of transcript.

46. See, for example, Friedman's November 6, 1975, testimony, in Committee on Banking, Housing, and Urban Affairs (1975, 38).

47. Early statements by Friedman about the absence of reliable information on economic dynamics included those in Friedman (1942a, 320; 1950a, 467; 1951b, 113). Latterday reaffirmations of this perspective included Friedman and Schwartz (1982a, 27, 343); Friedman (1987a, 17, point 11; 1992c, 31, 49); and Friedman's remarks in Darby et al. (1987, 22) and in Laidler (1995, 338).

48. From a letter (dated June 8, 1978) from Milton Friedman to Congressman Dawson Mathis, published in *Congressional Record*, July 18, 1978, 21530.

49. It is perhaps the effects of a constant-monetary-growth rule on nominal and real income variability that Friedman had in mind when he made his otherwise puzzling remark that he had selected that rule "with an eye primarily to short-run considerations" (Friedman 1969a, 48). This remark contrasts with Friedman's many observations that long-run considerations guided his consideration of monetary policy rules. (For example, he re-

marked in Taylor 2001, 119: "I'm sure I was thinking more of the long run. I've always had the view that you ought to try to design policies for the long run.") The point Friedman may have been communicating in Friedman (1969a) (as well as in Friedman 1987a, 18) was that the constant-monetary-growth rule was motivated by considerations of reducing economic variability as well as achieving a satisfactory mean outcome, while the optimum-quantity-of-money rule (the deflation rule) discussed in Friedman (1969a) was concerned solely with achieving the best mean outcome. If this interpretation is accepted, then the constant-monetary-growth rule can be seen as having been motivated by dynamic considerations and as a rule that was concerned with the short run. (Alternatively, one can view both rules as dictated by a long-run concept: the constant-monetary-growth rule by the need for a satisfactory outcome for the ergodic distribution of key macroeconomic data; the 1969 deflation rule by the criterion of optimizing welfare in the nonstochastic steady state.)

50. It would, consequently, not be appropriate to imply, as Kydland (1992, 379) did, that the notion that "contemporaneous private behavior depends on (expected) future policy" was absent from Friedman's case for rules.

51. Friedman (1962d). Earlier, Mints (1950, 169, 172) wrote in less specific terms about the favorable effects that a constant-monetary-growth rule might have on confidence and on private-sector expectations.

52. Friedman (1949b, 950).

53. Friedman made a similar observation in Friedman and Samuelson (1980, 29). For further discussion of the connections between Friedman's work and the literature on rational expectations, see chapter 15 below.

54. Friedman (1951c, 188).

55. See Friedman (1974a, 22; 1982b, 117).

56. In Ketchum and Strunk (1964, 42). This observation is consistent with Friedman's observation thirty years later (in CSPAN, November 20, 1994, p. 12 of hard-copy transcript) that "I've long been in favor of abolishing it [the Federal Reserve System]." See also the 1981 quotation given in the text presently.

57. For an example of this erroneous suggestion, see Hammond (2011b, 7).

58. See Friedman (1962d) in particular. See also *Human Events* (December 5, 1981, 6) and Friedman and Friedman (1985, 99).

59. Friedman (1984c, 44). Friedman wrote these words against a background in which Federal Reserve officials had occasionally laid the blame on failure to achieve monetary or other targets on large US budget deficits and in which he was himself concerned that federal debt-management policy could work at cross-purposes with the achievement of official monetary-growth targets.

60. See Friedman's remarks in his written submission in Committee on Banking, Currency and Housing (1976a, 2164).

61. In addition to what follows, see chapter 1 above.

62. Friedman (1951f, 227). Wallace (1988) instead cited Friedman (1960a, 5) as the source of the observation, but the latter discussion, although it does refer to digging up gold, does not provide a version of the remark. On the other hand, *Capitalism and Freedom* had essentially restated the Friedman (1951f) remark in question (Friedman 1962a, 40), as did Friedman (1962d, 221 [p. 175 of 1968 reprint] and a later exposition, that of Friedman (1992c, 42). See also Friedman (1962c, 30).

63. His major post-1951 discussions of the matter included Friedman (1961h; 1962a, 40–44).

64. Pigou (1917, 57) associated price-level targeting specifically with Fisher; Mervyn

King (1997b, 435) nominated Keynes, Fisher, and Wicksell as having propounded the idea; and O'Driscoll (1987, 404) argued that "Keynes was most responsible for promoting the new idea" of domestic price stability, although he also named Hawtrey as an advocate. Friedman's own discussions of the matter tended to emphasize Keynes, especially when Friedman was discussing the issue of fixed versus floating exchange rates. But Friedman's (1967a) discussion, among others, considered Simons's proposals for domestic monetary rules. See also chapter 2 above.

65. In addition, Friedman and Friedman (1980, 308) remarked that a return of the United States to the gold standard, or the establishment of a commodity-based standard, was "neither feasible nor desirable."

66. See also chapters 10 and 11 below. As noted in chapter 2, the position of Friedman and Schwartz (1963a) was that even the Federal Reserve's tightening in 1931, although set in train by the pound sterling's departure from gold, was not an action that was necessary to keep the United States on the gold standard.

67. Friedman (1985c, 60).

68. Among the authors who have attributed this position to Friedman have been early contributors to the vector autoregression literature, whose work is discussed below. A particularly forthright statement in this connection was Yoshikawa's (1993, 121) remark that Friedman numbered among the "monetarists . . . [who] consider unanticipated changes in the money supply exogenously caused by central banks to be the major shock driving economic fluctuations." Yoshikawa's remark appeared in the same volume in which Kenneth West (1993, 162) made the contrary—and far more well-taken— observation that the hypothesis "that the money supply . . . is set in total disregard to the state of the economy" is "not a view that Friedman or anyone else has advocated, as far as I know."

69. See also Brittan (1983, 147).

70. Friedman (1968c, 445). For similar remarks, see Friedman (1964b, 7 [p. 76 of 1969 reprint]; 1970i, 22); Friedman and Schwartz (1963a, 274, 474); and Friedman's statements in Ketchum and Kendall (1962, 50) and Instructional Dynamics Economics Cassette Tape 10 (January 1969).

71. See Friedman and Schwartz (1963a, 629-31) and chapter 10 below.

72. In the same vein, Schwartz (1969, 4) observed: "Most of the time the [monetary] growth rate has been inadvertent, a side effect . . . of monetary policy."

73. Friedman discussed the fact that the Federal Reserve from its inception managed market interest rates (in the process removing the seasonality from market rates) in Friedman (1960a, 92); Friedman and Schwartz (1963a, 292-93); and Instructional Dynamics Economics Cassette Tape 33 (August 21, 1969). His analyses of the Federal Reserve's interest-rate policy in the early 1920s included Friedman and Schwartz (1963a, 231-35; 1963b, 52; 1982a, 531); Friedman (1960a, 16-17); and Instructional Dynamics Economics Cassette Tape 34 (September 4, 1969).

He and Schwartz could, however, be criticized for not having been sufficiently explicit in their *Monetary History* about the Federal Reserve's use of short-term interest rates as an instrument—and as a criterion for judging monetary policy stance—during the 1930s. See the discussion in chapter 11 below.

74. See, for example, Friedman (1960a, 44).

75. A qualification to this statement is that, in the 1975-99 period, Friedman was more inclined to attribute public-choice-related motives to Federal Reserve policy makers. See the discussion under "Monetary Policy and the Theory of Public Choice" below.

76. Friedman (1970a, 26; p. 18 of 1991 reprint).

77. See also Friedman (1980a, 58, point 14; p. 54 of 1991 reprint).

78. For example, in Friedman (1957f, 68) he indicated that initially "tight money in general [is] reflected in a rising or high interest rate," while in Joint Committee on the Economic Report (1952d, 1019) Friedman had stated that "policies producing the rise in interest rates reduce the volume of currency or deposits." Also relevant in this connection is that, while Friedman often articulated his criticism of the Federal Reserve for tightening too late and too much in terms of the behavior of the monetary growth, in Friedman and Schwartz (1963a, 231, 239) this criticism was applied to the Federal Reserve Board's use of the discount rate as a policy instrument, and increases in that policy rate were taken as giving rise to a reduction in monetary growth.

79. See the previous chapter for a discussion of Friedman's views on nominal rigidity.

80. Friedman (1968b, 10).

81. In principle, an inappropriate monetary policy response may be one that stabilizes output but destabilizes the output gap (for example, by not allowing output to exhibit a short- or medium-run response to aggregate-supply shocks). In practice, this analytical point does not seem to have been a prominent part of Friedman's critique of the conduct of US monetary policy from 1914 to 1973. Although the evidence that can be gleaned from his writings does not all point in one direction, he seems to have regarded the behavior of potential output during peacetime as fairly smooth until the 1970s: see, for example, Friedman and Schwartz (1982a, 414). Even prior to the 1970s, however, Friedman was prone to see technology and demographics as changing the relationship between unemployment (and other labor-force variables), on the one hand, and potential output, on the other. See also the discussion of aggregate supply in chapter 7 above.

82. Recall that Friedman's (1953d) work had suggested that even a correctly signed policy response to nonpolicy shocks could be so large as to be destabilizing.

83. See Friedman's remarks in *Washington Post*, November 5, 1967; and in Friedman (1968c, 445).

84. Friedman (1973a, 39).

85. See especially Todd (1990, 21, 30).

86. See, for example, Sims (1998, 934).

87. Friedman and Schwartz (1982a, 552).

88. Friedman and Schwartz (1982a, 618, 620). See also Friedman and Schwartz's (1982a, 565) observation that real shocks could produce a response of the monetary base.

89. See, for example, Friedman (1964e, 12; p. 267 of 1969 reprint).

90. Friedman and Schwartz (1982a, 618). In a related vein, Friedman regarded the case of a rigid gold standard—when the money stock is made a function of other variables not by domestic stabilization policy but by the country's international obligations—as one in which money in a particular country may "be the conduit through which other forces determine" through its prices and nominal income (Friedman 1984b, 157; see also Friedman and Schwartz 1982a, 325).

91. Bennett McCallum has also been a prominent critic of this aspect of the VAR literature, including in McCallum (1983a). In addition, two early instances in which the fact that Friedman did not emphasize univariate policy-generated shocks in his monetary explanation of output deserve to be highlighted: Amacher and Sweeney's (1980, 340) correct attribution to Friedman of the view that monetary "policy often acted to make the recessions started by private-sector disturbances even more severe"; and Congdon's (1982, 15)

observation that "Friedman has . . . only contended that [monetary] targets prevent [the effects of] nonmonetary disturbances . . . from being exaggerated."

92. *The American Economy, Lesson 48: Can We Have Full Employment without Inflation?*, filmed for CBS College of the Air, circa June 5, 1962.

93. Thomas Cargill (interview, April 17, 2015) noted that in this analysis Friedman advanced a version of Kydland and Prescott's (1977) argument that the authorities would have an inflation bias. This is accurate. But a key difference between the analyses should be underlined: in Friedman's scenario, authorities unconsciously inflated because they misunderstood the nature of inflation; in the Kydland-Prescott analysis and later work, the inflationary policy was consciously and rationally promoted by the authorities as a by-product of the optimization of an objective function, whose specification made the authorities desire above-potential levels of output.

94. Here—at least until he adopted the public-choice perspective in the 1970s—Friedman was taking essentially the same position concerning his preferred rule as McCallum (1995, 208–9; 1999a, 1489–90) and Woodford (1999, 293, 298) would with regard to the status of monetary policy rules.

95. From Friedman's November 6, 1975, testimony, in Committee on Banking, Housing, and Urban Affairs (1975, 59).

96. Since the 1970s, the use of "discretion" to mean a totally unsystematic monetary policy has become rare, in part because of the research literature's intensified focus on policy rules but also importantly because, in the wake of Kydland and Prescott (1977), "discretionary" policy has come to be regarded as a type of optimal-control policy—one in which policy makers restart their optimization every period. In this later literature (with which Friedman had some familiarity, but to which he did not contribute), "discretionary" policy, far from being a totally unsystematic policy, is governed by a time-invariant first-order condition. Indeed, the time-invariant and systematic character of this policy led Lucas and Sargent (1981, xxxvii) to refer to discretion (in the Kydland-Prescott sense) as a monetary policy rule.

97. Similarly, Brunner (1981, 27) called for the debate on appropriate monetary policy to be understood as one about the merits of alternative policy rules, instead of as competition between a monetary policy rule and a wholly random policy.

98. Cowles Foundation (1964, 24). Not all Tobin's research worked in this direction, however, and, unlike some other critics of Friedman, Tobin attached considerable analytical importance to money and the monetary base. See later chapters, including the discussion in chapter 12.

99. Friedman (1960a, 89).

100. Notwithstanding his enhanced interest in later years in other financial markets, notably for long-term securities and equity claims, Tobin reaffirmed his wish for the short-term interest rate (specifically, the interest rate paid on commercial bank reserves at the central bank) to be the key monetary policy instrument in Tobin (1978c). To be clear: Friedman and Tobin *both* supported payment of interest on reserves. But they parted company on the issue of whether, under such an arrangement, the interest rate on reserves should be used as the policy instrument.

101. Friedman (1977c, 18).

102. See Friedman (1973a, 31; 1977c, 17–18); Friedman and Modigliani (1977, 26); and E. Nelson (2008a, 101).

103. The quotation is from the debate in *Free to Choose* (US television version), PBS, episode 3, "Anatomy of a Crisis," broadcast January 29, 1980, p. 16 of transcript.

104. See Friedman's November 6, 1975, testimony, in Committee on Banking, Housing, and Urban Affairs (1975, 40) and Friedman (1980a, 59, paragraph 18; p. 56 of 1991 reprint). See also *Newsweek*, December 8, 1975.

105. This feature of monetary-growth targeting was acknowledged by Romer and Romer (1994a, 23); Taylor (1996, 190); and Woodford (2003, 111, 298), among others.

106. Friedman (1971g, 5).

107. This criticism of Friedman was also voiced by a number of senior Federal Reserve officials in the late 1960s and the 1970s: for example, Gramley (1969, 5; p. 490 of 1970 printing); Wallich (1977, 293–94); and Federal Reserve Board governor Sherman Maisel (who, according to Federal Reserve Board records, registered the criticism at a meeting of the Board with its academic consultants on November 20, 1970).

108. Friedman and Schwartz (1963a, 683). Friedman made the same point in many other publications, including Friedman and Schwartz (1982a, 626) and Friedman (1984c, 34).

109. One early discussion that implied that interest-rate setting characterized all US monetary policy regimes from 1914 through 1979 as interest-rate-setting regimes was that of Brittan (1983, 147). Some of Friedman's own remarks to this effect were discussed above. See also the discussion of the *Monetary History* in chapter 11 below.

110. Phillip Cagan (interview, January 13, 1992) complained in the following terms about those economists who "say that endogeneity explains everything" about the money/income relationship: "If, for example, aggregate demand rose, and you prevented the money stock from expanding, you'd clearly get a different result in the economy. But these people pretend as though that's not the case; they ignore that case, on the grounds that [they believe that] the money stock is completely endogenous [that is, that its path cannot be altered by the monetary authorities]."

111. The quotation is from p. 2 of a May 17, 1971, memorandum, a copy of which Christopher Sims kindly supplied to the author. The memorandum was written by Sims to a list of readers (internal referees), including Friedman, of a manuscript version of Sims (1972) that Sims had proposed to issue as an NBER paper (Christopher Sims, personal communication, September 13, 2013). For more on the interaction between Friedman and Sims, see chapter 15.

112. Friedman (1969h, 4).

113. In a notable concession, Paul Samuelson acknowledged (see *Sunday Telegraph*, January 24, 1971, 20) that monetarists had made a valid point in stressing that much of the empirical evidence on the power of fiscal policy arose from episodes in which the fiscal action had been accommodated by monetary policy.

114. Friedman (1970i, 8–9).

115. *Wall Street Journal*, January 8, 1999. See also Friedman's article in *Wall Street Journal*, October 10, 2001.

116. See chapter 15.

117. Sargent and Wallace (1981, 9).

118. See Friedman (1987b).

119. See, in addition to the preceding discussion, chapter 4 above as well as McCallum (2001b) and McCallum and Nelson (2005).

120. Friedman (1960a, 52).

121. Friedman and Schwartz (1963a, 596).

122. Friedman (1980a, 59, paragraph 19, p. 56 of 1991 reprint; emphasis in original).

123. Friedman (1977c, 17).

124. Friedman (1951c, 187). Similarly, when Friedman presented his argument for the monetization rule at the 1947 Mont Pelerin Society meeting, it was in the face of criticism from Hayek that the rule was not politically feasible (see Hartwell 1995, 37).

125. See chapter 2. Also of note in this connection is Friedman's remark about analyzing matters "from a purely Machiavellian point of view" (Instructional Dynamics Economics Cassette Tape 9, January 1969).

126. From Friedman's June 21, 1973, testimony, in Joint Economic Committee (1973, 135).

127. Friedman and Friedman (1980, ix–x; xiii–xiv of later printings). In his various discussions of the public-choice literature, Friedman gave *specific* references only infrequently, but he clearly had in mind items such as Buchanan and Tullock (1962).

Burgin (2012, 281) contends that it was only in the mid-1980s that Friedman acknowledged the public-choice literature—and then only in an unpublished piece. But Friedman had in fact mentioned that literature prominently in Friedman (1976a, 3) and in his Nobel lecture of December 1976 (Friedman 1977e, 460) and did so again many times in publications in subsequent years, including in the *Free to Choose* discussion just quoted as well as Friedman (1982b, 114–15; 1986c, 2). (Some of these later public statements include the item that Burgin cites. For, although Burgin incorrectly implies that the Friedman remark in question is available only in an unpublished file stored in physical archives, the remark actually appeared in print more than once during the 1980s: see Friedman 1985e, 15; 1986b, 50.)

Congdon (1978, 83, 87) suggested that Friedman (1976k) was the earliest Friedman piece to reflect a strong influence of the public-choice literature. This article was adapted from a lecture (Friedman 1976i) given on December 11, 1975, approximately a year before his Nobel address. Other early Friedman discussions in this area included those in *Financial Times*, January 6, 1977; and *Milton Friedman Speaks*, episode 5, "What Is Wrong with the Welfare State?" (taped February 23, 1978, pp. 5–19 of transcript).

128. See Friedman and Friedman (1980, 307–8). As Dixit (1996, 16) noted, the public-choice literature tended to suggest that it is the writing of the national constitution, rather than the routine legislative process, that provides the main means through which economists' normative analysis can be put into practice. Consistent with this perspective, Friedman (1977c, 18) had implied that it was public-choice considerations that had impressed on him the need for "a constitutional provision to set monetary policy." By that point, he was also an advocate of constitutional restrictions on the size of state and federal budgets. Prior to taking that position, Friedman had regarded constitutional restrictions on peacetime income tax rates as a desirable step but doubted their political feasibility (see *Chicago Daily News*, July 29, 1970, 4).

129. Friedman (1957b, 99).

130. Friedman (1957f, 73). Still later, when Friedman (1961d, 466) suggested that actual policy "at times tends to be dominated by goals other than, and even contradictory to, stabilization," he cited the goals for bond prices and the balance of payments rather than political goals.

131. Quoted in Fischer (1990, 1181). Some years after it appeared, this quotation became widely repeated, in large part because it came to the attention of Mervyn King (at the time a senior official at the Bank of England). King used the quotation in a number of articles and speeches in the mid- and late 1990s (see, for example, Mervyn King 1997c, 94). Indeed, King mentioned the quotation in a dinner speech he gave in the presence of both Friedman and Fischer at the Federal Reserve Bank of San Francisco's annual monetary policy conference of March 1998, held at Stanford University.

132. See also Friedman (1985c, 61; 1986c, 3).

133. Friedman (1984c, 40).

134. See Friedman (1982b, 102–3; 1984i, 41).

135. Friedman (1972e, 13).

136. Friedman did make some apparent attempts to provide a reconciliation of the two perspectives. For example, he suggested that the bureaucratic structure of the Federal Reserve might be a factor preventing improvements in monetary analysis from being reflected in policy making (see *Newsweek*, December 8, 1975; and Friedman 1982b, 103). In addition, Friedman contended that Federal Reserve policy makers, although self-interested, regarded themselves as acting in the national interest (Friedman 1985c, 61; 1986c, 3). The latter contention may have been related to the interpretation—which Friedman articulated after he adopted the public-choice perspective—that the Federal Reserve in the 1970s believed that its formal independence would be jeopardized if it took more aggressive actions against inflation, an attitude that led it (Friedman implied) to postpone such actions and to focus on encouraging changes in fiscal policy that might create conditions more conducive for monetary restraint (*Newsweek*, October 3, 1977; *Newsweek*, January 9, 1978).

137. See chapter 15. Even in 1971, Friedman had suggested in his research that the short-term outlook of governments, motivated by the electoral timetable, might explain why governments inflated (see Friedman 1971c, 853–54. This perspective was more in line with the public-choice literature than it was with his prior work on monetary history. But the US public debates of 1970–71 disabused Friedman of the presumption, which had been embedded in his 1971 article, that governments consciously viewed inflation as a choice variable. Once, however, the public-choice perspective took hold of his thinking about monetary policy, Friedman frequently slipped back into the habit of treating it as obvious that policy makers knew that their monetary actions affected inflation.

138. Friedman (1982b, 115). See also Friedman and Schwartz's (1991, 42) statement that future researchers could go beyond their own work by modeling "the Federal Reserve as a political institution." It should be noted, however, that both Friedman (1982b) and Schwartz in her own writings did continue to emphasize the real bills doctrine (that is, a theoretical error) for the understanding of historical Federal Reserve policy.

139. This is a matter on which Meltzer's (2009b) analysis of inflation in the United States in the 1970s can be criticized. As discussed in C. Romer (2005) and E. Nelson (2012b), Meltzer's emphasis on political pressure as the source of US inflation is at the expense of a consideration of the flawed views with regard to the determination of inflation that were prevalent at the Federal Reserve during the 1970s. Interestingly, Meltzer's longtime coauthor Karl Brunner, while receptive to the public-choice literature and a contributor to it, stressed that the analytical framework used by the Federal Reserve was an important factor to take into account in understanding of its decisions during the 1970s (Brunner 1981, 22).

140. It therefore might well be appropriate to invoke public-choice theory for understanding US tax policy—as Friedman did in O'Driscoll et al. (1997, 8–9). In addition, regulatory capture was a theme of the public-choice literature that Friedman embraced. As noted in chapter 4, this notion, which had already appeared in Friedman's work in the 1960s, played a more prominent role in his commentaries during the 1970s.

There have also been indications that the public-choice perspective might be applicable to the analysis of central banking in certain countries and eras, even if (as argued in the present discussion) it is not very fruitful in understanding US monetary policy developments. For example, when criticizing monetary policy practice in Japan in the early

2000s, Lars Svensson remarked: "So far, Japanese authorities seem to have set myopic bureaucratic interests and technical details above the welfare of their country" (*Financial Times*, September 25, 2001). However, with regard to the specific question of whether the public-choice perspective is useful in understanding the behavior of monetary policy during the 1970s in *any* advanced economy, the present author would answer in the negative. See E. Nelson (2012b) for an extended discussion.

141. Prior to this, Laidler (1993b, 206) perceived in Friedman's (1992c) account some signs of a move away from the public-choice perspective.

142. This attitude was reflected in Friedman (1983a, 4) and in his favorable attitude during the 1990s to research on monetary policy rules produced by Bennett McCallum and Athanasios Orphanides. See also Friedman's affirmation in O'Driscoll et al. (1997, 9) of the need for normative policy analysis.

143. See, for example, Friedman's June 21, 1973, testimony, in Joint Economic Committee (1973, 134) as well as Friedman (1982b, 100). See also chapter 13 for an extended discussion.

144. From Friedman's October 30, 1959, testimony in Joint Economic Committee (1959b, 605).

145. Indeed, Okun (1972b, 134) speculated that Friedman may have, in effect, originated the practice of specifying the objective function as being quadratic.

146. See Friedman (1977c, 12). Sargent (1987a, 448) likewise characterized Friedman and Keynesians as having the same objective function.

147. See, for example, Friedman (1968b, 11; 1968c, 445).

148. Friedman (1973a, 40). See also note 49 above.

149. See, in addition to the discussions considered in section I above, Friedman (1963c, 18 [p. 39 of 1968 reprint]; 1975c, 16; 1980a, 60–61 [p. 59 of 1991 reprint]).

150. See, for example, Friedman (1960a, 23, 98; 1984c, 34). See also chapter 15 below.

151. Email from Milton Friedman to author, July 21, 2003; quoted in E. Nelson (2007, 172).

152. Friedman (1973c, 37). See also the *Economist* June 4, 1983, 37. In a panel appearance at the Federal Reserve Bank of San Francisco's March 1998 monetary policy conference, Stanley Fischer recalled that Friedman (who was in the audience) had made remarks to the same effect at the University of Chicago during the 1969–73 period, when the two had overlapped at the institution. Fischer implied that Friedman had done so during the course of discussions held in the money workshop.

153. Friedman (1970a, 27; p. 19 of 1991 reprint).

154. Friedman's interest in optimal-control approaches to stabilization policy might appear to receive confirmation in his statement in 1975 that "work . . . [on] the so-called problem of 'optimal control' . . . is important as well as intellectually fascinating" (from Friedman's written submission of November 6, 1975, in Committee on Banking, Housing, and Urban Affairs 1975, 47). Indeed, Woglom (1988, 694), in quoting this passage, basically took Friedman to be referring to optimal stabilization policy. However, a reading of the context of Friedman's statement indicates that he was referring to "the techniques of [monetary] control," that is, how to achieve a specified monetary-growth target. (The November 1975 testimony was specifically on this subject, as was a column, "How to Hit the Money Target," that Friedman produced a little later, for the December 8, 1975, edition of *Newsweek*.) Consequently, the passage is suggestive about, but *not* specifically concerned with, Friedman's attitude to the application of optimal-control methods to the stabilization of output and inflation.

155. Friedman (1973b, 9).

156. Mishkin (1995, 3) contended that, in 1973, Fischer himself became disillusioned with the optimal-control approach. Specifically, Mishkin stated that Fischer was "a prominent researcher who was working with optimal-control methods to do econometric policy evaluation, but immediately dropped this line of research upon reading [the 1973 version of] Lucas's [1976b] 'Econometric Policy Evaluation: A Critique.'" This does not appear to be an altogether accurate characterization of the evolution of Fischer's thinking. The Lucas research contributions would certainly have cautioned Fischer against working with the essentially backward-looking macroeconomic models that he and Cooper had examined; and Lucas's work, as well as that of Kydland and Prescott (1977), would have underlined the challenges associated with applying optimal-control analysis to macroeconomic models that *were* forward looking. But Fischer's own analysis and his examination of the literature of the 1970s left him with the conclusion that it *was* indeed possible to carry out both valid econometric policy evaluation and legitimate optimal-control analysis in models that had rational expectations and forward-looking agents. His discussion in Fischer (1980) delivered this conclusion.

Furthermore, the ending of the Cooper-Fischer joint research program did not signify a disavowal on Fischer's part of optimal-control analysis. Instead, it reflected the fact that the two authors both left the University of Chicago in mid-1973, with Cooper moving to the nonacademic private sector.

157. Treasury and Civil Service Committee (1980, 4).

158. Friedman (1980a, 61; also p. 61 of 1991 reprint).

159. In volume 2 of the 1990 *Handbook of Monetary Economics*, McCallum (1990c) tried to hold the line against the "Friedman rule" terminology, and he followed Niehans (1978, 93) in instead using the label "Chicago rule" for the prescription of deflation. The motivation for this alternative terminology was that the prescription had been mentioned by more than one figure associated with the University of Chicago and had also been derived in articles in the University of Chicago's *Journal of Political Economy* (*JPE*). (A similar terminology was advanced by Phelps 1973.) However, in the same volume of the 1990 *Handbook*, Michael Woodford—at the time himself a member of the economics department of the University of Chicago—used the "Friedman rule" terminology throughout his own chapter, which was specifically concerned with the deflation proposal (see Woodford 1990).

160. Friedman (1969a).

161. Harry Johnson is also sometimes named as a developer of the deflation rule. Indeed, the discussion in Moggridge (2008, 336, 429–30) appears to imply that a key issue is whether it was Friedman (1969a) or Johnson who launched the literature on the rule. However, the papers of Johnson's that have primarily been cited as developing the rule are Harry Johnson (1968, 1969a, 1970b) (see, for example, Moggridge 2008, 336; Townsend 1980, 266; Merrick and Saunders 1985, 692). These papers, of course, appeared after Phelps's (1965) published contribution on the matter. It therefore does not appear fruitful to proceed on the premise that the literature on optimal monetary growth was launched only in the later 1960s, or to suggest that Johnson spearheaded that literature.

162. That is, they indicated that the only relevant pre-1969 reference was Bailey (1956), and they did not cite Phelps (1965). These authors did, however, cite Phelps (1973).

Friedman himself did not mention Bailey (1956) in his 1969 paper, but he acknowledged its link to his "Optimum Quantity of Money" analysis when briefly recapitulating that analysis in Friedman (1971c, 854). See also Friedman and Schwartz (1963a, 568).

163. In a similar vein, Argy (1992, 44) referred to the Friedman (1969a) deflation rule as "Friedman's famous 'liquidity rule.'"

164. Phelps also considered "The Optimum Quantity of Money" to be a very poor title for Friedman's paper, as the analysis in the latter concerned the appropriate setting for the *growth rates* of money and prices. Notwithstanding its imprecision, however, the term "The Optimum Quantity of Money" became fairly widely used. It was deployed as the title of a *New Palgrave* economics dictionary entry (Howitt 1987, 744) and was used again as the title of Woodford's (1990) article on optimal monetary growth.

165. Friedman (1960a, 73). This early Friedman reference to the deflation rule was noted by, among others, Melitz (1972, 683); Howitt (1987); and McCallum (1987a, 326; 1990c, 978). (The very last of these references, however, gave an incorrect page reference for the passage.) Another early articulation of the deflation rule was that by Marty (1961).

166. Friedman and Schwartz (1963a, 219, 473) were, however, prepared to view monetary financing of government spending, if it did not generate inflation, as more akin to borrowing than to taxation.

167. See, for example, Friedman (1951c, 187) and NBC (1951b, 4, 11). As we have seen, just prior to the United States' entry into World War II Friedman endorsed using inflation, to some extent, as a method of wartime taxation. But, at the time, his position was that it was fiscal rather than monetary action that had the more reliable effect on inflation.

168. Friedman (1953f, 257). See also Phelps (1973, 82).

169. As well as Friedman, another figure who made recommendations along these lines was George Tolley, whose 1957 article is sometimes seen as an antecedent to the deflation-rule idea (see Howitt 1987, 744). Tolley recalled that Friedman "was very supportive of that [1957] work," and "Milton actually gave me full credit for it" in *A Program for Monetary Stability* (George Tolley, interview, November 14, 2014).

170. E. Nelson (2013a) contains an extensive discussion of Friedman's recommendation that interest be paid on commercial banks reserve balances.

171. Friedman's (1969a) use, in essence, of the Ramsey criterion was also noted by Lucas and Stokey (1983, 56) and Bewley (1983, 1487). The latter author also complained that "Friedman never speaks of Pareto optimality." Friedman's (1987a, 18) later discussion of the "Optimum Quantity of Money" analysis did refer briefly to Pareto efficiency, although it probably did not do so in a way that Bewley would have found satisfactory. See Woodford (1990) for a rigorous analysis of the relationship between the deflation rule and Pareto optimality.

172. Rotemberg and Woodford (1997) showed that, under certain conditions, maximization of intertemporal utility implied minimization of an objective function in which output-gap variability and inflation variability appeared. But Friedman's own work did not make these connections.

It should also be noted that Giannoni (2001, 10) and Woodford (2003, 417) argued that the particular money-in-the-utility-function considerations that Friedman emphasized in his 1969 paper pointed toward a need to add the variability of nominal interest rates to the policy makers' objective function. This was not an implication of the 1969 analysis that Friedman himself grasped; or, if he did grasp the implication, it apparently did not influence his own policy recommendations. For Friedman (1971g, 5) stated that interest rates were "neither an ultimate end of policy nor an effective means." What happened to interest rates, he suggested, was not material in itself; what mattered was the associated behavior of "income, employment, inflation."

173. On these matters, see chapter 6.

174. Friedman (1969a, 47–48).

175. In addition to what follows, see the discussion in chapter 15.

176. Friedman (1960a, 91).

177. Friedman (1984c, 37). The same article reaffirmed that the deflation rule derived in Friedman (1969a) should not be used for, or did not have immediate relevance for, policy prescriptions for the US economy (Friedman 1984c, 50).

178. This perspective seemingly contrasted with the (then) assessment of Michael Woodford: "the conclusions that Friedman [1969a] reaches are of apparent relevance to some of the most hotly debated issues of practical economic policymaking, and his proposed policy rule is of such striking simplicity that its implications for practical policy are quite clear" (Woodford 1990, 1068). (It should be mentioned that the analysis in Woodford 1990, did go on to take issue with the case for the deflation rule.)

179. Friedman (1987a, 18).

Chapter Nine

1. NBC (1952b, 4).

2. *Milton Friedman Speaks*, episode 13, "Who Protects the Worker?" (taped September 29, 1977), p. 4 of transcript.

3. *The Jay Interview*, ITN, July 17, 1976.

4. See, for example, Friedman's remarks in *Playboy* (February 1973, 66) (reprinted in Friedman [1975e, 31; 1983b, 49]); *The Jay Interview*, ITN, July 17, 1976; and *Donahue*, NBC, September 6, 1979.

5. The quotation is from Friedman's *Playboy* interview (February 1973, 68), reprinted in Friedman (1975e, 32; 1983b, 50).

6. Friedman (1985e, 18; 1986b, 55; 1997, 23).

7. CSPAN, November 20, 1994, p. 7 of hard-copy transcript.

8. Friedman (1958a, 22).

9. See, for example, *Milton Friedman Speaks*, episode 1, "What Is America?" (taped October 3, 1977; p. 14 of transcript); *Milton Friedman Speaks*, episode 15, "The Future of Our Free Society" (taped February 21, 1978; p. 10 of transcript); and Friedman (1984f, 8).

10. The study of Winch (1978) was mentioned in this connection in chapter 2.

As David Laidler stressed in comments on an earlier version of this chapter, Friedman likely had a wider conception than did Smith of the conditions under which a market exchange benefited both sides of the exchange. Although Friedman (1982a, 50) specifically attributed to Smith the notion that a market exchange between individuals must benefit both sides, in Friedman (1976c, p. 9; also p. 9 of 1977 version) he provided an example in which Smith departed from this notion, by endorsing usury laws. Although Friedman labeled this departure "highly uncharacteristic" for Smith, it may have been connected to the aspects of Smith's thinking stressed in Winch (1978) as well as Smith's favorable disposition—in contrast to many later economists, including Friedman—toward production-based theories of value.

11. See, for example, Friedman (1978d, 11; 1982a, 43, 62); *Milton Friedman Speaks*, episode 8, "Free Trade: Producer vs. Consumer" (taped April 27, 1978), p. 32 of transcript; and *Newsweek*, June 29, 1981. In the *Los Angeles Times* (December 14, 1986, 13), Friedman remarked, "Nobody who has ever looked at my work is going to accuse me of being a hired minion of the capitalist class."

12. Friedman argued that the case for expanding competition among firms could be

founded on the saying: "To catch a thief, set a thief to catch him" (*The Jay Interview*, ITN, July 17, 1976). Friedman made the same analogy in *Reason* (December 1974, 11); *Saturday Evening Post* (May/June 1977, 20; *Donahue*, NBC, April 16, 1980; Friedman (1982a, 62); and elsewhere.

13. For Friedman's articulation of this suspicion, see for example Friedman (1972c, 24).

14. See especially chapters 4, 10, and 15 of this book.

15. See, for example, Friedman and Friedman (1980, 45; 1985, 53, 118).

16. See, for example, Friedman (1958f, 508 [p. 85 of 1987 reprint]; 1964g, 170); *Business and Society Review* (Spring 1972) (12; excerpted in Friedman 1975e, 249); *Donahue*, NBC, September 6, 1979; and *Newsweek*, March 16, 1981.

17. Friedman (1964g, 170).

18. Examples of these criticisms included Friedman's opposition to a US government guarantee of a loan to Lockheed (*Business and Society Review*, Spring , 12; excerpted in Friedman 1975e, 249); a later (1980) US government guarantee of a loan to Chrysler; and Friedman's opposition to actual or prospective public-sector subsidization of supersonic air transport (see E. Nelson 2009a, 488; 2009b, 77–78).

19. See Friedman's remarks in *Speaking Freely*, WNBC, May 4, 1969 (p. 33 of transcript); Instructional Dynamics Economics Cassette Tape 132 (October 24, 1973); and Friedman (1984f, 15; 1990a, 71).

20. Other concerns that Friedman had about government-operated firms included the possibility that their decisions on staffing, wages, and prices would be obstructed from adjusting to market forces, as well as the likelihood that a situation in which there were many nationalized industries would lead the government to be directly involved in labor disputes. (See, for example, his remarks in Instructional Dynamics Economics Cassette Tape 141, March 12, 1974.)

21. For example, in 1984 Friedman stated that his belief in the economic efficiency of free markets was based on "historical evidence, and analysis alike" (*Tyranny of the Status Quo*, episode 3, "Politicians," March 28, 1984).

22. For Friedman's articulation of this argument, see for example *Newsweek*, October 28, 1968; and his remarks in Friedman, Porter, Gruen, and Stammer (1981, 23–24). In the latter discussion, Friedman also acknowledged that the greater monetary stability in the 1950–70 period than in prior eras had been conducive to economic development.

23. Friedman (1958e, 254; p. 36 of 1962 reprint).

24. See chapter 11 below for further discussion.

25. Friedman emphasized this point in Friedman (1962a, 45, 50; 1967a, 13; 1976j).

26. Friedman and Friedman (1988, 467).

27. From Friedman's remarks in Friedman and Kristol (1976, 26–27). See also Friedman's remarks in *The Open Mind*, PBS, December 7, 1975, p. 5 of transcript.

28. In particular, Friedman (1962a, 77) referred to "the widespread acceptance by intellectuals of the belief that government should play a larger role." See also his remarks in Friedman (1958e, 253; p. 35 of 1962 reprint) and in *Human Events*, July 2, 1966.

Leeson (2000b, 754) took Friedman's (1978f) criticism of intellectuals' role in fostering a climate for greater government intervention as reflecting the after-effects of the criticism by Harry Johnson (1971a) and Patinkin (1969, 1972a) of his work on monetary doctrine. But the similarity of Friedman's 1978 remarks to those he made during the 1960s refutes this interpretation.

The background of Leeson's remarks is the fact that, other than Friedman (1972a), there was a dearth of discussions by Friedman during the 1970s of the Johnson-Patinkin criticisms. Indeed, the record strongly suggests that he devoted far more time and energy to other debates—including his exchanges with Tobin on monetary analysis, the disputes with the Federal Reserve Board on monetary control and on responsibility for inflation, and the public policy debates (with Samuelson, Galbraith, and others) on the appropriate degree of government intervention in the economy. In the absence of an extensive post-1972 Friedman discussion of the Johnson-Patinkin critique, Leeson took the Friedman (1978f) discussion—which did not in fact mention that critique at all—as having been generated by that critique. Such an interpretation is not appropriate, for the reasons just given. In any event, Harry Johnson had, by the time of his death in 1977, largely adopted a perspective on government intervention of the kind that Friedman (1978f) articulated (see Harry Johnson 1978c, 32; Laidler 1984, 593).

29. See, for example, Friedman (1977b, 36; 1978f, xiv) and his remarks in *Business and Society Review* (Spring 1972, 16), as excerpted in Friedman (1975e, 256).

30. *Milton Friedman Speaks*, episode 8, "Free Trade: Producer vs. Consumer," taped April 27, 1978, p. 30 of transcript.

31. On this, see also Tobin (1987b, 371). See also Friedman and Friedman (1988, 459-60).

32. Similar remarks by Friedman appeared in Friedman (1977b, 42), *Times Higher Education Supplement*, September 3, 1976; and *Jerusalem Post*, November 11, 1987.

33. See, for example, Friedman (1977b, 42; 1986c, 9) and Friedman's remarks in Feldberg, Jowell, and Mulholland (1976, 42) and M. Anderson (1982, 200). See also the discussion of *Capitalism and Freedom* in chapter 11 below.

Similar sentiments have been expressed by other economists. For example, Mervyn King (2012) observed that "there seems no limit to the ingenuity of economists to identify such market failures."

34. See, for example, *Milton Friedman Speaks*, episode 1, "What Is America?" (taped October 3, 1977), p. 19 of transcript.

35. *Milton Friedman Speaks*, episode 2, "Myths That Conceal Reality" (taped October 13, 1977), p. 33 of transcript.

36. From *America's Drug Forum* 1991 television program, episode 223, "Milton Friedman: On Liberty and Drugs," printed in Trebach and Zeese (1992, 74).

37. *Saturday Briefing*, BBC2, March 12, 1983, p. 9 of transcript.

38. On Friedman's view of the courts' role, see his remarks in Friedman (1958f, 507; p. 85 of 1987 reprint; 1962a, 14, 145-46) and Ketchum and Strunk (1965, 13).

39. See chapters 8 and 12 for discussion.

40. See Friedman (1955b). See also Ealy and Enlow (2006).

41. Friedman also favored means-tested, government-provided loans for university education. See, for example, All Participants (1951, 258) and Friedman (1962a, 102-5).

42. See, for example, Friedman (1962a, 108-9, 164-66; 1962b, 11) and *Milton Friedman Speaks*, episode 1, "What Is America?" (taped October 3, 1977), p. 32 of transcript.

43. See, for example, Friedman (1966f; 1970o, 82-83).

44. See respectively Friedman (1962a, 201) *Newsweek*, August 22, 1977 and Friedman and Friedman (1980, 141-42). The perspective in the latter two discussions reflected Friedman's embrace—discussed in chapter 8—of the public-choice literature.

45. See chapter 14 below.

46. Friedman (1952d, 15).

47. See Friedman (1962a, 130, 132; 1981e, 26) and his remarks in Ketchum and Strunk (1965, 55) and Friedman and Kristol (1976, 39).

48. The quotation is from Friedman (1962a, 127). See also the discussions on pp. 127–28 and 147 of the same book.

49. The quotation is from *Donahue*, NBC, September 30, 1975. See also *Milton Friedman Speaks*, episode 12, "Who Protects the Consumer?" (taped September 12, 1977; pp. 36–37 of transcript), for a later affirmation by Friedman of his position on patents that he took in *Capitalism and Freedom*.

Van Horn and Klaes (2011, 182) contend that there was "a significant change in the Chicago School's attitude toward patents," with that attitude becoming favorable as the postwar decades progressed. Their analysis almost exclusively concerns figures other than Friedman and therefore has little relevance for the discussion in this chapter. But the authors' inclusion of a single Friedman reference in their bibliography—Friedman's (1982e) preface to a reprint of *Capitalism and Freedom*—might encourage the impression that Friedman favored patents in 1982 after having not done so in *Capitalism and Freedom* in 1962. Such an impression would be incorrect, as Friedman's 1962 discussion did endorse patents. The Friedman (1982e, viii–ix) passage referred to by Van Horn and Klaes (2011, 203–4) does not in fact pertain to patents at all. It is, instead, a statement that intellectuals serve to keep ideas alive during periods in which those ideas are out of favor in policy circles. This was a sentiment that Friedman expressed on numerous occasions. In particular—notwithstanding Van Horn and Klaes's claim (204) that he had this sentiment only in "hindsight"—Friedman articulated it many times before 1982 (see, for example, his remarks in *Wall Street Journal*, November 4, 1969, 1; and the *Guardian*, September 17, 1970).

50. *Playboy* (February 1973, 74), reprinted in Friedman (1975e, 37; 1983b, 57).

51. However, for a contrary position on patents, see Boldrin and Levine (2008). This article was published in the *Journal of Monetary Economics*—a location that may seem less incongruous in light of the fact that Friedman (whom the authors do not cite) contributed in his major writings both to monetary economics and the discussion of patents.

52. Friedman (1981e, 24). Similarly, Friedman (1981a, 21) stated that he had the "task of trying to make the public at large understand the costs of some of the policies that are being followed."

53. See chapter 15.

54. See Friedman (1962h, 4) for an early application of this argument, which became more central in his writings of the 1970s and 1980s (see, for example, Friedman and Friedman 1985, 56). In *Human Events*, July 2, 1966, Friedman indicated (8) that he had encountered the argument by reading Mitchell (1912).

55. *Milton Friedman Speaks*, episode 3, "Is Capitalism Humane?" (taped September 27, 1977), p. 26 of transcript.

56. See *Free to Choose* (US television version), PBS, episode 3, "Anatomy of a Crisis," debate portion, January 29, 1980, p. 15 of transcript.

57. Quoted in Friedman and Friedman (1998, 469). See also Friedman's remarks in *Forbes*, December 12, 1988, 176.

58. *Milton Friedman Speaks*, episode 3, "Is Capitalism Humane?," taped September 27, 1977, p. 15 of transcript. See also Friedman (1983c, 85).

59. *Free to Choose* (US television version), PBS, episode 5, "Created Equal" (debate portion), February 15, 1980, p. 18 of transcript. Friedman also described individual liberty as his "fundamental value" (*The Jay Interview*, ITN, July 17, 1976) and his "primary objective" (*Tyranny of the Status Quo*, episode 3, "Politicians," March 28, 1984).

60. Friedman (1983e, 17). See also Friedman (1958f, 511–12 [pp. 87–88 of 1987 reprint]). Chapter 1 of *Capitalism and Freedom* (Friedman 1962a) concerned itself specifically with the relationship between economic freedom and political freedom.

61. In this connection, it is noteworthy that one article that Friedman repeatedly praised, and that he cited as a reference on how the price system operated, was Hayek (1945)—see Friedman (1976a, 323–24; 1977e, 467; 1984f, 9) and chapter 11. Friedman also gave considerable attention in his Price Theory class in the early 1970s to Hayek's article (Victor Canto, interview, September 11, 2015). When it came to the ranking of the contributions of Marshall and Walras, Hayek had a view more similar to that of Hahn than to that held by Friedman.

62. See also Friedman (1957c, 72; 1962b, 10–11).

63. In a related vein, Hutchison (1977b, 86–87) explicitly criticized Hahn for characterizing the case for the price system and market arrangement as dependent on the verdict of general equilibrium analysis. Hutchison argued that the case for a market allocation could arise from a government-failure argument that did not rely on a general equilibrium analysis of economic efficiency.

64. For further discussion, see chapters 4 and 13.

65. Plosser observed: "I think the other interesting moment [other than the teaching] in that class for everybody, even Milton, was the final exam. . . . And it was a question in which we had to derive some demand curves from some preferences and budget constraints, etc., etc. It wasn't a difficult thing; it was kind of a straightforward, mechanical type of question. And everybody should have known how to do it, but we didn't. We couldn't figure it out; it wasn't working out right. Well, it turned out that Milton had given us a utility function for which he hadn't checked the second-order conditions. . . . And so it was a poorly designed question by Milton. And poor Milton had to announce to everybody that he was going to disregard this question, because it was his fault because he didn't check his second-order condition before he designed the question" (Charles Plosser, interview, April 2, 2015).

66. Friedman (1975e, 306). See also Friedman (1976a, 8) for a related discussion.

67. See Friedman (1949a, 469; 1953c, 8). See also Sargent (1981, 238).

68. Friedman (1962b, 35; 1976a, 33).

69. See chapter 6.

70. Friedman (1976a, 7). For similar criticisms that Friedman made around the same time, see Friedman (1975a, 176) and Instructional Dynamics Economics Cassette Tape 213 (May 1977, part 1).

71. Friedman (1976a, 7). In fact, the 1976 version did cover some macroeconomics.

72. See especially Friedman's remarks in Taylor (2001, 111). For an attempt to distinguish "price theory" from microeconomics, see Weyl (2015). Weyl's discussion overwhelmingly concerns contributions other than those of Friedman, however, and, as discussed below, the links between Friedman's work on price theory and those of economists at the University of Chicago have tended to be greatly overstated. Consequently, the relevance of Weyl's paper for the analysis of Friedman's economics is limited.

73. As Stigler joined the University of Chicago only after Becker was a graduate student at the university, Becker presumably encountered these labels during the 1969–76 period when he was a departmental colleague of both Friedman and Stigler.

74. The reticence about using "macroeconomics" was also not shared by Robert Lucas, who would refer to "research in my field of specialization—macroeconomics, or monetary and business cycle theory" (Lucas 1987, 1).

75. See chapter 13.

76. *John Maynard Keynes: Life, Ideas, Legacy*, Institute of Economic Affairs (London) documentary, 1988 (also in Blaug 1990, 89). See also the discussion in chapter 12 below of Friedman's 1965–66 exchange with *Time* magazine on this matter.

77. See also Friedman and Savage's (1952a, 464) reference to the "unfortunate connotations" of the term "utility."

78. Friedman (1958j, 3).

79. The published version was Friedman (1958i).

80. Friedman (1962b, 6).

81. Friedman and Friedman (1980, x; p. xiv of some later printings).

82. See, for example, Friedman and Schwartz (1986b, 37-38).

83. See, for example, Friedman (1962a, 200; 1977a, 10). As a related matter, Friedman's contended that philanthropic and charitable activity had strengthened during times in which the scope given to free enterprise expanded. See Friedman (1976j, 6; pp. 64-65 of 1983 reprint); Friedman and Friedman (1980, 36-37); and *Milton Friedman Speaks*, episode 3, "Is Capitalism Humane?" (taped September 27, 1977; pp. 16-17 of transcript).

84. *Milton Friedman Speaks*, episode 3, "Is Capitalism Humane?" (taped September 27, 1977), p. 7 of transcript.

85. *Free to Choose* (UK television version, debate portion), BBC2, episode "Created Equal," March 8, 1980, p. 11 of transcript. Friedman had also cited Nightingale in this connection in *Playboy* (February 1973, 66) (as reprinted in Friedman 1975e, 31; 1983b, 49-50).

86. From *America's Drug Forum* 1991 television program, episode 223, "Milton Friedman: On Liberty and Drugs," printed in Trebach and Zeese (1992, 73-74). Friedman had also cited Mother Teresa in a similar context in *Firing Line*, PBS, December 13, 1990, p. 10 of transcript.

87. *Milton Friedman Speaks*, episode 5, "What Is Wrong with the Welfare State?" (taped February 23, 1978), p. 32 of transcript.

88. *The Open Mind*, PBS, December 7, 1975, p. 7 of pdf transcript.

89. "Chicago price theory" is an undesirable label for the further reason that it embeds the parochial and factually incorrect notion that the word "Chicago" automatically means "University of Chicago." Use of the more accurate label "the Chicago School's price theory" would help matters somewhat.

90. Friedman maintained that Adam Smith's (1759) *The Theory of Moral Sentiments*, which he quoted and cited in Friedman (1977a, 11, 12 and elsewhere), was as important in understanding Smith's framework as was *The Wealth of Nations* (see his January 18, 2000, letter to Ben Cerruti, reprinted in Cerruti 2014, 60). In contrast, George Stigler (1960b, 44) contended that Smith's analysis in *Theory of Moral Sentiments* "bears scarcely any relationship to his economics."

91. See chapter 13.

Stigler's specialization in microeconomics also means that a very different interpretation is available of a Friedman remark from that made by Freedman, Harcourt, Kriesler, and Nevile (2013, 1-2). The latter authors treat Friedman's favorable reaction to the absence of a reference to Keynes in Stigler's microeconomics text as reflecting a sinister agenda on Friedman's part to erase Keynes from history. What that interpretation overlooks is that Stigler was a microeconomist, and Friedman's satisfaction at Stigler's lack of reference to Keynes might have reflected Friedman's belief (shared *very* widely among US economists—including James Tobin, as shown in Tobin 1987a, 105) that Keynes's *General Theory* did not amount to a shake-up of microeconomics. In no way did it imply a wish to deny Keynes's impact on *macroeconomics*.

92. That is, Becker (1955, 1957b).

93. *A Conversation with Milton Friedman*, 2002. This conversation occurred at a date close to the University of Chicago's November 2002 conference in Friedman's honor, an

event that had Friedman and many other guests in attendance. One guest, David Meiselman, recalled that "Gary Becker spoke at the dinner. I was really looking forward to Gary Becker's talk. [But] I thought he might have something more to say. It was OK, but it really wasn't anything [special]" (David Meiselman, interview, April 30, 2013).

94. See chapter 8.

95. See chapters 10 and 11 below.

96. That is, Friedman (1953c).

97. The exchange-rate and stabilization policy papers are, respectively, Friedman (1953a) and Friedman (1953d). See chapter 8 for a discussion of the latter paper.

98. A book-length study of Friedman's methodology is Hirsch and de Marchi (1990). These authors followed the laudable strategy of studying not only Friedman's article on methodology, but also his other writings, with their analysis of the latter drawing out further Friedman statements about methodology as well as information about Friedman's methodology in practice. Although the Hirsch–de Marchi study contains many valuable observations, its validity is somewhat vitiated by the fact that the authors were steeped in the literature on methodology but not the literature on monetary economics in which Friedman was most engaged. Their background in the methodological literature evidently led the authors to favor phrases that many monetary economists would find forbidding (an example being the reference on their p. 222 to the "supposed deductive-nomological character of satisfactory explanation"), while subjecting Friedman's choices of phrases to a forensic treatment that Schwartz (1992, 959) called a "critical interpretation of ordinary words" that bordered on "arrant pedantry." (That said, much of the Hirsch–de Marchi volume is highly readable, and their coverage includes some matters—such as the pre-1953 literature on methodology that anticipated Friedman's article, and to some of which he was likely exposed—not considered in the present chapter.)

Hirsch and de Marchi's (1990) lack of specialization in monetary economics was seemingly reflected in a number of misstatements about that field. Among these was their claim that in Friedman's analysis "a rise in M will have to raise desired cash balances by $(M \times V)$" (228), an incorrect chronology of Friedman's work on lags (265), and their poorly informed assertion that in every country M1 was "the narrowest measure among monetary aggregates in use" (268). The last error is related to the authors' failure—which was noted in chapter 2 of the present book—to grasp the concept of the monetary base adjusted for changes in reserve requirements (a concept for which two principal measures were regularly produced by the Federal Reserve System from 1980 through the early 2010s). Furthermore, judged from the standpoint of a study of Friedman's work on methodology, the Hirsch–de Marchi study suffered from the fact that they confined themselves (see 253) to those Friedman *Newsweek* columns reprinted in his 1970s collections. They thereby missed Friedman's columns of November 9, 1970, and May 18, 1981, both of which discussed alternative approaches to carrying out economic research.

99. From Tobin's remarks in Klamer (1983, 105).

100. See especially Friedman (1953c, 21–30). See also Friedman (1982b, 116) for a later restatement and reaffirmation of the argument. In this 1982 discussion (concerned with profit maximization), Friedman did not cite his 1953 article or associate the "as-if" argument specifically with himself. This may have reflected a judgment that his argument had become commonly accepted. Alternatively, it might suggest that in 1953 Friedman believed he was articulating what was already the standard, albeit largely tacit, position among economists regarding why they assumed profit maximization.

101. See chapter 2 above.

102. In this connection, Anna Schwartz wrote to the present author on March 6, 2008: "You are right, Friedman's essay on methodology had no connection with policymakers' behavior." See also Schwartz (1992, 961). This contention is corroborated by the fact of Friedman's (1961f, 1052) criticism of what he called the "unanalyzed assumption" about the monetary authorities' behavior made in Wilson's (1961) study of inflation.

103. See DiCecio and Nelson (2013, 395-96) for a related discussion.

104. Friedman (1953c, 8-9, emphasis in original).

105. Among the similar sentiments voiced by Friedman in print before 1953, see Friedman (1946, 631; 1951b, 107, 109). In addition, the discussion in Friedman (1952c, 456) was clearly adapted from his subsequently published 1953 article.

106. Another example is Layard and Walters's (1978, 409) statement, in a microeconomic context, that "we only approximate reality if we ignore it."

107. Friedman (1969c, 129).

108. Friedman (1953c, 14).

109. Shiller (1972, 19). An earlier instance in which Friedman's approach to assumptions was invoked in the context of a presentation of optimization-based financial economic analysis was in William F. Sharpe's 1970 monograph *Portfolio Theory and Capital Markets*, which stated, "A *positive* model is predictive in nature. . . . The realism of the assumptions matters little. If the implications are reasonably consistent with observed phenomena, the theory can be said to 'explain' reality" (Sharpe 1970, 2, 77; emphasis in original.) Sharpe had been exposed to Friedman's methodology article through Almen Archian's graduate teachings at the University of California, Los Angeles, in the 1950s (William F. Sharpe, interview, February 6, 2016). The connection between Sharpe's and Friedman's perspectives on methodology was made most overt in Sharpe, Alexander, and Bailey's (1995, 262) *Investments* text, which used a quotation from Friedman (1953c, 15) in their section titled "Assumptions."

110. This statement led to sharp criticism from Hahn (1988b). Hahn's attitude to Lucas's statement lined up with the hostility that, as already noted, Hahn displayed by the 1980s to Friedman's position on methodology.

111. Friedman (1976f, 310).

112. See, for example, Friedman (1988a, 225). See also chapters 2 and 12.

113. See *Reason* (June 1995, 38), Friedman and Friedman (1998, 222), and Friedman's remarks in Taylor (2001, 116).

114. A contrary judgment might seem to flow from Hammond (1996, 36-39). But Hammond's discussion rested heavily on lengthy quotations from the work of Stigler, not Friedman, and the present book has repeatedly stressed that Friedman and Stigler should *not* be regarded as having a wholly overlapping theoretical framework.

115. Friedman (1953c, 37). See also Friedman (1962a, 121-22).

116. Friedman (1953c, 34).

117. Friedman (1953c, 38).

118. Richard Muth, a student in Friedman's Price Theory class of the 1950s, came to see merit in that class's questioning of the rigor of monopolistic-competition theories. This was because, as Muth saw it, the imperfect-competition literature abounded with alternative theories and had not converged on an agreed framework (Richard Muth, interview, May 20, 2015). It should be stressed that this judgment was essentially one made about the literature as it stood *prior* to the appearance of the breakthrough Dixit-Stiglitz (1977) article.

119. Friedman (1953c, 30).

120. The same is true of Phelps and Taylor (1977, esp. 167).

121. *Milton Friedman Speaks*, episode 11, "Putting Learning Back in the Classroom" (taped September 15, 1977), p. 27 of transcript. See also Friedman's (1977c, 13) rejection of the notion that his work on the natural-rate hypothesis embedded the assumption of perfect competition.

It also deserves mention that cases in which Friedman took price as equal to marginal cost did not always signify a perfect-competition assumption on his part, because he was an advocate of *defining* total cost as equal to total receipts in equilibrium—that is, of taking variation in the markup as variation in a cost of production. See Friedman (1955h, 235; 1962b, 144; 1976a, 149).

122. See, for example, his remarks in Parkin (1990, 99) and in Friedman (2009).

123. For example, Friedman (1970c, 326) stated: "To quote again from my essay on methodology . . ."

124. See Friedman and Becker (1958a, 547). See also Friedman (1958k).

125. Friedman (1957f, 71).

126. See Friedman (1963c, 4; p. 25 of 1968 reprint). Friedman-supervised dissertations on various countries' inflation experiences appeared in Friedman (1956b) and Meiselman (1970). Friedman's (1952b) study, which looked to US wartime episodes for information on the behavior of inflation (see chapter 4), was alluded to in Friedman's methodology article (1953c, 11).

127. In this connection, see, in addition to the references given in section I, Friedman's March 25, 1957, testimony, in Special Committee to Study the Foreign Aid Program (1957, 126).

128. As indicated in chapters 4 and 8, this work on monetary history heavily shaped Friedman's policy prescriptions, although NBER rules restricted such prescriptions from appearing in the joint Friedman-Schwartz work.

129. Glaringly, however, the supporting documentation (like the citation itself) did not mention Anna Schwartz.

130. Friedman (1955f, 33).

131. For further discussion, see chapter 14 below.

132. Although it is discussed below, detailed analysis of this paper (as well as of the debate that it generated) is deferred until chapter 12.

133. Friedman (1951b, 107).

134. Friedman and Meiselman (1963, 169).

135. See the beginning of chapter 4 above, as well as Friedman's remarks in Friedman and Heller (1969, 53).

136. Friedman (1967a, 13).

137. See Friedman and Schwartz (1982a, 623).

138. As noted in chapter 2, Friedman also took issue with the approach of Henry Simons, who recognized velocity fluctuations but, in Friedman's view, did not appreciate the extent to which monetary stability could lower the tendency of velocity to fluctuate.

139. See, for example, Friedman (1967a, 12; 1968d, 10–11; 1977e, 468–69).

140. See chapter 12, as well as the discussions in chapters 2 and 5 above.

141. See, for example, Friedman's remarks in Friedman (1976a, 220); Snowdon and Vane (1997, 195); Parker (2002, 53); and *American Banker*, April 30, 1986, 20.

142. See Friedman's remarks in *Human Behavior*, November 1978, 31. See also Friedman and Meiselman (1965, 770) on the possibility of a "joint theory" containing elements of different theories. However, the particular broader model contemplated in

the Friedman-Meiselman discussion—one in which monetary and fiscal policy *each* had powerful effects on nominal aggregate demand—was not one to which, in Friedman's view, the economics profession would converge, as he doubted the effectiveness of non-monetized fiscal actions. See especially chapter 8 above.

143. The quotation is from Friedman (1953c, 33). See also the brief but negative reference to "institutionalism" in Friedman (1952c, 457).

144. Friedman (1970j, 53).

145. Friedman and Schwartz (1982a, 142).

146. See Friedman (1983a, 4). See also E. Nelson (2003, 1037) and McCallum and Nelson (2011, 111–12) for related discussions.

147. See chapter 12 below.

148. See Friedman (1956a, 12–13). The same passage raised the possibility of taking the simpler route of treating the trend as given, and it is for this route that Friedman and Schwartz (1982a, 217–21) eventually opted.

149. Another difference concerned the feasibility of control of the stock of money. But the Kaldor-Sayers position implied that monetary control was not useful for economic stabilization, even if feasible.

Important material concerning the positions of Sayers and Kaldor appears in Sayers (1960) and Kaldor (1970). The bottom line of these authors that velocity could vary without limit and that the demand for money was not well defined was essentially the same as that of Alvin Hansen, whose views were discussed in chapter 3. But, unlike Hansen, Sayers and Kaldor put stress on the idea that it was the advent of the modern commercial banking system that was responsible for rendering the money-demand function a useless concept.

150. This attitude to nonmonetary explanations for inflation was voiced even in his article on methodology (Friedman 1953c, 11). This passage, in conjunction with the favorable references to the quantity theory of money that appeared elsewhere in the article (and that were mentioned in chapter 6 above), makes the methodology article yet another demonstration that Friedman's adherence to the quantity theory of money was established in print well before 1956. See Hutchison (1954) for a discussion that emphasized (797) the article's support for the quantity theory of money.

151. CSPAN, November 20, 1994, p. 8 of hard-copy transcript.

152. Some claims have been made that Friedman was a master of technical economics, but these have tended to come from those outside economic research (see chapter 13 below).

153. The quotation is from Friedman (1958i, 991).

154. Specifically, Friedman (1976b) was reprinted in abridged form in *New York Times*, March 23, 1986.

155. After the news of Friedman's death, Friedman (2005c) was adapted rapidly into an article in *Wall Street Journal*, November 17, 2006.

156. Becker (1991a, 143). See also the discussion in chapter 11 below.

157. Initially, however, the prediction that Friedman was nonmathematical did not seem to have been borne out, as Valentine's first day at work consisted of typing up a draft chapter of *Monetary Trends*: "I was given a mostly handwritten copy . . . that was loaded with equations!! I rushed to the administrative assistant's office with the chapter and said as I showed her the chapter, 'I thought you said he wasn't mathematical!' She was stunned and we both laughed. I was in for the long haul and had no intention of leaving." Indeed, Valentine did not leave, and she noted that her tenure as Friedman's secretary involved

"starting in January 1972 and staying with Professor Friedman until his death" (Gloria Valentine, personal communication, November 4, 2014).

158. In addition to the discussion that follows, see that at the end of chapter 4 above.

159. Friedman and Friedman (1998, 262).

160. See, for example, his remarks on "mathematical economics, with its emphasis on Walrasian general equilibrium analysis" in Friedman (1952c, 457).

It is true that Friedman (1986a, 80) observed that the introduction to Euclidean geometry that he received in his sophomore year of high school imbued him with "a love and respect for and interest in mathematics that has remained with me ever since." But it is clear from the context of this remark that the highly positive attitude toward mathematics that Friedman claimed to have kept pertained primarily to the mathematics in which he had been trained—and not to the more abstract mathematics that would appear in the economic research of others. It is also clear from a multitude of Friedman statements that, notwithstanding the esteem in which he held mathematics, by the early 1950s his conviction was that many economic researchers were striking the wrong balance in their writings between mathematical sophistication and economic content.

161. From Friedman's remarks in Hammond (1992, 104).

162. See Friedman (1969c, 129).

163. Arrow and Friedman also had an affiliation with, and location at, the same university (Stanford University) from 1977 to 2006. However, they saw each other only infrequently over these years (Kenneth Arrow, interview, December 7, 2013).

164. See Friedman (1977e, 460). In addition, Friedman profited from Arrow's feedback on some of his own work. See, for example, Friedman (1969a, 49–50).

165. The contrast between Friedman's approach to economics and that of Debreu was brought out during 1991, a year in which both published articles in the *American Economic Review*. Debreu's (1991) was titled "The Mathematization of Economic Theory," while Friedman and Schwartz's (1991) paper (in the same issue) bore the title "Alternative Approaches to Analyzing Economic Data."

166. It is also possible that Friedman was still smarting from a negative review that Arrow had written (in the *New Republic*, March 22, 1980) of the book version of *Free to Choose*. Friedman had been incensed by this review, which he believed had implied that he lacked compassion (Kenneth Arrow, interview, December 7, 2013).

167. Friedman (1955g, 904). Friedman made this complaint in the context of an article, already mentioned in previous chapters, in which Walras (1954)—a new English translation of Walras's *Elements of Pure Economics*—was reviewed.

168. Friedman and Savage (1948, 294n29).

169. In a similar vein, Sargent (1987b, 21) cited Benveniste and Scheinkman (1979), as well as Lucas's University of Chicago graduate lectures, on the differentiability of value functions.

170. Friedman and Friedman (1980, 29–30). This discussion was in the context of the Friedmans' explanation of the need for the government to help enforce private contracts.

171. They specifically claim this is so for the version of the "survivor hypothesis" advanced in Friedman (1953c, 22). See also chapter 15 below.

172. See, for example, Friedman's statement about one analysis that "the mathematical form in which it is expressed serves to conceal its economic substance" (Friedman 1954c, 698). See also Friedman's (1991b, 35) contention that economic-research articles had come to present results in terms of mathematical and econometric language, at the expense of exposition in ordinary English.

173. Friedman (1955g, 908).

174. A similar criticism was applied by Grossman (1984, 337–38) to a result obtained by Hahn (1983b) as part of Hahn's critique of monetarism. See also Hutchison (1977, 86).

175. He did so in Friedman (1946, 625–26), whose stance was later described using measure-theory terminology in Baumol (1957, 265). Other economists who have pointed to instances in which the measure-zero case is the economically relevant one have included McCallum (1999c, 628)—in his case, in connection with the selection of the equilibrium in rational-expectations models.

176. The issue of mathematical versus economic criteria is also relevant for the treatment of the Marshall-Lerner condition in open-economy analysis. Friedman's (1953a, 162) "Case for Flexible Exchange Rates" analysis imposed this condition. Laffer and Miles (1982, 145–47, 327, 390–91), in the course of a book that contained a highly critical retrospective of Friedman (1953a), disputed his reasoning for the restriction but nonetheless supported imposing the restriction. Their own reasoning was that the restriction was a dynamic-stability condition. But, from the Friedman perspective, the original basis for the restriction was better, as Laffer and Miles had substituted a mathematical rationalization for the restriction (that is, dynamic stability) for an economic one (that is, a version of the postulate that demand curves slope downward).

177. See especially Friedman (1950a, 488).

178. See, for example, Friedman (1955g, 904; 1957a, 26; 1962b, 69; 1976a, 61) and Friedman and Savage (1948, 304).

179. See, for example, Friedman (1946, 614). In insisting that a theoretical model was useful only if it was specified in a manner that gave it specific predictive content, Friedman was not offering a view that was at variance with that of many users of general equilibrium models. Prescott (1991, 4), for example, took essentially the same perspective.

180. Lucas referred to a passage of Patinkin's *Money, Interest, and Prices* in which Patinkin acknowledged an observation from Friedman that, in Patinkin's analysis, the price of any one good depended on demand conditions in every single market (Patinkin 1965a, 235). Lucas inferred that Friedman's attitude was that Patinkin should have imposed more restrictions on the model to avoid this degree of generality. (In the index for Lucas 2013, this inference on Lucas's part is associated directly with Friedman, as it appears in Friedman's index entry (p. 530) as his "critique of Patinkin.")

181. On this matter, see section III of chapter 15.

182. See especially the discussion in chapter 5 above for documentation of this point.

183. See his remarks in Hammond (1992, 108).

184. Chapter 6 above discussed the fact that Friedman's joint work with Henry Schultz used Irving Fisher (1892). In addition, Friedman referred to Irving Fisher (1896) on many occasions, including in the *Monetary History* (Friedman and Schwartz 1963a, 70) and the 1961 unpublished draft of the *Monetary History*. In addition, Friedman (1949a) copiously cited another major contribution to general equilibrium theory, Hicks's *Value and Capital* (Hicks 1939).

185. See chapters 7 and 13, as well as the discussion that follows.

186. Friedman (1970b, 222). See also p. 219 of that paper.

187. Friedman (1961f, 1052).

188. See, for example, Friedman (1951b, 112).

189. See Friedman (1955g, 905).

190. Email from Milton Friedman to the present author, April 6, 2006.

191. For formalization of the concept of the natural rate of output in an economy with

monopolistic elements, see for example Woodford (2003), and for the explicit introduction of a nonzero unemployment rate into the flexible-price version of such an economy, see for example Christiano, Eichenbaum, and Trabandt (2016).

192. See Friedman (1966d, 79–82).

193. Along similar lines, the cash-in-advance literature of the 1980s developed dynamic general equilibrium models in which interest-elastic money demand coexisted with the neutrality of money. See Hodrick, Kocherlakota, and D. Lucas (1991) for a study of the properties of these models.

194. Friedman and Schwartz (1982a, 343).

195. Friedman (1977d, 413).

196. McCallum's procedure could be regarded as reflecting an insistence that the list of state variables used in the model solution be consistent with the model's transmission mechanism.

197. See Friedman (1952c, 457), perhaps referring in part to questionnaires.

198. Friedman (1961d, 460).

199. See, for example, Friedman (1948b, 140).

200. The quotation is from Friedman and Schwartz (1982a, 572).

201. This was the conference at which Friedman gave the remarks published as Friedman (1969c).

202. Friedman (1987a, 15).

Chapter Ten

1. See Friedman and Schwartz (1963a, 577–79, 605, 610) and Friedman (1982b, 104).

2. Letter from Governor Marriner Eccles, in draft and undated form (but—as it referred to NBC 1951a—probably written in mid-February 1951), available at https://fraser.stlouisfed.org/docs/historical/eccles/062_01_0002.pdf.

3. Friedman and Heller (1969, 61).

4. Harrod (1971, 58).

5. That is, as *Defense, Controls, and Inflation* (Director 1952). The conference was sponsored by the University of Chicago Law School and its written record edited by that school's Aaron Director (Friedman's brother-in-law). Friedman served on the committee in charge of the conference (Director 1952, v). Although it featured lengthy contributions from Friedman, the conference proceedings volume did not appear in Friedman's official bibliography and is therefore seldom referenced in discussions of Friedman's activities. Ebenstein (2007, 111), for example, does not cite the conference volume and closely follows, without actually citing, Harrod's (1971) description of the proceedings of the conference.

6. Harrod (1971, 58). Among Friedman's University of Chicago colleagues (not all from the economics department) at the conference were Friedrich Hayek, Frank Knight, Theodore Schultz, Jacob Viner, and Allen Wallis. Also present were several individuals whom Friedman had known from his earlier activities: his former boss Roy Blough (who was now economic adviser to President Truman), Homer Jones, Carl Shoup, and Beardsley Ruml. Additional attendees included Gardner Ackley (then at the Office of Price Stabilization), Eugene Rostow (who, although primarily a foreign policy expert, was active in economic policy discussions during the early 1950s, and whose brother Walt had worked on UK economic history with Anna Schwartz), Henry Hazlitt, Herbert Stein, George Stigler, and Alvin Hansen. See Director (1952, viii–x).

Another participant, whose presence reflected the fact that he was a junior member of the University of Chicago's economics department at the time, was Richard Goode. During the war, Goode had been coauthor of the Ensley and Goode (1943) paper that, as noted in chapter 3, drew fire from Clark Warburton for its dismissal of the quantity-theory analysis of inflation. Like Friedman, Goode made a postwar reappraisal of the importance of money; and, during his service from the 1950s onward as an International Monetary Fund official, Goode was known for pressing the importance of monetary aggregates on policy officials in various countries, including the United Kingdom during the late 1960s see Capie 2010, 374–75, 381). Goode's intervention in the UK discussions led him to be described in retrospect as one of the "monetarist disciples of Dr. Milton Friedman" (*Investor's Chronicle*, October 1, 1976, 16). However, it is not clear to what extent Goode's latter-day emphasis on money reflected the IMF's tradition of monetary analysis (see, for example, Polak and White 1955) rather than Friedman's influence.

7. In Director (1952, 48).

8. Friedman in Director (1952, 48).

9. Harrod in Director (1952, 31).

10. Harrod, as quoted in Director (1952, 194).

11. See the discussions in chapters 2, 4, and 7, as well as the coverage of cost-push debates in the next section and in chapter 15.

12. Harrod, as quoted in Director (1952, 31).

13. See, for example, Friedman (1966a, 39; p. 120 of 1968 reprint) and *Newsweek*, May 29, 1978.

14. Friedman as quoted in Director (1952, 65). In another passage (on p. 49), Friedman granted that Alvin Hansen had expressed a contrary view at the conference, one closer to the original cheap-money stance.

15. Friedman as quoted in Director (1952, 49).

16. Friedman (1951c, 190). The point that the money-demand function is redundant when discussing the relationship between interest rates and prices is, of course, one repeatedly made in the modern monetary policy literature, including Rotemberg and Woodford (1997, 309). This result does not, however, reflect a property special to New Keynesian models; it is present, for example, in any model in which monetary policy's effects can be summarized by a single interest rate. Consequently, the point about the redundancy of the money-demand function for the analysis has appeared in the pre–New Keynesian literature: see, for example, Robbins (1960, 103); Brunner (1973, 516); and the quotations in McCallum and Nelson (2011, 137).

17. See chapters 5 and 6. Friedman's shift in favor of a multiple-rate view of monetary policy's transmission would also have the effect of pushing him away from a belief in important wealth effects of monetary policy. He therefore became comfortable with ruling out the presence of a direct term involving money in the IS, or output-demand, equation, and instead emphasizing the effects of monetary policy on a variety of important yields (which, in turn, appeared in the IS equation). The consequence was that Friedman viewed money as appearing in term-structure and similar equations describing yields' determination.

18. Along similar lines, in NBC (1951a, 6), Friedman said that "one effect" of restrictive monetary policy actions was "higher interest rates."

19. Joint Committee on the Economic Report (1952b, 334).

20. Friedman in Director (1952, 66).

21. NBC (1951a, 9).

22. In Joint Committee on the Economic Report (1952c, 688).

23. In Joint Committee on the Economic Report (1952c, 732).

24. From Samuelson's remarks in *The American Economy, Lesson 48: Can We Have Full Employment without Inflation?*, CBS College of the Air, filmed circa June 5, 1962.

25. Reprinted in Joint Committee on the Economic Report (1952a, 1297–302).

26. Joint Committee on the Economic Report (1952a, 1302).

27. On the disagreement between Friedman and Samuelson about the 1980 credit controls, see E. Nelson and Schwartz (2008a, 847).

28. Joint Committee on the Economic Report (1952a, 1300).

29. See, for example, Friedman (1962a, 80–82; 1970a, 24, point 9 [p. 16 of 1991 reprint]) for examples of these later statements. See also the discussion in McCallum and Nelson (2005) of other expressions in the monetarist literature of related positions.

30. The indirect scenario amounted to the more likely of the two in the US institutional structure, under which direct subscription on the part of the Federal Reserve to new issues of government debt is heavily restricted by law.

31. Joint Committee on the Economic Report (1952b, 335).

32. See Director (1952, 175–76).

33. Friedman (1952b, 623).

34. NBC (1951b, 11). In addition, Friedman's January 1952 testimony in Joint Committee on the Economic Report (1952b, 334) called for a "rule" under which additional expenditures would lead to a commensurate increase in taxes (an arrangement that he had endorsed earlier in NBC 1950, 5).

35. In Director (1952, 96).

36. In Director (1952, 96).

37. NBC (1952a, 5).

38. NBC (1952b, 6).

39. See Friedman (1951c, 187).

40. As well as the references in chapters 4 and 8, see Friedman (1951f, 227–28).

41. See also his remarks in Joint Committee on the Economic Report (1952b, 334–35).

42. See, for example, Friedman (1951c, 188).

43. The date of the talk and its location (Stockholm) were given on p. 72 of the 1968 reprint of Friedman (1954a). In Friedman and Heller (1969, 79), Friedman (1968d, 12; 1982a, 29), and *Forbes* (December 29, 1997, 53), Friedman misremembered the talk as having been delivered in 1953.

44. Friedman (1954a; p. 76 of 1968 reprint). See also Friedman (1960a, 70, 75–76).

45. The downward trend in the share continued well into the 1970s. See, for example, Nordhaus and Wallich (1973, 16) and K. Kuttner and Lown (1999, 170).

46. See p. 76 of the 1968 reprint of Friedman (1954a).

47. See, in particular, Friedman's letter from 1986, as quoted in R. Phillips (1995, 174).

48. Friedman (1954a, p. 85 of 1968 reprint).

49. Thus, in *Business Week* (November 3, 1956, 188), Friedman listed "current attitudes toward monetary policy" as less important than deposit insurance and changes in bank asset structure as factors providing "something close to a guarantee against a monetary collapse." The last two factors, like fiscal stabilizers, provided reasons for the money stock to be resilient in the face of downward pressure on the economy and credit, and their operation did not require an appreciation of the importance of the money stock (which Friedman felt was still inadequate among economists and policy makers).

50. Cumulative postwar US experience would later persuade him, however, that this was not a good generalization (see *Wall Street Journal*, January 30, 1981; *Newsweek*, February 23, 1981; and chapter 15).

51. Friedman (1954a; pp. 88, 90 of 1968 reprint).

52. See Friedman (1951a, 230–31), a discussion given in 1950 that was also quoted in Friedman (1955a, 404–405).

53. See Friedman (1953d), an article discussed in chapter 8.

54. Again, see Friedman (1953d). Mayer (1999, 55) argued that policy makers' errors in estimates of policy lags had led them to be more inflationary, on average. But he did not provide a sound basis for accepting that this source of error should deliver the one-sided pattern of policy mistakes required by his argument.

55. Friedman (1954a; p. 84 of 1968 reprint).

56. NBC (1950, 8).

57. See Fand (1969a, 235–39).

58. Friedman (1980c, 82). Friedman (1975c, 1) made a similar remark, and in a television debate in 1980 he referred to "roller coaster of the kind we in America have had these past twenty years" (*Free to Choose*, UK television version, episode "How to Cure Inflation," BBC2, March 22, 1980, p. 11 of transcript). In addition, Friedman (1982b, 102) stated that the Federal Reserve had been an engine of inflation "since at least 1960," a formulation perhaps chosen in order to include the pre-Accord bond-price pegging policy in Friedman's indictment of Federal Reserve policy.

59. See Friedman (1977c, 16; 1982b, 105). See also Meltzer (2009a, 95, table 2.2) in which it is shown that the long-term US Treasury bond yield increased notably during the first half of 1953. Indeed, Culbertson (1973, 35) viewed "overly enthusiastic debt lengthening" by the authorities in 1953 as raising longer-term interest rates and playing a major part in producing the recession of 1953–54. (This could be reconciled with the Friedman-Schwartz *Monetary History* account of the 1953–54 recession, insofar as the debt-management operations also tended to reduce M2 growth. But Friedman 1977c granted that the effective demonetization of longer-term securities in 1953 meant that the behavior of M2 growth in that year understated the tightening of monetary conditions.)

60. For example, in January 1952, Friedman acknowledged that in recent years the federal budget had been near balance and that he expected that this would likely continue in the year ahead (NBC 1952b, 9; Joint Committee on the Economic Report 1952b, 334). Modern data give a federal deficit of 1.1 percent of GDP for fiscal 1950, followed by a surplus of 1.9 percent in fiscal year 1951, and deficits of 0.4 percent and 1.7 percent of GDP in fiscal years 1952 and 1953, respectively. In contrast, the budget deficit was over 20 percent of GDP for three of the heavily mobilized years in World War II (Council of Economic Advisers 2011, 284, table B-79).

61. Friedman recalled his dialogue with Burns on this matter in Instructional Dynamics Economics Cassette Tape 129 (September 13, 1973).

62. From Dewald's May 9, 1968, testimony, in Joint Economic Committee (1968a, 108). See Herbert Stein (1969, chapter 14) on the Eisenhower administration's push for a budget surplus in 1959–60.

63. For example, Friedman would list restraint in government spending as an example of Eisenhower being "willing to take the unpopular measures that stopped inflation" (*Milton Friedman Speaks*, episode 6, "Money and Inflation," taped November 7, 1977, p. 21 of transcript).

64. Friedman (1982c, 63). Friedman may have been including Franklin Roosevelt in the generalization on the grounds that Roosevelt in the 1932 election campaign advocated economic policies different from those he followed in office. President Roosevelt's economic actions as president might therefore be seen as having been driven by the trends in opinion that had become prevalent by 1933.

65. Herbert Stein (1969, 283, 298, 313, 335–36, 341, 349–50) and Congdon (1988, 33, 80) provided discussions of Eisenhower's lack of interest in moving fiscal policy in the direction suggested by Keynesian analysis.

66. Burns chaired the council for essentially the whole of Eisenhower's first term as president, serving from March 19, 1953, to December 1, 1956. See obamawhitehouse .archives.gov.

67. Instructional Dynamics Economics Cassette Tape 197 (mid-August 1976). See also *Newsweek*, December 6, 1976.

68. Friedman (1984c, 26).

69. See Friedman's remarks in his October 7, 1965, memorandum to the Board of Governors of the Federal Reserve System, as printed in Friedman (1968a, 148–49), and his commentaries in Instructional Dynamics Economics Cassette Tape 1 (October 1968) and *Newsweek*, December 9, 1968. See also the discussion in the next chapter.

70. The quotation is from Friedman (1973c, 33).

71. See Council of Economic Advisers (2011, 284, table B-79).

72. Debate between Milton Friedman and Senator Joseph S. Clark, "The Role of Government in Our Society," US Chamber of Commerce, Washington, DC, May 3, 1961.

73. *Milton Friedman Speaks*, episode 9, "The Energy Crisis: A Humane Solution" (taped February 10, 1978, pp. 15–16 of transcript); see also Friedman (1983b, 147). Furthermore, in *Expo* (Summer 1979, 20), Friedman traced the beginnings of the problems with US energy policy to the introduction of price controls on natural gas in the 1950s. See also Friedman (1962a, 126).

74. Friedman and Friedman (1985, 12).

75. The quotation is from Instructional Dynamics Economics Cassette Tape 92 (February 9, 1972). In addition, see Friedman's praise for Burns's conduct as CEA chair in Instructional Dynamics Economics Cassette Tape 6 (December 1968) and in the remarks he gave at Burns's memorial service (Friedman 1987c).

76. See E. Nelson (2009b, 67). The disdain that Friedman and Keyserling felt for each other was abundantly clear in their appearance together in a television special, *The Great Society: The Sizzling Economy*, NET, June 27, 1966.

77. Friedman (1955e, especially 361; 1958c).

78. These were advocated in the most famous item among Friedman's 1950s writings on free markets, 1955's "The Role of Government in Education" (Friedman 1955b).

79. Friedman (1955e, 362).

80. As was noted in chapter 4, Friedman's dissent from Simons on the merits of nationalization of natural or "technical" monopolies was also remarked on by R. D. Friedman (1976a, 30).

81. Occasionally, these were published alongside related written material by one of the panelists. For example, the printed version of the 1952 debate that is discussed presently was supplemented by a Friedman article, "Free Enterprise in the United States" (Friedman 1952d). This, like other *University of Chicago Round Table* contributions by Friedman, does not typically appear in Friedman's bibliographies, and previous accounts of Friedman's activities have tended to overlook them. For example, Ebenstein (2007, 138–39) takes Friedman (1951e, 1955e) as the antecedents to *Capitalism and Freedom* and does not refer to the 1952 discussions considered here.

82. In his remarks at the NBER's meeting in memory of Anna Schwartz on April 21, 2013, the current director of the NBER, James Poterba, recounted an incident in which Schwartz said she had never visited the premises of the University of Chicago during her collaboration with Friedman. (Likewise, David Meiselman, in an interview on July 16,

2014, stated that Schwartz never visited the university when Meiselman was a member of the money workshop.) A qualification, however, is that Jo Anna Gray (interview, August 8, 2013) recalled that Schwartz substituted for Friedman when he was out of town while Gray defended her dissertation at the University of Chicago in 1976. Taking these accounts together, it might be concluded that Friedman and Schwartz were never both present on the University of Chicago premises until November 2002 (when both of them attended an event held in Friedman's honor), but that Schwartz made a visit to the campus in 1976 on an occasion when Friedman was absent.

83. See Friedman and Friedman (1998, 197–98).

84. Probably the item most identified as criticism on Friedman's part of the Cowles agenda is Friedman (1951b). The NBER conference, held in late November 1949, at which Friedman delivered this critical comment, came to be regarded as featuring something of a showdown between Cowles Commission econometrics and NBER methods, with Friedman championing the latter (see Robert Gordon 1986, 26). Friedman himself recalled the event as an occasion on which he voiced his skepticism regarding econometric models (Instructional Dynamics Economics Cassette Tape 48, April 15, 1970). However, the published conference volume, as opposed to its unpublished floor discussions, likely did not bring out the scale of Friedman's hostility to econometric models. The negativity of his published comment was limited by the fact that the paper for which Friedman was the formal discussant was authored by Carl Christ, who was affiliated with the Cowles Commission but whose work Friedman greatly admired.

A more overt and representative example in print of Friedman's criticism of the Cowles Commission research agenda is in his discussion of identification in Friedman (1953c, 12–13). Although it appeared in a footnote, this Friedman discussion has been long remembered in the monetary-economics literature (see, for example, Sargent 1996, 540).

85. See also the discussion in chapter 12.

86. In particular, as indicated in Friedman and Schwartz (1991), Friedman had extravagant views—seemingly an outgrowth of his interaction with Harold Hotelling and Henry Schultz in the 1930s—about what could be achieved by running a regression both ways (i.e., Y on X, and X on Y). Friedman and Schwartz's (1991) discussion gave the impression that running an ordinary least-squares regression in both directions could resolve key identification problems and so bypass the need for estimation of structural relationships by simultaneous methods. Although Hammond (1996, 205–6) takes it for granted that Friedman and Schwartz were correct in arguing this point, the present author's view is that there would be essentially no support among researchers in the field of monetary policy or econometrics for the claims that Friedman and Schwartz (1991) made about identification via reverse regression.

87. Friedman and Schwartz (1982a, 34) referred to Koopmans's (1953) "classic" study of identification as well as to work in the same vein by Franklin Fisher (1966). Even in Friedman (1957a, 144n22), Friedman had given a nonargumentative discussion of the seriousness of the identification issue, and in Friedman (1963e, 63) he used, and accepted the validity of, the econometric literature's terminology regarding instrumental variables.

88. Hildreth (1986) alluded to, but did not cite, Friedman (1951b), while the remaining Friedman items referenced were from the 1940s (56, 145).

89. Hildreth and Friedman had good relations, and they had worked together as recently as 1976 on the Bach Committee on monetary aggregates (Bach et al. 1976).

90. That is, to Koopmans and Marschak. Furthermore, Marschak (1966) provided a foreword to the Christ textbook.

91. Friedman emphasized his proposal to test econometric models against a "naïve"

forecast when reflecting in Hammond (1992, 109) on his interaction with the Cowles Commission. This aspect of Friedman's critique of the Cowles Commission agenda was stressed also in Boumans (2013).

92. As described by Christ (1951, 56–57), Naïve Model II involves a projection for a next-year value of an endogenous variable, y_{t+1}, given by the formula: $y_t + \Delta y_t$. This resembles the random-walk-with-drift benchmark forecast for y_{t+1}, which corresponds to: $y_t + E[\Delta y_t]$. See also Friedman and Becker (1957, 68) for the usage of a version of Naïve Model II that was still closer to the random-walk-with-drift benchmark.

93. The lineage between Friedman's (1951b) use of random-walk forecasts as a criterion on which the forecasts of structural econometric models should be judged, and C. R. Nelson's (1972) comparison of univariate time-series forecasts with those generated by macroeconometric models was earlier noted by Zellner (1984, 101).

The connection between Friedman's earlier, 1940s work and the thrust of the much later literature on benchmarking econometric models is also close, as the following two quotations attest:

"Tinbergen's results cannot be judged by ordinary tests of statistical significance. The reason is that the variables with which he winds up, the particular series measuring these variables, the leads and lags, and various other aspects of the equations . . . have been selected after an extensive process of trial and error *because* they yield high coefficients of correlation. . . . But these attractive correlation coefficients create no presumption that the relationships they describe will hold in the future" (Friedman 1940, 659).

"It is scarcely surprising that both sets of predictors as well as their composites achieve reasonable accuracy during the period they were designed to explain. In the operational use of models, however, neither the forecaster nor the policy maker enjoys the luxury of working within the period of fit. Rather, from their point of view it is post-sample performance which is most relevant" (C. R. Nelson 1972, 914).

94. Over the years, Friedman referred to this workshop both as the Workshop *on* Money and Banking and the Workshop *in* Money and Banking. The former term is used in this book.

95. A 1951 date for the start of the workshop was given in Walters (1987, 424; 1991, viii). Emmett (2011, 104), citing Hammond (1999) as well as unpublished information from Hammond, suggests that the workshop did not really commence "fully" until 1953. Likewise, Becker (1991a, 144) stated that the workshop "was begun in 1953." (Specifically, this full-fledged launch was in the 1952–53 academic year—see Hammond 1999, xiii. As noted above, Friedman was in the United Kingdom for the 1953–54 academic year.) Stephen Axilrod, who was a graduate student in the economics department, confirmed that during 1951–52 Friedman organized a seminar series, at which students presented papers, that was a forerunner of the workshop (Stephen Axilrod, interview, April 24, 2013). Along similar lines, Horwich (1964, 245) recalled presenting as a graduate student in Friedman's spring 1951 class Economics 432, "the seminar in Monetary Dynamics." See also Hammond (1996, 222).

96. Friedman (1956b).

97. For example, George Kaufman of the Federal Reserve Bank of Chicago presented a version of Kaufman (1964) to the University of Chicago Workshop on Money and Banking on January 29, 1964, and, also around early 1964, William Gibson—who was then an undergraduate, or "college," student at the University of Chicago and who barely knew Friedman at this point—gave a talk to the workshop on banking issues (William Gibson, interview, March 6, 2013).

98. If Harrod's account is accepted, some version of the workshop evidently existed

even in the 1950–51 academic year, ahead of the 1951–52 date given in Hammond (1999, xiii) as the academic year in which a tryout version of the workshop began. Friedman was certainly inviting external speakers on a regular basis by the mid-1950s: Harry Johnson (1976a, 298) implied that Stanford University's Edward Shaw presented in the workshop in 1955, while a letter from Friedman in the spring of 1956 (held in the Friedman papers at the Hoover Institution's archives), invited Arthur Okun to visit the workshop to present his Columbia University PhD dissertation work.

99. Meiselman (1975, 295) similarly described the workshop as being held in the basement. David Laidler (personal communication, September 20, 2015) recalled the workshop location being shifted upstairs during Friedman's absence in the 1962–63 academic year.

100. Mehrling (2005, 157) gave the impression that academic staff who attended the Workshop on Money and Banking were, like the student attendees, required to present. (In particular, he implied that Fischer Black's presentation at the workshop in the early 1970s resulted from a mandatory condition associated with the right to attend.) But Friedman's "no representation without taxation" condition applied to students, not his teaching colleagues, and some University of Chicago personnel interviewed for this book (such as Eugene Fama, September 11, 2013) recalled years in which they attended the workshop without presenting a paper.

A further example that underscores the fact that a requirement to present was not imposed on academics attending the workshop is provided by Friedman's own presentation at the workshop (of a version of Friedman 1977d) in fall 1972. An unusually large number of department and business school members associated with the field of finance attended that workshop session (Benjamin Eden, interview, March 14, 2014). An earlier example of a nonpresenting attendee was that of Friedrich Hayek, as noted in the discussion that follows in the text.

101. Burgin (2012, 171) does, however, acknowledge that Friedman and Hayek's different positions at the University of Chicago meant that they did not interact very regularly.

102. Friedman (1954a, p. 78 of 1968 reprint).

103. Friedman (1955f, 32).

104. Friedman (1968d, 12).

105. Friedman (1962c, 12).

106. Friedman and Schwartz (1963a, 596).

107. *Fortune* (March 1955, 194), reprinted in Mulcahy (1957, 92).

108. Published as Friedman (1960a). See chapter 8.

109. See the quotation from a 1957 letter from Friedman to Burns in Hetzel (1998, 41). Hetzel interpreted Burns as advocating a nonmonetary view of inflation in his lectures and portrayed Friedman as offering a rebuttal to that view of inflation. However, as discussed in E. Nelson (2005b) and chapter 15 below, Burns's nonmonetary view of inflation actually materialized later, specifically in 1970; in particular, such a view is not implied by the discussion in Burns (1957). The Friedman/Burns disagreement in the 1950s appears to have centered on the channels linking monetary policy and aggregate demand, and not on the links between aggregate demand and inflation. It is the latter that are at the heart of the difference between monetary and nonmonetary views of inflation.

110. As noted, a passage in the letter was quoted in Hetzel (1998, 41).

111. This discussion will principally cover monetary policy in the period 1952–58, with the coverage of developments in 1959–60 reserved for the discussion of William McChesney Martin in section III of this chapter. This separation of 1952–58 from 1959–60 is con-

sistent with Romer and Romer's (2002a, 125) decision, when studying the monetary policy of the 1950s, to include only the first block of years in their estimated reaction function for the Federal Reserve.

112. Burns (1968, 3). A similar judgment was expressed in a *Fortune* magazine analysis (March 1955, 200, reprinted in Mulcahy 1957, 94), whose authors noted that President Eisenhower—his conservatism regarding budgetary matters notwithstanding—took more responsibility for economic stabilization than presidents had before the Great Depression.

113. This aspect of the pre-Keynesian version of the quantity theory was the subject of extensive documentation and analysis in Laidler (1999). Friedman (1972a, 937-41) made related observations when discussing the policy prescriptions that University of Chicago economists gave during the early 1930s.

114. Friedman (1957b, 75-76, 99-100).

115. Friedman (1957f, 73).

116. NBC (1955, 6). Benjamin Friedman (1980, 12, table 1.2) gave the decline in output (real GNP) in the 1953-54 recession as 3.3 percent. This made it one of the more severe postwar recessions, but also milder than many of the pre-1953 downturns that were necessarily Milton Friedman's basis for comparison in 1955.

117. Friedman (1975c, 4). Benjamin Friedman's (1980) table also indicated that the 1957-58 recession featured a decline in real GNP of 3.2 percent, that is, roughly the same as that in 1953-54. In modern real GDP data, however, the decline in output in the 1957-58 recession (3.6 percent) is larger than that in 1953-54 (2.5 percent) (quarterly data from FRED portal, Federal Reserve Bank of St. Louis). As for the 1960-61 recession (which is discussed in section III of this chapter), it was milder than either of the preceding two recessions.

118. Warburton, increasingly vocal again on monetary issues after several years of employer-imposed silence, was serving as a discussant for a session on December 28, 1958, of the meetings of the American Statistical Association.

119. See Benjamin Friedman (1980, 12, table 1.2).

120. On Friedman's generalization that deep recessions are followed by rapid recoveries in the United States, see for example Friedman and Schwartz (1963a, 493) and Friedman (1964e, 14-18; 1993).

121. Friedman (1977c, 15).

122. See, for example, Friedman (1960a, 94).

123. From Friedman's March 3, 1964, testimony, in Committee on Banking and Currency (1964, 1156).

124. Friedman (1973c, 36).

125. From Friedman's appearance on *The Great Challenge: How Strong Is Our Economy?*, CBS, March 23, 1958, p. 15 of transcript.

126. Friedman (1958a, 20).

127. See Friedman (1960a, 94). See also Friedman's testimony of October 30, 1959, in Joint Economic Committee (1959b, 3034).

128. Friedman (1960a, 94). See also Fischer (1980, 227) and E. Nelson (2007, 154-55).

129. James Tobin, too, would ultimately also come to this conclusion. See chapter 12.

130. See Friedman's footnote, appended on p. 83 of the 1968 reprint of Friedman (1954a).

131. Friedman and Schwartz (1963a, 628). See also Friedman's testimony of October 30, 1959 (in Joint Economic Committee 1959b, 3041), in which Friedman dated the Federal Reserve's interest in the money supply somewhat earlier (basically, to 1950-53). Brunner

and Meltzer (1964a, 4) referred specifically to the Federal Reserve's acknowledgment to Congress in 1952 of the importance of its actions "affecting the money supply."

132. Indeed, one of the Federal Reserve Board's senior staff during the 1950s—albeit with responsibilities concentrated in international affairs rather than in US monetary policy—was Arthur W. Marget, whose two-volume *The Theory of Prices* (Marget 1938, 1942) had defended the quantity theory of money against Keynes's criticisms.

Tavlas (1989, 247) stressed the connections between Marget's approach to monetary economics and that later taken by Friedman. However, the similarities between *The Theory of Prices* and Friedman's subsequent work were sharply limited. As its title implied, Marget's work did not have an appreciable empirical dimension and did not press the case for interpreting the Great Depression as a monetary phenomenon. Furthermore, Marget's (1938, 1942) discussion of theoretical matters included attacks on versions of the quantity theory of money in which Friedman saw merit, such as those that used income rather than transactions as the economic-activity variable (see, for example, Marget 1938, 403), while Marget's criticisms of Keynes were centered on the latter's interpretation of the preexisting literature rather than on specific hypotheses advanced by Keynes.

133. Friedman (1964b, 7; p. 76 of reprint). A qualification to this judgment is that there was an uptick in the Federal Reserve's discussion of monetary aggregates when Lauchlin Currie was a senior member of the Federal Reserve Board's staff during the later 1930s. See, for example, Bernanke (2006) and Rotemberg (2014).

134. See Friedman's remarks in his October 1965 memorandum to the Federal Reserve Board, printed in Friedman (1968a, 146).

135. NBC (1955, 7).

136. The memorandum was Friedman (1955d).

137. Brunner and Meltzer (1964b, 44) similarly judged that the Federal Reserve moved to ease ahead of the 1953 and 1960 cyclical peaks, and Sprinkel (1964, 43) acknowledged that the Federal Reserve shifted to ease ahead of or at the start of the 1960/61 recession.

138. Simple correlations calculated between (real and nominal) income growth and lagged monetary growth confirm this relationship. Using quarterly log differences to measure growth rates, real GNP growth for 1954:Q1–1960:Q4 has a maximum correlation of 0.51 with M2 growth two quarters earlier and of 0.55 with M1 growth one quarter earlier. Nominal GNP growth for 1954:Q1–1960:Q4 has a maximum correlation of 0.48 with M2 growth two quarters earlier and of 0.55 with M1 growth one quarter earlier.

139. Meltzer (2009a, 95) reported ninety-day Treasury bill rates (for new issues) as 1.68 percent at the end of June 1952 and 2.23 percent at the end of December 1952.

140. See Romer and Romer (2002a, 124), E. Nelson (2012b, 248–49), and chapter 6 above.

141. Evidence accumulated through studies of later sample periods, such as C. Evans and Marshall (1998, 68) and Chung, Laforte, Reifschneider, and Williams (2012), has suggested that a 100 basis point change in short-term rates is typically associated with a change of about 25 basis points in longer-term rates.

142. The quoted phrase is from Friedman and Schwartz (1963a, 593). In the same vein, Friedman (1977c, 16) contended that the discontinuation of the bond-price peg "didn't really become effective until 1953." See also Friedman (1982b, 105), as well as Wallich's (1983, 264) observation that the 1951 Accord ushered in only a "gradual withdrawal" from the bond-price pegging policy.

Tobin (1965a, 466), in noting that Friedman and Schwartz treated money and securities as equivalent under the peg, argued that they did not follow through on this logic, as the reasoning would imply that "the 1951 Accord would abruptly shrink [the effective stock of] money." There is some merit in this criticism. As discussed in chapter 4, it is true that Friedman and Schwartz did not provide a comprehensive discussion of the implications of the peg for monetary analysis. Nevertheless, in their account of developments following the Accord, Friedman and Schwartz did indeed follow the logic that Tobin sketched. In particular, they viewed the abandonment of the peg as a monetary contraction: see Friedman and Schwartz (1963a, 598, 672) and Friedman (1964f, 7–9). However, they dated this demonetization not to the establishment of the Accord in 1951 but to 1953, when the commencement of the bills-only policy meant that the pegging policy was abandoned decisively. See also the next note.

143. Friedman (1977c, 16). Friedman also recognized the looseness of the money/income relationship in the early to mid-1950s in Friedman (1973a, 23).

144. See Friedman's June 1966 remarks in Friedman (1968a, 162).

145. Friedman (1960a, 44).

146. Here are four examples of commentary to this effect:

McKim (1962, 282) characterized the post-Accord period as one in which the Federal Reserve attempted "to affect all interest rates by manipulations of the short rate."

Chapin (1959, 8.6) stated that "under the present monetary system . . . the rules of action . . . often use attempts [by the central bank] to change interest rates as devices to induce changes in bank reserves."

Carr (1959, 505) observed that "the appropriateness of the System's judgments may be less important than knowledge of the judgment, since the influence of credit policy—wrong or right—upon interest rates is dominant."

Finally, Paul Samuelson (in *Financial Times*, February 10, 1960a, 8) referred to the conditions under which "the Federal Reserve could safely lower interest rates."

The efforts by the Federal Reserve to obscure its influence on short-term interest rates were also noted from time to time: the *Financial Times* editorialized (February 10, 1960b), "Central bankers often talk about 'natural market movements' when for some reason they wish to avoid public discussion of a change in interest rates for which they are responsible." Likewise, Horwich (1965, 20) observed: "The Federal Reserve, in its official statements, repeatedly denies that it alters interest rates in a direction opposite to market forces. . . . [Doing so] is something that the Federal Reserve is unlikely to acknowledge publicly in this post-Accord era."

It would probably be fair to say that the Federal Reserve became more transparent about its use of a short-term interest rate when publicly discussing monetary policy in the 1960s and the 1970s. In 1982, however, when it returned to a short-term interest rate instrument (after a gap between 1979 and 1982), the FOMC initially exhibited a lack of clarity on the matter, much as it had in the 1950s. See, for example, Thornton (2006) and Bernanke (2013) for discussions of this point.

147. To reiterate, this was not the same as a claim that Federal Reserve policy makers overlooked the nominal/real rate distinction. As already mentioned, policy makers in the 1950s were aware of this distinction, and nominal and real interest rates largely moved together in the 1950s. Even in these circumstances, however, the use of the short-term nominal interest rate as a measure of policy stance is inappropriate if the natural short-term rate of interest (real and nominal) is undergoing sizable fluctuations. Friedman's (1955d) memorandum criticized policy makers' concentration on short-term interest rates on the grounds that a constant nominal interest rate was not a neutral policy. In effect, Friedman was arguing that the natural rate of interest was undergoing fluctuations, one

result of which was to make the nominal rate less valuable—compared with monetary growth—as a measure of policy stance.

148. Young (1958a, 205).

149. See also chapters 1 and 8.

150. Another example of Friedman's continuing skepticism about forecasts during this period was Friedman (1958a, 18).

151. Although Friedman's injunction to set policy without relying on forecasts did not catch on, his sentiments about humility are widely shared in policy circles. For example, Stacey Tevlin, at the time assistant director at the Division of Research and Statistics at the Federal Reserve Board (and later the division's director), was quoted in the *Washington Post* of January 3, 2012, as follows: "Forecasting the economy is a really challenging job. . . . You have to be pretty humble and comfortable with the fact that your projections don't always come through."

Similar sentiments have been expressed over the years by private-sector forecasters. For example, a financial market participant, Michael Bazdarich, when appearing alongside Friedman in a panel in July 1986, observed: "As a forecaster, I face humility and ignorance every day. And in trying to figure out interest rates, I have been especially humble and ignorant" (in Darby et al. 1987, 17).

152. The monograph was simply the in-print version of a University of Chicago Department of Economics doctoral dissertation (Friedman 1961c, 181; American Economic Association 1970, 293), and it reflected work instigated when Meigs attended Friedman's Workshop on Money and Banking during the 1958-59 academic year (Meigs 1962, ix).

153. In particular, Friedman (1960a, 41-42; 1961c). The latter reference (specifically, p. 181) is the source of the quotation in the text. This reference also cited the 1960 dissertation version of Meigs (1962).

154. Friedman and Schwartz (1963a, 396). See also Meltzer (2003, 401-2) and chapter 2 above.

155. See Friedman's November 14, 1963, testimony, in Joint Economic Committee (1963a), as well as the items discussed in the next chapter.

156. See Friedman (1980c, 83). See also Friedman (1953a, 171, 179) and his remarks in *Wall Street Journal*, June 30, 1975.

157. Friedman (1977e, 465). See also Friedman (1976a, 216) and Friedman and Schwartz (1982a, 570).

158. Friedman and Schwartz (1963a, 585, 597).

159. As well as the *Monetary History*, see Instructional Dynamics Economics Cassette Tape 109 (October 18, 1972).

160. NBC (1949, 17).

161. Friedman (1959b, 214).

162. Friedman (1959a). The article saw print in the *Journal of Political Economy* in August 1959. Somewhat pointlessly, just three months earlier Friedman had published a short preview of the article—bearing the same title as the full article—in the proceedings issue of the *American Economic Review* (see Friedman 1959c).

163. See Friedman (1959a, 335-37).

164. Benjamin Klein, interview, March 4, 2013. See Benjamin Klein (1975a, 1975b) for the main output of the research.

165. Hahn (1971, 62) and McCallum (1990a, 167) also criticized Friedman's permanent-prices concept. Rasche (1987, 1990) used Beveridge and Nelson's (1981) decomposition procedure to propose a generalization of Friedman's permanent-price-level concept to a nonstationary environment.

166. See Friedman and Schwartz (1982a, 451–52, 570–72).

167. Price Statistics Review Committee (1961). Stigler sketched the committee's findings (released in January 1961) at an April 1961 conference, attended by Friedman, hosted by the University of Chicago's Graduate School of Business (*Business Week*, May 6, 1961).

168. See, for example, Friedman (1963c, 20 [p. 41 of 1968 reprint]; 1969a, 47). In addition, in 1986 Anna Schwartz went so far as to assert that it was "commonly accepted that there was no inflation in the United States until 1966, since measured price increases until then could well have reflected inadequate allowance for quality changes in goods and services" (Schwartz 1986, 671). Notwithstanding this statement, the narrative and data analysis that appeared in Schwartz's prior work with Friedman largely took readings on inflation between 1954 and 1960 as bona fide. And it will be argued presently that this treatment was appropriate. In addition, it should be acknowledged that Schwartz (1986, 671) did take average inflation above 1.5 percent as bona fide inflation—and US inflation *did* exceed 1.5 percent over much of the period from 1954 to 1960.

169. In an interview for this book (March 21, 2013), Gordon said: "I don't think he ever integrated that. He had an enormously warm personal relationship with George Stigler. He would have referred to George Stigler's committee report in 1961 [by saying], you know, 'That's great work,' and stuff. Then he'll go off two months later and write about inflation and take the data at face value, for what it is, and not remember Stigler. I think that's very related to the fact that [later, when Gordon and Friedman were colleagues at the University of Chicago] he didn't pay any attention to half of what I was doing [that is, to the portion of Gordon's research program that concerned price measurement]." On the last point, see the section on Robert Gordon in chapter 14 below.

170. See Hallman, Porter, and Small (1991) and Rasche (1993a, 292, 303).

171. See, for example, Friedman (1988a) and Friedman and Schwartz (1982a, chapter 5). In some discussions (before the 1980 redefinition of M2), Friedman dated the leveling-off of velocity to 1960 rather than the 1950s (see, for example, Friedman 1973b).

172. Replacing the observed price-level pattern for the period 1954–63 with a flat line would imply removing from the data a price-level increase (by the criterion of the GDP deflator) of roughly 20 percent. It would also imply a decline in velocity by the same percentage—an adjustment likely to mean a less stable money-demand relationship over that period. (One could, alternatively, avoid this decline in velocity and still postulate that prices were flat by assuming that aggregate nominal income was accurately measured and classifying more of its rise as an increase in real output. But this alternative assumption would imply adding about 2 percentage points over the period 1954–63 to the annual average of real output growth, which was already recorded to be over 3 percent.)

173. Lucas (1996, 667) expressed doubt about the presence of a short-run Phillips-curve relationship in the data during the 1950s. But the seeming absence of a curve in Lucas's unemployment/inflation scatter for the 1950s (p. 667) reflected the inclusion in the scatter of the observations for the period 1950–53. Measured inflation for the early 1950s was clouded by the imposition of price controls in that period (see, for example, Shapiro 1994, 309, 311; and McCallum 1994b, 332).

174. See his remarks in Ketchum and Kendall (1962, 54). On this occasion, Friedman also stated that avoidance of the fluctuations in monetary growth would also have helped forestall some of 1958's increase in inflation expectations (an increase noted above and further discussed at the end of this chapter). Other discussions Friedman provided in which he took inflation as present in the United States during the 1950s included his reference (*Newsweek*, December 9, 1968) to the "burst of inflationary pressure in 1956 and 1957" (see also Friedman 1958a, 20); his statement (*Newsweek*, October 17, 1966) that

prices rose in 1957 and 1958; and Friedman and Schwartz's (1963a, 583) discussion of the "price rises . . . in 1955 to 1957." See also Friedman (1992b, vii). In a similar vein, James Tobin was quoted in a *Business Week* article (of January 1, 1966, reprinted in N. Marshall 1970, 105) referring to "the wage-price pressures we had then [the mid-1950s]."

175. *Milton Friedman Speaks*, episode 6, "Money and Inflation" (taped November 7, 1977), p. 21 of transcript.

176. Friedman (1980c, 81).

177. Among those in policy circles, Federal Reserve Board governor George Mitchell in 1969 gave the automatic tendency of the CPI to rise because of technological improvement as 1 to 1½ percent, adding: "When you get the inflation rate higher than 1½ percent or so, it begins to represent real inflation" (*U.S. News and World Report*, January 20, 1969, 25). A similar number was given, in a joint television appearance with Friedman in 1962, by Paul Samuelson, who suggested that a 1 percent per year increase in the CPI might reflect quality changes rather than genuine inflation. Friedman agreed about the existence of the bias described, but he neither endorsed nor rejected Samuelson's number of 1 percent, replying, "I wouldn't want to put a number on it but . . . on the general point we're in complete agreement" (*The American Economy, Lesson 48: Can We Have Full Employment without Inflation?*, CBS College of the Air, filmed circa June 5, 1962).

178. As discussed in chapter 7, other elements not in this list also entered the Phillips-curve relationship that was embedded in Friedman's framework. These other elements included roles for both lagged and forward-looking terms in the relationship and a stipulation that different information sets underlay wage and price decisions in any period.

179. See E. Nelson (2005b, 2009c) and DiCecio and Nelson (2013) for detailed discussions.

180. See Friedman (1977b, 12; also in Friedman 1978a, 52).

181. See, for example, Silk (1976, 113–14).

182. Friedman (1977b, 33), also in Friedman (1978a, 65).

183. Both quotations are from NBC (1953, 8). See also Friedman's (1962a, 122) criticism (reaffirmed in Ketchum and Strunk 1965, 55) of what he regarded as overstatement of the implications of monopoly power. For related discussions, see chapters 4 and 7 above.

184. See Friedman (1951a, 1955a) as under Friedman and Kuznets (1945).

185. See, for example, Friedman (1962a, 123; 1971f, 23).

186. Friedman and Friedman (1980, 262).

187. A corollary of this position was that Friedman resisted using "labor" as a synonym for the organized labor-union movement (see, for example, *San Jose Mercury News*, February 13, 1979; and *Newsweek*, January 17, 1983).

188. See especially Friedman (1959b, 212–13).

A colleague of Friedman's at the University of Chicago in the 1950s, Albert Rees, was also a critic of cost-push views, and union wage-push views in particular, during this period (see especially Rees 1962—a book that appeared in the *Cambridge Economic Handbook* series for which Friedman was a general editor, and whose text acknowledged Friedman's comments). Ashenfelter and Pencavel (2010) provide coverage of some of Rees's work in the field. These authors do not relate Rees's work to Friedman's research; however, in an interview for this book, John Pencavel noted that Friedman looked to Rees as an authority on labor issues, to such an extent that Rees became known as "Milton Friedman's Secretary of Labor" (John Pencavel, interview, May 12, 2014).

Other accounts, both in the 1950s (for example, Schlesinger 1958, 296) and subsequently (for example, Macesich 1997, 66–67, 69) did note the solidarity of Friedman and

Rees in their rejection of cost-push ideas. A Rees statement in congressional testimony on May 22, 1958, given when he was an associate professor in the University of Chicago's economics department, laid out some of the main points of this critique: "There is no firm evidence that unions are a cause of inflation, and there is a good deal of evidence that in rapid inflations wages set by collective bargaining lag behind other wages. The view that gradual inflation results from a 'wage push' is based on casual observation, which can be highly misleading" (in Joint Economic Committee 1958a, 401). Among these points, the one that wages of unionized workers frequently lag those of nonunionized workers was one Friedman spotlighted on several occasions (including in Friedman 1971f, 23; 1975d, 33 [p. 83 of 1991 reprint]; 1981a, 13; Instructional Dynamics Economics Cassette Tape 67, February 10, 1971; and *Monday Conference*, ABC Television, Australia, April 14, 1975, p. 15 of transcript). See also Fischer (1985, 42) and chapter 15 below.

Although they concurred on the endogeneity of wages, Friedman and Rees parted company on whether there was a permanent inflation/unemployment relationship. Rees maintained that a nonvertical relation prevailed even in the long run (see Rees 1970a; Friedman 1976a, 221; and chapter 13 below). This disagreement underscores the fact emphasized here that Friedman's differences with other economists on inflation covered multiple areas, including the issue of the endogeneity of inflation (the heart of the cost-push debate) and the issue of whether, conditional on inflation being endogenous, there existed a long-term inflation/unemployment relationship. (And, as discussed presently, a third position that Friedman contested consisted of a hybrid of the cost-push and nonvertical-Phillips-curve views—with this hybrid view implying a permanent trade-off between inflation and unemployment.)

189. Friedman (1959b, 212). Cherrier (2011, 360), in challenging positions taken in the recent history-of-thought literature to the effect that Friedman's basic position was pro-business, offers Friedman's defense of unions from the accusation of causing inflation as a counterexample. In so doing, she treats Friedman's position on this matter as little known. It may well be little known in the history-of-thought literature, but Friedman's position that unions were being unjustly blamed for inflation has been very heavily discussed in the monetary economics literature and also became a talking point in popular discussions of Friedman's views (as in, for example, *Fortune*, June 1, 1967, 150; and *Sunday Times*, January 22, 1978; as well as Trevithick 1977, 15). And as detailed in E. Nelson (2007, 2009a, 2009b) and in subsequent chapters, this was an aspect of his views that Friedman himself highlighted repeatedly during the Great Inflation of the 1970s.

190. Friedman (1938b, 129).

191. Friedman (1962a, 168). See also Friedman (1962b, 197).

192. See Friedman and Schwartz (1963a, 498-99) as well as chapter 7 above.

193. The restriction that $E[u_t] = 0$ can be thought of as a restriction that nominal stickiness vanishes in the long run. In the case of New Keynesian models with price stickiness, this restriction is consistent with the notion that the steady-state markup is the same under sticky and flexible prices, with the sticky-price economy featuring zero-mean markup shocks (a standard property in these models: see, for example, Galí, Gertler, and López-Salido 2001; and Walsh 2003). See also chapter 7 above for a related discussion of the basis for the $E[u_t] = 0$ restriction.

194. As in much of Friedman's discussions (for example, Friedman 1968b), it will be taken for granted here that output fluctuations have a counterpart in unemployment variations, even though that relationship is not literally implied by most New Keynesian models, nor by Friedman's (1968b) discussion. (Taken at face value, these frameworks

imply, as noted, that labor-input fluctuations solely take the form of variations in hours worked and do not take the form of variations in the number of employed workers.)

195. If the long-run Phillips curve is nonvertical, $\beta < 1$, $E[u_t] > 0$ creates a long-run trade-off between inflation and the output gap even if the policy makers' target output level is the natural level of output (so that their implied unemployment target is the natural rate). For $\beta = 1$ and $E[u_t] > 0$, there is no long-run trade-off (i.e., the long-run Phillips curve is vertical), but there is a permanent output gap (i.e., unemployment is permanently above the natural rate, and the vertical Phillips curve is positioned to the right of the natural rate of unemployment).

196. Friedman (1958b). The publication in which this appeared (Joint Economic Committee 1958b) was identified as produced on March 31, 1958. Friedman was originally scheduled to testify in person to the Joint Economic Committee on the subject of this submission. On the day of his scheduled testimony (May 15, 1958), however, Representative Richard Bolling opened the hearing by stating: "We will miss, this morning, the stimulating presence of Dr. Milton Friedman, professor of economics at the University of Chicago. Dr. Friedman has for the past year been [visiting] with the center for advanced study in the behavioral sciences at Stanford University. We are sorry that unexpected complications prevent his being with us this morning" (Joint Economic Committee 1958a, 127).

197. Friedman (1958b, 252; pp. 182–83 of 1969 reprint).

198. Lerner (1958). The very title of Lerner's article—"Inflationary Depression and the Regulation of Administered Prices"—indicates that the cost-push advocates in the 1950s had their own explanation for what in subsequent decades would be called "stagflation."

199. Solow (1976, 3–4) and Phelps (1968b, 679) identified Robinson (1937) as an early statement in the Keynesian literature of a Phillips-curve relationship, with Phelps further pointing to Dunlop (1938). See also the discussion in chapter 13 below.

200. Friedman (1970b, 220). See also Friedman (1977e, 469) and chapter 7 above.

201. Samuelson and Solow (1960, 194). Samuelson had, in fact, expressed his belief in a Phillips curve trade-off well before the writing of the Samuelson-Solow paper and the publication of A. W. Phillips (1958): see, for example, Samuelson (1953, 551; 1956, 130). Indeed, as we have seen, Samuelson would credit Alvin Hansen's work with the trade-off idea. In one such discussion, Samuelson (1976, 30) indicated that both he and Hansen viewed free wage/price arrangements as unlikely to be consistent with a situation of full employment alongside price stability, and therefore pointing to "the need for an incomes policy." In addition, a colleague of Hansen's at Harvard University, Seymour Harris, was described in a 1963 Federal Reserve Board memorandum as having "argued that 'some' inflation is tolerable and perhaps even necessary to achieve socially acceptable levels of employment" (Young 1963, 3).

See also chapter 13 for further discussion of Samuelson and Solow (1960) and its relationship to the subsequent Phillips-curve literature.

202. From the appearance by Friedman and Samuelson on *The American Economy, Lesson 48: Can We Have Full Employment without Inflation?*, CBS College of the Air, filmed circa June 5, 1962.

203. Alan Blinder recalled the paper in these terms in the floor discussion of DiCecio and Nelson (2013) at the September 2008 NBER conference on the Great Inflation in Vermont. Indeed, even in the 1970s an extract from Schultze's monograph appeared in a macroeconomics readings book (see W. Smith and Teigen 1970, 163–69).

204. Schultze (1959, 6), summarized the issue as follows: "The controversy between the demand-pull and cost-push theorists is in reality, therefore, a debate about the con-

sistency of full employment and price stability." A qualification to this statement is that a *mixed* demand-pull/cost-push theory of the type Schultze, and Samuelson and Solow advocated is sufficient to render full employment and price stability inconsistent objectives.

205. Friedman (1951a). Schultze 91939, 6) also cited All Participants (1951).

206. Schultze was a lecturer at Indiana University from 1959 to 1961 (information from Brownings Institution).

207. Friedman (1958a, 21–22). This was also reported in the *Odessa American*, November 11, 1958.

208. For further documentation of Friedman's concerns about the Eisenhower administration's receptiveness toward cost-push and wage-push theories of inflation during its second term, see S. Gordon (1974). See also Friedman (1962b, 281–82).

209. From Eisenhower's State of the Union address of February 2, 1953 (Eisenhower 1953, 7). The reference to controls on credit, in this context, simply referred to the use of standard monetary policy tools. It did not mean deployment of direct credit controls of the kind Friedman opposed.

210. Instructional Dynamics Economics Cassette Tape 51 (May 27, 1970). See also chapter 15.

211. Friedman (1982b, 104–5).

212. See Friedman and Schwartz (1963a, 595).

213. Friedman (1982b, 105). Another retrospective in which Friedman praised Douglas for helping end the bond-price support program was that in Instructional Dynamics Economics Cassette Tape 163 (February 1975, part 1).

214. Subcommittee on Monetary, Credit, and Fiscal Policies (1950a, 17). A similar passage, appearing on p. 2 of the report, was quoted in Friedman and Schwartz (1963a, 595).

215. Subcommittee on Monetary, Credit, and Fiscal Policies (1950a, 1).

216. For example, Orphanides (2003, 634), in discussing the fact that "Burns' [1957] proposed price stability amendment was never enacted," apparently accepted Burns's premise that the price-stability mandate was not present in the Employment Act of 1946.

Burns evidently changed his view on this matter, because he later took the maximum-purchasing-power component of the employment act's remit as a price-stability objective. On this change in position, see DiCecio and Nelson (2013, 413) as well as Burns's statement (July 26, 1977) that the "actual practice of the Board and the Federal Open Market Committee" had been to interpret the Employment Act of 1946 as including a price-stability mandate, in line with "the Board's understanding of the intent of Congress" (Burns 1977b, 717).

Some treatments (for example, Kohn 2005, 347) have taken the Federal Reserve as having a legislated price-stability goal only with the passage of the Federal Reserve Reform Act of 1977. In the same vein, prior to the passage of that legislation, Warburton (1976, 542) questioned whether the Federal Reserve had a legislative responsibility for maintaining the value of money. On the interpretation offered here, however, treatments such as these concentrated unduly on legislation pertaining specifically to the Federal Reserve Act and neglected the remit to the Federal Reserve embodied in the Employment Act of 1946, which did essentially relay a price-stability mandate.

217. See Eisenhower (1959, 7) and Friedman's May 25, 1959, testimony in Joint Economic Committee (1959a, 627).

218. See, for example, Representative Reuss's discussions on several occasions in the late 1950s, including in Joint Economic Committee (1958a, 29, 262; 1959d, 20). Earlier in

the 1950s, the Council of Economic Advisers (1952, 847), stated: "While price stability is not specifically mentioned as an objective in the Employment Act, there is no doubt that it is implicit in several of the stated objectives."

219. On the former point, C. Walker (1960, 55) referred to the "conviction on the part of [the] Federal Reserve authorities that the Employment Act includes an implicit mandate with respect to price stability," quoting in this connection a 1957 submission from Federal Reserve chairman Martin (in Committee on Finance 1957, 1256) in which Martin stated "it would be impossible to 'foster and promote . . . the general welfare' and 'to maintain maximum employment, production, and purchasing power' if prices were highly unstable." See also Romer and Romer (2002b) and C. Romer (2007) for evidence that US policy maker objectives have not changed appreciably over the postwar period.

220. Subcommittee on Monetary, Credit, and Fiscal Policies (1950a, 17).

221. What the statement did not entirely capture was the fact that part of the problem with the bond-price peg was that it was capable of generating either easy or tight conditions, depending on how the economic outlook changed the equilibrium nominal interest rate. As discussed in chapter 4, the fact that a policy of holding the interest rate constant produced wide variation in economic conditions was a major part of Friedman and Schwartz's (1963a) narrative of the bond-price pegging policy, and it was also reflected in Warburton's (1958, 211) dictum, "interest rates need to be flexible in order that monetary policy may be stable." See also Brunner (1971b, 44).

222. From Douglas's remarks in the December 3, 1949, hearing, in Subcommittee on Monetary, Credit, and Fiscal Policies (1950b, 494), also quoted in Friedman and Schwartz (1963a, 622).

223. The position of chair of the Joint Economic Committee rotates between members of the House of Representatives and the Senate. Douglas was chairman of the committee in 1955–56, 1959–60, and 1963–64 (information provided to author by the Joint Economic Committee, July 24, 2014).

224. See Tavlas (1977b)—a paper for which Friedman served as referee (see Tavlas 1998, 19). Douglas's positions during the 1920s and 1930s on economic fluctuations and monetary management were also considered in detail in Laidler (1999, 222–28).

225. From Friedman's appearance of May 25, 1959, in Joint Economic Committee (1959a, 626). Friedman had earlier indicated his rejection of a trade-off in 1952 congressional testimony. See E. Nelson (2009a, 2009b) and chapter 7 above.

226. Friedman (1958e, 255; p. 36 of 1962 reprint).

227. Friedman (1958b, 256; p. 187 of 1969 reprint).

228. See, for example, Instructional Dynamics Economics Cassette Tape 42 (January 15, 1970).

229. Friedman and Schwartz (1970a). The modern official Federal Reserve Board series on M1 and M2 start only in January 1959, and so comparable twelve-month changes cannot be generated for these series.

230. See, for example, Friedman and Schwartz (1963a, 629–31); Friedman (1970d, 23); and Rotemberg (2014). In congressional testimony on August 13, 1957, Chairman Martin stated that, in defining the money supply, "we usually eliminate time deposits from these figures" (Committee on Finance 1957, 1307).

231. See the following chapters for further discussion.

232. Federal Reserve Bank of Chicago (1958, 12).

233. Eugene Lerner worked at the Federal Reserve Bank of Chicago for a few years in the 1950s after completing his doctoral work with Friedman, but he found the atmosphere hostile to Friedman and to the study of money (Eugene Lerner, interview, July 29, 2016).

234. Einzig (1959, 4–5).

235. R. Turner (1957, 103), discussing Friedman (1957b).

236. Culbertson (1964, 375). Culbertson also labeled their causality discussion "pathetic" (378). On Friedman's initial reaction, see Hammond (1996, 115–18). In later years, however, Friedman would cite Culbertson (1964) and accept criticisms other than those in the offending passages. See, in particular, Friedman and Schwartz (1982a, 16).

237. Gramley (1969, 2; p. 489 of 1970 printing). Gramley gave the speech while serving as full-time adviser in the Federal Reserve Board's Division of Research and Statistics.

238. Friedman (1960a, 43).

239. Abbott (1959, 3). The items being referred to were Federal Reserve Board (1953) and Young (1958b). The latter appeared in revised form as Young (1964).

240. What were labeled the "Minutes" for FOMC meetings up to 1967 (and the "Memoranda of Discussion" for the period between 1967 and 1976) were the counterpart to the "Transcripts" from 1976 onward. See Romer and Romer (2002b), Lindsey (2003), and Meltzer (2009a, 2009b).

241. Roosa (1956, 76). Likewise, Young (1964, 60) described periods of expansionary monetary policy as those in which "monetary policy is designed to encourage, rather than restrain, credit expansion and spending."

242. See Friedman (1970d, 19). The discussion in this article indicated that, by the end of the 1960s, Friedman had concluded that the Federal Reserve was largely interested in money due to its alleged status as a noisy indicator of credit (an interpretation also advanced by Rotemberg 2014). This assessment of the Federal Reserve's views contrasted with the earlier discussion in Friedman and Schwartz (1963a, 628), which took the opposite tack, viewing Federal Reserve discussions of bank credit magnitudes as a sign of growing Federal Reserve interest in money. The latter interpretation was understandable because the Federal Reserve routinely discussed monetary and credit aggregates in the same breath. Examples included the Federal Reserve Board's (1953, 234) reference to the need to avoid "an excessive and unstabilizing growth of credit and money"; Abbott's (1960, 1102) statement in a *Federal Reserve Bulletin*, "The Federal Reserve regulates the supply of reserves so as to keep the amount of bank credit and money consonant with the changing needs of the economy"; and Axilrod and Young's (1962, 1113) remark (also in a *Federal Reserve Bulletin* piece) that, following the Accord, US "monetary policy became free to regulate bank credit and monetary expansion in the interest of sustainable economic growth and a stable value for the dollar."

243. Here Friedman and Schwartz's (1970a) monthly data on the money series are used. Friedman cited the Federal Reserve's reliance on an interest-rate instrument as the source of the 1959 decline in the money stock in Instructional Dynamics Economics Cassette Tape 52 (June 10, 1970). Note that the key point here is not that interest rates and monetary growth did not both register a tightening in the late 1950s. In fact, they both did so, and, as noted earlier in the chapter, interest rates and monetary growth did have an inverse relationship from the mid-1950s to the mid-1960s. But, by the same token, the two series did disagree in the late 1950s on the pace and degree of the monetary tightening.

244. For the later Friedman discussions of this issue, see, for example, Friedman (1973b; 1980a, 59 [p. 57 of 1991 reprint]; 1988a, 224). See also chapter 6 above, in which the relevance of the issue for the recent monetary policy research literature was stressed.

245. As the modern definition of M2 begins only in January 1959, it cannot be used in generating a velocity series for much of the period covered in figure 10.6.

246. As was noted in section II, Romer and Romer (2002a, 126) suggested that the steep tightening may have been motivated by an uptick in inflation forecasts. The analysis of

the late Julio Rotemberg (2013, 71) also pointed in this direction. Such behavior of inflation forecasts would help explain why short-term nominal interest rates were allowed to become so high in relation to *actual* inflation in 1959.

247. Instructional Dynamics Economics Cassette Tape 42 (January 15, 1970).

248. Instructional Dynamics Economics Cassette Tape 89 (December 26, 1971). Friedman also recalled the 1960 concerns in his letter to Burns of December 13, 1971, which is available in digitized form on the Federal Reserve Bank of St. Louis's FRASER website at https://fraser.stlouisfed.org/archival/?id=1193.

249. Nixon's book *Six Crises* credited Burns with accurately warning him of the recession danger. Nixon's (1962, 309–10) narrative, which did not mention Friedman, was the source for the accounts in Wells (1994, 18) and Matusow (1998, 18–19). The *Six Crises* account was earlier drawn on in Meigs's (1972, 27–28) and Blinder's (1979, 143–44) discussions of the 1960–61 recession, and Nixon's book may also have served as the basis for Paul Samuelson's reference to Burns's 1960 warning in *Newsweek*, November 21, 1977. Friedman himself referred to Burns's warning in Instructional Dynamics Economics Cassette Tape 88 (December 15, 1971).

250. Nixon recalled this in a January 28, 1972, letter to Burns, which is available in digitized form on the Federal Reserve Bank of St. Louis's FRASER website.

251. Friedman referred to this visit in general terms in Instructional Dynamics Economics Cassette Tape 42 (January 15, 1970), and he gave further details in Instructional Dynamics Economics Cassette Tape 89 (December 26, 1971).

252. Instructional Dynamics Economics Cassette Tape 89 (December 26, 1971).

253. From Friedman's 1966 letter in Board of Governors of the Federal Reserve System (1970, 60), referring to Friedman (1960a).

254. Friedman (1960a, 30–35).

255. Friedman and Schwartz (1963, 511–12); Friedman (1970a, 10; p. 4 of 1991 reprint).

256. Quoted in McKinley (1960, 99). Martin made this remark in the question-and-answer portion of his June 12, 1956, testimony in Subcommittee on Economic Stabilization (1956, 33).

257. Instructional Dynamics Economics Cassette Tape 89 (December 26, 1971). Friedman made a similar remark, to the effect that a superpenal discount rate would remove it as a source of variations in the monetary base, in Friedman (1962c, 29).

258. See, for example, Friedman (1982b, 117). As discussed in E. Nelson (2013a, 64–65), although his preference was to abolish discounting, Friedman often accepted that it would likely continue and made policy recommendations in that context. An example of this practice was provided by Friedman's (1955d) memorandum to the Federal Reserve Board, in which he conditioned his analysis on the continuation of discounting.

259. See, for example, Pecchenino and Rasche (1990).

260. Friedman would seem to have first used the M1 and M2 terms publicly in Friedman and Meiselman (1963). Earlier, Friedman and Meiselman had used the terms in a limited-circulation 1959 preliminary version of the work (discussed in chapter 12). R. G. Anderson and Kavajecz (1994, 4) cited Abbott (1960, 1962) as the first public use of the "M1" label in an official Federal Reserve publication. The first of these Abbott articles laid out monthly series for M1; Anderson and Kavajecz considered this "the first modern monetary aggregate based on averages of daily data." The Federal Reserve Board did not have an official M2 aggregate until 1971 (R. G. Anderson and Kavajecz 1994, 21).

Gregory Chow (in Pagan 1995, and in a July 1, 2013, interview for this book) observed that Friedman introduced the terms "M1" and "M2," seemingly off the cuff, in a money workshop presentation in 1953 (Gregory Chow, interview, July 1, 2013) or 1954 (Pagan 1995, 599). Chow (interview, July 1, 2013) recalled that many years later he suggested to Friedman that the M1 and M2 terms were due to Friedman. When Friedman expressed doubts about this attribution, Chow challenged him to find an earlier author using those terms. Friedman could not do so, and in 1977 he credited himself with coining the terms "M1" and "M2" (*Milton Friedman Speaks*, episode 6, "Money and Inflation," taped November 7, 1977, p. 22 of transcript). Around the same time, the Federal Reserve Board itself also credited Friedman with originating the terminology: see Wallich's (1977, 279) remarks.

Albert Hart (1948, 275) narrowly missed out on pioneering the terminology. Unfortunately, he used M2 to refer to the *narrower* aggregate, with M1 used to designate the broader total. It would seem that Friedman could claim, with Meiselman, to be the first to use in print the term "M2" for an aggregate that covered currency, demand deposits, and time deposits.

261. Friedman (1960c). In his public statements, too, Friedman criticized 1959 Federal Reserve monetary policy for being destabilizing. See, for example, his remarks in *Business Week*, May 6, 1961.

262. See the April 12, 1960, FOMC Minutes (Federal Open Market Committee 1960, 40).

263. Friedman and Schwartz (1963a, 619).

264. See Friedman's March 3, 1964, testimony, in Committee on Banking and Currency (1964, 1155).

265. From Friedman's remarks in *The American Economy, Lesson 48: Can We Have Full Employment without Inflation?*, CBS College of the Air, filmed circa June 5, 1962.

266. Friedman and Schwartz (1963a, 638).

267. See *Business Week*, July 16, 1960; and *New York Times*, June 20, 1960. Both these items were referred to in Dewald (1963).

268. Friedman and Schwartz (1963a, 638).

269. Benjamin Friedman (1980, 12) gave the real GNP decline in the recession as 1.2 percent. Modern real GDP data indicate a 1.3 percent decline in real output in the recession.

270. Friedman (1962c, 24). Similarly, in February 1, 1968, congressional testimony, Friedman stated that the expansion was "cut short in mid-passage" by the Federal Reserve's tightening (Committee on Banking and Currency, US Senate, 1968, 155). He expressed a similar view in Instructional Dynamics Economics Cassette Tape 85 (November 3, 1971).

271. Instructional Dynamics Economics Cassette Tape 42 (January 15, 1970). Friedman voiced the same sentiment in Instructional Dynamics Economics Cassette Tape 77 (June 30, 1971). Earlier, in Instructional Dynamics Economics Cassette Tape 6 (December 1968), Friedman cited the decline in M1 during 1960 as "one of the major reasons" for Kennedy's election victory.

Bibliography

This bibliography consists of two parts: a chronological listing of the media items (pieces in sound, television, newspaper, and magazine sources) that have been cited in this study, and a reference list, in alphabetical order, consisting of the research papers and books that have been cited.

I. Newspaper Articles, Periodical Articles, and Electronic Media Items Cited

Special to the *New York Times*. "Wins Logic Prize at Rutgers." *New York Times*, April 25, 1932, 17.

Special to the *New York Times*. "Four Women Named to Rutgers Board: Election by Trustees Is Made Possible by Revision of University Charter; Clothier Inaugural Today; Moore to Preside at Installation of President after Which 600 Degrees Will Be Conferred." *New York Times*, June 11, 1932, 16.

"Engineers' Income Tops Five Groups: Consultants' Average Leads That of Doctors, Dentists, Lawyers and Accountants." *New York Times*, February 5, 1939, 16.

AP. "'Pay-as-You-Go Tax' Brings U.S. Offer: Treasury Suggests Possible Modification of the Plan for Canceling '42 Income Levy." *New York Times*, August 20, 1942, 40.

"News of the Classes." *University of Chicago Magazine*, January 1946, 24–33.

Jeannette Lowrey. "News of the Quadrangles." *University of Chicago Magazine*, June 1946, 10–13.

Special to the *New York Times*. "Prof. H. C. Simons Dead: Chicago Economist Is Reported Victim of Sleeping Pills." *New York Times*, June 20, 1946, 25.

"Henry Calvert Simons." *University of Chicago Magazine*, July 1946, 16.

AP. "Lange Says Poland Shuns Lackey Role: Envoy Holds His Country Is Not Satellite of Any Country, but Needs Financial Credits." *New York Times*, August 18, 1946, 24.

Special to the *New York Times*."Statistics Urged as Liberal Study: Committee Would Teach It to All as Preparation for the Making of Decisions." *New York Times*, September 5, 1947, 21.

Aaron Director, Milton Friedman, Abram L. Harris, Frank H. Knight, H. Gregg Lewis, Lloyd W. Mints, Russell T. Nichols, and W. Allen Wallis. "Control of Prices: Regulation of Money Supply to Halt Inflation Advocated." *New York Times*, January 11, 1948, E8.

Editorial, "Prices." *Financial Times* (London), February 10, 1951, 4.

"An Important Opportunity!" (advertisement for new 3¼-percent-coupon 30-year Treasury bonds). *Ada Evening News* (OK), April 24, 1953, 12.

"Operational Economics." *Economist* (London), May 8, 1954, 450.

Gilbert Burck and Charles E. Silberman. "Why the Depression Lasted So Long." *Fortune* 51, no. 3 (March 1955): 84–88, 189–90, 192, 194, 196, 199, 200 and 202. (Reprinted in Mulcahy 1957, 88–94.)

P.E. "Some Shorter Notices: *John Maynard Keynes—Economist and Policy-Maker* by Seymour Harris." *Financial Times* (London), May 23, 1955, 10.

Don J. Lenhausen. "Inflation, Not Bust, Held Biggest Threat." *Sunday Journal-Star* (Peoria, IL), January 29, 1956, D-12.

"What's Wrong with the Top U.S. Economists. . . ." *Newsweek*, January 30, 1956, 78–79.

First National City Bank of New York Monthly Economic Newsletter, April 1956.

P.E. "Shorter Notices: *Introduction to Keynesian Dynamics* by Kenneth K. Kurihara." *Financial Times* (London), October 15, 1956, 10.

"The Boom-Bust Cycle: How Well Have We Got It Tamed?" *Business Week*, November 3, 1956, 176–88.

First National City Bank of New York Monthly Economic Newsletter, December 1956.

First National City Bank of New York Monthly Economic Newsletter, April 1957.

Lombard. "Banking and Finance: The Real Rate of Interest." *Financial Times* (London), June 6, 1957, 3.

"Unemployment and Wages." *Financial Times* (London), October 11, 1957, 3.

Milton Friedman appearance on *The Great Challenge: How Strong Is Our Economy?*, CBS television, March 23, 1958; transcript in Milton Friedman papers, box 44, folder 44, Hoover Institution archives.

First National City Bank Monthly Letter: Business and Economic Conditions, July 1958.

UPI. "Enterprise Risk: Economist Objects to Ike's Wage-Price Plea." *Austin American* (TX), July 22, 1958, A20.

AP. "McCollom Tells API 'Industry Must Improve.'" *Odessa American* (TX), November 11, 1958, 19.

Edith Kermit Roosevelt. "A Specialist on Theory of Earnings and Savings." *Newark Sunday News* (NJ), February 22, 1959, magazine section, 12–14.

Edith Kermit Roosevelt. "How Rich, How Poor Scale Doesn't Apply to Savings." *Cleveland News*, May 25, 1959, 2.

Paul A. Samuelson. "Why Has Wall Street Got the Jitters?" *Financial Times* (London), February 10, 1960a, 8 and 14.

Editorial, "U.S. Interest Rates." *Financial Times* (London), February 10, 1960b, 8.

Richard E. Mooney. "Reserve Puzzled by Money Decline." *New York Times*, June 20, 1960, 43.

"The Trend: Why Isn't Money Getting Easier?" *Business Week*, July 16, 1960, 148.

Richard Hammer. "Will Trading Stamps Stick?" *Fortune*, August 1960, 116–19. (Reprinted in R. Clifton Andersen and Philip R. Cateora, eds., *Marketing Insights: Selected Readings.* New York: Appleton-Century-Crofts, 1963. 343–55.)

"Interview: Money 'Stayed Tight Too Long.'" An interview (pp. 62–63) with Allen Wallis appearing as part of "Interviews with Leading Experts On: What Caused Today's Recession? What Comes Next?" *U.S. News and World Report*, February 13, 1961, 60–66.

"How Goes the Recession?" *Time*, March 3, 1961, 12.

Debate between Milton Friedman and Senator Joseph S. Clark (D-PA). "The Role of Government in Our Society." US Chamber of Commerce, Washington, DC, May 3, 1961. (Audiotape of debate held in Hoover Institution archives; information on date, title, and location of debate available in worldcat.org and in coverage of the debate in afternoon editions of newspapers: UPI, "CoC Reviews Code of Ethics." *Philadelphia*

Inquirer, May 3, 1961; AP, "U.S. CoC Boos Clark: 'Grow Up,' He Retorts." *Philadelphia Evening Bulletin*, May 3, 1961; and AP, "CoC Delegates Boo Democratic Senator's Speech." *Racine Journal-Times* [WI], May 3, 1961, 1. A next-day report also appeared as AP, "U.S. Chamber Group Raps Kennedy Plan, Boos Senator." *Abilene Reporter-News* [TX], May 4, 1961, 12-B.)

"What Chronic Slack?" *Business Week*, May 6, 1961, 112–13 and 116.

"Debate over Controls Begins." *Business Week*, September 30, 1961, 84–86 and 90–94.

Milton Friedman. "An Alternative to Aid: An Economist Urges U.S. to Free Trade, End Grants of Money." *Wall Street Journal*, April 30, 1962, 12.

Milton Friedman appearance on *The American Economy, Lesson 41: How Important Is Money?*, presented by Learning Resource Institute, cosponsored by American Economic Association and Joint Council on Economic Education; filmed for CBS College of the Air on June 4, 1962; broadcast on November 19, 1962.

Milton Friedman and Paul A. Samuelson appearance on *The American Economy, Lesson 48: Can We Have Full Employment without Inflation?*, presented by Learning Resource Institute, cosponsored by American Economic Association and Joint Council on Economic Education; filmed for CBS College of the Air, circa June 5, 1962; broadcast on November 30, 1962.

Lex. "A Prosperous New Year? Equities v. Gilts for 1963." *Financial Times* (London), December 29, 1962, 1.

First National City Bank of New York Monthly Economic Letter, February 1963.

"Theorizing for Goldwater?" *Business Week*, November 23, 1963, 106 and 108.

"Speaker Cites Government as Consumer Injury Cause." *Gazette-Telegraph* (Colorado Springs), December 18, 1963, 11.

Chesly Many. "U.C. Economic Experts Advise Goldwater: Many to Aid Campaign of Conservative." *Chicago Tribune*, April 12, 1964, 8.

Emerson P. Schmidt. "Massive Evidence." *Business Week*, January 11, 1964, 6.

Albert L. Kraus. "Economist Is Foe of U.S. Controls: Views of Chicago Educator Admired by Goldwater." *New York Times*, July 26, 1964, F1 and F13.

Milton Friedman. "The Goldwater View of Economics." *New York Times* (*New York Times Magazine* section), October 11, 1964, 35 and 133–37.

Paul A. Samuelson. "The New Economics in the U.S. Faces Some Old Problems." *Financial Times* (London), December 31, 1965, 9.

"The Slippery Path of Prosperity." *Business Week*, January 1, 1966, 70–73. (Reprinted in N. Marshall 1970, 104–9.)

Milton Friedman. "Friedman and Keynes." *Time*, February 4, 1966, 13.

Sylvia Porter. "Your Money's Worth: When Does Inflation Start to Hurt?" *Detroit Free Press*, February 24, 1966, 13B.

Milton Friedman and Leon Keyserling appearance on *The Great Society: The Sizzling Economy*, NET (National Educational Television), June 27, 1966.

Milton Friedman. "Why Does the Free Market Have Such a Bad Press?" *Human Events*, July 2, 1966, 8 and 14.

Milton Friedman. "Inflationary Recession." *Newsweek*, October 17, 1966, 92.

Milton Friedman. "Friedman on U.S. Monetary and Fiscal Policy." *Banker* (London) 117, no. 491 (January 1967): 68–70.

Milton Friedman. "Myths That Keep People Hungry." *Harper's Magazine*, April 1967, 16–24.

Karl Brunner and Allan H. Meltzer. "Tobin Article Challenged." *Washington Post*, April 30, 1967, C6.

"Outgrowing the Business Cycle." *Business Week*, May 6, 1967, 119–20.

John Davenport. "The Radical Economics of Milton Friedman." *Fortune*, June 1, 1967, 131–32, 147–48, 150, and 154.

Paul A. Samuelson. "American Pause and Revival." *Financial Times* (London), June 14, 1967, 17.

Milton Friedman. "Current Monetary Policy." *Newsweek*, October 30, 1967, 80.

Milton Friedman. "Taxes, Money and Stabilization." *Washington Post*, November 5, 1967, H1 and H3.

Milton Friedman appearance on *Firing Line*, syndicated, episode "The Economic Crisis," January 8, 1968; transcript available on Hoover Institution website.

Gerald R. Rosen. "Has the New Economics Failed? An Interview with Milton Friedman." *Dun's Review*, February 1968, 38–39, 92–94, and 96.

Milton Friedman. "The Gold Requirement." *Newsweek*, February 19, 1968, 78.

Milton Friedman appearance on National Educational Television's *Great Decisions 1968 #7: The Dollar in Danger*, broadcast Washington, DC, March 17, 1968, WETA/channel 26; transcript.

Milton Friedman. "Monetary Policy." *Newsweek*, June 3, 1968, 85.

Louis Dombrowski. "Ask Money Supply Equal to Growth Rate." *Chicago Tribune*, July 5, 1968, C8.

Milton Friedman. "Customers Go Home." *Newsweek*, August 26, 1968, 75.

Milton Friedman. "Negative Income Tax—I." *Newsweek*, September 16, 1968, 86.

Instructional Dynamics Economics Cassettes (audiotaped series of commentaries by Friedman), various dates October 1968–December 1978. Most tapes available in digitized form on Hoover Institution website.

Instructional Dynamics Economics Cassettes (Paul Samuelson series) (audiotaped series of commentaries by Paul A. Samuelson), various dates October 1968–October 1977.

Milton Friedman. "Because or Despite?" *Newsweek*, October 28, 1968, 104.

"Friedman's Hard Line: U.S. Controls over Business Challenged by Nixon Adviser." *St. Louis Post-Dispatch*, November 11, 1968, 5B.

Milton Friedman. "After the New Economics." *Newsweek*, December 9, 1968, 83.

UPI. "Interest Rate Hits New High." *Beaver County Times* (PA), January 8, 1969, A1 and A4.

"The New Attack on Keynesian Economics." *Time*, January 10, 1969, 64–65.

"Inflation Crackdown Begins: 'Trying to Slow the Economy'; Exclusive Interview with George W. Mitchell, Member, Federal Reserve Board." *U.S. News and World Report*, January 20, 1969, 25–28.

Milton Friedman appearance on *Speaking Freely*, NBC television (WNBC, New York), taped April 4, 1969, broadcast May 4, 1969; WNBC transcript.

Milton Friedman. "Invisible Occupation." *Newsweek*, May 5, 1969, 94.

Milton Friedman and Paul A. Samuelson appearance on *The Great Economics Debate*, WGBH Boston, May 22, 1969 (listed in "TV Highlights Today," *Boston Globe*, May 22, 1969, 61). (This was a live transmission of the Friedman/Samuelson seminar dialogue "Old, New, and Correct Economics," in the Karl Compton Lecture Series, Kresge Auditorium, Massachusetts Institute of Technology.)

Laurence Harris. "The Chicago School of Thought." *Bankers' Magazine* 28, no. 7 (July 1969): 5–11.

Milton Friedman. "Monetary Overkill." *Newsweek*, August 18, 1969, 75.

Alfred L. Malabre Jr. "Influential Economist: Milton Friedman's Ideas Gain Wider Acceptance among Policy-Makers." *Wall Street Journal*, November 4, 1969, 1 and 15.

"'Through the Windshield:' Nixon Adviser Warns of Severe Recession." *Phoenix Gazette* (AZ), November 24, 1969, 26.

Milton Friedman. "How to Free TV." *Newsweek*, December 1, 1969, 82.

Roy F. Harrod. "Keynes: The Arrested Revolution." *New Statesman* (London) 78, no. 2021 (December 5, 1969): 808–10.

"The Intellectual Provocateur." *Time*, December 19, 1969, 71.

Milton Viorst. "Friedmanism, n[oun]. Doctrine of Most Audacious U.S. Economist, Esp. Theory 'Only Money Matters.'" *New York Times* (*New York Times Magazine* section), January 25, 1970, 22–23, 80 and 82–84.

Milton Friedman. "A New Chairman at the Fed." *Newsweek*, February 2, 1970, 68.

Peter Malken. "Hysterics Won't Clean Up Pollution: Economist Milton Friedman Appraises an Old Problem and the Cost of Solving It." *Chicago Tribune*, magazine section, April 12, 1970, 66–67, 69, 71–72, 77, 80, and 82.

Milton Friedman appearance on *NET Journal Presents Conservative Viewpoint*, PBS, May 4, 1970.

Milton Friedman. "Burns and Guidelines." *Newsweek*, June 15, 1970, 86.

Milton Friedman appearance on *Meet the Press*, NBC, June 28, 1970; NBC transcript.

Rob Warden. "What Really Causes Inflation? Milton Friedman, Top White House Adviser, Puts the Blame on Washington and Nowhere Else." *Chicago Daily News*, July 29, 1970, 3–4.

"Miscellany: Freedom Fighter." *Guardian* (London and Manchester, UK), September 17, 1970, 19.

Malcolm Crawford. "Milton Friedman on the Only Way to Halt Inflation." *Sunday Times* (London), September 20, 1970, 54.

Milton Friedman. "Inflation and Wages." *Newsweek*, September 28, 1970, 77.

Milton Friedman. "Paul Samuelson." *Newsweek*, November 9, 1970, 80.

Paul A. Samuelson. "Milton Friedman Is Wrong—So Wrong." *Sunday Telegraph* (London), January 24, 1971, 19–20.

Henry C. Murphy. "Fiscal Policy: Guardian of the Economy." *South China Morning Post* (Hong Kong), January 29, 1971, "Banking and Finance" section, 1 and 10.

Milton Friedman. "Money—Tight or Easy?" *Newsweek*, March 1, 1971, 80.

Milton Friedman. "Which Crystal Ball?" *Newsweek*, July 5, 1971, 62.

Milton Friedman. "Why the Freeze Is a Mistake." *Newsweek*, August 30, 1971, 22–23.

Milton Friedman. "Will the Kettle Explode?" *Newsweek*, October 18, 1971, 30.

Milton Friedman. "First Readings on the New Game Plan." *Newsweek*, November 8, 1971, 100.

Milton Friedman. "Inflation and How to Control It." *New York Times*, November 24, 1971, 34.

Milton Friedman appearance on *Firing Line*, PBS, episode "American Conservatives Confront 1972," PBS, taped January 5, 1972, broadcast January 7, 1972; PBS transcript, available on Hoover Institution website.

Milton Friedman, Paul A. Samuelson, and Henry C. Wallich. "Three Views of Nixonomics and Where It Leads [panel Q&A]." *Newsweek*, January 31, 1972, 74–75.

Milton Friedman. "The Case for a Monetary Rule." *Newsweek*, February 7, 1972, 67.

John McClaughry. "Milton Friedman Responds: A *Business and Society Review* Interview." *Business and Society Review* 1, no. 1 (Spring 1972): 5–16. (Excerpted in Friedman 1975e, 240–56.)

Paul A. Samuelson. "Frank Knight, 1885–1972." *Newsweek*, July 31, 1972, 55.

Milton Friedman. "The Fed on the Spot." *Newsweek*, October 16, 1972, 98.

"Friedman: Budget Deficit May Upset Money Policy." *National Journal*, January 13, 1973, 57.

Michael Laurence and Geoffrey Norman. "*Playboy* Interview: Milton Friedman—a Candid Conversation in Which the Maverick Economist Advocates the Abolition of Welfare, Social Security and the Graduated Income Tax." *Playboy* 28, no. 2 (February 1973): 51–54, 56, 58–60, 62, 64, 66, 68 and 74. (Reprinted in Friedman 1975e, 1–38, and Friedman 1983b, 9–59.)

Milton Friedman. "A Frightening Parallel." *Newsweek*, August 6, 1973, 70.

Milton Friedman. "Public Spending and Inflation." *The Times* (London), August 29, 1973, 15.

Milton Friedman. "The Voucher Idea." *New York Times* (*New York Times Magazine* section), September 23, 1973, 22–23, 65, 67, and 69–72. (Reprinted in Friedman 1975e, 270–84.)

Frederick C. Klein. "A New Discipline: Chicago Business School Shuns the Case Method and Comes into Its Own." *Wall Street Journal*, October 30, 1973, 1 and 30.

Milton Friedman. "Why Now?" *Newsweek*, December 31, 1973, 29.

Long-Term Solutions to the Energy Crisis (symposium of Morris A. Adelman, Milton Friedman, and William Nordhaus at the National Conference on Government Response to the Energy Crisis), Washington, DC, January 24, 1974; audiotape.

John Vaizey. "Whatever Happened to Equality?—5. Equality and Income [Interview with Milton Friedman]." *Listener* (London), May 30, 1974, 688–90.

Milton Friedman. "Perspective on Inflation." *Newsweek*, June 24, 1974, 73.

Milton Friedman appearance on *Newsday* (BBC2 television program), September 20, 1974.

Milton Friedman. "Inflation Prospects." *Newsweek*, November 4, 1974, 84.

Tibor Machan, Joe Cobb, and Ralph Raico. "An Interview with Milton Friedman." *Reason*, December 1974, 4 and 7–14.

Dennis V. Waite. "A Monetarist Talks Tough on Recession." *Philadelphia Sunday Bulletin*, March 2, 1975, 25.

Milton Friedman appearance on *Monday Conference*, ABC Television (Australia), April 14, 1975; ABC Television (Australia) transcript.

Milton Friedman. "Two Economic Fallacies." *Newsweek*, May 12, 1975, 83.

Paul A. Samuelson. "Alvin H. Hansen, 1887–1975." *Newsweek*, June 16, 1975, 72.

Milton Friedman. "Subsidizing OPEC Oil." *Newsweek*, June 23, 1975, 75.

Milton Friedman. "Six Fallacies." *Wall Street Journal*, June 30, 1975, 11.

Milton Friedman. "Five Examples of Fed Double-Talk." *Wall Street Journal*, August 21, 1975, 6.

Tom Oliver. "Ingrid Bergman: In Search of a Good Movie." *Photoplay Film Monthly* (UK) 26, no. 9 (September 1975): 20–21 and 51.

Milton Friedman appearance on *Donahue*, NBC, September 30, 1975.

Theodore Kurrus. "*Laissez Faire*: Friedman against Government Control." *Dallas Morning News*, October 17, 1975, 13B.

Milton Friedman appearance on *The Open Mind*, PBS, December 7, 1975; transcript.

Milton Friedman. "How to Hit the Money Target." *Newsweek*, December 8, 1975, 85.

"In His Own Words: Economist Milton Friedman Calls the Income Tax 'an Unholy Mess' and Wants to Reform It." *People Weekly*, April 5, 1976, 49–52.

Milton Friedman appearance on *The Jay Interview* (hosted by Peter Jay), ITN, videotaped May 11, 1976; UK broadcast date July 17, 1976.

Lindley H. Clark, "Speaking of Business: The Skeptic." *Wall Street Journal*, August 23, 1976, 8.

"Economists Are Schizophrenic, Friedman Says." *Times Higher Education Supplement* (London), September 3, 1976, 20.

David Sinclair. "Inflation: 'The Tax That Never Has to Be Passed by Parliament.'" *Times* (London), September 13, 1976, 7.

Milton Friedman. "Money and Inflation." *Newsweek*, September 20, 1976, 77.

Christopher Fildes. "City Notebook—the Toast Is: Absent Chancellors." *Investor's Chronicle* (London), October 1, 1976, 16–17.

James Tobin. "The Nobel Milton." *Economist* (London), October 23, 1976a, 94–95.

Harry G. Johnson. "The Nobel Milton." *Economist* (London), October 23, 1976b, 95.

Milton Friedman appearance on *Meet the Press*, NBC, October 24, 1976; NBC transcript.

"Medal for a Monetarist." *Time*, October 25, 1976, 58.

Paul A. Samuelson. "Milton Friedman." *Newsweek*, October 25, 1976a, 89 (41 of UK edition). (Reprinted in Samuelson 1983a, 130–32).

Larry Martz. "A Nobel for Friedman." *Newsweek*, October 25, 1976b, 86 and 89 (40–41 of UK edition).

James Eisener. "Sorry He Spoke Out? Not Milton Friedman." *Chicago Tribune*, November 28, 1976, A17.

Milton Friedman. "To Jimmy from James." *Newsweek*, December 6, 1976, 87.

Milton Friedman. "How to Denationalize." *Newsweek*, December 27, 1976, 54.

Milton Friedman. "An Open Reply from Milton Friedman." *Financial Times* (London), January 6, 1977, 17.

Milton Friedman. "Steady as You Go." *Newsweek*, January 10, 1977, 58–59.

Milton Friedman appearance on *Dinah!* (Dinah Shore talk show), broadcast March 30, 1977. Clip of appearance available on *Free to Choose* website; recording of full appearance purchased from Hoover Institution.

Milton Friedman. "Tax Gimmickry at Its Finest." *Newsweek*, April 11, 1977, 90.

Fred Kutchins. "Leaning against Next Year's Wind" (interview with Milton Friedman), *Saturday Evening Post* (New York), May/June 1977, 16 and 18–20.

Milton Friedman. "Monetary Policy and the Inflation Rate." *The Times* (London), May 2, 1977, 13.

Milton Friedman. "When Is a Tax Cut Not a Tax Cut?" *Newsweek*, May 17, 1977, 72.

"Letters Follow-Up: An Exchange among Nobel Laureates [on] Milton Friedman, the Chilean Junta and the Matter of Their Association" (with contributions from Milton Friedman, David Baltimore, and S. E. Luria). *New York Times*, May 22, 1977, sec. 4, p. 18.

Friedman appearance on *The Open Mind*, episode titled "A Nobel Laureate on the American Economy," PBS, May 31, 1977; transcript.

"*Reason* Interview: Milton Friedman." *Reason*, August 1977, 24–29.

Milton Friedman. "Israel's Other War." *Newsweek*, August 22, 1977, 57.

Milton Friedman Speaks, episode 12, "Who Protects the Consumer?," taped September 12, 1977.

Milton Friedman Speaks, episode 11, "Putting Learning Back in the Classroom," taped September 15, 1977.

Milton Friedman Speaks, episode 3, "Is Capitalism Humane?," taped September 27, 1977.

Milton Friedman Speaks, episode 13, "Who Protects the Worker?," taped September 29, 1977.

Milton Friedman. "Why Inflation Persists." *Newsweek*, October 3, 1977, 54.

Milton Friedman Speaks, episode 1, "What Is America?," taped October 3, 1977.

Milton Friedman Speaks, episode 2, "Myths That Conceal Reality," taped October 13, 1977.

Celeste Durante. "John Wayne, Two Winners of Nobel Prize Honored." *Los Angeles Times*, November 7, 1977, C1.

Milton Friedman Speaks, episode 6, "Money and Inflation," taped November 7, 1977.

AP wire photo. *Irish Times* (Dublin), November 9, 1977, 9.

Paul A. Samuelson. "Reappoint Burns?" *Newsweek*, November 21, 1977, 81.

Hugh Sidey. "The Importance of Being Arthur." *Time*, December 26, 1977.

Peter Lilley. "Keynes' *General Theory*." *Listener* (London), January 5, 1978, 21.

Milton Friedman. "Burns on the Outside." *Newsweek*, January 9, 1978, 52–53.

Thomas Balogh. "The Ghost of Montagu Norman Is in Business." *Sunday Times* (London), January 22, 1978, 62.

Milton Friedman Speaks, episode 7, "Is Tax Reform Possible?," taped February 6, 1978.

Milton Friedman Speaks, episode 9, "The Energy Crisis: A Humane Solution," taped February 10, 1978.

Milton Friedman Speaks, episode 15, "The Future of Our Free Society," taped February 21, 1978.

Milton Friedman Speaks, episode 5, "What Is Wrong with the Welfare State?," taped February 23, 1978.

Milton Friedman. "Inflationary Recession." *Newsweek*, April 24, 1978, 81.

Milton Friedman Speaks, episode 8, "Free Trade: Producer vs. Consumer," taped April 27, 1978.

Milton Friedman Speaks, episode 10, "The Economics of Medical Care," taped May 19, 1978.

Milton Friedman and Paul A. Samuelson. "Answering the Big Questions [panel Q&A]." *Newsweek*, May 29, 1978, 80–81.

Milton Friedman, letter to Representative Dawson Mathis of June 8, 1978, published in *Congressional Record* 124, July 18, 1978, 21530–31.

Milton Friedman. "Inertia and the Fed." *Newsweek*, July 24, 1978, 70.

Robert Edward Brown. "Profile: Milton Friedman." *Human Behavior* 7, no. 11 (November 1978): 28–33.

Milton Friedman appearance on *Meet the Press*, NBC, November 12, 1978; NBC transcript.

Milton Friedman. "Borrowing Marks." *Newsweek*, January 8, 1979, 56.

John Burton. "There Will Have to Be Changes—VI: The Unions Must Be Brought Back within the Law." *Daily Telegraph* (London), February 12, 1979, 14.

Harry Farrell. "Who Gains from Inflation? The Politicians, Says Milton Friedman." *San Jose Mercury News*, February 12, 1979, 7B.

Henry Farrell. "Friedman's Choice: Inflation with Recession or Recession Without." *San Jose Mercury News*, February 13, 1979, 7B.

Mervyn A. King. "Reality: A Charter for Avoidance." *New Statesman* (London), April 13, 1979, 505–8.

Rich Thomas. "A Talk with Arthur Burns." *Newsweek*, May 14, 1979, 90.

Vivian Gray. "Milton Friedman Speaks Out: An Exclusive *Expo* Interview with America's Best-Known Economist." *Expo: The Contemporary Jewish Magazine* 1, no. 3 (Summer 1979): 16–20 and 112.

Patrick Minford. "A Return to Sound Money." *Banker* 129, no. 641 (July 1979): 29–31.

Otto Eckstein. "Value of Econometric Models." *Wall Street Journal*, August 27, 1979, 14.

Milton Friedman appearance on *Donahue*, NBC, September 6, 1979 (Chicago broadcast date; the syndication broadcast date was October 10, 1979). A videotape including this episode was released commercially in 1994–96 as *Interviewing the Great Minds of America*. Also available on YouTube.

Milton Friedman. "Inflation and Jobs." *Newsweek*, November 12, 1979, 97.

Free to Choose (US television version), PBS, episode 1, "The Power of the Market," broadcast dates in US areas included January 12, 1980; transcript available online on *Free to Choose* website.

Free to Choose (US television version), PBS, episode 2, "The Tyranny of Control," broadcast dates in US areas included January 19, 1980; transcript available online on *Free to Choose* website.

Free to Choose (US television version), PBS, episode 3, "Anatomy of a Crisis," broadcast dates in US areas included January 29, 1980; transcript available online on *Free to Choose* website.

Free to Choose (US television version), PBS, episode 5, "Created Equal," broadcast dates in US areas included February 15, 1980; transcript available online on *Free to Choose* website.

Anthony Holden. "The Free Market Man." *Observer* (London), February 17, 1980, 33 and 35.

Free to Choose (UK television version, debate portion), BBC2, episode "From Cradle to Grave," broadcast March 1, 1980; BBC transcript.

Milton Friedman. "Monetarism: A Reply to the Critics." *The Times* (London), March 3, 1980, 19.

Philip Corrigan. "'Free to Choose?'" *Listener* (London), March 6, 1980, 307.

Free to Choose (UK television version, debate portion), BBC2, episode "Created Equal," March 8, 1980; BBC transcript.

Milton Friedman. "Things That Ain't So." *Newsweek*, March 10, 1980, 79.

Free to Choose (UK television version, debate portion), BBC2, episode "How to Cure Inflation," broadcast March 22, 1980; BBC transcript.

Kenneth J. Arrow. "*Free to Choose* by Milton and Rose Friedman." *New Republic*, March 22, 1980, 25–28.

Milton Friedman. "The Case for Free Trade." *Listener* (London), March 27, 1980, 393–94.

Milton Friedman. "The Myth of Equality." *Listener* (London), April 10, 1980, 457–58.

Milton Friedman appearance on *Donahue*, NBC, April 16, 1980 (Chicago broadcast date; New York broadcast date April 18, 1980). Available on YouTube.

Milton Friedman. "The Corporate Clout." *Newsweek*, May 5, 1980, 82.

Peter T. Maiken. "Milton Friedman—the Free-Market Monetarist Thrives in a New Locale." *Chicago Tribune*, July 20, 1980, magazine setion, 20–24.

Brian Vine. "Yes, It *Will* Work If Maggie Doesn't Waver: Verdict on the Tory Strategy So

Far—by the Economist Who Virtually Invented It." *Daily Express* (London), August 6, 1980, 8.

Milton Friedman. "A Simple Tax Reform." *Newsweek*, August 18, 1980, 68.

Tom James. "Friedman Scolds Treasury 'Failure.'" *Scotsman* (Edinburgh), October 20, 1980, 1.

Milton Friedman. "A Biased Double Standard." *Newsweek*, January 12, 1981, 68.

Milton Friedman. "A Memorandum to the Fed." *Wall Street Journal*, January 30, 1981, 20.

Milton Friedman. "Deficits and Inflation." *Newsweek*, February 23, 1981, 70.

Milton Friedman. "Autos and Import Curbs." *Newsweek*, March 16, 1981, 84.

Milton Friedman. "An Open Letter on Grants." *Newsweek*, May 18, 1981, 99.

John Curley. "MBA Students Learn the Cost of Education." *Wall Street Journal*, May 18, 1981, 29 and 36.

Milton Friedman. "Regulatory Schizophrenia." *Newsweek*, June 29, 1981, 65.

Milton Friedman. "Closet Keynesianism." *Newsweek*, July 27, 1981, 60.

Patrick Bedard. "Someone Doesn't Want You to Have the Car of Your Dreams, and It Isn't the United States Government." *Car and Driver* 27, no. 3 (September 1981): 79–83.

Milton Friedman. "Reaganomics and Interest Rates." *Newsweek*, September 21, 1981, 39.

Lester C. Thurow. "A Disastrous Recession?" *Newsweek*, November 16, 1981, 88.

"Exclusive Interview: Milton Friedman on Reaganomics." *Human Events* 51, no. 49 (December 5, 1981): 1 and 6–9.

Milton Friedman. "The Yo-Yo Economy." *Newsweek*, February 15, 1982, 72.

Milton Friedman. "Tax, Tax; Spend, Spend." *Newsweek*, May 31, 1982, 63.

Scott M. Sedam. "Engineering: Next in Line for Productivity Push?" *Professional Engineer* 52, no. 2 (June 1982): 8–11.

Milton Friedman. "Defining 'Monetarism.'" *Newsweek*, July 12, 1982, 64.

Iain Fraser Grigor. "Unrepentant at 70—Monetarism's High Priest." *Glasgow Herald* (Scotland), July 30, 1982, 8.

Milton Friedman. "An Aborted Recovery?" *Newsweek*, August 23, 1982, 59.

Peter Brimelow. "Talking Money with Milton Friedman: He Isn't Particularly Bullish on the Fed or Interest Rates." *Barrons*, October 25, 1982, 6–7.

Family Ties, season 1, episode "Summer of '82," NBC, US broadcast date October 27, 1982.

Milton Friedman. "The Wayward Money Supply." *Newsweek*, December 27, 1982, 58.

Milton Friedman. "Some Pet Peeves." *Newsweek*, January 17, 1983, 58.

Milton Friedman. "Washington: Less Red Ink." *Atlantic*, February 1983, 18, 20–24, and 26.

Milton Friedman appearance on *Saturday Briefing*, BBC2, March 12, 1983; BBC transcript.

Sidney Blumenthal. "Economic Navigator for the Right." *Boston Globe* (magazine section), April 3, 1983, 10, 11, 20–21, 24–25, 40, and 42–43.

Milton Friedman. "High Taxes, Low Security." *Newsweek*, April 18, 1983, 64.

Milton Friedman. "The Keynes Centenary: A Monetarist Reflects." *Economist* (London), June 4, 1983, 17–19 of US edition; 35–37 of London edition.

Tim Congdon. "Has Friedman Got It Wrong?" *Banker* (London) 133, no. 689 (July 1983): 117–25.

Milton Friedman. "Why a Surge of Inflation Is Likely Next Year." *Wall Street Journal*, September 1, 1983, 24.

"Correction." *Wall Street Journal*, September 7, 1983, 30.

Tyranny of the Status Quo television program, episode 3, "Politicians," US broadcast dates including March 28, 1984, on channel 16 in Pennsylvania (as given in "Today's Television Listings." *Beaver County Times* [PA], March 28, 1984, B8).

Milton Friedman. "Inflation Isn't Beaten." *New York Times*, April 3, 1984, A31.

Milton Friedman appearance on *Donahue*, NBC, April 25, 1984 (Chicago broadcast date; New York broadcast date April 29, 1984).

Milton Friedman. "The Taxes Called Deficits." *Wall Street Journal*, April 26, 1984, 28.

Milton Friedman. "Monetarist Can Be a Supply-Sider, Too." *Wall Street Journal*, August 31, 1984, 13.

Ken Kelley. "The Interview: Outspoken Economists Milton and Rose Friedman." *California*, October 1984, 70–79 and 160–64.

"Schools Brief: Beefing Up Demand." *Economist*, October 27, 1984, 70–71 of US edition; 42–43 of London edition.

Lindley H. Clark Jr. and Laurie McGinley. "Money's Role: Monetarists Succeed in Pushing Basic Ideas but Not Their Policies." *Wall Street Journal*, December 10, 1984, 1 and 16.

Nicholas Kaldor. "The Views of Keynes." *Financial Times* (London), June 3, 1985, 15.

"*The Margin* Interview: Milton Friedman." *Margin*, January 1986, 3–5.

Milton Friedman. "Homer Jones, a Reminiscence." *New York Times*, March 23, 1986, F13.

Milton Friedman appearance on *Firing Line*, PBS, episode "Resolved: We Should Move toward Privatization, Including the Schools," taped April 10, 1986; PBS transcript, available on Hoover Institution website.

Mike Robinson. "Milton Friedman Reprises Monetarist Views, Discusses Cause and Effect of His Nobel Prize." *American Banker*, April 30, 1986, 20 and 23.

James Srodes. "The New Galbraith." *Daily Telegraph* (London), June 30, 1986, 17.

Jonathan Peterson. "The Captain of Capitalism: Even as Milton Friedman's Theories Have Gone Out of Vogue in Washington, His Ideas Have Come to Shape the Way Nations Manage Their Money." *Los Angeles Times* (*Los Angeles Times Magazine* section), December 14, 1986, 12–18 and 54. (Also appeared as Jonathan Peterson, "Defining Friedman Takes a Lifetime." *San Francisco Chronicle*, December 26, 1986, 39; and Jonathan Peterson, "Now, the Friedman Revival." *Sydney Morning Herald*, December 27, 1986, 27.)

Idea Channel. *Milton Friedman*. Videotaped interview, 1987.

Benjamin Stein and Victoria A. Sackett. "The 25 Most Important Americans." *Penthouse*, January 1987.

Milton Friedman. "Monetary History, Not Dogma." *Wall Street Journal*, February 12, 1987, 24.

Milton Friedman appearance on *Nightline*, ABC, March 17, 1987, show 1516 ("Semiconductors: Japanese Hegemony?"); ABC transcript.

Milton Friedman. "Ice-Cream Cone Challenge Scooped Up." *Wall Street Journal*, July 2, 1987, 19.

Milton Friedman appearance on *Nightline*, ABC, show 1685 ("A National Town Meeting on Wall Street and the Economy"), November 6, 1987; ABC transcript.

Daniel Doron. "Part Five of an Interview with Milton Friedman: 'Is the Private Sector Really Privatized?'" *Jerusalem Post*, November 11, 1987, 8.

John Maynard Keynes: Life, Ideas, Legacy. Institute of Economic Affairs (London) video documentary, 1988.

Samuel Brittan. "Money Supply: Anchors Past and Present." *Financial Times* (London), February 15, 1988, 41–42 of centennial supplementary section.

Milton Friedman. "Floating Rates vs. Monetary Standard." *Wall Street Journal*, March 4, 1988, 29.

Milton Friedman. "The Fed Has No Clothes." *Wall Street Journal*, April 15, 1988, 28.

Peter Brimelow. "Why Liberalism Is Now Obsolete [interview with Milton Friedman]." *Forbes*, December 12, 1988, 161–65, 168, 170, 174, and 176.

Milton Friedman. "What Is the 'Right' Amount of Saving?" *National Review*, June 16, 1989a, 25–26.

Robert M. Solow. "What Is the 'Right' Amount of Saving? [Discussion]." *National Review*, June 16, 1989b, 27–28.

Milton Friedman. "Whither Inflation?" *Wall Street Journal*, July 5, 1989, A10.

Milton Friedman. "The Fed, a Bastion of Inflation." *Wall Street Journal*, November 17, 1989, A15.

Milton Friedman appearance on *This Week with David Brinkley*, ABC, December 17, 1989; ABC transcript.

Milton Friedman. "Fed's Arsenal Has Only One Big Gun." *Wall Street Journal*, April 5, 1990, A19.

Warren T. Brookes. "The Gospel According to Knut Wicksell." *Forbes*, July 9, 1990, 66–69.

Milton Friedman and Paul A. Samuelson appearance on *MacNeil/Lehrer NewsHour*, PBS, August 27, 1990; PBS transcript.

Milton Friedman appearance on *Firing Line*, PBS, December 13, 1990; PBS transcript available on Hoover Institution website.

Milton Friedman. "In Eastern Europe: The People vs. the Socialist Elite." *Wall Street Journal*, January 8, 1991, A14.

Milton Friedman and Paul A. Samuelson appearance on *Wall Street Week with Louis Rukeyser*, PBS, episode 2134, "Two Nobel Economists." February 21, 1992; Maryland Public Television transcript.

John Lichfield. "Interview—Freedom's Demon King: Milton Friedman." *Independent on Sunday* (London), July 26, 1992, 23.

Milton Friedman appearance, May 6, 1993, at House Republican Conference Task Force on the Economy, Washington, DC. Broadcast on CSPAN, May 7, 1993, and released as a videotape by CSPAN educational video. Also viewable on CSPAN website.

Timothy Devinney. "Why the Jobless Will Wake in Fright." *Sydney Morning Herald*, August 12, 1993, 13.

Paul Sheehan. "Friedman's Fundamentals." *Australian Business Monthly*, October 1993, 52–55.

Milton Friedman and Anna J. Schwartz. "A Tale of Fed Transcripts." *Wall Street Journal*, December 20, 1993, A12.

Interview with Milton Friedman conducted by Brian Lamb for *Booknotes*, CSPAN, November 20, 1994. Transcript available on CSPAN website; transcript was also issued in hard-copy form by CSPAN in 1994.

Amanda Bennett. "Business and Academia Clash over a Concept: 'Natural' Jobless Rate." *Wall Street Journal*, January 24, 1995, A1 and A8.

Brian Doherty. "Best of Both Worlds: Interview with Milton Friedman." *Reason*, June 1995, 32–38.

Milton Friedman. "Taxing Battle." *Reason*, November 1995, 10.

Peter Robinson. "Rose and Milton Friedman: Our Early Years—Interview." *Hoover Digest*, no. 2 (1996): 126-35.

Milton Friedman appearance, April 18, 1996, at Claremont McKenna College, broadcast on CSPAN on December 26, 1996; viewable on CSPAN website.

Milton Friedman talk, November 21, 1996, at Indiana University, broadcast on CSPAN on December 1, 1996; viewable on CSPAN website.

Peter Brimelow. "Milton Friedman at 85." *Forbes*, December 29, 1997, 52-55.

Robert J. Samuelson. "The Age of Friedman." *Newsweek*, June 15, 1998, 44-45.

Milton Friedman. "Monetary Policy Dominates." *Wall Street Journal*, January 8, 1999, A18.

Amity Shlaes. "The Greedy Hand in a Velvet Glove." *Wall Street Journal*, April 15, 1999, A22.

Lars E. O. Svensson. "How Japan Can Recover." *Financial Times* (London), September 25, 2001, 13.

Milton Friedman. "No More Economic Stimulus Needed." *Wall Street Journal*, October 10, 2001, A17.

A Conversation with Milton Friedman. 2002 interview with Milton Friedman conducted by Gary S. Becker; issued commercially as a DVD by the Liberty Fund in 2003.

John A. Tatom. "Policymakers Fixated on Use of Nominal Interest Rates." *Financial Times* (London), June 14, 2002, 18.

Milton Friedman. "The Fed's Thermostat." *Wall Street Journal*, August 19, 2003, A8.

Milton Friedman appearance on television special *Election 2004: The Economy*, WQED San Francisco, broadcast live on October 15, 2004.

John T. Ward. "The View from Up There: Economist Milton Friedman, RC '32, Reflects on a Long Life as a Contrarian." *Rutgers* magazine, Fall 2006, 22-27 and 48.

Holcomb B. Noble. "Milton Friedman, the Champion of Free Markets, Is Dead at 94." *New York Times*, November 17, 2006, A1 and B10.

Milton Friedman. "Why Money Matters." *Wall Street Journal*, November 17, 2006, A20.

Mary Ruth Yoe. "Market Force." *University of Chicago Magazine* 99, no. 3 (January/February 2007): 30.

The Partnership for Public Service. "Monitoring and Predicting the Economy's Future Path." *Washington Post*, January 3, 2012. https://www.washingtonpost.com/politics/monitoring-and-predicting-the-economys-future-path/2012/01/01/gIQAnPjPWP_story.html.

Paul Krugman. "America Isn't a Corporation." *New York Times*, January 13, 2012, A23.

Jon Hilsenrath. "Reporter's Journal: A Close Bond and a Shared Love for 'Dismal Science'—Correspondence between Famously Brash Summers and His Uncle, a Nobel Economist, Reveals Flashes of Humility and Tenderness." *Wall Street Journal*, September 14, 2013, A4.

John B. Taylor. "The Economic Hokum over 'Secular Stagnation.'" *Wall Street Journal*, January 2, 2014, A17.

John B. Taylor, "Family Economics and Macro Behavior at a Gary Becker Memorial," economicsone.com, September 2, 2014.

Paul Krugman. "Business vs. Economics." *New York Times*, November 3, 2014, A31.

Paul Romer. "Protecting the Norms of Science in Economics." *PaulRomer* blog entry, May 18, 2015.

II. References

Abbott, William J. 1959. Money Supply Statistics." In Ad Hoc Committee on Money Supply Statistics (William J. Abbott, Harry Brandy, Robert S. Einzig, Roland I. Robinson [Committee Chairman], and Clarence W. Tow), *Recommendations for Statistics of Money Supply and Member Bank Reserves*. Washington, DC: Federal Reserve Board. October 8.

———. 1960. "A New Measure of the Money Supply." *Federal Reserve Bulletin* 46, no. 10 (October): 1102-23.

———. 1962. "Revision of Money Supply Series." *Federal Reserve Bulletin* 48, no. 8 (August): 941-51.

Abel, Andrew B. 1979. *Investment and the Value of Capital*. New York: Garland.

———. 1983. "Optimal Investment under Uncertainty." *American Economic Review* 73, no. 1 (March): 228-33.

———. 1987. "Optimal Monetary Growth." *Journal of Monetary Economics* 19, no. 3 (May): 437-50.

Abel, Andrew B., and Ben S. Bernanke. 1992. *Macroeconomics*. Reading, MA: Addison-Wesley.

Abel, Andrew B., and Olivier J. Blanchard. 1986. "The Present Value of Profits and Cyclical Movements in Investment." *Econometrica* 54, no. 2 (March): 249-73.

Abel, Andrew B., Rudiger Dornbusch, John Huizinga, and Alan Marcus. 1979. "Money Demand during Hyperinflation." *Journal of Monetary Economics* 5, no. 1 (January): 97-104.

Abramovitz, Moses. 1948. "Business Cycles." In Arthur F. Burns, ed., *The Cumulation of Economic Knowledge: Twenty-Eighth Annual Report of the National Bureau of Economic Research*. New York: National Bureau of Economic Research. 34-36.

Ahearn, Daniel S. 1963. *Federal Reserve Policy Reappraised, 1951-1959*. New York: Columbia University Press.

Alford, R. F. G. 1956. "Marshall's Demand Curve." *Economica* 23, no. 89 (February): 23-48.

All Participants. 1951. "Selections from the Discussion of Friedman's Paper." In David McCord Wright, ed., *The Impact of the Union: Eight Economic Theorists Evaluate the Labor Union Movement*. New York: Harcourt Brace. 235-59.

Altman, Oscar L. 1941. *Saving, Investment, and National Income*. Washington, DC: Temporary National Economic Committee.

Amacher, Ryan C., and Richard James Sweeney. 1980. *Principles of Macroeconomics*. Cincinnati, OH: South-Western.

American Bankers Association. 1963. *Proceedings of a Symposium on Economic Growth*. New York: American Bankers Association.

American Economic Association. 1937. "Thirty-Fourth List of Doctoral Dissertations in Political Economy in Progress in American Universities and Colleges." *American Economic Review* 27, no. 3 (September): 638-57.

———. 1948. *The 1948 Directory of the American Economic Association (as of June 15, 1948)*. Evanston, IL: American Economic Association.

———. 1952. "Annual Business Meeting, December 29, 1951, Hotel Statler, Boston, Massachusetts." *American Economic Review (Papers and Proceedings)* 42, no. 2 (May): 709-11.

———. 1970. "Biographical Listings of Members." In American Economic Association,

1969 Handbook of the American Economic Association. Nashville, TN: American Economic Association. 1–492. Archived in jstor.org as an issue of the *American Economic Review* (59, no. 6 [January 1970]).

———. 1981. "Biographical Listing of Members." In American Economic Association, *Nobel Lectures and 1981 Survey of Members*. Nashville, TN: American Economic Association. 33–456. Archived in jstor.org as part of an issue of the *American Economic Review* (71, no. 6 [December 1981]).

American Enterprise Institute. 1974. *Indexing and Inflation*. Washington, DC: American Enterprise Institute.

American Statistical Association. 1950. "Proceedings: American Statistical Association 109th Annual Meeting: Hotel Biltmore, New York, New York: Minutes of the Annual Business Meeting." *Journal of the American Statistical Association* 45, no. 250 (June): 270–86.

Anderson, Benjamin M., Jr. 1929. "Commodity Price Stabilization: A False Goal of Central Bank Policy." *Chase Economic Bulletin* 9, no. 3 (May): 3–24.

Anderson, Martin, ed. 1982. *Registration and the Draft: Proceedings of the Hoover-Rochester Conference on the All-Volunteer Force*. Stanford, CA: Hoover Institution Press.

Anderson, Oliver D. 1976. "Discussion of the Paper by Dr. Prothero and Dr. Wallis." *Journal of the Royal Statistical Society, Series A (General)* 139, no. 4, 487–90.

Anderson, Richard G., Michael D. Bordo, and John V. Duca. 2016. "Money and Velocity during Financial Crises: From the Great Depression to the Great Recession." NBER Working Paper no. 22100, March.

Anderson, Richard G., and Kenneth A. Kavajecz. 1994. "A Historical Perspective on the Federal Reserve's Monetary Aggregates: Definition, Construction and Targeting." *Federal Reserve Bank of St. Louis Review* 76, no. 2 (March/April): 1–31.

Anderson, R. L. 1946. "Review: *Income from Independent Professional Practice*." *Journal of the American Statistical Association* 41, no. 235 (September): 398–401.

Ando, Albert, and Franco Modigliani. 1963. "The 'Life Cycle' Hypothesis of Saving: Aggregate Implications and Tests." *American Economic Review* 53, no. 1 (March): 55–84.

Andrade, Philippe, Jordi Galí, Hervé Le Bihan, and Julien Matheron. 2018. "The Optimal Inflation Target and the Natural Rate of Interest." NBER Working Paper no. 24328, February.

Andrés, Javier, David López-Salido, and Edward Nelson. 2004. "Tobin's Imperfect Asset Substitution in Optimizing General Equilibrium." *Journal of Money, Credit and Banking* 36, no. 4 (August): 665–690.

Angell, James W. 1941. "Taxation, Inflation and the Defense Program." *Review of Economics and Statistics* 78, no. 2 (May): 78–82.

Archibald, G. C., and Richard G. Lipsey. 1958. "Monetary and Value Theory: A Critique of Lange and Patinkin." *Review of Economic Studies* 26, no. 1 (October): 1–22.

Argy, Victor. 1992. *Australian Macroeconomic Policy in a Changing World Environment*. Sydney: Allen and Unwin.

Arrow, Kenneth J. 1950. "A Difficulty in the Concept of Social Welfare." *Journal of Political Economy* 58, no. 4 (August): 328–46.

———. 1963. "Uncertainty and the Welfare Economics of Medical Care." *American Economic Review* 53, no. 5 (December): 941–73.

———. 1964. "The Role of Securities in the Optimal Allocation of Risk-Bearing." *Review of Economic Studies* 31, no. 2 (April): 91–96.

Arrow, Kenneth J., and Mordecai Kurz. 1970. *Public Investment, the Rate of Return, and Optimal Fiscal Policy*. Baltimore: Johns Hopkins University Press.

Arrow, Kenneth J., and Marcel Priebsch. 2014. "Bliss, Catastrophe, and Rational Policy." *Environmental Resource Economics* 58, no. 4 (August): 491–509.

Ashenfelter, Orley, and John Pencavel. 2010. "Albert Rees." In Ross B. Emmett, ed., *The Elgar Companion to the Chicago School of Economics*. Cheltenham, UK: Edward Elgar. 311–14.

Atkeson, Andrew, V. V. Chari, and Patrick J. Kehoe. 1999. "Taxing Capital Income: A Bad Idea." *Federal Reserve Bank of Minneapolis Quarterly Review* 23, no. 3 (Summer): 3–17.

Atkeson, Andrew, and Lee E. Ohanian. 2001. "Are Phillips Curves Useful for Forecasting Inflation?" *Federal Reserve Bank of Minneapolis Quarterly Review* 25, no. 1 (Winter): 2–11.

Auerbach, Alan J., and Kevin Hassett. 2015. "Capital Taxation in the Twenty-First Century." *American Economic Review (Papers and Proceedings)* 105, no. 5 (May): 38–42.

Auerbach, Alan J., and Laurence J. Kotlikoff. 1995. *Macroeconomics: An Integrated Approach*. Cincinnati, OH: South-Western College Publishing.

Axilrod, Stephen H., and Ralph A. Young. 1962. "Interest Rates and Monetary Policy." *Federal Reserve Bulletin* 48, no. 9 (September): 1110–37.

Bach, George L. 1950. *Federal Reserve Policy-Making: A Study in Government Economic Policy Formation*. New York: Alfred A. Knopf.

Bach, George L., Phillip Cagan, Milton Friedman, Clifford G. Hildreth, Franco Modigliani, and Arthur M. Okun. 1976. *Improving the Monetary Aggregates: Report of the Advisory Committee on Monetary Statistics*. Washington, DC: Federal Reserve Board.

Backhouse, Roger E., and Andrea Salanti, eds. 2000. *Macroeconomics and the Real World*. Vol. 2, *Keynesian Economics Unemployment and Policy*. Oxford: Oxford University Press.

Bailey, Martin J. 1954. "The Marshallian Demand Curve." *Journal of Political Economy* 62, no. 3 (June): 255–61.

———. 1956. "The Welfare Cost of Inflationary Finance." *Journal of Political Economy* 64, no. 2 (April): 93–110.

———. 1957. "Saving and the Rate of Interest." *Journal of Political Economy* 65, no. 4 (August): 279–305.

———. 1962. *National Income and the Price Level*. New York: McGraw-Hill.

———. 1992. "Introduction." In Martin J. Bailey, *Studies in Positive and Normative Economics*. Aldershot, UK: Edward Elgar. xi–xx.

Bailey, Martin J., Mancur Olson, and Paul Wonnacott. 1980. "The Marginal Utility of Income Does Not Increase: Borrowing, Lending, and Friedman-Savage Gambles." *American Economic Review* 70, no. 3 (June): 372–79.

Baily, Martin Neil, and James Tobin. 1977. "Macroeconomic Effects of Selective Public Employment and Wage Subsidies." *Brookings Papers on Economic Activity* 8, no. 2 511–41.

Baker, Scott R., Nicholas Bloom, and Steven J. Davis. 2013. "Measuring Economic Policy Uncertainty." Manuscript, Stanford University, May.

Balbach, Anatol, and Denis S. Karnosky. 1975. "Real Money Balances: A Good Forecasting Device and a Good Policy Target?" *Federal Reserve Bank of St. Louis Review* 57, no. 9 (September): 11–15.

Balke, Nathan S., and Robert J. Gordon. 1986. "Appendix B: Historical Data." In

Robert J. Gordon, ed., *The American Business Cycle: Continuity and Change*. Chicago: University of Chicago Press. 781–850.

Ball, Laurence, and N. Gregory Mankiw. 1995. "Relative-Price Changes as Aggregate Supply Shocks." *Quarterly Journal of Economics* 110, no. 1 (February): 161–93.

Ball, R. J. 1985. "Demand Management and Economic Recovery: The United Kingdom Case." *National Westminster Bank Review* 18, no. 3 (August): 2–17.

Baran, Paul A. 1963. "*Capitalism and Freedom* by Milton Friedman." *Journal of Political Economy* 71, no. 6 (December): 591–94.

Barro, Robert J. 1974. "Are Government Bonds Net Wealth?" *Journal of Political Economy* 82, no. 6 (November/December): 1095–117.

———. 1977. "Unanticipated Money Growth and Unemployment in the United States." *American Economic Review* 67 (March): 101–15.

———. 1979a. "On the Determination of the Public Debt." *Journal of Political Economy* 87, no. 5 (October): 940–71.

———. 1979b. "Money and the Price Level under the Gold Standard." *Economic Journal* 89, no. 353 (March): 13–33.

———. 1981. "Output Effects of Government Purchases." *Journal of Political Economy* 8, no. 6 (December): 1086–21.

———. 1982. "United States Inflation and the Choice of Monetary Standard." In Robert E. Hall, ed., *Inflation: Causes and Effects*. Chicago: University of Chicago Press. 99–110.

———. 1986. "The Behavior of United States Deficits." In Robert J. Gordon, ed., *The American Business Cycle: Continuity and Change*. Chicago: University of Chicago Press. 361–87.

———. 1987. "Government Spending, Interest Rates, Prices, and Budget Deficits in the United Kingdom, 1701–1918." *Journal of Monetary Economics* 20, no. 2 (September): 221–47.

Barro, Robert J., and Stanley Fischer. 1976. "Recent Developments in Monetary Theory." *Journal of Monetary Economics* 2, no. 2 (April): 133–67.

Barro, Robert J., and Robert G. King. 1984. "Time-Separable Preferences and Intertemporal-Substitution Models of Business Cycles." *Quarterly Journal of Economics* 99, no. 4 (November): 817–39.

Barro, Robert J., and Charles J. Redlick. 2011. "Macroeconomic Effects from Government Purchases and Taxes." *Quarterly Journal of Economics* 126, no. 1 (February): 51–102.

Barrow, Lisa, Julia Campos, Neil R. Ericsson, David F. Hendry, Hong-Anh Tran, and William Veloce. 1997. "Cointegration." In David Glasner, ed., *Business Cycles and Depressions: An Encyclopedia*. New York: Garland. 101–5.

Batini, Nicoletta, and Edward Nelson. 2005. "The U.K.'s Rocky Road to Stability." Federal Reserve Bank of St. Louis Working Paper 2005-020A, March.

Baumol, William J. 1951. "The Neumann-Morgenstern Utility Index—an Ordinalist View." *Journal of Political Economy* 59, no. 1 (February): 61–66.

———. 1952. "The Transactions Demand for Cash: An Inventory Theoretic Approach." *Quarterly Journal of Economics* 66, no. 4 (November): 545–56.

———. 1954. "*Essays in Positive Economics* by Milton Friedman." *Review of Economics and Statistics* 36, no. 4 (November): 462–65.

———. 1957. "Speculation, Profitability, and Stability." *Review of Economics and Statistics* 39, no. 3 (August): 263–71.

———. 1961. "Pitfalls in Contracyclical Policies: Some Tools and Results." *Review of Economics and Statistics* 43, no. 1 (February): 21–26.

———. 1978. "Smith versus Marx on Business Morality and the Social Interest." In Fred R. Glahe, ed., *Adam Smith and "The Wealth of Nations": 1776–1976 Bicentennial Essays*. Boulder: Colorado Associated University Press. 111–22.

———. 1983. "*Essays on and in the Chicago Tradition*, by Don Patinkin." *Journal of Political Economy* 91, no. 6 (December): 1080–82.

Bazdarich, Michael. 1982. "A Natural Rate Approach to Potential Output." In Federal Reserve Bank of San Francisco, ed., *Proceedings of Fifth West Coast Academic/Federal Reserve Economic Research Seminar, December 1981, Published by the Federal Reserve Bank of San Francisco, November 1982*. San Francisco: Federal Reserve Bank of San Francisco. 174–214.

Bean, Charles R. 1988. "Sterling Misalignment and British Trade Performance." In Richard C. Marston, ed., *Misalignment of Exchange Rates: Effects on Industry and Trade*. Chicago: University of Chicago Press. 39–69.

Becker, Gary S. 1955. "The Economics of Racial Discrimination." PhD diss., Department of Economics, University of Chicago, June.

———. 1957a. "A Proposal for Free Banking." Mimeographed paper, University of Chicago. (Cited in Rockoff 1975, 141.)

———. 1957b. *The Economics of Discrimination*. Chicago: University of Chicago Press.

———. 1960. "Underinvestment in College Education?" *American Economic Review (Papers and Proceedings)* 50, no. 2 (May): 346–54.

———. 1964. *Human Capital*. New York: Columbia University Press.

———. 1975. *Human Capital*. 2nd ed. New York: Columbia University Press.

———. 1991a. "Milton Friedman." In Edward Shils, ed., *Remembering the University of Chicago: Teachers, Scientists, and Scholars*. Chicago: University of Chicago Press. 138–46.

———. 1991b. *A Treatise on the Family*. Enlarged ed. Cambridge, MA: Harvard University Press.

———. 1993. "A Proposal for Free Banking." In Lawrence H. White, ed., *Free Banking*. Vol. 3. Cheltenham, UK: Edward Elgar. 20–25.

———. 2007. "Afterword: Milton Friedman as a Microeconomist." In Milton Friedman, *Milton Friedman on Economics: Selected Papers*. Chicago: University of Chicago Press. 181–86.

Belongia, Michael T., and Peter N. Ireland. 2014. "The Barnett Critique after Three Decades: A New Keynesian Analysis." *Journal of Econometrics* 183, no. 1 (November): 5–21.

———. 2016. "Money and Output: Friedman and Schwartz Revisited." *Journal of Money, Credit and Banking* 48, no. 6 (September): 1223–66.

Benston, George J., and George G. Kaufman. 1993. "Deposit Insurance Reform: A Functional Approach—a Comment." *Carnegie-Rochester Conference Series on Public Policy* 38, no. 1, 41–49.

Benveniste, Lawrence M., and José A. Scheinkman. 1979. "On the Differentiability of the Value Function in Dynamic Models of Economics." *Econometrica* 47, no. 3 (May): 727–32.

Bernanke, Ben S. 1981. "Bankruptcy, Liquidity, and Recession." *American Economic Review (Papers and Proceedings)* 71, no. 2 (May): 155–59.

———. 1982. "The Real Effects of Financial Crises: Theory and Evidence." In Federal Reserve Bank of San Francisco, ed., *Proceedings of Sixth West Coast Academic/Federal*

Reserve Economic Research Seminar November 1982. San Francisco: Federal Reserve Bank of San Francisco. 134–62.

———. 1983. "Nonmonetary Effects of the Financial Crisis in the Propagation of the Great Depression." *American Economic Review* 73, no. 3, 257–76.

———. 1986. "Alternative Explanations of the Money-Income Correlation." *Carnegie-Rochester Conference Series on Public Policy* 25, no. 1, 49–99.

———. 2002a. "Deflation: Making Sure 'It' Doesn't Happen Here." Speech before the National Economists Club, Washington DC, November 21.

———. 2002b. "On Milton Friedman's Ninetieth Birthday." Remarks at the Conference to Honor Milton Friedman, University of Chicago, November 8.

———. 2004. "Friedman's Monetary Framework: Some Lessons." In Mark A. Wynne, Harvey Rosenblum, and Robert L. Formaini, eds., *The Legacy of Milton and Rose Friedman's "Free to Choose": Economic Liberalism at the Turn of the 21st Century*. Dallas: Federal Reserve Bank of Dallas. 207–17.

———. 2006. "Monetary Aggregates and Monetary Policy at the Federal Reserve: A Historical Perspective." Remarks at the Fourth ECB Central Banking Conference, "The Role of Money: Money and Monetary Policy," November 10. www.federalreserve.gov.

———. 2011. "Transcript of Chairman Bernanke's Press Conference, June 22, 2011." www.federalreserve.gov.

———. 2012a. "Transcript of Chairman Bernanke's Press Conference [of] September 13, 2012." www.federalreserve.gov.

———. 2012b. "The Federal Reserve and the Financial Crisis, Lecture 1: Origins and Mission of the Federal Reserve." Transcript of lecture given at the George Washington University School of Business, Washington, DC, March 20. www.federalreserve.gov.

———. 2013. "A Century of U.S. Central Banking: Goals, Frameworks, Accountability." *Journal of Economic Perspectives* 27, no. 4 (Fall): 3–16.

Bernanke, Ben S., and Mark Gertler. 2001. "Should Central Banks Respond to Movements in Asset Prices?" *American Economic Review (Papers and Proceedings)* 91, no. 2 (May): 253–57.

Bernanke, Ben S., Mark Gertler, and Mark W. Watson. 2004. "Reply: Oil Shocks and Aggregate Macroeconomic Behavior: The Role of Monetary Policy." *Journal of Money, Credit and Banking* 36, no. 2 (April): 287–91.

Bernanke, Ben S., and Ilian Mihov. 1998. "The Liquidity Effect and Long-Run Neutrality." *Carnegie-Rochester Conference Series on Public Policy* 49, no. 1 (December): 149–94.

Beveridge, Stephen, and Charles R. Nelson. 1981. "A New Approach to Decomposition of Economic Time Series into Permanent and Transitory Components with Particular Attention to Measurement of the 'Business Cycle.'" *Journal of Monetary Economics* 7, no. 2, 151–74.

Bewley, Truman. 1983. "A Difficulty with the Optimum Quantity of Money." *Econometrica* 51, no. 5 (September): 1485–504.

Beyer, Andreas, Vitor Gaspar, Christina Gerberding, and Otmar Issing. 2013. "German Monetary Policy after the Breakdown of Bretton Woods." In Michael D. Bordo and Athanasios Orphanides, eds., *The Great Inflation: The Rebirth of Modern Central Banking*. Chicago: University of Chicago Press. 301–46.

Black, Fischer. 1972. "Active and Passive Monetary Policy in a Neoclassical Model." *Journal of Finance* 27, no. 4 (September): 801–14.

———. 1974. "Uniqueness of the Price Level in Monetary Growth Models with Rational Expectations." *Journal of Economic Theory* 7, no. 1 (January): 53–65.

Blanchard, Olivier J. 1985. "Debt, Deficits, and Finite Horizons." *Journal of Political Economy* 93, no. 2 (April): 223–47.

Blanchard, Olivier J., and Stanley Fischer. 1989. *Lectures on Macroeconomics*. Cambridge, MA: MIT Press.

Blanchard, Olivier J., and Nobuhiro Kiyotaki. 1987. "Monopolistic Competition and the Effects of Aggregate Demand." *American Economic Review* 77, no. 4 (September): 647–66.

Blanchard, Olivier J., and Lawrence H. Summers. 1986. "Hysteresis and the European Unemployment Problem." *NBER Macroeconomics Annual* 1, no. 1, 15–78.

Blatt, John Markus. 1983. *Dynamic Economic Systems: A Post-Keynesian Approach*. Armonk, NY: M. E. Sharpe.

Blaug, Mark. 1976. "The Empirical Status of Human Capital Theory: A Slightly Jaundiced Survey." *Journal of Economic Literature* 14, no. 3 (September): 827–55.

———, ed. 1986. *Who's Who in Economics: A Biographical Dictionary of Major Economists 1700–1986*. 2nd ed. Cambridge: MA, MIT Press.

———. 1990. *John Maynard Keynes: Life, Ideas, Legacy*. London: Palgrave Macmillan.

Blinder, Alan S. 1979. *Economic Policy and the Great Stagflation*. New York: Academic.

———. 1986. "Ruminations on Karl Brunner's Reflections." In R. W. Hafer, ed., *The Monetary versus Fiscal Policy Debate: Lessons from Two Decades*. Totowa, NJ: Rowman and Allanheld. 117–26.

Blume, Lawrence, and David Easley. 2006. "If You're So Smart, Why Aren't You Rich? Belief Selection in Complete and Incomplete Markets." *Econometrica* 74, no. 4 (July): 929–66.

Blume, Lawrence, David Easley, and Maureen O'Hara. 1982. "Characterization of Optimal Plans for Stochastic Dynamic Programs." *Journal of Economic Theory* 28, no. 2 (December): 221–34.

Boag, Harold. 1916. "Human Capital and the Cost of the War." *Journal of the Royal Statistical Society* 79, no. 1 (January): 7–17.

Board of Governors of the Federal Reserve System. 1945. *Annual Report of the Board of Governors of the Federal Reserve System, 1945*. Washington, DC: Federal Reserve Board.

———. 1970. *Academic Views on Improving the Federal Reserve Discount Mechanism*. Washington, DC: Federal Reserve Board.

———. 1976. *Banking and Monetary Statistics, 1941–1970*. Washington, DC: Federal Reserve Board.

Bodkin, Ronald G. 1995. "The Discussion among Future Nobel Laureates Becker, Friedman, and Klein, on Macro Models and Consumption Functions, in 1957 and 1958." In M. Dutta, ed., *Economics, Econometrics and the LINK: Essays in Honor of Lawrence R. Klein*. Amsterdam: Elsevier. 45–57.

Bohn, Henning. 1998. "The Behavior of U.S. Public Debt and Deficits." *Quarterly Journal of Economics* 113, no. 3 (August): 949–63.

Boianovsky, Mauro. 2016. "Wicksell, Secular Stagnation and the Negative Natural Rate of Interest." CHOPE Working Paper No. 2016-25, September.

Boldrin, Michele, and David K. Levine. 2008. "Perfectly Competitive Innovation." *Journal of Monetary Economics* 55, no. 3 (April): 435–53.

Bordo, Michael D. 1972. "The Effects of the Sources of Change in the Money Supply on the Level of Economic Activity: A Historical Essay." PhD diss., Department of Economics, University of Chicago.

———. 1975. "The Income Effects of the Sources of Monetary Change: An Historical Approach." *Economic Inquiry* 13, no. 4 (December): 505–25.

———. 1981. "The Classical Gold Standard: Some Lessons for Today." *Federal Reserve Bank of St. Louis Review* 63, no. 5 (May): 2–17.

———. 1987. "Equation of Exchange." In John Eatwell, Murray Milgate, and Peter Newman, eds., *The New Palgrave: A Dictionary of Economics*. Vol. 2, *E to J*. London: Macmillan. 175–77.

———, ed. 1989a. *Money, History, and International Finance: Essays in Honor of Anna J. Schwartz*. Chicago: University of Chicago Press.

———. 1989b. "The Contribution of *A Monetary History of the United States, 1867–1960* to Monetary History." In Michael D. Bordo, ed., *Money, History, and International Finance: Essays in Honor of Anna J. Schwartz*. Chicago: University of Chicago Press. 15–70.

Bordo, Michael D., Ehsan U. Choudhri, and Anna J. Schwartz. 1995. "Could Stable Money Have Averted the Great Contraction?" *Economic Inquiry* 33, no. 3 (July): 484–505.

Bordo, Michael D., Christopher J. Erceg, and Charles L. Evans. 2000. "Money, Sticky Wages, and the Great Depression." *American Economic Review* 90, no. 5 (December): 1447–63.

Bordo, Michael D., Owen Humpage, and Anna J. Schwartz. 2012. "Epilogue: Foreign-Exchange-Market Operations in the Twenty-First Century." NBER Working Paper no. 17984, April.

Bordo, Michael D., and John Landon Lane. 2010. "Exits from Recessions: The U.S. Experience 1920–2007." NBER Working Paper no. 15731, February.

Bordo, Michael, and Angela Redish. 2004. "Is Deflation Depressing? Evidence from the Classical Gold Standard." In Richard C. K. Burdekin and Pierre L. Siklos, eds., *Deflation*. New York: Cambridge University Press. 191–217.

Bordo, Michael D., and Hugh Rockoff. 2011. "The Influence of Irving Fisher on Milton Friedman's Monetary Economics." NBER Working Paper no. 17267, August.

———. 2013a. "Not Just the Great Contraction: Friedman and Schwartz's *A Monetary History of the United States, 1867–1960*." *American Economic Review (Papers and Proceedings)* 103, no. 3 (May): 61–65.

———. 2013b. "The Influence of Irving Fisher on Milton Friedman's Monetary Economics." *Journal of the History of Economic Thought* 35, no. 2 (June): 153–77.

Bordo, Michael D., and Anna J. Schwartz. 1979. "Clark Warburton: Pioneer Monetarist." *Journal of Monetary Economics* 5, no. 1 (January): 43–65.

———. 1983. "The Importance of Stable Money: Theory and Evidence." *Cato Journal* 3, no. 1 (Spring): 63–82.

Boskin, Michael J. 1987. *Reagan and the Economy: The Successes, Failures, and Unfinished Agenda*. San Francisco: Institute for Contemporary Studies.

———. 2005. "Testimony of Michael Boskin." In *President's Advisory Panel on Federal Tax Reform: Sixth Meeting, Thursday, March 31, 2005*. http://govinfo.library.unt.edu /taxreformpanel/meetings/meeting-03312005.html.

Boulding, Kenneth E., and George J. Stigler, eds. 1952. *Readings in Price Theory*. Chicago: Richard D. Irwin.

Boumans, Marcel J. 2013. "Friedman and the Cowles Commission." Manuscript, University of Amsterdam, November.

Bowen, William G. 1960. "'Cost Inflation' versus 'Demand Inflation': A Useful Distinction?" *Southern Economic Journal* 26, no. 3 (January): 199–206.

Brady, Dorothy S., and Rose D. Friedman. 1947. "Savings and the Income Distribution." In National Bureau of Economic Research, ed., *Studies in Income and Wealth, no. 10.* New York: National Bureau of Economic Research. 247–65.

Brainard, William C. 1967. "Uncertainty and the Effectiveness of Policy." *American Economic Review (Papers and Proceedings)* 57, no. 2 (May): 411–25.

Braun, Anne Romanis. 1986. *Wage Determination and Incomes Policy in Open Economies.* Washington, DC: International Monetary Fund.

Breit, William, and Roger L. Ransom. 1971. *The Academic Scribblers: American Economists in Collision.* New York: Holt, Rinehart and Winston.

Brittan, Samuel. 1976. "Full Employment Policy: A Reappraisal." In G. D. N. Worswick, ed., *The Concept and Measurement of Involuntary Unemployment.* London: Allen and Unwin. 249–78.

———. 1978. "Inflation and Democracy." In Fred Hirsch and John H. Goldthorpe, eds., *The Political Economy of Inflation.* London: Martin Robertson. 161–85.

———. 1983. *The Role and Limits of Government: Essays in Political Economy.* Minneapolis: University of Minnesota Press.

———. 2005. *Against the Flow: Reflections of an Individualist.* London: Atlantic Books.

Brock, William A. 1974. "Money and Growth: The Case of Long-Run Perfect Foresight." *International Economic Review* 15, no. 3 (October): 750–77.

Brothwell, John F. 1975. "A Simple Keynesian's Response to Leijonhufvud." *Bulletin of Economic Research* 27, no. 1 (May): 3–21.

Brown, Alan, and Angus Deaton. 1972. "Surveys in Applied Economics: Models of Consumer Behaviour." *Economic Journal* 82, no. 328 (December): 1145–236.

Brown, T. M. 1952. "Habit Persistence and Lags in Consumer Behavior." *Econometrica* 20, no. 3 (July): 355–71.

Brozen, Yale, and Milton Friedman. 1966. *The Minimum Wage Rate: Who Really Pays?* Washington, DC: Free Society Association.

Brunie, Charles H. 2007. "My Friend, Milton Friedman." *City Journal* 23, no. 1, online edition.

Brunner, Karl. 1960. *"Money, Credit, and Public Policy* by Lawrence Smith." *Journal of Finance* 15, no. 4 (December): 605–6.

———. 1961a. "Some Major Problems in Monetary Theory." *American Economic Review (Papers and Proceedings)* 51, no. 2 (May): 47–56.

———. 1961b. "The Report of the Commission on Money and Credit." *Journal of Political Economy* 69, no. 6 (December): 605–20.

———. 1969a. "Monetary Analysis and Federal Reserve Policy." In Karl Brunner, ed., *Targets and Indicators of Monetary Policy.* San Francisco, CA: Chandler. 250–82.

———. 1969b. "'Assumptions' and the Cognitive Quality of Theories." *Synthese* 20, no. 4 (December): 501–25.

———. 1971a. "A Survey of Selected Issues in Monetary Theory." *Swiss Journal of Economics and Statistics* 107, no. 1 (March): 1–146.

———. 1971b. "The Monetarist View of Keynesian Ideas." *Lloyds Bank Review* 26, no. 102 (October): 35–49.

———. 1973. "A Diagrammatic Exposition of the Money Supply Process." *Swiss Journal of Economics and Statistics* 109, no. 4 (December): 481–533.

———. 1980a. "A Fascination with Economics." *Banca Nazionale del Lavoro Quarterly Review* 33, no. 135 (December): 403–26.

———. 1980b. "Theories of Inflation and the Explanation of Intractable Inflation." In

Artur Woll, ed., *Inflation: German Contributions to the Debate*. London: John Martin. 97–143.

——. 1980c. "The Control of Monetary Aggregates." In Federal Reserve Bank of Boston, ed., *Controlling Monetary Aggregates III*. Boston: Federal Reserve Bank of Boston. 1–65.

——. 1981. "The Case against Monetary Activism." *Lloyds Bank Review* 36, no. 139 (January): 20–39.

Brunner, Karl, and Allan H. Meltzer. 1963. "Predicting Velocity: Implications for Theory and Policy." *Journal of Finance* 18, no. 2 (May): 319–54.

——. 1964a. *Analysis of Federal Reserve Policy-Making [Part 1:] Some General Features of the Federal Reserve's Approach to Policy: A Staff Analysis*. Printed for the use of the Committee on Banking and Currency, US House of Representatives. Washington, DC: US Government Printing Office.

——. 1964b. *Analysis of Federal Reserve Policy-Making [Part 2:] The Federal Reserve's Attachment to the Free Reserve Concept: A Staff Analysis*. Printed for the use of the Committee on Banking and Currency, US House of Representatives. Washington, DC: US Government Printing Office.

——. 1964c. *Analysis of Federal Reserve Policy-Making [Parts 6 to 8:] An Alternative Approach to the Monetary Mechanism*. Printed for the use of the Committee on Banking and Currency, US House of Representatives. Washington, DC: US Government Printing Office.

——. 1966. "A Credit-Market Theory of the Money Supply and an Explanation of Two Puzzles in U.S. Monetary Policy." In Tullio Bagiotti, ed., *Essays in Honor of Marco Fanno: Investigations in Economic Theory and Methodology*. Vol. 2. Padova, Italy: Cedam. 151–76.

——. 1973. "Mr. Hicks and the 'Monetarists.'" *Economica* 40, no. 157 (February): 44–59.

——. 1983. "Strategies and Tactics for Monetary Control." *Carnegie-Rochester Conference Series on Public Policy* 18, no. 1, 59–103.

——. 1993. *Money and the Economy: Issues in Monetary Analysis*. Cambridge: Cambridge University Press.

Bryant, John. 1995. "Does a Constant Money-Growth Rule Help Stabilize Inflation? Experimental Evidence: A Comment." *Carnegie-Rochester Conference Series on Public Policy* 43, no. 1 (December): 157–62.

Buchanan, James M., and Gordon Tullock. 1962. *The Calculus of Consent: Logical Foundations of Constitutional Democracy*. Ann Arbor: University of Michigan Press.

Budd, Alan. 1979. "The Future of Demand Management: Reviewing the Choices." In S. T. Cook and P. M. Jackson, eds., *Current Issues in Fiscal Policy*, Oxford, UK: Martin Robertson. 198–210.

Burgin, Angus. 2012. *The Great Persuasion: Reinventing Free Markets since the Depression*. Cambridge, MA: Harvard University Press.

Burman, J. P. 1969. "Discussion on the Paper by Mr. Coen, Mr. Gomme and Dr. Kendall." *Journal of the Royal Statistical Society, Series A (General)* 132, no. 2, 154–55.

Burmeister, Edwin, and Edmund Phelps. 1971. "Money, Public Debt, Inflation and Real Interest." *Journal of Money, Credit and Banking* 3, no. 2 (May): 153–82.

Burns, Arthur F. 1929. "The Quantity Theory and Price Stabilization." *American Economic Review* 19, no. 4 (December): 561–79.

——. 1934. *Production Trends in the United States since 1870*. New York: National Bureau of Economic Research.

——, ed. 1946. *Twenty-Sixth Annual Report of the National Bureau of Economic Research.* New York: National Bureau of Economic Research.

——. 1947. "Keynesian Economics Once Again." *Review of Economics and Statistics* 29, no. 4 (November): 252–67.

——, ed. 1948. *The Cumulation of Economic Knowledge: Twenty-Eighth Annual Report of the National Bureau of Economic Research.* New York: National Bureau of Economic Research.

——, ed. 1949. *Wesley Mitchell and the National Bureau: Twenty-Ninth Annual Report, National Bureau of Economic Research.* New York: National Bureau of Economic Research.

——. 1952a. "The Instability of Consumer Spending." In Arthur F. Burns, ed., *The Instability of Consumer Spending, 32nd Annual Report, National Bureau of Economic Research.* New York: National Bureau of Economic Research. 3–20.

——. 1952b. "Introductory Sketch." In Arthur F. Burns, ed., *Wesley Clair Mitchell: The Economic Scientist.* New York: National Bureau of Economic Research. 3–54.

——. 1957. *Prosperity without Inflation.* New York: Fordham University Press.

——. 1960. "Progress towards Economic Stability." *American Economic Review* 50, no. 1 (March): 1–19.

——. 1965. "Wages and Prices by Formula?" *Harvard Business Review* 43, no. 2 (March/April): 55–64. Reprinted as "Wages and Prices by Formula," in Arthur F. Burns, *The Business Cycle in a Changing World.* New York: Columbia University Press, 1969. 232–53.

——. 1968. "The New Economics and Our Current Needs." Address at the Commonwealth Club of California, San Francisco, June 7. Abridged version published as Arthur F. Burns, "'To Stabilize, [and] Promote, Economy We Must Stop Inflation Which Pauperizes People'—Burns," Commonwealth (Commonwealth Club of California, San Francisco) 62, no. 25 (June 17): 165–67. Unabridged typescript version appears in Arthur F. Burns, *Addresses, Essays, Lectures of Arthur Frank Burns. Vol. 1, 1962–1970.* Washington, DC: Federal Reserve Board Library.

——. 1977a. "Statement before the Committee on Banking, Finance and Urban Affairs, U.S. House of Representatives, July 29, 1977." *Federal Reserve Bulletin* 63, no. 8 (August): 721–28.

——. 1977b. "Statement before the Committee on Banking, Finance and Urban Affairs, U.S. House of Representatives, July 26, 1977, on the Views of the Board on H.R. 8094, the 'Federal Reserve Reform Act of 1977.'" *Federal Reserve Bulletin* 63, no. 8 (August): 717–21.

Burns, Arthur F., and Wesley C. Mitchell. 1946. *Measuring Business Cycles.* New York: National Bureau of Economic Research.

Burton, John. 1981. "Positively Milton Friedman." In J. R. Shackleton and Gareth Locksley, eds., *Twelve Contemporary Economists.* New York: John Wiley and Sons. 53–71.

Butler, Eamonn. 1985. *Milton Friedman: A Guide to His Economic Thought.* New York: Universe Books.

Caballero, Ricardo J. 1994. "Notes on the Theory and Evidence on Aggregate Purchases of Durable Goods." *Oxford Review of Economic Policy* 10, no. 2 (Summer): 107–17.

Cabral, Luís M. B. 2000. *Introduction to Industrial Organization.* Cambridge, MA: MIT Press.

Cagan, Phillip. 1956. "The Monetary Dynamics of Hyperinflation." In Milton Friedman, ed., *Studies in the Quantity Theory of Money*. Chicago: Chicago: University of Chicago Press. 25–117.

———. 1965. *Determinants and Effects of Changes in the Stock of Money, 1875-1960*. New York: Columbia University Press.

———. 1971. "Discussion [of George D. Green, 'The Economic Impact of the Stock Market Boom and Crash of 1929']." In Federal Reserve Bank of Boston, ed., *Consumer Spending and Monetary Policy: The Linkages*. Boston: Federal Reserve Bank of Boston. 222–28.

———. 1972a. *The Channels of Monetary Effects on Interest Rates*. New York: National Bureau of Economic Research.

———. 1972b. "Monetary Policy." In American Enterprise Institute, ed., *Economic Policy and Inflation in the Sixties*. Washington, DC: American Enterprise Institute. 89–153.

———. 1974. *The Hydra-Headed Monster: The Problem of Inflation in the United States*. Washington, DC: American Enterprise Institute.

———. 1979a. *Persistent Inflation: Historical and Policy Essays*. New York: Columbia University Press.

———. 1979b. "Financial Developments and the Erosion of Monetary Controls." In William Fellner, ed., *Contemporary Economic Problems*. Washington, DC: American Enterprise Institute. 117–51.

———. 1987. "Monetarism." In John Eatwell, Murray Milgate, and Peter Newman, eds., *The New Palgrave: A Dictionary of Economics*. Vol. 3, *K to P*. London: Macmillan. 492–97. Reprinted in John Eatwell and Murray Milgate, eds., *Money: New Palgrave*. New York: W. W. Norton, 1989. 195–205.

Calomiris, Charles W., Joseph Mason, and David C. Wheelock. 2011. "Did Doubling Reserve Requirements Cause the Recession of 1937-1938? A Microeconomic Approach." NBER Working Paper no. 16688, January.

Calvo, Guillermo A. 1978a. "On the Time Consistency of Optimal Policy in a Monetary Economy." *Econometrica* 46, no. 6 (November): 1411–28.

———. 1978b. "On the Indeterminacy of Interest Rates and Wages with Perfect Foresight." *Journal of Economic Theory* 19, no. 2 (December): 321–37.

———. 1983. "Staggered Prices in a Utility-Maximizing Framework." *Journal of Monetary Economics* 12, no. 3 (September): 383–98.

Campbell, John Y., and N. Gregory Mankiw. 1990. "Permanent Income, Current Income, and Consumption." *Journal of Business and Economic Statistics* 8, no. 3 (July): 265–79.

Capie, Forrest. 2010. *The Bank of England: 1950s to 1979*. Cambridge: Cambridge University Press.

Cargill, Thomas F. 1979. "Clark Warburton and the Development of Monetarism since the Great Depression." *History of Political Economy* 11, no. 3: 425–49.

———. 1981. "A Tribute to Clark Warburton, 1896-1979." *Journal of Money, Credit and Banking* 13, no. 1 (February): 89–93.

Cargill, Thomas F., and Thomas Mayer. 2006. "The Effect of Changes in Reserve Requirements during the 1930s: The Evidence from Nonmember Banks." *Journal of Economic History* 66, no. 2 (June): 417–32.

Carlson, Keith M., and Roger W. Spencer. 1975. "Crowding Out and Its Critics." *Federal Reserve Bank of St. Louis Review* 57, no. 12 (December): 2–17.

Carr, Hobart C. 1959. "Why and How to Read the Federal Reserve Statement." *Journal of Finance* 14, no. 4 (December): 504–19.

Carroll, Christopher D., and Lawrence H. Summers. 1991. "Consumption Growth Parallels Income Growth: Some New Evidence." In B. Douglas Bernheim and John B. Shoven, eds., *National Saving and Economic Performance*. Chicago: University of Chicago Press. 305–43.

Cerruti, Ben. 2014. *Dear Milton Friedman: A Decade of Lessons from an Economic Master*. Brentwood, CA: A Rational Advocate.

Chamberlin, Edward H. 1933. *The Theory of Monopolistic Competition*. Cambridge, MA: Harvard University Press.

Chapin, Ned. 1959. "An Appraisal of the One Hundred Per Cent Money Plan." PhD diss., Illinois Institute of Technology, Chicago, June.

Chen, Han, Vasco Cúrdia, and Andrea Ferrero. 2012. "The Macroeconomic Effects of Large-Scale Asset Purchase Programmes." *Economic Journal* 122, no. 564 (November): F289–F315.

Cherrier, Beatrice. 2011. "The Lucky Consistency of Milton Friedman's Science and Politics, 1933–1963." In Robert Van Horn, Philip Mirowski, and Thomas A. Stapleford, eds., *Building Chicago Economics: New Perspectives on the History of America's Most Powerful Economics Program*. Cambridge: Cambridge University Press. 335–67.

Chick, Victoria. 1973. *The Theory of Monetary Policy*. London: Gray-Mills.

Christ, Carl F. 1951. "A Test of an Econometric Model for the United States, 1921–1947." In NBER, ed., *Conference on Business Cycles*. New York: National Bureau of Economic Research. 35–107.

———. 1966. *Econometric Models and Methods*. New York: John Wiley and Sons.

———. 1994. "The Cowles Commission's Contributions to Econometrics at Chicago, 1939–1955." *Journal of Economic Literature* 32, no. 1 (March): 30–59.

Christiano, Lawrence J., and Martin Eichenbaum. 1992. "Current Real-Business-Cycle Theories and Aggregate Labor-Market Fluctuations." *American Economic Review* 82, no. 3 (June): 430–50.

Christiano, Lawrence J., Martin Eichenbaum, and Charles L. Evans. 2005. "Nominal Rigidities and the Dynamic Effects of a Shock to Monetary Policy." *Journal of Political Economy* 113, no. 1 (February): 1–45.

Christiano, Lawrence J., Martin Eichenbaum, and Sergio Rebelo. 2011. "When Is the Government Spending Multiplier Large?" *Journal of Political Economy* 19, no. 1 (February): 78–121.

Christiano, Lawrence J., Martin Eichenbaum, and Mathias Trabandt. 2016. "Unemployment and Business Cycles." *Econometrica* 84, no. 4 (July): 1523–69.

Christiano, Lawrence J., Roberto Motto, and Massimo Rostagno. 2003. "The Great Depression and the Friedman-Schwartz Hypothesis." *Journal of Money, Credit and Banking* 35, no. 6 (supplement): 1119–97.

Chung, Hess, Jean-Philippe Laforte, David Reifschneider, and John C. Williams. 2012. "Have We Underestimated the Likelihood and Severity of Zero Lower Bound Events?" *Journal of Money, Credit and Banking* 44, no. 1 (supplement) (February): 47–82.

Clarida, Richard, Jordi Galí, and Mark Gertler. 1999. "The Science of Monetary Policy: A New Keynesian Perspective." *Journal of Economic Literature* 37, no. 2 (December): 1661–707.

Clark, John J., and Morris Cohen, eds. 1963. *Business Fluctuations, Growth, and Economic Stabilization: A Reader*. New York: Random House.

Clark, Kim B., and Lawrence H. Summers. 1982. "Labour Force Participation: Timing and Persistence." *Review of Economic Studies* 49, no. 5 (December special issue): 825–44.

Clements, Kenneth W. 2012. "Notes on Milton Friedman." Manuscript, Business School, University of Western Australia.

Coase, Ronald H. 1991. "George J. Stigler." In Edward Shils, ed., *Remembering the University of Chicago: Teachers, Scientists, and Scholars.* Chicago: University of Chicago Press. 469–78.

Cochrane, John H. 1989. "The Return of the Liquidity Effect." *Journal of Economics and Business* 7, no. 1 (January): 75–83.

———. 1994. "Permanent and Transitory Components of GNP and Stock Prices." *Quarterly Journal of Economics* 109, no. 1 (February): 241–65.

———. 2013. "The New-Keynesian Liquidity Trap." NBER Working Paper no. 19476, September.

Cogley, Timothy, Thomas J. Sargent, and Viktor Tsyrennikov. 2014. "Wealth Dynamics in a Bond Economy with Heterogeneous Beliefs." *Economic Journal* 124, no. 575 (March): 1–30.

Cole, Harold L., and Lee E. Ohanian. 2004. "New Deal Policies and the Persistence of the Great Depression: A General Equilibrium Analysis." *Journal of Political Economy* 112, no. 4 (August): 779–816.

———. 2013. "The Impact of Cartelization, Money, and Productivity Shocks on the International Great Depression." NBER Working Paper no. 18823, February.

Coleman, John R., and Kenneth O. Alexander. 1962. *Study Guide for "The American Economy."* New York: McGraw-Hill.

Committee for Economic Development. 1947. *Taxes and the Budget: A Program for Prosperity in a Free Economy.* New York: Committee for Economic Development.

Committee on Appropriations, US House of Representatives. 1943. *Treasury Department Appropriation Bill for 1944: Hearings.* Washington, DC: US Government Printing Office.

Committee on Banking and Currency, US House of Representatives. 1964. *The Federal Reserve System after Fifty Years: Hearings.* Washington, DC: US Government Printing Office.

———. 1968a. *Removal of Gold Cover: Hearings, January 23, 25, 30 and 31; February 1, 1968.* Washington, DC: US Government Printing Office.

———. 1968b. *Compendium on Monetary Policy Guidelines and Federal Reserve Structure, Pursuant to H.R. 11.* Washington, DC: US Government Printing Office.

Committee on Banking and Currency, US Senate. 1968. *Gold Cover: Hearings, January 30, 31, and February 1, 1968.* Washington, DC: US Government Printing Office.

Committee on Banking, Currency and Housing, US House of Representatives. 1976a. *Financial Institutions and the Nation's Economy (FINE): Discussion Principles: Hearings, Part 3.* Washington, DC: US Government Printing Office.

———. 1976b. *The Impact of the Federal Reserve's Money Policies on the Economy: Hearings, June 8–24, 1976.* Washington, DC: US Government Printing Office.

Committee on Banking, Finance and Urban Affairs, US House of Representatives. 1990. *H.R. 3512 and H.R. 3066: Hearing, November 9, 1989.* Washington, DC: US Government Printing Office.

Committee on Banking, Housing, and Urban Affairs, US Senate. 1975. *Second Meeting on the Conduct of Monetary Policy: Hearings on Oversight on the Conduct of Monetary Policy*

Pursuant to House Concurrent Resolution 133, November 4 and 6, 1975. Washington, DC: US Government Printing Office.

Committee on Finance, US Senate. 1942a. *Withholding Tax: Hearing before a Subcommittee of the Committee on Finance, United States Senate, Seventy-Seventh Congress, Second Session, on Data Relative to Withholding Provisions of the 1942 Revenue Act, Wednesday, August 19, 1942.* Washington, DC: US Government Printing Office.

———. 1942b. *Withholding Tax: Hearing before a Subcommittee of the Committee on Finance, United States Senate, Seventy-Seventh Congress, Second Session, on Data Relative to Withholding Provisions of the 1942 Revenue Act, August 21 and 22, 1942.* Washington, DC: US Government Printing Office.

———. 1957. *Investigation of the Financial Condition of the United States Hearings, Part 3: August 13, 14, 15, 16, and 19, 1957.* Washington, DC: US Government Printing Office.

Committee on the Judiciary, US House of Representatives. 1980. *Constitutional Amendments to Balance the Federal Budget: Hearings.* Washington, DC: US Government Printing Office.

Committee on the Working of the Monetary System. 1959. *Report* [Radcliffe Report]. Command 827. London: Her Majesty's Stationery Office.

Comstock, Alzada. 1942. "Role of Income and Profits Taxes in the Control of Inflation." In Tax Institute, ed., *Financing the War: Symposium Conducted by the Tax Institute December 1–2, 1941, Philadelphia.* New York: J. J. Little and Ives. 93–104.

Conference on Research in National Income and Wealth. 1937. *Studies in Income and Wealth.* Vol. 1. New York: National Bureau of Economic Research.

———. 1938. *Studies in Income and Wealth.* Vol. 2. New York: National Bureau of Economic Research.

———. 1939. *Studies in Income and Wealth.* Vol. 3. New York: National Bureau of Economic Research.

Congdon, Tim. 1978. *Monetarism: An Essay in Definition.* London: Centre for Policy Studies.

———. 1982. *Monetary Control in Britain.* London: Macmillan.

———. 1988. *The Debt Threat: The Dangers of High Real Interest Rates for the World Economy.* Oxford, UK: Basil Blackwell.

———. 1994. "An Economic Program for the 1990s." *Economic Affairs* 15, no. 1 (Winter): 15–21.

———. 2011. *Money in a Free Society: Keynes, Friedman, and the New Crisis of Capitalism.* New York: Encounter Books.

———. 2014. "What Were the Causes of the Great Recession? The Mainstream Approach vs. the Monetary Interpretation." *World Economics* 15, no. 2 (April–June): 1–32.

Cooley, Thomas F., and Lee E. Ohanian. 1997. "Postwar British Economic Growth and the Legacy of Keynes." *Journal of Political Economy* 105, no. 3 (June): 439–72.

Cooper, J. Phillip, and Stanley Fischer. 1972. "Simulations of Monetary Rules in the FRB-MIT-Penn Model." *Journal of Money, Credit and Banking* 4, no. 2 (May): 384–96.

———. 1973. "Stabilization Policy and Lags." *Journal of Political Economy* 81, no. 4 (July/August): 847–77.

———. 1974. "Monetary and Fiscal Policy in the Fully Stochastic St. Louis Econometric Model." *Journal of Money, Credit and Banking* 6, no. 1 (February): 1–22.

Cooper, J. Phillip, and Charles R. Nelson. 1975. "The Ex Ante Prediction Performance of the St. Louis and FRB-MIT-PENN Econometric Models and Some Results on Composite Predictors." *Journal of Money, Credit and Banking* 7, no. 1 (February): 1–32.

Council of Economic Advisers. 1952. "Reply by the Council of Economic Advisers."
In Joint Committee on the Economic Report, US Congress, *Monetary Policy and the
Management of the Public Debt: Their Role in Achieving Price Stability and High-Level
Employment, Replies to Questions and Other Material for the Use of the Subcommittee on
General Credit Control and Debt Management, Part 2*. Washington, DC: US Govern-
ment Printing Office. 847–93.

———. 1969. *The Economic Report of the President, 1969*. Washington, DC: US Government Printing Office.

———. 1974. *The Economists Conference on Inflation: September 5, 1974, Washington D.C.;
September 23, 1974, New York*. Washington, DC: US Government Printing Office.

———. 2011. *The Economic Report of the President, 2011*. Washington, DC: US Government
Printing Office.

Cowles Foundation. 1964. *Report of Research Activities July 1, 1961–June 30, 1964*. New
Haven, CT: Cowles Foundation for Research in Economics at Yale University.

Cox, Albert H., Jr. 1966. *Regulation of Interest on Bank Deposits*. Ann Arbor: University of
Michigan Press.

Cripps, Francis. 1977. "The Money Supply, Wages and Inflation." *Cambridge Journal of
Economics* 1, no. 1 (March): 101–12.

———. 1979. "Wages and Unemployment—a Non-monetarist Rejoinder." *Cambridge
Journal of Economics* 3, no. 2 (June): 175–77.

Cross, Rod. 1984. "Monetarism and Duhem's Thesis." In Peter Wiles and Guy Routh,
eds., *Economics in Disarray*. Oxford, UK: Basil Blackwell. 78–99.

Crowder, William J., Dennis L. Hoffman, and Robert H. Rasche. 1999. "Identification,
Long-Run Relations, and Fundamental Innovations in a Simple Cointegrated System." *Review of Economics and Statistics* 81, no. 1 (February): 109–21.

Culbertson, John M. 1964. "United States Monetary History: Its Implications for Monetary Theory." *National Banking Review* 1, no. 3 (March): 359–79.

———. 1973. "Alternatives for Debt Management: Discussion." In Federal Reserve Bank
of Boston, ed., *Issues in Federal Debt Management: Proceedings of a Conference Held at
Melvin Village, New Hampshire, June, 1973*. Boston: Federal Reserve Bank of Boston.
31–38.

Currie, Lauchlin B. 1934. *The Supply and Control of Money in the United States*. Cambridge, MA: Harvard University Press. Rev. ed., 1935.

Dacey, W. Manning. 1947. "The Cheap Money Technique." *Lloyds Bank Review* 2, no. 3
(January): 49–63.

Darby, Michael R. 1975. "Book Review: *Permanent Income, Wealth, and Consumption*,
by Thomas Mayer." *Journal of Money, Credit and Banking* 7, no. 1 (February): 122–24.

Darby, Michael R., Milton Friedman, William Poole, David E. Lindsey, and Michael J.
Bazdarich. 1987. "Recent Behavior of the Velocity of Money." *Contemporary Policy
Issues* 5, no. 1 (January): 1–33.

Darby, Michael R., and James R. Lothian. 1983. "British Economic Policy under Margaret Thatcher: A Midterm Examination." *Carnegie-Rochester Conference Series on
Public Policy* 18, no. 1, 157–207.

David, Paul A., and John L. Scadding. 1974. "Private Savings: Ultrarationality, Aggregation, and 'Denison's Law.'" *Journal of Political Economy* 82, no. 2, part 1 (March/April):
225–49.

Davidson, Paul. 1970. "Monetary Policy and the Clearing Banks: Discussion Paper." In
David R. Croome and Harry G. Johnson, eds., *Money in Britain, 1959–1969: The Papers*

of the "Radcliffe Report: Ten Years After" Conference at Hove, Sussex, October, 1969. London: Oxford University Press. 189-99.

Davis, Richard G. 1969. "How Much Does Money Matter? A Look at Some Recent Evidence." *Federal Reserve Bank of New York Monthly Review* 51, no. 6 (June): 119-31.

Debreu, Gerard. 1959. *Theory of Value: An Axiomatic Analysis of Economic Equilibrium.* New Haven, CT: Yale University Press.

———. 1991. "The Mathematization of Economic Theory." *American Economic Review* 81, no. 1 (March): 1-7.

Dennis, Geoffrey E. J. 1981. *Monetary Economics.* London: Longman.

Despres, Emile, Albert G. Hart, Milton Friedman, Paul A. Samuelson, and Donald H. Wallace. 1950. "The Problem of Economic Instability." *American Economic Review* 40, no. 4 (September): 501-38.

Dewald, William G. 1963. "Free Reserves, Total Reserves, and Monetary Control." *Journal of Political Economy* 71, no. 2 (April): 141-53.

———. 1966. "Money Supply versus Interest Rates as Proximate Objectives of Monetary Policy." *National Banking Review* 3, no. 4 (June): 509-22.

DiCecio, Riccardo, and Edward Nelson. 2013. "The Great Inflation in the United States and the United Kingdom: Reconciling Policy Decisions and Data Outcomes." In Michael D. Bordo and Athanasios Orphanides, eds., *The Great Inflation: The Rebirth of Modern Central Banking.* Chicago: University of Chicago Press. 393-438.

Director, Aaron. 1948. "Prefatory Note." In Henry C. Simons, *Economic Policy for a Free Society.* Chicago: University of Chicago Press. v-vii.

———, ed. 1952. *Defense, Controls, and Inflation: A Conference Sponsored by the University of Chicago Law School.* Chicago: University of Chicago Press.

Dixit, Avinash K. 1976. "Public Finance in a Keynesian Temporary Equilibrium." *Journal of Economic Theory* 12, no. 2 (April): 242-58.

———. 1992. "Theory and Policy: Reply to Tanzi." *IMF Staff Papers* 39, no. 4 (December): 967-70.

———. 1996. *The Making of Economic Policy: A Transaction-Cost Politics Perspective.* Cambridge, MA: MIT Press.

———. 2014. *Microeconomics: A Very Short Introduction.* Oxford: Oxford University Press.

Dixit, Avinash K., and Joseph E. Stiglitz. 1977. "Monopolistic Competition and Optimum Product Diversity." *American Economic Review* 67, no. 3 (June): 297-308.

Dolan, Edwin G., and David E. Lindsey. 1977. *Basic Economics.* Hinsdale, IL: Dryden.

Dormen, Leslie, and Mark Zussman. 1984. *The Secret Life of Girls.* New York: Plume.

Dornbusch, Rudiger, and Stanley Fischer. 1978. *Macroeconomics.* New York: McGraw-Hill.

———. 1979. *The Determinants and Effects of Changes in Interest Rates: A Study Prepared for the Trustees of the Banking Research Fund.* Chicago: Association of Reserve City Bankers.

———. 1981. *Macroeconomics.* 2nd ed. New York: McGraw-Hill.

———. 1994. *Macroeconomics.* 6th ed. New York: McGraw-Hill.

Dornbusch, Rudiger, and Alberto Giovannini. 1990. "Monetary Policy in the Open Economy." In Frank H. Hahn and Benjamin M. Friedman, eds., *Handbook of Monetary Economics.* Vol. 2. Amsterdam: North-Holland. 1231-303.

Dornbusch, Rudiger, and Alejandro Reynoso. 1989. "Financial Factors in Economic Development." *American Economic Review (Papers and Proceedings)* 79, no. 2 (May): 204-9.

Duesenberry, James S. 1949. *Income, Saving, and the Theory of Consumer Behavior*. Cambridge, MA: Harvard University Press.

———. 1962. "The Co-ordination of Policies for Full Employment and Price Stability." In Douglas C. Hague, ed., *Inflation: Proceedings of a Conference Held by the International Economic Association*. New York: St. Martin's. 129–46.

———. 1972. *Money and Credit: Impact and Control*. Third edition. Englewood Cliffs, NJ: Prentice Hall.

———. 1983. "The Political Economy of Central Banking in the United States or *Quis Custodiet Ipsos Custodes*." In Donald R. Hodgman, ed., *The Political Economy of Monetary Policy: National and International Aspects—Proceedings of a Conference Held in July 1983*. Boston: Federal Reserve Bank of Boston. 123–40.

Dunlop, John T. 1938. "The Movement of Real and Money Wage Rates." *Economic Journal* 48, no. 191 (September): 413–34.

Dupraz, Stéphane, Emi Nakamura, and Jón Steinsson. 2018. "A Plucking Model of Business Cycles." Manuscript, University of California, Berkeley, December.

Dynan, Karen, Jonathan Skinner, and Stephen Zeldes. 2004. "Do the Rich Save More?" *Journal of Political Economy* 112, no. 2 (April): 397–444.

Ebenstein, Lanny. 2007. *Milton Friedman: A Biography*. New York: Palgrave Macmillan.

Eccles, Marriner S. 1944. "Possibilities of Postwar Inflation and Suggested Tax Action." In Tax Institute, *Curbing Inflation through Taxation: Symposium Conducted by the Tax Institute, February 7–8, 1944, New York*. New York: Tax Institute. 225–38.

Eckstein, Otto. 1983. *The DRI Model of the U.S. Economy*. New York: McGraw-Hill.

Econometric Society. 1948. "Report of the Washington Meeting, September 6–18, 1947." *Econometrica* 16, no. 1 (January): 33–111.

Edey, Malcolm, and Mark Britten-Jones. 1990. "Saving and Investment." In Stephen Grenville, ed., *The Australian Macroeconomy in the 1980s*. Sydney: Reserve Bank of Australia. 79–145.

Eggertsson, Gauti B. 2008. "Great Expectations and the End of the Depression." *American Economic Review* 98, no. 4 (September): 1476–516.

———. 2012. "Was the New Deal Contractionary?" *American Economic Review* 102, no. 1 (February): 524–55.

Eggertsson, Gauti B., and Neil R. Mehrotra. 2014. "A Model of Secular Stagnation." NBER Working Paper no. 20574, October.

Eichenbaum, Martin. 1995. "Some Comments on the Role of Econometrics in Economic Theory." *Economic Journal* 105, no. 433 (November): 1609–21.

Eichenbaum, Martin, Lars Peter Hansen, and Kenneth J. Singleton. 1988. "A Time Series Analysis of Representative Agent Models of Consumption and Leisure Choice under Uncertainty." *Quarterly Journal of Economics* 103, no. 1 (February): 51–78.

Eichengreen, Barry. 1992. *Golden Fetters: The Gold Standard and the Great Depression, 1919–1939*. Oxford: Oxford University Press.

Einzig, Robert S. 1959. "The Behavior of the Active Money Supply as a Guide to Federal Reserve Policy Formation." In Ad Hoc Committee on Money Supply Statistics (William J. Abbott, Harry Brandy, Robert S. Einzig, Roland I. Robinson [Committee Chairman], and Clarence W. Tow), *Recommendations for Statistics of Money Supply and Member Bank Reserves*. Washington, DC: Federal Reserve Board, October 8. 1–10.

Eisenhart, Churchill, Millard W. Hastay, and W. Allen Wallis, eds. 1947. *Selected Techniques of Statistical Analysis for Scientific and Industrial Research and Production and*

Management Engineering by the Statistical Research Group, Columbia University. New York: McGraw Hill.

Eisenhower, Dwight D. 1953. "Annual Message to the Congress on the State of the Union, February 2nd, 1953." http://www.eisenhower.archives.gov/all_about_ike /speeches/1953_state_of_the_union.pdf.

———. 1959. "Annual Message to the Congress on the State of the Union, January 9, 1959." http://www.eisenhower.archives.gov/all_about_ike/speeches/1959_state_of _the_union.pdf.

———. 1963. *The White House Years: Mandate for Change, 1953-1956*. Garden City, NY: Doubleday.

———. 1965. *The White House Years: Waging Peace, 1956-1961*. Garden City, NY: Doubleday.

Eisner, Robert. 1958. "The Permanent Income Hypothesis: A Comment." *American Economic Review* 48, no. 5 (December): 972-90.

———. 1963. *"Money, Trade and Economic Growth: Survey Lectures in Economic Theory* by Harry G. Johnson." *American Economic Review* 53, no. 1, part 1 (March): 151-54.

———. 1967. "A Permanent Income Theory for Investment: Some Empirical Explorations." *American Economic Review* 57, no. 3 (June): 363-90.

———. 1986. *How Real Is the Federal Deficit?* New York: Free Press.

Ekelund, Robert B., Jr., E. G. Furubotn, and W. P. Gramm, eds. 1972a. *The Evolution of Modern Demand Theory: A Collection of Essays*. Lexington, MA: Lexington Books.

———. 1972b. "The State of Contemporary Demand Theory." In Robert B. Ekelund Jr., E. G. Furubotn, and W. P. Gramm, eds., *The Evolution of Modern Demand Theory: A Collection of Essays*. Lexington, MA: Lexington Books. 57-93.

Emmett, Ross B. 2011. "Sharpening Tools in the Workshop: The Workshop System and the Chicago School's Success." In Robert Van Horn, Philip Mirowski, and Thomas A. Stapleford, eds., *Building Chicago Economics: New Perspectives on the History of America's Most Powerful Economics Program*. Cambridge: Cambridge University Press. 93-115.

Enders, Walter. 1995. *Applied Econometric Time Series*. New York: John Wiley and Sons.

Engen, Eric M., Thomas Laubach, and David Reifschneider. 2015. "The Macroeconomic Effects of the Federal Reserve's Unconventional Monetary Policies." Federal Reserve Board Finance and Economics Discussion Series Paper no. 2015-005, January.

Engle, Robert F., and C. W. J. Granger. 1987. "Co-integration and Error Correction: Representation, Estimation, and Testing." *Econometrica* 55, no. 2 (March): 251-76.

Enlow, Robert C., and Lenore T. Ealy, eds. 2006. *Liberty and Learning: Milton Friedman's Voucher Idea at Fifty*. Washington, DC: Cato Institute.

Ensley, Grover W., and Richard Goode. 1943. "Mr. Warburton on the Gap." *American Economic Review* 33, no. 4 (December): 897-99.

Epstein, Larry G., and Stanley E. Zin. 1989. "Substitution, Risk Aversion, and the Temporal Behavior of Consumption and Asset Returns: A Theoretical Framework." *Econometrica* 57, no. 4 (July): 937-69.

Erceg, Christopher J., and Andrew T. Levin. 2003. "Imperfect Credibility and Inflation Persistence." *Journal of Monetary Economics* 50, no. 4 (May): 915-44.

———. 2006. "Optimal Monetary Policy with Durable Consumption Goods." *Journal of Monetary Economics* 53, no. 7 (October): 1341-59.

Ericsson, Neil R. 2004. "The *ET* Interview: Professor David F. Hendry." *Econometric Theory* 20, no. 4 (August): 743-804.

Eshag, Eprime. 1983. *Fiscal and Monetary Policies and Problems in Developing Countries.* Cambridge: Cambridge University Press.

Europa Publications. 2003. *The International Who's Who 2004.* London: Europa.

Evans, Charles L., and David A. Marshall. 1998. "Monetary Policy and the Term Structure of Nominal Interest Rates: Evidence and Theory." *Carnegie-Rochester Conference Series on Public Policy* 49, no. 1 (December): 53–111.

Evans, Michael K. 1983. *The Truth about Supply-Side Economics.* New York: Basic Books.

Evans, Paul. 1982a. "The Effects of General Price Controls in the United States during World War II." *Journal of Political Economy* 90, no. 5 (October): 944–66.

———. 1982b. "*The Supply-Side Effects of Economic Policy*, edited by Laurence H. Meyer." *Journal of Money, Credit and Banking* 14, no. 3 (August): 429–31.

———. 1983. "What Does a Tax Cut Do?" In Victor A. Canto, Douglas H. Joines, and Arthur B. Laffer, eds., *Foundations of Supply-Side Economics: Theory and Evidence.* New York: Academic. 207–23.

———. 1986. "Is the Dollar High Because of Large Budget Deficits?" *Journal of Monetary Economics* 18, no. 3 (November): 227–49.

Evers, Williamson M., ed. 1990. *National Service: Pro and Con.* Stanford, CA: Hoover Institution Press.

Fabricant, Solomon, ed. 1958. *Investing in Economic Knowledge: Thirty-Eighth Annual Report—a Record for 1957 and Plans for 1958, National Bureau of Economic Research, Inc.* New York: National Bureau of Economic Research.

Fama, Eugene F., and Merton H. Miller. 1972. *The Theory of Finance.* New York: Holt, Rinehart and Winston.

Fand, David I. 1969a. "Some Issues in Monetary Economics." *Banca Nazionale Quarterly Review* 22, no. 90 (September): 215–47.

———. 1969b. "A Monetary Interpretation of the Post-1965 Inflation in the United States." *Banca Nazionale del Lavoro Quarterly Review* 22, no. 89 (June): 99–127.

Federal Open Market Committee. 1960. Historical Minutes for Meeting of April 12, 1960. Scan www.federalreserve.gov.

Federal Reserve Bank of Chicago. 1958. "Another Look at the Money Supply." *Business Conditions* (Federal Reserve Bank of Chicago) 43, no. 3 (March): 12–16.

Federal Reserve Board. 1924. *Tenth Annual Report of the Federal Reserve Board, Covering Operations for the Year 1923.* Washington, DC: US Government Printing Office. Scan available at https://fraser.stlouisfed.org/files/docs/publications/arfr/1920s/arfr_1923 .pdf.

———. 1953. "Influence of Credit and Monetary Measures on Economic Stability." *Federal Reserve Bulletin* 39, no. 3 (March): 219–34.

Feibes, Walter. 1974. *Introduction to Finite Mathematics.* Santa Barbara, CA: Hamilton.

Feldberg, Meyer, Kate Jowell, and Stephen Mulholland, eds. 1976. *Milton Friedman in South Africa.* Johannesburg: Creda.

Feldstein, Martin S. 1979. "The Welfare Cost of Permanent Inflation and Optimal Short-Run Economic Policy." *Journal of Political Economy* 87, no. 4 (August): 749–68.

Fellner, William J. 1956. "The Balancing of Objectives under the Employment Act of 1946." In Gerhard Colm, ed., *The Employment Act, Past and Future: A Tenth Anniversary Symposium.* Washington, DC: National Planning Association. 87–91.

———. 1976. *Towards a Reconstruction of Macro-economics: Problems of Theory and Policy.* Washington, DC: American Enterprise Institute.

Fellner, William J., et al. 1967. *Ten Economic Studies in the Tradition of Irving Fisher*. New York: John Wiley and Sons.

Fischer, Stanley. 1975. "Recent Developments in Monetary Theory." *American Economic Review (Papers and Proceedings)* 65, no. 2 (May): 157-66.

———. 1976. "Comments on Tobin and Buiter." In Jerome L. Stein, ed., *Monetarism*. Amsterdam: North-Holland. 322-26.

———. 1977. "Long-Term Contracts, Rational Expectations, and the Optimal Money Supply Rule." *Journal of Political Economy* 85, no. 1 (February): 191-205.

———. 1980. "On Activist Monetary Policy with Rational Expectations." In Stanley Fischer, ed., *Rational Expectations and Economic Policy*. Chicago: University of Chicago Press. 211-35.

———. 1981. "Relative Price Shocks, Relative Price Variability, and Inflation." *Brookings Papers on Economic Activity* 12, no. 2, 381-431.

———. 1985. "Contracts, Credibility and Disinflation." In Victor Argy and John W. Nevile, eds., *Inflation and Unemployment: Theory, Experience and Policy-Making*. London: George Allen and Unwin. 39-59.

———. 1990. "Rules versus Discretion in Monetary Policy." In Benjamin M. Friedman and Frank H. Hahn, eds., *Handbook of Monetary Economics*. Vol. 2. Amsterdam: Elsevier/North-Holland. 1155-84.

Fischer, Stanley, and Rudiger Dornbusch. 1983. *Economics*. New York: McGraw Hill.

Fishburn, Peter C. 1970. *Utility Theory for Decision Making*. New York: Wiley.

Fisher, Franklin M. 1966. *The Identification Problem in Econometrics*. New York: McGraw-Hill.

Fisher, Irving. 1892. "Mathematical Investigations in the Theory of Value and Prices." *Transactions of Connecticut Academy of Arts and Sciences* 27, no. 1, 1-124.

———. 1896. *Appreciation and Interest*. New York: Macmillan.

———. 1907. *The Rate of Interest*. New York: Macmillan.

———. 1911a. *The Purchasing Power of Money: Its Determination and Relation to Credit, Interest and Crises*. New York: Macmillan.

———. 1911b. *Elementary Principles of Economics*. New York: Macmillan.

———. 1926. "A Statistical Relation between Unemployment and Price Changes." *International Labour Review* 13, no. 6 (June): 785-92.

———. 1930. *The Theory of Interest*. New York: Macmillan.

———. 1935. *100% Money*. New York: Adelphi.

———. 1973. "I Discovered the Phillips Curve." *Journal of Political Economy* 81, no. 2, part 1 (March/April): 496-502.

Forbes, William. 2009. *Behavioural Finance*. New York: John Wiley and Sons.

Fraser, Bernie. 1994. "The Art of Monetary Policy." *Reserve Bank Bulletin* 57, no. 10 (October): 17-25.

Frazer, William. 1988a. *Power and Ideas: Milton Friedman and the Big U-Turn I; The Background*. Gainesville, FL: Gulf-Atlantic.

———. 1988b. *Power and Ideas: Milton Friedman and the Big U-Turn II; The U-Turn*. Gainesville, FL: Gulf-Atlantic.

———. 1994. *The Legacy of Keynes and Friedman: Economic Analysis, Money, and Ideology*. Westport, CT: Praeger.

———. 1997. *The Friedman System: Economic Analysis of Time Series*. Westport, CT: Praeger.

———. 2002. "Friedman, Milton." In Brian Snowdon and Howard R. Vane, eds., *An Encyclopedia of Macroeconomics*. Cheltenham, UK: Edward Elgar. 271-84.

Freedman, Craig D. 2008. *Chicago Fundamentalism: Ideology and Methodology in Economics.* Hackensack, NJ: World Scientific.

Freedman, Craig D., Geoffrey C. Harcourt, Peter Kriesler, and John W. Nevile. 2013. "Milton Friedman: Constructing an Anti-Keynes." University of New South Wales Australian School of Business Research Paper no. 2013-35.

Freeman, H. A., Milton Friedman, Frederick Mosteller, and W. Allen Wallis, eds. 1948. *Sampling Inspection: Principles, Procedures, and Tables for Single, Double, and Sequential Sampling in Acceptance Inspection and Quality Control Based on Percent Defective by the Statistical Research Group, Columbia University.* New York: McGraw Hill.

Friedman, Benjamin M. 1980. "Postwar Changes in the American Financial Markets." In Martin S. Feldstein, ed., *The American Economy in Transition.* Chicago: University of Chicago Press. 9–78.

——. 1986. "Money, Credit, and Interest Rates in the Business Cycle: Reply." In Robert J. Gordon, ed., *The American Business Cycle: Continuity and Change.* Chicago: University of Chicago Press. 450–55.

——. 1988. "Monetary Policy without Quantity Variables." *American Economic Review (Papers and Proceedings)* 78, no. 2 (May): 440–45.

——. 2004. "Commentary on 'Is Inflation Targeting Best-Practice Monetary Policy?'" *Federal Reserve Bank of St. Louis Review* 86, no. 4 (July/August): 145–49.

——. 2013. "Comment [on Andreas Beyer, Vitor Gaspar, Christina Gerberding, and Otmar Issing, 'German Monetary Policy after the Breakdown of Bretton Woods']." In Michael D. Bordo and Athanasios Orphanides, eds., *The Great Inflation: The Rebirth of Modern Central Banking.* Chicago: University of Chicago Press. 346–54.

Friedman, Milton. 1933. "An Empirical Study of the Relationship between Railroad Stock Prices and Railroad Earnings for the Period 1921–1931." MA thesis, Department of Economics, University of Chicago, December.

——. 1935a. "Professor Pigou's Method for Measuring Elasticities of Demand from Budgetary Data." *Quarterly Journal of Economics* 50, no. 1 (November): 151–63.

——. 1935b. "*Seasonal Variations in Industry and Trade* by Simon Kuznets." *Journal of Political Economy* 43, no. 6 (December): 830–32.

——. 1936. "Marginal Utility of Money and Elasticities of Demand: II." *Quarterly Journal of Economics* 30, no. 3 (May): 532–33.

——. 1937a. "The Use of Ranks to Avoid the Assumption of Normality Implicit in the Analysis of Variance." *Journal of the American Statistical Association* 32, no. 200 (December): 675–701.

——. 1937b. "Discussion." In Conference on Research in National Income and Wealth, *Studies in Income and Wealth.* Vol. 1. New York: National Bureau of Economic Research. 159–62.

——. 1938a. "Mr. Broster on Demand Curves." *Journal of the Royal Statistical Society* 101, no. 2, 450–54.

——. 1938b. "Comment [on M. A. Copeland and E. M. Martin, 'The Correction of Wealth and Income Estimates for Price Change']: III." In Conference on Research in National Income and Wealth, *Studies in Income and Wealth.* Vol. 2. New York: National Bureau of Economic Research. 123–30.

——. 1939. "Discussion: Charles Stewart, 'Income Capitalization as a Method of Estimating the Distribution of Wealth by Size Groups.'" In Conference on Research in National Income and Wealth, *Studies in Income and Wealth.* Vol. 3. New York: National Bureau of Economic Research. 129–41.

———. 1940. "*Business Cycles in the United States of America, 1919-1932* by J. Tinbergen." *American Economic Review* 30, no. 3 (September): 657-60.

———. 1941. "*Monopolistic Competition and General Equilibrium Theory* [by] Robert Triffin." *Journal of Farm Economics* 23, no. 1 (February): 389-91.

———. 1942a. "The Inflationary Gap: II. Discussion of the Inflationary Gap." *American Economic Review* 32, no. 2 (February): 314-20.

———. 1942b. "Exhibit 66. Statement by Milton Friedman, May 7, 1942, on the Relation of Taxation to Inflation." In Treasury Department and the Staff of the Joint Committee on Internal Revenue Taxation, *Data on Proposed Revenue Bill of 1942, Submitted to the Committee on Ways and Means, House of Representatives.* Washington, DC: US Government Printing Office.

———. 1942c. "The Danger of Inflation." Memorandum, Division of Tax Research, US Treasury, July 23. Text available on Hoover Institution website, Robert Leeson and Charles G. Palm, Milton Friedman Collected Work Project (CWP).

———. 1943a. "The Spendings Tax as a Wartime Fiscal Measure." *American Economic Review* 33, no. 1 (March): 50-62.

———. 1943b. "Methods of Predicting the Onset of 'Inflation.'" In Carl S. Shoup, Milton Friedman, and Ruth P. Mack, *Taxing to Prevent Inflation: Techniques for Estimating Revenue Requirements.* New York: Columbia University Press. 111-53.

———. 1944. "*Saving, Investment, and National Income* by Oscar L. Altman." *Review of Economics and Statistics* 26, no. 2 (May): 101-2.

———. 1946. "Lange on Price Flexibility and Employment: A Methodological Criticism." *American Economic Review* 36, no. 4 (September): 613-31.

———. 1947. "Lerner on the Economics of Control." *Journal of Political Economy* 55, no. 5 (October): 405-16.

———. 1948a. "A Monetary and Fiscal Framework for Economic Stability." *American Economic Review* 38, no. 3 (June): 245-64.

———. 1948b. "*Cycles: The Science of Prediction* by Edward R. Dewey [and] Edwin F. Dakin." *Journal of the American Statistical Association* 43, no. 241 (March): 139-41.

———. 1949a. "The Marshallian Demand Curve." *Journal of Political Economy* 57, no. 6 (December): 463-95.

———. 1949b. "Professor Friedman's Proposal: Rejoinder." *American Economic Review* 39, no. 5 (September): 949-55.

———. 1949c. "'Liquidity and Uncertainty'—Discussion." *American Economic Review (Papers and Proceedings)* 39, no. 2 (May): 196-201.

———. 1950a. "Wesley Mitchell as an Economic Theorist." *Journal of Political Economy* 58, no. 6 (December): 465-93.

———. 1950b. "Does Monopoly in Industry Justify Monopoly in Agriculture?" *Farm Policy Forum* 3, no. 6 (June): 5-8.

———. 1951a. "Some Comments on the Significance of Labor Unions for Economic Policy." In David McCord Wright, ed., *The Impact of the Union: Eight Economic Theorists Evaluate the Labor Union Movement.* New York: Harcourt Brace. 204-34.

———. 1951b. "Comment [on Carl F. Christ, 'A Test of an Econometric Model for the United States, 1921-1947.']" In NBER, ed., *Conference on Business Cycles.* New York: National Bureau of Economic Research. 107-14.

———. 1951c. "Comments on Monetary Policy." *Review of Economics and Statistics* 33, no. 3 (August): 186-91.

———. 1951d. "Comment [on George Katona and Janet A. Fisher, 'Postwar Changes in

Income of Identical Consumer Units.']" In Conference on Research in Income and Wealth, *Studies in Income and Wealth*, vol. 13. New York: National Bureau of Economic Research. 119–22.

———. 1951e. "Neo-liberalism and Its Prospects." *Farmand* (Oslo, Norway), February 17, 89–93. Reprinted in Lanny Ebenstein, ed., *The Indispensable Milton Friedman: Essays on Politics and Economics*. Washington, DC: Regnery, 2012. 3–9.

———. 1951f. "Commodity-Reserve Currency." *Journal of Political Economy* 59, no. 3 (June): 203–32.

———. 1952a. "A Method of Comparing Incomes of Families Differing in Composition." In Conference on Research in Income and Wealth, *Studies in Income and Wealth*, Vol. 15. New York: National Bureau of Economic Research. 9–20.

———. 1952b. "Price, Income, and Monetary Changes in Three Wartime Periods." *American Economic Review (Papers and Proceedings)* 62, no. 2 (May): 612–25.

———. 1952c. "Comment on 'Methodological Developments.'" In Bernard F. Haley, ed., *A Survey of Contemporary Economics*. Vol. 2. Homewood, IL: Richard D. Irwin. 455–57.

———. 1952d. "Free Enterprise in the United States." In NBC, *The Transformation of British and American Capitalism*. University of Chicago Round Table no. 740, June 1. 12–17.

———. 1952e. "The 'Welfare' Effects of an Income Tax and an Excise Tax." *Journal of Political Economy* 60, no. 1 (February): 25–33.

———. 1952f. "'Welfare' Effects: A Reply." *Journal of Political Economy* 60, no. 4 (August): 334–36.

———. 1952g. "The Economic Theorist." In Arthur F. Burns, ed., *Wesley Clair Mitchell: The Economic Scientist*. New York: National Bureau of Economic Research. 237–82.

———. 1953a. "The Case for Flexible Exchange Rates." In Milton Friedman, *Essays in Positive Economics*. Chicago: University of Chicago Press. 157–203.

———. 1953b. *Essays in Positive Economics*. Chicago: University of Chicago Press.

———. 1953c. "The Methodology of Positive Economics." In Milton Friedman, *Essays in Positive Economics*. Chicago: University of Chicago Press. 3–43.

———. 1953d. "The Effects of a Full-Employment Policy on Economic Stability: A Formal Analysis." In Milton Friedman, *Essays in Positive Economics*. Chicago: University of Chicago Press. 117–32.

———. 1953e. "Choice, Chance, and the Personal Distribution of Income." *Journal of Political Economy* 61, no. 4 (August): 277–90.

———. 1953f. "Discussion of the Inflationary Gap [revised version]." In Milton Friedman, *Essays in Positive Economics*. Chicago: University of Chicago Press. 251–62.

———. 1954a. "Why the American Economy Is Depression Proof." *Nationalekonomiska Föreningens Förhandlingar*, no. 3, 58–77. Reprinted in Milton Friedman, *Dollars and Deficits: Living with America's Economic Problems*. Englewood Cliffs, NJ: Prentice Hall, 1968. 72–96.

———. 1954b. "The Marshallian Demand Curve: A Reply." *Journal of Political Economy* 62, no. 3 (June): 261–66.

———. 1954c. "The Reduction of Fluctuations in the Incomes of Primary Producers: A Critical Comment." *Economic Journal* 64, no. 256 (December): 698–703.

———. 1955a. "Marshall and Friedman on Union Strength: Comment." *Review of Economics and Statistics* 37, no. 4 (November): 401–6.

———. 1955b. "The Role of Government in Education." In Robert A. Solo, ed., *Economics and the Public Interest*. New Brunswick, NJ: Rutgers University Press. 123–44.

——. 1955c. "What All Is Utility?" *Economic Journal* 65, no. 259 (September): 405–9.

——. 1955d. "Credit and Monetary Policy, 1952–1954." Report on [Federal Reserve Board] Staff Studies by Review Panel, no. 6, Federal Reserve Board, May 20. Federal Reserve Board records.

——. 1955e. "Liberalism, Old Style." In William T. Couch, ed., *Collier's 1955 Year Book: Covering National and International Events of the Year 1954*. New York: P. F. Collier and Son. 360–63.

——. 1955f. "Money and Banking." In Solomon Fabricant, ed., *Government in Economic Life: National Bureau of Economic Research Thirty-Fifth Annual Report, May 1955*. New York: National Bureau of Economic Research. 30–33.

——. 1955g. "Leon Walras and His Economic System." *American Economic Review* 45, no. 5 (December): 900–909.

——. 1955h. "Comment [on Caleb A. Smith, 'Survey of the Empirical Evidence on Economies of Scale']." In George J. Stigler, ed., *Business Concentration and Price Policy: A Conference of the Universities—National Committee for Economic Research*. Princeton, NJ: Princeton University Press. 230–38.

——. 1956a. "The Quantity Theory of Money—a Restatement." In Milton Friedman, ed., *Studies in the Quantity Theory of Money*. Chicago: University of Chicago Press. 3–21.

——, ed. 1956b. *Studies in the Quantity Theory of Money*. Chicago: University of Chicago Press.

——. 1956c. "Monetary Policy, Domestic and International." Lecture, Wabash College, June. Available on Hoover Institution website, CWP.

——. 1957a. *A Theory of the Consumption Function*. Princeton, NJ: Princeton University Press.

——. 1957b. "Consumer Credit Control as an Instrument of Stabilization Policy." In Federal Reserve Board, ed., *Consumer Instalment Credit, Part 2*. Vol. 2, *Conference on Regulation*. Washington, DC: Federal Reserve Board. 73–103.

——. 1957c. "Discussion of 'The Indian Alternative' by John Strachey." *Encounter* 8, no. 1 (January): 71–73.

——. 1957d. "Comment on John Strachey." In University of Chicago, the College, ed., *Introduction to the Civilization of India: India and Pakistan in the Modern World; Syllabus Readings, March 1957*. Chicago: University of Chicago Press (Syllabus Division). 362–67.

——. 1957e. "Savings and the Balance Sheet." *Bulletin of the Oxford University Institute of Statistics* 19, no. 2 (May): 125–36.

——. 1957f. "Government Control of Consumer Credit." *University of Pennsylvania Bulletin* 62, no. 13 (March 25): 65–75.

——. 1958a. "What Price Inflation?" *Finance and Accounting* 38, no. 7, 18–27.

——. 1958b. "The Supply of Money and Changes in Prices and Output." In Joint Economic Committee, *The Relationship of Prices to Economic Stability and Growth: Compendium of Papers Submitted by Panelists Appearing before the Joint Economic Committee*. Washington, DC: US Government Printing Office. 241–56. Reprinted in Milton Friedman, *The Optimum Quantity of Money and Other Essays*. Chicago: Aldine, 1969. 171–87.

——. 1958c. "Capitalism and Freedom." In Felix Morley, ed., *Essays on Individuality*. Philadelphia: University of Pennsylvania Press. 168–82.

——. 1958d. "Inflation." Paper delivered at the Ninth Meeting of the Mont Pelerin Society, Princeton, NJ, September 3 to 8.

——. 1958e. "Minimizing Government Control over Economic Life and Strengthening Competitive Private Enterprise." In Committee for Economic Development, *Problems of United States Economic Development*. Vol. 1, January. New York: Committee for Economic Development. 251-57. Reprinted as "Strengthening Competitive Private Enterprise," in Shelley M. Mark and Daniel M. Slate, eds., *Economics in Action: Readings in Current Economic Issues*, 2nd ed. Belmont, CA: Wadsworth, 1962. 33-38.

——. 1958f. "Foreign Economic Aid: Means and Objectives." *Yale Review* 47, no. 4 (June): 500-516. Reprinted in Kurt R. Leube, ed., *The Essence of Friedman*. Stanford, CA: Hoover Institution Press. 79-91.

——. 1958g. "Money Supply." In Solomon Fabricant, ed., *Investing in Economic Knowledge: Thirty-Eighth Annual Report—a Record for 1957 and Plans for 1958, National Bureau of Economic Research, Inc*. New York: National Bureau of Economic Research. 39-41.

——. 1958h. "Reply to Comments on *A Theory of the Consumption Function*." In Lincoln H. Clark, ed., *Consumer Behavior: Research on Consuemr Reactions*. New York: Harper and Brothers. 463-70.

——. 1958i. "The Permanent Income Hypothesis: Comment." *American Economic Review* 48, no. 5 (December): 990-91.

——. 1958j. "The Permanent Income Hypothesis." Manuscript, University of Chicago.

——. 1958k. "Supplementary Comment." *Journal of Political Economy* 66, no. 6 (December): 547-49.

——. 1959a. "The Demand for Money: Some Theoretical and Empirical Results." *Journal of Political Economy* 67, no. 4 (August): 327-51.

——. 1959b. "Discussion of 'Wage-Push Inflation' by Walker A. Morton." In *Proceedings of the Eleventh Annual Meeting of the Industrial Relations Research Association, December 28-29, 1958*. Chicago: Industrial Relations Research Association. 212-16.

——. 1959c. "The Demand for Money: Some Theoretical and Empirical Results." *American Economic Review (Papers and Proceedings)* 49, no. 2 (May): 525-27.

——. 1960a. *A Program for Monetary Stability*. Fordham, NY: Fordham University Press.

——. 1960b. "Comments." In Irwin Friend and Robert Jones, eds., *Conference on Consumption and Saving: Proceedings*. Vol. 2. Philadelphia: University of Pennsylvania Press. 191-206.

——. 1960c. "Recent Behavior of Stock of Money and Its Relation to Past Behavior." Memorandum to Secretary of the Treasury Robert B. Anderson, April 19. Milton Friedman papers, box 34, folder 22, Hoover Institution archives.

——. 1961a. "The Demand for Money." *Proceedings of the American Philosophical Society* 105, no. 3 (June): 259-64.

——. 1961b. "Monetary Data and National Income Estimates." *Economic Development and Cultural Change* 9, no. 3 (April): 267-86.

——. 1961c. "Vault Cash and Free Reserves." *Journal of Political Economy* 69, no. 2 (April): 181-82.

——. 1961d. "The Lag in Effect of Monetary Policy." *Journal of Political Economy* 69, no. 5 (October): 447-66.

——. 1961e. "Economic Aid Reconsidered: A Reply." *Yale Review* 50, no. 4 (Summer): 533-40.

——. 1961f. "*Inflation* by Thomas Wilson." *American Economic Review* 51, no. 5 (December): 1051-55.

———. 1961g. "Money and Banking." In Solomon Fabricant, ed., *Towards a Firmer Basis of Economic Policy: Forty-First Annual Report—a Record for 1960 and Plans for 1961, National Bureau of Economic Research, Inc.* New York: National Bureau of Economic Research. 41–43.

———. 1961h. "Real and Pseudo Gold Standards." *Journal of Law and Economics* 4, no. 1 (October): 66–79.

———. 1962a. *Capitalism and Freedom.* Chicago: University of Chicago Press.

———. 1962b. *Price Theory: A Provisional Text.* Chicago: Aldine.

———. 1962c. "A Program for Monetary Stability: Part I." In Marshall D. Ketchum and Leon T. Kendall, eds., *Proceedings of the Conference on Savings and Residential Financing: 1962 Proceedings, May 10 and 11, 1962, Chicago, Illinois.* Chicago: US Savings and Loan League. 11–32.

———. 1962d. "Should There Be an Independent Monetary Authority?" In Leland B. Yeager, ed., *In Search of a Monetary Constitution.* Cambridge, MA: Harvard University Press. 219–43. Reprinted in Milton Friedman, *Dollars and Deficits: Living with America's Economic Problems.* Englewood Cliffs, NJ: Prentice Hall, 1968. 173–94.

———. 1962e. "Foreword." In A. James Meigs, *Free Reserves and the Money Supply.* Chicago: University of Chicago Press. v–viii.

———. 1962f. "The Interpolation of Time Series by Related Series." *Journal of the American Statistical Association* 57, no. 300 (December): 729–57.

———. 1962g. "The Report of the Commission on Money and Credit: An Essay in *Petitio Principii.*" *American Economic Review (Papers and Proceedings)* 52, no. 2 (May): 291–301.

———. 1962h. "Is a Free Society Stable?" *New Individualist Review* 2, no. 2 (Summer): 3–10.

———. 1963a. "The Present State of Monetary Theory." *Economic Studies Quarterly* 14, no. 1 (September): 1–15.

———. 1963b. "Windfalls, the 'Horizon,' and Related Concepts in the Permanent-Income Hypothesis." In Carl F. Christ et al., *Measurement in Economics: Studies in Mathematical Economics and Econometrics in Memory of Yehuda Grunfeld.* Stanford, CA: Stanford University Press. 3–28.

———. 1963c. *Inflation: Causes and Consequences.* Bombay: Asia Publishing House. Reprinted in Milton Friedman, *Dollars and Deficits: Living with America's Economic Problems.* Englewood Cliffs, NJ: Prentice Hall, 1968. 21–71.

———. 1963d. "More on Archibald versus Chicago." *Review of Economic Studies* 30, no. 1 (February): 65–67.

———. 1963e. "Note on Nissan Liviatan's Paper." In Carl F. Christ et al., *Measurement in Economics: Studies in Mathematical Economics and Econometrics in Memory of Yehuda Grunfeld.* Stanford, CA: Stanford University Press. 59–63.

———. 1964a. "Comments by Milton Friedman on Testimony of George W. Mitchell and J. Dewey Daane." In Committee on Banking and Currency, US House of Representatives, *The Federal Reserve after Fifty Years: Hearings.* Vol. 2. Washington, DC: US Government Printing Office. 1220–22.

———. 1964b. "Post-war Trends in Monetary Theory and Policy." *National Banking Review* 2, no. 1 (September): 1–9. Reprinted in Milton Friedman, *The Optimum Quantity of Money and Other Essays.* Chicago: Aldine, 1969. 69–79.

———. 1964c. "A Dissent of Prominency . . ." *Challenge* 12, no. 10 (July): 2.

———. 1964d. "Comment on 'Collusion in the Auction Market for Treasury Bills.'" *Journal of Political Economy* 72, no. 5 (October): 513–14.

———. 1964e. "The Monetary Studies of the National Bureau." In NBER, ed., *The National Bureau Enters Its 45th Year*. 44th Annual Report. New York: National Bureau of Economic Research. 7-25. Reprinted in Milton Friedman, *The Optimum Quantity of Money and Other Essays*. Chicago: Aldine, 1969. 261-84.

———. 1964f. "Reply to James Tobin." Remarks at American Bankers Association Conference of University Professors, Princeton, NJ, September 1.

———. 1964g. "Can a Controlled Economy Work?" In Melvin R. Laird et al., *The Conservative Papers*. Garden City, NY: Anchor Books, Doubleday. 162-74.

———. 1964h. "Note on Lag in Effect of Monetary Policy." *American Economic Review* 54, no. 5 (September): 759-60.

———. 1965. "Transfer Payments and the Social Security System." *National Industrial Conference Board Record* 2, no. 9 (September): 7-10.

———. 1966a. "What Price Guideposts?" In George P. Shultz and Robert Z. Aliber, eds., *Guidelines: Informal Controls and the Market Place*. Chicago: University of Chicago Press. 17-39. Reprinted in Milton Friedman, *Dollars and Deficits: Living with America's Economic Problems*. Englewood Cliffs, NJ: Prentice Hall, 1968. 97-121.

———. 1966b. "The Schizophrenic Businessman: Friend and Enemy of Free Enterprise." Panel discussion, International University for Presidents, Young Presidents' Organization, Phoenix, AZ, April 25. Published in Leonard S. Silk, ed., *Readings in Contemporary Economics*. New York: McGraw-Hill, 1970. 27-36.

———. 1966c. "Discussion and Comments on Paper by Professor Meade ['Exchange-Rate Flexibility']." In American Enterprise Institute, ed., *International Payments Problems: A Symposium Sponsored by the American Enterprise Institute for Public Policy, Washington, D.C., September 23 and 24, 1965*. Washington DC: American Enterprise Institute. 87-90.

———. 1966d. "Interest Rates and the Demand for Money." *Journal of Law and Economics*, no. 1 (October): 71-85.

———. 1966e. "Comments [on Robert M. Solow, 'The Case against the Case against the Guideposts']." In George P. Shultz and Robert Z. Aliber, eds., *Guidelines: Informal Controls and the Market Place*. Chicago: University of Chicago Press. 55-61.

———. 1966f. "The Case for the Negative Income Tax: A View from the Right." Address at the National Symposium on Guaranteed Income sponsored by the US Chamber of Commerce, Washington, DC, December 9, 1966. Printed in US Chamber of Commerce, *The National Symposium on Guaranteed Income*. Washington, DC: US Chamber of Commerce, 1967. 49-55. Reprinted in Committee on Government Operations, US Senate, *Federal Role in Urban Affairs: Hearings before the Subcommittee on Executive Reorganization of the Committee on Government Operations, December 18, 1966*. Washington, DC: US Government Printing Office, 1967. 2732-39. Also reprinted in John Harvey Bunzel, ed., *Issues of American Public Policy*. Englewood Cliffs, NJ: Prentice Hall, 1968. 111-20.

———. 1967a. "The Monetary Theory and Policy of Henry Simons." *Journal of Law and Economics* 10, no. 1 (October): 1-13.

———. 1967b. "Comments by the Panelists: Milton Friedman." In American Bankers Association, ed., *Proceedings of a Symposium on Money, Interest Rates and Economic Activity*. Washington, DC: American Bankers Association. 100-103.

———. 1967c. "Must We Choose between Inflation and Unemployment?" *Stanford Graduate School of Business Bulletin* 35, no. 3 (Spring): 10-13, 40, and 42.

———. 1968a. *Dollars and Deficits: Living with America's Economic Problems*. Englewood Cliffs, NJ: Prentice Hall.

———. 1968b. "The Role of Monetary Policy." *American Economic Review* 58, no. 1 (March): 1–17.

———. 1968c. "Money: Quantity Theory." In David L. Sills, ed., *The International Encyclopedia of the Social Sciences*. Vol. 10. New York: Macmillan. 432–47.

———. 1968d. "Why Economists Disagree." In Milton Friedman, *Dollars and Deficits: Living with America's Economic Problems*. Englewood Cliffs, NJ: Prentice Hall. 1–16.

———. 1968e. *Dollars and Deficits: Inflation, Monetary Policy and the Balance of Payments.* Englewood Cliffs, NJ: Prentice Hall.

———. 1968f. "Factors Affecting the Level of Interest Rates." In Donald P. Jacobs and Richard T. Pratt, eds., *Proceedings of the 1968 Conference on Savings and Residential Financing*. Chicago: US Savings and Loan League. 11–27.

———. 1968g. "Money and the Interest Rate." In University of Miami, *Savings Institutions Forum, March 11–12, 1968: Proceedings*. Miami: University of Miami. Chapter 4.

———. 1968h. "The Case for the Negative Income Tax." In Melvin R. Laird, ed., *Republican Papers*. Garden City, NY: Anchor Books, Doubleday. 202–20.

———. 1968i. "[Remarks by] Milton Friedman." In Lawrence Fertig, ed., *What's Past Is Prologue: A Commemorative Evening to the Foundation for Economic Education on the Occasion of Leonard Read's Seventieth Birthday, October 4, 1968, the Starlight Roof, Waldorf-Astoria Hotel.* New York: Foundation for Economic Education. 22–31.

———. 1969a. "The Optimum Quantity of Money." In Milton Friedman, *The Optimum Quantity of Money and Other Essays*. Chicago: Aldine. 1–50.

———. 1969b. *The Optimum Quantity of Money and Other Essays*. Chicago: Aldine.

———. 1969c. "Miguel Sidrauski." *Journal of Money, Credit and Banking* 1, no. 2 (May): 129–30.

———. 1969d. The Euro-Dollar Market: Some First Principles." *Morgan Guaranty Survey*, no. 10 (October): 4–15. Also appeared as Graduate School of Business Selected Papers no. 34, University of Chicago, 1969.

———. 1969e. "Discussion of Charles P. Kindleberger, 'The Case for Fixed Exchange Rates, 1969.'" In Federal Reserve Bank of Boston, ed., *The International Adjustment Mechanism: Proceedings of a Conference Held at Melvin Village, New Hampshire, October 8–10, 1969*. Boston: Federal Reserve Bank of Boston. 109–19.

———. 1969f. "Round Table on Exchange Rate Policy." *American Economic Review (Papers and Proceedings)* 59, no. 2 (May): 364–66.

———. 1969g. "The International Adjustment Mechanism: Panel Discussion." In Federal Reserve Bank of Boston, ed., *The International Adjustment Mechanism: Proceedings of a Conference Held at Melvin Village, New Hampshire, October 8–10, 1969*. Boston: Federal Reserve Bank of Boston. 15–20.

———. 1969h. "Fiscal and Monetary Policy." Transcript of talk given at Bache Institutional 1969 Seminar, Geneva, Switzerland, April 25.

———. 1970a. "The Counter-revolution in Monetary Theory." Institute of Economic Affairs Occasional Paper no. 33. London: Institute of Economic Affairs. Reprinted in Milton Friedman, *Monetarist Economics*. Oxford, UK: Basil Blackwell, 1991. 1–20.

———. 1970b. "A Theoretical Framework for Monetary Analysis." *Journal of Political Economy* 78, no. 2, 193–238.

———. 1970c. "Comment on Tobin." *Quarterly Journal of Economics* 84, no. 2 (May): 318–27.

———. 1970d. "Controls on Interest Rates Paid by Banks." *Journal of Money, Credit and Banking* 2, no. 1 (February): 15–32.

———. 1970e. "Monetarism: A Counter-revolution in Economic Thought." Lecture at Florida Presbyterian College, February 21.

———. 1970f. "Money Management and Economic Growth." In Business Week, ed., Money and the Corporation: "Business Week" Conference. New York: McGraw Hill. 37–45.

———. 1970g. "Special Interest and the Law." Chicago Bar Record 51, no. 9 (June): 434–41.

———. 1970h. "Protecting Free Institutions from Our Noble Impulses." Lecture at Florida Presbyterian College, February 19.

———. 1970i. "The Proof of the Monetarist Pudding." Manuscript, July 1; held in Milton Friedman papers, box 43, folder 8, Hoover Institution archives.

———. 1970j. "The New Monetarism: Comment." Lloyds Bank Review 25, no. 98 (October): 52–53.

———. 1970k. "Address Commemorating the 80th Anniversary of Halle and Stieglitz." Plaza Hotel, New York City, March 5. Available on Hoover Institution website, CWP.

———. 1970l. Address to Provident National Bank, April 24. Available on Hoover Institution website.

———. 1970m. "Current Monetary Policy." Memorandum for Federal Reserve Board Consultants Meeting, June 19.

———. 1970n. "Errata: A Theoretical Framework for Monetary Analysis." Journal of Political Economy 78, no. 6 (November/December): 1385–86.

———. 1970o. The Market vs. the Bureaucrat." In Abraham Kaplan, ed., Individuality and the New Society. Seattle: University of Washington Press. 69–88.

———. 1971a. "In Memoriam: Jacob Viner, 1892–1970." American Economic Review 61, no. 1 (March): 247–48.

———. 1971b. "The Euro-Dollar Market: Some First Principles." Federal Reserve Bank of St. Louis Review 53, no. 7 (July): 16–24.

———. 1971c. "Government Revenue from Inflation." Journal of Political Economy 79, no. 4 (July/August): 846–56.

———. 1971d. "A Monetary Theory of Nominal Income." Journal of Political Economy 79, no. 2 (March/April): 323–37.

———. 1971e. "A Note on the U.S. and U.K. Velocity of Circulation." In George Clayton, John C. Gilbert, and Robert C. Sedgwick, eds., Monetary Theory and Monetary Policy in the 1970s: Proceedings of the 1970 Sheffield Money Seminar. London: Oxford University Press. 151–52.

———. 1971f. "Have Monetary and Fiscal Policy Failed?" Speech before the Economic Club of Detroit, March 8.

———. 1971g. "Monetary Aggregates and Monetary Policy." Memorandum for Federal Reserve Board Consultants Meeting, June 9.

———. 1971h. "Introduction." In Beryl W. Sprinkel, Money and Markets: A Monetarist View. Homewood, IL: Richard D. Irwin. xix–xxiii.

———. 1971i. "Money, Economic Activity, Interest Rates: The Outlook." In United States Savings and Loan League, ed., Savings and Loan Annals, 1970. Chicago: United States Savings and Loan League. 60–68.

———. 1972a. "Comments on the Critics." Journal of Political Economy 80, no. 5 (September/October): 906–50.

———. 1972b. "Monetary Policy." Proceedings of the American Philosophical Society 116, no. 3 (June): 183–96.

———. 1972c. "A Libertarian Speaks [Interview]." Trial Magazine 8, no. 1 (January/February): 22–24.

——. 1972d. *An Economist's Protest: Columns in Political Economy*. Glen Ridge, NJ: Thomas Horton.

——. 1972e. "Have Monetary Policies Failed?" *American Economic Review (Papers and Proceedings)* 62, no. 1-2 (March): 11-18.

——. 1972f. "The Need for Futures Markets in Currencies." In International Monetary Market of the Chicago Mercantile Exchange, ed., *The Futures Market in Foreign Currencies*. Chicago: International Monetary Market of the Chicago Mercantile Exchange. 6-12.

——. 1973a. *Money and Economic Development: The Horowitz Lectures of 1972*. New York: Praeger.

——. 1973b. "How Much Monetary Growth?" *Morgan Guaranty Survey* 15, no. 2 (February): 5-10.

——. 1973c. "Facing Inflation." *Challenge* 16, no. 5 (November/December): 29-37.

——. 1974a. "Letter on Monetary Policy." *Federal Reserve Bank of St. Louis Review* 56, no. 3 (March): 20-23.

——. 1974b. "Money." In *The New Encyclopaedia Britannica*. 15th ed. Chicago: Encyclopaedia Britannica. 349-56.

——. 1974c. "Using Escalators to Help Fight Inflation." *Fortune* 91, no. 7 (July): 94-97 and 174-76. Reprinted in Friedman 1975e, 148-61.

——. 1974d. "Short-Term and Long-Term Economic Outlook." Talk at O'Hare Executive's Club, March 14. Available on Hoover Institution website, CWP.

——. 1974e. "Inflation, Taxation, Indexation." In Institute of Economic Affairs, ed., *Inflation: Causes, Consequences, Cures*. London: Institute of Economic Affairs. 71-88.

——. 1974f. "Schools at Chicago." *University of Chicago Magazine* 67, no. 1 (Autumn): 11-16.

——. 1974g. *Monetary Correction: A Proposal for Escalator Clauses to Reduce the Costs of Ending Inflation*. London: Institute of Economic Affairs.

——. 1974h. "Statement on Indexing as a Tool for Economic Stabilization." In Committee on Banking, Housing and Urban Affairs, US Senate, *Indexing: Hearings before the Subcommittee on Production and Stabilization of the Committee on Banking, Housing and Urban Affairs*. Washington, DC: US Government Printing Office. 62-68.

——. 1975a. "Twenty-Five Years after the Rediscovery of Money: What Have We Learned? Discussion." *American Economic Review (Papers and Proceedings)* 65, no. 2 (May): 176-79.

——. 1975b. "Critique of Guideposts." In John E. Elliott and Arthur L. Grey, eds. *Economic Issues and Policies: Readings in Introductory Economics*. 3rd ed. New York: Houghton-Mifflin. 113-18.

——. 1975c. "The National Business Outlook for 1975 [address of December 16, 1974]." In Portland State University School of Business Administration, *Proceedings of the 12th Annual Business and Economic Outlook for 1975*. Portland, OR: Portland State University of Business Administration. 1-27.

——. 1975d. "Unemployment versus Inflation?—An Evaluation of the Phillips Curve." IEA Occasional Paper no. 44. London: Institute of Economic Affairs. Reprinted in Milton Friedman, *Monetarist Economics*. Oxford, UK: Basil Blackwell, 1991. 63-86.

——. 1975e. *There's No Such Thing as a Free Lunch*. LaSalle, IL: Open Court.

——. 1975f. *Milton Friedman Speaks to CEDA: A Report on the Visit of Professor Milton Friedman to the Committee for Economic Development of Australia on April 11, 1975, at the Great Hall, the National Gallery of Victoria, Melbourne.* Melbourne: Committee for Economic Development of Australia.

———. 1975g. *Is Inflation a Curable Disease?* Pittsburgh: Pittsburgh National Bank, Alex C. Walker Educational and Charitable Foundation, and University of Pittsburgh Graduate School of Business. Reprinted in Committee on the Budget, US House of Representatives, *Impact of Inflation on the Economy: Hearings before the Task Force on Inflation.* Washington, DC: US Government Printing Office, 1979. 693-712.

———. 1975h. "Gold, Money and the Law: Comments." In Henry G. Manne and Roger LeRoy Miller, eds., *Gold, Money and the Law.* Chicago: Aldine. 71-81.

———. 1975i. *Milton Friedman in Australia 1975.* Sydney: Constable and Bain and the Graduate Business Club.

———. 1976a. *Price Theory.* 2nd ed. Chicago: Aldine.

———. 1976b. "Homer Jones: A Personal Reminiscence." *Journal of Monetary Economics* 2, no. 4 (November): 433-36.

———. 1976c. *Adam Smith's Relevance for 1976.* In *The Adam Smith Lectures*, Graduate School of Business, University of Chicago Selected Paper no. 50. Reprinted in Fred R. Glahe, ed., *Adam Smith and "The Wealth of Nations": 1776-1976 Bicentennial Essays.* Boulder: Colorado Associated University Press, 1978. 7-20. A version also appeared as Milton Friedman, "Adam Smith's Relevance for Today." *Challenge* 20, no. 1 (March/April 1977): 6-12.

———. 1976d. "Rejoinder by Milton Friedman to 'Federal Reserve Staff Comments on Prof. Friedman's Statement before Senate Committee on Banking, Housing, and Urban Affairs (Nov. 6, 1975).'" In Committee on Banking, Housing, and Urban Affairs, US Senate, *Third Meeting on the Conduct of Monetary Policy: Hearings, May 3, 4, and 5, 1976.* Washington, DC: US Government Printing Office. 130-32.

———. 1976e. "Foreword." In Fritz Machup, ed., *Essays on Hayek.* New York: New York University Press. xxi-xxiv.

———. 1976f. "Comments on Tobin and Buiter." In Jerome L. Stein, ed., *Monetarism.* Amsterdam: North-Holland. 310-17.

———. 1976g. Letter to Rep. Stephen L. Neal, Chairman, Subcommittee on Domestic Monetary Policy, October 2, 1976. In Committee on Banking, Currency and Housing, US House of Representatives, *Maintaining and Making Public Minutes of Federal Reserve Meetings: Hearings.* Washington, DC: US Government Printing Office, 1977. 201-2.

———. 1976h. "The Milton Friedman View." *University of Cape Town Graduate School of Business Journal* 3, no. 1, 15-18.

———. 1976i. "The Fragility of Freedom." *Brigham Young University Studies* 16, no. 4 (Summer): 561-74.

———. 1976j. "Economic Myths and Public Opinion." *The Alternative: An American Spectator* 9, no. 4 (January): 5-9. Reprinted in Milton Friedman, *Bright Promises, Dismal Performance: An Economist's Protest.* New York: Harcourt Brace Jovanovich, 1983. 60-75.

———. 1976k. "The Line We Dare Not Cross." *Encounter* 47, no. 5 (November): 8-14.

———. 1977a. "The Invisible Hand." In Milton Friedman et al., *The Business System: A Bicentennial View.* Hanover, NH: University Press of New England. 2-13.

———. 1977b. *From Galbraith to Economic Freedom.* IEA Occasional Paper no. 49. London: Institute of Economic Affairs.

———. 1977c. "Discussion of 'The Monetarist Controversy.'" *Federal Reserve Bank of San Francisco Economic Review* 59 (supplement) (Spring): 12-19.

——. 1977d. "Time Perspective in Demand for Money." *Scandinavian Journal of Economics* 79, no. 4, 397-416.

——. 1977e. "Nobel Lecture: Inflation and Unemployment." *Journal of Political Economy* 85, no. 3 (June): 451-72.

——. 1978a. *Tax Limitation, Inflation and the Role of Government*. Dallas: Fisher Institute.

——. 1978b. Submission dated August 21, 1978. In Committee on Banking, Housing, and Urban Affairs, US Senate, *Federal Reserve Requirements Act of 1978: Hearings*. Washington, DC: US Government Printing Office. 280-82.

——. 1978c. "How Stands the Theory and Practice of Monetary Policy?" Paper presented at Mont Pelerin Society meeting, Hong Kong.

——. 1978d. "The Future of Capitalism." In Milton Friedman, *Tax Limitation, Inflation and the Role of Government*. Dallas: Fisher Institute. 1-13.

——. 1978e. "The Limitations of Tax Limitation." *Policy Review* 2, no. 5 (Summer): 7-14.

——. 1978f. "Preface." In William E. Simon, *A Time for Truth*. New York: McGraw Hill. xiii-xvi.

——. 1979. "Prepared Statement [October 30, 1979]." In Committee on the Judiciary, US Senate, *Proposed Constitutional Amendment to Balance the Federal Budget: Hearings*. Washington, DC: US Government Printing Office, 1980. 412-13.

——. 1980a. "Memorandum: Response to Questionnaire on Monetary Policy, June 11, 1980." In Treasury and Civil Service Committee, House of Commons, ed., *Memoranda on Monetary Policy*. London: Her Majesty's Stationery Office. 55-61. Reprinted in Milton Friedman, *Monetarist Economics*. Oxford, UK: Basil Blackwell, 1991. 49-62.

——. 1980b. "Prices of Money and Goods across Frontiers: The £ and the $ over a Century." *World Economy* 2, no. 4 (February): 497-511.

——. 1980c. "Comment: The Changing Character of Financial Markets." In Martin S. Feldstein, ed., *The American Economy in Transition*. Chicago: University of Chicago Press. 78-86.

——. 1981a. "An Address by Professor Milton Friedman, Wellington, New Zealand, April 22nd, 1981." Wellington, New Zealand: Buttle Wilson and Broadbank.

——. 1981b. "Foreword." In Thomas Sowell, *Markets and Minorities*. New York: Basic Books. viii-ix.

——. 1981c. *The Invisible Hand in Economics and Politics*. Singapore: Institute of Southeast Asian Studies.

——. 1981d. "Introduction." In William R. Allen, *The Midnight Economist: Choices, Prices and Public Policy*. New York: Playboy Press. xiii-xvi.

——. 1981e. Address to the National Press Club of Australia. Canberra, Australia, April 7.

——. 1982a. *On Milton Friedman*. Vancouver, British Columbia: Fraser Institute.

——. 1982b. "Monetary Policy: Theory and Practice." *Journal of Money, Credit and Banking* 14, no. 1 (February): 98-118.

——. 1982c. "Supply-Side Policies: Where Do We Go from Here?" In Federal Reserve Bank of Atlanta, ed., *Supply-Side Economics in the 1980s: Conference Proceedings*. Westport, CT: Quorum Books. 53-63.

——. 1982d. "Monetary Policy: Theory and Practice: A Reply." *Journal of Money, Credit and Banking* 14, no. 3 (August): 404-6.

——. 1983a. "Monetarism in Rhetoric and in Practice." *Bank of Japan Monetary and Economic Studies* 1, no. 2 (October): 1-14.

———. 1983b. *Bright Promises, Dismal Performance: An Economist's Protest*. Introductions and selections by William R. Allen. New York: Harcourt Brace Jovanovich.

———. 1983c. "Is Capitalism Humane?" In Milton Friedman, *Bright Promises, Dismal Performance: An Economist's Protest*. New York: Harcourt Brace Jovanovich. 83–90.

———. 1983d. "Who Protects the Consumer?" In Milton Friedman, *Bright Promises, Dismal Performance: An Economist's Protest*. New York: Harcourt Brace Jovanovich. 161–68.

———. 1983e. "A Monetarist View." In Alan Horrox and Gillian McCredie, eds., *Money Talks: Five Views of Britain's Economy*. London: Thames Methuen. 1–17.

———. 1984a. *The Suicidal Impulse of the Business Community: Based on Remarks Delivered at the Hoover Pacific Coast Seminar Dinner, October 25, 1983*. Stanford, CA: Hoover Institution.

———. 1984b. "Comment [on 'The Success of Purchasing-Power Parity: Historical Evidence and Its Implications for Macroeconomics.']" In Michael D. Bordo and Anna J. Schwartz, eds., *A Retrospective on the Classical Gold Standard, 1821-1931*. Chicago: University of Chicago Press. 157–62.

———. 1984c. "Monetary Policy for the 1980s." In John H. Moore, ed., *To Promote Prosperity: U.S. Domestic Policy in the Mid-1980s*. Stanford, CA: Hoover Institution Press. 23–60.

———. 1984d. "Lessons from the 1979-82 Monetary Policy Experiment." *American Economic Review (Papers and Proceedings)* 74, no. 2 (May): 397–400.

———. 1984e. "Has Monetarism Failed?" *Manhattan Report* 4, no. 3, 3–4.

———. 1984f. *Market or Plan? An Exposition of the Case for The Market*. London: Centre for Research into Communist Economies.

———. 1984g. "Capitalism and the Jews." *Encounter* 62, no. 6 (June): 74–79.

———. 1984h. "Currency Competition: A Sceptical View." In Pascal Salin, ed., *Currency Competition and Monetary Union*. The Hague: Martinus Nijhoff. 42–46.

———. 1984i. *Politics and Tyranny: Lessons in Pursuit of Freedom*. San Francisco: Pacific Institute for Public Policy Research.

———. 1985a. "Monetary Policy in a Fiat World." *Bank of Japan Monetary and Economic Studies* 3, no. 2 (September): 11–18.

———. 1985b. "Quantity Theory of Money." Manuscript, Hoover Institution.

———. 1985c. "How to Give Monetarism a Bad Name." In James K. Galbraith and Dan C. Roberts, eds., *Monetarism, Inflation and the Federal Reserve: Essays Prepared for the Use of the Joint Economic Committee, Congress of the United States*. Washington, DC: US Government Printing Office. 51–61.

———. 1985d. "Is Hyperinflation Inevitable? [Talk on June 28, 1985]." *Commonwealth* (Commonwealth Club of California, San Francisco) 79, no. 27 (July 8): 213–14 and 217.

———. 1985e. "Comment on Leland Yeager's Paper on the Keynesian Heritage." In Center for Research in Government Policy and Business, ed., *The Keynesian Heritage*. Center Symposia Series no. CS-16, University of Rochester Graduate School of Management. 12–18.

———. 1986a. "My Evolution as an Economist." In William Breit and Roger W. Spencer, eds., *Lives of the Laureates: Seven Nobel Economists*. Cambridge, MA: MIT Press. (Paperback edition, 1988.) 77–92.

———. 1986b. "Keynes' Political Legacy." In John Burton, ed., *Keynes' General Theory: Fifty Years On*. London: Institute of Economic Affairs. 47–55.

———. 1986c. "Economists and Economic Policy." *Economic Inquiry* 24, no. 1 (January): 1–10.

———. 1987a. "Quantity Theory of Money." In John Eatwell, Murray Milgate, and Peter Newman, eds., *The New Palgrave: A Dictionary of Economics*. Vol. 4, *Q to Z*. London: Macmillan. 3–20.

———. 1987b. "*Rational Expectations and Inflation* by Thomas J. Sargent." *Journal of Political Economy* 95, no. 1 (February): 218–21.

———. 1987c. "Arthur Burns." In American Enterprise Institute, ed., *In Memoriam: Arthur F. Burns, 1904–1987*. Washington, DC: American Enterprise Institute. 7–11.

———. 1987d. "Free Markets and Free Speech." *Harvard Journal of Law and Public Policy* 10, no. 1 (Winter): 1–9.

———. 1987e. "Simon Newcomb." In John Eatwell, Murray Milgate, and Peter Newman, eds., *The New Palgrave: A Dictionary of Economics*. Vol. 3, *K to P*. London: Macmillan. 651–52.

———. 1988a. "Money and the Stock Market." *Journal of Political Economy* 96, no. 2 (April): 221–45.

———. 1988b. "A Proposal for Resolving the U.S. Balance of Payments Problem: Confidential Memorandum [dated October 15, 1968, submitted December 1968] to President-Elect Richard Nixon." In Leo Melamed, ed., *The Merits of Flexible Exchange Rates: An Anthology*. Fairfax, VA: George Mason University Press. 429–38.

———. 1989. "Collaboration in Economics." In Michael D. Bordo, ed., *Money, History, and International Finance: Essays in Honor of Anna J. Schwartz*. Chicago: University of Chicago Press. 247–50.

———. 1990a. *Friedman in China*. Hong Kong: The Chinese University Press for the Hong Kong Centre for Economic Research.

———. 1990b. "The Crime of 1873." *Journal of Political Economy* 98, no. 6 (December): 1159–94.

———. 1991a. "Economic Freedom, Human Freedom, Political Freedom." Smith Center Inaugural Lecture, November 1.

———. 1991b. "Old Wine in New Bottles." *Economic Journal* 101, no. 404 (January): 33–40.

———. 1992a. "Do Old Fallacies Ever Die?" *Journal of Economic Literature* 30, no. 4 (December): 2129–32.

———. 1992b. "Preface." In Milton Friedman, *A Program for Monetary Stability*. 10th printing with new preface. Fordham, NY: Fordham: University Press. vii–xii.

———. 1992c. *Money Mischief: Episodes in Monetary History*. New York: Harcourt Brace Jovanovich.

———. 1992d. "Parental Choice: The Effective Way to Improve Schooling [Talk on August 7, 1992]." *Commonwealth* (Commonwealth Club of California, San Francisco) 86, no. 31 (August 31): 514–16 and 521–23.

———. 1993. "The 'Plucking Model' of Business Fluctuations Revisited." *Economic Inquiry* 31, no. 2 (April): 171–77.

———. 1995. "Monetary System for a Free Society." In Kevin D. Hoover and Steven M. Sheffrin, eds., *Monetarism and the Methodology of Economics: Essays in Honour of Thomas Mayer*. Cheltenham, UK: Edward Elgar. 167–77.

———. 1997. "John Maynard Keynes." *Federal Reserve Bank of Richmond Economic Quarterly* 83, no. 2 (Spring): 1–23.

———. 1998. "The Suicidal Impulse of the Business Community." Remarks at luncheon address, San Jose, California, November 21.

——. 2001. "How to Cure Health Care." *Public Interest* 36, no. 142 (Winter): 3–30.

——. 2005a. "How Not to Stop Inflation." *Region Focus* (Federal Reserve Bank of Richmond), Summer, 2–7.

——. 2005b. "Comment: Inflation, Unemployment and the Pound." In Subroto Roy and John Clarke, eds., *Margaret Thatcher's Revolution: How It Happened and What It Meant*. London: Continuum. 66.

——. 2005c. "A Natural Experiment in Monetary Policy Covering Three Episodes of Growth and Decline in the Economy and the Stock Market." *Journal of Economic Perspectives* 19, no. 4 (Fall): 145–50.

——. 2007. *Milton Friedman on Economics*. Chicago: University of Chicago Press.

——. 2009. "Final Word." In Uskali Mäki, ed., *The Methodology of Positive Economics: Reflections on the Milton Friedman Legacy*. Cambridge, UK: Cambridge University Press. 335.

Friedman, Milton, and Gary S. Becker. 1957. "A Statistical Illusion in Judging Keynesian Models." *Journal of Political Economy* 65, no. 1 (February): 64–75.

——. 1958a. "The Friedman-Becker Illusion: Reply." *Journal of Political Economy* 66, no. 6 (December): 545–49.

——. 1958b. "Reply to Kuh and Johnston." *Review of Economics and Statistics* 40, no. 3 (August): 298.

Friedman, Milton, and Rose D. Friedman. 1980. *Free to Choose: A Personal Statement*. New York: Harcourt Brace Jovanovich.

——. 1984. *Tyranny of the Status Quo*. New York: Harcourt Brace Jovanovich.

——. 1985. *The Tyranny of the Status Quo*. Harmondsworth, UK: Penguin.

——. 1988. "The Tide in the Affairs of Men." In Annelise G. Anderson and Dennis L. Bark, eds., *Thinking about America: The United States in the 1990s*. Stanford, CA: Hoover Institution Press. 455–68.

——. 1998. *Two Lucky People: Memoirs*. Chicago: University of Chicago Press.

Friedman, Milton, and Walter W. Heller. 1969. *Monetary vs. Fiscal Policy*. New York: W. W. Norton.

Friedman, Milton, Homer Jones, George Stigler, and Allen Wallis, eds. 1935. *The Ethics of Competition*. New York: George Allen and Unwin.

Friedman, Milton, and Irving Kristol. 1976. "Dialogue: The Relationship between Business and Government: Collaboration or Confrontation?" In Alan Heslop, ed., *Business-Government Relations*. New York: New York University Press. 11–45.

Friedman, Milton, and Simon Kuznets. 1945. *Income from Independent Professional Practice*. New York: National Bureau of Economic Research.

Friedman, Milton, and David Meiselman. 1959. "Judging the Predictive Abilities of the Quantity and Income-Expenditure Theories." Manuscript, University of Chicago, for discussion at Workshop on Money and Banking session of October 27, 1959.

——. 1963. "The Relative Stability of Monetary Velocity and the Investment Multiplier in the United States, 1897–1958." In Commission on Money and Credit, ed., *Stabilization Policies*. Englewood Cliffs, NJ: Prentice Hall. 165–268.

——. 1964. "Keynes and the Quantity Theory: Reply to Donald Hester." *Review of Economics and Statistics* 46, no. 4 (November): 369–76.

——. 1965. "Reply to Ando and Modigliani and to DePrano and Mayer." *American Economic Review* 55, no. 4 (September): 753–85.

Friedman, Milton, Lloyd A. Metzler, Frederick H. Harbison, Lloyd W. Mints, D. Gale Johnson, Theodore W. Schultz, and H. G. Lewis. 1951. "The Failure of the Present

Monetary Policy." In Joint Committee on the Economic Report, US Congress, *January 1951 Economic Report of the President: Hearings.* Washington, DC: US Government Printing Office. 458-60.

Friedman, Milton, and Franco Modigliani. 1977. "Discussion of 'The Monetarist Controversy' [dialogue portion]." *Federal Reserve Bank of San Francisco Economic Review* 59 (supplement) (Spring): 19-26.

Friedman, Milton, Michael Porter, Fred Gruen, and Don Stammer. 1981. *Taxation, Inflation and the Role of Government.* Sydney: Centre for Independent Studies.

Friedman, Milton, and Paul A. Samuelson. 1980. *Milton Friedman and Paul A. Samuelson Discuss the Economic Responsibility of Government.* College Station: Texas A&M University Center for Education and Research in Free Enterprise.

Friedman, Milton, and Leonard J. Savage. 1947. "Planning Experiments Seeking Maxima." In Churchill Eisenhart, Millard W. Hastay, and W. Allen Wallis, *Selected Techniques of Statistical Analysis for Scientific and Industrial Research and Production and Management Engineering by the Statistical Research Group, Columbia University.* New York: McGraw Hill. 363-82.

———. 1948. "The Utility Analysis of Choices Involving Risk." *Journal of Political Economy* 56, no. 4 (August): 279-304.

———. 1952a. "The Expected-Utility Hypothesis and the Measurability of Utility." *Journal of Political Economy* 60, no. 6 (December): 463-74.

———. 1952b. "The Utility Analysis of Choices Involving Risk [revised version]." In Kenneth E. Boulding and George J. Stigler, eds., *Readings in Price Theory.* Chicago: Richard D. Irwin. 57-96.

Friedman, Milton, and Anna J. Schwartz. 1963a. *A Monetary History of the United States, 1867-1960.* Princeton, NJ: Princeton University Press. (Also appeared as trade paperback edition, 1971.)

———. 1963b. "Money and Business Cycles." *Review of Economics and Statistics* 45, no. 1 (February): 32-64.

———. 1965. *The Great Contraction, 1929-1933.* Princeton, NJ: Princeton University Press.

———. 1966. "Trends in Money, Income, and Prices, 1867-1966." Book manuscript. New York: National Bureau of Economic Research.

———. 1967. "Trends in Money, Income, and Prices." In Geoffrey Moore, ed., *Contributions to Economic Knowledge through Research: Annual Report, National Bureau of Economic Research.* New York: National Bureau of Economic Research. 36-40.

———. 1970a. *Monetary Statistics of the United States: Estimates, Sources, Methods.* New York: Columbia University Press.

———. 1970b. "Money." In NBER, ed., *Economics—a Half Century of Research, 1920-1970: 50th Annual Report, September 1970, National Bureau of Economic Research, Inc.* New York: National Bureau of Economic Research. 79-81.

———. 1976. "From Gibson to Fisher." *Explorations in Economic Research* 3, no. 2 (April): 288-91.

———. 1982a. *Monetary Trends in the United States and the United Kingdom: Their Relation to Income, Prices, and Interest Rates, 1867-1975.* Chicago: University of Chicago Press.

———. 1982b. "The Effect of Term Structure of Interest Rates on the Demand for Money in the United States." *Journal of Political Economy* 90, no. 1 (February): 201-12.

———. 1986a. "The Failure of the Bank of United States: A Reappraisal—a Reply." *Explorations in Economic History* 23, no. 2 (April): 199-204.

———. 1986b. "Has Government Any Role in Money?" *Journal of Monetary Economics* 17, no. 1 (January): 37–62.

———. 1991. "Alternative Approaches to Analyzing Economic Data." *American Economic Review* 81, no. 1 (March): 39–49.

Friedman, Milton, and George J. Stigler. 1946. *Roofs or Ceilings? The Current Housing Problem*. Irvington-on-the-Hudson, NY: Foundation for Economic Education. Reprinted in Milton Friedman, *Monetarist Economics*. Oxford, UK: Basil Blackwell, 1991. 169–83.

Friedman, Rose D. 1976a. "Milton Friedman: Husband and Colleague (1): Early Years." *Oriental Economist* 44, no. 787 (May): 28–32.

———. 1976b. "Milton Friedman: Husband and Colleague (2): The Beginning of a Career." *Oriental Economist* 44, no. 788 (June): 18–22.

———. 1976c. "Milton Friedman: Husband and Colleague (4): The Years 1946–1953." *Oriental Economist* 44, no. 790 (August): 21–26.

———. 1976d. "Milton Friedman: Husband and Colleague (5): A Spokesman for Libertarianism." *Oriental Economist* 44, no. 791 (September): 22–27.

———. 1976e. "Milton Friedman: Husband and Colleague (6): Milton Friedman and Monetarism." *Oriental Economist* 44, no. 792 (October): 22–26.

———. 1976f. "Milton Friedman: Husband and Colleague (8): First Nixon Administration." *Oriental Economist* 44, no. 794 (December): 28–32.

———. 1977a. "Milton Friedman: Husband and Colleague (9): Heights and Depths." *Oriental Economist* 45, no. 1 (January): 24–32.

———. 1977b. "Milton Friedman: Husband and Colleague (10): The Nobel Award." *Oriental Economist* 45, no. 796 (February): 24–28.

Frydman, Roman, and Michael D. Goldberg. 2011. *Beyond Mechanical Markets: Asset Price Swings, Risk, and the Role of the State*. Princeton, NJ: Princeton University Press.

Fuhrer, Jeffrey C., and George R. Moore. 1995a. "Inflation Persistence." *Quarterly Journal of Economics* 110, no. 1 (February): 127–59.

———. 1995b. "Monetary Policy Trade-Offs and the Correlation between Nominal Interest Rates and Real Output." *American Economic Review* 85, no. 1 (March): 219–39.

Fuhrer, Jeffrey C., Giovanni P. Olivei, and Geoffrey M. B. Tootell. 2012. "Inflation Dynamics When Inflation Is Near Zero." *Journal of Money, Credit and Banking* 44, supplement no. 1 (February): 83–122.

Galbraith, John Kenneth. 1952. *A Theory of Price Control*. Cambridge, MA: Harvard University Press.

———. 1958. *The Affluent Society*. Boston: Houghton Mifflin.

Gale, Douglas. 1982. *Money: In Equilibrium*. Cambridge, UK: Cambridge University Press.

———. 1983. *Money: In Disequilibrium*. Cambridge, UK: Cambridge University Press.

Galí, Jordi, Mark Gertler, and J. David López-Salido. 2001. "European Inflation Dynamics." *European Economic Review* 45, no. 7 (June): 1237–70.

Georgescu-Roegen, Nicholas. 1936. "Marginal Utility of Money and Elasticities of Demand: III." *Quarterly Journal of Economics* 30, no. 3 (May): 533–39.

———. 1970. "Structural Inflation-Lock and Balanced Growth." *Economies et Societes* 4, no. 3 (March): 557–605.

———. 1988. "An Emigrant from a Developing Country: Autobiographical Notes—I." *Banca Nazionale Del Lavoro Quarterly Review* 41, no. 164 (March): 3–31.

Gertler, Mark. 1979. "Money, Prices, and Inflation in Macroeconomic Models with

Rational Inflationary Expectations." *Journal of Economic Theory* 21, no. 2 (October): 222–34.

———. 1985. *"Money, Expectations, and Business Cycles* by Robert J. Barro." *Journal of Money, Credit and Banking* 17, no. 2 (May): 284–87.

Giannoni, Marc P. 2001. "Model Uncertainty and Optimal Monetary Policy." PhD diss., Department of Economics, Princeton University, June.

Giannoni, Marc P., and Michael Woodford. 2005. "Optimal Inflation-Targeting Rules." In Ben S. Bernanke and Michael Woodford, eds., *The Inflation-Targeting Debate*. Chicago: University of Chicago Press. 93–162.

Gisser, Micha. 1966. *Introduction to Price Theory*. Scranton, PA: International Textbook.

Goldberger, Arthur S. 1964. *Econometric Theory*. New York: John Wiley.

Goldenweiser, E. A. 1945. "Postwar Problems and Policies." *Federal Reserve Bulletin* 31, no. 2 (February): 112–21.

Goldfeld, Stephen M. 1973. "The Demand for Money Revisited." *Brookings Papers on Economic Activity* 4, no. 3, 577–638.

———. 1976. "The Case of the Missing Money." *Brookings Papers on Economic Activity* 7, no. 3, 683–730.

Goldfeld, Stephen M., and Daniel E. Sichel. 1987. "Money Demand: The Effects of Inflation and Alternative Adjustment Mechanisms." *Review of Economics and Statistics* 69, no. 3 (August): 511–15.

Goodhart, Charles A. E. 1982. *"Monetary Trends in the United States and the United Kingdom*: A British Review." *Journal of Economic Literature* 20, no. 4 (December): 1540–51.

———. 1989a. "The Conduct of Monetary Policy." *Economic Journal* 99, no. 396 (June): 293–346.

———. 1989b. "Keynes and Monetarism." In Roger Hill, ed., *Keynes, Money and Monetarism: The Eighth Keynes Seminar Held at the University of Kent at Canterbury, 1987*. London: Macmillan. 106–20.

———. 1992. "The Objectives for, and Conduct of, Monetary Policy in the 1990s." In Adrian Blundell-Wignall, ed., *Inflation, Disinflation and Monetary Policy*. Sydney: Ambassador. 314–34.

———. 2005. "Allan Meltzer, *A History of the Federal Reserve*." *Macroeconomic Dynamics* 9, no. 2 (April): 267–75.

Goodhart, Charles A. E., and Andrew D. Crockett. 1970. "The Importance of Money." *Bank of England Quarterly Bulletin* 10, no. 2 (June): 159–98.

Gordon, Robert J. 1974a, ed. *Milton Friedman's Monetary Framework: A Debate with His Critics*. Chicago: University of Chicago Press.

———. 1974b. "Introduction." In Robert J. Gordon, ed., *Milton Friedman's Monetary Framework: A Debate with His Critics*. Chicago: University of Chicago Press. ix–xii.

———. 1975. "The Demand for and Supply of Inflation." *Journal of Law and Economics* 18, no. 3 (December): 807–36.

———. 1976a. "Comments on Modigliani and Ando." In Jerome L. Stein, ed., *Monetarism*. Amsterdam: North-Holland. 52–66.

———. 1976b. "Recent Developments in the Theory of Inflation and Unemployment." *Journal of Monetary Economics* 2, no. 2 (April): 185–219.

———. 1977. "The Theory of Domestic Inflation." *American Economic Review (Papers and Proceedings)* 67, no. 1 (February): 128–34.

———. 1982. "Price Inertia and Policy Ineffectiveness in the United States, 1890–1980." *Journal of Political Economy* 90, no. 6 (December): 1087–117.

———. 1986. "Introduction: Continuity and Change in Theory, Behavior, and Method-ology." In Robert J. Gordon, ed., *The American Business Cycle*. Chicago: University of Chicago Press. 1-33.

Gordon, Robert J., and Robert E. Hall. 1980. "Arthur M. Okun 1928-1980." *Brookings Papers on Economic Activity* 11, no. 1, 1-5.

Gordon, Scott. 1974. *The Development of Wage-Price Policy in the United States: The Eisen-hower Administration; The Doctrine of Shared Responsibility*. Manuscript prepared for a conference on November 1 and 2, 1974, sponsored by the Brookings Institution and the Office of Presidential Libraries.

Gramley, Lyle E. 1969. "Guidelines for Monetary Policy: The Case against Simple Rules." Speech at the Financial Conference of the National Industrial Conference Board, New York, February 21. https://fraser.stlouisfed.org/docs/historical/federal %20reserve%20history/bog_members_statements/gramley_19690221.pdf. Also appeared in Warren L. Smith and Ronald L. Teigen, eds., *Readings in Money, National Income, and Stabilization Policy*. 2nd ed. Homewood, IL: Irwin, 1970. 488-95.

Gramlich, Edward M. 1970. "Monetary Influences on Consumption." In National Plan-ning Association, Center for Economic Projections, ed., *Consumption Issues in the Seventies: Proceedings; Tenth Annual Conference of the Center for Economic Projections, March 12-13, 1970*. National/Regional Economic Projections Series, Report no. 70-J-1, July. Washington, DC: National Planning Association. 95-103.

Gray, Jo Anna. 1976a. "Wage Indexation: A Macroeconomic Approach." *Journal of Monetary Economics* 2, no. 2 (April): 221-35.

———. 1976b. "Essays on Wage Indexation." PhD diss., Department of Economics, University of Chicago.

Greenspan, Alan. 1959. "Stock Prices and Capital Evaluation." *Proceedings of the Business and Economic Statistics Section of the American Statistical Association* 6, no. 1, 2-26.

Gregory, Nathaniel. 1980. "Relative Wealth and Risk Taking: A Short Note on the Friedman-Savage Utility Function." *Journal of Political Economy* 88, no. 6 (Decem-ber): 1226-30.

Greider, William. 1987. *Secrets of the Temple: How the Federal Reserve Runs the Country*. New York: Simon and Schuster.

Groenewegen, Peter. 2003. *Classics and Moderns in Economics*. Vol. 2, *Essays on Nine-teenth and Twentieth Century Economic Thought*. New York: Routledge.

Grossman, Herschel I. 1975. "Tobin on Macroeconomics: A Review Article." *Journal of Political Economy* 83, no. 4 (August): 829-48.

———. 1984. "Book Review: Frank Hahn, *Money and Inflation*." *Journal of Political Econ-omy* 92, no. 2 (April): 337-340.

Grossman, Herschel I., and John B. Van Huyck. 1986. "Seigniorage, Inflation, and Repu-tation." *Journal of Monetary Economics* 18, no. 1 (July): 21-31.

Guillebaud, C. W., and Milton Friedman. 1957. "Introduction to the Cambridge Eco-nomic Handbooks by the General Editors." In Peter T. Bauer and Basil S. Yamey, *The Economics of Under-developed Countries*. Chicago: University of Chicago Press. v-vii.

Gurley, John G., and Edward S. Shaw. 1960. *Money in a Theory of Finance*. Washington, DC: Brookings Institution.

Haavelmo, Trygve. 1943. "The Statistical Implications of a System of Simultaneous Equations." *Econometrica* 11, no. 1 (January): 1-12.

Hahn, Frank H. 1954. "Review: *Essays in Positive Economics*." *Econometrica* 22, no. 3 (July): 399-401.

———. 1971. "Professor Friedman's Views on Money." *Economica* 38, no. 149 (February): 61–80.

———. 1980. "Monetarism and Economic Theory." *Economica* 47, no. 185 (February): 1–17.

———. 1983a. "Comment [on Allan H. Meltzer, 'On Keynes and Monetarism']." In David Worswick and James Trevithick, eds., *Keynes and the Modern World: Proceedings of the Keynes Centenary Conference, King's College, Cambridge.* Cambridge: Cambridge University Press. 72–75.

———. 1983b. *Money and Inflation.* Cambridge, MA: MIT Press.

———. 1987. "Information, Dynamics and Equilibrium." *Scottish Journal of Political Economy* 34, no. 4 (November): 321–34.

———. 1988a. "On Market Economies." In Robert Skidelsky, ed., *Thatcherism.* London: Chatto and Windus. 107–24.

———. 1988b. "*Models of Business Cycles* by Robert E. Lucas." *Economica* 55, no. 218 (May): 283–84.

———. 1990. "Liquidity." In Frank H. Hahn and Benjamin M. Friedman, eds., *Handbook of Monetary Economics.* Vol. 1. Amsterdam: North-Holland. 63–80.

Hall, Robert E. 1977. "Investment, Interest Rates, and the Effects of Stabilization Policies." *Brookings Papers on Economic Activity* 8, no. 1, 61–103.

———. 1978. "Stochastic Implications of the Life Cycle–Permanent income hypothesis: Theory and Evidence." *Journal of Political Economy* 86, no. 6 (December): 971–87.

———. 1979. "A Theory of the Natural Unemployment Rate and the Duration of Employment." *Journal of Monetary Economics* 5, no. 2 (April): 153–69.

———. 1980. "Labor Supply and Aggregate Fluctuations." *Carnegie-Rochester Conference Series on Public Policy* 12, no. 1, 7–34.

———. 1981. "Comments [on Stanley Fischer, 'Relative Price Shocks, Relative Price Variability, and Inflation']." *Brookings Papers on Economic Activity* 12, no. 2, 432–34.

Hall, Robert E., and Paul R. Milgrom. 2008. "The Limited Influence of Unemployment on the Wage Bargain." *American Economic Review* 98, no. 4 (September): 1653–74.

Hall, Robert E., and John B. Taylor. 1997. *Macroeconomics.* 5th ed. New York: W. W. Norton.

Hall, Stephen G., P. A. V. B. Swamy, and George S. Tavlas. 2012. "Milton Friedman, the Demand for Money, and the ECB's Monetary Policy Strategy." *Federal Reserve Bank of St. Louis Review* 94, no. 3 (May/June): 153–85.

Hallman, Jeffrey J., Richard D. Porter, and David H. Small. 1991. "Is the Price Level Tied to the M2 Monetary Aggregate in the Long Run?" *American Economic Review* 81, no. 4 (September): 841–58.

Hallowell, Burton C. 1950. *A Study of British Interest Rates, 1929–50.* Philadelphia: Connecticut General Life Insurance.

Hamburger, Michael J. 1971. "The Lag in the Effect of Monetary Policy: A Survey of Recent Literature." *Federal Reserve Bank of New York Monthly Review* 53, no. 12 (December): 289–98.

Hammond, J. Daniel. 1989. "An Interview with Milton and Rose Friedman, July 24, 1989." Manuscript, Wake Forest University.

———. 1992. "An Interview with Milton Friedman on Methodology." *Research in the History of Economic Thought and Methodology* 10, no. 1, 91–118.

———. 1996. *Theory and Measurement: Causality Issues in Milton Friedman's Monetary Economics.* Cambridge: Cambridge University Press.

———. 1999. "Introduction." In J. Daniel Hammond, ed., *The Legacy of Milton Friedman as Teacher*. Vol. 1. Cheltenham, UK: Edward Elgar. i–xli.

———. 2011a. "Friedman and Samuelson on the Business Cycle." *Cato Journal* 31, no. 3 (Fall): 643–60.

———. 2011b. "Milton Friedman and the Federal Reserve: Then and Now." Manuscript, Wake Forest University.

Hammond, J. Daniel, and Claire H. Hammond, eds. 2006. *Making Chicago Price Theory: Friedman-Stigler Correspondence 1945-1957*. London: Routledge.

Hanes, Christopher. 2006. "The Liquidity Trap and U.S. Interest Rates in the 1930s." *Journal of Money, Credit and Banking* 38, no. 1 (February): 163–94.

———. 2013. "Monetary Policy Alternatives at the Zero Bound: Lessons from the 1930s U.S." Manuscript, State University of New York at Binghamton, March.

Hansen, Alvin H. 1932. *Economic Stabilization in an Unbalanced World*. New York: Harcourt Brace.

———. 1938a. *Full Recovery or Stagnation?* New York: W. W. Norton.

———. 1938b. "The Consequences of Reducing Expenditures." *Proceedings of the Academy of Political Science* 17, no. 4 (January): 60–72.

———. 1939a. "Economic Progress and Declining Population Growth." *American Economic Review* 29, no. 1 (March): 1–15.

———. 1939b. "Capital Formation and Its Elements: Some Introductory Observations." In National Industrial Conference Board, ed., *Capital Formation and Its Elements: A Series of Papers Presented at a Symposium Conducted by the Conference Board*. New York: National Industrial Conference Board. 1–13.

———. 1941. *Fiscal Policy and Business Cycles*. New York: W. W. Norton.

———. 1945. "Stability and Expansion." In Paul T. Homan and Fritz Machlup, eds., *Financing American Prosperity: A Symposium of Economists*. New York: Twentieth-Century Fund. 199–265.

———. 1946. "Notes on Mints' Paper on Monetary Policy." *Review of Economics and Statistics* 28, no. 2 (May): 69–74.

———. 1947a. *Economic Policy and Full Employment*. New York: McGraw Hill.

———. 1947b. "Burns on Keynesian Economics." *Review of Economics and Statistics* 29, no. 4 (November): 247–52.

———. 1947c. "*The General Theory* (2)." In Seymour E. Harris, ed., *The New Economics: Keynes' Influence on Theory and Public Policy*. New York: Alfred A. Knopf. 133–44.

———. 1949. *Monetary Theory and Fiscal Policy*. New York: McGraw-Hill.

———. 1951a. *Business Cycles and National Income*. Expanded edition. New York: W. W. Norton.

———. 1951b. "Monetary Policy and the Control of Inflation." *Review of Economics and Statistics* 33, no. 3 (August): 191–94.

———. 1953. *A Guide to Keynes*. New York: McGraw-Hill.

———. 1957. *The American Economy*. New York: McGraw-Hill.

Hansen, Lars Peter, and Thomas J. Sargent. 2000. "Wanting Robustness in Macroeconomics." Manuscript, University of Chicago.

———. 2011. "Wanting Robustness in Macroeconomics." In Benjamin M. Friedman and Michael Woodford, eds., *Handbook of Monetary Economics*. Vol. 3B. Amsterdam: Elsevier/North-Holland. 1097–157.

———. 2014. "Four Types of Ignorance." Manuscript, New York University, May.

Hansen, Lars Peter, Thomas J. Sargent, and Thomas D. Tallarini Jr. 1999. "Robust

Permanent Income and Pricing." *Review of Economic Studies* 66, no. 4 (October): 873–907.

Harberger, Arnold C. 1954. "Monopoly and Resource Allocation." *American Economic Review (Papers and Proceedings)* 44, no. 2 (May): 77–87.

———, ed. 1960. *The Demand for Durable Goods.* Chicago: University of Chicago Press.

———. 1963. "The Dynamics of Inflation in Chile." In Carl F. Christ et al., *Measurement in Economics: Studies in Mathematical Economics and Econometrics in Memory of Yehuda Grunfeld.* Stanford, CA: Stanford University Press. 219–50.

———. 1978. "On the Use of Distributional Weights in Social Cost-Benefit Analysis." *Journal of Political Economy* 86, no. 2, part 2 (April): S87–S120.

Harcourt, G. C. 1977. "[Floor] Discussion of the Paper by Professor Streissler." In G. C. Harcourt, ed., *The Microeconomic Foundations of Macroeconomics: Proceedings of a Conference Held by the International Economic Association, at S'Agaro, Spain.* Boulder, CO: Westview. 133–43.

Harrigan, Frank, and Peter G. McGregor. 1991. "The Macroeconomics of the Chicago School." In Douglas Mair and Anne Miller, eds., *A Modern Guide to Economic Thought: An Introduction to Comparative Schools of Thought in Economics.* Aldershot, UK: Edward Elgar. 109–44.

Harris, Seymour E. 1951. "Introductory Remarks." *Review of Economics and Statistics* 33, no. 3 (August): 179–84.

Harrison, Richard. 2012. "Asset Purchase Policy at the Effective Lower Bound for Interest Rates." Bank of England Working Paper no. 444, January.

Harrod, Roy F. 1937. "Mr. Keynes and Traditional Theory." *Econometrica* 5, no. 1 (January): 74–86.

———. 1951. *The Life of John Maynard Keynes.* London: Macmillan.

———. 1970. "Reassessment of Keynes's Views on Money." *Journal of Political Economy* 78, no. 4, part 1 (July/August): 617–25.

———. 1971. "Discussion Papers: (*a*)." In George Clayton, John C. Gilbert, and Robert C. Sedgwick, eds., *Monetary Theory and Monetary Policy in the 1970s: Proceedings of the 1970 Sheffield Money Seminar.* London: Oxford University Press. 58–63.

Hart, Albert Gailord. 1935. "The 'Chicago Plan' of Banking Reform: A Proposal for Making Monetary Management Effective in the United States." *Review of Economic Studies* 2, no. 2 (February): 104–16.

———. 1948. *Money, Debt, and Economic Activity.* New York: Prentice Hall.

———. 1953. "Monetary Policy for Income Stabilization." In Max F. Millikan, ed., *Income Stabilization for a Developing Democracy: A Study of the Politics and Economics of High Employment without Inflation.* New Haven, CT: Yale University Press. 303–45.

Hart, Albert Gailord, and Edward Douglass Allen. 1941. *Paying for Defense.* Philadelphia: Blakiston.

Hart, Oliver D. 1982. "A Model of Imperfect Competition with Keynesian Features." *Quarterly Journal of Economics* 97, no. 1 (February): 109–38.

Hartley, Roger, and Lisa Farrell. 2002. "Can Expected Utility Theory Explain Gambling?" *American Economic Review* 92, no. 3 (June): 613–24.

Hartwell, Ronald Max. 1995. *A History of the Mont Pelerin Society.* Indianapolis: Liberty Fund.

Harvey, Andrew C. 1990. *The Econometric Analysis of Time Series.* 2nd ed. Cambridge, MA: MIT Press.

Hausman, Joshua K. 2016. "Fiscal Policy and Economic Recovery: The Case of the 1936 Veterans' Bonus." *American Economic Review* 106, no. 4 (April): 1100–1143.

Hayek, Friedrich A. 1944. *The Road to Serfdom.* Chicago: University of Chicago Press.

———. 1945. "The Use of Knowledge in Society." *American Economic Review* 35, no. 4 (September): 519–30.

———. 1960. *The Constitution of Liberty.* Chicago: University of Chicago Press.

———. 1976. *Denationalisation of Money.* London: Institute of Economic Affairs.

Hazlitt, Henry. 1959. *The Failure of the 'New Economics': An Analysis of the Keynesian Fallacies.* Princeton, NJ: D. Van Nostrand.

Heller, H. Robert, Andrew D. Crockett, Milton Friedman, William A. Niskanen, and Allen Sinai. 1984. "Economic Outlook." *Contemporary Policy Issues* 3, no. 1 (Fall): 15–52.

Hellyer, Paul. 2010. *Light at the End of the Tunnel: A Survival Plan for the Human Species.* Bloomington, IN: AuthorHouse.

Hendry, David F. 1972. "*The Analysis and Forecasting of the British Economy* by M. J. C. Surrey." *Economica* 39, no. 155 (August): 346.

———. 1985. "Monetary Economic Myth and Econometric Reality." *Oxford Review of Economic Policy* 1, no. 1 (Spring): 72–84.

Hendry, David F., and Neil R. Ericsson. 1983. "Assertion without Empirical Basis: An Econometric Appraisal of *Monetary Trends in . . . the United Kingdom* by Milton Friedman and Anna Schwartz." In Bank of England, ed., *Monetary Trends in the United Kingdom.* London: Bank of England. 45–101.

———. 1991a. "Modeling the Demand for Narrow Money in the United Kingdom and the United States." *European Economic Review* 35, no. 4 (May): 833–81.

———. 1991b. "An Econometric Analysis of U.K. Money Demand in *Monetary Trends in the United States and the United Kingdom* by Milton Friedman and Anna J Schwartz." *American Economic Review* 81, no. 1 (March): 8–38.

Hendry, David F., and Mary S. Morgan. 1995. *The Foundations of Econometric Analysis.* Cambridge: Cambridge University Press.

Hettinger, Albert J., Jr. 1963. Director's Comment. In Milton Friedman and Anna J. Schwartz, *A Monetary History of the United States, 1867–1960.* Princeton, NJ: Princeton University Press. 809–814.

Hetzel, Robert L. 1998. "Arthur Burns and Inflation." *Federal Reserve Bank of Richmond Economic Quarterly* 84, no. 1 (Winter): 21–44.

Heukelom, Floris. 2014. *Behavioral Economics: A History.* New York: Cambridge University Press.

Hicks, John R. 1937. "Mr. Keynes and the 'Classics': A Suggested Interpretation." *Econometrica* 5, no. 2 (April): 147–59.

———. 1939. *Value and Capital: An Inquiry into Some Fundamental Principles of Economic Theory.* Oxford: Oxford University Press.

———. 1946. *Value and Capital: An Inquiry into Some Fundamental Principles of Economic Theory.* 2nd ed. Oxford, UK: Clarendon.

———. 1963. "Review: *Capitalism and Freedom* by Milton Friedman," *Economica* 30, no. 119 (August): 319–20.

———. 1980. "'IS-LM': An Explanation." *Journal of Post Keynesian Economics* 3, no. 2 (Winter): 139–54.

Hildreth, Clifford G. 1986. *The Cowles Commission in Chicago, 1939–1955.* Berlin: Springer-Verlag.

Hirsch, Abraham, and Neil de Marchi. 1990. *Milton Friedman: Economics in Theory and Practice*. Ann Arbor: University of Michigan Press.

Hodrick, Robert J. 1978. "An Empirical Analysis of the Monetary Approach to the Determination of the Exchange Rate." In Jacob A. Frenkel and Harry G. Johnson, eds., *The Economics of Exchange Rates: Selected Studies*. Reading, MA: Addison-Wesley. 97–116.

Hodrick, Robert J., Narayana Kocherlakota, and Deborah Lucas. 1991. "The Variability of Velocity in Cash-in-Advance Models." *Journal of Political Economy* 99, no. 2 (April): 358–84.

Holden, Anthony. 1984. *Of Presidents, Prime Ministers, and Princes: A Decade in Fleet Street*. New York: Atheneum.

Holmes, James M. 1970. "A Direct Test of Friedman's Permanent Income Theory." *Journal of the American Statistical Association* 65, no. 331 (September): 1159–62.

Horn, Karen Ilse. 2009. *Roads to Wisdom: Conversations with Ten Nobel Laureates in Economics*. Cheltenham, UK: Edward Elgar.

Horne, Alistair. 1989. *Harold Macmillan*. Vol. 2, *1957–1986*. New York: Viking Penguin.

Horwich, George. 1964. *Money, Capital, and Prices*. Homewood, IL: R. D. Irwin.

———. 1965. *Tight Money, Monetary Restraint and the Price Level*. Institute Paper no. 98 (Institute for Research in the Behavioral, Economic, and Management Sciences), Herman C. Krannert Graduate School of Industrial Administration, Purdue University, Lafayette, IN, February.

Hotelling, Harold. 1929. "Stability in Competition." *Economic Journal* 39, no. 153 (March): 41–57.

———. 1931. "The Economics of Exhaustible Resources." *Journal of Political Economy* 39, no. 2 (April): 137–75.

———. 1933. "Review of *The Triumph of Mediocrity in Business* by Horace Secrist." *Journal of American Statistical Association* 28, no. 184 (December): 463–65.

Hotson, John H. 1985. "Response: Professor Friedman's Goals Applauded, His Means Questioned." *Challenge* 28, no. 4 (September): 59–61.

House Republican Research Committee. 1984. *Candid Conversations on Monetary Policy*. Washington, DC: House Republican Research Committee.

Howitt, Peter. 1987. "Optimum Quantity of Money." In John Eatwell, Murray Milgate, and Peter Newman, eds., *The New Palgrave: A Dictionary of Economics*. Vol. 3, *K to P*. London: Macmillan. 744–45.

Hume, David. 1752. "Of Interest." In David Hume, *Political Discourses*. Edinburgh, UK: Fleming. Included in David Hume, *Essays: Moral, Political and Literary*. Modern edition: London: Oxford University Press, 1963.

Humphrey, Thomas M. 1971. "Role of Non-Chicago Economists in the Evolution of the Quantity Theory in America 1930–1950." *Southern Economic Journal* 38, no. 1 (July): 12–18.

———. 1982a. "The Real-Bills Doctrine." *Federal Reserve Bank of Richmond Economic Review* 68, no. 5 (September/October): 3–13.

———. 1982b. "Of Hume, Thornton, the Quantity Theory, and the Phillips Curve." *Federal Reserve Bank of Richmond Economic Review* 68, no. 6 (November/December): 13–18.

Hutchison, Terence W. 1954. "*Essays in Positive Economics* by Milton Friedman." *Economic Journal* 64, no. 256 (December): 796–99.

———. 1977a. *Keynes versus the 'Keynesians' . . . ? An Essay in the Thinking of J. M. Keynes and the Accuracy of Its Interpretation by His Followers*. London: Institute of Economic Affairs.

———. 1977b. *Knowledge and Ignorance in Economics*. Chicago: University of Chicago Press.

Hynes, J. Allan. 1998. "The Emergence of the Neoclassical Consumption Function: The Formative Years, 1940-1952." *Journal of the History of Economic Thought* 20, no. 1 (March): 25-49.

Ireland, Peter N. 2015. "Monetary Policy, Bond Risk Premia, and the Economy." NBER Working Paper no. 21576, September.

Israelsen, L. Dwight. 1985. "Marriner S. Eccles, Chairman of the Federal Reserve Board." *American Economic Review (Papers and Proceedings)* 75, no. 2 (May): 357-62.

Jacobs, Donald P., and Richard T. Pratt, eds. 1968. *Proceedings of the 1968 Conference on Savings and Residential Financing*. Chicago: US Savings and Loan League.

Jalil, Andrew, and Gisela Rua. 2015. "Inflation Expectations and Recovery from the Depression in 1933: Evidence from the Narrative Record." Federal Reserve Board Finance and Economics Discussion Series Paper no. 2015-029, April.

Johnson, Harry G. 1968. "Problems of Efficiency in Monetary Management." *Journal of Political Economy* 76, no. 5 (September/October): 971-90.

———. 1969a. "Inside Money, Outside Money, Income, Wealth, and Welfare in Monetary Theory." *Journal of Money, Credit and Banking* 1, no. 1 (February): 30-45.

———. 1969b. "The Case for Flexible Exchange Rates, 1969." *Federal Reserve Bank of St. Louis Review* 51, no. 6 (June): 12-24.

———. 1970a. "Recent Developments in Monetary Theory—a Commentary." In David R. Croome and Harry G. Johnson, eds., *Money in Britain, 1959-1969: The Papers of the "Radcliffe Report: Ten Years After" Conference at Hove, Sussex, October, 1969*. London: Oxford University Press. 82-114.

———. 1970b. "Is There an Optimal Money Supply?" *Journal of Finance* 25, no. 2 (May): 435-42.

———. 1971a. "The Keynesian Revolution and the Monetarist Counterrevolution." *American Economic Review (Papers and Proceedings)* 61, no. 2 (May): 1-14.

———. 1971b. *Macroeconomics and Monetary Theory*. London: Gray-Mills. (US edition: New York: Aldine, 1972.)

———. 1974. "Review: *Money and Economic Development*." *Economica* 41, no. 163 (August): 346-47.

———. 1976a. "Comment [on Michael G. Porter, 'International Financial Integration: Long-Run Policy Implications']." In Ronald I. McKinnon, ed., *Money and Finance in Economic Growth and Development: Essays in Honor of Edward S. Shaw*. New York: Marcel Dekker. 298-301.

———. 1976b. "What Is Right with Monetarism." *Lloyds Bank Review* 31, no. 120 (April): 13-17.

———. 1978a. "Cambridge as an Academic Environment in the Early Nineteen-Thirties: A Reconstruction from the Late Nineteen-Forties." In Elizabeth S. Johnson and Harry G. Johnson, *The Shadow of Keynes: Understanding Keynes, Cambridge and Keynesian Economics*. Chicago: University of Chicago Press. 84-105.

———. 1978b. "Introduction." In Harry G. Johnson, *Selected Essays in Monetary Economics*. London: George Allen and Unwin. i-iv.

———. 1978c. "The Individual and the State: Some Contemporary Problems." In Fred R. Glahe, ed., *Adam Smith and "The Wealth of Nations": 1776-1976 Bicentennial Essays*. Boulder: Colorado Associated University Press. 21-34.

Johnson, Kirk, and Marianne Johnson. 2009. "Incomplete Course Notes from Milton

Friedman's Price Theory, Economics 300B, University of Chicago, Spring 1947." *Research in the History of Economic Thought and Methodology* 27C, no. 1, 159–99.

Johnson, Marianne, and Warren J. Samuels. 2008. "Glenn Johnson's Notes from Milton Friedman's Course in Economic Theory, Economics 300A, University of Chicago, Winter Quarter 1947." *Research in the History of Economic Thought and Methodology* 26C, no. 1, 63–117.

Johnston, J. 1958a. "A Statistical Illusion in Judging Keynesian Models: Comment." *Review of Economics and Statistics* 40, no. 3 (August): 296–98.

———. 1958b. "Statistical Cost Functions: A Re-appraisal." *Review of Economics and Statistics* 40, no. 4 (November): 339–50.

———. 1958c. "*A Theory of the Consumption Function* by Milton Friedman." *Review of Economics and Statistics* 40, no. 4 (November): 431–35.

Joines, Douglas H. 1981. "Estimates of Effective Marginal Tax Rates on Factor Incomes." *Journal of Business* 54, no. 2 (April): 191–226.

Joint Committee on the Economic Report, US Congress. 1952a. *Monetary Policy and the Management of the Public Debt: Their Role in Achieving Price Stability and High-Level Employment.* Vol. 2. Washington, DC: US Government Printing Office.

———. 1952b. *January 1952 Economic Report of the President: Hearings, January 23, 24, 25, 26, 28, 30, 31, February 1, 1952.* Washington, DC: US Government Printing Office.

———. 1952c. *Monetary Policy and the Management of the Public Debt: Hearings, March 10, 11, 12, 13, 14, 17, 18, 19, 20, 21, 24, 25, 26, 27, 28, and 31, 1952.* Washington, DC: US Government Printing Office.

———. 1952d. *Monetary Policy and the Management of the Public Debt: Their Role in Achieving Price Stability and High-Level Employment: Replies to Questions and Other Material for the Use of the Subcommittee on General Credit Control and Debt Management, Part 2.* Washington, DC: US Government Printing Office.

Joint Economic Committee, US Congress. 1958a. *Relationship of Prices to Economic Stability and Growth: Hearings* [Vol. 1], *May 12, 13, 14, 15, 16, 19, 20, 21, and 22, 1958.* Washington, DC: US Government Printing Office.

———. 1958b. *The Relationship of Prices to Economic Stability and Growth: Compendium of Papers Submitted by Panelists Appearing before the Joint Economic Committee.* Washington, DC: US Government Printing Office.

———. 1959a. *Employment, Growth, and Price Levels, Hearings, Part 4.* Washington, DC: US Government Printing Office.

———. 1959b. *Employment, Growth, and Price Levels, Hearings, Part 9A.* Washington, DC: US Government Printing Office.

———. 1959c. *Relationship of Prices to Economic Stability and Growth: Hearings, Continued: December 15–18, 1958.* Washington, DC: US Government Printing Office.

———. 1959d. *Amending the Employment Act of 1946 to Include Recommendations on Monetary and Credit Policies and Hearings on Proposed Price and Wage Increases: Hearings.* Washington, DC: US Government Printing Office.

———. 1963a. *The United States Balance of Payments: Hearings, Part 3.* Washington, DC: US Government Printing Office.

———. 1963b. *January 1963 Economic Report of the President: Hearings, January 28, 29, 30, 31, February 1, 4, 5, and 6, 1963.* Washington, DC: US Government Printing Office.

———. 1967a. *Economic Outlook and Its Policy Implications: Hearings, June 27, 28, and 29, 1967.* Washington, DC: US Government Printing Office.

———. 1967b. *The 1967 Economic Report of the President: Hearings, Part 3: February 15, 16, and 17, 1967.* Washington, DC: US Government Printing Office.

——. 1968a. *Standards for Guiding Monetary Action: Hearings, May 8, 9, 15, and 16, 1968.* Washington, DC: US Government Printing Office.

——. 1968b. *The 1968 Economic Report of the President: Hearings, Part 1: February 5, 6, 7, 14, 15, 1968.* Washington, DC: US Government Printing Office.

——. 1969. *The 1969 Economic Report of the President: Hearings, Part 2: February 17-20, 24, 1969.* Washington, DC: US Government Printing Office.

——. 1970a. *Economic Analysis and the Efficiency of Government: Hearings, Part 3: September 25, 30, October 6, 1969.* Washington, DC: US Government Printing Office.

——. 1970b. *The Federal Budget, Inflation, and Full Employment: Hearings.* Washington, DC: US Government Printing Office.

——. 1970c. *The 1970 Economic Report of the President: Hearings, Part 1, February 16, 17, 18, and 19, 1970.* Washington, DC: US Government Printing Office.

——. 1971a. *The 1971 Economic Report of the President: Hearings, Part 2: February 22, 23, 24, 25, and 26, 1971.* Washington, DC: US Government Printing Office.

——. 1971b. *The President's New Economic Program: Hearings, Part 4: September 20, 21, 22, and 23, 1971.* Washington, DC: US Government Printing Office.

——. 1973. *How Well Are Fluctuating Exchange Rates Working? Hearings of the Subcommittee on International Economics.* Washington, DC: US Government Printing Office.

——. 1995. *The Balanced Budget Amendment: Hearings before the Joint Economic Committee, Congress of the United States, One Hundred Fourth Congress, First Session, Part 1, January 20, 1995.* Washington, DC: US Government Printing Office.

Jones, Daniel Stedman. 2012. *Masters of the Universe: Hayek, Friedman, and the Birth of Neoliberal Politics.* Princeton, NJ: Princeton University Press.

Jones, Larry E., and Rodolfo E. Manuelli. 2001. "On the Taxation of Human Capital." Manuscript, University of Minnesota.

Jorgenson, Dale W. 1963. "Capital Theory and Investment Behavior." *American Economic Review (Papers and Proceedings)* 53, no. 2 (May): 247-59.

Juster, F. Thomas, Joseph P. Lupton, James P. Smith, and Frank Stafford. 2004. "The Decline in Household Saving and the Wealth Effect." Federal Reserve Board Finance and Economics Discussion Series Paper no. 2004-32, April.

Kaldor, Nicholas. 1955. *An Expenditure Tax.* London: Allen and Unwin.

——. 1970. "The New Monetarism." *Lloyds Bank Review* 25, no. 97 (July): 1-18.

Kaldor, Nicholas, and James A. Trevithick. 1981. "A Keynesian Perspective on Money." *Lloyds Bank Review* 36, no. 139 (January): 1-19.

Kareken, John H., and Neil A. Wallace. 1977. "Portfolio Autarky: A Welfare Analysis." *Journal of International Economics* 7, no. 1 (February): 19-43.

Karnosky, Denis S. 1974a. "Real Money Balances: A Misleading Indicator of Monetary Actions." *Federal Reserve Bank of St. Louis Review* 56, no. 2 (February): 1-10.

——. 1974b. "Another Recession, but Different." *Federal Reserve Bank of St. Louis Review* 56, no. 12 (December): 15-18.

Kashyap, Anil K., and Jeremy C. Stein. 2000. "What Do a Million Observations on Banks Say about the Transmission of Monetary Policy?" *American Economic Review* 90, no. 3 (June): 407-28.

Kaufman, George G. 1964. "The Supply of Money: A Supply Function Explaining Federal Reserve Behavior." Manuscript, Federal Reserve Bank of Chicago.

Kay, John A., and Mervyn A. King. 1978. *The British Tax System.* Oxford: Oxford University Press.

Keller, Peter M. 1977. "Controlling Fluctuations in Credit." *IMF Staff Papers* 24, no. 1 (March): 128-53.

Ketchum, Marshall D., and Leon T. Kendall, eds. 1962. *Proceedings of the Conference on Savings and Residential Financing: 1962 Proceedings, May 10 and 11, 1962, Chicago, Illinois.* Chicago: US Savings and Loan League.

Ketchum, Marshall D., and Norman Strunk, eds. 1964. *Proceedings of the Conference on Savings and Residential Financing: 1964 Proceedings, May 7 and 8, 1964, Chicago, Illinois.* Chicago: United States Savings and Loan League.

———, eds. 1965. *Conference on Savings and Residential Financing: 1965 Proceedings.* Chicago: United States Savings and Loan League.

Keynes, John Maynard. 1923. *A Tract on Monetary Reform.* London: Macmillan.

———. 1925. *The Economic Consequences of Mr. Churchill.* London: Hogarth.

———. 1930. *A Treatise on Money.* 2 vols. London: Macmillan.

———. 1936. *The General Theory of Employment, Interest and Money.* London: Macmillan.

———. 1939a. "Official Papers: The League of Nations—Professor Tinbergen's Method." *Economic Journal* 49, no. 195 (September): 558-68.

———. 1939b. "The Income and Fiscal Potential of Great Britain." *Economic Journal* 49, no. 196 (December): 626-38.

———. 1940. *How to Pay for the War: A Radical Plan for the Chancellor of the Exchequer.* London: Macmillan.

Khan, Aubhik, Robert G. King, and Alexander L. Wolman. 2003. "Optimal Monetary Policy." *Review of Economic Studies* 70, no. 4 (October): 825-60.

Kiley, Michael T. 2003. "Why Is Inflation Low When Productivity Growth Is High?" *Economic Inquiry* 41, no. 3 (July): 392-406.

———. 2014. "The Aggregate Demand Effects of Short- and Long-Term Interest Rates." *International Journal of Central Banking* 10, no. 4 (December): 69-104.

Kilponen, Juha, and Kai Leitemo. 2008. "Model Uncertainty and Delegation: A Case for Friedman's *k*-percent Money Growth Rule?" *Journal of Money, Credit and Banking* 40, nos. 2-3 (March/April): 547-56.

Kim, Chang-Jin, and Charles R. Nelson. 1999. "Friedman's Plucking Model of Business Fluctuations: Tests and Estimates of Permanent and Transitory Components." *Journal of Money, Credit and Banking* 31, no. 3 (August): 317-34.

Kindleberger, Charles P. 1985. *Keynesianism vs. Monetarism and Other Essays in Financial History.* London: George Allen and Unwin.

———. 1986. *The World in Depression, 1929-1939.* Berkeley, CA: University of California Press.

King, Mervyn A. 1977. *Public Policy and the Corporation.* London: Chapman and Hall.

———. 1994. "The Transmission Mechanism of Monetary Policy." *Bank of England Quarterly Bulletin* 34, no. 3 (August): 261-67.

———. 1997a. "Monetary Stability: Rhyme or Reason?" *Bank of England Quarterly Bulletin* 37, no. 1 (February): 88-97.

———. 1997b. "The Inflation Target Five Years On." *Bank of England Quarterly Bulletin* 37, no. 4 (November): 434-42.

———. 1997c. "Changes in UK Monetary Policy: Rules and Discretion in Practice." *Journal of Monetary Economics* 39, no. 1 (June): 81-97.

———. 2003. "No Money, No Inflation: The Role of Money in the Economy." In Paul Mizen, ed., *Central Banking, Monetary Theory and Practice: Essays in Honour of Charles Goodhart.* Vol. 1. Cheltenham, UK: Edward Elgar. 62-89.

———. 2012. "Twenty Years of Inflation Targeting." Stamp Memorial Lecture, London School of Economics, October 9.

King, Robert G. 1991. "Value and Capital in the Equilibrium Business Cycle Programme." In Lionel McKenzie and Stefano Zagmani, eds., *"Value and Capital"—Fifty Years Later: Proceedings of a Conference Held by the International Economic Association at Bologna, Italy*. New York: New York University Press. 279-309.

———. 2009. "Comments [on Bartosz Maćkowiak and Frank Smets, 'Implications of Microeconomic Data for Macroeconomic Models']." In Jeffrey C. Fuhrer, Jane S. Little, Yolanda K. Kodrzycki, and Giovanni P. Olivei, eds., *Understanding Inflation and the Implications for Monetary Policy: A Phillips Curve Retrospective*. Cambridge, MA: MIT Press. 333-50.

King, Robert G., and Charles I. Plosser. 1981. *"Rational Expectations and Monetary Policy*, by Jac J. Sijben." *Journal of Money, Credit and Banking* 13, no. 3 (August): 404-7.

King, Robert G., and Mark W. Watson. 1998. "The Solution of Singular Linear Difference Systems under Rational Expectations." *International Economic Review* 39, no. 4 (November): 1015-26.

King, Robert G., and Alexander L. Wolman. 1996. "Inflation Targeting in a St. Louis Model of the 21st Century." *Federal Reserve Bank of St. Louis Review* 78, no. 3 (May/June): 83-107.

Kitch, Edmund W., ed. 1983. "The Fire of Truth: A Remembrance of Law and Economics at Chicago, 1932-1970." *Journal of Law and Economics* 26, no. 1 (April): 163-234.

Klamer, Arjo. 1983. *The New Classical Macroeconomics: Conversations with the New Classical Economists and Their Opponents*. Totowa, NJ: Rowman and Allanheld.

Klein, Benjamin. 1970. "The Payment of Interest on Commercial Bank Deposits and the Price of Money: A Study of the Demand for Money." PhD diss., Department of Economics, University of Chicago.

———. 1974. "Competitive Interest Payments on Bank Deposits and the Long-Run Demand for Money." *American Economic Review* 64, no. 6 (December): 931-49.

———. 1975a. "Our New Monetary Standard: The Measurement and Effects of Price Uncertainty, 1880-1973." *Economic Inquiry* 13, no. 4 (April): 461-84.

———. 1975b. "The Impact of Inflation on the Term Structure of Corporate Financial Investments: 1900-1972." In William L. Silber, ed., *Financial Innovation*. Lexington, MA: D. C. Heath. 125-49.

———. 1976a. "Competitive Interest Payments on Bank Deposits and the Long-Run Demand for Money: Reply." *American Economic Review* 66, no. 5 (December): 958-60.

———. 1976b. "Competing Monies: Comment." *Journal of Money, Credit and Banking* 8, no. 4 (November): 513-19.

———. 1977. "The Demand for Quality-Adjusted Cash Balances: Price Uncertainty in the U.S. Demand for Money Function." *Journal of Political Economy* 85, no. 4 (August): 691-715.

———. 1978. "Competing Monies, European Monetary Union and the Dollar." In Michele Fratianni and Theo Peeters, eds., *One Money for Europe*. London: Macmillan. 69-94.

Klein, Lawrence R. 1950. *Economic Fluctuations in the United States, 1921-1941*. Cowles Commission Monograph no. 11. New York: Wiley.

———. 1958. "The Friedman-Becker Illusion." *Journal of Political Economy* 66, no. 6 (December): 539-45.

Kneeland, Hildegarde, Erika H. Schoenberg, and Milton Friedman. 1936. "Plans for a

Study of the Consumption of Goods and Services by American Families." *Journal of the American Statistical Association* 31, no. 193 (March): 135-40.

Kneeland, Hildegarde, et al. 1939. *Consumer Expenditures in the United States: Estimates for 1935-1936.* Washington, DC: National Resources Committee.

Knight, F. H. 1933. *The Economic Organization.* Manuscript, University of Chicago. Expanded edition: New York: A. M. Kelley, 1951.

———. 1937. "Unemployment: And Mr. Keynes's Revolution in Economic Theory." *Canadian Journal of Economics and Political Science* 3, no. 1 (February): 100-23.

Koenig, Evan F. 1987. "A Dynamic Optimizing Alternative to Traditional IS-LM Analysis." University of Washington Institute for Economic Research Discussion Paper no. 87-07, May.

Kohn, Donald L. 1990. "Making Monetary Policy: Adjusting Policy to Achieve Final Objectives." In W. E. Norton and Peter Stebbing, eds., *Monetary Policy and Market Operations.* Sydney: Reserve Bank of Australia. 11-26.

———. 2005. "Comment [on Marvin Goodfriend, 'An Inflation Target for the United States?']." In Ben S. Bernanke and Michael Woodford, eds., *The Inflation-Targeting Debate.* Chicago: University of Chicago Press. 337-50.

Koopmans, Tjalling C. 1947. "Measurement without Theory." *Review of Economics and Statistics* 29, no. 3 (August): 161-72.

———. 1953. "Identification Problems in Economic Model Construction." In William C. Hood and Tjalling C. Koopmans, eds., *Studies in Econometric Method, by Cowles Commission Research Staff Members.* New York: Wiley. 27-48.

Koyck, L. M. 1954. *Distributed Lags and Investment Analysis.* Amsterdam: North-Holland.

Krugman, Paul. 1980. "Oil and the Dollar." NBER Working Paper no. 554, September.

———. 1990. "Equilibrium Exchange Rates." In William H. Branson, Jacob A. Frenkel, and Morris Goldstein, eds., *International Policy Coordination and Exchange Rate Fluctuations.* Chicago: University of Chicago Press. 159-87.

———. 1999. "Domestic Policies in a Global Economy." *Brookings Trade Forum* 2, no. 1, 73-93.

———. 2007. "Who Was Milton Friedman?" *New York Review of Books* 54, no. 2, February 15, 27-30.

Krusell, Per, and Anthony A. Smith Jr. 2015. "Is Piketty's 'Second Law of Capitalism' Fundamental?" *Journal of Political Economy* 123, no. 4 (August): 725-48.

Kuttner, Kenneth N., and Cara C. Lown. 1999. "The Composition of Bank Portfolios and the Transmission of Monetary Policy." In K. Alec Chrystal, ed., *Government Debt Structure and Monetary Conditions.* London: Bank of England. 165-89.

Kuttner, Robert. 2005. "Agreeing to Disagree: Robert Kuttner Speaks with Milton Friedman." December 18. prospect.org.

Kuznets, Simon. 1934. *National Income, 1929-1932.* New York: National Bureau of Economic Research, Bulletin no. 49.

———. 1937. *National Income and Capital Formation, 1919-1935.* New York: National Bureau of Economic Research.

———. 1941. *National Income and Its Composition, 1919-1938,* Vols. 1 and 2. New York: National Bureau of Economic Research.

———. 1942. "Use of National Income in Peace and War." National Bureau of Economic Research Occasional Paper no. 6.

———. 1946. *National Product since 1869.* New York: National Bureau of Economic Research.

———. 1952. "Proportion of Capital Formation to National Product." *American Economic Review (Papers and Proceedings)* 42, no. 2 (May): 507-26.

Kuznets, Simon, and Milton Friedman. 1939. "Incomes from Independent Professional Practice, 1929-1936." *National Bureau of Economic Research Bulletin*, nos. 72-73 (February 5): 1-31.

Kydland, Finn E. 1992. "Rules versus Discretion." In John Eatwell, Murray Milgate, and Peter Newman, eds., *The New Palgrave Dictionary of Money and Finance*. Vol. 3, *K to P*. London: Macmillan. 379-81.

Kydland, Finn E., and Edward C. Prescott. 1977. "Rules Rather Than Discretion: The Inconsistency of Optimal Plans." *Journal of Political Economy* 85, no. 3 (June): 473-92.

———. 1982. "Time to Build and Aggregate Fluctuations." *Econometrica* 50, no. 6 (November): 1345-70.

———. 1988. "The Workweek of Capital and Its Cyclical Fluctuations." *Journal of Monetary Economics* 21, nos. 2-3 (March-May): 343-60.

Laffer, Arthur B., and Marc A. Miles. 1982. *International Economics in an Integrated World*. Oakland, NJ: Scott, Foresman.

Laidler, David. 1976. "Expectations and the Phillips Trade Off: A Commentary." *Scottish Journal of Political Economy* 23, no. 1 (February): 55-72.

———. 1981. "Monetarism: An Interpretation and an Assessment." *Economic Journal* 91, no. 361 (March): 1-28.

———. 1982. "Friedman and Schwartz on Monetary Trends: A Review Article." *Journal of International Money and Finance* 1, no. 1, 293-305.

———. 1984. "Harry Johnson as a Macroeconomist." *Journal of Political Economy* 92, no. 4 (August): 592-615.

———. 1985. *The Demand for Money: Theories, Evidence, and Problems*. 3rd ed. New York: Harper and Row.

———. 1989. "Dow and Saville's *Critique of Monetary Policy*—a Review Essay." *Journal of Economic Literature* 27, no. 3 (September): 1147-59.

———. 1990. "The Legacy of the Monetarist Controversy." *Federal Reserve Bank of St. Louis Review* 72, no. 2 (March): 49-64.

———. 1991a. *The Golden Age of the Quantity Theory*. Princeton, NJ: Princeton University Press.

———. 1991b. "Karl Brunner's Monetary Economics—an Appreciation." *Journal of Money, Credit and Banking* 23, no. 4 (November): 633-58.

———. 1993a. "Hawtrey, Harvard, and the Origins of the Chicago Tradition." *Journal of Political Economy* 101, no. 6 (December): 1068-103.

———. 1993b. "Book Review: *Money Mischief: Episodes in Monetary History* by Milton Friedman." *Journal of Political Economy* 101, no. 1 (February): 203-6.

———. 1995. "Some Aspects of Monetarism circa 1970: A View from 1994." *Kredit und Kapital* 28, no. 3, 323-45.

———. 1999. *Fabricating the Keynesian Revolution: Studies of the Inter-war Literature on Money, the Cycle and Unemployment*. Cambridge: Cambridge University Press.

———. 2012. "Milton Friedman's Contributions to Macroeconomics and Their Influence." University of Western Ontario Economic Policy Research Institute Working Paper 2012-2, February.

———. 2013a. "The Fisher Relation in the Great Recession and the Great Depression." University of Western Ontario Economic Policy Research Institute Working Paper 2013-2, March.

———. 2013b. "Reassessing the Thesis of the *Monetary History*." University of Western Ontario Economic Policy Research Institute Working Paper 2013-5, October.

Laidler, David, and A. Robert Nobay. 1976. "International Aspects of Inflation: A Survey." In Emil Maria Claassen and Pascal Salin, eds., *Recent Issues in International Monetary Economics: Third Paris-Dauphine Conference on Money and International Monetary Problems, March 28-30, 1974*. Amsterdam: North-Holland. 291-307.

Lange, Oskar R. 1936. "On the Economic Theory of Socialism, Part I." *Review of Economic Studies* 4, no. 1 (October): 53-71.

———. 1937. "On the Economic Theory of Socialism, Part II." *Review of Economic Studies* 4, no. 2 (February): 123-42.

———. 1939. "Is the American Economy Contracting?" *American Economic Review* 29, no. 3 (September): 503-13.

———. 1942. "Say's Law: A Restatement and Criticism." In Oskar R. Lange, Francis McIntyre, and Theodore Otto Yntema, eds., *Studies in Mathematical Economics and Econometrics*. Chicago: University of Chicago Press. 49-68.

———. 1944. *Price Flexibility and Employment*. Bloomington, IN: Principle.

———. 1970. *Papers in Economics and Sociology, 1930-1960*. Oxford: Pergamon.

Lange, Oskar R., and Fred M. Taylor. 1938. *On the Economic Theory of Socialism*. Minneapolis: University of Minnesota Press.

Laurent, Robert D. 2000. "Monetarist Thoughts." *Journal of Economic Perspectives* 14, no. 4 (Fall): 225-27.

Layard, P. R. G., and Alan A. Walters. 1978. *Microeconomic Theory*. New York: McGraw Hill.

Leeper, Eric M. 2010. "Monetary Science, Fiscal Alchemy." In Federal Reserve Bank of Kansas City, ed., *Macroeconomic Challenges: The Decade Ahead*. Kansas City, MO: Federal Reserve Bank of Kansas City. 361-434.

Leeson, Robert. 1996. "How Chicago Overcame Cambridge." Murdoch University Department of Economics Working Paper no. 151, July.

———. 1997a. "The Political Economy of the Inflation-Unemployment Trade-Off." *History of Political Economy* 29, no. 1, Spring, 117-56.

———. 1997b. "The Trade-Off Interpretation of Phillips's Dynamic Stabilization Exercise." *Economica* 64, no. 253 (February): 155-71.

———. 1998. "'The Ghosts I Can't Get Rid of Now': The Keynes-Tinbergen-Friedman-Phillips Critique of Econometrics." *History of Political Economy* 30, no. 1 (Spring): 51-94.

———. 2000a. *The Eclipse of Keynesianism: The Political Economy of the Chicago Counterrevolution*. New York: Palgrave.

———. 2000b. "Patinkin, Johnson, and the 'Shadow of Friedman.'" *History of Political Economy* 32, no. 4 (Winter): 733-64.

———. 2003a. "From Keynes to Friedman via Mints: A Resolution of the Dispute." In Robert Leeson, ed., *Keynes, Chicago and Friedman*. Vol. 2. London: Pickering and Chatto. 483-525.

———, ed. 2003b. *Keynes, Chicago and Friedman*. Vol. 1. London: Pickering and Chatto.

———, ed. 2003c. *Keynes, Chicago and Friedman*. Vol. 2. London: Pickering and Chatto.

———. 2003d. "The Debate Widens." In Robert Leeson, ed., *Keynes, Chicago and Friedman*. Vol. 1. London: Pickering and Chatto. 283-309.

———. 2003e. "The Initial Controversy." In Robert Leeson, ed., *Keynes, Chicago and Friedman*. Vol. 2. London: Pickering and Chatto. 1-30.

Leeson, Robert, and Charles G. Palm. 2017. *Milton Friedman on Freedom: Selections from the Collected Works of Milton Friedman*. Stanford, CA: Hoover Institution Press.

Leijonhufvud, Axel (1977). "Costs and Consequences of Inflation." In G. C. Harcourt, ed., *The Microeconomic Foundations of Macroeconomics: Proceedings of a Conference Held by the International Economic Association, at S'Agaro, Spain*. Boulder, CO: Westview Press. 264–312.

Lerner, Abba P. 1944. *The Economics of Control*. New York: Macmillan.

———. 1953. "On the Marginal Product of Capital and the Marginal Efficiency of Investment." *Journal of Political Economy* 61, no. 1 (February): 1–14.

———. 1958. "Inflationary Depression and the Regulation of Administered Prices." In Joint Economic Committee, US Congress, *The Relationship of Prices to Economic Stability and Growth: Compendium of Papers Submitted by Panelists Appearing before the Joint Economic Committee*. Washington, DC: US Government Printing Office. 257–68.

Lettau, Martin, and Sydney C. Ludvigson. 2004. "Understanding Trend and Cycle in Asset Values: Reevaluating the Wealth Effect on Consumption." *American Economic Review* 94, no. 1 (March): 276–99.

Leube, Kurt R. 1987. "Preface." In Kurt R. Leube, ed., *The Essence of Friedman*. Stanford, CA: Hoover Institution Press. xiii–xviii.

Levacic, Rosalind. 1984. "Keynes Was a Monetarist." *Economic Affairs* 4, no. 3 (April–June): 19–23.

Levin, Andrew T., Alexei Onatski, John C. Williams, and Noah Williams. 2005. "Monetary Policy under Uncertainty in Micro-Founded Macroeconometric Models." *NBER Macroeconomics Annual* 20, no. 1, 229–87.

Levin, Fred J., and Ann-Marie Meulendyke. 1982. "Monetary Policy: Theory and Practice: Comment." *Journal of Money, Credit and Banking* 14, no. 3 (August): 399–403.

Levy, David. 1992. "Interview with Milton Friedman." *Region* (Federal Reserve Bank of Minneapolis) 6, no. 2 (June): 6–13. https://www.minneapolisfed.org/publications/the-region/interview-with-milton-Friedman.

Library of Congress, Legislative Reference Service. 1942. *The War Production Program: Selected Documentation on the Economics of War*. Washington, DC: Division of Information, War Production Board.

Lindsey, David E. 2003. "A Modern History of FOMC Communication: 1975–2002." Division of Monetary Affairs, Federal Reserve Board, June 24. Authorized for public release by the FOMC Secretariat on August 19, 2009, and available for public download on the website of the Federal Reserve Bank of St. Louis.

Lipsey, Richard G., and M. D. Steuer. 1961. "The Relation between Profits and Wage Rates." *Economica* 28, no. 110 (May): 137–55.

Littleboy, Bruce. 1990. *On Interpreting Keynes: A Study in Reconciliation*. London: Routledge.

Liviatan, Nissan. 1963. "Tests of the Permanent-Income Hypothesis Based on a Reinterview Savings Survey." In Carl F. Christ et al., *Measurement in Economics: Studies in Mathematical Economics and Econometrics in Memory of Yehuda Grunfeld*. Stanford, CA: Stanford University Press. 29–59.

Longbottom, Andrew, and Sean Holly. 1985. "Monetary Trends in the U.K.: A Reappraisal of the Demand for Money." London Business School Discussion Paper no. 147, April.

Lothian, James R., Anthony Cassese, and Laura Nowak. 1983. "Data Appendix." In

Michael R. Darby and James R. Lothian, eds., *The International Transmission of Inflation*. Chicago: University of Chicago Press. 525–718.

Lothian, James R., and George S. Tavlas. 2018. "How Friedman and Schwartz Became Monetarists." *Journal of Money, Credit and Banking* 50, no. 4 (June): 757–87.

Lowe, Philip. 1992. "The Term Structure of Interest Rates, Real Activity and Inflation." Reserve Bank of Australia Research Discussion Paper no. 9204, May.

Lucas, Robert E., Jr. 1967. "Optimal Investment Policy and the Flexible Accelerator." *International Economic Review* 8, no. 1 (February): 78–85.

———. 1972a. "Econometric Testing of the Natural Rate Hypothesis." In Otto Eckstein, ed., *The Econometrics of Price Determination: Conference, October 30–31, 1970*. Washington, DC: Federal Reserve Board. 50–59.

———. 1972b. "Expectations and the Neutrality of Money." *Journal of Economic Theory* 4, no. 2 (April): 103–24.

———. 1973. "Some International Evidence on Output-Inflation Tradeoffs." *American Economic Review* 63, no. 3 (June): 326–34.

———. 1976a. Letter to Rep. Stephen L. Neal, Chairman, Subcommittee on Domestic Monetary Policy, September 21, 1976. In Committee on Banking, Finance, and Urban Affairs, US House of Representatives, *Maintaining and Making Public Minutes of Federal Reserve Meetings: Hearings*. Washington, DC: US Government Printing Office, 1977. 223.

———. 1976b. "Econometric Policy Evaluation: A Critique." *Carnegie-Rochester Conference Series on Public Policy* 1, no. 1, 19–46.

———. 1977. "Understanding Business Cycles." *Carnegie-Rochester Conference Series on Public Policy* 5, no. 1, 7–29.

———. 1980a. "Rules, Discretion, and the Role of the Economic Advisor." In Stanley Fischer, ed., *Rational Expectations and Economic Policy*. Chicago: University of Chicago Press. 199–210.

———. 1980b. "Methods and Problems in Business Cycle Theory." *Journal of Money, Credit and Banking* 12, no. 4, part 2, 696–715.

———. 1980c. "Two Illustrations of the Quantity Theory of Money." *American Economic Review* 70, no. 5 (December): 1005–14.

———. 1987. *Models of Business Cycles*. Oxford, UK: Basil Blackwell.

———. 1988a. "On the Mechanics of Economic Development." *Journal of Monetary Economics* 22, no. 1 (July): 3–42.

———. 1988b. "Money Demand in the United States: A Quantitative Review." *Carnegie Rochester Conference on Public Policy* 29, no. 1, 137–67.

———. 1994a. "Comments on Ball and Mankiw." *Carnegie-Rochester Conference Series on Public Policy* 41, no. 1 (December): 153–55.

———. 1994b. "Review of Milton Friedman and Anna J. Schwartz's *A Monetary History of the United States, 1867–1960*." *Journal of Monetary Economics* 34, no. 1 (August): 5–16.

———. 1996. "Nobel Lecture: Monetary Neutrality." *Journal of Political Economy* 104, no. 4 (August): 661–82.

———. 2001. "Professional Memoir." Manuscript, University of Chicago, April 15.

———. 2004a. "Keynote Address to the 2003 *HOPE* Conference: My Keynesian Education." *History of Political Economy* 36 (supplement): 12–24.

———. 2004b. "Robert E. Lucas, Jr." In William Breit and Barry T. Hirsch, eds., *Lives of the Laureates: Eighteen Nobel Economists*. 4th ed. 273–97.

———. 2013. *Collected Papers on Monetary Theory*. Max Gillman, ed. Cambridge, MA: Harvard University Press.

Lucas, Robert E., Jr., and Edward C. Prescott. 1974. "Equilibrium Search and Unemployment." *Journal of Economic Theory* 7, no. 2 (February): 188–209.

Lucas, Robert E., Jr., and Leonard A. Rapping. 1969. "Real Wages, Employment, and Inflation." *Journal of Political Economy* 77, no. 5 (September/October): 721–54. Reprinted with additional appendix in Edmund S. Phelps, ed., *Microeconomic Foundations of Employment and Inflation Theory*. New York: W. W. Norton, 1970. 257–305.

Lucas, Robert E., Jr., and Thomas J. Sargent. 1981. "Introduction." In Robert E. Lucas Jr. and Thomas J. Sargent, eds., *Rational Expectations and Econometric Practice*. Vol. 1. Minneapolis: University of Minnesota Press. xi–xl.

Lucas, Robert E., Jr., and Nancy L. Stokey. 1983. "Optimal Fiscal and Monetary Policy in an Economy without Capital." *Journal of Monetary Economics* 12, no. 1, 55–93.

Lutz, Friedrich A., and Lloyd W. Mints, eds. 1951. *Readings in Monetary Theory, Selected by a Committee of the American Economic Association*. Homewood, IL: Richard D. Irwin; Philadelphia: Blakiston.

Lydall, H. F. 1958. "Milton Friedman, *A Theory of the Consumption Function*." *Kyklos* 11, no. 4 (November): 563–64.

Lynn, Jonathan, and Antony Jay. 1988. *The Complete Yes Minister*. New York: Harper and Row.

Macesich, George. 1997. *The United States in the Changing Global Economy: Policy Implications and Issues*. Westport, CT: Praeger.

Macfarlane, Ian. 2006. *The Search for Stability*. Sydney: ABC Books.

Machina, Mark J. 1987. "Expected Utility Hypothesis." In John Eatwell, Murray Milgate, and Peter Newman, eds., *The New Palgrave: A Dictionary of Economics*. Vol. 2, *E to J*. London: Macmillan. 232–39.

Machlup, Fritz. 1943. *International Trade and the National Income Multiplier*. Philadelphia: Blakiston.

Mäki, Uskali. 1985. "Rhetoric at the Expense of Coherence: A Reinterpretation of Milton Friedman's Methodology." *Research in the History of Economic Thought and Methodology* 4, no. 1, 127–43.

———, ed. 2009. *The Methodology of Positive Economics: Reflections on the Milton Friedman Legacy*. Cambridge: Cambridge University Press.

Makinen, Gail E. 1977. *Money, the Price Level, and Interest Rates: An Introduction to Monetary Theory*. Englewood Cliffs, NJ: Prentice Hall.

Mankiw, N. Gregory. 1986. "Comment on 'Do Equilibrium Real Business Cycle Theories Explain Postwar U.S. Business Cycles?'" *NBER Macroeconomics Annual* 1, no. 1, 139–45.

Mankiw, N. Gregory, Julio J. Rotemberg, and Lawrence H. Summers. 1985. "Intertemporal Substitution in Macroeconomics." *Quarterly Journal of Economics* 100, no. 1 (February): 225–51.

Manuelli, Rodolfo E., and Ananth Seshadri. 2014. "Human Capital and the Wealth of Nations." *American Economic Review* 104, no. 9 (September): 2736–62.

Marget, Arthur W. 1938. *The Theory of Prices: A Re-examination of the Central Problems of Monetary Theory*. Vol. 1. New York: Prentice Hall.

———. 1942. *The Theory of Prices: A Re-examination of the Central Problems of Monetary Theory*. Vol. 2. New York: Prentice Hall.

Markowitz, Harry. 1952. "The Utility of Wealth." *Journal of Political Economy* 60, no. 2 (April): 151–58.

Marquis Who's Who, Inc. 1950. *Who's Who in America, 1950/1951.* Chicago: Marquis Who's Who.

———. 1964. *Who's Who in America, 1964/1965.* Chicago: Marquis Who's Who.

———. 1972. *Who's Who in the Midwest, 1972/1973.* Chicago: Marquis Who's Who.

———. 1976. *Who's Who in America 1976/1977.* 39th ed. Vol. 1. Chicago: Marquis Who's Who.

Marschak, Jacob. 1966. "Foreword: A Remark on Econometric Tools." In Carl F. Christ, *Econometric Models and Methods.* New York: John Wiley and Sons. vii–xi.

Marshall, Alfred. 1920. *Principles of Economics: An Introductory Volume.* 8th ed. London: Macmillan.

Marshall, Natalie J., ed. 1970. *Keynes: Updated or Outdated?* Lexington, MA: D. C. Heath.

Martin, George R. 1983. *Thread of Excellence.* Chicago: Martin Hughes Publishers.

Martin, Justin. 2001. *Greenspan: The Man behind Money.* New York: Basic Books.

Marty, Alvin L. 1961. "Gurley and Shaw on Money in a Theory of Finance." *Journal of Political Economy* 69, no. 1 (February): 56–62.

———. 1994. "What Is the Neutrality of Money?" *Economics Letters* 44, no. 4 (April): 407–9.

Matusow, Allen J. 1998. *Nixon's Economy: Booms, Busts, Dollars, and Votes.* Lawrence: University Press of Kansas.

Mayer, Thomas. 1972. *Permanent Income, Wealth, and Consumption: A Critique of the Permanent Income Theory.* Los Angeles: University of California Press.

———. 1999. *Monetary Policy and the Great Inflation in the United States: The Federal Reserve and the Failure of Macroeconomic Policy, 1965–1979.* Cheltenham, UK: Edward Elgar.

McCallum, Bennett T. 1979. "The Current State of the Policy-Ineffectiveness Debate." *American Economic Review (Papers and Proceedings)* 69, no. 2 (May): 240–45.

———. 1980. "Rational Expectations and Macroeconomic Stabilization Policy: An Overview." *Journal of Money, Credit and Banking* 12, no. 4, part 2 (November): 716–46.

———. 1982. "Macroeconomics after a Decade of Rational Expectations: Some Critical Issues." *Federal Reserve Bank of Richmond Economic Review* 68, no. 6 (November/December): 3–12.

———. 1983a. "A Reconsideration of Sims' Evidence Concerning Monetarism." *Economics Letters* 13, nos. 2–3, 167–71.

———. 1983b. "On Non-uniqueness in Rational Expectations Models: An Attempt at Perspective." *Journal of Monetary Economics* 11, no. 2, 139–68.

———. 1984a. "A Linearized Version of Lucas's Neutrality Model." *Canadian Journal of Economics* 17, no. 1 (February): 138–45.

———. 1984b. "Credibility and Monetary Policy." In Federal Reserve Bank of Kansas City, ed., *Price Stability and Public Policy.* Kansas City, MO: Federal Reserve Bank of Kansas City. 105–26.

———. 1986a. "Monetary versus Fiscal Policy Effects: A Review of the Debate." In R. W. Hafer, ed., *The Monetary versus Fiscal Policy Debate: Lessons from Two Decades.* Totowa, NJ: Rowman and Allanheld. 9–29.

———. 1986b. "Some Issues concerning Interest Rate Pegging, Price Level Determinacy, and the Real Bills Doctrine." *Journal of Monetary Economics* 17, no. 1 (January): 135–60.

———. 1987a. "The Optimal Inflation Rate in an Overlapping-Generations Economy with Land." In William A. Barnett and Kenneth J. Singleton, eds., *New Approaches to Monetary Economics: Proceedings of the Second International Symposium in Economic Theory and Econometrics*. New York: Cambridge University Press. 325-39.

———. 1987b. "The Development of Keynesian Macroeconomics." *American Economic Review (Papers and Proceedings)* 77, no. 2, 125-29.

———. 1989a. "New Classical Macroeconomics: A Sympathetic Account." *Scandinavian Journal of Economics* 91, no. 2 (June): 223-52.

———. 1989b. *Monetary Economics: Theory and Policy*. New York: Prentice Hall.

———. 1990a. "Comment [on Robert H. Rasche, 'Demand Functions for Measures of U.S. Money and Debt']." In Peter Hooper, Karen H. Johnson, Donald L. Kohn, David E. Lindsey, Richard D. Porter, and Ralph W. Tryon, eds., *Financial Sectors in Open Economies: Empirical Analysis and Policy Issues*. Washington, DC: Board of Governors of the Federal Reserve System. 167-72.

———. 1990b. "Could a Monetary Base Rule Have Prevented the Great Depression?" *Journal of Monetary Economics* 26, no. 1 (August): 3-26.

———. 1990c. "Inflation: Theory and Evidence." In Frank H. Hahn and Benjamin M. Friedman, eds., *Handbook of Monetary Economics*. Vol. 2. Amsterdam: North-Holland. 963-1012.

———. 1993a. "Specification and Analysis of a Monetary Policy Rule for Japan." *Bank of Japan Monetary and Economic Studies* 11, no. 2 (November): 1-45.

———. 1993b. "Specification and Analysis of a Monetary Policy Rule for Japan: Reply to Comments by Kunio Okina." *Bank of Japan Monetary and Economic Studies* 11, no. 2 (November): 55-57.

———. 1993c. "Unit Roots in Macroeconomic Time Series: Some Critical Issues." *Federal Reserve Bank of Richmond Economic Quarterly* 79, no. 2 (Spring): 13-43.

———. 1994a. "Identification of Inflation-Unemployment Tradeoffs in the 1970s: A Comment." *Carnegie-Rochester Conference on Public Policy* 41, no. 1, 231-41.

———. 1994b. "Comment [on Matthew D. Shapiro, 'Federal Reserve Policy: Cause and Effect']." In N. Gregory Mankiw, ed., *Monetary Policy*. Chicago: University of Chicago Press. 332-34.

———. 1995. "Two Fallacies concerning Central-Bank Independence." *American Economic Review (Papers and Proceedings)* 85, no. 2 (May): 207-11.

———. 1998. "An Interview with Allan Meltzer." *Macroeconomic Dynamics* 2, no. 2 (June): 238-83.

———. 1999a. "Issues in the Design of Monetary Policy Rules." In John B. Taylor and Michael Woodford, eds., *Handbook of Macroeconomics*. Vol. 1C. Amsterdam: Elsevier. 1483-530.

———. 1999b. "An Interview with Robert E. Lucas Jr." *Macroeconomic Dynamics* 3, no. 2 (June): 278-91.

———. 1999c. "Role of the Minimal State Variable Criterion in Rational Expectations Models." *International Tax and Public Finance* 6, no. 4 (November): 621-39.

———. 2001a. "Monetary Policy Analysis in Models without Money." *Federal Reserve Bank of St. Louis Review* 83, no. 4 (July): 145-60.

———. 2001b. "Indeterminacy, Bubbles, and the Fiscal Theory of Price Level Determination." *Journal of Monetary Economics* 47, no. 1 (February): 19-30.

———. 2004. "Long-Run Monetary Neutrality and Contemporary Policy Analysis." *Bank of Japan Monetary and Economic Studies* 22, no. S1 (December): 15-28.

———. 2008. "Monetarism." In *The Concise Encyclopedia of Economics*. http://www.econlib.org/library/Enc/Monetarism.html.

———. 2014. "History of Money and Monetary Policy." Book manuscript, Tepper School of Business, Carnegie Mellon University, July 14.

McCallum, Bennett T., and Marvin Goodfriend. 1987. "Demand for Money: Theoretical Studies." In John Eatwell, Murray Milgate, and Peter Newman, eds., *The New Palgrave: A Dictionary of Economics*. Vol. 2, *E to J*. London: Macmillan. 775-81.

McCallum, Bennett T., and Edward Nelson. 1998. "Nominal Income Targeting in an Open-Economy Optimizing Model." NBER Working Paper no. 6675, August.

———. 1999. "An Optimizing IS-LM Specification for Monetary Policy and Business Cycle Analysis." *Journal of Money, Credit and Banking* 31, no. 3 (August): 296-316.

———. 2005. "Monetary and Fiscal Theories of the Price Level: The Irreconcilable Differences." *Oxford Review of Economic Policy* 21, no. 4 (Winter): 565-83.

———. 2011. "Money and Inflation: Some Critical Issues." In Benjamin M. Friedman and Michael Woodford, eds., *Handbook of Monetary Economics*. Vol. 3A. Amsterdam: Elsevier. 97-153.

McCloskey, D. N. 1985. *The Applied Theory of Price*. 2nd ed. New York: Macmillan.

———. 2000. *How to Be Human*: *Though an Economist*. Ann Arbor: University of Michigan Press.

McKean, Roland Neely. 1948. "Fluctuations in Our Private Claim-Debt Structure and Monetary Policy." PhD diss., Department of Economics, University of Chicago, September.

McKim, Bruce Turner. 1962. "Income Velocity and Monetary Policies in the United States, 1951-1960." PhD diss., State University of Iowa, August.

McKinley, David H. 1960. "The Discount Rate and Rediscount Policy." In H. V. Prochnow, ed., *The Federal Reserve System*. New York: Harper and Brothers. 90-112.

McKinney, George W., Jr. 1967. "New Sources of Bank Funds: Certificates of Deposit and Debt Securities." *Law and Contemporary Problems* 32, no. 1 (Winter): 71-99.

Medema, Steven G. 2007. "Aldine Transaction Introduction." In Milton Friedman, *Price Theory*. New Brunswick, NJ: Transaction. vii-xiii.

Meghir, Costas. 2004. "A Retrospective on Friedman's Theory of Permanent Income." *Economic Journal* 114, no. 496 (June): F293-F306.

Mehrling, Perry. 2005. *Fischer Black and the Revolutionary Idea of Finance*. New York: Wiley.

———. 2014. "MIT and Money." *History of Political Economy* 46 (supplement): 177-97.

Meigs, A. James. 1962. *Free Reserves and the Money Supply*. Chicago: University of Chicago Press.

———. 1972. *Money Matters: Economics, Markets, Politics*. New York: Harper and Row.

Meiselman, David. 1962. *The Term Structure of Interest Rates*. Englewood Cliffs, NJ: Prentice Hall.

———, ed. 1970. *Varieties of Monetary Experience*. Chicago: University of Chicago Press.

———. 1975. "Discussion [of Phillip Cagan and Anna Jacobson Schwartz, 'How Feasible Is a Flexible Monetary Policy?']." In Richard T. Selden, ed., *Capitalism and Freedom—Problems and Prospects: Proceedings of a Conference in Honor of Milton Friedman*. Charlottesville: University Press of Virginia. 294-302.

Melitz, Jacques. 1972. "On the Optimality of Satiation in Money Balances." *Journal of Finance* 27, no. 3 (June): 683-98.

Meltzer, Allan H. 1963. "The Demand for Money: The Evidence from the Time Series." *Journal of Political Economy* 71, no. 3 (June): 219-46.

———. 1965. "Monetary Theory and Monetary History." *Swiss Journal of Economics and Statistics* 101, no. 4 (December): 404-22.

——. 1969a. "The Role of Money in National Economic Policy: Panel Discussion." In Federal Reserve Bank of Boston, ed., *Controlling Monetary Aggregates: Proceedings of a Conference Held in June, 1969*. Boston: Federal Reserve Bank of Boston. 25–29.

——. 1969b. "Tactics and Targets of Monetary Policy: Discussion." In Federal Reserve Bank of Boston, ed., *Controlling Monetary Aggregates: Proceedings of a Conference Held in June, 1969*. Boston: Federal Reserve Bank of Boston. 96–103.

——. 1977. "Monetarist, Keynesian and Quantity Theories." *Kredit und Kapital* 10, no. 2 (June): 149–82. Reprinted in Thomas Mayer et al., *The Structure of Monetarism*. New York: W. W. Norton, 1978. 145–75.

——. 1992. "Patinkin on Keynes and Meltzer." *Journal of Monetary Economics* 29, no. 1 (February): 151–62.

——. 2001a. "Money and Monetary Policy: An Essay in Honor of Darryl Francis." *Federal Reserve Bank of St. Louis Review* 83, no. 4 (July/August): 23–32.

——. 2001b. "The Transmission Process." In Deutsche Bundesbank, ed., *The Monetary Transmission Process: Recent Developments and Lessons for Europe*. London: Palgrave. 112–30.

——. 2003. *A History of the Federal Reserve*. Vol. 1, *1913–1951*. Chicago: University of Chicago Press.

——. 2009a. *A History of the Federal Reserve*. Vol. 2, bk. 1, *1951–1969*. Chicago: University of Chicago Press.

——. 2009b. *A History of the Federal Reserve*. Vol. 2, bk. 2, *1970–1986*. Chicago: University of Chicago Press.

——. 2011. "Milton Friedman: Non-research Activities, 1976–89." Manuscript, Tepper School of Business, Carnegie Mellon University, January.

Meltzer, Allan H., and Saranna Robinson. 1989. "Stability under the Gold Standard in Practice." In Michael D. Bordo, ed., *Money, History, and International Finance: Essays in Honor of Anna J. Schwartz*. Chicago: University of Chicago Press. 163–95.

Merrick, John J., Jr., and Anthony Saunders. 1985. "Bank Regulation and Monetary Policy." *Journal of Money, Credit and Banking* 17, no. 4, part 2 (November): 691–717.

Merton, Robert C. 1987. "In Honor of Nobel Laureate, Franco Modigliani." *Journal of Economic Perspectives* 1, no. 2 (Fall): 145–55.

Meulendyke, Ann-Marie. 1988. "A Review of Federal Reserve Policy Targets and Operating Guides in Recent Decades." *Federal Reserve Bank of New York Quarterly Review* 13, no. 3 (Autumn): 6–17.

——. 1998. *U.S. Monetary Policy and Financial Markets*. New York: Federal Reserve Bank of New York.

Meyer, Laurence H. 2001. "Does Money Matter?" *Federal Reserve Bank of St. Louis Review* 83, no. 5 (September/October): 1–16.

Meyer, Laurence H., and Chris Varvares. 1981. "A Comparison of the St. Louis Model and Two Variations: Predictive Performance and Policy Implications." *Federal Reserve Bank of St. Louis Review* 63, no. 12 (December): 13–25.

Miles, Marc A. 1984. *Beyond Monetarism: Finding the Road to Stable Money*. New York: Basic Books.

Mints, Lloyd W. 1945. *A History of Banking Theory in Great Britain and the United States*. Chicago: University of Chicago Press.

——. 1950. *Monetary Policy for a Competitive Society*. New York: McGraw Hill.

Miron, Jeffrey A. 1994. "Empirical Methodology in Macroeconomics: Explaining the Success of Friedman and Schwartz's *A Monetary History of the United States, 1867–1960*." *Journal of Monetary Economics* 34, no. 1 (August): 17–25.

Mirrlees, James. 1989. "Discussion [of Alberto Alesina, 'Politics and Business Cycles in Industrial Democracies']." *Economic Policy* 4, no. 8 (April): 87–90.

Mishkin, Frederic S. 1982. "Does Anticipated Monetary Policy Matter? An Econometric Investigation." *Journal of Political Economy* 90, no. 1 (February): 22–51.

———. 1983. "Recent Velocity Behavior, the Demand for Money and Monetary Policy: Discussion." In Federal Reserve Bank of San Francisco, ed., *Proceedings of the Conference on Monetary Targeting and Velocity*. San Francisco: Federal Reserve Bank of San Francisco. 129–32.

———. 1986. "Comments [on Jeffrey A. Frankel, 'International Capital Mobility and Crowding-Out in the U.S. Economy: Imperfect Integration of Financial Markets or of Goods Markets?']." In R. W. Hafer, ed., *How Open Is the U.S. Economy?* Lexington, MA: Lexington Books. 69–74.

———. 1989. *The Economics of Money, Banking and Financial Markets*. 2nd ed. Glenview, IL: Scott, Foresman.

———. 1995. "The Rational Expectations Revolution: A Review Article of Preston J. Miller, ed., *The Rational Expectations Revolution, Readings from the Front Line*." NBER Working Paper no. 5043, February.

Mitchell, Wesley C. 1896. "The Quantity Theory of the Value of Money." *Journal of Political Economy* 4, no. 2 (March): 139–65.

———. 1912. "The Backward Art of Spending Money." *American Economic Review* 2, no. 2 (June): 175–208.

Modigliani, Franco. 1944. "Liquidity Preference and the Theory of Interest and Money." *Econometrica* 12, no. 1 (January): 45–88.

———. 1964a. "How to Make a Burden of the Public Debt: A Reply to Mishan." *Journal of Political Economy* 72, no. 5 (October): 483–85.

———. 1964b. "Some Empirical Tests of Monetary Management and of Rules versus Discretion." *Journal of Political Economy* 72, no. 3 (June): 211–45.

———. 1971. "Monetary Policy and Consumption: Linkages via Interest Rate and Wealth Effects in the FMP Model." In Federal Reserve Bank of Boston, ed., *Consumer Spending and Monetary Policy: The Linkages*. Boston: Federal Reserve Bank of Boston. 9–84.

———. 1975a. "The Life Cycle Hypothesis of Saving Twenty Years Later." In Michael Parkin and A. Robert Nobay, eds., *Contemporary Issues in Economics: Proceedings of the Conference of the Association of University Teachers of Economics, Warwick, 1973*. Manchester, UK: Manchester University Press. 2–36.

———. 1975b. "Monetary Policy and the World Economic Crisis: Roundtable Discussion." Remarks from August 8 session in "Conference on 'The Monetary Mechanism in Open Economies,' Helsinki, Finland, August 4–9." Unpublished conference transcript. 7–12.

———. 1977. "The Monetarist Controversy; or, Should We Forsake Stabilization Policies?" *American Economic Review* 67, no. 2 (March): 1–19.

———. 1986a. "Life Cycle, Individual Thrift, and the Wealth of Nations." *American Economic Review* 76, no. 3 (June): 297–313.

———. 1986b. *The Debate over Stabilization Policy*. Cambridge: Cambridge University Press.

———. 1986c. "Comment on R. J. Barro, 'U.S. Deficits since World War I.'" *Scandinavian Journal of Economics* 88, no. 1 (March): 223–34.

———. 1988. "The Monetarist Controversy Revisited." *Contemporary Policy Issues* 6, no. 4 (October): 3–18.

Modigliani, Franco, and Albert Ando. 1957. "Tests of the Life Cycle Hypothesis of Savings: Comments and Suggestions." *Bulletin of the Oxford University Institute of Statistics* 19, no. 2 (May): 99-124.

———. 1960. "The 'Permanent Income' and the 'Life Cycle' Hypothesis of Saving Behavior: Comparison and Tests." In Irwin Friend and Robert Jones, eds., *Consumption and Saving*. Vol. 2. Philadelphia: University of Pennsylvania Press. 49-174.

Modigliani, Franco, and Richard E. Brumberg. 1954. "Utility Analysis and the Consumption Function: An Interpretation of Cross Section Data." In Kenneth K. Kurihara, ed., *Post Keynesian Economics*. New Brunswick, NJ: Rutgers University Press. 388-436.

Modigliani, Franco, and Lucas Papademos. 1976. "Monetary Policy for the Coming Quarters: The Conflicting Views." *New England Economic Review* 58, no. 2 (March/April): 2-35.

Modigliani, Franco, Robert H. Rasche, and J. Phillip Cooper. 1970. "Central Bank Policy, the Money Supply, and the Short-Term Rate of Interest." *Journal of Money, Credit and Banking* 2, no. 2 (May): 166-218.

Modigliani, Franco, and Arlie Sterling. 1986. "Government Debt, Government Spending and Private Sector Behavior: Comment." *American Economic Review* 76, no. 5 (December): 1168-79.

———. 1990. "Government Debt, Government Spending and Private Sector Behavior: A Further Comment." *American Economic Review* 80, no. 3 (June): 600-603.

Modigliani, Franco, and Richard C. Sutch. 1966. "Innovations in Interest-Rate Policy." *American Economic Review* 56, no. 1-2 (March): 178-97.

Moggridge, Donald. 2008. *Harry Johnson: A Life in Economics*. Cambridge: Cambridge University Press.

Morgan, E. Victor. 1969. *Monetary Policy for Stable Growth*. Revised edition. London: Institute of Economic Affairs.

Morgenstern, Oskar. 1972. "Foreword." In Robert B. Ekelund Jr., E. G. Furubotn, and W. P. Gramm, eds., *The Evolution of Modern Demand Theory: A Collection of Essays*. Lexington, MA: Lexington Books. ix-x.

Morris, Frank E. 1968. "The Chicago School as Viewed from Boston." *Business Economics* 3, no. 2 (Spring): 23-26.

Mulcahy, Richard E., ed. 1957. *Readings in Economics from "Fortune."* New York: Holt.

Mulligan, Casey B. 1998. "Pecuniary Incentives to Work in the United States during World War II." *Journal of Political Economy* 106, no. 5 (October): 1033-77.

Murphy, Brian, and Michael Wolfson. 2013. "Income Trajectories of High Income Canadians 1982-2010." Manuscript, Statistics Canada, May.

Musgrave, R. A., and M. H. Miller. 1948. "Built-In Flexibility." *American Economic Review* 38, no. 1 (March): 122-28.

Muth, John F. 1960. "Optimal Properties of Exponentially Weighted Forecasts." *Journal of the American Statistical Association* 55, no. 290 (June): 299-306.

———. 1961. "Rational Expectations and the Theory of Price Movements." *Econometrica* 29, no. 3 (July): 315-35.

Muttitt, Kathleen. 1948. "*Income from Independent Professional Practice* by Milton Friedman [and] Simon Kuznets." *Canadian Journal of Economics and Political Science* 12, no. 4 (November): 538-39.

Nathan, Otto, and Milton Fried. 1942. "Consumer Spending, Inflation, and the Wage Earner in the United States." *International Labour Review* 45, no. 2 (February): 125-41.

NBC. 1943. *Prices and Your Pocketbook: A Radio Discussion*. University of Chicago Round Table no. 275, June 27.

———. 1946a. *What Can Be Done about Inflation?* University of Chicago Round Table no. 420, April 7.

———. 1946b. *Can World-Wide Income Inequalities Be Lessened?* University of Chicago Round Table no. 457, December 22.

———. 1947a. *What Can Be Done about Rising Prices?* University of Chicago Round Table no. 508, December 14.

———. 1947b. *How Can We Get Housing?* University of Chicago Round Table no. 462, January 26.

———. 1949. *What Do We Know about Economic Stability?* University of Chicago Round Table no. 570, February 20.

———. 1950. *Must We Have a Deficit?* University of Chicago Round Table no. 632, April 30.

———. 1951a. *Can the Control of Money Stop Today's Inflation?* University of Chicago Round Table no. 672, February 11.

———. 1951b. *Should Taxes Be Bigger and How Can They Be Better?* University of Chicago Round Table no. 705, September 30.

———. 1952a. *The Military Budget.* University of Chicago Round Table no. 725, February 17.

———. 1952b. *The State of the Union.* University of Chicago Round Table no. 720, January 13.

———. 1952c. *The Transformation of British and American Capitalism.* University of Chicago Round Table no. 740, June 1.

———. 1953. *What Is American Capitalism?* University of Chicago Round Table no. 794, June 28.

———. 1954. *Anti-Americanism and the Atlantic Alliance.* University of Chicago Round Table no. 860, October 3.

———. 1955. *Dollars across the Border.* University of Chicago Round Table no. 877, January 30.

Neiss, Katharine S., and Edward Nelson. 2001. "The Real Interest Rate Gap as an Inflation Indicator." Bank of England Working Paper no. 130, April.

———. 2003. "The Real Interest Rate Gap as an Inflation Indicator." *Macroeconomic Dynamics* 7, no. 2 (April): 239–62.

———. 2005. "Inflation Dynamics, Marginal Cost, and the Output Gap: Evidence from Three Countries." *Journal of Money, Credit and Banking* 37, no. 6 (December): 1019–45.

Nelson, Charles R. 1972. "The Prediction Performance of the FRB-MIT-PENN Model of the U.S. Economy." *American Economic Review* 62, no. 5 (December): 902–17.

———. 1981. "Adjustment Lags versus Information Lags: A Test of Alternative Explanations of the Phillips Curve Phenomenon." *Journal of Money, Credit and Banking* 13, no. 1 (February): 1–11.

Nelson, Edward. 2002a. "What Does the U.K.'s Monetary Policy and Inflation Experience Tell Us about the Transmission Mechanism?" In Lavan Mahadeva and Peter J. N. Sinclair, eds., *Monetary Transmission in Diverse Economies.* Cambridge: Cambridge University Press. 137–55.

———. 2002b. "Direct Effects of Base Money on Aggregate Demand: Theory and Evidence." *Journal of Monetary Economics* 49, no. 4 (May): 687–708.

———. 2003. "The Future of Monetary Aggregates in Monetary Policy Analysis." *Journal of Monetary Economics* 50, no. 5 (July): 1029–59.

———. 2004a. "An Interview with Anna J. Schwartz." *Macroeconomic Dynamics* 8, no. 3 (June): 395–417.

———. 2004b. "News-Magazine Monetarism." In Patrick Minford, ed., *Money Matters: Essays in Honour of Alan Walters*. Cheltenham, UK: Edward Elgar. 123-47.

———. 2004c. "Money and the Transmission Mechanism in the Optimizing IS-LM Specification." *History of Political Economy* 36 (supplement 1) (December): 271-304.

———. 2005a. "Paul Samuelson and Monetary Analysis." *Monetary Trends/Economic Synopses* (Federal Reserve Bank of St. Louis), no. 8 (April): 1. https://files.stlouisfed.org/files/htdocs/publications/es/05/ES0508.pdf.

———. 2005b. "The Great Inflation of the Seventies: What Really Happened?" *Advances in Macroeconomics* 5, no. 1, article 3, 1-50.

———. 2007. "Milton Friedman and U.S. Monetary History: 1961-2006." *Federal Reserve Bank of St. Louis Review* 89, no. 3 (May/June): 153-82.

———. 2008a. "Friedman and Taylor on Monetary Policy Rules: A Comparison." *Federal Reserve Bank of St. Louis Review* 90, no. 2 (March/April): 95-116.

———. 2008b. "Why Money Growth Determines Inflation in the Long Run: Answering the Woodford Critique." *Journal of Money, Credit and Banking* 40, no. 8 (December): 1791-814.

———. 2009a. "Milton Friedman and U.K. Economic Policy, 1938-1979." *Federal Reserve Bank of St. Louis Review* 91, no. 5, part 2 (September/October): 465-506.

———. 2009b. "Milton Friedman and U.K. Economic Policy, 1938-1979." Federal Reserve Bank of St. Louis Working Paper 2009-017A, April.

———. 2009c. "An Overhaul of Doctrine: The Underpinning of U.K. Inflation Targeting." *Economic Journal* 119, no. 538 (June): F333-F368.

———. 2011. "Friedman's Monetary Economics in Practice." Federal Reserve Board Finance and Economics Discussion Series Paper no. 2011-026, April.

———. 2012a. "Book Review: *Milton Friedman* by William Ruger and *Milton Friedman: A Concise Guide to the Ideas and Influence of the Free-Market Economist* by Eamonn Butler." *Journal of Economic Literature* 44, no. 4 (December): 1106-9.

———. 2012b. "A Review of Allan H. Meltzer's *History of the Federal Reserve, Volume 2*." *International Journal of Central Banking* 8, no. 2 (June): 241-66.

———. 2013a. "Friedman's Monetary Economics in Practice." *Journal of International Money and Finance* 38, no. 1 (November): 59-83.

———. 2013b. "The Correlation between Money and Output in the United Kingdom: Resolution of a Puzzle." Manuscript, Federal Reserve Board, September; presented at Bank of Canada Workshop on Money and Liquidity, October 18, 2013.

———. 2013c. "Key Aspects of Longer-Term Asset Purchases in U.S. and U.K. Monetary Policy." *Oxford Economic Papers* 65, no. 1 (January): 92-114.

———. 2013d. "Milton Friedman and the Federal Reserve Chairs, 1951-1979." Manuscript, Federal Reserve Board, October; presented at University of California, Berkeley, Economic History seminar, October 28, 2013. http://eml.berkeley.edu//~webfac/cromer/Nelson.pdf.

———. 2016. "Milton Friedman and the Federal Reserve Chairs in the 1970s." In Robert Cord and J. Daniel Hammond, eds., *Milton Friedman: Contributions to Economics and Public Policy*. Oxford: Oxford University Press. 313-33.

———. 2018. "Milton Friedman and the Debate on Indexation." Manuscript, August. SSRN: https://ssrn.com/abstract=3229236 or http://dx.doi.org/10.2139/ssrn.3229236.

Nelson, Edward, and Kalin Nikolov. 2003. "U.K. Inflation in the 1970s and 1980s: The Role of Output Gap Mismeasurement." *Journal of Economics and Business* 55, no. 4 (July/August): 353-70.

Nelson, Edward, and Anna J. Schwartz. 2008a. "The Impact of Milton Friedman on Modern Monetary Economics: Setting the Record Straight on Paul Krugman's 'Who Was Milton Friedman?'" *Journal of Monetary Economics* 55, no. 4 (May): 835–56.

———. 2008b. "Rejoinder to Paul Krugman." *Journal of Monetary Economics* 55, no. 4 (May): 861–62.

Newman, Peter. 1954. "Book Review: *Essays in Positive Economics*." *Economica* 21, no. 83 (August): 259–60.

Neyman, Jerzy. 1938. "Contribution to the Theory of Sampling Human Populations." *Journal of the American Statistical Association* 33, no. 201 (March): 101–16.

———. 1952. *Lectures and Conferences on Mathematical Statistics and Probability*. Rev. ed. Washington, DC: US Department of Agriculture.

———. 1971. "Foundations of Behavioristic Statistics." In V. P. Godambe and D. A. Sprott, eds., *Foundations of Statistical Inference: Proceedings of the Symposium on the Foundations of Statistical Inference Prepared under the Auspices of the René Descartes Foundation and Held at the Department of Statistics, University of Waterloo, Ont., Canada, from March 31 to April 9, 1970*. René Descartes Foundation, University of Waterloo Department of Statistics. Toronto: Holt, Rinehart and Winston of Canada. 1–13.

Niehans, Jürg. 1978. *The Theory of Money*. Baltimore: Johns Hopkins University Press.

Nielsen, Peter Erling. 1992. "*Does Debt Management Matter?* by Jonas Agell, Mats Persson, Benjamin M. Friedman." *Scandinavian Journal of Economics* 94, no. 4 (December): 625–28.

Nixon, Richard M. 1962. *Six Crises*. Garden City, NY: Doubleday.

Nobay, A. Robert, and Harry G. Johnson. 1977. "Monetarism: A Historic-Theoretic Perspective." *Journal of Economic Literature* 15, no. 2 (June): 470–85.

Nordhaus, William D., and Henry C. Wallich. 1973. "Alternatives for Debt Management." In Federal Reserve Bank of Boston, ed., *Issues in Federal Debt Management: Proceedings of a Conference Held at Melvin Village, New Hampshire, June, 1973*. Boston: Federal Reserve Bank of Boston. 9–25.

Noyes, C. Reinold. 1945. Director's Comment. In Milton Friedman and Simon Kuznets, *Income from Independent Professional Practice*. New York: National Bureau of Economic Research. 405–10.

Nutter, G. Warren. 1951. *The Extent of Enterprise Monopoly in the United States: 1899–1939*. Chicago: University of Chicago Press.

O'Driscoll, Gerald P., Jr. 1977. *Economics as a Coordination Problem: The Contributions of Friedrich A. Hayek*. Kansas City, KS: Sheed Andrews and McMeel.

———. 1987. "*Money, Capital, and Fluctuations: Early Essays* by F. A. Hayek, edited by Roy McCloughry." *Journal of Money, Credit and Banking* 19, no. 3 (August): 402–4.

O'Driscoll, Gerald P., Jr., Thomas R. Saving, Herbert G. Grubel, Arnold C. Harberger, Milton Friedman, and W. Lee Hoskins. 1997. "Tax Reform." *Contemporary Economic Policy* 15, no. 1 (January): 1–20.

Ohanian, Lee E. 1998. *The Macroeconomic Effects of War Finance in the United States: Taxes, Inflation, and Deficit Finance*. New York: Garland.

Okun, Arthur M. 1971. "Rules and Roles for Fiscal and Monetary Policy." In James J. Diamond, ed., *Issues in Fiscal and Monetary Policy: The Eclectic Economist Views the Controversy*. Chicago: DePaul University. 51–74.

———, ed. 1972a. *The Battle against Unemployment*. 2nd ed. New York: W. W. Norton.

———. 1972b. "Fiscal-Monetary Activism: Some Analytical Issues." *Brookings Papers on Economic Activity* 3, no. 1, 123–63.

———. 1981. *Prices and Quantities: A Macroeconomic Analysis.* Washington, DC: Brookings Institution Press.

Olkin, Ingram. 1991. "A Conversation with W. Allen Wallis." *Statistical Science* 6, no. 2 (May): 121-40.

Orphanides, Athanasios. 2002. "Monetary-Policy Rules and the Great Inflation." *American Economic Review (Papers and Proceedings)* 92, no. 2 (May): 115-20.

———. 2003. "The Quest for Prosperity without Inflation." *Journal of Monetary Economics* 50, no. 3 (April): 633-63.

Orphanides, Athanasios, and John C. Williams. 2002. "Robust Monetary Policy with Unknown Natural Rates." *Brookings Papers on Economic Activity* 33, no. 2, 63-118.

———. 2013. "Monetary Policy Mistakes and the Evolution of Inflation Expectations." In Michael D. Bordo and Athanasios Orphanides, eds., *The Great Inflation: The Rebirth of Modern Central Banking.* Chicago: University of Chicago Press. 255-88.

Pagan, Adrian. 1995. "The *ET* Interview: Gregory C. Chow." *Econometric Theory* 11, no. 3 (August): 597-624.

Paish, F. W. 1941. "The Budget and the White Paper." *London and Cambridge Economic Service Bulletin* 19, no. 4 (April): 40-43.

Parker, Randall E. 2002. *Reflections on the Great Depression.* Northampton, MA: Edward Elgar.

Parkin, Michael. 1982. "Mrs. Thatcher's Monetary Policy: 1979-1981." *ORDO: Jahrbuch für die Ordnung von Wirtschaft und Gesellschaft* 33, no. 1: 61-80.

———. 1984a. *Macroeconomics.* Englewood Cliffs, NJ: Prentice Hall.

———. 1984b. "Discriminating between Keynesian and Classical Theories of the Business Cycle: Japan 1967-1982." *Bank of Japan Monetary and Economic Studies* 2, no. 2 (December): 23-60.

———. 1990. *Economics.* New York: Addison Wesley.

———. 1993. "Inflation in North America." In Kumiharu Shigehara, ed., *Price Stabilization in the 1990s: Domestic and International Policy Requirements.* London: Macmillan. 47-83.

Patinkin, Don. 1956. *Money, Interest, and Prices: An Integration of Monetary and Value Theory.* Evanston, IL: Row, Peterson.

———. 1965a. *Money, Interest, and Prices: An Integration of Monetary and Value Theory.* 2nd ed. New York: Harper and Row.

———. 1965b. "An Indirect-Utility Approach to the Theory of Money, Assets, and Savings." In Frank H. Hahn and Frank P. R. Brechling, eds., *The Theory of Interest Rates.* London: Macmillan. 52-79.

———. 1969. "The Chicago Tradition, the Quantity Theory, and Friedman." *Journal of Money, Credit and Banking* 1, no. 1 (February): 46-70.

———. 1972a. "Friedman on the Quantity Theory and Keynesian Economics." *Journal of Political Economy* 80, no. 5 (September/October): 883-905.

———. 1972b. "On the Short-Run Non-neutrality of Money in the Quantity Theory." *Banca Nazionale del Lavoro Quarterly Review* 25, no. 100 (March): 3-22.

———. 1973a. "Frank Knight as Teacher." *American Economic Review* 63, no. 5 (December): 787-810.

———. 1973b. "On the Monetary Economics of Chicagoans and Non-Chicagoans: Comment." *Southern Economic Journal* 39, no. 3 (January): 454-59.

———. 1976a. *Keynes' Monetary Thought: A Study of Its Development.* Durham, NC: Duke University Press.

———. 1976b. "Keynes and Econometrics." *Econometrica* 44, no. 6 (November): 1091–123.

———. 1979. "Keynes and Chicago." *Journal of Law and Economics* 22, no. 2 (October): 213–32.

———. 1981a. "Introduction, Reminiscences of Chicago, 1941–47." In Don Patinkin, *Essays on and in the Chicago Tradition.* Durham, NC: Duke University Press. 3–20.

———. 1981b. "Postscript: Further Comment on Friedman." In Don Patinkin, *Essays on and in the Chicago Tradition.* Durham, NC: Duke University Press. 264–65.

———. 1981c. "Some Observations on the Inflationary Process." In M. June Flanders and Assaf Razin, eds., *Development in an Inflationary World.* New York: Academic. 31–34.

———. 1982. *"Anticipations of the 'General Theory'?" and Other Essays on Keynes.* Chicago: University of Chicago Press.

———. 1983. "Monetary Economics." In E. Cary Brown and Robert M. Solow, eds., *Paul Samuelson and Modern Economic Theory.* New York: McGraw-Hill, 1983. 157–67.

———. 1984. "Keynes and Economics Today." *American Economic Review (Papers and Proceedings)* 74, no. 2, 97–102.

———. 1986. *"Essays on and in the Chicago Tradition* by Don Patinkin—a Review Essay: A Reply." *Journal of Money, Credit and Banking* 18, no. 1 (February): 116–21.

———. 1990. "In Defense of IS-LM." *Banca Nazionale del Lavoro Quarterly Review* 43, no. 172 (March): 119–34.

———. 1993. "Israel's Stabilization Program of 1985, or Some Simple Truths of Monetary Theory." *Journal of Economic Perspectives* 7 (no. 2) (Spring): 103–28.

———. 1995. "Concluding Comments." In Mark Blaug et al., *The Quantity Theory of Money: From Locke to Keynes and Friedman.* Cheltenham, UK: Edward Elgar. 120–33.

Patinkin, Don, and J. Clark Leith, eds. 1977. "Discussion." In Don Patinkin and J. Clark Leith, eds., *Keynes, Cambridge, and "The General Theory": The Process of Criticism and Discussion Connected with the Development of "The General Theory": Proceedings of a Conference.* London: Macmillan. 115–26.

Pecchenino, R. A., and Robert H. Rasche. 1990. "P^*-Type Models: Evaluation and Forecasts." *International Journal of Forecasting* 6, no. 3 (October): 421–40.

Pelloni, Gianluigi. 1987. "A Note on Friedman and the Neo-Bayesian Approach." *Manchester School of Economic and Social Studies* 55, no. 4 (December): 407–18.

———. 1996. "De Finetti, Friedman, and the Methodology of Positive Economics." *Journal of Econometrics* 75, no. 1 (November): 33–50.

Pesek, Boris P. 1988. *Microeconomics of Money and Banking and Other Essays.* New York: Harvester Wheatsheaf.

Phelps, Edmund S. 1965. "Anticipated Inflation and Economic Welfare." *Journal of Political Economy* 73, no. 1 (February): 1–17.

———. 1968a. "Notes on Optimal Monetary Growth and the Optimal Rate of Growth of Money: Comment." *Journal of Political Economy* 76, no. 4, part 2 (July/August): 881–85.

———. 1968b. "Money-Wage Dynamics and Labor-Market Equilibrium." *Journal of Political Economy* 76, no. 4, part 2 (July/August): 678–711.

———. 1970a. "The New Microeconomics in Employment and Inflation Theory." In Edmund S. Phelps, ed., *Microeconomic Foundations of Employment and Inflation Theory.* New York: W. W. Norton. 1–26.

———, ed. 1970b. *Microeconomic Foundations of Employment and Inflation Theory.* New York: W. W. Norton.

———. 1971. "Inflation, Expectations and Economic Theory." In Neil Swan and David A. Wilton, eds., *Inflation and the Canadian Experience*. Kingston, Ontario: Industrial Relations Centre, Queen's University. 31-47.

———. 1973. "Inflation in the Theory of Public Finance." *Swedish Journal of Economics* 75, no. 1 (March): 67-82.

———. 1979. "Introduction [to Section III]." In Edmund S. Phelps, *Studies in Macroeconomic Theory: Employment and Inflation*. New York: Academic. 121-23.

———. 1989. "Overview of Chapters 2 and 3." In Marcello De Cecco and Alberto Giovanni, eds., *A European Central Bank? Perspectives on Monetary Unification after Ten Years of the EMS*. Cambridge: Cambridge University Press. 90-94.

Phelps, Edmund S., and John B. Taylor. 1977. "Stabilizing Powers of Monetary Policy under Rational Expectations." *Journal of Political Economy* 85, no. 1 (February): 163-90.

Philippon, Thomas. 2009. "The Bond Market's *q*." *Quarterly Journal of Economics* 124, no. 3 (August): 1011-56.

Phillips, A. W. 1954. "Stabilisation Policy in a Closed Economy." *Economic Journal* 64, no. 254 (June): 290-323.

———. 1958. "The Relation between Unemployment and the Rate of Change of Money Wage Rates in the United Kingdom, 1861-1957." *Economica* 25, no. 100 (November): 283-99.

Phillips, Peter C. B. 1991. "Bayesian Routes and Unit Roots: *De Rebus Prioribus Semper Est Disputandum*." *Journal of Applied Econometrics* 6, no. 4 (October–December): 435-73.

Phillips, Ronnie J. 1995. *The Chicago Plan and New Deal Banking Plan*. Armonk, NY: M. E. Sharpe.

Phipps, Cecil G. 1952. "Friedman's 'Welfare' Effects." *Journal of Political Economy* 60, no. 4 (August): 332-34.

Pigou, A. C. 1910. "A Method of Determining the Numerical Value of Elasticities of Demand." *Economic Journal* 20, no. 80 (December): 636-40.

———. 1917. "The Value of Money." *Quarterly Journal of Economics* 32, no. 1 (November): 38-65.

———. 1928. *A Study in Public Finance*. London: Macmillan.

———. 1932. *The Economics of Welfare*. 4th ed. London: Macmillan.

———. 1936. "Marginal Utility of Money and Elasticities of Demand: III." *Quarterly Journal of Economics* 30, no. 3 (May): 532.

———. 1950. *Keynes's "General Theory": A Retrospective View*. London: Macmillan.

Plosser, Charles I. 1979. "Response to Discussants." In Arnold Zellner, ed., *Seasonal Analysis of Economic Time Series*. Washington, DC: US Government Printing Office. 406.

Polak, J. J., and William H. White. 1955. "The Effect of Income Expansion on the Quantity of Money." *IMF Staff Papers* 4, no. 3 (August): 398-433.

Poole, William. 1970. "Optimal Choice of Monetary Policy Instruments in a Simple Stochastic Macro Model." *Quarterly Journal of Economics* 84, no. 2 (May): 197-216.

Portes, Richard. 1983. "Central Planning and Monetarism: Fellow Travelers?" In Padma Desai, ed., *Marxism, Central Planning and the Soviet Economy: Economic Essays in Honor of Alexander Erlich*. Cambridge, MA: MIT Press. 149-65.

Posner, Richard. 2011. "Keynes and Coase." *Journal of Law and Economics* 54, no. 4 (November): S31-S40.

Powell, Alan. 1966. "A Complete System of Consumer Demand Equations for the Australian Economy Fitted by a Model of Additive Preferences." *Econometrica* 34, no. 3 (July): 661–75.

Powell, Jim. 2003. *FDR's Folly: How Roosevelt and His New Deal Prolonged the Great Depression.* New York: Crown Forum.

Prescott, Edward C. 1975. "Efficiency of the Natural Rate." *Journal of Political Economy* 83, no. 6 (December): 1229–36.

———. 1991. "Real Business Cycle Theory: What Have We Learned?" *Revista de Análisis Economico* 6, no. 2 (November): 3–19.

President's Advisory Panel on Federal Tax Reform. 2005. "Sixth Meeting, March 31, 2005." govinfo.library.unt.edu/taxreformpanel/meetings/meeting-03312005 .html.

Presley, John R. 1986. "Modern Monetarist Ideas: A British Connection?" In R. D. Collison Black, ed., *Ideas in Economics.* Totowa, NJ: Barnes and Noble Books. 191–209.

Prest, A. R. 1956. "A Tax on Expenditure?" *Lloyd's Bank Review* 11, no. 42 (October): 35–49.

Price Statistics Review Committee. 1961. *The Price Statistics of the Federal Government: Review, Appraisal, and Recommendations: A Report to the Office of Statistical Standards, Bureau of the Budget, Together with Twelve Staff Papers.* New York: National Bureau of Economic Research.

Purvis, Douglas D. 1980. "Monetarism: A Review." *Canadian Journal of Economics* 13, no. 1 (February): 96–122.

Rachev, Svetlozar T., Stoyan V. Stoyanov, and Frank J. Fabozzi. 2008. *Advanced Stochastic Models, Risk Assessment, and Portfolio Optimization: The Ideal Risk, Uncertainty, and Performance Measures.* New York: Wiley.

Ramey, Valerie A. 2011. "Identifying Government Spending Shocks: It's All in the Timing." *Quarterly Journal of Economics* 126, no. 1 (February): 1–50.

Ramsey, F. P. 1927. "A Contribution to the Theory of Taxation." *Economic Journal* 37, no. 145 (March): 47–61.

Rasche, Robert H. 1981. "Comments on the Size of Macroeconomic Models." In Jan Kmenta and James Bernard Ramsey, eds., *Large-Scale Macroeconometric Models.* Amsterdam: North-Holland. 265–77.

———. 1987. "M1-Velocity and Money Demand Functions: Do Stable Relationships Exist?" *Carnegie-Rochester Conference Series on Public Policy* 27, no. 1, 9–88.

———. 1990. "Demand Functions for Measures of U.S. Money and Debt." In Peter Hooper, Karen H. Johnson, Donald L. Kohn, David E. Lindsey, Richard D. Porter, and Ralph W. Tryon, eds., *Financial Sectors in Open Economies: Empirical Analysis and Policy Issues.* Washington, DC: Board of Governors of the Federal Reserve System. 113–61.

———. 1993a. "Indicators of Inflation." In Kumiharu Shigehara, ed., *Price Stabilization in the 1990s: Domestic and International Policy Requirements.* London: Macmillan. 277–318.

———. 1993b. "Monetary Policy and the Money Supply Process." In Michele U. Fratianni and Dominick Salvatore, eds., *Monetary Policy in Developed Economies.* Westwood, CT: Greenwood. 25–54.

Rayack, Elton. 1987. *Not So Free to Choose: The Political Economy of Milton Friedman and Ronald Reagan.* New York: Praeger.

Reder, Melvin W. 1982. "Chicago Economics: Permanence and Change." *Journal of Economic Literature* 20, no. 1 (March): 1–38.

Rees, Albert. 1962. *The Economics of Trade Unions*. Chicago: University of Chicago Press.

———. 1970a. "The Phillips Curve as a Menu for Policy Choices." *Economica* 37, no. 147 (August): 227–38.

———. 1970b. "On Equilibrium in Labor Markets." *Journal of Political Economy* 78, no. 2 (March/April): 306–10.

Reid, Gavin C. 1990. "Analysing Rankings, with an Application to the Financing of Small Entrepreneurial Firms." *Economic Journal* 100, no. 400, 200–205.

Reid, Margaret G. 1934. *The Economics of Household Production*. New York: John Wiley and Sons.

———. 1952. "Effect of Income Concept upon Expenditure Curves of Farm Families." In Conference on Income and Wealth, *Studies in Income and Wealth*. Vol. 15. New York: National Bureau of Economic Research. 133–74.

Robbins, Lionel. 1960. "Monetary Theory and the Radcliffe Report." Revision of paper presented at the University of Rome, Spring 1960. Reprinted in Lionel Robbins, *Money, Trade, and International Relations*. London: Macmillan, 1971. 90–119.

Roberts, John M. 1993. "The Sources of Business Cycles: A Monetarist Interpretation." *International Economic Review* 34, no. 4 (November): 923–34.

———. 1995. "New Keynesian Economics and the Phillips Curve." *Journal of Money, Credit and Banking* 27, no. 4 (November): 975–84.

Roberts, Russell. 2006. "An Interview with Milton Friedman." *EconLib* (Library of Economics and Liberty), September 4. https://www.econlib.org/library/Columns/y2006/Friedmantranscript.html.

Robinson, Joan. 1933. *The Economics of Imperfect Competition*. London: Macmillan.

———. 1937. *Essays in the Theory of Employment*. New York: Macmillan.

Rockoff, Hugh. 1975. *The Free Banking Era: A Re-examination*. New York: Arno.

———. 1984. *Drastic Measures: A History of Wage and Price Controls in the United States*. Cambridge: Cambridge University Press.

———. 2015. "Henry Simons and the Quantity Theory of Money." Manuscript, Rutgers University, March.

Romer, Christina D. 1992. "What Ended the Great Depression?" *Journal of Economic History* 52, no. 4 (December): 757–84.

———. 1993. "The Nation in Depression." *Journal of Economic Perspectives* 7, no. 2 (Spring): 19–39.

———. 2005. "Comment [on 'Origins of the Great Inflation' by Allan H. Meltzer]." *Federal Reserve Bank of St. Louis Review* 87, no. 2, part 2 (March/April): 177–86.

———. 2007. "Macroeconomic Policy in the 1960s: The Causes and Consequences of a Mistaken Revolution." Economic History Association Annual Meeting, September.

Romer, Christina D., and David H. Romer. 1989. "Does Monetary Policy Matter? A New Test in the Spirit of Friedman and Schwartz." *NBER Macroeconomics Annual* 4, no. 1, 121–84.

———. 1994a. "What Ends Recessions?" *NBER Macroeconomics Annual* 9, no. 1, 13–57.

———. 1994b. "Monetary Policy Matters." *Journal of Monetary Economics* 34, no. 1 (August): 75–88.

———. 2002a. "A Rehabilitation of Monetary Policy in the 1950's." *American Economic Review (Papers and Proceedings)* 92, no. 2 (May): 121–27.

———. 2002b. "The Evolution of Economic Understanding and Postwar Stabilization Policy." In Federal Reserve Bank of Kansas City, ed., *Rethinking Stabilization Policy*. Kansas City, MO: Federal Reserve Bank of Kansas City. 11–78.

———. 2013a. "The Missing Transmission Mechanism in the Monetary Explanation of the Great Depression." *American Economic Review (Papers and Proceedings)* 103, no. 3 (May): 66–72.

———. 2013b. "The Most Dangerous Idea in Federal Reserve History: Monetary Policy Doesn't Matter." *American Economic Review (Papers and Proceedings)* 103, no. 3 (May): 55–60.

———. 2013c. "Transfer Payments and the Macroeconomy: The Effects of Social Security Benefit Changes, 1952–1991." Manuscript, University of California, Berkeley.

Romer, Paul M. 1990. "Endogenous Technological Change." *Journal of Political Economy* 98, no. 5, part 2 (October): S71–S102.

Roosa, Robert V. 1956. *Federal Reserve Operations in the Money and Government Securities Markets*. New York: Federal Reserve Bank of New York.

Roose, Kenneth. 1954. *The Economics of Recession and Revival: An Interpretation of 1937–38*. New Haven, CT: Yale University Press.

Rosen, Sherwin. 1981. "The Economics of Superstars." *American Economic Review* 71, no. 5 (December): 845–58.

———. 1997. "Manufactured Inequality." *Journal of Labor Economics* 15, no. 2 (April): 189–96.

Rostow, Eugene V. 1960. "To Whom and for What Ends Is Corporate Management Responsible?" In Edward S. Mason, ed., *The Corporation in Modern Society*. Cambridge, MA: Harvard University Press. 46–71.

Rotemberg, Julio J. 1982. "Monopolistic Price Adjustment and Aggregate Output." *Review of Economic Studies* 49, no. 4 (October): 517–31.

———. 1987. "The New-Keynesian Microfoundations." *NBER Macroeconomics Annual* 2, no. 1, 69–104.

———. 2013. "Shifts in U.S. Federal Reserve Goals and Tactics for Monetary Policy: A Role for Penitence?" *Journal of Economic Perspectives* 27, no. 4 (Fall): 65–86.

———. 2014. "The Federal Reserve's Abandonment of Its 1923 Principles." NBER Working Paper no. 20507, September.

Rotemberg, Julio J., and Michael Woodford. 1997. "An Optimization-Based Econometric Framework for the Evaluation of Monetary Policy." *NBER Macroeconomics Annual* 12, no. 1, 297–346.

———. 1999a. "Interest Rate Rules in an Estimated Sticky Price Model." In John B. Taylor, ed., *Monetary Policy Rules*. Chicago: University of Chicago Press. 57–119.

———. 1999b. "The Cyclical Behavior of Prices and Costs." In John B. Taylor and Michael Woodford, eds., *Handbook of Macroeconomics*. Vol. 1, part B. Amsterdam: Elsevier. 1051–135.

Rothbard, Murray. 1971. "Milton Friedman Unraveled." *Individualist* 3, no. 2 (February): 3–7.

Rotwein, Eugene. 1959. "On 'The Methodology of Positive Economics.'" *Quarterly Journal of Economics* vol. 73, no. 4 (November): 554–75.

Rowan, D. C. 1980. *Australian Monetary Policy 1950–1975*. Sydney: Allen and Unwin.

Rudebusch, Glenn D., Brian P. Sack, and Eric T. Swanson. 2007. "Macroeconomic Implications of Changes in the Term Premium." *Federal Reserve Bank of St. Louis Review* 89, no. 4 (July/August): 241–69.

Ruffin, Roy J. 1979. "Tariffs, the Balance of Payments, and the Demand for Money." *Journal of International Economics* 9, no. 2 (May): 287–302.

Ruger, William. 2011. *Milton Friedman*. New York: Continuum Books.

Ruml, Beardsley, and H. Christian Sonne. 1944. *Fiscal and Monetary Policy*. National Planning Pamphlet no. 35, July. Washington, DC: National Planning Association.

Samuelson, Paul A. 1941. "Appendix: A Statistical Analysis of the Consumption Function." In Alvin H. Hansen, *Fiscal Policy and Business Cycles*. New York: W. W. Norton. 250-60.

———. 1946. "Lord Keynes and the *General Theory*." *Econometrica* 14, no. 3 (July): 187-200.

———. 1947. *Foundations of Economic Analysis*. Cambridge, MA: Harvard University Press.

———. 1948. *Economics: An Introductory Analysis*. New York: McGraw-Hill.

———. 1953. "Full Employment versus Progress and Other Economic Goals." In Max F. Millikan, ed., *Income Stabilization for a Developing Democracy: A Study of the Politics and Economics of High Employment without Inflation*. New Haven, CT: Yale University Press. 547-80.

———. 1955. *Economics: An Introductory Analysis*. 3rd ed. New York: McGraw Hill.

———. 1956. "Economic Forecasting and National Policy." In Gerhard Colm, ed., *The Employment Act, Past and Future: A Tenth Anniversary Symposium*. Washington, DC: National Planning Association. 130-36.

———. 1960. "Reflections on Monetary Policy." *Review of Economics and Statistics* 42, no. 3 (August): 263-69.

———. 1961. *Economics*. 5th ed. New York: McGraw Hill.

———. 1963a. "Reflections on Central Banking." *National Banking Review* 1, no. 1 (September): 15-28.

———. 1963b. "Problems of Methodology—Discussion." *American Economic Review (Papers and Proceedings)* 53, no. 2 (May): 231-36.

———. 1968. "What Classical and Neoclassical Monetary Theory Really Was." *Canadian Journal of Economics* 1, no. 1 (February): 1-15.

———. 1969a. "The Role of Money in National Economic Policy." In Federal Reserve Bank of Boston, ed., *Controlling Monetary Aggregates: Proceedings of a Conference Held in June, 1969*. Boston: Federal Reserve Bank of Boston. 7-13.

———. 1969b. "Nonoptimality of Money Holding under *Laissez Faire*." *Canadian Journal of Economics* 2 (May): 303-8.

———. 1970a. *Economics*. 8th ed. New York: McGraw Hill.

———. 1970b. "Reflections on Recent Federal Reserve Policy." *Journal of Money, Credit and Banking* 2, no. 1 (February): 33-44.

———. 1970c. "Monetarism Objectively Evaluated." In Paul A. Samuelson and Felicity Skidmore, eds., *Readings in Economics*. 6th ed. New York: McGraw Hill. 145-54.

———. 1971. "Reflections on the Merits and Demerits of Monetarism." In James J. Diamond, ed., *Issues in Fiscal and Monetary Policy: The Eclectic Economist Views the Controversy*. Chicago: DePaul University. 7-21.

———. 1973a. "Discussion [of Assar Lindbeck, 'Some Fiscal and Monetary Experiments in Sweden']." In Federal Reserve Bank of Boston, ed., *Credit Allocation Techniques and Monetary Policy: Proceedings of a Conference Held at Melvin Village, New Hampshire, June, 1973*. Boston: Federal Reserve Bank of Boston. 224-28.

———. 1973b. *The Samuelson Sampler*. Glen Ridge, NJ: Thomas Horton.

———. 1975. "Addendum." In Committee on Banking, Housing and Urban Affairs, US Senate, *Second Meeting on the Conduct of Monetary Policy*. Washington, DC: US Government Printing Office. 74-75.

———. 1976. "Alvin Hansen as a Creative Economic Theorist." *Quarterly Journal of Economics* 90, no. 1 (February): 24-31.

———. 1980. "The Public Role in the Modern American Economy." In Martin S. Feldstein, ed., *The American Economy in Transition*. Chicago: University of Chicago Press. 665–71.

———. 1983a. *Economics from the Heart: A Samuelson Sampler*. San Diego, CA: Harcourt Brace Jovanovich.

———. 1983b. "My Life Philosophy." *American Economist* 27, no. 2 (Fall): 5–12.

———. 1997. "Credo of a Lucky Textbook Author." *Journal of Economic Perspectives* 11, no. 2 (Spring): 153–60.

Samuelson, Paul A., and Robert M. Solow. 1960. "Analytical Aspects of Anti-inflation Policy." *American Economic Review (Papers and Proceedings)* 50, no. 2 (May): 177–94.

Sanderson, Allen R. 2012. "Chicago Remembers Milton Friedman: Personal Reflections and Professional Intersections." Manuscript, Department of Economics, University of Chicago.

Sandilands, Roger J. 1990. *The Life and Political Economy of Lauchlin Currie: New Dealer, Presidential Adviser, and Development Economist*. Durham, NC: Duke University Press.

Sargent, Thomas J. 1971. "A Note on the 'Accelerationist' Controversy." *Journal of Money, Credit and Banking* 3, no. 3 (August): 721–25.

———. 1972. "Rational Expectations and the Term Structure of Interest Rates." *Journal of Money, Credit and Banking* 4, no. 1, part 1 (February): 74–97.

———. 1973a. "Rational Expectations, the Real Rate of Interest, and the Natural Rate of Unemployment." *Brookings Papers on Economic Activity* 4, no. 2, 429–72.

———. 1973b. "Interest Rates and Prices in the Long Run: A Study of the Gibson Paradox." *Journal of Money, Credit and Banking* 5, no. 1, part 2 (February): 383–449.

———. 1978. "Rational Expectations, Econometric Exogeneity, and Consumption." *Journal of Political Economy* 86, no. 4 (August): 673–700.

———. 1979. *Macroeconomic Theory*. New York: Academic.

———. 1980. "Tobin's q and the Rate of Investment in General Equilibrium." *Carnegie-Rochester Conference Series in Public Policy* 12, no. 1, 107–54.

———. 1981. "Interpreting Economic Time Series." *Journal of Political Economy* 89, no. 2 (April): 213–48.

———. 1982a. "Nongradualist Approaches to Eliminating Inflation." In Federal Reserve Bank of Atlanta, ed., *Supply-Side Economics in the 1980s: Conference Proceedings*. Westport, CT: Quorum Books. 107–13.

———. 1982b. "Beyond Demand and Supply Curves in Macroeconomics." *American Economic Review (Papers and Proceedings)* 72, no. 2 (May): 382–89.

———. 1986. "Interpreting the Reagan Deficits." *Federal Reserve Bank of San Francisco Economic Review* 68, no. 4 (Fall): 5–12.

———. 1987a. *Macroeconomic Theory*. 2nd ed. New York: Academic.

———. 1987b. *Dynamic Macroeconomic Theory*. Cambridge, MA: Harvard University Press.

———. 1987c. *Some of Milton Friedman's Scientific Contributions to Macroeconomics*. Stanford, CA: Hoover Institution.

———. 1996. "Expectations and the Nonneutrality of Lucas." *Journal of Monetary Economics* 37, no. 3 (June): 535–48.

———. 2014. "The Evolution of Monetary Policy Rules." *Journal of Economic Dynamics and Control* 49, no. S1 (December): 147–50.

Sargent, Thomas J., and Neil A. Wallace. 1973. "The Stability of Models of Money and Growth with Perfect Foresight." *Econometrica* 41, no. 6 (November): 1043–48.

———. 1981. "Some Unpleasant Monetarist Arithmetic." *Federal Reserve Bank of Minneapolis Quarterly Review* 5, no. 1 (Winter): 1–17.

Saunders, Anthony. 1979. "The Short-Run Causal Relationship between U.K. Interest Rates, Share Prices and Dividend Yields." *Scottish Journal of Political Economy* 26, no. 1 (February): 61–71.

Savage, Leonard J. 1954. *The Foundations of Statistics*. New York: John Wiley and Sons.

———. 1972. *The Foundations of Statistics*. 2nd ed. New York: John Wiley and Sons.

Sayers, R. S. 1960. "Monetary Thought and Monetary Policy in England." *Economic Journal* 70, no. 280 (December): 710–24.

Sbordone, Argia M. 2002. "Prices and Unit Labor Costs: A New Test of Price Stickiness." *Journal of Monetary Economics* 49, no. 2 (March): 265–92.

Scadding, John L. 1979. "Estimating the Underlying Inflation Rate." *Federal Reserve Bank of Economic Review* 61, no. 2 (Spring): 7–18.

Schlesinger, James R. 1956. "After Twenty Years: *The General Theory*." *Quarterly Journal of Economics* 70, no. 4 (November): 581–602.

———. 1958. "Market Structure, Union Power and Inflation." *Southern Economic Journal* 24, no. 3 (January): 296–312.

———. 1960. "The Friedman Proposal of a Fixed Monetary Rule." *Rivista di Diritto Finanziario e Scienza della Finance* 19, no. 8, 357–69.

Schmalansee, Richard. 1983. "George Stigler's Contributions to Economics." *Scandinavian Journal of Economics* 85, no. 1, 77–86.

Schultz, Henry. 1938. *The Theory and Measurement of Demand*. Chicago: University of Chicago Press.

Schultz, Theodore W. 1961. "Investment in Human Capital." *American Economic Review* 51, no. 1 (March): 1–17.

———. 1963. *The Economic Value of Education*. New York: Columbia University Press.

Schultze, Charles L. 1959. *Recent Inflation in the United States*. Study Paper no. 1, Joint Economic Committee, US Congress. Washington, DC: US Government Printing Office.

Schwartz, Anna J. 1969. "Why Money Matters." *Lloyds Banks Review* 24, no. 94 (October): 1–16.

———. 1976. "Comments on Modigliani and Ando." In Jerome L. Stein, ed., *Monetarism*. Amsterdam: North-Holland. 43–49.

———. 1981. "Understanding 1929–33." In Karl Brunner, ed., *The Great Depression Revisited*. Boston: Martinus Nijhoff. 5–48.

———. 1984. "Comments on the Paper by Alan Budd, Sean Holly, Andrew Longbottom and David Smith." In Brian Griffiths and Geoffrey E. Wood, eds., *Monetarism in the United Kingdom*. New York: St. Martin's. 129–36.

———. 1986. "*World Inflation since 1950: An International Comparative Study* by A. J. Brown." *Economic History Review* 39, no. 4 (November): 670–72.

———. 1992. "Review: *Milton Friedman: Economics in Theory and Practice*." *Economic Journal* 102, no. 413 (July): 959–61.

———. 1998. "Schwartz on Friedman: 'Who Is Milton? What Is He?': Reflections on *Two Lucky People*." *Region* (Federal Reserve Bank of Minneapolis) 12, no. 3 (September): 4–8.

Schwartz, Anna J., and Elma Oliver. 1947. "Currency Held by the Public, the Banks, and the Treasury, Monthly, December 1917–December 1944." NBER Technical Paper no. 4.

Seater, John J. 1993. "Ricardian Equivalence." *Journal of Economic Literature* 31, no. 1 (March): 142–90.

Selden, Richard T. 1962. Stable Monetary Growth. In Leland B. Yeager, ed., *In Search of a Monetary Constitution.* Cambridge, MA: Harvard University Press. 322–55.

Seligman, Ben B. 1964. "The Search for a Working Theory." *Challenge* 12, no. 8 (May): 10–13.

Sen, Amartya. 1970. "The Impossibility of a Paretian Liberal." *Journal of Political Economy* 78, no. 1 (January/February): 152–57.

Shapiro, Matthew D. 1994. "Federal Reserve Policy: Cause and Effect." In N. Gregory Mankiw, ed., *Monetary Policy.* Chicago: University of Chicago Press. 307–32.

Sharpe, William F. 1970. *Portfolio Theory and Capital Markets.* New York: McGraw-Hill.

Sharpe, William F., Gordon J. Alexander, and Jeffery V. Bailey. 1995. *Investments.* 5th ed. Englewood Cliffs, NJ: Prentice Hall.

Shaw, Edward S. 1950. *Money, Income, and Monetary Policy.* Chicago: Richard D. Irwin.

———. 1964. "Money Supply and Stable Economic Growth." In Neil H. Jacoby, ed., *United States Monetary Policy.* Rev. ed. New York: Praeger. 73–93.

Sheffrin, Steven M. 1982. "Discussion [of 'The Real Effects of Financial Crises: Theory and Evidence']." In Federal Reserve Bank of San Francisco, ed., *Proceedings of Sixth West Coast Academic/Federal Reserve Economic Research Seminar November 1982.* San Francisco: Federal Reserve Bank of San Francisco. 163–68.

Shiller, Robert J. 1972. "Rational Expectations and the Term Structure of Interest Rates." PhD diss., Massachusetts Institute of Technology.

———. 1978. "Rational Expectations and the Dynamic Structure of Macroeconomic Models: A Critical Review." *Journal of Monetary Economics* 4, no. 1 (January): 1–44.

———. 1982. "Consumption, Asset Markets and Macroeconomic Fluctuations." *Carnegie-Rochester Conference Series on Public Policy* 17, no. 1, 203–38.

Shiller, Robert J., and Franco Modigliani. 1979. "Coupon and Tax Effects on New and Seasoned Bond Yields and the Measurement of the Cost of Debt Capital." *Journal of Financial Economics* 7, no. 3 (September): 297–318.

Shimer, Robert. 1996. "Essays in Search Theory." PhD diss., Massachusetts Institute of Technology, June.

———. 2010. *Labor Markets and Business Cycles.* Princeton, NJ: Princeton University Press.

Shoup, Carl S., Milton Friedman, and Ruth P. Mack. 1941. "Amount of Taxes Needed in June 1942 to Avert Inflation." US Treasury Department, October 15.

———. 1943. *Taxing to Prevent Inflation: Techniques for Estimating Revenue Requirements.* New York: Columbia University Press.

Shove, G. F. 1942. "The Place of Marshall's *Principles* in the Development of Economic Theory." *Economic Journal* 52, no. 208 (December): 294–329.

Siegel, Jeremy J. 2005. *The Future for Investors: Why the Tried and True Triumph over the Bold and New.* New York: Crown Business.

Silber, William L. 1969. "Monetary Channels and the Relative Importance of Money Supply and Bank Portfolios." *Journal of Finance* 24, no. 1 (March): 81–87.

Silk, Leonard S. 1976. *The Economists.* New York: Basic Books.

Simons, Henry C. 1934. *A Positive Program for Laissez Faire.* Chicago: University of Chicago Press.

———. 1936. "Rules versus Authorities in Monetary Policy." *Journal of Political Economy* 44, no. 1 (February): 1–30.

———. 1942. "Hansen on Fiscal Policy." *Journal of Political Economy* 50, no. 2 (April): 161–96.

———. 1948. *Economic Policy for a Free Society*. Chicago: University of Chicago Press.

Simons, Henry C., Aaron Director, Frank H. Knight, Garfield V. Cox, Lloyd W. Mints, Henry Schultz, Paul H. Douglas, Albert G. Hart, et al. 1933. "Banking and Currency Reform, Long-Time Objectives of Monetary Management, and Business Cycles." University of Chicago, November 17.

Sims, Christopher A. 1972. "Money, Income, and Causality." *American Economic Review* 62, no. 4 (September): 540–52.

———. 1982. "Scientific Standards in Econometric Modeling." In Michiel Hazelwinkel and A. H. G. Rinnooy Kan, eds., *Current Developments in the Interface: Economics, Econometrics, Mathematics; State of the Art Surveys Presented on the Occasion of the 25th Anniversary of the Econometric Institute*. Boston: D. Reidel. 317–40.

———. 1991. "Comment by Christopher A. Sims on 'To Criticize the Critics,' by Peter C. B. Phillips." *Journal of Applied Econometrics* 6, no. 4 (October–December): 423–34.

———. 1992. "Interpreting the Macroeconomic Time Series Facts: The Effects of Monetary Policy." *European Economic Review* 36, no. 5 (June): 975–1000.

———. 1998. "Comment on Glenn Rudebusch's 'Do Measures of Monetary Policy in a VAR Make Sense?'" *International Economic Review* 39, no. 4 (November): 933–41.

———. 2012. "Statistical Modeling of Monetary Policy and Its Effects." *American Economic Review* 102, no. 4 (June): 1187–205.

Sinclair, Tara M. 2009. "Asymmetry in the Business Cycle: Friedman's Plucking Model with Correlated Innovations." Manuscript, George Washington University, June.

Skidelsky, Robert. 1992. *John Maynard Keynes*. Vol. 2, *The Economist as Saviour, 1920–1937*. London: Macmillan. US edition: New York, Penguin, 1994.

———. 2000. *John Maynard Keynes*. Vol. 3, *Fighting for Britain, 1937–1946*. London: Macmillan.

Skidelsky, Robert, and Edward Skidelsky. 2013. *How Much Is Enough? Money and the Good Life*. Rev. ed. New York: Other.

Skousen, Mark. 2001. *The Making of Modern Economics: The Lives and Ideas of the Great Thinkers*. Armonk, NY: M. E. Sharpe.

Smith, Adam. 1759. *The Theory of Moral Sentiments*. London: A. Millar. Reprint ed.: New York: Garland, 1971.

———. 1776. *An Inquiry into the Nature and Causes of the Wealth of Nations*. Reissued version: Edwin Cannan, ed., New York: Modern Library, 1937.

Smith, David. 1987. *The Rise and Fall of Monetarism*. Middlesex, UK: Penguin.

Smith, Gary. 1982. "Monetarism, Bondism, and Inflation." *Journal of Money, Credit and Banking* 14, no. 2 (May): 278–86.

Smith, Harlan M. 1951. "Classified Bibliography of Articles in Monetary Theory." In Friedrich A. Lutz and Lloyd W. Mints, eds., *Readings in Monetary Theory, Selected by a Committee of the American Economic Association*. Homewood, IL: Richard D. Irwin; Philadelphia: Blakiston. 457–505.

Smith, Warren L., and Ronald L. Teigen, eds. 1970. *Readings in Money, National Income, and Stabilization Policy*. 2nd ed. Homewood, IL: Richard D. Irwin.

Snowdon, Brian, and Howard R. Vane. 1997. "Modern Macroeconomics and Its Evolution from a Monetarist Perspective: An Interview with Professor Milton Friedman." *Journal of Economic Studies* 24, no. 4 (July/August): 191–221 (192–222 of some printings).

Snowdon, Brian, Howard R. Vane, and Peter Wynarczyk. 1994. *A Modern Guide to*

Macroeconomics: An Introduction to Competing Schools of Thought. Cheltenham, UK: Edward Elgar.

Solow, Robert M. 1966a. "The Case against the Case against the Guideposts." In George P. Shultz and Robert Z. Aliber, eds., *Guidelines: Informal Controls and the Market Place.* Chicago: University of Chicago Press. 41–54.

———. 1966b. "Comments." In George P. Shultz and Robert Z. Aliber, eds., *Guidelines: Informal Controls and the Market Place.* Chicago: University of Chicago Press. 62–66.

———. 1969. *Price Expectations and the Behavior of the Price Level.* Manchester, UK: Manchester University Press.

———. 1976. "Down the Phillips Curve with Gun and Camera." In David A. Belsley, Edward J. Kane, Paul A. Samuelson, and Robert M. Solow, eds., *Inflation, Trade and Taxes: Essays in Honor of Alice Bourneuf.* Columbus: Ohio State University Press. 3–22.

———. 1986. "Unemployment: Getting the Questions Right." *Economica* 53, no. 210 (supplement issue): S23–S34.

———. 2012. "The Serfdom Scare." *New Republic* 243, no. 18 (December 6): 40–43.

Special Committee to Study the Foreign Aid Program. 1957. *The Foreign Aid Program: Hearings.* Washington, DC: US. Government Printing Office.

Speers, Michael F. 1982. "NSA Revealed." *Foreign Service Journal* 59, no. 11 (December): 10–12.

Sprinkel, Beryl W. 1964. *Money and Stock Prices.* Homewood, IL: Richard D. Irwin.

Stallings, Penny. 1991. *Forbidden Channels: The Truth They Hide from "TV Guide."* New York: Harper Perennial.

Stein, Herbert. 1969. *The Fiscal Revolution in America.* Chicago: University of Chicago Press.

Stein, Jerome L., ed. 1976a. *Monetarism.* Amsterdam: North-Holland.

———. 1976b. "Introduction: The Monetarist Critique of the New Economics." In Jerome L. Stein, ed., *Monetarism.* Amsterdam: North-Holland. 1–16.

Steindl, Frank G. 2004. "Friedman and Money in the 1930s." *History of Political Economy* 36, no. 3 (Fall): 521–31.

Stevenson, Andrew, Vitantonio Muscatelli, and Mary Gregory. 1988. *Macroeconomic Theory and Stabilisation Policy.* Hertfordshire, UK: Philip Allan.

Stigler, George J. 1949. *Five Lectures on Economic Problems.* London: Longman, Green.

———. 1960a. "*Selected Papers on Economic Theory* by Knut Wicksell." *Econometrica* 28, no. 3 (July): 719–20.

———. 1960b. "The Influence of Events and Policies on Economic Theory." *American Economic Review (Papers and Proceedings)* 50, no. 2 (May): 36–45.

———. 1966. *The Theory of Price.* 3rd ed. New York: Macmillan.

———. 1988. *Memoirs of an Unregulated Economist.* New York: Basic Books.

Stigler, Stephen. 1996. "The History of Statistics in 1933." *Statistical Science* 11, no. 3 (August): 244–52.

———. 2007. "Milton Friedman and Statistics." Manuscript, University of Chicago.

Stock, James H. 1988. "A Reexamination of Friedman's Consumption Puzzle." *Journal of Business and Economic Statistics* 6, no. 4 (October): 401–7.

Stokey, Nancy L., Robert E. Lucas, Jr., and Edward C. Prescott. 1989. *Recursive Methods in Economic Dynamics.* Cambridge, MA: Harvard University Press.

Subcommittee on Economic Stabilization of the Joint Committee on the Economic Report, US Congress. 1956. *Conflicting Official Views on Monetary Policy: April 1956; Hearing, June 12, 1956.* Washington, DC: US Government Printing Office.

Subcommittee on Monetary, Credit, and Fiscal Policies of the Joint Committee on the Economic Report, US Congress. 1950a. *Monetary, Credit, and Fiscal Policies: Report of the Subcommittee on Monetary, Credit, and Fiscal Politics of the Joint Committee on the Economic Report, Congress of the United States, Pursuant to S. Res. 26.* Washington, DC: US Government Printing Office.

———. 1950b. *Monetary, Credit, and Fiscal Policies: Hearings,* September 28, November 16, 17, 18, 22, 23 and December 1, 2, 3, 5, 7, 1949. Washington, DC: US Government Printing Office.

Sugden, Robert. 2004. "Alternative to Expected Utility: Foundations." In Salvador Barbera, Peter J. Hammond, and Christian Seidl, eds., *Handbook of Utility Theory.* Vol. 2, *Extensions.* Netherlands: Kluwer Academic. 685-756.

Summers, Lawrence H. 1986. "Estimating the Long-Run Relationship between Interest Rates and Inflation: A Response to McCallum." *Journal of Monetary Economics* 18, no. 1 (July): 77-86.

———. 1991. "The Scientific Illusion in Empirical Macroeconomics." *Scandinavian Journal of Economics* 93, no. 2, 129-48.

———. 2015. "Have We Entered an Age of Secular Stagnation? IMF Fourteenth Annual Research Conference in Honor of Stanley Fischer, Washington, D.C." *IMF Economic Review* 63, no. 1 (April): 277-80.

Svensson, Lars E. O. 2015. "Cost-Benefit Analysis of Leaning against the Wind: Are Costs *Always* Larger Than Benefits, and Even More So with a Less Effective Macroprudential Policy?" Manuscript, Stockholm School of Economics, September.

Swenson, John, ed. 1981. *The Year in Rock 1981-82.* New York: Delilah Books.

Szyr, Eugeniusz, ed. 1964. *Twenty Years of the Polish People's Republic.* Warsaw: Warszawa Panstwowe Wydawnictwo Ekonomiczne.

Tavlas, George S. 1977a. "Chicago Schools Old and New on the Efficacy of Monetary Policy." *Banca Nazionale del Lavoro Quarterly Review* 30, no. 120 (March): 51-73.

———. 1977b. "The Chicago Tradition Revisited: Some Neglected Monetary Contributions: Senator Paul Douglas (1892-1976)." *Journal of Money, Credit and Banking* 9, no. 4 (November): 529-35.

———. 1989. "Interpreting Keynes: Reflections on the Leijonhufvud-Yeager Discussion." *Cato Journal* 9, no. 1 (Spring/Summer): 237-52.

———. 1998. "More on the Chicago Tradition." *Journal of Economic Studies* 25, no. 1 (January): 17-21.

———. 2015. "In Old Chicago: Simons, Friedman and the Development of Monetary-Policy Rules." *Journal of Money, Credit and Banking* 47, no. 1 (February): 99-121.

Taylor, John B. 1980. "Aggregate Dynamics and Staggered Contracts." *Journal of Political Economy* 88, no. 1 (February): 1-23.

———. 1981. "On the Relation between the Variability of Inflation and the Average Inflation Rate." *Carnegie-Rochester Conference Series on Public Policy* 15, no. 1, 57-85.

———. 1986. "Improvements in Macroeconomic Stability: The Role of Wages and Prices." In Robert J. Gordon, ed., *The American Business Cycle: Continuity and Change.* Chicago: University of Chicago Press. 639-59.

———. 1993. "Discretion versus Policy Rules in Practice." *Carnegie Rochester Conference Series on Public Policy* 39, no. 1, 195-214.

———. 1996. "How Should Monetary Policy Respond to Shocks While Maintaining Long-Run Price Stability?—Conceptual Issues." In Federal Reserve Bank of Kansas City, ed., *Achieving Price Stability.* Kansas City, MO: Federal Reserve Bank of Kansas City. 181-95.

——. 2001. "An Interview with Milton Friedman." *Macroeconomic Dynamics* 5, no. 1 (February): 101–31.

Teichgraeber, Richard, III. 1979. *"Adam Smith's Politics: An Essay in Historiographic Revision,* by Donald Winch." *Eighteenth-Century Studies* 12, no. 4 (Summer): 566–69.

Telser, Lester G. 2001. "Higher Member Bank Reserve Ratios in 1936 and 1937 Did Not Cause the Relapse into Depression." *Journal of Post Keynesian Economics* 24, no. 2 (Winter): 205–16.

——. 2003. "The Veterans' Bonus of 1936." *Journal of Post-Keynesian Economics* 26, no. 2 (Winter): 227–43.

——. 2007. *The Core Theory in Economics: Problems and Solutions.* London: Routledge.

Temin, Peter. 1976. *Did Monetary Factors Cause the Great Depression?* New York: W. W. Norton.

Thomas, Woodlief. 1947. "The Heritage of War Finance." *American Economic Review (Papers and Proceedings)* 37, no. 2 (May): 205–15.

Thornton, Daniel L. 2006. "When Did the FOMC Begin Targeting the Federal Funds Rate? What the Verbatim Transcripts Tell Us." *Journal of Money, Credit and Banking* 38, no. 8 (December): 2039–71.

Thygesen, Niels. 1977. "The Scientific Contributions of Milton Friedman." *Scandinavian Journal of Economics* 79, no. 1, 56–98.

Tinbergen, Jan. 1939. *Statistical Testing of Business-Cycle Theories: II, Business Cycles in the United States of America, 1919-1932.* New York: Columbia University Press.

Tobin, James. 1947. "Liquidity Preference and Monetary Policy." *Review of Economics and Statistics* 29, no. 2 (May): 124–31.

——. 1956. "The Interest Elasticity of the Transactions Demand for Cash." *Review of Economics and Statistics* 38, no. 3 (August): 241–47.

——. 1958a. "Liquidity Preference as Behavior towards Risk." *Review of Economic Studies* 25, no. 2 (February): 65–86.

——. 1958b. "Discussion of Milton Friedman's [Summary Paper] 'A Theory of the Consumption Function.'" In Lincoln H. Clark, ed., *Consumer Behavior: Research on Consumer Reactions.* New York: Harper and Brothers. 447–54.

——. 1960. "Towards Improving the Efficiency of the Monetary Mechanism." *Review of Economics and Statistics* 42, no. 3 (August): 276–79.

——. 1961. "Money, Capital, and Other Stores of Value." *American Economic Review (Papers and Proceedings)* 51, no. 2 (May): 26–37.

——. 1963a. "An Essay on the Principles of Debt Management." In Commission on Money and Credit, ed., *Fiscal and Debt Management Policies.* Englewood Cliffs, NJ: Prentice Hall. 143–218.

——. 1963b. "Commercial Banks as Creators of 'Money.'" In Deane Carson, ed., *Banking and Monetary Studies.* Homewood, IL: Richard D. Irwin. 408–19.

——. 1965a. "The Monetary Interpretation of History." *American Economic Review* 55, no. 3 (June): 464–85.

——. 1965b. "Money and Economic Growth." *Econometrica* 33, no. 4 (October): 671–84.

——. 1969a. "A General Equilibrium Approach to Monetary Theory." *Journal of Money, Credit and Banking* 1, no. 1 (February): 15–29.

——. 1969b. "The Role of Money in National Economic Policy: Panel Discussion." In Federal Reserve Bank of Boston, ed., *Controlling Monetary Aggregates: Proceedings of the Monetary Conference Held on Nantucket Island, June 8-10, 1969.* Boston: Federal Reserve Bank of Boston. 21–25.

——. 1969c. "Monetary Semantics." In Karl Brunner, ed., *Targets and Indicators of Monetary Policy*. San Francisco: Chandler. 165-74.

——. 1970a. "Money and Income: Post Hoc Ergo Propter Hoc?" *Quarterly Journal of Economics* 84, no. 2 (May): 301-17.

——. 1970b. "Rejoinder." *Quarterly Journal of Economics* 84, no. 2 (May): 328-29.

——. 1974a. "Monetary Policy in 1974 and Beyond." *Brookings Papers on Economic Activity* 5, no. 1, 219-32.

——. 1974b. "Friedman's Theoretical Framework: Postscript." In Robert J. Gordon, ed., *Milton Friedman's Monetary Framework: A Debate with His Critics*. Chicago: University of Chicago Press. 88–89.

——. 1975. "Keynesian Models of Recession and Depression." *American Economic Review (Papers and Proceedings)* 65, no. 2 (May): 195-202.

——. 1976a. "Review: *Issues in Monetary Economics* [edited] by H. G. Johnson, A. R. Nobay." *Journal of Finance* 31, no. 1 (March): 169-72.

——. 1976b. "Reply: Is Friedman a Monetarist?" In Jerome L. Stein, ed., *Monetarism*. Amsterdam: North-Holland. 332-36.

——. 1978a. "Comments from an Academic Scribbler." *Journal of Monetary Economics* 4, no. 3 (August): 617-25.

——. 1978b. "Monetary Policies and the Economy: The Transmission Mechanism." *Southern Economic Journal* 44, no. 3 (January): 421-31.

——. 1978c. "Correspondence [August 8, 1978] Relating to Legislative Proposals concerning the Federal Reserve's Monetary Control and the Membership Problem." In Committee on Banking, Finance, and Urban Affairs, US House of Representatives, *Monetary Control and the Membership Problem: Hearings*. Washington, DC: US Government Printing Office. 792-95.

——. 1980. *Asset Accumulation and Economic Activity: Reflections on Contemporary Macroeconomic Theory*. Chicago: University of Chicago Press.

——. 1981a. "Book Review: *Keynes' Monetary Thought: A Study of Its Development* by Don Patinkin." *Journal of Political Economy* 89, no. 1, 204-7.

——. 1981b. "The Monetarist Counter-revolution Today—an Appraisal." *Economic Journal* 91, no. 361 (March): 29-42.

——. 1981c. "Comment on Michael Bruno and Jeffrey Sachs, 'Supply versus Demand Approaches to the Problem of Stagflation.'" In Herbert Giersch, ed., *Macroeconomic Policies for Growth and Stability: A European Perspective, Symposium 1979*. Tübingen: Institut für Weltwirtschaft an der Universität Kiel; J. C. B. Mohr (Paul Siebeck). 61-69.

——. 1981d. "Comment on Albert Ando, 'On a Theoretical and Empirical Basis of Macroeconometric Models.'" In Jan Kmenta and James Bernard Ramsey, eds., *Large-Scale Macroeconometric Models*. Amsterdam: North-Holland. 391-92.

——. 1987a. "Keynesian Economics and Its Renaissance." In David A. Reese, ed., *The Legacy of Keynes*. New York: Harper and Row. 94-121.

——. 1987b. "Irving Fisher." In John Eatwell, Murray Milgate, and Peter Newman, eds., *The New Palgrave: A Dictionary of Economics*. Vol. 2, *E to J*. London: Macmillan. 369-76.

——. 1995. "The Natural Rate as New Classical Macroeconomics." In Rod Cross, ed., *The Natural Rate of Unemployment: Reflections on 25 Years of the Hypothesis*. Cambridge: Cambridge University Press. 32-42.

Tobin, James, and William C. Brainard. 1977. "Asset Markets and the Cost of Capital."

In Bela Balassa and Richard Nelson, eds., *Economic Progress, Private Values, and Public Policies: Essays in Honor of William Fellner.* Amsterdam: North-Holland. 235-62.

Tobin, James, and Willem H. Buiter. 1976. "Long-Run Effects of Fiscal and Monetary Policy on Aggregate Demand." In Jerome L. Stein, ed., *Monetarism.* Amsterdam: North-Holland. 273-309.

———. 1980. "Fiscal and Monetary Policies, Capital Formation, and Economic Activity." In George M. Von Furstenberg, ed., *The Government and Capital Formation.* Cambridge, MA: Ballinger. 73-151.

Todd, Richard M. 1990. "Vector Autoregression Evidence on Monetarism: Another Look at the Robustness Debate." *Federal Reserve Bank of Minneapolis Quarterly Review* 14, no. 2 (Spring): 19-37.

Tolley, George S. 1957. "Providing for Growth of the Money Supply." *Journal of Political Economy* 65, no. 6 (December): 465-85.

Townsend, Robert M. 1980. "Models of Money with Spatially Separated Agents." In John H. Kareken and Neil A. Wallace, eds., *Models of Monetary Economies.* Minneapolis: Federal Reserve Bank of Minneapolis. 265-303.

Treasury and Civil Service Committee, House of Commons. 1980. "Questionnaire on Monetary Policy." In Treasury and Civil Service Committee, House of Commons, ed., *Memoranda on Monetary Policy.* London: Her Majesty's Stationery Office. 1-4.

Trebach, Arnold S., and Kevin B. Zeese, eds. 1992. *Friedman and Szasz on Liberty and Drugs.* Washington, DC: Drug Policy Foundation Press.

Trevithick, James A. 1977. *Inflation: A Guide to the Crisis in Economics.* Harmondsworth, UK: Penguin.

Triffin, Robert. 1940. *Monopolistic Competition and General Equilibrium Theory.* Cambridge, MA: Harvard University Press.

Turner, Philip. 2011. "Is the Long-Term Interest Rate a Policy Victim, a Policy Variable or a Policy Lodestar?" BIS Working Paper no. 367, December.

Turner, Robert C. 1957. "Comment [on 'Consumer Credit Control as an Instrument of Stabilization Policy']." In Federal Reserve Board, ed., *Consumer Instalment Credit, Part 2: Conference on Regulation.* Washington, DC: Federal Reserve Board. 103-11.

University of Chicago Press. 1941. "*Incomes from Independent Professional Practice, 1929-1936*, by Simon Kuznets, Milton Friedman." *American Journal of Sociology* 46, no. 4 (January): 636-37.

Vaizey, John, ed. 1975. *Whatever Happened to Equality?* London: British Broadcasting Corporation.

Valentine, Gloria. 1987. "Complete Bibliography of Milton Friedman." In Kurt R. Leube, ed., *The Essence of Friedman.* Stanford, CA: Hoover Institution Press. 527-51.

Van Horn, Robert. 2009. "Reinventing Monopoly and the Role of Corporations: The Roots of Chicago Law and Economics." In Philip Mirowski and Dieter Plehwe, eds., *The Road from Mont Pèlerin: The Making of the Neoliberal Thought Collective.* Cambridge, MA: Harvard University Press. 204-37.

Van Horn, Robert, and Matthias Klaes. 2011. "Intervening in Laissez-Faire Liberalism: Chicago's Shift on Patents." In Robert Van Horn, Philip Mirowski, and Thomas A. Stapleford, eds., *Building Chicago Economics: New Perspectives on the History of America's Most Powerful Economics Program.* Cambridge: Cambridge University Press. 180-207.

Van Overtveldt, Johan. 2007. *The Chicago School: How the University of Chicago Assembled the Thinkers Who Revolutionized Economics and Business.* Evanston, IL: Agate B2.

Viner, Jacob. 1927. "Adam Smith and *Laissez Faire*." *Journal of Political Economy* 35, no. 2 (April): 198–232.

———. 1933. *Balanced Deflation, Inflation, or More Depression*. Minneapolis: University of Minnesota Press.

———. 1936. "Mr. Keynes on the Causes of Unemployment." *Quarterly Journal of Economics* 51, no. 1 (November): 147–67.

———. 1945. *The United States in a Multi-national Economy*. New York: Council on Foreign Relations.

Volcker, Paul A. 1977. "A Broader Role for Monetary Targets." *Federal Reserve Bank of New York Quarterly Review* 59, no. 1 (Spring): 23–28.

———. 1978. "The Role of Monetary Targets in an Age of Inflation." *Journal of Monetary Economics* 4, no. 2 (April): 329–39.

von Neumann, John, and Oskar Morgenstern. 1944. *Theory of Games and Economic Behavior*. Princeton, NJ: Princeton University Press.

Wachter, Susan M. 1976. *Latin American Inflation: The Structuralist-Monetarist Debate*. Lexington, MA: Lexington Books.

Wald, Abraham. 1947. *Sequential Analysis*. New York: John Wiley and Sons.

Walker, Charles E. 1960. "Monetary Policy and Economic Stability." In Herbert V. Prochnow, ed., *The Federal Reserve System*. New York: Harper and Brothers. 54–74.

Walker, Francis A. 1893. "Value of Money." *Quarterly Journal of Economics* 8, no. 1 (October): 62–76.

———. 1895. "The Quantity-Theory of Money." *Quarterly Journal of Economics* 9, no. 4 (July): 372–79.

Wallace, Neil A. 1977. "Why the Fed Should Consider Holding Mo Constant." *Federal Reserve Bank of Minneapolis Quarterly Review* 1, no. 1 (Summer): 2–10.

———. 1988. "A Suggestion for Oversimplifying the Theory of Money." *Economic Journal* 98, no. 390 (supplement): 25–36.

Wallechinsky, David, Amy Wallace, and Irving Wallace. 1981. *The "People's Almanac" Presents the Book of Predictions*. New York: Bantam.

Wallich, Henry C. 1977. "From Multiplier to Quantity Theory." In Bela Balassa and Richard Nelson, eds., *Economic Progress, Private Values, and Public Policy: Essays in Honor of William Fellner*. Amsterdam: North-Holland. 279–95.

———. 1983. "Samuelson and Trends in Monetary Policy." In George R. Feiwel, ed., *Samuelson and Neoclassical Economics*. Boston: Kluwer. 263–70.

Wallich, Henry C., and Stephen H. Axilrod. 1964. "Postwar United States Policy Appraised." In Neil H. Jacoby, ed., *United States Monetary Policy*. Rev. ed. New York: Praeger. 116–54.

Wallis, Kenneth F. 1980. *Topics in Applied Econometrics*. Rev. 2nd ed. London: Gray-Mills.

Wallis, W. Allen. 1942. "How to Ration Consumers' Goods and Control Their Prices." *American Economic Review* 32, no. 3, part 1 (September): 501–12.

———. 1947. "Preface." In Churchill Eisenhart, Millard W. Hastay, and W. Allen Wallis, eds., *Selected Techniques of Statistical Analysis for Scientific and Industrial Research and Production and Management Engineering by the Statistical Research Group, Columbia University*. New York: McGraw Hill. vii–x.

———. 1948. "Preface." In H. A. Freeman, Milton Friedman, Frederick Mosteller, and W. Allen Wallis, eds., *Sampling Inspection: Principles, Procedures, and Tables for Single, Double, and Sequential Sampling in Acceptance Inspection and Quality Control Based on Percent Defective by the Statistical Research Group, Columbia University.* New York: McGraw Hill. v–x.

Wallis, W. Allen, and Milton Friedman. 1942. "The Empirical Derivation of Indifference Functions." In Oskar Lange, Francis McIntyre, and Theodore Otto Yntema, eds., *Studies in Mathematical Economics and Econometrics.* Chicago: University of Chicago Press. 175–89.

Walras, Leon. 1954. *Elements of Pure Economics.* Translated by William Jaffe. Homewood, IL: Richard Irwin.

Walsh, Carl E. 2003. *Monetary Theory and Policy.* 2nd ed. Cambridge, MA: MIT Press.

Walters, Alan A. 1968. *Introduction to Econometrics.* London: Macmillan.

———. 1987. "Milton Friedman." In John Eatwell, Murray Milgate, and Peter Newman, eds., *The New Palgrave: A Dictionary of Economics.* Vol. 2, *E to J.* London: Macmillan. 422–27.

———. 1991. "Introduction." In Milton Friedman, *Monetarist Economics.* Oxford, UK: Basil Blackwell. vii–x.

Warburton, Clark. 1943a. "Measuring the Inflationary Gap." *American Economic Review* 33, no. 2 (June): 365–69.

———. 1943b. "Who Makes the Inflationary Gap?" *American Economic Review* 33, no. 3 (September): 607–12.

———. 1944. "Monetary Expansion and the Inflationary Gap." *American Economic Review* 34, no. 2 (June): 303–27.

———. 1946a. "Effect of Wartime Monetary Expansion on the Postwar Price Level." Manuscript, Division of Research and Statistics, FDIC, July 25.

———. 1946b. "The Misplaced Emphasis in Contemporary Business-Fluctuation Theory." *Journal of Business* 19, no. 4 (October): 199–220.

———. 1950a. "Co-ordination of Monetary, Bank Supervisory, and Loan Agencies of the Federal Government." *Journal of Finance* 5, no. 2 (June): 148–69.

———. 1950b. "The Theory of Turning Points in Business Fluctuations." *Quarterly Journal of Economics* 64, no. 4 (November): 525–49.

———. 1951. "An Additional Note on Co-ordination of Banking and Monetary Agencies." *Journal of Finance* 6, no. 3 (September): 338–40. Reprinted (as "An Additional Note") in Clark Warburton, *Depression, Inflation, and Monetary Policy: Selected Papers, 1945–1953.* Baltimore: Johns Hopkins University Press, 1966. 412–14.

———. 1952. "How Much Variation in the Quantity of Money Is Needed?" *Southern Economic Journal* 18, no. 4 (April): 495–509.

———. 1958. "Discussion." *Proceedings of the Business and Economic Statistics Section of the American Statistical Association* 5, no. 1, 210–12.

———. 1963. "Money and Business Cycles: A Comment." *Review of Economics and Statistics* 45, no. 1 (February): 77–78.

———. 1966. *Depression, Inflation, and Monetary Policy: Selected Papers, 1945–1953.* Baltimore: Johns Hopkins University Press.

———. 1976. "*Gold, Money and the Law*, edited by Henry G. Manne and Roger LeRoy Miller." *Journal of Money, Credit and Banking* 8, no. 4 (November): 542–43.

Ward, Richard A., ed. 1966. *Monetary Theory and Policy.* Scranton, PA: International Textbook.

Watson, Mark W. 1988. "Comment [on 'A Reexamination of Friedman's Consumption Puzzle']." *Journal of Business and Economic Statistics* 6, no. 4 (October): 408–9.

———. 1993. "Measures of Fit for Calibrated Models." *Journal of Political Economy* 101, no. 6 (December): 1011–41.

Weinstein, Michael M. 1980. *Recovery and Redistribution under the NIRA*. Amsterdam: North-Holland.

Weintraub, Robert. 1967. "The Stock of Money, Interest Rates and the Business Cycle, 1952–1964." *Western Economic Journal* 5, no. 3 (June): 257–70.

———. 1969. "The Time Deposit-Money Supply Controversy." In Karl Brunner, ed., *Targets and Indicators of Monetary Policy*. San Francisco: Chandler. 300–312.

Weintraub, Sidney. 1964. "Supplement: Theoretical Economics." *Annals of the American Academy of Political and Social Science* 352, no. 1 (March): 152–64.

Wells, Wyatt C. 1994. *Economist in an Uncertain World: Arthur F. Burns and the Federal Reserve, 1970–1978*. New York: Columbia University Press.

West, Kenneth D. 1993. "An Aggregate Demand–Aggregate Supply Analysis of Japanese Monetary Policy, 1973–1990." In Kenneth J. Singleton, ed., *Japanese Monetary Policy*. Chicago: University of Chicago Press. 161–88.

Weyl, E. Glen. 2012. "Introduction: Simon Kuznets, Cautious Empiricist of the Eastern European Jewish Diaspora." In Simon Kuznets, *Jewish Economies: Development and Migration in America and Beyond*. Vol. 1, *The Economic Life of American Jewry*, ed. Stephanie Lo and E. Glen Weyl. New Brunswick, NJ: Transaction. xv–liv.

———. 2015. "Price Theory." Manuscript, University of Chicago, July.

White, Lawrence H. 1987. "Competitive Money, Inside and Out." In James A. Dorn and Anna J. Schwartz, eds., *The Search for Stable Money: Essays on Monetary Reform*. Chicago: University of Chicago Press. 339–57.

Wicksell, Knut. 1935. *Lectures on Political Economy*. Vol. 2, *Money*. London: George Routledge and Sons.

Williamson, Stephen, and Randall Wright. 2011. "New Monetarist Economics." In Benjamin M. Friedman and Michael Woodford, eds., *Handbook of Monetary Economics*. Vol. 3A. Amsterdam: Elsevier/North-Holland. 25–96.

Wilson, Thomas. 1961. *Inflation*. Cambridge, MA: Harvard University Press.

———. 1976. "The 'Natural' Rate of Unemployment." *Scottish Journal of Political Economy* 23, no. 1 (February): 99–107.

Winch, Donald. 1969. *Economics and Policy: A Historical Study*. New York: Walker.

———. 1978. *Adam Smith's Politics: An Essay in Historiographic Revision*. Cambridge: Cambridge University Press.

———. 1981. "Jacob Viner." *American Scholar* 50, no. 4 (Autumn): 519–25.

———. 1983. "Jacob Viner as Intellectual Historian." *Research in the History of Economic Thought and Methodology* 1, no. 1, 1–17.

Woglom, Geoffrey. 1988. *Modern Macroeconomics*. Glenview, IL: Scott, Foresman.

Wonnacott, Paul, and Ronald J. Wonnacott. 1979. *Economics*. New York: McGraw Hill.

Wonnacott, Ronald J., and Thomas H. Wonnacott. 1979. *Econometrics*. 2nd ed. New York: John Wiley and Sons.

Woodford, Michael. 1990. "The Optimum Quantity of Money." In Benjamin M. Friedman and Frank H. Hahn, eds., *Handbook of Monetary Economics*. Vol. 2. Amsterdam: Elsevier/North-Holland. 1067–152.

———. 1994. "Monetary Policy and Price Level Determinacy in a Cash-in-Advance Economy." *Economic Theory* 4, no. 3 (May): 345–80.

———. 1998. "Comment [on John H. Cochrane, 'A Frictionless View of U.S. Inflation']." *NBER Macroeconomics Annual* 13, no. 1, 390–418.

———. 1999. "Commentary: How Should Monetary Policy Be Conducted in an Era of Price Stability?" In Federal Reserve Bank of Kansas City, ed., *New Challenges for Monetary Policy*. Kansas City, MO: Federal Reserve Bank of Kansas City. 277-316.

———. 2003. *Interest and Prices: Foundations of a Theory of Monetary Policy*. Princeton, NJ: Princeton University Press.

———. 2008. "How Important Is Money in the Conduct of Monetary Policy?" *Journal of Money, Credit and Banking* 40, no. 8 (December): 1561-98.

———. 2010. "Financial Intermediation and Macroeconomic Analysis." *Journal of Economic Perspectives* 24, no. 4 (Fall): 21-44.

———. 2012. "Methods of Policy Accommodation at the Interest-Rate Lower Bound." In Federal Reserve Bank of Kansas City, ed., *The Changing Policy Landscape*. Kansas City, MO: Federal Reserve Bank of Kansas City. 185-288.

Wouk, Herman. 1951. *The Caine Mutiny*. New York: Doubleday.

Wright, David McCord. 1951. "Concluding Commentary." In David McCord Wright, ed., *The Impact of the Union: Eight Economic Theorists Evaluate the Labor Union Movement*. New York: Harcourt Brace. 379-85.

Yeager, Leland B. 1960. "*Methodenstreit* over Demand Curves." *Journal of Political Economy* 68, no. 1 (February): 53-64.

———. 1981. "Clark Warburton, 1896-1979." *History of Political Economy* 13, no. 2 (Summer): 279-84.

Yntema, Dwight B. 1946. "*Income from Independent Professional Practice* by Milton Friedman and Simon Kuznets." *American Economic Review* 36, no. 4 (September): 682-83.

Yoshikawa, Horoshi. 1993. "Monetary Policy and the Real Economy in Japan." In Kenneth J. Singleton, ed., *Japanese Monetary Policy*. Chicago: University of Chicago Press. 121-59.

Young, Ralph A. 1958a. "The Statistical Foundation for Policy Formation in the Federal Reserve System." *Proceedings of the Business and Economic Statistics Section of the American Statistical Association* 5, no. 1, 202-7.

———. 1958b. "Tools and Processes of Monetary Policy." In Neil H. Jacoby, ed., *United States Monetary Policy: Its Contribution to Prosperity without Inflation*. New York: American Assembly. 13-48.

———. 1963. Memorandum to Chairman William McChesney Martin on Seymour Harris. October 31. Federal Reserve Board. fraser.stlouisfed.org/docs/historical/martin/21_04_19631031.pdf.

———. 1964. "Tools and Processes of Monetary Policy." In Neil H. Jacoby, ed., *United States Monetary Policy*. Rev. ed. New York: American Assembly. 24-72.

Zellner, Arnold. 1984. *Basic Issues in Econometrics*. Chicago: University of Chicago Press.

———. 1985. "Bayesian Econometrics." *Econometrica* 53, no. 2 (March): 253-69.

Index

In what follows, "MF" refers to Milton Friedman.